OPERATIONS MANAGEMENT

Production of Goods and Services

Third Edition

John O. McClain **L. Joseph Thomas**

Cornell University

Joseph B. Mazzola

Duke University

PRENTICE HALL, Englewood Cliffs, New Jersey 07632

Library of Congress Cataloging-in-Publication Data

McClain, John O.
Operations management: production of goods and services/John O. McClain, L. Joseph Thomas, Joseph B. Mazzola.—3rd ed.
p. cm.

Includes bibliographical references and index.
ISBN 0-13-636135-8
1. Industrial management—Mathematical models. 2. Production management—Mathematical: models. 3. Operations research.
I. Thomas, L. Joseph, 1942- . II. Mazzola, Joseph B. III. Title.
HD30.25.M38 1992
658.4—dc20 91-39076
CIP

Acquisition Editor: Valerie Ashton
Production Editor: Pat Reynolds/Caliber
Cover and Interior Design: Thomas Nery
Prepress Buyer: Trudy Pisciotti
Manufacturing Buyer: Robert Anderson

Printed in the United States of America
10 9 8 7 6 5 4 3 2 1

ISBN 0-13-636135-8

Prentice-Hall International (UK) Limited, London
Prentice-Hall of Australia Pty. Limited, Sydney
Prentice-Hall Canada Inc., Toronto
Prentice-Hall Hispanoamericana, S.A., Mexico
Prentice-Hall of India Private Limited, New Delhi
Prentice-Hall of Japan, Inc., Tokyo
Prentice-Hall of Southeast Asia Pte. Ltd., Singapore
Editora Prentice-Hall do Brasil, Ltda., Rio de Janeiro

Contents

Preface

This text is designed to introduce upper-level undergraduate or first-year graduate students to the problems and techniques encountered in the production and delivery of goods and services—that is, operations management. Our purpose is to give future managers an understanding of the variety and importance of the management decisions faced in the operations area in different organizations and to help them learn how to approach operations management problems. It is also our purpose to provide the foundation for further study in more specialized courses in production and operations management. Finally, by emphasizing the importance of operations in making firms and countries competitive in our global economy, we hope to interest students in further study in the fascinating field of operations management.

To accomplish our objectives, the book is oriented toward both problem recognition and problem solving. Several chapters use large, integrative examples to illustrate the problems that can arise in actual situations. Analytical methods are used, but their limitations and potential misuse are also stressed. The examples, caselets, and problem materials are designed to give the student not only an understanding of the details of many operational decisions, but also a broad view of operations. We also stress the similarities and differences of operations management in different settings.

The changes in the third edition reflect shifts of emphasis encountered in practice as managers seek better ways to respond to international competition. Although some of the new material is technical, most is focused on matters of judgment and strategy. This is particularly evident in the discussions of quality and productivity, two areas that are inextricably linked, and where choice of managerial philosophy and commitment to goals are vital.

In the third edition, we have expanded the discussion of work flow analysis and tied this discussion to new software tools such as XCELL+, available from Scientific Press. Simulation tools such as this are revolutionizing the modeling of operations, making even complex models easy to build and analyze.

We have also expanded the discussion of total quality management, just-in-time production, and technology. The connection of operations to accounting and finance is examined in discussions of new methods of management accounting and justification of expenditures in new technology. Finally, new material has been added on operations strategy, including the interaction of marketing and operations.

In most organizations, production and delivery operations account for the majority of the expenditures and investments. The opportunities this creates makes operations management an interesting career, requiring an integrated (systems) view of the organization, a knowledge of marketing, finance and accounting, a knowledge of the application of mathematical and computer methods, and a high degree of interpersonal skills. We have found that an emphasis on the importance and complexity of operations management makes study in the area more enjoyable and challenging.

A WORD TO THE INSTRUCTOR

Several different types of courses can be based on this book. The extensive use of both manufacturing and service examples and problems has allowed us to use this book both as part of an MBA program and, in conjunction with some outside reading, for a graduate course in the management of services, including health-care operations. We have expanded the number of caselets in this edition. Because of the caselets and integrative examples used in several chapters, the text can be used either by itself, or supplemented by cases, or as background reading for a case-oriented course. The book can be used for a two-quarter course, or a two-semester course if some cases and outside readings are used.

The operations research techniques of queuing, simulation, and linear programming are treated in technical appendices. Each of these topics can be a significant part of the course, used only for reference, or deleted entirely. Sections in the text that require one of the appendices are indicated by a footnote, and can be skipped. Thus, the course can be designed to fit the backgrounds of the students as well as the desires of the instructors.

If the analytical topics are included, they can be covered with or without mathematical detail. As stated above, our discussion can be tied to easy-to-use computer tools. Key ideas from the three technical appendices can be covered without recourse to mathematics. In fact, we believe that some of the concepts (e.g., Little's Law in Appendix A, model building in Appendix B, and shadow prices for constrained resources in Appendix C) are crucial to the study of operations management.

We have designed the book so that chapters do not have to be used sequentially. The sequence of chapters can easily be varied to suit the individual preferences of the instructor. (Of course, we have placed the chapters in a sequence that we find useful in our own teaching.) By design the book contains more material than can be included in a one-semester course. This allows for the book to be used in different types of operations management courses (e.g., manufacturing or service-oriented courses), as well as for its continued use as the basic text in an operations management elective, perhaps supplemented by additional readings or cases.

At Cornell, for example, operations management is a one-semester course. Students have had introductory courses in statistics, economics, and accounting. Material from all three technical appendices is included. Several cases and outside readings are used to supplement the text. Several chapters are covered quickly. For example, Chapters 1, 2, and 3 can be covered in one week, and Chapter 5 can be covered in one day. A first-year course in service operations (such as health-care operations) might omit Chapters 10, 11, 12, and 14. An elective in service operations could cover in depth the material in Chapters 2, 5, 6, 7, 13, 15, and Appendices A, B, and C.

A WORD TO THE STUDENT

Material, especially in examples and problems, should be examined using both analysis and common sense. You should develop an appreciation for management issues even while you are learning technical material.

Each section in the book is followed by review problems designed to help you test your mastery of the material. You should complete them after reading each section before proceeding. After reading an entire chapter, try the problems assigned by the instructor. You should expect to need to re-read portions of the chapter as you are working on the problems. The problems range from easy to difficult, and cover both analytical techniques and the managerial concepts of the chapter. Working on problems and cases is the best way to solidify your knowledge.

In this revision, we have added many new references so that readers can do further study in a topic of special interest. Some of these references are technical in nature, but the majority are intended for a managerial audience. Since references can interrupt the flow, students are urged to read past references during a first reading of any topic. For term papers, subsequent courses, or research, the up-to-date references should prove useful.

ACKNOWLEDGMENTS

We are indebted to our past students for the improvements they have suggested. In addition, many of our colleagues have provided valuable comments. In particular, we would like to thank Professors Peter Billington of the University of Southern Colorado, Gabriel Bitran of MIT, Robert Machol of Northwestern University, Kavindra Malik of Cornell University, Lawrence Robinson of Cornell University, Jeff Rummel of Duke University, Linda Sprague of the University of New Hampshire, Mihkel Tombak of the University of British Columbia, and Elliott Weiss of the University of Virginia. The Johnson Graduate School of Management of Cornell University and the Fuqua School of Business of Duke University provided us with an excellent environment, challenging students, and clerical support, with special acknowledgment to the outstanding assistance of Donna Phoenix of Cornell and Cheryl Baxley of Duke. Finally, we would like to thank our families for supporting our work and helping us to escape from it, too.

chapter

1

Managing Operations

Global competition is a reality, with winners and losers that are constantly changing. International trade is growing significantly as a fraction of the world economy, but countries and companies are not sharing equally in this growth. For example, the U.S., U.K. and Canadian share of manufacturing exports has declined, while the French, Italian, West German and Japanese share has increased. Exports have fallen and imports have risen, *as a percent*, in many different industries in the United States (see Hill 1989, appendix, for data).

Winning and losing is not forever, for countries or companies. The Netherlands led the world in productivity for 85 years, followed by the United Kingdom for 105 years, followed by the United States for 100 (see Grayson 1988). Currently, many developed countries have similar productivity overall (see Baumol 1989); consequently, competition will be tougher than ever before.

Examples of corporate success and failure abound. Xerox dominated the copying machine market, only to lose then regain profitability and market share (see Jacobson and Hillkirk 1986). Ford Motor Company's imminent demise was trumpeted in the early 1980's, but they regained share and profits through good design and commitment to quality. Harley-Davidson was in danger of being swept away by Japanese competition, but by improving customer contact and manufacturing methods, it regained leadership in its market segment (see Holusha 1990). Entire indusries can win and lose. In 1988 seven of the top ten banks were Japanese, whereas ten years before the United States dominated the list (Grayson 1988). In semiconductor equipment United States market share slipped sharply from 1980 to 1990, dropping from over 80% to half that amount (see U.S. Congress 1990).

Even the basis of competition can change, creating winners and losers. Whereas comfort and visual attraction once sold cars, quality, safety, and innovation do now. As customers demand higher quality and more innovation, the automobile industry, throughout the world, has responded. The quality of automobiles from the United States improved from 1980 to 1990, from 8 to 1.75

defects per car (see Stertz 1990). Compared with the 1980 Japanese average of 3.0, the 1.75 figure is impressive. However, Japanese cars averaged 1.25 defects per car in 1990. (See Stertz 1990. Also see U.S. Congress 1989 for other comparative statistics, including data from other parts of the world.) In addition to quality, automobile companies are speeding up innovation (responding to customers' desires) by reducing the design time, the time between product concept and finished automobile. The importance of this new basis of competition, *speed*, is discussed in depth with many examples in *Fortune* (February 13, 1989).

If the basis of competition can change, and if both old and new competitors can be counted on to lower cost, improve quality, and find other ways to serve the customer, what can a company do? The answer is very simple but very hard to execute. First, all organizations must stay in touch with their customers so that they can know what the customers want at the present time. Second, organizations must aggressively improve cost, quality, design time, or other key factors because today's winner may be tomorrow's loser.

This book is about ways in which such improvements can be obtained. Constant improvement is required for all operations, and to achieve this an organization must have a clear definition of what customer needs they are serving. The *strategy* must be clear. To manage daily operations well, the product and process must be designed to facilitate achieving strategic goals. Finally, everyone must be involved in the never-ending search for *constant improvement* (often referred to by the Japanese word *kaizen*).

These ideas are not only simple, they are also old. Hayes et al. (1988, chapter 2) give some historical perspective and some old quotes that sound very current. Operations managers in the past contributed to the current high standard of living. From 1870 to 1979, output per labor-hour increased by 1100% in the United States, allowing a 40% reduction in the workweek and an eightfold increase in output per year (see Maddison 1982). The growing world trade opens markets to new competitors, many of whom are improving faster than United States and European companies. Managers in the United States, in particular, are sometimes charged with resting on their laurels rather than aggressively continuing to improve (for example see Berger et al. 1989).

Improvements in production methods go back to the wheel, lever, and inclined plane. The last two centuries have seen several major improvements, beginning with the development of interchangeable parts by Eli Whitney, between 1798 and 1800, while working on a government contract for muskets. In 1913 Henry Ford instituted the first assembly line, allowing specialization of tasks and faster rates of production. Ford's accomplishment reshaped the United States by providing a "car for the masses," whereas before the automobile had been a luxury item. The impressive production rate and quality (for the time) of the automobile industry was transferred to military use in World War II, and to other industries in the postwar period (see Hayes et al. 1988).

Throughout the time period preceding Ford's accomplishment (1895–1913), Frederick Taylor (the "father of scientific management") was investigating ways of improving workers' output by analyzing the methods and tools involved in a work assignment. Taylor's efforts were followed by many other industrial engineers, notably Frank and Lillian Gilbreth. Controversy surrounds Taylor's work even today (see *IIE Focus*, October 1989). Taylor introduced statistical time studies and obtained more output by working people harder. The Gilbreths focused on detailed work analysis also but tried to improve the ways jobs were done. Taylor used "rather tough talk" in dealing with people, causing a negative reaction that survives today. The Gilbreths used work improvements including new equipment and work methods. Their advice to ''combine, simplify, and eliminate . . .'' steps of a process is still valid.

During the 1940s, 1950s, and 1960s, many managers and academics rejected detailed analysis of work, stressing the individual's motivation and creativity. They pointed out, correctly in our opinion, that the best ideas for improvement come from people doing the work. Agreeing with that, we still believe that detailed analysis of a statistical nature should be used to improve quality and productivity. Throwing out detailed measurements of jobs, the basis of ''scientific management,'' was one of the biggest management errors of this century. However, the focus of detailed analysis must be on assisting the person doing the work; the worker must be empowered to make decisions and assisted in doing so. The synthesis of employee involvement and statistical analysis is evident in the work of ''total quality'' pioneers like W. E. Deming and J. M. Juran, who are given significant credit for upgrading Japan's manufacturing quality during the period from 1950 to 1970.

In addition to working on detailed operations, managers must also concentrate on bigger, more strategic questions. The recent past has taught us that both the small and the large issues matter. Small improvements add up to major strategic advantage. But if we are improving operations for an out-of-date product (or process), our organization will fail. Finding ways to manage operations effectively from strategy to details is the goal of this book, and it is an exciting opportunity for organizations and managers.

1-1 OPERATIONS MANAGEMENT: DEFINITIONS AND EXAMPLES

The constant improvement that will be necessary to survive in the 1990s can be good for all of us, since products will be cheaper and better. It will also insure that the job of *operations manager* will continue to be important and exciting.

Operations management is crucial to the success of all organizations. Banks are profitable if they perform the mechanics of financial transactions correctly and at low cost. Airlines are successful if their scheduling, maintenance, and flight operations are of very high quality and if costs are kept low. In general, operations managers must manage to produce high-quality, low-cost goods and services. The goods and services must meet *customer* needs and have quality and cost characteristics better than the *competitors'*. To meet customer needs and provide services and goods at higher quality and lower cost than competitors, operations managers must understand and help to shape the organization's overall strategy. How will we serve our customers, now and in the future? What sustainable advantage will we have over our competitors?

Operations managers must obtain and utilize resources to produce useful goods and services and thus meet the goals of the organization. The organization can be a manufacturer, a hospital, a university, or a department store. The goals can be to maximize profit, provide the best possible service within a budget, or simply ensure existence. The resources used can be quite different, ranging from drill presses, classrooms, and cardiac care units to doctors, mechanics, professors, and unskilled laborers.

Operations managers must also schedule work assignments, plan inventory levels, and make many decisions and plans regarding what work will be done and when it will be done. Because these tasks entail an immense amount of detail, managers often find it difficult to keep in mind the overall goals of the organization. Yet it is extremely important to maintain a larger view. For example, purchasing low-cost materials is not really cost-effective if poor quality or delivery performance forces inefficiencies on production.

We define *operations* to include any *process* that accepts *inputs* and uses *resources* to change those *inputs* (see Figure 1-1). For example, an outpatient health clinic accepts patients and utilizes doctors, nurses, drugs, and equipment to treat the patients. A mail-order house accepts physical goods and customer orders and utilizes material handling equipment, delivery capability, computers, and people to fill the orders. In the Postal Service, the inputs and outputs are identical (or are supposed to be) with only the time and place having been transformed. A bank accepts money, checks, and other forms of paper input and changes them to transactions on an account record. A steel plant has inputs of iron ore and coal (plus several others depending on the product) and produces steel of several types.

The operations manager must control the flow of inputs and outputs and the use of the resources involved. An effective manager must pinpoint and control day-to-day important problems such as assuring adequate supplies of the resources that are most limited. The operations manager must also think ahead, laying plans to acquire and use resources, and coordinate the implementation of the plan. For example, a manufacturer's plan might be to produce 5000 toasters, based on a sales forecast, during a month. The plan would include predictions of contribution to fixed costs and profit and end-of-month inventory. The day-to-day operations are then based on the plan, including detailed decisions on production quantities for each model of toaster, work force schedules, material ordering, and many other details of operation. If the longer-term plan is good, detailed operations will be easier to control. On the other hand, if day-to-day operations are well managed, it will be easier to plan.

Finally, managers must design the physical facilities, including the location and capacity, as well as the staffing and work flow to be used. For example, a rural area with one hospital may choose to add satellite outpatient clinics in other locations in order to meet the health needs of the area. For each satellite, the number of examination rooms, the staff size (doctors, nurses, aides, secretaries), and the location must be planned, considering not only patient convenience but also problems of coordination with and access to the parent facility.

In the preceding two paragraphs, we described three levels of operational

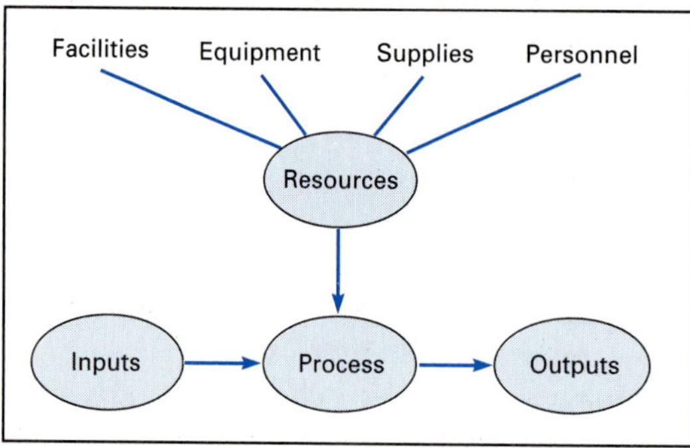

Figure 1-1 Model of the Operations Process

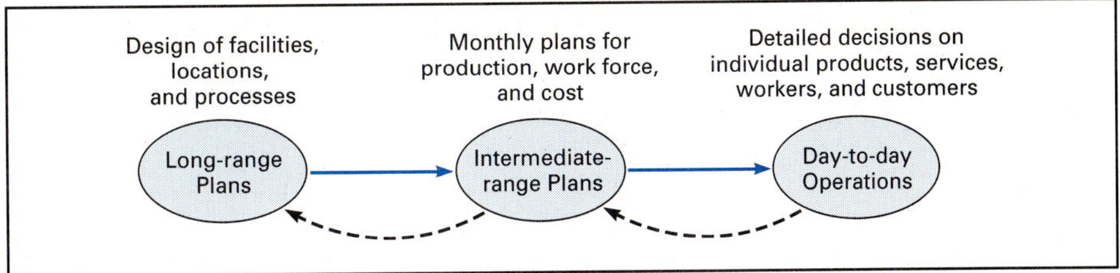

Figure 1-2 The Interaction of Day-to-day Operations and Longer-term Plans.

control: design, planning, and day-to-day control (see Figure 1-2). These different levels always vie for the manager's attention, with day-to-day control often winning. We believe that all three levels must be done well or none of them will be. Good day-to-day control requires good designs and plans.

Each of the problems raised previously for the toaster and clinic organizations is discussed in this book—facility and job design, capacity and location analysis, forecasting, work-force planning, inventory ordering procedures, material requirements planning, quality control—as well as many others.

Operations can be categorized in several ways. For example, service and manufacturing operations have some differences, the basic one being that service organizations often cannot inventory their service for later use. However, this is not always true. Examples of firms inventorying a service include restaurants buying portion-sized entrées rather than basic raw materials, pharmacies purchasing medications in "unit doses," and our writing this book rather than discussing operations management with you in person.

All organizations have the problem of coordinating the supply of their goods or services with the demands. When inventory is not available, other methods must be used. Table 1-1 gives some methods of coordinating supply and demand. Notice the parallel arrangement of ideas. For example, a waiting customer is, in a sense, an inventory of demand.

Nearly all the items in Table 1-1 can be used by both service and manufacturing organizations. Table 1-2 lists some typical manufacturing organizations and some operations management problems. Table 1-3 does the same for some service organizations.

Table 1-1 Actions to Coordinate Supply and Demand for Physical Goods and for Services

Supply Modifications	Demand Modifications
1. Inventory the good or service	1. Have the customers wait
2. Schedule workers according to demand (time of day, season, etc.)	2. Schedule customers by appointment
3. Subcontract to another organization	3. Provide substitute goods or services
4. Diversify work (e.g., do maintenance or preparation during a slack time)	4. Diversify demands by entering new markets to balance seasonal demand patterns
5. Provide excess capacity so that peak demand can be met	5. Turn some customers away during peak demand periods

Table 1-2 Manufacturing Organizations and Some of Their Operations Management Problems

Organization	Typical Problems: Before Operation	Typical Problems: During Operation
Air-conditioner manufacturer	Design building and assembly line, including task assignments	Plan material requirements; plan seasonal inventory accumulation and work-force patterns; maintain quality control system; maintain material-flow system
Cosmetic manufacturer	Design facility for "batch" operations	Obtain raw materials and packaging; make sequence and batch-size decisions for various items
Multilocation food product manufacturer	Design all facilities; choose location, capabilities, and capacity of plants, warehouses, and transportation links	Obtain raw materials (perhaps entering into long-term contracts with suppliers); determine which products are to be made at which plants; determine shipment patterns; plan "safety stocks" and seasonal inventories
Building contractor	Purchase capital equipment and obtain skilled work force	Sequence activities; obtain materials; perform quality checks; schedule work crews (perhaps at several locations)
Computer manufacturer	Design facility to be flexible for future products, to accept design changes easily, and to produce verifiably high-quality products	Plan production of each product line; schedule modifications requested by customers; manage quality control to guarantee good finished products
Manufacturer of specialty steel products, such as structural members for buildings	Design facility, with emphasis on production capabilities and material flow	Maintain materials inventory; sequence different jobs in the facility; manage "work-in-process" inventory; plan completion times

Even though Table 1-3 describes service operations, manufacturing organizations face essentially all these problems. In fact, manufacturing firms spend more on internal services than on labor to manufacture products. DeMeyer (1986) gives 13.5% as direct labor and 29.5% as manufacturing overhead for North American firms. The manufacturing overhead expenditures all provide some service. An IBM effort to improve quality and cost (Kane 1986) revealed that the biggest improvements may come in internal services rather than in making the product.

In the United States, productivity in manufacturing has grown at an average of approximately 3% per year since the 1950s. In services, productivity has grown less than 1% annually. The United States economy is composed of nearly 70% services, and manufacturing firms have more internal services than direct labor. For these reasons, today's operations manager is striving to bring

Table 1-3 Service Organizations and Some of Their Operations Management Problems

Organization	Typical Problems: Before Operation	Typical Problems: During Operation
Outpatient Clinic	Design facility and staffing plan	Schedule patients and employees
Hospital	Design facility and staffing plan	Schedule operating room; schedule elective patients; staff emergency room; schedule employees; maintain quality audit; maintain inventories of blood and supplies
Public school administration	Design or modify facilities and geographic coverage	Design bus routes; schedule classes; operate lunch programs
Mail-order house	Design distribution system (capacity and location of warehouses and transportation links); design order-entry system	Maintain inventories; expedite late orders; develop transportation plans
Banks	Design information-flow system; locate and design branch banks	Maintain and audit quality of information; plan employee schedules

productivity improvement in the service sector up to the level of the manufacturing sector.

Operations can also be categorized by demand type and process type (see Table 1-4).

Although the two breakdowns in Table 1-4 help us to think about different characteristics of problems, we must not be limited in our thinking by the table. Some ''batch'' manufacturers are trying to maintain quasi-continuous manufacturing by proper equipment selection and management techniques. (IBM calls their version of this ''Continuous Flow Manufacturing.'' We will discuss these approaches in Chapter 12.) Also, some organizations buy computer capability and other equipment that allows them to provide specialized products and services at a cost similar to that for high-volume operations. For example, flexible manufacturing systems (FMSs) are designed to do this.

Table 1-4 Two Categorizations for Types of Operations

Demand types	One-time	Special, but similar and frequent	High volume
Example	Construction	Health clinic	Film production

	CONTINUOUS		BATCH	
Process type	Distribution	Manufacturing	Producing standard products	Producing special products
Example	Postal Service	Oil refinery	Cosmetic production	Super-computer research installation

REVIEW PROBLEMS[1]

1. Refer to Table 1-1 and indicate which methods of demand–supply coordination would most likely be used in each of the following organizations:
   a. a large public accounting firm
   b. a furniture manufacturing firm with nationwide distribution
   c. a doctor's office

2. What type of demands and processes do universities have? List some operations management problems that universities have in delivering their services.

Solutions

1. In all three examples, the methods used will vary from one organization to another. Thus, answers other than those given here are possible.
   a. The accounting firm managers would certainly plan vacations at low demand times, and they might hire some extra clerical assistance for peak demand periods. They probably have some excess capacity on average, and they would attempt to enter other markets (management consulting) to partially balance the work load.
   b. The furniture manufacturing managers would inventory their products and would also frequently make customers wait for a particular color-fabric combination. They might use seasonal employees, and they would do maintenance and preparatory work during low-demand periods. They might diversify demand by entering (say) the institutional furniture market, which is less seasonal than retail sales.
   c. The doctor's office would use a queue and a customer schedule. They might turn some customers away, perhaps to another doctor's office. They would schedule support personnel to match demand patterns. They might choose not to have excess M.D. capacity because of the high cost of such capacity.

2. Universities have many different demands, but the most common type is ''special but similar and frequent'': students requiring specialized but similar degree programs. Most university processes are batch type, in which several students attend a class at a given time, for example. Universities have many operations: billing, dining, classroom scheduling, student information services, and so on.

1-2 MAJOR THEMES OF THIS BOOK

Three main themes will be revisited many times throughout this text. In this section we will introduce these themes and give illustrative examples.

[1]Review problems should be completed before proceeding to the next section. Nearly all sections in the book will have review problems, followed by a solution.

Theme 1:
Organizational Strategy Must Include Operations; Operations Strategy Must Consider Benefits Outside of Operations

Strategic aims for the operations area must begin with the customers and competitors. What business are we in, and who are the customers? Who are the competitors? How will these answers change in the future? Now and in the future, how can operations add value to the customers in a way that gives us a sustainable competitive advantage over our competitors?

The focus on customers and competitors implies that product design is part of operations strategy. Both marketing and operations must be considered in designing the product line. What segment of the market do we want? Can operations deliver the products desired at competitive cost and quality levels?

Continuing innovation must also be part of strategy. Operations cannot be measured only by cost and quality, but must be measured by the ability to change, to meet new customer needs, and to stay ahead of competitors.

Theme 2:
Organizations Must Integrate Strategy, Design, and Operations (SDO)

The methods for managing day-to-day operations (O) cannot be selected appropriately without knowing what the operating system is designed (D) to do and is capable of doing. The operating system design (and redesign) must be selected based on the organization's strategy (S). In turn, strategy must be determined considering both what our operating system is capable of accomplishing and the detailed methods of operating at which we can outperform our competitors. Strategy must guide design and operations; conversely, strategy must be guided by what we do well.

A second part of Theme 2 is that all three elements (SDO) matter. Not only must they fit together well, but the details must be handled well, every day in every way. Focusing only on strategy or only on operating details, or ignoring the design of the operating system and its effects on strategy and operating details, are three different ways to fail. Managing the details well will lead to success if the details are part of a solid strategy, and if the design of the operating system allows the firm to achieve its strategic aims.

Theme 3:
Quality is Fundamental in All Activities

Every function in every organization must be carried out with high quality. Otherwise, a competitor with higher quality will take your customers. Quality applies to manufactured products, but quality improvements must also be obtained in service organizations and in the services provided within manufacturing organizations. (Several references to this chapter and in Chapter 6 describe quality improvement methods applied to services, within both service and manufacturing organizations; see Kane 1986 and Tucker et al., 1987, for example.)

For a textbook, quality means that there are no (or few) errors, such as arithmetic mistakes and misspelled words. It also means that wording is clear, and that the main ideas are communicated well. It also means that the main ideas are the right ideas. Narrow definitions of quality are not acceptable today. We accept the challenge of producing a high quality book, one that adds value to the customer. (As with other products, the customer must accept responsibility for the use of the product.)

Quality must be carefully integrated into strategy, operating system design, and detailed management of operations in both service and manufacturing organizations. The entire organization must believe that striving for perfect quality in their work is essential to success.

SUMMARY: THREE THEMES

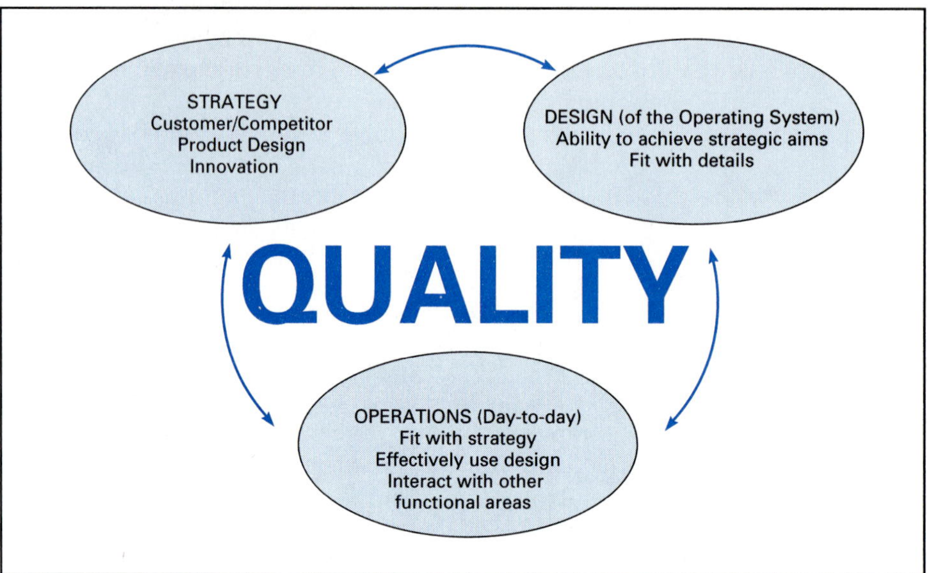

Figure 1-3 Three Themes of the Book.

A strategy must be selected by focusing on the customer and the competition, and operations must be part of the process. Strategic aims will be met only if design and operations fit well with the strategic aims. Quality must permeate all three of these areas, as well as the interaction of operations with other functional areas. Quality must be broadly defined, and everyone must be involved.

EXAMPLE: STRATEGY (WHAT BUSINESS ARE WE IN?)

The most well-known strategic failures are organizations that did not know what business they were in. Railroad companies in the early part of this century thought they were in the railroad business. In fact, they were in the transportation business, with trucks as an important competitor. The *customer's* need was for point-to-point transportation, and the railroads provided only the long-haul portion of that. Even though trucking was more expensive for the long-haul portion of the service, they could offer complete point-to-point service, faster and at competitive prices. The review problems ask you to consider other examples.

EXAMPLE: STRATEGY, DESIGN AND OPERATIONS (SDO)

Flexible automation, including flexible manufacturing systems (FMSs), is designed to allow companies to introduce new products, to produce individually designed products, and to respond quickly to individual customer needs. However, some companies have not achieved their goals with these systems because of a failure to integrate the strategy, design, and operations (SDO). (See Jaikumar 1986 for a discussion.) Suppose that a firm has a strategy to respond quickly to customer needs; a design consistent with that strategy is to purchase an FMS. At the operating level, some companies measure their FMS managers on the percent of time the system is up and running, or ''uptime.'' This measure may cause a manager to produce only a few items that he or she can manage well rather than utilize the flexibility of the equipment and obtain the strategic advantage that flexibility can give: Do not experiment to see how to add new products because trial runs cause lost production time; do not try to deal with individualized customer needs. Producing standard items in large batches can give nearly 100% uptime. This is but one example of how the operating details can determine the success or failure of a strategy and the strategic value of the operating system design.

EXAMPLES: QUALITY BROADLY DEFINED

Universities have many operations, including billing, class scheduling, and bus operations. As an example, quality for billing should be measured by correctness and timeliness of bills. (The fact that the bills are perceived as too high is a separate, but important, issue.) Poor-quality billing services lead not only to frustrated customers but also to late collections for the University, and large amounts of time spent by university employees to reconcile incorrect bills.

Banks get high marks for correctness. (They do not have 100% correct accounts, but nearly so.) To achieve this, some banks use quality assurance processes similar to methods used in manufacturing organizations. However, not all banks get high marks for quality, more broadly defined. Are reports easy to read, saving the customer time? Are computer systems and organizational practices designed to allow customers easy access to additional information? Do automated teller machines work when they are needed, such as on weekends and holidays? Increasingly, market share is determined by how easy it is for customers to obtain financial services, and correctness is not the only measure of quality.

REVIEW PROBLEMS

1. CAC, Inc., a producer of coated abrasives (sandpaper), is third in the industry in market share. Cost and quality for each of the five major companies in the industry is very similar. However, the top company has the fastest

and most reliable service time (from order placement to shipment arrival at the customer), and the general manager of CAC feels that service time is the key to increasing market share.

a. Briefly discuss the SDO approach that the firm might use. (There are many ways to answer this question, and it requires you to imagine how such an industry might operate.)

b. How might the firm measure the quality of its customer service? Give a few possible measures.

2. What business is the airline industry in, particularly with regard to the business traveler? What customer needs do they fulfill? What new competitors may exist in the near future?

3. Briefly discuss SDO for a hospital emergency room.

Solutions

1. This question can be answered in many, very different ways. This is true so often in this book that we will refrain from saying it in most cases.

   a. *Strategy*: A strategic goal might be that ''We will match the top company for average service time and be more reliable (have a smaller variation around promised times), and continue to match the cost and product quality of all competitors.''

      Design: One way to design the operating system to produce and deliver products faster (as implied by the above strategy) is to buy more equipment, or more flexible equipment, so that the production lead time is small. A second idea is to use a faster means of transportation.

      Operations: Managers, including production managers, must be measured on meeting target dates. This should be as important as cost and quality.

   b. Correctness of the shipment, with regard to product type and quantity. Average service time. Fraction of promised shipment dates that are met. Customer satisfaction, as measured by survey, compared with the competition.

2. They facilitate face-to-face meetings. Their customers need to be in the same location so that they can have better communication. Potential future competitors include trains (if superconductivity allows 300–mile-per-hour travel) and telecommunications companies (if we get used to seeing just an image instead of a person).

3. A strategic goal might be always to provide initial care within 15 minutes and always to have a bed to admit emergency patients to the hospital. The design might include extra capacity, in both beds and emergency-room facilities. The detailed operations might include not admitting elective surgery patients into the last few beds, instead saving them for emergencies. Also, the emergency room might have additional personnel on call, in case of heavy loads.

1-3 SUMMARY

Operations management has the responsibility for the production and delivery of physical goods and services. Consequently, it is an important topic of study for a potential manager, especially considering the broad definition of the field that we use. This book will discuss many significant operations problems and management tools that have been applied to them. Our examples will include challenges and opportunities that arise in service and manufacturing organizations, in profit-making and not-for-profit organizations.

The differences between manufacturing industries and service industries are not as strong as they would seem at first. Table 1-1 and the associated discussion indicate ways to coordinate supply and demand, and we found that each method can be used by either a manufacturing or a service organization. The subsequent chapters take advantage of this substantial overlap whenever possible. Only a few chapters are specifically limited to either service or manufacturing problems. In studying this material, we must learn to consider the applicability or lack of applicability of each approach in the context of the particular situation.

In this book we will discuss detailed operating problems such as forecasting, inventory control, work-force scheduling, and production planning. We will also analyze design issues such as equipment selection, facility location, and capacity analysis. Strategic issues will be presented in several parts of the book, including Chapter 17. Each of these, and the connections among them, are crucial to an organization's success.

No area is more important than operations management. Operations management requires the ability to manage people and invest in facilities; it requires the ability to handle many details, each of which matter, and to have a broader strategic focus. Productivity and quality improvements over the past 100 years have dramatically improved standards of living. Operations managers have the opportunity to do the same for the future.

PROBLEMS

*1. Name some operations management problems that occur in a bank.

2. Name some operations management problems that occur in constructing a building.

*3. Why is efficiency important to an agency that has a specified budget that cannot be exceeded and must be spent?

4. How are operations decisions affected by policies in marketing? In human resources? In finance?

5. Select an organization that you know. Discuss SDO. Are there failures of coordination of SDO that you can describe?

*6. Name one key difference between service and manufacturing operations management. How does this difference impinge on decisions?

7. What three demand types were discussed in this chapter? Name at least one example of each, other than the example given in Table 1-4.

---

*Problems with an asterisk have answers in the back of the book.

*8. The Postal Service has an essentially continuous process. Yet some of their key decisions involve batch decisions: how often to make deliveries (of a batch of mail), how often to pick up mail from collection points, and how many collection points to have. What major considerations are involved in these batching decisions?

9. What capacity-related design considerations and demand modifications are most important to a city that is planning to build a sports arena?

*10. Name an operation in which the basic method of demand–supply coordination is to inventory the product during periods of relatively low demand.

*11. Name three strategic goals that a hospital might have, and state some ways in which they conflict with each other.

12. What are the three major themes of this book? How might they be applied to a consulting firm specializing in manufacturing management?

13. State three concepts of quality for a textbook. Which is most important, in your opinion?

14. In what businesses is a major state university engaged? What do their customers need from the university? What new competitors might exist in the future?

*15. Place yourself in the position of manager of production for a medium-size consumer goods manufacturer that introduces several new products each year. As manager you are part of a new product committee. Marketing has suggested a new product for introduction next year called a flubscrub.

   a. Why would you be asked to serve on a new product committee?
   b. Other members of the committee include representatives from the marketing and finance areas. What information will you need from them concerning the flubscrub?
   c. What information will you have to provide the committee to aid in the decision whether to market the flubscrub?

16. For each of the following organizations, give a few examples of inputs, resources, and outputs. State whether the operation would be labor or capital intensive.

   a. telephone company
   b. restaurant
   c. book publisher
   d. furniture reupholstery shop
   e. steel mill

17. For the organizations listed in problem 16, describe some production manipulations and demand modifications that would be used to coordinate supply and demand. Refer to Table 1-1.

18. Labor saving devices have provided an important source for productivity increases in manufacturing. Compare the growing service sector with the manufacturing sector in terms of methods and rate of productivity increases.

REFERENCES

BAUMOL, W.J., "Is There a U.S. Productivity Crisis?" *Science*, February 3, 1989.

BERGER, S., M.L. DERTOUZOS, R.K. LESTER, R.M. SOLOW, AND L.C. THUROW, "Toward a New Industrial America," *Scientific American*, June, 1989.

DEMEYER, A., "The Use of Manufacturing as a Competitive Weapon in the International Markets," *Gestion 2000*, 2, pp. 123–136, 1986.

Fortune, "How Managers Can Compete through Speed," February 13, 1989.

GRAYSON, C.J., "Productivity for All Seasons: Yesterday, Today, and Tomorrow," in *Competing through Productivity and Quality*, Y.K. Shetty and V.M. Buehler, eds., Cambridge, Mass.: Productivity Press, 1988.

HAYES, R.H., S.C. WHEELWRIGHT, AND K.B. CLARK, *Dynamic Manufacturing: Creating the Learning Organizations*, New York: Free Press, 1988.

HILL, T., *Manufacturing Strategy: Text and Cases*, Homewood, Ill.: Irwin, 1989.

HOLUSHA, J., "How Harley-Davidson Outfoxed the Imports," *The New York Times*, August 12, 1990.

IIE Focus, October, 1989. Published by the Institute of Industrial Engineers.

JACOBSEN, G., AND J. HILLKIRK, *Xerox: American Samurai*, New York: Macmillan, 1986.

JAIKUMAR, R., "Postindustrial Manufacturing," *Harvard Business Review*, November–December, 1986.

KANE, E., "IBM's Quality Focus on the Business Process," *Quality Progress*, April, 1986.

MADDISON, A., *Phases of Capitalist Development*, Oxford: Oxford University Press, 1982.

STERTZ, B., "Big Three Boost Car Quality But Still Lag," *The Wall Street Journal*, April 4, 1990.

TUCKER, F.G., S.M. ZIVAN, and R.C. CAMP, "How to Measure Yourself against the Best," *Harvard Business Review*, January–February, 1987.

U.S. CONGRESS, OFFICE OF TECHNOLOGY ASSESSMENT, *Making Things Better: Competing in Manufacturing*, OTA-JTE-443, Washington, D.C.: U.S. Government Printing Office, February, 1990.

chapter

2

The Strategic Role of Production Processes in Manufacturing and Services

Virtually every organization depends on the production (or operations) function to transform inputs such as raw materials, labor, capital, technology, and energy into usable outputs, which are bundles of goods and services. How effectively the organization manages this transformation often determines the success of the company in the competitive marketplace. This chapter explores different kinds of production processes in both manufacturing and service organizations.

To understand the role of the production process, it is first necessary to become familiar with basic process characteristics and to identify fundamental differences among types of processes. Then we can address the strategic relationship between the *product* (a good or a service) and the *process* by which it is produced.

It is important to understand the unique properties of services that make them different from manufacturing operations. There are also many similarities between manufacturing and service processes, and we can often improve the management of service operations by adopting manufacturing process ideas and technology. For similar reasons, it is useful to be able to distinguish among different types of services. This can be accomplished by examining classifications of service operations.

2-1 THE PRODUCTION PROCESS

Consider a small service organization, The Yuppie Car Wash Company.

Jane Dow (known by her friends as "the Dow") recently opened a new car wash in an affluent suburb of a major metropolitan area. Dow decided to cater to the high-priced segment of the car-wash market and to try as much as possible to service expensive cars that are highly pampered by their owners. The Yuppie Car Wash, as Dow chose to name her enterprise, uses a two-stage wash and cleaning process. In the first stage, cars are washed using state-of-the-art automatic car-wash machines with brushes that are "baby-bumper smooth." The second-stage of the process involves the cleaning of the interior of the cars.

Yuppie has two automatic car-wash machines, each of which costs $150,000. To be cleaned, a car need only go through one of the machines. Both machines are identical and can process cars in parallel. These machines are fed from a single common waiting line. They are imported from Italy and use extremely fine brushes that are guaranteed not to scratch even the most delicate paint finishes. Each machine requires 130 seconds to wash a car. It also takes an additional 20 seconds for one car to exit the machine while another car simultaneously enters it. This standard is set sufficiently high so that there is comfortable spacing between the two cars.

The second stage of Yuppie's process, which concentrates on cleaning the car's interior, is labor intensive and is performed in one of two interior cleaning centers (ICC). Each ICC is staffed by at most three employees. In each ICC the cleaning process for a car requires a total of 6 labor-minutes; that is, this job can be performed by one person in 6 minutes, by two persons in 3 minutes, and so on. (This standard includes the time required to move the car into and out of the ICC.) Dow has found that four or more persons tend to get in each other's way and do not save a proportional amount of time.

Yuppie's production process is illustrated in Figure 2-1 using what is commonly referred to as a *process-flow diagram* (see, for example, Marshall 1974 or Bohn et al. 1986). The diagram illustrates the general flow of product or service from input to final output. In addition to showing the different stages of the production process (shown as rectangles), the diagram includes the various kinds of *inventory* designed into the process (shown as inverted triangles). The inventory of cars that have driven up to Yuppie and are awaiting service is directly comparable to the inventory of raw materials typically encountered immediately prior to the initial stages of a manufacturing process. This analogy extends to the *work-in-process* (*WIP*) inventory of cars that have been washed and will soon enter one of the two ICCs. This is much like the WIP inventory found between work centers in a manufacturing process. Finally, there is the *finished-goods inventory* of cars that have been cleaned and parked, and await being picked up by their owners.

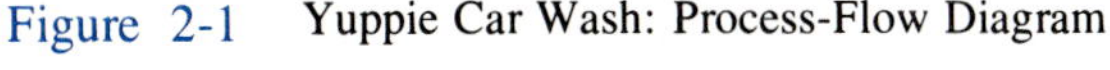
Figure 2-1 Yuppie Car Wash: Process-Flow Diagram

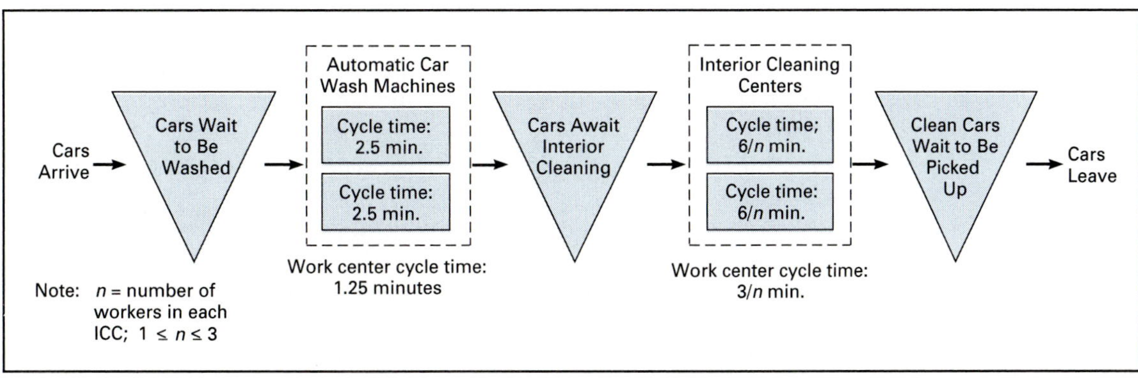

There are two stages to Yuppie's process, so we refer to it as a *multistage* production process. The first stage, which is performed by a relatively expensive machine and requires very little direct labor, is *capital intensive*, whereas the second stage is *labor intensive*. Whenever a process involves multiple stages, it must be designed and managed to take into account the relationship between product flows in each of the various stages. For example, the time required for each car—that is, the *cycle time* of a car in each automatic car-wash machine—is equal to 130 + 20 = 150 seconds, or 2.5 minutes. Thus, the *capacity* of each automatic car-wash machine is 1/2.5 = 0.4 car per minute, or equivalently, 24 cars per hour. Since there are two automatic car-wash machines, the capacity of the first stage of Yuppie's process is 2(24) = 48 cars per hour. In this manner we see that capacity provides a measure of potential *rate of production*.

Similarly, we see that the cycle time per car in each ICC is $6/n$ minutes, where n is the number of people assigned to work in the ICC. Thus, if Dow schedules two workers in each ICC, the capacity of each ICC is one car every 3 minutes, or 20 cars per hour; since there are two ICCs, the resulting capacity of the interior cleaning process is 2(20) = 40 cars per hour. In this case the capacity of the two ICCs is less than that of the first stage; thus, the ICCs are the *limiting* (or *bottleneck*) *resource*. Therefore, the capacity of the total process is 40 cars per hour, the capacity of the bottleneck process.

By increasing the number of workers assigned to each ICC, Dow can increased the capacity of the second stage of the process. This gives her the capability to manage the bottlenecks. For example, if three workers are assigned to each ICC, the capacity of the second stage increases to 60 cars per hour. Now the first stage is the bottleneck process, and the capacity of the system is 48 cars per hour.

Even if Dow schedules enough workers in each ICC to achieve a theoretically perfect balance between the two stages of the process, it is important to realize that at times either work-in-process inventory will occur between the two stages or the ICCs may be waiting (or *starved*) for work even though one or both automatic car-wash machines may be running. This is due to the variability in processing times. Because it is automatic, there will be relatively little variability in automatic car-wash service time. There will, however, be greater variability in ICC service time because of the inherent nature of the interior cleaning process, which is a function of the type and size of the car (sports car versus full size), type of interior, the state of the interior (has it been one week or one year since the last cleaning?) and the efficiency of the particular crew assigned to the ICC (how experienced are they? how rigidly are their jobs defined by management? will they be as fast on Saturday at 7:00 A.M. as they will be in the early afternoon?) Dow can reduce the average level of work-in-process inventory by scheduling the capacity of the ICCs to be greater than 48 cars per hour. However, if she plans the capacity to be too large, she then incurs the tangible and intangible costs of idle workers. These intangible costs include the carryover of inefficient work ethic, as well as the potential cost of irritating customers who are waiting seemingly long periods of time for their cars to enter the first stage of the process while seeing workers standing around doing nothing!

In the process-flow diagram for the Yuppie Car Wash Company, we see three different types of *queues* (that is, waiting lines) corresponding to the various types of inventory occurring in this system. The effective management of queues is an essential part of the study of production systems. This applies to planning for queues, which addresses issues such as the physical location of the queue and the capacity of the queue. It also applies to controlling the queue, for which we must determine in what order goods will be produced or customers will be served, and manage the flow of information about products (or customers) in the queue.

Although the process flow for Yuppie Car Wash is straightforward, it enabled us to consider important aspects of the process and to understand better the way in which the various components of the process combine to produce the service. The systematic application of ''combine, simplify, and eliminate'' to process-flow analysis of large-scale operations has vast potential to increase overall process effectiveness and efficiency.

It is the management of the production process that is the topic of this book, and throughout the chapters that follow we will learn considerably more about this challenging task. For now, let us continue to focus on the basic types of production processes.

REVIEW PROBLEMS

1. a. Even though different types of inventory are pictured separately in the process-flow diagram for the Yuppie Car Wash Company, it is common for different types of inventory (and hence, queues) to occupy the same physical waiting area. Looking at Yuppie's process-flow diagram as shown in Figure 2-1, which waiting areas should be kept separate and which might be combined? Explain your answer.
   b. Planning the size of each waiting area is also a significant issue concerning the design of production processes. Briefly discuss factors affecting the size of Yuppie's waiting areas, and provide some indication of their size relative to one another.
   c. What sequencing rule (also referred to as the *queue discipline*) should Yuppie use to set the order in which cars will be processed?

2. The points that were addressed in the preceding question were discussed primarily within the context of a service organization. Briefly discuss similarities and differences between these points as they pertain to both manufacturing and service operations.

Solutions

1. a. Yuppie may wish to combine the parking area for arriving (dirty) cars and finished (clean) cars. In fact, displaying ''before'' and ''after'' may be good advertising. In addition, the cost of two separate parking lots may be prohibitive.

   On the other hand, it may not be desirable to combine cars awaiting interior cleaning with either of the other two queues. The time required to drive a car from the automatic car-wash machines to the main parking lot and then drive it back to the ICCs may lengthen considerably the time required to service the car. Also, some confusion about the quality of interior cleaning may arise from customers seeing partially clean cars parked in the main lot.
   b. Assuming that the incoming and clean cars are parked in the same lot, Yuppie should plan this lot to be large enough to handle its periods of peak business. There is, of course, a trade-off in regard to this decision,

since Yuppie will not want to run out of parking space for arriving customers, but more space is costly.

We would expect the WIP waiting area to be relatively small. It should, however, be large enough to accommodate differences in service times in the automatic car-wash machines and the ICCs. It would be undesirable to have cars *blocked* from leaving the automatic car-wash machines as a result of a lack of space.

c. Since customers will presumably wait for their cars to be cleaned, Yuppie will probably follow the first-come, first-served priority sequencing rule. This rule is common among service operations of this type.

2. The points mentioned in the solution to review problem 1 need to be addressed in both manufacturing and service operations. Because customers are generally not present in the manufacturing process, we typically enjoy greater flexibility in resolving these issues. The location of waiting areas, for instance, can be selected to make the production process more efficient, allowing for physical constraints arising from the nature of the product. (For example, when processing food, cooked food must be kept away from raw ingredients.) On the other hand, in a service operation, we must plan for and continually manage the process with an awareness of the customers' presence. The customers' experience while waiting may directly affect their perception of the quality of service.

Determining the relative size of waiting areas is an important decision concerning both types of operations. As the size increases, we are generally faced with the challenge of managing and controlling the inventory. When this ''inventory'' consists of people, we need to plan carefully such issues as how customers are treated while waiting, how long customers wait, and how customers are kept informed of their status in line. The effective management of this task encompasses many behavioral issues.

Finally, manufacturing operations usually offer much greater latitude in sequencing jobs, provided the finished good is produced in a reasonable amount of time. For instance, if a sophisticated piece of machinery has been set up with intricate tooling to produce a particular type of part, the manager may choose to select all goods in the queue that require that particular part and advance them through that stage of the process. An entire theory of scheduling has evolved over the past several decades, and we will address some of these ideas in Chapters 11 and 13.

2-2 WAYS TO COMPETE

As a consumer of goods and services, think about the differences in products (that is, goods and services) that result in your selection of one product over another. Often we purchase simply on the basis of *low cost*, especially for products that we use in high volume and that vary relatively little across suppliers. Alternatively, we sometimes require a *customized* product that is tailored to fit our unique needs. This occurs when we seek the services of a highly-trained professional, such as a physician or management consultant, or a special custom-made product, such as contact lenses. Beyond seeking a customized product, we sometimes look for an *innovative* good or service.

Consider, for example, the architect who is very good at putting together a home or office building that is customized to meet our particular needs, and contrast this against the architect who develops an entirely new design concept that not only meets our needs, but offers an innovative approach to building design. Also, there are certain goods and services that we select on the basis of their *quality,* and we may be willing to pay a premium for them. This applies, for example, to top-notch services or extremely reliable consumer products. Finally, we select goods and services on the basis of other factors as well. For example, we often base purchasing decisions on *time*-related attributes, ranging anywhere from the time required to develop or produce a product to the time required to deliver a service (see Blackburn 1991).

Competing on the basis of low cost, customization, innovation, quality, and time have direct implications on the design and management of the process that delivers the product. We can design the process to produce a high-volume, low-cost good or service. Alternatively, we can design the system to be *flexible,* so that it is capable of handling a high degree of customization and, if desired, innovation, as well as of adjusting to changing levels of demand. Many fast-food restaurants offer a limited menu and compete primarily on the basis of cost, whereas expensive gourmet restaurants may offer a broader range of menu choices and thereby compete on flexibility. (Both may be high quality, but in different senses.)

It is useful to differentiate among processes on the basis of their strategically planned degree of standardization or customization (see Sari 1981). The firm that produces to finished-goods inventory and supplies its customers from this inventory operates in a *make-to-stock* environment. Since goods are produced to inventory, there is usually little or no customization. Alternatively, organizations that produce to customer order, thus allowing for customization, operate in a *make-to-order* environment. There are varying degrees of customization within this strategy. When component parts and subassemblies of a product are produced and stored in inventory, and assembly of the final product is delayed until a customer order is placed, the process is referred to as *assemble-to-order*. By operating within an assemble-to-order strategy, the customer is afforded some degree of customization. When the item is produced to meet the customer order, and production begins in the early stages of the physical construction of the product, the strategy is one of *make-to-order*. Finally, if customization is required in the design stages of the good or service, the environment is one of *engineer-to-order*.

The notion of competing on quality is also extremely important. ''Quality'' in its common usage takes into account a variety of attributes. As we will see in Chapter 6, it is useful to explore the definition of quality so that we know exactly what it encompasses. For example, quality is often defined as ''fitness for use'' or ''conformance to requirements.'' It is common in everyday usage, however, to include the ''grade'' of a product or a service within the assessment of its quality. In this regard, the high-priced, U.S. made car is commonly viewed as a ''high quality'' car while the standard model, bottom of the line Japanese car is often viewed as a ''lower quality'' car. The comparison of these two products is actually being made on the basis of grade rather than quality. As we well know, it is quite possible (and often the case) that someone might pay twice as much for the American made car, only to have it require repair considerably more often and last a shorter time than the ''cheaper'' car. Quality also includes notions of reliability, dependability, and responsiveness. For this reason, it is useful to keep separate the concepts of grade and quality.

Types of Production Processes

We now examine different types of production processes. First we consider two fundamentally different types of processes, known as *job shops* and *flow shops*. The various types of processes are further refined and then situated along a continuum. Each process type enables the organization to compete in a different manner. The choice of process can be effectively employed within the company's strategic plan for competing in the marketplace.

A job shop is a production process that is designed for low-volume production of highly customized products or services. Since job shops are geared for low-volume, customized production, they are typically labor intensive, and moreover, require a relatively highly skilled work force. Also, job shops utilize a production layout that is more process oriented. *Process layouts* are arranged on the basis of the various processes and tasks that are typical of the general good or service that the process is responsible for delivering. For example, in a machine shop, which is a classic job shop, the workplace is often arranged according to the type of machine; that is, drill presses are located in one area, and milling machines are arranged together in another part of the facility.

Each job within the job shop follows its unique path (or *route*) through the facility. This random routing of jobs is a function of the degree of customization, low volume, and the high skill level required to produce the product. The challenges of managing a job shop relate directly to the skill level of the workers and the scheduling of product through the shop, together with the vast amount of information that is required to produce highly varying items to desired specifications and to keep track of each item in the system.

A flow shop is a production system that is designed for high-volume production of a standardized product. The automobile assembly line is the classic example of a flow shop. Because of the standard nature of the good or service, the skill level required of the workers need not be high, and there is often opportunity for specialization of labor, as well as automation of part or all of the process. Thus, flow shops often exhibit more of a capital-intensive nature.

Since the demands for customization that are placed on the process are low, it is common for products in a flow shop to follow a *serial* or straight-line routing through the shop. Hence, the layout of the process is essentially determined by the manner in which the product is constructed; that is, flow shops employ a *product layout*. Managers of flow shops are concerned with problems arising from a relatively low skilled work force performing narrowly defined jobs, as well as with the effective utilization of expensive equipment that is not readily adaptable to changes in the environment.

In addition to "job shop" and "flow shop," there are other terms that can be used to identify production processes. For example, a *project* is a one-time, usually large task that is made up of a set of activities that must be performed subject to precedence requirements. The construction of a building or the development and introduction of a new product are common examples of projects. Since projects are highly customized and unique, we can view their corresponding process as an extreme case of a job shop. (Projects are addressed in Chapter 4, where we discuss techniques that have been developed for managing and controlling the many tasks that constitute the project.)

The *batch process* lies between the job shop and the flow shop. As suggested by the name, products move through the production facility and are produced at each work center in *batches* (or *lots*), which can range in size from a handful to several thousand. The batch process allows for some degree of customization, but considerably less than in a pure job shop.

As noted earlier, the assembly line is an example of a flow shop. The extreme version of a flow shop is a *continuous-flow* process. Continuous-flow processes are extremely capital intensive and are encountered, for example, in the petroleum and chemical industries. In this setting the process is set up to run for a relatively long period of time and once set into motion requires little direct labor and allows for little change in the specified production.

These different processes can be placed along a continuum ranging from low volume, high customization to high volume, low customization (see Figure 2-2).

In today's globally competitive environment, it is essential that upper-level management view the selection of process as a strategic decision. It is not enough simply to be able to distinguish among the various types of processes. Rather, as Hayes and Wheelwright (1984) point out, the selection of a particular process type must be made in conjunction with the nature of the product (good or service) produced by the firm. In addition, this strategic decision must be viewed as being *dynamic*; that is, it changes over time in response to factors in the environment.

Within the study of marketing, the concept of the *product life cycle* is extremely helpful in planning strategy for a product or service over time (Levitt 1965; Kotler 1988). The ''product'' to which the life cycle concept applies can range anywhere from an entire industry to a specific product brand, although the nature of the life cycle usually differs between these extremes. It is often useful to apply the concept to an intermediate level, such as a product class (Day 1986). For example, instead of looking at the entire automobile industry or a particular brand of car, we may wish to apply the concept to sports cars.

The behavior of a typical product life cycle is illustrated in Figure 2-3. Observe that the product begins in the introduction (or *incubation*) stage, characterized by a high rate of product innovation and change, together with a low sales volume. As acceptance of the product increases, the demand for the product increases rapidly, and the product is said to be in the *growth* stage. As this stage continues, the rate of product innovation begins to slow as the product features become more standardized. The product then reaches the *mature* stage in which a few changes are made to the basic design of the product as demand peaks. As the cycle progresses, some products enter the *decline* phase, in which demand begins to decrease.

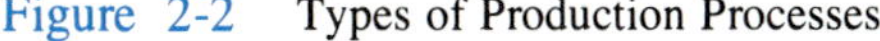

Figure 2-2 Types of Production Processes

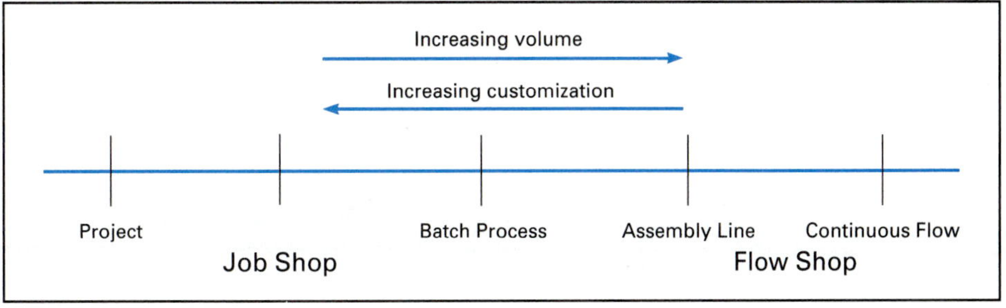

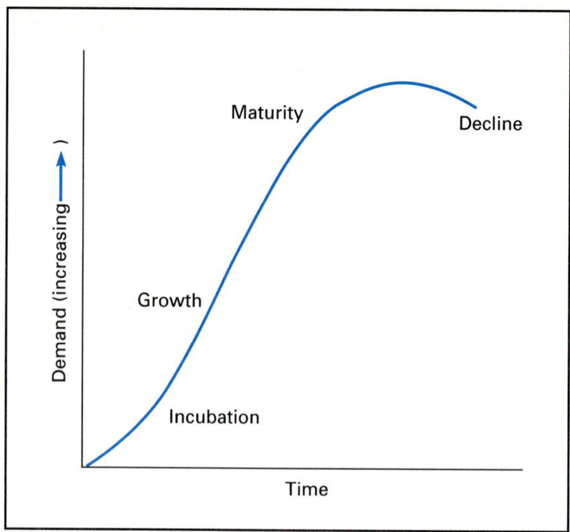

Figure 2-3 Product Life Cycle

Hayes and Wheelwright (1984) observe that from a strategic perspective the choice of process must be viewed in conjunction with the product life cycle. Their product–process matrix is depicted in Figure 2-4. In this matrix the product life cycle is measured along the top of the matrix, and process type is indicated along the left side. The levels of demand and degree of customization serve as a useful measure of the position of the product in its life cycle. In this manner, low volume and high customization typify products in the early stage, whereas high volume and low customization characterize products in the mature stage. Notice that process types range from job shop (toward the top of the matrix) to flow shop.

Figure 2-4 Product–Process Matrix.

(Adapted from R. Hayes and S. Wheelwright, *Restoring Our Competitive Edge: Competing through Manufacturing*, New York: John Wiley & Sons, 1984. With permission.)

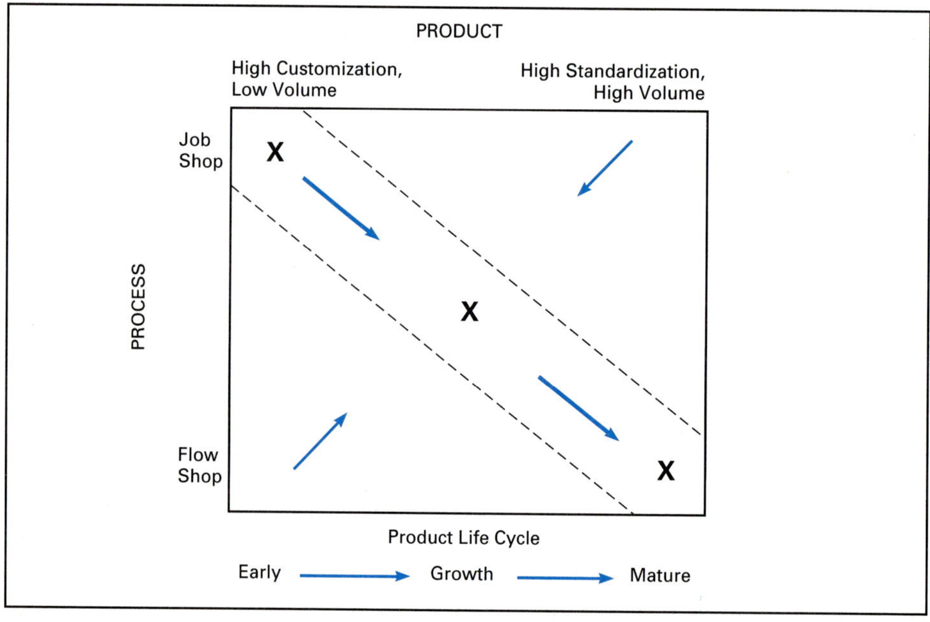

In their strategic analysis, Hayes and Wheelwright observe that by positioning itself along the main diagonal, a company is able to match the nature of the product with the most effective process type. That is, job shops are best suited for low volume, highly customized production, whereas flow shops are better able to handle high-volume mass production. Moreover, as the product evolves along its life cycle, a corresponding strategic change in process should occur; that is, movement should occur down the main diagonal.

Manufacturing and corporate strategy will be discussed in greater detail later (Chapter 17). We mention product–process strategy here so that we can begin to think about how the operations management decision concerning which type of process to implement can be viewed within the framework of the organization's competitive strategy. It is necessary to recognize some additional ramifications of the product–process relationship. Not all companies must situate themselves along the main diagonal. Some companies have deliberately chosen to position themselves off the main diagonal to achieve a specific competitive advantage in the marketplace. For example, Volvo chooses to produce its automobile, a very mature product, using a process that is more like a job shop than a typical assembly line (Gyllenhammar 1977; Kapstein and Hoerr 1989). The company must realize exactly what it is doing and be able to justify it on a strategically determined competitive basis.

What drives this decision—the product or the process? The answer to this question must ultimately be decided by top-level management in the strategic plan for the firm. It is important, however, that the choice of product and process be consistent. As the company considers expansion into new products, it must look carefully into whether existing process capability adequately matches the new products. Also, as the company becomes more diverse in its product offerings, it must choose carefully where each product will be produced throughout its production facilities (see, for example, Hayes and Wheelwright 1984 or Skinner 1974).

REVIEW PROBLEMS

1. Consider the Yuppie Car Wash example presented earlier in this chapter. On what basis does Yuppie compete?

2. Provide examples of make-to-stock, assemble-to-order, make-to-order, and engineer-to-order in both manufacturing and service organizations.

3. The *lead time* of a product is the length of time required from the moment when an order is placed until the time the item is delivered to the customer. Which would have shorter lead times, make-to-stock, make-to-order, or assemble-to-order? Explain why.

Solutions

1. Yuppie competes on the basis of grade of service, quality of service, and speed of service. Customers will go to Yuppie expecting appropriate treatment of expensive cars (and temperamental owners). Quality of service will be measured by achieving and maintaining a consistent level of (high-grade) cleaning, as well as dependability of the service.

2. Among manufacturing organizations, producers of consumer products (such as packaged food and clothing) are typically make-to-stock producers. The automobile industry provides an example of both make-to-stock and assemble-to-order. In the first instance, companies produce cars with prespecified options and ship them to car dealers. Alternatively, prior to building the car, consumers can specify the combination of options they would like included in the car. The consumer generally selects from among existing options, which are produced and stocked to inventory independently of, and prior to, the customer's order.

   An example of a make-to-order manufacturing company is a small furniture manufacturer for which customers select furniture from a catalog; production of the furniture from the raw materials begins after the order is placed. The aerospace contractor that designs and builds equipment to be used in the space program is an example of engineer-to-order.

   McDonald's restaurants have designed their service operations to follow a make-to-stock strategy, whereas Burger King has traditionally been more assemble-to-order. McDonald's serves customers from stores of finished-goods inventory, whereas Burger King stores the cooked hamburger patty and then assembles the completed burger to customer specifications (no onions, extra pickle, and so on). Traditional, sit-down gourmet restaurants with waiter service are usually make-to-order. The management consulting firm that develops an innovative solution approach to a complex business problem facing one of its clients is an engineer-to-order service.

3. Make-to-stock has shorter lead times. One merely has to retrieve items from finished-goods inventory to satisfy customer demand. In make-to-order operations, the lead time encompasses the time required to fabricate and assemble the item through all stages of production. It may also include lead times for purchasing component parts from outside suppliers. Assemble-to-order production is between these two extremes. It offers some degree of customization with smaller lead times than make-to-order.

2-3 SERVICE OPERATIONS

Services have become the predominant component of the U.S. economy, accounting for over 70% of the gross national product. As indicated in Chapter 1, productivity growth in the service sector has been much lower than in manufacturing for many years. It is therefore no surprise that there is a growing interest concerning the effective management of the production function in service organizations.

Service organizations and their operations have some characteristics that differentiate them from manufacturing organizations (Fitzsimmons and Sullivan 1982). Perhaps the key characteristic is that the customer of a service organization is a participant in, as well as a direct recipient of, the service. The process must be designed and managed to reflect the customer's presence in the system. For example, jobs should be designed with a sensitivity toward the manner in which workers and customers interact. Facilities often need to be located near the customer to facilitate customer access and convenience. Also, the customer's presence contributes to the uncertainty and variability in the delivery of the operation.

Another distinctive characteristic of services is that a service typically cannot be inventoried. For many services, production and consumption occur simultaneously, and it is not possible to produce in advance for later consumption. This has a direct effect on managing the capacity of the process. Manufacturing firms, in anticipation of a period of peak demand, can produce to inventory in advance of the peak demand. This affords them the opportunity to level production over the year. Services, however, often must plan capacity to meet peak demand. The Yuppie Car Wash, for example, must design its process to be able to accommodate peak demand, which will probably occur on Friday evenings and Saturdays. During periods of low demand, the excess capacity will remain idle. This property places heavy emphasis on the importance of managing capacity in conjunction with managing demand. Since demand management is typically the responsibility of the marketing function, service organizations frequently require careful coordination and critical cooperation between marketing and operations.

Services are often labor intensive. While this is not true of all services, labor intensiveness requires that we pay particular attention to the work force and the manner in which they interact with the customer. Quality control becomes crucial and also a little more difficult as we attempt to control the interaction of the worker and the customer. Levitt (1972) claims that ''discretion is the enemy of order, standardization, and quality.''

Service operations frequently employ various techniques to limit discretion on the part of both customers and workers. By offering a limited menu or by not allowing substitutions in the menu, a restaurant seeks to reduce customer discretion. As Levitt notes, McDonald's restaurants limit worker discretion in the preparation and serving of french fries by using a standard input of precut, partially cooked frozen potatoes, a specially designed fryer, which is strategically situated in the layout of the operation, and a special-purpose wide-mouth scoop that is designed to deliver a standard-size serving.

Finally, services are often intangible in nature. For instance, it is not unusual for two or more persons to perceive the outcome of the same service on the same day quite differently. (Have you ever discussed one of your classes with your classmates and found, much to your surprise, that you hold dramatically different, sometimes conflicting views on the overall quality of that same class?) This makes it extremely difficult to measure the output and quality of the service. The classic case of a telephone operator illustrates this point nicely. Often telephone companies attempt to measure the effectiveness of an operator by monitoring the number of phone calls that can be handled on a per-hour basis. This may adversely affect the perception of operator-service quality for someone who requires assistance, since the operator might choose to terminate a long inquiry prematurely.

This intangibility of a service also leads to a unique relationship between the product and the process. That is, the process and, in particular, the customer's role in the process actually become part of the service that is delivered. Classroom teaching, especially the case method, provides an excellent example. The learning on the part of the student is not only a function of the information that is conveyed by the teacher, but also depends on the students' participation and role in the process.

The customer's assessment and attitude toward perceived risk also enter into the intangible nature of services. Heskett (1986) notes that research suggests ''that customers associate risk more highly with the purchase of services than with goods.'' Customers are sometimes willing to pay a premium for services to overcome this increased perception of risk. By utilizing a carefully designed service process, companies can seek to manage risk perception.

To enable us to study the effective design and operation of the production process in a service organization, we must be able to distinguish between different types of service organizations. Several classifications of service operations have been proposed for this purpose. Chase and Aquilano (1989) differentiate between service operations by using a one-dimensional taxonomy based on the degree of *customer contact* in the creation of the service. In this context, customer contact is "the physical presence of the customer in the system," and creation of the service means "the work process that is entailed in providing the service itself."

Using this concept of customer contact, services are classified along a continuum that ranges from low contact to high contact, as shown in Figure 2-5. Appropriately, low-contact services are referred to as *quasi-manufacturing* services, since they exhibit many of the characteristics of manufacturing operations. High-contact services are called *pure services*. For ease in classification, companies falling between the two extremes are referred to as *mixed services*. Looking at Figure 2-5, we see that different parts of the same organization can fall into different categories. For example, the home office of a bank can experience very little customer contact, while the branch office has a greater degree of customer contact. Activities such as loan application processing and account-servicing paperwork that occur in a bank have a lower degree of customer contact than those occurring in a pure service, such as a hairstyling shop for example.

Low-contact service operations have a greater potential to apply productivity-enhancing principles developed for manufacturing operations. Efficiency-improving concepts have been studied in relation to manufacturing systems since the onset of the industrial revolution, and low-contact services are well positioned to take advantage of this existing technology. Although it follows that high-contact services do not enjoy the same potential, there is often a *technical core* of the operation which can indeed benefit from the adoption of

Figure 2-5 Classification of Services Based on Extent of Customer Contact.

(From R.B. Chase and N.J. Aquilano, *Production and Operations Management: A Life Cycle Approach*, Fifth Edition, Homewood, IL.: Irwin, 1989, p. 99. With permission.)

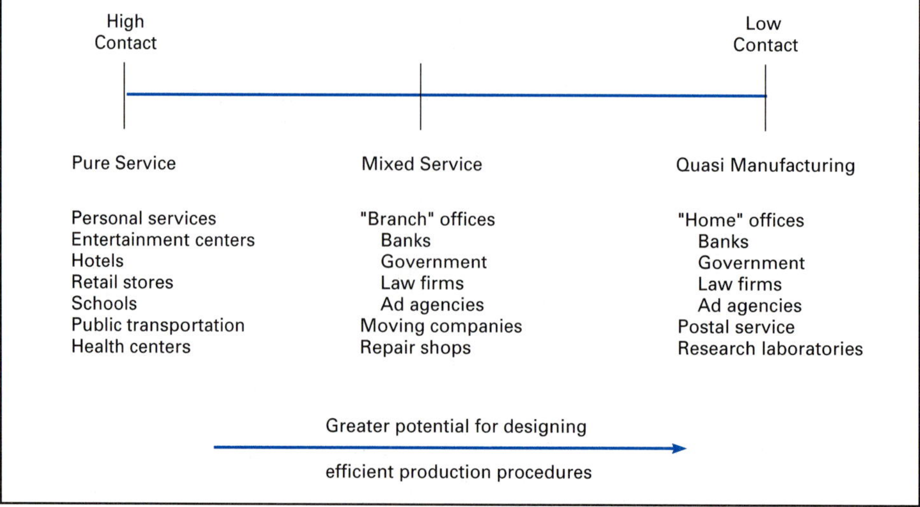

manufacturing technology (Thompson 1967; Chase 1981; and Chase and Aquilano 1989).

In almost every organization, there are functions that do not require the presence of the customer. There are usually corresponding sets of workers who are responsible for performing these activities. Often these functions are highly technical in nature. For example, in a company that develops customized accounting-information-system software for corporate clients, there is typically a field team that is responsible for working directly with the client while the system is being designed and implemented. There is also a technical group that develops the computer programs that make up the software. This group's activities are quite different from those performed by field-team members; entirely different skills are needed.

Figure 2-6 illustrates the concept of the technical core within the operations function. In manufacturing operations and in low-contact service operations, the technical core is distinct, and it also constitutes most of the production function. In this environment the technical core is easily sealed off from unnecessary customer contact without interfering with the nature of the operation. In a high-contact service organization, however, it becomes more difficult to seal off the operation of the core from the customer. Hence, in this setting the technical core is less easily identifiable and constitutes a smaller portion of the total production process. Nevertheless, a technical core usually exists, and it is advantageous to identify it and manage it efficiently.

It is necessary to examine each activity within a service operation and ensure that relevant technical-core activities are indeed performed within the core. Once the technical core is established, the firm should take advantage of the productivity-enhancing potential in the core. At the same time, we must realize that noncore activities, by their nature, involve customer contact. Thus, it is necessary to concentrate on improving the interpersonal skills and establishing the desired behavior of high-contact workers (Chase and Aquilano 1989).

We should be careful not to push the efficiency-enhancing potential of the technical core to the extreme by recommending that service organizations continually seek to enlarge their technical core. This can have an adverse effect on the strategically planned competitive nature of the service. (This idea is discussed further in review question 2.) In addition, even though the technical core can operate in the absence of the customer, it must remain sensitive to the needs of the customer, and it must add value for the customer (Chapter 17).

Because of the high degree of customer contact in pure services (or in the high-contact side of other services), they pose an intrinsically challenging operations management environment. In a high-contact service, the operations function is faced with the decision of planning adequate capacity to meet day-to-day and even hour-to-hour variations in demand. Since the level of customer

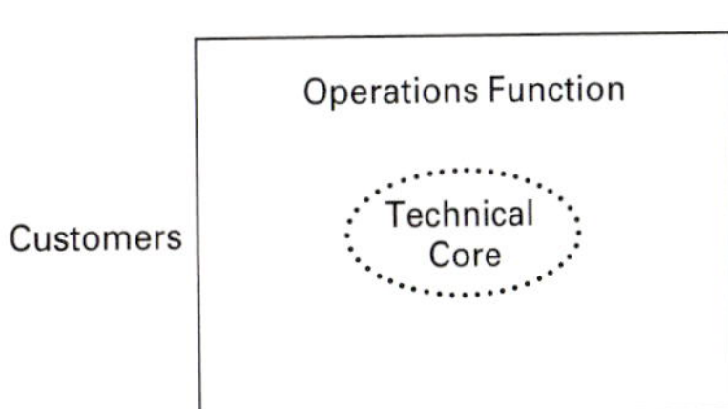

Figure 2-6 The Technical Core

contact is high and the demand behavior of customers is often hard to forecast, it is difficult to match capacity and demand.

As we noted earlier, the nature of each customer's request, and to some extent the personality of the customer (or server), can contribute considerably to the variability in demand. This adds to the total amount of uncertainty. (Have you ever stood in line at a bank while the person in front of you argues with the teller?)

Furthermore, because the customer is present in the system, the operations function must be sensitive to the customer's needs and possible demands. This means that the workers in high-contact jobs require public relations skills. Many high-quality service organizations devote considerable effort to enhancing employee–customer encounters. It is common, for example, for workers to wear uniforms and follow standard operating procedure, which often includes a standard greeting and closing (''Good morning. Welcome to . . . May I take your order? . . . Thank you.'').

In high-contact systems we must be sensitive to the fact that customers will probably be required to wait for service. Many clever ways have been devised to manage the customer waiting process. For example, when visiting a medical clinic, a long wait frequently occurs between the time when a patient enters the clinic and the time when he or she finally sees the physician. In the interim, however, if the patient is directed to an office where vital signs are checked by a nurse and then returns to the waiting area (or perhaps ''proceeds'' to a different waiting area), the perceived total waiting time is reduced.

Disney World has some excellent queue-management methods. For many of the attractions, signs are posted along the waiting area telling visitors of the expected wait from that point. Also, the queue configurations are adroitly managed by a series of rails and (adjustable) ropes. As the line advances, it typically moves from the outside to the inside of the exhibit. Thus, upon entering the building, the change in environment signals that significant progress has been made in advancing toward the front of the line. In actuality, there may be a considerable wait inside. Finally, the waiting areas themselves are lined with interesting or humorous paintings or signs.

Service organizations offer unique challenges to the operations manager. Other classifications of service operations have been suggested (see, for example, Schmenner 1986). We will use the classification given in Figure 2-5 throughout this text, since it provides a convenient way to relate services and manufacturing. In the chapters that follow, whenever manufacturing ideas are presented, it is important to also think of them as they apply to the technical core of a service. We will also consider issues that arise in the high-contact side of the operations function.

REVIEW PROBLEMS

1. Provide specific examples of high-, medium-, and low-contact service operations. For each, discuss high-contact activities, as well as technical-core activities.

2. It was mentioned previously that although service operations should seek to identify and seal off the technical core, it is not necessarily wise to expand its size even though it offers productivity-enhancing benefits. Explain why this is the case.

3. Provide other examples of ways in which service operations control worker discretion in the delivery of the service.

Solutions

1. An exclusive retail clothing store provides an example of a high-contact service. As customers enter the store, they are greeted by a salesperson who is responsible for assisting the customer in locating and selecting the desired clothing. Finally, the customer may have to be fitted for the clothing by the tailor, or in the case of minor alterations, by the salesperson.

   In this setting the technical core consists of activities in the tailor's shop (other than fitting customers) and activities involved in ordering, receiving, and stocking new items of clothing. Activities occurring in the general office also form part of the core (although some workers may have to call customers to communicate account information or handle special inquiries). Activities of the clothing buyers may be viewed as part of the core from the point of view of the customer, but buyers interact with clothing designers and wholesalers.

   A small office dealing in the preparation of relatively straightforward individual tax returns is an example of a medium-contact service. In this setting clients meet with front-office workers who provide general information concerning the service, talk with the client about the nature of the return, screen clients by forwarding complex returns to an accountant's office, and inform clients of the necessary information required to complete the return. The technical core consists of those activities required in the processing and preparation of returns, which include making the appropriate number of copies and handling the necessary correspondence. Some of these technical-core activities are now supported, and in some cases replaced, by automation in the form of personal computers and specialized software.

   A mail-order house is an example of a low-contact service. Customers phone or mail in orders, which are received by a staff of customer-service employees who are trained to communicate with the customer, gather information of the correct type, and place it in the correct form for processing. This group also handles customer complaints. The technical-core activities are warehouse receiving, stocking, order retrieval, order sequencing, packaging and shipping, and materials handling.

2. The design of the service operation, including the relative size of the technical core, is largely determined by the nature of the service and by the specific dimensions along which the organization wishes to compete. If an organization desires to compete on its warm, friendly, customized service but places more aspects of its service delivery into the core, the resulting effect could easily conflict with the desired competitive strategy.

3. Educational institutions have developed a number of ways to control worker (that is, teacher) discretion in the delivery of the service (teaching). This is frequently accomplished by establishing a required curriculum, requiring teachers to follow a standard syllabus, and using common exams.

   Examples occur in the health services as well. The discretion of nurses and physician's assistants is limited by using standard operating procedures and strict specification of illnesses that can be treated without the direct involvement of a physician. Physician discretion is also limited through the use of established treatment procedures, common certification, control of prescription drugs, and hospital procedures.

2-4 SUMMARY

The operations function in an organization is responsible for converting the inputs of raw materials, labor, technology, capital, and energy into the desired output, which is a specified bundle of goods and services. This chapter has sought to increase our familiarity with the production process. In addition to studying basic types of production processes, we have seen that one of the keys to achieving a competitive position in the marketplace is the management of the organization in a manner that simultaneously takes into consideration the nature of the product (that is, the good or service) and the process that is used to make or deliver it.

We began our discussion by looking at the example of the Yuppie Car Wash Company. This discussion introduced many of the concepts relevant to multistage production processes. It also enables us to realize how operations management decisions can affect the way in which the process runs, as well as the ability of the process to either facilitate or hinder achievement of the strategic competitive goals established by top management. Firms can compete on the basis of low cost, high quality, customization, innovation, or time. Although it may appear obvious, the importance of the production process in achieving these goals was perhaps one of the most significant (and, in many instances, painful) lessons learned by United States manufacturing companies in the 1980s.

Job shops and flow shops represent two extreme stereotypes of production environments. Along the continuum ranging from job shops to flow shops, there are other well-known types of production processes, which include projects, batch processes, and continuous-flow processes. We have also seen that it is useful to distinguish between make-to-stock and make-to-order production environments and that there are different degrees of make-to-order. The product–process matrix of Hayes and Wheelwright provides a convenient way to compare process capability with product demands. It also provides a basis upon which a company can consider whether it is pursuing a coherent competitive strategy.

The chapter concludes with a discussion of services. Although the study of operations management traditionally has been dominated by manufacturing, the significant presence of the service sector in the economies of developed nations has brought about a critical need to explore and realize the productivity-enhancing potential in service operations. We began our study of services by identifying characteristics that make them different from manufacturing operations. We also discussed a one-dimensional classification of services based on the concept of degree of customer contact. By observing the nature of the technical core as it changes from low contact (quasi-manufacturing services) to high contact (pure services), we are better able to understand the similarities and differences between manufacturing and service operations. This understanding will prove to be invaluable in our study of operations management in the chapters that follow.

CASELET

HALL RUNNERS*

Robert Hall was a marathon runner. Earlier in his running career, Bob had some problems with his feet because of the running. Dr. Baines, an orthopedist, diagnosed Bob's problem as one requiring special running shoes. While in graduate school, Bob started making running shoes for himself, and later for a few friends. These shoes were designed by Bob in consultation with Dr. Baines. During the first few years, Bob made the shoes in the garage of his parents' home using their sewing machine. For other processing equipment, he invented methods and processes to get the job done cheaply.

Bob's method of manufacture was to purchase what he could and make whatever he could not purchase. At the beginning he purchased all his material in flat sheets or in rolls and cut out the patterns with scissors. He made some wooden shoe lasts (forms) on which he constructed the shoe after he had all the necessary parts. He converted an old clothes dryer into a drying oven (by removing the drum drive) to dry the glues and solvents that held most of the shoe together.

Bob had started this business just before the ''jogging craze'' began sweeping the country. He was now selling some of his shoes through independent shoe stores in three large cities within 200 miles of his home. With the help of Dr. Baines, he developed three master patterns for the majority (85%) of the shoes that he now makes. The remaining shoes continue to be made for specific customers in consultation with Dr. Baines.

Bob currently rents a 2000 square foot facility, which houses his operation. The current manufacturing operation differs little from that which Bob started in his parents' garage, except for larger production runs and some heavier-duty equipment (including two industrial sewing machines). The layout of the shop is shown in Figure 2-7. In addition to himself, Bob's shop now employs one full-time worker, who is an experienced garment maker, and five part-time workers, who received on-the-job training. All the basic ''Hall Runners'' are made in the same style except for the tread design. As was noted previously, there are three of these: one for street, one for cross-country, and one for track. The only other variation is in size. To facilitate scheduling, shoes are produced in lots consisting of the same size and style shoe. Bob has also noted that more and more people are wearing running shoes as casual attire or as everyday shoes. This trend may warrant developing different styles and colors. Bob feels that the market potential is great for quality running shoes, and he intends to enlarge his production capacity.

Required

This case contains many aspects of the product-process operations concepts discussed in this chapter. Discuss briefly all such concepts that are applicable to Robert Hall's operation. Be as thorough as possible, and be sure to include in your discussion concepts such as process characteristics, relevant product characteristics, and product-process interaction and evolution.

*Reprinted by permission of Macmillan Publishing Company from *Production/Operations Management: Concepts and Situations*, by R.W. Schmenner. Copyright © 1981 Science Research Associates, Inc.

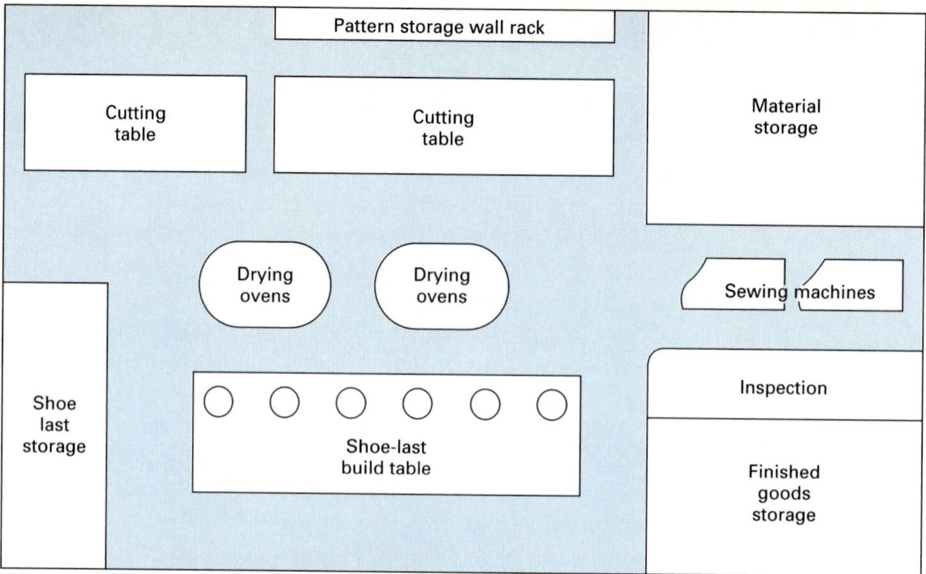

Figure 2-7 Shop Layout for Hall's Running Shoes

PROBLEMS

1. Answer each of the following questions concerning multistage production processes.
   a. What is a multistage production process?
   b. What is meant by the capacity of the process?
   c. What does it mean for one of the stages to be a bottleneck?

*2. a. Is it possible for there to be more than one bottleneck in a process? Explain.
   b. For a given process, must the bottleneck(s) always remain at the same stage(s) of the process or can it (they) "move around"? Explain.

*3. In the Yuppie Car Wash Company example of Section 2-1, we saw that if Yuppie uses two workers in each of the ICCs, the resulting capacity of the total process is 40 cars per hour.
   a. If Yuppie assigns one worker to each ICC, what is the capacity of the ICCs, and what is the resulting capacity of the entire process? Identify the bottleneck work center(s).
   b. Answer the questions in part a assuming that Yuppie assigns three workers to each ICC.

4. Consider a production process consisting of three workstations (Stations 1, 2, and 3). All goods enter the process immediately prior to Station 1, where they await processing at Station 1. All goods flow sequentially through each of the stations in the same order (Station

*Problems with an asterisk have answers in the back of the book.

1 to Station 2 to Station 3). Upon leaving Station 3, finished goods are stored in inventory until they are eventually sold to customers.

The workstations operate independently of one another. Stations 1 and 3 are each machine controlled. Station 1 has a cycle time of 0.5 minute per good, and Station 3 has a cycle time of 20 seconds per good. Station 2 is labor intensive, and its capacity depends on whether there are two, four, or six workers assigned to it. (Workers must work in pairs because of the nature of the work performed at the station.) The capacity of Station 2 is 100 goods per hour if it is staffed by two workers, and its capacity increases by 50 goods per hour for each additional pair of workers. There are work-in-process storage bins between consecutive workstations. The cycle times at each workstation include the average time required to move the good into and out of the storage bins.

a. Draw the process-flow diagram for this operation.
b. Determine the hourly capacity of this process assuming that (i) two, (ii) four, and (iii) six workers are assigned to Station 2.
c. Determining the bottleneck workstation(s) for each assumption in part b.

5. Consider the production process defined in problem 4. Suppose now that the company purchases another machine of the type that is used in Station 1. This machine would be used in parallel with the machine currently in Station 1 and would effectively double the capacity of that work center. The machines would be fed by a common queue. Answer parts a, b, and c of problem 4 for the modified process.
6. List and define the different types of inventory discussed in this chapter.

*7. Consider a two-stage production process in which ten different parts are fabricated from raw materials in the first stage (using only one machining center) and are then assembled, in the second stage, into the finished product. Four of the ten parts come in different (but interchangeable) styles and colors. Also, each of the ten parts is made in the first stage from a unique raw material, and only one part can be made at a time. A finished assembly contains one of each of the ten parts.

a. Would you expect to see work-in-process inventory between the two stages of this process? Why?
b. Assuming that the company operates in a make-to-stock environment, draw the process-flow diagram for this manufacturing process.
c. Assuming that the company operates in an assemble-to-order environment, draw the process-flow diagram and explain the differences between this diagram and the one occurring in part b.
d. Assume that the company operates in a make-to-order environment. Draw the product-flow diagram and discuss differences between it and the ones arising in parts b and c.

8. Describe a few ways in which a company may compete. How does this relate to the operations function? Provide examples to support your answer.

9. One way in which a firm may choose to compete is on the basis of "quality." Sometimes the quality of a good or service is confused with its "grade." What is meant by the grade of a product (good or service)? Provide examples that illustrate a high-grade product that may be of low quality and a low-grade product that may be of high quality.
10. a. What is the difference between a make-to-stock and a make-to-order production environment?
    b. Explain differences in competitive advantage offered by these two environments.
    c. Identify the various types of make-to-order processes, and explain the differences between them.
11. a. Define the term "job shop," and discuss the general characteristics of a job shop.
    b. Define the term "flow shop," and discuss the general characteristics of a flow shop.
    c. What is a project?
    d. What is a batch process?
    e. What is a continuous-flow process?
12. Summarize the basic ideas contained in the Hayes and Wheelwright product–process matrix. Be sure to discuss the strategic implications of this concept.
13. In what ways do services differ from manufacturing organizations?
14. What does Levitt mean when he asserts that "discretion is the enemy of order, standardization, and quality" in service organizations? Provide examples to support your response.
15. Discuss the classification of service operations based on customer contact. In your response, be sure to include and define each of the following terms:
    a. customer contact
    b. creation of the service
    c. pure services
    d. quasi-manufacturing services
    e. mixed services
16. What is the technical core of a service operation? How does the nature of the technical core change as the operation ranges from a quasi-manufacturing to a pure service?
17. a. Why is it helpful to be able to distinguish between different types of services using a taxonomy such as the classification based on the degree of customer contact?
    b. What are the implications regarding the design, planning, and control of service operations that result from understanding the concept of the technical core, as well as the nature of the service based on the degree of customer contact?
18. Think of your favorite (or least favorite) food service. In general terms, what type of production process does it employ? On what basis does it compete? Can you think of any characteristics of its production process or general operations that support or run counter to this competitive strategy?

*19. In the calculation of the cycle time for the two ICCs in the Yuppie Car Wash Company example of Section 2-1, it was assumed that an equal number of workers would be assigned to each ICC. In reality, Jane Dow is free to assign to each ICC, independently of the number assigned to the other ICC, any number of workers (including none) up to the maximum of three workers allowed per ICC.

For each allowable combination of workers in the ICCs, answer the following questions. (Assume that cars waiting to enter the ICC are serviced first come, first served and that each car is serviced by the ICC that first becomes available.)

a. Compute the cycle time and capacity of the ICCs (i.e., the subsystem defined by both ICCs).
b. Determine the capacity of the entire process.
c. Identify the process bottleneck(s).

20. The discussion of the Yuppie Car Wash Company in Section 2-1 purposely focused on the flow of cars through the process and did not take into account what happens to the customer. This is reflected in the process-flow diagram shown in Figure 2-1. Consider now what happens to the customer at the Yuppie Car Wash.

Upon arriving at Yuppie, customers park their cars in the large parking lot in front of the car wash and proceed into a separate building adjacent to the car wash. The building is nicely furnished in contemporary design, with an attractive combination of natural wood paneled walls, ceramic tile, and plush carpeted floors, with light music in the background. Customers wait in line in front of the reception desk. At the reception desk, the customer provides basic information on the type of car and any special washing or cleaning instructions. (For example, upon request, Yuppie will use a special-formula Bavarian-made soap for extremely delicate paints; of course, Yuppie charges extra for this.) The customer then hands the ignition key to the employee and proceeds to a large waiting room. Reception-desk employees wear standard uniforms that are primarily dark colored.

The waiting room is amply equipped with comfortable furniture, a minilibrary of investment magazines, and two large-screen TVs, with one tuned to a cable news station and the other tuned to a financial information network. A large window runs along the wall of the waiting area facing the car wash so that customers can watch the progress of their cars through the process and also monitor the careful handling of cars by Yuppies' employees.

When servicing of the car is complete, an employee returns the keys to the customer checkout desk. The customer checkout desk is located at the opposite end of the waiting area from the location of the reception desk, and the room is designed so that a large wall obstructs direct vision between the reception and checkout desks. Customer checkout representatives are required to wear standard uniforms that are predominantly white in color. The customer is paged over the public address system in the standard manner: "Mr. (or Ms.) Smith, your car has been serviced; please proceed to the customer checkout area." The customer then approaches the checkout area and, if necessary, joins a single line that is formed in a winding pattern by a series of velvet-covered ropes. After paying the customer checkout representative, the customer receives his or her key back and then proceeds to the large parking lot, picks up his or her car, and drives away.

Given this additional information, answer each of the following questions:

a. Expand the process-flow diagram in Figure 2-1 so that it also takes into account the customer flow throughout the system. To distinguish between car and customer flow, use solid lines to represent the flow of cars and dashed lines to indicate the flow of customers.
b. Process-flow diagrams are also useful in indicating the flow of information in the process. Augment your answer to part a by now including the flow of information in the system. Use dotted lines to indicate information flows.
c. This example illustrates many of the points mentioned in the chapter concerning the planning, design, and control of service operations. Discuss instances of this pertaining to each of the following:
   (i) limiting customer discretion
   (ii) the design of waiting areas
   (iii) the technical core
   (iv) the customer's presence in the system
   (v) intangibility
d. Suggest minor changes to the process flow that could reduce the total amount of time a customer spends in the system.

REFERENCES

BLACKBURN, J., "Time Based Competition: JIT as a Weapon," *APICS—The Performance Advantage*, July, 1991, pp. 30–34.

BOHN, R., K. SOMERS, and G. GREENBERG, "Kristen's Cookie Company (A1, A2)," HBS Case Services, Harvard Business School, 9-686-093, 9-686-094, revised, 1986.

CHASE, R.B., "The Customer-Contact Approach to Services: Theoretical Bases and Practical Extensions," *Operations Research*, vol. 29, no. 4, 1981, pp. 698–706.

CHASE, R.B., and N.J. AQUILANO, *Production and Operations Management: A Life Cycle Approach*, 5th ed., Homewood, Ill.: Irwin, 1989.

DAY, G.S., *Analysis for Strategic Market Decisions*, St. Paul, Minn.: West, 1986.

FITZSIMMONS, J.A., and R.S. SULLIVAN, *Service Operations Management*, New York: McGraw-Hill, 1982.

GYLLENHAMMAR, P.G., "How Volvo Adapts Work to People," *Harvard Business Review*, July–August, 1977, pp. 102–113.

HAYES, R.H., and S.C. WHEELWRIGHT, *Restoring Our Competitive Edge: Competing through Manufacturing*, New York: Wiley, 1984.

HESKETT, J.L., *Managing in the Service Economy*, Boston: Harvard Business School Press, 1986.

KAPSTEIN, J., and J. HOERR, "Volvo's Radical New Plant: 'The Death of the Assembly Line'?," *Business Week*, August 28, 1989, pp. 92–93.

KOTLER, P., *Marketing Management: Analysis, Planning, Implementation, and Control*, 6th ed., Englewood Cliffs, N.J.: Prentice Hall, 1988.

LEVITT, T., "Exploit the Product Life Cycle," *Harvard Business Review*, November–December, 1965.

LEVITT, T., "Production-Line Approach to Service," *Harvard Business Review*, September–October, 1972, pp. 41–52.

MARSHALL, P.W., "A Note on Process Analysis," Harvard Business School Teaching Note 1-645-038, Intercollegiate Case Clearing House, Boston, Mass., 1974.

SARI, F.J., "The MPS and the Bill of Material Go Hand-in-Hand," Winston-Salem, N.C.: Ling, 1981.

SCHMENNER, R.W., "How Can Service Businesses Survive and Prosper?" *Sloan Management Review*, Spring, 1986, pp. 21–32.

SKINNER, W., "The Focused Factory," *Harvard Business Review*, May–June, 1974, pp. 113–121.

THOMPSON, J.D., *Organizations in Technologies*, New York: McGraw-Hill, 1967.

chapter 3

Analyzing Operations: Building Models and Obtaining Cost Information

To manage an operating system well, one must understand what the system does and how well it is performing. To gain this knowledge, managers use models of the system and cost information about its performance. For example, a production schedule such as ''Produce the components on Monday and Tuesday and assemble them on Wednesday'' is implicitly based on a model of a factory. The model contains information about work currently under way, available people and equipment, expected processing times, and so on. As another example, when a grocery store manager receives a report that says costs are too high in the dairy department, he or she assumes that the cost figure is correct and has a standard value in mind as a goal, based on some simple model of the operation. In this chapter we will discuss how models can be used and misused and how cost information can help or mislead.

Studying methods of analysis for operations management is of crucial importance because analysis can be done well or poorly in several different ways. Four basic mistakes have occasionally placed analytical methods in bad repute: (1) solving the wrong problem[1]; (2) using incorrect inputs; (3) choosing a model or method that does not fit the situation; and (4) using the results of the analysis incorrectly. An example of solving the wrong problem is examining the wrong organizational unit. If we examine a distribution system one warehouse at a time, it is possible to develop a solution that is good for the warehouse but bad for the overall system's effectiveness. The second mistake is referred to by the acronym ''GIGO'' (garbage in, garbage out). If incorrect data are used, the analysis will lead to bad solutions. Of course, even good data cannot save an

[1]In statistics courses Type I and Type II errors play an important role. The former is believing that an assertion is true when it is in fact false, and the latter is believing that the assertion is false when it is in fact true. In the real world, the Type III error—solving the wrong problem—is more common and typically more costly. The Type IV error—solving the right problem but too late to be useful—is sometimes called paralysis by analysis, and we must be careful not to make this error by overanalyzing operational problems.

incorrect analytical approach (mistake 3). Finally, all analysis, from problem definition to data gathering to implementation of the solution, should be viewed as an aid to managerial judgment. Good analysis and good judgment are supportive of each other. Managers gain intuition about their operations from viewing the results of analysis, but their judgment is tempered by understanding the limitations inherent in all analytical methods.

Example: Farm Supply Corporation

Harry LaRoe is in charge of production and distribution for the Farm Supply Corporation. Farm Supply (a fictitious name, but a real company) sells over 20,000 items, but most of their business comes through sales of heavy machinery such as silo loaders, baling machines, and milking machines, called big-ticket items, of which they have about three hundred. Total annual sales of all items is $2.8 billion.

As part of the firm's marketing strategy, they provide a parts-supply service designed to quickly respond to customers' needs. Many of their products are items that their users cannot do without for an extended period of time. For this reason the firm had over $88 million of its $306 million inventory (as of January 1, 1991) in spare parts. The percentage of the total inventory allocated to spare parts has grown significantly in the last fifteen years. In addition, they have received an increasing number of complaints from their customers about the lack of spare-parts support. These two symptoms caused LaRoe to commission a study, involving internal people as well as external consultants, of the spare-parts distribution system. In preparation for the study, he wrote a brief description of the system:

> Farm Supply has one plant that produces the spare parts made by the company. The company also purchases some parts from outside vendors. However, the plant maintains a very small inventory of spare parts. Instead, parts are produced and shipped to three distribution centers (DCs) when it fits the plant's production schedule. The DCs ship spare parts on demand to a total of 250 stores, each of which maintains a spare-parts inventory. The current breakdown of the $88 million inventory is as follows: $35 million at the stores, $49 million at the DCs, and $4 million at the plant.

LaRoe asked the study group to describe areas for potential improvements in the service system. He was specifically interested in the following questions:

1. How could inventory be reallocated to provide better service, or, alternatively, how could the same level of service be obtained with less total inventory?
2. How can production be scheduled and throughput improved in the production of spare parts?
3. Until a possible expansion, how should stores be assigned to DCs, considering the capacity constraint on throughput at each DC?
4. What information on inventories and costs of distribution is currently available, and what information should be available? How can this information, including accounting numbers, be used to better manage distribution?

We will use this example throughout Chapter 3.

3-1 MODELS IN OPERATIONS MANAGEMENTS

A model is an abstract representation of reality. Automobile designers build clay models of their car designs to see how the finished car will look. This type of model is a *physical* model. Economists build computer models of the economy to predict future economic trends or the effect of a tax reduction. This type of model is referred to as a *conceptual* model. Operations managers use both types of models to help them choose inventory levels, design a facility layout, choose warehouse locations, and to make many other decisions.

Models are used for several reasons:

1. to eliminate the myriad of details surrounding a problem and allow concentration on the key factors
2. to perform ''experiments'' (see what would happen if . . .) without altering the real system (thus lowering the cost of experimentation)
3. to choose an ''optimal'' solution from among the large number of alternatives

A manager's job in using any model is to avoid the four mistakes listed in paragraph two of the introduction. Stated positively, managers must

1. see that the model is being used to ask the right question(s)

2,3. see that the model, its assumptions, and the data inputs accurately represent the key factors in the real system

4. use the information obtained from the model, along with managerial judgment and other inputs, in reaching the decision

Some models allow us to find an ''optimal'' solution to the question posed. Of course, the solution may be optimal only for the abstract version of the question as captured in the model. The manager's role in assessing the validity of a model is vital. Judgment regarding factors not included in the model must be incorporated into the actual decision. One way in which managers exercise judgment is that they usually ''satisfice'' rather than ''optimize''; that is, a satisfactory solution is sought rather than an optimal one. (In doing so, managers are considering the cost of seeking a better solution.) Herbert A. Simon, who won the 1978 Nobel Prize in economics, did the pioneering work in dealing with managerial decisions in this more realistic way. Managers can use models as an information source in seeking a solution. In simple situations, a model can be programmed to make the decision, with the possibility of managerial intervention if necessary. In complex situations, such as strategy formulation, a model should be only one of several sources of information.

The Economic Order Quantity (EOQ) Model

As an example of a model, Farm Supply's manufacturing plant is analyzing the production schedule for one expensive spare part. Part B64 is demanded at an average rate of 100 units per week, nationwide. The product cost of $250 per unit consists of $190 for materials and purchased components and $60 for labor (2 hours at a full cost of $30 per hour). The cost to begin a new batch of B64 is $90 (3 hours of labor at $30 per hour). Finally, Farm Supply believes that money tied up in inventory costs 13% of the dollar value per year, or 1/4% per week.

The model we will use to analyze this problem is called the *Economic Order Quantity (EOQ)*, developed by Harris (1913). We will use this to illustrate trade-off analysis, incorrect data inputs, and solving the wrong problem. We will also discuss the model's appropriate use.

If Farm Supply produces B64 once per week, the size of each batch will be 100 units, on the average. Upon completion, each batch will become 100 units of inventory, but the average lot-size inventory will be half that (50) since demand will reduce inventory from 100 to 0 before the next production run. The inventory cost per week would be the average inventory in units times the cost per unit times the 1/4% per week cost of inventory dollars, or (50)($250)(0.0025) = $31.25. The weekly cost to begin a new batch is $90, since one batch is begun each week. The total of these two costs will be $31.25 + $90, on the average. As one alternative, if Farm Supply orders 200 units once every two weeks (twice as much, half as often), weekly inventory cost will double to $61.50, and the average weekly cost of beginning batches will be half as much, or $45. With a batch size of 200, average inventory would be 100 (200/2), and Farm Supply would have one setup every two weeks (1/2 setup per week). Total weekly cost would be $62.50 + $45.

When we order twice as much, inventory cost increases and setup cost declines. There is a trade-off between these two costs. We want to find the batch size that makes the sum of the two costs as small as possible. Table 3-1 gives the total of inventory and setup costs for four different batch sizes, including the two just discussed, 100 and 200.

The numbers in Table 3-1 are based on a model of this particular inventory decision. We did not really produce 100 units and observe the costs. Rather, we have a model in mind that says

$$\text{Total cost per week} = (0.0025)(250)\left(\frac{Q}{2}\right) + \frac{100}{Q}(90) \tag{1}$$

where Q = the order size.

The model in equation 1 gives total cost as a function of order size Q. To verify the equation, plug in $Q = 100$ and see if total cost is equal to $121.25. Equation 1 allows us to compute costs for any Q.

Equation 1 can be generalized if we use symbols for the cost of money, value per unit, and weekly demand:

$$TC(Q) = F_I C_u \left(\frac{Q}{2}\right) + \frac{D}{Q} C_S \tag{2}$$

Table 3-1 Trade-off of Inventory Cost Against the Cost of Beginning a New batch

Order Size	Average Inventory	Orders per Week	Weekly Inventory Cost	Weekly Cost of Beginning New Batches	Total Cost per Week
100	50	1	$ 31.25	$90.00	$121.25
200	100	1/2	62.50	45.00	107.50
300	150	1/3	93.75	30.00	123.75
400	200	1/4	125.00	22.50	147.50

where

$TC(Q)$ = total cost, as a function of order size

F_I = cost of money tied up for one period in inventory (an interest charge)

C_u = variable cost of 1 unit of the item

D = demand rate per period; this period and the period referred to in F_I must be the same period (week, year, month, etc.)

C_S = cost of beginning a batch (setup cost)

Equation 2 has been used and misused for many years. We will discuss it in more detail in Chapter 8. Here we will discuss several very important ideas about the use of models, using equation 2 as an example.

QUESTION 1: *What is the optimal order size?*

If equation 2 is an appropriate model of reality, costs will be minimized by selecting

$$Q^* = \sqrt{\frac{2DC_S}{F_I C_u}} \tag{3}$$

This formula, the economic order quantity equation, is derived in Chapter 8. For the Farm Supply example $Q^* = \sqrt{2(100)(90)/(.0025)(250)} = 170$ units. The cost for $Q^* = 170$ will be less than any cost value in Table 3-1.

QUESTION 2: *Why are there only two cost terms in "total cost"?*

The implication is that only two costs are affected in an important way by the selection of Q. For example, if unit cost is always $250, average production cost per week (or per year or another period) is fixed at $25,000 for 100 units per week. Fixed costs should not affect decisions. (This is discussed later in this chapter.) However, if there is a quantity discount for ordering 200 units or more, should we increase the order quantity from 170 to 200? (Quantity discounts will be analyzed in Chapter 8.) Here the point is that it is the manager's job to include all important components in a model. At the same time, models should be kept as simple as possible.[2]

QUESTION 3: *Is minimizing cost as stated in equation 2 the right problem?*

The "just-in-time" system for controlling production is discussed in Chapter 12. Many Japanese companies popularized this method in which, among other things, setup time and cost are reduced so that small batch sizes are appropriate. If setup cost could be reduced to $1, from $90, for B64, the appropriate order quantity is less than 20 units. This would allow very fast response to customers since, even if Farm Supply were out of stock, the item could be produced the day of demand. (Weekly demand of 100, divided by 20 units order size, gives 5 orders per week or 1 per working day.)

---

[2]Albert Einstein said, "Every problem should be simplified as far as possible—and no further."

Reducing the setup cost may be the right problem to solve. Spence and Porteus (1987) discuss the value of reducing setup cost, and Shingo (1989) gives ways to do it. However, equation 2 does not adequately represent this problem since the value of faster response to customers is not included.

There are other ways in which minimizing equation 2 may be inappropriate. B64 may have to share production facilities with other components, or it may have to be scheduled so that components are available for assembly, with other parts, into finished products. When a single item is being produced or ordered, and when setup cost and inventory cost are the main variable cost components, equation 2 is an appropriate model to use.

QUESTION 4: *Are the cost inputs correct?*

Probably not. Obtaining cost estimates is very difficult, as will be discussed in Section 3-2. For example, both inventory and setup costs often include large amounts of allocated fixed costs; consequently their value may be overstated.

QUESTION 5: *What implicit assumptions are lurking in the model?*

In equation 2 we use average inventory equal to $Q/2$. What if weekly demand of 100 arrives all at once, on Thursday morning? (Then Farm Supply should try to produce on Thursday morning; if they produce once per week, inventory can be approximately 0, not 100/2.) If demand arrives in ''chunks,'' a different approach is needed, as discussed in Chapter 10.

You may be wondering, how can a simple model like the EOQ give rise to so many questions and concerns? Our point is that each model you will encounter in this book and in actual operations can be misused in many ways. Managers must ask and answer questions such as the foregoing before using any model. In particular, managers must ask:

- Are we using the correct objectives?
- Have we considered all key items and interrelationships (and omitted unimportant ones) in the model?
- Are the input values correct?
- What explicit and implicit assumptions are made by the model? Are these assumptions reasonable?

Other Models: Mathematical Programming and Simulation

Equation 2 is an *abstract or mathematical model* in that the costs are modeled using only mathematical symbols. It is a model that can be optimized; that is, we can find the best decision from among the infinite number of possible production quantities. We will study several models of this type, using calculus and mathematical programming techniques to perform the optimization. However, it is possible to include more realism in models, to make the model act like the real system in several important ways. Such models can be called *analog* models or *simulation* models. The distinction between a mathematical model and a simulation model is frequently unclear. Typically, large simulation models are not optimized owing to their complexity, but they are used to evaluate alternatives specified by management.

Example: Mathematical Programming

Harry LaRoe's third question regarding the Farm Supply Corporation distribution system was, until a possible expansion, how should stores be assigned to distribution centers, considering the capacity constraints of the DCs? With 250 stores, several thousand products, and 3 DCs, the number of possible shipping patterns is huge—too large for even a large computer to examine all possibilities. Problems of this type (minimize cost or maximize profit, subject to several constraints) can frequently be modeled using a mathematical program. The mathematical program will then find the optimal solution to the problem as modeled. (This type of model is discussed extensively in Appendix C.) Here we will give an example of the approach, without many details.

> The objective is to minimize costs. The constraints are of two kinds: (1) the amount of throughput in any DC is limited, and (2) the demands of each store must be met. Any model involves simplifying reality. Here we are going to assume that the demands at each store, measured in truckloads, are known and are constant throughout the year. Since we are only seeking an assignment of stores to DCs rather than a detailed trucking schedule, this assumption may be reasonable. Given our assumptions, a model of the following form would result:
>
> Let
>
> X_{ij} = truckloads shipped from DC i to retail store j, where $i = 1, 2,$ or 3 and $j = 1, \ldots, 250$
>
> CAP_i = weekly throughput capacity in truckloads, at DC i, where $i = 1, 2,$ or 3
>
> DEM_j = demand per week in truckloads, at store j, where $j = 1, \ldots, 250$
>
> C_{ij} = cost of shipping one truckload from DC i to store j, where $i = 1, 2,$ or 3 and $j = 1, \ldots, 250$

Then the mathematical programming formulation is

$$\text{minimize} \sum_{i=1}^{3} \sum_{j=1}^{250} C_{ij}X_{ij} \text{ (minimize the sum of all shipment costs)} \tag{4}$$

subject to

$$\sum_{i=1}^{3} X_{ij} = \text{DEM}_j \quad \text{for each store, } j = 1, \ldots 250 \tag{5}$$

$$\sum_{j=1}^{250} X_{ij} \leq \text{CAP}_i \quad \text{for each DC, } i = 1, 2, \text{ or } 3 \tag{6}$$

$$X_{ij} \geq 0 \quad \text{for all DCs, } i = 1, 2, \text{ or } 3, \text{ and stores, } j = 1, \ldots, 250 \tag{7}$$

The first constraint, equation 5, says that in total, enough truckloads must be shipped to each store to satisfy the demand. The second constraint, equation 6, says that in total, each DC must ship no more than its capacity. The third constraint, equation 7, reminds the computer that negative shipment is not allowed in this model. There are 3 × 250 = 750 variables. There are 250 constraints of the first kind, 3 constraints of the second kind, and 750 nonnegativity constraints. A computer can solve this model quickly, finding a shipping pattern that gives the minimum possible value of the objective function (4). (How this is done is discussed in Appendix C.) The output of the program would be the number of truckloads to be shipped from each DC to each store. A manager would use the solution as a significant input into the actual decisions to be made.

A simulation of an operating system is a model that acts like the system in some important ways. A simulation allows a manager to try different decisions without making mistakes on the real system. Most of the simulations we will discuss will be computer programs, although several other types of simulation have been used to solve operations management problems.

New tools exist that make computer simulation models very easy to build and use. For example, XCELL+ (see Conway et al., 1987) is a factory simulation system that will be used in several places in this book. (Thomas et al., 1989 give case studies that use XCELL+, including both manufacturing and service situations.)

Example: Simulation

Farm Supply produces B64 in four stages. The process is new, and they have had difficulty making it reliable; production time per piece has been variable. For this reason they maintain some work-in-process (WIP) inventory between each stage. Figure 3-1 shows the production flow.

Farm Supply wants to maximize the throughput rate so that they can respond quickly to spare-part requests. To do that there are two approaches. First, they can reduce the variability in the process. If each process step took exactly 10 minutes, they could produce, in lockstep, one B64 every 10 minutes, with no WIP inventory. If some variability remains, but the process steps take the same amount of time on the average, WIP inventory can improve throughput. (When W1 is slow, W2 can begin work on a unit in inventory; since they are the same speed on the average, W1 will be fast at some later time and build up the WIP inventory to its former level.)

Currently, each stage requires an average of 10 minutes ($\mu = 10$) to process one unit, and the standard deviation of process time is also 10 minutes ($\sigma = 10$). (That is, the coefficient of variation CV $= \sigma/\mu = 1$. They think process times are *exponentially* distributed.) They maintain space for 20 units of inventory between each workstation, and they would like to reduce that amount.

A simulation model of Figure 3-1 using XCELL+ is easily built in a few minutes time. The model then generates task times for each process, randomly, and moves the item to the next buffer (if there is room for it) or to shipment when it is done. During the simulation, the computer looks over all task times to see which one will finish next. It then attempts to move the item, keeps track of the state of the system, and looks for the next task completion time. Here we want only to illustrate simulation, and the ability to model systems that

Figure 3-1 Production Process for Farm Supply's B64

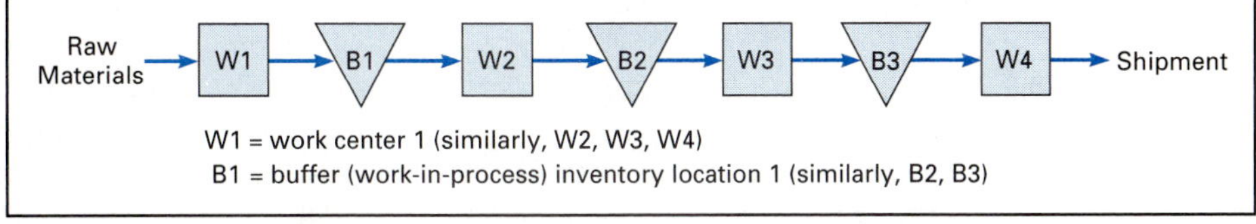

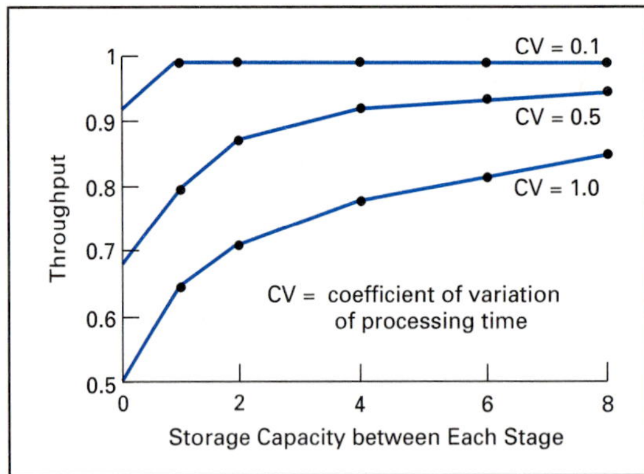

Figure 3-2 Throughput of a Four-Stage Line to Produce B64

contain complex interactions and randomness. (Simulation is discussed in Appendix B.)

Figure 3-2 shows the results of several different experiments. In Figure 3-2, 1.0 = throughput implies 100% of ''maximum,'' and maximum = 1 unit every 10 minutes.

1. With CV = 1, how much output would we obtain if buffer inventory space were eliminated? (Answer: 51% of maximum.)
2. If we could reduce CV to 0.1 (a dramatic reduction) through engineering analysis, how much output could be obtained? (Answer: 92% of maximum.)
3. With CV = 0.1, 0.5, or 1.0, how much buffer inventory space is needed to get 80% of the maximum output? (Answer: 0, 1, and 5.)

Each of the 15 points in Figure 3-2 represents average throughput for a simulated period of 10,000 minutes, or 20.8 eight-hour days. To do these experiments in the factory would be inconvenient to say the least, since that would require 15 (20.8) = 312 working days of the production line. A simulation model is very helpful here.

As in the previous example, the simulation model does not make the decision. A manager must consider the cost of inventory, the cost and value of reducing variability, and the value of increased throughput before deciding how to proceed. Figure 3-2 gives very important *trade-off* information. For a given CV, higher throughput must be paid for with higher inventory. As inventory increases, there are diminishing returns to adding more inventory. Trade-offs are basic to many managerial situations.[3] Models can give the proper information to the manager.

REVIEW PROBLEMS

1. Compute the EOQ for B64 if C_S = \$1. Verify that the answer is less than 1/5 of a week's demand.

[3]In some cases, it is possible to improve two or more things at once, so that trade-offs are not needed. The most important such case involves productivity and quality, discussed in Chapters 5 and 6. In many cases, improving quality reduces rework and repair so much that productivity also improves.

2. For B64 production (Figure 3-1), if reduction of CV to 0.5 (with no WIP inventory) costs the same as having space for 4 units of inventory (with CV = 1.0), which would you choose? How do you know?

3. In this section we analyzed the production schedule and throughput rate for B64. Farm Supply also needs to determine where to stock B64 and in what quantities. They want to minimize the average length of time it takes to deliver a spare part to a customer. (This is zero if they have it at the store, a few hours if they have it at the DC.)
   a. Should they build a separate model to study each store, one at a time? Why or why not?
   b. Suppose that some items will be carried only at the DC. For these items there will be no stock at the retail stores, and customers will have some delay in getting these items. What type of items will they be? Why?

Solutions

1. $Q^* = \sqrt{\frac{2DC_S}{F_I C_u}} = \sqrt{\frac{2(100)(1)}{(0.0025)(250)}} = 17.9.$

   This is $\frac{17.9}{100} = 0.179$, less than 1/5 of a week's demand.

2. From Figure 3-2 we can see that CV = 1.0 with space for 4 units of inventory between each stage gives approximately 77% of maximum output, compared with 69% for CV = 0.5 with no buffer inventory.

3. a. No, because the amount of inventory at the DC affects the level of inventory needed at each store to achieve a specified level of service. The entire system must be studied.
   b. The low demand items should be carried centrally (i.e., at the DC). Even though there are many such items, they are a small part of total demand. Inventory will be significantly reduced, and average service will not be degraded significantly. (This topic will be discussed in Chapter 14.)

3-2 OBTAINING AND USING COST AND PERFORMANCE DATA FOR OPERATIONS MANAGEMENT

Managers must have numbers with which to manage the business. Improvements can only be verified if you can show numerical change.[4] However, invalid numbers can cause serious mistakes. In particular, models can be dangerous if the cost inputs are inappropriate. In this section we discuss the key problems that operations managers face in getting good cost information, and we present some approaches to these problems.

We assume that readers are familiar with financial terms such as *contribution* (contribution margin, contribution to fixed costs and profits) and *fixed*

[4]Lord Kelvin said, "Until you can (numerically) measure a phenomenon, your knowledge about it is at best rudimentary."

and variable costs. We will very briefly review *break-even analysis* and *net present value* calculations in Section 3-3. (Many readers will be able to skip Section 3-3.) These topics are covered in depth in books on management accounting and finance (see for example, Bierman et al. 1990 and Brealey and Myers 1988). Some of the problems at the end of the chapter give the opportunity for practice using these concepts.

Data for Management: Incentives and Transfer Prices

We will continue to use the Farm Supply Corporation to illustrate basic concepts. Because Farm Supply Corporation had some problems with spare-parts distribution, Harry LaRoe commissioned a study of the distribution system, including a discussion of data problems. The lengthy report contained many technical details and some new ways of optimizing the inventory. Following are some brief excerpts:

''Farm Supply owns most of its stores, but it allows almost total autonomy in their operation. Thus, there is no consistent method of inventory control. Farm Supply supports their managers by allowing them to ''pay'' for merchandise when it is sold, not when it is shipped to the store. The stores are profit centers, and they are not charged any inventory carrying cost as part of their profit computation. (A profit center is a unit of a business organization that buys and sells products within and from outside the firm. A profit computation for the subunit is made, and the manager of the profit center is evaluated using that profit.)

''Many of the store managers stock only one to two hundred of the spare parts. (There are over 20,000 stock-keeping units—SKUs—in Farm Supply. An SKU is simply a product for which an inventory record is maintained.) In our opinion this is because of the complexity of managing more items than this and because spare parts is not the store's main business. However, of the items carried, many items are carried to excess. We found up to 50 times last year's sales of some items at some locations. (While 50 was an unusually large value, 5 years' worth of many items was carried at some locations.) This is because there is no perceived cost to the store manager of having inventory, but there is a cost to being out of an item when it is needed, in that one of the customers is upset.

''In an emergency situation, a part from the DC is shipped by bus or air-freight. For regular shipments, company-owned trucks make weekly shipments to each store. In either case, the cost of the part to the store is the same. The store is never supposed to receive spare parts from a source other than their own DC, but they frequently call around to other stores in their vicinity to find spare parts (or other items) that they do not have in stock.

''Based on our examination of the system, we have several suggestions for your consideration:

1. The profit centers should be assessed an inventory charge based on a percentage of the value of the inventory, valued at store cost. The percentage should include a cost of the money tied up and a charge for the risk of obsolescence.
2. Technical assistance in establishing inventory levels should be given by the corporate office. A central responsibility for corporate inventory control, under Hary LaRoe, should be established. The person assigned should set DC inventory policy, both overall and detailed, and recom-

mend inventory policies to store managers. The latter responsibility would be the only change over the present system.

3. Many items, including many spare parts, are strongly seasonal and have only a short selling period per year. We recommend that such items be identified, and that the inventory charge until the next selling season be assessed within one month after the current season. The implication would be that managers would closely watch inventories of seasonal items and have an incentive to reduce prices at the end of the season. We feel these changes would reduce the overall inventory in an appropriate manner.
4. Emergency ordering costs should be charged to the individual stores.''

To make proper decisions, managers must have good information and the proper goal. Farm Supply's store managers have not properly managed the inventories, partially because of poor information and improper incentives. One of the most important tasks for LaRoe is to establish incentive systems for the store managers. Currently, the store managers are measured on the profit they make, but they are, in essence, given interest-free loans to purchase inventory. Also, they are not charged the emergency ordering cost. The first of these two facts gives a store manager an incentive to carry excessive inventory. The second gives them a reason to ignore many low-demand items and to count on expensive emergency shipments.

Interdepartmental charges in an organization should be designed to make managers properly consider the organization's goals. The report given to LaRoe explains one way to improve the incentive system. (There are several other ways, and there would not be general agreement in Farm Supply about which methods should be used.) Notice that the changes will not all cause reduced inventory. Suggestions 1 and 3 are incentives to reduce inventory, whereas suggestion 4 is an incentive for managers to increase inventory. The point is that the managers will be making more appropriate trade-offs.

One common charge used in operations management is a transfer price; that is, a physical item flows from one unit in an organization to another, and the receiving unit is charged a transfer price for the item. There has been much written on transfer pricing, but the basic notion is, again, that transfer prices should cause managers to act in accordance with overall goals. (See Bierman et al. 1990 for a discussion of transfer pricing methods.)

REVIEW PROBLEM

Analyze the preceding excerpts from the Farm Supply report, from the point of view of a store manager. Which ideas do you accept and which do you reject? Why?

Solution

Many answers are possible. One idea is that a store manager should be charged inventory costs and emergency ordering costs only if everyone understands that the ''profit'' measure will be adversely affected. They should not be expected to achieve the same profit level as if those charges were not imposed.

The "Irrelevance" of Fixed Costs

One of the key ideas in management education is that fixed costs are irrelevant to decisions. The difficulty with applying this notion is that it is not clear what costs are really fixed: all costs are variable in the long run.

For example, in considering how many units to produce at a time, the heat for the building, the plant manager's salary, and the cost of the water treatment facility are not relevant since they will not change based on the order size used. In considering whether to close the plant, all these costs are relevant.

In both service and manufacturing, fixed costs are increasing as a percentage of total costs. Direct labor is being reduced through automation, and capital requirements are increasing. If a firm follows a "no-firing" policy, even the direct-labor-force cost is fixed in the short run. This makes it imperative to get a return on fixed assets but makes it more dangerous to allocate fixed costs. Consider the following oversimplified example:

A firm with three divisions shared one production facility. There were no costs other than the fixed cost of running the facility, which was $30 million per year. The three divisions had revenues of $20 million, $12 million, and $8 million, respectively, a total of $40 million. The $10 million profit made everyone happy. Then someone decided that fixed costs should be allocated to the divisions, so each division was charged $10 million. The divisions then had profits of 20 − 10 = +10, 12 − 10 = +2, and 8 − 10 = −2. The third division was eliminated. However, after that, each of the two divisions "owed" $15 million. They had profits of 20 − 15 = +5 and 12 − 15 = −3. The second division also had to go. And then . . .

Often fixed costs are more difficult to spot than in the foregoing example. For example, in some manufacturing settings there is a setup crew that does not produce items but prepares production equipment for running the next batch. Sometimes this is done overnight on the third shift or on the weekend. If the setup crew is busy only half of the time (as is sometimes the case), the marginal cost of one additional setup is zero as far as labor cost is concerned. The accounting cost for a setup may include a labor cost that contains several hours of time at a fully allocated rate. Similarly, what is the cost of using an additional hour of time of a machine that is only utilized 20% of the time? On the other hand, consider the cost of using one hour of time of the machine that is the bottleneck in a production process. This machine may keep us from producing, say, a $5 million computer. The marginal cost of time for this machine is very high indeed. The marginal cost of time for an underutilized machine may be zero.

The accounting system cannot maintain true marginal costs in every situation. The situation changes from time to time. An underutilized machine may become fully utilized, for example. Operations managers must be aware of the idea of marginal costs (the irrelevance of fixed costs), and they must make decisions accordingly. When we study mathematical programming in Appendix C and in several chapters that use it, we will see that the notion of *shadow prices* helps us see the true marginal cost of a constrained resource.

The basic message is to be careful when allocating fixed costs and when estimating the value of a fixed (perhaps capacity-constrained) facility. These questions are discussed at more length in the next subsection (see also Goldratt and Cox 1984; the ideas from Goldratt and Cox are discussed in Chapter 11).

New Approaches to Cost Accounting for Operations Management

Cost figures are necessary for management, but they can be so flawed that they lead to serious errors. How can managers spot potential problems, and what can they do about them? Several recent works, including those of Johnson and Kaplan (1987), Kaplan (1988), Cooper and Kaplan (1988), and Cooper (1989), address these questions. We will summarize some of their key ideas here. Again, the main concerns are (1) the allocation of fixed costs, and (2) the value of a fixed (perhaps constrained) facility.

QUESTION 1: *What symptoms should tell a manager that there are problems with the cost system?* (See Cooper 1989.)

- "Functional managers want to drop products that are profitable according to the cost system." (The managers may know that the "profitable" products use more scarce resources than their allocation of fixed costs implies.) This is often true for low-demand products.
- "Hard-to-make products show big profits."
- "You have a high-margin niche all to yourself." (Why are your competitors so stupid?)
- "Customers don't mind a price increase." (They know that they have been getting a bargain.)

Cooper (1989) gives several other symptoms. He also argues that several new situations can make the old cost system obsolete, including increased automation or the use of other new technologies.

QUESTION 2: *How can we measure costs correctly?* (See Cooper and Kaplan 1988.)

"Activity-based costing" is a method that tries to allocate support costs (that are usually considered fixed or semifixed) to products. The process often shows that low-demand items use more than their "share" of many support activities. By attempting to charge back (to products) distribution, service, computer usage, marketing effort, financial control effort, and other support services, activity-based accounting estimates actual profitability of products. Some costs may be related to the number of stock-keeping units (SKUs) rather than to the amount of sales. Allocating these costs on a dollar-sales basis will overstate the cost for high-demand items and understate the cost for low-demand items. Activity-based accounting attempts to determine the actual total cost, and then unit cost, of a product by charging nearly all costs to some product. Cooper and Kaplan (1988) present an example in which seven SKUs have manufacturing overheads and gross margins that vary dramatically, old system to new (activity-based) system. For a high-volume item, manufacturing overhead per unit went from \$5.44 to \$4.76, and gross margin went from 41% to 46%. For a low-volume item, manufacturing overhead per unit went from \$7.30 to \$77.64, and gross margin went from 47% to −258%.

As an example, suppose that Farm Supply produces B64 and B65 in one production facility. They are identical except that B64 is green and B65 is orange. B64 sells 100 per week; B65, 1 per week.

Current cost estimates:

B64: \$190 material + \$30/hour (2 hours) = \$250
B65: \$190 material + \$30/hour (2 hours) = \$250

The \$30 per hour figure comprises \$12 per hour direct labor cost plus \$18 per hour of allocated overhead. The \$18 figure is computed by adding all overhead costs and dividing by the number of direct labor hours. For simplicity, assume that overhead consists only of the purchasing and production-control departments, and that the direct cost of an hour of labor in these departments is \$20. Activity-based estimates of actual usage of overhead departments by B64 and B65 are

B64: 12 hours per week (at \$20 per hour direct cost)
B65: 6 hours per week (at \$20 per hour direct cost)

Now manufacturing overhead is estimated to be

B64: \$240/week = 240/100 = \$2.40 per item (since weekly demand is 100 units)
B65: \$120/week = 120/1 = \$120 per item (since weekly demand is 1 unit)

and the (activity-based) product cost estimates are

B64: \$190 material + 2 hours (\$12 per direct labor hour) + \$2.40 overhead = \$216.40 (lower than the previous \$250 estimate)
B65: \$190 material + 2 hours (\$12 per direct labor hour) + \$120 overhead = \$334 (higher than the previous \$250 estimate)

QUESTION 3: *Does activity-based costing have limitations?*

Yes. Cooper and Kaplan (1988) say that two costs should not be allocated to products. These are (1) the cost of underutilized capacity and (2) the cost of R & D. Basically, underutilized capacity is not a product's ''fault.'' Allocating the fixed costs over a smaller base will lead to high costs. Although it is true that in the long run all costs must be covered, if a firm acts as if unit costs were increased during a slow period, they might raise the price until demand drops even further.

R & D is a long-term investment (regardless of how governments make companies account for it). In companies with large R & D budgets, *life-cycle costing*, in which a product's viability is examined over its entire life, may be appropriate. Considering R & D costs, the costs of preparing for manufacturing, and the costs of making it, can we make money during the product's life? This is difficult to determine because predictions of cost, demand, and price are needed (and then must be tracked) for the several-year life.

In addition to these limitations of activity-based accounting, there are others. First, the cost of assigning support services to products can be significant. Second, there are services that really are fixed. (They are needed, but they are hard to assign to an individual product.) Any allocation of fixed costs may produce distorted information.

Finally, even if the allocation makes sense, the decision is not automatically made by the numbers. Having B65 may make Farm Supply a ''full-line supplier,'' and customers may come to Farm Supply first because of that. They may choose to raise the price on B65 or not, and only the managers who know the market can decide. Activity-based accounting is another, often better, way to look at product costs, but management still must apply their judgment.

QUESTION 4: *What other cost information might be needed?*

Kaplan (1988) argues that there are three separate purposes for cost systems, and different methods are needed to obtain information for these purposes. The three different functions are as follows:

1. *Inventory valuation.* Done for legal reasons, using standard accounting methods. The standard costs used are updated infrequently, say once per year.
2. *Operational control.* Management needs to make decisions frequently regarding corrections to the operating process. Waiting for monthly cost statements is a mistake. Information for operational control should be collected frequently, including nonfinancial measures such as number of defects and variability of process times. These systems must be tailored to the precise nature of the company's products or services and processes.
3. *Product cost.* Product costs can be developed using activity-based accounting. Product costs are by their nature approximate, but knowing the approximate value is important. Product costs take a lot of effort, but they need to be developed only infrequently, say once per year.

QUESTION 5: *Are changes needed in the basic data collection?*

Many cost systems do not capture the basic data needed for management decisions. Courses and books on cost accounting (see, for example, Bierman et al., 1990) discuss this issue. We will only note here that transactions can be captured in a way that supports the multiple uses of cost information.

REVIEW PROBLEMS

The cost analysis for B64 and B65 revealed the following:

	Old Figures	New Figures
B64	$250	$216.40
B65	$250	$334.00

The weekly demands are 100 for B64 and 1 for B65. Harry LaRoe of Farm Supply has discovered another overhead item, ''the president's time.'' On the average, the president spends (1/100) hour/week on each of these items. The direct cost of the president's time is $500/hour.

1. Recompute the activity-based cost estimates, including this new overhead item.

2. The theory behind activity-based cost estimates is that even ''fixed'' costs are variable in the long run. Or the fixed resources could be put

to other use at least equal in value to the direct cost if we dropped a product. How does the theory apply in question 1, in your opinion?

Solutions

1. B64: cost/unit = \$216.40/unit
   + (0.01 hour/week)(\$500/hour)/(100 units/week)
   = \$216.40/unit + \$0.05/unit = \$216.90/unit.

   B65: cost/unit = \$334.00/unit
   + (0.01 hour/week)(\$500/hour)/(1 unit/week)
   = \$334.00/unit + \$5.00/unit = \$339.00/unit.

2. The president's salary, while not fixed, is not easy to reduce. Thus, we might choose not to allocate this activity. However, since the president's time presumably does have value, dropping B65 and saving a few minutes might be useful.

3-3 BREAK-EVEN ANALYSIS AND INVESTMENT ANALYSIS*

Break-even analysis determines the number of units we must sell to cover fixed costs. This is relevant, for example, if we are considering buying a new facility.

Suppose that a small hospital is considering a radiology unit. The unit would cost \$80,000 per year for equipment rental and maintenance, \$120,000 per year for a radiologist, and \$80,000 per year in other salaries. The total, \$280,000 per year, is all fixed cost. The average charge for each service the radiology unit performs is \$40, and the average variable cost, for materials such as film, is \$4. Symbolically,

$$\begin{aligned} \text{FC} &= \text{Fixed cost} = \$280{,}000 \text{ per year} \\ \text{VC} &= \text{variable cost per unit} = \$4 \\ \text{REV} &= \text{revenue per unit} = \$40 \\ N &= \text{units (number of radiology visits) per year} \end{aligned}$$

The total revenue per year is

$$(\text{REV})N = \$40N$$

The total cost per year is

$$\$280{,}000 + (\text{VC})N = \$280{,}000 + \$4N$$

These two relationships are graphed in Figure 3-3.

The fixed costs of \$280,000 are the key to the economic side of the decision whether to begin a radiology unit. (Medical considerations must be included, of course.) The point where the two lines cross in Figure 3-3 is the *break-even point*, the minimum N (number of radiology visits) necessary to cover the fixed costs. Symbolically,

$$\text{FC} + (\text{VC})N = (\text{REV})N \text{ at the break-even point}$$

*This section can be skipped by readers with basic accounting and finance background.

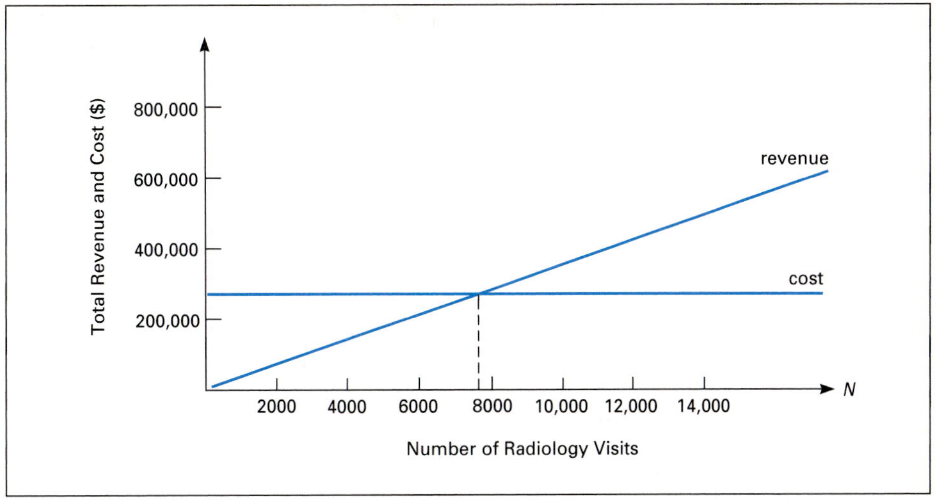

Figure 3-3 Graph of Total Revenue and Total Cost, Radiology Problem

Solving yields

$$N = \frac{\text{FC}}{\text{REV} - \text{VC}} = \frac{280{,}000}{40 - 4} = 7778$$

If more than 7778 visits to radiology are made per year, the radiology unit will make money for the hospital.

It may be that the amount of fixed costs depends on the number of visits, or on output of the product in a manufacturing setting. For example, at 10,000 visits, another radiologist plus some other paraprofessionals, at a total cost of $160,000, may be necessary. The extra expense is referred to as a *semifixed* cost. The new cost relationships are shown in Figure 3-4.

The second break-even point occurs at $N = 12{,}222$. Between 10,000 visits and 12,222 visits, the hospital would again lose money on the radiology unit. Whether to start the unit and whether to hire a second radiologist will depend on their estimate of N, the demand for the service.

Figure 3-4 Costs and Revenues of Radiology Unit, Including Semifixed Costs

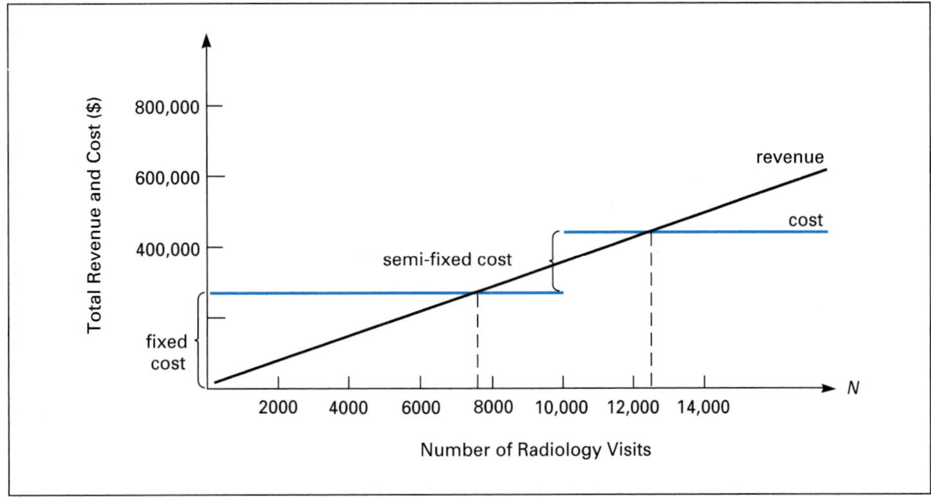

A final point about break-even analysis is that cost curves often are not really linear as shown. In a production situation, people learn how to produce an item as they make it; thus, the cost per unit may decrease. However, since unit costs are an output of engineering estimates or a cost accounting system, linear cost functions (constant unit costs) are typically used. It is a manager's job to be alert to any glaring errors in the cost assumptions of a break-even analysis.

REVIEW PROBLEM

Show how the second break-even point in Figure 3-4, at $N = 12{,}222$, can be computed.

Solution

The fixed and semifixed costs must both be recovered past $N = 10{,}000$. Thus FC = 440,000, REV = 40, and VC = 4, and the second break-even point is 440,000/(40 − 4) = 12,222.

Investment Analysis

A break-even analysis as just described does not take into account the fact that a dollar today is worth more than a dollar next year. That is, future revenues should be *discounted;* they are worth less than current revenue. Analyzing capital investment projects is a well-developed science (see Bierman and Smidt 1988). In this text we will give only a brief introduction to the topic, considering again the Farm Supply Corporation.

Harry LaRoe of Farm Supply believes that the New York distribution center should be expanded. There are two plans, A and B, under consideration. A report from the consulting team indicates that shipment costs would decrease in the entire distribution system by $475,000 per year, for each of the next 10 years, if the facility is expanded using plan A. The 10-year period represents the expected time before major refurbishing is needed for the distribution center, at which time the net value of the investment will be zero. The investment required for the expansion using plan A is $1.4 million. Plan B would save $550,000 per year and cost $2.1 million. Which, if either, of these investments should be made?

The simplest method of investment analysis is to determine a *payback period*. This has serious flaws and should be used only for a quick calculation to indicate obvious acceptability or unacceptability. The payback period is the time by which the investment is recovered.

For example, plan A pays back $475,000 per year. The investment cost is $1.4 million. By the end of the third year, plan A will have returned $1,425,000; thus, plan A's payback is 3 years (or slightly less). Plan B takes slightly less than 4 years to pay back the $2.1 million investment.

An organization such as Farm Supply might use a maximum payback period of anywhere between 2 and 5 years, depending on their capital situation and the perceived riskiness of a venture. Suppose that the criterion level is 4 years. That means that any investment with a payback period less than or equal to 4 years is acceptable. Thus, both plans are acceptable, and we do not know how to choose between them. If we were using payback with a 4-year criterion level, we would know that some expansion is appropriate.

A preferable method for investment analysis involves *net present value* (NPV). In an NPV analysis, cash flows are *discounted* back to the present in a manner analogous to the compounding done by the bank to figure the future value of a current bank account.

The total saving of $475,000 times 10 or $4,750,000, must be discounted back to time zero and compared against the $1.4 million investment. (We will treat the saving as if it occurred entirely at the end of the year rather than as if it were spread evenly throughout the year. Using integral calculus, it can be done assuming a constant rate throughout the year, but the result is essentially the same.) The rate of discount to use is discussed extensively in finance texts (see, for example, Brealey and Myers 1988). For business organizations with access to capital markets, the cost of debt and the cost of equity capital must be considered. For nonprofit organizations, the cost of debt, if debt is available, must be considered. If any type of organization is under capital constraints, a discount rate must be set high enough that only available funds are invested.

Discounting of future cash flows is accomplished by multiplying them by

$$\left(\frac{1}{1+i}\right)^t$$

where i is the discount rate and t the number of years in the future. (If monthly periods are used for t, a monthly discount rate must be used.)

A proper analysis of an investment problem should consider the tax benefits (investment tax credits and tax effects of depreciation). Before illustrating such complexities, we will show a before-tax analysis. This is used by many profit-making organizations and by nonprofit organizations. A firm such as Farm Supply might use $i = 0.18$ on a before-tax basis. Then the present value of the cost savings would be

$$(475{,}000)\left(\frac{1}{1+0.18}\right)^1 + (475{,}000)\left(\frac{1}{1+0.18}\right)^2 + \ldots + (475{,}000)\left(\frac{1}{1+0.18}\right)^{10}$$

$$= (475{,}000)\left[\sum_{t=1}^{10}\left(\frac{1}{1.18}\right)^t\right]$$

$$= (475{,}000)(0.84746 + 0.71819 + \ldots + 0.19107)$$

$$= \$2{,}134{,}700$$

The net present value of plan A is the present value of the cost saving minus the investment cost. Thus, for plan A, using a discount rate of 18%,

$$\text{NPV} = 2{,}134{,}700 - 1{,}400{,}000 = \$734{,}700$$

A positive NPV implies that an investment is worthwhile since it earns more than the required rate of return, which was 18% in the example.

Two comments are in order here. First, there is an easy formula to use in evaluating an *annuity*, which is a stream of equal payments for T periods, as in the foregoing. When A is the annual amount, i the discount rate, and T the number of years for which the payments will occur, the present value of an annuity is

$$\text{PV} = A\left[\frac{1-(1+i)^{-T}}{i}\right] \tag{8}$$

For plan A we obtain

$$PV = (475{,}000)\left[\frac{1 - (1.18)^{-10}}{0.18}\right] = (475{,}000)(4.494) = \$2{,}134{,}700$$

We will use equation 8 several times in the following discussion. There are, in fact, formulas for many such situations, and these can be looked up in books on the mathematics of finance or engineering economics. Also, inexpensive calculators can compute present values.

Second, we can find, by trial and error or search procedures using calculators or computers, the discount rate that causes NPV to be zero. This rate is the *internal rate of return* of the investment. For plan A, this value is approximately 31.8%. An investment that returns 31.8% is an attractive investment for most organizations. Having seen the foregoing calculations, LaRoe made the same calculations for Plan B, using equation 8. First, using $i = 0.18$, he obtained

$$NPV = 550{,}000\left[\frac{1 - (1.18)^{-10}}{0.18}\right] - 2{,}100{,}000 = \$371{,}700$$

The discount rate that gives NPV = 0 is 22.8%, or 0.228. Based on this analysis, Farm Supply should select plan A. They should select the plan with the larger net present value. The internal rate of return is useful management information, but it should not be used to select between plans in a situation such as the present one. The reasons for this are discussed in finance texts.

After-Tax Analysis

After-tax analysis depends on the investment tax credit in effect at the time, the depreciation method used, the firm's tax rate, and the firm's after-tax cost of capital. All these topics are discussed by Bierman and Smidt (1988), as well as in courses and texts on finance and accounting. This method is preferable in profit-making organizations because it properly measures the actual monetary effect on the firm. There are four steps:

1. Deduct the investment tax credit (if any) from the investment.
2. Deduct taxes that must be paid on all returns.
3. Include the tax saving due to depreciation as a new stream of cash flows.
4. Find the net present value of the investment using the foregoing and the after-tax discount rate. (The after-tax discount rate is lower than the before-tax rate, but it will not in general be the before-tax rate times 1 minus the tax rate. Ways of computing before- and after-tax discount rates are discussed in finance texts.)

For example, suppose that $i = 0.13$ is the after-tax discount rate for Farm Supply, and the tax rate is 0.34. An investment tax credit of 8% applies to the entire investment in either plan A or plan B. Finally, we will use straight-line depreciation over the 10-year life of the investment, still assuming zero value 10 years from now. This implies that 1/10 of the investment is deducted from income in each of the 10 years. For plan A, this means that (1/10)(1,400,000) = \$140,000 depreciation expense is incurred every year, and the tax rate times that amount, (0.34)(140,000) = \$47,600, is saved each year in taxes. There are other methods of depreciation that allow a firm to obtain the tax benefits faster, thus favoring the capital investment. These methods will not be discussed here.

The after-tax analysis for plan A is as follows:

$$\begin{aligned}\text{Net investment after deducting tax credit} &= (1{,}400{,}000)(1 - 0.08)\\ &= \$1{,}288{,}000\\ \text{After-tax yearly saving} &= (475{,}000)(1 - 0.34)\\ &= \$313{,}500\\ \text{Yearly tax saving due to depreciation} &= (1/10)(1{,}400{,}000)(0.34)\\ &= \$47{,}600\\ \text{Total saving per year} &= 313{,}500 + 47{,}600\\ &= \$361{,}100\end{aligned}$$

Using equation 8, with $A = 361{,}100$, $T = 10$, and $i = 0.13$, the net present value of the saving is

$$(361{,}100)\left[\frac{1 - (1.13)^{-10}}{0.13}\right] = (361{,}100)(5.426) = \$1{,}959{,}000$$

The net value, after taxes, of plan A, is

$$\$1{,}959{,}000 - \$1{,}288{,}000 = \$671{,}000$$

Properly accounting for the time value of money is crucial for an operations manager. In business firms, obtaining a high rate of return is a primary objective. In public organizations, which nearly always have limited capital, the dollars that are available must be used in the most advantageous way. Still, financial analysis is only part of the decision process, as we will discuss in subsequent chapters.

REVIEW PROBLEM

Find the net present value, after taxes, of plan B. The annual saving is \$550,000, and the investment required is \$2.1 million. Use $i = 0.13$, a tax rate of 0.34, an investment tax credit of 0.08, and straight-line depreciation over a 10-year life.

Solution

$$\begin{aligned}\text{Net investment after deducting tax credit} &= (2{,}100{,}000)(1 - 0.08)\\ &= \$1{,}932{,}000\\ \text{After-tax yearly saving} &= (550{,}000)(1 - 0.34)\\ &= \$363{,}000\\ \text{Yearly tax saving due to depreciation} &= (1/10)(2{,}100{,}000)(0.34)\\ &= \$71{,}400\end{aligned}$$

$$\text{Total saving per year} = 363{,}000 + 71{,}400 = \$434{,}400$$

Using equation 8, the net present value of the saving is

$$434{,}400\left[\frac{1-(1.13)^{-10}}{0.13}\right] = (434{,}400)(5.426) = \$2{,}357{,}000$$

The net present value, after taxes, of plan B, is

$$\$2{,}357{,}000 - 1{,}932{,}000 = \$425{,}000$$

The company should select the larger net present value—plan A. In this case both a before-tax and an after-tax analysis suggested the same decision; this will not always be so.

SUMMARY

Models are useful in operations management because experimenting with the actual system can be very expensive. However, using bad models or inappropriately using a good model can lead to serious mistakes.

For a model to be "good," the manager must be involved to see that (a) the right problem is being solved, (b) the important items are included (the right "system" definition is being used), and (c) any assumptions made are reasonable for the purpose at hand. Models cannot be perfect; they can be useful. For a model to be useful, the output of a good model must be scrutinized by a manager, as input to the decision. Very rarely should models actually *make* a decision in an operations management situation.

Both for use in models and, more importantly, for day-to-day decisions, managers must develop cost estimates that are appropriate. Commonly used cost accounting methods give poor cost figures in many cases. First, managers must know this and not use inappropriate cost estimates. Second, they must examine the management accounting system, from basic data gathering to developing cost estimates to using those values. Three distinct uses of cost figures (inventory valuation, operational control, and product costing) require different accounting methods. Activity-based costing can be very helpful for product costing. Operational control is discussed in Chapter 5. Standard accounting methods can be used to value inventory.

Even the new methods can lead to bad estimates. The basic difficulty arises out of the allocation of "fixed" costs, and it is unclear what costs are really fixed. All cost estimates require that management judgment be applied after the estimate is made, before decision making.

Operations management requires the use of complicated mathematical and computer models. It requires advanced cost estimating methods. And it requires an experienced manager who both knows the marketplace and the people and the facilities in his or her organization and can effectively combine that experience with analysis to obtain good decisions. That last sentence is good news. It means that operations management is interesting and challenging, and that the managers cannot be replaced by a computer.

PROBLEMS

*1. The Farm Supply Corporation has 250 stores, 3 distribution centers, and 1 plant. In analyzing the layout for one store, is it reasonable to build a model of only that one store and ignore the rest of the system? Why or why not?

2. In determining the long-term staffing plan for one fire station in a metropolitan fire department, should our model(s) consider the entire metropolitan system, or only this one station? Why?

3. One of the questions managers must ask about models is, are we using the correct objectives? Suggest two alternatives to
   a. minimizing the average time a customer waits for a spare part, in Farm Supply (see problem 1)
   b. minimizing the average time to first truck arrival, after a call, in a municipal fire system (see problem 2)

4. In addition to considering the objectives used in a model, managers must consider whether (a) key items are included in the model, (b) input values (such as costs) are correct, and (c) any assumptions made are reasonable.
   For the mathematical programming model described in Section 3-1, briefly discuss possible difficulties of each of these three types.

5. (Refer to problem 4.) For the four-station simulation model described in Section 3-1, briefly discuss difficulties of each of the three types.

*6. Farm Supply Corporation currently maintains its own trucking operation. Shipments are made from the DC to each store twice per week. They are considering making daily shipments to each store. What tradeoffs are involved in this decision?

7. A regional blood bank makes daily shipments of fresh blood to each hospital in the region. They are considering shipping every other day. What trade-offs are involved in this decision?

8. A publisher is considering how many copies of a new book to print in a first printing. What trade-offs are involved in this decision?

*9. In Section 3-1 the following equation was introduced:

$$TC(Q) = F_I C_u \frac{Q}{2} + \frac{D}{Q} C_S$$

   A firm is considering order quantities for a \$5 item. They use $F_I =$ 0.15 per year and $C_S =$ \$2.50. The annual demand is 4000 units. They are considering order quantities of 200, 500, or 1000. Which should the firm choose?

10. (This problem uses the data introduced in problem 9.) If the unit cost is \$5 in batches of 200, \$4.96 in batches of 500, and \$4.91 in batches of 1000, what order quantity should the firm use?

*11. Consider the mathematical program of equations 4 to 7. Suppose that we change equation 5 to

$$\sum_{i=1}^{3} X_{ij} \leq \text{DEM}_j \quad \text{for each store, } j = 1, \ldots, 250$$

   What solution would the computer think is optimal?

*Problems with an asterisk have answers in the back of the book.

12. Consider the mathematical program of equations 4 to 7. Suppose that we change equation 6 to

$$\sum_{j=1}^{250} X_{ij} = \text{CAP}_i \quad \text{for each DC, } i = 1, 2, \text{ or } 3$$

What problems may the computer encounter?

13. Consider the following production-scheduling problem, with only one product:

Period	1	2	3
Demand	10	20	50
Capacity	40	40	40

Production cost per unit is thought to be $20; inventory cost per unit, $0.50 per period; setup cost, $300 per setup. They are considering several different production plans, with production patterns of (10, 20, 50), (10, 30, 40), (40, 0, 40), and (25, 25, 30), respectively.

a. Compute the cost of each of these plans. Are there any problems in doing so? If so, make some reasonable assumption that allows you to proceed.

b. Discuss ways in which the foregoing cost estimates might be incorrect.

14. (Refer to problem 13 for basic data.) On reconsideration, management feels that the marginal cost of a setup is 0, and that inventory cost is only $0.30 per unit per period. Further, production cost is $20 and overtime cost is $25.

a. Which of the proposed production plans is best, using this cost structure?

b. Explain why you might really choose a different solution. Notice that your reasons are weaknesses in the cost model; some items must be considered qualitatively, by the manager.

15. In Section 3-2, four suggestions were given for improving the management of Farm Supply's inventory system. Do you agree with the suggestions? How would you modify them? Would your answer change if Farm Supply were a *cooperative*, whose stated goal was to provide the best service possible, subject to a constraint of breaking even each year?

*16. An accounting firm is considering opening an office in a new city. The annual fixed cost of operating a new office is $115,000. The average revenue from a client is $18,000 per year, and the average marginal cost of a client is $9,000. How many clients do they need in order to break even? How might an analysis of this type be improved?

17. In Section 3-3 two break-even points were computed for a radiology unit: one to cover the $280,000 fixed cost and one to cover the $160,000 semifixed cost. The semifixed cost must be paid if N (the number of visits) exceeds 10,000. Suppose that if N exceeds 20,000 visits, another $160,000 must be expended. The revenue from one

visit is $40 and the marginal cost is $4. What value of N would be required to break even and cover the 280,000 + 160,000 + 160,000 = $600,000 fixed and semifixed costs? What does the answer mean?

*18. Compute the net present value of a $1,000,000 investment that will return $400,000 at the end of 1 year, $500,000 at the end of 2 years, $600,000 at the end of 3 years, and no other returns. Use a discount rate of $i = 0.15$.

*19. The manager of traffic and distribution for a large firm is considering renting trucks rather than purchasing them. The rental agreement would cost $2 million per year for the next 5 years. The purchase cost would be $5 million. Maintenance would be the same under either plan, and the trucks would be worthless after 5 years of intensive use. Ignoring the tax effects and using a discount rate of $i = 0.16$, should the manager buy the trucks?

20. (This problem uses the data from problem 19.) The investment tax credit is 10% of the investment. The tax rate is 0.48. The firm is using straight-line depreciation. Using an after-tax analysis with a discount rate of $i = 0.09$, should the manager buy the trucks?

*21. (This problem refers to problems 19 and 20.) Would the following changes tend to make buying the trucks look more or less attractive than shown in the analysis in Problem 20? Why?
   a. a salvage value at the end of the 5 years
   b. a faster depreciation method, such as the sum of years' digits or double declining balance.

22. A machine shop manager has two machines that can do the same milling operation. Machine B, which is designed for high volume, has a larger initial setup cost but lower per-unit variable costs.

Machine	Setup Costs	Variable Cost per Unit
A	$ 8	$0.24
B	80	0.09

The manager wants to determine which machine to schedule to minimize total cost when an order requires milling.
   a. Determine the total cost equation for each machine.
   b. Plot these two equations on one graph.
   c. At what volume do machines A and B have the same total cost?
   d. What decision rule should the manager use when determining which machine to use for a particular order requiring milling?

23. What three different purposes of cost systems are suggested by Kaplan (1988)? With what frequency is each one needed?

24. What basic information is required to develop activity-based cost estimates?

*25. Brellum Publications Corporation (BPC) produces advertising brochures and supplements, and a few business periodicals. Currently, they have three monthly publications. Some cost information is as follows:

	Per Unit		Per Issue				
	Cost of Raw Materials	Usage of Direct Labor	Usage of Editorial Time	Usage of Artist Time	Usage of Other Professional Time	Sales per Month	Selling Price
Ithaca Business Monthly	$0.20	0.05 hr	30 hrs	5 hrs	20 hrs	700	$3.00
Tompkins County Tourism	$0.36	0.08 hr	50 hrs	30 hrs	20 hrs	300	$4.50
Rutabaga Farming	$0.18	0.04 hr	15 hrs	20 hrs	20 hrs	400	$2.50

Direct labor cost is $12 per hour for salary and fringe benefits, or $45 per hour "fully loaded," with all overhead costs allocated to direct labor. Editorial, artist, and other professional time has a direct cost of $15 per hour.

a. Using only the cost of materials and the fully loaded cost of direct labor, estimate product cost and gross margin. (That is, do not use any "per-issue" costs.) Comment briefly on the validity of these estimates.

b. Including the per-issue costs, and using the $12 and $15 direct costs, develop activity-based estimates of product cost and gross margin. Comment briefly on the differences between the estimates in parts a and b.

26. (Refer to problem 25 for basic information.) For all three publications, management believes that they could get a $0.50 increase in price if they upgraded the paper and ran an extra color in printing. These changes would not affect any overhead items. Raw-materials cost would go up by $0.12 per publication. Direct labor would increase by 0.01 hour.

a. Using the fully allocated cost for labor ($45), does gross margin increase if we make these changes?

b. Using the direct cost of labor ($12), does gross margin increase if we make these changes?

If they make the changes but leave the selling price the same, management believes that they can increase sales of each magazine by 300 units over current levels. Use this information for parts c and d.

c. Are these changes profitable, based on standard cost procedures, using the $45 fully allocated cost of labor?

d. Are these changes profitable, based on activity-based cost estimates, for each product? (Refer to the answers in the back of the book for activity-based cost estimates from problem 25 part b.)

27. (This problem requires solutions to problems 25 and 26 as input.) Consider the option of deleting products and the price-increase and demand-increase options described in problem 26. What do you think they should do? Why? Support your suggestions with calculations.

REFERENCES

BIERMAN, H., and S. SMIDT, *The Capital Budgeting Decision*, 7th ed., New York: Macmillain, 1988.

BIERMAN, H., T. DYCKMAN, and R. HILTON, *Cost Accounting: Concepts and Applications*, Boston: PWS-Kent, 1990.

BREALEY, R., and S. MYERS, *Principles of Corporate Finance*, 3rd ed., New York: McGraw-Hill, 1988.

CONWAY, R., W.L. MAXWELL, J.O. MCCLAIN, and S.L. WORONA, *The XCELL + Factory Modeling System*, Palo Alto, Calif.: Scientific Press, 1987.

COOPER, R., and R.S. KAPLAN, "Measure Costs Right: Make the Right Decisions," *Harvard Business Review*, September–October, 1988.

COOPER, R., "You Need A New Cost System When . . . ," *Harvard Business Review*, January–February, 1989.

GOLDRATT, E., and J. COX, *The Goal: Excellence in Manufacturing*, Croton-on-Hudson, New York: North River Press, 1984.

HARRIS, F.W., "How Many Parts to Make At Once," *Factory, The Magazine of Management*, 10, 135–136, 152, 1913.

JOHNSON, H.T., and R.S. KAPLAN, *Relevance Lost: The Rise and Fall Of Management Accounting*, Cambridge, Mass.: Harvard Business School Press, 1987.

KAPLAN, R.S., "One Cost System Isn't Enough," *Harvard Business Review*, January–February, 1988.

SPENCE, A., and E. PORTEUS, "Setup Reduction and Increased Effective Capacity," *Management Science*, 33, 10 (October), 1987.

SHINGO, S., *Study of the Toyota Production System from an IE Viewpoint*, Revised, Cambridge, Mass.: Productivity Press, 1989.

THOMAS, L.J., D.B. EDWARDS, and J.O. MCCLAIN, *Cases in Operations Management: Using the XCELL Factory Modeling System*, Palo Alto, Calif.: Scientific Press, 1989.

c h a p t e r

4

Project Management

Task forces or special-purpose teams are effective ways to complete projects. Developing new long-range strategies, bringing out a new service or product, building and moving into new facilities, implementing new quality assurance procedures, finding ways to increase productivity—these are but a few of the many common managerial activities that can be described as projects.

New—that is the common element. A project is typically a one-of-a-kind task. Project management is therefore very different from management of continuing (repetitive) operations such as a retail store or a factory. Activities that have never been done before are commonly undertaken as projects. Usually the manager can draw on experience with similar activities. However, some activities are so new and different that the only transferable experience is that of managing unique undertakings. Project management is a profession that specializes in this uncertain environment.

Projects typically cut across organizational boundaries. For example, consider the design and implementation of an information system. Many people typically share such a system, so effective design requires their cooperation and active participation. The diversity of points of view can be extreme. Sales representatives need to know which products are currently available, lead times for other products, prices, discounts, and so forth. Most of this information depends on the activities of other people. Lead times, for example, depend on how manufacturing priorities are set, but the information requirements of manufacturing are very different (availability of raw materials, equipment, personnel, skills, schedules, etc.) A project to design an information system must address these diverse but overlapping needs.

Brunies (1989) suggests that project management approaches are most beneficial for undertakings that

- are concerned with an identifiable end product
- are complex in scope

- require significant contribution by more than two functional organizations
- require quick response to change
- are unique or infrequent
- have a high degree of interdependence among the tasks
- are vital to a company's reputation or have unusually high rewards for success or penalties for failure.

As you can see, projects are likely to have high visibility; this is why effective project management is often an important step in career advancement.

The field of project management has advanced rapidly in the past twenty years. Journals, books, and conferences abound for the professional project manager. Much of the material for this introduction has been drawn from the book *Project Management: A Reference for Professionals* (Kimmons and Lowree 1989), a collection of over one hundred articles by experienced project managers and educators. We spend most of one chapter describing a technique for planning and management, whereas that book spends over three hundred pages describing what goes into a project before formal planning begins. In other words, there is much more to project planning than can be conveyed in one chapter. The references at the end of this chapter will guide you to further reading.

Elements of a Project

Projects have four interrelated elements: goals, timing, resources, and environment. Goals can be quite diverse. The goal of a construction project might be on-time completion at minimum cost. In contrast, installing a new inventory system with minimum disruption may be more important than meeting a set deadline or minimizing cost. Low cost is usually one of the goals of a project, but it is not always paramount.

The time element of a project includes deadlines, lead times to procure resources, and schedules of activities, personnel, and equipment. The sequence in which activities may be done is also important. For example, furniture should not be installed in a new office until the floor covering is in place.

Resources include personnel, equipment, and materials. Identifying needed resources is important, and coordinating their use through time can be difficult because of conflicting schedules and the sequence requirements.

The environment in which a project is carried out includes both the physical environment (such as weather) and the characteristics of the organization. Environment can strongly influence timing, availability of resources, and even the choice of goals. Much of the uncertainty faced by a project manager arises in the environment.

History of Network Planning Methods

The United States Navy was faced with an immense coordination problem in the development of Polaris, the first weapons system that could launch a long-range ballistic missile from a submerged submarine. To coordinate the activities of 11,000 contractors, a new method was invented, now known as PERT (from Program Evaluation and Review Technique). This method was used to evaluate proposed changes in schedule to prevent delays in the ultimate completion date. The application was considered very successful (Malcolm et al. 1959), and led to widespread use of the technique.

At about the same time, the Critical Path Method (CPM) was developed at Du Pont, in consultation with Remington-Rand. It was soon recognized that PERT and CPM were the same idea. Since that time both have evolved substantially, but the essential concept remains the same.

PERT/CPM is based on a diagram that represents the entire project as a network of arrows and nodes. In the diagram method we will use, nodes are boxes or circles representing activities, and arrows show *precedence relationships* among activities. A precedence relationship states that (for example) activity X must be completed before activity Y can begin. The resulting diagram can be used to identify potential scheduling difficulties, to estimate the time needed to complete the entire project, and to improve the project's coordination. For large projects, PERT/CPM diagrams may cover whole walls with information such as when each activity is scheduled to begin and notes such as "continued in corridor G, second floor."

PERT and CPM are easy to understand and use. Computerized versions are available for both small- and large-scale projects, but manual calculation is quite suitable for many situations in everyday management. The trade literature abounds with applications, ranging from new product introduction to opening a new hospital.

Unfortunately, some managers have placed too much reliance on PERT/CPM, at the expense of good management (Vazsonyi 1970). For example, when activities are scheduled for a designated time slot, there is a tendency to try to meet the schedule at all costs. These time pressures may lead to inadequate work in some activities, the results of which may not be felt until near the scheduled project completion time. For example, in developing a new product, if tests are shortened or eliminated as a result of time pressure, design flaws may be discovered much later in the project. Correcting the design may require many activities to be repeated. As a consequence, a project that appeared to be under control is suddenly several months behind schedule and substantially over the planned budget. When this happens, it is convenient to blame PERT/CPM even though the real cause is poor management.

Properly used, network planning methods can yield spectacular results. For example, new product development times have been shortened dramatically (Clark and Fujimoto 1989) by careful study of the activities with three goals: elimination, simplification, and simultaneity. Elimination of activities is possible because procedures have developed gradually over many years, and steps that once had a useful purpose often survive after becoming outmoded. Simplification is usually the result of new ideas. Simultaneity refers to doing many activities at the same time. For example, the design of a new product logically precedes the testing of it. However, if part of the testing can take place at the same time as design, the project can be completed earlier. Simultaneity requires examining activities and rearranging them to permit overlapping them in time.

In this chapter project planning will be described in three phases: *planning, scheduling,* and *control*. Planning consists of identifying the important elements of the project, preliminary data gathering, constructing a PERT/CPM diagram, and using it to identify critical elements of the project. Scheduling makes use of this information to coordinate the project, taking into consideration where changes in personnel or other resources will have the most beneficial effect. Once the project is under way, PERT/CPM can be used to *monitor* and *control* the project's progress.

4-1 PROJECT PLANNING AND ANALYSIS

"Now I feel we have a good overall view of the project. Even if we stopped right here, this activity analysis has been worthwhile." This is a typical comment of a manager engaged in the project-planning phase, during which the project is described as a list of activities, each with a responsible person and an estimated duration. The definition of each activity is obtained in consultation with the person responsible, who provides time estimates based on previous experience.

Time estimation should be approached carefully. One method is to ask for "worst-case" and "best-case" estimates before requesting the "most likely" activity duration. This allows a person to express concerns and uncertainty about the future before making a forecast. In addition, the difference between the worst and best cases can be a useful measure of uncertainty, as we will see later.

In addition to defining activities and estimating the required time, a list of *predecessors* is constructed for each activity. Predecessors are activities that must be finished before an activity can begin. (For example, electrical wiring must be completed before lighting fixtures can be installed.) The list is kept as short as possible by excluding all but the immediate predecessors[1]. Otherwise activities near the end of the project would have gigantic predecessor lists.

Other details of the activity are also recorded, such as the number and type of personnel and equipment required, procurement lead times for materials, and special requirements such as dust-free environment or clear weather. The result of an activity analysis of a project to implement a new office procedure is presented in Table 4-1.

Table 4-1 Installing a New Office Procedure

Activity	Activity Code	Duration (days)	Predecessors
Preliminary training	A	5	none
Procure full supply of forms	B	8	D
Train personnel to use new forms	C	6	A, D
Modify forms for new system	D	11	none
Train personnel on new equipment	E	7	A, C

The Network (Arrow) Diagram

All the information in Table 4-1 is represented in the last diagram in Figure 4-1. This is an activity-on-node diagram. Each box (node) represents an activity and the arrows show precedence.[2] A procedure for drawing a network diagram follows, using the data in Table 4-1 as an illustration.

[1]If A precedes B and B precedes C, then A is not an immediate predecessor of C.

[2]Another version will be described later in which arrows represent both activities and precedence.

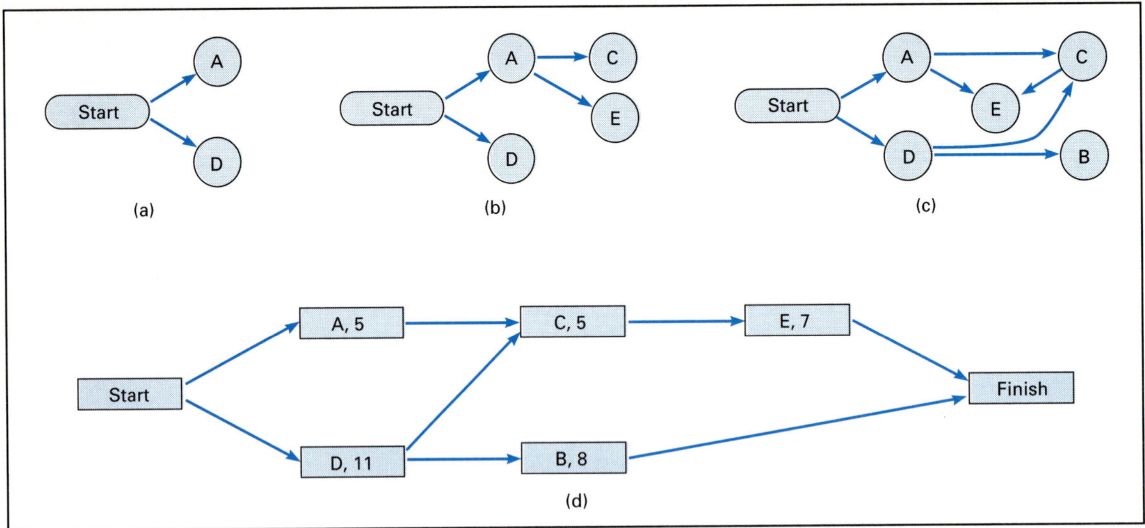

Figure 4-1 Constructing an Activity-on-Node Diagram for the Project in Table 4-1

How to Draw an Activity-on-Node Diagram

1. First, draw a node (box or circle) called START, at the left-hand side of the page.
2. Draw a node for each activity that has no predecessors, and draw an arrow from START to each node. (Since activities A and D have no predecessors, they are added first. See Figure 4-1a.)
3. Consider the first activity node that you drew (A); study the right-hand column in Table 4-1 to see whether it is a predecessor for other activities. Since A precedes both C and E, we need two arrows, one from A to C and the other from A to E. Nodes C and E are added to the diagram, and the two arrows are drawn as in Figure 4-1b. Now, all the information concerning activity A is on the chart, so we put a check mark (✓) beside A in Table 4-1.
4. Now choose any other activity that is already in the diagram and draw arrows wherever that activity is a predecessor, adding new nodes as necessary. Then put a ✓ beside it in the table. For example, activity D is on the chart now, and the right-hand column of Table 4-1 show that D precedes both C and B. C is already in the diagram, so we draw an arrow from D to C. B is not yet in the diagram, so we add node B and then draw an arrow from D to B. Then we ✓ activity D.
5. Repeat step 4 until every activity has a ✓ beside it in the table. At this point the diagram will resemble Figure 4-1c.
6. Draw a FINISH node. Look for ''dead-end'' nodes (those with no arrows pointing outward) and connect them to the FINISH node. In Figure 4-1c activities B and E need this finishing touch.
7. Now go back and clean up the mess you have made. This time, use rectangular nodes, and reduce the number or arrows that cross each other to a minimum. Eliminate any redundant arrows, such as from A to E in Figure 4-1d. (Can you explain why this arrow is not needed?)
8. On each node write in the estimated activity time.

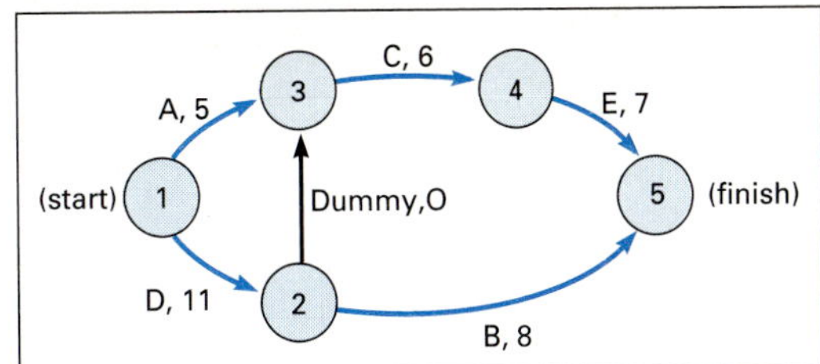

Figure 4-2 Activity-on-Arrow Diagram Equivalent to Figure 4-1d.

Activity-on-Arrow Diagrams. As was mentioned earlier, another common network diagramming method uses arrows to represent both activities and precedence. However, this method requires two kinds of arrows, as illustrated by the ''dummy'' arrow between nodes 2 and 3 in Figure 4-2. The dummy is needed to show that both D and A must be completed before C can begin.

The ''nodes'' (circles) in this diagram are numbered only for reference. Each node signifies an event. For example, node 3 signifies that activities A and D are both finished. Focusing on events has certain advantages, and this technique is widely used.[3] In the next section, we will develop time-scale charts in which the length of the arrow shows the activity's duration. This removes the distinction between activity-on-arrow and activity-on-node.

Precedence Diagramming. Notice that all arrows in Figure 4-1 are from the end of one activity to the start of another (end-to-start). Precedence diagramming allows arrows to be drawn from end-to-end, start-to-start and start-to-end. The computations and interpretation are very similar to the usual PERT/CPM method. Wiest (1981) describes this method and some unusual characteristics that it has. No further discussion of precedence diagramming is given in this chapter.

Calculations Using the Network Diagram

Earliest Start and Finish Times. Time zero is defined to be the earliest start time of the project. Each activity has an earliest start (ES) and an earliest finish (EF) time. The earliest start time depends on the predecessors. *An acivity can start when all its predecessors are finished;* it must wait for the *last* of its predecessors. Thus,

$$ES_i = \max \{\text{EF of the predecessors of activity } i\} \qquad (1)$$

in which ''max'' means maximum, or in this case, the last predecessor to finish. The earliest finish time of an activity is simply the earliest start time plus the activity time (AT):

$$EF_i = ES_i + AT_i \text{ for each activity } i \qquad (2)$$

To use these formulas, we work from left to right in the diagram. For example, in Figure 4-3 activities A and D both have earliest start times of 0. (They have no predecessors.) Since activity A takes 5 days, its earliest finish time is $EF_A = 0 + 5 =$ day 5; D can be done by $EF_D = 0 + 11 =$ day 11. However, when we come to activity C, the situation is more complicated. Look at Figure 4-3 to see why C cannot begin at time 5 (when A is completed) but

[3]Activity-on-arrow diagrams are usually associated with PERT, whereas CPM commonly uses nodes as activities and arrows for precedence.

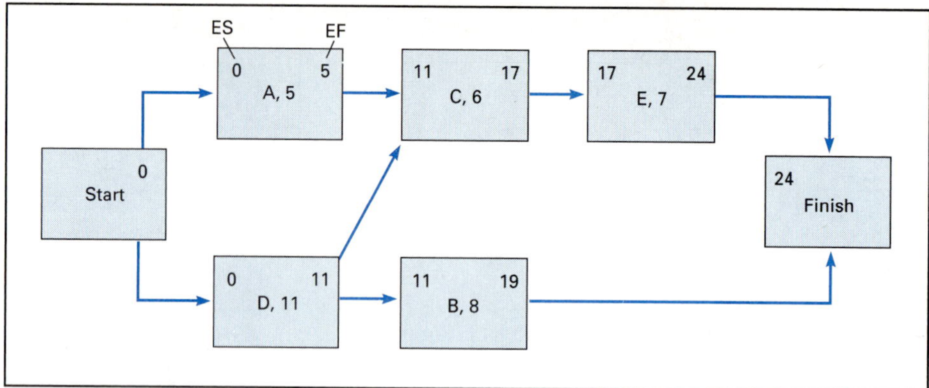

Figure 4-3 Calculating Earliest Start (ES) and Earliest Finish (EF) Times

must wait until time 11 to begin (after both A and D are completed). *All predecessors have to be done before the activity can begin.* Using equations 1 and 2,

$$ES_C = \max\{5, 11\} = 11$$

$$EF_C = ES_C + AT_C = 11 + 6 = 17$$

We work from left to right in the diagram because we cannot calculate the start time for an activity until we know the finish times for all its predecessors. The ES and EF times are written in the top corners of the nodes. The ES time for the FINISH node is 24, indicating that the whole project can end by time 24 *at the earliest*.

Latest Start and Finish Times. In a small diagram like Figure 4-3, it is easy to see that the path D—C—E is longer than any other and is therefore the one that determines when the project can be completed. The longest path is known as the *critical path*. (Later we will show how to find the critical path in a larger diagram.) Activity B is not on the critical path. How late could B start without delaying project completion? The latest start (LS) and latest finish (LF) times are calculated by working backward (right to left) through the diagram, with the following formulas:

$$LF_i = \min(\text{LS of the successors of activity } i\} \quad (3)$$

$$LS_i = LF_i - AT_i \quad (4)$$

First, we must choose a target completion time for the entire project. Since we already know that 24 is the earliest time that the project can be completed, whatever time we use for the project deadline should be no earlier than 24. For now, let us use 24 as the project deadline. (Review problem 5 asks you to use 30 instead.)

Both E and B must be done by time 24 since they are the last activities in the project. Hence, they both have LF = 24. The LS times are 24 − 7 = 17 for E and 24 − 8 = 16 for B. These numbers appear in the bottom corners of the nodes in Figure 4-4. (Notice that the project deadline of 24 appears at the bottom of the FINISH node.)

Working backward, activity C is next. Its only successor, E, must start by 17 (its LS time); therefore, equations 3 and 4 give

$$LF_C = \min\{17\} = 17$$

$$LS_C = 17 - 6 = 11$$

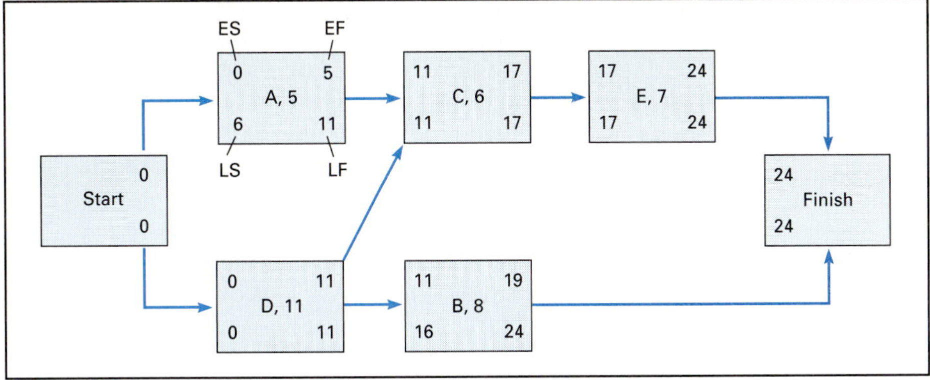

Figure 4-4 Activity-on-Arrow Diagram with ES, EF, LS, and LF Times

Next, activity D has two successors, C and B. Applying formulas 3 and 4,

$$LF_D = \min\{11, 16\} = 11$$

$$LS_D = 11 - 11 = 0$$

That is, if we start D later than time 0, it will delay activity C beyond its latest start time of 11, forcing a delay in E, which delays project completion. This ''chain reaction'' occurs because of the precedence relationships along the path D—C—E—FINISH.

You may compute the remaining LF and LS times using equations 3 and 4.

Slack (Float) and Critical Path. Notice that there are several activities in Figure 4-4 for which the earliest times are the same as the latest times. There is no *slack* for delaying any of these activities without causing a chain reaction that will delay the project. *Total slack* (TS) for an activity is defined as the difference between LS and ES. (Slack is often called *float*.) That is,

$$TS_i(\text{total slack of activity } i) = LS_i - ES_i \tag{5}$$

There is no slack on the path D—C—E. However, activity B has a total slack of 16 − 11 = 5 days. It could start as early as 11 or as late as 16 without changing the project completion.

The critical path is easy to identify now by calculating TS for each activity. In our example the critical activities had no slack at all because the project deadline of 24 was also the earliest possible project completion time. In general, critical activities are the ones with the smallest total slack. Together, the critical activities will form at least one path from START to FINISH. *Critical paths are the longest paths in the network—the ones with the least total slack.* (There is often more than one critical path, but all critical activities have the same total slack.)

Project Planning with PERT/CPM Diagrams

Elimination, simplification, and simultaneity, as discussed earlier, can shorten the duration of a project, often lowering cost as well. Critical path, total slack, and the diagram itself help to anticipate the effects of such changes.

For example, in the office procedure example of Table 4-1, are there any activities that are candidates for elimination? One possibility would be to use the existing forms. This would eliminate activity D and reduce or eliminate activity C. Suppose (to keep the example simple) that D were eliminated. What effect would that have on the project completion time?

D is an 11 day activity and is on the critical path. Since that is the longest chain from Start to Finish, getting rid of D would certainly shorten the project. However, the reduction is only 6 days rather than 11. Can you see why? Without D the new critical path is A—C—E which takes 18 days instead of 24. Activity A previously had 6 days of slack, so its successors cannot move more than 6 days earlier.

By contrast, if it were possible to eliminate A instead of D, the project's finish time would not change. A is not on the critical path, and D—C—E still requires 24 days.

Now consider simultaneity. Figure 4-4 shows that activities A and D may be carried out simultaneously but that C and E cannot; E must wait until C is finished. Upon closer inspection, however, the project's manager realized that part of E need not await completion of C. Some personnel will not use the new forms but will use the new equipment. Hence, their training (part of E) does not depend on activity C at all. Suppose that we can divide E into two activities:

F = equipment training not involving new forms (3 days, no predecessors)

G = equipment training involving new forms (4 days, predecessor = C)

This will shorten the project by 3 days because F may be done simultaneously with C.

The review problems ask you to use the diagram and the concepts of critical path and slack to deal with some other planning issues.

REVIEW PROBLEMS

1. In the example of this section, activity A is ''preliminary training'' and D is ''modify existing forms for the new system.'' The training instructor wishes to have at least a preliminary draft of the new forms to use in the introductory sessions. How long can A be delayed, to procure these drafts, without affecting the project completion time?

2. The supplier of the forms considers 8 days (the activity time of B) a ''rush'' order and is charging a premium price. An additional 5 working days would eliminate the premium. Should we continue the rush-order status?

3. Path A—C—E is the shortest path through the network. Why not follow that path rather than D—C—E?

4. What happens to the numbers in Figure 4-4 if the project deadline were 30 rather than 24? (Put 30 at the bottom of the FINISH node and recalculate.)

Solutions

1. The LS of activity A is 6. Therefore, if preliminary forms are available by day 6, waiting for them will not delay the project completion date.

2. Because activity B has 5 days of slack, we could cancel the rush order. However, there would no longer be any slack for activity B, and any unanticipated delay in delivery would delay project completion. Depending on the costs, one might wish to continue the rush-order status, just for protection.

Notice that if B takes 13 days, there would be two critical paths, D—C—E and D—B.

3. We do not follow a path through this type of network. We must perform all the tasks to complete the project.

4. The ES and EF numbers do not change. All LS, LF, and TS (slack) values increase by 6 days. That is, if we build in 6 days of slack between the fastest possible project completion and the project deadline, that slack will be added to every activity in the network. Consequently, the critical activities will have 6 days of total slack rather than 0.

4-2 SCHEDULING WITH PERT/CPM

Schedules are often developed at two levels: a master schedule and a series of detailed schedules. Hartley (1989) describes the master schedule as consisting of a few activities and major milestones (targets for completing portions of the project). The activities actually represent broad functional categories such as procurement, construction, and design. Within each activity of the master schedule, a detailed schedule is developed.

Scheduling activities is easier if the network diagram has a time scale. Figure 4-5 shows one way to do this with the example from the preceding section. Notice that each rectangular box has been expanded to a length proportional to the activity time; START and FINISH have been reduced to vertical lines, since they have zero activity time. Figure 4-5 shows each activity beginning as early as possible. The arrows show some of the precedence relationships. For example, the vertical arrow from D to C is a reminder that D must precede C as well as B. Most of the arrows from Figure 4-4 have been eliminated; they were squashed between the expanding blocks.

The time-scale diagram presents an improved picture of the project. Slack is visible in the form of horizontal arrows. For example, after A there is an arrow 6 time units long; therefore, A has a total slack of 6 days. This makes critical paths easy to identify. (In Figure 4-5, path D—C—E is critical.) The effects of changes are also easier to interpret. (To illustrate this, you can do review problem 3 in Section 4-1 using the time-scale diagram.)

Coordination of resources is also facilitated by the time-scale chart. Figure 4-6 shows a chart of a construction project; each activity has a list of the required number of carpenters, plumbers, and unskilled laborers. At the bottom

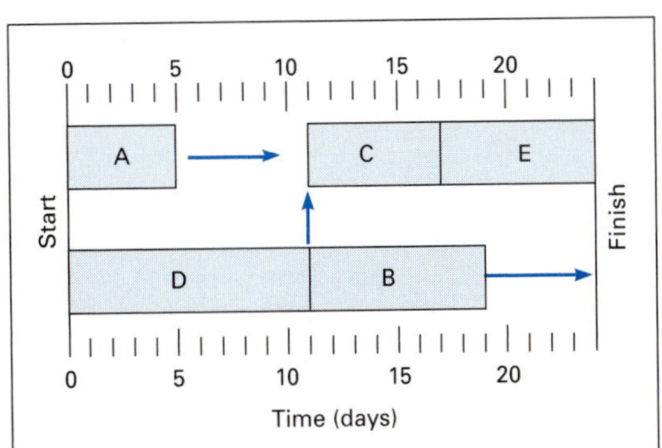

Figure 4-5 Time-Scale Chart for the New Office Procedure Project

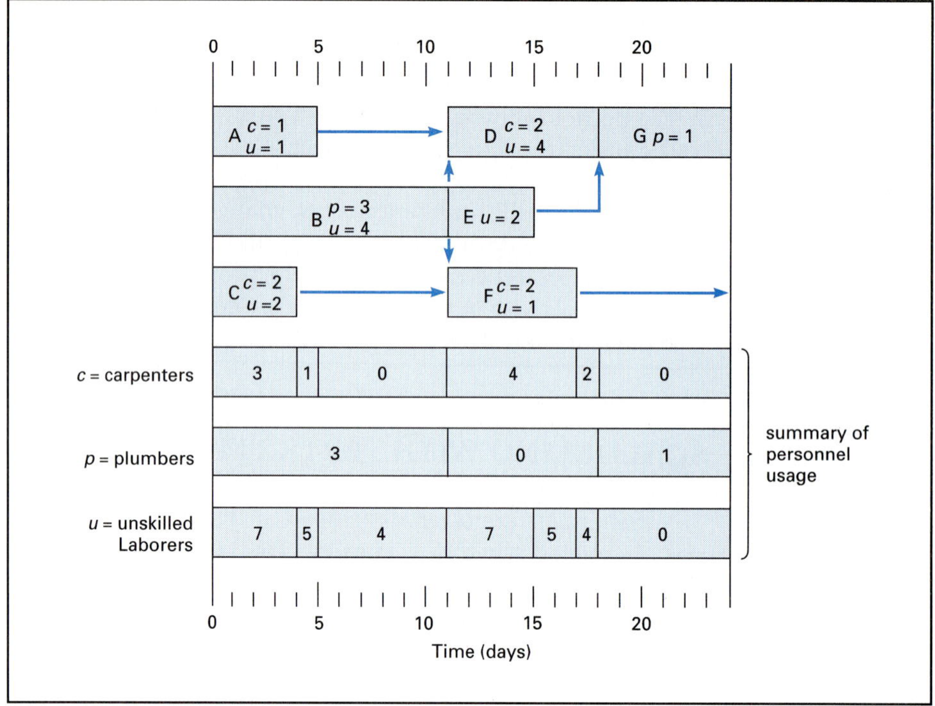

Figure 4-6 Construction Project with Limited Resources

are three bar-charts that show how many workers are needed and when. This information may be used to improve the schedule. For example, delaying the start of activity C until day 5 would reduce the peak number of carpenters from 3 to 2 during the first 11 project days, and would also reduce the peak number of laborers from 7 to 6. This move would cause activity C to begin at 5 and end at 9; activity F is not delayed by the shift. Further analysis will be left for a review problem.

The preceding is an example of *resource leveling*. A nearly constant usage of resources is easier to manage and less costly than an uneven schedule with widely varying peaks of activity. Coordinating resources over several projects at the same time is even more complicated. This is common in management of construction projects. Some of the contractors may have workers and equipment on several jobs. Weiss (1988) describes a computer model for this kind of situation. Computer routines for resource leveling are based on heuristics, which are rules designed to develop good plans. (Heuristics do not guarantee an optimal solution.) The Project Management Institute (Webster 1991) publishes surveys of project management computer software and other project control programs.

Time-versus-cost trade-offs are also common in the use of PERT/CPM. An example was given as review problem 2 in the preceding section—a rush order at extra cost. Since resources are usually limited, accelerating one activity may be at the expense of slowing down another. However, since some activities are ''more critical'' than others, such trade-offs may improve the overall project performance.

The simplest situation is one in which there is a single resource that can be used to change some activity times. Whether the resource is personnel,

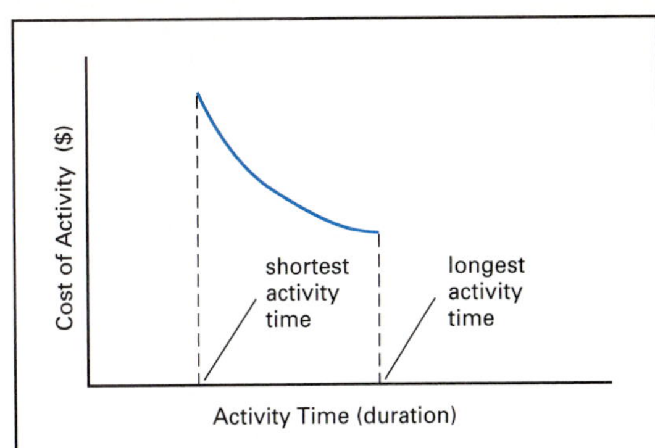

Figure 4-7 Typical Time-Versus-Cost Trade-off for an Activity

equipment, or something else, the cost of reducing activity times can often be expressed in dollar terms. The solid curve in Figure 4-7 is typical; shortening the activity increases the cost, but there are upper and lower limits on activity time.

As an example, suppose that an activity could be shortened from 12 days to 7 days by doubling the number of personnel working on it. This doubles the hourly cost but does not cut the time in half; thus the activity would cost more in its shortened version. Some activities speed up in direct proportion to resources expended; for those, cost is unaffected by accelerating or slowing down the activity. Of course, some activities cannot be shortened at all (concrete takes a certain time to set); no amount of money can reduce those activity times.

Time-versus-cost trade-offs can be generated by hand in small problems if the cost of reduction is linear. Begin by solving for the critical path using normal times, then reduce the critical path sequentially by finding the activity (or set of activities) that is cheapest (per unit time) to speed up. When there are multiple critical paths, as there will be as reductions are made, they must all be reduced simultaneously. When a critical path is composed of activities at their crash times, no further reduction is possible.

REVIEW PROBLEMS

1. Rearranging Figure 4-6, smooth the utilization of personnel as much as possible within the 24-day limit. Once a carpenter or plumber is on the job, it is best to keep that worker there as long as possible.

2. In time-versus-cost trade-offs, why is it not necessarily true that doubling the personnel on an activity will cut the activity time in half?

3. In Figure 4-6 suppose that activity D can be crashed, cutting its duration from 7 days to 3 days. By how much will this shorten the critical path?

Solutions

1. The following start times smooth the usage of carpenters: B = 0, A = 2, C = 7, D = 11, E = 11, F = 18, G = 18. One carpenter begins at time 2, a second at time 7, and both remain until F is completed at time 24. Three plumbers are needed for B and one for G, but between the end of B and the start of G there is a gap during which no plumbers are needed. There is no way to close the gap because of the precedence relationships (B → D → G).

2. There may be other factors, such as limited equipment or waiting for the paint to dry, that limit the effectiveness of additional personnel.

3. The following figure shows that crashing D from 7 to 3 days shifts the critical path to B—E—G, which requires 21 days, a saving of only 3 days compared with the 4-day reduction in D. The extra day becomes slack for D.

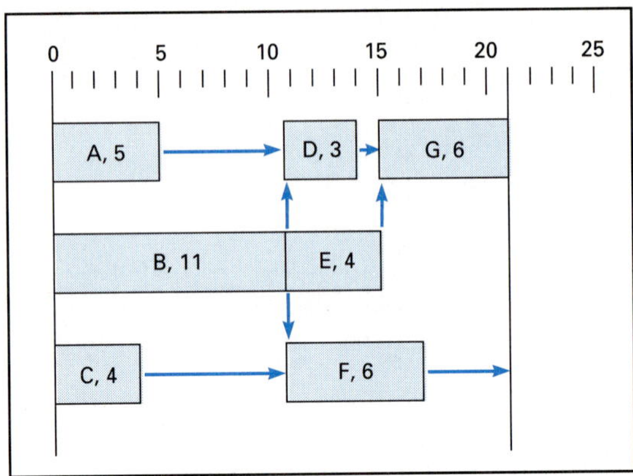

Construction Project with D Crashed

4-3 UNCERTAIN ACTIVITY TIMES

All the analyses in the earlier sections have relied on the time estimates obtained in the early phase of planning. But these are not always reliable, particularly if an activity involves new product development or depends on uncertain elements such as the weather. Some authors distinguish between PERT and CPM by noting that variability in activity times is an integral part of the PERT methodology but was not included in CPM as described by its developers. However, as the methods have evolved, the emphasis on the formal use of probabilities has diminished among PERT users, and elements of randomness have been adopted in many CPM-based approaches.

Today the formal use of probabilistic methods in PERT/CPM is not common. However, two alternative approaches are used and are discussed here. The first represents uncertainty on a time-scale graph. The second uses computer-supported simulation techniques.

One method of eliciting a forecast of activity time is to ask first for an optimistic time, a, and a pessimistic time, b, and then ask for the most likely time, m. The range, $b - a$, is one indicator of the expected precision of the forecast. The developers of PERT went one step further and converted these three time estimates into an expected time (ET) and a standard deviation (σ) for each activity. These formulas[4] are

$$\text{ET} = (a + 4m + b)/6 \text{ (expected activity time)} \quad (6)$$

$$\sigma = (b - a)/6 \text{ (standard deviation of activity time)} \quad (7)$$

[4]These formulas are based on the assumption that activity time has a beta probability distribution. However, the mathematical development is unimportant for our purposes. (See Malcolm et al. 1959, and MacCrimmon and Ryavec 1964).

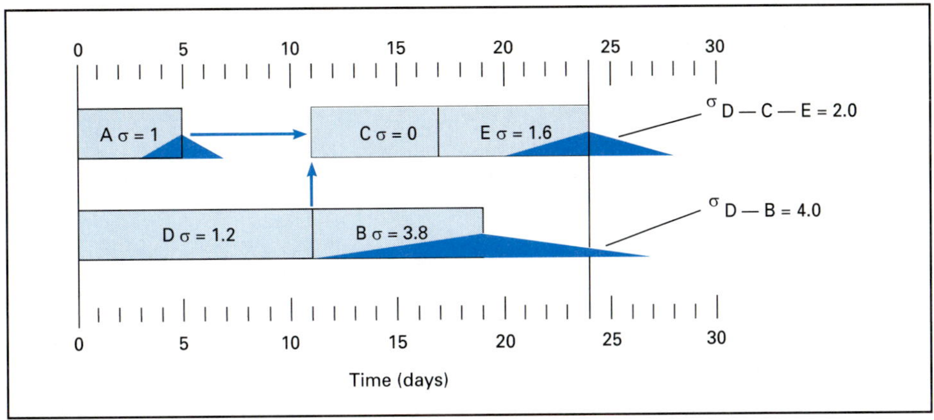

Figure 4-8 Time-Scale Diagram with 2σ Confidence Intervals (the Triangles)

The expected time, ET, may be used instead of AT (activity time) in the critical path calculations. However, the standard deviations enter the picture in a more complicated fashion.

For example, in Figure 4-8 uncertainty in activity times has been represented by attaching triangles to the activity blocks. The triangle extends two standard deviations in each direction, indicating (very roughly) that there is about a 95% probability of the actual time staying within the triangle. We will discuss how the numbers were derived later, after interpreting the significance of the triangles.

First, consider activity A. We now see that the slack time following A is substantial enough that we may expect A to remain non-critical, because the horizontal arrow extends beyond the triangle (there is more slack than uncertainty). However, since the triangle following B extends well beyond the arrow, it is possible that the project will be delayed beyond day 24 because of a delay in B, *even though B was not on the original critical path*. Some ''non-critical'' activities are more likely to become critical than others. It depends on how large σ is compared with slack time.

The triangle following the critical path, D—C—E, also extends beyond 24 days and, in fact, extends beyond the D—B triangle. This indicates that D—C—E is more likely the D—B to be the longest path, but there is no way to know for certain which one will be longer.

Based on the discussion so far, one should be cautious about treating 24 days as a target completion time for the project, particularly if the firm's reputation were hanging in the balance. Attempting to convert the triangles into numbers (probabilities) requires assumptions that are often unrealistic. This analysis has gone about as far as it should.[5] Many attempts have been made to refine this approach, but most have fallen into disfavor because of added expense or poor performance.

Now to explain the triangles. First, σ is estimated for each activity using equation 7. For example, if the optimistic estimate for activity A is 2.0 and the pessimistic estimate is 8.0, $\sigma_A = (8.0 - 2.0)/6 = 1.0$. (The other values, cal-

[5]MacCrimmon and Ryavec (1964) carefully analyzed the PERT assumptions and the calculations. They concluded that the overall project completion time, as estimated by PERT (or CPM), is always biased optimistically (actual time is likely to be longer than the PERT estimate). In their examples, the bias ranged from 10% to 30%.

culated the same way, are $\sigma_B = 3.8$, $\sigma_C = 0$, $\sigma_D = 1.2$, and $\sigma_E = 1.6$). Second, these standard deviations are combined along each path using a statistical formula:

$$\sigma^2_{\text{path}} = \Sigma_i \sigma_i^2 \text{ (summation is over activities on the path only)} \quad (8)$$

That is, for the path D—B,

$$\sigma^2_{\text{D—B}} = \sigma^2_{\text{D}} + \sigma^2_{\text{B}} = 1.2^2 + 3.8^2 = 15.9$$

Therefore, $\sigma_{\text{D—B}} = \sqrt{15.9} \approx 4.0$. The triangle at the end of path D—B extends 2σ or 8 days in each direction. This formula is valid only if the activity times of B and D are statistically independent. There are many situations that violate this assumption; therefore, the length of the triangle must be taken only as a rough indicator of variability.

Many projects are more complex than a PERT/CPM diagram indicates. For example, Taylor and Moore (1980) describe a research and development (R & D) project in which some activities may need to be repeated, or may fail altogether. They applied Q-GERT to model the complex and random character of R & D projects. Q-GERT is a type of simulation program (simulation is described in Appendix B) designed for modeling projects. Simulation is the only reliable method available for managers of such projects who want good estimates of project duration and the probabilities of delay. Unfortunately, this requires much more extensive data than is usually required for PERT/CPM. Nevertheless, computer simulation is finding wider application in project planning as well as other areas of management.

REVIEW PROBLEMS

1. In Figure 4-8 compute σ for the critical path D—C—E. Using this σ value, an estimated duration of 24 days for the path, and the normal probability distribution (Table 2, Appendix D), what is the probability that D—C—E will be completed within 25 days? Within 28 days?

2. Explain why activity B in Figure 4-8 could turn out to be on a critical path, even though it is shown as ending before E and its "triangle" (2σ confidence interval) also terminates first.

3. What complication would be introduced if the triangle following activity A were to extend beyond day 11, the early start of activity C, in Figure 4-8?

Solutions

1. $\sigma^2_{\text{D—C—E}} = 1.2^2 + 0^2 + 1.6^2 = 4$; therefore, $\sigma_{\text{D—C—E}} = 2$ days. With a mean of 24 days and $\sigma = 2$ days, we compute $z = (25 - 24)/2 = 0.5$. Using Table 2, Appendix D, the result is a probability of 0.692 or 69.2% that path D—C—E will take 25 days or less. For 28 days, $z = (28 - 24)/2 = 2.0$, and the probability is 97.7%. (These probabilities are rough estimates, based on guesses about activity times and some questionable assumptions.)

2. There are several reasons. Activity E may progress normally and B may encounter delays. Or E might be finished ahead of schedule.

3. This would suggest that A might delay activity C. The triangle following C would then be understated, since it was calculated from path D—C—E, assuming that A did not intervene.

4-4 PROJECT CONTROL

Once the project begins, the nature of the game changes. Effective project control requires quick and reliable feedback of the progress to date. Experience has shown that the simplest reporting methods are usually the best, since more complex reports are generally more expensive, more likely to be late, and more prone to being ignored because of their length and complexity.

One method of control is to require weekly revisions of estimated activity completion time. These estimates are used to update the network diagram to help anticipate upcoming "bottlenecks." An activity qualifies as a bottleneck if it has several successor activities and appears likely to become critical. Such an activity would be a prime candidate for management attention, perhaps requiring a *contingency plan* for diverting resources to alleviate the bottleneck, if necessary. (Management of contingencies is discussed in Avots 1989.)

PERT-COST was developed as a management control tool, to report on the cost and time performance of the responsibility centers as the project progresses (see Wiest and Levy 1977). The Department of Defense has since promulgated a set of thirty five Cost/Schedule Control System Criteria (C/SCSC) that are applied to the management systems of its contractors (see Chacko 1989). Both PERT-COST and C/SCSC require continual monitoring of actual and planned spending, which are then compared on the basis of the amount of work actually performed. For example, consider a $10 million, twelve month project. At the end of six months, actual spending was $5 million although only $4 million was budgeted for the first six months. The real picture does not emerge until the work actually performed is taken into account. In this example, the project had fallen one month behind schedule, and work actually completed was supposed to have cost only $3 million. Hence, in the sixth month the project was $2 million above budget and one month behind schedule.

These ideas are relatively simple and extremely useful. However, continual monitoring imposes significant requirements on the cost-accounting system as well as on the organizational structure used in project management. Using PERT-COST or conforming to C/SCSC can be quite expensive.

Time-scaled network diagrams are also useful tools for project control. To reflect the ever-changing nature of a project, the diagram needs to be easy to modify. For example, if the activities are represented by strips of plastic or heavy paper, changes in the schedule are shown by moving the appropriate strips. When a computer is being used, new diagrams can be printed with each revision. In any case, visual representation allows a quick and accurate view of the project and focuses attention on potential trouble spots.

REVIEW PROBLEMS

1. In Figure 4-8, which activity qualifies as a potential bottleneck? Why?

2. Suppose that, after 6 days had elapsed, we found that activity D could not be finished until day 14 rather than day 11, as scheduled.

   a. What does this do to the critical path?

   b. Where would you expend resources to try to meet a deadline of day 26 for project completion?

Solutions

1. Activity D is on the critical path and has two immediate successors on the critical path. Its delay would have the most significant effects on the project as a whole.

2. a. The accompanying figure shows that path D—C—E remains critical since paths D—C—E and D—B are both delayed. The length of the critical path is increased by 3 days.

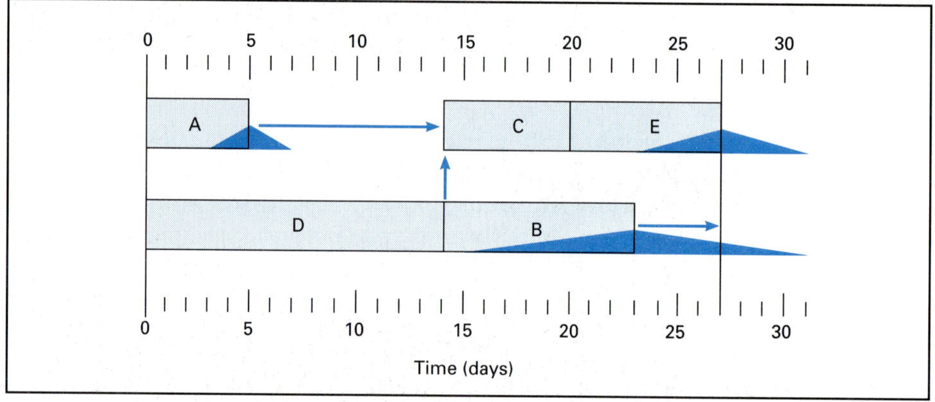

Project of Figure 4-8 with Completion of D Delayed to Day 14

   b. This depends on costs and feasibility. It is tempting to concentrate on D. However, day 6 may be too late to implement effective changes for D. The next most likely candidate is path C—E since it has no slack. However, Figure 4-8 indicates that the manager may also want to speed up B, since it has a high degree of uncertainty. Of course, the cost of reduction should be considered.

SUMMARY

It is unusual when a single method addresses both the overall picture and the details of an operation, but network analysis does. The diagram provides both a broad overview of project phases and a detailed schedule of individual activities. Indeed, it is common to have at least two levels of charts, with the highest-level chart having "activities" that are actually subprojects, and with the second level consisting of detailed diagrams for each subproject.

As part of an information system, PERT/CPM transforms data from individual activities into information about the project as a whole. The most fundamental information is identification of the critical path or paths, pinpointing where slack time and potential trouble spots exist in the system and monitoring changes. These serve to focus management's attention on key problems and opportunities, suggesting activities that are primary candidates for contingency planning and crash programs (critical or near-critical activities) and pointing out activities that can be rescheduled to improve resource utilization. At the same time, the system provides a forecast of overall project completion time, and it can be used to summarize the projected utilization of key resources through time.

PERT/CPM is a valuable tool for planning and control but is not a substitute for good judgement, with attention to organizational and behavioral implications. It is common practice, for example, to build in a certain amount of slack at various stages of a project, to allow for unpredictable delays. The network diagram can be used to decide where to locate the slack.

Judgment is central to every phase of project management with PERT/CPM: deciding what version of network planning to use, assigning responsibilities, estimating requirements, scheduling, contingency planning, and so on. PERT/CPM helps the manager to keep on top of the situation, to focus attention on the most significant decisions, and to sort out the implications of a decision.

CASELET

CORINTH MEDICAL SCHOOL SCIENCE BUILDING

"Construction costs jumped 10.4% last year. I'm afraid that we may be facing a cost overrun if we don't get this project under way quickly. I know that many of the local contractors are facing contract negotiations with their employees this year. You know what that means!" Marney Joseph had just opened the meeting of the Alterations Planning Committee. She continued, "The sooner we get this project out to bid, the better our chance of staying within budget. The NIH Grant, if we get it, will not cover additional costs." She then called on Douglas Molly of the NIH Grant Subcommittee.

"The problem is that there is a long chain of activities that have to be done before NIH (the National Institutes of Health) will consider our grant proposal. And until we know whether this funding will be available, we can't go out to bid with the contractors. I have listed all the tasks (see the accompanying table) and estimated how long each one will take. As you can see, the total is ninety five working days."

"Have you considered some parallel operations, Doug?" asked Ms. Joseph. "For example, couldn't we speed things up by having the architects develop their design immediately after we have approved the schematic, and then go to final drawings?"

"Yes, that is possible, but we face the possibility of having paid for design work that becomes obsolete. If the grant proposal is denied by NIH, the alterations will have to be scaled back,'' replied Mr. Molly. ''Activities, I, J, and K will each cost about $100,000.''

''But Doug, we have a $10 million project that might become an $11 million project if we don't act quickly. Let's at least follow up all of the options for shortening your ninety five days and then evaluate the risks. Are there any other activities that might be done simultaneously?''

At this point, Cynthia Dempster spoke up. ''Yes, I think that the building and sidewalk approval applications (activity M) can go out as soon as the design development is complete. The city departments do not require the final drawings. All the information we need comes from design development (activity J).''

''Good idea, Cindy,'' said Ms. Joseph. ''Doug, what about preparation of the narrative (activity C)? What is the earliest point when the grant writers could start that task?''

''I suppose they could start work as soon as the preliminary application is approved (activity B), but about half of their work depends on the cost estimates, and the cost estimates can't be done until the architects finish programming and schematics (activity I). But let me change the subject for a moment. At the end of the site visit, the team meets to decide on their recommendation to NIH. Before they leave, they will tell us what their recommendation will be. NIH accepts their recommendation almost every time.

Activity	Duration (days)	Predecessors[a]
A. Preparation of preliminary application to NIH for funding alteration to medical science building	4	none
B. Approval of preliminary application by NIH and subsequent request for detailed application	8	A
C. Preparation of narrative for application	4	B, E
D. Review and submission of application by medical center board of trustees; request for site visit	3	C
E. Development of cost estimates for grant application	4	I
F. Revision of application following site visit by NIH	3	G
G. Site visit by NIH team	1	L
H. Approval of grant application	16	F, G
I. Programming and schematic design by architects	8	B
J. Design development by architects	12	I, H
K. Final drawings by architects	12	J
L. ``Rehearsal'' of medical school faculty by planning committee for NIH site visit	2	D
M. Application for (and approval of) alterations in building and sidwalk to City Building Department and Traffic Department	16	J, K
N. Out to bid to contractors	2	K, M, H
	Total = 95	

[a]Predecessors as defined before the committee meeting.

Maybe we could minimize our risk by waiting to give the architects the go-ahead until the site visit team approves our project.''

''Let's consider that as a third alternative. I think we have a least a 90% chance of getting this grant; we might therefore be better off getting the work done as soon as possible so we don't get hit by the cost increase. So that's it. The three alternatives are to run the ninety five day project as you have it now, to use parallel activities as much as possible, or to use parallel activities but delay activities I and J until after the site visit.'' With this, Ms. Joseph closed the meeting.

Required

1. Prepare time-scale diagrams for the three alternatives. Alternatives 2 and 3 require changes to the table.
2. Evaluate the potential costs and benefits, as far as possible, of the three alternatives. You may also consider others if you wish.
3. Prepare a report to Ms. Joseph, based on your evaluations. Recommend one alternative and support your choice.

PROBLEMS

1. a. How does one recognize the critical path in a PERT or CPM diagram?
   b. Define ''total slack.''
   c. Explain, in one sentence, the advantage of knowing the critical path.
   d. Explain how knowledge of the total slack can be useful in managing a project.
   e. For what type of network would the PERT estimate of expected project duration be biased? In what direction might it be biased?
2. a. Draw an activity-on-node diagram for the following project.
   b. Calculate ES, EF, LS, LF, and total slack for each activity.
   c. Indicate the critical path.
   d. Draw a time-scale PERT diagram, with activities starting at their ES times.

Activity	Time Required (weeks)	Predecessors
A	2	C, B
B	2	C
C	3	none
D	3	C, F
E	3	C, D, F, G
F	4	none
G	4	F

*3. Examine the following time-scale PERT chart:

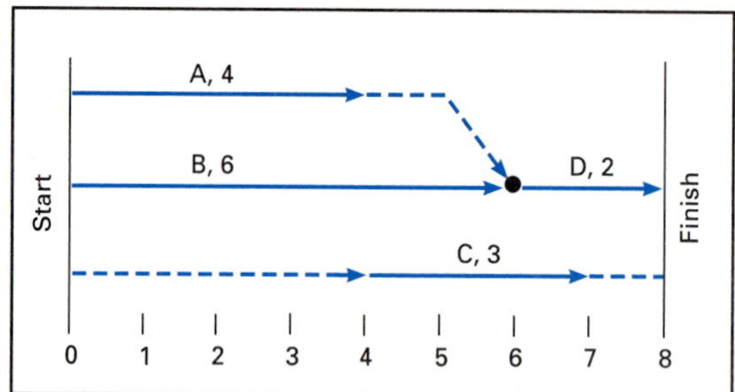

a. What is unusual about the placement of activity C on the chart? How much slack is there for delaying this activity as shown? Why is that different from the total slack for C?

b. As manager, which of the activities would you monitor most closely for possible delays of the project? Which activity is least worrisome? Why?

*4. (Refer to the accompanying activity-on-arrow diagram)

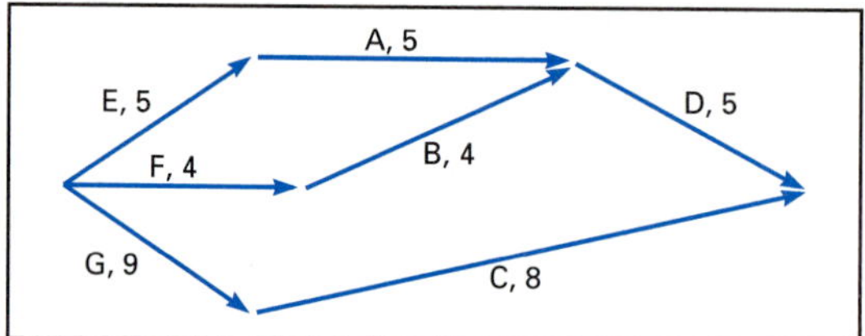

a. Calculate ES, EF, LS, LF, and total slack for each activity, using a deadline of 20 days for project completion.

b. Indicate the critical path and its completion time.

c. Management is worried that the start of activity D might be delayed beyond day 12. Discuss briefly how we could decide which activities would be most likely to cause such a delay.

d. What is the earliest finish time for the project? Discuss briefly the accuracy of this number for planning purposes, and the sources of possible errors.

5. The BPA Distribution Company has obtained exclusive rights, nationwide, for the sale of a new product. They want to plan its introduction and set up a plan for inventory control. The new product introduction requires the following steps:

Activity	Time Required (weeks)	Predecessors
A. Laboratory tests	3	none
B. Home tests	6	A
C. Design advertising campaign	5	A, B
D. Implement advertising campaign	4	C
E. Test market in a small region	6	B
F. Make decision whether to continue	1	E
G. Ship supplies to all regional warehouses	3	F
H. Deliver supplies to retail outlets	3	D, G

*Problems with an asterisk have answers in the back of the book.

a. How long, at a minimum, will the project take, and what items are on the critical path? (Draw an activity-on-node diagram.)

b. How much total slack does task C have?

c. The project manager has proposed a schedule in which all activities that have earliest start times before task F's completion should begin as late as possible. What items would be affected and what would the new start times be? Give arguments for and against the project manager's policy.

*6. The curriculum committee of a well-known MBA program has decided that MBA programs are too long. They have decided to try a modular approach to curriculum planning, in which each person proceeds at his or her own pace through the modules, but there is a system of prerequisites. Some of the activities, average times, and prerequisites are as follows:

Activity	Average Number of Time Modules[a]	Predecessors
1. Accounting	3	none
2. Quantitative Methods	4	none
3. Economics	4	none
4. Finance	3	1, 3
5. Operations Management	2	2
6. Business Policy	2	4, 5

[a]Average times are in terms of 5-week modules.

a. Draw an activity-on-node diagram, and find the critical path and its expected time. Show the earliest and latest finish times on the diagram.

b. Is the critical-path time a good estimate of the average time a student would take to complete the program? Explain.

7. The accompanying diagram describes a project to develop new microcomputer software, complete with documentation. Activities A, B, D, E, and F involve writing and testing code, whereas G and H involve developing the manuals and other documents. Activity C is "approval of work to date" and F involves integrating and testing the code developed in A, B, D, and E. (Note the ***simultaneity*** in A, B, D, and E.)

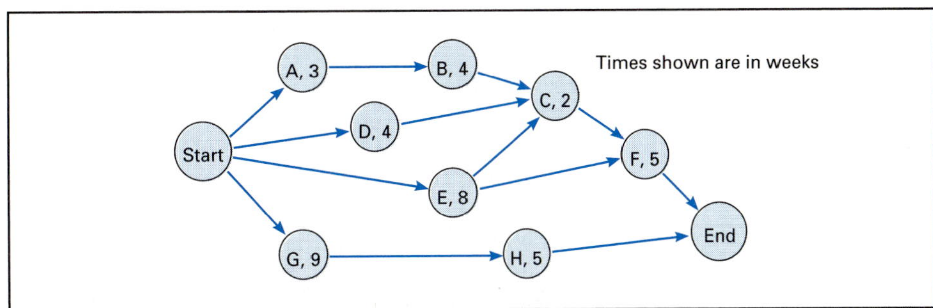

a. What is the critical path? How long does it take?

b. What activity is least likely to delay completion of the project?

c. Of the activities on the critical path, which one is most likely to be delayed beyond its ES time because of precedence relationships?

d. What happens to the critical path if E takes 7 weeks instead of 8 weeks?

Elimination: Activity C is ''approval of work done to date.'' Management has decided to eliminate this step, giving the go-ahead responsibility to the individual activity managers. Nonetheless, activity F must still await completion of activities B, D, and E.

e. What effect does elimination of C have on project completion?

f. How does this affect your answer to part d?

Simultaneity: Instead of eliminating activity C, management has decided to carry it out in parallel with activity F. However, activity C sometimes results in disapproval so that some earlier steps must be repeated.

g. Ignoring the possibility of disapproval, what effect would this change have on project completion?

h. What new risk does parallel operation of C and F carry?

*8. The accompanying diagram shows the network representation of a project to rearrange the machine shop in a manufacturing firm.

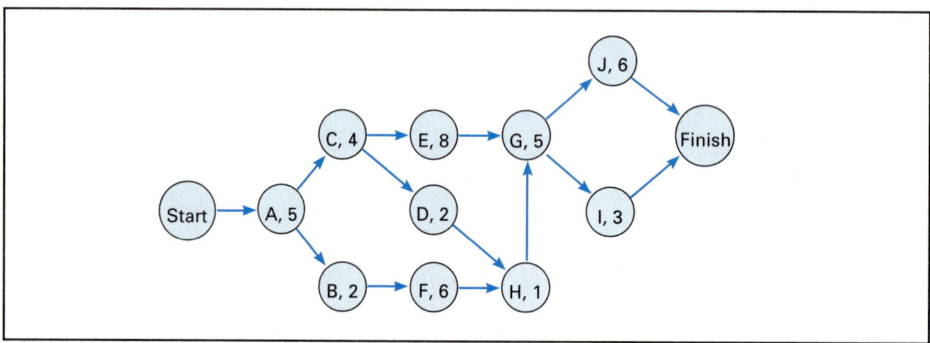

The foreman is almost satisfied with the diagram, but he has a couple of problems.

a. He understands that activities on the critical path are the ones most likely to cause a delay. Which other activities should he be watching carefully because of their potential for delaying project completion?

b. How much does the duration of D have to increase in order to change

(i) the early start time of H?

(ii) the early start time of I?

(iii) the early completion time of the project?

c. He feels that activity C should be a predecessor to activity F. If this is done,

(i) which earliest start times change and by how much?

(ii) which latest start times change and by how much?

9. PERT/CPM can be adapted to handle target completion times (deadlines) for portions of the project. Consider the following project:

Activity	Time Required (days)	Predecessors	Deadline for Completion
A	1	none	none
B	3	A	none
C	7	A	none
D	2	B	7
E	2	C, D	none

   a. What is the EF time for D without considering the deadline? Can the deadline be met?
   b. How would you modify the formula for LF to accommodate deadlines?

*10. The accompanying table describes a project to implement a new manufacturing process. Management is eager to complete this project as soon as possible, but not at the expense of carelessness.
   a. Of all the activities, which is the least critical (least likely to delay the project's completion)?
   b. Activity G can be shortened, but each day that its duration is decreased adds $500 to the cost of the project. Management is willing to pay this price to shorten the project. How many days should they trim from activity G?
   c. Activity D depends on the arrival of a particular piece of equipment. The news has just arrived that the equipment may not be available until day 12. If this delay does occur, would it affect the project completion time?

   Simultaneity: The predecessor relationships for activities H and D have been reexamined. For H, it was found that the first 6 days do not depend on completion of activity G; they may be done at any time. For D, it is customary, but not necessary, to do activity C first.
   d. Ignoring part b (i.e., G remains a 14-day activity), what effect do these changes have on the completion time of the project?
   e. Answer part b taking into account the new precedence requirements.

Activity	Time Required (days)	Predecessors
A	14	D
B	9	none
C	7	none
D	7	C, B
F	12	D
G	14	C
H	14	G

*11. American Bottle Company (ABC) produces several types of glass containers. They have recently reduced capacity at several of their plants. Glass manufacturing involves large, expensive machines (including ovens), several of which were turned off in the capacity reduction. The start-up process is described in the following table. How quickly can they start a new oven using normal times? What is the fastest time in which a new oven can be started, and how much additional cost is involved?

Cost per Unit Time Reduction	Activity	Normal Time (hours)	"Crash Time" (hours)	Predecessors
—	A. Preheat glass	8	8	C
—	B. Preheat oven	12	12	D
$40/hr	C. Obtain materials	4	2	none
$20/hr	D. Check valves	4	2	none
$20/hr	E. Check pressure seals	2	1	B
—	F. Add glass to oven	2	2	A, E
$50/hr	G. Prepare bottlemaker	6	3	E
—	H. Run test production	4	4	F, G
$50/hr	I. Examine test quantity and make adjustments	4	2	H
—	J. Refill oven with glass	2	2	H

*12. Metropolis General Hospital is installing a linear accelerator in their radiology department, replacing a cobalt unit. The accompanying table represents the main phases of the project (excluding training of personnel, which has already been completed). Today is June 1. Delivery of the accelerator is scheduled for June 12. Once the cobalt unit is removed, every day that the unit is out of operation means a net revenue loss of $500. However, of the activities shown, only the wiring may be speeded up, and this may be accomplished by working the electricians overtime, up to 3 hours per day (a normal day is 8 hours), at an additional cost of $50 per hour of overtime for the crew.

Activity	Duration (days)	Predecessors
B. Install new floor mounts for accelerator	8	D
C. Install new wiring	14	none
D. Remove cobalt unit	2	none
E. Install accelerator	7	B, C, D
F. Test accelerator	14	E

a. Draw a critical path diagram and calculate ES, EF, LS, LF, and slack for each activity. Identify the critical path.

b. Should the electricians work overtime? If so, how much overtime, and what saving results? If not, explain why not. State any assumptions that you must make.

13. A division of Generous Motors has decided to install a computer to record and collate test results. It has been projected that the plant will save $300 per day with the new system. All activities can be shortened (except E) by using overtime. The electricians are employed by the company at a rate of $20 per hour for a normal 8-hour day. They may work 4 hours overtime at an additional cost of $80 per hour for the crew. The carpentry work is done by contract. This crew may work overtime at a cost of $40 per hour for the crew for a maximum of 4 hours. The computer is expected to arrive on day 14.

Activity	Duration (days)	Predecessors	Crew
A. Build a raised floor	4	none	carpenter
B. Wire auto analyzers to feed results into computer	5	C	electrician
C. Wire computer room	6	none	electrician
D. Install air-conditioning	2	G, B	electrician
E. Wait to take delivery of computer	(see problem)	none	administrator
F. Install computer	10	A, C, D, E	electrician
G. Build vents	3	A	carpenter
H. Connect to auto analyzer wiring	4	C, B, F	electrician

a. Draw an activity-on-node diagram and calculate ES, EF, LS, LF, and total slack for each activity. Identify the critical path.

b. Construct a time-scale chart, unless you already did so in part a.

c. Should overtime labor be used? If not, why not? If so, how many hours of overtime for what activity? What saving results?

14. The Eljay Samoht Construction Company builds houses. They want you to do a network analysis of their construction process. The data are given in the accompanying table.

Activity	Normal Time (days)	Crash Time (days)	Cost of Crashing	Predecessors	Standard use of Bulldozers	Standard use of Workers
A. Rough in driveway	2	1	$200	none	1	2
B. Dig foundation	4	2	500	A	1	2
C. Finish driveway	2	1	100	A	1	3
D. Pour foundation	6	6	—	B	—	4
E. Construct framing	10	6	200	D	—	4
F. Construct roof	10	6	400	E	—	2
G. Siding	8	4	200	E	—	2
H. Plumbing	8	6	200	F, G	—	2
I. Wiring	6	5	100	F, G	—	2
J. Interior walls	10	6	300	H, I	—	3
K. Interior carpentry	14	8	800	J	—	3
L. Flooring	8	6	200	J	—	3
M. Finish lawn grading	2	1	200	G	1	2
N. Exterior painting	12	8	160	G	—	2
O. Interior painting and finishing	18	14	240	K	—	3
P. Landscaping	6	4	300	M	—	4

a. Using all normal times, find the critical path, the earliest start times, the latest start times, the length (in days) of the critical path, and the planned usage of workers and bulldozers, starting all activities at earliest start times.

b. Develop time-versus-cost trade-offs to reduce the length of the project by at least 24 days.

c. In part b an assumption was necessary. Comment on the validity of the assumption in this case. Would a reexamination make any changes in your answer to part b? Be brief.

d. Assuming that skills are transferable, it makes sense to lower peak usage of both workers and bulldozers to minimize the number of workers on the payroll and the number of bulldozers and operators the company needs. State a simple heuristic to lower peak usage and use it. After applying the heuristic, do you see any better solution? If so, state it.

*15. A project manager has done a PERT/CPM analysis and found that the critical path contains the following tasks:

	Time Estimates		
Activities	**Optimistic**	**Most likely**	**Pessimistic**
A	3	4	5
D	7	7	7
G	5	10	21
H	2	5	8

a. What is the estimated time for completion of the critical path, and what is the standard deviation?

b. What is the probability of completion by time 30? (Assume the normal probability distribution.)

c. Consider that the project has more activities than the critical-path ones shown in the table, the answer to part b is a biased estimate of project duration. Is it too high or too low? Why?

16. A project manager has the following activity-on-node diagram of her project:

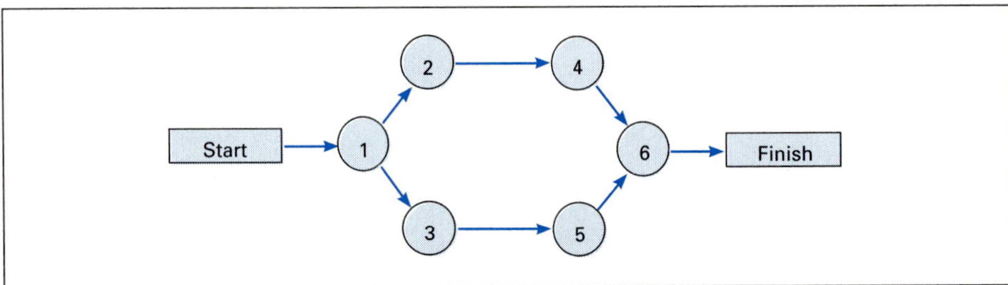

The time estimates are as follows:

Activity	Time Estimates		
	Optimistic	Most Likely	Pessimistic
1	3	3	3
2	4	6	8
3	2	3	10
4	5	7	15
5	1	3	11
6	4	4	4

a. Find the critical path and its mean and variance using the PERT assumptions. (You may use inspection to find the critical path.)

b. Using the PERT method, what is the probability that the project will finish within 25 time units? Which way is this probability biased?

c. As an estimate of total project duration, what can you say about the mean value calculated in part a?

17. The accompanying activity-on-arrow chart is not drawn with a time scale. Activity J has been identified as a potential bottleneck because it has many successor activities. Management has set a target of starting activity J by time 20.

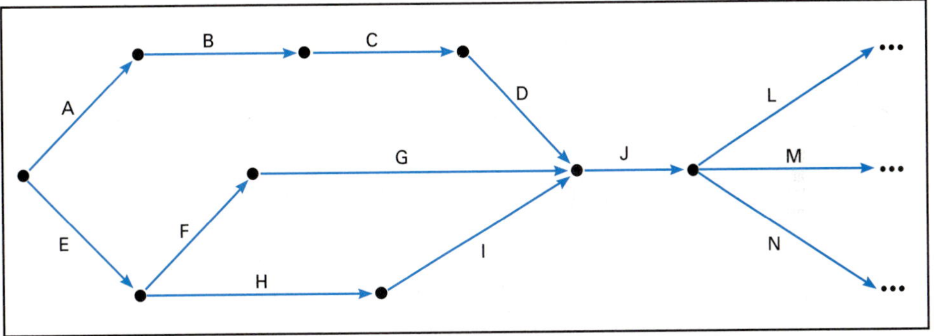

The data in the following table show that there is substantial uncertainty in the start time for J because several of its predecessors

Activity	Expected Activity Time (weeks)	Variance σ^2
A	4	1.0
B	4	1.0
C	4	1.0
D	4	1.0
E	5	3.0
F	1	0.5
G	1	0.5
H	5	3.0
I	5	10.0

have uncertain durations. Analysis of that data has led to an apparent contradiction: Considering the portion of the project prior to J, the critical path is A—B—C—D. However, when considering the probability of being finished by time 20, another path appears to be "more critical" than A—B—C—D.

a. Calculate the ES time of J based on expected activity times.
b. Explain the contradiction.
c. What is the probability that all of the activities A through I will be finished by time 16?
d. Given your answer to part b, should you expect J to start before or after the ES time you calculated in part a? Explain.

REFERENCES

AVOTS, I., "Contingency Reserves: A Management Control Tool," in *Project Management: A Reference for Professionals*, R.L. Kimmons and J.H. Lowree, eds., New York: Marcel Decker, 1989.

BRUNIES, R.A., "Suitable Applications of Project Management," in *Project Management: A Reference for Professionals*, R.L. Kimmons and J.H. Lowree, eds., New York: Marcel Decker, 1989.

CHACKO, G.K., *Dynamic Program Management*, New York: Praeger, 1989.

CLARK, K.B., and T. FUJIMOTO, "Overlapping Problem Solving in Product Development," in *Managing International Manufacturing*, K. Ferdows, ed., New York: North Holland, 1989.

HARTLEY, K.O., "The Project Schedule," in *Project Management: A Reference for Professionals*, R.L. Kimmon and J.H. Lowree, eds. New York: Marcel Decker, 1989.

KERZNER, H. *Project Management: A Systems Approach to Planning, Scheduling and Controlling*, 3rd Ed., New York: Van Nostrand Reinhold, 1989.

KIMMONS, R.L. and J.H. LOWREE (eds.), *Project Management: A Reference for Professionals*, New York: Marcel Decker, 1989.

MACCRIMMON, K.R., and C.A. RYAVEC, "An Analytical Study of the PERT Assumptions," *Operations Research*, vol. 12, no. 1, 1964.

MALCOLM, D.G., J.H. ROSENBLOOM, C.E. CLARK, and W. FAZAR, "Application of a Technique for Research and Development Program Evaluation," *Operations Research*, vol. 7, no. 5, 1959.

MODER, J.J., C.R. PHILLIPS, and E.W. DAVIS, *Project Management with CPM and PERT*, 3rd ed., New York: Van Nostrand Reinhold, 1983.

RANDOLPH, W.A., and B.Z. POSNER, *Effective Project Planning and Management: Getting the Job Done*, Englewood Cliffs, N.J., Prentice-Hall, 1988.

SCOTT, D., C. ALSOP, and R.L. CHANDLER, "Planning the Opening of a New Hospital," *The Hospital and Health Services Review*, March, 1974.

TAYLOR, B.W. and L.J. MOORE, "R&D Project Planning with Q-GERT Network Modeling and Simulation," *Management Science*, vol. 26, no. 1, 1980.

VAZSONYI, A., "The History of the Rise and Fall of the PERT Method," (Title in French, text in English), *Management Science*, vol. 16, no. 8, 1970.

WEBSTER, F.M., *Survey of CPM Scheduling Software Packages and Related Project Controls Programs*, Drexel Hill, Pa.; Project Management Institute, 1991.

WEISS, E.N., ''An Optimization Based Heuristic for Scheduling Parallel Project Networks with Constrained Renewable Resources,'' *IIE Transactions*, vol. 20, no. 2, (June), 1988.

WIEST, J.D., ''Precedence Diagramming Method: Some Unusual Characteristics and Their Implication for Managers,'' *Journal of Operations Management*, vol. 1., no. 3, (February), 1981.

WIEST, J.D., and F.K. LEVY, *A Management Guide to PERT/CPM with GERT/PDM/DCPM and other Networks*, 2nd ed., Englewood Cliffs, N.J.: Prentice-Hall, 1977.

chapter

5

Measurement and Management of Productivity

Productivity will always be of major importance to organizations. Increased productivity allows all of us to be more cost competitive, have more leisure time, provide more and better service, or achieve other objectives. From 1870 to 1979, output per labor-hour increased 1100% in the United States (see Maddison 1982), allowing the workweek to shrink by 40% while obtaining an eightfold increase in per capita output. The division of the wealth generated by productivity increases is an appropriate and important politico-economic issue that countries and companies must deal with, but the long-term value of productivity improvement is obvious. Dividing the pie is an easier task when there is a large pie with enough to go around.

If this is true, why have labor and management often fought about productivity improvement? There are many reasons, but two important ones are (1) that management has occasionally taken too narrow a view of the needs and abilities of labor, and (2) that labor has occasionally assumed that increased productivity will benefit shareholders, not labor, and may even lead to elimination of some jobs.

Wages are not only the issue of interest to employees. In a 1973 study it was found that pay was the fifth of eight key items desired in a "good job" (*Work in America* 1973):

1. interesting work
2. enough help and equipment to get the job done
3. enough information to get the job done
4. enough authority to get the job done
5. good pay
6. opportunity to develop special abilities (self-development)
7. job security
8. seeing the results of one's work (feedback and recognition)

In 1988 the president of the United Steelworkers listed five items (Williams 1988) paraphrased as follows:

1. decent wages
2. safe workplace
3. voice in decisions
4. job security
5. help (retraining, income security) for persons who unavoidably lose their job

The exact items and order depend heavily on the experiences of the people being asked. The points we draw from both lists are (1) that wages are important, but only as one of several items; (2) that involvement in decisions is also important; and (3) that self-development, including access to training, is necessary and beneficial to all.

Job security is important to most people. Lack of job security has often kept people (including managers) from making productivity improvements. Productive organizations find a way to utilize employees' talents, providing as much security as possible and involving people in major decisions and efforts. Very detailed engineering-type methods can lead to significant improvements in productivity if they are applied with an understanding of human behavior and the needs of the employees. Resistance to efficiency methods can be avoided.

Of course, productivity improvement involves more than efficiency. In Chapter 1 we quoted Peter Drucker: "Efficiency is doing things right; effectiveness is doing the right things." Working smarter is often more important than working harder. Eliminating the causes of waste is better than efficiently cleaning up the scrap, for example. In general, eliminating an unnecessary step, streamlining the process, is better than performing that step quickly.

Productivity improvements are required of all organizations if they are to compete in worldwide markets. Any company that does not improve will be left behind. If enough companies are left behind, an entire country's economy can be affected.

Someone reading the popular press during the 1970s and 1980s might come to the conclusion that the United States is lagging far behind the rest of the world in productivity. In fact, the United States has lagged behind in productivity *growth*, but is at or near the top in absolute productivity. McKee and Sessions-Robinson (1989) make the distinction between productivity and change in productivity: the United States had a huge lead, and others have gained. Baumol (1989) showed that several industrialized countries have very similar absolute productivity; the competition among them is fierce. The real test, of course, is organization by organization. Many companies in the United States are the best in the world in their industry, and many others are far behind.

Productivity is as important in service organizations as it is in manufacturing. During the last thirty years, manufacturing productivity has improved over three times as fast as service productivity. Since services provide 70% of the jobs, operations managers must find ways to use the successful manufacturing ideas in the service sector. Even in manufacturing firms most employees provide services, either to the firm itself or to customers. Billing, order entry, and customer records are service activities for both internal purposes and for the customer. An 800-number phone system for product information is a service for potential customers. A central engineering department is an internal service organization assisting manufacturing. In Europe, Japan, and the United States, manufacturing overhead (people providing services) is much larger than direct labor, as a fraction of total product cost (see de Meyer 1986).

All countries need productivity improvements to improve the standard of living. Also, there will be fewer workers entering the U.S. work force during the remainder of this century (see Wolfbein 1982 and Johnston and Packer 1987). We must plan to use less labor content in future products. Improving productivity has many benefits for society, and we can reduce or eliminate many of the negative aspects.

In this chapter we will examine methods for motivating people (Section 5-1), an industrial-engineering approach to analyzing work (Section 5-2), and some methods of measuring and improving productivity (Section 5-3). The field is far too broad to allow us to treat these topics extensively, but the references can be used to find follow-up reading. Much of the book discusses ways of improving productivity. In particular, topics covered in Chapter 2 (process analysis), Chapter 6 (quality), and Chapter 12 (just-in-time) are important to our discussion.

5-1 DESIGNING JOBS AND ORGANIZATIONS FOR PRODUCTIVITY

The design of jobs and organizations has a major influence on productivity. First, people must be able to get the job done: the organization and managers must facilitate this. Second, workers must also want to get the job done. Research shows that most workers believe that productivity is a problem and want to do something about it. Organizations must tap into this *motivation*. Finally, individuals and organizations must *learn* in order to continually improve: jobs and organizations must be designed to foster learning. This section discusses these three topics, beginning with motivation.

Motivation is often used to describe the desire to want to be productive (see Organ and Bateman 1986 or Werther et al. 1986 for a more complete discussion). When productivity is seen as the best path to achieve an important personal goal, people will want to be productive. The list of eight ''good job'' characteristics from the *Work in America* list gives managers insight into what can be used as *work incentives*.

Item 1, interesting work, has led to significant changes in some industries, leading to sociotechnical systems, quality-of-work-life programs, job enrichment, job enlargement, semiautonomous teams, and similar approaches. We will discuss these approaches to motivation in the next subsection. The next three items are requirements for effective job performance; these are the direct responsibility of management.

Pay (item 5) is an obvious incentive. Achieving a bonus or a raise provides short-run satisfaction, but the desire for higher pay continues. Successful plans reward superior performance with higher pay but also guarantee decent wages for average performance. Some are designed for very quick feedback, whereas others have monthly or yearly bonuses. They also differ as to whether rewards go to individuals, groups, or the entire company, through some kind of profit-sharing scheme. Successful examples can be cited for each of these approaches, although the nature of the product and the work force strongly influence the appropriate choice of plan.

The trend in financial rewards above base pay is toward group incentives, for two reasons. First, people have a need to be part of, and to contribute to, a group. Second, small, local goals can be counterproductive: if we are not selling our product, producing more is not a neutral but a negative factor.

One important approach is *gainsharing*, which characterizes systems based on overall goals such as profitability or total cost. Improvements in total cost are shared according to a formula such as 60% to employees, 40% to the corporation. These systems have a historic root in *Scanlon plans*, in which productivity improvements were shared by all workers. Bullock and Bullock (1982) describe two gainsharing operations (see also Fein 1983, Organ and Bateman 1986, and Werther et al. 1986, for additional examples and discussion). Changes in management style are sometimes needed to reflect the commonality of interest of all parties. Bullock and Bullock (1982) describe success stories, but they caution that the plans must be evaluated over time rather than immediately.

Individual (rather than group) goal setting is also used in many organizations. The goals should be specific (rather than, say, ''do your best''), high but achievable, and agreed to by the employee. It is acceptable to have high goals, but only if rewards are given for performance that is progressing toward the goal. (Goal setting, together with the difficulties of implementation, is discussed in Werther et al. 1986, pp. 194–197.)

Self-development is often a major motivating factor for some people. The steps of a carrier ladder present short- to medium-run goals (the next promotion) that are self-renewing unless the career path is a short, dead-end street. Unfortunately, many jobs do not have much potential for self-improvement. However, the use of self-improvement as an incentive tends to bring talented people to higher positions and therefore to encourage them to make better use of their talents.

The search for motivating factors has extended beyond the foregoing. *Pride and loyalty* are familiar slogans in company campaigns to motivate people. However, it is difficult to convince somebody to be proud of a narrow, repetitive job with no responsibility. Increases in pride and loyalty can result from meaningful changes, but exhortations to be proud and loyal are not effective motivators by themselves.

Accountability has been found to be a key motivator, but it cannot stand alone. When accompanied by authority, increased accountability for quality and productivity provides a positive stimulus. However, in the absence of authority and access to necessary equipment and information, responsibility for outcomes will not be accepted. Thus, accountability encourages productivity when the worker feels that the necessary elements have been provided to do the job well.

Finally, individual goals must be consistent with organizational goals. Organizational goals must be understood by all and seen as important. The goal of providing outstanding products and services to customers, at low cost, must be understood if the continued growth or existence of the firm is to be ensured. This requires careful selection of individual goals and communication of organizational goals to motivate employees. As we will see in Chapters 6 and 12, the concepts of just-in-time (JIT) and total quality management (TQM) derive strength by focusing heavily on worker motivation, pride, and common objectives.

Designing Good Jobs

Good jobs are designed through both behavioral and engineering methods, by selecting the best work pattern and equipment and by motivating the person or group. In this subsection we will discuss the behavioral methods, leaving engineering job design to the next section.

Employee involvement (EI) or total employee involvement (TEI) is the most important trend today in job design (or redesign). The basic idea, to which we subscribe, is that employees have more to offer than just physical labor, and organizations should involve them directly in job design and in finding ways to make firms competitive. (In Chapter 6, EI will be discussed as one of the keys to assuring quality.) So many companies now consider EI crucial to their success that any list is incomplete, but we have personally discussed EI effort with managers from organizations as diverse as Eli Lilly, P&G, Ford, Alcoa, Hershey Foods, Kodak, Xerox, Corning, Florida Power and Light, GTE, AT&T, Hewlett-Packard, Travelers' Insurance, Cornell University, and Duke University. Each of these organizations believes that major improvements have been made as a result of EI.

Job redesign refers to efforts to improve jobs, to improve performance. Either of the lists of good-job characteristics given in the introduction can help managers understand what changes might make workers feel better about their job. (See Organ and Bateman 1986 and Werther et al. 1986 for further discussion of these topics.)

Job enlargement and ***job enrichment*** are two methods of job redesign. Job enlargement provides each worker with a more varied set of tasks, each requiring more or less the same level of skill and responsibility; working in teams on a wider range of tasks than before is one way to accomplish this. Job enrichment adds responsibility and accountability, such as in giving a worker responsibility for his or her own quality inspection.

One example of job enrichment is given by Herzberg (1976), in which he describes a group charged with responding to shareholder inquiries in a corporation:

Diminish role of supervisor:

1. Less frequent supervisor proofreading.
2. Outgoing mail bypasses supervisor.
3. Experienced workers were designed as subject-matter experts, serving as first-line consultants to the other workers.

Increase authority/accountability:

1. Correspondents sign their own names.
2. More personalized letters encouraged.
3. Accuracy and quality of letters reflect on individual rather than supervisor.

In a similar case, a worldwide multibillion-dollar publishing company replaced a six-stage copy-editing process for proofreading advertisements (their major source of income) with a single person, responsible for correctness. The person enjoyed the job more, productivity obviously improved, *and* errors declined dramatically.

Quality of work life *(QWL)* is another term that has been used to describe methods of improving the work setting from the employee's point of view (see Lawler and Ledford 1982 and Copenhaver and Guest 1983). These programs change many aspects of a work situation, often beginning with minor annoyances, such as insufficient changing or washing space for workers. QWL programs are long-term efforts to unlock the employee's abilities for the good of both the organization and the individual. If the program has management commitment, QWL programs lead to more satisfaction for the employees. Sometimes, improvement in productivity also occurs, but the link of QWL or satisfaction to productivity remains unclear.

Organizational behavior modification *(OB mod)* is a related area (see Organ and Bateman 1986). OB mod entails rewarding improved performance swiftly. The desired behavior must be precisely defined, and the reward must be directly linked to the behavior. For example, to encourage supervisors to respond quickly to employee suggestions, set the goal of "answer all suggestions within three days" and reward the supervisors as they achieve the goal. Positive reinforcement is more powerful than negative reinforcement, but both work only if they are swift and precise. Blanchard and Johnson (1982) discuss the value of "catching employees doing something right" and praising the effort. The reward need not be monetary; formal and informal recognition are also powerful tools.

Several important points must be made about the job-design changes that we have discussed, particularly EI. First, fewer supervisors (and middle managers) are needed, and their roles must change dramatically. Second, the characteristics of a good job change through time, as the needs of workers change. Finally, as we discussed in Chapter 2, the "learning organization" that is able to change quickly will be successful and productive in the future. We will now comment briefly on each of these points.

One of the key similarities in successful job improvement programs is the redefinition of the role of the managers, particularly supervisors. Bringing accountability to the worker reduces substantially the role of the supervisor as "checker and slave driver." Management's role becomes more supportive of the worker, one of ensuring that the tools, equipment, and information necessary to do the job are available. In addition, the need for training is increased to facilitate self-development; the position of supervisor is ideal for this training function, assuming that superior experience and skill are some of the qualities that lead to promotion to supervisory levels.

Employee involvement implies that workers have a say over matters of strategic importance. This implies that management must communicate the competitive priorities to all employees, and indicate how well the firm is doing. Joint management-labor teams can address topics of strategic importance. Klingel and Martin (1988) describe three major efforts, each involving a strong union, centered on "cost study teams" addressing the question, "How can we match the competitor's cost?" There are many advantages to joint efforts, including bringing more good minds and different perspectives to the problem, as well as the commitment generated by the process.

Individuals' needs are different, and they change through time, for many reasons. Old plans must be modified if they are to remain effective. As one example, the demographics of the U.S. work force are changing dramatically. We are getting older. There will be a shortage of many skills. Minorities and women will constitute 85% of the net new entrants to the job market during the 1990s (See *Workforce 2000* 1987 and Naisbett and Aburdene 1990 for numbers and discussion.) Each of these changes implies changes in appropriateness of job design. For example, more women in the work force implies more employees who have two-career families; flexible hours will become more important. Also, successful organizations will incorporate minorities and women at all levels. Finally, older workers' skills cannot be lost if skills are in short supply. Greater use of part-time jobs has been used by service organizations to lure retirees back to the work force. Facing these job-design issues now can help organizations succeed during the upcoming years.

Swift feedback is part of good management and job design because it helps an organization to learn quickly. The JIT philosophy (Chapter 12) relies heavily on finding errors quickly and improving the operation at once. The productivity improvement that results from avoiding the repetition of errors is dramatic (see Schmenner 1988). Jobs must be designed to allow this; everyone must be involved in the team effort, and rewards must be given for improvement, rather than punishment for mistakes.

In summary, job design with careful attention to the desires of workers has been shown to benefit both labor and management. However, certain warnings occur repeatedly in the literature.

1. An effective, long-lasting scheme requires changes in attitudes as well as in behavior, at all levels.
2. Middle-level management is most likely to cause problems, as job enrichment will be encroaching on their domain. (Their job usually can be enriched as well.)
3. Careful diagnosis must precede action. Projects often fail because the wrong problem was addressed.
4. Implementation must proceed slowly but deliberately, beginning with small projects. Employees need to learn how to improve, and management must demonstrate its long-run commitment to the new system.
5. Approaching the problem as though attitude change is the major goal is inadvisable, since the program may be dismissed as another public relations gimmick.
6. Even implementation of a small demonstration project must take a system-wide view. The new roles of supervisors, for example, must be carefully spelled out to avoid slipping back into the old ways.
7. As a result of all the preceding potential difficulties, top-level management must be solidly behind the program and fully prepared to invest for the long term in the new training, equipment, and personnel.

REVIEW PROBLEMS

1. It is often argued that effecting job changes to improve worker satisfaction will result in lower productivity as a result of less pressure on the workers, less specialization, and so on. Review some of the broader issues that tend to counter this argument.

2. Describe how the role of middle management must change to develop a learning organization.

Solutions

1. Changes in the fundamental nature of jobs have the potential to achieve the following:

   a. reduction in the requirements for personnel whose role is pushing the workers (for example, expediters and some supervisors)

b. reduction in employee grievances and union difficulties
c. reduction in turnover, in costs of recruiting and training new workers, and in disruption of operations
d. improved product quality, with reductions in scrap cost, customer dissatisfaction, and the cost of quality control

2. Managers must evolve from bosses to helpers, trainers, and facilitators. Their new role is to ensure that employees have what they need to be effective and efficient.

5-2 WORK DESIGN AND INDUSTRIAL ENGINEERING

Jobs can be made easier, more pleasant, and more efficient through careful attention to detail and the proper design and use of equipment. A classic experiment in work improvement was carried out by Gilbreth (Taylor 1919) in the bricklaying trade. The changes were as follows:

1. A helper placed bricks with the best edge facing up, in a position convenient for the bricklayer.
2. A new scaffold was used to keep the worker at the proper height relative to the wall.
3. Mortar was carefully mixed to the proper consistency to avoid the need for excessive tapping of the bricks to properly secure them.
4. Careful observations allowed many motions to be eliminated altogether.
5. Workers were trained to work with both hands at the same time. For example, with proper positioning of materials, one should scoop mortar with one hand while picking up a brick with the other.

The result of this effort was an increase from 120 to 350 bricks laid per worker per hour. Moreover, the bricklayers did not have to work harder, since the new method eliminated the heaviest tasks, such as bending over to pick up bricks and mortar, which requires lifting both the materials and the 150 pounds or more of the worker's own body more than 1000 times per day.

This example illustrates the major elements of task design:

1. careful observation of the task
2. obtaining or designing equipment most suited to the task
3. optimal preparation of materials
4. design of the workplace to make the task easier and quicker
5. training the worker
6. providing lower-skilled labor to support and facilitate the work

The returns from higher productivity have to cover the expenses of the design project as well as the additional labor required for support. The almost trebled output in this case left a substantial surplus, from which bricklayers were given a large raise.

The theme of this example is improved efficiency. Although bricklaying has been practiced for thousands of years, such a dramatic improvement was made possible through systematic observation by someone who was not a bricklayer! Similar improvements continue to be possible and should certainly be welcomed, for example, by a work team that has the authority to select work methods and is paid according to the results.

To be proficient in work methods an industrial engineer (IE) must be familiar with a wide variety of processes and machines as well as with the methods for getting the most from each machine. In addition, principles of motion economy have been developed to aid in streamlining a job. A third area is understanding the capabilities of people as they operate on a job, including their interactions with other people and with machines. Environmental effects are a crucial consideration, with regard to both the health and safety of the workers and the impact on the community in which the organization is situated.

Most of these topics are highly technical in nature; consequently, the ''efficiency expert'' has typically received an education with little emphasis on the organizational and human factors discussed earlier. This has been cited as a contributing factor to labor-management strife over productivity measures.

In Chapter 1 we discussed the controversy over the ''scientific management'' techniques of Taylor and others. Our opinion is that very simple techniques, applied with attention to detail *and* to the needs of the work force, can make dramatic improvements in productivity. Analyzing work methods can be done in a way that ignores human needs; it should not be. As Organ and Bateman (1986) have observed, ''the productivity increases registered by Taylor, Gilbreth, and countless other industrial engineers and efficiency experts are especially impressive when compared to the reasonable gains produced by various kinds of motivational techniques.'' They compare the gains of 200% from Gilbreth's methods to several smaller (but still meaningful) gains from other methods.

The most important part of a work improvement study, *operations analysis*, is observing the process in detail, to understand the nature and purpose of each operation. The observer must take notes on how to *combine, simplify*, or *eliminate* steps of the process. The easiest way to improve productivity is to eliminate a task that is unnecessary; it is surprisingly common to find such tasks. Earlier in this chapter, we described a publishing company that reduced the number of proofreaders on advertising copy from six to one, increasing productivity and reducing errors. Other successful examples in our experience include the following:

1. A large consumer goods company had a flow chart for new product launches that contained 172 steps. Using ''combine, simplify, and eliminate,'' that number was reduced by 90%. Productivity improved, but more important, the total elapsed time was compressed dramatically.
2. A multibillion-dollar U. S. manufacturing firm has an ongoing joint venture with a multibillion-dollar Japanese company. Noting that the U.S. firm's finance department was many times the size of the Japanese firm's department, the U. S. firm asked for advice on how to improve productivity. The response: ''Your finance department is amazingly productive. We believe that no one could generate the reports and analyses you do with fewer people. However, we do not understand why you need all the analyses and reports.''

Each of the foregoing examples involved a service. We used these examples to emphasize the fact that productivity improvement is possible in all settings, and that operations analysis can be used in essentially all settings.

The tools for systematic operations analysis include many kinds of charts (for example, flow diagrams, process charts, layout schematics, and Gozinto charts, described elsewhere in this book). These devices help to visualize the process in detail and thereby provide a means for working out improvements. At the same time, such a systematic approach minimizes the chance of an unforeseen outcome of a suggested change.

Combining or subdividing operations is one place where operations analysis overlaps with job enlargement or job enrichment. Whether in manufacturing or service, combining two steps can save setup time (preparing to do the operation) but requires more skills of the operator and perhaps more equipment.

Motion study was developed around the turn of the century by Frank and Lillian Gilbreth and others. In its present form (Niebel 1982), it is an important part of the design of jobs and the layout of the workplace. Information has been cataloged on human capabilities in terms of the kinds of motions that are easiest (most natural and least tiring are smooth, continuous motions), physical capabilities (force that can be applied by a person sitting or standing, pushing or pulling, etc.), and coordination of effort (both hands should begin and end their tasks simultaneously). The kinds of basic hand motions are called therbligs (Gilbreth spelled backward), and include search, select, grasp, reach, and thirteen other elements, each of which has a standard abbreviation, color code, and pictorial symbol for use in charting. With these elements an engineer can describe an existing operation or design a new one. The symbols are used to construct process flowcharts, which describe the task assigned to each hand.

Micromotion study is carried out with videotape pictures, which are viewed in slow motion to categorize, study, and criticize the elemental motions of an operation. This very expensive form of analysis is not justifiable for most situations, but the fine tuning it achieves can recover the investment for high-volume operations.

Information has also been cataloged relating various work conditions (noise, pace, vibration, rest periods, etc.) to fatigue and performance. The interface between human beings and machines is also approached in part from this point of view. For example, attention span is important in monitoring patients and equipment in an intensive care unit, loads on a municipal electrical system, or flows and heat in a chemical factory. Innovations such as installing warning lights and orienting dials so that normal position of the indicator is straight up (the twelve o'clock position) have immensely improved the reliability and ease of monitoring.

Time studies

Time studies have been used for many purposes, including measuring travel times for layout design, measuring task times for job design, setting standards for evaluating worker performance, estimating job times for production planning and scheduling (see Chapters 9, 10, 11, and 12), and estimating the number of personnel needed for scheduling the work force (see Chapters 9 and 13). Time studies require not only accurate time measurement but also reliable methods for rating the performance of the person being observed. Ratings and standards will be discussed later.

Stopwatch techniques can be used after careful observation has divided a task into its elements. Once a carefully selected operator has agreed to participate, the observer remains on the site, timing elements of the operation without interfering in the actual process. In most cases it is advisable for the observer to remain inconspicuous, but those parties to be observed must be willing, notified participants. Each element is timed repeatedly until the desired accuracy is obtained.

Times can be estimated without a stopwatch through a technique called *work sampling*. In this technique an observer takes data at preselected times of day. Each observation consists of a notation of what work element was being performed at the preselected instant of time. After a large number of such observations, the fraction of observations that noted activity i being performed becomes the estimate of the proportion of the day being spent on activity i. To be valid, the observation times must be selected randomly, using a table of random numbers[1] or some other randomizing method, to avoid the possibility of the observations being taken in a cycle that may coincide with work patterns. For example, observations "on the hour" might be biased because of the pattern of work breaks.

Both the stopwatch method and work sampling require at least a two-phase study, with the first (pilot) phase used to iron out the methods and to estimate the variability of the process elements. From the results of the pilot study, the number of observations required in phase 2 is estimated. Table 5-1 summarizes the formulas used for each method. The first phase is carried out using an arbitrarily chosen sample size, typically around 30 for the stopwatch method and 50 to 100 or more for work sampling. The results are used in the formula for sample size, which determines the extent of the data to be collected in the second phase.

For example, in a pilot stopwatch study, a work element was timed n = 30 times. The average was $\bar{x} = 0.372$ minute, and the standard deviation was $s = 0.123$ minute. For 95% confidence we find that $z = 1.96$ (Table 2, Appendix D). Therefore, using the appropriate formula from Table 5-1, the precision of

[1]There is a list of random numbers in Table 1, Appendix D.

Table 5-1 Summary of Statistical Formulas for Work Measurement

STOPWATCH	WORK SAMPLING
Estimates	
$\bar{x}$ = average measured time of the activity	p_i = fraction of observations that noted activity i
s = standard deviation of the measurements	n = total number of observations
n = number of measurements taken on the activity	
Approximation Precision of Estimate (confidence interval)	
$\dfrac{zs}{\sqrt{n}}$	$z\sqrt{\dfrac{p_i(1-p_i)}{n}}$
z = standard normal statistic[a]	z = standard normal statistic[a]
Approximate Sample Size Needed	
$n \approx \left(\dfrac{zs}{\epsilon \bar{x}}\right)^2$	$n \geq \left(\dfrac{z}{L_i}\right)^2 p_i(1-p_i)$ for all activities i
ϵ = acceptable error, as a fraction of $\bar{x}$	L_i = acceptable numerical error in p_i

[a]See Table 2, Appendix D, to find a z value for the desired level of confidence. For example, z = 1.96 for 95% confidence. This is only a rough approximation if the sample size is less than 30.

the estimate is

$$\frac{zs}{\sqrt{n}} = \frac{(1.96)(0.123)}{\sqrt{30}} = 0.044$$

which is about 11.8% of $\bar{x}$. A 95% confidence interval is $\bar{x}$ plus and minus the precision; in this case we are 95% sure that the true average time for this work element is 0.372 ± 0.044, or from 0.328 to 0.416.

Management desired 2% precision, so the required sample size, using the appropriate formula from Table 5-1, is

$$n = \left[\frac{(1.96)(0.123)}{(0.02)(0.372)}\right]^2 = 1050$$

Standards

Many wage incentive systems require performance evaluation for each worker or for a small group involved in a particular task. (Some large group incentives, such as gainsharing, discussed in Section 5-1, examine overall outcomes such as total plant cost.) When evaluation of an individual operation is desired, a *standard time* (the time in which the operation should be completed) is necessary.

Time-study observers are trained to rate their subjects according to their observed work pace. For example, a stopwatch study might result in $\bar{x} = 0.372$ minute for a worker whose pace was rated 110% of normal; thus, the estimated standard would be (0.372)(1.10) = 0.409 minute. The ability of observers to give accurate ratings has been studied. An average error of less than ±5% is desirable, but a study of 599 trained time-study observers by the Society for Advancement of Management (see Niebel 1982) showed that 59% of the observers had error rates exceeding 10%, with one person as high as 22%.

The conclusion is that there is no way to be sure of a correct standard. Therefore, standards are themselves open to negotiation. The accuracy of time-study numbers is often substantially overstated, since they must be adjusted for pace using a factor that averages greater than 10% error.

Nevertheless, standard time data have been collected over many years and are available in tables, classified according to type of operation. With reference to these tables, standards can be constructed for jobs that have never been done before, and in turn, labor costs per item may be estimated for purposes of product planning. Although these must be treated as rough estimates (for reasons that should now be clear), they are better than a seat-of-the-pants estimate, which would be the only alternative.

Learning curves

It has been observed in a variety of settings that the amount of time an operation takes should decline as workers learn how to do the task better. This idea can also be applied to entire organizations and whole products (rather than single operations). There is a huge body of research on industrial applications of *learning curves* (see Conway and Schultz 1959, Argote and Epple 1990, and Argote, Beckman, and Epple 1990 for a discussion of this research).

Cost estimates over a long period of time are often based on learning curve assumptions. It is common for the 100th unit made to take a small fraction of the time the first unit took, and accurate cost estimates must take that into account. The most common learning curve model is

$$Y_i = ai^{-b} \tag{1}$$

where:

Y_i = the number of direct labor hours required to produce the ith unit
a = the number of direct labor hours required to produce the first unit
i = the cumulative number of units produced
b = a learning parameter

If $b = 0$, there is no learning. If $b > 0$, we assume that the organization learns better how to produce the item, through time. Equation 1 implies that the time required per unit decreases by the same percentage each time the cumulative production (i) doubles. A value of $b = 0.322$ implies that the time required decreases by 20% each time the quantity doubles. If the first unit takes 10 hours, the second takes 8; then the fourth takes (.80)(8) = 6.4 and the eighth takes (.8)(6.4) = 5.12.

The parameters of equation 1, a and b, can be estimated by taking logarithms of both sides, resulting in $\ln(Y_i) = \ln(a) - b\ln(i)$, an equation that is linear in b, the learning parameter. Using $\ln(Y_i)$ as the dependent variable and $\ln(i)$ as the independent variable, linear regression can be used to obtain estimates of b and $\ln(a)$.

Research shows that there is considerable variation in learning rates, but it is unclear why. Also, organizations can forget some of what they learned if there is a hiatus in production. (See Argote and Epple 1990 and Argote, Beckman, and Epple 1990.) Obviously, a slight increase in the learning rate has a dramatic effect on the firm's competitive posture. Just-in-time (Chapter 12) and other techniques can help improve an organization's learning rate. In the next section, we will briefly suggest some methods that help an organization transfer learning from one division to another.

Either learning more quickly than competitors or being the largest firm in an industry (thereby producing more units and moving further down the learning curve) can lead to a lower cost position and to a sustainable competitive advantage. Hayes and Wheelwright (1984) describe the applicability of learning curves to manufacturing strategy.

The effect of the learning parameters is significant. When $b = 0.152$, labor-hours drop to 90% (decrease by 10%) each time the quantity doubles. For 80%, $b = 0.322$, and for 70%, $b = 0.515$. If the first unit takes 100 hours of labor, the 1000th unit will require

35 hours if $b = 0.152$ (90% learning rate)
11 hours if $b = 0.322$ (80% learning rate)
3 hours if $b = 0.515$ (70% learning rate)

The learning rate (90%, 80%, or 70%) is related to the learning parameter, b, by

$$\text{Learning rate} = R = 2^{-b} \tag{2}$$

A firm with a faster learning rate or a firm with the same learning rate but higher market share can obtain a large competitive advantage. (Learning is discussed further in Chapter 12, and competitive advantage in Chapter 17.)

To illustrate the power of learning rates, consider two firms, A and B, with equal production rates (and market shares) for widgets. Firm A's first widget took 360 hours to produce. Firm B's first widget took 150 hours. Firm A has an 80% learning rate ($b = 0.322$) and firm B has a 90% learning rate ($b = 0.152$). The graphs of direct labor hours are shown in Figure 5-1. Although firm A

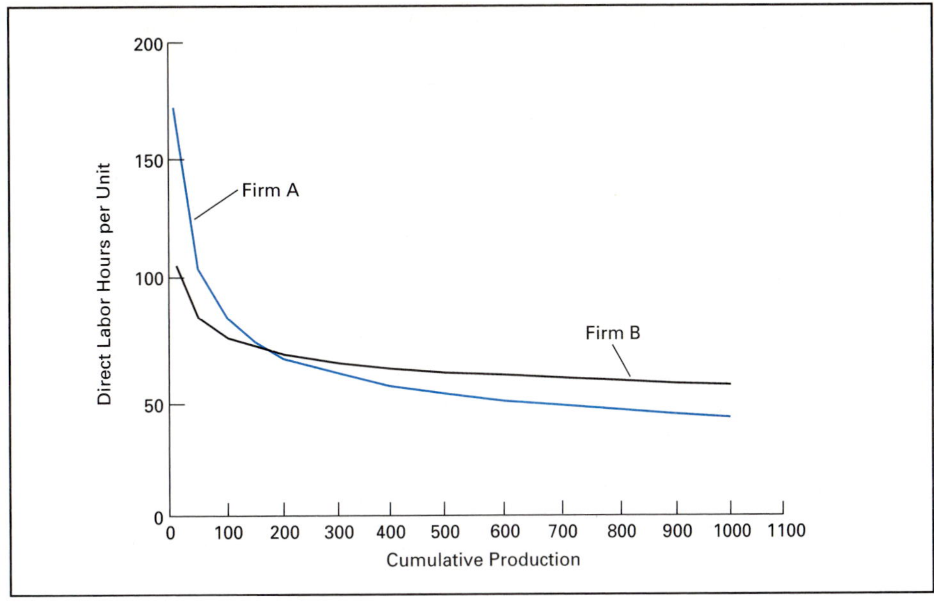

Figure 5-1 Learning Curves for Two Firms

started with a higher cost, which firm will be in a better competitive position in the long run?

REVIEW PROBLEMS

1. In the stopwatch method example in this section, suppose that the observer rated the worker at 80% of normal pace in the pilot study.
   a. Was the worker faster or slower than normal?
   b. What is the adjusted estimate of the normal task time? (The observed time was $\bar{x}$ = 0.372 minute.)

2. In the stopwatch example in this section the sample size of 1050 was judged to be unacceptably large (too expensive). What sample size should be used if the allowable error is increased to 4%?

3. In the learning curve example, at which cumulative production value does firm A catch up, in direct labor hours per unit, to firm B?

Solutions

1. a. Slower.
   b. Adjusted $\bar{x}$ = (0.372)(0.80) = 0.298 minute.

2. Sample size = 263. Notice that reducing the accuracy by a factor of 2 cuts the required sample size by a factor of 4.

3. Find i such that $360i^{-0.322} = 150i^{-0.152}$

$$\frac{360}{150} = \frac{i^{-0.152}}{i^{-0.322}} = i^{-0.152+0.322} = i^{0.17}$$

$$\text{Then } (i^{0.17})^{(1/0.17)} = i = \left(\frac{360}{150}\right)^{(1/0.17)} = 172.$$

5-3 MEASURING AND IMPROVING PRODUCTIVITY

As was discussed in the introduction to this chapter, improvements in productivity can lead to benefits for the individual, the organization, and society. Consideration of productivity should not be limited to factories, since 75% of the labor force in the United States is in the service sector. Productivity measurement in the service sector is often more difficult, but many articles and books have been written regarding productivity in areas such as banking, research and development, offices, urban transit, school districts, and white collar workers in general (see, for example, Werther et al. 1986, chapter 17). In this section we will discuss both service and manufacturing examples, beginning with the *measurement* of productvity. There are two basic reasons for computing and tracking productivity measures: to evalute an individual or an organization, and to learn, as an organization, what methods work to improve productivity. Each measure must serve one or both of these purposes.

Measurement

What gets measured gets done. This means that if you compute a productivity statistic and evaluate people using it, you will improve on that measure. Unfortunately, this is both good news and bad news. Kopelman (1983) has shown that objective feedback "virtually always works. In all cases, results were positive." That is, if a firm uses quantitative measures and feeds these directly back to employees, the measure will improve. Das and Shikdar (1990) have obtained similar results. The bad news is that many productivity measures, when "improved," actually hurt the organization. A simple example is that more production is bad if we cannot sell the units. Son (1990) gives several examples of firms with increasing productivity but poor profitability. In this section we will discuss how to select appropriate measures and use them appropriately.

Measuring productivity is simple in concept but difficult in practice. A productivity index in basic form is defined as

$$\text{Productivity index (P.I.)} = \frac{\text{(outputs/inputs) in the current period}}{\text{(outputs/inputs) in a base period}} \tag{3}$$

For example, suppose that a firm produced 4 units of an item using 2 labor-hours, in the base period. In the current period, the firm produces 6 units in 2.5 labor-hours. Then the productivity index is

$$\text{P.I.} = \frac{6/2.5}{4/2} = \frac{2.4}{2.0} = 1.2$$

The index shows a 20% improvement in productivity, but the improvement may be illusory. Perhaps the item has been redesigned, so that the units are not exactly comparable. Perhaps a capital investment has resulted in the improvement, and the 20% increase does not show whether the investment was justified or not. Perhaps there is a setup time of 1 hour; the labor force produced 4 units in 1 hour after setup in the base period and 6 units in 1.5 hours after setup in the current period.

This example illustrates several important points about productivity measurement. We will now highlight each main point with some examples from Mundel (1978).

First, the quantity to be measured must be selected carefully; it must reflect what the organization wishes to improve. For example, in measuring the productivity of hospital nursing staffs, it would be shortsighted to measure only nursing hours per patient-day. If more nursing hours results in patients who heal faster, productivity may have improved, even though the nursing-hours-per-patient-day ratio has increased. In measuring the effectiveness of a government agency charged with ensuring compliance with pollution standards, the number of citations issued per inspector day would be inappropriate; inspectors should strive to increase the fraction of firms in compliance with the regulation. Productivity measures can be counterproductive unless they are selected carefully. In the two preceding cases, it is easy to see how nursing hours per patient-day might decline or the number of citations issued might increase while not improving the real goal of the organization.

A productivity measure must also represent something that is at least partially controllable by the people being measured. This dictum was not followed when a weather department was measured using the number of typhoons tracked. Unless they had failed to track some typhoons, this measure was not controllable by the department.

Several difficulties plague productivity measurement. For example, how should a productivity ratio handle products that change over time? (Consider how different computers or cars are today than they were twenty-five years ago.) Also, how can a firm measure the input due to capital equipment? How can a productivity measure for a plant or company be developed when there are many outputs (such as cars, spark plugs, and ignition systems) and many inputs (such as unskilled labor, skilled labor, engineers, and capital equipment)? Finally, while measures may be taken for individuals or for an organization, different measures should be used for different purposes. In the remainder of this section, we will discuss these issues.

Most productivity measures are *partial productivity measures;* they measure the amount of output per unit of a single input. For example, tons of steel per worker is a common measure in the steel industry. Partial productivity measures, by their nature, fail to consider the effect of other inputs. For example, tons of steel per worker can be increased by investing in new, automated plants. This may be either right or wrong, depending on the return on the investment. There are two common ways around the problem. A manager can use either (1) a small set of productivity measures, combined with judgment applied after examining the results, or (2) a ''total factor'' productivity measure.

As an example of a set of measures, consider measuring the effectiveness of a new product development group in a computer manufacturing company. This group is charged not only with product design, but also with defining the product concept (before design) and interacting with manufacturing (after design). Several measures have been proposed:

1. average time to develop a new product
2. number of new products developed per person-year

3. company sales from products developed in the last five years
4. quality, measured in frequency of repair of new products during their first year in the field

Any one of these measures by itself can cause the group to "improve" the measure while hurting the organization. If "average time to develop" is to be minimized, for example, the way to do that is to develop only modestly new (similar to previous) products. "Company sales from new products" can cause us to replace old products before the appropriate time. Also, this measure is difficult to use as an evaluation tool; it takes so long for a product to go from idea to market to success that the developer may have moved on.

Taken as a *set*, the foregoing measures might be appropriate, depending on the goals of the organization. Judgment must always be used in interpreting the data. To emphasize this, some firms use the term "indicators of performance," rather than "productivity measures." The idea is that if a group develops products faster than before, at the very least we should investigate to find out why.

To measure the productivity of a company, or a subunit entirely responsible for producing and selling some goods or services, *total factor productivity (TFP)* models can be used. These models attempt to use all major inputs, and to aggregate the outputs, in a single measure. (See Haves et al. 1988 for a discussion of the advantages of TFP in evaluating manufacturing organizations.)

TFP begins with equation 3, but includes many inputs (for example, energy, capital, labor, and materials) and outputs. Both inputs and outputs must be in monetary terms if they are to be summed. (What would two cars plus three spark plugs equal?) Then the inflation effect must be removed by restating all inputs and outputs in the same prices. For example, base-period prices can be used. TFP provides a good feeling for how an organization is doing overall. If the organization uses more labor, saving even more in materials by doing so, TFP would increase while labor-hours per unit would look worse (higher). Still, even TFP measures can give an incorrect impression. Consider the following example, for manufacturing firms, from Taylor and Davis (1978).

Total factor productivity = (value added in sales + change in inventory + additions, produced by the firm, to plant and equipment) ÷ [wages and benefits + (fraction of return on assets in base year) × (working + fixed capital)]. Symbolically,

$$\text{TFP} = \frac{(S + C + P_m) - E}{(W + B) + (K_w + K_f)F_b \cdot d_f} \tag{4}$$

where

S = sales
C = change in inventory
P_m = manufactured plant (adding value to our own facilities)
E = purchases and other exclusions, so that the numerator is value added
$W + B$ = wages plus benefits
$K_w + K_f$ = working plus fixed capital assets employed (plant, equipment, inventory, etc.)
F_b = return on assets earned in the base year (against which we are comparing)
d_f = a price deflator to adjust capital assets to base-year values

All parts of the measure are in monetary terms, adjusted for inflation. This measure is a good way to analyze productivity, but it can also lead to misconceptions. For example, if inventory is growing dramatically, our productivity measure can look good, but the company can be in bad shape.

In summary, we must measure productivity if we are to improve it, but no one measure of productivity is flawless. Total factor productivity can include many different inputs and outputs, but even so it can be misleading. (See the review problems for this section.) Several productivity measures may be needed, and they must be interpreted by a manager who understands the organization being measured. Since productivity measurement, from goal selection to final computation to interpretation, requires management judgment, managers must be aware of both the value and the difficulty of measuring productivity.

Improving Productivity

There are three major ways to improve productivity:

1. Motivation and teamwork: Change the attitudes of managers, government, and workers.
2. Investment: Invest in properly selected technology and equipment, and in improving the organization's human-resource base.
3. Manage day-to-day operations, using labor and capital, more effectively.

Motivation is discussed briefly in Section 5-1 and in many organizational behavior texts (see, for example, Organ and Bateman 1986). Teamwork must exist in many different settings. The functional areas of a firm must work together toward common goals. (See Kane 1986 for one technique.) And management, labor, and governments must work together. To foster cross-functional and labor-management cooperation, proper productivity and performance measures must be used. Narrow measures will cause suboptimization, but measuring two departments on something they both affect will help to foster cooperation. Top management commitment is required to maintain motivation for productivity improvement. (See Whitman 1990 for a discussion of this issue in a health-care setting.)

Investment in new technologies is discussed in Chapter 15. Here we want to stress that training people is also a long-term investment in human resources. Marshall (1988) indicates that the return on investments in human capital exceeds that of investments in equipment. Companies will need to invest more in human capital as the pace of change quickens. Investments that make a company a learning organization will typically pay off handsomely.

In the third area, managers must schedule operations to avoid idle time, reduce assets employed, and still provide the service desired by customers. Methods for obtaining improvements such as these form the core of this book. One technique we will discuss in this chapter is *benchmarking*. (Xerox's benchmarking efforts are described in Tucker et al. 1987.) Benchmarking is based on the idea that looking inward is not enough: 10% improvement per year is sufficient if we are 50% behind.

In benchmarking, operations such as billing or warehousing are selected for comparison and improvement. Competitors *or* companies in other industries known to be good at the operation being examined are used for the study. Some organization can nearly always be found to cooperate, for mutual benefit. Once the study begins, specific measures (for example, dollar value moved out of the warehouse per employee) are selected, and methods are studied in detail. Methods that lead to improved operations are analyzed and implemented. Follow-up procedures are used to see that the expected improvements really occur. The purpose of benchmarking is both to compare against and learn from other organizations. Any improvement must be rewarded (not necessarily financially), even if on reflection we think that the improved method is obvious and should have been in use before.

In summary, productivity measurement is commonplace but nevertheless elusive. Careless application of productivity incentives can lead to grave errors. Difficult as measurement is, it is very useful to monitor the effects of managerial changes. Each of the three areas for potential productivity improvement can be very important. Motivation and teamwork require managers to be sensitive to the needs of others, stressing the importance of cooperation. Investment and more effective operations management require careful operations analysis, understanding both the broad view and the details of the problem.

REVIEW PROBLEMS

Refer to the total factor productivity formula (equation 4) in this section. Suppose that a manager wants to maximize the productivity rating.

1. Why might inventories grow?

2. What other factor might be used to improve the productivity rating?

Solutions

1. If capacity is underutilized, the marginal cost of the next unit of production is probably lower than the average cost. Since inventory additions count as much as sales, the firm's productivity index will go up if we produce extra units, even though they are not needed. (The inventory will increase the numerator more than it increases the denominator.)

2. Several answers are possible here. For example, the firm can add to its plant (P_m). If capacity is limited, the productivity rating can be increased by producing only high-margin items, perhaps causing long-term marketing difficulties. For a while, the firm can allow fixed capital to decline, thereby obtaining a short-term productivity increase by borrowing from the future.

SUMMARY

All organizations should try to be more productive. Lower production costs make a manufacturing firm more competitive. Less time spent on routine work gives a social-service agency more time for contact with people needing their services. Productivity improvements have been good for our society, dramatically improving our standard of living, and they can often be good for all members of an organization.

Unfortunately, productivity improvement efforts do not always lead to improved productivity. There are several reasons for this. First, productivity measures are not perfect; they can be improved without making the organization better off. Second, workers may not take productivity improvement seriously unless a program is applied carefully and consistently over a long period of time. Third, some changes, such as quality-of-work-life (QWL) programs have not been clearly shown by research studies to improve productivity. What does improve productivity? We will cite one study, and then give our opinions.

Studying manufacturing organizations, Schmenner (1988) found that throughput time (cycle time) reduction, quality improvement, and inventory reduction improved productivity. He noted that "all three of these are clearly in the JIT (just-in-time) camp." (See Chapter 12, as well as Chapter 6 on total quality management.) Employee involvement is "somewhat supported," as is investment in new equipment.

Our judgment generally agrees with these observations. We would also like to share some additional opinions.

1. Measurements must be taken. Things will not improve until you measure them quantitatively. (Of course, measurement is only the beginning.)
2. The implementation of numerical measures must not be seen as antiworker, but rather as cooperatively working to improve.
3. No one measure will suffice. A set of measures must be used, and judgment must always be applied to the numbers. Measures must not be so narrow as to defeat cross-functional cooperation.
4. Teamwork throughout the organization is crucial, and it requires careful selection of measures and dedicated management effort to foster teamwork; we favor group incentives over individual incentives where feasible.
5. Quality improvement (Chapter 6), and just-in-time (Chapter 12) can also improve productivity if applied appropriately.
6. Very significant productivity improvements are gained by detailed process analysis. "Combine, simplify, and (especially) eliminate" are important ideas.
7. Investment in automation helps only after the process is carefully thought out; investment in human capital is likely to lead to larger payoffs.
8. Building up the human capital in an organization will require that the firm utilize the talents of women, minorities, and older workers, flexibly and at all levels.
9. Learning from others both within the organization and outside is crucial.
10. Rewards for improvement are effective motivators. Both financial and nonfinancial rewards work. Everyone likes to be appreciated; no one is above enjoying positive feedback, a "pat on the back."

Improving productivity calls on the manager to use his or her analytical ability, interpersonal skills, knowledge of the particular system being managed, and judgment. Improving productivity is often difficult, but there is no more important management task.

PROBLEMS

*1. A software development group in a very large company developed a productivity improvement program (PIP). They decided to use three basic measures: (i) thousands of lines code per programmer year (KLOC/PY), (ii) proven errors per thousand lines of code, found after the program is shipped to an internal or external customer (PE/KLOC), and (iii) average time to develop a new program.

   a. What is your opinion about these measures when applied to an individual programmer? To a large 100-person department?

   b. The development group claims that (i) is a quantity measure, that (ii) is a quality measure, and that (iii) is a market measure. Why is the third measure a ''market'' measure? What do you think about the basic idea of including a quantity, a quality, and a market measure?

   c. Suggest an improved set of three measures for the department.

2. A work incentive may be thought of as a motivation factor that is at least partially withheld from workers, so that it may be ''earned'' by workers who perform well. In the introduction to this chapter, there is a list of ''good job'' characteristics. Which of these do you feel are commonly used as work incentives?

3. How does employee involvement (EI) change the role of a supervisor?

*4. a. What is the fundamental difference between the stopwatch method and work sampling?

   b. Why are ratings of work pace necessary for both methods?

5. a. What are the roles of operations analysis and motion study in the design of jobs?

   b. Why is it that time-and-motion studies are well received by the workers in some settings but not in others?

*6. A work sample is being conducted. The observer randomly samples 60 times a day and notes that a particular element is performed 12 times.

   a. Estimate the percentage of the time that workers spend on this element.

   b. Calculate the precision of the estimate (a 95% confidence interval).

   c. Determine the appropriate sample size required for a second set of observations if the acceptable numerical error in p_i is 0.02.

7. In a work study, the basic tasks for assembling a can opener were timed. The raw data are shown in the table on page 119.

   a. Calculate the precision (95% confidence) of the average task times.

   b. How many additional observations are needed to reduce the error in the average task time to $\pm 1\%$ for task 6?

8. There are five different work groups in a plant, and we want to design a work-sampling plan to ascertain what percentage of time is

*Problems with an asterisk have answers in the back of the book.

Task	Number of Observations	Average Task Time (minutes)	Standard Deviation (minutes)
1	20	0.50	0.04
2	100	1.00	0.50
3	10	0.70	0.03
4	20	0.30	0.06
5	100	2.00	0.80
6	10	1.00	0.04
7	20	0.70	0.01

being spent by each worker in each of eight general activity categories. Our prior estimates range from a low of 5% for activity category C to a high of 25% for category F.

a. What sample size is needed to achieve an accuracy of ±3 percentage points (or better) for all categories with 95% confidence?

b. The plan is to visit the work groups at randomly selected times over a 4-hour period, each day, until a sufficiently large sample size is achieved. There will be at least 15 minutes between observations, and one worker will be observed in each visit. Show how to randomly assign 15-minute observation intervals among the five work groups, using one die.

c. How many days will be required to take the sample? Suggest a way to reduce this time.

d. How many observations would be required to double the accuracy?

*9. How can management successfully solicit laborsaving suggestions from employees?

10. A firm makes nails in 20 sizes. Suppose that a productivity goal is given in (a) number of nails or (b) pounds of nails. What products might they make in each case, and why? (This question is based on an old Russian cartoon about central planning goals.)

*11. The MTM company had 50 employees in the base year, during which it produced 20 large computers. In the current year, the firm produced 25 computers with 60 employees.

a. Compute a labor productivity index.

b. Why might this partial productivity index be misleading?

*12. Suppose that the MTM company, described in problem 11, makes two models of computer. Product 1 (P1) requires 2 labor-years, and product 2 (P2) requires 3 labor-years. In the current year they produced 15 P1's and 10 P2's.

a. Next year they believe they can sell up to 20 P1's and 20 P2's. They will have 60 employees. How many of each should they produce if they want to maximize the productivity ratio from problem 11?

b. Why might the answer to part a be bad for the company?

13. (This problem requires information from problem 12.) Suppose that P1 sells for \$1 million and P2 sells for \$2 million.
    a. If the company wants to maximize revenue, what products should they make next year with 60 employees, assuming that they can sell up to 20 of each?
    b. Why might this not be the right thing to do?
14. The company in problems 11 to 13 (you must read those problems for information) has decided to use the total factor productivity model from equation 4 in Section 5-3, and to purchase rather than manufacture some subsystems. That is, they will add less value to their products than before. They will not fire people, but they may allow the work force to be reduced over time through attrition. Their capital assets will be unchanged, at least in the short run.
    a. If they produce 15 P1's and 10 P2's next year (as they did this year), describe what will happen to their total factor productivity index, indicating the terms that will cause the change.
    b. If they are going to purchase 60% of the sales value of each product, and if they can now produce P1 with 1 labor year and P2 with 2 labor years, what products should they produce to maximize their value added? (They can sell up to 20 of each product.)
    c. In equation 4, the TFP formula in Section 5-3, $C = P_m = 0$; $W + B = 60$ times $100{,}000 = \$6$ million; $K_w + K_f = \$40$ million; $F_b = 0.20$; and $d_f = 1$. Compute the value of TFP based on your decision in part b. Comment briefly on the meaning and validity of the value of TFP.
15. List four reasons why good productivity measurements are difficult to obtain.

*16. Discuss reasons for favoring group incentives. What arguments favor individual incentives?

*17. In benchmarking their student registration and room-scheduling system, to whom might a university look in addition to other universities? What goals might be used in the study?

*18. In Section 5-2 two firms were described that had different learning rates. Firm A's production hours were given by $360i^{-0.322}$; the production hours for firm B were given by $150i^{-0.152}$. (i is the total number of units produced since the product was introduced.)
    a. When $i = 200$ for both, how much advantage does firm A have over firm B? When $i = 1000$?
    b. Verify that firm A does not catch up to firm B on a total-labor-hours-expended basis until $i = 643$, even though they catch up on a marginal basis at $i = 172$. (Hint: As a close approximation, total labor-hours expended equals the integral of marginal labor-hours:

$$\int_0^i ax^b\,dx = ai^{1-b}/(1-b)$$

The constants are $a = 360$, $b = 0.322$ for firm A, and $a = 150$, $b = 0.152$ for firm B.)

19. Managers in a company are using the concept of the learning curve in estimating production labor-hour requirements for a product. They estimate that by the time the 10th unit is produced, learning will have occurred to the point that this unit will require 75 direct labor hours. From previous experience with this type of product, they estimate that it will follow a 90% learning rate.
    a. Determine the learning parameter.
    b. Determine the number of direct labor hours required to produce the first unit.
    c. How many labor hours will be required to produce the eightieth unit?
20. In what way does improvement of quality also increase productivity? Give an example in manufacturing and in service.
21. Investment in improved computer reservation systems can improve the productivity of airline ticket agents.
    a. Describe productivity measures that would capture the effects of this kind of improvement.
    b. One productivity measure might be "average time required to gain access to a customer's existing reservation." What disadvantages might accrue if this were the only measure?

REFERENCES

ARGOTE, L., S. BECKMAN, and D. EPPLE, "The Persistence of Learning in Industrial Settings," *Management Science*, vol. 36, no. 2, 1990.

ARGOTE, L., and D. EPPLE, "Learning Curves in Manufacturing," *Science*, February 23, 1990.

BAUMOL, W., "Is There a U.S. Productivity Crisis?" *Science*, February 3, 1989.

BECKER, J.G., JR., *Productivity Plus*, Houston: Gulf, 1987.

BLANCHARD, K., and S. JOHNSON, *The One Minute Manager*, New York: Morrow, 1982.

BOUCHER, T., "Adam Smith and the Humanists: An Enquiry into the Productivity of Labor Controversy," *IIE Transactions*, March, 1988.

BULLOCK, R.J., and P.F. BULLOCK, "Gainsharing and Rubik's Cube: Solving System Problems," *National Productivity Review*, vol. 1, no. 4, 1982.

CONWAY, R., and A. SCHULTZ, "The Manufacturing Progress Function," *The Journal of Industrial Engineering*, January–February, 1959.

COPENHAVER, L., and R. GUEST, "Quality of Work Life: The Anatomy of Two Successes," *National Productivity Review*, vol. 2, no. 1, 1983.

DAS, B., and A.A. SHIKDAR, "Applying Production Standards and Feedback to Improve Worker Productivity and Satisfaction in a Repetitive Production Task," *IIE Transactions*, June, 1990.

DE MEYER, A., "The Use of Manufacturing as a Competitive Weapon in the International Markets," *Gestion 2000*, 2, 123–131, 1986.

FEIN, M., "Managing Philosophy Affects Productivity Improvement Programs," *Industrial Engineering*, vol. 15, no. 10 (October), 1983.

HAYES, R., and S. WHEELWRIGHT, *Restoring our Competitive Edge: Competing Through Manufacturing*, New York: Wiley, 1984.

HAYES, R., S. WHEELWRIGHT, and K. CLARK, *Dynamic Manufacturing: Creating the Learning Organization*, New York: The Free Press, 1988.

HERZBERG, F., *The Managerial Choice: To Be Efficient or to Be Human*, Homewood, Ill.: Irwin, 1976.

JOHNSTON, W. AND A. PACKER, *Workforce 2000: Work and Workers for the 21st Century*, Indianapolis, Indiana, Hudson Institute, 1987.

KANE, E., ''IBM's Quality Focus on the Business Process,'' *Quality Progress*, April, 1986.

KLINGEL, S., AND A. MARTIN (eds.), *A Fighting Chance to Save Jobs*, Ithaca, NY: ILR Press, Cornell University, 1988.

KOPELMAN, R., ''Improving Productivity Through Objective Feedback: A Review of the Evidence,'' *National Productivity Review*, Winter, 1983.

LAWLER, E., III, AND G. LEDFORD, JR., ''Productivity and the Quality of Work Life,'' *National Productivity Review*, vol. 1, no. 1, 1982.

MADDISON, A., *Phases of Capitalist Development*, Oxford: Oxford University Press, 1982.

MARSHALL, R., ''New Skills and Productivity,'' in Shetty and Buehler, eds., *Competing Through Productivity and Quality*, Cambridge, Mass.: Productivity Press, 1988.

MAY, J., AND R. JACKSON, ''Industrial Engineering Philosophies and Practices Can Increase Shop Floor Productivity . . . And Our Own,'' *Industrial Engineering*, June, 1989.

MCKEE, K., AND C. SESSIONS-ROBINSON, ''Manufacturing Productivity and Competitiveness,'' *The Journal of Manufacturing*, Spring, 1989.

MUNDEL, M., ''Measures of Productivity,'' in *Productivity: A Series from Industrial Engineering*, M. Mundel, ed., Atlanta: Institute of Industrial Engineers, 1978.

NAISBETT, J., AND P. ABURDENE, ''Megatrends 2000,'' *Best of Business Quarterly*, vol. 11, no. 4, 1990.

NIEBEL, B., *Motion and Time Study*, 7th ed., Homewood, Ill.: Irwin, 1982.

ORGAN, D., AND T. BATEMAN, *Organizational Behavior*, 3rd ed., Plano, Tex.: Business Publications, 1986.

SCHMENNER, R., ''Behind Labor Productivity Gains in the Factory,'' *Journal of Manufacturing and Operations Management*, vol. 1, no. 4, 1988.

SHETTY, Y.K., AND V.M. BUEHLER, EDS., *Competing Through Productivity and Quality*, Cambridge, Mass.: Productivity Press, 1988.

SON, Y.K., ''A Performance Measurement Method Which Remedies the 'Productivity Paradox','' *Production and Inventory Management*, vol. 31, no. 2, 1990.

TAYLOR, F.W., *Shop Management*, New York: Harper & Row, 1919.

TAYLOR, B.W., III, AND K.R. DAVIS, ''Corporate Productivity—Getting It All Together,'' in *Productivity: A Series from Industrial Engineering*, M. Mundel, ed., Atlanta: Institute of Industrial Engineers, 1978.

TUCKER, F., S. ZIVAN, AND R. CAMP, ''How to Measure Yourself Against the Best,'' *Harvard Business Review*, January–February, 1987.

WERTHER, W., W. RUCH, AND L. MCCLURE, *Productivity Through People*, St. Paul, Minn.: West, 1986.

WHITMAN, A.R., ''Productivity Implementation Management Needs Commitment from the Top,'' *Industrial Engineering*, August, 1990.

WILLIAMS, L., ''Competitiveness and the Union,'' in Shetty and Buehler, eds., *Competing Through Productivity and Quality*, Cambridge, Mass.: Productivity Press, 1988.

WOLFBEIN, S., ''Planning for the U.S. Labor Force of the '80s,'' *National Productivity Review*, vol. 1, no. 2, 1982.

Work in America, report of a special task force to the Secretary of Health, Education and Welfare, Cambridge, Mass.: MIT Press, 1973.

chapter

6

Total Quality Management

Quality is the key to making American products. We are in the midst of a technological revolution, and our work to build quality products will be a crucial link to the long-term success of the United States in the global marketplace.

*George Bush, 1989**

Quality and price are fundamental in competitive markets for goods and services. In a 1987 Gallup survey, top executives gave quality improvement top priority, ahead of productivity, product liability, and many other issues (Skrzycki 1987). Major corporations include quality in strategic planning. Quality has been a major factor in the success of Japanese products, particularly in automotive and electronic markets.

High quality does not necessarily mean high price. Many quality improvements actually reduce cost. For example, the Cadillac division of General Motors achieved a 29% decrease in warranty-related costs in four years even though the warranty was extended from 1 year or 12,000 miles to 4 years or 50,000 miles (Holusha 1990). This is why quality is of such strategic importance. Having low price and high quality is a tremendous competitive advantage. According to an IBM senior vice-president, ''This is one of the single most important things we can do to improve our financial performance and become more competitive'' (Schwartz 1990).

In the service industry superior quality is a winning corporate strategy. Leading service companies use high quality to be different from their competitors, to increase productivity, to earn customer loyalty, to gain positive word-of-mouth advertising, and to seek some shelter from price competition (Zeithaml et al. 1990).

*Malcolm Baldrige National Quality Award. Quote appeared in the 1989 Application Guidelines.

Experience has shown that quality problems have many apparent sources, but underlying them all are *root causes*. A root cause contributes to many problems, not just the one that brought it to light. Therefore, removing a root cause is the most effective way to improve both quality and productivity. For example, we will explore situations in which quality problems in one part of an organization impede work (increase cost) in another part. When a root cause is removed, many problems simply disappear. This translates to higher productivity and lower cost.

Finding and eliminating root causes requires skill and resources. Investing in workers through training and incentives is a hallmark of *total quality management* (*TQM*). However, training is not enough. Organizations naturally resist change, and change is the heart of total quality management. Many of the needed changes are easily understood, and often well-known among the workers. Then why don't they happen? Organizational inertia is probably the best explanation of why so many opportunities for improvement remain untouched. To improve, an organization must be designed and managed to encourage experimentation and change.

Every aspect of an organization can be improved. Eliminating root causes is very effective in a surprising variety of situations. In total quality management, every part of an organization is viewed as both a supplier and a customer. Everyone who depends on your work is your customer, and everyone on whom you depend is your supplier. Neither producing nor accepting defective product should be the goal of every employee. Total quality management emphasizes that quality is everyone's job.

The power of total quality management is not completely revealed without a look at its performance through time. Figure 6-1 illustrates that the improvement process is a never-ending cycle of discovery and change.

The heart of the improvement process is learning. Each improvement teaches you how to find root causes and how to make sure that they are permanently eliminated. This increases the speed with which the next improvement can be made. Figure 6-2 illustrates this. An organization that has learned how to learn is a very tough competitor. Accelerating improvement is the true power of TQM.

The Malcolm Baldrige National Quality Award, sponsored by the U.S. Department of Commerce, is an important force in spreading the knowledge gained by companies that have achieved excellence in quality. "We are defining

Figure 6-1 Quality Improvement Cycle in a Learning Organization

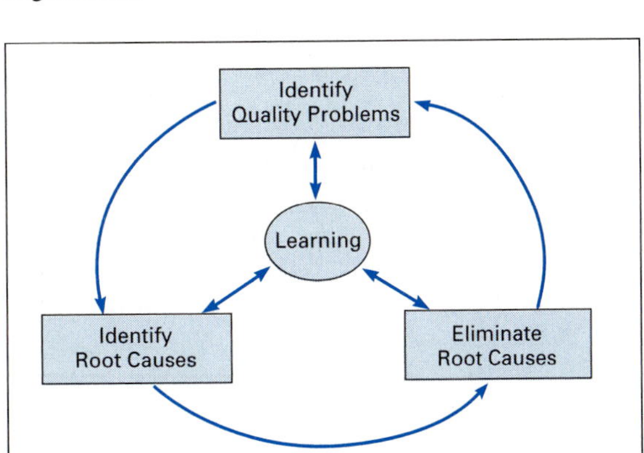

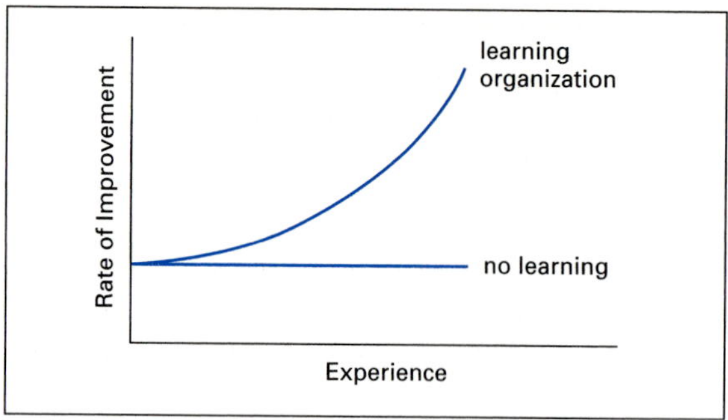

Figure 6-2 Accelerating Improvement in a Learning Organization

what quality is for the nation. Companies are using these criteria as a self-assessment tool'' (C.W. Reimann, quoted in Holusha 1990). In fact, winners of this prestigious prize are required to share their knowledge, and do so in a variety of ways. This includes guided tours and talks that may be attended by some of their competitors. The philosophy is that American industry needs a major overhaul, and improvements in the industry as a whole will be to everyone's benefit because it will preserve a marketplace for American products.

Higher Quality and Lower Cost

If this introduction sounds like an exaggeration, consider the following examples, abstracted from real situations.

Example: Food Services Incorporated

Food Services, Incorporated, supplies restaurants with fresh vegetables. By establishing direct links with growers, and by operating its own fleet of refrigerated trucks, FSI can move produce to its customers in one tenth the time required by normal distribution channels. FSI's customers do not have to inspect their produce. FSI's inspection and prepackaging operations virtually eliminate unsatisfactory product, and the rapid delivery by their own trucking fleet maintains the quality level for the customers. FSI charges a higher price than its competitors. However, in balance, the cost is reduced for the restaurants. Avoided are the wages of inspectors and the cost of scrap. The ultimate consumer (the diners) receive a higher-quality product at the same price.

Improving operations is one way to increase quality and lower costs. The following example illustrates that the design of the product itself is equally important.

Example: Snappy Printer

Snappy Printer Company eliminated inspectors at the final stage of assembly for their latest printer. This was possible because the product was designed so that if it fit together, it would work. Each component snaps into place (no screws). No two components are of the same size. All components are asymmetrical, so that they can snap in in only one orientation: They cannot be mounted backward or in the wrong location. All the final assembly steps are easy, and it is obvious to the workers when something goes wrong. The final assembly step is to plug the machine in, insert a piece of paper, and push one button. If the machine works, it passes.

This is an example of "mistake-proof" operations, described later. The new Snappy printer has higher quality than its predecessors, but the cost is lower. They eliminated some inspection and no longer need to fix final assembly errors. Eliminating rework is an obvious cost saver, but other benefits also accrue, such as improved production scheduling, reduced inventory, and higher customer satisfaction.

Example: Snappy Printer (continued)

> In the past, Snappy printers that failed the final test were sent to a rework area to be fixed. The work load in that area was unpredictable because of the random nature of defects. Therefore, the time to produce a batch of printers was highly variable. Since the printers are scheduled for delivery along with other components of a personal computer system, completing printers on schedule substantially improved delivery performance of the PCs and increased customer satisfaction. And the inventory of PCs waiting for printers was virtually eliminated.

Many similar results may be found in the trade journals on quality. Although the results have been impressive, the methods are not particularly complicated. (Try making a list of the quality-improving steps illustrated in the foregoing examples.) However, if it is so easy, why is quality still an important problem? A little history will help to illustrate the current dilemma.

A Brief History

Although W. A. Shewhart proposed the use of statistics in quality control in 1924, it was not until World War II that quality control was established as a way of life in American industry. Military procurement led the way, establishing a set of quality-control procedures and requiring contractors to follow them.

The link between quality and productivity became apparent at about this time. For example, Deming (1986) had observed this effect when working as a consultant in postwar Japan in the late 1940s. His explanation is simple. Improving quality decreases rework costs and reduces mistakes, delays and snags, resulting in better use of time and materials. And that is higher productivity. Unfortunately, that lesson was lost to much of American industry during the seller's markets that followed. International competition, mainly from the Japanese, brought the lesson home during the 1970s and 1980s.

Crosby emphasized the quality-productivity link in his book entitled *Quality is Free:* "Quality is not only free, it is an honest-to-everything moneymaker. Every penny you don't spend on doing things wrong, over, or instead of, becomes half a penny right on the bottom line. . . . If you concentrate on making quality certain, you can probably increase your profit by an amount equal to 5% to 10% of your sales" (Crosby 1979, p. 1). "IBM, Caterpillar, Michelin, Procter and Gamble, and Ford are some of the many companies that use this concept of quality in their overall strategy." (Johnson and Winchell 1989, p. 3).

Major organizational changes are necessary before substantial quality improvements will be achieved. Juran (1989, p. 324) recommends that the changes begin at the top: "Upper managers should be the first to acquire the new training." This not only sets an important example but also qualifies the managers to plan and evaluate training programs for the rest of the company.

A word of caution: Quality-improvement programs have a long history of failure. In many companies employees have seen program after program intended to change the way things are done, but after the excitement dies down, nothing changes. With good reason, employees say, "Here comes another program. Ignore it and it will go away."

The major implementation problem seems to be the urge to achieve a "quick fix." Ideas painstakingly worked out in one setting can be successfully transplanted, but all too often the most important elements are missed. The "program" is reduced to superficial things like signs, slogans, and progress charts: "Make Every Day ZERO DEFECTS DAY!" While these tools can help to motivate employees, they are of no use by themselves. History shows that quality-improvement programs without fundamental organizational change are doomed to failure.

TQM and the Systems View

Where do these opportunities for quality and productivity improvement reside? Quality begins at the product concept stage and extends throughout the development, production, delivery, and use of a good or service. Causes of poor quality can occur any place in the organization, from top management to janitorial staff, in accounting, production, sales, service, or any of the functional areas. The irony of the Snappy Printer example is that quality control (inspection and rework) had damaged the quality of the delivery schedule.

Causes of poor quality extend beyond the organization. On the input side, poor quality can be caused by supplies that are defective, late, or simply received in the wrong quantity. (Consider the impact of these three elements on a hospital's emergency room!) On the output side, inappropriate activities by those who sell or service a product are poor quality in the eyes of the consumer.

Total quality management requires us to look at the entire system, seeking new and imaginative ways to improve quality and productivity at the same time. Since the problems and the solutions cross organizational boundaries, the responsibility for total quality management must reside at the highest levels. For example, at Federal Express, "executive bonuses rest on the performance of the whole organization in meeting performance goals. . . . [These] bonuses are suspended if employees do not rate management leadership at least as high as the previous year" (Holusha 1990). Although designing and operating a continually changing organization is difficult, the payoff can be enormous in the long run.

The next section describes how organizations manage quality improvement, giving examples of methods that are used to spot opportunities and to make major improvements. Later sections detail some of the statistical methods used to assess and control quality.

REVIEW PROBLEMS

1. Make a list of ideas for quality improvements that lower cost, based on the examples in this section.

2. Illustrate the fact that causes of poor quality can occur anywhere in an organization, using marketing (sales, advertising, etc.) as an example.

3. In a hospital, the medical record contains all of the information about a patient. Consider the system effects of a one-day delay in reporting all diagnostic test results. How can that affect the patient? The productivity of the hospital? The cost of the medical care system?

Solutions

1. (a) Shorten the flow time from raw material to delivered product to reduce spoilage. (b) Prepackage and preinspect to eliminate tasks for the customer and increase quality. (c) Design the product for easy assembly to eliminate the potential for errors. Reducing rework saves money. (d) Eliminate defects to improve on-time delivery performance, part of quality of the service. (e) Improve the reliability of a process. This reduces inventory by allowing tighter coordination between production of components (e.g., printer and computer) that are needed at the same time.

2. (a) Inaccurate advertising gives customers unrealistic expectations, which can lead to dissatisfaction with the product. (b) Incorrect assessment of customer preferences can lead to designing the wrong product. (c) If customers are promised a delivery date that the production department cannot meet, the ''sales pitch'' was of poor quality.

3. Delays in reporting lab findings could delay treatment, and that could cause sicker patients. It can also cause overcrowding in the hospital, since the patients must stay longer. The unnecessary days require extra nursing care, reducing the productivity of the staff. Additional resources such as meals and linen also increase costs. In the long run, the overcrowding will lead to construction of more facilities, and that increases the cost of the medical system.

6-1 MANAGEMENT FOR QUALITY IMPROVEMENT

What is quality? Quality has so many dimensions that it is difficult to agree on one simple definition. One aspect is reliability, the ability to perform without failure. Quality also refers to the grade of a good or service, such as prime, choice, good, standard, and commercial (grades of meats). Safety and quality are closely related in most people's minds, and safety standards are set by federal agencies such as the Consumer Products Safety Commission. Consistency is also valued by consumers, as variation in quality can cause confusion and disappointment. You can undoubtedly list several other dimensions of quality of goods or services.

Sometimes high quality in one dimension may degrade performance on another. For example, high-performance automobiles often require more expensive service than standard models. Purchasers of high-performance vehicles understand and expect this trade-off. The perception of quality depends, to a large extent, on the consumer's expectations.

The definitions that best embody quality from the consumer's point of view are ''fitness for use'' and ''conformance to customer requirements.'' Does the product act (smell, look, feel) as the customer expects it to? If not, we have a quality problem. Either the product is deficient or the customer's expectations are misplaced. Both of these are the producer's problem. Adopting this definition has many implications, to which we will return presently.

Several other terms are frequently used to describe the management of quality. ''Quality assessment'' is measuring the level of quality. ''Quality control'' is action taken during production to avoid or eliminate unacceptable quality. ''Quality assurance'' includes all activities that eliminate poor quality. This includes quality design of products, processes, and jobs, as well as quality in personnel selection and training.

Assessment, control, and assurance all fit together. Assessment is needed for control, which is part of quality assurance. And quality assurance is the goal of total quality management.

Quality as ''Conformance to Requirements''

Many companies define quality as ''conformance to requirements.'' If a good or service lives up to expectations, it is of high quality. Unfortunately, expectations are not always accurately expressed by a written set of requirements.

Example: More Motors Company

> More Motors Company obtains gears from two different suppliers. Specifications set by More Motors regarding size, shape, materials, and so on, are met by both suppliers. However, customer complaints about gear noise led to an investigation that showed that the quiet transmissions had gears from supplier 1. Close inspection revealed that these gears had almost no variation from the target dimensions. They were right in the middle of the allowable range. Supplier 2 also stayed within the range, but often sent gears that were near the tolerance limits. More Motors revised their specifications (tightened the tolerance limits) and the problem disappeared.

Obviously, More Motors Company had a quality problem. Their consumers were not satisfied. What was the cause? The gears? The suppliers? The fundamental cause was defective specifications. The design engineers who specified how much variation would be acceptable made an error. Their specifications did not reflect the customers' expectations of low noise level.

Using conformance to requirements only works if it is applied at every stage of production. This forces every sector of a company to take a system view.

Definition: Who is your Customer?

> We start by making sure that everyone is clear about the objectives. IBM defines quality as ''meeting the requirements of our customers, both internal and external, for defect-free products and services.'' The most important customer will always be the user of products, but the most important customer to any individual employee will be the person who receives his or her work product. The objective is to neither pass on defective work nor accept it. (Kane 1986)

For example, in a product development department, new designs are the product, and the production department is one of their customers. If a new product design makes production unnecessarily difficult, that design is defective; Development has not met the requirements of Production, its immediate customer. By the same token, the design must also accurately reflect consumer requirements. Using conformance to customer requirements as the criterion for acceptable operation, and carefully defining who the customers are, is one mechanism for implementing total quality management.

Design Specifications for Goods and Services

Specifications (specs) are documents that prescribe the requirements to which goods or services must conform. Tolerances are part of specifications, expressing how much variation from the ideal values is acceptable. High quality depends on goods and services conforming to specifications, and on specifications accurately reflecting customer requirements.

Performance specifications tell what a product is supposed to do rather than how it is to be produced. This gives the producers and suppliers a chance to use their knowledge to increase quality and reduce cost.

Example: Speedy Pizza

Speedy Pizza guarantees delivery in thirty minutes or less. Drivers are given detailed instructions for reaching every neighborhood in the service area. However, based on experience, drivers modify their routes to suit the current traffic situation. Even faster delivery has resulted.

Speedy has two products: Pizza (a good) and fast delivery (a service). Thirty-minute delivery is a performance spec. Quality of service was increased by giving the producer (driver) autonomy to change production methods (routes).

Suppliers can also increase quality, as Snappy Printer discovered:

Example: Snappy Printer (continued)

When Snappy Printer was designing its new product, the specifications called for a specific plastic for the base. The supplier convinced Snappy to change to a different plastic with superior elastic properties. This allowed some of the spring clips to be an integral part of the base rather than added later. The cost of the steel springs was avoided, but more important, one source of defects was eliminated: missing or improperly installed springs.

In many cases both performance and dimensional specifications are given. For example, Snappy Printer Company could specify the dimensions and required strength of the base and leave the choice of material and production technology to the supplier. (A good discussion of performance specifications may be found in Grieco et al. 1988.)

Maintaining accurate specifications is no easy task. For example, automobile design occurs several years ahead of production. How can we know what customer requirements will be in three years? Even if customer requirements are known, there are usually many different designs that can achieve them, and trade-offs often occur. Greater acceleration may adversely affect both the noise and the fuel economy of an automobile, for example.

Specifications must change to reflect new customer requirements or improvements to the product. But change can damage quality or increase costs. For example, introducing a new processing method may cause more defects, at least temporarily. Even though each disruption is temporary, frequent changes cause perpetual turmoil. Flexibility to change specifications is important, but keeping such changes to a minimum is equally important.

Designing new goods and services is an ongoing process. Managing the design process is an important part of total quality management. Designs must satisfy several customers; their interests need to be represented during the design process. The *House of Quality* (Hauser and Clausing 1988) is a design tool for reconciling customer specifications with product and process attributes.

(More on this later.) Design teams with broad representation can be very effective. Sales or service people may understand the consumer's interests. Vendors have special knowledge about materials that will be used. Producers know things about production that may influence the design. Using design teams is a powerful method for quality assurance.

The Cost of Quality (COQ)

We have emphasized that increasing quality often reduces cost and increases productivity. Several examples have already been given. The following lists (Pall 1987) point out many costs related to quality and where to look for them. Each of these costs also represents an opportunity: Reduce or eliminate it.

Costs of Prevention

Quality education. Process design. Defect cause removal. Quality audit or assessment. Preventive maintenance.

Costs of Appraisal

Testing. Measurements. Evaluations and assessments. Problem analysis. Detection. Inspection. Maintenance of test equipment.

Costs of Failure (internal)

Reinspection and testing. Scrap. Rework. Repairs. Service. Defect removal. Lost production.

Costs of Failure (external)

Returned products. Legal exposure and costs. Liability and damage claims. Replacement. Complaint administration and warranty. Lost reputation and sales.

The *costs of conformance* are incurred to assure quality, the *costs of nonconformance* occur because of failures. Kane (1986) has estimated that nonconformance represents 75% of the total cost of quality. Some of the costs of conformance may be viewed as an investment, with reduced costs of nonconformance as part of the return on that investment. For example, consider the cost of inspecting computer equipment at the factory (conformance) compared with the cost of repair under warranty after delivery and installation (nonconformance). ''The leverage in finding an error at its source versus waiting until it occurs in the field can be over 100-to-1 in many cases'' (Kane 1986).

Analysis of quality improvement must take this ratio into account. For example, an assembly line was analyzed on which defects were sometimes discovered during production (Robinson et al. 1990). One alternative was to repair the defects immediately so that no defects would be passed on to the next stage; unfortunately, the next stage might fall idle while the repair was being made, lowering productivity. Another alternative was to tag the defective items and repair them after they left the assembly line. This avoided the disruption of on-line repair but suffered from the cost ratio just mentioned: the item must be partially disassembled to effect repair. Which policy was more effective depended on how expensive this disassembly was, and on how disruptive on-line repair was.

The cost of quality (COQ) can be very large. Crosby (1979) suggests that 20% of sales is a good estimate in many situations, and that reducing COQ to as low as 2.5% of sales is a realistic target. Obviously there must be substantial change to achieve a saving of this magnitude. The key is a systematic approach to finding and removing the causes of poor quality. The remainder of this section illustrates some tools and approaches for quality improvement that have proven very effective in practice.

Tools for Quality Improvement

Quality Teams. A quality team (or quality circle) is a group of employees whose assignment is to identify problems, formulate solutions, and present their results to management with suggestions for implementation. Although simple in concept, successful implementation of quality teams requires a support structure:

Steering committee: Provide overall guidance, suggest problems, receive recommendations, and follow up on implementation.

Facilitators: Train team leaders and help train members. Get information that circles request.

Team leaders: Train team members in problem identification and solution methods. Moderate team meetings. Prepare presentations to management.

Team members: Volunteers from regular work force, given company time to carry out quality improvement projects. Responsible for selecting an important problem, identifying an effective solution, and recommending implementation strategy.

At Hughes Aircraft, more than five hundred quality circles had been established by 1982 (see Kohler and Wells 1982), and the president encouraged middle managers to "make this a top priority of their job."

The Quality-Improvement Cycle. As we emphasized in Figure 6-1, quality improvement is a never-ending cycle. Formally describing the cycle as a management process helps to assure its effectiveness. Alcoa (1989) views quality improvement as a never-ending cycle divided into eight steps:

1. *Define problems and quality improvement opportunities:* Describe problems and opportunities clearly and concisely.
2. *Select the problem or opportunity:* Decide which problem is likely to yield the greatest benefit, if solved.
3. *Analyze causes and effects:* Search for "root causes." Keep asking, "But what caused that?"
4. *Generate potential actions:* Look for novel as well as conventional solutions.
5. *Evaluate and select actions:* Identify needed resources and potential side effects. Estimate how customers will like the solution.
6. *Test effectiveness of actions:* Try out solution before full-scale implementation. Obtain a critical outside review of your plan.
7. *Implement:* Develop an implementation plan for communication, training, changing procedures, and measuring results. Then do it.
8. *Monitor:* Learn from successes and mistakes. Make sure that this problem "stays solved."

Analytical Tools. Most of the suggested tools are very simple. Their effectiveness lies in their ease of use and their systematic application.

Check sheet (or tally sheet): Records the frequency with which each problem is encountered. When a problem is encountered, place a mark beside it on a list. After a period of observation, the problem with the most marks is the one that happens most frequently. The results are useful in problem selection.

Process flowchart: Documents how a process actually works and can help pinpoint weak spots (see Chapter 2).

Statistical tools: Histograms, scatter diagrams and control charts are used to analyze variations in a process. (Control charts are described in detail later in this chapter.)

Cause-and-effect diagrams: Used to find the root causes of a quality problem. For example, Ishikawa (1985) describes three different types of cause-and-effect diagrams. Figure 6-3 illustrates the production-process-classification type, in which potential causes of variation are indicated for each production step. Branches represent causes, and twigs represent finer and finer definitions of the causes. For example, in the bead-removing step, if the bench moves, the workpiece may be damaged. Two causes of bench movement are shown.

Reassessing Customer Requirements. We like to call this avoiding Type III errors (solving the wrong problem). For example, redesigning a 300-page installation manual for a computer system is the wrong problem if the customer really wants a computer that works as soon as it is plugged in.

Product Design for Producibility. Snappy Printers (described in the introduction) were designed to make assembly rapid and nearly error free. Design teams that include people responsible for producing the good or service can influence the design with a view toward ease of production.

Process Simplification. Using process flowcharts, look for steps that can be eliminated entirely or multiple steps that can be combined. For example, a manufacturer of soap products examined the procedure for developing new artwork for its soap boxes. The flowchart describing artwork development covered a large page. Despite the fact that there were five different sign-off steps (in which a manager's signature of approval was required), production began on a new box with some of the lettering applied backward. Applying process simplification, many steps were eliminated or redesigned. Now there is only one sign-off, and one manager is responsible. A faster and more effective cycle for new artwork has resulted.

Mistake-Proof Operations. How can mistakes be eliminated? Sounds impossible, doesn't it? But it is not impossible. Here are some examples of Japanese companies that have completely eliminated some mistakes (Shingo 1981):

Examples: Mistake-Proof Operations

Matsushita Electric found that parts were sometimes missing from a packaged item. Their solution was to install detectors under each item to be packed. Until exactly one of each required item had been removed from its hopper, the box would not be released.

Arakawa Shatai Company found that the lining plate installed on the inside of an automobile door occasionally had fewer retaining clips than specified. About two million clips were installed per month. The assembly error was completely eliminated by installing twenty proximity switches to detect missing clips at the next assembly stage.

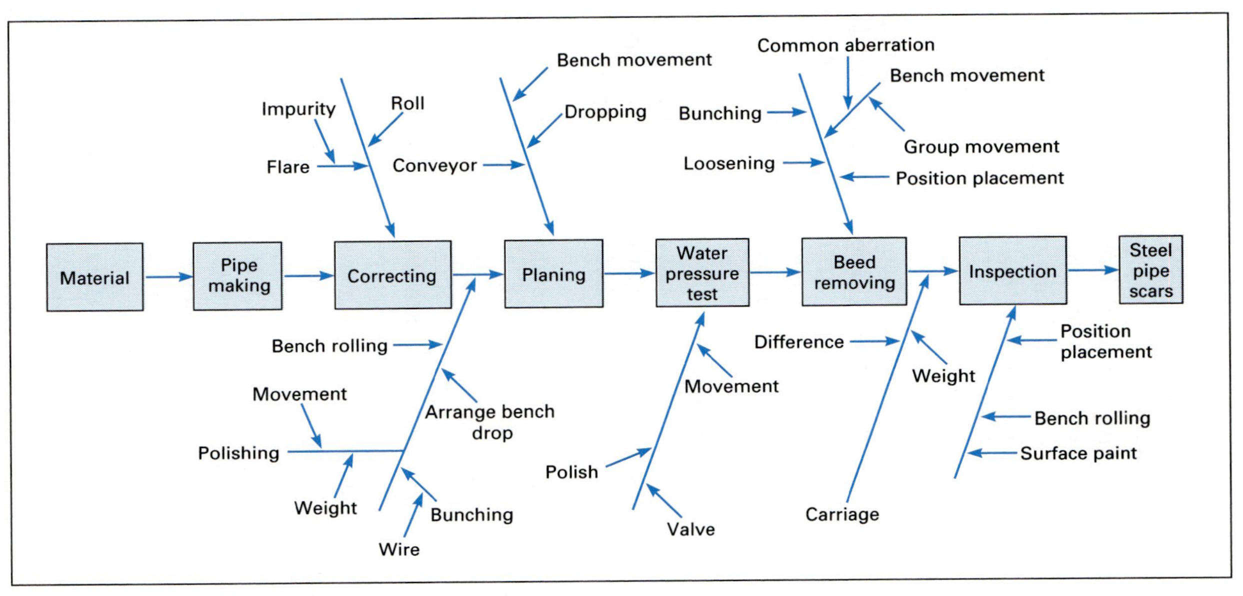

Figure 6-3 Cause-and-Effect Diagram for Steel Pipe Scars.
(Reprinted from *Guide to Quality Control* by Dr. Kaoru Ishikawa. Reprinted by permission of Asian Productivity Organization. Distributed in the U.S., Canada, and Western Europe by Quality Resources, White Plains, New York.)

> The same company eliminated errors in assembling seats by using a machine-readable label. The electronic controller scanned the label, opened the correct parts bins, and turned on indicator lights to call the worker's attention to the correct bins.

The Japanese term *poka-yoke* refers to mistake proofing an operation. Besides improving the quality of products, *poka-yoke* can reduce the need for caution and thus reduce strain on the worker. The effects are like hitting "two birds with one stone" (Shingo 1981). Without the worry of forgetting one or two retaining clips out of two million, the worker can concentrate on other aspects of the job.

In the preceding examples, inspection was not eliminated, but it was automated and nearly instantaneous, so that little if any time was wasted. In hospitals, pharmaceuticals are often packaged in "unit doses" so that nurses are responsible only for administering the correct medicine, not measuring it. Quantity errors are eliminated and the nurse has more time to concentrate on other needs of the patient. Many more examples are given in Shingo (1986). It may be impossible to eliminate all errors, but clever thinking and design can eradicate many of them.

Coordinating Customer Requirements with Product and Process Design. As was previously mentioned, The *House of Quality* (Hauser and Clausing 1988) is a design tool for reconciling customer specifications with product and process attributes. Part of a management approach known as quality function deployment (QFD), this tool was developed by Mitsubishi in 1972 and refined by Toyota and its suppliers. The "house of quality" is a house-shaped table that lists customer specifications down the side and engineering characteristics across the top. A survey of customer perceptions about several competing products allows the organization to measure whether the engineers are using design criteria that measure what the customers want. For example, customers want car doors that close easily but also stay open even when the car is parked on a hill. How well do the laboratory measures used by the engineers correlate with the customers' level of satisfaction? Answering questions like this substantially improves the likelihood that the product will actually please the customer. It also lowers preproduction costs by eliminating many design changes, especially late in the development process, at which point changes are most costly. The same approach is used to design manufacturing operations. The house of quality helps assure that the process characteristics are properly designed and controlled to meet specifications.

To conclude, enormous improvements in quality were made by many companies during the second half of the 1980s. For the most part, tools like the ones we have listed were sufficient. Continual improvement is a process, a never-ending part of doing business. Although many of the quality improvement tools and skills are simple, people learn valuable lessons every time they go through an improvement cycle. Converting employees into experienced process improvers is an important strategic move. Each new problem is solved more rapidly and implemented more smoothly if this process is well managed. Progress accelerates because of learning, and total quality management becomes ever more effective.

REVIEW PROBLEMS

1. In a hospital's kitchen, meals for patients are placed onto trays in assembly-line fashion. The trays move on a conveyer, and a series of food service personnel place the items on the tray according to the patient's order. What quality effects might result if the food orders were difficult to read? Suggest a system to avoid such mistakes. Describe how this improvement would also reduce the cost of the food service.

2. Why is longer product life not necessarily higher quality?

3. Speedy Pizza is a vertically integrated corporation. Pizza dough and toppings are manufactured centrally and delivered to the pizzerias in refrigerated trucks. Pizza is assembled and baked at the pizzeria and delivered in oven-equipped trucks. For each stage of this system, who are the suppliers and who are the immediate customers? How can quality problems of one stage affect quality and cost at the other stages?

Solutions

1. Wrong food items could make a patient sicker, or at least unhappy. Large-print patient menus with large boxes for checking preferred items would make ordering easier and the servers' jobs easier and less error prone. Tray loading would be more efficient because less time would be spent trying to read orders. Efficiency would rise for food delivery personnel and nurses because they would have fewer complaints to handle and fewer extra trips to the kitchen.

2. For example, an automobile wheel bearing that lasts for 500,000 miles is not of lower quality than one that's lasts for 1 million miles if the car is designed for at most 200,000 miles.

3. The factory's suppliers are vendors who sell flour, eggs, salt, and other ingredients. The factory's customers are the refrigerated trucks. (The factory's job is to get the right materials to the truck at the appropriate time, with packaging designed to maintain quality.) In turn, these trucks have the pizzerias as customers. The pizzerias have two customers: delivery trucks and consumers who come to the restaurant. The customers of the delivery trucks are the pizza eaters. Viewed in this way, it is the responsibility of each stage to neither accept nor pass on defective product. This places a great responsibility on the truck drivers, for example.

   Raw-material problems can result in bad pizza dough (cost for the factory) or delayed deliveries that cause pizzerias to run out of dough.

   Poor-quality pizza preparation makes customers unhappy. This affects the whole company regardless of whether it occurs at the factory or at the pizzeria. For example, if a pizza is improperly prepared, the customer may demand a replacement. Dealing with this situation wastes time and ingredients. This affects the factory as as well as the pizzeria because wasted ingredients consume factory resources.

Excessive waste of materials is a process-quality problem that increases cost. In addition, the random nature of this kind of error imposes more variable demands on the delivery of ingredients, which makes the control of inventory more difficult and expensive.

6-2 ACCEPTANCE SAMPLING

When an item is purchased in large quantities, quality is often assessed by inspecting samples rather than by examining every item. The advantage is lower cost of inspection. The disadvantage is that sampling causes errors. Why these errors occur is described in this section, and methods are given for assuring that errors are rare. Because these errors do occur, many companies do not use acceptance sampling.

Example: Mugwump Assemblers

Mugwump Assemblers purchases parts and components from several vendors. One of the items, which arrives in batches of 1000 units, sometimes has an unacceptably high percentage of defects. Mugwump is working with the supplier to eliminate the source of the defects. Meanwhile, acceptance sampling is being used to control quality. From each batch, 175 randomly chosen units are inspected. If the number found to be defective is 3 or more, the batch is rejected and returned to the supplier.

This is called *single sampling* and is the most commonly used procedure for batch inspection.[1] The procedure is illustrated in Figure 6-4.

[1]Some sampling plans have several levels of errors, with "critical defect" being the worst. It is also possible to base a sampling plan on one or more measurements on each item, without necessarily judging the item defective or acceptable. These plans, known as acceptance sampling by variables, will not be discussed here.

Figure 6-4 Acceptance Sampling

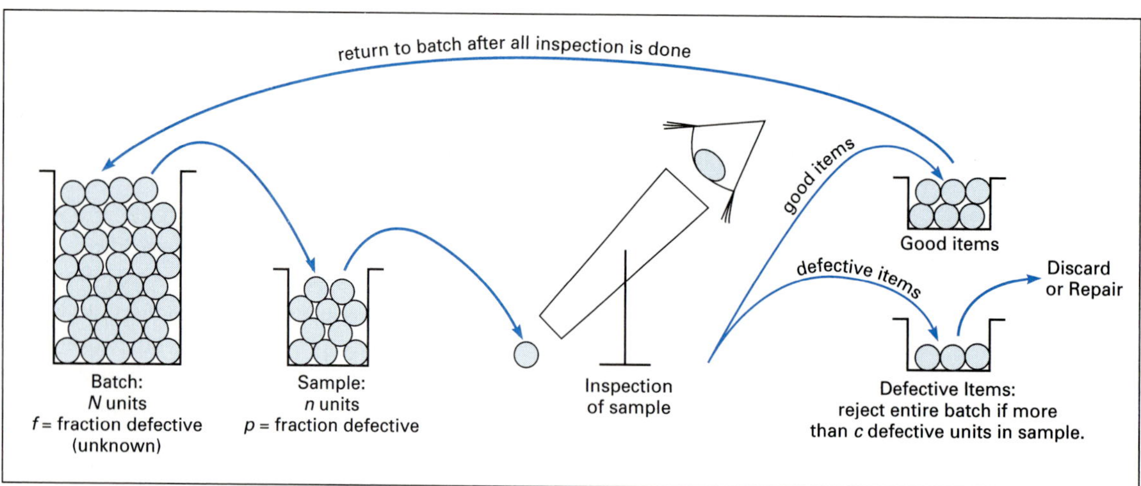

Description of the Batch

N = batch size, the total quantity received.

f = fraction defective in the batch. This is unknown, and varies from batch to batch.

Description of the Sample

n = sample size, the number inspected. These items are randomly selected from the batch.

p = fraction defective in the sample. This is a random variable because the sample is randomly selected. After the sample is inspected, p is the number of defective items divided by n. Then p becomes an estimate of f.

Description of the Decision Rule

c = acceptance number (or cutoff number) in the sample. If c or fewer are defective in the sample, accept the batch. Reject the batch if c + 1 or more are defective in the sample.

$p_c = (c + 0.5)/n$ = cutoff fraction defective for the sample. Reject if p exceeds p_c; accept if $p \leq p_c$. (We use $c + 0.5$ because it is halfway between acceptance, c, and rejection, $c + 1$.)

A sampling plan is denoted as either (n, c) or (n, p_c). It specifies both the sample size and the decision rule.

Errors in Acceptance Sampling

Sampling causes errors. For example, suppose that we have two of Mugwump's batches. Each consists of $N = 1000$ parts. Unbeknownst to the inspector, the first batch has 40 defective items ($f = 4\%$) and the second has 5 ($f = 0.5\%$); therefore, the second batch is ''better.'' Now the inspector randomly draws $n = 175$ from each batch and applies the decision rule $c = 2$. (Mugwump rejects if 3 or more are defective, so the acceptance level is 2.) Although it is improbable, there might be only 2 defective items in the first sample and 3 in the second. With these ''unlucky draws'' we would accept the wrong batch.

There are two types of errors: accepting bad batches and rejecting good ones. Before we can measure the probabilities of these errors, we need definitions of ''good'' and ''bad'' batches:

AQL = acceptance quality level, expressed as a fraction defective. This is the value of the batch fraction defective, f, that would make management happy. It defines a ''good'' batch. Mugwump is accustomed to 0.5% or fewer defectives. They use AQL = 0.005 to design sampling plans.

α = probability of rejecting ''good'' batches. Probability of large p when f = AQL.

LTPD = lot tolerance percent defective. This is the f value that defines a ''bad'' batch. Mugwump will not tolerate batches with 4% or more defectives, so they use LTPD = 0.04.

β = probability of accepting ''bad'' batches. Probability of small p when f = LTPD.

Good sampling plans have low values for both α and β. Designing a sampling plan is not an exact science because the definitions of ''good'' and ''bad'' batches are somewhat arbitrary. Management must decide, somehow, what level of defectives is acceptable (AQL) and what level is intolerable (LTPD). Then they must designate target values for the error probabilities. Based on this information, a sampling plan can be chosen.

Sampling Plans Based on AQL, α, LTPD, and β

Mugwump has decided that 0.5% defective is "good" and that 4% is "bad". The key to designing a sampling plan is to make sure that the accept-or-reject cutoff *for the sample* lies somewhere between these values. It also stands to reason that larger samples should have lower error probabilities. There are several methods for determining the sample size and decision rule. The following method is based on an approximation to the probability distribution of p, the fraction defective in the sample.[2]

The Normal Approximation for Single Sampling Plans

Step 1: Look up z-values corresponding to α and β. (Call them z_α and z_β.) Use the normal probability distribution. Table 6-1 has commonly used values.

Step 2: Compute a tentative sample size, which we will call $\tilde{n}$:

$$\tilde{n} = \frac{\left(z_\beta\sqrt{\text{LTPD}\,(1 - \text{LTPD})} + z_\alpha\sqrt{\text{AQL}\,(1 - \text{AQL})}\right)^2}{(\text{LTPD} - \text{AQL})^2} \tag{1}$$

Step 3: Compute p_c, c and n as follows:

$$p_c = \text{AQL} + z_\alpha\sqrt{\text{AQL}\,(1 - \text{AQL})/\tilde{n}} \tag{2}$$

$$c = \tilde{n}p_c \quad \text{(round off)} \tag{3}$$

$$n = (c + 0.5)/p_c \quad \text{(round off)} \tag{4}$$

(*Note:* Equation 2 places the cutoff fraction p_c above AQL. A similar formula [equation 5] would keep it below LTPD. You don't need to use equation 5, however, because it is "built into" step 2: equation 1 was derived by solving equations 2 and 5 simultaneously.)

$$p_c = \text{LTPD} - z_\beta\sqrt{\text{LTPD}(1 - \text{LTPD})/\tilde{n}} \tag{5}$$

Mugwump's sampling plan was derived as follows:

Step 1: Management has decided that both error probabilities should be 5%. Table 6-1 shows that z_α and z_β are both 1.645.

Step 2: Equation 1 gives 156.9 as a tentative sample size.

[2]Sampling from a batch is described by the hypergeometric distribution. If the batch size is large, the binomial distribution is a good approximation. We use the normal distribution to approximate the binomial (see any statistics text), so our formulas are "twice removed" from the correct distribution. In practice, the formulas based on the normal distribution give satisfactory sampling plans, especially considering that the design criteria of AQL, LTPD, α, and β are never precise.

Table 6-1 Commonly Used z-Values from the Normal Distribution

Probability	z-value	Probability	z-value
0.005	2.576	0.050	1.645
0.010	2.327	0.060	1.555
0.015	2.171	0.070	1.476
0.020	2.054	0.080	1.405
0.025	1.960	0.090	1.341
0.030	1.881	0.100	1.282
0.040	1.751		

Step 3: Equation 2 gives p_c = 0.0143. Equation 3 gives c = (156.9)(0.0143) = 2.24, which rounds to c = 2. Equation 4 gives n = (2 + 0.5)/ 0.0143 = 174.8, which rounds to n = 175. Conclusion: n = 175, c = 2.

Operating Characteristics of a Single Sampling Plan

A sampling plan should have a high probability of accepting good batches and a low probability of accepting bad ones. This desirable property can be represented by a graph known as the operating characteristics (OC) curve. The downward-sloping OC curves in Figure 6-5 show that the acceptance probability decreases as the fraction defective in the batch grows. The worse the batch (high f-value), the lower the probability that the sample will pass the acceptance test.

Mugwump's sampling plan (n = 175, c = 2) is displayed as one of the OC curves in Figure 6-5. "Bad" batches are represented on the right side of the graph; at f = 0.04 (the LTPD) the curve for n = 175, c = 2 passes well below the 5% level, so our target for β is satisfied. At the left end of the graph, we see that their plan has a very high acceptance probability for good batches; when f is exactly 0.005 (the AQL) the likelihood of acceptance is slightly below 95%, so the plan just misses our target of 5% for α. (Remember that our formulas are just an approximation.)

The four OC curves in Figure 6-5 all have one feature in common: They all have the same cutoff fraction, p_c = 0.0143. The way these curves cross reveals an important property: *Larger samples cause lower error probabilities, if the cutoff*

Figure 6-5 Operating Characteristics Curves

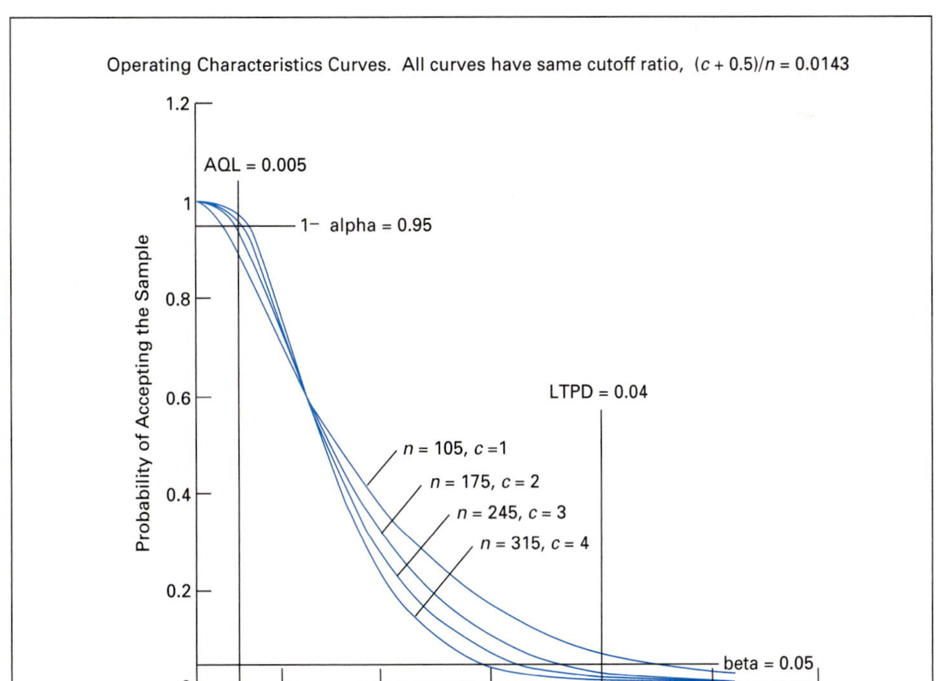

fraction, p_c, is held constant. That is, for good batches (near $f = 0.005$), larger samples are more likely to be accepted than small samples. In the bad-batch region (near $f = 0.04$), the reverse is true. Intuitively, since larger samples should be more accurate, this property certainly makes sense.

All sampling plans have an OC curve. In one book (Dodge and Roming 1959) an entire section is devoted to these visual displays, allowing the reader to see quickly whether a plan under consideration is suitable.

Other Acceptance Sampling Methods

Double and multiple sampling plans use a small initial sample. Additional inspection is done only if the first sample gives inconclusive results. The early decisions reduce the average number of units that are inspected.

Sequential sampling takes this one step further. After each unit is inspected, an accept-reject-or-continue decision is made, based on the total number of items inspected. It has been estimated that sequential sampling may reduce the average number inspected by approximately 50% compared with single sampling. However, applying an accept-or-reject rule after each item is inspected can be very time consuming.

Military Standard (Mil. Std.) 105d is an international military standard that is widely used. It is based on an automatic method of vendor rating. A ''normal'' sampling plan is chosen from a set of tables, depending primarily on the acceptable quality level. However, any time that two out of five consecutive batches have been rejected, a tighter plan is instituted. Moreover, if the quality level doesn't improve quickly, sampling is suspended entirely, and 100% inspection is required. The vendor has been decertified. On the other hand, if a string of ten batches in a row have been accepted by the normal sampling plan, a reduced plan is put into effect. Thus, good performance leads to less inspection.

Average outgoing quality is the name of another criterion for designing sampling plans. It recognizes that the process of inspection improves the quality of the batch for the simple reason that every defective item in the sample is either discarded or repaired. Furthermore, rejected batches are either sent back to the supplier or are subjected to 100% inspection. Tables are available to select plans based on this concept (Dodge and Romig 1959).

Cost minimization is the final method that we will describe. Inspection is costly. We have to pay the inspectors and provide the necessary equipment, training, and floor space to do the job; and sometimes the items that are inspected are damaged or destroyed. (How do you find out whether something is strong enough? You break it!) On the other hand, too little inspection allows defects to escape detection; their presence represents a cost as well. For example, defective parts can cause disruption of a production process, or customer dissatisfaction and field repair costs later on. Estimating the cost of undetected defective items is difficult.

Even if these two costs are available, finding a plan that minimizes the long run average cost is not easy. First we need more information about the batch fraction defective, f. For an individual batch, f is unknown. To minimize costs, we have to know how f varies—we need its probability distribution. Given all of this information, a computer program can be designed to search for the best sampling plan. (An example is included in problem 24.)

The following rules do not minimize costs, but they do allow us to determine whether we should inspect 100% of the items, inspect a sample of some sort, or simply accept all batches without inspection. In these rules, C_{ins} is the cost of inspecting one unit, C_{def} is the cost if a defective unit escapes detection, and f_{min} and f_{max} are the best-case and worst-case batch fraction defective.

Rule 1: If $C_{ins} < f_{min} C_{def}$, 100% inspection is optimal. (6)

Rule 2: If $C_{ins} > f_{max} C_{def}$, accept all batches without inspection. (7)

Rule 3: If C_{ins} is between these values, find a sampling plan. (8)

For example, suppose that the unit costs are $0.50 for inspection and $8.00 for undetected defective items. Further, suppose that some batches have no defectives ($f_{min} = 0$), and that the fraction defective never exceeds 8% ($f_{max} = 0.08$). Then rule 1 tells us that 100% inspection is not optimal (since $0.50 exceeds 0 times $8), and rule 2 tells us that no inspection is also a bad idea (since $0.50 is lower than 0.08 times $8 = $0.64). Hence, this company should use a sampling plan of some sort.

REVIEW PROBLEMS

1. If inspection costs $0.20 per unit and each defective item that gets by the inspectors costs $10, what kind of guarantee (regarding batch fraction defective) would justify accepting without inspection?

2. A company is using the single sampling plan $n = 105$, $c = 1$.

   a. Using the OC curve in Figure 6-5, what is the probability that an incorrect decision will be made for a batch in which 5% of the units are defective?

   b. If the batch size is 1000, how many defective items are in the batch when $f = 5\%$? How many would be defective in the sample if it is accepted?

   c. What would the fraction defective be in the sample if it is accepted? How can p be so low even when f is as high as 5%?

3. The following table gives a number of sampling plans designed around AQL = 0.005 and LTPD = 0.04. Each plan was designed using the three-step method of this section, which is based on an approximation.

Some Sampling Plans for AQL = 0.005, LTPD = 0.04

Target Values				Sampling Plan	
α	β	p_c	$\tilde{n}$	c	n
0.005	0.005	0.0143	384.8	5	386
0.01	0.01	0.0143	313.9	4	315
0.02	0.02	0.0143	244.6	3	245
0.05	0.05	0.0143	156.9	2	175
0.10	0.10	0.0143	95.2	1	105
0.03	0.05	0.0152	169.1	3	230
0.04	0.04	0.0143	177.8	3	245
0.05	0.03	0.0134	191.8	3	262

   a. Looking at the first five plans, what generalization can you make about the effect of increasing the size of the sample?

   b. Looking at the last three plans, what can you say about varying the cutoff fraction, p_c?

Solutions

1. Use rule 2: \$0.20 > (f_{max})(\$10) when f_{max} is below 0.20/10 or 0.02, so ''zero inspection'' is optimal if f is guaranteed never to exceed 2% in any batch.

2. a. At $f = 0.05$, the batch is ''bad'' by definition (LTPD = 4%). Accepting would be an error. The OC curve shows that the acceptance probability is about 3% at $f = 0.05$.
   b. If $N = 1000$ and $f = 5\%$, there are 50 defective items in the batch (5% of 1000). If the sample is accepted by the plan $n = 105$, $c = 1$, the number of defective items in the sample is 1 or 0.
   c. The fraction defective in the sample is 1/105 = 0.0095 or lower. It is this low because of an ''unlucky draw.'' Random sampling sometimes causes errors.

3. a. Both error probabilities drop as n increases, providing that c increases as well to keep p_c constant.
   b. Changing p_c causes a trade-off in the error probabilities. Decreasing p_c causes α to increase and β to decrease.

6-3 STATISTICAL PROCESS CONTROL

Maintaining quality while a good or service is being produced requires careful attention. Knowing when to intervene (and when not to) is crucial. Stopping a process to ''fix'' it halts output. That can mean longer waiting times for customers or lost sales. Not stopping can be even worse. A ''broken'' process produces faulty output, and that can be worse than no output at all. The key to process control is monitoring variations in the product.

Example: The Sweet Sugar Company

The Sweet Sugar Company uses an automatic machine to fill 1-pound boxes of sugar. Specifications call for no less than 1.000 pound and no more than 1.050. The manufacturer of the filling machine states that the machine is capable of operating at any average fill level, and that the standard deviation will be 0.003 pound when the machine is properly maintained. To maintain boxes within the specifications, Sweet sets the machine for 1.025 pounds.

''Process capability'' is the term for the standard deviation just mentioned. It measures how variable the process will be under optimal conditions. Variation beyond 3 standard deviations (3-sigma, or 3σ) are rare.[3] Therefore, boxes of Sweet Sugar should weigh within 0.009 pounds of the setting, or between 1.016 and 1.034 pounds (that is, 1.025 $\pm$ 0.003 pounds).

Figure 6-6 shows the weights of 80 individual boxes. Most of the boxes fall within the process capability limits represented by the 3-sigma lines. However, 9 boxes are outside the limits. One of these is actually defective: Box 78 violates the specification of ''no more than 1.050 pounds.'' Because of these abnormalities, an investigation of the filling process was conducted.

Two possible explanations were proposed. First, perhaps the filling machine was gradually drifting out of adjustment. Second, maybe something

[3]See the Tchebychev Inequality in any standard statistics text. No more than 1/9 of the observations can fall outside 3-sigma limits in the long run. In most realistic situations, the probability is much smaller.

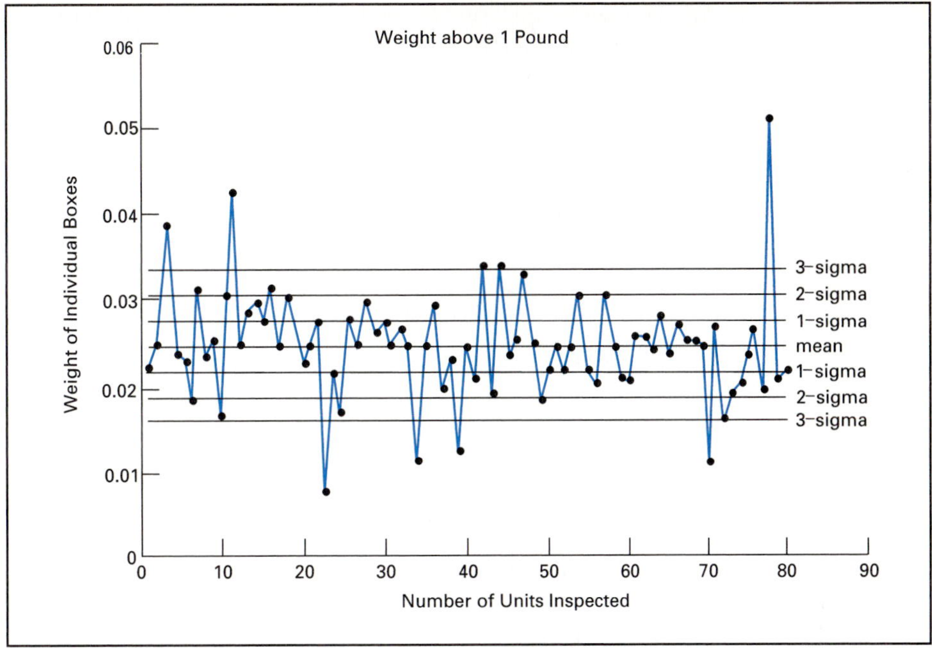

Figure 6-6 Excess Weights of 80 Individual Boxes of Sweet Sugar

about the filling process was inconsistent, causing weights to vary substantially. Both explanations were explored as follows.

The 80 boxes were divided into 16 subgroups, each having 5 boxes, as shown in Table 6-2. The average weight was computed for each subgroup; a process drift should show up as a trend in the average weight. The range (heaviest weight in the subgroup minus lightest) was also computed to measure process variability. Table 6-2 also shows these averages and ranges for each of

Table 6-2 Excess Weights of 80 One-Pound Boxes of Sugar

Actual weight = table value plus 1 pound								
Boxes:	**1–5**	**6–10**	**11–15**	**16–20**	**21–25**	**26–30**	**31–35**	**36–40**
	.0226	.0185	.0308	.0280	.0249	.0276	.0253	.0298
	.0263	.0317	.0426	.0318	.0274	.0252	.0269	.0197
	.0387	.0238	.0251	.0250	.0081	.0302	.0253	.0232
	.0237	.0255	.0291	.0307	.0224	.0262	.0115	.0122
	.0232	.0169	.0301	.0229	.0171	.0274	.0250	.0250
Averages:	.02690	.02328	.03154	.02768	.01998	.02732	.02280	.02198
Ranges:	.0161	.0148	.0175	.0089	.0193	.0050	.0154	.0176
Boxes:	**41–45**	**46–50**	**51–55**	**56–60**	**61–65**	**66–70**	**71–75**	**76–80**
	.0208	.0256	.0249	.0200	.0258	.0272	.0270	.0267
	.0344	.0329	.0225	.0313	.0256	.0255	.0163	.0192
	.0188	.0251	.0251	.0250	.0244	.0254	.0190	.0508
	.0345	.0185	.0311	.0211	.0286	.0250	.0204	.0209
	.0240	.0223	.0224	.0208	.0240	.0114	.0238	.0217
Averages:	.02650	.02488	.02520	.02364	.02568	.02291	.02128	.02787
Ranges:	.0157	.0144	.0087	.0113	.0046	.0158	.0106	.0316

the 16 subgroups. In Figure 6-7 the $\overline{X}$ (or X-bar) chart shows the subgroup averages, and the *R* chart plots the ranges. The horizontal lines are called control limits. Formulas for the control limits are given later.

The $\overline{X}$ chart shows that the third and fifth points are outside the 3-sigma limit; *something is causing the mean to shift significantly over time.* In the *R* chart,

Figure 6-7 Subgroup Averages and Ranges, 80 boxes of Sweet Sugar Divided into 16 Subgroups with 5 Boxes per Subgroup

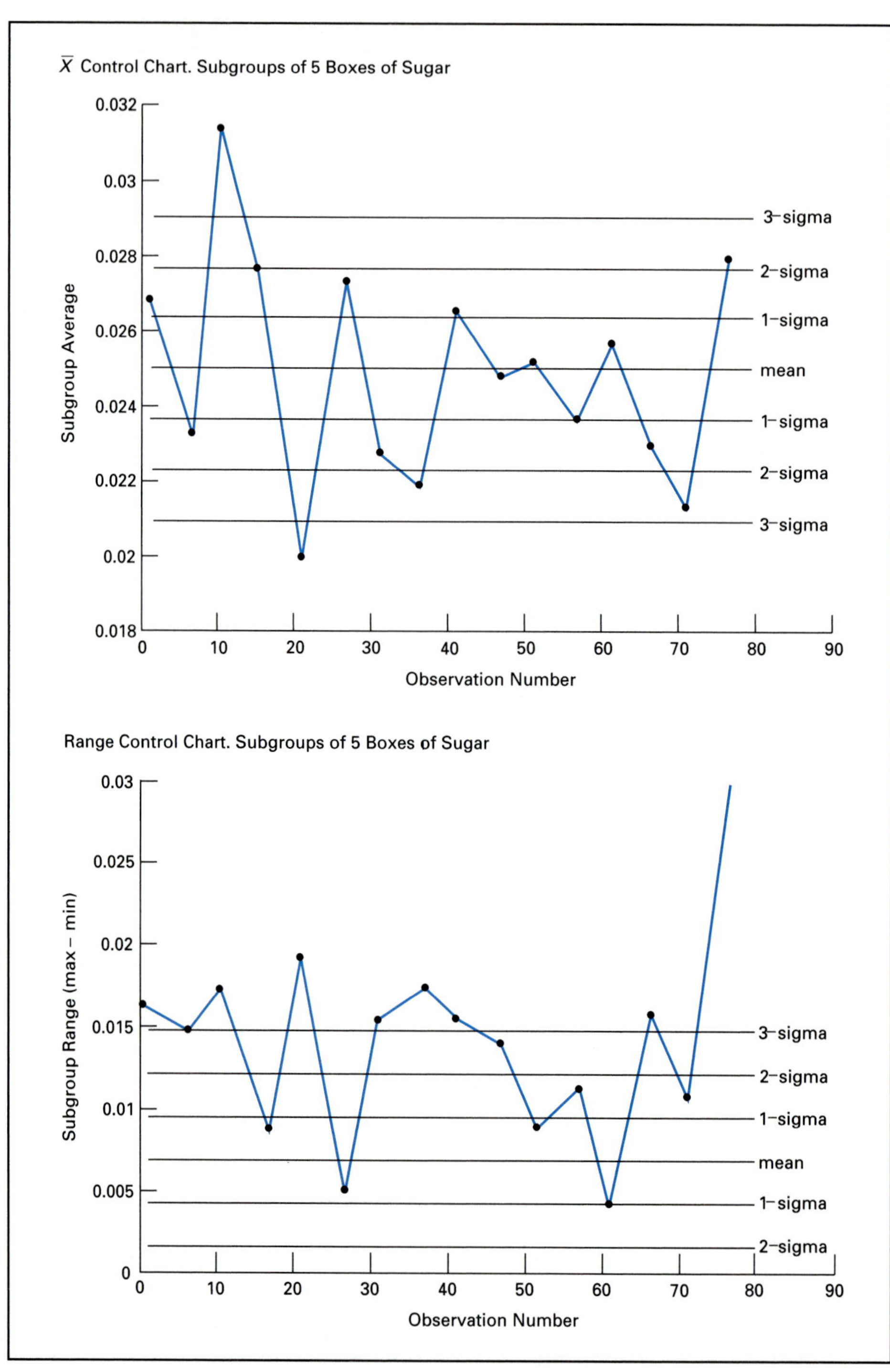

many of the subgroups are outside the 3-sigma limits; *the process variability is significantly higher than the manufacturer's stated process capability.*

In consultation with the service representative of the filling machine's manufacturer, Sweet discovered one cause of the problem: The sugar itself was not consistent. Small lumps caused the weight to vary. Steps were taken to improve the sugar's consistency and a new set of charts was prepared (Figure 6-8). The new *R* chart shows improvement. However, two points are above the

Figure 6-8 Sweet Sugar's Control Charts after the First Improvement

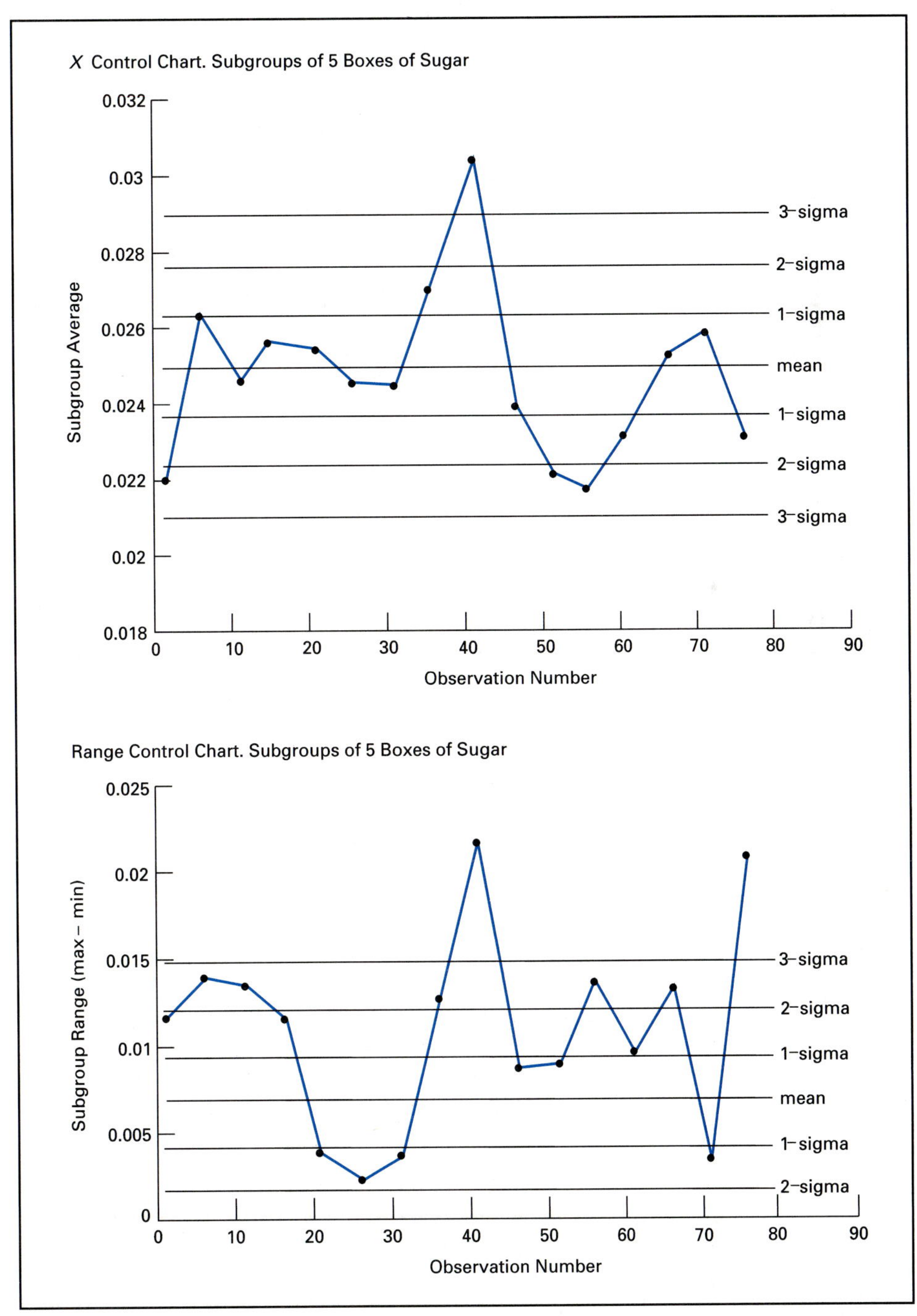

3-sigma limits, and well over half of the subgroup ranges are above the mean; thus, the filling process was still too variable.

A second round of study and improvement was undertaken. This included a modification of the filling machine itself, suggested by its operator. Figure 6-9 shows the control charts after these improvements were made. The *R* chart shows that the variability is finally reduced to the level claimed by the machine's manufacturer; attention was then turned to the $\overline{X}$ chart.

In Figure 6-9 one subgroup average is outside the 3-sigma limits in the $\overline{X}$ chart, one is between 2-sigma and 3-sigma, and the rest are within two standard deviations of the mean. This is fairly typical of a process that is in control. Any point outside the 3-sigma limits is cause for concern, and the filling machine was stopped after the second subgroup. Finding nothing wrong, the process was restarted.

Figure 6-9 Sweet Sugar's Control Charts after the Second Improvement

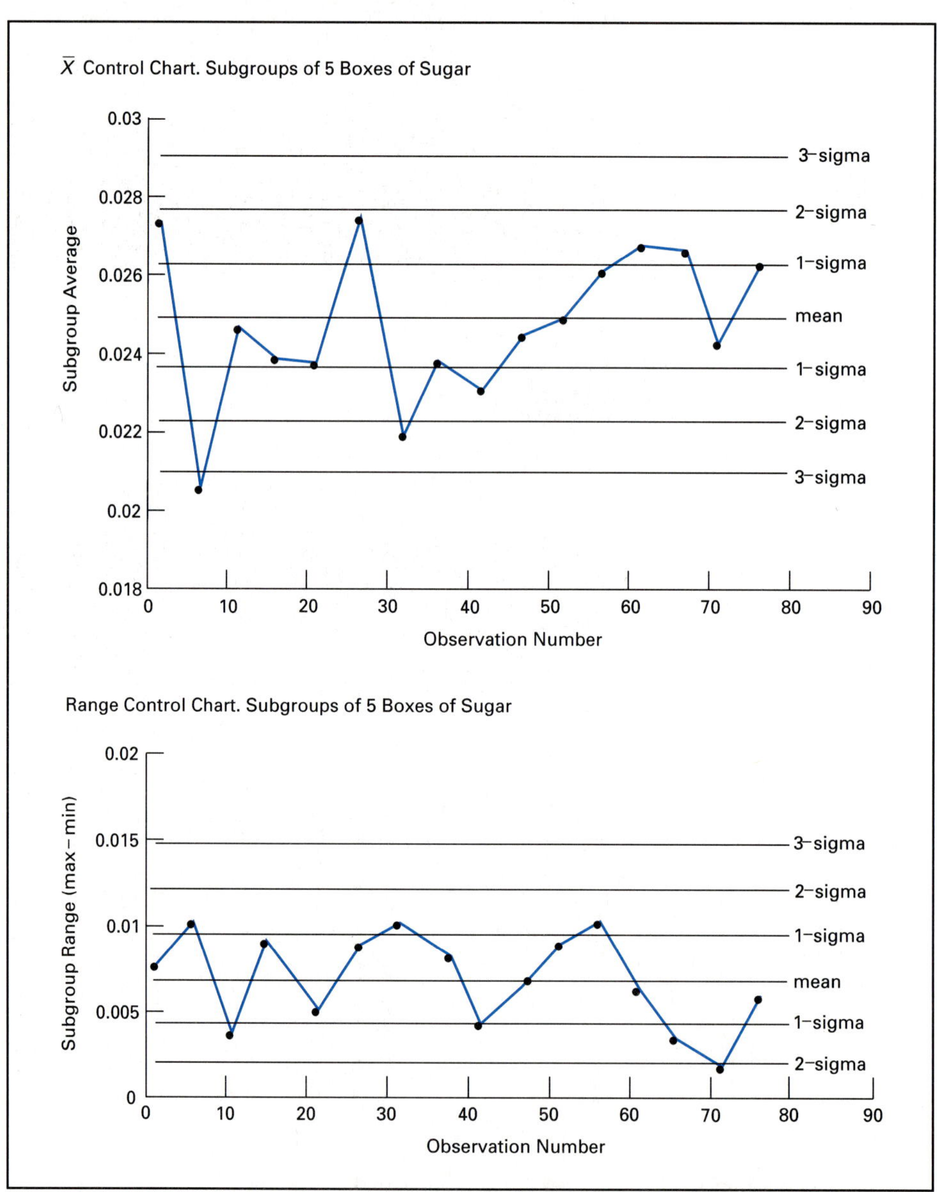

Example: The Sweet Sugar Company (continued)

A plot of individual box weights (Figure 6-10) showed that all boxes were substantially above the 1-pound specification. The operator suggested that the machine setting be lowered to 1.020 pounds from the current value of 1.025. This suggestion was evaluated by monitoring weights of thousands of boxes. While the machine was set at 1.025 pounds, no weight was found below 1.015 pounds. Therefore, the suggestion was implemented and the employee was given an award. Quality was not compromised, but the amount of sugar per box was reduced by 0.5%, saving Sweet Sugar Company thousands of dollars every week.

Interpreting Control Charts

Patterns may be evident in control charts. Caution must be used, however, because some patterns may occur by chance and therefore may signify nothing about the process. Some commonly applied indications that a process may be out of control are as follows (Duncan 1986):

1. One or more points outside the 3-sigma limits.
2. One or more points in the vicinity of a 3-sigma limit. This suggests immediately taking more data.
3. A run of seven or more points. This may be a run up, or a run down, or simply seven or more in a row on the same side of the center line.
4. Cycles or other nonrandom patterns.
5. Two or three points in a row outside of 2-sigma limits.
6. Four or five points in a row outside of 1-sigma limits.

These rules apply to any control chart. For example, after Sweet Sugar's first improvement, the *R* chart of Figure 6-8 caused them to continue seeking improvement. Two values are above 3-sigma limits (rule 1), and seven subgroups in a row were above the center line (rule 3). (One other rule is violated. Can you find it?)

It is extremely important to follow a recommended set of criteria such as the preceding one. Making up your own criteria can be dangerous, since you

Figure 6-10 Individual Sweet Sugar Boxes after the Second Improvement

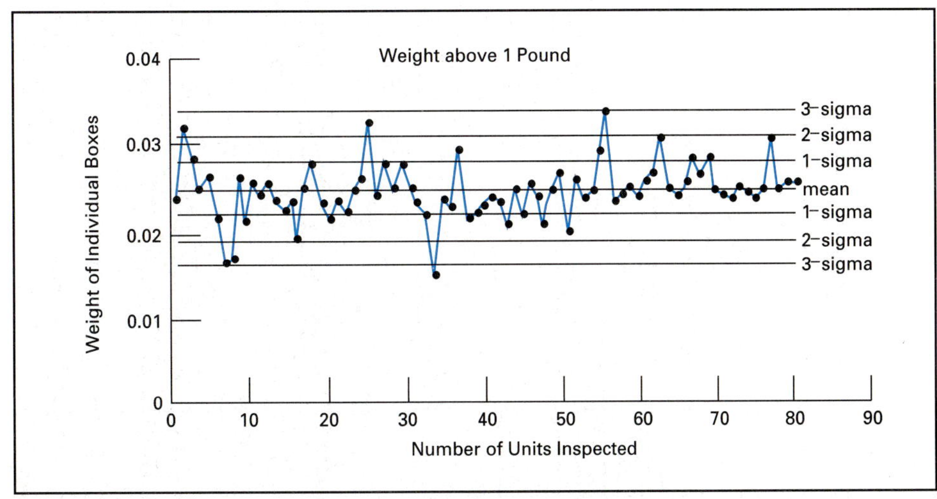

might design criteria that will cause you to stop your process without cause, as the following example illustrates.

Example: Overcompensating for Variability

Nashua Corporation manufactures carbonless paper. Quality control was found to have a negative effect on production. As Deming (1982) described it, the operator was overcompensating for the variability of the process. By adjusting the flow rate too often, he added to the process variability rather than controlling it. When statistical methods were introduced, the overcompensation ceased. Adjustments were made only when the operator had statistically sound evidence that the machine had strayed from its proper setting. This reduced the variability to the point that the average coating thickness could be reduced, saving $800,000 per year in the cost of the coating material.

Setting Statistical Control Limits When σ Is Known

Dividing the data into subgroups allows nearly continuous monitoring of both the process average and variability. In the Sweet Sugar example, the process standard deviation was known to be 0.003 pounds under ideal conditions. This information was used in both the $\overline{X}$ and R charts.

The limits in the $\overline{X}$ chart are based on the standard error of the subgroup averages (a subgroup consists of n units):

$$\text{Standard error of } \overline{X} = \sigma/\sqrt{n} \tag{9}$$

$$\text{3-sigma limits for } \overline{X} = \text{process mean } \pm 3\sigma/\sqrt{n} \tag{10}$$

For Sweet Sugar, this is 1.025 ± 3(0.003)/2.236, giving 3-sigma limits of 1.021 and 1.029. The other control limits are set in a similar manner. Because of the central limit theorem (see any statistics text), the normal probability distribution describes the subgroup averages. Table 2 in Appendix D shows that the probability of exceeding the upper 3-sigma limit is 0.00135. The same probability applies to the lower 3-sigma limit. Therefore, fewer than 3 subgroups per thousand should lie in the region beyond the 3-sigma limits.

The R chart also depends on the process standard deviation. Statisticians have developed a mathematical relationship between σ and the range, expressed through Table 6-3 and the following formulas:

$$\text{Mean of subgroup range} = d_2\sigma \tag{11}$$

$$\text{Standard deviation of subgroup range} = d_3\sigma \tag{12}$$

$$\text{3-sigma limits for } R = d_2\sigma \pm 3d_3\sigma \tag{13}$$

Sweet Sugar Company's R chart 3-sigma limits are 2.326(0.003) ± 3(0.864)(0.003) or −0.0008 to 0.0148. However, since a range cannot be negative, the lower 3-sigma limit is set to zero. The other limits are set in a similar manner.

Setting Statistical Control Limits When σ Is Not Known

The process standard deviation, σ, measures variability under ideal circumstances. If σ is not known, it must be estimated from the data. This can

Table 6-3 Control Limit Factors for *R* Charts and *S* Charts

Subgroup Size	d_2	d_3	c_4
2	1.128	0.853	0.798
3	1.693	0.888	0.886
4	2.059	0.880	0.921
5	2.326	0.864	0.940
6	2.534	0.848	0.952
7	2.704	0.833	0.959
8	2.847	0.820	0.965
9	2.970	0.808	0.969
10	3.078	0.797	0.973

be tricky because (as we have seen) the data may not be reliable; process control may not have been attained. Using the standard deviation from Sweet Sugar's first data set would have been inappropriate. Those data included variability due to lumpy sugar.

Process capability studies are conducted to estimate σ. The objectives are to seek out causes of variation, to estimate how much variability they cause, and to estimate how much variation would be left if the causes were eliminated. The "left over" or "residual" variation is called the *process capability*, or the process standard deviation, σ.

Sweet Sugar Company did not do a process capability study because σ was supplied by the manufacturer of the filling machine. Knowing σ gave them the ability to use $\overline{X}$ and R charts to show that improvement was needed. But how would they have known whether improvement was possible if the manufacturer had not supplied σ?

Designed experiments are one way to determine what is causing fluctuations. Possible causes are found by careful study of the process, often by the operators themselves with help from process engineers. Then experiments are designed to test these potential causes. Statistical methods such as analysis of variance (ANOVA) are used to decide which effects are significant. These methods also yield an estimate of the residual variation that would remain if all the identified causes of variation were removed. The residual standard deviation may be used as an estimate of the process capability, σ.

A process capability study also shows which causes of variation are most important. Some of the causes may be easier to eliminate than others, but all else being equal, we would start process improvement by attacking the greatest source of variation.

When ANOVA or other sophisticated analyses are not used, another method for estimating σ is based on the subgrouped data. Since each subgroup has a range, we can calculate the average range, $\overline{R}$. Then equation 11 is reversed to estimate σ:

$$\text{Estimate of } \sigma = \overline{R}/d_2 \qquad (14)$$

In Table 6-2 there are 16 subgroups, and the average of the 16 ranges is 0.0142 (not given in the table). Thus, the estimate of σ would be 0.0142/2.326 = 0.00611. This estimate of σ is almost twice as high as the 0.003 pounds stated by the manufacturer. It is large because the other sources of variation had yet not been eliminated. In the third data set, taken after two improvements had been made, $\overline{R}$ is 0.0069, yielding an estimate of 0.0031 for σ.

Once σ has been estimated accurately, equations 10 and 13 may be used to set the control limits.

Using *S* Charts Instead of *R* Charts

Process control charts are easily computerized. Spreadsheet programs generated the figures in this chapter, for example. When this is done, it is preferable to use the subgroup standard deviation, *S*, rather than the range:

$$S = \sqrt{\sum_{i=1}^{n} (X_i - \overline{X})^2/(n-1)} \tag{15}$$

Each subgroup has a standard deviation, calculated from this formula, where X_i is the weight of box *i* and $\overline{X}$ is the average for that subgroup. For example, back in Table 6-2, the first subgroup had $\overline{X} = 0.02690$. Using equation 15, the *S* for the first subgroup is 0.01298. The *S* chart has similar appearance and interpretation as the *R* chart.[4]

$$\text{3-sigma limits for } S = c_4\sigma \pm 3\sigma\sqrt{1 - c_4^2} \tag{16}$$

Values for c_4 are given in Table 6-3. For example, given that the process σ is 0.003, Sweet Sugar would use an *S* chart with center line 0.940(0.003) = 0.0028, and the 3-sigma limits would be above and below the center line by $3(0.003)\sqrt{1 - 0.8836} = 0.0031$. (This leads to a negative lower limit, so it is set to zero.)

If σ is not known, it may be estimated by calculating the average of the subgroup standard deviations, $\overline{S}$, and using the following formula:

$$\text{Estimate of } \sigma = \overline{S}/c_4 \tag{17}$$

Subgroup Size and Sampling Frequency

Small samples of $n = 4$ or 5 are commonly used to obtain fast, low-cost feedback to the production process. However, sometimes larger samples are needed to increase the accuracy of the feedback. For example, consider Sweet Sugar's situation. If they produce boxes below 1 pound, they are violating the truth-in-packaging law. The box label says 1 pound, so it must contain at least that much product. Sweet's improved process never produced a box below 1.015 pounds, so they reduced the process average. The risk of doing that is that some boxes may fall below the legal limit. They continue using the control charts to guard against this.

If the process average were to shift downward, would they know it? The $\overline{X}$ chart should indicate such a shift by producing lower subgroup means. The likelihood of an $\overline{X}$ below the 3-sigma limit would increase, as would the likelihood of a run of seven below the center line. But how long would it be before the process shift produced such a pattern? The answer depends on how large the shift was.

General Rule for Sample Size

As a general rule, if the process mean shifts by 2σ or more, samples of five are large enough to virtually assure that the next subgroup mean will fall outside the 3-sigma control limit. However, to be sure of detecting a shift of only 1σ, subgroups of at least fifteen to twenty are needed.

[4] For $E[S] = c_4\sigma$, see Shewhart 1931, p. 184. For $\text{Var}[S] = \sigma^2(1 - c_4^2)$, see Duncan 1986, p. 144.

To see how to apply this rule, we will ask whether $n = 5$ was sufficient at Sweet Sugar's old process setting of 1.025 pounds. The rule says that if the setting were to (accidentally) shift downward by $2\sigma = 2(0.003) = 0.006$ pounds or more, we would quickly detect the change and stop the machine. But Sweet wants to detect drift *before it becomes large enough to produce boxes below the legal limit.* So the question Sweet faces is, If the process mean drops by 2σ (or 0.006 pounds), would we be producing boxes below 1 pound? That is, how serious is a 2σ drop in the mean for Sweet Sugar?

Sweet's improved process produced no boxes below 1.015 pounds when the process was set at 1.025. A 2σ drop would reduce the minimum box weight to $1.015 - 0.006 = 1.009$, still well above the legal limit. Therefore subgroups of five are large enough; Sweet Sugar can absorb a 2σ drop without producing defective boxes.

Frequency of sampling is a related issue. How often should Sweet Sugar inspect a subgroup of five boxes? The cost of inspection is determined by sample size and frequency. This must be balanced against the cost of allowing an out-of-control situation to continue until the next measurement. The frequency of sampling should be proportional to the frequency of quality problems. If the process mean reliably remains fixed for at least 1000 boxes of sugar, measurements need not be taken any more frequently. We do not have a simple rule for frequency. The arguments become fairly complex. (Further discussion may be found in Duncan 1986 or Meske 1976.)

P Charts for Process Control by Attributes

Inspection may not result in a quantitative measure such as weight. For example, a shirt might be classified as either defective or acceptable depending on whether any flaws are found. The fraction of defective items in a subgroup is denoted P. The P chart shows P for each subgroup. (It is analogous to acceptance sampling, applied to an ongoing production process rather than to batches that arrive from another source.)

The appearance and interpretation of a P chart is similar to those of an R chart. In both cases the focus is on values that are "too high." However, P charts need much larger subgroup sizes. The reason for large subgroups is that defects are supposed to be rare in a well-functioning production process. If the acceptable defect rate is 0.005, we need a very large subgroup if we expect to see any defects at all. For example, subgroups of 200 would have an *average* of only one defective item, since $200(0.005) = 1$.

Using AQL as the acceptable fraction defective, the 3-sigma control limits for a P chart are

$$\text{3-sigma limits for } P = \text{AQL} \pm 3\sqrt{\text{AQL}(1 - \text{AQL})/n} \qquad (18)$$

REVIEW PROBLEMS

One of the important functions of a hospital laboratory is to perform tests on blood samples. The quality of this process is tested periodically by selecting five blood specimens and dividing each specimen into two equal parts. Approximately one half hour after the first batch of five has been processed, its twin is submitted and the results are compared. (This procedure is sometimes used to test quality-control inspectors, too.) For example, concentrations of total serum cholesterol were measured twice for each sample, and percent differences were recorded. The following data were taken at four different times over one 8-hour shift.

Percent Difference between Readings on Two Identical Blood Samples

	9:30 A.M.	11:00 A.M.	2:00 P.M.	4:00 P.M.
	1.2	0.6	0.6	2.1
	1.8	0.3	1.5	0.6
	1.5	0.3	1.0	0.6
	0.9	0.0	0.0	2.7
	0.3	0.6	1.9	2.7
$\overline{X}$ = averages	1.14	0.36	1.00	1.74
R = ranges	1.50	0.60	1.90	2.10

1. Calculate the upper and lower 3-sigma control limits for an $\overline{X}$ chart, assuming that the normal process average is 0.9%, and that the normal process standard deviation is $\sigma = 0.5\%$.

2. Calculate the 3-sigma upper control limit for an R chart.

3. Does the process seem to be in control?

Solutions

1. Using equation 10, the 3-sigma limits are 0.9% ± 3(0.5%)/2.236, which gives 0.23% for the lower limit and 1.57% for the upper limit.

2. Using Table 6-3 and equation 13, the upper 3-sigma limit is 2.326(0.5%) + 3(0.864)(0.5%) = 2.46%.

3. The last batch (subgroup) average falls above the 3-sigma limit from review problem 1. Since this batch came near the end of the day, it would be worthwhile to determine whether operator fatigue is a factor.

SUMMARY

There are many opportunities to improve both quality and productivity simultaneously. This observation has encouraged firms to undertake massive campaigns to improve quality. The most successful programs bring about permanent changes in attitude, organizational structure, and work methods; and they heavily involve top management. Missing any of these elements is likely to lead to temporary improvements that are lost in the long run.

Many quality problems have causes that cross departmental boundaries or even come from outside the organization. Methods such as cause-and-effect diagrams are intended to uncover the root causes. Viewing quality improvement as a process—a never-ending cycle—increases the likelihood that effective changes can be implemented and will be maintained.

Any quality-control program requires information. Statistical methods are important in this regard because they are designed to separate random variations from real, assignable causes of deviation from normal. However, statistics can be complicated and confusing. Effective training is required for all employees who are expected to make appropriate use of statistical control.

Inspection serves both a statistical purpose and a behavioral one. In addition to detecting errors, an inspection system may be designed to assure that quality production continues. Recognition and rewards for good performance are an important part of total quality management.

Acceptance sampling is inspection of part of a batch to form a judgment about the entire lot. Several methods are available for finding an acceptance-sampling plan. However, sampling (rather than inspecting everything) causes errors. Sometimes defective product will slip through. Sampling is not a substitute for process improvement and mistake-proofing operations; many companies consider acceptance sampling an inappropriate quality-control tool.

Quality-control charts display the results of inspecting a continuous process. This provides convenient and rapid feedback, suggesting when adjustment, overhaul, or retraining may be needed. Properly used, control charts will detect process deviations before they are serious enough to cause defects.

The statistical methods discussed in this chapter are widely used in manufacturing and service industries, as well as in other applications, such as the auditing of financial information. Furthermore, they are the basis for many of the commonly used, but more complex, schemes described in our references.

The amount of quality assurance an organization engages in is a policy-level decision. The image a firm desires, the selling price, and the customer it wishes to attract depend strongly on product quality. Successful quality-assurance programs must therefore have a long-range focus and be a permanent part of an organization.

Quality and productivity are closely related. Quality-improvement programs often more than pay for themselves in the long run by reductions in the cost of quality and increases in the real output rate. Proper evaluation of COQ is difficult because it contains such elements as lost market opportunities. Nevertheless, learning how to evaluate COQ and how to estimate productivity increases are necessary parts of total quality management. Without this understanding, the benefits of quality improvements are always understated.

With a clear understanding of the broad impact of the quality of goods and services, avenues are opened for savings that may be as great as 20% of the cost of sales, a better market image, and a leaner, healthier operation. Quality assurance is certainly one of the most important tasks in operations management, requiring analytical and other managerial skills.

CASELET

THE COMPUTER PRINTER DIVISION

The Computer Printer Division (CPD) manufactures printers for sale to another division of the same company. The printers are used in several types of systems sold to small to medium-sized firms. The printer is a small part of the total cost of the systems they sell, but an important and visible part of how the product is perceived.

CPD has encountered quality problems: Up to 5% of the printers have proven to be defective when received by customers. Given the high quality of some competitors' products, this level of quality is unacceptable. Mary Smith was given the job of improving the monitoring and reporting of quality. In her investigation of the current system, she found that the production process was very simple. The components were purchased from outside vendors. Assembly was done by groups of five workers. During assembly each unit was passed back and forth among all the workers. It was thought to be impossible to check quality during this process. The assembly workers' performance evaluations were primarily based on the number of units completed, without consideration of defects.

Quality was monitored by a group of four quality inspectors, after the product was completed. They did some simple tests on each unit, and extensive tests on a sample. The simple tests were not perfect, leading to the failure rate found later in systems using the printer. The procedure was also tedious, and inspection steps were often omitted. The quality inspectors had a goal of turning back as many units as they could, and found satisfaction in stopping the process when defects were too frequent. Ms. Smith noted that relations between the assemblers and the quality-control workers were terrible. In addition, no one was responsible for the level of quality; 95% sounded pretty good, even though the competitors had over 99% acceptable quality. No long-term data were available to identify trends or causes for defects.

When finished items were received by the other division of the company, a sample was inspected to see whether to pass or to reject the batch. If the batch was rejected, 100% inspection was used, and bad items returned to CPD for credit. The user division was very concerned about quality since they thought their reputation in their markets was slipping. They had threatened to go to another vendor.

Mary posed several questions which she thought should be investigated:

1. What could be done to improve relations between assembly and quality-control personnel?
2. Since purchased materials constitute such a large fraction of the value of the product, should some inspection be done before assembly?
3. How could the two divisions cooperate to solve the quality problems?
4. How could they work with the vendors on the quality of purchased materials?
5. How can the competitive pressures faced by the client division be internalized by CPD? Should the user division be allowed to solicit an outside vendor?

In developing solutions, Ms. Smith was to avoid suggesting additional quality-control expense. Also, she needed to do something quickly. Some short-run expense would be allowed, as long as it was clear that total costs would not increase in the long run.

Required: Write a report containing suggestions for Ms. Smith. You should deal with a short-run solution and a long-run quality program. Include comments on each of Ms. Smith's five questions.

PROBLEMS

1. Define and contrast customer requirements, product specifications, and tolerances.

2. Explain the following ideas:
   a. As a quality improvement program begins to take hold, cost may temporarily increase.
   b. Quality is free, but it is not a gift.
3. Figure 6-1 (in the introduction to this chapter) shows a quality-improvement cycle. In Section 6-1 an eight-step quality-improvement cycle (Alcoa's) was described. Think about the eight steps and draw a diagram showing how each of them contributes to the four elements of Figure 6-1. Use your diagram to evaluate Figure 6-1 critically. What are its major shortcomings?

*4. a. What is the fundamental difference between the use of acceptance sampling plans and process control charts?
   b. In which situation (acceptance sampling or process control) is the quality-control inspector more likely to be in close contact with the people whose work is being examined?
   c. Under what circumstances is inspection by sampling from completed batches not a good idea?

5. List two or three causes of product variation for each of the following products:
   a. baked goods
   b. vaccinations
   c. street cleaning
   d. bookkeeping
6. One step in automobile manufacturing is painting the body. Flawless painting is difficult, and sometimes a car will have to be repainted as many as three times. Consider the system effects of this quality problem.
   a. A factory has 10 identical paint booths. On the average, each car needs to be painted 1.1 times. How many paint booths would be needed if no repainting were needed? How much additional volume could the existing booths handle if repainting were eliminated? Discuss the implications for the company.
   b. There are many stages of assembly that follow after painting. The flow of cars out of the paint booths is, to some extent, random because of repainting. Why does the company need to keep an inventory of correctly painted cars between painting and the next assembly stage? What saving will result if this inventory can be eliminated?
   c. Down the assembly line, many stages after the paint booth, seats are installed. The combination of seat colors, fabric, and configuration are specified by customer orders and must be matched to a particular car with a specific paint job. The flow of the assembly

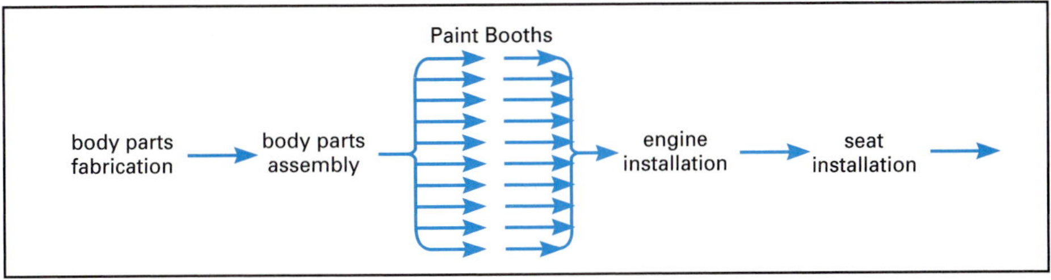

*Problems with an asterisk have answers in the back of the book.

plant is described (roughly) in the accompanying diagram. Describe the difficulties that the seat installer may face because of repainting and how that affects quality and cost.

7. The preceding problem described some of the effects that defects in painting caused in the rest of an automobile assembly system. The costs included extra paint booths, inventory, and productivity loss.
   a. Are these costs of conformance or nonconformance? Explain.
   b. Does ''painting defects'' qualify as a root cause because it causes disruptions and inefficiency in so many other places? Explain.
   c. Defects may be classified as chips, drip (run) marks, scratches, or ''other.'' Describe a simple method to determine which of these is most prevalent. Why would this be useful information?

*8. Laser bar-code readers are widely used in grocery checkouts. Items are scanned by a laser beam, and the bar code on the item is read. A computer then looks up the item, registers its price and quantity on the customer receipt, and notes the removal of the item from inventory. In some stores, even the discount coupons are scanned, and the computer matches them against items actually purchased in this transaction and computes the customer's discounts.
   a. What does this have to do with quality? What sort of quality improvement is the laser scanner? What process steps does it simplify or eliminate?
   b. What financial advantages can this system have for the customer?
   c. Some customers consider the speed of this system a partial disadvantage, as they cannot keep up with the system to assure its accuracy. Based on your experience (or imagination) describe a high-tech solution to this concern.

9. This problem is best done by working in small groups. You, the student, are a customer of your school.
   a. Consider the services that your school provides to you and make a short list of quality problems you have encountered. For example, when you applied to the school, were you satisfied with the communication process? What kinds of things do you encounter in registration that are an irritating waste of time?
   b. Using the Alcoa eight-step process as a guide, work through to step 5. In each step, write down what kind of information you would need to gather and how you would go about it. When you get to step 3, try to identify causes, even if you have to guess. But be sure to reject superficial causes and look for root causes.
   c. Describe briefly how your school should carry out step 8, monitoring the solution you have proposed, assuming that it were implemented. What should be measured? How can they make sure the problem stays fixed? Address the issue of cost. Would your suggestion improve the productivity of the people working for your school? How?

10. Meals for hospital patients must be carefully temperature-controlled to preserve both palatability and safety. For example, if hot food is stored below a certain temperature, bacterial growth is encouraged and food poisoning can result. However, keeping it hot too long turns it to mush. Most meals involve both hot and cold dishes. Meals are delivered on trays. A cart carrying twenty trays is transported by

elevator to a designated area of the hospital, and meals are then distributed.

Consider technological solutions to the food quality problems related to delivery. You may wish to address the design of the food containers, trays, or carts, or some other aspect of the distribution system. If the preceding description is not adequate, you may need to add some "facts," either by a visit to a library or hospital or by making them up (i.e., pretending that you did the necessary research).

a. Select and define one problem.
b. Identify one or more root causes.
c. Describe a solution and show how it addresses the root cause.
d. Discuss the costs and benefits of your solution, paying particular attention to productivity.

*11. The accompanying cause-and-effect diagram was used to analyze the reason for delays in hiring new employees to fill empty positions (see Juran 1988, p. 21.17, for a more complete description). The time required to fill a position ranged from 1 month to 31 months, averaging 5 months.

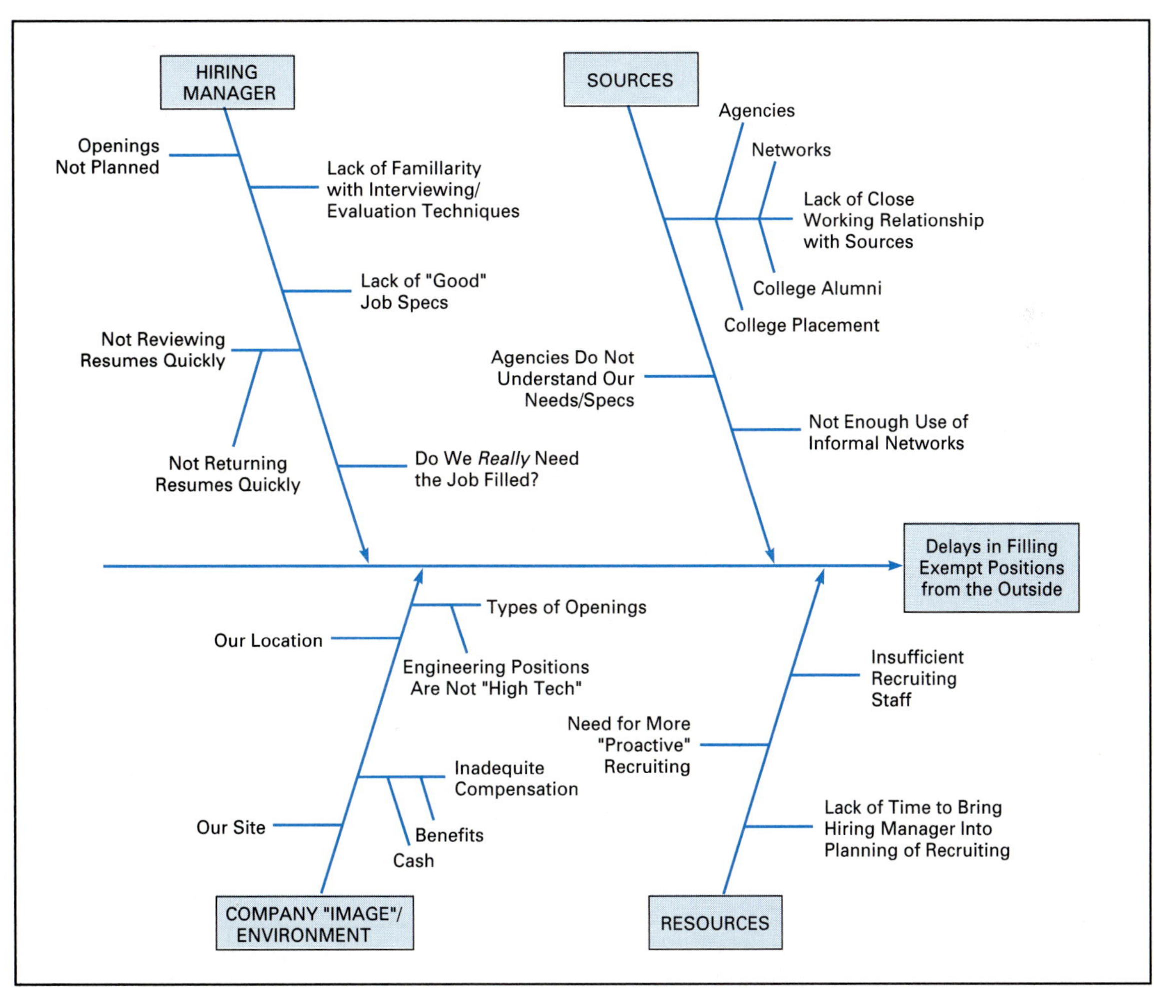

a. What does this problem have to do with quality? Productivity?
b. Explain the ''sources'' branch. In particular, explain the ''bushy twig'' on the branch concerning working relationships.
c. Consider the ''company image/environment'' branch. In what ways could the elements on this branch contribute to long delays? To highly variable delays?

12. The hiring process described in the previous problem was studied in greater depth (see Juran 1988, p. 21.19). The cause-and-effect diagram had suggested the hiring manager as one possible cause of delay in filling positions. The following diagram describes an analysis of the ''flow'' of the hiring process. The boxes represent ''events'' or ''milestones'' in the process, and the numbers represent the time that passes between the events. For example, an average of 3.0 days passes between receipt of a resume and passing the resume on to the hiring manager. However, the range (longest minus shortest time) is 10 days.

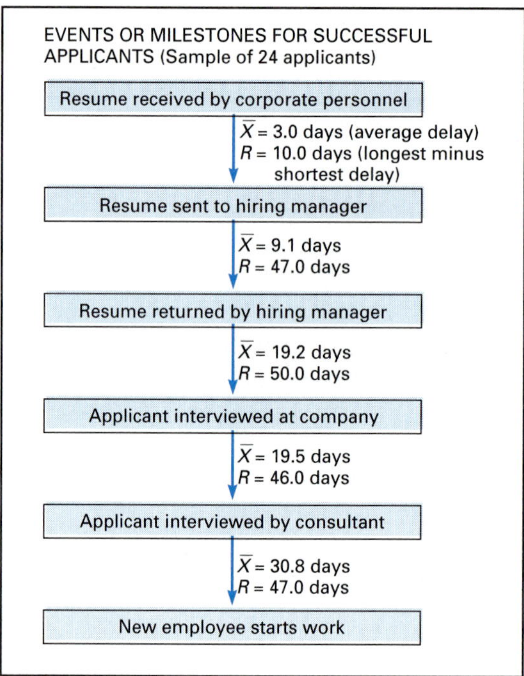

a. What does this problem have to do with quality?
b. Do these data support the hypothesis that the hiring manager is the cause of the delay in filling positions?
c. The 30.8 day delay at the end is somewhat misleading. Why?
d. Suggest a method to shorten the process.

13. Damage to the taillights of light trucks prior to customer receipt was investigated. (See Juran 1988, p. 21.18). The trucks are shipped on large trailers. They are loaded and unloaded by driving them, and they are secured on the trailers by chains fastened to the undercar-

riage. A brainstorming session resulted in the following list of possible causes of taillight breakage:

brittle taillight material
poor driver training
vandalism
chains snap during transport
loading ramp improperly positioned
trailer improperly positioned
taillight position extends beyond frame rails of truck
ice and snow during winter
collision in storage yard at factory
collision in delivery yard

a. Define a small number (four to six) of categories and sort these items into your categories. Add more items if you think of them.
b. Draw a cause-and-effect diagram using your categories from part a to define the branches.

14. Why are averages of small subgroups used in control charts rather than individual measurements or large-sample averages?

*15. A recent graduate was asked to look over the quality-control program at his new company. The first thing that he noticed was that the quality-control charts were labeled as having 99% confidence limits, but that 4% of the points plotted on them fell outside the limits. He claimed that the limits should be moved out until only 1% of the points fell outside. *But he is wrong.* Explain why you might expect more than 1% of the points to fall outside the 99% control limits, even in the long run.

16. In setting up an $\overline{X}$ chart for the weight of 1-pound boxes of sugar, an argument arose. The question concerned the correct method for determining the central line of the control chart. The two contenders were (i) the long-run average weight, and (ii) the desired weight of 1.020 pounds. Discuss both of these alternatives and explain the situations in which each is appropriate.

*17. An automobile manufacturer buys roller-bearing subassemblies in large batches for use in assembly. Each bearing unit is inspected just before it is installed. If there are too many defectives, the assembly line must be slowed down because of the added inspection operations. Therefore, management has decided to inspect a sample from each batch upon receipt. The foreman has estimated that the assembly-line slowdown is likely to occur if there are more than 5% defective parts. When the batch has 1% or fewer defective bearings, the pressure on the assembly line is considerably relieved. Because of the economics of sampling versus slowing down the line, they want the probability of rejecting a bad batch to be 0.975 or higher, but are willing to reject a good batch 10% of the time.

a. What values would you suggest for AQL and LTPD for this manufacturer? Why?
b. From the description, what target values should be used for α and β? Explain.
c. Design a sampling plan (n, c) using the normal approximation formulas.

d. Describe how your sampling plan works. In particular, what fraction defective *in the sample* would cause the inspector to reject the batch? What should be done with a batch that has been rejected?

e. Suppose that the target α is 2.5%. Design a new sampling plan, and interpret the difference from your previous answers. In particular, describe what happens to n and p_c and why these changes are appropriate.

18. Sampling plans may be described by either (n, c) or (n, p_c).
   a. What is the difference between c and p_c?
   b. Why should p_c be between AQL and LTPD?

19. This problem concerns the managerial implications of choice of AQL, LTPD, α, and β in acceptance sampling.
   a. Review problem 3 in Section 6-2 gave a table that showed several sampling plans. Draw a graph of sample size as a function of error probability α for the cases where $\alpha = \beta$. (Put α on the x-axis and n on the y-axis.) Interpret the graph in managerial terms.
   b. What happens to sample size as LTPD is decreased? To explore this question, use four values of LTPD (0.04, 0.03, 0.02, and 0.01) and hold AQL, α, and β constant at 0.5%, 5%, and 5%, respectively. Compute sampling plans, and interpret the results. Be sure to explain what ''decreasing LTPD'' means.

20. The Mortimer McSnarf Manufacturing Company (the M^3 Co.) makes balloons for promotional purposes in lots of 1000. Milton McSnarf is the plant manager. He says the cost of inspection is \$0.01 per item, and the per-unit contribution to fixed cost and profit is \$0.02, excluding the cost of inspection. He also says that he wants to be 95% sure of accepting a lot that has a fraction defective of 0.01. The sales manager, Lowd Roar, says that he wants to be 90% sure of rejecting a lot with 0.025 fraction defective. The controller, Hierman Bass, says that they must make an average of \$0.015 per balloon to cover their fixed costs, after subtracting inspection costs of a sampling plan. The personnel director, Marilyn McCool, says that an inspector should not be assigned a task of inspecting more than 200 per lot owing to boredom problems. (At present they have one inspector.)
   a. Find a sampling plan, if possible, to satisfy both McSnarf and Roar.
   b. Are the constraints by Bass and McCool met? Show your computations and state your reasons.
   c. What do you suggest they do?

21. A transistor manufacturing firm has found that the cost of inspection of each transistor is \$0.021. The cost of an undetected defect is \$7. They know that the process is in one of two states: in control with $f = 0.005$ or out of control with $f = 0.020$. They currently use a sampling plan with $n = 100$, $c = 1$. They believe that the process is in control most, but not all, of the time, and it is never in any state other than $f = 0.005$ or $f = 0.020$.
   a. How can they improve the acceptance sampling scheme?
   b. What sampling plan would achieve $\alpha = 0.1$, $\beta = 0.1$?

*22. The XYZ Corporation produces widgets in lots of 1000. They know beyond a shadow of a doubt that their fraction defective is between 0.01 and 0.08, and their costs of inspection and of an undetected defect are \$1 and \$20, respectively.

a. Is either 0% or 100% inspection optimal? Why or why not?
b. Further study disclosed the batches with fraction defective above 4% almost never occur; only 1 out of the past 1000 batches exceeded this level. What kind of sampling plan do you suggest?

23. The accompanying figure shows operating-characteristic curves for three sampling plans $n = 100$, $c = 3$; $n = 100$, $c = 4$; and $n = 78$, $c = 3$.

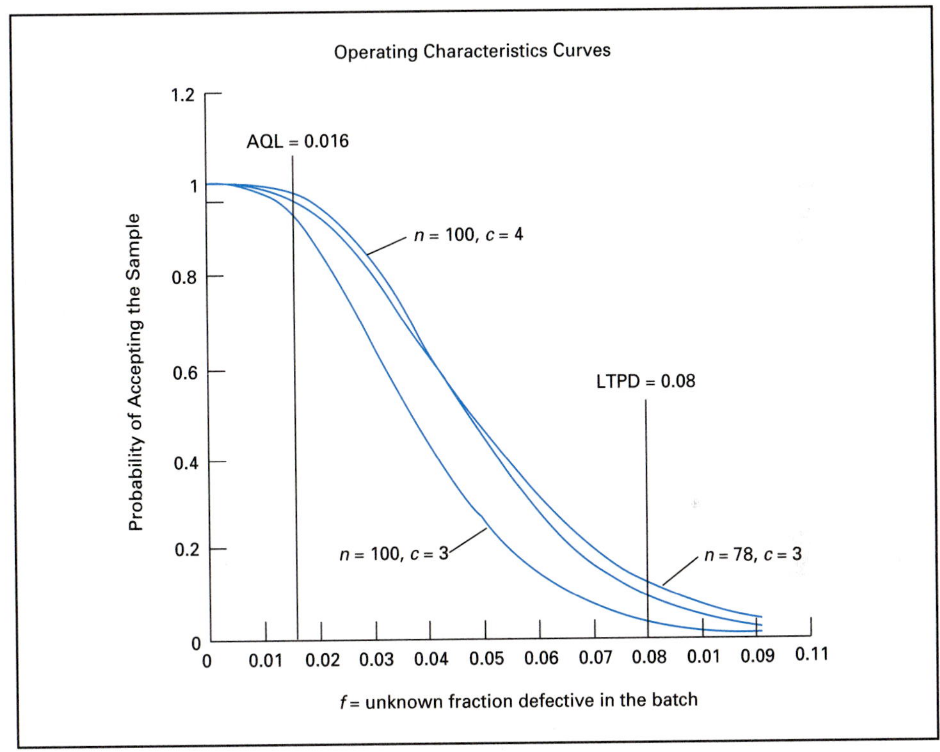

a. From the OC curves, estimate α and β for each of the three sampling plans if AQL = 1.6% and LTPD = 8%.
b. Study the results of part a to answer the following: Suppose that you already have a sampling plan in operation but that it has been determined that β is too high and α is lower than required; what change would you suggest in the sampling plan? (Change n or change c? Up or down?)
c. Calculate the cutoff ratio $(c + 0.5)/n$ for each plan. Two of the plans have almost identical cutoff ratios. What can you say about the changes in α and β as n is changed but the cutoff ratio does not change?

24. Gargantuous Motors buys headlight dimmer switches from Sure Lee, Incorporated. The president of Sure Lee is concerned about the average long-run cost of conformance and of nonconformance. She has gathered the following information about the the production process:

 Dimmer switches are shipped in lots of 1000 units.

 Prior to shipping, the sampling plan $n = 100$, $c = 3$ is applied. (An OC curve for this plan is given in problem 23.)

 Fraction defective in the batches varies between 1% and 8%.

 Inspection costs $0.10 per switch, and those found to be defective are replaced by good ones. Each defective switch passed on is thought to cost $3.

 If a batch is rejected by the sampling plan, every item in the batch is inspected and all defective switches are replaced by good ones.

a. Should a sampling plan be used at all?

(The remainder of this question requires the student to go beyond the material presented in the text.)

b. Suppose that $f = 0.03$ for all batches. Use the OC curve in problem 23 to estimate what fraction of batches will fail inspection (be rejected). If $f = 0.03$, what would the long-run average cost of inspection be, per batch? (This would be the cost of conformance.)

c. Using the acceptance probability from part b ($f = 0.03$ still assumed), what would the long-run average cost of nonconformance (defectives shipped out) be for this plan? Also use your answer from part b to compute the average cost of conformance.

In actuality the fraction defective, f, varies randomly. The accompanying table shows the frequency with which different f values occur, based on a large sample.

Relative Frequency with Which Different f Values Have Been Observed by Sure Lee, Inc.

f^a	Relative Frequency
0.01	0.60
0.02	0.20
0.03	0.10
0.04	0.05
0.05	0.02
0.06	0.01
0.07	0.01
0.08	0.01
Total	1.00

[a] f = batch fraction defective for headlight dimmer switches.

d. Explain in words how the long-run average cost of conformance and of nonconformance could be computed, using methods similar to those used in parts b and c.

e. Carry out the calculations you described in part d.
f. How could one find a sampling plan that minimizes these costs?

25. The Red Canners Corporation is concerned about the quality of their whole canned tomatoes. They produce tomatoes in batches, and one batch contains 10,000 cans, each of which sells to the wholesaler for \$0.20. Unfortunately, to inspect a can of tomatoes, they must destroy the can and its contents. Since they can sell any cans they are able to produce, the quality-control manager, Mack Cann, says that the cost of inspection is the selling price (\$0.20) plus the labor cost of inspection (\$0.10). Thus, he says that total inspection cost is \$0.30 per can. The cost of shipping a defective is deemed to be high, but they are unwilling to specify a value.
    a. Is Cann's cost of inspection value reasonable? Why?
    b. If the firm knew for sure that the true fraction defective was 0.02 or lower, they would not inspect any items, but if it was 0.10 or higher, they would inspect every item. What can you say about their implied cost of shipping a defective?

26. Some companies use ''zero defects'' acceptance sampling plans, in which $c = 0$, so that any defective items at all will cause the batch to be rejected. The acceptance probability for a zero defects plan has a very simple formula:

$$P_{\text{accept}} = (1 - f)^n$$

which is the probability of drawing n perfect items in a row if the true fraction defective is f. (This is an approximation. It is quite accurate as long as the sample size n is small compared with the batch size N.)
    a. If $n = 50$, what is the probability of accepting a batch with $f = 0.01$? $f = 0.02$? $f = 0.05$?
    b. Use the three answers from part a to draw (roughly) an OC curve for the plan $n = 50$, $c = 0$.
    c. Why does this so-called zero defects plan sometimes accept batches that have some defective items (f greater than 0)?
    d. How large should n be to assure a 95% probability of rejecting whenever $f \geq 0.01$?

*27. In a city fire department, the number of labor-hours lost each day because of accidents and work-related injuries is a normally distributed random variable with mean = 30 and standard deviation = 8. At the end of each day, the number of lost hours is recorded. At week's end the five daily observations are treated as a subgroup, and the average and range are plotted on control charts.
    a. For the $\overline{X}$ chart, what values should be used for the center line and the 1-sigma, 2-sigma, and 3-sigma limits? What assumptions must you make to use the data given previously in setting up an $\overline{X}$ chart?
    b. Answer part a for the R chart.
    c. What limits would be appropriate if they want to plot each day's lost hours rather than weekly averages? Would these control limits be accurate in this case? Explain.

d. If daily labor-hours lost were not normally distributed, what limits should be used for the weekly $\overline{X}$ chart? Could they use a daily chart? Explain.

28. The consistency of a manufacturing process is being investigated. The following data were taken at four different times of day. Each time, five finished items were removed from the conveyor and the specific gravity was measured for each one.

Subgroup 1	Subgroup 2	Subgroup 3	Subgroup 4
1.025	1.036	1.011	1.022
1.042	1.016	1.029	1.027
1.013	1.028	1.031	1.046
1.027	1.023	1.021	1.033
1.018	1.025	1.019	1.034

a. Calculate mean, range, and standard deviation for each subgroup.
b. Calculate the average of the four means, of the four ranges, and of the four standard deviations.
c. Use the average range to estimate σ.
d. Use the average standard deviation to estimate σ.
e. Set up an $\overline{X}$ chart and plot the four points.
f. Set up an R chart and plot the four points.
g. Calculate the control limits for an S chart.

*29. The diameter of roller bearings must be within a tolerance of ± 0.010 millimeter of the designated diameter. A production process is selected that has a normal process standard deviation of 0.003. Is a subgroup size of five sufficient to reliably detect a shift in the process mean that is large enough to produce significant numbers of out-of-tolerance bearings?

*30. The process standard deviation in the manufacture of roller bearings is 0.003 millimeter.
a. What should the upper 3-sigma control limit be for an R chart when the subgroup size is six?
b. Why should a roller-bearing manufacturer be interested in an R chart?

31. Apply the six rules for interpreting control charts to the accompanying charts. Mark with an X every point (or the last point in a series) that indicates that the process may be out of control. Give reasons for each mark.

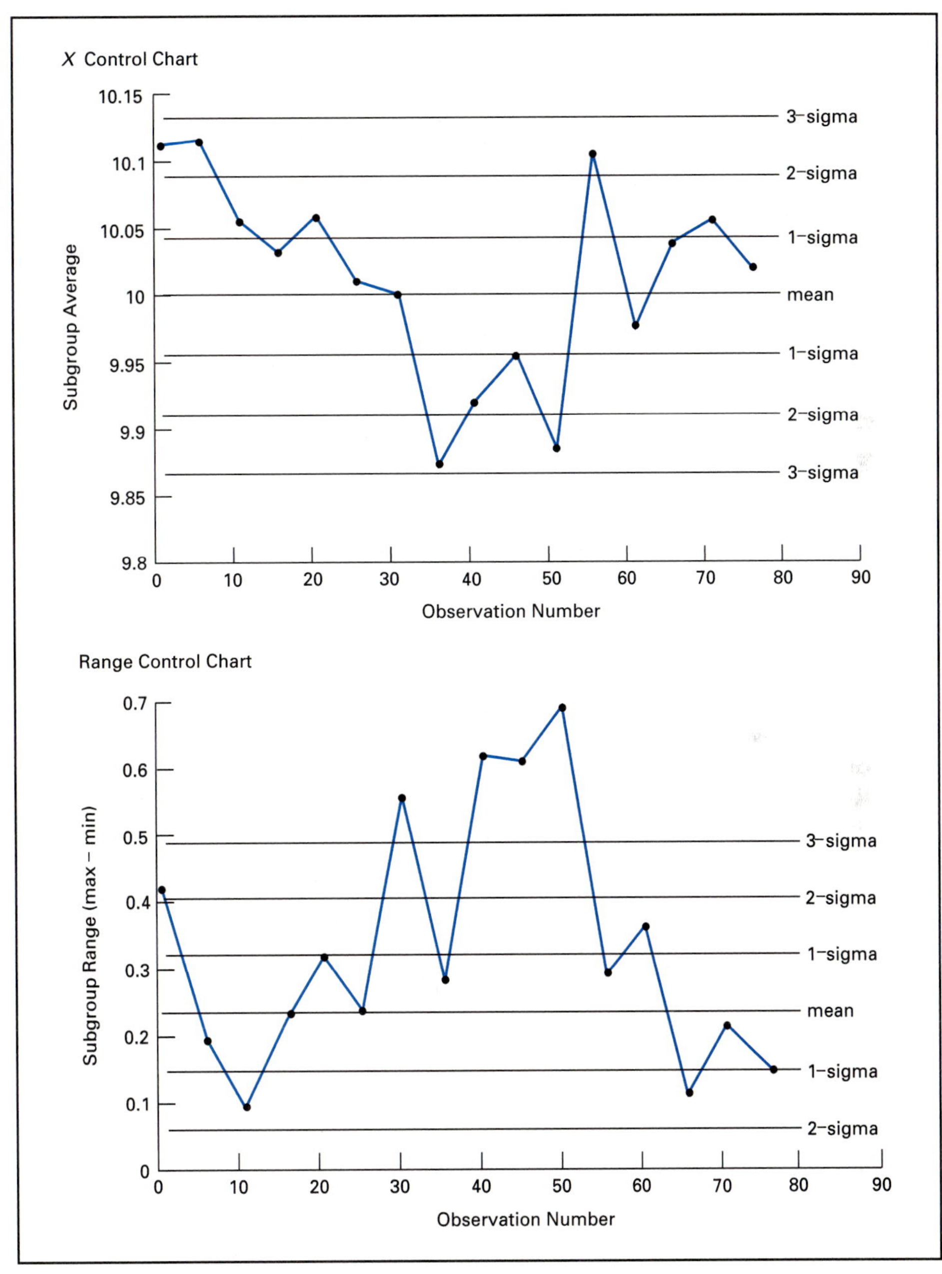

32. Apply the six rules for interpreting control charts to the accompanying charts. Also look for any suspicious patterns. Mark with an X every point (or the last point in a series) that indicates that the process may be out of control. Give reasons for each mark.

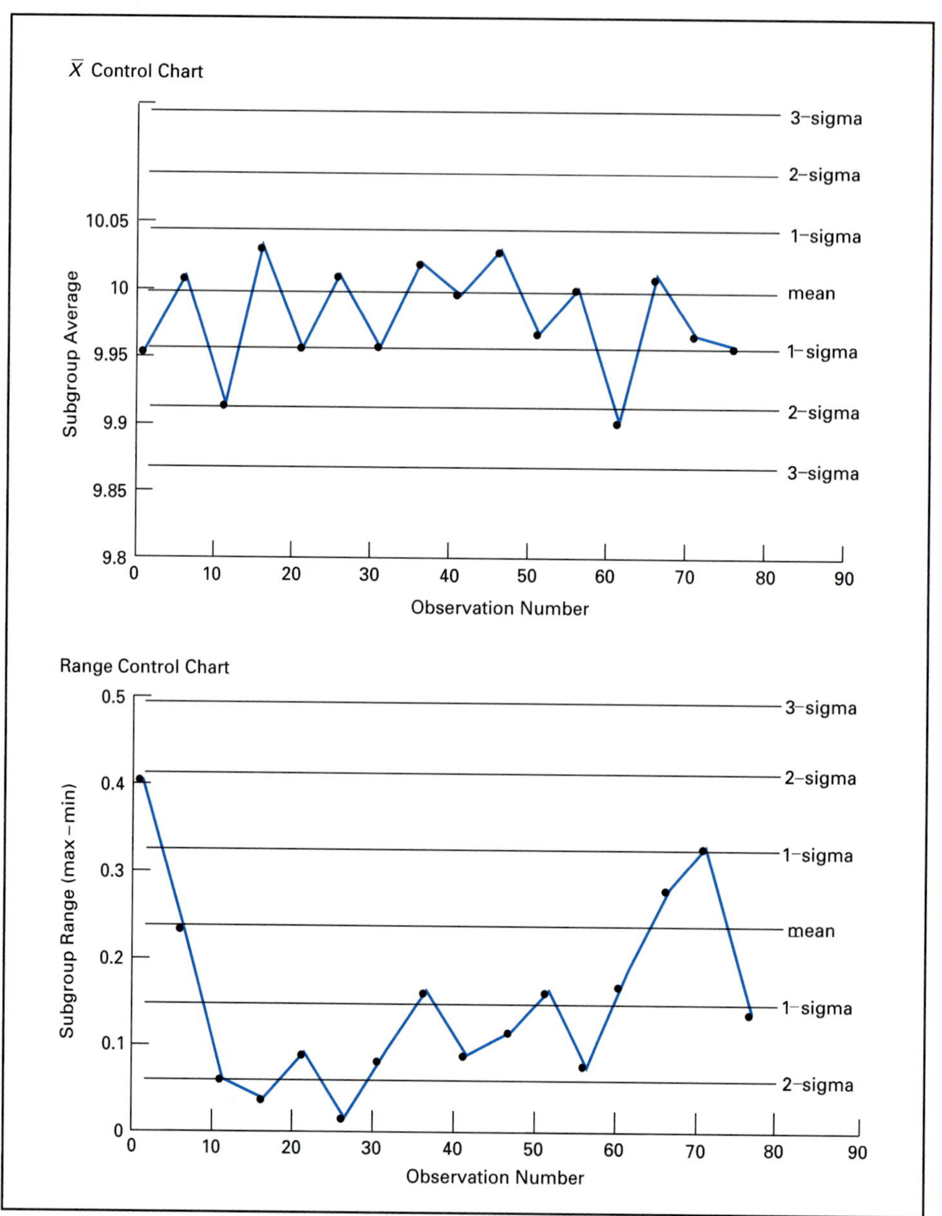

REFERENCES

ALCOA, "The Alcoa Eight Step Quality Improvement Process," pamphlet, Aluminum Company of America, 1989.

BARRA, R., *Putting Quality Circles to Work*, New York: McGraw-Hill, 1983.

CROSBY, P.B., *Quality Is Free*, New York: McGraw-Hill, 1979.

DEMING, J.E., "Out of the Crisis," MIT Center for Advanced Engineering Study, Cambridge Mass., 1986.

DEMING, W.E., "Improvement of Quality and Productivity through Action by Management," *National Productivity Review*, vol. 1 no. 1, 1982.

DODGE, H.F., and G.G. ROMIG, *Sampling Inspection Tables—Single and Double Sampling*, New York: Wiley, 1959.

DUNCAN, A.J., *Quality Control and Industrial Statistics*, 5th ed., Homewood, Ill.: Irwin, 1986.

GRIECO, P.L., M.W. GOZZO, and J. CLAUNCH, *Just-in-Time Purchasing: In Pursuit of Excellence*, Plantsville, Conn.: PT Publications, 1988.

HAUSER, J.R., and D. CLAUSING, "The House of Quality," *Harvard Business Review*, May–June, 1988.

HILLIARD, J.E., and H.A. LASATER, "Type I Risks When Several Tests Are Used Together on Control Charts for Means and Ranges," *Industrial Quality Control*, August, 1966.

HOLUSHA, J. "The Baldrige Badge of Courage—and Quality," *New York Times*, October 21, 1990.

INGLE, S., and N. INGLE, *Quality Circles in Service Industries*, Englewood Cliffs N.J.: Prentice-Hall, 1983.

ISHIKAWA, K., *Guide to Quality Control*, 15th printing, Tokyo: Asian Productivity Organization, 1985.

JOHNSON, R., and W.O. WINCHELL, *Production and Quality*, The American Society for Quality Control, 310 W. Wisconsin Ave., Milwaukee, Wis., 1989.

JURAN, J.M. *Juran on Leadership for Quality*, New York: Free Press, 1989.

JURAN, J.M., and GRYNA, F.M., eds., *Juran's Quality Control Handbook*, 4th ed., New York: McGraw-Hill, 1988.

KANE, E.J., "IBM's Quality Focus on the Business Process," *Quality Progress*, April, 1986.

KOHLER, M.T., and E.R. WELLS, "Quality Circles at Hughes Aircraft," *National Productivity Review*, vol. 1, no. 3, 1982.

MESKE, H., "A Management Standard for Economic Inspection," *Quality*, January, 1976.

MONDEN, Y., "What Makes the Toyota Production System Really Tick?" *Industrial Engineering*, January, 1981.

PALL, G.A., *Quality Process Management*, Englewood Cliffs, N.J., Prentice-Hall, 1987.

ROBINSON, L.W., J.O. MCCLAIN, and L.J. THOMAS, "The Good, the Bad and the Ugly: Quality on an Assembly Line," *International Journal of Production Research*, vol. 28, no. 5, 1990.

SCHONBERGER, R.J., "Work Improvement Programmes: Quality Control Circles Compared with Traditional Western Approaches," *International Journal of Operations and Production Management*, vol. 3, no. 2, 1983.

SCHWARTZ, S., quoted in *USA Today*, September 4, 1990.

SHEWHART, W.A., *Economic Control of Quality of Manufactured Product*, New York: Van Nostrand Reinhold, 1931.

SHINGO, S., *Report on Study of 'Toyota' Production System from Industrial Engineering Viewpoint* (English translation), Japan Management Association, 1981.

SHINGO, S. *Zero Quality Control: Source Inspection and the Poka-yoke System*, Cambridge, Mass: Productivity Press, 1986.

SKRZYCKI, C., ''Making Quality a Priority,'' *Washington Post*, October 11, 1987.

WERTHER, W.B., Jr., ''Quality Circles and Corporate Culture,'' *National Productivity Review*, vol. 1, no. 3, 1982.

ZEITHAML, V.A., A. PARASURAMAN, and L.L. BERRY, *Delivering Quality Service*, New York: Free Press, 1990.

chapter

7

Forecasting

I hope you'll keep in mind that economic forecasting is far from a perfect science. If recent history's any guide, the experts have some explaining to do about what they told us had to happen but never did.

Ronald Reagan, January 21, 1984

The preceding quote from President Reagan was used to introduce an article entitled "Are Economic Forecasters Worth Listening To?" (Bernstein and Silbert 1984), which concluded that "at one time or another, every professional forecaster is wrong. Taken as a group, however, forecasters have a good record." The message is that we cannot expect forecasts to be perfect. In a sense, forecasts should be expected to be wrong; it is impossible to guarantee a perfect forecast.

Forecasting is a difficult subject. There are many methods, both quantitative and qualitative. Deciding which is best for a particular situation is difficult. Moreover, the success that a given method has depends on the skill (and luck) of the person who uses it. There is a measure of "art" in the science of forecasting. You cannot just plug numbers into a formula and expect to get a good forecast. Judgment is always required.

This chapter introduces forecasting with several examples. This is followed by an in-depth look at exponential smoothing, a method that is widely used in operations management. The chapter closes with a discussion of a variety of other methods, indicating their advantages and disadvantages, and the kinds of situations in which they are most useful.

7-1 FORECASTING EXAMPLES

Forecasts are used to support decision making. The kind of forecast needed depends on the nature of the decision. The following example involves long-range plans for major construction projects.

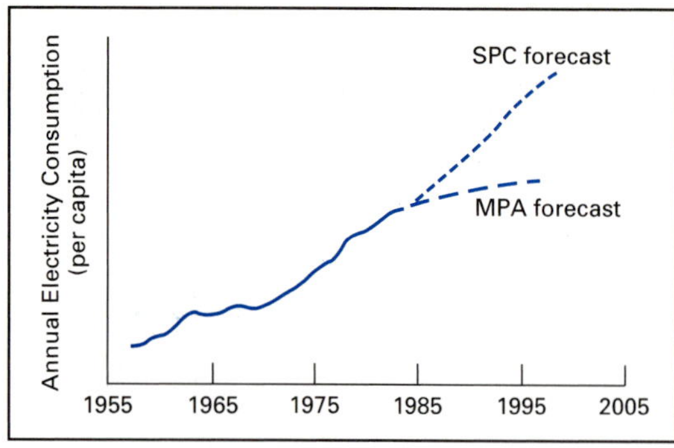

Figure 7-1 Southnorthern Power Company Energy Forecasts

Example: Southnorthern Power Company

Southnorthern Power Company (SPC) forecasts demand for electricity many years into the future because of the long lead time for approval and construction of power plants. At a meeting with the Public Utility Commission in 1985, these forecasts were called into question. Figure 7-1 shows the history of per capita consumption along with the SPC forecast and an alternative forecast prepared by Maria P. Angelo from the Utility Commission. The discussion revealed that both forecasts used the same methodology, but SPC put substantial weight on the historical trend, whereas Angelo assumed that the moderation of this trend in the early 1980s was a new pattern and therefore substantially discounted the pre-1980 data. Each forecasting model showed a very good ability to fit the prior data.

SPC and the Public Utility Commission faced a difficult situation: Two forecasters used the same methodology but arrived at very different forecasts. The reason was that they used different assumptions. Judgment is required to decide which assumptions are more realistic.

The following example concerns short-range decision making, where staffing plans are finalized one day in advance.

Example: Podunk Hospital

Podunk Hospital has a call-in system of patient admissions that is intended to smooth out the daily fluctuations of inpatient census. Each afternoon, a work sheet (Figure 7-2) is used to prepare a forecast of patient discharges for the following day. This is subtracted from the current census. Then the admissions scheduled for the next day are added, along with an allowance for emergency admissions and forecast error. The resulting census forecast is compared to a target, to determine how many patients can be offered the opportunity for an earlier-than-planned admission. The head nurse also uses the forecast while making last-minute adjustments in nursing work schedules.

Recently, the head nurse asked her nurses to prepare a daily census forecast based on their knowledge of the patients and their doctors. After some time had passed, the two forecasting methods were compared. The study revealed that

1. neither forecast was always correct
2. the nurses' reports were better at predicting exceptionally low discharge rates
3. a combination of the two performed slightly better, overall, than either separately

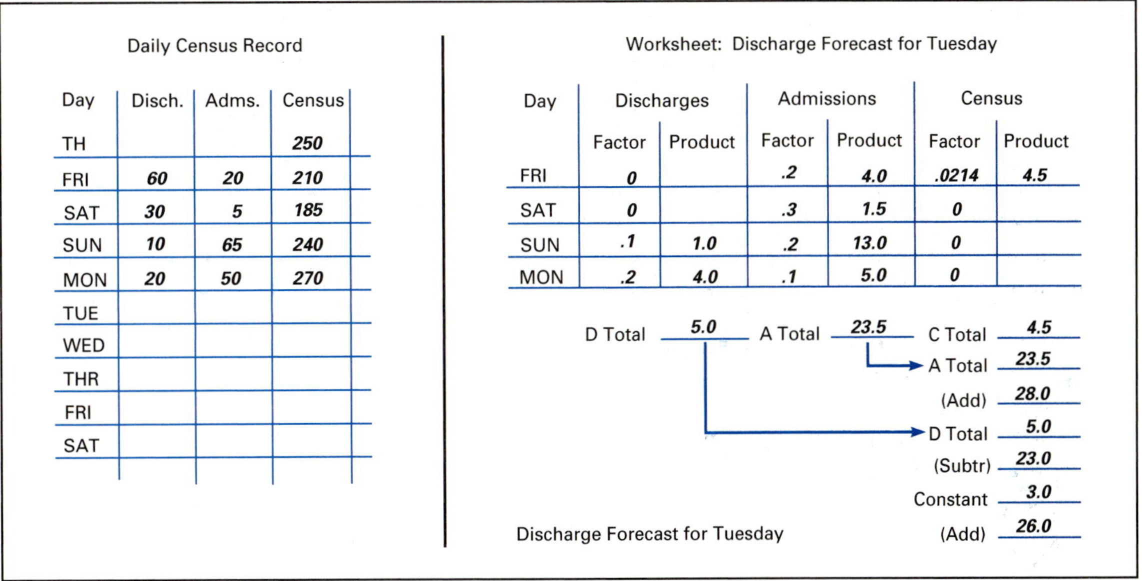

Daily Census Record

Day	Disch.	Adms.	Census
TH			250
FRI	60	20	210
SAT	30	5	185
SUN	10	65	240
MON	20	50	270
TUE			
WED			
THR			
FRI			
SAT			

Worksheet: Discharge Forecast for Tuesday

Day	Discharges		Admissions		Census	
	Factor	Product	Factor	Product	Factor	Product
FRI	0		.2	4.0	.0214	4.5
SAT	0		.3	1.5	0	
SUN	.1	1.0	.2	13.0	0	
MON	.2	4.0	.1	5.0	0	

D Total 5.0 A Total 23.5 C Total 4.5

A Total 23.5

(Add) 28.0

D Total 5.0

(Subtr) 23.0

Constant 3.0

Discharge Forecast for Tuesday (Add) 26.0

Figure 7-2 Podunk Hospital Discharge Forecasting Method

The preceding two examples point out a number of important principles, which will now be summarized.

Forecasts Are an Integral Part of Decision Making. Accordingly, they must be timely (daily for Podunk Hospital) and dependable. SPC and the Utility Commission had a difficult time making a decision because of the very different forecasts.

Forecasts Are Always Wrong! Systems that incorporate forecasts must be designed to allow adjustments to plans and schedules, to allow for imperfect forecasts. Different forecasting methods may give similar results and may complement one another. Moreover, the same forecasting method may give different results, depending on the assumptions of the forecaster.

Forecasting Methods Should Be Chosen to Fit the Need. Podunk Hospital cannot afford to spend days or weeks obtaining and justifying the forecasts, whereas SPC must. As another example, Gardner (1990) showed that the choice of a forecasting method is very important in inventory control systems. In general, we should use the simplest method that will provide satisfactory forecasts. It is often the case that a very simple model will provide forecasts that are good enough so that even the most complex methods cannot substantially improve the quality of the forecast (Armstrong 1986).

A Forecast Is Often Confused with a Goal. Sales forecasts, for example, are sometimes biased toward the high side when they are reported to sales personnel (to encourage them to work hard), and biased toward the low side when reported to higher levels of management (so that the actual achievements will appear to have exceeded expectation). This may explain, in part, why the SPC forecast was higher than the Utility Commission's. At the time, SPC saw their business as generating and selling power, whereas the Utility Commission was responsible for energy conservation.

All forecasting requires judgment. At Podunk Hospital the nurses were making their own forecasts based solely on judgment. In the power company example, judgment was required to decide between two sets of assumptions. Even extremely sophisticated mathematical forecasting methods require judgment and are affected very strongly by choices made by the forecaster.

We will return to the use of judgment in each section of this chapter. The next several sections introduce exponential smoothing, showing how the equations work and describing the decisions that a manager will encounter in their use. At the end of the chapter, we discuss how to choose among many available methods.

1. If forecasts are always wrong, of what use are they?

2. How is judgment used in statistical forecasting?

Solutions

1. Planning requires some estimate of the future. Forecasts are useful if they can be relied on to provide an estimate of the future, within a known level of error.

2. Selecting the statistical method to use requires judgment. Whether or not to believe a forecast, how large a safety margin to allow above the forecast, and whether to seek additional information are also management decisions.

7-2 SIMPLE EXPONENTIAL SMOOTHING (NO TREND OR SEASONALS)

Most forecasting methods recognize at least three components of a data series: trend, seasonality, and randomness (sometimes called noise).

Trend: a tendency for the data to increase (or decrease) steadily.

Seasonality: a pattern that repeats periodically.

Noise: the unpredictable (random) part of the data.

Some data series have no trend or seasonality. For example, Figure 7-3 shows monthly demand for staple pullers made by Robinson Removers, Incorporated. The demand for this item averages approximately 150,000 units per month, seldom growing or declining; it is a ''mature'' market.

Without trend or seasonality there is no real pattern to the data; it is purely random noise. By definition, randomness cannot be predicted. The best we can hope for is an accurate estimate of the average. In an average, high and low data values cancel each other, so the result tends to stay near the middle, as shown in Figure 7-3. As you can see, the average only predicts the ''level'' of the demand, not the variation. Some degree of forecast error is inevitable and must be allowed for when Robinson uses the forecast to decide how many staple pullers to produce (see Section 7-5).

Computing an average of all the data is not usually a good idea. Although there may no apparent trends, subtle changes may be occurring. Simply

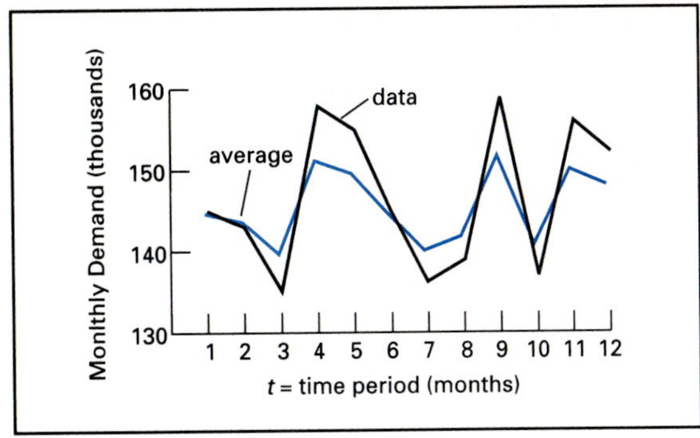

Figure 7-3 Demand for Staple Pullers: Robinson Removers, Inc.

ignoring data that are "too old" is one way to deal with this issue. The result is called a *moving average*. Table 7-1 shows a four-month moving average. The first four-month average, 145.25, is a forecast for month 5. Of course, that forecast was not available until the end of month 4. Later, at the end of month 5, the average of months 2 through 5 (147.75) is a forecast for month 6, and so on. In practice, more than four periods are typically used in a moving average. We used four months for ease of illustration.

Exponential smoothing is a different way to calculate an average. Each period, the average is "updated" by calculating a weighted average of only two numbers: the new data point and the old average.

$$\text{New average} = (\text{weight})(\text{new data}) + (1 - \text{weight})(\text{old average})$$

$$S_t = \alpha D_t + (1 - \alpha) S_{t-1} \tag{1}$$

in which α (alpha) is the weight, a fraction between 0 and 1. The current time period is denoted by the subscript t, S_t is the new exponentially smoothed

Table 7-1 A Moving Average and Two Exponentially Smoothed Averages: Staple Pullers Manufactured by Robinson Removers, Inc.

Period	Demand (thousands)	4-Month Moving Average	Exponentially Smoothed Averages $\alpha = 0.4$	Exponentially Smoothed Averages $\alpha = 0.1$
1	145			
2	143			
3	135			
4	158	145.25	145.25[a]	145.25[a]
5	155	147.75	149.15	146.23
6	145	148.25	147.49	146.10
7	136	148.50	142.89	145.09
8	139	143.75	141.34	144.48
9	159	144.75	148.40	145.93
10	137	142.75	143.84	145.04
11	156	147.75	148.70	146.14
12	152	151.00	150.02	146.72

[a] Initialized with a 4-month average (see text)

average, D_t is the new data value, and S_{t-1} is the old exponentially smoothed average.

The two exponentially smoothed averages in Table 7-1 are different because they have different α values. The calculations for months 11 and 12 using $\alpha = 0.4$ are

$$S_{11} = 0.4(156) + 0.6(143.84) = 148.70 \quad \text{(forecast for month 12)}$$

$$S_{12} = 0.4(152) + 0.6(148.70) = 150.02 \quad \text{(forecast for month 13)}$$

Notice that when month 12 ended, the new data point (152) was combined with the average computed in the previous month (148.70). The unique advantage of exponential smoothing is that you never have to go back more than one time period to calculate a new average.

Judgment In the Use of Exponential Smoothing

As we emphasized in the previous section, judgment is needed to use a forecasting method properly. In what follows, you will learn four important facts that will help you apply exponential smoothing wisely. In a subsequent example we put these ideas to work.

Similarity to Moving Averages. In all the time periods of Table 7-1, the exponentially smoothed average for $\alpha = 0.4$ is very similar to the four-month moving average. However, using $\alpha = 0.1$ gives very different results. The following formulas tell how to choose α so that the exponentially smoothed average is roughly similar to a moving average of N periods:

$$N = \frac{2 - \alpha}{\alpha} \quad \text{or} \quad \alpha = \frac{2}{N + 1} \tag{2}$$

Plugging in $\alpha = 0.4$ gives $N = 1.6/0.4 = 4$, whereas $\alpha = 0.1$ gives $N = 1.9/0.1 = 19$. Thus, exponential smoothing with $\alpha = 0.4$ emulates a four-period moving average, whereas $\alpha = 0.1$ will act like an average that looks back nineteen periods. But in each case, you only have to look back one period to compute the average.

Discounting by Increasing α. Exponential smoothing discounts data as they age: Old data are gradually ''forgotten.'' Larger α values discount more rapidly, much like using fewer periods in a moving average. This is because equation 1 multiplies the old average by $(1 - \alpha)$; thus, the weight accorded to the old data decreases when α is made larger. The larger α is, the less influence old data (represented by S_{t-1}) have on the forecast. (Problems 17 and 19 show that this influence decreases exponentially as the data age. Hence the name ''exponential smoothing.'')

Smoothness versus Responsiveness. Decreasing α causes ''smoother'' averages (less variation). Increasing α makes the average ''more responsive'' to new data points. The averages in Table 7-1 change very slowly for the smaller α value; they are smoother. For example, the largest data point is 159 in month 9. For $\alpha = 0.4$, the average jumps up from 141 to 148 in response to the large data point. By contrast, the average only moves up by about one point for $\alpha = 0.1$. Smoothness and responsiveness are opposites, but they both have advantages. We will return to this issue several times.

Initial Values. Calculating the first (or initial) value requires you to do something other than exponential smoothing. Since we need an "old average" in equation 1, what do we do when there are no old data? This is called initialization, and it is often given very little attention in explanations of exponential smoothing. However, we will show later that it is extremely important. For now, note that we used the four-month average as the first value for exponential smoothing in Table 7-1.

In the following example, each of the foregoing ideas are used to help understand what to do when the demand pattern changes, spoiling the forecasting model.

Example: Robinson Removers

Robinson Removers sells staple pullers under several different brand names. Demand is fairly steady, but now and then a customer is added or lost, causing a shift in demand. Robinson recently began using exponential smoothing, and Figure 7-4 shows the first thirty months. In the beginning there was no trend, but somewhere around month 20 demand began to increase, only to level out again later.

The reason for the increase was the gradual entry of a new customer, Weiss & Malik, Incorporated. W&M had indicated that they expected to buy approximately twenty units per month. The first order from W&M was received in month 17. By month 23, W&M had transferred all their business to Robinson Removers. Robinson wondered how to incorporate this information into their forecasting system.

The two exponentially smoothed averages ($\alpha = 0.1$ and $\alpha = 0.4$) are shown in Figure 7-4. There are two differences between Table 7-1 and the figure. First, there are thirty time periods in the figure instead of twelve. Second, in the figure the exponentially smoothed averages have been offset by one time period to show that they are forecasts of demand that is to occur in the following period. That is, each average appears in the time period *after* it was calculated,

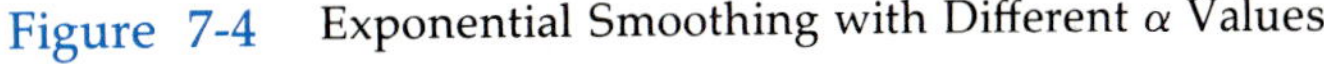

Figure 7-4 Exponential Smoothing with Different α Values

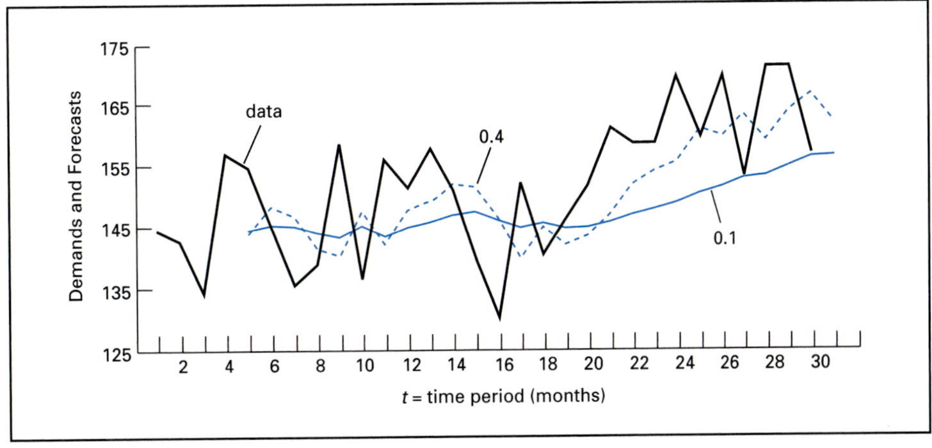

and the vertical distance between the forecast and the actual demand is the forecast error:

$$\text{Error} = \text{actual data} - \text{forecast} \quad \text{(general definition)} \tag{3}$$

$$e_t = D_t - S_{t-1} \quad \text{(for simple exponential smoothing)} \tag{4}$$

We will now apply some judgment to Robinson's problem. Figure 7-4 shows that $\alpha = 0.4$ causes the forecast to move rapidly toward the new demand level. In fact, it seems to have achieved the new level by the end of the data set. In contrast, $\alpha = 0.1$ moves much more slowly. This illustrates the issue of *smoothness versus responsiveness:* the lower α gives a smoother forecast, and the higher one is more responsive.

Why is $\alpha = 0.4$ more responsive? Applying equation 2, the slow-moving forecast is equivalent to a moving average of nineteen periods. No wonder it has not yet achieved the new level. By period 30, it is still making use of data as far back as period 11, before the new customer entered. By contrast, $\alpha = 0.4$ is like a four-month average and has therefore ''forgotten'' the data prior to the new customer. From this point of view, $\alpha = 0.4$ seems preferable, based on its greater ''responsiveness'' to the new customer.

On the other hand, $\alpha = 0.1$ gives better forecasts prior to period 17. Table 7-2 shows the calculations for the first sixteen periods. At the end of the table, the average and standard deviation of errors are shown; both of these measures show that $\alpha = 0.1$ gives forecast errors closer to zero, on the average.

A careful examination of Figure 7-4 shows that $\alpha = 0.4$ causes the forecast to follow the ups and downs of the data, but always one period too late; the

Table 7-2 Exponentially Smoothed Averages Used to Forecast Demand for Staple Pullers with Lead Time = 1 Period[a]

		$\alpha = 0.4$			$\alpha = 0.1$		
Period	**Demand (thous.)**	**S_t = Avg.**	**Fcst.**	**Error**	**S_t = Avg.**	**Fcst.**	**Error**
1	145						
2	143						
3	135						
4	158	145.25			145.25		
5	155	149.15	145.25	9.75	146.23	145.25	9.75
6	145	147.49	149.15	−4.15	146.10	146.23	−1.22
7	136	142.89	147.49	−11.49	145.09	146.10	−10.10
8	139	141.34	142.89	−3.89	144.48	145.09	−6.09
9	159	148.40	141.34	17.66	145.93	144.48	14.52
10	137	143.84	148.40	−11.40	145.04	145.93	−8.93
11	156	148.70	143.84	12.16	146.14	145.04	10.96
12	152	150.02	148.70	3.30	146.72	146.14	5.86
13	158	153.21	150.02	7.98	147.85	146.72	11.28
14	152	152.73	153.21	−1.21	148.27	147.85	4.15
15	140	147.64	152.73	−12.73	147.44	148.27	−8.27
16	131	140.98	147.64	−16.64	145.80	147.44	−16.44
			140.98			145.80	
Average Error				−0.89			0.45
Standard Deviation				11.10			10.27

[a]Data correspond to the first 16 periods in Figure 7-4.

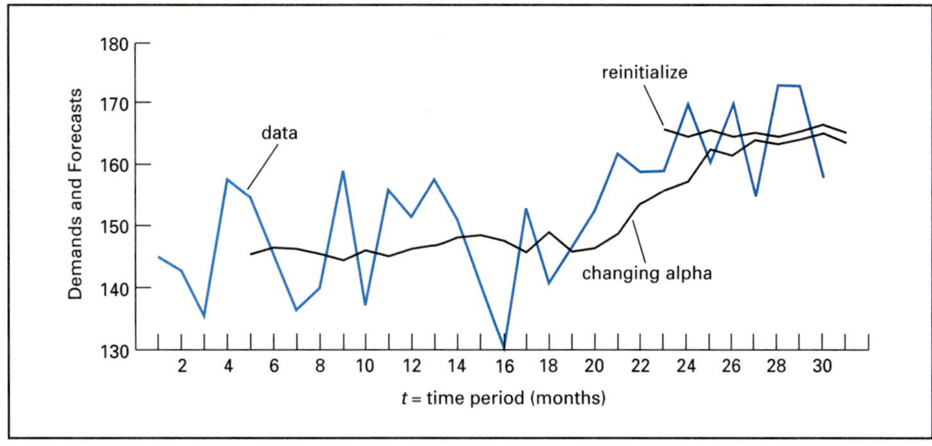

Figure 7-5 Two Methods for Intervening When Demand Jumps to a New Level

forecast is trying to track a random pattern. Decreasing α to 0.1 causes the average to be smoother. It responds less to the random fluctuations and thereby achieves a smaller forecast error prior to the entry of the new customer. From this alternative point of view, $\alpha = 0.1$ seems preferable, based on its greater smoothness.

But here we have a dilemma: Both forecasts have strong and weak points. We will describe two ways to deal with this dilemma.

The first way is to use $\alpha = 0.1$ most of the time, but to increase α when something unusual occurs, such as when a new customer enters or leaves. In Figure 7-5, the curve labeled ''changing alpha'' uses $\alpha = 0.1$ through period 16, $\alpha = 0.4$ for periods 17 through 26, and then returns to $\alpha = 0.1$. Note that 23, 24, 25, and 26 are the first four periods in which W&M was giving Robinson all their business, and 0.4 corresponds to a moving average of $N = 4$ periods. Hence, the exponentially smoothed average should be just about ''caught up'' by the time α is returned to 0.1.

The second way, depicted by curve labeled ''reinitialize,'' uses only $\alpha =$ 0.1 but disregards periods 17 through 22. Instead, it reinitializes (starts over) at period 22 using $S_{22} = 20 + S_{16}$. The logic is that S_{16} represents the demand before W&M's entry, and 20 is the additional demand that W&M will cause. Exponential smoothing resumes in period 23.

Both these methods require management intervention. They use the information about W&M in a way that exponential smoothing (by itself) cannot do. ''Changing alpha'' uses what we know about the timing of W&M's entry. ''Reinitialize'' uses both timing and W&M's estimated demand. Deciding which to use is a matter of judgment.

REVIEW PROBLEMS

1. One question to ask in deciding between ''reinitialize'' and ''changing alpha'' is, How reliable is M&W's estimated monthly demand of twenty units? Describe how an answer to this question would affect your choice.

2. ''Reinitialize'' uses 165.8 for S_{22}. Explain why this is a reasonable value.

3. Using $S_{22} = 165.80$ and $D_{23} = 159$, calculate S_{23} for the "reinitialize" method. Verify your answer against Figure 7-5.

4. Beginning with $S_{16} = 145.80$ and demand of 153 for month 17, calculate S_{17} for the "changing alpha" method. Verify your answer against Figure 7-5.

5. The accompanying table shows the Robinson Remover forecasts calculated through period 30. Is it possible to decide which of these methods would be better to use in general, based on this information? Explain.

Period	Demand	Changing Alpha		Reinitialize	
(t)	(D_t)	S_t	Fcst.	S_t	Fcst.
16	131	145.80		145.80	
17	153	148.68	145.80		
18	141	145.61	148.68		
19	147	146.16	145.61		
20	152	148.50	146.16		
21	162	153.90	148.50		
22	159	155.94	153.90	165.80	
23	159	157.16	155.94	165.12	165.80
24	170	162.30	157.16	165.60	165.12
25	160	161.38	162.30	165.04	165.60
26	170	164.83	161.38	165.54	165.04
27	155	163.84	164.83	164.49	165.54
28	173	164.76	163.84	165.34	164.49
29	173	165.58	164.76	166.10	165.34
30	158	164.83	165.58	165.29	166.10
			164.83		165.29

Solutions

1. If M&W's estimate is very reliable, "reinitialize" is preferable, since it uses all the information to improve the forecasts. If the demand is likely to vary substantially from twenty units, "changing alpha" may be preferable, since it requires only timing information and incorporates new data very rapidly.

2. S_{16} + estimated new demand = 145.80 + 20 = 165.80. This is reasonable because 145.80 is an estimate of the demand level before W&M entered, and 20 is the estimated amount that they will order.

3. For "reinitialize," $S_{23} = 0.1(159) + 0.9(165.8) = 165.12$. This is the forecast for period 24 in Figure 7-5.

4. For "changing alpha," $S_{17} = 0.4(153) + 0.6(145.8) = 148.7$. This is the forecast for period 18 in Figure 7-5.

5. No, for two reasons. First, there are only four data points after α is changed back to 0.1, and that is too few for a reliable choice to be made. Second, choosing between the methods in general would depend on when the forecasts are needed. The "reinitialize" option ignored several periods. This is reasonable if the periods have already passed. However, if the current

period were, say, 18 (rather than 31) and Robinson needed a forecast, the "reinitialize" method as described would not have helped. Period 18 is during the time that W&M's orders were increasing, so adding 20 would be inappropriate.

7-3 EXPONENTIAL SMOOTHING WITH TREND

An average makes a poor forecast for a data series that is increasing or decreasing. What is your forecast of the next number in the sequence 9, 8, 7, 6, 5? The average is 7, but most people would predict 4. Since the last point in the series represents the newest data, we say that the "current level" is 5. Its "trend" (slope) is -1. Forecasts with trend allow a pattern to be projected into the future for as many periods as desired.[1] For example, a two-period linear projection of the foregoing series would be $5 + 2(-1) = 3$. In general,

Linear trend forecast = current level + (lead time)(trend)

$$F(t, k) = a_t + kb_t \tag{5}$$

in which a_t (current level) is an estimate of the average demand level at time t, k is the lead time (or look-ahead interval), and b_t is the trend (or slope).

Exponential smoothing can be used to estimate both level and trend, but some new equations are required. Since there are two terms to estimate, we use two alpha values:

R_a = alpha value for estimating the current level, a_t
R_b = alpha value for estimating the trend (slope), b_t

As before, the forecast error is defined as the difference between the actual data and the forecast. For a one-period lead time, the forecast error is

Forecast error = new data − old forecast

$$e_t = D_t - (a_{t-1} + b_{t-1}) \tag{6}$$

Level and slope are calculated as follows:

New level = old forecast + (weight)(forecast error)

$$a_t = (a_{t-1} + b_{t-1}) + R_a e_t \tag{7}$$

New slope = old slope + (weight)(forecast error)

$$b_t = b_{t-1} + R_b e_t \tag{8}$$

These formulas may look different from equation 1 for simple exponential smoothing, but setting $b_t = 0$ makes equation 7 exactly the same as equation 1, with a_t playing the role of S_t, and R_a equal to α (see problem 20).

Choosing Values for R_a and R_b

As with simple exponential smoothing, small values of the smoothing parameters R_a and R_b give "smoother" forecasts, and large values increase the "responsiveness."[2] However, it takes longer for a trend model to "catch up"

[1] Gardner and McKenzie (1985) warn against projecting a linear trend too far into the future. They propose a "damped trend" forecast that "levels off" at longer lead times, and show that it is more accurate than linear trend models.

[2] The parameters are called R_a and R_b because they adjust the responsiveness of the terms a_t and b_t, respectively. Problem 18 demonstrates this numerically.

when there is a major change in the demand. In the Robinson Remover example of the last section, demand grew between periods 17 and 23; temporarily, there was a trend. If a trend model had been used, the slope, b_t, would have increased in response to that growth. However, after period 23 demand stopped increasing, but the model requires some time to gets its slope, b_t, back to zero. The trend model has to "forget" both the level of demand prior to period 17 and the slope that occurred between periods 17 and 23.

Recall that simple exponential smoothing (no trend) is similar to a moving average of N periods if N and α satisfy equation 2. The trend model of exponential smoothing is similar to an unweighted analysis (such as linear regression) of N periods if

$$N = \frac{2(2 - R_a)}{R_a} \quad \text{or} \quad R_a = \frac{4}{N + 2} \tag{9}$$

As a guideline, allow N periods for a trend model to forget the initial estimates.

Caution should be used when setting the trend's smoothing parameter, R_b. It must be substantially smaller than R_a. It has been shown that setting R_b too large causes the forecast to behave erratically (McClain and Thomas 1973). We recommend the following value[3] for R_b:

$$R_b = (R_a)^2 \tag{10}$$

Initial Values for a_t and b_t

The choice of initial values is very important. We will give an example before suggesting a method for initialization. The demand pattern in Figure 7-6 has an increasing trend. Both forecasts include trend, but the initial trend value is 0, ($b_0 = 0$) for one of the models and $b_0 = 5.418$ for the other. (Obtaining initial values is described presently.) Zero slope is clearly a poor choice for the data in Figure 7-6, and the model with $b_0 = 0$ underforecasts demand for about half the data set.

[3]Some commonly available packages use different values for R_b. Equation 10 is equivalent to using Winters' model (1960) with equal smoothing parameters, whereas the following reproduces Brown's (1963) model:

$$R_b = 2 - R_a - 2\sqrt{1 - R_a}$$

Figure 7-6 Forecasts with Trend: Sensitivity to Initial Values

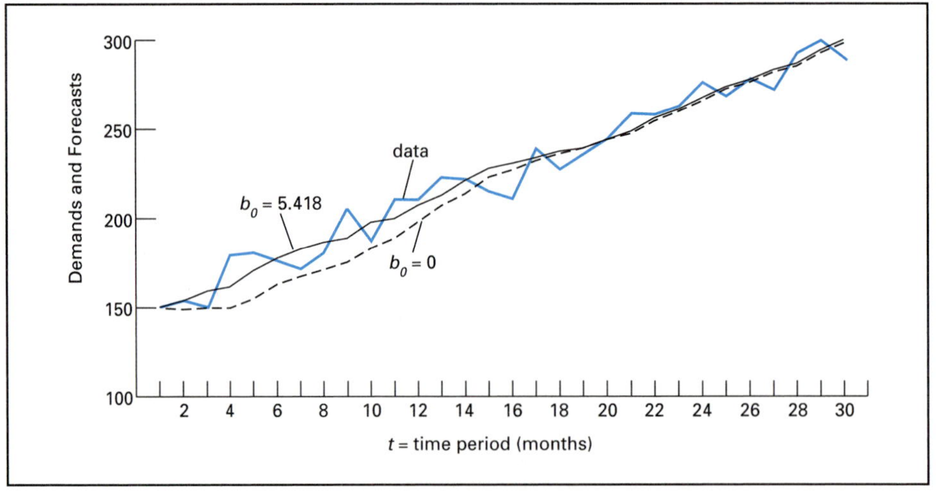

Note that the two models are about the same in periods 19 and beyond. Apparently the different *initial* trend values do not affect the forecasts near the end of the data set. Indeed, according to our guideline of equation 9, the initial estimates should be forgotten after $N = 2(2 - 0.2)/0.2 = 18$ periods.

Table 7-3 gives the first 11 calculations. In period 11, the two models have nearly equal slopes, b_t, but very different levels, a_t. Think about that! The slope and the level affect each other. Poor choice of b_t at time 0 causes bad values for a_t in later periods. Good initial estimates of both a_t and b_t are needed.

To obtain initial values $a_0 = 143.67$ and $b_0 = 5.418$, linear regression was carried out on the first eleven data points, using demand as the dependent variable and time as the independent variable.[4] (The equations are given in problem 11.) The intercept from the regression becomes a_0 and the slope becomes b_0. (The other model used $b_0 = 0$ and the first demand as a_0.)

Initialization consists of more than calculating a_0 and b_0. All the calculations in Table 7-3 are part of initializing the forecasting model. By the time the eleven periods of data have been exponentially smoothed, the initial values of 143.67 and 5.418 have been substantially discounted. The values $a_{11} = 203.13$ and $b_{11} = 5.442$ are initial values for forecasting in periods 12 and beyond. We recommend the following procedure for initializing a trend model:

1. Collect a set of data for initialization. (Let m = the number of observations in the initialization data set.)
2. Use the data to estimate a_0 and b_0. (Linear regression may be used, as in problem 11.)
3. Calculate a_t and b_t for each period of the initialization data, as in Table 7-3, using smoothing parameters consistent with the amount of data. For example, $R_a = 4/(m + 2)$ and $R_b = R_a^2$ as suggested by equations 9 and 10.

[4]An alternative method is described by McClain (1981) in which linear regression is not used. Instead, exponential smoothing begins with very high R_a and R_b, thereby avoiding undue weight on the initial values. R_a and R_b are gradually reduced as time passes, using a special formula.

Table 7-3 Two Trend Models: Different Initial Slopes. $R_a = 0.2$ and $R_b = 0.04$

		Initial Trend = 5.418				Initial Trend = 0.0			
	Data	Fcst.	e_t	a_t	b_t	Fcst.	e_t	a_t	b_t
				143.67	5.418			150.00	0.000
1	150	149.09	0.91	149.27	5.455	150.00	0.00	150.00	0.000
2	153	154.73	−1.73	154.38	5.385	150.00	3.00	150.60	0.120
3	150	159.77	−9.77	157.81	4.995	150.72	−0.72	150.58	0.091
4	178	162.81	15.19	165.85	5.602	150.67	27.33	156.13	1.185
5	180	171.45	8.55	173.16	5.944	157.32	22.68	161.85	2.092
6	175	179.10	−4.10	178.28	5.780	163.95	11.05	166.16	2.534
7	171	184.06	−13.06	181.45	5.258	168.69	2.31	169.15	2.626
8	179	186.71	−7.71	185.17	4.949	171.78	7.22	173.22	2.915
9	204	190.12	13.88	192.89	5.505	176.14	27.86	181.71	4.030
10	187	198.40	−11.40	196.12	5.049	185.74	1.26	185.99	4.080
11	211	201.17	9.83	203.13	5.442	190.07	20.93	194.26	4.917
12		208.58				199.17			

4. Use the last values of a_t and b_t to begin actual forecasting. You may wish to choose new values for R_a and R_b at this time.

REVIEW PROBLEMS

1. The demand in period 12 is 212. Update a_t and b_t using equations 6 to 8 and the data from the first model in Table 7-3. Then compute a forecast for period 13 using equation 5.

2. At the end of period 12, forecasts may be needed for several periods ahead, rather than just for period 13. Compute forecasts for periods 14, 15, and 16.

3. As we saw in Figure 7-6, there are really thirty periods of data. The eleven periods in Table 7-3 were used for initialization.
   a. What values of R_a and R_b should have been used, according to the recommended initialization procedure?
   b. Since $R_\alpha = 0.2$ and $R_b = 0.04$ were actually used, how many periods will pass before a_0 and b_0 are forgotten?
   c. Drawing an analogy to the "changing alpha" example given in Section 7-2, explain why the forecaster should consider changing R_a and R_b after the initialization data set.

Solutions

1. The forecast for period 12 (from period 11) is 203.13 + 5.442 = 208.58. The forecast error is 212 − 208.58 = 3.42. The new level is a_{12} = 203.13 + 5.442 + 0.2(3.42) = 209.26. The new trend is b_{12} = 5.442 + 0.04(3.42) = 5.579. The forecast for period 13 is 209.26 + 5.579 = 214.84.

2. Using equation 5, with k = 2, 3, and 4,

$$a_{12} + 2b_{12} = 209.26 + 2(5.579) = 220.42 \quad \text{for period 14}$$

$$a_{12} + 3b_{12} = 209.26 + 3(5.579) = 226.00 \quad \text{for period 15}$$

$$a_{12} + 4b_{12} = 209.26 + 4(5.579) = 231.58 \quad \text{for period 16}$$

3. a. In step 3, using m = 11 observations, $4/(m + 2) = 4/13 = 0.3077$ is recommended for R_a and $(0.3077)^2 = .0947$ for R_b.
   b. Initial values will have a negligible effect after $N = 2(2 - 0.2)/0.2 = 18$ periods.
   c. The first part of the data is a period of initialization. A high value of R_a is needed to discount the initial estimates. After N periods, a lower value for R_a could be used to make the forecasts smoother, decreasing the effect of the random component. R_b should also be reduced to comply with equation 10.

7-4 SEASONALITY

Many goods and services have seasonal demand, with predictable rises and falls caused by seasonal influences such as weather and holidays. Seasonality is often the most important aspect of a forecast. For example, at a time of year when demand is always low, hospitals schedule renovations, manufacturers schedule preventive maintenance, and retailers schedule inventory counts. Vacation planning is also affected by seasonality.

Fortunately, rather simple methods are available to quantify seasonal patterns. One of the simplest is illustrated in the following example.

Example: Tomasco Apple Wines

Sales of Tomasco Apple Wines has a pronounced seasonal pattern. Figure 7-7 shows that third-quarter sales are low, followed by a strong fourth quarter. Four seasonal factors are used to describe this pattern: 1.053, 0.952, 0.798, and 1.196 for quarters 1 to 4, respectively. A seasonal factor of 1.0 is ''normal'' or ''average.'' Hence, Tomasco's first quarter tends to be 5.3% higher than average for the year (1.053 is 5.3% above 1.0) and their second-quarter sales are usually 4.8% below average.

This same approach can be used to quantify day-of-the week variation. A ''Friday factor'' of 1.37 in a forecast of demand for emergency services would indicate that 37% more people need emergency services on Fridays, compared with the average for the week.

Now let us look at how seasonal factors are used. Then we will show you how Tomasco calculated their seasonal factors.

Using Seasonal Factors

Seasonal factors are used in two ways: to remove seasonal effects from data (deseasonalizing) and to introduce seasonality into an average or trend forecast. The following steps describe how to use seasonal factors. Any fore-

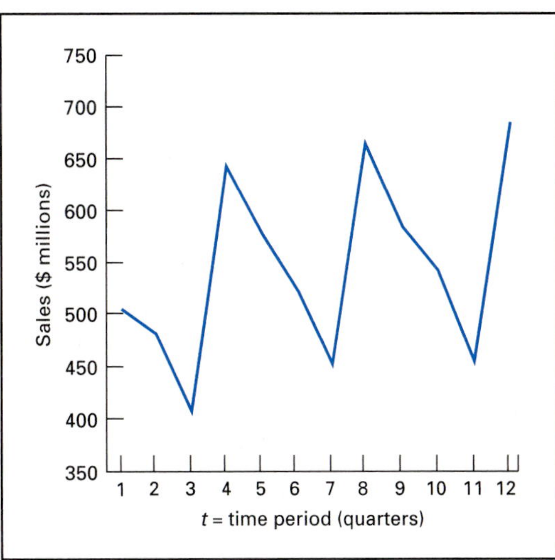

Figure 7-7 Quarterly Sales of Tomasco Apple Wines: A Seasonal Pattern

casting method may be used in steps 3 and 4, including exponential smoothing with or without trend.

1. At the end of time period t, observe a new data point, D_t.
2. ***Deseasonalize the data:*** $D_t^* = D_t$ divided by the seasonal factor for period t.
3. Use the deseasonalized data, D_t^*, in the exponential smoothing equations in place of D_t (equations 6, 7, and 8, or equation 1).
4. Use the results to make a forecast with lead time k (e.g., equation 5.)
5. ***Seasonalize the forecast:*** Multiply by the seasonal factor for the period being forecast, period $t + k$. That is,

   Seasonal forecast = (trend or no-trend forecast)(seasonal factor)

$$F(t, k) = (S_t)(\text{factor}_{t+k}) \quad \text{(without trend)} \tag{11}$$

$$F(t, k) = (a_t + kb_t)(\text{factor}_{t+k}) \quad \text{(with trend)} \tag{12}$$

Tomasco uses exponential smoothing with seasonal factors. Their smoothing parameters are $R_a = 0.25$ and $R_b = 0.06$. To illustrate how seasonality is integrated with exponential smoothing, consider the calculations they would have made at the end of period 6 (the second quarter of year 2). Assume that the values $a_5 = 550.7$ and $b_5 = 1.70$ are left over from the previous quarter. Sales of $D_6 = 523$ (\$ millions) occurred in period 6. Tomasco wants forecasts for the next four quarters. Using the preceding five steps and recalling the seasonal factors of 1.053, 0.952, 0.798, and 1.196 results in the following:

1. $t = 6$ is the current time, and $D_6 = 523$ has just been observed.
2. Period 6 is a second quarter (year 2), so the seasonal factor is 0.952; deseasonalized sales = $D_6^* = 523/0.952 = 549.4$.
3. Using equations 6, 7, and 8 with $R_a = 0.25$ and $R_b = 0.06$,

$$e_6 = 549.4 - (550.7 + 1.70) = -3.0 \quad \text{(we use } D^* \text{ instead of } D\text{)}$$

$$a_6 = 550.7 + 1.70 + 0.25(-3.0) = 551.7$$

$$b_6 = 1.70 + 0.06(-3.0) = 1.52$$

4 and 5.

Time Period	Lead Time	Season (quarter)	Trend Projections	Seasonalized Forecasts
7	$k = 1$	3	551.7 + 1(1.52) = 553.2	(553.2)(0.798) = 441.5
8	$k = 2$	4	551.7 + 2(1.52) = 554.7	(554.7)(1.196) = 663.4
9	$k = 3$	1	551.7 + 3(1.52) = 556.3	(556.3)(1.053) = 585.8
10	$k = 4$	2	551.7 + 4(1.52) = 557.8	(557.8)(0.952) = 531.0

The forecasts for periods 7 to 10 reflect the same seasonality evident in Figure 7-7. Period 7 is predicted to show a strong decrease to \$441.5 million. Nevertheless, the trend projection shows that sales are expected to grow by b_6 = \$1.52 million each quarter, on the average.

Table 7-4 Computing Seasonal Factors for Tomasco Apple Wines Sales

Period	Sales ($ millions)	Centered Average	Ratio[a]	Average Ratio[a]	Normalized Seasonal Factor[a]
1	504				
2	484				
3	409	519.88	0.7867	0.7997	0.798
4	644	534.38	1.2051	1.1980	1.196
5	581	544.63	1.0668	1.0547	1.053
6	523	552.75	0.9462	0.9539	0.952
7	452	556.13	0.8128		
8	666	559.25	1.1909		
9	586	562.00	1.0427		
10	543	564.63	0.9617		
11	454				
12	685		Averages =	1.0016	1.000

[a] See description in accompanying text.

Computing Seasonal Factors: Ratio-to-Centered-Averages Method

In the Tomasco example the seasonal pattern of apple wine sales is examined by itself. The reader should note that more reliable estimates are often obtained by working with groups of products that share a common seasonal pattern. This also reduces the computational task, since there may be only a few seasonal patterns in a product line with 50,000 items. The ratio-to-centered-averages method is easily modified to consider groups of items.

Table 7-4 is a work sheet for computing quarterly seasonal factors for Tomasco Apple Wines sales. The data are the same as in Figure 7-7. Note the strong contrast between the data and the centered averages: centered averages estimate what sales would have been without seasonality.

The centered averages cover one year,[5] but an entire year cannot have seasonality, by definition. However, to be truly representative of a given quarter, equal amounts of data should come from before and after that quarter. Then if there is a trend, the higher level at one end of the year will be canceled out by the lower level at the other end. Consider period 4. To place period 4 exactly in the center of a year, we need to include 1.5 periods before and 1.5 periods after (1.5 + 1 + 1.5 = 4 periods, which is one year.) The centered average for period 4 is 534.38, calculated as $(0.5D_2 + D_3 + D_4 + D_5 + 0.5D_6)/4$. The weight of 0.5 on D_2 and D_6 in effect takes the average from midperiod 2 to midperiod 6.

The ratio column in Table 7-4 is the sales divided by the centered average. Note that this number is quite low for periods 3 and 7, which are both third quarters. In the average ratio column, all ratios for a given quarter are averaged (for example, the number 0.7997 is the average of periods 3 and 7, both third quarters). The last column contains the seasonal factors, computed by dividing the average ratios by 1.0016 (their overall average). This causes the average of the four seasonal factors to be 1.0.

[5] Or one whole week for day-of-week patterns.

In summary, seasonal factors quantify a repeating cycle in a data set. Quarterly and monthly factors are used for cycles based on the seasons of the year. Day-of-week patterns require seven factors. There are a number of other ways to estimate seasonal factors, but the ratio-to-centered-averages method is the easiest to understand.

REVIEW PROBLEMS

1. Qwikkie Car Wash gets crowded around noon (11:45 A.M. to 1:15 P.M.), commuting time (4:00 to 5:30 P.M.), and after dinner (7:00 to 8:30 P.M.). Could they use seasonal factors to quantify this pattern? Discuss briefly.

2. Tomasco's sales for periods 7 and 8 were 452 and 666, respectively. Deseasonalize these numbers. You will note that 452 increases and 666 decreases when you deseasonalize them. Why does that make sense?

3. When the five steps were used on the period 6 data, why was the seasonal factor 0.952 used in step 2 whereas different seasonal factors were used in step 5?

4. Plot the centered averages from Table 7-4 on the graph in Figure 7-7. What does the centered-average graph tell you about the demand pattern, and specifically about the trend (slope) in demand?

Solutions

1. They could use time-of-day factors. They should divide the day into time intervals (similar to seasons of the year) and record the demands for each time interval. The ratio-to-centered-averages method would yield the time-of-day factors.

2. 452/0.798 = 566.4, 666/1.196 = 556.9. Period 8 is a fourth quarter. It is expected to be above average. Dividing it by 1.196 reduces it so that it may be compared with other periods. Period 7 sales are normally low, and dividing by 0.798 increases it. The two deseasonalized values reveal a ten-unit decline in seasonally adjusted sales, even though actual sales increased.

3. In step 3 the goal is to remove the seasonal effect from the period 6 data, and period 6 is a second quarter. In step 5, the goal is to forecast periods 7 through 10, and they are quarters 3, 4, 1, and 2, respectively. The trend projections from step 4 are deseasonalized and step 5 reseasonalizes with the seasonal factor appropriate to the period being forecast.

4. Your plot should show centered averages smoothly increasing, passing between the actual data points without showing the seasonal rises and falls. The centered averages reveal the upward trend of demand, but the pattern appears to be curved rather than linear. Apparently growth is slowing. Perhaps the market is maturing or Tomasco's rate of market penetration is slowing.

7-5 ERROR DETECTION AND SAFETY MARGINS

Many retailers, wholesalers, and manufacturers have thousands of different items in inventory. Delegating forecasting responsibility for most items to an automatic system frees management to concentrate on items for which forecast errors are of greatest consequence. However, even an automatic system must have human intervention from time to time. For example, if there is a significant change in the demand pattern, it takes time for an exponential smoothing system to fully incorporate the new situation. Meanwhile, serious forecast errors will occur. There are two approaches to dealing with this dilemma: *automatic error detection* and *self-adaptive methods* that provide automatic adjustments in the response rate.

Automatic error detection produces a signal when human intervention and judgment is needed. This would have been very useful to Robinson Removers, for example, when their new customer changed the level of demand. Errors are detected statistically by looking for a pattern in the forecast error, e_t, defined in equations 3, 4, and 6. A measure of average forecast error is the mean absolute deviation (MAD), which may be estimated by exponentially smoothing the forecast errors without regard to sign:

$$\text{MAD}_t = \alpha|e_t| + (1 - \alpha)\,\text{MAD}_{t-1} \tag{13}$$

in which $|e_t|$ is the absolute value of the forecast error (the sign is dropped). If the forecast error is normally distributed, MAD is theoretically related to the standard deviation, σ, by

$$\sigma = \sqrt{\frac{\pi}{2}}\,\text{MAD} \approx 1.25\ \text{MAD} \tag{14}$$

Because of this relationship, about 95% of the time (if errors are normally distributed) the forecast should be within 2 standard deviations, or 2.5 MAD, of the actual demand, and within 3 MAD about 98% of the time.

MAD can be used *to provide a safety margin for a forecast.* For example, to be (approximately) 99% certain that supplies will be adequate to satisfy all customers, a retailer should have an inventory equal to the demand forecast plus 3 MAD. Or a forecaster can quote a "probable margin of error" as "plus or minus 2.5 MAD" and expect to be correct about 95% of the time.

MAD can also be used *to detect spurious data.* For example, sales figures may have been incorrectly entered into the computer. Or sales may have been influenced by a one-time promotion. In either case the large forecast error is not an indication of trouble with the forecast, and e_t *should not be incorporated into next month's forecast unless it is first corrected for the event.* A spurious data detector can be constructed as follows:

$$\text{Possibly spurious data if } |e_t| > n_1\text{MAD}_t$$

The parameter n_1 determines the sensitivity of the filter. A common value for n_1 is 4, but experience may suggest a higher or lower value.

A third use of MAD is as part of a tracking signal *to detect forecast bias.* A forecast is said to be biased upward if it tends to be too high, and downward if too low. Forecasts can be biased for two reasons: incorrect model and changed data pattern. Simple (no-trend) exponential smoothing gives biased forecasts if there is a trend in the data—an example of an incorrect model. A sudden change in the demand pattern causes biased forecasts with any model. For example, Robinson Removers experienced biased forecasts for several periods after they acquired a major new customer (look back to Figure 7-4).

One method of bias detection uses MAD in combination with the *smoothed average error*, E_t:

$$E_t = \alpha e_t + (1 - \alpha)E_{t-1} \tag{15}$$

The sign *does* matter in this formula, allowing E_t to be positive, negative, or zero. By contrast, MAD must be positive because of the absolute value in equation 13. Trigg (1964) proposed the following tracking signal as a forecast bias detector:

$$\text{Tracking signal} = \frac{E_t}{\text{MAD}_t}$$

$$\text{Possibly biased forecast if } |\text{tracking signal}| > n_2 \tag{16}$$

For a simple (no trend) exponential smoothing system, Gardner (1983) recommends that n_2 be set between 0.36 and 0.47 for $\alpha = 0.1$ and somewhat larger for higher α values. However, he also found that larger values of α can lead to poorer performance of this error detector and suggested alternative methods.

The tracking signal works better if different α values are used for MAD_t and E_t. McClain (1988) recommends $\alpha = 0.05$ for MAD_t and $\alpha = 0.2$ for E_t. With this modification, the value of n_2 should be between 0.65 and 0.83 for $R_a = 0.1$ and somewhat smaller for higher R_a values. Using these α values leads to faster detection of sudden changes in the data.

Regardless of the method used for tracking signals, the purpose is to allow an automatic forecasting system to signal for help. Whether the problem is an incorrect model or a change in the data pattern, the forecaster can usually find out what caused the problem and fix it. Reinitializing a no-trend model (discussed in Section 7-2) and initializing with a trend (Section 7-3) are two possible actions. Increasing the smoothing parameters to allow the model to adapt quickly to the new pattern is another.

Self-adaptive methods automatically increase the responsiveness of the model when the forecast seems to be inaccurate, and reduce it again as the forecast realigns itself. The method of Trigg and Leach (1967) is the simplest: The smoothing constant α (or the response rate R_a) is set equal to the tracking signal (dropping the sign). Adaptive models are most useful when the time series is relatively smooth (low noise) but subject to abrupt changes (Fliedner et al. 1986). If there is substantial randomness, holding the smoothing parameters constant works better, particularly if tracking signals are used to signal the need for reinitialization.

REVIEW PROBLEMS

1. Contrast the actions that a manager should take when spurious data is detected with those that are appropriate in response to an indication of forecast bias from a tracking signal.

2. Given that actual demand should be within 3 MAD of the forecast about 98% of the time, why can we say that a stock level equal to the forecast plus 3 MAD will be sufficient to satisfy demand 99% (rather than 98%) of the time?

3. Explain why the Trigg-Leach method will quickly improve a forecast that has been biased for a period of time.

Solutions

1. The manager would either correct spurious data or delete it from the data set altogether. Forecast bias can be eliminated only by more extensive intervention such as reinitialization or increasing the response rates.

2. The first statement is two-sided: It says that the forecast will be above or below demand by 3 MAD or more about 2% of the time. The protection against high demand is one-sided: All that we are worried about is a forecast that is too low by more than 3 MAD, and that should occur half as often, or 1% of the time.

3. When bias is present, all the recent errors will (tend to) have the same sign. That is, if the forecast is biased high, e_t will be negative, and conversely. The smoothed average error, E_t, is a weighted average of recent forecast errors. When the forecast is not biased, the errors tend to alternate in sign and E_t stays near zero. When the forecast is biased, consistently positive or negative errors will cause E_t to move away from zero. This causes the tracking signal to grow. If α (or R_a) is set equal to the tracking signal, it too will grow when the forecast is biased. This increases the responsiveness of the forecast, causing it to forget old data more rapidly, and hence allowing it to accommodate rapidly to a new data pattern.

7-6 OTHER FORECASTING METHODS

In *Manager's Guide to Forecasting,* Georgoff and Murdick (1986) describe twenty forecasting techniques in four categories: judgment methods, counting methods, time-series methods, and association or causal methods. This section presents a brief description of some methods in each category.

The Box-Jenkins Method for Time Series

Exponential smoothing is a time-series method because it projects a pattern from past data into the future. A more complex time-series analysis method is that of Box and Jenkins (1970). This approach is more powerful than exponential smoothing in some applications. It also has some drawbacks: (1) The tools of analysis are difficult to master; (2) large amounts of data are required to properly use the method; and (3) the data must be transformed to achieve ''stationarity'' before the forecasting model can be developed. The major steps in the preparation of a Box-Jenkins model are as follows:

1. *Data transformation to achieve stationarity.* If necessary use a function (such as the logarithm or the first difference) to eliminate trends in the average level of demand and in the variability.

2. *Model identification*. Analyze the remaining variability (using some cleverly derived rules of thumb) to determine one or more models that account for the autocorrelation[6] in the transformed data.
3. *Parameter estimation*. Find the optimal values for the unknown parameters in the model(s) selected in step 2.
4. *Checking*. Repeat steps 2 and 3 as many times as necessary until no further improvements are found.

A Box-Jenkins model bases its forecasts on two sources of information: previous forecast errors and the previous values of the data. As an example, consider the following equation for the one-period-ahead forecast for the (natural logarithm of the) monthly number of automobile registrations in the United States (Nelson 1973):

$$\text{Forecast} = D_t + D_{t-11} - D_{t-12} - 0.21e_t - 0.26e_{t-1} - 0.85e_{t-11} + 0.18e_{t-12} + 0.22e_{t-13} \quad (17)$$

Thus, the forecast for the next month's registrations is based on the value observed this month (D_t), the seasonal change observed between the same two months last year ($D_{t-11} - D_{t-12}$), and five different forecast errors. Sophisticated methods are required to derive an equation like this. However, the resulting model is quite easy as long as 25 data points are retained for easy access (12 months of auto registration and 13 months of forecast errors). A comparable exponential smoothing model requires 14 data points (12 seasonal factors plus the intercept and slope terms).

Research indicates that the Box-Jenkins method is superior when there is low randomness in the data. This is the case with highly aggregated data such as industry-wide statistics. However, greater accuracy has been reported using simpler methods such as exponential smoothing when randomness is a large factor (Carbone et al. 1983 and Lawrence 1983), as is the case with forecasts of single-item demand.

Judgmental Methods

Human judgment is often used to obtain forecasts. For example, many manufacturers and distributors routinely collect opinions from their sales force and use this information to construct a forecast. The forecast is not necessarily the sum of the individual projections, however. Management may have additional information, such as a consumer survey, knowledge of an impending strike in a related industry, or plans for an upcoming promotional effort.

It can be very frustrating to try to bring judgmental information together into a single quantitative forecast. A reliable, systematic procedure must be established for collecting the opinions. Yet the process must also be rapid, since the usefulness of the information diminishes with age. (Georgoff and Murdick 1986 describe several useful procedures.)

A common judgmental method is referred to as BFE (bold, freehand extrapolation) or SWAG (sophisticated, wild guess). The information contained in these forecasts is substantial because of the experience of the managers who provide them. They suffer, however, from various human weaknesses, such as the tendency to overreact to perceived changes and to give too much credence to the most forceful presentation (the squeaky-wheel effect). Delphi is one of

[6]Autocorrelation is a correlation between a variable and its own previous values.

the formal methods that are designed to reduce these effects by careful control of personal contact during a session when forecasts are being elicited.

The major advantages of judgmental methods are their relative simplicity and the possibility of predicting rare events. The first advantage explains why these methods are widely used: Managers feel comfortable with a method that is straightforward and easily understood. Predicting rare events is sometimes simple for people but impossible for statistical methods. There is, in classical statistics, no counterpart to private conversations that transmit information about an impending event that has never occurred before.

A disadvantage of judgmental methods is the time required. Many firms have thousands of items subject to inventory control, and forecasts of usage are very important in preventing shortages. It has been shown in an experimental environment that judgmental forecasting can be at least as accurate as ''black box'' statistical computer programs, and sometimes better (Lawrence 1983). However, it also appears that judgmental modification of statistical forecasts makes little difference in their accuracy (Carbone et al. 1983). We believe that the best system uses a combination of statistical and judgmental methods. Using tracking signals to indicate when judgment is needed is that sort of combination.

Counting Methods

When a new product or service is being considered, potential demand is often estimated by consumer surveys. By careful design of survey instruments, researchers can find out not only what the consumer prefers but also which *attributes* are the most significant in the consumer's decision. For example, in a survey concerning health care, McClain and Rao (1974) identified three groups of consumers who could be distinguished not only by their choice of a health plan but also by what they regarded as the most important aspect of a health plan. The attributes were ''method of payment,'' ''hours of operation,'' and ''use of physician's assistants''; by asking the consumers to choose among health plans, the researchers were able to discover, indirectly, how each attribute was valued, without asking the respondents. The name *conjoint measurement* is applied to this kind of approach because two things are jointly estimated from the same data: overall preferences for different alternatives (for example, different health plans) and the underlying values (or utilities) of the attributes that describe the alternatives.

Market testing is another counting method. A new product is introduced to a selected market to assess its potential sales. To be realistic, a market test should include advertising and other promotions.

The two major advantages of counting methods are that historical data are not required and that the detailed understanding of the consumer's preferences may lead to new ideas, such as a new product or service that combines some of the most preferred attributes. However, they are among the most expensive approaches.

Association or Causal Methods

The most common method for quantifying an association between variables is linear regression. For example, a company that sells hair cream collected sales data for several districts. Using regression, they can determine whether there is an association between sales and certain characteristics of the districts. Sales is the dependent variable, whereas population of the district and per capita discretionary income were chosen as predictor (independent) variables. Information for twelve districts was analyzed using a regression program on a computer, and the following equation resulted:

$$\text{Sales (\$ millions)} = 2.34 + 0.051(\text{population in thousands}) + 0.12(\text{income in \$ thousands})$$

That equation can be used to forecast sales in a district where the population is 100,000 and income is \$20,000:

$$\text{Forecast} = 2.34 + 0.051(100) + 0.12(20) = \$9.84 \text{ million}$$

In addition to the forecast, most regression programs calculate a prediction interval (margin for error).

Regression is a very useful and powerful tool. A large number of predictor variables can be included in the same equation. This includes so-called indicator or dummy variables (to represent seasonality or other categorical effects) and nonlinear terms to represent properties like diminishing marginal returns. However, it is also a very complex topic with pitfalls too numerous to list in brief. Suffice it to say that at least one full semester of coursework is required to become proficient in the use of this tool.

SUMMARY

There are many forecasting models to choose from. Not only do they differ in techniques but also in effort and cost of implementation. Forecasting methods should be selected to suit the need.

Exponential smoothing is one of the simplest quantitative techniques for forecasting from historical data. With or without trend and seasonal terms, exponential smoothing has the effect of discounting older data and placing more emphasis on newer data. It is reasonably accurate for short lead times, at least until some significant event causes the underlying pattern to change. After such a change, unless there is human intervention, forecasts will be biased for a time until the old patterns are forgotten, as a result of the discounting inherent in the system. Most exponential-smoothing systems currently in use have an error-detection system to signal when human intervention is needed.

The Box-Jenkins method, although far more difficult to implement, is easy to use once the correct model has been identified and parameters have been estimated. However, experience has shown that even highly trained forecasters can make significant errors in implementing a Box-Jenkins model.

It is well to remember that forecasts are always wrong. Because of this, it may be difficult to decide among the many alternative forecasting methods. The acid test is to try the candidates, using historical data as though it were just occurring. One should select the simplest model among those that perform best for the application.

It is not an exaggeration to say that most important decisions are based on forecasts, either implicitly or explicitly. Every decision that has an element of planning requires some estimate of what is to be expected in the future. This includes long-range decisions such as capacity and location planning, intermediate-range production and work-force plans, and short-range personnel and other scheduling decisions. The All-Sports caselet that follows asks you to estimate the value of a forecasting model for control of inventory in a distribution company.

CASELET

ALL-SPORTS DISTRIBUTION COMPANY

The All-Sports Distribution Company distributes sporting goods to retail stores and schools in a four-county area in Ohio. They cover a mostly rural area, with a total population of 450,000. There are several cities in the range of 20,000 to 50,000 population but no larger cities. All-Sports has about 20% of the market, sharing the market with one larger competitor and two smaller competitors.

All-Sports has not been using any forecasting techniques. Rather they have relied on yearly average sales and maximum monthly sales to make their decisions on how many units to carry. They have not had a problem with lost sales, but they believe that they are carrying too much inventory. Recently their warehouse has been full at all times, and some units have been stored in the receiving room, causing some difficulties in handling.

The firm has 120 product lines, and each line has several sizes or styles. For example, the Wilson Profile tennis racquet is a line that has nine combinations of weight and grip. The mix of demands for various weight–grip combinations is relatively stable; they assume that the mix will continue to be constant and that they can ignore the problem of what weight–grip combinations to order.

They want to study the sales of Wilson Profile racquets to see if better forecasting can reduce their inventory sufficiently to warrant the expense.

Costs: An outside company has proposed to operate a forecasting system for All-Sports. The forecasting system would require a computer terminal, at a cost of $120 per month. The computer time and storage is estimated to cost $160 per month. The data necessary are already available in a central location, and it is estimated that the additional time to enter the data and receive the output would be only 3 or 4 hours once a month. The employee who would do that task is paid $12 per hour gross salary, but the office manager feels that the employee can perform that task without affecting other work. Thus they feel there is no additional cost. (It is important to note that no in-house computer expertise is required for this application.) Some initial expense would be incurred in setting up the system. The firm estimates this expense to be $5000 plus two days of management time, including one day for the warehouse superintendent and one day for the executive vice-president.

The cost of a Wilson Profile racquet to distributors is $94. They sell it to their customers at $120, who, in turn, sell it for $180. Since other distributors are available, they do not want to be out of stock. The president of All-Sports says that it is impossible to say what the cost of capital is for the inventory, since the company uses long-term debt, short-term debt, and current receipts to finance its operations.

Current Policy: The company places an order for each product line in each month. They order an amount so that their inventory (on hand plus on order) is equal to the maximum monthly demand last year plus 10 units. They began each month in 1990 with 140 + 10 = 150 tennis racquets, since the maximum 1989 demand was 140 in April. The orders arrive very quickly; they do not have a problem with lead time.

The firm knows that this policy is too conservative, but they have not had time to make separate monthly forecasts of each product line. They have stated that they believe a policy of ordering up to next month's forecast plus 20 units would yield customer service as good as the present system.

Data: As of the time of this analysis, July 1991, the firm had 5 1/2 years of data available for Wilson Profile. As was mentioned previously, no breakdown by weight-grip combinations is given or deemed necessary.

Month	1986	1987	1988	1989	1990	1991
Jan.	72	75	80	78	84	82
Feb.	71	77	78	76	81	81
Mar.	102	110	120	131	124	128
Apr.	115	110	136	140	142	140
May	81	74	78	84	85	91
June	60	68	76	71	75	78
July	58	54	58	61	66	
Aug.	61	64	66	68	72	
Sept.	75	78	74	91	88	
Oct.	92	97	105	101	110	
Nov.	120	124	121	130	145	
Dec.	115	116	117	122	128	

Required: Evaluate costs and benefits of the proposed forecasting system.

PROBLEMS

1. Describe how forecasts with confidence intervals would be useful for
   a. ordering office supplies
   b. planning maintenance of equipment
   c. preparing a budget for a school district
   d. scheduling employee vacations
   e. planning an employee recruitment and training program
2. Would exponential smoothing be an appropriate forecasting method to supply information for capacity and location decisions? For intermediate-range production and work-force planning? Explain your answers, briefly.

*3. Mary and George are having a forecasting contest. For the past twelve months, each has been using no-trend exponential smoothing with $\alpha = 0.2$, but George has been calculating his forecasts monthly, whereas Mary updates weekly. Three months ago there was a substantial drop in demand. Prior to that time, demand had been fluc-

*Problems with an asterisk have answers in the back of the book.

tuating around an average of 200 per week, but now it seems to be nearer 100. Who is more likely to have an accurate forecast, given the recent drop? Why?

4. The Amalgamated Battery Company distributes a large-capacity battery that has been used for some industrial processes. They know that electric cars are now in production and they think that a jump (a permanent, one-time increase) has occurred in their demand. They are forecasting by simple exponential smoothing (equation 1 in the text), since there has been no trend. The battery costs $25 to produce. At the end of December, the exponentially smoothed average was 150. The recent demands are January = 230, February = 250.
   a. Which is more appropriate, $\alpha = 0.05$ or $\alpha = 0.30$? Why?
   b. Incorporate January and February into the exponentially smoothed average, using equation 1 and the α you selected in part a.
   c. Compute forecasts for March and April based on the data available at the end of February.
   d. They are using these forecasts as a basis for deciding on production quantities. What difficulties do you foresee in using this method in this situation? What should they do to improve the forecasts?

*5. A manufacturer of commercial upholstery sewing machines has decided to implement a new method to forecast demand for its finished products. There are four different models of this product. Spare parts for these machines are their only other products. Their production policy for sewing machines has recently changed from producing only to fill firm orders to producing to fill forecasted orders.

   Orders for one type of sewing machine have been averaging 16 per month with no trend or seasonality. The MAD has been 2.1. The most recent sales figure, since new delivery promises went into effect, was 24.
   a. Compute a forecast for next month using exponential smoothing with no trend and compute the new MAD value. Use $\alpha = 0.3$.
   b. Describe how the company should forecast sales for the upcoming period. First, if they are going to use exponential smoothing, how should they use it? Second, what other information should they collect?

*6. It is the end of February and Joe Schmoe has been working on a forecast for March. There is no seasonal pattern. So far, he has calculated

$$a_{\text{Feb}} = 180 \qquad b_{\text{Feb}} = 3 \qquad \text{MAD}_{\text{Feb}} = 10$$

   using smoothing parameters $R_a = 0.2$ and $R_b = 0.011$, and $\alpha = 0.2$ for MAD.
   a. What is the forecast for March? Put a 95% confidence interval around the forecast.
   b. A month has passed since part a and the March demand turned out to be 200 units. What is the April forecast? The 95% confidence interval?

7. The accompanying table is an excerpt from the records of a company that had been using exponential smoothing for a long time. They are not using seasonal factors.

EXPONENTIAL SMOOTHING CALCULATIONS

t	Deseasonalized Demand	a_t ($R_a = 0.36$)	b_t ($R_b = 0.04$)	$a_t + b_t$	MAD_t ($\alpha = 0.2$)	E_t ($\alpha = 0.2$)
108	555.3	563.8	8.095	571.9	11.26	−8.10
109	558.3	567.0	7.551	574.6	11.73	−9.20
110	571.7	573.5	7.437	581.0	9.96	−8.00

a. In month 109, what was the forecast for month 110?
b. In month 109, what was the forecast for month 112?
c. In month 110, what was the forecast for month 112?
d. Explain why the answer to part c is lower than the answer to part b. (What happened in month 110 that would suggest that the forecast should be revised downward?)
e. It is now the end of month 111. The demand in month 111 was 567.9. What is the forecast for month 112?
f. Put a 95% confidence interval around your answer to part e.
g. Calculate tracking signals for each period from 108 to 111.

8. After a new product is introduced a firm believes that its sales will follow a pattern of the form shown in the accompanying graph. After maturation, the same rate of sales will continue for the foreseeable future. (Eventually sales will drop off, but we do not have to plan for that now.) Since there is uncertainty in sales, the firm must use forecasting techniques. They are concerned first about forecasting during the growth phase of the demand pattern.

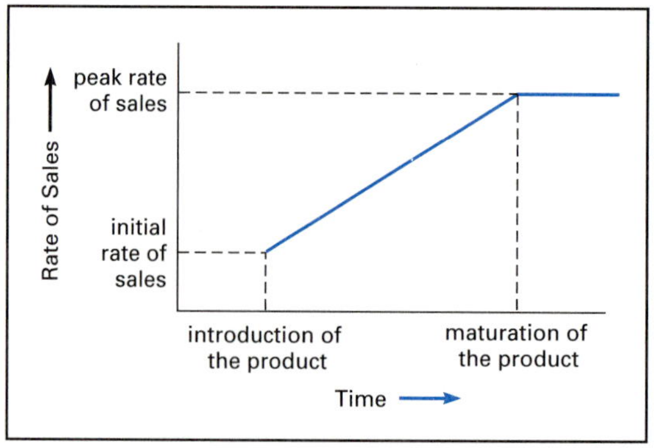

a. The sales manager believes that the slope will be some specific value, say b_0, during introduction and that the maturation point will come in approximately two years. How should she include this in the forecasting system? (Be sure to answer both parts of the question, b_0 and maturation point.)

b. Part way into the introductory period, the exponential-smoothing values are $a_t = 156$ and $b_t = 4$, computed using $R_a = 0.1$ and $R_b = 0.01$. Also, $\text{MAD}_t = 20$ using $\alpha = 0.1$. What is the forecast for the next period's demand?

c. If the next period's demand turns out to be $D_{t+1} = 150$, calculate a_{t+1}, b_{t+1}, and MAD_{t+1}.

*9. The demand for egg agitators has recently changed dramatically. As is shown in the accompanying figure, there has been an upswing in what had been a downward trend in the sales of this nonseasonal item. Using your eyeball (and perhaps a straightedge) you are to determine reasonable values for a_6, and b_6, to be used as initial values for an exponential-smoothing forecasting system

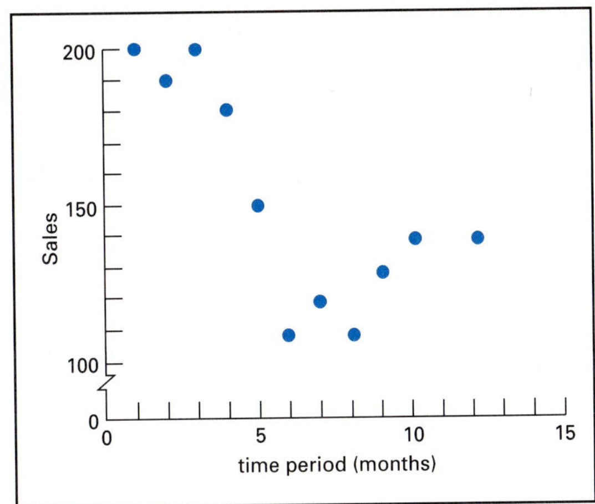

a. Given the data for periods 1 to 6 only (forget that you ever saw the data after period 6), what are reasonable values for b_6 and a_6? Why?

b. Given what you can see from the entire data set, give reasonable values for a_6 and b_6. Explain.

c. If you ignore the data prior to period 7, and wish to exponentially smooth the rest of the data to reinitialize your forecasting system (i.e., calculate a_{12} and b_{12} to use as new data arrive), what values of R_a and R_b would be appropriate? Why?

d. Carry out exponential smoothing for periods 7 to 12, using your answers to parts b and c to get started. Read the sales data from the figure.

10. Southern Barnesville Distribution Company purchases small gift items in bulk, packages them, and sells them to retail stores. They are conducting an inventory-control study of all their items. The following data are for item number IC-42A, which is not seasonal:

Monthly Sales During 1990

Month	1	2	3	4	5	6	7	8	9	10	11	12
Sales	51	55	54	57	50	68	66	59	67	69	75	73

Using linear regression, the forecasting equation "sales $= a + b \cdot t$" was estimated from the foregoing data, with $t = 1$ representing January 1990. Regression results: $a = 48.3$ (intercept), $b = 2.1$ (slope), and MAD $= 2.8$.

a. Based only on these results, calculate forecasts for the first four months of 1991.
b. During January, February, and March of 1991, the firm expects demand to be 10 units higher than normal, as the result of a promotional campaign. Use this information to modify the forecasts in part a.
c. The inventory manager wants to use exponential smoothing, beginning in January 1991, but does not wish to use the 1990 data for initialization. Instead, you have been instructed to calculate initial values from the regression results $a = 48.3$, $b = 2.1$, and MAD $= 2.8$. What values should you use for a_{12}, b_{12}, and MAD_{12} to represent the old values left over from December 1990?
d. At the end of month 13, demand for January 1991 was reported to be 80. Use exponential smoothing to forecast demand for February, March, and April. Be sure to decide how to make allowance for the "extra" demand of 10 units. Use $R_a = 0.1$, $R_b = 0.01$, and your answer from part c for a_{12} and b_{12}.
e. Calculate a confidence interval for the February forecast in part d. Use $\alpha = 0.1$ for MAD. What can you say about confidence intervals for the March and April forecasts in part d?

*11. a. The linear regression formulas for the slope b and the intercept a are

$$b = \frac{\sum x_i y_i - n\bar{x}\bar{y}}{\sum x_i^2 - n\bar{x}^2}$$

$$a = \bar{y} - b\bar{x}$$

Treating time as x and sales as y, compute the coefficients a and b from the data in problem 10 for the Southern Barnesville Distribution Company. (You need not work problem 10 to complete this problem.)

b. Calculate how accurately the regression line "sales $= a + b \cdot t$" fits the data. Do this by computing values for $a + b \cdot t$ for each month and subtracting them from the sales data. Ignoring the signs of these deviations, calculate their average. (That is, calculate the unweighted mean absolute deviation.)

12. Demand for Markov Chains (tire chains for traction on snow and ice) follows a seasonal pattern, which has been quantified by calculating a multiplicative factor for each quarter of the year.

Quarter	Seasonal Factor
First	1.1
Second	0.5
Third	0.4
Fourth	2.0

Demand per year has been growing at a rate of about 15%. Last year, total sales were $5 million.

a. Prepare a numerical forecast for the next eight quarters from the foregoing information. (Do not use regression or exponential smoothing.)

b. If you were going to forecast quarterly sales with exponential smoothing, would a *linear* trend model be appropriate for Markov Chains? Explain briefly.

*13. The following data show a pronounced day-of-week "seasonal" pattern:

	Week 1	Week 2	Week 3	Week 4	Week 5
Sun.	103	95	104	96	105
Mon.	124	118	113	124	116
Tue.	131	125	136	121	137
Wed.	126	118	117	128	118
Thu.	120	115	124	119	127
Fri.	108	96	102	102	106
Sat.	81	74	88	73	85

a. Calculate a seasonal factor for Wednesday.

b. Suggest a method for computing seasonal coefficients that would put greater emphasis on recent data and less on older data.

*14. Two products, frosting mix and cake mix, share the same seasonal pattern but have different trends. We are now at the beginning of September, and the exponential-smoothing calculations have been carried out to include August sales, except for the forecasts themselves.

a. Given the following information, construct forecasts for the next five months.

		Cake Mix		Frosting Mix	
Month	Seasonal Factors	Intercept a_t	Trend b_t	Intercept a_t	Trend b_t
Aug.	0.9	90,000	0	51,000	1,000
Sept.	1.1				
Oct.	1.2				
Nov.	1.4				
Dec.	1.3				
Jan.	0.8				
Feb.	0.7				

b. Compute a forecast for the final quarter (total for three months) of the year, for each product.

c. Time passes. It is now October 1, and September sales were 94,000 cases of cake mix and 58,000 cases of frosting mix. Compute new forecasts for October. Use $R_a = 0.1$ for both products, but $R_b = 0$ for cake and $R_b = 0.01$ for frosting.

d. These two items have the same seasonal pattern. How should this affect the method by which seasonal factors are calculated?

15. For two years, Risky Parts Company has been using an exponentially smoothed forecast, with trend and seasonal factors. They are using smoothing constants of $R_a = 0.05$ and $R_b = 0.05$; they update the slope and intercept terms monthly and the seasonal factors annually.

a. It is now May 1, and the slope and intercept terms have been updated by the forecasting department with the following results. Use this information to forecast demand for May, June, and July.

Forecasting terms, updated to include April's demand:

$$a_t = 178.3 \qquad b_t = 1.2$$

Seasonal factors:

0.90 (April) 0.95 (May) 1.05 (June) 0.85 (July) 1.02 (August)

b. It is now May 31, and May's demand was 205. Use this new information to forecast June, July, and August demands.

c. Risky Parts has not been happy with the performance (accuracy) of this forecasting model. Suggest why poor performance might be expected, given the previous description of the model used.

*16. The following data are the natural logarithms of the number of U.S. automobile registrations (in thousands) for fourteen months beginning in January 1967. Also shown is the Box-Jenkins forecast made in the previous month. Use equation 17 to construct a forecast for March 1968.

Data	6.42	6.29	6.51	6.67	6.71	6.69		
Forecast	6.29	6.56	6.55	6.52	6.60	6.67		
Error	0.13	−0.27	−0.04	0.15	0.11	0.02		
Data	6.62	6.59	6.31	6.57	6.47	6.60	6.49	6.40
Forecast	6.79	6.33	6.60	6.47	6.56	6.33	6.47	6.71
Error	−0.17	0.26	−0.29	0.10	−0.09	0.27	0.02	−0.31

17. This problem shows you what is "exponential" about exponential smoothing, how S_t automatically discounts each data point as it ages, and what effect α has on these matters.

a. Using exponential smoothing without trend, calculate S_t for the following data set. Begin with $S_0 = 100$ and use $\alpha = 0.40$.

Period, t	1	2	3	4	5	6
Data, D_t	100	200	100	100	100	100

b. Graph the data and S_t from part a using a format similar to Figure 7-3.

c. The data have a 100-unit "spike" in period 2. What fraction of that spike was incorporated in S_2? How does that relate to the value of α?

d. Describe the "shape" of the graph of S_t in periods 2 and later.

e. The "gap" between S_t and D_t decreases each period after period 2. How large is the gap in period 3 as a fraction of the gap in period 2? How does that relate to the value of α?

f. Repeat part e but compare period 4's gap to period 3's.

g. Based on your answers to parts e and f, at what rate does exponential smoothing "discount" data as they age? Express your answer as a function of α.

h. Has the 100-unit spike been "forgotten" within N periods, where N is given by equation 2?

18. This problem addresses how long it takes a trend model to "catch up" when the demand level suddenly increases, how long it takes to "forget" initial values, and what the smoothing parameters R_a and R_b really mean.

The following table contains a data set with no randomness; there is a linear trend, but at time 0 there is a permanent increase (i.e., a step) in the level. The table also summarizes the calculations of a_t and b_t for two different values of R_b.

		Brown's Model (R_a = 0.4, R_b = 0.0508)				**Winters' Model (R_a = 0.4, R_b = 0.16)**			
	Data	**Fcst.**	e_t	a_t	b_t	**Fcst.**	e_t	a_t	b_t
−4	80			80.00	10.000			80.00	10.000
−3	90	90.00	0.00	90.00	10.000	90.00	0.00	90.00	10.000
−2	100	100.00	0.00	100.00	10.000	100.00	0.00	100.00	10.000
−1	110	110.00	0.00	110.00	10.000	110.00	0.00	110.00	10.000
0	220	120.00	100.00	160.00	15.081	120.00	100.00	160.00	26.000
1	230	175.08	54.92	197.05	17.871	186.00	44.00	203.60	33.040
2	240	214.92	25.08	224.95	19.145	236.64	3.36	237.98	33.578
3	250	244.10	5.90	246.46	19.445	271.56	−21.56	262.94	30.128
4	260	265.90	−5.90	263.54	19.145	293.06	−33.06	279.84	24.837
5	270	282.69	−12.69	277.61	18.501	304.68	−34.68	290.81	19.289
6	280	296.11	−16.11	289.67	17.682	310.09	−30.09	298.06	14.474
7	290	307.35	−17.35	300.41	16.800	312.53	−22.53	303.52	10.869
8	300	317.21	−17.21	310.33	15.926	314.39	−14.39	308.63	8.567
9	310	326.25	−16.25	319.75	15.100	317.20	−7.20	314.32	7.415
10	320	334.85	−14.85	328.91	14.346	321.73	−1.73	321.04	7.138
11	330	343.26	−13.26	337.95	13.672	328.18	1.82	328.91	7.429
12	340	351.63	−11.63	346.98	13.082	336.34	3.66	337.80	8.015
13	350	360.06	−10.06	356.03	12.571	345.82	4.18	347.49	8.685
14	360	368.61	−8.61	365.16	12.133	356.17	3.83	357.70	9.297
15	370	377.30	−7.30	374.38	11.763	367.00	3.00	368.20	9.776
16	380	386.14	−6.14	383.68	11.451	377.98	2.02	378.79	10.100

a. Which model corresponds to the R_b value recommended in the text? Characterize the difference you would expect in the behavior of these two models, based on their different R_b values. Which should be more responsive? More stable?

b. Plot the data and both forecasts in a graph similar to Figure 7-6.

c. How well have the forecasts ''forgotten'' the prestep data points after N periods, as expressed in equation 9?

d. The data show a 100-unit ''step'' in period 0, as though a new, permanent customer began to buy a constant amount each period. Both models have a 100-unit error in period 0, and a smaller error in period 1. What fraction of the 100-unit step was incorporated in the forecast for period 1? (Answer for each model.) Relate your answer to the values of the smoothing parameters.

19. This problem uses algebra to explain what is ''exponential'' about S_t. Consider the following three equations.

$$S_7 = \alpha D_7 + (1 - \alpha) S_6 \tag{i}$$

$$S_8 = \alpha D_8 + (1 - \alpha) S_7 \tag{ii}$$

$$S_9 = \alpha D_9 + (1 - \alpha) S_8 \tag{iii}$$

a. Solve for S_9 as a function of D_9, D_8, D_7, and S_6. (Hint: substitute [ii] into [iii] and [i] into the result.

b. Given your answer to part a, what ''weights'' do D_9, D_8, and D_7 have in S_9? If you were to continue to substitute older and older terms in part a, what weight would you find for the demand that is n periods old (i.e., the weight for D_{9-n} in S_9)?

c. What weight would S_0 have if you continued substituting?

d. Consider the weights of D_1 and S_0. Which has the larger influence on S_9? What does this say about the importance of initial values? Use $\alpha = 0.2$ to illustrate.

*20. This problem shows that exponential smoothing with trend reduces to simple exponential smoothing if you force b_t to be 0.

a. Show that the following is the same as equation 1:

$$S_t = S_{t-1} + \alpha(D_t - S_{t-1})$$

b. Show that the following is the same as equation 6 if the trend is 0:

$$a_t = a_{t-1} + R_a(D_t - a_{t-1})$$

c. Suppose that $S_{t-1} = 100 = a_{t-1}$ and $\alpha = 0.1 = R_a$. Then use $D_t = 110$ and calculate S_t and a_t using the equations in parts a and b.

*21. In the example of Section 7-4, Tomasco Apple Wines had seasonal factors of 1.053, 0.952, 0.798, and 1.196 for the four quarters of the calendar year. Sales for period 7 was 452.

a. Carry out exponential smoothing on period 7's deseasonalized sales. Use $R_a = 0.25$, $R_b = 0.06$, $a_6 = 551.7$, and $b_6 = 1.52$ to calculate a_7 and b_7.

b. Construct forecasts for periods 8 and 9 based on your answer to part a.

c. In Section 7-4 the forecasts constructed at the end of period 6 were 441.5 for period 7, 663.4 for period 8, and 585.8 for period 9. Why are those forecasts for periods 8 and 9 different from your answer to part b?

22. The accompanying graph shows Tomasco Apple Wines sales, both actual and deseasonalized.

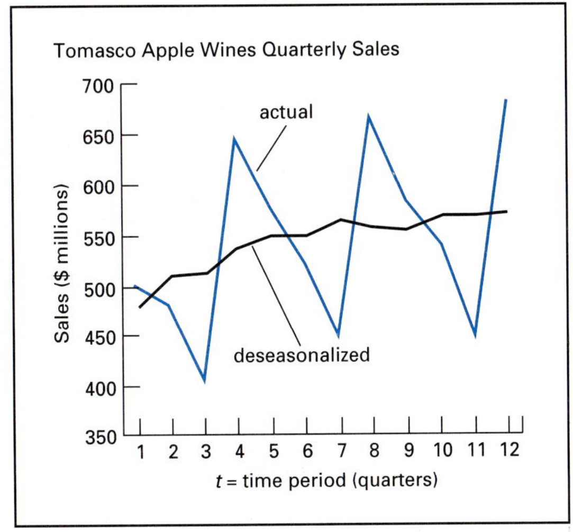

a. Should Tomasco be using a trend model (a_t and b_t) or a no-trend model (S_t) to forecast sales? Why?

The sales data and the seasonal factors for Tomasco Apple Wines are given in Table 7-4. The following parts are most easily done using a spreadsheet program on a computer.

b. Deseasonalize all the sales data. (As a check, you should get 478.6 for period 1, a first quarter.)

c. Beginning with S_0 = the average of the first four deseasonalized data points, calculate S_t for all twelve periods. Use $\alpha = 0.1$. Do your results show any evidence that simple exponential smoothing is the wrong model for Tomasco? Explain. (A graph of deseasonalized sales and S_t for all twelve periods may be useful to you here.)

23. (*Problem 22 should be done first.*) This problem asks you to calculate tracking signals to detect the forecast bias caused by using the wrong model. Two alternative ways of calculating the tracking signal are described after equation 16 in the text. You are asked to try both of them. A spreadsheet computer program will make the changes easy.

a. Calculate the forecast errors for all twelve periods using your model from problem 22, part c. Be sure to offset S_t by one period to show that it is a forecast for D_{t+1}. (Use only deseasonalized data.)

b. Beginning with $MAD_0 = 17.52$ and $E_0 = 0$, calculate MAD_t, E_t and the tracking signal for all twelve periods. Use $\alpha = 0.1$ in equation 13 for MAD and $\alpha = 0.1$ in equation 15 for E_t. What is the earliest time period that the tracking signal detects forecast bias using $n_2 = 0.47$?

c. Change α to 0.05 for MAD and 0.2 for E_t and use $n_2 = 0.83$. Now when does the tracking signal detect the bias?

d. Characterize the difference between parts b and c regarding both MAD and E_t.

24. (*Problem 22 should be done first.*) This problem asks you to initialize a_t and b_t for the deseasonalized sales of Tomasco Apple Wines. A spreadsheet computer program will make the calculations easier. You should use the regression equations given in problem 11 for the initialization.

The accompanying diagram shows the deseasonalized sales data. A strong trend is evident in the first half of the data, but it moderates in the second half. Tomasco wonders how much of the data should be used for initialization. Two options are being considered: initialize over the entire data set or ignore the first four points altogether.

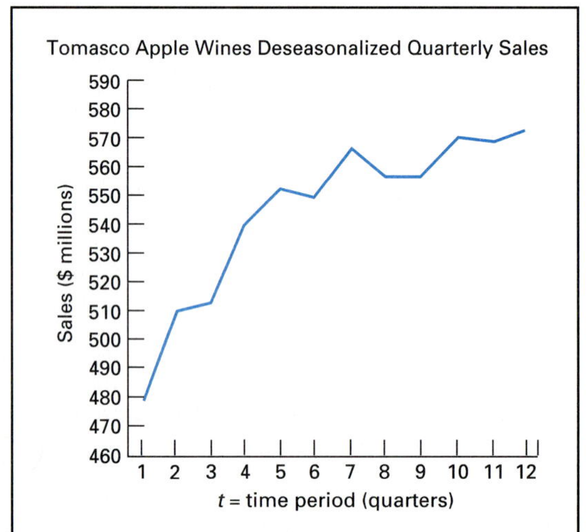

a. Using linear regression for the entire data set, calculate the intercept a and the slope b. Calculate how accurately the regression line "sales = $a + b \cdot t$" fits the data. Do this by computing values for $a + b \cdot t$ for each period and subtracting them from deseasonalized sales. Ignoring the signs of these deviations, calculate their average. (We will use that to initialize MAD.)

b. Using $a_0 = a$, $b_0 = b$, and MAD_0 = the average absolute error from part a, calculate exponentially smoothed forecasts (for lead time $k = 1$, updated after each data point) for the entire data set, and compute a 95% confidence interval for each forecast. Be sure to offset the forecasts and confidence intervals by one period from the actual data. Use $R_a = 0.1$, $R_b = 0.01$, and $\alpha = 0.05$ for MAD. Based on your results, do you think that this would be a good forecast for the periods to come? Explain.

c. Change the forecasting parameters to $R_a = 0.25$, $R_b = 0.0625$, and $\alpha = 0.05$ for MAD. Compare with part b. Which forecast would you recommend? Why?

d. Repeat parts a and b using only the data from periods 5 and later. Compare the results and make a recommendation for Tomasco.

REFERENCES

ARMSTRONG, J.S., "The Ombudsman: Research on Forecasting: A Quarter-Century Review, 1960–1984," *Interfaces*, vol. 16, no. 1, 1986.

BERNSTEIN, P.L., and T.H. SILBERT, "Are Economic Forecasters Worth Listening To?" *Harvard Business Review*, September–October 1984.

BOX, G.E., and G.M. JENKINS, *Time Series Analysis*, San Francisco: Holden-Day, 1970.

BROWN, R.G., *Smoothing, Forecasting and Prediction of Discrete Time Series*, Englewood Cliffs, N.J.: Prentice-Hall, 1963.

CARBONE, R., A. ANDERSEN, Y. CORRIVEAU, and P.P. CORSON, "Comparing for Different Time Series Methods the Value of Technical Expertise, Individualized Analysis, and Judgmental Adjustment," *Management Science*, vol. 29, no. 5, 1983.

FLIEDNER, E.B., B. FLORES, and V.A. MABERT, "Evaluating Adaptive Smoothing Models: Some Guidelines for Implementation," *International Journal of Production Research*, vol. 24, no. 4, 1986.

GARDNER, E.S., JR., "Automatic Monitoring of Forecast Errors," *Journal of Forecasting*, vol. 2, no. 1, 1983.

GARDNER, E.S., JR., "Exponential Smoothing: The State of the Art," *Journal of Forecasting*, vol. 4, no. 1, 1985.

GARDNER, E.S., JR., "Evaluating Forecasting Performance in an Inventory Control System," *Management Science*, vol. 36, no. 4, 1990.

GARDNER, E.S., and E. MCKENZIE, "Forecasting Trends in Time Series," *Management Science*, vol. 31, no. 10, 1985.

GEORGOFF, D.M., and R.G. MURDICK, "Manager's Guide to Forecasting," *Harvard Business Review*, vol. 64, no. 1, 1986.

LAWRENCE, M.J., "An Exploration of Some Practical Issues in the Use of Quantitative Forecasting Models," *Journal of Forecasting*, vol. 2, no. 2, 1983.

MAKRIDAKAS, S., and S.C. WHEELRIGHT, *Forecasting Methods and Applications*, New York: Wiley, 1978.

MCCLAIN, J.O., "Dynamics of Exponential Smoothing with Trend and Seasonal Terms," *Management Science*, vol. 20, no. 9, 1974.

MCCLAIN, J.O., "Restarting a Forecasting System When Demand Suddenly Changes," *Journal of Operations Management*, vol. 2, no. 1, 1981.

MCCLAIN, J.O., "Dominant Tracking Signals," *International Journal of Forecasting*, vol. 4, no. 4, 1988.

MCCLAIN, J.O., and V.R. RAO, "Tradeoffs and Conflicts in Evaluation of Health Systems Alternatives," *Health Services Research*, Spring 1974.

MCCLAIN, J.O., and L.J. THOMAS, "Response Variance Tradeoffs in Adaptive Forecasting," *Operations Research*, vol. 21, no. 2, 1973.

NELSON, C.R., *Applied Time Series Analysis*, San Francisco: Holden-Day, 1973.

TRIGG, D.W., "Monitoring a Forecasting System," *Operational Research Quarterly*, vol. 15, 1964.

TRIGG, D.W., and A.G. LEACH, "Exponential Smoothing with an Adaptive Response Rate," *Operational Research Quarterly*, vol. 18, 1967.

WINTERS, P.R., "Forecasting Sales by Exponentially Weighted Moving Averages," *Management Science*, vol. 6, 1960.

c h a p t e r

8

Inventory Control: Ordering Systems for Independent Demand

"Zero inventory" became a common phrase in the 1980s. Although it may not be an attainable (or even desirable) goal in some processes, it clearly represents a shift in attitude. At a minimum, it serves to emphasize the many bad managerial practices that inventory can be used to conceal. In this and subsequent chapters, we describe some of the beneficial functions of inventory, as well as the costs. As an introduction, it is instructive to consider why people work toward zero inventory.

Inventories held in the United States exceed $650 billion in value (see U.S. Department of Commerce 1987). That is, well over one-half trillion dollars are tied up in goods stockpiled for one reason or another. If even half of these dollars could be freed for investment, a modest return of 10% would yield $32.5 billion annually. It is no wonder that reduction of inventory is sometimes viewed by managers as a potential source of capital.

Companies differ dramatically in their use of inventory. The *turnover rate* is a common measure, being defined as the annual cost of sales divided by the average value of inventory. Inventory turnover provides a measure of how long the average item remains in inventory. As an example of the contrast, Toyota achieves 22 turns per year compared with nine for General Motors (see the annual reports for Toyota and GM). Although the turnover rate can be criticized as a measure, it is clear that such a large difference must reflect greatly differing methods of operation. Indeed, Toyota's just-in-time production system has become a model for study and imitation by other firms. (Methods used in this and other inventory-lean systems are described in Chapters 1, 2, 6, 10, and 12.)

Contrasts such as this lead people to believe that a sizable portion of the huge investment in inventory can be eliminated. Reduction in inventory, however, requires careful analysis of the relevant cost trade-offs. In the automotive example, reducing inventories requires investments in new production techniques, robots, facility layouts, vendor contracts, and even reorganization of work-force management. Even at the micro level, controlling cost is not the same as minimizing inventory. For example, consider the quantity discount. If you have to buy more than immediate requirements to obtain a cost-saving discount, then inventory increases. This and other inventory-related trade-offs are described in this chapter, including methods for controlling the associated costs.

Uses and Abuses of Inventory

Inventory is an important component of virtually every system that produces goods or services. As we saw in the example of the Yuppie Car Wash Company in Chapter 2, there are several types of inventory, each serving a different purpose in the production system. Silver and Peterson (1985) suggest five broad categories that can be used to classify aggregate inventory: cycle stock, safety stock (also referred to as buffer stock), pipeline inventory (including work-in-process inventory), decoupling inventory, and anticipation inventory. (In Chapter 14 we will describe another type: obsolete or dead stock.)

Cycle stock is the inventory occurring throughout the process that results from ordering or producing in batches (or lots). Because of fixed costs associated with ordering or producing a batch, it is often economical to procure more than one item at a time. This results in obtaining more product than is currently needed, and cycle stock results. Later in this chapter we explore optimal order quantities within the context of the various costs affecting the inventory decision.

Since a product's supply and demand are often uncertain, additional inventory is sometimes carried to protect the process from this uncertainty. Such inventory is called *safety (buffer) stock*. Determining appropriate levels of safety stock involves the trading off of costs arising from carrying the buffer inventory against the costs resulting from not being able to meet demand (that is, shortage costs). As we will see in Section 8-5, the establishment of desired service levels is useful in modeling this trade-off.

Pipeline inventory, discussed in Chapter 14, includes work-in-process inventory as well as inventories of goods that are in transit between facilities in a multilocation distribution system. For example, if the distribution system contains factories, warehouses, and retail sales outlets, the quantity of pipeline inventory existing throughout the system on a day-to-day basis can be substantial. Managing this pipeline inventory can be a formidable task, but if done effectively, can result in a sizable cost saving. As we saw in Chapter 2, work-in-process inventory occurs between workstations. It plays an important role in the design and operation of the process in that it allows separate stages of the process greater freedom to operate independently.

Decoupling inventory arises in distribution systems and is part of pipeline inventory. To allow for the decentralized operation of the various facilities constituting the distribution network, inventory is often maintained at each facility. The resulting inventory is called decoupling inventory. A vast distribution system can require large quantities of decoupling inventory. Careful strategic management and planned coordination of this inventory can result in considerable cost savings.

Finally, *anticipation inventory* consists of inventories that are purposely accumulated because of an anticipated supply shortfall or demand increase. If demand for a manufactured product is seasonal, for example, rather than increase production capacity in the periods of peak demand, the manufacturer can elect to follow a level production strategy by taking advantage of excess capacity in periods of low demand and building anticipation inventory that can be used when demand increases. The effectiveness of this strategy depends on the relevant costs and is addressed in detail in the discussion of aggregate production planning in Chapter 9. Anticipation inventory is also used when the availability of necessary supplies or inputs to the production process is seasonal, as well as in the presence of pending supply uncertainty. For instance, if we expect an interruption in supply from a vendor as a result of factors such as a looming labor problem, forecasted bad weather conditions, or an uncertain political or social climate in the country in which the supplier is located, anticipation inventory provides a way of protecting against such uncertainties.

In light of these important categories of inventory, each serving a useful purpose within the production system, it may be puzzling to hear continually that "zero inventory" or "stockless production" is ideal. How can inventory be so "bad" while simultaneously serving such useful purposes? The answer to this critical question is perhaps one of the most important issues facing production systems that seek to achieve a globally competitive position in the world marketplace.

Significant insight into the answer to this key question is gained by highlighting some of the ways in which inventory has been abused by companies (and managers) to conceal ineffective management. Inventory can be used (that is, abused) to hide quality problems in the production process. If quality-related problems arise frequently during production and substantial rework or rejection of product results, the manager can hide the problem by maintaining high levels of work-in-process and finished-goods inventory. Inventory can be used to cover up a multitude of worker-related problems such as absenteeism, turnover, poor training, or drug abuse. Problems with suppliers (such as low quality or reliability) can be camouflaged by inventory. Ineffective, outdated, or improper process design, poor production control, and bad organizational design can also be compensated for (typically at huge expense) by inventory.

These are abuses because they avoid real opportunities for long-run success. Fixing the problems eliminates these ongoing costs, whereas covering them up with inventory adds to the costs. This realization is a fundamental principle behind just-in-time production and total quality management (see Chapters 6 and 12).

Rather than view all inventory as "bad," it is better to recognize fully *both* the uses and abuses of inventory in designing, planning, and controlling the production system. With this awareness, the concepts and tools presented in this chapter constitute an essential component of the operations manager's repertoire.

Independent and Dependent Demand

When there are plans and schedules that are either under your control or known to you for some other reason, the demand for supplies is said to be *dependent* on those plans and schedules. For example, if item A is used exclusively as a component part in product B, the demand for A is directly dependent on the production schedule for B. In this situation the demand can be accurately anticipated in both amount and timing. Material requirements planning (MRP) is appropriate for this kind of situation and is the subject of Chapter 10.

An example of *independent* demand is retail sale of waterproof boots. Demand is highly seasonal for this product, but the quantity needed for any given week or month is not perfectly predictable. Demand arises from many sources, each of which has its own plans or schedules that are unknown to the store manager.

Differentiating between dependent and independent demand is useful, since it suggests a different approach to management of the inventory system. Independent demand requires a statistical forecast, such as the ones described in Chapter 7, whereas dependent demand is estimated by working backward from the known production schedule. The incorrect utilization of independent-demand statistical methods on dependent demand items can result in needless expense because of the levels of safety stocks that are typically maintained for independent demand items.

Sometimes, however, it is practical to use independent-demand models even when (dependent) demand can be calculated from known schedules. For instance, consider an item used in many different products. Its demand arises from a large number of known schedules, requiring a substantial amount of calculation to predict the demand by working backward from the schedule. Because the item has so many different uses, its *overall* demand rate is likely to be moderately steady; therefore, it may be more appropriate to treat the demand as independent and use a statistical forecasting method. This is particularly so when there are likely to be changes in many of the schedules that give rise to the demand.

Independent demand describes only a part of the inventory of a manufacturing firm, but it predominates in service-oriented firms such as hospitals, many distributors, and retailers. This chapter discusses materials management for independent demand.

Functions of the Materials Manager

Materials management is a combination of ordering, receiving, and supply operations. The goal of a material-management system is to make sure that the items are available when and where they are needed, and that the total cost associated with the supply system is kept to a minimum. This requires familiarity with sources of supply, price negotiations, methods of shipment, bulk discounts, budgeting, physical handling and record keeping, and inspection of shipments. In addition, an integrated system is required to coordinate all these functions. The materials manager also relies on established inventory control principles and procedures to achieve the goals of the system.

The study of inventory control requires that we address the following three questions (Silver and Peterson 1985): (1) How often should the status of the inventory be monitored? (2) When should a replenishment order be placed? and (3) How large should each replenishment order be? There are well-known statistical and economic principles that can be applied to inventory control, and it is on these principles that this chapter concentrates.

Inventory control systems can be and are circumvented by employees. ''Unofficial inventory'' is a label given by Rakowski (1981) to quantities that have been issued by a stockroom but have not yet been used. This applies to materials in the nursing supply cabinets of a hospital, or many other analogous circumstances. Knowledge of the quantity and location of these supplies can substantially reduce the need for stock in other locations. The advent of computerized materials-management systems (see Shore 1981, for example) makes multilocation inventory coordination increasingly common.

The reduction and control of costs is an important part of the materials manager's job. However, under normal circumstances, the rate of usage of an inventory item is not under the materials manager's control. Instead, it is dictated by those who use the materials. Among the exceptions to this rule are antiwaste campaigns and standardization efforts (an attempt to eliminate some items by substituting one that is similar and perhaps less expensive). For the most part, however, annual usage will be estimated through some kind of forecasting method. The three costs that directly affect materials management are (1) the cost of holding inventory, (2) the transaction cost associated with placing an order, and (3) the cost of shortages. It is the materials manager's objective to minimize these costs.

Sometimes it is not possible to specify all the costs. For example, shortages may cause bad feelings, which are difficult to measure in dollar terms. We will explore several approaches to this kind of problem and show how the tradeoffs can be presented to management in an informative manner.

8-1 INVENTORY CONTROL: THE A-B-Cs OF INVENTORY

The A-B-C system of inventory classification (sometimes called Pareto analysis) is a useful concept and is still widely used to separate items into groups that are controlled differently. The basis of this scheme is the recognition that the total variable cost associated with inventory control of a given item is primarily a function of its annual dollar volume, $D^{\$}$ (unit price times annual demand). Therefore, the greatest cost reductions may be achieved by concentrating inventory efforts on items with high $D^{\$}$ (category A) while building slack in the system to avoid problems for other items (categories B and C).

The great practical value of this scheme becomes clear by the following observation: If one studies a list of stock-keeping units (SKUs, or item names) and picks off those with the highest $D^{\$}$, by the time the top 20% of the SKUs have been tallied, about 80% of the annual cash outlay will have been accounted for. Thus we have identified category A as the minority of stock-keeping units that account for the majority of cash flow. Similarly, category C, containing items having the lowest $D^{\$}$, comprises about 50% of the SKUs, and they account for only 5% of the sales; B items are the rest.

This phenomenon occurs frequently and was first observed in the eighteenth century by Vilfredo Pareto when he observed that most of the economic wealth was controlled by a relatively small percentage of the population. This concept is thus also known as the Pareto principle. In addition, it is sometimes referred to as the 80-20 rule, even though the 80%-20% combination varies across applications. This concept comes up repeatedly in this chapter. It has also found application in total quality management (discussed in Chapter 6) with the use of Pareto diagrams to improve quality by focusing attention on the "vital few" process characteristics that account for most of the quality problems.

It is often necessary to physically count items stored in inventory. Tax laws require annual (or more frequent) physical counts. In addition, there are often discrepancies between stock on hand and stock on record, and a physical count is needed to set the record straight. Reasons for discrepancies vary from record-keeping errors to theft and spoilage. Efforts to reduce these discrepancies are an important part of inventory control. A physical count can be done all at once or by *cycle counting*, whereby SKUs are counted in an annual sequence to minimize disruptions and smooth the work load. In some instances we may vary the frequency of counts for different items according to their importance in the A-B-C classification, with the A items counted more frequently. *Event-based* cycle counting is a further refinement. If counting is initiated by an event such as the placement of a replenishment order, total work may be reduced, since inventory is typically near its lowest levels when an order is placed.

As was mentioned earlier, turnover rate is a measure of inventory and can be applied both to individual SKUs and to an organization's total inventory. The conventional wisdom is that a high turnover rate is good and a low one is bad. Although it is true that low turns might indicate an excessive amount of stock on hand, one must recognize the trade-off as the turnover rate is increased: shortages may increase, and more frequent handling may be required because of smaller order quantities. Therefore, the turnover rate should be used with caution. Many companies have made management errors because of a mandate to achieve a specific number of inventory turns.

Inventory Control Policies

Two common methods for monitoring inventory status are *periodic review* and *continuous review*. Periodic review involves establishing a fixed period of time for each SKU and then observing the inventory position at the end of each period. Continuous review (also known as perpetual inventory) systems require constant monitoring of inventory positions and, consequently, more record keeping. The *inventory position* is defined as the stock on hand *plus* stock previously ordered from the supplier but not yet received *minus* stock backordered (promised to customers but not yet delivered). We consider the inventory position of an SKU, rather than the amount physically on hand, since it is necessary to keep track of orders that have already been placed, as well as goods that have already been promised.

Periodic review systems are used widely but have several limitations: (1) the lack of positive control between reviews; (2) the need for large safety cushions of extra inventory because of possible surges in demand between reviews; and (3) variability in order quantity, which sometimes precludes the negotiation of certain quantity discounts. Nonetheless, this type of system will continue to be used for some items because it avoids the increased cost of constant monitoring and reporting that are required by continuous review. It also offers the convenience of coordinating orders from the same supplier by establishing common review periods for SKUs supplied by that vendor.

The record-keeping disadvantage of continuous-review inventory systems has been addressed in some firms by attaching machine-readable tags to items as they are received. Then with the brush of an electronic pen, or the flash of a laser, the inventory tally is made automatically when the item is withdrawn. An example of this kind of system is the laser bar-code readers found in many supermarkets. Such a system can be programmed to produce a purchase order, addressed to the appropriate supplier, when the reorder point is reached.

A commonly used periodic review system involves placing an order at the end of every review period,[1] ordering enough to increase the inventory posi-

[1]Another version of this system does not necessarily place an order each period. Instead, an order is placed at the end of each review period only if the inventory position has dropped to or below a specified reorder level. Once the reorder level is reached, the quantity ordered is sufficient to restore the inventory position to its original level. The advantage of this system is the elimination of small orders.

tion to a level that will satisfy demand until the *next* order arrives. Thus, the inventory position must cover demand for one period plus an allowance for shipping time.

In the most common continuous-review inventory control system, each withdrawal of an SKU from inventory is recorded, and the resulting inventory position is checked against a reorder level R. A new order is triggered whenever the inventory position falls to or below R. In contrast with the periodic review policy, the order is for a fixed amount Q, alleviating the variability in order quantity mentioned previously. Sometimes referred to as a (Q, R) inventory system, this policy gives continuous protection against demand variation. For example, surges in demand automatically trigger the order sooner by drawing inventory below the reorder point.

Standing-order systems offer an alternative to the inventory control systems just discussed. Rosenshine and Obec (1976) describe a scheme in which a contract with a supplier guarantees delivery of an order of fixed size on a regular schedule. This eliminates the portion of the transaction costs attributable to placing orders. More important, an annual contract gives more leverage to negotiate for discounts and preferential treatment in promptness of delivery. This approach is consistent with the concept of just-in-time purchasing (see, for example, Grieco, et al. 1988, as well as Chapter 12).

Two new costs are introduced by standing orders. Since the delivery schedule and the order quantity are fixed, it is necessary to establish a special method to protect against running short when demand is unexpectedly high. Rosenshine and Obec's model assumes that shortfalls are handled by placing an emergency order (at extra cost) when inventory drops below a prespecified level. The second new cost is incurred if the long-range forecast turns out to be too high, resulting in an oversupply. The contractual nature of the deliveries specifies that a penalty will be incurred when unused items are returned. Alternatively, the excess supply can be sold, presumably at a net loss. Consequently, a standing order is likely to be preferable when usage is highly predictable, so that these emergency measures need not be used very often.

Standing orders do not eliminate the need for monitoring inventory levels. Indeed, both emergency orders and item returns are triggered by unanticipated changes in the amount of stock. Either periodic or continuous review of inventories may be used.

Information Requirements and Cost Trade-offs

Inventory control requires more than just knowing the current inventory position. We have already mentioned the need for information on suppliers, discounts, and so on. Effective inventory control also requires (1) demand forecasts, (2) knowledge of the reorder *lead time* (time required from the moment an order is placed until it is delivered and ready for use), and (3) accurate measures of the three basic costs (holding, transaction, and shortage). Forecasting methods such as those discussed in Chapter 7 are included in most of the various commercially available inventory control computer programs. Reorder lead time will be discussed later, in conjunction with safety stocks. The costs must be carefully defined, as we will now discuss.

Inventory holding costs accrue from several sources. Most significant is the opportunity cost of capital invested in the inventory. This is usually specified as a required rate of return on investment (sometimes called a *hurdle rate*) and serves to assure that capital is put to its best use throughout an organization.

In addition, there are costs of storage, including operation and depreciation (or rental) of the warehouse, taxes, insurance, obsolescence, breakage, pilferage, and any special costs such as refrigeration. This is summed up in the symbol C_I which is the annual holding cost per unit of inventory. This differs across items, owing primarily to differing unit price. Although it is not strictly correct to do so, inventory holding cost is often expressed as a percentage of the per unit purchase price of an item, resulting in what we shall term F_I (fractional holding cost). That is, F_I equals C_I divided by unit price. Since holding cost is usually between 10% and 40% of purchase price, F_I is usually between 0.10 and 0.40. Opportunity cost is usually the primary component.

Inventory can be viewed as a hedge against inflation; that is, capital invested in inventory may hold its worth when the value of the dollar drops. To account for this an estimate of the annual rate of inflation should be *subtracted* from the cost of capital in computing C_I. In economic terms, we should use the real cost of capital, corrected for inflation of the cost of the items. (This adjustment is explained in Bierman and Thomas 1977.)

In estimating C_I, it is important to follow the principles of *fixed* versus *avoidable* costs. For example, much of the cost of owning and operating a warehouse is fixed, unaffected by the quantity of inventory. However, if inventory is growing, C_I must eventually reflect part of these fixed costs, or else inventory, being underpriced, will grow until a new warehouse cannot be avoided. The manager must be careful to exclude any costs that will be fixed no matter what inventory level is chosen.

Holding cost is often overstated because firms include fixed costs and use a hurdle rate that is too high. The hurdle rate should be close to the borrowing rate less inflation. On the other hand, obsolescence rates can be quite high, particularly in high-technology industries. The obsolescence rate is a function of the size of the inventory and is, therefore, not constant, but a constant rate is used as a matter of practicality.

A similar principle applies to C_T, *the cost associated with the transaction of a single replenishment order, independent of the order quantity*. This includes avoidable costs such as paperwork in ordering and receiving the item, but does not include costs that are a function of the annual volume of usage. For example, the cost of attaching machine-readable tags to each item should not be included in C_T because changing the frequency of replenishment transactions will not change the number of tags per year. In a manufacturing setting, C_T is also referred to as the *setup cost*, denoted C_S, since it is incurred each time we set up to make a production run. The notation C_T and C_S can be used interchangeably; whenever possible, we will limit the use of C_S to applications involving a physical process setup.

The cost of a transaction depends in part on the technology employed. Computer-assisted ordering, for example, may substantially affect the cost. It is important to be able to allocate avoidable costs of administrative use of a computer as part of C_T. On the other hand, if labor is a fixed cost over the entire possible range for number of orders, labor cost should not be included in the analysis.

Shortage costs (or *stockout costs*) are more difficult to measure. If estimated at all, they are often subjective, that is, guesswork. (This issue will be discussed more thoroughly in the section concerning safety stock.) The cost of a shortage occurs when an item is needed but unavailable (out of stock). There are two common responses: The item may be *backordered* (delivery promised as soon as possible, perhaps at the cost of a rush order), or the request may be canceled (which may represent a *lost sale*, with a corresponding opportunity cost). The symbol used is C_B, *which refers to the per-unit cost associated with either backordering an item when it is not in stock or losing the sale.*[2] In the literature on inventory control, there are two ways to specify this cost. Some models assume that the shortage cost is proportional to the duration of the shortage. In this chapter, however, the other view is taken: C_B does not include a time factor. It denotes a one-time cost accrued at the time of the shortage and assumes that the duration of the shortage is irrelevant. These two approaches can give very different results. (Refer to Chapter 14 and texts such as Silver and Peterson 1985 for the development of models with time-weighted backorder cost).

Inventory control is achieved by a trade-off of these costs. For example, as we increase the order quantity, Q, the quantity of cycle stock increases, and hence, the cost of holding this cycle stock increases. On the other hand, a larger Q decreases the frequency of replenishment orders, so that the transaction cost is reduced. A similar trade-off occurs between inventory and shortage costs as the reorder level, R, is changed. The next section explores these trade-offs in detail and examines just how the A-B-C classification scheme is useful in cost control.

REVIEW PROBLEMS

1. A fixed order quantity, Q, is commonly used in both continuous-review (perpetual) and standing-order inventory systems. Why do standing-order systems require special measures not normally encountered under continuous review?

2. Why are better prices often available for standing orders?

3. In the A-B-C classification, explain how it is possible for category C to constitute as much as 50% of the items, yet only 5% of annual dollar volume.

4. A manager computed the fractional holding cost as $F_I = 0.25$ (or 25%) per dollar invested in inventory per year. However, the annual rate of inflation was 5% and was not factored in. What adjustment should be made to F_I?

Solutions

1. The continuous review system is self-adjusting. If demand slows down, new orders are automatically delayed, since inventory falls more slowly toward the reorder level R. In contrast, a standing order would continue to build inventory until some special action is taken to change the contract. A similar argument applies if demand increases.

2. A smooth delivery schedule is easier for the vendor.

3. Each category C item has a small annual dollar volume, attributable either to low price or to low usage (or both). Most organizations have a wide variety of such items in stock.

4. F_I should be reduced by the inflation rate; thus, $F_I = 0.20$.

[2]Theoretically, the economics of lost sales is modeled differently from that of backordered demand. However, for the purposes of this text we will treat them the same.

8-2 THE ECONOMIC ORDER QUANTITY

One of the oldest (Harris 1913) methods of scientific inventory control, the *economic order quantity* (*EOQ*), has endured because of its ability to balance some major costs and to be very flexible and adaptable for many situations. The EOQ is the major focus of this chapter, not only because of its wide use but also because the relatively simple analysis brings out the nature of the trade-offs that must be faced in any inventory system. (See Erlenkotter 1990 for a discussion of the early history of the EOQ Model.)

All the important terms and formulas used in the following discussion (as well as in Sections 8-3 and 8-5) have been collected in Table 8-1 for handy reference. The reader may wish to attach a paper clip to this page, as the table will be used many times.

The key aspects of the EOQ system are shown in Figure 8-1. The EOQ system assumes continuous review of the inventory position and a constant average rate of demand. The decision variables are Q (the number of units ordered) and R (the reorder level). Inventory is controlled by placing a replenishment order of size Q whenever the inventory position drops to or below R units. This leads to the sawtooth pattern exhibited in the figure.

When to Order?

Since the reorder level, R, is the inventory position at the time at which we order more material from the vendor, it must satisfy the demand that will occur during the lead time, LT, while we are waiting for the shipment to arrive. Conceptually, R has two components: $\overline{U}$, which is the average quantity that will be used or demanded during the average lead time; and SS (safety stock), which is the extra quantity needed to protect against the possibility of higher-than-average demand or longer-than-average lead time. This is illustrated in Figure 8-1. The vertical axis shows these two components of the reorder level. The first two shipments shown in the figure were received after part of the safety stock had been used; U_1 and U_2 were both greater than average. Since the third shipment had a short lead time, less demand (U_3) occurred during LT_3, and inventory was still above the safety-stock level when the shipment arrived.

Setting R involves a trade-off between the cost of inventory and the quality of service, as measured by the likelihood of shortage. That is, increasing the reorder level increases the safety stock, and that means more inventory and a lower probability of running short. Practical methods of setting safety-stock levels are described in Sections 8-5 and 8-6.

How Much to Order?

The EOQ model assumes that a fixed quantity, Q, is ordered each time an order is placed. Study of Figure 8-1 reveals that the safety stock (SS) is the average low point of inventory.[3] The high point is Q units higher, resulting in an average inventory of SS + $Q/2$, for an average annual cost of $(C_I)(\text{SS} + Q/2)$. This equation shows that inventory cost may be reduced by ordering in small quantities, since the cycle stock, $Q/2$, is changed proportionally. How-

[3]There are R units on hand when the procurement order is placed, and $\overline{U}$ units are used (on the average) by the time the shipment arrives. The remaining inventory therefore averages $R - \overline{U}$, which is the safety stock.

Table 8-1 Symbols and Formulas for Inventory Control[a,b]

I. Inventory Quantities

D = annual[c] usage (demand in units per year)

$D^\$$ = annual[c] dollar volume (\$ per year) = (unit price) · (D)

d = daily usage (demand)

U = usage during replenishment order lead time

LT = length of the lead time (lag until order is actually received)

n = number of replenishment orders placed each year[c] for an item

Q = quantity of each order = D/n

$Q^\$$ = dollar value of the order = (unit price) · (Q)

R = reorder level, or quantity on hand when an order is placed

SS = safety stock to protect against stockout in case of unexpected increase in lead-time usage, U. By definition, $SS = R - \overline{U}$

P = probability of running out of stock before Q arrives (per reorder cycle)

SO/yr = average number of times per year[c] that inventory reaches zero (a stockout condition). By definition, SO/yr = nP

II. Per-Unit Costs

C_I = annual[c] cost of holding 1 unit in inventory. Cost of capital, insurance, obsolescence, storage, etc.

F_I = fractional holding cost = C_I divided by the unit purchase price of the item

C_T = transaction cost for each replenishment order placed and received; this includes paperwork and handling but excludes the cost of the item

C_B = backorder cost, incurred each time an item is needed but out of stock (as noted in the text, this may be the opportunity cost of a lost sale)

III. Economic Order Quantity Formulas

TVC = total annual[c] variable cost

A. Order Quantity (Sections 8-2 and 8-3)

$$\text{TVC} = C_IQ/2 + C_TD/Q + C_ISS = F_ID^\$/2n + C_Tn + C_ISS \quad (1)$$

$$Q^* = \sqrt{2DC_T/C_I} = D/n^* \quad (2)$$

$$n^* = \sqrt{C_ID/2C_T} = D/Q^* = \sqrt{(F_I/2C_T)(D^\$)} \quad (3)$$

B. Statistics of Lead-Time Demand (Section 8-5)

$\overline{U} = \overline{d}\,\overline{\text{LT}}$, where $\overline{U}$ denotes the average of U (4)

$$\text{Var } U = (\text{Var } d)(\overline{\text{LT}}) + (\text{Var LT})(\overline{d})^2 \quad (5)$$

$$\sigma_u = \sqrt{\text{Var } U} \quad (6)$$

C. Safety Stock When Backorder Costs Are Unknown

P^* = (desired SO/yr)/n (7)

z = value from normal table to achieve P^* (8)

$SS^* = z\sigma_u$ (9)

$R^* = \overline{U} + SS^*$ (10)

Implied backorder cost (Section 8-5)

C_B (implied) = C_I/(desired SO/yr) (11)

D. Safety Stock When Backorder Costs are Known

Optimal SO/yr = C_I/C_B (12)

P^* = (optimal SO/yr)/n (13)

R^* = same as equations 8, 9, and 10 (14)

E. Stockout Protection When a Reorder Level Is Prespecified

SS(actual) = $R - \overline{U}$ (15)

z(actual) = SS(actual)/σ_u (16)

P(actual) = value from normal table given z(actual) (17)

SO/yr(actual) = nP(actual) (18)

[a] Equations 8 and 16 assume that demand has a normal probability distribution.

[b] An asterisk indicates the optimal value. Thus, Q^* is the optimal order quantity, and n^* is the number of orders placed annually if Q^* is the order quantity.

[c] One year is used as the measure of time in this table. Any other period could be used (e.g., 1 week), but the *same* time period must be used for D, C_I, F_I, n, SO, and TVC.

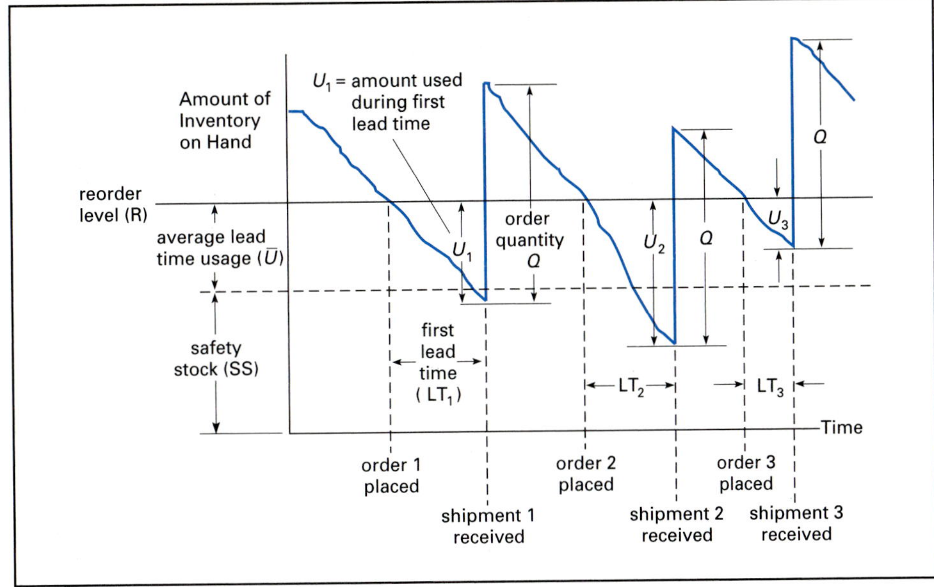

Figure 8-1 Level of Inventory through Time in a Continuous Review (Perpetual) System, with Replenishment Order Quantity Q and Reorder Level R

ever, ordering in small quantities necessitates more frequent order transactions to keep up with demand (usage). The annual number of orders placed, n, must satisfy the annual demand, D; therefore, $n = D/Q$, and the annual transaction cost is nC_T or $(C_T)(D/Q)$. A company that reduces its order quantities will therefore suffer increased transaction costs.

The economic order quantity determines the best trade-off between holding and transaction costs. By the preceding discussion, the *total variable cost* (*TVC*) is the annual cost of holding inventory plus the annual transaction cost (equation 1 in Table 8-1). The economic order quantity, Q^*, is the cost that minimizes TVC and can be found by calculus.[4] Observe that Q^* has a square-root relationship with annual demand (equation 2 in Table 8-1). For example, if demand for an item were to double, one would increase the order quantity but not double it.[5] Accordingly, to keep up with demand, the order frequency

[4]The formula for the total variable cost in Section III of Table 8-1 is

$$\text{TVC} = \frac{C_I Q}{2} + \frac{C_T D}{Q} + C_I \text{SS}$$

Taking the first derivative,

$$\frac{\partial \text{TVC}}{\partial Q} = \frac{C_I}{2} + C_T D\left(-\frac{1}{Q^2}\right) + 0$$

Setting the first derivative equal to 0 and solving for Q^*, we obtain

$$Q^* = \sqrt{\frac{2DC_T}{C_I}}$$

The second derivative is greater than 0, so Q^* is the minimum cost value of Q.

[5]If demand goes up by a factor of 2 (100%), the EOQ formula indicates that the order quantity should increase by a factor of $\sqrt{2}$ (only 41.4%). Therefore, since the order size does not fully reflect the increased demand, orders must be placed more frequently.

(n) must also increase. Therefore, inventory and transaction costs remain in balance, both having increased somewhat.

It is instructive to contrast the EOQ to another order quantity rule, "days of supply." In this rule, a common target value of t days of supply is used for a group of items, and the rule is applied by setting Q = (daily demand rate) times (t). With this rule, order quantity is directly proportional to demand, in contrast to the EOQ's square-root relationship. Therefore, a days-of-supply system does not minimize holding plus transaction cost. Nevertheless, it is widely used for other reasons. For example, coordination of orders can be accomplished by such a rule, and this can lead to quantity discounts. (This is pursued further in Section 8-4.)

REVIEW PROBLEMS

1. Demand for widgets occurs at an absolutely constant rate totaling $D = 10{,}000$ units per year. No safety stock is kept. $C_I = \$5$ per unit per year, and $C_T = \$9.25$ per order. Evaluate the cost of the current policy of ordering batches of 1000 units, and compare it with the optimal policy.

2. How important is it to follow the optimal policy precisely? For example, what happens to TVC if Q is 50% above or below the EOQ in review problem 1?

Solutions

1. From equation 1 in Table 8-1,

$$\begin{aligned}\text{TVC} &= \frac{C_I Q}{2} + \frac{C_T D}{Q} + C_I\text{SS} \\ &= (5)(500) + (9.25)(10) + 0 = \$2593 \text{ per year}\end{aligned}$$

From equation 2 each order should be for

$$Q^* = \sqrt{\frac{2DC_T}{C_I}} = \sqrt{37{,}000} = 192.4, \text{ or } 192 \text{ units}$$

Using equation 1, the optimal cost is TVC = \$962 per year. Thus, using the optimal ordering policy should save about 63% of inventory-related costs.

2. Try $Q = 288$ and $Q = 96$ in equation 1. The result is TVC = \$1041 and TVC = \$1204, which are different from the optimum by only 8% and 25%, respectively.

8-3 USING EOQ WITH ROUGH COST ESTIMATES

Example: Podunk Hospital Revisited

Podunk Hospital orders supplies from many different distributors. Order quantities have been determined with very little thought to cost trade-offs. Table 8-2 shows current policy for a random sample of items from Podunk's inventory. For now assume that Podunk does not maintain safety stock for these items.

Table 8-2 Summary of Ordering Policy for a Sample of Podunk's Inventory

Item	Current Order Quantity	Annual Usage	Price	Annual Dollar Volume
A	500	1,000	$30	$30,000
B	30	360	5	1,800
C	72	432	50	21,600
D	10,000	5,000	0.42	2,100
E	600	1,800	3	5,400
			Total	$60,900

The hospital administrator has read about inventory control several times in recent journals. Those sources suggested that annual holding costs for hospital supplies are generally between 15% and 30% of the unit cost of an item, attributable mainly to the opportunity cost of capital.

An investigation to determine the transaction cost met with some difficulty. Careful study pointed out that the major portion of the costs was salaries, but the allocation of the salaries among the many functions performed by the personnel was, at best, a guess. The transaction cost was estimated to be somewhere between $1 and $10 per order placed.

QUESTION 1: *Can we do anything at all, given such rough cost estimates?*
Analysis: Perform the analysis with midrange values for the costs. Then do a sensitivity analysis. Use F_I = 20% and C_T = $3.50 initially. Table 8-3 summarizes the results.
Sensitivity Analysis: The suggested new policy (Q^*) cuts gross average inventory cost from $12,375 to $1413 by increasing orders per year from 23.5 to 82.1. Since the number of orders was increased and the inventory decreased, we can make the new policy look its worst (relative to the old policy) by using the lowest estimate of inventory cost (15%) and the highest transaction cost ($10). That would change the result to TVC(Q^*)

Table 8-3 Variable Cost Using Podunk's EOQ and Current Q

		Costs Using Q^*				Costs Using Old Q			
Item	Q^*		(Price) × ($Q^*/2$)		$D/Q^* = n^*$		(Price) × ($Q/2$)		$D/Q = n$
A	34		$ 510		29.4		$ 7,500		2
B	50		125		7.2		75		12
C	17		425		25.4		1,800		6
D	645		135.5		7.7		2,100		0.5
E	145		217.5		12.4		900		3
Totals			$1,413		82.1		$12,375		23.5
Multiplied by:		F_I =	0.20	C_T =	$3.50	F_I =	0.20	C_T =	$3.50
Costs			$282.6		$287.4		$2,475		$82.3
TVC			$570				$2,557		

= (0.15)(1413) + (10)(82.1) = \$1033, compared with \$2091 for the present policy.

Conclusion: If F_I = 20% and C_T = \$3.50 are correct, total annual variable cost (associated with order quantities) may be reduced by about 75% (from \$2557 to \$570) for this random sample of items. More important, the saving is still 50% even if these cost estimates are incorrect in the worst possible way.

QUESTION 2: Switching to Q^* would more than triple the number of orders per year, according to the preceding analysis. This may not be feasible over the next few years, because it would require a large staff increase in the ordering and receiving departments. *Can we achieve any saving without increasing the annual number of orders placed?*

Analysis: Adjust all the Q^* values upward until n drops to its original value of 23.5 per year for the sample. (This method is discussed in Plossl 1985.) Table 8-3 shows that n^* totals 82.1 using Q^*, whereas n totals 23.5 for the current order quantities. Since 82.1/23.5 = 3.49, we multiply all Q^* by 3.49. The new Q values will be denoted by Q^+ and are shown in Table 8-4.

Conclusion: The Q^+ policy costs \$1068.80 compared with \$2257 for the current policy, a saving of 53%. Q^+ accomplishes this without changing the work load in the ordering department.

QUESTION 3: *What happens if we round off the order quantities to make more natural order sizes?*

Analysis: There are many ways this could be done. As an illustration, consider the following set of order quantities, all of which are within 20% of Q^*: A =30, B = 50, C = 20, D = 600, E = 150. You may show that TVC = \$574, a trivial difference.

Conclusions on the Use of the EOQ

The preceding example illustrates several important points about the economic order quantity. Perhaps most striking is the success of the Q^+ policy, which appears to be an arbitrary modification of the EOQ. It is instructive to compare the last two columns in Table 8-4 to the "old Q" portion of Table 8-3. Major differences occur in items A and B. Q^+ achieves its saving by reducing

Table 8-4 Variable Costs Using Podunk's Q^+

Item	$Q^+ = 3.49Q^*$		(Price) × (Q^+/2)		$D/Q^+ = n^+$
A	119		\$1,785		8.4
B	175		437.5		2.1
C	59		1,475		7.3
D	2,253		473.1		2.2
E	507		760.5		3.6
Totals			\$4,931		23.6
Multiplied by:		F_I =	0.2	C_T =	\$3.50
Costs			\$ 986.2		\$82.6
TVC			\$1,068.8		

the order quantity of item A, which has by far the greatest cycle stock ($7500). A smaller order quantity means more frequent orders; thus, item A's transactions increase from 2 to 8.4 per year. Item B has only $75 tied up in cycle stock and is ordered 12 times per year under the old policy. Q^+ increases B's cycle stock at very little cost and achieves a reduction in annual transactions from 12 to 2.1. This offsets the increase in item A's transaction cost.

In short, the Q^+ policy is efficient because it breaks up the demand for high-dollar-volume items into very frequent orders, and does the opposite for low-dollar-volume items. This property is shared by the EOQ. Therefore, the idea of multiplying all EOQ values by a constant is not as arbitrary as it first appears. In fact, it is the most efficient method for achieving a target for annual transactions (as in the example) or a target for cycle stock. (A review problem and problem 27 pursue this point further.)

The following notes summarize the conclusions from the example.

Robustness. The EOQ formula gets you in the right ball park, even with shaky cost estimates. Within that ballpark, deviations of up to 20% in order quantities will cause only small penalties, owing to the fact that marginal transaction and holding costs are balanced at Q^*. Figure 8-2 summarizes how TVC varies as the order quantity changes; it shows that oversized orders are a less serious error than ordering too few.

Annual Dollar Volume. According to the A-B-C idea, $D^\$$ is the key to costs, and therefore to cost reduction. Table 8-5 illustrates that the Q^* and Q^+ policies explored in the example share the following property: The annual ordering frequency (n), the dollar value of the order ($Q^\$$), and the cost (TVC) are all highest for items of high annual dollar volume.

Practicality. Even if EOQ cannot be used directly, a straightforward modification of the EOQ can significantly reduce costs without imposing major changes on the current system. The Q^+ method is an example. Other practical modifications can be made. Several are described in the next section, and other versions of the Q^+ modification are considered in the problems at the end of the chapter.

The robustness property is the principal factor contributing to the importance and longevity of the EOQ model, and it is what makes this material worth studying even though the assumptions underlying EOQ are almost never totally realistic. For example, demand rates are often random and may vary seasonally. Or in the other extreme, demand may be totally predictable but lumpy (rather than uniform) over time. The latter is often faced when the supplies are to be used in a scheduled production process. (This will be considered exten-

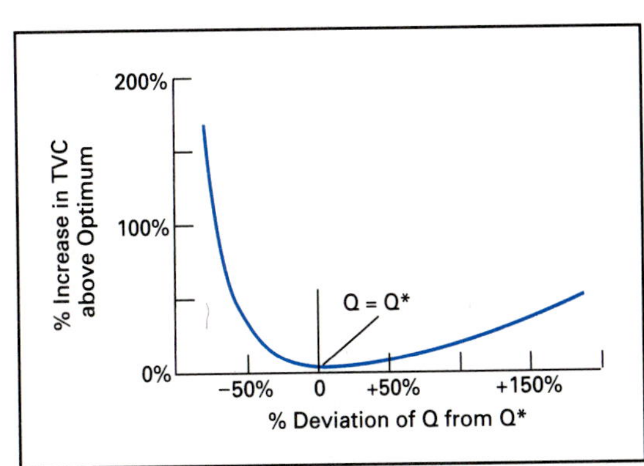

Figure 8-2 Total Variable Cost (TVC) Expressed as a Deviation from the Optimal Value

Table 8-5 Relationship Between $D^{\$}$ and Optimal Ordering Policy

Item	Annual Dollar Volume ($D^{\$}$)	n^*	$Q^{\$*}$	TVC	n^+	$Q^{\$+}$	TVC$^+$
A	\$30,000	29.4	\$1,020	\$205	8.4	\$3,570	\$386
C	21,600	25.4	850	173	7.3	2,950	321
E	5,400	12.4	435	87	3.6	1,521	165
D	2,100	7.7	271	54	2.2	946	102
B	1,800	7.2	250	50	2.1	875	95

sively in Chapters 10 and 11, where it will be seen that EOQ still plays an important role.)

Keying on annual dollar volume is the basis of the A-B-C analysis discussed earlier. We have now seen that A items will be ordered more frequently than others, which is part of the additional effort we are willing to undertake to keep these items under tight control.

Finally, the EOQ has fallen into bad repute because of the way in which it has been misused. Just-in-time or zero inventory is advocated. The value of EOQ in a zero-inventory world is discussed in Section 8-4.

REVIEW PROBLEMS

1. Are the potential savings for Podunk Hospital due to reduced inventory or fewer transactions? How do you know? What is the implication for personnel?

2. The last inventory count revealed that Podunk had \$12 million tied up in supplies. Of this, \$8 million was estimated to be cycle stock and the rest safety stock. If the EOQ policy were implemented in the entire supply system, what would the dollar value of inventory be? State your assumptions.

3. Suppose that Podunk wanted to achieve a reduction of 70% in the cash tied up in cycle stock. Describe a method of modifying the EOQ values to achieve this goal.

Solutions

1. The analysis in Table 8-3 showed that, if the optimal quantities (Q^*) were used, inventory would drop in dollar value from \$12,375 to \$1413, and annual transactions would increase from 23.5 to 82.1. This change would require substantial increases in the work load of those involved in ordering and receiving. The modified policy (Q^+) achieved its savings from inventory alone.

2. Using Q^*, the dollar value of cycle stock would be only 11.4% of its current value in the sample of five items. If the sample is representative and if the latest inventory count is accurate and representative of the usual situation, we could expect cycle stock to drop from \$8 million to \$0.9 million. Using

20% as the holding cost, the annual cost of inventory would drop by $1.42 million. (We have assumed that safety stock remains constant.)

3. Target cycle stock = 30% of $12,375 = $3712.50. The EOQ has a cycle stock of $1413; therefore, multiply each EOQ by 3712.5/1413 = 2.627. This will achieve 82.1/2.627 = 31.2 transactions per year.

8-4 ADAPTING EOQ TO FIT THE REAL SITUATION

Quantity Discounts

If lower prices are offered for buying an item in larger quantities than the EOQ, a simple analysis will determine whether it is worthwhile to order a larger quantity. By systematically calculating the increase in TVC due to ordering the minimum-cost quantity within each price range and then adjusting for the annual saving due to the discount, we can determine the optimal quantity to be ordered.

The vendor of Podunk's item A offers an ''*all-units*'' discount: unit price is $32 if you buy fewer than 100; for order quantities of 100 to 499, each unit purchased costs $31; the price of each unit is $30 for order quantities $Q \geq 500$. Assuming that $F_I = 0.20$ and $C_T = \$3.50$, what is the best order quantity?

The pricing structure is equivalent to three different TVC curves, one for each price. Table 8-6 shows three different Q^* values; they differ because the holding cost depends on the unit price (that is, $C_I = F_I \cdot$ unit price). However, in two of the price ranges the EOQ values are infeasible. In range 3, the best you can do is to order 500, because 500 is as close to 34.2 as you can get at this price, and the TVC increases steadily for any quantity above $Q^* = 34.2$. Similarly, the best quantity in price range 2 is 100. However, in range 1, ordering $Q^* = 33$ is best, since that quantity minimizes TVC and is in the range within which $32 applies.

Thus, there are three candidate values for the optimal Q^*: 33, 100, and 500. To decide which of these candidates is best, we must take into account both the TVC and how much would be saved by the discount. Table 8-7 summarizes all the costs, assuming that Podunk carries a safety stock of 100 units of this item. The safety stock is included in the calculation, since the change in price affects the holding cost of safety stock as well as cycle stock (see Aucamp 1981).

Thus, the optimal order quantity under this quantity discount is 100 units, which achieves the minimum total annual cost of $31,965. Notice how we must take into account the cost saving from the discount as well as the change in

Table 8-6 EOQ and Best Feasible Quantity in Each Price Range

Range	Unit Price	Order Quantity	$C_I = F_I \cdot$ Price	EOQ (Q_i^*)	Best Feasible Quantity (Q_i)
1	$32	$0 \leq Q < 100$	$6.4	33.1 → 33	33
2	31	$100 \leq Q < 500$	6.2	33.6 → 34	100
3	30	$500 \leq Q$	6	34.2 → 34	500

Table 8-7 Calculation of Total Annual Cost for Each Price Range

Range	Feasible Q_i	C_I	$C_IQ_i/2$	C_TD/Q_i	C_ISS	TVC	Annual Purchase Cost	Total Annual Cost
1	33	$6.4	$ 105.6	$106.06	$640	$ 851.66	$32,000	$32,851.66
2	100	6.2	310	35	620	965	31,000	31,965
3	500	6	1,500	7	600	2,107	30,000	32,107

Annual Purchase Cost = (purchase price)(annual demand)
= ($32)(1000) for Price Range 1
= ($31)(1000) for Price Range 2
= ($30)(1000) for Price Range 3

TVC. For this example, the annual saving from taking advantage of the discount in the third price range is not sufficient to offset the accompanying increase in TVC.

This is sometimes referred to as an all-units discount because once the size of the order exceeds the break point for a price range, the discount applies to all units purchased. If Podunk Hospital's discount had applied only to the additional items above the break point, it would be called an *incremental discount*. Then the first ninety-nine items would cost $32 each, regardless of how large the total purchase is. In this case there is no incentive to order "just enough" to obtain the discount, in strong contrast with the situation described previously. The potential saving is much smaller in this case, and the computations are more complicated (see Johnson and Montgomery 1974).

Announced Price Increases

The price of Podunk's item B is $5 (see Table 8-2), but it is about to increase by $1, permanently. How much more than the EOQ should we order? Each unit added to the order will incur inventory holding cost until it is eventually used. If we order Q units, the last one will be used $t = Q/D$ years from now; thus, the holding cost of the last item used is $(C_I)(t) = C_IQ/D$. The main saving on that last item is $1 by avoiding the price increase. (Some reduction in the number of replenishments is also achieved, but it is usually a small saving.) Should we have bought that last unit? Or should Q have been smaller? The marginal costs and benefits of the last unit will offset each other if $\$1 = C_IQ/D$; thus, the optimal one-time order quantity is $Q = (\$1)(D/C_I)$. Since the order will be placed at the $5 price, $C_I = (0.2)(5) = \$1$, and $Q = (1)(360/1) = 360$ units, compared with an EOQ of 50 under the old price and 46 under the new price. The result, stated in general terms, is

$$Q = (\$\text{ price increase})\left(\frac{D}{C_I}\right) \text{ or current EOQ (whichever is larger)} \quad (19)$$

This simple formula is quite different from the EOQ and is included here both to increase your arsenal of handy tools and to show clearly that a permanent price change is different from a constantly available quantity discount. (A complete, more complicated analysis is given in Love 1979.)

Multi-Item Orders

Often, many items are supplied by the same vendor. For items that are ordered with similar frequency, it may be beneficial to combine them on one order. The savings that accrue include a smaller transaction cost per item (placing three items on one order takes less time than writing three separate orders) and possibly a quantity discount based on the dollar value of the order. One difficulty that arises is that the items may not necessarily hit their reorder levels simultaneously, which results in excess inventory for those that are ordered prematurely.

A simple method for determining joint order quantities is to conceptually combine all the items into a single entity and compute its optimal ordering frequency, n^*. The correct method is to add together the annual dollar volumes ($D^\$$) and use the square-root formula for n^* (see Table 8-1, equation 3). For example, Podunk Hospital's items B and D have annual demands of 360 and 5000 and prices of \$5 and \$0.42, respectively (Table 8-2). If they are ordered jointly the annual cash outlay is $D^\$ = \$1800 + \$2100 = \$3900$. Suppose that ordering two items instead of one only adds \$0.50 to the \$3.50 transaction cost. Then $C_T = \$4$, and using $F_I = 0.2$, we obtain

$$n^* = \sqrt{\left(\frac{F_I}{2C_T}\right)D^\$}$$

$$= \sqrt{\left(\frac{0.2}{8}\right)(3900)} = 9.9$$

Using $n^* = 9.9$, we can compute

$$Q = \frac{D}{n^*} = \frac{360}{9.9} = 36 \quad \text{for item B}$$

$$= \frac{5000}{9.9} = 505 \quad \text{for item D}$$

Excluding safety stock, the total variable cost for joint ordering (derived from equation 1 in Table 8-1) is

$$\text{TVC} = \frac{F_I D^\$}{2n} + C_T n = \$79 \quad \text{(excluding safety stock)}$$

Compared with the TVC of \$50 for B and \$54 for D when ordered separately (Table 8-3), this is a saving of \$25 per year.

In dollar terms, the joint order quantity is (\$5)(36) = \$180 for B and (\$0.42)(505) = \$212 for D, for a total of \$392 per order. If a (dollar-valued) quantity discount also exists, the analysis should proceed in a manner similar to that described in the earlier discussion. That is, consider increasing the size of the order to achieve the discount, and compare the increases in TVC with the discount saving.

EOQ and Zero Inventory

The recent emphasis on zero inventory has caused some production and inventory control researchers and practitioners to question the appropriateness of the EOQ model. The basis of this concern arises from the observation that low inventory levels (''zero inventory'') have been extremely beneficial in many instances, but the EOQ model may not advocate the small order quantities that would be required to support such inventory levels. Because of these seemingly contradictory observations, some specialists have gone so far as to assert that the EOQ model is no longer valid and recommend that its use be discontinued.

The key to understanding this apparent contradiction lies in understanding the assumptions and limits of the basic EOQ model. Recall that in addition to other parameters, the EOQ model assumes that the transaction cost per order (C_T) is given. However, the classic EOQ formula (equation 2 in Table 8-1) shows that one way to reduce the order quantity (and hence, cycle stock; and therefore move toward zero inventory) is to reduce C_T.

Recognizing this, Porteus (1985b) generalized the EOQ model by broadening the decision-making framework so that it considers the optimal transaction cost as well as determines the optimal order quantity. In this setting it can be seen that reduced inventory is consistent with optimal EOQ policy.

Assuming that transaction, or as in the case of the Porteus (1985b) model, manufacturing setup cost can be reduced through investment in relevant technology such as new equipment or procedures, let $a(C_T)$ be the investment required to reduce transaction cost to C_T. For example, suppose that it currently costs \$100 each time an order is placed, but that the computer package used by the ordering department can be upgraded at a one-time cost of \$200,[6] resulting in a 10% reduction in C_T. Further, assume that an additional 10% improvement in C_T can be accomplished by an additional \$200 investment. Then $a(100) = 0$, $a(90) = \$200$, $a(81) = \$400$. and so on. The *total annual cost with setup reduction* (TCS), including the inventory and transaction costs and the opportunity cost of the investment in reducing C_T, is

$$\text{TCS}(C_T, Q) = ia(C_T) + C_I Q/2 + C_T D/Q$$

in which i is the annual opportunity cost of capital. Note that the last two terms are the same as TVC in equation 1 (with SS = 0), whereas the first term converts the one-time investment into an equivalent annual cost.

Porteus discusses a number of ways to proceed, all of which require assumptions about the opportunities and costs of reducing C_T. We will illustrate by continuing with the example. To find the best solution, we can compute Q^* for each of the different possible values of C_T and choose the alternative with the lowest value of TCS. Table 8-8 shows the evaluation of three alternatives. Note that Q^* differs because the alternatives have different transaction

[6]Presumably this technology would be used for a large number of items. The following analysis would include the TVCs of all relevant items. For simplicity of calculation, we are using only one item and a fairly low cost of improvement.

Table 8-8 Calculation of TCS for Three Investment Alternatives

Investment ($a(C_T)$)	C_T	Q^*	TCS
0	100	158	1264.91
200	90	150	1230.00
400	81	142	1198.42

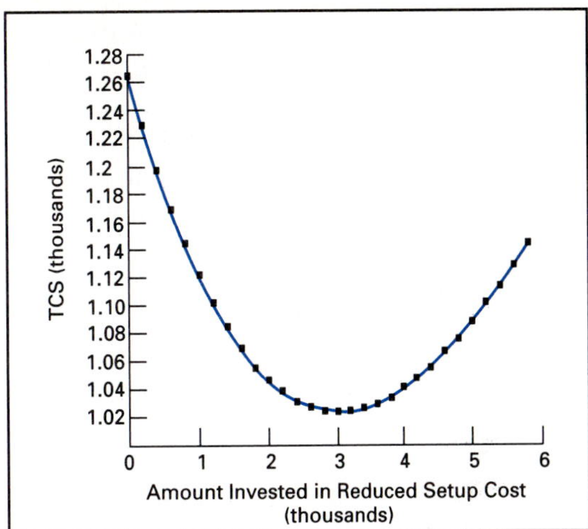

Figure 8-3 EOQ Model with Investment in Reduced Replenishment Costs

costs. We have used C_I = \$8 per year holding cost, D = 1000 units demanded per year, and i = 0.15 per year cost of capital.

As expected, Q^* decreases as the transaction cost decreases. Also, in this example the total cost decreases despite the increasing cost of investment. Therefore, this company should invest in lowering C_T because the cost of the investment is more than offset by the saving in inventory and transaction costs.

Figure 8-3 shows what happens if this analysis is continued. Eventually the cost begins to increase, so that additional investment is no longer justified. The optimal investment is \$3000, and that corresponds to a transaction cost of \$20.59. (Problem 18 continues this analysis.)

The EOQ is consistent with current trends toward zero inventory if reducing C_T is included in the analysis. In Chapters 11 and 12 this idea is discussed in the context of manufacturing. By approaching the problem in a broader setting, we gain considerable insight into those situations in which inventory reduction (toward zero) is appropriate. It is also clear that there is a limit beyond which additional reduction is impractical unless more effective technology becomes available. (For other articles dealing with optimal C_T reduction see Porteus 1986, which also incorporates quality improvement, and Zangwill 1987.)

REVIEW PROBLEMS

1. When items B and D are jointly ordered, a quantity discount of 5% is available if the order size is \$1000 or more. Should the order be increased to \$1000 to obtain the reduced price?

2. In the previous example on EOQ and zero inventory, verify the calculations for an investment of \$400 in reducing C_T.

Solutions

1. If the order size is \$1000 instead of \$392, the order quantities are multiplied by 1000/392 = 2.551, and the transaction frequency is divided by the same number. Therefore, the average inventory is \$1000/2 = \$500, representing a cost of (0.2)(\$500) = \$100 per year. There are 3.9 transactions per year at C_T

= \$4 each, so that $n \cdot C_T$ = \$15.6. Therefore, the total variable cost is TVC = \$100 + \$15.6 = \$115.6. Compared with \$79, which was the TVC at n^*, this is an increase of \$36.6 per year. The annual saving from the discount is 5% of the \$3900 total annual dollar volume, or \$195. If we include SS in the calculation, the saving would be even greater with the discount; in this instance, it is certainly worthwhile to increase the size of the order to realize the saving.

2. In the example, \$400 buys two 10% reductions; therefore, $C_T = (0.9)(0.9)(100) = 81$. Equation 2 gives $Q^* = \sqrt{2(1000)(81)/8} = 142$; then TCS = 0.15(400) + 8(142)/2 + 81(1000)/142 = \$1198.42.

8-5 Safety Stock

The economic order quantity is useful in a variety of situations. However, the discussion so far has made no reference to the possibility of running short of stock. This issue will now be addressed through the use of safety stock.[7]

There are two difficult issues with respect to safety stock. The first is, What is the optimal level of protection? or, stated another way, How often will we tolerate running out of stock? This is a theoretical issue, based on the trade-off between holding costs and shortages. The second is, What reorder level should we set to achieve this theoretically optimal protection? This is a practical question and is handled through statistics. Because the discussion of each of these issues is complex, they are considered one at a time, beginning with the practical one.

Practical Methods for Setting Safety Stock

In this section we must assume that a criterion has been set for an acceptable quality of service. One way to do this is to determine an acceptable average number of stockouts[8] per year (SO/yr). This criterion is often specified through management intuition; a cost analysis will be discussed later. The goal is to find the appropriate reorder level R, one that achieves the target value of SO/yr. This problem focuses on the lead time (LT), its variability, and the demand that occurs during the lead time.

Lead time begins when the inventory position descends to R and ends when the resulting shipment arrives on the shelves, ready for use. Numerous opportunities for delay arise during the lead time. The critical events are

1. It is discovered that inventory is at or below R.
2. An order is placed.
3. The supplier receives the order.
4. The supplier fills the order.
5. The supplier ships the order.

[7]Strictly speaking, when shortages are included in the analysis, the EOQ should be reexamined, since larger Q means less frequent ordering and therefore fewer times per year when inventory is near the stockout level. However, because of the robustness of EOQ, the resulting increase in the optimal order quantity usually has negligible effects on total cost. Johnson and Montgomery (1974) describe an algorithm that allows for this effect.

[8]A stockout is an occasion when (on-hand) inventory reaches zero. Any demands that occur during a stockout are called shortages. That is, during one stockout, if, for example, seven units are demanded, there are seven shortages.

6. The shipment is received.
7. The stock is on the shelf.

Control of these events often pays handsome dividends, since unreliability in any of these stages translates directly into the need for extra safety stock.

The word *unreliability* deserves special emphasis. Variability in lead time is expensive. To see why, consider suppliers X and Y, each of whom averages 5 weeks delivery time. Supplier X always delivers in exactly 5 weeks, but Y randomly varies from 4 to 6 weeks. To avoid shortages, we need at least 6 weeks' supplies on hand when we place an order with Y, of which 0 to 2 weeks' supply will still be on hand when the order arrives. If X is our supplier, inventory can be reduced by 1 weeks' supply, on the average. As discussed in Chapters 6 and 12, reduction in process variability is a critical component of total quality management and just-in-time production.

Even if lead time does not vary, there is still a need for safety stock, because of fluctuations in the rate at which supplies are used. Suppose that the usage of an item is between 60 and 80 per working day, averaging 70. Then if we use supplier X, lead time is 5 weeks, the average lead time usage ($\overline{U}$) is (5 weeks)(5 days per week)(70 units per day) = 1750 units. To this we must add safety stock, in case there are more high-usage days than low-usage days during the lead time. (Safety stock is discussed further presently.) This discussion is encapsulated in the following formula (equation 8 in Table 8-1):

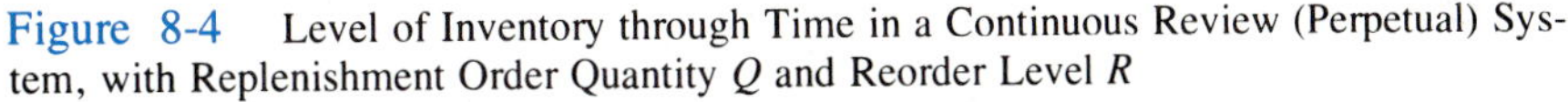

$$\text{Reorder level} = \text{average lead-time demand} + \text{safety stock}$$

$$R = \overline{U} + SS$$

A few details from Figure 8-4 will help to fix this relationship firmly in mind. The term $\overline{U}$ is the average depletion of inventory during lead time. (In

Figure 8-4 Level of Inventory through Time in a Continuous Review (Perpetual) System, with Replenishment Order Quantity Q and Reorder Level R

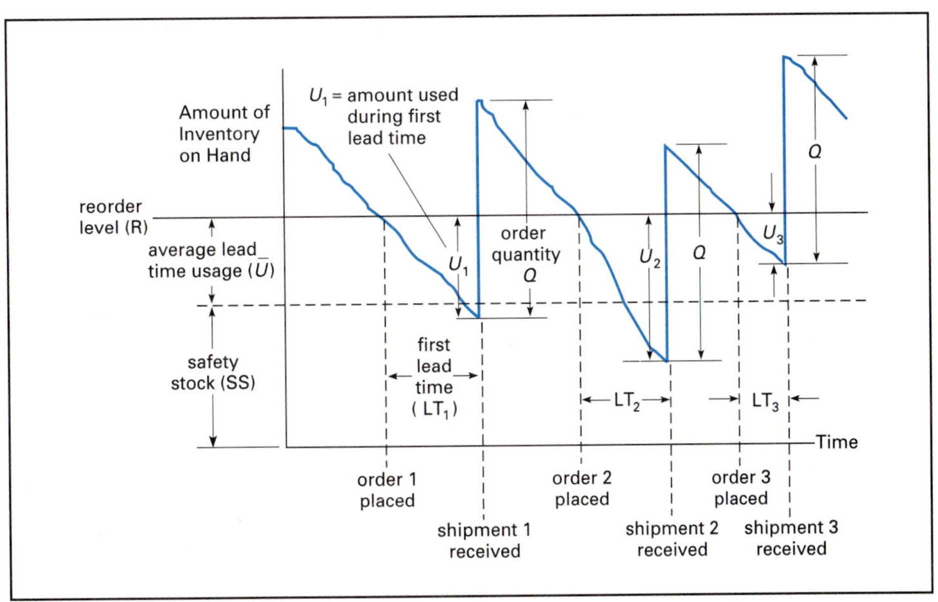

Figure 8-4, U_1, U_2, and U_3 represent actual depletion during the three lead times shown in the figure.) The safety stock is an excess built into R, to protect against heavy depletion (such as during lead time 2 in the figure) arising from an unexpectedly long lead time or an unusually heavy usage rate.

The *worst-case method* is to set the reorder point equal to the largest lead-time demand ever experienced for the item in question. If an item has never stocked out, a quick saving may be attained by scanning the inventory records, finding the *lowest* inventory level over the past few years, and reducing the reorder level by that amount. (Caution and judgment must be used, as always, when basing your decision on data that are several years old. There may have been changes in usage, suppliers, or even in safety stock.) If data on lead time demand (U) are available, the worst-case method would set R equal to the largest U encountered in the relevant history.

The *nth worst-case method* applies if a criterion has been specified for an acceptable number of stockouts per year (SO/yr). Suppose that we have data on 30 reorder cycles spanning 6 years, and the criterion was to allow one stockout every 2 years. Then the reorder level should be set somewhere between the third and fourth largest lead-time demands encountered over the 6 years. (That would have resulted in three stockouts in 6 years, equaling one in 2 years.)

Theoretical distributions are often useful, especially if only limited relevant information is available on lead-time demand. We present, for your toolbox, two formulas (equation 4 and 5 from Table 8-1) that will be used shortly in an example.

$$\overline{U} = \bar{d}\,\overline{\text{LT}} \tag{4}$$

$$\text{Var } U = (\text{Var } d)(\overline{\text{LT}}) + (\text{Var LT})(\bar{d})^2 \tag{5}$$

As before, U refers to lead-time demand, LT to lead time (working days), and d to daily demand. Var is the statistical variance, which is the square of the standard deviation.

The first formula is easily understood: Average lead-time demand is the product of average demand rate and average lead time. The second formula takes us back to our earlier discussion of unreliability in lead time. If Var(d) (the variance of daily demand) is not zero, the daily demand is not always the same. Similarly, Var(LT) measures the unreliability of lead time. The formula shows that both these uncertainties combine to give the variance in lead-time demand, Var (U), against which the safety stock is to protect.

These formulas are important because they help one estimate the two components of the reorder level R. In particular, *safety stock (SS) is directly proportional to the standard deviation of lead-time demand* (σ_u). That is,

$$\sigma_u = \sqrt{\text{Var } U}$$

and

$$\text{SS} = z\sigma_u$$

in which z is a constant of proportionality, to be defined presently. Therefore, the formula that relates the reorder level R to lead-time demand is

$$R = \overline{U} + z\sigma_u$$

which is equation 10 in Table 8-1.

The *normal probability distribution* is sometimes used as an approximation for the probability distribution of lead-time demand. When this is done, the constant z is taken from the normal tables (Table 2, Appendix D). The value is chosen to achieve a prespecified service-level criterion (see the following example).

Poisson and *exponential* are two other probability distributions that are sometimes used in inventory control. Carlson (1982) combines these two distributions for items with short and variable lead times and derives simple formulas for order quantities and safety stocks. Regardless of the probability distribution, one cardinal rule is to test the resulting reorder levels carefully, against old data if possible, and in actual use. It is not too difficult to determine, for example, whether stockouts are occurring more often than planned if one observes the performance over many items.

Example: Safety Stock

Podunk Hospital is changing suppliers for item G, which has a per-unit holding cost of C_I = \$1 per year. They plan to continue ordering it four times per year, and have specified a target service level of one stockout every 3 years (SO/yr = 0.33). The history of reorder lead times (based on Podunk's experience on other items purchased from this new supplier) is shown in Table 8-9. A similar table (not included here) compiled daily demands during the last 6 months. From that table, it was calculated that $\bar{d}$ = 40 units per day, and Var(d) = 30 (units/day)^2.

QUESTION: *What is the appropriate reorder level, R?*

Analysis: Referring to equations 4 through 10 in Table 8-1, we see that the average and the variance of lead time are needed. They are calculated as follows:

$$\overline{\text{LT}} = \frac{7 + 12 + 25 + 16 + 14 + 15}{6} = 14.83 \text{ days}$$

$$\text{Var(LT)} = \frac{(7 - 14.83)^2 + (12 - 14.83)^2 + \cdots + (15 - 14.83)^2}{6 - 1}$$

$$= 34.97 \text{ (days)}^2$$

These numbers, with $\bar{d}$ and Var(d) (given previously), are substituted in equations 4 to 10 as follows:

$$\bar{U} = (40)(14.83) = 593.3 \text{ units demanded per lead time} \quad (4)$$

$$\text{Var}(U) = (30)(14.83) + (34.97)(40)^2 = 56{,}397 \quad (5)$$

$$\sigma_u = \sqrt{56{,}397} = 237.5 \text{ units per lead time} \quad (6)$$

$$\text{Desired SO/yr} = 0.33 \text{ (as stated previously)}$$

$$\text{Order cycles/year} = 4 \text{ (given)} = n$$

$$P^* = \text{desired probability of stockout per order cycle}$$

$$= \frac{\text{SO/yr}}{n} = \frac{0.33}{4} = 0.083 \quad (7)$$

Table 8-9 Lead Times for Similar Items Obtained From This Supplier

Order placed (date):	1/7	2/3	3/16	4/6	5/2	6/2
Order received:	1/18	2/21	4/20	4/28	5/20	6/23
Lead times						
Calendar days	11	18	35	22	18	21
Working days	7	12	25	16	14	15

From Table 2, Appendix D, $P = 0.083$ corresponds to $z = 1.39$ (8)

$$SS^* = (1.39)(237.5) = 330.1 \quad (9)$$

$$R^* = 593.3 + 330.1 = 923.4 \quad (10)$$

Conclusion: Assuming that these data are representative of what we can expect in the future, orders should be placed whenever inventory drops to 923 units of item G. This allows for the average usage of 593 units, plus a safety stock of 330. Using $R = 923$, Podunk will experience approximately one stockout every 3 years, which was the target they specified.

Sensitivity Analysis: Should we be concerned with the unreliability of lead time in this case? Suppose that Var(LT) could (somehow) be eliminated. Repeating the calculations, safety stock is only 29 units, compared with 330 previously. The reorder level is reduced from 923 to 622; therefore, the inventory is lowered by 301 units, on the average. Because C_I is \$1 for this item, the annual saving is \$301. In addition, we would presumably reap a similar saving for the other items ordered from this supplier. Consequently, it may be worthwhile to expend some effort to improve the reliability of lead time.

Optimal Stockout Frequency and Implied Backorder Costs

Most safety-stock decisions are based on a more or less arbitrary level of protection. (One stockout every 3 years in the preceding example is a case in point.) The following analysis shows how to minimize cost by considering the cost and saving of a one-unit change in the reorder level.

Suppose that we considered reducing the reorder level by one unit for a given item. *What will it save?* Referring to Figure 8-4, if R is lowered, the entire graph moves down, indicating a lower average inventory. The saving is therefore C_I dollars per year from each one-unit reduction in R. *What will it cost?* The answer depends on the number of times per year we are out of stock (SO/yr). Each time we were out of stock last year, if R had been lower we would have had greater shortages. Thus, lowering R by one unit will cost us one more unit of shortage for each out-of-stock condition; hence, the average cost per year is

$$(1 \text{ shortage}) \cdot (\text{average SO/yr}) \cdot (\text{cost per item short, } C_B)$$

If the cost is less than the saving, we should reduce R. If the cost exceeds the saving, R should be higher. Therefore, at the optimal R, the cost of a marginal change should equal the saving, or

$$(\text{SO/yr})(C_B) = C_I$$

From the previous analysis (rearranging the last equation) the reorder level R should be set in such a way that the average annual number of stockouts is numerically equal to C_I/C_B, or

$$\text{Optimal SO/yr} = \frac{C_I}{C_B}$$

(This is equation 12 in Table 8-1.)

To apply this result to Podunk Hospital, suppose that the shortage cost for item G is estimated to be $C_B = \$10$ per unit, because of the expediting required to procure the item if it is needed when out of stock. As before, $C_I = \$1$, $\overline{U} = 593.3$ units demanded during lead time, $\sigma_u = 237.5$, and $n = 4$ replenishment orders per year.

QUESTION 1: *What is the optimal reorder level R?*

Analysis: $C_I/C_B = \$1/\$10 = 0.10$, so the optimal reorder policy should average one-tenth stockout per year (10 years between stockouts). The service level specified in the preceding example was one stockout in 3 years, which is too frequent according to this analysis. (Refer to Table 8-1 for the following equations.) The reorder-level calculations are

$$\text{Optimal SO/yr} = \frac{C_I}{C_B} = \frac{\$1}{\$10} = 0.10 \tag{12}$$

$$P^* = \frac{\text{SO/yr}}{n} = \frac{0.10}{4} = 0.025 \tag{13}$$

$$\left\{\begin{array}{l} z = 1.96 \quad \text{(from the normal probability table, for } P = 0.025) \\ R^* = 593.3 + (1.96)(237.5) = 593.3 + 465.5 = 1058.8 \end{array}\right\} \tag{14}$$

Conclusion: The optimal reorder level is 1059. This is 132 units higher than the reorder level calculated earlier, based on the value 0.33 SO/yr, specified subjectively by management.

QUESTION 2: The inventory manager is adamant, claiming that it is a waste of money and storage space to increase R above 926, which was the level that achieved one stockout per 3 years. *Can this dispute be mediated?*

Analysis: Knowing that $C_I = \$1$, suppose that we assume that the optimal SO/yr is 0.33, as the manager is insisting. What value of C_B is implied? Solve equation 12 for C_B:

$$\text{SO/yr} = \frac{C_I}{C_B}$$

$$0.33 = \frac{\$1}{C_B}$$

$$C_B = \frac{\$1}{0.33} = \$3$$

or in general terms,

$$\text{Implied } C_B = \frac{C_I}{\text{desired SO/yr}}$$

Conclusion: The dispute comes down to the correct valuation of a shortage. Unless C_B is substantially lower that \$10, the inventory manager is wrong; that is, allowing 0.33 stockout per year is optimal only if $C_B = \$3$. However, perhaps the manager has some less expensive method of dealing with shortages. The argument can be resolved by finding out whether \$10 or \$3 more realistically represents all the tangible and intangible costs of being short of item G by one unit.[9]

---

[9] A caveat: The method just described for setting the optimal safety stock is an approximation. Porteus (1985a) describes situations in which significantly better results can be obtained using more complex models. In general, the equations developed here are useful when the backorder cost (C_B) is high relative to the inventory cost. We assumed that inventory status is monitored continuously and that orders can be placed at any time. However, if these events take place only once per week, or once per month, serious errors can be incurred by using this model. Porteus (1985a) gives examples of several models that are designed for periodic-review inventory control and compares their effectiveness.

Safety Stock and A-B-C

The A-B-C concept is applicable to safety stock as follows: high-dollar-volume items need more safety stock, in absolute terms, than low-dollar-volume items. This can be seen by reviewing the equations in Table 8-1. Specifically, high-dollar-volume ($D^\$$) items are ordered most frequently (high n^*, equation 3), but a high n^* necessitates a low stockout probability per cycle (low P^*, equations 7 and 13) to keep the frequency of stockouts at its optimal annual level. This, in turn, requires extra safety stock. This conclusion confirms the idea that effort spent on controlling lead time, or anything else to make possible lower safety stock, should be concentrated on the A items. This will yield the biggest saving for the effort.

A practical concern that Podunk Hospital must face has often been expressed in the question, Should a lifesaving item ever be considered a C item? The answer is definitely yes, if it has a low annual dollar volume. A lifesaving C item may achieve stockout protection at very little cost through increased safety stock. Of course, some lifesaving items may have high $D^\$$ and therefore belong in category A. In that case more elaborate methods of avoiding shortages may be employed to cut down on the safety stock. This could be done through a sharing agreement with another hospital or a hot line to the supplier, for example.

As with order quantities, the largest safety-stock-related costs are incurred with high-dollar-volume items. We have studied two approaches to controlling these costs: statistics and economics. The statistical method begins with management's specification of a reasonable number of stockouts per year, and sets a reorder level through the analysis of average lead times and demands and their variability. The economic analysis can supply an optimal level for the stockout criterion if an accurate value of backorder cost is available. When backorder cost is not well defined, one may ascertain whether management's target stockout level is in the right ball park by calculating the backorder cost *implied* by the current policy.

REVIEW PROBLEMS

1. Safety stocks protect against two aspects of variability, either of which can cause shortages. What are they? Give two examples of possible causes for each.

2. A manager has decided that once in five years is a reasonable target for the frequency of stockouts for each item maintained in inventory. Information on three items for which this manager is responsible is as follows:

Item	Annual Demand	Order Quantity	$\bar{U}$	σ_u
X	5000	2500	1000	30
Y	4000	2100	800	28
Z	300	300	60	10

a. How long (what part of a year) will one order of item X last, given the rate of demand? Also answer for Y and Z. How many times per year will each of these items be ordered, on the average?

b. What target should this company use for the stockout probability for one reorder cycle, given their annual stockout goal and your answer to part a?

c. Use Table 2, Appendix D, to find z values for each of the three products, and then calculate the reorder levels that will achieve the company's annual stockout target for each item.

d. If all these items have unit prices of $10, does the A-B-C concept seem to apply? That is, do high-$D^{\$}$ items have more safety stock and more frequent orders?

Solutions

1. *Variability of Lead Time:* This can be caused by delays or changes in any of the seven critical events listed at the beginning of this section. For example, a supplier backlog in filling orders could increase the time required to process the order. Shipment could be delayed because of a truck breakdown. *Variability of Demand:* This also has a variety of causes. Customer sales are typically random. Internal usage of the item may also be difficult to predict.

2. a. 2500 units will last half of a year. For Y, 2100/4000 = 0.525 year. Each order of Z is a 1-year supply. For X, n = 5000/2500 = 2 orders per year; for Y, n = 1.9, and for Z, n = 1.

   b. Since X is ordered twice per year, it has 10 reorder cycles in 5 years, so this item should experience 1 stockout per 10 cycles or $P^* = 0.1$ to meet the criterion. In a similar manner, we can calculate $P^* = 0.105$ for Y, and $P^* = 0.2$ for Z.

   c.

Item	P^*	z	$\overline{U}$	σ_u	R
X	0.1	1.282	1000	30	1038.5
Y	0.105	1.25	800	28	835.0
Z	0.2	0.84	60	10	68.4

   d. Yes. SS (measured in dollars) is $385 for X, $350 for Y, and $84 for Z; the n values are 2, 1.9, and 1.0 per year, respectively.

8-6 OTHER INVENTORY CONTROL SYSTEMS

The periodic review system was briefly described earlier in this chapter. The key variables are T, the *review period* (fixed time between reviews of inventory records), and TI, the *target inventory level* on which orders are based. Figure 8-5 summarizes the operation of a *forced-ordering* periodic review system, so called because an order *must* be placed at the end of each review period. Each review period is exactly T days long; at the end of this period, an order is placed for a quantity sufficient to replenish inventory to the target level, TI. After the reorder lead time (LT), the shipment arrives and goes into inventory. The order

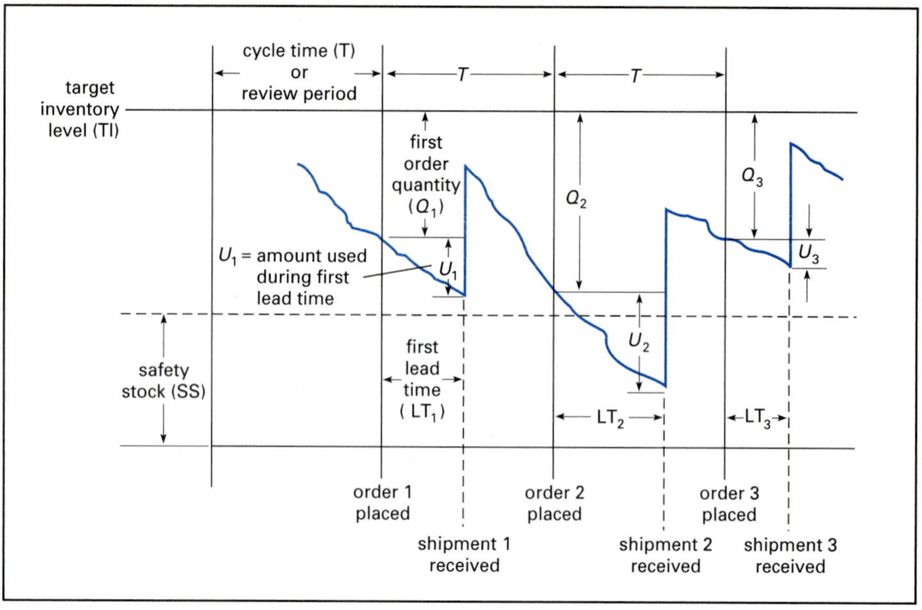

Figure 8-5 Level of Inventory through Time in a Periodic Review System: Order Quantity = Target Inventory − Inventory Position

quantities are different each period, being calculated as Q = TI − inventory position. The formula for TI for a fixed interval T is as follows:

$$\begin{aligned} \text{TI} &= \text{average review-period demand} + \text{average lead-time demand} \\ &\quad + \text{safety stock} \\ &= (T)(\bar{d}) + \bar{U} + z\sqrt{(T)(\text{Var } d) + \text{Var } U} \end{aligned} \tag{20}$$

In comparison with a continuous-review reorder-level system (such as the one studied in the preceding section), the periodic forced-ordering system requires more safety stock. The clue to understanding this statement is in the comparison of equation 20 with equation 9 in Table 8-1. (This is explored in problem 21.)

Perishable supplies and obsolescence present a new set of problems. The most important rule in inventory management of perishables is "First in, first out." That is, the first item to arrive should be used first. Sometimes this is difficult to enforce. For example, a blood bank may be required to supply their freshest blood for certain surgical procedures in which the quantity of blood needed is high or the patient is in very poor condition. In the retail grocery business, dairy and baked goods will often be selected on a freshest-first basis by the customer, contrary to the desires of the grocer.

One method for reducing spoilage is to *share the risk* with other users. Thus, there will be a smaller percentage of spoilage in a blood bank that serves three hospitals than if each hospital has its own. Unfortunately, this leads to the need for complex organizational arrangements, and the models we present in this book do not apply. (Further reading and references on this problem can be found in Nahmias 1982.)

There are two simple approaches that work for some situations. An EOQ model with a reorder level may be used if the shelf life is of the same order of magnitude as the turnover time, $(Q + \text{SS})/\bar{d}$. In this approach, a factor is added to the inventory cost (C_I) to reflect the average amount of spoilage that has been experienced. This results in somewhat smaller Q^* and SS and therefore less spoilage, at a cost of more frequent orders and a higher likelihood of shortage.

The other approach is referred to as the *newsperson problem*. This is useful when spoilage or obsolescence is almost immediate, so that there is no inventory carried over between orders. End-of-season ordering is another important application, encountered in automobiles, clothing, chocolate Easter bunnies, and many other markets. In this model we assume that a one-time order is placed, and the size of the order is based on the probability that total demand will exceed the amount ordered.

The newsperson model may be developed by examining the cost and saving of a one-unit change in the order quantity, Q. If we order one unit less than Q, and if demand (d) subsequently is greater than or equal to Q, we have lost the net revenue of that unit, and we have incurred the cost of one shortage (perhaps the loss of goodwill). Thus, the expected loss is (net revenue + shortage cost) times the probability that $d \geq Q$. On the other hand, if demand turns out to be less than Q, the reduction of the order quantity represents a saving equal to the cost of the item less its salvage value.

If the expected cost and expected saving are equal, there is no incentive to change the order quantity. Therefore, Q is optimal if

$$\begin{aligned}&(\text{Net revenue} + \text{shortage cost})\,[\text{Prob}(d \geq Q)]\\&\quad = (\text{cost} - \text{salvage value})\,[1 - \text{Prob}(d \geq Q)]\end{aligned}$$

The optimal probability of stockout (rearranging the foregoing equation) is the *newsperson formula*;

$$\begin{aligned}&\text{Optimal stockout probability} = \text{Prob}(d \geq Q)\\&\quad = \frac{\text{cost} - \text{salvage value}}{\text{net revenue} + \text{shortage cost} + \text{cost} - \text{salvage value}}\end{aligned} \tag{21}$$

in which all these costs are on a per-unit basis. The optimal order quantity, therefore, is just high enough to achieve this stockout probability. The usefulness of this result is limited by the ability to specify the shortage cost. Therefore, another useful form of this equation is obtained by solving for the implied shortage cost:

$$\begin{aligned}&\text{Implied shortage cost}\\&\quad = \frac{\text{cost} - \text{salvage value}}{\text{stockout probability}} - \text{net revenue} - \text{cost} + \text{salvage value}\end{aligned} \tag{22}$$

The managerial use of this kind of formula (implied shortage cost) was described in the previous section (safety stock).

REVIEW PROBLEMS

Christmas tree retailers must place their orders three months in advance of the holiday season. The average cost of a tree is \$18, and they sell for an average of \$25. It costs \$1.50 to dispose of each leftover tree.

1. What is the optimal ordering policy in terms of planned stockout probability?

2. If demand follows the normal probability distribution, and the forecast is for 500 trees (with a standard deviation of 50 trees), how many should be ordered?

Solutions

1. The salvage value is negative (i.e., −\$1.50) because of the disposal cost. Net revenue = \$25 − \$18 = \$7. Using equation 21, the stockout probability should be

$$P = \frac{\$18 - (-\$1.50)}{\$7 + \text{shortage cost} + \$18 - (-\$1.50)}$$

If there is no cost assigned to running short (other than the lost profit), this is $P = 19.50/26.50 = 0.736$, or 73.6%. Therefore, one should carry *fewer* trees than the expected value of demand.

2. From the normal probability table (Table 2, Appendix D), to have a stockout probability of 73.6% we must have $z = -0.63$. Therefore, $Q = 500 + (-0.63)(50) = 469$ trees.

SUMMARY

In this chapter we have explored the many useful roles of inventory, as well as techniques that can be used to effectively manage inventory. Inventory serves an important service function. The goal of this function is to provide an acceptable level of service (availability) at minimum cost. The level of service is adjusted through safety stocks, and the costs are minimized by ordering in the proper quantity. When costs are balanced at the margin, suprisingly large deviations may be taken from the optimal order quantities at very little cost penalty. This property of robustness is due to the fact that increases in holding cost (as Q increases) are almost exactly offset by decreases in transaction costs when Q is near Q^*.

There is a major interaction between this facet of operations management and both finance and marketing. The financial aspect of these models requires careful attention to the allocation of fixed costs. For example, the cost of a new warehouse may be avoidable if there are major shifts in inventory policy. In this situation, therefore, the fixed costs of warehousing must be allocated correctly to the holding cost, C_I. Furthermore, inventory, just as all other uses of capital, must show an acceptable return through cost reductions and service. This is assured by including the cost of capital (hurdle rate) in C_I. Forecasting demand is one of many interactions of inventory management with marketing. Of particular importance is the coordination of supplies with sales promotion schemes. The marketing department should provide information concerning customers' plans and competitors' schemes that will affect demand and therefore inventory. These observations join the growing list of reasons why it is important that the operations manager establish and maintain close ties with other areas of management.

We have also seen that there is considerable potential for abuse of inventory. For example, there are squirrels in most organizations, whose instincts require them to fill closets with supplies "just in case" the central supply system fails. This often results in far more safety stock than is actually necessary.

However, capital is tied up in these stocks, and their protection against damage and pilferage is less than ideal. Further, they often contribute to general disarray and clutter. Consequently, one of the major goals in inventory control is to install a system that can be relied on and implement it in such a way that the users believe in it. Then, and only then, can the squirrel nests be eliminated. The dollar benefit of this is difficult to measure, but this kind of tidying up is often a major improvement. This basic philosophy is captured by the desire to move toward zero inventory and is discussed further in the chapters on just-in-time production and total quality management.

A major cost saving comes from getting a good handle on lead time and lead-time demand. Monitoring late deliveries is a very important materials management function. The mathematical models we have presented allow us to carry out sensitivity analyses (such as the example in Section 8-5) to pinpoint major sources of inventory cost. Decreasing the procurement lead time substantially reduces the safety stock required, for example. A quantitative estimate of this saving is useful in deciding whether to pursue new vendor contracts, or whether to hire an order expediter. A major saving is also achieved through the elimination of low-use items, concentration on multiuse items, and the reduction of duplicate purchasing (go to a single brand when possible). A good information system is very important for this aspect of operations management, allowing rapid access to the data needed for the kinds of analyses we have discussed.

Most computer manufacturers and many other firms sell software packages that are designed for inventory control in various situations. One advantage of using this software is that it reflects experience obtained from other implementations, and, of course, we also avoid reinventing the wheel. The disadvantages are the cost and the fact that no prepackaged routine ever fits a situation completely. Nevertheless, a well-implemented computerized inventory control system goes a long way toward minimizing the major cost sources, such as orders being placed late, out-of-date stock quantities, and time-consuming manual order processing.

CASELET

VENERABLE DISTRIBUTORS

"Twenty million dollars of inventory is simply too high! We are getting only three turns per year while our competitors are getting from four to ten. As I see it, there are two ways to reduce our inventory of supplies. One way is to order in smaller quantities, and the other is to cut down on safety stock. Ms. Place, both purchasing and inventory control report to you. I want you to find ways to increase our inventory turnover."

Apparently finished, Mr. Topp sat back in his chair and puffed on his unlighted cigar. Ms. Place thought for a moment and then replied, "I've been telling you for months that my departments are understaffed. We need more personnel if we are to control inventory more carefully. Suppose we reduced the size of every order by half. Then we would have to process twice as many orders."

"True," replied Mr. Topp, "but I think there may be some avenues you have not yet explored. I want you to have a chat with Mr. Byte in the data processing department and see if there is any way that your ordering operation can be made more productive by using the computer more effectively. Maybe you should get a microcomputer. I want you to increase turnover without adding to your budget. I'm sure you can find ways to control inventory more efficiently.''

After the meeting, Ms. Place went to see Ms. Dee Olds, her predecessor as vice-president for materials management. ''Vendor control,'' said Olds. ''That's the secret. Our biggest reason for safety stock is to cover for late deliveries. If the vendors were more reliable with lead time, we could save a bundle. I had dinner with Charlie Young over at Consolidated the other day, and he told me about the deal he had worked out with one of his best vendors. He called it 'favorable status.' Charlie explained that from now on vendors would be evaluated on delivery reliability as well as on price and quality. Vendors with good delivery records would be more likely to be chosen. Consolidated expects to reduce substantially the number of vendors they deal with.''

''Much to his surprise, Charlie found out that the vendor liked the idea. They worked out a deal that covered a large number of items. I didn't get all the details, but he did say that by putting all the items into a single package they were able to work out some favorable prices.''

''In addition, they agreed on a different delivery arrangement. Rather than waiting for an order from Consolidated, the vendor delivers items on a weekly basis, although slow-moving items are delivered less frequently. Charlie set limits so that if an item gets too low or too high, its order is modified. The change is guaranteed to be implemented on the next delivery. Now most of the deliveries occur with virtually no transaction cost. The paperwork is standardized, so only the changes require any special attention.''

''It sounds like Charlie killed three birds with one stone,'' said Ms. Place. ''But tell me, Dee, how much time and expense went into making all these arrangements? Does he have to set up a unique agreement with each vendor, or is there one system that fits all?''

''I don't have a good answer. All I know is that he has been working on it for a year already and is still ironing out the details with some of his vendors.''

Required

1. What are the ''three birds'' that Charlie bagged? Discuss how they relate to Ms. Place's problem.
2. How much of a reduction in inventory does she have to achieve? Given what you know about the cost of holding inventory, how much will the annual saving be is she succeeds?
3. Describe in detail how Ms. Place could estimate the reduction in cycle stock if she adopted Consolidated's ''favored vendor'' idea.
4. How does Consolidated's delivery schedule arrangement affect the calculation of safety stock? Make reference to the equations in the chapter, and describe how Ms. Place could evaluate the potential saving.
5. The purchasing manager is evaluated on the basis of costs, including cash outlays for purchasing, as well as wages and other operating expenses. How might this manager react to including reliability of delivery as a criterion for vendor selection?

PROBLEMS

1. Define the various types of inventory that occur within an organization and briefly describe their uses.
2. Discuss some of the ways in which inventory can be abused in covering up ineffective management.
3. What determines the time at which an order is placed and the quantity ordered in
   a. periodic-review forced-ordering systems?
   b. continuous-review (perpetual) inventory systems?
4. Under the A-B-C classification, comparing the A and C categories, which has
   a. the greater number of types of items?
   b. the greater capital tied up in inventory per SKU?
   c. the greater physical quantity of inventory?
5. A company has a warehouse for storing the supplies purchased for company use. The warehouse is typically one-half to two-thirds full. In deciding on values of the unit costs to be used in setting inventory control policies, the manager was having difficulty with certain items. Decide how to allocate the costs listed below between the parameters C_I and C_T, defined in Table 8-1. Indicate which costs should not be included in either of the two parameters.
   a. the cost of heat and lights in the warehouse
   b. wages paid for the annual physical count of inventory
   c. wages paid for inspecting the quality of items when they are received
   d. janitorial wages
   e. wages of the materials-handling crew (warehouse and receiving dock)
   f. wages paid for paperwork involved in ordering and receiving
6. Scan the equations in Table 8-1 and point out where forecasts must be used, including a measure of forecast accuracy such as the standard deviation.

*7. An inventory system for supplies (independent demand) has been using a continuous-review (perpetual) inventory (Q, R) system, but with arbitrarily defined order quantities. Recently the paperwork due to order transactions has begun to increase, and the boss is looking for a way to control (minimize) this trend. One suggestion was an across-the-board increase in order quantities of 25% for all items.
   a. Explain briefly why this will reduce the paperwork.
   b. Explain briefly why this will increase inventory.
   c. Suggest a method for reducing the paperwork due to transactions *without* increasing total inventory costs.

8. Both of the following situations could be characterized as dependent demands.

---

*Problems with an asterisk have answers in the back of the book.

Situation I: A production line is devoted to one product and operates at a steady pace all year (excluding nights, weekends, etc.). One of the raw materials is ordered with $Q = 200$, $R = 200$. Delivery occurs 1 week after ordering. The average usage of raw material is 175 units per 4-week period.

Situation II: A production line is used for many products. Product A is manufactured once every 4 weeks, and the production run requires 1 day. One of the raw materials for A is also used in six other products, but their production schedules are occasional and sporadic. The raw material is ordered using $Q = 200$ and $R = 200$, delivery occurs 1 week after ordering, and 150 units of it are used in each product A run. The average total usage of the raw material in the other six products is 25 units per 4-week period.

a. Explain why Situation I is a suitable application for the methods of this chapter, whereas Situation II is not, by noting a very simple ordering policy that is a substantial improvement over the reorder quantity, reorder level (Q, R) system for Situation II.

b. What is it about Situation II that allows this improvement?

*9. An aircraft company uses rivets at an approximately constant rate of 5000 pounds per year; rivets cost $2 per pound, and it costs $20 to place an order. The annual carrying cost of inventory is 10% of the price of the item, and the cost of storage is negligible. Assume zero safety stock for this problem.

a. What is the economic order quantity (EOQ) for rivets?

b. Another item, a titanium alloy, costs $40 per pound. Demand is also 5000 pounds per year, and other costs are the same as for rivets. Calculate its EOQ, $D^{\$}$, TVC, and n.

c. Explain why it is best to order titanium more frequently than rivets in this problem.

10. A retailing firm has a constant demand rate of 70 units per month for a certain product. The ordering cost is $14 per order, and they use 1% per month as the cost of capital. The cost of capital is the only relevant inventory cost, since this product takes very little storage space. The purchase cost is $10 per unit up to a quantity of 200 and $9.90 per unit if 200 or more units are purchased. Safety stock is 80 units. Management wants to know how many units to order.

*11. Find an order quantity that minimizes annual cost, given the following information:

Annual inventory holding cost = 20% of item price
Cost of placing an order = $3.00
Price of the item = $20 each in lots < 200
$19.50 in lots ≥ 200
Forecasted annual usage = 50,000 units

12. Using the following table of discounts, what is the best order quantity, and why? (The EOQ number were calculated using the corresponding prices.)

Quantity	Prices per Unit	EOQ
0–99	$10.00	490
100–499	9.80	495
500 and up	9.40	505

*13. You are the manager of the supplies department of a manufacturer. The annual usage of part MB014 is 4000 cases, compared with 16,000 for part XZ201. They come from different manufacturers, and each is used in many different assembly operations in your company. The cost of placing an order is the same for both items, and their prices are very nearly equal. Each is ordered in quantities of 400. They are *not* substitutes for each other.

a. Show that this ordering policy is not consistent with the principles of EOQ.

b. Does this imply that one or the other (or both) order quantities should be changed? Why or why not?

14. Parts MB014 and MB213 are ordered from the same supplier at prices of $1 and $4 per case, respectively. The transaction cost of placing an order is $0.75, but if both items are ordered at the same time, the transaction cost is only $1 instead of $1.50. Annual holding cost is 20% of the price, and annual demands are 4000 cases for each item.

a. Calculate an EOQ for each item.

b. How many orders per year would there be for MB014 using the EOQ? For MB213?

c. If you order them both *every time an order is placed,* which one should have the larger order quantity? Explain your answer. (You can answer this without any calculations.)

d. What is the optimal number of orders per year if they are ordered jointly, as in part c?

e. What are the order quantities and the TVC corresponding to your solution in part d?

*15. A $20 item has a usage rate of 500 per year and is normally ordered in quantities of 40. A 10% price increase is expected in 6 weeks. The annual holding cost is 20% of the price. How much should we order and when?

16. The city of Harpo has a small department devoted to ordering supplies. The clerks in that department are fire proof (cannot be fired). Because they are only working at about 60% of their capacity, morale is sagging. They would like to be busier, but their job definitions do not allow them to accept work from other departments. A similar situation prevails in the receiving department. A study of the items ordered in this department showed that quantity discounts are not available for most items. Economic order quantities and the current

order quantities are shown in the accompanying table for a random sample of items.

Item	Annual Demand	Order Quantities	
		Current	EOQ
1	20,000	5,000	3,487
2	14,000	7,000	2,521
3	27,000	1,000	5,112
4	2,340	2,340	206
5	576	1,000	200
6	40	10	5
7	4,521	500	567
8	5,000	1,000	392

a. What order quantities should be used? Why?

b. Would savings be obtained by ignoring EOQ but scaling down the current order quantities? Explain.

*17. An item is used in an assembly operation at a constant rate of 16 per day (5 days per week, 50 weeks per year). This item is procured from an outside vendor at a cost of $12.50 each. The unit holding cost is $2.50 per year, and the transaction cost is $50 per transaction.

a. What is the optimal order quantity?

b. How many transactions will there be per year?

c. Lead time is normally distributed with a standard deviation of 3 days. How much safety stock should be maintained for 99% protection against stockouts, per order cycle?

d. What is the annual cost of this safety stock?

e. How much could be saved by reducing the average lead time by 50%? By reducing the standard deviation of lead time by 50%?

18. Consider the example of Section 8-4 in which the EOQ model is generalized so that it also takes into account the reduction of transaction (or manufacturing setup) cost, C_T.

a. Verify that the total annual cost with setup reduction (TCS) decreases as the transaction cost decreases to $20.59 by computing the values of Q^* and TCS(C_T, Q^*) for setup-investment values of $1000 ($C_T = 59.05$), $2000 ($C_T = 34.87$), and $3000 ($C_T = 20.59$). Check to see if your answers agree with the graph in Figure 8-3.

b. Verify that for a setup investment of $4000 ($C_T = \$12.16$) the total annual cost with setup reduction has begun to increase.

c. Figure 8-3 shows that the TCS curve is flat near the optimum value of the amount to invest in reducing C_T. Consider your calculations for investments of $2000, $3000, and $4000 in parts a and b. Use this information to fill in the blanks:

"Underinvesting by ____% (compared with the optimum investment) results in annual costs that are ____% higher than the minimum value, whereas overinvesting by the same percentage incurs a cost penalty of ____%.

19. Again consider the example of Section 8-5, which addresses the transaction-cost–reduction generalization of the EOQ model. Suppose now that each 10% (compound) reduction costs $400 (instead of $200); that is, $a(100) = 0$, $a(90) = 400$, $a(81) = 800$, etc. (You may wish to use a spreadsheet program to solve this problem.)
    a. Determine the optimal amount to invest in transaction reduction, as well as the optimal order quantity.
    b. You have now tried both $200 and $400 incremental investments in this problem setting. How large must this value be before the optimal solution is to not invest? (Continue to assume a 10% compound reduction in transaction cost.)
20. Weekly demand has been forecast, using exponential smoothing, for an item with independent demand. The demand forecast is 300 units per week, 52 weeks per year, and the MAD of the forecast is 20. (As we learned in Chapter 7, $\sigma \approx 1.25$ MAD.) The item is purchased from a vendor with a lead time of exactly 2 weeks. Orders are placed about twice per year.
    a. What is the standard deviation of the weekly forecast error?
    b. What are the estimates of the mean and the standard deviation of lead-time demand?
    c. What should the reorder level be to achieve an average of one stockout in 10 years? (Assume the normal probability distribution.)
    d. How much safety stock is included in the answer to part c?
    e. How much reduction would there be in safety stock if the average lead time were reduced by 50%?
    f. How much reduction would there be in safety stock if the forecast error (MAD) were reduced by 50%?
    g. What significance do the answers to parts e and f have for a manager?
21. (Problem 20 should be done in conjunction with this one.) Management is considering a periodic-review forced-ordering system for the item described in problem 20, ordering twice per year on the first day of January and July.
    a. Compute the appropriate target inventory level (TI), assuming that $z = 1.645$ for a 95% level of protection against stockouts.
    b. Using the new policy, what would the order quantity be if inventory is 1000 at the time the order is placed? At the average rate of demand, when would the inventory position (which includes this order) reach zero if no additional orders were placed?
    c. What is the safety stock associated with this policy? Why must the safety stock be larger in this problem than with a (Q, R) system, as in problem 20?

*22. An item with annual demand of 10,000 is ordered 10 times per year, on the average. An order is placed whenever inventory falls below 600. The item is used in a production line, so the daily usage is always the same, 50 weeks per year, 5 days per week. However, the delivery time varies, averaging 10 working days with a standard deviation of 2 days. C_I is \$2 per year.

a. How often should a stockout be expected?

b. After considerable debate, it was determined that the backorder cost of this item should be between \$200 and \$500, owing to its importance in the production process. Is the current reorder level reasonable? If not, suggest a better one.

23. There are 30 raw materials used at Wacko Manufacturers. The service level has been specified: an average of one stockout per year is acceptable for the entire system (i.e., 1/30 = 0.033 SO/yr for each raw material). The inventory holding cost is \$1 per unit per year for all raw materials. The unit price is \$2.50 higher when Wacko special orders raw materials, and the lead time for a special order is 2 days.

    a. Compute the implied backorder cost.

    b. Compare part a to the \$2.50 special-order charge. How might this difference be justified?

*24. The Happy Grocery receives baked goods twice each week, on Monday and Thursday. They sell the items as day old if they remain on the shelf the afternoon before the new shipment arrives. Day-old items sell at 10% below the wholesale cost and all day-old items are sold very quickly. Markup on all items is 30% above wholesale.

    a. Assuming that this is a newsperson problem with zero shortage cost, find a rule for determining order quantity. The rule is independent of the actual wholesale cost.

    b. Demand for pumpernickel bread averages 10 loaves per order cycle, and the Poisson probability distribution is applicable. How many should be ordered? Wholesale cost is \$0.40 per loaf.

    c. Is this really a newsperson problem? What is the most questionable assumption of the newsperson problem as applied to this situation?

25. The production plans for Hurtin Shoe Manufacturer are based in part on the annual style change in a large number of their products. During most of the year, the plans are based on a forecast of demand plus a safety stock. The actual demand seems to vary from the forecasts according to a normal probability distribution, with a standard deviation that is approximately 80% of the square root of the forecast (e.g., if the forecast is 100 units, the standard deviation is 80% of $\sqrt{100}$ or $0.8 \times 10 = 8$). Items not sold during their style year are sold at a discount during the annual end-of-season sale. These sales yield a return that is 5% below cost. In contrast, normal sales return 50% above cost. Inventory holding cost is 25% of item cost (per unit per year) and setup cost is \$50 per production run.

    a. What should the size of the *final production order* be for an item that costs \$20 with demand forecasted to be 4900 units during the remainder of the model year?

    b. How should this be modified if current inventory on hand consists of 1200 units?

*26. The accompanying table gives a record of actual daily demands of a stock item at Central City Hospital for a 6-week period. Inventory on hand at the beginning of week 1 is 600 units.

	Week 1	Week 2	Week 3	Week 4	Week 5	Week 6
Mon.	33	42	39	21	33	41
Tue.	27	39	33	44	69	43
Wed.	41	33	21	42	39	27
Thu.	15	26	18	33	42	36
Fri.	61	44	65	51	22	66
Sat.	38	48	41	68	38	62
Sun.	39	50	40	18	40	21

a. Estimate what value of D should be used in an EOQ formula.

b. Construct an inventory and backorder record assuming that a continuous-review (perpetual) inventory system was in use with $Q = 550$ and $R = 550$. Show when orders were placed and when they were received, as well as a day-by-day record of the quantity of inventory and the number of units for which backorders have been issued. Assume that the lead time was 1 week for the first order, 2 weeks for the second, and 3 weeks for the third.

c. Repeat part b using a periodic-review forced-ordering system with a review period of 2 weeks (every second Monday, beginning in week 1) and TI = 1100.

d. Using the average demand rate from part a and an average lead time of 2 weeks, how much safety stock is there for the policies in parts b and c?

27. The example of Section 8-3 computed two ordering policies, Q^* and Q^+. The Q^+ policy simply multiplied each Q^* by 3.49 to decrease the annual number of orders placed from 82.1 if Q^* were implemented to 23.6 for Q^+.

a. Using the same approach, what multiplier would be used to achieve 20 orders per year? 40? 60? 80?

b. Compute the dollar value of inventory for each answer in part a and plot a trade-off curve of dollar inventory against orders per year when a Q^+ type of policy is used. Join the points with a smooth curve. (Hint: You do not have to compute inventory for each item.)

c. Now plot a single point that describes the current operating policy (before EOQ or Q^+ was considered).

d. Which section of the curve represents changes that would be easiest to sell to management as improvements?

e. Suppose that we want to have about 50 orders per year. What should the order quantities be for each item, A, B, C, D, and E? You may wish to use your graph from part b to help you.

28. In Section 8-3, the Q^+ order quantities were 3.49 times Q^*. Verify that the same result would be obtained by multiplying the transaction cost by $(3.49)^2$ and using the result in the EOQ formula. Compare this idea with the implied backorder cost concept.
29. The derivation of the EOQ (see footnote 4) is only an approximation to a complete economic analysis. Let r be the discount rate and i be the inflation rate, so that all costs incurred at time t are discounted by e^{-rt} and inflated by e^{it}. Let C_H be the inventory holding cost excluding the cost of capital, and p be the price of the item.
    a. Write an expression for the present value of the cost of using an EOQ system (ignoring safety stock).
    b. Take the first derivative to find the condition for an optimal solution.
    c. Use the approximation $e^x = 1 + x + x^2/2 + \ldots$ to derive the EOQ from part b.
    d. Show that the EOQ is a reasonable formula if $C_I = C_H + (r - i)(p)$ and if $(r - i)Q/D$ is not too large.

REFERENCES

AUCAMP, D.C., ''A Caveat on the Inventory Price-Break Model,'' *International Journal of Operations and Production Management*, vol. 2, no. 2, 1981.

BIERMAN, H., and L.J. THOMAS, ''Inventory Decisions under Inflationary Conditions,'' *Decision Sciences*, vol. 8, no. 1, 1977.

CARLSON, P.G., ''An Alternate Model for Lead-Time Demand: Continuous-Review Inventory Systems,'' *Decision Sciences*, vol. 13, no. 1, 1982.

CHASE, R.B., and N.J. AQUILANO, *Production and Operations Management: A Life Cycle Approach*, 5th ed., Homewood, Ill.: Irwin, 1989.

ERLENKOTTER, D., ''Ford Whitman Harris and the Economic Order Quantity Model,'' *Operations Research*, vol. 38, no. 6, 1990.

GRIECO, P.L., JR., M.W. GOZZO, and J.W. CLAUNCH, *Just-in-Time Purchasing: In Pursuit of Excellence*, Plantsville, Conn.: CT Publications, 1988.

HARRIS, F.W., ''How Many Parts to Make at Once,'' *Factory, The Magazine of Management*, vol. 10, no. 2, 1913. (Reprinted in *Operations Research*, vol. 38, no. 6, 1990.)

JOHNSON, L.A., and D.C. MONTGOMERY, *Operations Research in Production Planning, Scheduling, and Inventory Control*, New York: Wiley, 1974.

LOVE, S.F., *Inventory Control*, New York: McGraw-Hill, 1979.

NAHMIAS, S., ''Perishable Inventory Theory: A Review,'' *Operations Research*, vol. 30, no. 4, 1982.

PLOSSL, G.W., *Production and Inventory Control: Principles and Techniques*, 2nd ed., Englewood Cliffs, N.J.: Prentice-Hall, 1985. First edition coauthored with O.W. Wight, 1967.

PORTEUS, E.L., ''Numerical Comparisons of Inventory Policies for Periodic Review Systems,'' *Operations Research*, vol. 33, no. 1, 1985a.

PORTEUS, E.L., ''Investing in Reduced Setups in the EOQ Model,'' *Management Science*, vol. 31, no. 8, 1985b.

PORTEUS, E.L., "Optimal Lot Sizing, Process Quality Improvement and Setup Cost Reduction," *Operations Research*, vol. 34, no. 1, 1986.

RAKOWSKI, J.P., "Unofficial Inventory," *Journal of Purchasing and Materials Management*, vol. 17, no. 3, 1981.

ROSENSHINE, M., and D. OBEC, "Analysis of a Standing Order Inventory System with Emergency Orders," *Operations Research*, vol. 24, no. 6, 1976.

SHORE, B., "A Micro-computer Based Purchasing Information System," *Journal of Purchasing and Materials Management*, vol. 17, no. 2, 1981.

SILVER, E.A., and R. PETERSON, *Decision Systems for Inventory Management and Production Planning*, 2nd ed., New York: Wiley, 1985.

U.S. DEPARTMENT OF COMMERCE, *Business Statistics 1986*, supplement to *Survey of Current Business*, 25th ed., 1987.

ZANGWILL, W.I., "From EOQ Towards ZI," *Management Science*, vol. 33, no. 10, 1987.

chapter

9

Intermediate-Range Planning and Scheduling

The goal of intermediate-range planning is to arrive at overall production and work-force decisions for a number of months to come. The importance of these plans cannot be overstated. For example, policies concerning the use of overtime have an effect on the national unemployment level. Brennan et al. 1982, studying this issue in the European Economic Community, pointed out that reduced use of overtime could create jobs but would also lead to increased capital costs. At the individual company level, the intermediate-range plans determine the ability to respond to opportunities in the marketplace as well as influence the delivery lead time of manufactured products. The quality of a firm's intermediate-range planning has a substantial effect on its competitive position.

Intermediate-range plans provide guidelines for detailed scheduling decisions in the immediate future; therefore, they must satisfy certain criteria. The overall plans must (1) meet demand requirements, (2) be within capacity restrictions, (3) be consistent with company policy, (4) leave the firm in a good position at the end of the plan, and (5) minimize costs.

The planning process consists of three phases. Anticipating future requirements is the first phase; it consists of forecasting demand month by month over the planning period and setting safety margins to allow for the possibility of the forecast error. Seasonality of demand and future economic trends are usually important in intermediate-range forecasts.

In the second phase, work-force and production plans are made on an overall, or aggregate, basis for the entire operation (firm, division, etc.). This process begins by comparing anticipated demand with production capability through time. A detailed study of production and work-force plans is then carried out over a future span of time (the *planning horizon*), trading off the costs of the various alternatives, such as work-force changes, subcontracting, overtime, and the use of inventory. Of particular importance is whether to plan seasonal work-force layoffs corresponding to seasonal demand patterns. In the second phase, production planning for service industries differs from planning for manufacturers, in that it is usually impossible to produce a service in advance of demand, whereas a physical product may be stored in inventory. Even so, manufacturers of expensive or perishable goods produce only when orders have been received. Make-to-order producers, including most service and some manufacturing organizations, do not include inventory in their intermediate-range plans. (See Thomas and McClain 1991 for an overview of production planning.)

The third phase is implementation of the plan, in which preparations are begun for planned future changes and the immediate plans are disaggregated into detailed work-force and production schedules, product by product.

Intermediate-range plans must be coordinated with both short- and long-range decisions. The time scale of intermediate range planning is usually measured in months, and the production plans are made in aggregate production units. Longer-range decisions, with the time scale measured in years, include capacity planning and product design. Both these longer-range decisions interact with intermediate-range planning by placing restrictions on it, including capacity restrictions and production requirements. At a lower level, with a time scale in days or weeks, are the scheduling decisions for individual items and decisions involving the individual workers. The intermediate-range plan places constraints on the short-range decisions by specifying the overall level of production and work force.

Intermediate-range planning is facilitated by aggregating the many products of a company into a single unit of output, referred to as the *aggregate production unit*. Some companies aggregate their sales and production levels on the basis of a common output measure, such as barrels in the oil industry. Others use dollars, labor-hours, or machine-hours. When correctly implemented, plans for this aggregate product can be disaggregated at a later date into detailed plans for individual products. The advantages of aggregation include more accurate forecasting than for individual items and simplification of the planning process, dealing with a few aggregate items rather than thousands of separate items.

Bitran and Hax (1977) have proposed a scheme for aggregating production units:

1. *Items* are the final products to be delivered to customers.
2. *Families* are groups of items that share a common manufacturing setup.
3. *Types* are groups of families whose production quantities are to be determined by an aggregate production plan. Items within a type share a common seasonal demand pattern.

Under this scheme there are several aggregate products (the types) rather than just one. This added complexity is not serious, however, since the Bitran-Hax scheme (discussed further in Chapter 11) includes a method for automatically generating the aggregate production plans for each product type, using linear programming (to be discussed later). The major advantage of using this multilevel (that is, hierarchical) approach is the natural way in which the aggregate plans (for types) may later be broken down into specific production schedules for families, and for items.

Production smoothing, a common goal of intermediate-range planning, means avoiding large changes in the overall production level. There are several reasons for wanting to smooth production. A steady production rate allows a constant work force without major layoffs. Moreover, it avoids the use of large amounts of overtime or subcontracting and avoids the cost of setting up or shutting down a new operation to meet peaks in demand. There are two ways to avoid the cost of changing production levels. The first way is to use inventory, which represents production in advance of demand. The second way (the only way available to high-contact service industry and make-to-order manufacturers) is through *demand management,* modification of the demand pattern itself (see Sasser 1976). This can be accomplished by several means, including promotional effort to encourage demand during slack periods and deliberate underproduction during peak demand, resulting in backlogs and possible loss of sales. Some companies allow long-term capacity shortages to exist as a way of obtaining smooth growth and uniform labor requirements.

The aggregate production planning problem may be viewed as searching for the optimal trade-off of the cost of changing production levels against the cost of avoiding the changes. A production plan that changes production levels to meet demand is called a *chase-demand* production strategy. As was mentioned previously, service organizations, for example, often employ a chase-demand strategy because of the inability to inventory a service. At the other extreme, some firms achieve an optimal cost trade-off by smoothing production and following a *constant-rate* or *level* production strategy.

Before explaining the techniques used to develop aggregate production and work-force plans, two additional concepts should be understood: *rolling schedules* and *frozen horizon*. The term "rolling schedule" reflects the recognition that aggregate plans are by no means final. That is, the methods we are about to study must be repeated monthly, even if the aggregate plans extend many months into the future. The reason for this is that demand will often turn out to be different from the forecast, leaving the company in a different inventory position than had been planned. Consequently, after the first period the entire problem is rolled forward one period, and new aggregate plans are made. The sequence of first-period aggregate plans is referred to as a rolling schedule. (See Baker 1977.)

"Frozen horizon" refers to the fact that it may already be too late to modify the plans for the first month, or maybe the second or third months, because of lead times for acquiring material, scheduling personnel, and so on. Periods that cannot be changed are referred to as the frozen horizon and need not appear in a production-planning chart. Throughout our discussion, period 0 refers to the end of the frozen horizon and period 1 refers to the first month in which plans can be changed.

In the first four sections of this chapter, we follow the case of the Smooth Products Company through two planning phases (anticipating requirements and developing work-force and production plans). This discussion includes a graphical method as well as a spreadsheet model for developing aggregate production plans. Section 9-5 presents a linear programming approach to aggregate production planning. The last section of the chapter discusses production planning, incorporating the use of the learning curve in determining capacity needs.

Example: The Smooth Products Company

The Smooth Products Company recently initiated several projects to improve efficiency and cut costs. One of these efforts involves a study of the possibility of cutting inventory by the use of seasonal layoffs. In this study production was measured in aggregate units equivalent to 100 worker-days of labor. That is, the regular-time production capacity per worker is 0.01 aggregate production unit per day. Regular-time production can be increased by up to 10% by scheduling overtime, but overtime production costs $2000 (per aggregate unit) more than regular time. There are currently 450 production workers, resulting in a regular-time production rate of 4.5 aggregate units per day.

The maximum daily production rate is 7.0 aggregate units, owing to physical limitations. This limit applies to total daily output; therefore, it may not be exceeded by use of overtime. However, additional production can be subcontracted to another firm at a cost that is $3500 higher per aggregate unit than regular-time production.

The average cost of hiring and training a worker is $400, whereas reducing the work force costs $200 per worker laid off. By company policy, a minimum of 400 workers is always retained.

It costs $12,000 per year to hold, in inventory, products equivalent to 1 aggregate unit of production. Currently (at the end of December) there are 80 aggregate units on hand. The annual demand is 1200 aggregate units. The seasonal demand pattern (column 2 of Table 9-1) has peaks in late spring and in December. There is an annual two-week shutdown in July, a slack month.

9-1 ANTICIPATING REQUIREMENTS

Required production consists of two elements: demand and inventory requirements. Demand is anticipated through forecasting methods such as those described in Chapter 7. It is significant that aggregate forecasts are more accurate than forecasts for individual items. This is because the randomness in the demand for individual items is reduced when the items are aggregated. However, because forecasts inevitably differ from actual demand, there is a

Table 9-1 Cumulative Production Requirements for Smooth Products Company

(1) Period (t)	(2) Demand (Forecast) (D_t)	(3) Cumulative Demand $\left(\sum_{i=1}^{t} D_i\right)$	(4) Minimum Inventory (MI_t)	(5) Cumulative Requirements [(3) + (4)] (CR_t)	(6) Production Days ($DAYS_t$)	(7) Cumulative Production Days (CD_t)
0. Dec.			40	40		0
1. Jan.	70	70	15	85	22	22
2. Feb.	50	120	10	130	18	40
3. Mar.	100	220	30	250	22	62
4. Apr.	200	420	40	460	21	83
5. May	150	570	35	605	22	105
6. June	50	620	10	630	21	126
7. July	50	670	10	680	12	138
8. Aug.	50	720	10	730	22	160
9. Sept.	90	810	30	840	21	181
10. Oct.	90	900	30	930	21	202
11. Nov.	100	1000	30	1030	20	222
12. Dec.	200	1200	40	1240	18	240

need to specify a margin of safety. In the case of manufacuring, this is done by specifying a required minimum level of inventory, referred to as safety stock. In addition to meeting all the demands, production must be sufficient to keep inventory at or above the safety-stock level.

As we saw in Chapter 8, cycle stock presents another inventory requirement. For example, if several items were to reach their safety-stock levels at the same time, it might not be possible to schedule production so that none of the items falls below its safety-stock level (or even incurs shortages). Consequently, the inventory requirement will usually be above the safety-stock level. (See Chapter 11 for a discussion of production cycles.) The minimum inventory (MI_t) for a time period t is the sum of safety stock, cycle stock, and any other required inventory.

We will now formalize the concept of requirements. At the end of period t, the *cumulative requirement* (CR) is defined as the minimum allowable ending inventory for that period plus the cumulative demand through period t. This is summarized in equation 1, in which D_j is the forecast of demand during period j:

$$CR_t = MI_t + \sum_{j=1}^{t} D_j \tag{1}$$

Demand and minimum inventory levels are given in columns 2 and 4 of Table 9-1 for the Smooth Products Company. The cumulative demand is shown in column 3. Cumulative requirements in column 5 is simply the sum of columns 3 and 4.

The reason for calculating cumulative requirements is to place a lower limit on production. As we consider alternative production plans, we are only interested in plans that meet or exceed CR_t, so that demand can be met with at least the extra margin of inventory given by MI_t. Of course, if production exceeds requirements, the inventory will exceed MI_t. Although excess inventory represents a cost to the company, production that exceeds requirements during part of the planning horizon may have advantages such as a more constant production rate, leading to less overtime or reduction in hiring or layoffs.

For purposes of illustration, a cumulative production plan is plotted in Figure 9-1 together with cumulative requirements and cumulative demand. Note that at time $t = 0$ the production curve is at a level of 80 units. This is the initial inventory, I_0, which represents leftover production from the past. The production rate in this plan is 3.87 per day through day 62, increases to 6.63 until day 105, then is 4.07 until day 202, and finishes the year at a rate of 6.32 per day. These values are represented by the slopes of the top line.

A general relationship between inventory and production is

Inventory in period t = initial inventory + cumulative production − cumulative demand

or equivalently,

$$I_t = I_0 + \sum_{j=1}^{t} P_j - \sum_{j=1}^{t} D_j \tag{2}$$

in which P_j is production during period j. That is, inventory is the difference between the cumulative production (including initial stocks) and cumulative demand. In the graph, this difference is the vertical distance from the cumula-

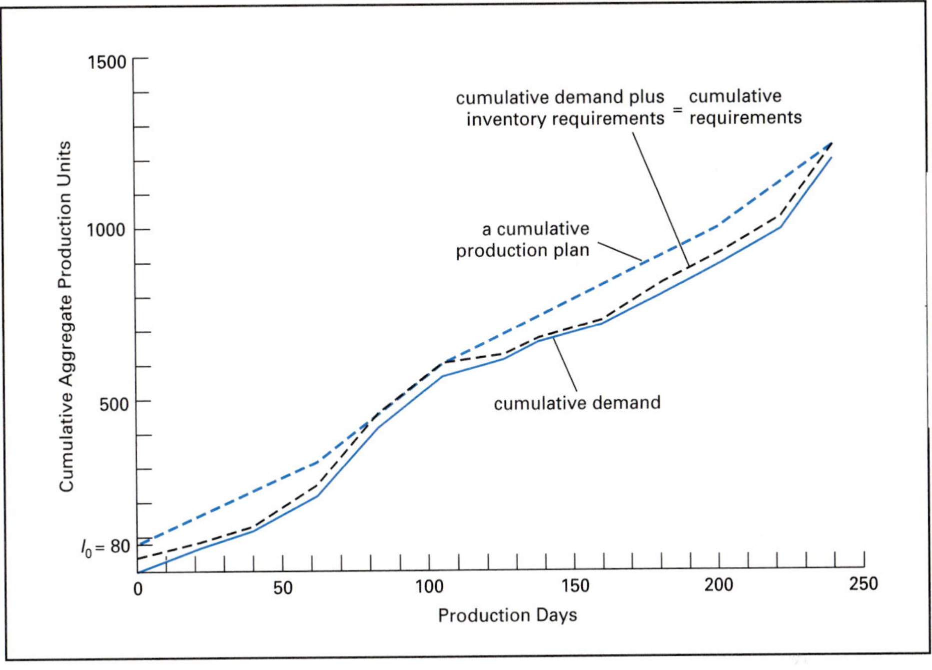

Figure 9-1 Demand and Inventory Requirements for the Smooth Products Company

tive demand to the cumulative production. Therefore, if the cumulative production graph dips below the cumulative requirements, inventory is less than MI_t, indicating an unacceptable plan. *The cumulative requirements represent a minimum for cumulative production plus initial inventory.*

Backlogging Demand

High-contact services and make-to-order organizations can use these same concepts with a slight modification. In these firms, production occurs at the same time as or later than demand. When production lags behind, demand is said to be *backlogged*, and the amount of the backlog is equal to the difference between the cumulative demand and the cumulative production. That is, backlog equals negative inventory. Equations 1 and 2 still hold. In situations when it is not possible to carry inventory, we require inventory to be zero or negative.

If the minimum inventory (MI) is a negative number, it represents the *maximum* allowable backlog. For example, in Table 9-1, if $I_0 = -80$ and all the MI_t terms were given negative signs, it would mean that we currently have a backlog of 80 aggregate units of demand, but our goals would be to cut the backlog to 15 by the end of January, to 10 in February, and so on. In this case, the rationale for allowing the backlog to grow again (as high as 40 in April) would be that a larger backlog during high-demand months may allow us to avoid drastic changes in the work force.

When inventory is not possible but backlogging is allowed, the relationship of the lines in Figure 9-1 is changed. The cumulative-requirements curve will be below the cumulative-demand curve, as may be seen in equation 1 with MI_t negative. Since inventory is not allowed, the cumulative-production curve must lie below the cumulative demand, between the demand and requirements curves. Because of this, a company with demand that is as seasonally varying as that of the Smooth Products Company would have to face wide fluctuations in production rate unless the allowable backlogs were larger than (the negative of) the MI_t numbers used in Figure 9-1.

Some manufacturers use both inventory and backlogging (during slack and peak months, respectively). In a month when backlogging is allowed, MI_t will be negative, but it can be positive during slack-demand months. Likewise, the inventory variable, I_t, represents a backlog when it is negative and inventory when positive.

Interpreting negative inventory as backlogged demand allows us to use equations 1 and 2 for all the situations we have discussed. However, for the sake of simplicity, backlogging of demand will not be allowed for the remainder of this chapter. The calculations are very similar to the ''inventory only'' model, as will be seen in the problems at the end of the chapter.

REVIEW PROBLEMS

1. If the Smooth Products Company continues at 450 workers with no overtime or subcontracting, what will the inventory be at the end of January? At the end of February? (Use the data in Table 9-1, and recall that there are 80 units of inventory currently on hand.)

2. What is the first period in which inventory will not meet the required MI at this production rate?

Solutions

1. 450 workers produce 4.5 units per day, and there are 22 working days in January (see Table 9-1). Therefore, $P_1 = (22)(4.5) = 99$ units produced. $I_1 = I_0 + P_1 - D_1 = 80 + 99 - 70 = 109$. Similarly, $P_2 = (18)(4.5) = 81$, so $I_2 = 80 + (99 + 81) - (70 + 50) = 140$.

2. Continue the same calculation. In April, inventory is 6.5 units below the required level of 40.

9-2 PLAN DEVELOPMENT BY THE GRAPHICAL METHOD

In Figure 9-1 any curve that starts at 80 on the vertical axis and remains above the cumulative-requirements curve is a potential production plan. It is useful to narrow the choices somewhat. In the case of the Smooth Products Company, the minimum daily production rate is 4.0. On a cumulative graph, a production rate translates to the *slope*; hence, any portion of a production plan that has a slope less than 4.0 is not feasible. Since we were also given a maximum production rate of 7.0 per day, a slope steeper than 7.0 is also not allowed unless a subcontract is let to augment production.

The MCP (Minimum Constant Production Rate) Production Plan

Upper and lower limits of production still leave many possibilities. One alternative that may be attractive is to adopt a constant daily production rate. Figure 9-2 shows two production plans that have constant rates. The lower of

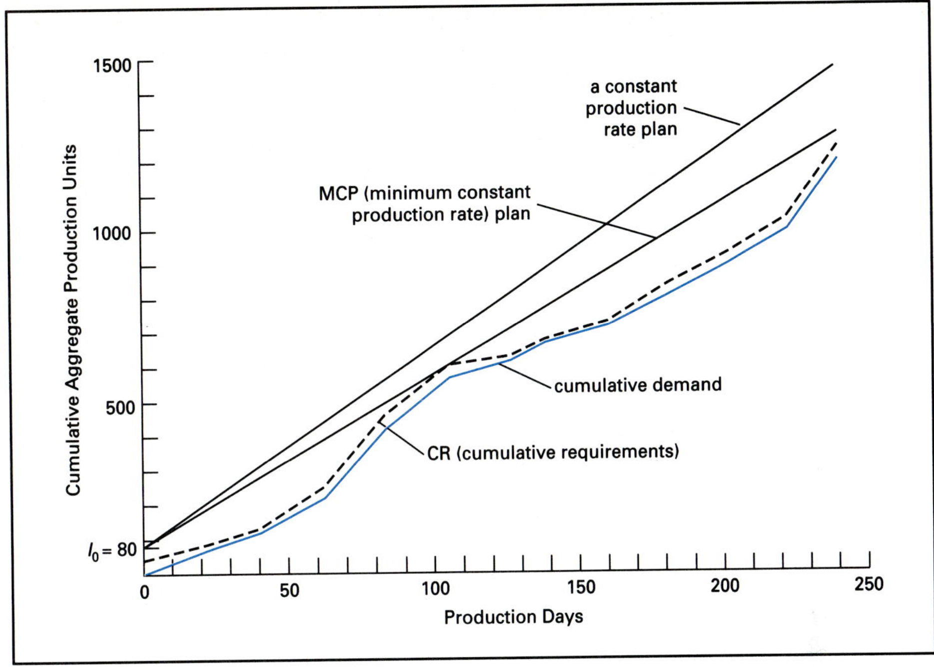

Figure 9-2 Cumulative Production Plans with Constant Daily Rates of Production

these two lines is more economical because it has less inventory. (Remember that on the graph, inventory is the distance between the production and requirements curves.) Furthermore, no constant-rate (or level) production plan can be lower in inventory than the one labeled *minimum constant production rate plan (MCP)*, since it would be below requirements at day 105 (the end of May). Therefore, ''MCP'' is a fitting label.

After May the MCP stays above the requirements curve. Perhaps a change to a new constant rate would be desirable at that time. That question will be left for later.

The production rate of the MCP is easily calculated because we know two points on the MCP, and it is a straight line. The MCP passes through 80 at time 0 and equals the CR of 605 at the end of May, day 105. Therefore, the daily production rate is (605 − 80)/(105 − 0) = 5 per day.

Table 9-2 illustrates another way of determining the MCP production rate. (Note that this table is a continuation of Table 9-1, and the columns are numbered accordingly.) Column 8 contains the same calculation we just performed but repeats it for all the months rather than just for May. The MCP rate stands out as the largest of these ''average requirements'' because the MCP line is tangent to the ''high point'' of the cumulative-requirements curve, as viewed from the initial inventory position of 80 units.

Before discussing other production plans, some additional evaluation of the MCP plan is in order. Table 9-2 illustrates how to compute the inventory on a monthly basis. The cumulative production in column 11 begins at 80, the initial inventory, and each month's production is added at the rate of 5 units per production day, using the production days per month from Table 9-1. Inventory is calculated as the difference between column 11 and column 5 from Table 9-1. This is simply carrying out equation 2. The calculations stop at May, for reasons to be discussed later.

Table 9-2 Calculating the MCP (Minimum Constant Production) Plan

(1) Period	(8) Average Requirements[a]	(9) Production Rate[b]	(10) Production[c]	(11) Cumulative Production Plus I_0	(12) Inventory[d]
				80 = (I_0)	
Jan.	0.23	5	110	190	120
Feb.	1.25	5	90	280	160
Mar.	2.74	5	110	390	170
Apr.	4.58	5	105	495	75
May	5.00	5	110	605	35
June	4.37		Beyond the natural horizon		
July	4.35				
Aug.	4.06				
Sept.	4.20				
Oct.	4.21				
Nov.	4.28				
Dec.	4.83				

[a] Average requirements = $(CR_t - I_0)/(CD_t - CD_0)$, all from Table 9-1.

[b] Choose the largest average requirement.

[c] Rate times DAYS ("DAYS" is column 6, Table 9-1).

[d] Inventory = cumulative production plus I_0 minus cumulative demand (from column 3, Table 9-1).

To complete the evaluation, consider how the production plan could be implemented. The current rate of production at Smooth Products Company is 4.5 per day. To achieve the MCP rate of 5 per day, there must be either hiring or overtime until May. It appears from the graph that a slowdown after May might be desirable, so some of the newly hired might be laid off again. Nevertheless, some hiring must take place, since the maximum amount of overtime was given as 10%, which would increase the current rate to 4.95. To complete the evaluation, one would have to specify how the production rate would change, and apply the appropriate costs.

As an example, suppose that the entire increase is met by hiring additional workers. (Refer back to the description of the Smooth Products Company just before Section 9-1.) Also, assume that the work force will return to its original size at the end of the five-month horizon. The costs of the MCP are as follows.

Inventory: Monthly cost is \$12,000/12 = \$1000 per aggregate unit. Total unit-months of inventory = 120 + 160 + 170 + 75 + 35 = 560 at \$1000 per unit = \$560,000, where 120 = 80 + 5(22) − 70, 160 = 80 + 5(18 + 22) − (70 + 50), etc.

Hiring: Increasing production by 0.5 aggregate unit per day requires the addition of 0.5/0.01 = 50 workers at \$400 per worker for hiring and training = \$20,000.

Overtime premiums: Zero.

Subcontracting premiums: Zero.

Layoffs: None through May, but assuming the work force will be reduced to 450 in June: 50(200) = \$10,000.

Normal cost of production: Not a variable cost. It will be the same under all plans because we account separately for additional costs (i.e., premiums) due to overtime and subcontracting.

Total variable cost: $590,000.

Plans with Varying Production Rates: Some Restrictions

If the production rate remains at 4.5 rather than 5 for a while, the total inventory will be reduced. Eventually production must increase, however, so that the increased demands of April and May can be met and the minimum inventory levels satisfied. Since the MCP rate of 5 was just enough to meet the May peak, it stands to reason that if the 4.5 rate is maintained for a month or more, a rate above 5 must be achieved to make up the difference.

Figure 9-3 shows two plans of this sort. Both plans retain a rate of 4.5 during the first three months. Plan X increases the production rate substantially at that point, whereas plan Y increases production more modestly, only enough to achieve the May requirements. We can see that the graphs of both plans are steeper after March than the MCP, confirming that the production rates are both in excess of 5.

Rather than carry out a numerical evaluation of these plans, consider the following arguments:

Plan X has higher hiring costs, because it is steeper during April and May.

Plan X has higher inventory costs because it is either the same or above plan Y in the diagram.

Figure 9-3 Cumulative Production Plans with Hiring and Layoffs

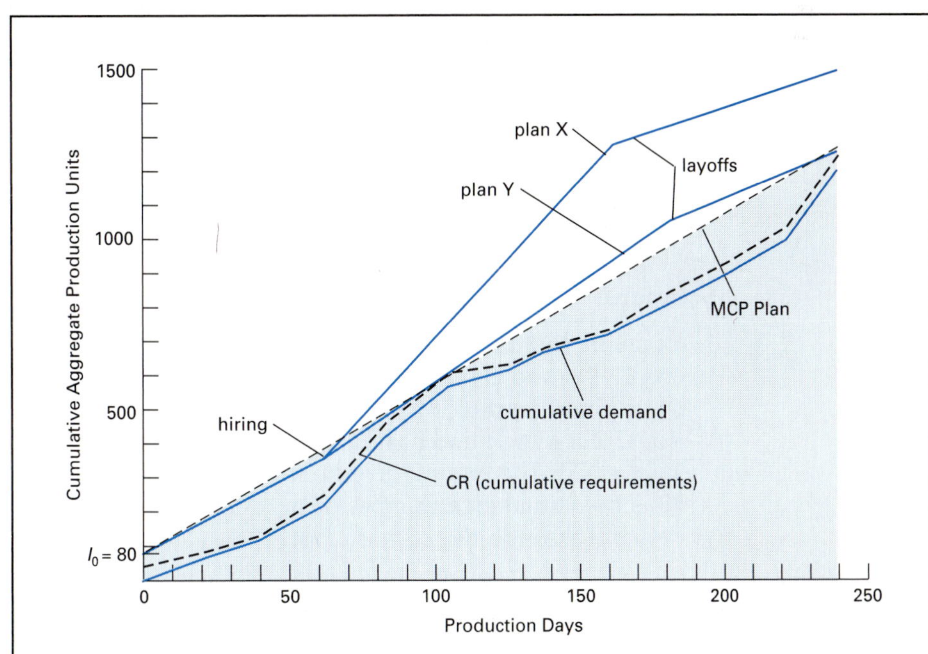

Both plans will require layoffs after May to avoid overproduction unless demand after the end of the horizon (day 240) is very high. Plan X, having the higher production rate, requires a greater layoff.

It is easy to see from these arguments that plan Y dominates plan X unless there is a dramatic increase in demand beyond day 240. If no such increase is expected, we can drop plan X from consideration without checking the exact costs. In fact, assuming costs are linear and using a similar argument, it follows that:

If the objective is to minimize costs within the planning horizon, we can drop any plan that has any segment above the MCP.

This idea is extremely important. We can now restrict our attention to production plans whose graphs fall between the cumulative-requirements curve and the MCP (inclusive).

The Natural Planning Horizon

The point where the MCP touches the cumulative-requirements curve is called the *natural planning horizon*. (Problem 6 suggests the reason for this label.) We need not concern ourselves with any production plan that does not pass through this point. A plan passing below that point does not meet the minimum inventory requirement. A plan passing above the natural horizon can be ruled out by an argument similar to that in the preceding paragraphs.

Now the reason why the calculations of Table 9-2 stopped at the end of May is clear. The "after May" decisions can be separated from the "before May" decisions, since every "before May" plan must lead to the same point, the natural planning horizon.

In the next section, guidelines that use the costs of inventory, overtime, hiring, and firing are described.

REVIEW PROBLEMS

1. Use equation 2 to calculate the inventory at the end of months 3 and 4 of the MCP.

2. When May arrives, given the data we have, what will the new MCP be, and when will the next natural planning horizon occur?

Solutions

1. Recalling that (a) the initial inventory level is 80 (aggregate) units, (b) there are 22, 18, and 22 production days, respectively, in January, February, and March, and (c) the constant production rate is 5 units per day, using equation 2 the March ending inventory is $80 + 5(22 + 18 + 22) - (70 + 50 + 100) = 170$. The ending inventory in April is $80 + 5(83) - 420 = 75$, where 83 is the cumulative number of production days and 420 is the cumulative demand through the end of April.

2. Using Figure 9-2, starting from the CR curve at May, a straight-line tangent to CR in December represents the next MCP. The production rate will be $(1240 - 605)/(240 - 105) = 4.70$ units per day. Unless data beyond December change this picture, December will be the next natural planning horizon.

9-3 DEVELOPING ALTERNATIVE PLANS: ECONOMIC GUIDELINES

In this section we will study how to develop and evaluate good plans using principles that are based on the relevant costs. As always, an analysis based entirely on costs is narrow in scope, and management may wish to use additional criteria to finally decide on a plan. For example, many firms believe that the long-term cost of firing people is so high in terms of loss of morale that they will do almost anything to avoid firing.

Research has resulted in a set of rules that are useful in the search for a minimum-cost plan. The rules we will use apply only to linear costs, but more general forms are given in the original papers (Kunreuther and Morton 1973 and McClain and Thomas 1977). Careful use of these rules leads to good plans but does not guarantee that the least-cost plan will be found. Table 9-3 contains a summary of the rules and of the symbols used for costs and time periods; this should be read carefully before continuing.

The easiest rules to understand involve temporary production increases: Should one use overtime or would temporary hiring be better? Suppose that a production plan requires the use of overtime for L consecutive months. It might be more attractive to hire a worker for the same time span, thereby reducing the amount of overtime needed. The cost of processing the temporary worker into and out of the work force is $C_H + C_F$. This worker produces p units per day for n days per month for L months, which reduces the required overtime cost by $L \cdot n \cdot p \cdot C_0$. Temporary hiring would be worthwhile if the cost $(C_H + C_F)$ is less than the saving $(L \cdot n \cdot p \cdot C_0)$, or if $L > (C_H + C_F)/npC_0$. The ratio is called l^*, and we have just derived rule 5 from Table 9-3.

Another useful result is the inventory-versus-overtime trade-off used in rules 4 and 6. Suppose that a production plan called for hiring in the third month, but the number of people to be hired was not large enough to avoid overtime during a peak demand month that occurs K periods later. Would it be worthwhile to move some or all of the hiring to one period earlier? If one person is hired in month 2 instead of month 3, there will be np more units in inventory at the end of month 2. These units can be carried for K months and then used to satisfy some of the peak demand, thereby reducing the overtime required by np units. Hiring earlier is worthwhile if the added inventory cost of $K \cdot n \cdot p \cdot C_I$ is less than the saving in overtime premium of $n \cdot p \cdot C_0$, which is true if $K < C_0/C_I = k^*$. We have just derived part of rule 6. Rule 4 also refers to k^*, and that relationship is obtained similarly.

Notice that these rules suggest certain things you should or should not do in developing a plan. They do not guarantee that you will find the best plan, but they do help eliminate many alternatives.

The other rules involve m^*. While we will use these, it is considerably more difficult to explain how they are derived. Instead, we will return to our example and consider production plans for the entire year.

For the Smooth Products Company, there are 240 production days per year, and the average is $n = 20$ days per month. The costs and other parameters are summarized in Table 9-4. By rule 1, since $m^* = 2$, the use of a seasonal layoff is economically feasible. Therefore, we should consider when to schedule a layoff.

The natural planning horizon at the end of May is a good time to schedule a layoff because every plan of interest has inventory at the MI level in May, and rule 3 says that this is a precondition for a planned layoff. Review problem

Table 9-3 Rules for Aggregate Planning

DEFINITIONS

C_H = cost of increasing production by hiring one worker

C_F = cost of decreasing production by firing one worker

C_O = overtime premium per unit (i.e., additional cost of producing one aggregate unit in overtime)

C_I = cost of holding one aggregate unit in inventory for 1 month

n = average number of production days per month

p = productivity, or daily output of aggregate units per worker

m^* = largest integer less than $-0.5 + [0.25 + 2(C_H + C_F)/(npC_I)]^{1/2}$

l^* = largest integer in $(C_H + C_F)/(npC_O)$

k^* = largest integer in C_O/C_I

seasonal layoff = reduction in work force for which the next scheduled work-force change is an increase (hiring)

RULES

1. Two seasonal layoffs should be at least $2(m^* + 1)$ months apart. Therefore, if $2(m^* + 1) > 12$ months, seasonal peaks should not be met through planned layoffs and hiring.
2. Inventory should be at the minimum level at least once in every $2(m^* + 1)$ periods. If a plan violates this rule, it can be improved by an immediate layoff, with hiring at some future time. An exception to this occurs when the work force is currently at its minimum level.

Layoffs

3. Work-force reductions should only occur in period 1 (i.e., immediately) or when inventory is at the minimum level, MI (e.g., at the end of a peak season).
4. After a layoff do not use overtime within $k^* + 1$ months or hiring within $m^* + 1$ months. (If necessary, a smaller layoff should be planned to avoid such premature increases in production.)

Hiring and Overtime

5. Temporary production increases of l^* or fewer months' duration should be accomplished through overtime. For longer time spans, temporary hiring (i.e., followed by layoff) is cheaper.
6. After hiring people, do not plan a layoff within $m^* + 1$ months, or use overtime within k^* months. Avoid these by hiring sooner. (This does not apply to first-period hiring, since hiring sooner is impossible.)

Timing of Production

7. Within the restrictions above, produce as late as possible to minimize inventory costs.

2 from the preceding section suggests that December is also a natural planning horizon, so we might consider a layoff there as well. However, one of these two layoffs can be ruled out. Since $2(m^* + 1) = 6$ and there are only 5 months from January to May, rule 1 prohibits scheduling both these layoffs. The interval from May to December is longer; therefore, a layoff at the end of May is more attractive than one in January. Even if there is no layoff in January, there must be some hiring before May. We know this because the average production rate through May is 5.0 (the MCP rate), which cannot be achieved with the present work force because of the 10% limit on overtime (4.5 plus 10% is 4.95). Furthermore, since $l^* = 1$, rule 5 prohibits using overtime in more than one consecutive month.

Table 9-4 Planning Parameters for the Smooth Products Company

n = 240/12 = 20 working days per month
p = 0.01 aggregate unit per worker per day
C_H = \$400 per worker hired
C_F = \$200 per worker fired
C_O = \$2000 per unit produced in overtime
C_I = \$12,000/12 = \$1000 per month per unit of inventory
m^* = integer less than 2.23, or 2 months
l^* = integer part of 1.5, or 1 month
k^* = integer part of 2.4, or 2 months
I_0 = 80 units of inventory on hand
W_0 = 450 workers currently on the payroll
MCP = 5.0 units per day through May (105 days), or 525 units total

Based on these observations, two plans have been proposed:

Plan 1. Allow 10% overtime in May, and hire immediately (in January) the smallest number of workers to meet the May peak. Since May has 22 days, we have 2.2 overtime days and 105 regular-time days to achieve 525 units of production ($CR_5 - I_0$). The daily rate must therefore be 525/107.2 = 4.897 units per day. With a daily productivity of 0.01 unit per worker, 4.897 may be achieved with 490 workers; therefore, 490 − 450 = 40 must be hired immediately. We assume that they will be laid off after May.

Plan 2. Postpone hiring as long as possible under rule 6, and use 10% overtime in May. Because of the layoff at the end of May, rule 6 requires us to hire at the beginning of March (or earlier) so that the workers are retained at least $m^* + 1 = 3$ months. Therefore we will have 450 workers (the present level) through February and 514 through May. (This may be verified using the same method as in plan 1.) The reader should be able to predict which plan will be best by reviewing rules 5, 6, and 7.

Table 9-5 shows the calculation of inventory for plan 1, and the costs of both plans are summarized in Table 9-6. By hiring more temporary workers

Table 9-5 Inventory for Plan 1

Period	Work Force	Days	Production: Regular[a]	Production: Overtime[b]	Cumulative Production Plus I_O	Cumulative Demand[c]	Inventory[d]
	450 = (W_0)				80 = (I_0)	0	
Jan.	490	22	107.8		187.8	70	117.8
Feb.	490	18	88.2		276.0	120	156.0
Mar.	490	22	107.8		383.8	220	163.8
Apr.	490	21	102.9		486.7	420	66.7
May	490	22	107.8	10.5	605.0	570	35.0
June	450 (assumed)						Total = 539.3

[a] Regular time production = (work force) · (productivity) · (days), in which productivity is 0.01.

[b] Overtime ≤ 10% of regular time, just enough to satisfy requirements in May.

[c] Cumulative demand from Table 9-1.

[d] Inventory = cumulative production + I_0 − cumulative demand. Note that inventory is measured in aggregate production units, or 100 worker-days worth of product.

Table 9-6 Costs for Plans 1 and 2

Source	Cost per Unit	Plan 1		Plan 2	
		Units	Cost	Units	Cost
Inventory	$1,000	539.3	$539,300	498.1	$498,100
Hiring	400	40	16,000	64	25,600
Firing	200	40	8,000	64	12,800
Overtime	2,000	10.5	21,000	10.9	21,800
Subcontracting	3,500	0	0	0	0
Total			$584,300		$558,300

later in the year, plan 2 achieved lower overall cost because the increased hiring and firing is more than offset by decreased inventory.

REVIEW PROBLEMS

1. Modify plan 2 by hiring two fewer people (lower daily production by 0.02) in March, instead hiring those two plus one more person in April. Layoffs occur at the end of May, as before. Compare the new plan to plan 2.

2. Modify (the original) plan 2 by hiring three people in February, and reducing the March-to-May work force by one. Evaluate the new plan. (Be careful. The March hiring is reduced by four people, since the three hired in February will remain on the job.)

3. Presuming that a subcontract is for at least one month, why should production never be subcontracted unless in-house production is already at capacity of 7.0 per day?

Solutions

1. Compared with plan 2, March inventory drops by two workers' output, or (2)(0.01)(22) = 0.44 aggregate unit; the extra person replaces (0.01)(21) = 0.21 unit in April, leaving the April inventory 0.44 − 0.21 = 0.23 unit below the plan 2 level. By the end of May, the inventory is back to plan 2, with 0.22 unit produced by the extra peron and 0.01 produced at overtime. Since C_I is $1000 per month, the saving in inventory cost amounts to (0.44 + 0.23 + 0)($1000) = $670. The cost of hiring and laying off the extra person is $600, together with the $20 cost of an additional 1% of overtime (0.01 × $2000), yields a net cost decrease of $50. This change is desirable.

2. The February inventory goes up by (3)(0.01)(18) = 0.54, but this excess is reduced to 0.54 − 0.22 = 0.32 in March, 0.11 in April, and is eliminated at the end of May; thus, inventory cost increases by (0.54 + 0.32 + 0.11 + 0)($1000) = $970. Plan 2 hires 64 in March, but the new plan hires 3 in February and 60 in March, for a total of 63 hired; thus, both hiring and firing drop by 1 person, saving $600. The additional inventory cost already exceeds the saving from reduced hiring and firing, even without including the slight increase in overtime; therefore, the change is not worth it.

3. To hire 1 worker for a month and then fire the worker costs \$600, for an average of 20 days of production, or 0.20 unit. To subcontract for the same amount would cost (0.20)(\$3500) = \$700.

9-4 A SPREADSHEET MODEL FOR AGGREGATE PLANNING

This section discusses how the graphical approach to aggregate planning can be augmented by the use of spreadsheet software. Looking at Tables 9-5 and 9-6, it is easy to see that the various calculations can be performed by systematically adding and multiplying values appearing in the tables. This is precisely the type of application to which spreadsheet analysis can be applied effectively. Moreover, once the spreadsheet has been developed, the ''what if'' (that is, sensitivity analysis) capability of spreadsheet software can be used to facilitate the aggregate planning decision process.

We will illustrate this approach with a LOTUS 1-2-3 spreadsheet model of the Smooth Products Company aggregate planning problem, repeating some of the previous discussion using the spreadsheet terminology. (See Fischer and Mazzola 1987 for a spreadsheet approach to a two-product example.)

The basic spreadsheet model, developed for the MCP plan, is shown in Figure 9-4. The rows of the spreadsheet (labeled with numbers) correspond to various quantities, decisions, and costs arising in the aggregate planning problem, and the columns (labeled with letters) generally correspond to each month in the five-month planning horizon. The last column is used to collect costs, and the total cost of the MCP is shown in the bottom right-hand corner of the spreadsheet.

Figure 9-5, containing each of the cell definitions, is also provided to aid in understanding the underlying logic behind the spreadsheet. Proceeding down column B in Figures 9-4 and 9-5, we see that *Demand* for the month of June is 70 (aggregate) units. Next, the *Net Production Requirement* for January, defined as this month's demand minus the previous month's ending inventory (in this case, B2 − 80, since the initial inventory is 80). The negative value for the net production requirement means that we begin the month with more units in inventory than would be needed to satisfy January's demand. The *Number of Production Days* (22) is specified in row 4, and in row 5, the *Units per Month per Worker*, which is equal to the aggregate production units per worker per day multiplied by the number of production days (0.01*B4).

The *Number of Workers* is specified in row 6. Notice that rows 6, 11, and 13 are indicated in boxes and highlighted. The reason for singling out these rows is that once the spreadsheet model is built, the aggregate-planning decision options will be explored by changing (only) values within these rows. That is, the values that we specify in these rows will determine the size of the work force (and hence hiring and firing), the amount of overtime, and the number of units subcontracted in each period. (In LOTUS 1-2-3, all cells outside these rows may be protected from being changed.)

Once the number of workers is specified in row 6 (which is 500 for the MCP), the number of units produced by *Regular Time Production* (row 7) is computed as the number of units per month per worker times the number of workers (B5*B6).

The next three rows concern the change in the size of the work force, and the corresponding hiring or firing cost. Row 8 computes the *Change in Work Force* by taking the number of workers this month and subtracting from it the

A	B	C	D	E	F	G	H
1 Month	Jan	Feb	Mar	Apr	May	Hiring/Firing	Cost Totals
2 Demand	70	50	100	200	150		
3 Net Production Requirement	−10	−70	−60	30	75		
4 Number of Production Days	22	18	22	21	22		
5 Units per Month per Worker	0.22	0.18	0.22	0.21	0.22		
6 Number of Workers	500	500	500	500	500	450	
7 Regular Time Production (units)	110	90	110	105	110		
8 Change in Work Force	50	0	0	0	0	−50	
9 Hiring Cost	$20,000.00	$0.00	$0.00	$0.00	$0.00	$0.00	$20,000.00
10 Firing Cost	$0.00	$0.00	$0.00	$0.00	$0.00	$10,000.00	$10,000.00
11 Overtime (units)	0	0	0	0	0		
12 Overtime Cost	$0.00	$0.00	$0.00	$0.00	$0.00		$0.00
13 Subcontract (units)	0	0	0	0	0		
14 Subcontracting Cost	$0.00	$0.00	$0.00	$0.00	$0.00		$0.00
15 Total Monthly Production	110	90	110	105	110		
16 End-of-Month Inventory	120	160	170	75	35		
17 Inventory Cost	$120,000.00	$160,000.00	$170,000.00	$75,000.00	$35,000.00		$560,000.00
18 Total Cost							$590,000.00

Figure 9-4 Smooth Products Company Spreadsheet for the MCP Plan

A	B	C	•••	F	G	H
1 Month	Jan	Feb		May	Hiring/Firing	Cost Totals
2 Demand	70	50		150		
3 Net Production Requirement	+B2−80	+C2−B16		+F2−E16		
4 Number of Production Days	22	18		22		
5 Units per Month per Worker	0.01*B4	0.01*C4		0.01*F4		
6 Number of Workers	500	500	•••	500	450	
7 Regular Time Production (units)	+B5*B6	+C5*C6		+F5*F6		
8 Change in Work Force	+B6−450	+C6−B6		+F6−E6	+G6−F6	
9 Hiring Cost	400*@MAX(B8,0)	400*@MAX(C8,0)		400*@MAX(F8,0)	400*@MAX(G8,0)	@SUM(B9..G9)
10 Firing Cost	200*@MAX(− B8,0)	200*@MAX(− C8,0)		200*@MAX(− F8,0)	200*@MAX(− G8,0)	@SUM(B10..G10)
11 Overtime (units)	0	0	•••	0		
12 Overtime Cost	2000*B11	2000*C11		2000*F11		@SUM(B12..F12)
13 Subcontract (units)	0	0	•••	0		
14 Subcontracting Cost	3500*B13	3500*C13		3500*F13		@SUM(B14..F14)
15 Total Monthly Production	+B7+B11+B13	+C7+C11+C13		+F7+F11+F13		
16 End-of-Month Inventory	+B15− B3	+C15− C3		+F15− F3		
17 Inventory Cost	1000*@MAX(B16,0)	1000*@MAX(C16,0)	•••	1000*@MAX(F16,0)		@SUM(B17..F17)
18 Total Cost						+H9+H10+H12+H14+H17

Figure 9-5 Smooth Products Company Spreadsheet: Cell Definitions

number of workers last month (B6-450, because the initial work-force size is 450). If this difference is positive, the *Hiring Cost* is computed by multiplying the hiring cost per worker by this increase (400*@MAX(B8,0), where @MAX(x, y) is equal to the maximum of x or y). Alternatively, if there is a decrease in the size of the work force (that is, the value in cell B8 is negative), the *Firing Cost* is computed as the firing cost per worker times the decrease in the number of workers (200*@MAX(−B8,0)).

Continuing down column B, in row 11 we specify the number of units produced in *Overtime,* which equals 0 for the MCP. The *Overtime Cost* is computed in row 12 by multiplying the overtime cost per unit by the number of units produced in overtime (2000*B11). Rows 13 and 14 perform the corresponding calculations for the number of units obtained through subcontracting.

The *Total Monthly Production* is calculated in row 15 by adding regular-time production plus overtime production plus units subcontracted (B7 + B11 + B13). The *End-of-Month Inventory* is then computed by subtracting the net production requirement for the month from the total monthly production. (For the MCP, the January end-of-month inventory [120] is greater than January's total production, since we started with a negative net production requirement.) A negative end-of-month inventory means that demand is backlogged. The monthly *Inventory Cost* is computed in row 17 by multiplying the inventory cost per aggregate unit by the (nonnegative) end-of-month inventory (1000*@MAX(B16,0)).

The calculations for subsequent months are basically identical, with the slight modification that the *Net Production Requirement* (row 3) for each month is computed by taking the demand for the month and subtracting from it the previous month's ending inventory (row 16). Similarly, the *Change in Work Force* is computed by taking the difference between the specified number of workers for that month and the previous month's number of workers.

Column G is used to account for the cost of adjusting the work force to its desired end-of-horizon level. For the Smooth Products Company example, we assume that the work force will return to 450 workers at the end of May (as specified in cell G6). The resulting change in the work force is computed in cell G8 (G6-F6), and the corresponding hiring or firing cost is computed in cells G9 and G10 using the same calculations discussed previously.

In column H, the costs are summed across each of rows 9, 10, 12, 14, and 17, resulting in the *Cost Totals* for hiring, firing, overtime, subcontracting, and inventory, respectively. These cost components are then summed down column H, yielding the *Total Cost* for the aggregate plan in cell H18. As calculated earlier, we see that the MCP has a total cost of $590,000.

Plan 2 from the preceding section is shown in Figure 9-6. To evaluate this plan using the spreadsheet model, the only changes in the spreadsheet occur in row 6 (*Number of Workers*) and row 11 (*Overtime*). Specifically, the entries in row 6 are changed to 450, 450, 514, 514, and 514, corresponding to the number of workers in January through May, respectively; and row 11 was changed to reflect the 10.9 units of overtime in May. With these small changes, the spreadsheet immediately shows that the *Total Cost* of this plan is $558,300.

The use of the spreadsheet model is not limited to these specific plans. The power of the model, in fact, lies in its ability to facilitate the search for low-cost production plans. This is accomplished by exploring combinations of values in the decision rows (rows 6, 11, and 13), in conjunction with the rules in Table 8-3. As the user explores the ''total-production-cost surface'' by testing these various combinations, the model also provides helpful insight into the sensitivity of changes in total cost to the various decision variables. (Problem 20 asks you to do this for the Smooth Products Company and to compare your answer with the optimal solution obtained using linear programming, discussed in the next section.)

In its present form the spreadsheet model does not directly account for the specified minimum inventory (MI_t) levels each month. Rather, as the user evaluates various production plans by changing values in the three decision rows, it is the user's responsibility to ensure that *End-of-Month Inventory* values do not go below the stated MI_t values. For example, in plan 2 notice how the overtime production specified in May brings the end-of-month inventory to the desired MI value of 35. (Problem 21 at the end of the chapter explores how this requirement might be incorporated directly into the spreadsheet.)

The spreadsheet model is easily expanded to handle more general situations. By adding one additional row, the model can accommodate backlogging of demand (see review problem 3). Also, the model can be generalized to consider more than one product type or family, or to allow for nonlinear costs (reflecting, for example, economies or diseconomies of scale). In addition, the model can be expanded to take into account learning-curve effects. The use of the learning curve in aggregate production planning is discussed in Section 9-6.)

REVIEW PROBLEMS

1. What changes would have to be made to the spreadsheet model in Figure 9-4 to evaluate plan 1 from the previous section?

	A	B	C	D	E	F	G	H
1	Month	Jan	Feb	Mar	Apr	May	Hiring/Firing	Cost Totals
2	Demand	70	50	100	200	150		
3	Net Production Requirement	−10	−59	−40	46.92	88.98		
4	Number of Production Days	22	18	22	21	22		
5	Units per Month per Worker	0.22	0.18	0.22	0.21	0.22		
6	Number of Workers	450	450	514	514	514	450	
7	Regular Time Production (units)	99	81	113.08	107.94	113.08		
8	Change in Work Force	0	0	64	0	0	−64	
9	Hiring Cost	$0.00	$0.00	$25,600.00	$0.00	$0.00	$0.00	$25,600.00
10	Firing Cost	$0.00	$0.00	$0.00	$0.00	$0.00	$12,800.00	$12,800.00
11	Overtime (units)	0	0	0	0	10.9		
12	Overtime Cost	$0.00	$0.00	$0.00	$0.00	$21,800.00		$21,800.00
13	Subcontract (units)	0	0	0	0	0		
14	Subcontracting Cost	$0.00	$0.00	$0.00	$0.00	$0.00		$0.00
15	Total Monthly Production	99	81	113.08	107.94	123.98		
16	End-of-Month Inventory	109	140	153.08	61.02	35		
17	Inventory Cost	$109,000.00	$140,000.00	$153,080.00	$61,020.00	$35,000.00		$498,100.00
18	Total Cost							$558,300.00

Figure 9-6 Smooth Products Company Spreadsheet for Plan 2

2. In the computation of inventory cost in row 17 of Figures 9-4 and 9-5, explain why we compute 1000*@MAX(B16,0) instead of simply calculating 1000*B16?

3. What modifications would have to be made to the basic model in Figures 9-4 and 9-5 to allow for backlogging of demand?

Solutions

1. To evaluate plan 1 in the basic spreadsheet model (Figure 9-4), change the entries in row 6 (*Number of Workers*) to 490 in columns B through F, and change the overtime amount in cell F11 to 10.5.

2. If total monthly production is too low, the value of end-of-month inventory (B16) will be negative, meaning that demand has been backlogged. If B16 has a negative value and we do not compute @MAX(B16,0), the negative value will be multiplied by the monthly inventory carrying cost per unit, yielding a negative cost, which is incorrect.

3. The spreadsheet model is easily expanded to accommodate backlogging by inserting a row between rows 17 and 18 (in which case the current row 18 [*Total Cost*] becomes row 19). The new row 18 is labeled ''*Backlogging Cost,*'' and the backlogging cost is computed in each column (month) as C_B*@MAX(−B16,0), where C_B is the backlogging cost per unit per month. These values would then be summed across the row, and their sum placed in column H. Finally, this backlogging-cost total would be added to the *Total Cost* amount in cell H19.

9-5 AGGREGATE PLANNING BY LINEAR PROGRAMMING

As we saw in the previous section, the calculations required to analyze aggregate plans may be implemented on a computer, giving the manager instantaneous feedback on the cost of alternatives. With more sophisticated programs, the computer can make suggestions or even find a minimum-cost solution, within the specified limitations. In this section, a linear programming (LP) formulation is used as an example. It should be no surprise that the formulation is rather lengthy, considering all the options and calculations we have been through in Section 9-3. (You should understand the material in Appendix C on linear programming before proceeding with this section.)

The complete LP formulation is shown in Table 9-7. The first equation is the cost over the T months of the planning horizon. The terms C_H, C_F, and so on, are the per unit costs of the variables representing hiring, firing, and so on, which will now be described.

The work-force variables at the beginning of each period are the number of workers (W_t), the number hired (H_t), and the number fired (F_t). Equation 4 accounts for the hiring and firing by increasing or decreasing W_t compared with the previous period's work force (W_{t-1}).

The production variables during each period are total ''within-firm'' production (P_t), overtime production (O_t), and undertime (U_t), which is the amount by which production falls short of the normal amount of regular time ($n_t p W_t$) for the given work force. Equation 5 forces the LP to pay an overtime premium

Table 9-7 Aggregate-Planning LP

$$\text{Minimize} \sum_{i=1}^{T} (C_H H_t + C_F F_t + C_O O_t + C_U U_t$$

$$+ C_S S_t + C_I I_t) + C_H H_{T+1} + C_F F_{T+1} \qquad (3)$$

subject to the following constraints for each period $t = 1, 2, \ldots, T$

Work force

$W_t = W_{t-1} + H_t - F_t$ (this equation also holds for period $T + 1$) (4)
Minimum work force $\leq W_t \leq$ maximum work force
$0 \leq H_t \leq$ allowable monthly hiring
$0 \leq F_t \leq$ allowable monthly firing
W_0 = current work force (period 0 only)
W_{T+1} = required ending work force (period $T + 1$ only)

Production

$P_t = n_t p W_t + O_t - U_t$ (5)
$0 \leq P_t \leq n_t \times$ (daily plant capacity)
$0 \leq O_t \leq (n_t p W_t) \times$ (allowable fraction of overtime)
$0 \leq U_t \leq (n_t p W_t) \times$ (allowable fraction of undertime)
$0 \leq S_t \leq$ available subcontracting

Inventory

$I_t = I_{t-1} + P_t + S_t -$ (demand in period t) (6)
(safety + cycle stock) $\leq I_t \leq$ storage capacity
I_0 = inventory currently on hand
I_T = required ending inventory

Note: In these constraints, n_t is the number of productive days available in period t, and p is the daily worker productivity (aggregate production units per worker per day). Both of these are constants. The other variables are defined in the first several paragraphs in the text of this section.

or an undertime opportunity cost if production is above or below $n_t p W_t$, respectively. Production subcontracted to an outside firm (S_t) is added to the within-firm production in equation 6, to be discussed next.

Inventory at the end of each period (I_t) is the remaining set of variables, and equation 6 adjusts the inventory between periods by the difference between total production (both within firm and subcontracted) and demand. (Note that this period-by-period adjustment gives exactly the same result as subtracting cumulative demand from cumulative production, as in the earlier sections.)

The rest of the formulation consists of more or less self-explanatory restrictions (or constraints). Note that every phrase expressed in words in Table 9-7 represents a number that must be obtained before the LP can be run. They are a mixture of hard facts (such as daily plant capacity) and softer numbers, representing policies that may be flexible (such as allowable hiring or firing).

The two variables I_0 and W_0 tie the LP to the current status of the firm, expressed as actual inventory and work force at the present time. The variables I_T and W_{T+1} represent the desired status of the firm (targets) after the T periods have expired. Normally, their values are unimportant to the period 1 decision, since a natural planning horizon is likely to exist between periods 1 and T. However, it is advisable to perform a sensitivity analysis on these target values. If they have no effect on the first-period decisions, a horizon has been encountered somewhere in the planning period. (One way of dealing with these targets when a planning horizon does not exist has been described in McClain and Thomas 1977.)

Many different computer packages exist for solving linear programming problems, and aggregate-planning LP models are readily solved using standard LP packages. Research has shown, however, that many types of aggregate-planning LPs can be solved with algorithms that are more efficient than general LP packages. For example, Posner and Szwarc (1983) developed a one-pass method for solving the aggregate-planning LP problem in the more general case in which backorders are allowed (at a cost). Also, Aronson, Morton, and Thompson (1984) define an algorithm for the production-smoothing problem without inventory. Their algorithm is shown to run faster than the corresponding LP model, and it is useful for planning the production of perishable commodities (for example, newspapers and fresh produce), as well as for certain types of services.

Using LP for Aggregate Planning

To use the LP, demand forecasts must be obtained, along with each of the cost coefficients of equation 3, the productivity factor (p), working days (n_t), and the upper and lower limits shown in Table 9-7. For a twelve-month model, this could be a sizable task. Fortunately, only the demand forecasts and initial inventory and work force will change each time the model is used; there will be only occasional changes in the other parameters. Consequently, only fourteen numbers are needed as a regular input, and the LP will find a minimum-cost plan.

A word of caution is in order. The solution recommended by the LP minimizes the cost equation 3, which is not necessarily an accurate reflection of the actual cost. Thus, although the solution is *optimal for the model*, there may be solutions that are better in that they achieve lower actual cost or because the LP model does not capture some quantitative or qualitative requirements that could not be expressed in the linear constraints and objective function. A discussion of four of the expected difficulties follows.

Costs Are Not Linear. Fortunately, in aggregate planning, costs can usually be approximated by either linear costs or by increasing marginal costs. If the curvature of the actual cost function is not extreme, linear functions provide satisfactory approximations. Methods are available to improve the accuracy of the model by approximating an increasing marginal cost curve with a series of straight-line segments. In LP texts, this is referred to as "separable programming" or "piecewise-linear approximation."

The Productivity of Workers Changes with Time. For new employees, learning while on the job causes an increase in productivity. This is sometimes represented by using a learning curve (Ebert 1976). However, disruptions caused by breaking in new workers can degrade the performance of experienced employees. The combination of these two effects can remove aggregate planning from the realm of LP (see, for example, Reeves and Sweigart 1982, Khoshnevis and Wolfe 1983, Hiller and Shapiro 1986, and Dada and Srikanth 1990).

Production Rates Cannot Always Be Changed Continuously. This presents a more difficult problem. Usually, small variations in production can be achieved through overtime or hiring and firing, but large changes are accomplished by adding an entire work shift. Thus H_t and F_t may be restricted to a few discrete values. There are two approaches to this problem: (1) Interact with the computer, varying the lower and upper bounds on work force among possible values until a satisfactory solution is obtained; or (2) use a more complex computer code that will restrict some variables to discrete values (see the discussion of mixed-integer LP in Hillier and Lieberman 1986).

The Effects of Other Company Decisions Are Not Recognized in the Standard LP Formulations. For example, advertising may change the demand pattern. Also, financial considerations such as cash budgeting are related to employment, production, and inventory patterns, since these are the largest users of cash in many companies. (Models that attempt to tie these different planning areas together in an LP are given in Thomas 1971.)

REVIEW PROBLEMS

1. In equation 5, explain what $n_t pW_t$ means, and restate the equation in words. Also explain the two constraints that follow equation 5.

2. How could the formulation be changed to take into account natural attrition in the work force? Specifically, suppose that on the average some fraction r of the work force leaves each month as a result of natural attrition, and this fraction is independent of the number of workers hired or fired. Assume that attrition occurs between periods.

3. How would the formulation change if there were three aggregate products (e.g., three types, in the terminology of Bitran and Hax [1977], discussed in the introduction)?

Solutions

1. W_t is the work force, p is the regular-time daily production output per worker, and n_t is the number of days in time period t; thus, $n_t pW_t$ is the regular-time production capacity in period t. For time t, equation 5 reads ''production equals regular-time capacity plus overtime production minus undertime production.'' The last term accounts for reduced output if production is set below the normal output of the work force. The next constraint keeps production between zero and the monthly plant capacity. In the next constraint, the right-hand side is the regular-time capacity multiplied by the fraction of overtime allowed by policy. The constraint therefore keeps overtime production between zero and the maximum allowed by company policy for the time period.

2. If a fraction r of the work force leaves at the end of each period because of attrition, constraint 4 would have to be modified to $W_t = (1 - r)W_{t-1} + H_t - F_t$. It is necessary to multiply the size of the previous month's work force by $(1 - r)$, since that will be the fraction of workers returning.

3. In each period there would have to be three inventory, three production, and three subcontracting variables. Equation 6 would be repeated for each product. Equation 5 would be modified so that total production of the three products was covered by the work force, with adjustments for overtime and undertime.

9-6 THE USE OF THE LEARNING CURVE IN PRODUCTION PLANNING

As we saw in Chapter 5, the learning curve provides a useful tool for modeling the decrease in the time required to make a product as the production system gains experience. Recall that the basic learning-curve formula, $Y_i = ai^{-b}$, gives the direct labor hours (Y_i) required for production of the ith cumulative unit. The parameter a is the time required to produce the first unit, and the learning parameter, b, is determined by the rate of learning.

Incorporating the learning curve in production planning can be important in strategic planning. By accounting for the learning effect in planning future capacity, we can formulate competitive production plans and attempt to make optimal use of capacity. (See, for example, the HBS case "Insight Optical Equipment Company.") The following example will help to illustrate this application of the learning curve in intermediate-range capacity planning.

Example: The Strategic Learning Company

The Strategic Learning Company (SLC) produces expensive high-technology industrial robots. Their most recent line of robot is the ROB1, which is designed for materials-handling applications in high-temperature environments (such as feeding material into and retrieving it from a blast furnace). Although modified for each customer, all ROB1 robots are similar in design and construction and are considered to be one model. SLC produces ROB1s strictly on a make-to-order basis, and to date SLC has produced four ROB1s. The last of these required a total of 2900 labor hours to produce and rolled off the production floor near the end of June. SLC management was pleased with this, since they had assumed that the ROB1 was following an 80% learning curve, and the fourth unit came close to the estimated production time.

SLC has received an invitation to bid on an order for five ROB1s. They can begin production on these on the first production day in July. (Any remaining production days in June are used for equipment repair, preventive maintenance, layout improvement, and so forth.) There are 10 production workers assigned to the ROB1 project team. ROB1 project-team members are the only workers permitted to work on this project, and they do not perform work on any jobs outside the project. SLC assumes that there are 20 production days per month (to allow for unanticipated interruptions, absences, and so forth), and that there are 8 hours per workday. All work is performed in one production shift. Because of the highly skilled nature of the work, SLC avoids having the ROB1 team work overtime.

SLC must quote a competitive delivery time if it wishes to win this order. However, the customer is a major purchaser of equipment, and SLC desires to keep them as customers well into the future. It is therefore essential that SLC quote a realistic delivery time for the entire order of five robots.

We begin our analysis by calculating the delivery time for the order. Recalling the basic formulas for the learning curve from Chapter 5, we have $b = -(\log 0.8)/(\log 2) = 0.3219$. Also, since $Y_4 = 2900$, it follows that $2900 = a(4)^{-0.3219}$. Solving, we obtain $a = 4531.073$.

We next compute the total hours required to complete the five-robot order. In particular, total production time (in labor hours) = $Y_5 + Y_6 + \cdots + Y_9 = 4531.073(5^{-0.3219} + 6^{-0.3219} + \cdots + 9^{-0.3219}) = 12{,}219.87$ labor-hours.

Using the existing project team consisting of 10 production workers, the time required to produce all five ROB1s will be 12,219.87/[(10)(20)(8)] = 7.63 months. SLC can promise delivery in a little over 7.5 months. Compare this with the "no-learning" delivery time, which is equal to [(5)(2900)]/[(10)(20)(8)] = 9.06 months.

Now suppose that the customer is willing to pay a $10,000 bonus if the entire order can be filled by the end of December. SLC can assign additional workers to the ROB1 project. Training and present-job replacement cost is approximately $1000 per new worker. Because of potential disruption, only one new worker can be added to the project team per month. Assume that new workers are transferred to the project from within the existing company-wide work force and that they are added at the beginning of the month. They are sufficiently skilled to produce at the same rate as the other team members. (This assumes that new workers do not slow down the learning process. Problem 24 extends this analysis so that new workers are allowed a training period at a slower production rate.)

To address the issue of whether or not to seek the bonus, we must calculate how many additional workers will be required to bring the completion date within the six-month limit. Using the present project team, a total of 10(20)(8) = 1600 labor-hours are available each month. We thus need to obtain an additional 12,219.87 − 6(1600) = 2619.87 labor-hours over the six-month period spanning July through December.

In the following table we compute the additional labor-hours obtained by a policy of bringing in one new worker at the beginning of each month as quickly as possible. For example, if we decide to bring in two new workers, one will arrive at the beginning of July and work for 6 months, and the other will arrive at the beginning of August and work for 5 months; each will work 160 hours per month.

Additional Workers Added	Additional Labor-Hours Obtained over Six Months
1	8(20)(6) = 960
2	160(6 + 5) = 1760
3	160(6 + 5 + 4) = 2400
4	160(6 + 5 + 4 + 3) = 2880
5	160(6 + 5 + 4 + 3 + 2) = 3200
6	160(6 + 5 + 4 + 3 + 2 + 1) = 3360

From this we see that SLC will have to bring in four additional workers (because 2880 > 2619.87) at a cost of $4000. This is well below the $10,000 bonus; SLC should plan to obtain the bonus. Notice also that this schedule will provide some slack (2880 − 2619.9 = 260.1 labor-hours) for unanticipated occurrences.

The preceding example points out the usefulness and importance of the learning curve in planning future capacity needs. Before establishing their final production plan, SLC should perform a sensitivity analysis on the various parameters. For example, by how much could the learning rate vary before SLC encountered serious difficulty meeting the deadline date (see, for example, review problem 1)? Also, how sensitive is the plan to minor disruptions in the work force?

As with the graphical approach, this analysis lends itself readily to a spreadsheet model. The spreadsheet model has the advantage of quickly obtaining answers to questions relating to sensitivity analysis.

REVIEW PROBLEMS

1. If SLC were to find out that production of the ROB1s was actually following an 85% learning curve, how long would it take to complete the five-robot order, assuming that no additional workers were hired?

2. Is it reasonable for SLC to assume the presence of a learning-curve effect in planning production for the ROB1s?

Solutions

1. With an 85% learning rate, b = 0.2345 and a = 4014.034. The time required to produce the five robots is $Y_5 + Y_6 + \cdots + Y_9 = 4014.034(5^{-0.2345} + 6^{-0.2345} + \cdots + 9^{-0.2345})$ = 12,795.19 labor-hours. With 10 production workers, 12795.19/[(10)(20)(8)] = 8.00 months will be required to fill the order. This is relatively close to the 7.6 months required for the (faster) 80% learning rate, and SLC may want to quote a conservative order time closer to 8 months to allow for this.

2. This question is difficult to answer without knowing more about SLC's production environment, and in particular, its past experience with using the learning curve. Note, however, that SLC plans to use remaining production capacity in June for equipment repair, preventive maintenance, and layout improvement, all of which contribute to learning.

SUMMARY

The techniques available for intermediate-range planning are suitable for either hand computation (using graphs such as Figure 9-3) or computer-assisted planning. The computations are complicated by the existence of many options in meeting requirements, multiple time periods, and restrictions handed down from higher-level decisions. Using graphs helps to visualize differences between production plans and may suggest good alternatives. The alternatives must then be analyzed for their cost performance and effect on company policies. Using an optimizing scheme such as linear programming takes the process one step further by isolating a plan that minimizes a cost model.

To use the graphical method, products must be aggregated into a single measure of output. With more advanced methods such as linear programming, several aggregate product types may be used. After aggregate plans have been determined, the first period becomes the basis for the short-range, detailed plans of individual products. That is, the plan's first period is disaggregated. At the conclusion of that period, aggregate plans may be reconsidered using new forecasts and recognizing the amount by which actual experience deviated from the plan. Thus the most recent experience may affect plans over the entire planning horizon. Plans made in this manner are called rolling schedules.

A substantial portion of this chapter has been devoted to presenting rules and principles for constructing aggregate plans. It is important to stress that methods such as those presented in this chapter should be used not as the sole decision criteria but rather for generating valuable information. For example, a cost basis for justifying actions such as layoffs was presented. Of course, decisions such as these are not based on short-run cost minimization alone. The company's commitment to its work force or its position in the community may overrule the cost-based policies.

Regardless of the method used for finding and comparing alternatives, one of the problems of implementation is obtaining the needed data. The costs and demands are estimated by commonly available cost accounting and forecasting methods. However, many of the planning restrictions are subjective; but at the same time they are important to future labor or community relations. It is important to include as many realistic restrictions as possible in developing alternative plans.

The function of a medium-range plan is to anticipate upcoming changes in work force and production, and to set overall output rates that may be translated into a detailed schedule at least for the first planning period. It is important, therefore, to use the best information available in setting these plans. For example, more elaborate (and expensive) forecasting methods are justified for aggregate planning than for individual product decisions.

The Handicraft Jewelry caselet (which follows) requires one to make an informed judgment about what kind of product mix will be held in inventory. It also provides an example in which the structure of the work force is somewhat different than in the Smooth Products example.

CASELET

THE HANDICRAFT JEWELRY COMPANY

The Handicraft Jewelry Company makes four handmade items on a fairly large scale. The items are all 24-carat gold, so inventory is expensive. Their demand forecast is as follows:

Period	Item 1	Item 2	Item 3	Item 4
March	800	1000	1000	600
April	800	800	600	800
May	1200	1400	500	1000
June	1200	1600	500	1500
July	400	400	500	1000
August	800	1000	500	400

Items 1, 2, and 3 are rings (class, wedding, and other), and they each take 1 hour to produce. Item 4 takes 2 hours to produce. Items 1, 2, and 3 have a unit variable cost (direct labor plus materials) of $20 each, while item 4 costs $76. Monthly inventory cost is 1% of the value of the items in inventory.

The regular work force consists of highly skilled artisans who have worked for the company an average of 22 years. Accordingly, the use of seasonal layoffs has been ruled out. This results in a regular work-force capacity of 4000 worker-hours per month at $16 per hour, with the possibility of up to 800 overtime worker-hours at $24 per hour.

There is, in the community, a cadre of people who are pleased to work for part of a year, to supplement family income. Over the years, 15 people have received enough training to qualify for this short-term employment. When such a person is hired, he or she is always employed full-time for full calendar months. In the first month, productivity is only 50%, compared with a regular worker, increasing to 75% in the second month, and 100% thereafter. For temporary workers, the month is 160 hours long, and no overtime is allowed. The pay is $12 per hour. The total cost of hiring and eventually laying off each temporary worker is $800, including a certain amount of catch-up training. (The training cost is in addition to the lower productivity in the first 2 months.)

Operating policy has been to produce only as necessary to meet each month's demand. Hiring decisions are postponed to the last possible date. Recently Handicraft began serious consideration of smoothing out the production process by building up inventory in anticipation of peak demands.

With very little promotional effort, June demand can be increased by 400 units for item 1. However, this has not been done because the month of June is already quite hectic because of the high sales rate. Passing up opportunities such as this is one of the main reasons for considering the use of inventory.

Required

1. Convert the demand forecasts into an aggregate measure, month by month.
2. Find the MCP solution, and determine its inventory.
3. Determine at least one work-force plan to achieve the MCP production rates.
4. Compare the cost of your MCP plan with that of the current plan.
5. Determine at least one plan that is better, and evaluates its cost.
6. Modifying your plan from (5), evaluate the cost of meeting the increased June demand, and compare that with the cost under current policy.

PROBLEMS

1. What is production smoothing? In what ways is it desirable? What problems can it cause?

*2. How can production smoothing be accomplished in a service organization?

3. What kinds of organizations are not likely to use inventory in intermediate-range planning?

*Problems with an asterisk have answers in the back of the book.

4. Is forecasting accuracy enhanced or lessened by the aggregation of products for intermediate-range planning? Explain.

*5. The Red Wine Producers face a demand pattern with a peak in December. All their wine is produced within a few weeks after the autumn harvest. It is stored in vats until it is needed for the bottling process. Currently their bottling policy is to run one shift from January to September and to add a second shift for each of the 3 months in advance of the December peak, to build enough inventory to avoid shortages. They are considering the possibility of smoothing out the bottling process to a uniform rate for the entire 12 months with one shift.

   a. Make a list of the costs that would be incurred if they went to the 12-month level-production bottling system but that are not currently incurred.

   b. List the costs they are incurring now that would be avoided or reduced by the level-production system.

   c. What new risks would be incurred under 12-month level production?

   d. What risks would be reduced or eliminated under 12-month level production?

6. Mentally place yourself into Figure 9-2. You are standing at time zero and your height is 80 aggregate production units. The dotted-line cumulative-requirements curve represents a hillside you must climb. From where you stand, what is the farthest point you can see? (Remember, the ground is opaque.) What does this have to do with the concepts we have discussed?

*7. In Figure 9-2 and Table 9-2, the natural planning horizon occurs in May (at day 105), but the MCP very nearly meets the requirements curve again in December (day 240).

   a. How much higher can the December forecast be before December becomes the natural horizon?

   b. Because the requirements curve is plotted on a cumulative basis, increases in June's forecast will increase cumulative requirements for June and each month thereafter. Show that an increase of 50 in June's forecast will shift the natural planning horizon to December.

   c. How much higher can the August forecast be before the natural horizon is no longer in May? If such an increase occurs, when will the natural horizon be?

   d. Suppose that several of the forecasts were changed at the same time. What impact would the following combination of forecast changes have on the period 1 (January) production rate? June, down 20; July, up 40; October, down 10; and December, up 20.

8. Smooth Products Company is considering a constant production rate of 4.90 per day. Calculate inventory at the end of each month through July. (The Smooth Products data are given in Table 9-1.) What is the maximum inventory? Is there any backlogging?

*9. Alprodco uses 4-week ''months'' for its aggregate-planning time periods, and each month has 20 working days (ignore holidays for this problem). The monthly demands in aggregate units are 110, 110, 140, and 100 for the next 4 months and will then remain at or below 110 for the rest of the year. Inventory is currently 20 aggregate units, and this is the minimum level allowed by company policy.

a. Using months (rather than days) as the time unit, plot the cumulative requirements.

b. Their production plan is 115, 130, 115, and 100, for the next 4 months, respectively. Will this meet requirements?

c. What costs would change if 5 units of production were shifted from month 2 to month 3? Will this be an improvement?

*10. The accompanying graph shows a cumulative-requirements curve and a cumulative-production plan for 10 months. (Notice that cumulative demand has not been drawn.)

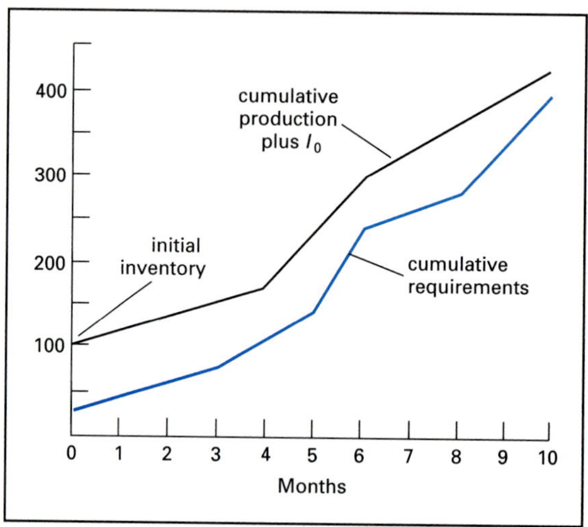

a. What time period has the highest planned production rate? How do you know?

b. What is the production rate for month 1?

c. Find the natural planning horizon by plotting the MCP with a straightedge.

d. Suggest a production plan that will save money, compared with the one shown in the graph. (Hint: Try to cut down on the inventory in month 6 without increasing other costs.)

11. Farmer Milton McSnarf grows rutabagas, selling some immediately and storing others in his root cellar. They can be stored indefinitely, and he has one growing season per year. Because of the increasing popularity of rutabaga milkshakes, he predicts the following demands:

Year	Forecast of Demand (thousands of bushels)
1	100
2	120
3	200
4	250
5	300

Workers are hired for at least 1 year. He currently has 3 workers. He had 110,000 bushels of rutabaga production last year, and he has a total of 20,000 bushels in inventory. He makes no attempt to maintain a minimum inventory. Workers are paid only for work actually done. (They are not compensated for undertime.) Overtime costs $1 per bushel more than regular time. Inventory cost is $0.10 per bushel per year. Hiring one person costs $1000, and one person can produce 30,000 bushels per year in regular time and 10,000 bushels per year in overtime.

a. Find the MCP solution and evaluate its total cost (over and above the regular-time wages) over the natural planning horizon, without using overtime.
b. The solution to part a requires some hiring. Consider the timing of the hiring decisions, and suggest a better plan, still without using overtime. Explain why your plan is better. (This can be answered with no calculations. However, you may use numbers if you wish.)
c. Does overtime look like an attractive alternative in this case? Why or why not?

12. (This problem is based on Milton McSnarf's farm, problem 11, but you need not have completed problem 11.) The crop of year 1 proved to be quite rewarding for farmer McSnarf. He planned to produce 190,000 bushels, but the crop was actually 220,000. Rutabaga milkshake popularity also exceeded expectations, and demand for rutabagas was 150,000 bushels. McSnarf has adjusted his forecasts upward by 25% and forecasts 400,000 for year 6.
    a. Calculate his starting inventory for year 2. Why should it be different from the *planned* year 1 ending inventory?
    b. Find the MCP production rate.

*13. Fancy Furniture, Incorporated, has a small production facility that has been characterized as machine limited. That is, the production output cannot be increased by adding personnel because the furniture is assembled and finished on a production line with a fixed number of workstations. However, they do have the capability of adding a second shift or of working overtime to meet demand in the peak summer months. If a new shift is added by hiring workers, production capacity is doubled, and the new workers must be retained for either 2 months, 4 months, or permanently. Fancy Furniture never produces at reduced capacity. The production rate is 5000 units per shift per month. Demand forecasts for the next 8 months are shown in the accompanying table along with other necessary information.
    a. Find the MCP solution, and find its cost.
    b. Evaluate the cost of a solution that hires a second shift for months 6 and 7.
    c. Being careful to account property for the fact that the preceding two plans will have different ending inventories, which one would you recommend and why? The data are as follows:

Inventory holding cost = $40 per unit per month
Regular-time pay = $80,000 per month per shift
Overtime pay = 50% more than regular time pay

Fringe benefits = \$30,000 per month per shift
Hiring cost = \$10,000 to hire a new shift
Firing cost = \$40,000 to lay off an entire shift
Monthly production capacity = 5000 units per shift
Monthly overtime capacity = 1250 units per shift
Minimum inventory = constant at 500 units
Inventory entering first period = 1500 units

Month	1	2	3	4	5	6	7	8
Demand (thousands)	5	5	4	4	7	7	8	8

14. The Knudsen Boltz Company produces three high-quality fabricated parts for the automotive industry. Since their main customers are companies that produce expensive cars, their sales have not been hurt by economic slowdowns as much as some other firms in the industry. Some data concerning the firm are given in the accompanying table.

	Sales Forecasts (thousands)							
	Year 1 (Current Year)			Year 2				Year 3
Quarter	**2**	**3**	**4**	**1**	**2**	**3**	**4**	**1**
Item 1	40	50	55	50	80	90	80	60
Item 2	35	35	40	35	50	60	50	40
Item 3	20	15	15	20	20	20	25	25

Based on their experience and the data, the firm notes that quarter 3 (July, August, and September) is usually their highest sales period, but that the industry is expected to enjoy a large increase in sales beginning late this year. Item 3 is sold as a spare part through independent dealers, whereas items 1 and 2 are sold to the automotive companies for assembly and to both the automotive companies and independent dealers as spares. Each item is sold in several different styles, and the figures given are totals for each type of item. Each of the three items requires 0.10 hour of labor per unit.

The firm has a policy of not using layoffs or overtime in their aggregate plans. They currently have 11,000 labor-hours per month capacity, and the plant is capable of using up to 15,000 labor-hours per month. (To exceed 15,000 hours, the firm would have to add new facilities, since 15,000 would require three shifts, 7 days per week.) Inventory cost is 20% of the item value per year. The unit values are \$10, \$8, and \$4 for items 1, 2, and 3, respectively. The cost of hiring is \$2000 for the first 1000 labor-hours hired in a quarter. They currently have an aggregate inventory equivalent to 5000 labor-hours, and they feel that the optimal MI_t inventory to have during the entire 2-year planning horizon is 4000 labor-hours.

a. Compute the aggregate demand forecast, by quarter, using 1000 labor-hours as the unit of measure.

b. When they are producing to build up an aggregate inventory, which item(s) should they be producing for inventory?

c. Given your answer to part b, what should one use for the per-unit cost of holding aggregate inventory?

d. Calculate the MCP solution and evaluate its total cost, using C_I = \$3000 per aggregate unit of inventory per quarter.

e. They are considering hiring 500 labor-hours in each of quarters 2 through 7, so that they will have labor-hours (in thousands) of 11.0, 11.5, 12.0, 12.5, 13.0, 13.5, 14.0, and 14.0 in the eight quarters of the planning horizon. Calculate the aggregate inventory of this option. Evaluate the total cost over the eight quarters.

f. Compare the MCP to the plan proposed in part e. Show how the differences in cost arise. Which plan do you recommend?

g. If the firm had a natural attrition of employees (because of resignations, retirements, etc.) of 200 labor-hours each quarter, discuss how this would change your recommended work-force levels.

*15. The U.R. Truckin Company produces 38 types of shirts for sale to organizations. Their forecasts for the next 6 months, in aggregate form are as follows:

Month	1	2	3	4	5	6
Forecast	4000	5000	4000	8000	5000	4000

After month 6 demand will remain at the 4000 to 5000 level until next year's peak (month 16).

All shirts take exactly the same time to produce. With their 10-person work force, they have a regular time capacity for 5000 shirts per month and overtime capacity for 1000 shirts per month. Each shirt costs \$7 to produce in regular time, including \$4 labor and \$3 material. Overtime labor is \$6, therefore, a shirt costs \$9 to produce in overtime. They can hire people at a cost of \$600 each, and each person can produce 500 shirts per month in regular time and 100 in overtime. New workers are paid the same amount as regular workers, and the \$600 cost of hiring includes training cost so that they are as efficient as regular workers. It costs \$600 to fire someone. They want always to meet demand, and they think the carrying-cost rate for inventory is 2% per month (based on regular-time cost). No minimum inventory has been specified, and they are currently out of stock (have no inventory). First, Truckin managers want to decide whether to use seasonal hiring and layoffs as an ongoing policy.

a. Show that a seasonal hiring-layoff cycle is economically justifiable for U.R. Truckin, using rule 1, Table 9-3. During which month would a seasonal layoff take place?

b. If they lay off people in month 4, how soon should they consider adding to the work force again?

c. When they hire seasonal workers, how long should they be kept?

d. Given the previous answers, only one seasonal hiring-layoff schedule should be considered. When should hiring occur?

Truckin has decided on a seasonal layoff after period 4, adding again to the work force in period 11. Now they want to focus on what to do right now, considering the current inventory and work-force situation. Workers are available to be hired immediately, and they expect this situation to prevail indefinitely.

e. Show that the present work force cannot meet demands without using overtime or hiring more workers.

f. What is the most economical way to increase production: overtime or hiring and then firing later? You may wish to use the rules in Table 9-3.

g. Truckin management is considering hiring workers at the beginning of period 4. What is your advice to them?

h. Calculate the total cost over a 4-month horizon of each of the following three plans. Don't forget the cost of layoffs at the end of period 4.

	Plan 1		Plan 2			Plan 3		
Month	**Regular-time Production**	**Over-time Production**	**Regular Time**	**Over-time**	**Hiring**	**Regular Time**	**Over-time**	**Hiring**
1	5000	0	5000	0	0	5000	0	0
2	5000	0	5000	0	0	5000	0	0
3	5000	0	5500	0	1	5000	0	0
4	5000	1000	5500	0	0	5500	500	1
			(layoff)		−1	(layoff)		−1

i. The personnel manager is arguing that temporary help should not be hired for a period of less than 6 months, since it is too expensive to train such a person and short-term employment may give the company a bad name in the community. How much will it cost the company to go along with personnel's advice, based on your answer to part h?

16. a. Formulate problem 15 as a linear program (LP). Assume that pay is on a "per shirt produced" basis.

b. Suppose that on the average one person per month resigns, retires, or is fired for poor performance. Show how to include that in your LP.

c. What do you think the effect might be of having no cost of undertime in the objective function?

*17. A company that produces fire trucks follows a make-to-order policy. That is, no trucks are produced until a firm order has been received. They currently have orders for 10 fire trucks, and they desire to keep the backlog between 5 and 15 trucks. They currently have 100 workers and can produce 10 trucks per month. Their demand forecasts are as follows, using 4-week months:

Month (4-week period)	1	2	3	4	5	6
Forecast	10	5	9	13	15	9

a. What constant production rate would bring the backlog to its maximum level at the end of 6 months?

b. Show that the production plan in part a does not meet their backlog policy.

c. Following the method used in Table 9-2 except using months in place of days, calculate the MCP solution. Note that the maximum backlog of 15 corresponds to a minimum inventory of $MI_t = -15$. Does the MCP stay within the backlog limits?

d. Would you recommend that they adopt the MCP plan or stay with the current rate of 10 trucks per month? Why?

18. The medical-surgical department in City Hospital occupies eight floors. They desire to schedule a complete shutdown of one floor for maintenance, which will require 2 weeks. The maintenance needs to be done within the next 8 weeks.

Demands for hospital beds are measured in patient-days. A patient who stays 6 days has consumed 6 patient-days. Each floor can produce up to 100 patient-days per week. The demand forecast for patient-days is shown in the accompanying table. Of course, a patient-day may not be inventoried, but can be backlogged within limits, since 40% of the patients are admitted for elective procedures, which can be delayed.

Week	1	2	3	4	5	6	7	8
Forecast of patient-days demanded	700	800	1000	700	700	800	600	700

Experience has shown that the efficiency of production is reduced when the backlog of patient-days is low, simply because empty beds are more likely to remain unfilled as a result of mismatches between the schedules of the physicians, patients, and operating rooms. As a guide, 100 patient-days can be produced per floor per week if the average backlog is 50 or more patient-days per floor (400 total), but production drops to 95 if the average backlog is between 1 and 50 patient-days per floor. (The average backlog is the beginning-of-the-week backlog plus the ending backlog divided by 2.) When there is no backlog, production does not exceed 90 per week. The present backlog is 500 patient-days, which is considered quite high.

The current plan is to shut down the floor right after the peak demand, so that it would be closed in weeks 4 and 5.

a. Evaluate their plan.

b. Suggest and evaluate an alternative.

c. What will the production rate be in week 9 of their plan if demand is 700?

19. Develop a spreadsheet model for problem 15.

a. Evaluate the three plans in problem 15, part h, using the spreadsheet.

b. Use the spreadsheet model, together with the rules in Table 9-3 (and the insight gained in problem 15), to search for a low-cost production plan. (If you answered problem 16, part a, compare your production plan with the optimal LP plan found in problem 16.)

20. Implement the spreadsheet model of Section 9-4 for the Smooth Products Company, and use it to do the following:

a. Verify the solutions to review problems 1 and 2 in Section 9-3, pertaining to modifications of plan 2.

b. Attempt to find the least-cost production plan by systematically exploring feasible combinations of the values in the three decision rows (corresponding to the number of workers, overtime, and subcontracting). Be sure your production plan is within the maximum daily production rate of 7 aggregate units per day, avoids backlogging, and satisfies all minimum inventory (MI_t) requirements.

c. Compare your solution with the optimal solution obtained by formulating and solving the Smooth Products Company production-planning problem as a linear program (LP). Compare the production plans. Does the LP plan differ substantially from the best solution you were able to find using the spreadsheet? If so, why?

21. The spreadsheet model in Section 9-4 does not explicitly capture the requirement that the minimum inventory level (MI_t) must be satisfied each month. Devise a way in which the model will account for this requirement. (Hint: Modify the model so that whenever one of these requirements is violated an extremely large cost is incurred, indicating an error.)

*22. The Small Yacht Company produces medium-priced fiberglass sailboats. They have recently introduced a new 17-foot model, the Sleek Sloop. The hull number on the last Sleek Sloop was 16, and it required 3750 labor-hours to make. Small Yacht has just received an order from a large theme park in the southeastern United States for 8 Sleek Sloops. Small Yacht has 15 full-time employees, each working 8 hours per day, 20 days per month.

a. How long will it take for Small Yacht to fill the 8-sailboat order?

b. Assuming that the Sleek Sloop is following an 85% learning curve, how long will it take to fill the order?

23. Consider the Strategic Learning Company production-planning problem of Section 9-6, involving the use of the learning curve. This question performs sensitivity analysis on the rate of learning. (You may wish to develop a spreadsheet model to answer this question.)

a. For each of the following learning rates, compute the time required to complete the 5-robot order: 70%, 75%, 80%, 85%, and 90%. (Assume that no additional workers are hired.) Graph these values by plotting completion time as a function of learning rate.

b. For each of the learning rates in part a, determine whether it is worthwhile for SLC to seek the extra bonus for completing the project by the end of December.

24. In the Strategic Learning Company problem of Section 9-6, we assumed that a new worker could be added to the project team each month, and that new workers were able to produce at the same rate as other team members. It is possible, however, that a new worker might require a training period before being able to produce at the same rate as an experienced worker. One way to incorporate this into the analysis is by assuming that each new worker performs at a specified fraction of the regular production rate, after which the worker performs at the regular rate.

Modify the analysis of the SLC problem assuming now that a new worker performs at 85% of the regular rate during the first month on the project team. (Hint: Model this by assuming that a new worker works only 85% of the available time during the first month.) Should SLC still try to obtain the bonus?

25. The Personalized Computers Corporation (PCC) has recently introduced its top-of-the-line customized personal computer, which is purchased primarily by company presidents and CEOs. They have produced 20 units to date, with the last unit requiring 1800 labor-hours. PCC has had good success using the learning curve in planning production and feels that the rate of learning for this new model is 75%. The demand forecast for the new model over the next four months is as follows.

Oct.	Nov.	Dec.	Jan.
7	10	7	3

Because the new model is custom-made, PCC assigns a single work crew to produce them. PCC employees compete for placement on this crew, and PCC therefore likes to make changes to the crew only a few times per year (October 1, February 1, and June 1). PCC has the flexibility to increase, decrease, or not make a change in the size of the crew on these dates. New crew members begin working immediately in the morning on the day they are assigned to the crew. There are 8 hours each workday, 20 workdays per month, and there are currently 50 workers assigned to the crew working on this model.

Because of the premium payed to crew members, PCC uses the minimum crew size possible to meet its demand, according to the objective specified by management. (Hint: You may wish to use a spreadsheet model to solve this problem. If you do not use a spreadsheet model, it may be helpful to approximate $Y_m + Y_{m+1} + \cdots + Y_n$ by

$$a \int_m^n i^{-b}\, di = a\left(\frac{n^{1-b} - m^{1-b}}{1 - b}\right)$$

a. Assuming that the PCC workers do not work overtime, how many workers should be added to or removed from the crew so that cumulative demand is met by the end of January. (Demand for months prior to January may be backlogged.)

b. Supposing that all crew members can work up to 10% overtime per month, how should the size of the crew be changed on October 1 so that cumulative demand is met by the end of January?

c. Assuming that no overtime is used, how should the crew size be changed on October 1 so that demand is not backlogged in either December or January?

d. Assuming that no overtime is used, how should the crew size be changed on October 1 so that demand is not backlogged in any month?

REFERENCES

ARONSON, J.E., T.E. MORTON, and G.L. THOMPSON, "A Forward Algorithm and Planning Horizon Procedure for the Production Smoothing Problem without Inventory," *European Journal of Operational Research*, vol. 15, 1984.

BAKER, K., "An Experimental Study of the Effectiveness of Rolling Schedules in Production Planning," *Decision Sciences*, vol. 8, no. 1, 1977.

BITRAN, G., and A. HAX, "On the Design of Hierarchical Production Planning Systems," *Decision Sciences*, vol. 8, no. 1, 1977.

BRENNAN, L., J. BROWNE, B.J. DAVIES, M.E.J. O'KELLY, and A.R. GAULT, "An Analysis of the Overtime Decision," *International Journal of Operations and Production Management*, vol. 2, no. 3, 1982.

DADA, M., and K.N. SRIKANTH, "Monopolistic Pricing and the Learning Curve: An Algorithmic Approach," *Operations Research*, vol. 38, no. 4, 1990.

EBERT, R.J., "Aggregate Planning with Learning Curve Productivity," *Management Science*, vol. 23, 1976.

FISCHER, W.A., and J.B. MAZZOLA, *Fischtale Enterprises* (and Instructor's Manual), 2nd ed., Glenview, Ill.: Scott, Foresman, 1987.

HBS CASE SERVICES, "Insight Optical Equipment Company," Harvard Business School, 9-675-168, revised, 1979.

HILLER, R.S., and J.F. SHAPIRO, "Optimal Capacity Expansion Planning When There are Learning Effects," *Management Science*, vol. 32, no. 9, 1986.

HILLIER, F.S., and G.J. LIEBERMAN, *Introduction to Operations Research*, 4th ed., San Francisco: Holden-Day, 1986.

KHOSHNEVIS, B., and P.M. WOLFE, "An Aggregate Production Planning Model Incorporating Dynamic Productivity," in 2 parts, *IIE Transactions*, vol. 15, nos. 2 and 4, 1983.

KUNREUTHER, H.C., and T.E. MORTON, "Planning Horizons for Production Smoothing with Deterministic Demands. I," *Management Science*, vol. 20, no. 1, September, 1973.

MCCLAIN, J.O., and L.J. THOMAS, "Horizon Effects in Aggregate Production Planning with Seasonal Demand," *Management Science*, vol. 23, no. 7, March, 1977.

POSNER, M.E., and W. SZWARC, "A Transportation Type Aggregate Production Model with Backordering," *Management Science*, vol. 29, no. 2, February, 1983.

REEVES, G.R., and J.R. SWEIGART, "Multiperiod Resource Allocation with Variable Technology," *Management Science*, vol. 28, no. 12, December, 1982.

SASSER, W.E., "Match Supply and Demand in Service Industries," *Harvard Business Review*, November–December, 1976.

THOMAS, L.J., "Linear Programming Models for Production-Advertising Decisions," *Management Science*, April, 1971.

THOMAS, L.J., and J.O. MCCLAIN, "An Overview of Production Planning," in GRAVES, S., A. RINNOOYKAN, and P. ZIPKIN, eds., *Handbook in Operations Research*, Amsterdam: North-Holland-Elsevier, 1991.

c h a p t e r

10

Multistage Manufacturing Systems: Material Requirements Planning

Coordinating manufacturing when there are several different stages of production and storage requires inventory-management tools different from those in Chapter 8. Product structure, process design, and management control of the system determine what demands are placed on each stage of production. Several approaches are available to deal with this complex coordination problem. In this chapter we will discuss *material requirements planning* and *manufacturing resource planning* (both referred to as MRP), as well as other approaches to multistage production systems, including recent research models.

Material requirements planning (MRP) is a method for coordinating detailed production plans in multistage production systems that involve many products, subassemblies, components, and materials. The basic idea of MRP is simple. One begins with a *master production schedule* for the finished product (or *end item*) and works backward to determine when and how much of each component will be needed. Because the requirements for subassemblies, components, and raw materials are calculated from the production schedule of the end product, they are said to have *dependent demand*. That is, demand for subassemblies and component parts depends on the production schedule for the end item. Once the master production schedule is established, we can anticipate these demands with considerable accuracy.

In contrast, the inventory control methods discussed in Chapter 8 are applicable to situations with *independent demand*. They apply when there are many small orders for an item arriving at random times. One of the most significant errors in the use of quantitative approaches to operations management has been the use of independent-demand inventory methods to control items with dependent demand.

To illustrate this, suppose that an end item is assembled using 100 components. (Many items are more complex than this.) The components are also used in other end items. If we treat the 100 components as if they had independent demand, we will need to carry safety stock for each component. Suppose that enough safety stock is maintained for each component to provide for a 98% chance of having the component in sufficient quantity to begin a batch. This will result in a large amount of safety stock. Nevertheless, since there is a 2% stockout probability per item, one or more of the 100 inputs will usually be out of stock, and we will often experience delays.

Alternatively, in an MRP approach the aim would be to have the exact amount needed of each component when it is time to begin a batch, thereby reducing work-in-process inventories and improving efficiency. MRP also provides a priority planning system, which helps management to allocate time on the productive facilities in an organized and effective manner.

Another method of dealing with dependent demand is the just-in-time (JIT) system, in which an end-item order causes a succession of cards to be sent back through the factory to *pull* the necessary inputs to the end item through the factory. The system is also simple in principle, and it has been effective at reducing lead times and work-in-process inventory. (We will discuss the JIT system in Chapter 12, where it will also be compared with MRP.) In Section 10-4 we will discuss other methods of dealing with the dependent demand in multistage manufacturing systems.

As an example of dependent demand we will consider the KB company (KBC), whose president and founder is Knudsen Boltz.

Example: The KB Company

KBC produces several products for sale to other manufacturing companies. Among their products are steering assemblies and other products for the automobile industry. The products involve several manufacturing steps, including raw-materials procurement, component production, and final assembly. Figure 10-1 shows the production process for three of KBC's products, which are referred to as *end items*. The three diagrams contained in the figure are called *product-structure diagrams*.

To illustrate, consider end item FA1. Using the diagram you can determine that each unit of FA1 requires 18 units of the raw material RM1, although they "arrive" at FA1 by two different routes. Ten units go into two COMP1s. Eight go into two COMP4s, which are used to make COMP3. Finally, FA1 is assembled using the indicated quantities of its three components.

KBC has a contract with their major customer that calls for a flexible production rate of finished products. They have just received notice of an increase in the requirements for FA1, FA2, and FA3, to

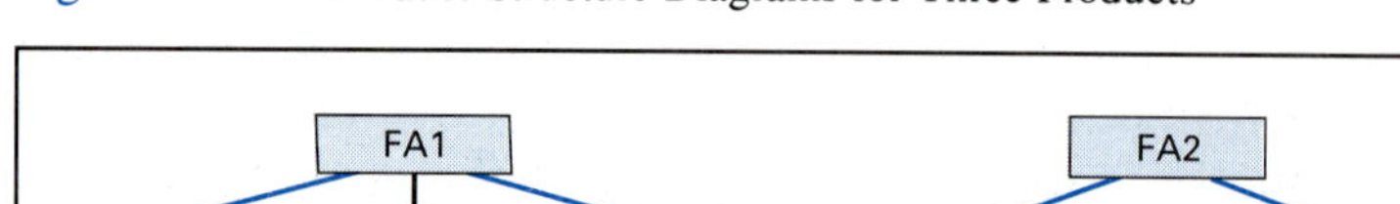

Figure 10-1 Product-Structure Diagrams for Three Products

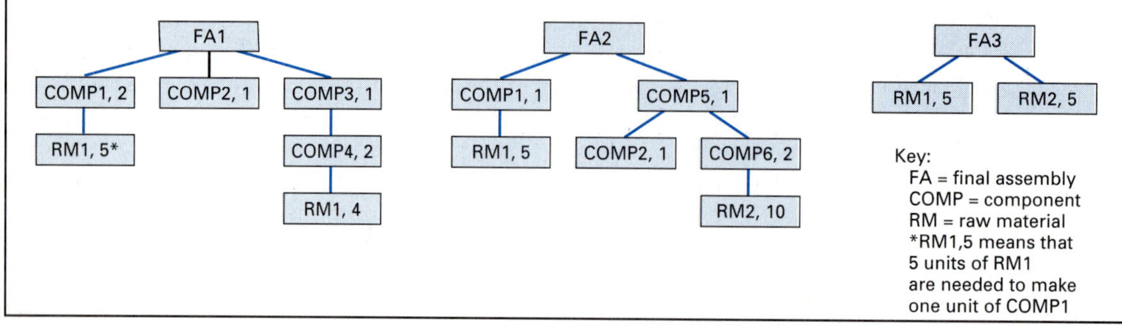

100 units of each per week. This rate of requirements is expected to hold for the next six months. Current inventories are 700, 900, and 1600 units for FA1, FA2, and FA3, respectively. KBC assembles end items in batches of 1000. The assembly facility is also used for other products, but enough capacity is available to allow for a batch to be shipped within two weeks after the required materials arrive.

KBC has a component-production facility that makes COMP1, COMP3, COMP4, COMP5, and COMP6. (COMP2 is purchased from an outside vendor, as are RM1 and RM2.) The component facility is capable of producing up to 1000 components per week. (All components require the same amount of productive capacity.) Since the facility is usually busy and a batch may have to wait, KBC plans production of components using a three-week lead time. A one-week lead time is used for the purchase of COMP2, RM1, and RM2. They currently have 1000 units of COMP1 and 1000 units of COMP6, but they do not have any inventory of the other components or raw materials at the present time. KBC has ''released'' an order for 2000 units of COMP4, which the component facility is expected to deliver to the final assembly area in week 3.

Boltz would like us to schedule production and procurement for the next few months using MRP.

10-1 REQUIREMENTS COMPUTATION

If we know the production schedule for a finished product, as well as the amount of inventory on hand of component parts and raw material, component and material demand may be computed directly. No statistical forecast is necessary. There are two aspects to this computation: quantities (based on bills of materials) and timing (based on planned lead times). Although quantity and timing are done simultaneously in MRP, we will explain them separately in the next two subsections.

The *master production schedule* for all end items is the basis for all requirements computation. It is convenient to think of end items appearing in the master schedule as being completely finished items; however, there may be options (such as color or fabric) that await a firm customer order, or the product may be only an input to another system. (This is discussed further in Section 10-3.) In any case, the master schedule is the top level of the MRP system. The master schedule for KBC is simply to produce batches of 1000 for each finished item, beginning two weeks before inventory would otherwise become negative.

The Bill of Materials

The *bill of materials* (BOM) gives the ingredients for a product. It does not explain the process or list the required tools. That information is kept in other files. The BOM file lists an item's inputs and their quantities. Six examples are shown in Figure 10-2. It can also contain *where-used* information, so that we can examine all the uses of a particular component. Other methods of representing the data include an *indented BOM*, a *summarized BOM*, and a *matrix BOM*. (The definition of each of these items is given in Wallace and Dougherty 1987.) The details of the data processing will not be covered here (see Vollman et al.,1988 for more discussion).

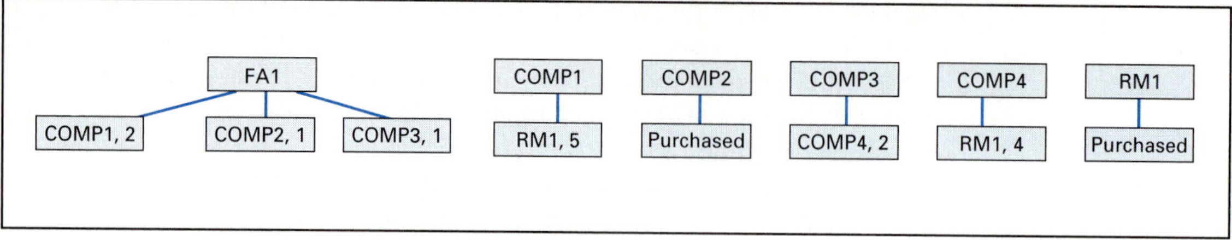

Figure 10-2 Bills of Materials for FA1 and Its Inputs

Using sequential processing, an MRP system explodes the bills of materials to obtain the complete requirements that result from end-item demand. *Level-by-level processing* is used to convert the master schedule for end products into a schedule for all components and raw materials. The production schedule at one level generates the demands for the next level through the bills of materials. At KBC the master schedule is a period-by-period plan for production of the three finished products (level 0, the top level). Using the BOMs, this schedule generates a period-by-period requirement (dependent demand) for components (level 1). Once a production schedule is formed to meet these level-1 requirements, the BOMs are used to calculate the level-2 requirements, and so forth. (This will be illustrated in detail later.) Because each product generates demands for several components in several time periods, this process is often referred to as *BOM explosion*.

To implement level-by-level processing, each component must be assigned to only one level.[1] Otherwise the total requirements for a component cannot be considered all at once. *Low-level coding* is used to avoid incorrectly assessing the need for production. For example, a component that is used on level 2 and level 3 will be designated as a level 3 component. Thus, when level 3 is processed (after level 2), all requirements for that component can be considered simultaneously.

Figure 10-3 displays KBC's product structure using low-level coding. As before, the numbers after a comma indicate the number of units of a component or material used to make one unit of the immediate successor. To illustrate low-level coding we can examine COMP2 and RM1. COMP2 goes directly into finished product FA1, but it is also required by COMP5 as part of FA2. Thus, it must be coded as a level-2 item. RM1 is used on level 1 (for FA3), level 2 (for

[1]The level refers to the depth of the part in the bill of materials. Thus, a low-level part occurs deep in the BOM, but its level is designated by a high number. (See Figure 10-3.)

Figure 10-3 Low-Level Coding for FA1, FA2, and FA3

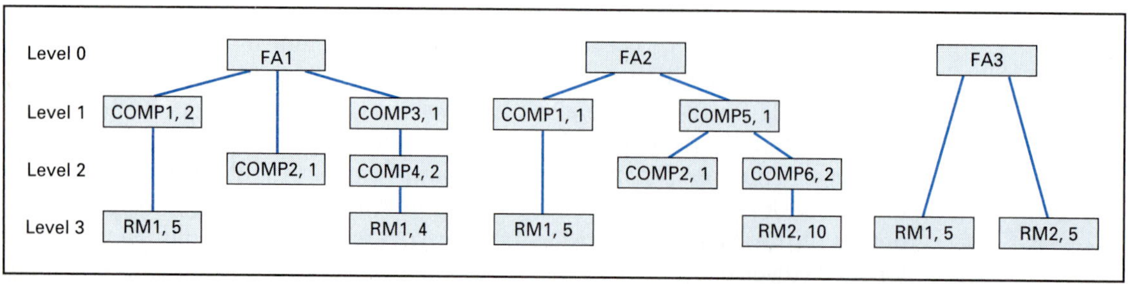

FA2 and FA1), and level 3 (as part of COMP4 in FA1). Thus, it must be coded as level-3 item.

A complete and accurate bill of materials is needed if an MRP system is to be used effectively. The task of initially organizing these data requires a large amount of effort from engineers, systems analysts, and management, in spite of the fact that the required information must be available and in daily use to operate the production process with or without MRP. We will not discuss all the potential difficulties, leaving those to texts on MRP (such as Orlicky 1975) and to your future experience. However, we will mention two problems that occur.

First, different levels of detail may have been used by different design engineers, making the bills inconsistent and hard to use for overall planning. Second, the same part frequently has several different numbers in the same company (a number may have been assigned each time it was used in a new location or product). Renumbering can be a difficult task, although at first it may seem easy. This is true because people are accustomed to the current system, and it may be hard to find all duplications in a large plant. Unless management is willing to invest the effort to produce a complete and accurate bill of materials, the MRP system will not perform up to its full potential.

Demand Computation with Time Phasing

An MRP system computes not only how many units of an item are needed but when they are needed. Units can be ordered or produced so that they arrive only when needed, rather than carrying the units in inventory and withdrawing them when needed. To facilitate this, computer records are maintained in *time buckets*, which are the small periods of time for which production plans are made. Typically, they are one day or one week in length. For KBC, the time-bucket size is one week, since they produce end items in large batches that are planned to take two weeks to complete, and since all lead times are one or more weeks in length.

MRP maintains at least four kinds of information for each part, namely *gross requirements, planned order receipts, projected available inventory balance,* and *planned order releases*. These concepts are illustrated for product FA1 in Figure 10-4.

Gross requirements are the total amount needed during each period. For FA1, the weekly requirement is 100 units, as specified by their major customer. For level 1, the gross requirements include the dependent demands derived from level-0 production plans (summed over all user items) plus any independent demand, such as for spare-parts sales.

Figure 10-4 MRP Information for FA1

Week number:		1	2	3	4	5	6	7	8	9	10	11	12
Gross Requirements		100	100	100	100	100	100	100	100	100	100	100	100
Planned Order Receipt									1000				
Projected Available Inventory	700*	600	500	400	300	200	100	0	900	800	700	600	500
Planned Order Release							1000						

*There are 700 units on hand at the beginning of week 1.

Planned order receipts are recorded for time periods in which an order is scheduled to arrive. The size of the order is indicated in the appropriate time bucket. These orders include anticipated orders that are required to prevent the inventory from becoming negative, as well as *scheduled receipts*, which correspond to firm orders that have already been placed.[2] Figure 10-4 shows that an order for 1000 units is scheduled for receipt in week 8. The quantity is 1000 units because that is the batch size specified by Mr. Boltz for finished items; the timing is week 8 because the cumulative gross requirements will have exhausted the inventory (projected inventory would become negative). If a longer planning horizon were used, a second scheduled receipt would occur in week 18, and a third in week 28.

Projected available inventory balance is the quantity of the item expected to remain after the production and demand have occurred for a period. As just discussed, the 700 units of FA1 on hand initially will all be gone after week 7. The projected available inventory in week 8 is 900 units because (a) 0 units will be carried over in inventory from the previous week, (b) an order for 1000 units is scheduled for receipt in week 8, and (c) 100 units will be required (demanded) in week 8.

The planned order release is generated by moving backward from the planned order receipt. This is called *time phasing*. For FA1, 1000 units are scheduled to be received in week 8; since the lead time is two weeks, KBC plans to keep this order in a file until week 6 and then ''release'' it to the final-assembly facility.

We are following the *midpoint convention* for determining order release dates. All receipts and requirements are assumed to take effect in the middle of the time bucket. Inventory is measured in the middle of the time bucket. If significant errors arise from lumping all record keeping at one point in the period, a smaller time bucket is appropriate.

It is often useful to calculate net requirements for determining the timing and quantity of planned order receipts (and corresponding planned order releases). *Net requirements* are computed by allocating inventory to gross requirements. If 100 units are needed in period 1 and 40 units are in inventory, there is a net requirement of 60 units. Planned order receipts must cover net requirements.

All the level-0 products are scheduled in this manner. The time-phased planned order releases are a level-0 production schedule, since they occur at just the right times to prevent shortages. MRP now uses the bills of materials to compute the quantities of level-1 products that will be needed to carry out this schedule. For example, the planned order releases for FA1 are ''exploded'' back to determine the gross requirements for COMP1, COMP2, and COMP3, which are the direct inputs to FA1. (It is sometimes helpful to refer to FA1 as the parent item to COMP1, COMP2, and COMP3, which in turn are referred to as its children.)

Planned order releases for FA1 and other level-0 products generate the gross requirements for level 1. Then planned order releases for level 1 products are computed, with respect to both time and quantity, in the manner previously discussed. For example, the production order for 1000 units of FA1 to be released in week 6 causes a planned order release for 1000 units of COMP1 in

[2]In many MRP applications, information on scheduled receipts is maintained separately from planned order receipts. This allows the user to identify easily those additional orders that must be placed to avoid product stockouts.

week 3, since (a) 2 units of COMP1 are used in each FA1, creating a gross requirement of 2000 units of COMP1 in week 6, (b) there are 1000 units of COMP1 in on-hand inventory, and (c) component manufacture requires a three-week lead time.

Because the planned order releases have been time-phased to allow for lead times, the level-1 planned order releases occur earlier than the level-0 order releases, and those in each subsequent level occur earlier still. The planning horizon must be long enough to ensure that there is time to obtain all materials and produce all components before specifying a planned order release for finished items.

The MRP system allows management input. For example, Mr. Boltz has specified the 1000-unit lot sizes that are to be used in the master schedule. Similarly, he could specify lot sizes for level-1 order releases. Those batches, in turn, cause gross requirements at level 2, which can be grouped into batches. This process is then repeated through all levels of the product structures.

For a given *lot-sizing* policy, the MRP system will report the corresponding suggested production schedule. Lot sizing is a major decision in a production setting. In an MRP environment it consists of grouping requirements (demand) occurring in discrete time periods into production batches. Batching rules can have a profound effect on the timing of production requirements, and therefore on the effective utilization of production capacity. (Lot-sizing methods are discussed in Section 10-3.)

For now, we know the lot sizes to be used by KBC at level 0. Thus, all components and materials will be needed in multiples of 1000 (the level-0 batch size); Boltz has decided that each gross requirement at levels 1, 2, and 3 will cause a planned order release once the initial on-hand inventory has been depleted. (This is referred to as *lot-for-lot scheduling* and is discussed further in Section 10-3.) Knowing these decisions allows us to give an overall view of the operation of this system through time. Figure 10-5 illustrates the operation of KBC's MRP system through week 20.

In Figure 10-5 the order release for 1000 units of FA1 in week 6 causes projected available inventory to equal 900 in week 8. It also causes a planned order receipt for COMP1, COMP3, and COMP2 to occur in week 6, since there is a gross requirement at that time and not enough inventory on hand to cover the requirements. The order releases for COMP1 and COMP3 occur in week 3, time phased three weeks earlier than their planned order receipts to allow for the three-week component lead time. The order release for COMP2 can occur in week 5, since it is a purchased part with a one-week lead time. The reader should trace the effects of each of the end-item production runs in Figure 10-5, using Figure 10-3 to obtain the inputs needed at each level. For example, consider RM2. The planned receipt of 10,000 units in week 2 is needed because of the planned order release of 1000 COMP6 units in week 2.

It should be emphasized that this 20-week plan would not stay unchanged for 20 weeks. A key advantage of MRP is the ability to change the production plan easily when there are demand changes, scrap, lost days of production, or other changes.

REVIEW PROBLEMS

1. Explain why the gross requirement for RM1 in week 10 is 8000 units.
2. What would have happened if an order for COMP4 had not already been scheduled for receipt in week 3?

Level	Week number:		1	2	3	4	5	6	7	8	9	10	11	12	13	14	15	16	17	18	19	20
Level 0	FA1: Gross Requirements		100	100	100	100	100	100	100	100	100	100	100	100	100	100	100	100	100	100	100	100
	Planned Order Receipt[a]									1000										1000		
	Projected Avaliable Inventory[b]	700	600	500	400	300	200	100	0	900	800	700	600	500	400	300	200	100	0	900	800	700
	Planned Order Release							1000										1000				
	FA2: Gross Requirements		100	100	100	100	100	100	100	100	100	100	100	100	100	100	100	100	100	100	100	100
	Planned Order Receipt											1000										1000
	Projected Avaliable Inventory	900	800	700	600	500	400	300	200	100	0	900	800	700	600	500	400	300	200	100	0	900
	Planned Order Release									1000										1000		
	FA3: Gross Requirements		100	100	100	100	100	100	100	100	100	100	100	100	100	100	100	100	100	100	100	100
	Planned Order Receipt																		1000			
	Projected Avaliable Inventory	1600	1500	1400	1300	1200	1100	1000	900	800	700	600	500	400	300	200	100	0	900	800	700	600
	Planned Order Release																1000					
Level 1	COMP1: Requirements		0	0	0	0	0	2000	0	1000	0	0	0	0	0	0	0	2000	0	1000	0	0
	Planned Order Receipt							1000		1000								2000		1000		
	Projected Avaliable Inventory	1000	1000	1000	1000	1000	1000	0	0	0	0	0	0	0	0	0	0	0	0	0	0	0
	Planned Order Release				1000		1000								2000		1000					
	COMP3: Gross Requirements							1000										1000				
	Planned Order Receipt							1000										1000				
	Projected Avaliable Inventory	0																				
	Planned Order Release				1000										1000							
	COMP5: Gross Requirements									1000										1000		
	Planned Order Receipt									1000										1000		
	Projected Avaliable Inventory	0																				
	Planned Order Release						1000										1000					
Level 2	COMP2: Gross Requirements						1000	1000									1000	1000				
	Planned Order Receipt						1000	1000									1000	1000				
	Projected Avaliable Inventory	0																				
	Planned Order Release					1000	1000									1000	1000					
	COMP4: Gross Requirements				2000										2000							
	Planned Order Receipt				(2000)[c]										2000							
	Projected Avaliable Inventory	0																				
	Planned Order Release											2000										
	COMP6: Gross Requirements						2000										2000					
	Planned Order Receipt						1000										2000					
	Projected Avaliable Inventory	1000	1000	1000	1000	1000	0															
	Planned Order Release			1000										2000								
Level 3	RM1: Gross Requirements				5000		5000					8000			10000		10000					
	Planned Order Receipt				5000		5000					8000			10000		10000					
	Projected Avaliable Inventory	0[d]																				
	Planned Order Release			5000		5000					8000			10000		10000						
	RM2: Gross Requirements			10000										20000			5000					
	Planned Order Receipt			10000										20000			5000					
	Projected Avaliable Inventory	0																				
	Planned Order Release		10000										20000			5000						

[a] Most zeros are omitted.

[b] Amount indicated in the box is the amount of inventory currently on hand at the beginning of week 1.

[c] Circled amount indicates a sceduled receipt for which an order has already been released.

[d] Assume that the 8000 units of RM1 that are required to produce the 2000 units of COMP4 currently in process have already been removed from inventory.

Figure 10-5 Material Requirements Planning System for KBC

3. On the average, is a weekly production rate of 1000 enough capacity in the component facility?

4. Even though capacity is sufficient on the average, short-term capacity problems could arise as a result of a temporarily heavy load. How does this relate to lead-time planning?

Solutions

1. From Figure 10-3, we see that the parent items for RM1 are FA3, COMP1, and COMP4. Of these, only COMP4 has a planned order release in week 10. This planned order is in the amount of 2000 units; since 4 RM1s are required for each COMP4, the resulting gross requirement for RM1 is 8000.

2. The gross requirement for COMP4 in week 3 is 2000 units; because there are no units in on-hand inventory and the lead time is three weeks, we would have to place an order for 2000 units immediately and try to have it completed in the remaining two weeks (i.e., we would have to expedite the order). We should not be surprised, however, that the order has already been placed. The MRP system picked up the planned order release last week, and the order was placed on time.

3. In total, KBC needs to produce 900 components each week, 500 for assembly into FA1 and 400 for FA2. (Remember that COMP2 is purchased.) Thus, the 1000-per-week capacity is sufficient on the average.

4. The actual lead time is a function of the current load on the facility. For example, suppose that the order releases for FA1, FA2, and FA3 happened to occur in the same week. This would generate requirements for large numbers of components, all needed at the same time, overloading the component facility. To accommodate this temporary load, some of the component orders might be released *earlier* than the stated three-week lead time.

10-2 CLOSED-LOOP MRP (MRP II)

MRP systems work properly only if the lead times assumed can actually be met within available capacity. Good system management requires that a realistic schedule be given to the MRP system and that any deviations from the schedule be fed back to make the next period's schedule realistic. This is called ''closing the loop,'' and it allows management to use MRP in a broader context, for business planning. This is referred to as MRP II (or *Manufacturing Resource Planning*). In this section we examine MRP II, beginning with an analysis of lead times and capacity planning.

Planned Lead Times

Actual lead time depends on (1) system capacity, (2) the amount of work loaded into the system, (3) the way in which work is scheduled through the system, and (4) uncertainties affecting the system (such as variable unit production times and system breakdown). Lead times are incorporated in production plans for three reasons. First, time must be allowed for the production process to be carried out. Second, since there is often a queue of jobs competing for a facility's time, waiting time must be expected. Third, since both production and waiting time may be highly variable because of breakdowns, interruptions for higher-priority work, and so on, safety time may be needed to make sure that an item is produced by the time it is needed.

MRP assumes that lead times are known in advance and then uses these *planned lead times* to calculate requirements. Planned lead times include actual production time, expected time waiting in queue, and some safety time margin. Using only the MRP logic discussed in the previous section, however, can cause actual lead times to differ dramatically from planned lead times because the MRP calculations do not take into account the finite capacity of the various centers into which work is loaded.[3]

As a product moves through a typical plant, well over 50% and often as much as 90% of its time is spent waiting. During this time, money is tied up in work-in-process inventory. Properly setting planned lead times in MRP systems (and in other production systems as well) can help to reduce that inventory and yield other benefits.

There is sometimes a temptation to inflate planned lead times in MRP systems in an attempt to allow some slack for scheduling. Consider the case of a billion-dollar manufacturing firm. In a 16-stage production process, the average lead time had grown from one week to three weeks per stage. The shorter lead times had been inflated because they had occasionally been insufficient. But as total planned lead time moved from 16 weeks to 48 weeks, work-in-process inventory tripled, the factory floor became cluttered with stock waiting to be processed, and huge amounts of money became tied up. Worse yet, the firm found that it could make very good four-month forecasts, but very bad 12-month forecasts. Thus, when the total lead time is nearly a year, they often started the wrong amounts of the wrong products. Then the necessary changes in production plans exacerbated their capacity problems. A 16-week production cycle is often easier to maintain than a 48-week cycle. Inflated planned lead times become self-fulfilling, and actual lead times will be longer than necessary.

Managing lead times, that is—keeping actual lead times, and thus the total production cycle, as short as possible—is one of the most beneficial things a manufacturing firm can do. (As we will see in Chapter 12, this is a benefit and on going goal of just-in-time production systems.) In MRP systems this is done by reducing capacity-caused delays by careful scheduling and minimizing the use of safety time.

Capacity Requirements Planning (CRP)

Capacity planning occurs on several levels in organizations. With a long planning horizon, firms decide whether to build new facilities. With a medium planning horizon they decide what changes, if any, need to be made to the labor force. In the short run, firms try to anticipate which facilities and work centers will have capacity difficulties and authorize overtime or modify the production plan. This detailed short-range planning, called *capacity requirements planning*, is the subject of this subsection. Later we will examine how long-,

[3]The practice of ignoring work-center capacity constraints is sometimes referred to as *infinite loading*. MRP specialists, however, discourage the use of this phrase because any good MRP system should account for limited production capacity.

medium-, and short-range capacity planning can be incorporated into a broader MRP framework.

Using a computerized MRP system, a manager can obtain a *load projection* or *capacity requirements plan (CRP)* for that unit. This is done by examining orders that are currently in production or waiting for production, together with orders planned for production by the MRP system. A "bill of labor" is sometimes used by the MRP system to explode capacity requirements at work centers. The result is a summary of the future activity of the productive unit. Capacity is then "planned" by scheduling overtime, extra shifts, subcontracting, or modifying the master production schedule.

Some industries plan for long periods of time, and the plan may therefore include *expected orders*. Although listed as planned orders in developing a load projection, expected orders should be removed from the system after the projection is made, to maintain the system's validity. A capacity requirements plan might be reported as shown in Figure 10-6. Such a picture helps management to see when a capacity problem is coming. The detailed scheduling tool (MRP) feeds into the higher-level problem of capacity planning. (An example is discussed in the review problems for this section.)

In many production systems a relatively small percentage of work centers are bottlenecks, or capacity-constrained work centers. For example, in the KBC example, the component facility is a bottleneck because its capacity is often not sufficient to meet the MRP-generated schedule. Since full-scale CRP requires a complete MRP explosion, it is time-consuming and may not provide sufficiently fast feedback for checking the feasibility of the master schedule.

Rough-cut capacity planning is often used to determine the feasibility of the production plan at key bottleneck work centers. Prior to implementing CRP, loads on these key work centers (or facilities) are examined, and if necessary, adjustments are made to the master schedule and short-term capacity. If the production plan still remains infeasible, a large change is needed. Once the production plan clears these critical work centers, CRP can be used to examine capacity-usage projections across the entire system, if desired.

Closed-Loop MRP

The basic idea of *closed-loop* MRP is that the master schedule must be a feasible plan throughout the system. Capacity usage is fed back to the master

Figure 10-6 Capacity Usage (or "Load") Projection for One Productive Unit

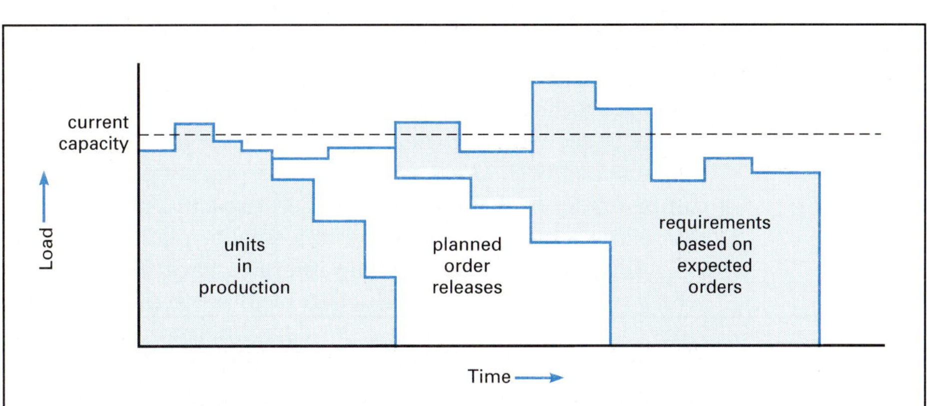

schedule, as are the details of how the plan is (or is not) carried out on the shop floor. The MRP system identifies any requests that cannot be completed during the lead time allowed. As changes occur, adjustments must be made to capacity or to the master schedule so that it remains feasible. Even if the master schedule is realistic in a planning sense, it is still necessary to monitor both capacity and materials during the actual execution of the production-scheduling plans. As problems arise during execution of the plans, or as new information is gathered, information is fed back in an attempt to resolve any short-term problems, as well as to modify the system so that future plans will reflect this new information.

Information must also be fed back to the aggregate production planning problem discussed in Chapter 9. Experience at meeting the schedules, as well as load projections, is fed back to indicate how facilities (work centers) are faring within the overall aggregate plan. Prior to that, the aggregate plan was used as input to the MRP system in two ways: First, the work-force decisions set the capacity level. Second, seasonal-inventory plans led to large production orders to build up the required seasonal inventory. The MRP system responds to this in the same way it responds to any demand. The two-way interaction allows the coordination of the aggregate plan and the detailed MRP. This planning approach, going from aggregate planning to master schedule to detailed plans, with feedback, is similar to a hierarchical planning system (discussed in Chapter 11).

It is possible to use linear or integer programming methods to plan lead times and stay within capacities, including the potential use of overtime. (Billington et al. 1983, Karmarker 1987, and Kanet 1982 discuss the relationship between capacity planning and lead times.) The use of mathematical programming methods to compute feasible lead times, within capacity constraints, is discussed in Section 10-4.

Manufacturing resource planning (MRP II) is a system of business planning for manufacturing companies, using MRP. It involves the use of the closed-loop MRP system to plan resources and link the functions of the firm, including production planning, master scheduling, material requirements planning, capacity requirements planning, shop-floor control, and purchasing.

A comprehensive view of the closed-loop MRP system is reproduced in Figure 10-7 (Berry et al. 1979). This figure focuses on the role of master scheduling in the manufacturing planning and control system, and it highlights (1) the three levels of capacity planning (resource planning, rough-cut capacity planning, and CRP or capacity requirements planning), (2) demand management, and (3) feedback from the shop floor. It also points out the possibility of having an aggregate production plan and a separate final assembly schedule. We will discuss each of these.

Production planning refers to a plan in aggregate units such as the sales value of production. *Resource planning* involves long-term capacity planning and checks to see whether there is sufficient (or too much) capacity to serve future demand needs. If there is not enough capacity, plans for additional capacity can be made; or if there is unutilized capacity, plans can be made to reduce it (by selling a plant or relocating to a smaller plant for example).

Rough-cut capacity planning interacts with the master schedule to predict which work centers (or production facilities) represent potential capacity problems for the particular schedule. *Capacity requirements planning* (CRP) looks at the MRP schedule in detail and generates load projections. Problems at this level are also fed back to the master scheduling activity.

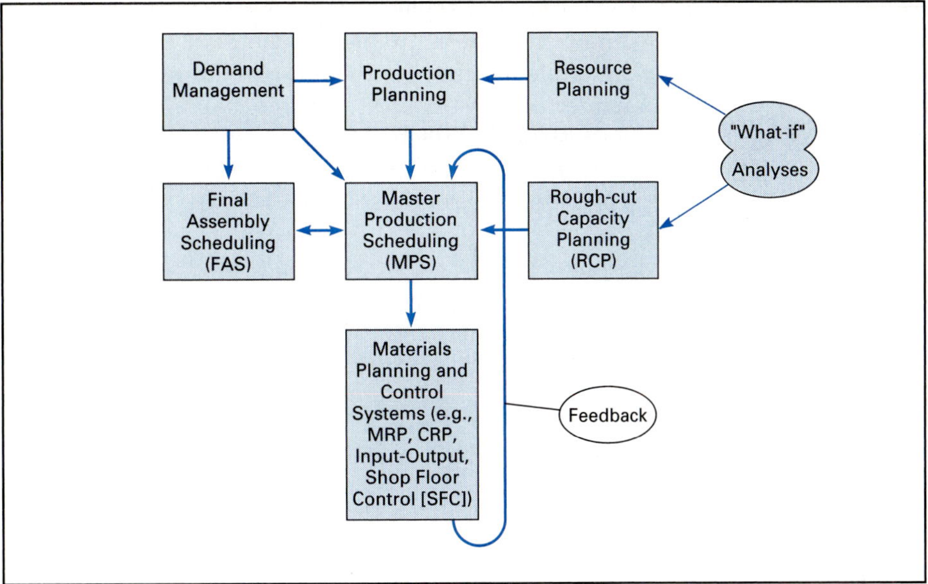

Figure 10-7 Relationship of Master Production Scheduling to Other Manufacturing Planning and Control Activities.
(Source: Reprinted with permission, American Production and Inventory Control Society, Inc., W. Berry, T. Vollman, and C. Whybark, *Master Production Scheduling: Principles and Practice*, 1979, p. 8.)

Demand management includes demand forecasting. However, it also involves working with the marketing function to manage the timing of demand, as well as deciding what demands will be accepted into the master schedule. (Practices such as off-peak pricing help to stimulate sales in periods of historically low demand and can help to utilize production capacity more effectively.) Order promising should be tied to the MRP II system, so that promises can be kept and one set of numbers is available to everyone. *Final assembly scheduling (FAS)* extends the application of MRP to assemble-to-order production systems, where the master schedule is done at a level below the finished product. FAS will not exist for some firms. (This is discussed further in Section 10-3.)

Scheduling problems do not end with the master schedule. For example, despite the best planning efforts, there are still likely to be disruptions that keep the firm from following the plan exactly. At any point in time, a facility may have several jobs from which a next job must be selected. MRP provides due dates to help in this decision and release dates so that the number to choose from will be small. Job-shop scheduling rules (discussed in Chapter 11) can be used in the selection process.

The relation of master scheduling and MRP to these details, referred to as *shop-floor control*, is described by Galligan and Hazarika (1982). The factory produces units based on MRP, as driven by the master schedule. Feedback from shop-floor control is essential because the plan probably will not be followed exactly. Future plans must take this into account.

It is useful at this point in our discussion to take a careful look at Figure 10-7. This figure unifies the many topics discussed in this text. Demand management (Chapter 7) and resource planning (Chapter 16) each provide input to the production plan (Chapter 9), which in turn serves as input to the master schedule. If the production system is one that involves dependent demand, MRP (this chapter) or JIT (Chapter 12), or some other multistage production system, can be used. If the system is characterized by independent demand, the inventory control techniques of Chapter 8 are appropriate. Once production plans are implemented, production scheduling (Chapter 11 for manufacturing and Chapter 13 for services) become important. Total quality management (Chapter 6) should permeate the entire system. It is also easy to use this framework to explain the other chapters of the text in regard to such things as the type of process, the overall strategy, and the use of automation and new technology.

In summary, the master schedule and the MRP bill of materials explosion are central elements in a closed-loop MRP II planning system. When implemented with feedback in the areas of capacity and resources, demand management, and shop-floor control, MRP II is an interactive management tool that helps coordinate the operations of a manufacturing firm. Management's effective use of this tool is dependent on understanding the system, a commitment to cross-departmental cooperation, the accuracy of data, and timely feedback.

REVIEW PROBLEMS

1. Why do companies use fixed planned lead times when the actual lead times are variable? Why do the planned lead times get inflated?

2. In Figure 10-5 a production plan for the next twenty weeks is given for KBC. Assume that each order release for COMP1, COMP3, COMP4, COMP5, and COMP6 is accomplished in equal thirds during the week of and each of the two weeks following the order release. (COMP2 is purchased rather than produced.) Develop a capacity usage (load) projection for the component facility's first twenty weeks. Use only information given in Figure 10-5.

3. The production plan in review problem 2 does not satisfy the weekly capacity limit of 1000 components. Try to generate a feasible production schedule for the component facility that meets order deadlines (as specified by the planned order receipts in Figure 10-5) and which satisfies the production capacity constraint. (Hint: Work backward from the deadline for the last order [week 18] and prepare a ''crash schedule,'' producing as late as possible, but always at the full capacity of 1000 per week.) For this problem, assume that we are about to begin production for week 1 and that production has not yet started on the order for 2000 units of COMP4, released last week.

4. Although the production schedule in Figure 10-9 satisfies the weekly capacity limit, there is still a good chance that some of the orders will not be completed on time. Why?

Solutions

1. It is too difficult to anticipate lead times exactly. A fixed lead time is set large enough to cover most situations. Inflation occurs when the plant cannot meet planned lead time.

2. The capacity is 1000 units per week. The component order releases during weeks 1 through 20, respectively, are 0, 1000, 2000, 0, 2000, 0, 0, 0, 0, 2000,

0, 2000, 3000, 0, 2000, 0, 0, 0, 0, and 0. We are assuming that one-third of each week's order releases are performed during that week and each of the next two weeks. Also, a 2000-unit order for COMP4 was released in the week prior to week 1, so one-third of it (667 units) will be produced in week 1, and the final third will be produced in week 2.

There will be 666.7 components produced in week 1, 1000 units produced in each of weeks 2 through 4, and 1333 units produced in week 5. (This exceeds the capacity of 1000 units per week.) Production capacity is also exceeded in week 12, and requirements climb to 1667 units during weeks 13 through 15. Requirements for all twenty weeks are shown in Figure 10-8.

3. The crash schedule is shown in Figure 10-9. Each block contains the component part number, the original release time, the deadline (three weeks later), and the total order quantity. Thus, a block with the data (1, 15, 18, 1000) denotes an order for 1000 units of component 1 that must be delivered by week 18 and was originally planned to be released in week 15. We can begin that order in week 17 and produce at full tilt for one week to obtain the 1000 units. Note that the second batch of 2000 units of component 4 was originally scheduled to be released in week 10; under this schedule, production begins in week 9, thus giving rise to a four-week lead time (since it is due in week 13).

4. For sixteen of the seventeen weeks in which production of components is scheduled, the planned capacity utilization is 100%. This does not leave room for any variability in processing time or order arrival. If production is delayed for any reason (a machine breaks down, employees are absent, or there is a delay in receipt of any of the requisite raw materials), the schedule will not be met.

Figure 10-8 Capacity Load for KBC Component Facility

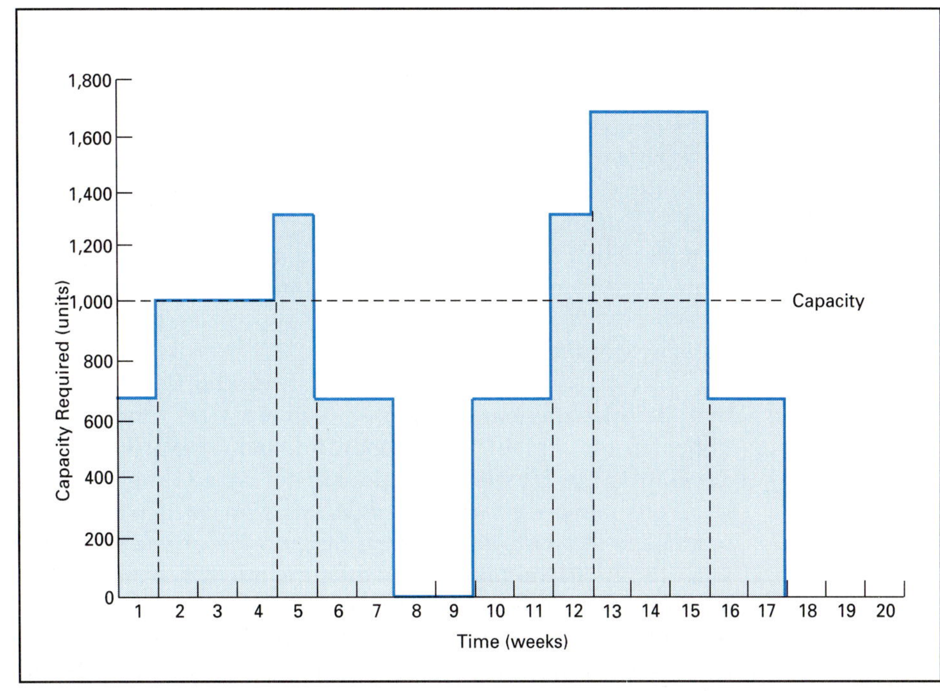

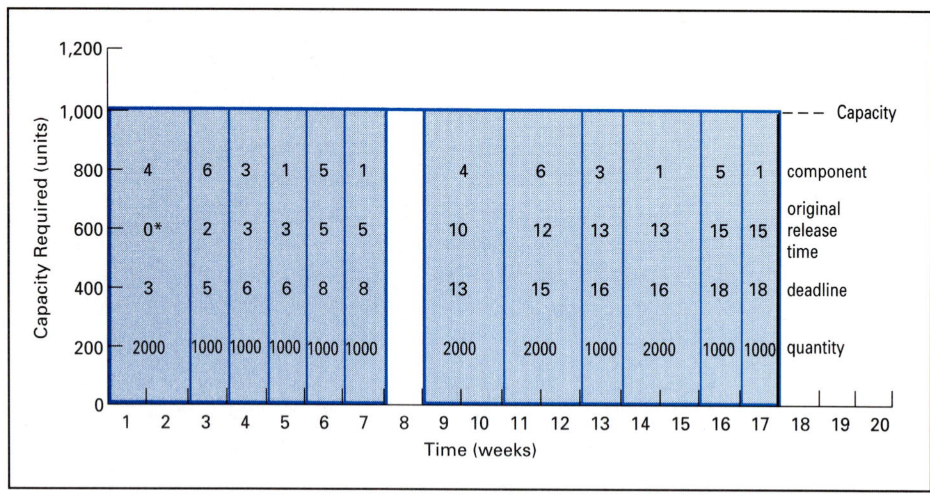

*Order released last week

Figure 10-9 "Crash" Schedule for KBC Component Facility

10-3 MANAGEMENT PLANNING AND OPTIONS IN MULTISTAGE SYSTEMS

Master Production Scheduling

Material requirements planning allows good management control of plant activities. It can be used as an information system to use in planning the business. At the heart of MRP II is the *master schedule,* which is a plan for the next several periods of what end products the firm will produce. One of the key ideas in master scheduling is that *marketing, production, and finance must all have the same plan!* Many companies have been led astray by poor coordination among these three areas. In MRP II a common saying is, "Plan the work and work the plan." This implies that all parties agree on what will happen in the next few periods. Then they all work to see that the plan is followed. If the plan is not followed for unforeseen reasons, adjustments are made to the next plan. *The master schedule must reflect a realizable goal. Everyone in the organization should be working with the same set of numbers.*

The master (production) schedule is a critical component of the MRP system. Because there are so many possible factors, and since the overall production plan for a plant is so important, managerial judgment must be used in developing the master schedule. Master scheduling should be the responsibility of one person, a *master scheduler,* who interacts with top management, other management functions, and the factory. He or she should know the business well. Inputs to the master schedule include a demand forecast, but the master schedule is different from the demand forecast. Forecasts are not automatically accepted into the master schedule. Instead, a meeting is held periodically with all interested parties to develop and approve the master schedule. Production, marketing, and finance all sign off, indicating their agreement to abide by the plan.

Time Fences for Planning and Scheduling

One policy input to master scheduling is a set of *time fences*. These describe the time intervals over which various actions will be considered. The first is the *frozen fence*. Before this time, the production plan will be changed only for emergencies (which should be rare). The frozen fence allows the plant to know what it is doing in the immediate future. The frozen fence is typically short, with production wanting a longer frozen period and marketing wanting a shorter one. The *planning fence* is the time to which the system looks ahead. This fence should be at least equal to the maximum cumulative lead time to make products, including raw-materials procurement. (If raw-materials procurement time is highly variable, materials may be maintained on an order point, order quantity basis, so that the planner can assume materials availability.) The planning fence may be longer if the firm builds up seasonal inventory. Firms often maintain a fence between frozen and planning fences, to schedule production for both firm and expected demands. The specific name and use depends on the nature of the business. This fence may be called a *demand fence* or *scheduling fence*.

Information Requirements

In forming a master schedule to drive the MRP system, the information system must collect all the required information inputs. The following is a modification of the list of such data sources (Orlicky 1975):

1. customer orders
2. forecasts
3. safety-stock requirements
4. seasonal inventory plans
5. orders placed by other parts of our own organization, including orders for interplant shipment and orders for company-owned dealers and distributors
6. service-part requirements

These six sources have varying levels of importance for different companies. Companies that work to backlog (where all customer orders are accepted for future delivery) may deal almost entirely with customer orders in forming the master schedule. A firm that produces to and sells from inventories will base a master schedule mainly on sources 2, 3, and 4.

In some organizations type 5 orders (within the organization) are the same as customer orders. In other organizations a central planning group determines what these orders will be, so that the level is known in advance. Finally, service-part requirements or spare parts (item 6) are independent demands for lower-level products. An example would be replacement compressors sold to persons who previously bought a refrigerator. This demand will be entered as a planned requirement at the appropriate level.

Safety Stock and Safety Time

Even though MRP uses dependent-demand calculations in planning requirements, provision must be made for uncertainty. In a multilevel system, however, safety margins at one level buffer against variations at other levels as well. Therefore, it is not correct to carry safety stock at all levels of an MRP system; that will cost a lot and it may not protect the firm. Safety stock should not be compounded but rather placed at strategic points to protect against uncertainties.

For example, suppose that a firm fabricates and assembles a single product using several hundred materials, components, and subassemblies. The value is added fairly evenly during the different stages of manufacture, and there is ample manufacturing capacity to plan lead times effectively. Purchased items are available with a short lead time and there are no large scrap rates. Finally, customer demand is erratic and immediate service is required. In such a situation, safety stock should be carried only at the finished product level. The master schedule must maintain that safety stock, but components will not require safety stock. The finished-product safety stock would also protect against minor disruptions in production.

In some situations safety stock is needed at carefully selected points other than the finished-goods level because of uncertainties not associated with the finished products. If, for example, raw materials sometimes arrive in batches that do not match the amounts ordered, some safety stock may be advisable. If a particular production facility often has a high fraction of rejects, safety stock immediately following that stage of the process may be useful. If there is a bottleneck resource, safety stock may be appropriate to guard against process disruptions.

Whybark and Williams (1976) point out that the need for safety margins arises when there is uncertainty in (1) supply timing, (2) supply quantity, (3) demand timing, or (4) demand quantity. Uncertainties (2) and (4) are related to quantity and therefore give rise to a need for a reserve of extra units (that is, *safety stock*). The location of the units depends on the location and degree of the uncertainty. On the other hand, Whybark and Williams claim that uncertainties (1) and (3) are related to timing and give rise to a need to include an extra *safety time* margin in planned lead time. This time margin leads to earlier production, with an attendant increase in the time inventory is held. This is the counterpart of safety stock. (As noted in Section 10-2, safety time should be used cautiously, since significant lead-time inflation could result.)

Grasso and Taylor (1984), however, suggest that safety stock is better than safety time in protecting against uncertainty arising from supply timing. A considerable amount of research has been performed on the use and placement of safety stock in MRP systems. Meal (1979) discusses the measurement of uncertainties in an MRP system, as well as the application of these measurements to establish safety stock and safety time in the MRP system. Graves (1988) provides an excellent discussion on the use of safety stocks in manufacturing systems.

In selecting where to put safety stock or time, the manager must consider several factors. First, buffering before and after machines that are capacity constrained can ensure that they are fully utilized and that they do not cause work stoppage downstream. Second, safety stock or safety time after an assembly point can protect against uncertainty up to that stage with less total stock. The *value-added profile* (cost at each stage) is another factor. (See Lambrecht et al. 1982). Given the variety of situations that occur, it is often helpful to perform a simulation study of the specific case at hand. (See Appendix B.)

Often companies sell components to outside customers (as spare parts, for example). In that event they have components that are subject to both *de-*

pendent and *independent* demand. If the dependent demand is predominant, an MRP system is still appropriate and the independent demand can be made to fit into the system. This is accomplished by including in each order for a component a quantity to meet expected spare-parts demand until the next production run, and safety stock to cover that same period of time. Then gross requirements arise not only because of finished items to be produced according to the master schedule but also to meet the independent demand.

Lot-Sizing Techniques

The economic order quantity, $Q^* = \sqrt{2DC_T/C_I}$, assumes that demand arrives in a continuous stream. That is not the case in an MRP environment, where it is typical to have large and unequal chunks of demand occur at irregular time intervals. In this situation it is necessary to determine an appropriate lot size that takes into account the amount and timing of demand, as well as production setup and holding costs.

For example, suppose that an end item for KBC is required, for shipment to customers, according to the following pattern:

	PERIOD								
	1	2	3	4	5	6	7	8	9
Net requirements	100	0	200	100	0	100	200	0	200
Cumulative requirements	100	100	300	400	400	500	700	700	900

The size of the production batch should be equal to the sum of the net requirements spanning some integer number of periods. Thus, a batch size of 100, 300, 400, 500, 700, or 900 would be considered for the initial batch, but no other value is appropriate (unless periods beyond period 9 are to be included). A batch size of 125, for example, would require a new setup in period 3 (to produce at least the remaining 175 units in that period), and it would also incur a larger inventory carrying cost than a lot size of 100. The extra 25 units, therefore, serve only to increase total cost.

In this context it is important to balance setup and holding costs in some way, as we did in deriving the economic order quantity in Chapter 8. Production setups are analogous to placing an order in a simple ordering situation. Thus, production setup cost, C_S, is much like the ordering or transaction cost, C_T; however, it also reflects costs due to factors such as the time required to clean and adjust machinery, initial waste if the first few units are rejects (which is quite common), and other labor costs that occur at the beginning of a production run. Thus, setup costs are generally larger than ordering costs.

Lot-sizing methods must be included in the MRP system, since the batch size at level 0 affects the timing and amount of requirements at level 1, and so on. Thus, all lot-size decisions on a given level must be made before passing to the next level. We will examine a few of the many lot-sizing techniques that can be applied to single-stage (that is, single-level) lot-sizing problems. These techniques are *heuristics* in that they provide approximate (rather than optimal) solutions. The nine-period KBC end-item example defined earlier in this subsection is used to illustrate the lot-sizing heuristics. For this problem, the holding cost is $0.50 per unit per period, and the setup cost is $180.

Lot-for-lot scheduling simply means plan to order the amount that is needed when it is needed. KBC used lot-for-lot scheduling for each of the components. Each time a net requirement arises, a planned order receipt is scheduled to meet the requirement for the period in which it occurs. In this way lots for the same component are scheduled independently of one another. This method is easy to implement and control, but it may lead to inefficient use of the production facility because of excessive setup time. The total cost of applying lot-for-lot scheduling to the KBC problem is 6($180) = $1080. (Note that six orders will be required during the nine-month horizon. Also, we assume that a holding cost is not incurred for an item produced and demanded in the same period.)

The concept of periodic review discussed in Chapter 8 can also be applied to this setting. Specifically, suppose that a review interval of three periods is established. At the beginning of each review period, an order is planned to cover all requirements during the three-period interval. Applying this to the KBC example, planned orders will be scheduled for receipt in periods 1, 4, and 7 for 300, 200, and 400 units, respectively. Setup costs then total 3($180) = $540, and holding cost is equal to $0.50[2(200) + 2(100) + 2(100)] = $400. (The 200 units required in period 3, for example, are planned for receipt in period 1 and are thus carried for two periods at $0.50 per period.) The total cost of this policy over the nine-week horizon is $940.

The EOQ discussed in Chapter 8 can be used to determine the length of the review period. From the EOQ formula, $Q^* = \sqrt{2DC_S/C_I}$, where C_S is used in place of C_T. Letting $D = 900/9 = 100$, which is equal to the average demand requirement per period (consistent with the holding cost specified as cost per unit per period), we have $Q^* = \sqrt{2(100)(180)/0.50} = 268.3$ units. Since there is a total requirement of 900 units, this suggests that the length of each review interval should be $Q^*/D = 268.3/100 = 2.68$, which rounds to 3 periods. The order quantity necessary to cover demand during this time interval is referred to as the *period order quantity* (POQ).

It is also possible to use the EOQ formula directly to determine a lot-sizing policy. In the *EOQ lot-sizing heuristic,* requirements are accumulated for each order so that they come as close to Q^* as possible. Recall that $Q^* = 268$ units (rounded to the nearest integer). For the first order, cumulative requirements are 100, 100, and 300 units for periods 1, 2, and 3, respectively. Since 300 > 268, there is no need to continue accumulating requirements for the first order. At this point we observe that 268 is closer to 300 than it is to 100 (the previous cumulative requirement), and a first order for 300 units is planned for period 1 (to cover periods 1, 2, and 3).

The procedure then advances to period 4, the first period not covered by the previous order, and repeats the process. Specifically, cumulative requirements (beginning with period 4) are 100, 100, 200, and 400 for periods 4, 5, 6, and 7, respectively. Again, 268 lies between 200 and 400, and since it is closer to 200 we plan an order in period 4 of size 200 units. Continuing in this manner, an order for 200 units will be planned in period 7, and an order for 200 units will be planned in period 9. The total cost of this lot-sizing policy is 4($180) + $0.50[2(200) + 2(100)] = $1020.

Silver and Meal (1973) have developed a heuristic that has proven to be quite effective on single-stage lot-sizing problems. To determine the size of an order, the Silver-Meal heuristic requires that we calculate the total cost per unit time (TCT) as a function of the number of time periods, T, covered by the order:

$$\text{TCT}(T) = \frac{\text{ordering cost} + \text{inventory carrying costs for a } T\text{-period order}}{T}$$

Beginning with $T = 1$, compute TCT(1); then, compute TCT(2), TCT(3), and so on, until we *first* reach a point N for which $\text{TCT}(N + 1) > \text{TCT}(N)$. At that point the order quantity is planned so that it covers requirements for N periods.

Illustrating the Silver-Meal heuristic on the KBC example, for the initial order we have

$$\text{TCT}(1) = \frac{\text{ordering cost}}{1} = \frac{180}{1}$$

$$\text{TCT}(2) = \frac{180 + 0.50(0)}{2} = 90$$

$$\text{TCT}(3) = \frac{180 + 0.50[0 + 2(200)]}{3} = 126.7$$

Since $\text{TCT}(3) > \text{TCT}(2)$, the initial order will cover the first two periods and will be in the amount of 100 units.

The heuristic then proceeds to period 3, where the calculations are repeated (beginning with period 3). For this order,

$$\text{TCT}(1) = \frac{180}{1}$$

$$\text{TCT}(2) = \frac{180 + 0.50(100)}{2} = 115$$

$$\text{TCT}(3) = \frac{180 + 0.50[100 + 2(0)]}{3} = 76.7$$

$$\text{TCT}(4) = \frac{180 + 0.50[100 + 2(0) + 3(100)]}{4} = 95$$

Thus, the second order covers three periods (periods 3 through 5) and will be in the amount of 300 units. Continuing this procedure for the next order (in period 6), an order quantity of 300 results. Finally, a fourth order planned for period 8 is also of size 300 units. The total cost of the Silver-Meal heuristic applied to this example is 4($180) + $0.50[0 + 100 + 200 + 100] = $920.

As noted previously, the lot-sizing procedures we have just discussed are not guaranteed to furnish an optimal solution to the single-stage lot-sizing problem. (An extensive review and evaluation of heuristics for single-stage lot-sizing problems without capacity constraints is provided in Baker 1989.) Wagner and Whitin (1958) developed an algorithm that will yield an optimal solution to this problem. This algorithm, discussed in more advanced texts (see, for example, Silver and Peterson 1985), is based on dynamic programming and requires more computational effort than the heuristics described here. When applied in a rolling-horizon environment (see Chapter 9), which is typically encountered in actual applications, the Wagner-Whitin algorithm is no longer guaranteed to provide an optimal solution; in fact, it has been shown (Blackburn and Millen 1980) that it often does not perform as well as the Silver-Meal heuristic in that environment. Kropp and Carlson (1984) present a modified Wagner-Whitin algorithm for the rolling-horizon setting. (Recently, researchers have developed optimal solution procedures for the single-item lot-sizing problem that are considerably faster than the Wagner-Whitin algorithm; see, for example, Federgruen and Tzur 1991.)

The preceding discussion considers single-stage lot sizing. MRP and other multistage production systems require that the effects and costs of lot sizing be evaluated *simutaneously* over many levels of the process. In addition to the complex optimization problem posed by multistage lot sizing, balancing setup and holding costs is difficult in multistage production systems because it is often unclear what those costs are, as well as how they interrelate. For example, a labor group may be maintained to do setups. They represent a fixed cost; if they are not fully occupied, the marginal cost of labor for a setup may be zero. Thus setup cost can be overstated by looking at the average cost. On the other hand, a setup for a subassembly may cause several of its inputs to be set up as well, so that the local setup cost may be only a fraction of the effective setup cost. Similarly, the effective inventory cost may vary. If all the inputs are available, only the value added at this stage contributes to inventory cost. If no inputs are available, we must build the item from scratch, and the cost of building the item as well as all its inputs contributes to inventory cost.

Since the appropriate costs to use are uncertain and may change over time, any lot-sizing method based on one level at a time may be wrong. Blackburn and Millen (1982) describe ways of modifying the costs to obtain better inputs for techniques such as the Wagner-Whitin algorithm. They are able to improve performance. Lot-sizing methods that consider the entire system are discussed in Section 10-4.

Production Yields

When producing a batch, a fraction of the total units may be defective; that is, it is common to experience yields of less than 100%. The *yield* is the proportion of usable parts obtained from a production run. In addition, production yields may also be variable in that they differ from one production run to the next.

Although low yields can sometimes be traced to poor quality, the presence of low yields does not necessarily mean that a particular industry or process suffers from low quality. Rather, there are industries in which the rejection rates are both high and unpredictable. In the production of silicon chips, for example, the cumulative-process yield of finished chips is often less than 25% because of the complex nature of the manufacturing process and the extremely demanding tolerances required to meet performance specifications.

Exact and heuristic solution procedures for single-stage variable-yield lot sizing have been defined by Mazzola, McCoy, and Wagner (1987). They found that heuristics based on modifications of the Wagner-Whitin and Silver-Meal procedures, together with an adjustment for imperfect yield and the inclusion of an extra production quantity (referred to as production safety stock) are effective in solving lot-sizing problems with variable yield. (A review of variable-yield lot-sizing problems is provided in Yano and Lee 1989.)

Since MRP plans material requirements from the bill of materials in a level-by-level manner based on dependent demand, the MRP logic must be modified to account for production yields of less than 100%. One way of doing this is by increasing the production quantity by a specified multiple, the *reject allowance*. For example, if the production yield of an item is 80% and 100 units are required as input to the next level, $100/0.8 = 125$ units might be produced, corresponding to a reject allowance of 1.25. The inventory records would be kept valid (eventually) by a receipt equal to the actual number of usable items.

The reject-allowance multiple must be determined considering the cost of extra units of inventory (and the potential scrap, mess, and handling cost they entail, as well as the capital tied up) against the cost of having to schedule a second batch to meet the upper-level requirements or to ship a partial order. If the multiple is chosen carelessly, the MRP system will lead to high production costs or high work-in-process inventories or both.

If lead times for customer orders are very long, it may be possible to use MRP with long lead times, to allow time to test items and to produce until enough usable items are obtained. However, if lead times are short, management may decide to maintain work-in-process inventories of completed parts to be used to fill out production batches of certain components. (Jaikumar 1989 refers to these as *contingent inventories*.) If the reject-allowance problem is severe, MRP may not be the appropriate way to control production. The value of MRP as an information system (discussed presently) should be considered, even though some of its advantage of reducing work-in-process inventory would be lost.

Selecting the Appropriate Master-Scheduling Level for MRP

MRP is not well adapted to systems that explode at the last step of production (into many options or colors). In such situations, master scheduling is not performed on final assembly or finished item. Rather, the master schedule occurs at a lower level in the bill of materials, and final assembly is managed in some other way.

In the KBC example, master scheduling was done on the finished-item level because of the structure of the bill of materials. In particular, several components or materials funneled down to finished products. As an alternative, suppose that each finished assembly comes with any one of 500 option packages. In that case, the production process would be as pictured in Figure 10-10 for FA1.

Predicting the demand for each option package would be difficult, making it hard to derive a master schedule based on completed items. In this situation it is likely that MRP should be used with a master schedule based on items without options. Then one unit of FA1 would have the options added (have the assembly completed) for a particular customer order. Some finished items with popular option packages might be stocked in finished form, but these would just be part of the demand placed on the master schedule.

The advantages of consolidating orders for all option packages is that the total inventory requirement will be reduced dramatically, since the total of all FA1 orders is easier to forecast than are individual option packages. One can then avoid the problem of a shortage of green units and leftover red ones. The disadvantages are that completely finished items are not ready for customers

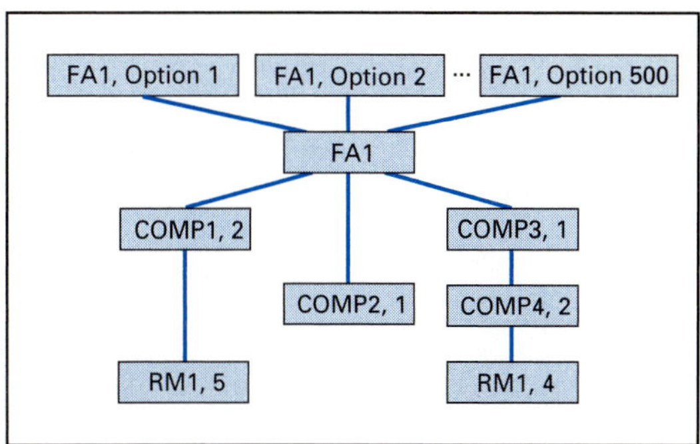

Figure 10-10 FA1 with Options

and that excess final assembly capacity must be maintained to respond quickly to customer demands.

There are other reasons for only performing MRP up to a semifinished product. For example, in the furniture industry, not only are chairs covered with many different fabrics, but semifinished chairs are much less damage prone. Thus, carrying semifinished items reduces deterioration. Some firms produce several basic components, then assemble many combinations from those components. Each of these situations leads to an assemble-to-order or finish-to-order approach as opposed to a make-to-stock approach. The proper method depends on costs and on the customer service required in the industry.

When the *master-scheduling level* for a product is established below that of the finished product, a bill of materials called a *super bill* can be used. For example, the master schedule might call for 1000 cars to be made, and the firm must begin immediately, without knowing the exact option package for each car. Based on historical data, the firm can begin to build 1000 statistical cars. That is, the average car has 0.6 automatic transmission and 0.4 standard transmission. Thus we start 600 automatic transmissions and 400 standard transmissions. Similarly, the firm begins building other components. As the end of the planning period approaches, we get data on which cars are to have a specific set of options, such as automatic transmission, six-cylinder engines, green paint, and bucket seats. Because of the uncertainty of the option mix, we may start a few extra of each long-lead-time item and include less and less safety stock as we refine our forecast (see Miller 1980 or Sari 1981).

MRP as a Management Information System

One function of a management information system (MIS) is to summarize the many details that are available about an organization in some manner that allows a manager to comprehend and control a situation easily. MRP is well designed to provide such information, if the appropriate inputs are available. MRP can provide a forward-looking production plan and capacity usage (load) information. This load projection can be used to help the manager determine work-force and other capacity variables, and thus to feed back to the MRP system and change the capacity load in the short to intermediate term. The production plan can be used to isolate trouble spots in meeting delivery schedules, material procurement, and so on, and thus allow management to expedite (or take other action) to avoid the problem. In both cases MRP can help to pinpoint future problems and allow the manager to act in time.

MRP systems should not make production decisions automatically; they are designed to accept management's decisions and plans and to reflect their likely impact on the production system. Production schedules can be changed; lead times can be modified; capacity can be modified. MRP's greatest value is the information it can provide. An MRP system can be used, for example, in a simulation mode: If a large order is anticipated, the manager can see how the system will be able to respond if the order materializes.[4]

An MRP system cannot function unless it has accurate bill-of-materials files, inventory files, and a master schedule. As input to the master schedule, forecasts for all independent demand items will be required, along with an inventory plan (lot size, seasonal accumulation, and safety stock) for those

[4]Systems that allow real-time checking of the effect of a new order or other schedule change are being developed currently. *Leitstands* in Germany are such systems. Conway and Maxwell (1989) have developed such a system, called the Production Reservation System.

items. Managers, in turn, use information from the MRP system to plan the lot size and seasonal accumulation policies, using the capacity plan as part of the analysis.

One key role for MRP is to provide input to management decisions. The manager controls the master production schedule, inventory policies, and detailed MRP decisions. However, the myriad of details is reduced for the manager by the MRP system, and if there is no intervention, the MRP system will proceed to make production decisions.

Chapter 12 discusses the just-in-time production system, which is an alternative to MRP. (MRP II can still be used to develop the master production schedule.) However, in Chapter 12 we also discuss the importance of selecting the production control system to match the production environment. We will see that there are some production environments that lend themselves to MRP, others that lend themselves to JIT, and yet others that require a hybrid mix of production systems (see Karmarkar 1989). In some instances in which MRP cannot be used for scheduling orders, its use as a management information system can be invaluable, and MRP II can be used for business planning in conjunction with several different scheduling methods.

Applications of MRP: Automation, Distribution, and Services

Because of its widespread use, MRP can serve an important role in the production planning of automated systems. (Automated production is discussed in Chapter 15.) In particular, we consider flexible manufacturing systems (FMS), which consist of computer-controlled machines with rapid changeover capability and automated material-handling devices, linked together by a computer-based planning and control system. The FMS usually does not comprise the entire plant; rather there are one or more FMS cells located within a production process.

Recently, Mazzola, Neebe, and Dunn (1989) defined a hierarchical framework for production planning of an FMS in an MRP environment. The FMS planning subsystem is designed to operate within the closed-loop MRP system. An important feature of this planning model is that the FMS-production-planning objectives are determined by the MRP system. Since the FMS is assumed to be a resource-constrained facility within the production process, it is essential that capacity planning and usage information flow in both directions between the FMS planning subsystem and the MRP system.

MRP is also helpful in the planning and coordination of large-scale distribution systems. Multilocation distribution systems (discussed further in Chapter 14) involve the simultaneous planning and control of inventory at all stages in the distribution chain, ranging from the factory through intermediate storage points (distribution centers) to the end user (retail outlets). *Distribution requirements planning* (*DRP*) uses MRP logic to coordinate activities throughout the chain.

Sales at the end of a distribution chain (retail stores, for example) are predicted as level 0 (corresponding to the master-scheduling level). These sales (requirements) are then exploded back through the distribution network. (A distribution system usually has a few plants, more warehouses, and many retail outlets. Thus, a picture of the process looks like disassembly.) Since there is a lower percent variation in total demand at a plant than there is in the demand at a retail store, we can estimate how many items to produce. It is not clear, however, where to ship them. The allocation of items to facilities can be made later, as time progresses, the units are moved through the system, and forecasts are refined.

DRP logic is the same as MRP. Thus, we will not describe details. (See Stenger and Cavinato 1979, for an example.) DRP, however, should be applied only when forecasts are reasonably good. This will be true for fairly high demand items. For low-demand items such as spare parts, other approaches are needed. (These are discussed in Chapter 14.) As with MRP, DRP provides a good way to keep track of the massive amounts of data involved. It does not help with allocation when demand is highly uncertain.

MRP was developed primarily for use in manufacturing processes. Two requirements for implementing MRP are that there is dependent demand for components and that work-in-process inventory occurs in discrete, identifiable parts. To the extent that a service exhibits these characteristics, MRP is applicable. As we discussed in Chapter 2, the technical core of a service operation reflects many manufacturing-like features, and MRP can be used to plan and control materials and scheduling. For example, MRP can be used to control supplies in a food service (see Jones 1979) or a hospital.

As service operations range from low contact to high contact, MRP becomes less amenable because it is either difficult or inconvenient to differentiate work in process or because lead times are too small. Khumawala, Hixon, and Law (1986) discuss the use of MRP II in intermittently processed services, which they define as having general-purpose equipment and low volume. They extend many of the ideas of MRP to services, including master service scheduling and the bill of labor.

REVIEW PROBLEMS

1. Why is the master production schedule for a product different from its demand forecast?

2. The gross requirements for one component, based only on the master schedule for finished items, are as follows. There is no inventory on hand for this item.

Period	1	2	3	4	5	6	7	8
Net requirements	400	0	800	400	0	0	1200	0

The setup cost, C_S, for this component is $36, and the inventory carrying cost is $0.02 per period.

a. What production quantities might be considered for production in period 1 if you wanted to try all possible appropriate order quantities?
b. What production quantity does the period order quantity suggest as the initial lot size?
c. Using the Silver-Meal heuristic, what is the size of the initial lot?

3. Marketing departments often want to expedite an order to satisfy a large customer. For example, when backlogs are five to six weeks in length, they

may want to place an order into the master schedule for completion in three weeks. How can an MRP system be used to determine if this is appropriate?

Solutions

1. The master production schedule must be established so that capacity requirements are met throughout the plant. The demand forecast for a product will be used as input to the production plan (within the intermediate-range planning decision). The production plan will then be disaggregated into short-term requirements, which then serve as input to the master production schedule, along with firm orders. The master schedule must then be adjusted to allow for adequate capacity.

2. a. Only 400, 1200, 1600, and 2800 would be appropriate, ignoring safety stock.

   b. $Q^* = \sqrt{2DC_S/C_I} = \sqrt{2(350)(36)/0.02} = 1122$; $Q^*/D = 1122/350 = 3.2$ or 3 periods. Thus, the first order should cover the first three periods, and the lot size is $(400 + 0 + 800) = 1200$ units.

   c. Applying the Silver-Meal heuristic for the first order, we have

$$\text{TCT}(1) = \frac{36}{1}$$

$$\text{TCT}(2) = \frac{36 + 0.02(0)}{2} = 18$$

$$\text{TCT}(3) = \frac{36 + 0.02[0 + 2(800)]}{3} = 22.7$$

   Since TCT(3) > TCT(2), the initial order should cover the first two periods and should thus be in the amount of 400 units.

3. The MRP system can be used in a simulation mode. If we schedule the item as requested, is there available capacity to meet all orders? If not, what products will be delayed, and how far? Then the marketing department or senior management can determine, based on judgment, if the disruptions to the plant *and* other customers are compensated for by meeting delivery for this one customer.

10-4 MULTISTAGE MANUFACTURING

In MRP systems there are some fundamental, unresolved issues. How do we choose production quantities when lot sizes on one level of the bill of materials may cause trouble on others? Lead times are often made far too long in practice because occasionally a capacity-constrained facility may need the extra time. How can we change lead times temporarily, only as needed? The opportunity cost of production time on a constrained facility varies dramatically depending on the current load. How can this be estimated? How should that affect the production schedule? Finally, when some uncertainty must be planned for, how can an overall system of management control be developed? We will briefly describe some recent research on these topics in this section.

Capacitated and Multistage Lot Sizing

In the preceding section we discussed techniques for lot sizing in a single-stage system when the capacity of the system was not a factor in determining the size of production batches. Determining optimal lot sizes in the presence of capacity constraints (known as *capacitated lot sizing*) is a complex problem, as is the problem of properly lot sizing a multistage production system, with or without capacity constraints. One special case is assembly systems, in which each component is used in at most one successor. (By definition, end products have no successors.)

In assembly systems with constant demand and without capacity constraints, a component will always be ordered in an integer multiple of the lot size of its successor (see Problem 27). Finding optimal lot sizes with constant or time-varying demand has been discussed by many authors, including Schwarz and Schrage (1975), McClain and Trigeiro (1983), and Afentakis, Gavish, and Karmarkar (1984). (Additional references are given in these papers and in Billington et al., 1983 and Maxwell et al., 1983.) The Afentakis, Gavish, and Karmarkar paper gives an effective computational scheme for time-varying demand. The McClain and Trigerio paper presents an easy-to-use method for constant demand.

Commonality, where an item is used in more than one successor item, is allowed in the papers by Blackburn and Millen (1982), Graves (1981), and Maxwell and Muckstadt (1985). These papers also do not allow capacity constraints.

Capacity constraints are included in Billington et al. (1983) in an integer linear programming formulation. This solution method incorporates the difficult-to-solve capacity-planning problem. It also computes tight, time-varying lead times, adding waiting time only when necessary to balance the load on a capacity-constrained facility. Thus, lead times are based on the anticipated load. Lot sizes can also vary with the anticipated load. The mathematical program gives the opportunity cost of using constrained facilities through shadow price information. This cost varies through time according to the facility load. Standard accounting costs do not contain the opportunity cost information that is necessary for good management in this situation. Billington et al. discuss ways of reducing the problem size to focus on the key capacity-constrained facilities. This *product structure compression* allows the manager to focus on scheduling the key facilities (with or without mathematical programming). Then other facilities follow directly. (Problems 25 and 26 present the pieces of a linear programming formulation.)

Recently, Billington, McClain, and Thomas (1986) presented a heuristic method for multistage lot sizing when there is a single bottleneck facility. They note that many capacity-limited production facilities are often constrained by one bottleneck facility, and the technique presented in their article is effective in finding good feasible solutions. Eppen and Martin (1987) developed models for the single- and multiple-item single-stage capacitated lot-sizing problem. These models employ a variable redefinition approach that gives rise to effective linear programming–based solution procedures. Trigeiro, Thomas, and McClain (1989) define a procedure for solving the single-stage, lot-sizing problem with capacity constraints, setup costs, and setup times. (The setup times are reflected in the capacity constraints in that the facility is not operating while it is in the process of being setup to run a new job.) They observe that when setup costs are present, the level of problem difficulty corresponds to the degree to which the capacity constraint actually limits production. Their research also suggests that good solutions are obtained more easily for problems having a large number of products or time periods than for smaller problems, although more solution time is required. This suggests that it might be possible to develop effective, easy heuristics for larger problems, which are indicative of those occurring in practice.

Each of the articles mentioned previously works with deterministic demand, treating setup cost or time as important. If setup cost or time is (or can be made) low, the JIT system (discussed in Chapter 12) may be appropriate. If uncertainties are large, the method must explicitly allow for it. A modeling framework proposed by Maxwell et al. (1983) suggests that a deterministic view such as that of Billington et al. (1983) should be used to determine the lot timing and overall work level for a long horizon. This is phase I. In phase II, a small amount of safety stock should be strategically placed to *protect* the phase I plan. Yield problems, constrained facilities, and uncertainty in final demand should be buffered against so that the plan can be implemented as closely as possible. Finally, in phase III, the day-to-day scheduling problems should be solved (1) considering the details of yields, broken machines, and so on, and (2) using the plan for overall production and safety stock as an ending target. The cost of deviating from the plan can be obtained as a shadow price from the mathematical program in phase I.

The modeling framework combines master scheduling, MRP, and capacity planning into phase I, for a long time horizon. Shop-floor control is accomplished by phase III, which can have better cost information on which to base detailed short-term decisions. Phase II explicitly recognizes the need to carefully buffer uncertainties that cannot be eliminated. This system allows the manager to connect planning and implementation, taking an overall-system viewpoint.

Other Multistage Production Systems

Throughout this chapter we have observed that it is difficult to plan production in a multistage system without simultaneously accounting for the large number of lot-sizing and scheduling decisions that must be made throughout each facility in the process. This results in an optimization problem that is too large to solve with current capability. MRP II attempts to address this problem in a hierarchical (top-down) manner with appropriate feedback loops to adjust higher-level decisions as necessary.

Because of the need for simultaneity between the production planning and scheduling activities in multistage processes, we consider production scheduling and control in the next chapter. In Chapter 12, we discuss the just-in-time production system, which offers an approach to multistage systems when setup costs can be reduced and when the demands placed on the system can be made relatively uniform.

Other approaches to multistage production have also been proposed. Goldratt (1980, 1988) defined optimized production technology (OPT), which is a multistage-production control system that offers an alternative to MRP. (See also Jacobs 1983.) OPT attempts to simultaneously plan and schedule production by focusing on bottleneck work centers.

Goldratt makes some very important observations about process bottlenecks. Among these is the idea that bottleneck facilities limit the output of the system and should therefore be treated differently than nonbottleneck facilities. That is, it is essential that a bottleneck facility be scheduled efficiently and that lost production time on bottlenecks be avoided as much as possible. Thus, bottlenecks determine the throughput of the system, as well as the quantity and location of inventory. It is important to buffer bottleneck facilities from the nonbottleneck facilities so that they are not, for example, starved for work. Confining attention to bottleneck facilities also offers the significant advantage of reducing the size of the problem that must be addressed.

The OPT approach to multistage production planning also uses the idea of distinguishing between a *transfer* batch and a *production* batch. A transfer batch is the size of a batch that is allowed to be moved from one workstation (or facility) to another. A production batch is the size of a lot that will be produced at a work center. The transfer batch can, and often should, be different from the production batch.

For example, suppose that machine A feeds machine B and that machine B is a process bottleneck. If machine A is currently running 100 units, there is no need to wait until all 100 units are completed before sending them to machine B. Suppose that the transfer-batch size between A and B is 25 units. Then, after each batch of 25 units is completed at machine A, they are immediately transferred to machine B, thus helping to ensure that machine B is not idle (which would lower throughput for the entire system). This idea can be very effective in a multiproduct, multistage environment.

Although OPT has met with mixed success in actual implementation, its approach has offered new insight into the dynamics and potential tractability of multistage production systems. Morton et al. (1988), for example, define a shop-scheduling module, called SCHED-STAR, that can be used in conjunction with an MRP planning system and that uses internal, dynamic, resource-utilization–based prices to establish scheduling priorities. Morton et al. note the contribution of OPT in helping to focus attention on important planning and scheduling issues. Managing bottlenecks is discussed further in Chapter 12, where we also discuss the importance of matching the production system to the production environment.

SUMMARY

Although MRP is not an ''optimal'' system in that it does not provide a best answer to every problem, MRP does provide excellent information to a production manager, and it does reduce a massive amount of information to comprehensible form. It can bring order out of chaos, reducing the work-in-process inventories and helping management to allocate production time. It may replace an informal production control system that has failed to keep track of all the interactions involved in the multistage production system. MRP provides tentative production schedules as well as input into the capacity-planning, aggregate-production-planning, and inventory-policy systems. It is a useful management tool for dealing with problems that are too complex for us to solve to optimality at the present time.

The basic ideas of MRP are simple. By specifying a master schedule for end products, we can obtain the quantity and time requirements for each of the preceding production stages. It may be difficult to tie down the master schedule, but by doing so we gain stability in running the plant. Further, if the master schedule must change, MRP provides the information to manage this change.

Finally, MRP does not apply to every situation, but it is widely used in many complex multistage production systems. MRP fits best if there are several stages to the production process under the firm's control, and if reject allowances and independent demand for spare parts are relatively small compared with the dependent demand for finished items. MRP will work most effectively if lead times are not highly variable and if forecasts of finished-item sales are good enough that a stable master production schedule can be developed. However, even in some situations in which these conditions are not met, MRP may allow better control of production than alternative approaches. Its value in providing timely management information must be considered in making this determination.

In practice, MRP may fail if capacity is not well managed and if lead times are overstated. Lead times must be kept as small as possible. Even the choice of the basic time bucket (week, day, or other) is important, since lead times must be stated as an integer number of periods.

In Chapter 12 we discuss the just-in-time (JIT) production system, which is useful in many types of multistage manufacturing settings. As we will see, some of the JIT concepts have been expanded into a general philosophy that is applicable across many production systems, manufacturing or service. Some of these concepts can be used in conjunction with MRP. Management must assess the important problems, whether they are in design or ongoing management, and use a system that will help to solve those problems. MRP and JIT have both proved very effective when used in the right situation with top-management commitment to making it work.

PROBLEMS

1. What is the difference between dependent and independent demand? Why can the inventory levels be significantly lower in a dependent-demand situation?

*2. MRP can often reduce work-in-process inventories significantly in a manufacturing situation, but its main function is in establishing a production schedule. It is used as a priority planning system to assist in the allocation of production time to different items. Briefly, how does it do this?

3. What is level-by-level processing, and why does it require low-level coding?

*4. a. What is the time-related counterpart of safety stock in an MRP system?

 b. Discuss situations that might lead to carrying safety stocks of component parts in an MRP system.

 c. In an MRP system with random demand for finished items, should safety stock of finished items be maintained? Why or why not?

5. a. How should the length of the time bucket be chosen in MRP systems?

 b. How is time phasing accomplished in MRP?

*Problems with an asterisk have answers in the back of the book.

6. a. Why shouldn't the EOQ formula be directly used in an MRP system?

   b. What modification makes the solution obtained using the EOQ reasonable?

*7. Why might the master schedule (level 0) of an MRP system not correspond to the finished item? State the conditions and give examples.

8. The production process for automobiles involves many stages, components, and subassemblies. The finished assembly rate is constant over significant periods of time. Is MRP appropriate? Why or why not?

*9. State the conditions under which MRP works best. How many of those conditions are met by the automotive example discussed in problem 8?

10. A cosmetic company makes products that are manufactured using a one-stage process. The lead times for raw-material procurement are long and highly variable. The production process is fast, and excess production capacity is maintained to avoid lost sales. Forecasts of finished-item sales are hard to produce and subject to large errors; the company maintains a large finished-goods inventory as a result. They have only one inventory point, since they sell directly to stores from their single plant. Is MRP appropriate? Why or why not?

11. a. In determining the amount of reject allowance to have, what trade-offs are involved?

    b. If the reject rate for each of 100 components varies between 0% and 5% (and has never exceeded 5%), how much reject allowance is necessary if we want to be rèasonably sure that we will have the necessary amount of each of the 100 components required for an assembly? Why?

*12. The assembly of a finished item requires four TM75s and six TM112s. TM75 and TM112 are subassemblies. The lead time to produce the subassemblies has been 1 to 3 months, with an average of 2 months. The two subassemblies each require 4 units of raw material RM-1 per unit. It has taken from 1 to 4 months to obtain the raw material, with an average of 2 months.

    a. Using maximum lead times, derive the order releases required by finished-item order releases of 25, 35, 40, 40, and 40 in months 1 through 5; include demand for times prior to the present. Compute the inventory that must be on hand or on order immediately prior to month 1 if we are to follow that plan. Assume lot-for-lot scheduling.

    b. The raw-material supplier claims that the lead time for that item will henceforth be exactly 3 months. That is both good news and bad news. Why?

13. Whiffen, Incorporated, manufactures a variety of items. Their most successful and steady seller is a fireplace bellows, sold under the name Whiffenpoofer. A component of a poofer is the nozzle. Nozzles are produced at the rate of 200 units per day. Having been scheduled under an MRP system, the average production run has been 2 days in length, and 10 runs have been scheduled per year. A year is 250

production days. Lead time is normally distributed with a standard deviation of 3 days.

a. How many days should be allocated as a safety margin for lead time, in order to achieve 99% protection against late delivery of nozzles (per order)?

b. How much inventory will be held on each day during this extra lead time?

c. If C_I = \$2.50 per item per year, what is the average annual inventory cost due to the variability of the lead time for the nozzle?

*14. The accompanying table gives a bill of materials for items A to F. For example, to manufacture 1 unit of C requires 1 unit of B and 2 units of F.

Product	Manufacturing Requirements (name, quantity)		
A (finished good)	(B, 2)	(C, 4)	(D, 1)
B	(E, 3)		
C	(B, 1)	(F, 2)	
D	(E, 1)	(F, 3)	
E	Purchased		
F	Purchased		

a. Using low-level coding, how many levels are required, and which items are on each level?

b. To make 100 units of A, how many units each of B to F are needed?

c. Each item has a 2-week lead time. Production of A is scheduled for week 10, and the quantity to be produced is 100. When must item E be ordered, and in what quantity, to meet the production schedule for A while avoiding any unnecessary inventory?

15. A frozen-dessert maker wishes to use MRP. Each frozen dessert requires 2 wooden sticks (with a 2-day lead time) and 2 ounces of flavored water (with a 1-day lead time). The master plan is to ship 100 units per day. Frozen desserts are produced and packaged in batches of 300 and take 2 days to process and ship. (An order is released 2 days before inventory would be negative.) There are currently 500 frozen desserts on hand and no inventory of sticks or flavored water.

a. Determine the production schedule and order-release days and quantities for frozen desserts, sticks, and flavored water for the next 10 days. Use lot-for-lot scheduling for the inputs.

b. It is now the middle of day 3. Engineering has determined that a third stick is required to prevent the dessert from falling apart while being eaten. If the production schedule for desserts is not altered, and additional sticks are ordered on the next stick order release, when will be the first day that three-stick desserts will be sold?

c. Management, in an economy move, has decided to decrease the quantity of flavored water in each dessert to 1.5 ounces immediately. If it is now the end of day 3, what impact will that decision have on the MRP schedule as determined in part a?

16. MRP is said to provide better management information than other systems. What types of information are obtainable, why are they useful, and what must the manager give to the MRP system to allow it to work?

*17. The Apartment Protection Company (APCO) produces two security systems designed for apartments. They sell the completed systems and spare parts for the units. The composition of the two systems is shown in the accompanying diagram. COMP3, COMP4, RM1, RM2, and RM3 are puchased from outside vendors.

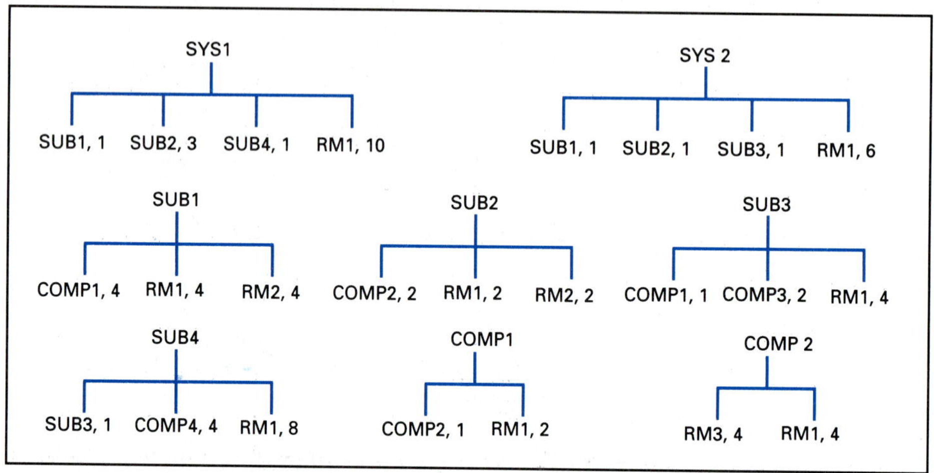

COMP3, COMP4, RM1, RM2, and RM3 are purchased from outside vendors.

a. Determine the level of each item, using low-level coding, and draw a bill of materials (product-structure diagram) for APCO, analogous to Figure 10-3.

b. How many RM1s are used in producing one SYS1?

*18. APCO, the firm described in problem 17, has independent demand for SYS1, SYS2, SUB1, SUB2, SUB3, and SUB4. (Problem 17 should be completed before attempting this question.) They have long-term contracts to supply several discount stores; the total amounts in units per week are

SYS1: 100	SUB2: 8
SYS2: 200	SUB3: 6
SUB1: 10	SUB4: 3

They currently have an inventory of 1500 units of SYS1, 1000 units of SYS2, and 40 units of each subassembly (SUB1 through SUB4). All production and procurement lead times are 2 weeks. When an order is released for any item, the firm produces enough to last for 10 weeks.

a. Using only the six items for which demand rates are given, give the complete MRP planning schedule for the next 17 weeks. Figure 10-5 can be used as a model to answer this problem. (Note: When computing the order quantity for an item, if the 10-week period extends beyond week 17, include the independent demand for that item occurring after week 17, but do not include any dependent demand that will occur after week 17. Although it is not necessary, you may wish to develop a spreadsheet to help in answering this question.)

b. How would the answer to part a change if each finished system had a steady reject rate of 10% and each subassembly had a reject rate of 20%?

*19. APCO, the firm described in problems 17 and 18, is concerned about their lot sizes. (Refer to Problems 17 and 18 for data, but you need not have worked problem 17 or 18 to do this problem.) The setup and inventory costs are as follows:

	C_S ($)	C_I ($/week)		C_S ($)	C_I ($/week)
SYS1	150	0.50	SUB2	60	0.20
SYS2	120	0.30	SUB3	50	0.25
SUB1	60	0.20	SUB4	50	0.30

a. What is the total weekly average expected demand for each item?

b. What is the standard EOQ for each item?

c. Using the EOQ formula, calculate the length of the review interval to be used in a periodic review lot-sizing policy for each item. What does the answer imply about how the items would be managed?

*20. This problem refers to APCO, described in problems 17, 18, and 19. (An answer to Problem 18 is required before this problem can be done.) In APCO, one production facility is devoted to manufacturing SYS1, SYS2, SUB1, SUB2, SUB3, and SUB4. Each subassembly requires 1.4 labor-hours and each system requires 1.8 labor-hours.

a. How many labor-hours are needed in each week to complete all these items, using the production schedule from problem 18? That is, develop a capacity (load) projection for these items. Assume that a released lot is equally divided between the order-release week and the week following.

b. Describe a manner in which they can develop a better schedule for capacity usage.

c. Can the firm operate over this period of 17 weeks with a capacity of 2400 labor-hours for these six items? How much average capacity do they need for these units in the long run?

21. Describe the numerical changes that would occur in the answers to problems 18 and 20 if the firm used the lot sizes found in problem 19, part c. (To complete this problem, answers to problems 18, 19, and 20 are required.)

22. The KB Company is described in the introduction to this chapter, and a summary of their expected production schedule is shown in Figure 10-5. The firm has just obtained a major new contract for FA2 and FA3, raising their demand rates to 200 units per week beginning in week 1.

The final-assembly facility has ample capacity for the new demands; its 2-week lead time and 1000 unit lot sizes remain unchanged. The capacity of the component facility will be doubled, becoming 2000 per week, by adding an extra shift. Consequently, management has reduced the planned component lead times (for all components except COMP2, which is purchased with a 1-week lead time) from 3 weeks to 2 weeks, which still leaves a margin of safety. Other lead times are 2 weeks (final assembly) and 1 week (procurement) as before. Lot-for-lot scheduling is used for all components.

a. Redo Figure 10-5 to reflect the preceding changes.
b. Describe any infeasibilities that occur.

23. (This problem requires an answer to problem 22.) A capacity plan for the component facility of KB Company is given in review problems 2 and 3 of Section 10-2. Remembering that COMP2 is purchased rather than produced, redo that analysis using the new situation described in problem 22. Give only two capacity plans: one splitting each batch between the order-release week and the next week and one that uses the "crash schedule."

24. The lot size of a component part is determined using the period-order-quantity heuristic with a period of 12 weeks. It is now time to place an order. If the next twelve demands are (4, 0, 4, 0, 4, 0, 4, 0, 4, 0, 4, 200), what order quantity does the period order quantity imply? Suggest a better order quantity and argue for its superiority.

25. (This problem and the next require a knowledge of linear programming, which is described in Appendix C.) Let

R_{it} = requirements for item i in period t (a decision variable)
D_{it} = external (independent) demand for item i in period t
P_{jt} = number of units of item j produced in period t (a decision variable)
a_{ij} = number of units of item i used in 1 unit of item j ($i = 1, \ldots, N$ and $j = 1, \ldots, N$)

There are N items (finished items and components) and T periods in the planning horizon.

a. Write an equation defining R_{it} in terms of the other variables. (Hint: Your equation should take the form: requirements = independent demand + dependent demand.)
b. Let

I_{it} = number of units of item i in inventory at the end of period t
F_i = scrap rate of a batch of item i (assumed known and constant)

Write an equation defining I_{it}. Assume that all (planned) lead times are zero. (The form should be: inventory = old inventory + amount produced − requirements.)

c. The capacity of a facility can be represented as

$$\sum b_i P_{it} \leq \text{capacity of facility K}$$

(The sum is taken over all items produced in facility K.) Even though planned lead times are zero, the capacity constraint may cause some nonzero lead times.

(i) Why is lead time not explicitly part of the capacity constraint?
(ii) In this constraint, what does b_i represent?

26. (Refer to Problem 25 for definition of symbols.)
    a. If lot-for-lot scheduling is used throughout the system and batch sizes are prescribed for finished goods, setup costs will be fixed and need not be considered. Then what objective function is appropriate in conjunction with the constraints listed in problem 25? Write it, defining any new symbols. If we minimize this objective function subject to the constraints in problem 25, is the model a linear program?
    b. If lot-size decisions (other than lot for lot) are to be made by the mathematical program, can ordinary linear programming be used?
    c. Comment on the size of the mathematical program described in problems 25 and 26, part a.
27. An end item has one input. The lead times for the end item and its input are both zero. The only costs are for setup and inventory. Capacity is not constrained. If the finished item will be produced in batches of 100, once per week, explain why lot sizes less than 100 make no sense for the input item. Might larger lot sizes be appropriate for the input item? Why? Does this logic carry over if there are several inputs? Why or why not?

REFERENCES

AFENTAKIS, P., B. GAVISH, and U. KARMARKAR, "Computationally Efficient Optimal Solutions to the Lot-Sizing Problem in Multistage Assembly Systems," *Management Science*, vol. 30, no. 2, 1984.

BAKER, K.R., "Lot-Sizing Procedures and a Standard Data Set: A Reconciliation of the Literature," *Journal of Manufacturing and Operations Management*, vol. 2, no. 3, 1989.

BERRY, W.L., T.E. VOLLMAN, and D.C. WHYBARK, *Master Scheduling: Principles and Practice*, Falls Church, Va.: American Production and Inventory Control Society, 1979.

BILLINGTON, P.J., J.O. McCLAIN, and L.J. THOMAS, "Mathematical Programming Approaches to Capacity-Constrained MRP Systems: Review, Formulation and Problem Reduction," *Management Science*, vol. 29, no. 10, 1983.

BILLINGTON, P.J., J.O. McCLAIN, and L.J. THOMAS, "Heuristics for Multilevel Lot-Sizing with a Bottleneck," *Management Science*, vol. 32, no. 8, 1986.

BLACKBURN, J., and R. MILLEN, "Heuristic Lot-Sizing Performance in a Rolling-Schedule Environment," *Decision Sciences*, vol. 11, no. 4, 1980.

BLACKBURN, J., and R. MILLEN, "Improved Heuristics for Multi-stage Requirements Planning Systems," *Management Science*, vol. 28, no. 1, January, 1982.

CONWAY, R., and W. MAXWELL, "PRS: A Production Reservation System," working paper, Malott Hall, Cornell University, 1989.

DAVIS, E.W., ed., *Case Studies in Material Requirements Planning*, Falls Church, Va.: American Production and Inventory Control Society, 1978.

EPPEN, G.D., and R.K. MARTIN, "Solving Multi-Item Capacitated Lot-Sizing Problems Using Variable Redefinition," *Operations Research*, vol. 35, no. 6, 1987.

FEDERGRUEN, A., and M. TZUR, "A Simple Forward Algorithm to Solve General Dynamic Lot Sizing Models with *n* Periods in *O*(*n log n*) or *O*(*n*) Time," *Management Science,* vol. 37, no. 8, 1991.

FISCHER, W.A., and J.B. MAZZOLA, *Fischtale Enterprises* (and Instructor's Manual), 2nd ed., Glenview, Ill.: Scott, Foresman, 1987.

GALLIGAN, S., and P. HAZARIKA, "Shop Floor Control in a Continuous Production Flow Environment," *Production and Inventory Management,* vol. 23, no. 4, 1982.

GOLDRATT, E.M., *OPT-Optimized Production Timetable,* Milford, N.Y.: Creative Output, 1980.

GOLDRATT, E.M., "Computerized Shop Floor Scheduling," *International Journal of Production Research,* vol. 26, no. 3, 1988.

GRASSO, E.T., and B.W. TAYLOR III, "A Simulation-Based Experimental Investigation of Supply/Timing Uncertainty in MRP Systems," *International Journal of Production Research,* vol. 22, no. 3, 1984.

GRAVES, S.C., "Multi-stage Lot Sizing: An Iterative Procedure," in *Multi-level Production/Inventory Systems: Theory and Practice,* L. Schwarz, ed., New York: Elsevier North-Holland, 1981.

GRAVES, S.C., "Safety Stocks in Manufacturing Systems," *Journal of Manufacturing and Operations Management,* vol. 1, no. 1, 1988.

JACOBS, F.R., "The OPT Scheduling System: A Review of a New Production Scheduling System," *Production and Inventory Management,* vol. 24, no. 3, 1983.

JAIKUMAR, R., Teaching Note (No. 5-688-075) for "Sturm, Ruger & Co., Inc. (A)," Harvard Business School, Boston, Mass., 1989.

JONES, J., "The Use of MRP in a Food Service Installation," *Production and Inventory Management,* Second Quarter, 1979.

KANET, J., "Toward Understanding Lead Time in MRP Systems," *Production and Inventory Management,* vol. 23, no. 3, 1982.

KARMARKAR, U.S., "Lot Sizes, Lead Times, and In-Process Inventories," *Management Science,* vol. 33, no. 3, 1987.

KARMARKAR, U.S., "Getting Control of Just-in-Time," *Harvard Business Review,* September–October, 1989.

KHUMAWALA, B.M., C. HIXON, and J.S. LAW, "MRP II in the Service Industries," *Production and Inventory Management,* Third Quarter, 1986.

KROPP, D., and R. CARLSON, "A Lot-Sizing Algorithm for Reducing Nervousness in MRP Systems," *Management Science,* vol. 30, no. 2, February, 1984.

LAMBRECHT, M., J. MUCKSTADT, and R. LUYTEN, "Protective Stocks in Multistage Production Systems," Technical Report 562, School of Operations Research and Industrial Engineering, Cornell University, Ithaca, N.Y., 1982.

MAXWELL, W.L., and J.A. MUCKSTADT, "Establishing Consistent and Realistic Reorder Intervals in Production-Distribution Systems," *Operations Research,* vol. 33, no. 6, 1985.

MAXWELL, W., J. MUCKSTADT, J. THOMAS, and J. VANDEREECKEN, "A Modeling Framework for Planning and Control of Production in Discrete Parts Manufacturing and Assembly Systems," *Interfaces,* vol. 14, no. 6, December, 1983.

MAZZOLA, J.B., W.F. MCCOY, and H.M. WAGNER, "Algorithms and Heuristics for Variable-Yield Lot Sizing," *Naval Research Logistics Quarterly,* vol. 34, 1987.

MAZZOLA, J.B., A.W. NEEBE, and C.V.R. DUNN, "Production Planning of a Flexible Manufacturing System in a Material Requirements Planning Environment," *International Journal of Flexible Manufacturing Systems*, vol. 1, no. 2, 1989.

MCCLAIN, J.O., and W.W. TRIGEIRO, "Cyclic Assembly Schedules," *IIE Transactions*, vol. 17, no. 4, 1983.

MEAL, H.C., "Safety Stocks in MRP Systems," Technical Report No. 166, Operations Research Center, Massachusetts Institute of Technology, 1979.

MILLER, J., "Hedging the Master Schedule," Graduate School of Business Administration, Harvard University, Cambridge, Mass., 1980.

MORTON, T.E., S.R. LAWRENCE, S. RAJAGOPOLAN, and S. KEKRE, "SCHED-STAR: A Price-Based Shop Scheduling Module," *Journal of Manufacturing and Operations Management*, vol. 1, no. 2, 1988.

ORLICKY, J., *Material Requirements Planning*, New York: McGraw-Hill, 1975.

SARI, F.J., "The MPS and the Bill of Material Go Hand-in-Hand," Winston-Salem, N.C.: Ling, 1981.

SCHWARZ, L.B., and L. SCHRAGE, "Optimal and System Myopic Policies for Multiechelon Production/Inventory Assembly Systems," *Management Science*, vol. 21, no. 11, July, 1975.

SILVER, E.A., and H.C. MEAL, "A Heuristic for Selecting Lot Size Requirements for the Case of a Deterministic Time-Varying Demand Rate and Discrete Opportunities for Replenishment," *Production and Inventory Management*, vol. 14, no. 2, 1973.

SILVER, E.A., and R. PETERSON, *Decision Systems for Inventory Management and Production Planning*, 2nd ed., New York: Wiley, 1985.

STENGER, A., and J. CAVINATO, "Adapting MRP to the Outbound Side—Distribution Requirements Planning," *Production and Inventory Management*, vol. 20, no. 4, 1979.

TRIGEIRO, W.W., L.J. THOMAS, and J.O. MCCLAIN, "Capacitated Lot Sizing with Setup Times," *Management Science*, vol. 35, no. 3, 1989.

VOLLMAN, T.E., W.L. BERRY, and D.C. WHYBARK, *Manufacturing Planning and Control Systems*, 2nd ed., Homewood, Ill.: Irwin, 1988.

WAGNER, H.M., and T. WHITIN, "Dynamic Version of the Economic Lot Size Model," *Management Science*, vol. 5, 1958.

WALLACE, T.F., and J.R. DOUGHERTY, *APICS Dictionary*, 6th ed., Falls Church, Va.: American Production and Inventory Control Society, 1987.

WHYBARK, D.C., and J.G. WILLIAMS, "Material Requirements Planning Under Uncertainty," *Decision Sciences*, October, 1976.

YANO, C.A., and H.L. LEE, "Lot-Sizing with Random Yields: A Review," Technical Report 89-16, Department of Industrial Engineering and Operations Research, University of Michigan, 1989.

chapter 11

Production Scheduling and Control

Production schedules are plans for near-future production. In this chapter plans for individual items are the initial focus, but most of the discussion concerns the problems encountered when multiple items share production resources. We also show how production-scheduling systems can consider aggregate plans (introduced in Chapter 9) as well as coordination of families of similar items. A schedule specifies when production is to take place and how much is to be produced. Production quantity is similar to order quantity (Chapter 8), but the issue of timing production of different items using the same facilities or resources makes scheduling much more difficult.

Production control concerns the present. Given all the plans and schedules, what shall we make right now? Control requires more than simply following the schedule, because unanticipated events occur. Equipment may fail. A customer may request early delivery. Orders may be canceled. Unexpected orders may arrive. Although scheduling and control have the same goals, they do not always have the same results.

A schedule is a bridge between intermediate-range plans and actual production, as illustrated in Figure 11-1. It must coordinate planned work with resource plans (plant capacity, equipment, etc.). It must assure that customer requirements can be met. If there are multiple production stages, the schedule must coordinate these stages. (MRP is one way to do this. See Chapter 10.)

The competitive advantages of good scheduling and control are many. Most obvious is that effective use of resources leads to high productivity. In addition, customers benefit when accurate scheduling leads to fast response and accurate delivery promises. Indeed, knowing the exact location of each order in a factory and being able to predict its future progress can be very useful in dealing with customers.

Even the simplest production-scheduling systems are complicated. Long production lead times make it difficult to forecast demand accurately; therefore, schedules must accommodate uncertainty. If a facility is tightly scheduled, mi-

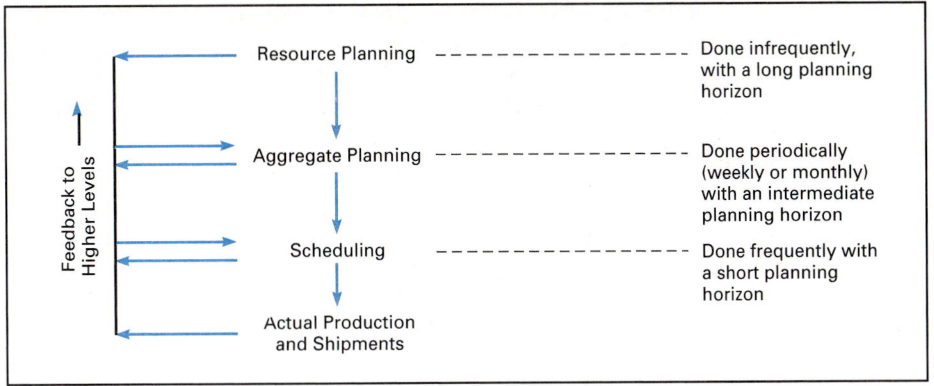

Figure 11-1 Scheduling as a Bridge between Intermediate-Range Plans and Actual Production

nor changes can disrupt the schedule. For example, suppose that a new order arrives for an item that is already scheduled for production. If the production quantity is increased to satisfy the new demand, it may take longer to finish the job. That delays all subsequent jobs. On the other hand, if the new order is scheduled later, we might lose the customer, and some efficiency will be lost since an extra setup of that item must be performed. This is but one example of what makes scheduling difficult. This chapter illustrates many more pitfalls faced by schedulers and some of the methods used to avoid them.

The first three sections address the *repetitive manufacturing* environment. Demand is presumed to be fairly stable, and a single facility is used to produce many products. We show how to develop a *cyclic schedule*, which is a repeating sequence of production. The cyclic schedule is imbedded in a system that includes a link to aggregate production plans, building inventory during low-demand seasons. In addition, safety time is included to protect against demand variations and other uncertain events. The third section concludes with a discussion of ''schedule busters,'' which are commonly encountered mistakes that make accurate scheduling difficult or impossible.

Section 11-4 describes the use of Gantt charts for scheduling more than one facility simultaneously. A computer-based system is briefly discussed. The examples in this section are quite different from the steady-demand environment of the earlier sections. Often called job shops, these facilities produce a variety of different products, often one of a kind, with demands that are unpredictable. Some control rules used in job shops are introduced and their effectiveness is compared. The chapter closes with a discussion of systems designed to integrate three levels of decision making into an effective production-management system. However, the discussion of production scheduling and control continues in the next chapter, where just-in-time production systems are described.

11-1 PRODUCTION SCHEDULING AND LOT SIZING

The purpose of a schedule is to assure that production goals can be met with the resources available. Scheduling is one of the most difficult tasks in operations management. In this section we address two issues: how much capacity is needed and what lot size (production quantity) to use. These are preliminary issues. Scheduling is addressed in the next section, followed by methods for protecting the schedule. Together, these topics constitute a *scheduling system*.

Repetitive manufacturing is the environment in the following example, which illustrates one scheduling system, *cyclic scheduling*. Although cyclic scheduling is one of the simplest methods, it illustrates many of the issues that make scheduling both important and difficult.

Example: National Carpet

National Carpet (NC) has three product categories (families): wool carpet, artificial-fiber carpet, and carpet backing. Both wool and artificial-fiber carpets come in a variety of colors, patterns, and other characteristics, but there is only one kind of backing. NC's manufacturing facility can only produce one item at a time, and changing to a different item requires a setup that stops production. The setup time and cost are small when changing between items in the same family (minor setup) but much larger between families (major setup). Because of this, the production schedule is organized around the families so that major setups will be less frequent than minor setups.

Despite the fact that production capacity exceeds demand, NC has been forced to decline some orders. The production control manager, Margaret Gill, has been asked to find out why. She began by reviewing NC's production-scheduling methods with the scheduling supervisor, Tom Louis.

"Boy, Gill," said Tom, "we haven't had much luck maintaining a production schedule. Demand can vary a lot, so items sometimes run out of stock before the family's turn arrives. Interrupting one family to produce an item from another family is very expensive. We try to avoid this with safety stocks, but top management has been after us to keep inventory low.

"Even worse is when we get conflicts between families. We decide which family to run next based on inventory. If two families are low on stock at the same time, one of them will have shortages no matter which family is produced next. Setting higher reorder levels helps, but that increases the inventory."

Looking at the records reminded Ms. Gill that demand for carpets peaks in late summer and early fall. NC has an aggregate plan that calls for a buildup of inventory during slack months. This allows them to meet the peak demand without increasing the capacity of their facility. Nevertheless, during the peak season they often use overtime because the items in inventory are not always the items that are demanded. Many special orders occur during peak, but production capacity is actually reduced because of the additional nonproductive setup time required to accommodate these orders.

The fundamental issue in scheduling is the limited capacity of the production facility. All of NC's items share the same production facility. Time devoted to production of any item has an effect on all the others. Simply put, the larger the production quantity, the longer the next item must wait for its turn. All future start times can be affected by any change in the schedule.

NC's production is repetitive. There are relatively few products and they all have continuing demand. NC schedules each item by setting start times and production quantities (lot sizes) large enough to satisfy demand between start times. However, lot sizes also influence inventory and setup costs. Later in this section, the economic production quantity (EPQ) is introduced to address this trade-off. Unfortunately, NC cannot schedule production with the EPQ. (Very few companies can.) Sections 11-2 and 11-3 describe practical modifications of the EPQ that maintain nearly minimal costs while achieving a realistic schedule.

Matching Lot Sizes to Production Capacity and Demand

The *production quantity* (lot size) determines

- production run time (how long it takes to produce the lot)
- production interval (how long until we must produce again)
- inventory
- frequency of setups, and therefore average setup cost and the proportion of production capacity that is lost because of setup time

The trade-off between inventory and setup costs is similar to the one described in the discussion of the economic order quantity (EOQ) in Chapter 8. Large quantity means high inventory but infrequent setups, and conversely. Production interval and run time are important scheduling concepts. They may be calculated as follows:

$$\text{Run time (excluding setup)} = \frac{\text{production quantity}}{\text{production rate}} = \frac{Q}{P} \tag{1}$$

$$\text{Production interval (if demand rate is constant)} = \frac{\text{production quantity}}{\text{demand rate}} = \frac{Q}{D} \tag{2}$$

At NC the production rate is P = 45,000 square meters per week, regardless of which item is being produced. This is the production capacity of the facility, ignoring setup time, equipment failures, overtime, and so forth. Carpet backing has a demand rate of D = 15,000 square meters per week. Consequently, a production lot of Q = 90,000 would satisfy demand for 90/15 = 6 weeks (production interval) and require 90/45 = 2 weeks (run time) to produce, once the setup is completed.

For scheduling purposes, the difference between these two numbers (6 − 2 = 4 weeks) is the time available for setups, maintenance, and production of other items before the next run of carpet backing. The ratio of these two numbers shows that carpet backing requires one third of the production capacity (2 weeks out of every 6) if demand is to be met. This result does not depend on the production schedule. In general,

$$\text{Fraction of capacity needed for production of one item} = \frac{\text{demand rate}}{\text{production rate}} = \frac{D}{P} \tag{3}$$

which is 15/45 or one third for carpet backing. This calculation is fundamental to scheduling. If we calculate D/P for all items and add the results, the total is the fraction of capacity needed to satisfy all demand. If the result exceeds 1.0, demand cannot be met. In fact, the result must be less than 1.0 if NC is to meet all demand because some of the production capacity is lost when setups occur. This is summarized as follows:

$$\text{Fraction of capacity needed for production} = \sum_i D_i/P_i \tag{4}$$

in which the subscript i refers to the different items and the sum is over all items.

The Economic Production Quantity (EPQ)

The ratio D/P is also important in determining the inventory caused by production. During the run time, inventory increases at the rate of production (P), and at the same time decreases at the demand rate (D). The net rate of increase is $P - D$. Since the run time is Q/P, the net amount added to inventory (rate multiplied by time) is

$$\text{Inventory increase during production} = (P - D)(Q/P) = Q(1 - D/P) \quad (5)$$

Figure 11-2 illustrates the sawtooth pattern of inventory. Note that the maximum height is $Q(1 - D/P)$ as in equation 5. The average inventory is half the peak value, or $(Q/2)(1 - D/P)$. We will use this fact to model the cost due to production lots.

Average setup cost depends on the production interval (Q/D), which determines how frequently setups occur. The cost of each setup can be difficult to determine. Direct costs may include the wages of specially trained mechanics who do the setup and the wages of the production workers idled during the setup, as well as damage or loss of material during tests of the new setup. In addition, setup time causes loss of production capacity. If that capacity is needed to satisfy demand, the setup time will either lead to lost sales or additional costs such as overtime. Therefore, the cost assigned to setup time depends on the situation.

The *economic production quantity* (*EPQ*) minimizes the sum of setup and holding costs. We will illustrate the formulas by continuing the example of carpet backing, for which $D = 15{,}000$ and $P = 45{,}000$ square meters per week. The unit costs are

$$\begin{aligned} C_I &= \text{inventory holding cost per unit time} \\ &= \$0.016 \text{ per square meter per week} \\ C_S &= \text{setup cost per production run} = \$650 \end{aligned}$$

The average total variable cost (TVC) is

$$\text{TVC} = C_I\,(Q/2)(1 - D/P) + C_S\,(D/Q) \quad \text{(average cost per unit time)} \quad (6)$$

Figure 11-2 Inventory Pattern with Production Rate P and Demand Rate D

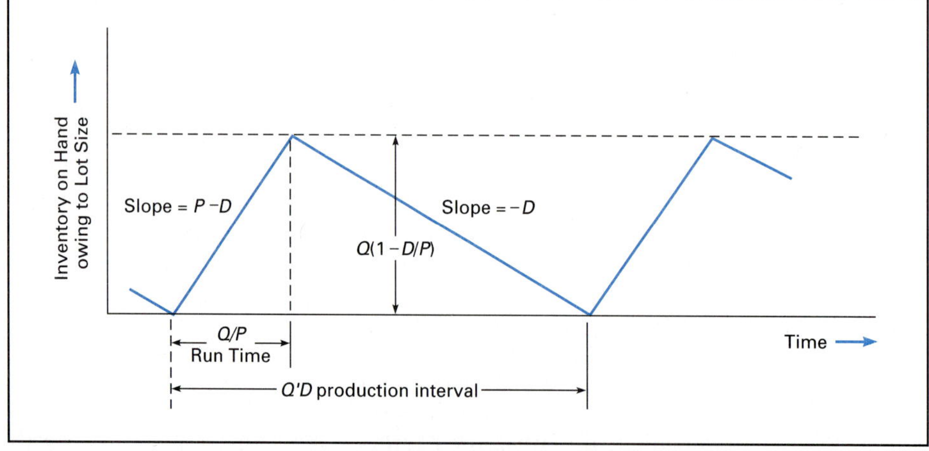

and the production quantity that minimizes TVC is

$$Q^* = \sqrt{\frac{2DC_S}{C_I(1 - D/P)}} \quad \text{(EPQ, the economic production quantity)} \tag{7}$$

$$= \sqrt{\frac{2(15{,}000)(650)}{0.016(1 - 15{,}000/45{,}000)}} = 42{,}757$$

$$T^* = Q^*/D \quad \text{(production interval for the EPQ)} \tag{8}$$

$$= 42{,}757/15{,}000 = 2.85 \text{ weeks}$$

If NC used this production quantity, they would produce carpet backing every 2.85 weeks (T^*), and the run time would be slightly less than a week (D/P = 42,757/45,000 = 0.95). As with the EOQ of Chapter 8, the EPQ can be changed at very little cost. Table 11-1 illustrates this property for carpet backing. This is extremely important for scheduling, because production run quantities *must* be modified to fit the schedule. We will use the EPQ as a guideline in forming schedules in later sections.

Other Lot-Sizing Methods

The EPQ is but one of many methods for computing lot sizes. If demand is not constant, other methods are more appropriate. Some of the lot-sizing methods used in MRP were described in Chapter 10, for example. Many lot-sizing methods are based on the EPQ. For example, if weekly demands are known but not constant, one way to determine the production quantity is to add up full weeks of demand until you get a number close to the EPQ. When demand is high, production will become more frequent using this approach, but lot size will be approximately the same for every run.

A similar approach is to compute the production interval (T^*) and then set the lot size equal to the total demand forecast over that period. This is known as the *period order quantity* (*POQ*) *heuristic*. For carpet backing, T^* was 2.85 weeks; assuming that demand forecasts are for whole weeks, POQ would suggest a production quantity equal to the demand forecast for the next three weeks. With this method, lot size rises and falls with demand, but the production interval remains constant at three weeks. (See Chapter 10 for additional discussion.) By itself, lot sizing does not produce a schedule to fit several items on the same facility. We will return to this issue after describing cyclic scheduling.

Table 11-1 Robustness[a] of the Economic Production Quantity

% deviation from EPQ	Q	TVC	% deviation from TVC*
−40%	25,654	516.88	13.33%
−20%	34,205	467.47	2.50%
0%	42,757	456.07	0.00%
20%	51,308	463.67	1.67%
40%	59,859	482.13	5.71%

[a] Robustness means that large deviations from the optimal *quantity* cause only small deviations from the minimum *cost*.

REVIEW PROBLEMS

1. Demand for carpet backing is 15,000 square meters per week, and the production capacity is 45,000 per week. A production schedule for carpet backing specifies production start times (weeks) of 1.0, 3.0, 5.0, etc. Each run is supposed to be one week long.

   a. Why are these run times inconsistent with the start times?
   b. To be consistent with these start times, how many square meters should they produce during each run? Why?
   c. At what times should the production runs be scheduled to stop?
   d. Using your answers to parts b and c, if inventory is zero at time 1.0, what is the maximum inventory reached between times 1.0 and 3.0? At what time is the maximum reached? When is the minimum reached?

2. NC's setup cost of \$650 includes an estimate of the profits (\$610) that could have been achieved by production if setup time could be avoided, and the cost (\$40) of labor and materials to adjust the equipment for carpet backing.

   a. Should the wages of workers who are idle during setup be added to this number? Explain.
   b. Is NC correct to include lost profits as an opportunity cost? Explain.

3. Suppose that demand for carpet backing were 40,000 (rather that 15,000) square meters per week.

   a. What fraction of the production capacity would be needed for carpet backing at this demand rate?
   b. Compute the EPQ and its cost (TVC).
   c. What run time and production interval would be appropriate for the EPQ?
   d. Increase the production quantity by 50% above the EPQ and compute the TVC. By what percentage does the TVC increase compared with using EPQ?

4. The following are weekly forecasts of demand for carpet backing. The EPQ is 42,757, the long-run average demand rate is 15,000 per week, and P = 45,000. In this question, assume that production intervals are required to be whole weeks (no fractional weeks).

Week	1	2	3	4	5	6	7	8
Demand	9000	8000	9500	10,000	8000	18,900	9000	9000

   a. Compute the production interval, T^*. What production quantity would the POQ heuristic suggest? What would the run time be?
   b. If a production quantity near the EPQ is desired, what quantity would you recommend? How long would the resulting production interval be?

Solutions

1. a. Demand during the two-week production interval is 2(15,000) = 30,000, but the one-week run produces 45,000. They would produce more than they can sell.
   b. 30,000 so that demand can be satisfied.
   c. Run time = 30,000/45,000 = 0.67 from equation 1. Stop times are 1.67, 3.67, 5.67, etc.
   d. Inventory is largest at the stop times. The number of units produced is 30,000, but demand during the 0.67-week run is 0.67(15,000) = 10,000; therefore, the net is 20,000 units of inventory. Equation 5 gives the same answer. Inventory will be gone just as the next run begins (at times 3.0, 5.0, 7.0, etc.)

2. a. No. Their wages have been included in the foregone profits. It would be double counting to include them again.
   b. Yes. NC is losing sales. Less setup time would allow more production.

3. a. D/P = 40,000/45,000 = 0.889 or 88.9% (equation 3).
   b. $Q^* = \sqrt{2(40{,}000)(650)/[0.016\ (1 - 40/45)]} = 171{,}026$.
   TVC = 0.016(171,026/2)(1 − 40/45) + 650(40,000/171,026) = \$304.05.
   c. Run time = 171,026/45,000 = 3.80 weeks (equation 1).
   Production interval = 171,026/40,000 = 4.28 weeks (equation 2).
   d. 1.5(171,026) = 256,539. TVC = 0.016(256,539/2)(1 − 40/45) + 650(40,000/256,529) = \$329.39. For the EPQ, the cost is \$304.05; thus, the 50% increase in Q caused weekly cost to increase by \$25.34 or 8.3%.

4. a. 42,757/15,000 = 2.85 weeks, which we round to 3 because the forecasts are for whole weeks. The quantity is Q = 9000 + 8000 + 9500 = 26,500. Run time = 26,500/45,000 = 0.59 weeks.
   b. The first five add to 44,500, which is as close to the EPQ as these numbers can get. The interval would be 5 weeks.

11-2 CYCLIC SCHEDULING

A *schedule* is a list of start and run times for each item. A *cyclic schedule* is a schedule that repeats. Cyclic schedules make sense for National Carpet because their product families have continuing demands, and the seasonal pattern is the same for all items. Establishing a repetitive manufacturing schedule is also fundamental to many just-in-time operations, described in Chapter 12.

The *production sequence* is the order in which items are produced. It is useful to consider the sequence prior to determining a schedule. For example, the setup costs for NC are sequence dependent. Changing between items in the same family is much easier than changing between families. There are other situations that lead to sequence-dependent setup costs. Production is less expensive for paints and cake mixes when the sequence progresses from light colors to dark. Sandpaper's natural progression is from fine to coarse grit. Since changing the tools on a large machine may be very time consuming, items with similar tooling requirements are often grouped together.

The problem of determining an optimal sequence is extremely difficult. (Mathematicians call it NP-hard. We will not go into any of the mathematics here.) NC's sequencing problem is made easier by the great disparity between major setups (between families) and minor setups (within a family). First, an optimal schedule must keep together items that are in the same family to avoid unnecessary major setups. Second, the sequence of families is unimportant because the major setup cost is the same going from wool to artificial fiber or to carpet backing. However, it may be desirable to produce some families more frequently than others because of different demands and inventory costs. For example, the sequence Wool–Artificial–Wool–Backing can be repeated indefinitely, and wool carpeting would be produced twice as often as the other two families.

NC's big cost element is the between-family setup. Therefore, the first target of the scheduling system is to control the number of these setups. Part of this is to assure that two or more families do not require production at the same time. This problem is attacked at two levels. First, a production interval is established for each family in a manner that allows a cyclic schedule to be formed. Within that schedule, actual run times for the families are allocated to avoid low-stock conditions occurring for two families at the same time. The EPQ formula, modified to apply to entire families, serves as a guide to setting these production intervals, thereby assuring that the major costs of setup and inventory are (nearly) minimized.

Second, production quantities for individual items are set in a manner designed to protect the integrity of the schedule of the major family setups, and to allow seasonal inventory accumulation consistent with an aggregate production plan. This part of the system is described in Section 11-3.

Family Production Intervals

Consider NC's family of wool carpets. There are $N = 10$ items in this family. One objective is to produce them sequentially, setting one production interval, T, for the entire family. To do this, the *average* production quantity for item i needs to be "a T-week supply," or $Q_i = D_i T$, where D_i is the average weekly demand rate. (The runout-time approach, shown later, gives time-varying quantities that match this average.) Using this relationship in the TVC formula and adding over all items in a family, the result is

$$\text{TVC} = (\text{family inventory cost})(T/2) + (\text{family setup cost})/T \qquad (9)$$

in which

$$\text{Family setup cost} = \text{major setup cost} + \sum_{\text{items in family}} (\text{minor setup cost}) \qquad (10)$$

$$\text{Family inventory cost}^1 = \sum_{\text{items } i \text{ in family}} (D_i C_{I,i})(1 - D_i/P_i) \qquad (11)$$

[1]The subscript i refers to different items. Otherwise the symbols are the same as defined earlier: C_I is inventory cost; D and P are demand and production rates, respectively. Multiplying this equation by $T/2$ is the same as multiplying $C_I(1 - D/P)$ by $Q/2$ in equation 6 in the EPQ discussion because we assume that $Q = DT$.

The optimal family production interval can be derived using calculus to minimize TVC in equation 9. The result is

$$T^* = \sqrt{\frac{2(\text{family setup cost})}{\text{family inventory cost}}} \tag{12}$$

The wool carpet family has 10 items. The major setup cost is \$650 to prepare the facility for the wool carpet family, and the minor setup cost is \$120 to begin production of any wool carpet item once the major setup is complete.

$$\text{Wool family setup cost} = \$650 + 10(\$120) = \$1850$$

The family inventory cost requires a little more work to calculate. All wool carpet items have production rates of P_i = 45,000 square meters per week and unit inventory costs of $C_{I,i}$ = \$0.12 per square meter per week. The weekly demand rate for item 1 is D_1 = 3,000, D_2 and D_3 are both 2,000, and the other seven each sell 1,000 square meters per week. The inventory costs for items i = 1 to 10 are

$$\begin{aligned}(D_iC_{I,i})(1 - D_i/P_i) &= (3000)(\$0.12)(1 - 3/45) = \$336.0 \quad \text{for } i = 1\\ &= (2000)(\$0.12)(1 - 2/45) = \$229.3 \quad \text{(each) for } i = 2, 3\\ &= (1000)(\$0.12)(1 - 1/45) = \$117.3 \quad \text{(each) for } i = 4 \text{ to } 10\end{aligned}$$

$$\begin{aligned}\text{Wool family inventory cost} &= \$336.0 + 2(\$229.3) + 7(\$117.3)\\ &= \$1616\end{aligned}$$

$$\text{Wool family production interval } T^* = \sqrt{2(1850)/1616} = 1.513 \text{ weeks}$$

Ideally, then, the wool family should be run once every 1.513 weeks. In the previous section, equation 4 states that the fraction of capacity needed for production is $\Sigma_i\ D_i/P_i$, which adds up to 0.311 for the wool family. Therefore, during the 1.513-week interval, 31.1% of the time (that is, 0.47 weeks) is needed for wool-carpet production, and the rest is available for setup times and for production of the other families.

However, as described earlier, the production cycle for the facility may not allow wool to be produced at exactly 1.513-week intervals. In fact, we may have to modify this value substantially to get a schedule that works for all three families. How much difference will this make to the cost? Table 11-1 (in the previous section) showed that production of carpet backing could vary by a large percentage at very little increase in cost. Problem 31 will show that, in general, T can be varied over a wide range at very little cost penalty.

Conflicts in Scheduling

NC has three families: wool, artificial-fiber and backing. Table 11-2 shows that the total demand is 35,000 square meters per week, substantially below the production capacity of 45,000. Since only 77.8% of capacity is needed for production, a schedule should be easy to find.

However, it isn't that simple. Table 11-3 shows an attempt to schedule the facility with each family achieving its ideal production interval, T^* (rounded to tenths of a week). Each family's run time is just sufficient to meet demand during its own T^*. The schedule begins with the wool family, immediately

Table 11-2 Time Required for Setup and Production of NC's Families of Products

Family	Demand Rate	Production Rate	Fraction of Capacity Needed for Production ($\Sigma_i D_i/P_i$)	Setup Time (minutes) Major	Minor	Total	(weeks) Total
Wool (10 items)	14,000	45,000	0.311	120	30	420	0.175
Artificial (10 items)	6,000	45,000	0.133	120	30	420	0.175
Backing (1 item)	15,000	45,000	0.333	120	30	150	0.063
Totals	35,000		0.778				0.413

followed by artificial and then backing. The first part of the schedule ends at time 2.37.

The difficulties begin as soon as the second run of wool is scheduled. It is supposed to start at time 1.5 (because $T^* = 1.5$ for wool), but the facility is producing the backing family at that time. By time 2.37, when the facility becomes available, the wool family will have substantial shortages because its run quantities were designed for its 1.5-week interval. The second runs of the other two families also have a problem: they overlap. We need to do something to prevent this kind of problem.

Cyclic Schedules with One Run of Each Family

Conflicts occurred because the ideal production intervals vary from 1.5 to 3.8 weeks; a compromise seems in order. For example, all families have production intervals of 3 weeks in Table 11-4. Notice that the run times are adjusted

Table 11-3 Attempt to Schedule using T^* for Each Family[a]

Family	T^*	First Run for Each Family: Start	Setup	Run	Finish	Second Run: Start	Finish
Wool	1.5	0.00	0.18	0.47	0.65	1.50	2.15
Artificial	3.8	0.65	0.18	0.51	1.34	4.45	5.14
Backing	2.9	1.34	0.06	0.97	2.37	4.24	5.27

[a] The T^* values and the associated costs are shown in Table 11-6.

Table 11-4 A Simple Cyclic Schedule Using $T = 3$ Weeks for Each Family

Family	T	First Production Cycle: Start	Setup	Run	Finish	Second Cycle: Start	Finish
Wool	3.0	0.00	0.18	0.93	1.11	3.00	4.11
Artificial	3.0	1.11	0.18	0.40	1.69	4.11	4.69
Backing	3.0	1.69	0.06	1.00	2.75	4.69	5.75
Totals			0.42	2.33			

to produce exactly the demand that is expected in 3 weeks. The second run of each family is a repetition of the first, beginning 3 weeks later. There is no overlap in the schedules. In fact, there is slack of 0.25 weeks between the end of the first cycle and the beginning of the second.

Other schedules can be produced by changing the production interval. There is no reason to believe that 3 weeks is the best length for the cycle. We will see later that the optimal cycle length is 2.067; therefore, if NC wants this kind of cycle, they should try 2 weeks rather than 3. First, another 3-week cycle will be discussed.

Cyclic Schedules with Multiple Runs of Some Families

Notice that the wool family's T^* is about half of the other two. That is, wool should be run about twice as often. A schedule using this fact is given in Table 11-5. The production interval is 1.5 for wool and 3.0 for the other two families. The length of the production cycle is 3 weeks, and the schedule starts over at that time. Figure 11-3 shows how this schedule compares with the one in Table 11-4.

Costs of Cyclic Schedules

Now that we have two alternative cyclic schedules, we can compare their costs. Table 11-6 contains the family setup and inventory costs, defined in the previous section, and shows the family T^* values that we have been using.

Table 11-5 A 3-Week Cyclic Schedule with Two Runs of the Wool Family

		First Production Cycle				Second Cycle	
Family	***T***	**Start**	**Setup**	**Run**	**Finish**	**Start**	**Finish**
Wool	1.5	0.00	0.18	0.47	0.65	3.00	3.65
Artificial	3.0	0.65	0.18	0.40	1.23	3.65	4.23
Wool	1.5	1.23	0.18	0.46	1.87	4.23	4.87
Backing	3.0	1.87	0.06	1.00	2.93	4.87	5.93
Totals			0.60	2.33			

Figure 11-3 Two 3-Week Cyclic Schedules

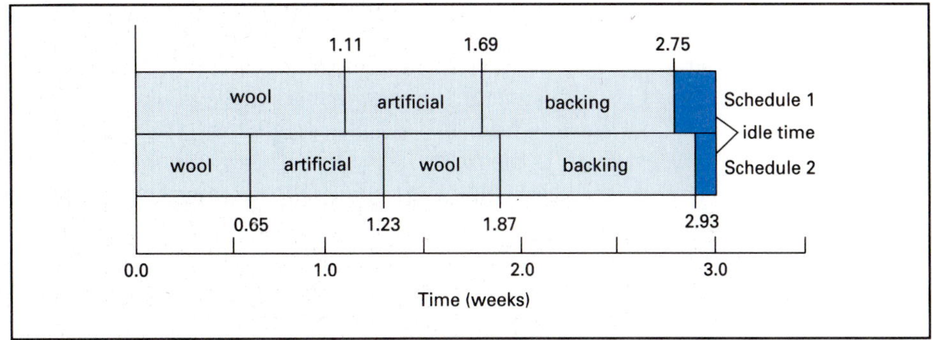

Table 11-6 "Optimal" Production Intervals, T^*

Family	Family Setup Cost	Family Holding Cost	Production Interval (T^*)	Minimum Cost if T^* Could Have Been Used (TVC*)
Wool	1,850	1616	1.513	2445.2
Artificial	1,850	260	3.772	980.8
Backing	650	160	2.850	456.1
Total				3882.1 (to be used later)

To calculate the optimal cycle length and the cost of the cycle, we need the following definitions, illustrated with the cycle in Table 11-5 that has two runs of the wool family:

$$\text{Family multiple } m_k = \text{number of runs of family } k \text{ in one production cycle} \tag{13}$$

(In the example, $m_1 = 2$, $m_2 = 1$, and $m_3 = 1$.)

$$\text{Cycle setup cost} = \sum_{\text{families in cycle}} (\text{family setup cost})(\text{family multiple}) \tag{14}$$

$$= 1850(2) + 1850(1) + 650(1) = 6200$$

$$\text{Cycle inventory cost} = \sum_{\text{families in cycle}} \frac{\text{family inventory cost}}{\text{family multiple}} \tag{15}$$

$$= 1616/2 + 260/1 + 160/1 = 1228$$

$$\text{Optimal cycle length} = \sqrt{\frac{2(\text{cycle setup cost})}{(\text{cycle inventory cost})}} \tag{16}$$

$$= \sqrt{2(6200)/1228} = 3.18 \text{ weeks}$$

The optimal length of this cyclic schedule is very close to the 3-week cycle length in Table 11-5. The total variable cost of the 3-week cycle is

$$\text{TVC} = (\text{cycle inventory cost})(T/2) + (\text{cycle setup cost})/T \tag{17}$$

$$= 1228(3/2) + 6200/3 = 3908.7$$

We can now compare the alternative schedules. The cyclic schedule in Table 11-4 has all family multiples equal to 1, so the cycle setup cost is 1850 + 1850 + 650 = 4350 and the cycle inventory cost is 1616 + 260 + 160 = 2036. This gives an optimal cycle length of 2.067 weeks.

Costs of several different cycles are evaluated in Table 11-7. Notice that TVC is lower when $m_1 = 2$. Also, all the schedules have TVC greater than \$3882, which is the value T^* would give if it weren't for the schedule conflicts. That is, the TVC calculated using T^* is a lower bound to what may actually be attained.[2]

[2]This fact helps us judge how near a schedule is to optimal, even though we do not know the optimal solution.

Table 11-7 Costs of Several Different Cyclic Schedules

Multiples			Cycle Length	TVC	Cycle Costs		Optimal Cycle Length
m_1	m_2	m_3			Inventory	Setup	
1	1	1	2	$4211	2036	4350	2.067
1	1	1	2.07	4209	2036	4350	2.067
1	1	1	3	4504	2036	4350	2.067
2	1	1	3	3909	1228	6200	3.18
2	1	1	3.18	3902	1228	6200	3.18
Using T^* for each family:				$3882	(Table 11-6. Not a feasible schedule.)		

Multiples by the Powers-of-2 Rule

Deciding how many times to run a family in a cycle can get rather complicated, particularly if there are many families. The following steps summarize one method that gives multiples that are easy to fit into a schedule and keep costs within about 6% of the minimum possible value. (Roundy [1989] shows this limit in a somewhat different context. Problem 31 demonstrates why this is so, and shows where the following rules come from. Zipkin [1991] describes an alternative method.)

1. Compute T^* for each family. Find the smallest of these and call it T_{min}.
2. For each family, compute its *production frequency*, $n = T^*/T_{min}$.
3. Round each n value to a power of 2 using the following rule:

From	To	Value	From	To	Value
0.707	1.414	1	5.657	11.314	8
1.414	2.828	2	11.314	22.627	16
2.828	5.657	4	22.627	45.255	32

4. Find the largest n value and call it N_{max}.
5. For each family, compute its multiple, $m = N_{max}/n$
6. Compute the optimal cycle length with these multiples. The optimal cycle length will be approximately equal to $N_{max}T_{min}$.

For National Carpet, these steps are applied as follows.

Step 1: For NC, the smallest T^* was 1.513 for the wool family; thus, T_{min} = 1.513.

Steps 2 and 3: For the artificial-fiber family, T^*/T_{min} is 3.772/1.513 = 2.493, which rounds to $n = 2$; for backing, 2.850/1.513 = 1.884 also rounds to n = 2. Artificial-fiber and carpet-backing family production intervals should be about twice as long as wool's.

Steps 4 and 5: $N_{max} = 2$; thus, the multiples are $m_1 = 2/1 = 2$ for wool, $m_2 = 2/2 = 1$ for artificial, and $m_3 = 2/2 = 1$ for backing.

Step 6: For these multiples the optimal cycle length is 3.18 weeks (computed earlier). Step 6 points out that a good approximation should be $N_{max} T_{min}$ = (2)(1.513) = 3.03 weeks, very close in this case. Furthermore, those two cycle lengths have almost equal costs (see the comparisons in Table 11-7).

Minimum Cycle Length: The Effect of Setup Time

Production run times are proportional to the cycle length because the longer the cycle, the more demand we must satisfy. However, setup times are not affected by cycle length; they depend only on the multiples (for example, the number of runs per family). To illustrate, look back to the two schedules in Tables 11-4 and 11-5. NC's cycle with all multiples equal to 1 has setup time totaling 0.42 week, whereas the cycle with two runs of wool has an additional 0.18 week setup time. Using a 3-week cycle length, production run times total 2.33 in both cases because it takes 2.33 weeks to produce enough stock to satisfy 3 weeks of demand, no matter how many setups there are. The difference in setup times causes the schedule with m_1 = 2 to take longer to complete (2.93 weeks versus 2.75). Nevertheless, both schedules finish in less than 3 weeks, leaving some slack before the second cycle begins.

Now consider a 3-week cycle in which both wool and artificial have multiples of two runs per cycle. This would add another setup time of 0.18 week; hence, the cycle would end at 2.93 + 0.18 = 3.11. A 3-week cycle time would not work for that sequence. There is not enough time for another family setup for artificial-fiber carpets.

The general principle is that both production time and setup time must fit into the cycle time. Recalling (from the previous section) that the fraction of capacity needed to satisfy demand is $\Sigma D_i/P_i$, the setup time must not consume more than $(1 - \Sigma D_i/P_i)$ of the cycle. That is,

$$\text{Cycle setup time} \le (\text{cycle length})\Big(1 - \sum_{\text{all items}} D_i/P_i\Big)$$

Turning this around,

$$\text{Cycle length} \ge \frac{\text{cycle setup time}}{1 - \sum_{\text{all items}} D_i/P_i} \tag{18}$$

In this formula, cycle setup time is calculated in the same way as cycle setup cost:

$$\text{Family setup time} = \text{major setup time} + \sum_{\text{items in family}} (\text{minor setup times}) \tag{19}$$

$$\text{Cycle setup time} = \sum_{\text{families}} (\text{family setup time})(\text{family multiple}) \tag{20}$$

For the schedule with two setups of wool, two of artificial, and one of backing, cycle setup time is 2(0.18) + 2(0.18) + 0.06 = 0.78 week. Table 11-2 shows that $\Sigma D_i/P_i$ = 0.778. Therefore, the cycle length must be at least 0.78/(1 − 0.778) = 3.51 weeks long to accommodate both production and setup time. As we saw earlier, this sequence will not fit the 3-week cycle. If NC wants shorter cycles, the setup time must be reduced. Methods for setup time reduction are described in Chapter 12.

REVIEW PROBLEMS

1. What advantages does cyclic scheduling have for National Carpet?

2. Verify that the production run time for the wool family in Table 11-4 is sufficient to meet demand until the next wool setup begins at 3.00.

3. The sum of the TVC values if each family were run at its ideal production interval, T^*, is $3882 (see Table 11-6).

   a. Why is this lower than the cost of any schedule shown in Table 11-7?

   b. Why are the last two schedules in Table 11-7 lower in cost than the others?

4. If there are five different families, and their T^* values are 3.2, 4.8, 9.2, 3.3, and 12.3, what multiples would you recommend in a cyclic schedule? How long would the optimal cycle be, approximately?

5. Calculate the minimum cycle lengths for the cycles in Tables 11-4 and 11-5. If demand were to increase by 10%, would 3-week cycles still fit these two schedules?

Solutions

1. It controls the major setup costs by timing family runs at approximately their ideal production intervals. A repeating schedule also makes planning easier. Orders of raw materials can be more easily coordinated with production, for example. If the cycle can be preserved, the finished-goods inventory can be reduced because they have previously found it necessary to keep stock on hand to prevent shortages due to schedule conflicts.

2. The production rate is 45,000 square meters per week; thus, the production quantity is 0.93(45,000) = 41,850. The family demand rate is 14,000 (Table 11-2); thus, 42,000 square meters are consumed during the 3-week interval. The difference is due to round-off error in computing 0.93.

3. a. T^* minimizes the total variable cost (TVC) but ignores the problems of scheduling conflicts. The schedules in Table 11-7 have to make some cost compromises to resolve those conflicts.

   b. In both of the last two schedules of Table 11-7, wool carpeting is run at about 1.5 week intervals (i.e., twice per cycle), which is much closer to T^* than the intervals in the first three schedules. The other families are also closer to their T^* values. The closer the intervals are to their respective T^* values, the closer TVC will be to $3882, its minimum possible value.

4. The smallest is 3.2, and the ratios are 1.0, 4.8/3.2 = 1.5, 9.2/3.2 = 2.88, 3.3/3.2 = 1.03, and 12.3/3.2 = 3.84. Using the power-of-2 table, these round off to frequencies of 1, 2, 4, 1, and 4. Since N_{max} = 4, the multiples are 4, 2, 1, 4, and 1. The optimal cycle length will be approximately 4(3.2) = 12.8 periods in length.

5. 0.42/0.222 = 1.89 weeks and 0.60/0.222 = 2.70 weeks, respectively. If demand increased by 10% in Table 11-2, the fraction of production capacity needed to satisfy demand would also increase by 10% to 0.778 + 0.1(0.778) = 0.886. This would increase the minimum cycle lengths to 0.42/(1 − 0.886) = 3.68 weeks and 0.60/0.114 = 5.26 weeks, respectively. Neither schedule would work with a 3-week cycle. The increase in demand would use up more than the available slack.

11-3 PROTECTING THE SCHEDULE

Repetitive manufacturing is an environment in which a production schedule can be found that is worth protecting. The cyclic schedules introduced in the previous section, for example, have the desirable property of minimizing the heavy cost of family setups. However, numerous forces are at work to undermine the schedule. Late delivery of materials, equipment failures, absenteeism, lower-than-expected yield of nondefective items, and unexpected variation in demand—any of these can cause a change in the production schedule. Notice that many of these are quality problems that can and should be addressed by methods such as those introduced in Chapter 6. As has been discussed, eliminating the source of a problem is often the most profitable solution. In this section we assume that the root causes have been exposed, studied, and reduced to the extent possible. Two ways are presented to use inventory to protect the schedule against what variation remains. These methods are most appropriate in repetitive manufacturing. The next section addresses a more complex environment, and the discussion of schedule integrity will continue.

Target Runout Times: Safety Time

Runout time is how long inventory (including planned production) can satisfy demand. In the wool family, demand for item 1 averages 3000 square meters per week. Suppose that NC has 6000 square meters in inventory and plans to produce 9000. They can expect stock to hit zero (run out) in (6000 + 9000)/3000 = 5 weeks, on average. That is, 15,000 units is 5 *weeks of supply*. Runout time is simply stock on hand plus the quantity to be produced, expressed as weeks of supply.

Figure 11-4 illustrates that a 5-week runout time provides enough stock to satisfy *average demand* during a 3-week production interval *plus* a 2-week *safety time*. Safety time is similar to safety stock (Chapter 10). The difference is that safety time's primary role is to protect the production sequence against variation in timing, whereas safety stock protects mainly against variation in demand. The figure makes it clear that safety time is achieved by increasing the inventory; thus, there is little difference between safety time and safety stock.

Runout times determine the success or failure of the production schedule. If runout occurs before the next scheduled family production, NC must choose between two bad alternatives: alter the schedule or accept shortages. Both of these are expensive. Shortages can be avoided by inserting an extra setup into the schedule, but setups are very expensive and time-consuming at NC. Moreover, an extra setup of one item would delay production of all the other items, leading to additional shortages. Overtime production is another alternative, but

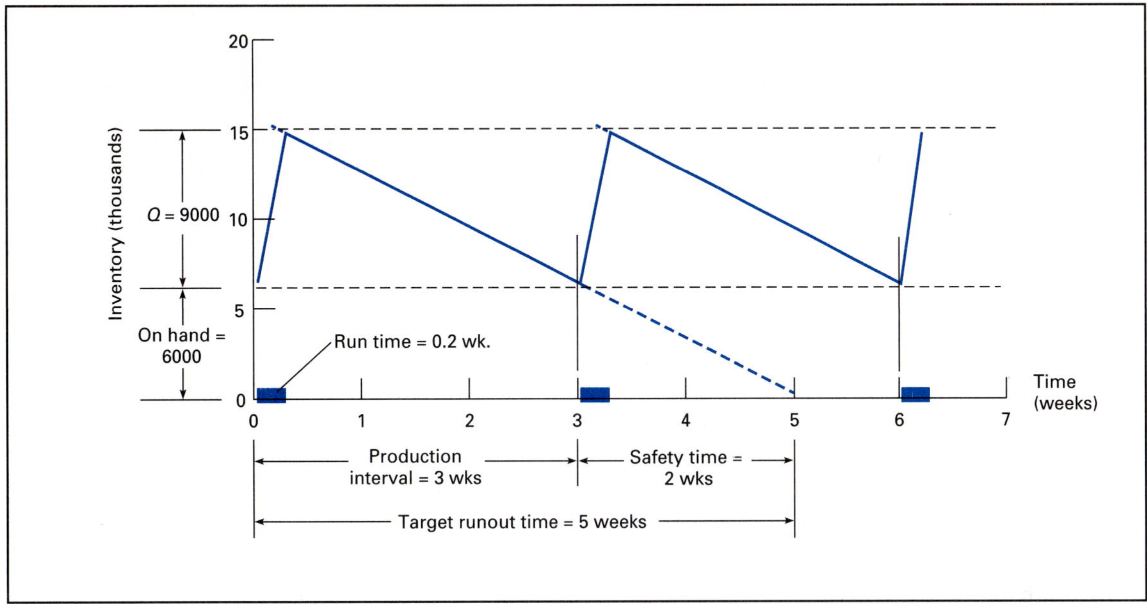

Figure 11-4 Runout Time, Production Interval, and Safety Time

that is also costly. Of course, shortages cause customer dissatisfaction that can result in lost sales. Because both alternatives are so costly, protecting the production schedule is important to NC's profitability.

NC uses *target runout times* to set production quantities. The targets are based on the schedule. For example, when it is time to produce wool carpets, NC makes enough of every wool item to last to a time *comfortably beyond the next planned start* of the wool family; the excess provides safety time. For example, if the wool family is scheduled to be produced every 1.5 weeks, the target runout time should be somewhat longer.

Three factors determine target runout times: production schedules, seasonal inventory plans, and safety margins. The production schedule determines *T*, the production interval for the item. In the NC case the same *T* applies for all items in a family; it is the family production interval. Seasonal planning, based on aggregate production plans (Chapter 9), sets inventory accumulation targets during the slack seasons, so that demands can be met during peak seasons without resorting to expensive production modes such as overtime or subcontracting. The resulting *seasonal-inventory target* is the planned level of stock to be held in anticipation of peak seasonal demand. Finally, safety margins allow for individual item variation in demand. These three factors are included as follows:

$$\text{Target runout time} = T + \text{the larger of ST and AT} \tag{21}$$

in which

T = production interval for the item (or family). In general, T is the interval until the *subsequent order* will first be available for use.

ST = safety time, added to protect against premature runout.

AT = accumulation time: seasonal-inventory target measured in weeks of supply. (For constant demand, AT = target seasonal inventory divided by demand rate.)

$$\text{Production quantity} = \text{demand forecast during target runout time} - \text{stock on hand} \quad (22)$$

These formulas make the runout time longer than the production interval to avoid premature runout and (if appropriate) to accumulate stocks for seasonal planning purposes. However, equation 21 avoids double counting: if the accumulation time is large enough, it provides the margin of safety. We will now illustrate for wool carpet item 1.

Example: National Carpet (continued)

The wool family setup has been completed, and item 1 is about to be run. Based on their intermediate-range aggregate production plan, NC's seasonal-inventory target is 12,500 square meters for the wool family. They have decided to concentrate seasonal stock in items 1 and 2, which are their most consistent sellers. (This is the *jellybean strategy*, described presently.) Based on the weekly demand rates of 3000 for item 1 and 2000 for item 2, the accumulation time is AT = 12,500/(3000 + 2000) = 2.5 weeks for items 1 and 2. The other items in the family have AT = 0.

Since wool is produced every 1.5 weeks, they feel that a safety margin of ST = 1 week is adequate to prevent premature runout. Current inventory of item 1 is 6000 and the production rate is 45,000 per week. Then, for item 1,

$$\text{Target Runout Time} = 1.5 + \text{larger of } (1, 2.5)$$
$$= 4 \text{ weeks (equation 21).}$$
$$\text{Production Quantity} = 4(3000) - 6000 = 6000 \text{ (equation 22).}$$
$$\text{Production Run Time} = 6000/45{,}000 = 0.13 \text{ weeks (equation 2).}$$

Using this method for all items, you may verify that target runout times would be 4 weeks for items 1 and 2, and 2.5 weeks for the other wool carpet items.

The concept of runout time is used in many other environments. For example, an electric utility has many locations where supplies are stored for use in maintaining and repairing the power distribution system. Usage is fairly steady for some of the items, and coordinating their delivery to match the schedule of a delivery truck helps to keep total system costs low. Avoiding special deliveries is the parallel of avoiding extra family setups. Also, many high-volume manufacturers do not use cyclic schedules but nevertheless form production schedules around product families and use target runout times. In this case the production interval (T) is determined from the production schedule. In all these examples, extra inventory is used to protect schedules against variations in time and quantity.

The Jellybean Strategy

This strange name is used to describe the following idea: if you are going to have inventory, concentrate it in items that are most sure to sell.[3] This idea finds application in a number of settings. Here we use it to decide which items are the best candidates to be kept in seasonal inventory.

Chapter 9 described aggregate planning methods that, among other things, determine inventory levels for different periods of the year. Production

[3]Other candies may come and go, but there is always demand for jellybeans.

capacity is taken into account in aggregate planning; therefore, it should be possible to find a production schedule that is consistent with the seasonal inventory plan. The jellybean strategy is one method for deciding which items should have those inventories.

The purpose of seasonal inventory is to avoid the expense of increasing the rate of production during peak demand seasons. As peak demand approaches, demand exceeds production and the seasonal inventories are depleted. However, since plans are never perfect, some stocks may be carried beyond the peak, whereas others may fall short. If the seasonal inventory is concentrated in the steady sellers, we can be sure that leftovers will be sold after the peak.

Another advantage accrues with this strategy. As the peak selling season approaches, setups may stop for the jellybean items because of their high stock levels. *Getting rid of these setup times gives extra production capacity just when it is most needed*. Since special orders often occur during the peak-demand season, that is when the production schedule is in greatest jeopardy. Eliminating setups of the jellybean items leaves more time to respond to both shortages and special orders without destroying the schedule.

The maximum saving of setup time and cost occurs if all the seasonal accumulation is concentrated in one item at a time. As soon as that item's runout time extends to the peak (plus a safety margin), setups stop for that item and accumulation shifts to another item. However, this is "putting all your eggs into one basket." Shifts in demand could leave large quantities of obsolete inventory and a shortage of capacity for other items. Therefore, this extreme version of the jellybean strategy is not often appropriate in practice.

Several other factors should be considered when deciding on accumulation targets. Inventory cost varies by product. Wool is more expensive than artificial fiber, so inventory cost is reduced if artificial-fiber items are the first to be produced for seasonal inventory. For some products, long-term storage can cause spoilage or other damage. The cost of raw materials may vary seasonally as well. For example, sheep shearing occurs at certain times of the year, whereas artificial-fiber production is not seasonal. There are many methods for protecting a schedule against sources of variation, and many different ways of implementing them.

Schedule Busters

This section focuses on situations in which it is desirable to protect the schedule rather than to change it in response to unexpected variation. Even in this environment, many companies find that production schedules are not actually followed. The Monday portion of a weekly schedule may be fairly accurate, but even Tuesday's production often bears no resemblance to the schedule. The purpose of this discussion is to bring to light some of the causes of "busted"[4] schedules. Particular attention goes to causes that can be avoided by improved management.

Reliability and Quality Problems. As was mentioned earlier, production schedules are disrupted by variations such as the late delivery of materials, equipment failures, absenteeism, and randomly occurring defects. For example, in a two-stage shop, undetected defects at the first stage can cause a shortage of materials at the second stage, disrupting the production schedule. If the shortage is rectified by a special production run at the first stage, the schedule

[4]That is, broken or destroyed schedules.

is damaged further because other items are preempted by the special run. (As you can see, problems quickly multiply.) Methods for eliminating defects (Chapter 6) are vital for protecting the schedule.

Misapplication of Dispatching Rules. In the next section we describe rules that are widely used to decide which item should be produced next. When applied in an environment like National Carpet's, many of these rules are schedule busters because they are not designed to maintain the schedule. For example, research has shown that selecting the shortest job reduces the number of waiting jobs as quickly as possible. However, the order in which jobs are completed bears no resemblance to the order in which they are scheduled. In contrast, rules that pay attention to due dates are designed to protect the schedule. Rules such as ''shortest job'' do have a place in manufacturing, but not in operations like National Carpet's, in which demand uncertainty is modest, production times are nearly deterministic, and maintaining a cyclic schedule is important. Misapplication of dispatching rules is a schedule buster that can be avoided by careful study of the conditions under which the rules are appropriate.

Overdependence on Expediters. The job of an expediter is to move designated jobs (hot orders) through the production system quickly. This is needed for two reasons: (1) The hot orders may be in imminent danger of being late. (2) The hot orders may represent work that has been given priority because of its importance. One way to expedite a job is to avoid congested areas, making use of alternative resources that are not as busy. Another is to ''encourage'' workers to change the order of processing. In that sense, the function of an expediter is to *change the schedule* ''on the fly.'' In some environments this is necessary and desirable. However, in repetitive manufacturing, in which variability is low, expediters are rarely needed. If rush orders are part of a business, the scheduling strategy should take that into account. For example, unassigned slack time may be built into the schedule. Or another version of the jellybean strategy may be used, in which steady sellers are built to stock, and their demand is satisfied from inventory whenever the schedule is interrupted by a high-priority job. Heavy use of expediters in a repetitive manufacturing environment indicates that the scheduling system itself needs to be improved.

Too Much Inventory. In this section we have proposed the use of inventory to protect the schedule. However, it can have the opposite effect. The simplest example is obsolescence. If we find that we have produced the wrong stuff, we are also probably short of the right stuff; therefore, the schedule has to be changed.

Long Production Runs. Suppose that NC's production cycle were three months rather than three weeks. Demand for three months may be difficult to forecast accurately, causing schedule changes to avoid shortages. Larger safety stocks may prevent shortages but will cause other problems (see ''Too Much Inventory''). In addition, if a special need arises, either the current production run must be interrupted (good bye schedule) or the special need must wait until the long production run is finished. Finally, large batches imply large inventories (see ''Too Much Inventory'').

Long Setup Times. Long setup times make minor schedule changes very disruptive. During a setup for an unanticipated need, production time is lost and all scheduled production is delayed. This can bring out the expediters (schedule busters) for jobs that would otherwise have been completed on schedule. Long setup times typically cause long production runs, which are themselves schedule busters.

Lack of Discipline. If there is no incentive to follow a schedule, it will not be followed. This is not as simple as it first seems. People who have worked in an environment in which the schedule has been inaccurate have no incentive to follow a schedule, no matter how carefully it is designed. It is hard to overcome an attitude that is based on such an experience.

Designing a scheduling system can be difficult. The preceding discussion points out that managing an operation according to a schedule is also difficult. To make a schedule worthwhile, the operation itself may need to be improved substantially. In Chapter 12 we will discuss methods that have successfully decreased setup times from hours to minutes. Chapter 6 described methods for eliminating quality problems. But even with these schedule busters eliminated, difficult problems remain that can be overcome only by skillful management.

REVIEW PROBLEMS

1. Explain how each of the three elements in the target-runout-time formula (equation 21) help to protect the schedule.

2. With a production schedule of wool–artificial–wool–backing, and a cycle length of 3 weeks, discuss how long the target runout time should be for artificial-fiber items. In particular, should the safety time be the same as for wool or not? Explain.

3. Seasonal inventory accumulation distributes production time over the year, avoiding a crunch during peak sales. Using the jellybean strategy to determine which items to accumulate can, in effect, increase the amount of time available for production.

   a. How does this occur?

   b. Why accumulate jellybeans instead of other items?

4. In what sense are expediters schedule busters in a repetitive manufacturing environment?

Solutions

1. T assures that the production quantity will satisfy demand during the scheduled production interval. ST provides extra inventory so that demand or timing variations will not disrupt the schedule. AT keeps production on track with the annual aggregate plan so that peak sales can be met without schedule changes.

2. The production interval is 1.5 weeks for wool and 3 weeks for the other two families. Therefore, the target runout time for artificial should be 3 weeks plus safety or accumulation time. Because of its longer production interval, artificial should have a longer safety time than wool. Presumably, 3-week demand forecasts are less accurate than 1.5-week forecasts.

3. a. Concentrating accumulation on a few items may cause enough inventory buildup to allow cancellation of production of those items as peak approaches. This cuts some setup time from the schedule, allowing more production.
   b. To minimize the risk of obsolete stock.

4. It is their job to pull a particular item through production. While this may be beneficial to the customer who is waiting for that item, it disrupts the schedule for other items and other customers.

11-4 SCHEDULING MULTIPLE FACILITIES

Coordinating production is more complicated when items require several stages of manufacture. As they move between stages, there are many opportunities for schedule conflicts. This is particularly true in a job shop, where a wide variety of items pass through the facility by different routes. This section introduces the *Gantt chart*, one of the most common devices for production scheduling. Computer-based scheduling systems that use Gantt charts as an interface are described. Research and practice in job-shop scheduling are then described.

Gantt Charts and Scheduling

Figure 11-5 shows two examples of the Gantt chart, developed by Henry Gantt early in the twentieth century. The examples show alternative schedules for three machines (M1, M2, and M3) for a 16-day period. There are three jobs (J1, J2, and J3) to be done by this hypothetical factory. Each job moves through the factory, receiving different operations at each machine. The jobs, described in Table 11-8, are very different from one another. For example, both J1 and J3 have three operations, but they move through the factory in opposite directions. These jobs cannot be "split" in any way. For example, a job cannot be on two machines at the same time.

Figure 11-5 Gantt Charts Showing Alternative Schedules for Three Machines

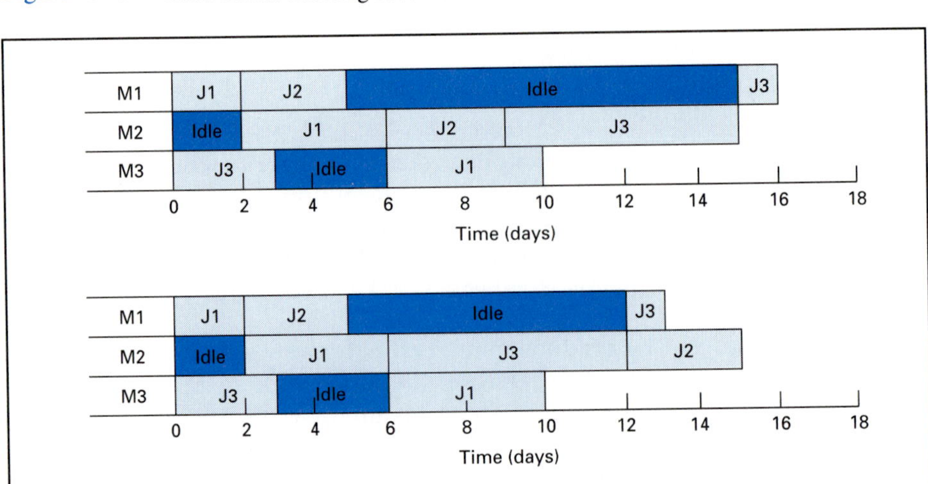

Table 11-8 Movement of Three Jobs through a Factory

Job	Required Sequence	Operation Times (days)
J1	M1, M2, M3	2 on M1, 4 on M2, 4 on M3
J2	No required sequence	3 on M1, 3 on M2
J3	M3, M2, M1	3 on M3, 6 on M2, 1 on M1

Which of the schedules is better? (Take a minute to examine the Gantt charts before continuing.) The interval needed to finish all three jobs (that is, the *makespan*) is shorter for schedule 2, but other criteria may also be important. There may be promised delivery dates, or perhaps other jobs need to use some of the machines. To choose among schedules, we have to specify what the objectives are.

For example, suppose that all three jobs are due on day 10. *Tardiness* is defined as the (positive) amount by which a job is late. The total tardiness in the first schedule is 6 days, since only J3 is late, but the second schedule has tardiness of 8 days (3 days for J3 and 5 for J2). Scheduling objectives may conflict. Schedule 2 is better with respect to makespan, but schedule 1 has lower tardiness and fewer late jobs. The choice of scheduling objectives is obviously very important. Sometimes multiple objectives are used (see, for example, Van Wassenhove and Baker 1982 and Nelson et al. 1986).

A Gantt chart makes the schedule visible, allowing people to see alternatives quickly. This is useful when the schedule needs to be changed, for example, because of equipment failure or the arrival of a high-priority job.

The *XACT Production Planning System* is a microcomputer scheduling program that uses Gantt charts as an interface (Conway and Maxwell 1991). When a scheduler moves an operation on the screen, the program automatically changes other parts of the schedule that are affected. For example, in Figure 11-5, if the start of J1 were delayed by 3 days on M1, this change would propagate to M2 and M3 (because J1 would arrive there later) and to the other jobs (for example, J2 would jump ahead of J1 on M1, and perhaps on M2 as well). XACT is designed to give real-time information similar to an airline reservation system so that when orders are being negotiated, the feasibility of meeting the customer's due date and quantity requirements can be accurately determined by tentatively fitting the order into the real schedule. Several similar systems have been developed in Germany, and are referred to as *leitstand* systems (Kanet and Sridharan 1990).

Job Shops

Job shops are often described as factories that can make anything. They are typically organized by functional area (for example, a process layout). For example, a machine shop may have all the lathes in one location, the grinders in another, and a separate area for all the screw machines. Jobs of many different kinds are accepted, and each job may have a unique routing through the shop.

Scheduling is difficult in this environment. It may be possible to forecast the *aggregate* load that the shop will experience, and those forecasts can be useful for planning capacity and work force in the functional areas. However, with such diversity of job types, schedules for *individual* jobs are difficult to maintain. A shop that has at least part of its work devoted to standard products has an advantage in this respect; producing those items to inventory helps smooth the work load.

A *job* is a customer order for one or more units of a specified item. A *task* is an individual operation required by a job, performed by a specific work area. That is, a job is a set of tasks to be done in a specified sequence. *Scheduling a job* is assigning a work area and a start time for each of its tasks. To schedule a job, a manager needs to know sequence requirements, operation times, the due date for delivery to the customer, and any penalties associated with being either early or late.

A *rolling schedule* is one that is changed periodically to reflect both new jobs and completed tasks. The nature of the job-shop environment virtually guarantees that schedules will change over time. As a consequence, the accuracy of a schedule depends on where you look, the near future being more reliable.

Dispatching refers to the last-minute decision of which job will be processed next when a facility becomes available. If several jobs are waiting, a *dispatching rule* may be applied to choose which should be done next. *Control of the dispatching decisions determines shop performance.* For example, if the dispatching rules pay no attention to the schedule, the schedule will (most likely) be very inaccurate. The performance of some commonly used rules will be described presently.

Information systems play an important role in job shops. Because of the large variety and customized nature of jobs, their routes through the shop may differ dramatically. Tracking the progress of a particular job is necessary to maintain good customer relations. Also, tracking the utilization of the work areas provides useful information for planning personnel work schedules. In addition, jobs often can have alternate routes, and avoiding overloaded work areas improves shop performance. Routing decisions are made at the time a job is first released to the shop; a good information system helps assign routes intelligently and allows them to be modified to take advantage of the changing shop environment. The XACT Production Planning System (described previously) adds the capability of simulating scheduling alternatives to test their effects on the real schedule.

Dispatching Rules for Job Shops

There are many ways to decide which job to start next (see Blackstone 1989). Some of the more important ones are as follows:

1. *FCFS (first come, first served), also known as FIFO (first in, first out):* Select the job that has been waiting longest at the current operation. (A variation selects the job that has been in the shop the longest.)
2. *EDD (earliest due date):* Select the job whose completion deadline is nearest or most overdue. (In one variation, due dates are assigned for each operation and they are used to select the next job.)
3. *SOT (shortest operation time), also known as SPT (shortest processing time):* Select the job whose pending operation can be most quickly finished.
4. *TSOT (truncated SOT):* Use SOT unless a job has been waiting longer than a specified *truncation time*. All jobs that have passed their truncation times are given top priority and are (usually) chosen among by FCFS.
5. *DS/RO (dynamic slack per remaining operation):* A priority ratio is calculated for each job as follows: DS (dynamic slack) = time until job due date minus processing time for all its unfinished tasks; RO (remaining operations) = number of unfinished tasks. Ratio = DS divided by RO. First priority goes to the smallest ratio.

6. *Critical ratio:* There are many forms of this rule. A common one is time until job due date divided by estimated remaining time in shop, in which the last term includes both processing and delay times, estimated based on a shop-load forecast.
7. *COVERT (cost over time):* Expected cost of tardiness divided by operation time. Priority is given to the job with the largest number. This rule emphasizes short jobs that are getting close to their due dates. (Formulas are given in Baker 1974.)

Research has shown that the performance of these dispatching rules depends on how well the shop is managed. If orders are accepted and due dates are set in a manner that is consistent with the capacity of the shop, rules that are based on due dates (such as EDD, DS/RO, critical ratio, and COVERT) work best. On the other hand, if the shop is frequently overloaded because of unrealistic delivery promises, the SOT rule outperforms the others on most criteria. This surprising result is easily explained: When the shop is overloaded, substantial lateness is unavoidable. Only the short jobs have a chance of meeting their due dates. By giving them priority, at least some of the jobs are not late. Moreover, moving a short job earlier in the schedule has little effect on the completion times of the jobs that follow.

Work-in-process inventory (WIP) is of particular interest in job shops. Substantial WIP helps to avoid idle time: There is always something to do. However, it also causes the system to be sluggish: The average time required for a job to make its way through the system is proportional to the average WIP. This is bad from the customer's perspective. It is common to see lead times measured in weeks or even months for jobs that have only hours of processing time required. Control of WIP is a very important competitive factor. (See Chapter 12 for further discussion.)

Planning realistic due dates is an important factor in controlling WIP. Overloading the shop causes large buildups of inventory and long lead times for customers. Using a good information system not only helps set realistic lead times, but also smooths out the work load and substantially reduces WIP because work is not released until the shop can absorb it. On-time delivery is also improved, enhancing customer satisfaction.

Among the schedule busters described in the previous section were reliability and quality problems, the misapplication of dispatching rules, overdependence on expediters, too much inventory, and lack of discipline. All of these are pertinent in job shops as well. The keys to good job-shop control are (1) minimizing sources of variation such as equipment failure, (2) setting realistic due dates so that the schedule can be followed (and using due-date–based dispatching rules to maintain the schedule), (3) controlling the release of jobs to the shop to keep inventory low, and (4) tracking jobs with a good information system, using expediters only to keep them on schedule.

REVIEW PROBLEMS

1. What is the difference between scheduling and dispatching?

2. In the Gantt charts of Figure 11-5, suppose that any job can be split into two partial runs. However, restarting the job requires an additional setup time of 1 day. Thus, if it is split, job J1 will require a total of 3 days rather than 2

on machine M1. Find a schedule that has one split job and finishes earlier (shorter makespan) than the second schedule in Figure 11-5. Also find one that finishes earlier without splitting.

3. A new job, J4 arrives at the beginning of day 4. It requires 4 days on M3, 5 days on M1 and 1 day on M2, in that sequence. Modify the second schedule in Figure 11-5 to incorporate the new job, trying to minimize makespan.

4. The jobs shown in the accompanying table are waiting at the number 4 milling machine in Elmer's job shop. The current time is 2:30 P.M. Which job would be chosen next using

   a. SOT?

   b. TSOT with truncation time of 3 hours?

   c. EDD?

   d. DS/RO?

   e. Compare the DS/RO priorities of jobs B and D. Which would be chosen first? Explain why this choice would be reasonable.

				After No. 4 Milling Machine	
Job	Operation Time (hours)	Arrival Time	Hours until Due Date	Number of Operations	Total Operation Time Remaining
A	3	8:00 A.M.	24	2	16
B	2	10:15 A.M.	20	3	14
C	4	11:10 A.M.	7	0	0
D	3	11:45 A.M.	40	9	28
E	4	12:02 P.M.	10	1	9
F	1	2:15 P.M.	20	0	0

Solutions

1. Scheduling is planning ahead. Dispatching is deciding what to do at the present time.

2. *Schedule with job splitting:* Using the second schedule, start J2 during the idle time on M2 at time 0 but interrupt it at time 2. Do the rest of that operation (J2 on M2) from time 12 to 14. The makespan is reduced to 14. *Schedule without splitting:* Begin J2 on M2 at 0, slide the second and third operations for J1 and J3 one day later and still finish the schedule by time 14.

3. Two modifications of schedule 2 are shown in the accompanying charts. In the first, J4 arrives at time 4 and starts on M3. This delays J1 by 2 days. The second operation of J4 delays J3 by 1 day. The third operation of J4 causes no delays and finishes at time 16. Although completions of J1 and J3 are delayed, the makespan for J1, J2, and J3 is not increased, since J2 still finishes at time 15. The makespan for the four-job schedule is 16. In the second schedule, a makespan of 14 days is achieved by starting J2 at time 0, as in review problem 2.

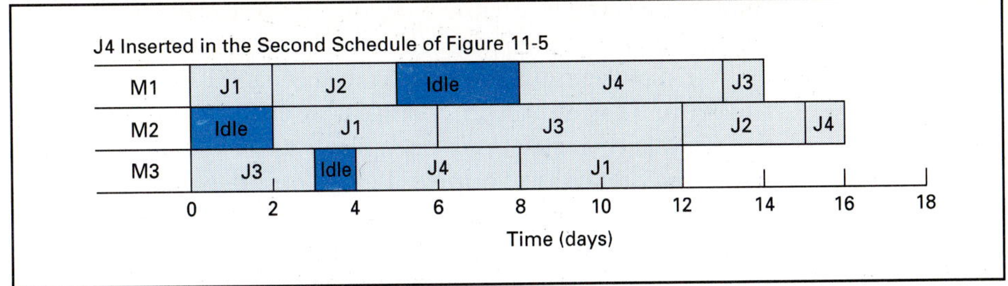

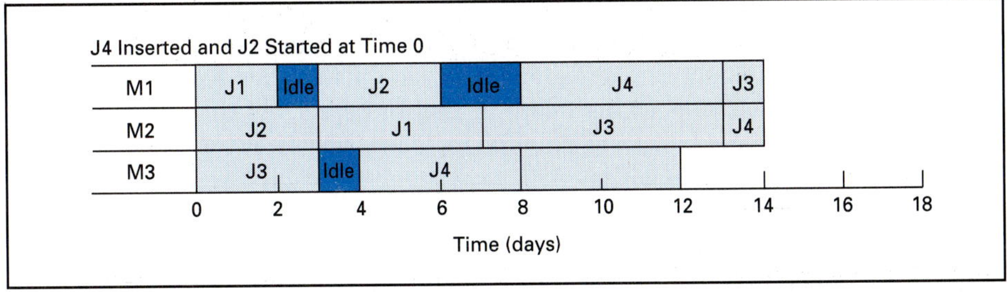

4. a. Job F has the shortest operation time and would come first, even though it arrived last.

   b. Jobs A, B, and C have passed the truncation time, so Job A is next (FCFS).

   c. Job C's due date is closest.

   d.

Job	**DS**	**RO**	**DS/RO**
A	24 − (3 + 16) = 5	1 + 2 = 3	5/3 = 1.67
B	20 − (2 + 14) = 4	1 + 3 = 4	4/4 = 1.00
C	7 − (4 + 0) = 3	1 + 0 = 1	3/1 = 3.00
D	40 − (3 + 28) = 9	1 + 9 = 10	9/10 = 0.90
E	10 − (4 + 9) = −3	1 + 1 = 2	−3/2 = −1.50
F	20 − (1 + 0) = 19	1 + 0 = 1	19/1 = 19.00

   Job E has the smallest ratio and would be chosen next.

   e. Job D has a smaller ratio than B and therefore has higher priority. This makes sense because it still faces 10 waiting lines, and the amount of slack time available to absorb those delays is lower, per waiting line, than for job B.

11-5 INTEGRATED PRODUCTION PLANNING, SCHEDULING, AND CONTROL SYSTEMS

There are many systems for coordinating large production/inventory systems. The two approaches described in this section are based on the concept of *hierarchical systems*, in which the decisions are arranged in a sequence reflecting their importance. Figure 11-1 (in the introduction to this chapter) shows a commonly used production-decision hierarchy. For example, plant capacity decisions are ''passed down'' to the aggregate planning level to set physical limits on the amount that can be produced each month. The arrows in that diagram indicate information flows between levels. The key to these systems is how decisions are linked. How are the higher-level decisions incorporated in the management of subsequent levels? How does information from lower levels influence higher-level decisions?

In a pioneering article, Hax and Meal (1975) proposed the structure shown in Figure 11-6, in which decisions at each level are passed to lower levels as constraints or restrictions on operations. Hax and Meal gave two reasons for using the hierarchical approach. The first reason is technical: A single model of the entire system would be too large to solve mathematically. The other reason is practical: The companies they were working with were organized for top-down decision making, so it was natural to use different models for different levels of decisions. In fact, it would have been impossible to implement a system that did not reflect the actual management structure of the firms. Their system helps management establish subgoals for every level that are consistent with decisions taken at higher levels. At the same time, the subgoals are not too restrictive: The subgoals are consistent with the management responsibilities at each level. Lower-level managers are allowed to use their specialized knowledge of the local situation, within guidelines that assure general conformance with the plan.

The sequence of decisions suggested by Hax and Meal for their example is (1) plant/production assignment, (2) seasonal planning, (3) product family scheduling, and then (4) item scheduling.

The first level is an annual decision. Product families are assigned to plants, considering the fixed cost of tooling up to produce a family and the variable cost of production and distribution. An integer mathematical program helps in this assignment. The results are also used to consider changing plant capacities to reduce costs in the long run.

The second level is seasonal planning, in which products are divided into "types" that share the same seasonal pattern. A seasonal inventory accumulation plan is developed using an aggregate planning LP, similar to the one described in Chapter 9. The demands and capacities for each plant, passed down from level-1 decisions, are reflected as constraints in the LP. The LP recommends which product types to accumulate.

Figure 11-6 Decision Sequence for the Hax-Meal Hierarchical System.

(*Source:* A. Hax and H. Meal, "Hierarchical Integration of Production Planning and Scheduling," in *Studies in the Management Sciences*, vol. I, *Logistics*, Murray Geisler, ed. [New York: North-Holland/American Elsevier, 1975].

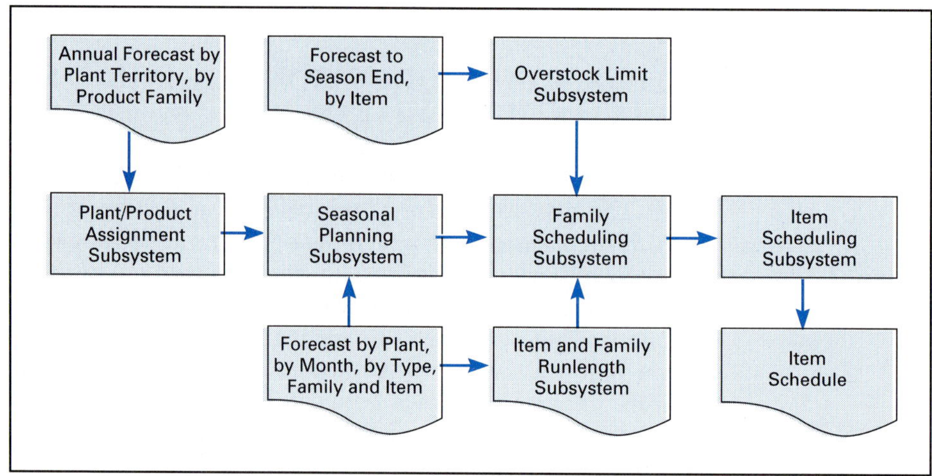

The third level, product family scheduling, is similar to the methods in Section 11-2. The model recommends family production intervals based on the EPQ computed with the *nonpeak demand rate.* Seasonal accumulation targets, passed down from level 2, are used to modify the family intervals. The manager uses this information to develop schedules (not necessarily cyclic schedules).

Finally, individual items are controlled using target runout times based on the family intervals from level 3. At this level it is the manager's responsibility to select the individual products to be used in building seasonal inventory.

Other Hierarchical Systems

Initially described for a single-level manufacturing environment, the Hax-Meal approach has been extended to two levels (Hax and Candea 1984). Other research on hierarchical systems includes Bitran et al. (1981 and 1982), Dempster et al. (1981), Caie and Maxwell (1981), and Maxwell et al. (1983).

In establishing a hierarchical planning system a company determines boundaries for each manager's problem. How large a view should be taken? What information flows in and out of each subsystem? How does the entire system fit together? (Volkema [1983] discusses problem boundaries for planning and design and gives a list of references to problem formulation in planning systems.)

Maxwell et al. (1983) discuss a hierarchical system in multilevel (MRP-type) manufacturing. Their system has three stages: (1) master production planning, (2) planning for uncertainty, and (3) real-time allocation.

Stage 1 consists of an aggregated, large-scale mathematical program to determine (a) assignment of products to facilities and to processes, (b) capacities for each facility, (c) batch sizes for each stage of production, and (d) what the production lead times *should be.* The new and important contribution is that *lead times are calculated, based on the actual capacity and schedule,* rather than determined in advance, as is the case with MRP.

Stage 2, planning for uncertainty, recognizes that even the best-run systems will occasionally have equipment failures, yield problems, order cancellation, or other unpredictable causes of variation. Safety stock and safety time are allocated to protect the stage-1 plan against uncertainty. The approach requires a careful analysis of the system to determine where these tools should be applied to give maximal protection with minimal investment. Specific suggestions for location of *small amounts* of safety stock include (a) before a bottleneck machine (so it will never fall idle), (b) after a low-yield process (to maintain downstream schedules), and (c) before a large-value-added production step (to minimize inventory costs).

Safety stock can be viewed as stored production capacity. In particular, this view suggests that safety stock would consist (where possible) of items with reliable demand so that the "stored" production capacity has been invested in something that will soon be needed. This is another application of the jellybean strategy described in Section 11-3.

Stage 3 is real-time resource allocation. Models used for these decisions are designed to work toward the goals set in the first two stages but consider current and local information regarding available resources and pending jobs. Managers at this level can use detailed information that is not available at the time the higher-level decisions are made, but their decisions are loosely guided by those decisions.

Many companies use systems similar to these. In Chapter 12 we will see that Toyota uses a hierarchical planning system to make sure that their just-in-time production system functions smoothly.

REVIEW PROBLEMS

1. What forecasts would be needed by each of the four steps described by Hax and Meal? At what level of aggregation and for what time horizon would they be?

2. How often would each of the four steps be carried out?

3. What kind of manager would be directly responsible for each step?

Solutions

1. The plant/product assignment phase would require total sales within each geographic region (''plant territory'') for at least the next year, by family. For capacity planning, a five year or longer forecast might be needed. For seasonal planning, the forecast must be broken down by months or weeks, by type and by plant. A forecast for at least a year would be necessary. For family and item scheduling, we would need the seasonal planning forecast to set EPQs, and a detailed short-term (next few months) forecast to establish run quantities.

2. The plant/product assignment phase would occur once a year, or more often if there were dramatic changes. The seasonal plan would probably be updated monthly to make small changes in the yearly plan. (A rolling schedule would be used.) Run-length decisions would be made frequently, whenever there is production for a family.

3. Each of these progressively lower-level decisions is strongly constrained by the less frequent but broader-scope decisions of higher-level management. Thus, an executive vice-president might be responsible for plant/product assignment and the associated capacity planning. Each plant manager, with help from central staff for forecasting, would be responsible for seasonal planning. Lower-level managers within plants would be responsible for the detailed run-length decisions.

SUMMARY

Excellence in production requires careful attention to scheduling. Forming a good schedule is difficult for many reasons. For example, changing either the lot size or the priority of a given job affects all the jobs that follow. In addition there are long-run plans that affect scheduling. Capacity, work force, and inventory decisions may be influenced by the seasonality of demand or by strategic competitive factors, and the schedule must be built around these plans. A scheduler must be able to deal with many variables simultaneously.

Integrated planning-scheduling-control systems afford flexibility to each level at which decisions are made, while imposing requirements or restrictions to assure that overall goals are met. For example, good aggregate plans can help to avoid scheduling crises when demand peaks, and good scheduling can avoid overtime or expediting. However, these benefits accrue only if production control actually uses the schedule, and the schedulers take into account the seasonal aggregate plans. Hierarchical planning systems are one approach to an integrated system.

This chapter introduced a number of scheduling tools. Gantt charts help by making the schedule visible. When there are multiple facilities, these graphs allow the scheduler to try alternative plans and see potential conflicts. A Gantt chart is also very effective as a graphical interface for computerized scheduling. In a job shop, for example, there are many different kinds of jobs following different paths through the facility, and quickly working out alternative routes is much easier with computer help.

When demand is stable, cyclic schedules (based on the economic production quantity) are useful. Heuristics such as the period order quantity can be used when demand is less stable. The costs of setup and inventory are kept near the minimum by these devices, while significant scheduling issues such as lead time and the allocation of capacity are being addressed by other means.

The important role that setup time plays in scheduling repetitive production was illustrated by some simple equations. Reducing setup time decreases both production quantities and inventory. The next chapter describes the just-in-time philosophy, in which setup-time reduction plays a crucial role.

Chapters 10 and 11 have described some scheduling methods and systems for effective production control. Which methods to use depends on the situation. The key is to develop a scheduling system that focuses on the major cost elements. The system should be internally consistent. For example, the failure to select dispatching rules that are consistent with the manufacturing environment guarantees an unreliable schedule. In the next chapter the focus shifts to improving the production system itself in ways that reduce the cost of operation and make scheduling more straightforward.

PROBLEMS

*1. Describe briefly why poor quality and long production runs are schedule busters.

2. Describe some of the productive activities that a worker may do during so-called idle time (i.e., periods when production has stopped and no items are scheduled to be made).

3. What is the basic idea of hierarchical planning, as described by Hax and Meal (1975)? What are their arguments against using a large, integrated model to solve all the production/distribution problems for a company at the same time? Finally, give your reasons for either agreeing or disagreeing with their general approach.

4. Describe the functions of the following subsystems from Figure 11-6.

   a. plant/product assignment subsystem
   b. seasonal planning subsystem
   c. family scheduling subsystem
   d. item scheduling subsystem

*Problems with an asterisk have answers in the back of the book.

*5. Define

a. lot size
b. run length
c. production interval
d. runout time
e. setup time
f. (b) through (e) when applied to a family of items

6. Cyclic scheduling is one of many approaches to production scheduling. Different manufacturing settings may require modifications of the methods given here, but the general approach can be adapted to many situations.

a. Describe the situation in which the methods of Sections 11-2 and 11-3 best apply.
b. Describe a modification that might be needed in some situation.

*7. Setup time consumes capacity. Use the following simple example to illustrate the trade-off between setup time and the maximum annual production that can be achieved. There are two products sharing the same production facility. If it were not for setup time, output could be as high as 10,000 units per year of either product. Management wants to produce them in equal quantities because customers tend to want ''one of each''; the objective is to produce as much as possible. Changing from one product to the other requires a new setup of the equipment, and each setup consumes a time equal to that required for producing 50 units.

a. What is the maximum annual output if we produce 10 lots (batches) of each item per year?
b. Describe the effect of changing the number of lots per year. (To illustrate, consider 1, 2, 5, 10, 20, and 50 lots of each item per year.) What happens to annual output? What happens to lot size? Explain.
c. If the company produces 10 lots of each item per year, describe the effect on annual output if we are able to reduce the setup time. (To illustrate, consider setup time equivalent to 5, 10, 20, 50, and 100 units of output.)
d. What costs other than setup may be affected if the number of setups per year is reduced to increase output? (Hint: Think of the whole system.)

8. (All of the scheduling examples in this chapter have very few items. This problem addresses the difficulty of scheduling with a larger number of jobs.) Suppose that you were asked to schedule production for one week. Forty jobs are currently in the queue for the facility, and your first job is to decide in what order (sequence) to process them. Some of the jobs are for the same product, but may differ as to customer and due date.

a. How many sequences are there of 40 jobs on one facility? What criteria might one use to decide which sequences are best?
b. Might it be reasonable to consider batching jobs (that is, combining two or more jobs into a single production lot) so that some or

all jobs that produce the same item are manufactured in a single run? Describe advantages and disadvantages.

c. The production capacity of the facility may be affected by your choice of sequence. How can this be? That is, how can changing the production sequence increase or decrease the time that it would take to finish all 40 jobs?

d. Recalling that your job was to make a schedule for the week, consider what you must do tomorrow if some new jobs arrive that you did not know about today. How can you take this possibility into account as you are planning the schedule today?

9. In Section 11-3 we described a strategy for selecting which items to use for accumulating seasonal inventories. Why does it make any difference which items are stored? Why not keep a mixture of all items?

*10. A manufacturer uses transistors of type TR-1 at the rate of 400 per day. The firm makes all its own transistors, and they are capable of producing 100 transistors per hour. Setup cost is $30 and the carrying cost of a transistor is $0.02 per year. Assume an 8-hour day and 365 days per year.

a. What is the EPQ?

b. What is the run time for the EPQ?

c. What would the production interval be if the EPQ were used?

d. Recalculate parts a, b, and c assuming a production rate of 1000 transistors per hour.

e. Compare the production quantities from parts a and d to the EOQ from the formula in Chapter 8. Under what conditions will the EPQ and the EOQ be nearly equal?

11. A production scheduler has been starting the production of a certain part every second month. The lot sizes are equal to 2 months of demand. The setup cost is $100, and the holding cost is $50 per year. If the production rate (capacity) is 2500 per year, and the demand is 1000 per year, what annual cost saving would result from using the EPQ instead of the scheduler's method?

*12. The Bland Packing Company has increased the length of their production runs so that they will have fewer production changeovers per year. As a result, two production supervisors were given some new tasks to fill the time that was made available because fewer setups need to be done. In their calculations, the consultants did not include a cost for the supervisors' time spent on changeovers.

a. The consultants have made an error in estimating the costs (either C_I or C_S). Explain what the error is and how you know it is wrong.

b. If this error is corrected, will there be an increase or decrease in the optimal lot sizes, production run lengths, and production intervals? Explain.

13. A machine shop specializes in aerospace fabrication jobs. One of their product families consists of two similar products. The production capacity is 100 per year for either product, and the demand rates are 10 and 5 per year. The use of rare metals causes the holding costs to

be $1000 per year per item. Because of intricate machining requirements, several units are destroyed while testing and adjusting the equipment setup for this family. Once that is accomplished the similarity of the two pieces allows rapid changeovers from one piece to the other. The result is a major family setup cost of $10,000 and a minor setup cost of $50 as each item begins its production run.

a. To minimize total cost, determine the family production interval.
b. How many units of each product will be produced in one family run, on the average, if your answer to part a is used?
c. After seeing your answers to parts a and b, the plant manager objected to the large production run and long time between runs. She was concerned about the high holding costs that would result. Explain why your answers are intuitively sound.
d. Why should both products be produced each time a run is made for the family?

*14. A manufacturer produces several families of products. One family consists of three items, A, B, and C. The major setup cost is $200. Other information is as follows:

Description	A	B	C
Minor setup cost ($)	10	20	30
Inventory holding cost ($/week)	2	3	1
Weekly demand (units)	300	200	100
Production rate per week (units)	2000	2000	2000

a. Determine the family production interval that minimizes total cost, assuming that each item is produced whenever the family setup occurs.
b. How many units of each product should be produced in one run, on the average?
c. On the average, what will be the production run times for each item? For the family in this example?

15. A corrugated board manufacturer uses a single facility to produce two families of board, double thickness and triple thickness. Each family can be produced in 4- or 6-foot widths. Major family setup cost is $1000 for either family. There are 50 working weeks per year. Other information is as follows:

Thickness:	**Double**		**Triple**	
Width:	**4-foot**	**6-foot**	**4-foot**	**6-foot**
Minor setup cost ($)	50	50	50	50
Inventory cost ($/linear foot/year)	0.02	0.02	0.02	0.02
Weekly demand (linear feet)	50,000	25,000	13,000	7,000
Production rate (linear feet/week)	144,000	144,000	144,000	144,000

a. Find the production intervals for each family that would minimize costs if scheduling conflicts did not happen.

b. How many units of each product would be produced in each run, on the average, using the intervals from part a?

c. What would be the production run times for each family?

d. A conflict arises between the families after these production intervals have been repeated several times. Use a Gantt chart to find out when the conflict first occurs. Assume that the double-thickness family begins production first.

16. (In this problem, if an answer cannot be derived precisely from the information given, give a numerical estimate and explain briefly.) In the accompanying diagram, several repetitions of a cyclic schedule for families A, B, and C are shown. Use the diagram to answer the following questions:

a. How long is the production cycle length for the facility?

b. How long is the production run time for family A?

c. How long is the runout time for family A?

d. What are the multiples for each family in the cyclic schedule?

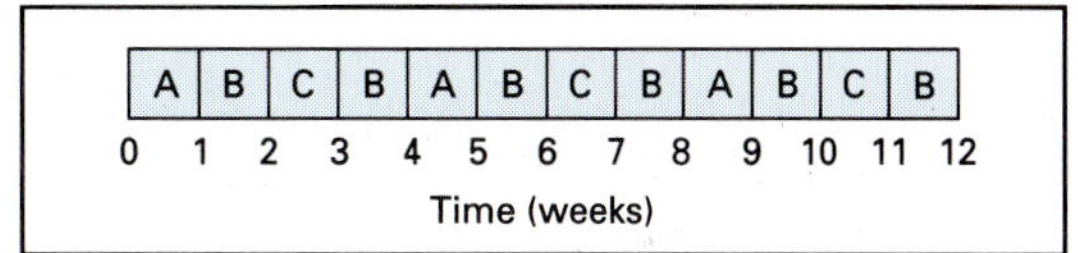

*17. A manufacturing facility produces only six items. These items belong to three families. Family A consists of items 1 and 2, and has an ideal cycle time of $T^* = 6$ weeks. Family B has $T^* = 14$ weeks, and C has $T^* = 10$ weeks.

Family:	**A**		**B**		**C**	
Item:	**1**	**2**	**3**	**4**	**5**	**6**
Demand, weekly	70	20	30	20	40	40
Production rate, weekly	250	250	250	250	250	250

a. Is the production capacity of 250 per week sufficient to meet demand? How much idle time will there be?

b. Using the six-step method in Section 11-2, calculate the total production time for each item for a complete production cycle. Use $N_{max}T_{min}$ for the cycle length.

c. Draw a Gantt chart showing one complete production cycle.

d. If each family has a one-week setup time, is it possible to use the cycle length from part b? What cycle length would you recommend? Explain.

18. The following data pertain to the production of a finished item: C_I = \$2.50 per year; C_S = \$200 per setup; annual demand = 750 units; daily demand = 3 units (there are 250 days/year); daily production rate = 25 units.

a. Compute the EPQ and its associated production interval.

This item shares a production facility with 11 other items. The facility schedule is cyclic and the cycle length is 25 days, during which there are three setups of this item as follows:

Day 1, produce 25; Day 11, produce 25; Day 21, produce 25.

b. Prove that inventory at the beginning of the first day cannot be zero if we are to satisfy demand during the foregoing schedule.

c. Modify the production quantities so that demand can be satisfied without initial inventory. (Do *not* change the times of the setups.)

d. Should the item be produced according to your schedule from part c? Why or why not?

*19. Consider the following data for a plant producing five families of items.

Family	Annual Demand	T^* (days)
A	10,000	30
B	30,000	10
C	50,000	12
D	40,000	11.25
E	20,000	15

a. What multiples would be appropriate for a cyclic schedule?

b. Develop a production sequence for a cyclic schedule of these families using your multiples from part a.

c. What daily production capacity is needed? (Assume 250 days per year.)

d. Assume that setup times are zero, that the length of your cyclic schedule is 30 working days, and that the production capacity is equal to your answer to part c. Put your production sequence from part b on a time scale.

20. Craters of the Moon, Incorporated, packs fruit into wooden crates. The production capacity is 2000 crates per day at full output, and only one product can be crated at a time. There are five families of fruit, and the optimal cycle times (T^*) for each family are shown in the following table:

Family	Current Inventory (crates)	Daily Demand (crates)	Family Production Interval (days)
A	5700	640	8.0
B	4100	400	8.7
C	1800	160	13.4
D	1500	160	11.5
E	1200	240	26.9

There are 5 days per week and 260 days per year.

a. What percentage of the time will the packing facility be idle?

b. If a 25-day cyclic schedule is used, how many days of production should be devoted to each family during each 25-day cycle on the average?

c. How many setups would you recommend for each family in the 25-day cycle?

d. For the next production cycle, the seasonal inventory accumulation target for family E is 2000 crates. What runout time should be used if we are required to have a safety stock equal to 15% of the demand for the 25-day cycle?

e. Repeat part d for inventory targets of 0, 500, 1000, and 1500. Explain what is different when the accumulation target is in the range 0 to 1000 than when it is above that range, and why it should be this way.

f. Given your answer to part d, how many days of production should be devoted to family E for the upcoming cycle?

g. How long can we delay the start of production for family A and still avoid running out?

h. Suppose that part f of this problem has been done for all families and the total production time exceeds the 25 days of the cycle. Discuss the alternative actions and their consequences.

*21. Among its many products, Cavity Candy Company produces four flavors of gum. These products constitute one family. The next run of this family will produce 2500 units. Additional information is as follows:

	Fruity	Wintergreen	Spearmint	Bubble Gum
Weekly demand	150	900	800	400
Current inventory	450	1200	1100	600

Assume that the run begins immediately.

a. How long would the current inventory plus the amount produced satisfy demand? (Base your answer on the family as a whole rather than on allocating production to individual items.)

b. Using your answer to part a as a runout time, calculate the production quantity for each flavor using the equal-runout-time approach with no seasonal accumulation or safety time targets.

c. Given the wide range of demand rates in this family, why might management wish to use unequal runout times? How might they decide which item will have the longest runout time? Why?

22. A glass manufacturer produces three different shapes in a family of soft drink bottles. Production of this family is scheduled to begin immediately. The firm always uses 1-week production runs, and they can produce 100,000 bottles in that time. Additional information:

	Short	Regular	Huge
Weekly demand	7,000	10,000	3,000
Current inventory	1,000	15,000	18,000

a. Calculate when the firm would run out of this family of products, assuming that a 100,000-unit production run of this family begins immediately.

b. Calculate the production quantity for each item using your answer to part a as a runout time.

c. In what order should the items be produced? Hint: consider current inventory measured in weeks of supply.

23. (Refer to problem 22 for data, but you need not have done problem 22 before doing this one.) Repeat parts a and b of problem 22 assuming that the production rates are 120,000, 100,000, and 80,000 per week for short, regular, and huge bottles, respectively. Remember that the company uses 1-week production runs.

*24. Consider the following Gantt chart for two jobs on two machines:

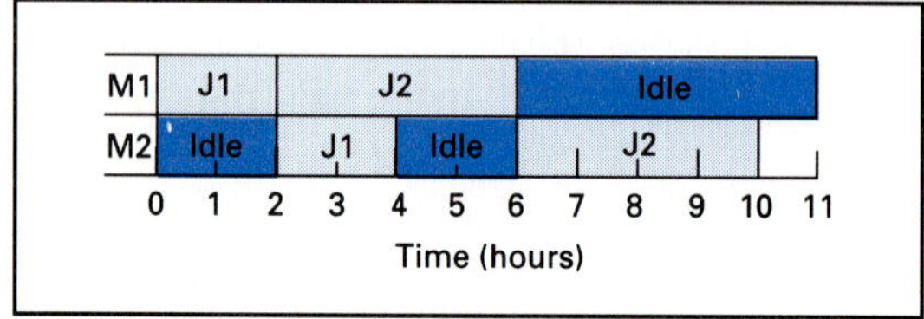

a. If both jobs require that the machine-1 operation be first, could the makespan be reduced? If so, draw a new Gantt chart. If not, why not?

b. If either operation can be first, could makespan be reduced? If so, draw a new Gantt chart. If not, why not?

c. If a job can be split with no loss of time (and there are no sequence requirements) what is the minimum makespan? That is, assume that job J2 could be done on machine 2 in two separate 2-hour time segments, for example.

25. The accompanying Gantt charts show two alternative schedules for two jobs on two machines. Both jobs must be processed first by machine 1. Since both schedules have a makespan of 5, what other factors may influence a choice of one over the other?

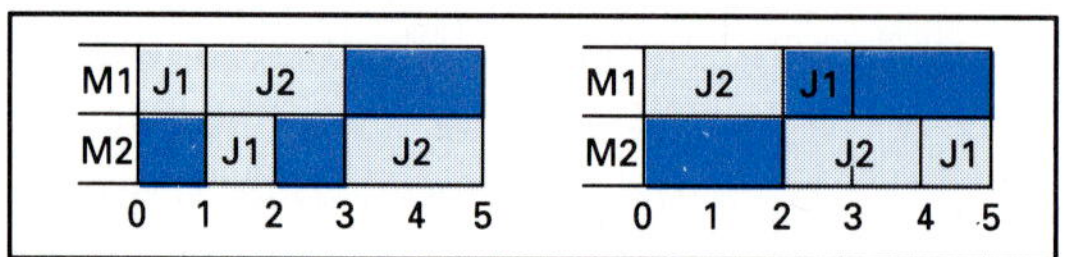

*26. A scheduling problem with the following jobs and sequencing requirements is discussed in the review problems of Section 11-4.

Job	Required Sequence	Operation Times (days)	Arrival Time
J1	M1, M2, M3	2 on M1, 4 on M2, 4 on M3.	0
J2	No required sequence	3 on M1, 3 on M2.	0
J3	M3, M2, M1	3 on M3, 6 on M2, 1 on M1	0
J4	M3, M1, M2	5 on M3, 4 on M1, 1 on M2	4

a. The production manager says that job J4 is unusual, but J1, J2, and J3 are common jobs that occupy most of the machine center's time, in roughly equal proportions. If the manager has approval to buy another machine (an M1, an M2, or an M3), what type should it be? Why?

b. On day 6 the new machine chosen in part a becomes available, and another order is received for one each of job types J1, J2, and J3. Thus, there are seven jobs in the system (J1 through J4, and the second orders for J1 through J3.) For day 0 to day 6, use the following schedule (taken from the solution to review problem 3). Building on that partial schedule, find a complete schedule that minimizes the makespan of the seven jobs. Show the Gantt chart.

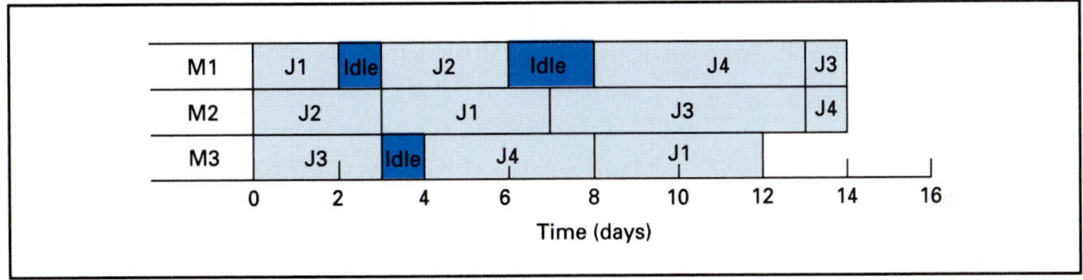

27. A print shop has the following jobs in queue at 7:00 A.M.:

Job (in order of arrival)	Operation Time on Machine 1 (hours)	Operation Time on Machine 2 (hours)
A	3	1
B	4	3
C	1	4

All jobs must have their first operation on machine 1 and then go to machine 2. The shop stays open until all jobs are completed, and no other jobs arrive during the day. Currently both machines are waiting for work.

a. For the following dispatching rules, determine the sequence for the three jobs and the time of completion for each job: (i) FCFS and (ii) SOT. Show your schedule on a Gantt chart.

b. Your schedule based on SOT has been given to the print shop manager, and she wants you to modify it to shorten the makespan so that the workers can go home as early as possible (to reduce overtime). Make a new schedule and show it on a Gantt chart.

*28. Bicycle Boutique's repairman has the following repair jobs. It is now 10:00 A.M.

Job (in order of arrival)	Estimated Time to Complete Repairs (hours)	Completion Time Promised to Customers
A	2.0	11:00 A.M.
B	1.5	4:00 P.M.
C	0.5	4:00 P.M.
D	1.5	6:00 P.M.
E	2.5	1:00 P.M.

a. Using each of the following dispatching rules, determine the sequence for the jobs, the number of jobs completed late, and the amount by which each late job will be late: (i) FCFS, (ii) SOT, and (iii) DS/RO (there is only one remaining operation for each job.)

b. If the repairman wants to minimize the total number of late jobs, which of the three dispatching rules from part a should he choose?

c. If total late time (summed over all jobs) is to be minimized, which rule should he choose?

d. Are the answers in parts b and c likely to hold in general, or do they just apply to this set of jobs?

29. The two jobs shown in the accompanying table are waiting to be processed at the same machine center. Assuming that we work 7 days per week, with no holidays, and that the current date is November 10, which job would be next, using

a. first come, first served (FCFS)?

b. shortest operating time (SOT)?

c. truncated SOT with $T = 6$ days?

d. dynamic slack per remaining operation?

	Job A	Job B
Deadline	November 30	November 30
Arrival date	November 5	November 3
Processing times:		
This operation	5 days	6 days
Next operation	2 days	6 days
Next operation	3 days	none (finished)
Next operation	none (finished)	

*30. (This problem requires a knowledge of queuing models from Appendix A.) Joe's Jobbers have a machine shop that is organized into twenty-five centers. Each center has several identical machines, and each machine is staffed by one operator. Jobs arriving at a machine center join a queue of waiting jobs and are assigned to the first available server. When an operation is completed, the job is sent to another work center to receive its next operation. When a job's last operation is completed, it is sent to the shipping department.

Machine center A has five machines. During a 5-week period when the shop was very busy, there was always a waiting line of jobs and the total output of center A was 10 jobs per day.

a. Estimate the service rate parameter (u) for a queuing model of this center.
b. What would be the average inventory of waiting jobs if the arrival rate of jobs to the center averaged 9.5 per day over a 1-year period, with no weekly or seasonal cycles?
c. List the assumptions used in obtaining the answer to part b.
d. If Joe's Jobbers use the SOT heuristic, would their inventory be more or less than your answer to part b? Why?

31. This problem addresses the idea of using powers-of-2 for the multiples in cyclic scheduling. It also demonstrates that the EPQ (and the production interval) can stray quite far from its optimal value at very little cost penalty.

All the cost equations in this chapter (equations 6, 9, and 17) are of the following form:

$$\text{TVC} = ax + b/x$$

where a is a measure of inventory cost and b is a measure of setup cost.

a. Show that the optimal solution to this equation is $x^* = \sqrt{b/a}$.
b. Show that the minimum TVC value is $\text{TVC}^* = 2\sqrt{ab}$.
c. Show that $\text{TVC}/\text{TVC}^* = 0.5(x/x^* + x^*/x)$. Use this formula to find how far x can vary from x^* before the TVC is 1% higher than TVC*. Trial and error is acceptable.

The round-off rules given in the six-step method in Section 11-2 are based on the square root of 2. For example, we round off to 4 if the number is between $4/\sqrt{2} = 2.828$ and $4\sqrt{2} = 5.656$.

d. How close is TVC to TVC* if x is within a factor of $\sqrt{2}$ of x^*? That is, use the formula in part c to show that both $x = x^*/\sqrt{2}$ and $x = \sqrt{2}x^*$ give TVC values that are approximately 6.1% above TVC*.
e. How is it that the six-step method keeps T values within a factor of $\sqrt{2}$ of T^* when the cycle length is $N_{\max}T_{\min}$?
f. If the "optimal-cycle-length" formula is used, will the cost still be within 6.1% of TVC*? Explain.

REFERENCES

BAKER, K.R., *Introduction to Sequencing and Scheduling*, New York: Wiley, 1974.

BAKER, K., and J.W.M. BERTRAND, "An Investigation of Due-Date Assignment Rules with Constrained Tightness," *Journal of Operations Management*, vol. 1, no. 3, February, 1981.

BITRAN, G., E. HAAS, and A. HAX, "Hierarchical Production Planning: A Single Stage System," *Operations Research*, vol. 29, no. 4, July–August, 1981.

BITRAN, G., E. HAAS, and A. HAX, "Hierarchical Production Planning: A Two Stage System," *Operations Research*, vol. 30, no. 2, March– April, 1982.

BLACKSTONE, J., *Capacity Management*, Cincinnati: South-Western, 1989.

BLACKSTONE, J.H., JR., D.T. PHILLIPS, and G.L. HOGG, "A State-of-the-Art Survey of Dispatching Rules for Manufacturing Job Shop Operations," *International Journal of Production Research*, vol. 20, no. 1, 1982.

CAIE, J., and W. MAXWELL, "Hierarchical Machine Load Planning," in *Multilevel Production/Inventory Systems: Theory and Practice*, L. Schwarz, ed., New York: North-Holland, 1981.

CONWAY, R., W. MAXWELL, and L. MILLER, *Theory of Scheduling*, Reading, Mass.: Addison-Wesley, 1967.

CONWAY, R., and W. MAXWELL, *Users' Guide for the XACT Production Planning System*, Lansing, N.Y.: C-Way Associates, 1991.

DELPORTE, C., and J. THOMAS, "Lot Sizing and Sequencing for N Products on One Facility," *Management Science*, June, 1977.

DEMPSTER, M.A.H., M.L. FISHER, L. JANSEN, B.J. LAGEWEG, J.K. LENSTRA, and A.H.G. RINNOOY KAN, "ANALYTICAL EVALUATION OF HIERARCHICAL PLANNING SYSTEMS," *Operations Research*, vol. 29, no. 4, July–August, 1981.

DOBSON, G., "The Economic Lot-Scheduling Problem: Achieving Feasibility Using Time-Varying Lot Sizes," *Operations Research*, vol. 35, no. 5, 1987.

DOBSON, G., U.S. KARMARKAR, and J.L. RUMMEL, "Batching to Minimize Flow Times on One Machine," *Management Science*, vol. 33, no. 6, 1987.

ELMAGHRABY, S., "The Economic Lot Scheduling Problem (ELSP): Review and Extensions," *Management Science*, February, 1978.

HAX, A., and D. CANDEA, *Production and Inventory Management*, Englewood Cliffs, N.J.: Prentice-Hall, 1984.

HAX, A., and H. MEAL, "Hierarchical Integration of Production Planning and Scheduling," in *TIMS Studies in the Management Sciences*, vol. 1, *Logistics*, M. Geisler, ed., New York: Elsevier, North-Holland, 1975.

KANET, J.J., and V. SRIDHARAN, "The Electronic Leitstand: A New Tool for Shop Scheduling," *Manufacturing Review*, vol. 3, no. 3 (September), 1990.

KARMARKAR, U.S., "Lot Sizes, Lead Times and In-Process Inventories," *Management Science*, vol. 33, no. 3, 1987.

MAXWELL, W., J. MUCKSTADT, J. THOMAS, and J. VANDEREECKEN, "A Modeling Framework for Planning and Control of Production in Discrete Parts Manufacturing and Assembly Systems," *Interfaces*, vol. 13, no. 6, December, 1983.

MAXWELL, W.L., and H. SINGH, "The Effect of Restricting Cycle Times in the Economic Lot Scheduling Problem," *IIE Transactions*, vol. 15, no. 3, 1983.

NELSON, R.T., R.K. SARIN, and R.L. DANIELS, "Scheduling with Multiple Performance Measures: The One-Machine Case," *Management Science*, vol. 32, no. 4, 1986.

PETERSON, R., and E.A. SILVER, *Decision Systems for Inventory Management and Production Planning*, New York: Wiley, 1979.

ROUNDY, R. "Rounding off to Powers of Two in Continuous Relaxations of Capacitated Lot Sizing Problems," *Management Science*, vol. 35, no. 12, December, 1989.

Van Wassenhove, L.N., and K.R. Baker, "A Bicriterion Approach to Time/Cost Trade-offs in Sequencing," *European Journal of Operational Research*, vol. 11, 1982.

Volkema, R., "Problem Formulation in Planning and Design," *Management Science*, vol. 29, no. 6, June, 1983.

Zipkin, P.H., "Computing Optimal Lot Sizes in the Economic Lot Scheduling Problem," *Operations Research*, vol. 39, no. 1, January–February, 1991.

chapter

12

Just-in-Time Production Systems

Just-in-time (JIT) is a manufacturing philosophy that has proven to be a powerful competitive tool. Combining intensive industrial engineering with enlightened personnel policies, Toyota Motors Company developed JIT over a period of several decades, during which they emerged as a world leader in the high-quality, low-cost production of automobiles. The name just-in-time derives from one of the most visible elements of the systems: factories that run with very little inventory; operations are carefully synchronized so that materials arrive just as they are needed.

Just-in-time factories operate at the brink of a scheduling disaster. Any deviation from the following formula will interrupt production: *delivery of the right material, in the correct quantity, with perfect quality, to the designated part of the factory, just slightly before it will be used.* Just-in-time is perilously close to just-too-late.

Taiichi Ohno, who is credited with the development of the Toyota system, notes that ''present capacity = work + waste'' (Ohno 1988). The just-in-time philosophy strives to maximize production effectiveness and efficiency by focusing on the continual reduction and eventual elimination of waste. ''The primary goal of the Toyota production system is to identify and eliminate waste and reduce costs. Inventories are eliminated by addressing and overcoming the hidden conditions that cause them'' (Shingo 1989, p. 95). This is a remarkable goal. Rather than ''making the best cars'' or ''maximizing daily output,'' this goal specifies **relentless waste elimination** as the major objective.

The definition of waste is also radical. Waste includes

warehouse storage and storage between operations

setup time

scrap and rework

operations that are unnecessary for making the product

fire fighting[1]

A major obstacle to JIT implementation is disbelief. Because of the extremely high standards of total waste elimination, people's initial reaction is that it cannot be done or it would be too expensive. Real experiences help to counter disbelief, and the examples in this chapter illustrate the following:

- Compared with current practice, enormous waste reductions are possible.
- Most changes use low technology, current knowledge, and current work force.
- Eliminating the source of a problem often creates a chain reaction of benefits.
- The full value of these benefits is difficult to measure.

Experience has also shown that the work force is the key strategic resource for JIT. Relentless pursuit of waste elimination is only possible if we

1. train workers in methods for identifying and eliminating waste
2. include process improvement as part of every employee's job description
3. reward new ideas and implement them quickly
4. establish discipline so that supervisors and workers will follow the system

These principles are deceivingly straightforward; they are not easy to implement (Vora et al. 1990). It takes both time and motivation to change existing company procedures (Bonito 1990). Fortunately, some JIT improvements can take place quickly and yield immediate benefits. For example, low-investment methods to mistake proof operations were described in Chapter 6. Many other tools are available. Some of them will be described, but they are far too numerous for us to discuss them all. Additional readings are included in the references at the end of the chapter.

Strategic Advantages of JIT

The true value of JIT becomes evident in the long run—a competitive advantage in the marketplace. First, eliminating waste lowers product cost, giving the JIT firm a price advantage. Second, the process improvements needed for JIT result in substantial improvement in product quality, which is very appealing to the consumer. Third, reducing inventory not only lowers costs but also shortens production lead time, allowing the company to be more responsive to changing customer demands. Finally, investing in worker training leads to a cycle of accelerating improvement, making it difficult for competitors to catch up (Melcher et al. 1990).

Each of these advantages will be illustrated in this chapter. The point is that JIT, applied in the right environment, is a strategic tool capable of reshaping a company into a lean, flexible, low-cost, world-class competitor.

---

[1]When a problem is encountered, *fire fighting* is solving the immediate problem without eliminating the cause. The JIT approach is analagous to *fire prevention*.

History of JIT

JIT can be traced to the introduction of the assembly line. Henry Ford has been credited with this fundamental idea, first implemented in a Model T Ford factory. Traditionally, vehicles (ships, coaches, and carriages, including the horseless variety) had been built one at a time. Ford developed an assembly line where the products moved through the factory and each worker performed a small set of tasks. Specialization of tasks permits study and improvement of each operation. Ford's goal was elimination of waste as well as production of a car that would actually start and run as soon as it reached the end of the line (a major achievement at the time).

As the car moved along the line, the parts (doors, seats, etc.) were supplied from the sides or from above. It was a monumental task to assure that parts were always available (to avoid stopping the line), and Ford achieved it through a number of methods, including stockpiling inventories.

Ford was enormously successful. Volume increased and price dropped. At one time the Model T held 55% of the market. General Motors finally made a major run on Ford's market when Alfred P. Sloan introduced the annual model change and product variety. Ford's plants had not been designed to accommodate change, and by 1930 Ford held only 30% of the market.

Toyota's strategy has been to extend and refine Ford's and Sloan's ideas, finding ways to increase both quality and flexibility and to reduce cost. Toyota's remarkable penetration of the American market parallels GM's triumph of the 1930s. American automotive manufacturers are responding to the challenge from Japan, but they have the ignominious task of importing ideas that were born in the United States but nurtured overseas.

JIT is widely applicable. Although it works best in high-volume discrete manufacturing, the payoffs can be high in both small and large companies (Golhar et al. 1990). Group technology and cellular manufacturing (discussed in Chapters 14 and 15) are sometimes used to bring JIT into the job-shop environment, where volume is low and variety high (Schonberger 1986). As application spreads, new information and methods come to light. In this chapter we present some of the fundamental ideas of the JIT philosophy, including examples of how improvements can be made and how they affect the work environment. In addition, we describe recent research findings addressing how to plan and control a factory that operates with extremely low inventory. Recall that inventory (safety stock and cycle stock) is required to make production schedules work. Fundamental changes are needed if these stocks are to be nearly eliminated. Some of the ideas behind the OPT (or synchronous manufacturing) philosophy are also described, and we indicate how they reinforce or improve on the JIT methods in the Toyota system.

12-1 WHY, WHERE, HOW, AND HOW MUCH TO REDUCE INVENTORY

Inventory reduction is a basic element of JIT. Introducing some of JIT's tenets serves to open the discussion of *why* and *how much*. Each of these points is then further illustrated by examples.

Inventory is waste. From the JIT point of view, inventory is "production too soon" and represents product that cannot be sold. As such, it is waste, and it wastes resources such as floor space, handling equipment and personnel, and capital.

Inventory hides problems. In factories inventory is used to ''solve'' problems such as unpredictable equipment failure, uncertainty of supply or process yield, and long setup times. The JIT view is that these problems are hidden rather than solved, and inventory only adds to the waste. In short, inventory is a bad solution.

To reduce inventory, solve the underlying problem. Many failed attempts at JIT have missed this point. JIT's benefits are largely due to the efficient production systems that result from relentless process improvement. Inventory reduction without process improvement can be a disaster.

Elimination of inventory is the target. The amount of reduction in inventory is a moving target. Experience has shown that a given project may achieve a reduction of (say) 60%, but when a fresh team is assigned the same problem, they find ways to reduce the new level by another 60%. At some point further reduction becomes uneconomical, but JIT proponents emphasize that this level is so low that ''elimination of inventory'' is not much of an overstatement.

The cost of inventory is drastically understated. Cost of capital and storage space are typically the largest components of the holding cost used in the EOQ and EPQ formulas. In Chapter 6 we argued that quality can suffer if inventory is too high; this cost is not included in C_I. The following two examples illustrate other missing elements.

Example: Overhead Conveyor

An automotive plant has an impressive conveyor system to move completed frames from welding to the area where body panels are attached. There, far overhead, are the gleaming frames of perhaps 100 future cars. What savings would accrue if the plant were reconfigured, replacing the overhead conveyor by a floor-level system containing only 1 car between these areas?

The conveyor is ''solving'' (hiding) the problem of poor factory layout:

1. Inventory reduction of 99 car frames would improve cash flow, since substantial funds are invested in each frame by that point.
2. Operation and maintenance expenses of the overhead conveyor would be eliminated.
3. Repair of that conveyor is difficult and requires stopping the entire line, so some lost production would be eliminated.
4. One-hundred cars is about one half of a day's production; therefore, the product flow time would be reduced by 0.5 day, shortening the lead time experienced by customers.
5. If an error causes welding to begin producing defective frames, the shorter conveyor allows the error to be discovered much sooner, potentially avoiding rework on 99 frames.

Example: Ceramic Tableware

A manufacturer of ceramic tableware produces 30 different product families. Several of these have low sales volume and are produced infrequently, in response to customer orders. High-volume items are produced according to a production schedule based on demand forecasts. Production occurs in stages. Raw clay is formed on rotating molds and then passed through a dryer. Glazing is applied and baked on. Decorations are applied and baked on. Production runs are long because substantial down-time occurs during each changeover while the equipment is adjusted to accept a different product. This causes large inventories of cycle stock. How can these be reduced and what saving would accrue?

Setup time is wasted production capacity. Long production runs ''solve'' (hide) the problem by making setups occur infrequently. Better engineering to lower setup time solves the problem directly:

1. Shorter setups allow frequent product changes, decreasing cycle stock.
2. This, in turn, shortens the time that one family must wait while another family is being produced. Each product's flow time through the factory is reduced, yielding faster response to customer demands.
3. Safety stocks are reduced because of shorter lead times.
4. Losses occur in each baking process, and shorter cycles increase the flexibility to add a production run if yield problems cause shortages.

Inventory in the first example is ''pipeline stock,'' present only because of the length of conveyor. In the second example, cycle-stock inventory is caused by long setup times. However, in both cases *inventory is causing long flow times*. This has two effects: Customers must wait longer before their orders pass through the factory, and larger safety stocks are needed. The relationship between inventory and flow time is called Little's law[2] and may be stated as follows:

$$\text{Flow time through the system} = \frac{\text{inventory in the system}}{\text{output rate of the system}}$$

That is, flow time is reduced by lowering inventory or increasing the output rate, or both. Since present capacity = work (output) + waste, reducing waste helps to increase the output rate and hence lower flow times. In this way, reduction in inventory has a compound effect, since it also lowers waste. Reducing work-in-progress inventory is viewed as a primary goal in JIT, yielding the strategic advantages of lower cost and better customer service.

How does C_I understate the cost of inventory in these examples? If C_I is the true cost of inventory, it should also represent the saving of reducing inventory. By classical accounting, the saving would be the reduction of the pipeline stock (the first example) or the cycle stock (the second example). The reduction of flow time and safety stock would be missed. In general, whenever inventory hides a problem, the opportunity cost of letting the problem continue should be viewed as part of the cost of inventory. This is the JIT point of view.

Note also that *inventory reduction causes further inventory reduction*. Less pipeline or cycle stock causes less safety stock because lead times become shorter. We saw the same effect while studying total quality management in Chapter 6: A chain reaction of improvements is common when a root cause is removed.

---

[2]In Appendix A, this law is expressed as $T_q = N_q/\lambda$, or the average time in the queue equals the size of the queue divided by the arrival rate.

The chain reaction is one reason why the full value of changes is difficult to measure. *Benefits include much more than just the inventory-cost reduction.* Improved responsiveness and other consumer benefits help increase market share in the long run, but estimating the magnitude of these effects with precision is nearly impossible.

A common element of the two examples is that the proposed changes are technical. The first involves the layout of the factory, a very expensive change. The second requires study and improvement of the setup process; this can often be done at little cost using methods that we will describe later. In both cases there is a clear and identifiable cause of the inventory in the current system, and removal of the cause is a one-time effort that will permanently improve the strategic position of the firm. The rest of this section addresses three kinds of inventory reduction: pipeline, cycle, and decoupling stocks.

Pipeline Stock: Transfer Lots

In many factories, material moves in batches. To make a factory operate more nearly like an assembly line, movement of material must approach the ideal of single piece, continuous flow. One impediment to this goal is *weekly planning and scheduling*. Figure 12-1a illustrates the inventory caused by weekly flow of material. A full week's supply of jobs arrives at a work center. During the week the pile of jobs is moved from input to output, and at the end of the week the entire batch is moved to the next operation. Figure 12-1b shows that inventory is reduced by a factor of 5 if material flow occurs daily, using a *transfer lot* that is smaller than the production lot. By the same reasoning, inventory can be reduced by more than 99% if transfers occur every 20 minutes rather than once per 40-hour week.[3] The potential cost reduction is enormous.

Material that is waiting for or receiving transport is called pipeline stock. More frequent transportation requires reducing the transfer lot size (or transfer batch size), as was noted in Chapter 10. *Separating the concepts of production lots and transfer lots is key in many just-in-time operations.* For example, the large supply

[3]Twenty minutes is 0.0083 of a 40-hour week.

Figure 12-1 Material Flow with Weekly versus Daily Transfers

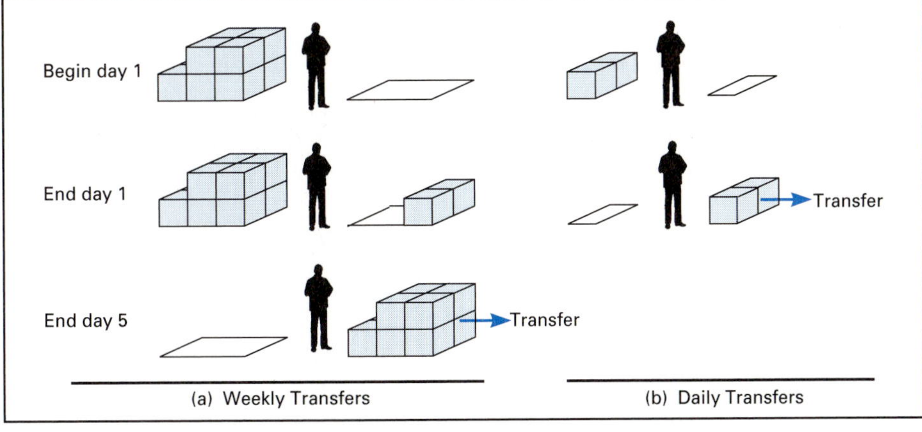

of material in Figure 12-1a may represent supplies for a week-long production run of one type of item. Does that rule out more frequent material flows? Not necessarily. Production can approach continuous flow by the simple expedient of moving partial batches, even if both processes use large production lots. The smaller the transfer batch, the lower the inventory.

Consider the effect on flow time. Figure 12-2 illustrates how much more quickly a production lot of 1000 units gets out of a three-stage factory if the transfer lot is reduced. Little's law strikes again! Lower inventory causes shorter flow time.

Another advantage of more frequent transfer is faster feedback between operations. For example, with transfers every 20 minutes, information about a quality deficiency can be passed back quickly, and the problem can be corrected before a large amount of defective product (waste) has been produced. In addition, because of the rapid feedback, the overall quality mission is reinforced, since it is more difficult for quality problems to be concealed.

Cycle Stock: Setup-Time Reduction

Cycle stocks occur because of large production lots. For example, consider a factory that produces five different items on the same equipment. If each item is run for one week, the resulting inventory must be large enough to satisfy demand for four more weeks until the production cycle returns to production of that item.

Large production lots are used when setup costs and times are high. Therefore, to reduce cycle stock, setup time and cost must be lowered. This fact

Figure 12-2 Smaller Transfer Batches Cause Shorter Flow Time for Production Lots

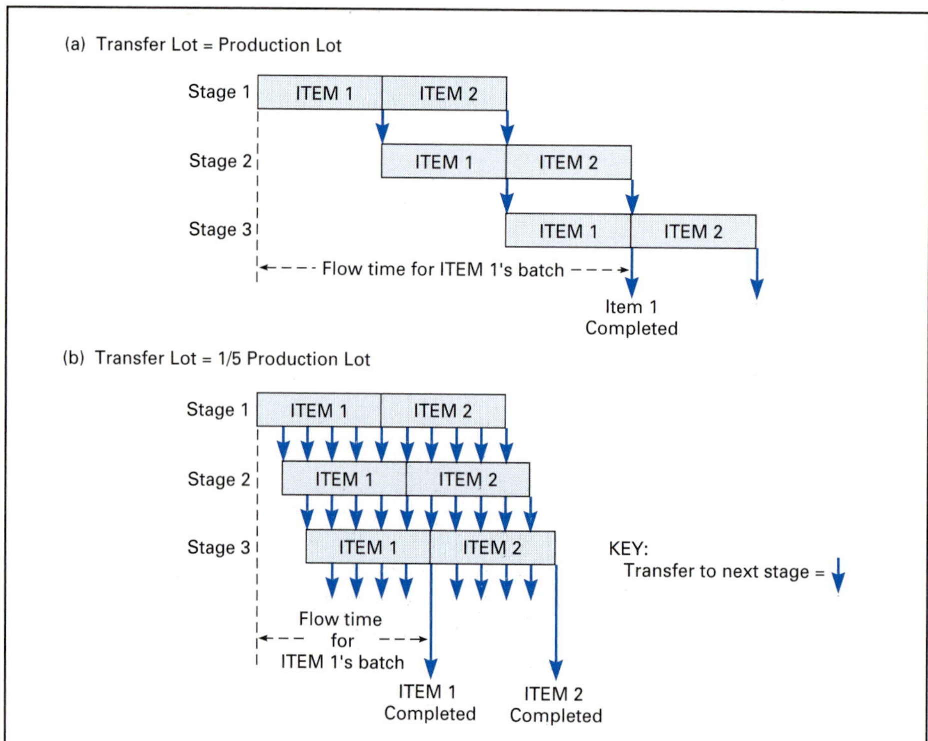

has been discussed in Chapter 8 for purchasing, Chapter 11 for production scheduling, and earlier in this section. There are some general principles for finding ways to reduce setup time, and their use has produced spectacular results.

The classic example is the changeover of dies in the metal-stamping industry. A die used to form an automobile fender can weigh several tons, and at one time it took as much as a full day to remove one, install another, and adjust it for production. These setup times have been reduced to a few minutes by careful engineering of the changeover process itself (Shingo 1990). We will illustrate setup-time reduction by continuing the ceramic tableware example.

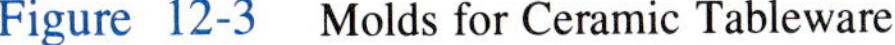

Example: Ceramic Tableware (continued)

In the first production stage, clay is placed on top of a mold made of gypsum. Mold and clay are placed on a spindle and held in place by suction while the spindle rotates (Figure 12-3a). From above, a metal mold is lowered against the rotating clay, squeezing it into the desired shape (Figure 12-3b). The item is removed from the spindle and passed through a dryer.

To change products, the spindle is exchanged with one that will fit the next product, and the metal mold is changed and adjusted. During the adjustment process, several trial pieces are used and then discarded. Setup occupies one worker for about forty-five minutes, during which time no pieces enter the dryer. To eliminate this wasted time requires faster changeover.

The following steps are the basis of the SMED[4] system developed by Shingo (1985) for reducing setup time.

Stage 1: Separate Internal and External Setup. Internal setup consists of *tasks that must occur while the machine is stopped*. External setup tasks can be done

[4]SMED is an acronym for single minute exchange of die, so named because of its roots in reducing the setup time for metal stamping.

Figure 12-3 Molds for Ceramic Tableware

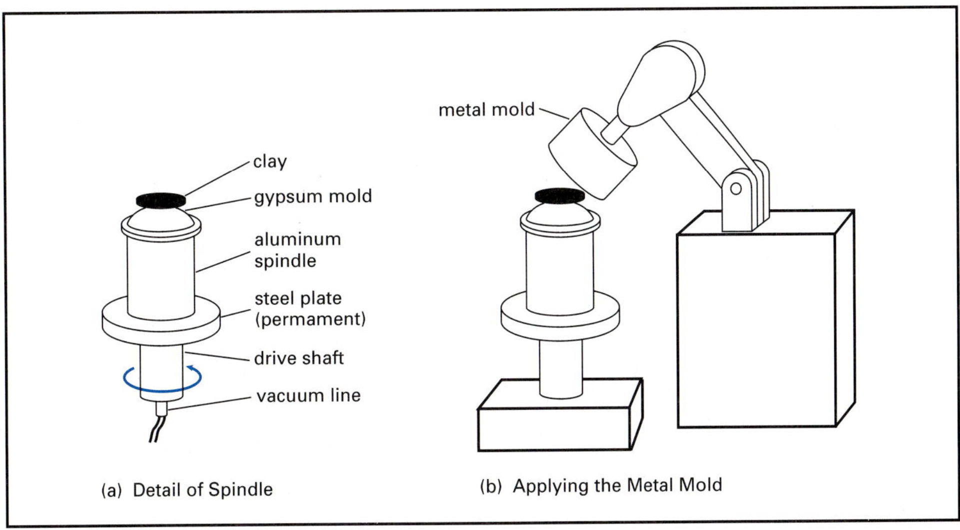

while the machine is producing the previous product. This distinction is fundamental. Production time is lost only during internal setup tasks. The spindle operator spent 10 minutes to get molds for the next run; during that time the equipment sat idle. This lost capacity was regained by transporting the new molds before the end of the previous run, a simple change of procedure. Mold transportation is an external setup task. In general, many tasks can be classified as preparation for setup, and they should be done externally.

Stage 2: Convert Internal to External Setup. Exchanging spindles required an average of 10 minutes. To convert this to external setup time, the company considered purchasing an extra machine; the setup of one machine could occur during production on the other machine. However, this method was not adopted because it was too expensive. In many operations, equipment duplication or alteration can move setup operations off-line. For example, if a mold requires heating before use, preheating before installing the mold converts that operation to external setup.

Stage 3: Streamline Setup Operation. Changing spindles required removing four bolts. Aligning the holes and threading the bolts to attach the next spindle required substantial trial and error. Exchange time was reduced from 10 minutes to one minute by eliminating the need to remove the bolts. The bolt holes in the bottom of the spindle were enlarged to a pear shape (Figure 12-4a). Now the bolts are loosened only one half turn, enough to allow the spindle to slip. A slight rotation of the spindle allows it to be lifted off—the bolts pass through the large ends of the holes. The process is reversed to install the next spindle.

Adjusting the machine to produce product of uniform thickness required 15 minutes. The applicable SMED principle is, *set, don't adjust*. To the extent possible, all adjustments are replaced by careful design: Once the process is set for a new product, no adjustments are necessary. Eliminating adjustment yields important additional benefits: improved quality and lower scrap. Trial pieces are no longer needed (reducing scrap) and overall product quality is improved because variation no longer occurs between lots as a result of slight difference in adjustments. The dinnerware manufacturer also made changes that elimi-

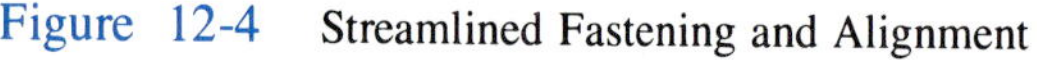
Figure 12-4 Streamlined Fastening and Alignment

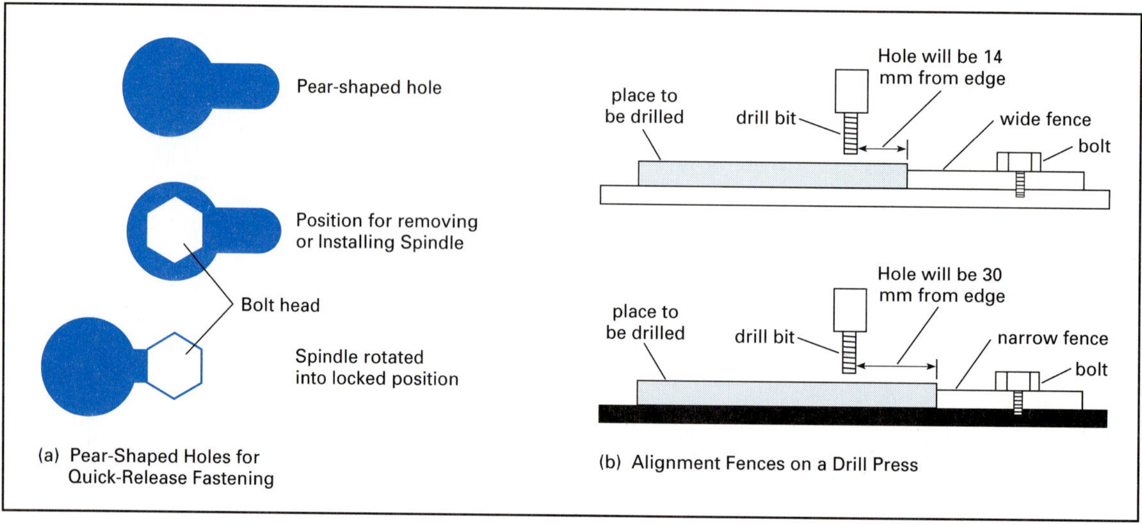

(a) Pear-Shaped Holes for Quick-Release Fastening

(b) Alignment Fences on a Drill Press

nated adjustments; the process-specific nature of those changes is too technical for this discussion.

A simpler example of eliminating adjustment is in drilling holes in a sheet of metal. The easy way to align the metal is to install a fence on the table of the drill press. Pushing the metal tightly against the fence assures that it is in the correct position. Realigning the fence for a new product can be time consuming. Most of that setup time can be eliminated by simplifying how the fence is fastened to the table. Suppose that the table has four holes in it. If all fences are designed to fasten into the same four holes, no adjustment is possible. Figure 12-4b shows that a wide fence places the drill near the edge of the metal, whereas narrow fences align the drill farther from the edge.

Stage 4: Mechanize. The dinnerware manufacturer used mechanical help in mounting the upper (metal) molds because they are heavy and dangerously hot. Carts were designed to present the molds at the required height and orientation for installation. In many situations, computer-controlled devices can be used to perform setups automatically. Mechanical aid (automated or not) will shorten setup time in situations in which danger or physical effort is extreme.

Setup time reduction follows a pattern that is similar to defect elimination (Chapter 6). The difference is that the focus is on preparation time rather than on the production process itself. The enormous gains bear testimony to years of neglecting procedures for setup. The tableware manufacturer brought the internal setup time down from 45 minutes to just under three minutes, a 96% reduction. Now it is economical to respond to small, infrequent orders, giving this company an advantage over its competitors.

Inventory to Decouple Production Stages

Figure 12-5 illustrates the simplest of multistage layouts: operations arranged serially. In the figure, the stages have been arrayed in a U shape. Although few factories are this simple, important parts of many factories have this layout. (Facility layout is discussed in Chapter 16.) This example serves to illustrate several points that are valid in more complex arrangements.

One important characteristic of this system is that material flow is *asynchronous*. When **W1** finishes a unit, it moves to storage area **B1** and waits until **W2** removes it for the next processing step. This is in sharp contrast to Henry Ford's *paced line*, where items all move together, much as the cars of a train. Inventory in the storage units (buffers **B1**, **B2**, etc.) serves to *decouple* the stages so that work may proceed more or less independently.

Inventory between stages helps to prevent idle time that can be caused by uneven performance. Without buffers, a machine failure at work area **W5**

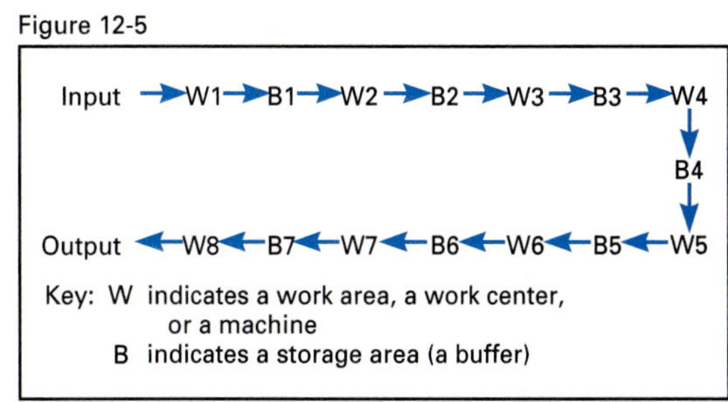

Figure 12-5 U-shaped Serial Facility with Storage Buffers for Work in Process

Table 12-1 Production Capacity of an Eight-Stage Serial Facility

Processing Time Distribution (minutes)				Average Production Rate (units/hour) for Various Buffer Capacities[a]		
Variability	Minimum	Mean	Maximum	$B = 0$	$B = 4$	$B = 8$
Low	8.27	10	11.73	5.41	5.96	5.96
Medium	4.8	10	15.2	4.53	5.76	5.84
High	1.34	10	18.66	3.88	5.43	5.67

[a] B is the storage capacity of each buffer. The total storage capacity in the production line is $7B$ because there are 7 buffers, B1 through B7.

would soon force **W6** to stop, since all its jobs come from **W5**. A buffer allows **W6** to continue working.

> *The function of in-process buffers is to smooth the flow of work, not (just) to store inventory. Buffer capacity should be as small as possible, consistent with this function.*

How large should the buffers be? Research has shown that small buffers work suprisingly well (Conway et al. 1988). Table 12-1 shows the results of simulation experiments (simulation is described in Appendix B) with an eight-stage line in which all the work centers have the same average processing time, but actual processing times vary randomly.

The "low-variability" factory was tested first. Processing time averages 10 minutes per stage, so, in theory, the output rate could be as high as one unit per 10 minutes[5] (six per hour). However, with no buffers the output rate was only 5.41 per hour, a loss of 9.8% of production capacity.[6] Installing $B = 4$ units of storage space between every stage increases output to almost six per hour. Increasing B to 8 has negligible additional benefit.

What causes loss of capacity with no buffers? Processing time varies randomly from 8.27 to 11.73 minutes for the low-variability factory. Every time **W2** finishes before **W1**, **W2** is *starved* (no input material). Likewise, when **W1** finishes first there is no storage for its finished piece; **W1** is *blocked. Interference* (blocking and starving) occurs throughout the line and causes loss of capacity.

Since variability causes loss of capacity, it should be no surprise that more variability is worse. Figure 12-6 shows that capacity loss is far more serious for the "high-variability" factory. Since improvement tapers off as buffer capacity increases, there must be a point at which the gain in output is offset by the cost of the buffers. Small buffers are very effective: Buffers that hold eight units obtain nearly all the benefit.

What causes variability in a factory? This question is important because eliminating variability at its source can reduce inventory by allowing smaller buffers. We will describe some of the more common sources of variability.[7]

Variability of processing time occurs when work has not been standardized. Industrial engineers can often improve both the efficiency and the consistency

[5]Stage 1 begins a new unit, on average, every 10 minutes; stage 2 receives them from stage 1 at the same average rate. Continuing this description, stage 8 also processes an average of one unit every 10 minutes, so the output is 6 per hour.

[6]That is, $6.0 - 5.41 = 0.59$ units per hour is the lost capacity, and $0.59/6.0 = 0.098$.

[7]A similar discussion occurs in Chapter 6 (Total Quality Management). As we will see throughout this chapter, JIT and TQM share many principles.

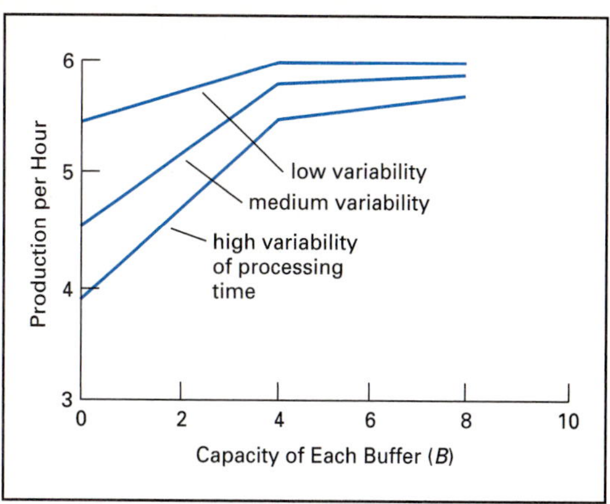

Figure 12-6 Output of an Eight-Stage Serial Line with Storage Buffers

of a process through careful study. However, in many high-tech industries, change occurs so fast that poorly understood production processes must be used. By the time a process is standardized, it may be near the end of its useful life.

Rework to eliminate defects causes large amounts of variability. For example, an item that takes 20 minutes to produce but has only a 95% chance of being defect free has a 5% chance of requiring additional time. *Poka-yoke* methods for mistake-proof operations (see Chapter 6) are important to inventory reduction.

Equipment failure adds unpredictably to processing time. Operator training can avoid some breakdowns. Better equipment is another solution. Preventive maintenance reduces the likelihood of failures.

These examples make it clear that lowering variability often requires process improvement. However, variability is sometimes inherent in production with product variety. For example, processing times vary when options are added to some units and not to others. Two adjacent workers cannot operate synchronously as a result. A buffer between the stages can smooth work flow. Alternatively, task sharing can be used. If the workers are cross-trained, worker 2 can help out when worker 1 falls behind, and vice-versa. Recent research (Ostolaza et al. 1990) has shown that buffer inventory can be substantially reduced in this manner. Cross-training of workers is another aspect commonly associated with JIT production.

Overview of Inventory Reduction

The title of this section posed the questions, Why, where, how, and how much should inventory be reduced? Many books have been written on these topics, and the answers given here are necessarily incomplete; but we can give a brief summary.

Why? The strategic value of inventory reduction, in the long run, far exceeds the classical estimate of inventory cost.

Where? Wherever stocks occur. We have focused on pipeline, cycle, and buffer stocks and described improvements that can eliminate the need for work-in-process stockrooms. The small inventories needed can be stored at the work areas themselves. The liberated floor space can be used for other purposes, and savings accrue in both personnel and information-system requirements. The next section furthers the discussion of *where* by introducing the concept of bottleneck facilities.

How? Look for root causes and eliminate them. Small transfer lots shrink work-in-process inventories. Setup-time reduction lowers cycle stocks. Process improvements reduce the need for buffer stocks, and simulation can help to determine how much is needed. Both flow time and safety stocks also decline whenever in-process inventory is reduced.

How Much? A fundamental principle of JIT is continual improvement. As with total quality management, perfection is the ultimate goal. ''Moving targets'' are commonly used. Each time one target is achieved, another one is adopted. In striving for complete waste elimination, the JIT philosophy requires that ''problems'' be viewed as opportunities to learn more about the process so that it can be improved. Avoiding the crisis-management mentality, the JIT philosophy takes a proactive stance toward exposing problems and eliminating their sources. One proactive approach is to deliberately cut work-in-process inventory until a new problem emerges that interferes with production. This has the advantage of answering *how much* and *where* at the same time, but the *where* refers to the next problem that must be solved. In this way improvement continually builds upon improvement as employees gain problem-solving skill and knowledge of the processes.

REVIEW PROBLEMS

1. A factory has seven production stages, arranged serially. Each stage has one machine. The factory operates 40 hours per week, but each machine is stopped for cleaning every 10 hours. They are stopped on a rotating schedule, so that no more than one machine is out of production. Cleaning requires 30 minutes and is done by an employee trained for that purpose. Taking into account the downtime for cleaning, each machine can process an average of 12 pieces per hour. There is ample buffer space between stages, and as soon as a job is completed at a machine, it is moved to the buffer. Total work-in-process inventory is 1200 pieces. This company is about to change the raw material used in one of their products.
   a. How long will it be before emergence of the first new-material item once they change raw material?
   b. How long, on average, does each unit spend in the factory, according to Little's law?
   c. Suggest a simple procedural change that would increase the output of the factory by about 5%. (Hint: Think of a parallel between the cleaning operation and internal setup time.)

2. What is the difference between a production lot and a transfer lot? Why does large setup time cause large production lots but not necessarily large transfer lots?

3. Table 12-1 gives the data from the simulation experiments on an eight-stage line discussed in this section.

a. By what percentage did the processing time vary from its mean value in each of the three types of factories?

b. Why is 6.0 per hour an upper limit on the average production capacity of this system?

c. How much production capacity is wasted each hour in the high-variability factory with no buffers ($B = 0$)? What causes this waste? How would one go about eliminating this waste?

Solutions

1. a. 1200/12 = 100 hours or 2.5 weeks.

   b. 1200/12 = 100 hours or 2.5 weeks (same answer).

   c. Perform the cleaning operations every eight hours, at night. The machines would be available 0.5 more hours every 10 hours, and that increases capacity by about 0.5/10 = 0.05 or 5%. (Cleaning becomes external.)

2. "Production lot" is the amount you make of one item before switching to another. "Transfer lot" is the amount you move between stages. If the units are produced one at a time, they are available to move as soon as they are produced. Transfer-lot size is determined by the economics of materials handling, and may be much smaller than production-lot size.

3. a. For low variability, (11.73 − 10)/10 = 0.173, and (8.27 − 10)/10 = −0.173; thus, the deviation is ±17.3%. For medium- and high-variability factories, the deviations are ±52% and ±86.6%, respectively.

   b. Six per hour is 1 per 10 minutes. If it were not for variability, that is how fast each stage could feed the next stage and therefore how fast the last stage could produce finished items.

   c. The lost capacity because of blocking and starving between stages is 6.0 − 3.88 = 2.22 pieces per hour. Process improvements might reduce the variability, thus reducing blocking and starving and increasing output. Another alternative is larger buffers.

12-2 BOTTLENECK OPERATIONS

Bottleneck is one of the most important concepts in designing and managing a factory.[8] To grasp this concept, consider a rubber garden hose. How can you adjust the flow of water? Turning the knob on the faucet is one way. An adjustable nozzle will also do the job. But if there is no nozzle and it is a hot day, how do you get a drink from a fast-flowing hose without drenching yourself? Make a loop in the hose and squeeze. The resulting "kink" is the bottleneck; it restricts the flow, much as the size of the neck of a bottle determines how fast you can pour.

Now apply this idea to a multistage, serial-flow process. Reducing the rate of input is like turning down the faucet. Slowing down any one of the work

[8] We first introduced the concept using the Yuppie Car Wash example in Chapter 2. Managing bottlenecks was discussed briefly in Chapter 10.

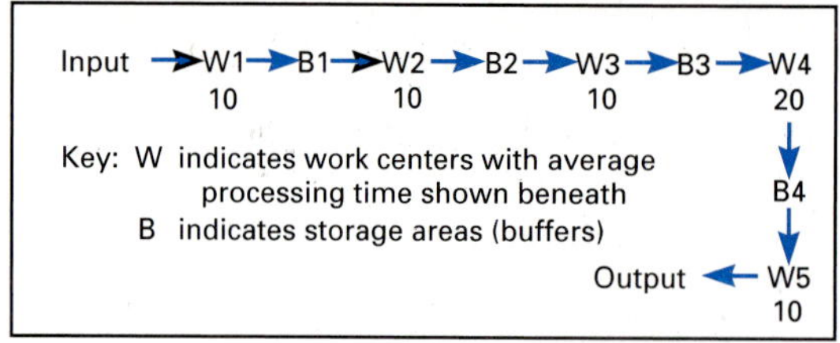

Figure 12-7 A Serial Facility with a Bottleneck

areas is like kinking the hose. Figure 12-7 shows a five-stage line with one bottleneck operation. Work center **W4** needs 20 minutes per unit to complete its assigned tasks, but the other work centers need only 10 minutes. What would the output rate of the factory be?

The answer is 1 piece per 20 minutes (3 per hour) because that is how fast **W4** can work. The other stages are not allowed to use their full capacities. The bottleneck is **W4**. Specifically,

> **W5** can produce 6 per hour, but its work comes from **W4** at a rate of three per hour; thus, **W5** will be idle 50% of the time.
>
> **W3** could produce 6 per hour, but inventory would grow indefinitely (six per hour would go into buffer **B3**, but only three per hour would go out to **W4**); therefore, **W3** must not be allowed to produce more than 3 per hour, in the long run.

The same reasoning applies to the rest of the line. In short, it doesn't matter where you kink the hose, only how firmly.

> *In a serial-flow facility, the slowest operation is the bottleneck, and the entire facility is constrained to operate at the rate of the bottleneck.*
>
> *In a general (not necessarily serial) facility, output is limited by the capacity of the bottleneck operation.*

These two principles show why the bottleneck concept is so important. To increase efficiency, we have to do something about the bottlenecks. The following properties help us find bottlenecks in a real factory:

> *Inventory tends to accumulate upstream of a bottleneck.*
>
> *Bottlenecks tend to be busy all the available time.*

The Importance of Managing Bottlenecks

Goldratt (1987) explains how to recognize and manage a bottleneck through the parable of Herbie, the slow hiker. A troop of scouts, unmanaged, spreads out along the hiking trail according to ability. At the lunch rendezvous it is a long time before the last scout (Herbie) arrives. Various methods are tried to keep the troop together, but all the successful ones require *the entire troop to walk at Herbie's pace.* Finally, in frustration, the faster hikers offer to take part of Herbie's load, and the troop stays together and moves faster.

How can we keep the stages of a factory together if some stages are slower than others? Small buffers limit how far the faster work centers can "get ahead," but the factory is forced to work at the bottleneck's pace. If some of the work currently assigned to the bottleneck is done elsewhere, factory output can increase.

For example, suppose that one of the tasks assigned to **W4** requires 4 minutes, but could be done at **W3** in 6 minutes. Is this less efficient or more efficient? Apparently **W3** is less well suited, since the task takes 50% longer there. However, **W3** is idle half the time. The added task would increase its processing time from 10 to 16 minutes per piece. Meanwhile **W4** would speed up from 20 to 16 minutes per piece by giving up that task; thus, the facility capacity is now higher (1 per 16 minutes rather than 1 per 20).

What is the cost of this improvement? That depends on several factors, but note that there is no fixed cost. Factory capacity was increased without buying new equipment. This apparently inefficient use of **W3** is efficient from the point of view of the factory.

Now consider the difficult task of scheduling production in a large factory that is not arranged serially. If there are hundreds of work centers, the task of scheduling them, taking into account all the routes by which items flow through the factory, is immense. But what if there are only three bottlenecks? Planning is greatly simplified if it is focused on the bottlenecks only. The management task is this: Schedule the most efficient use of the bottlenecks, and operate the rest of the facility to maintain this schedule. By definition, there is slack time at all work areas that are not bottlenecks, so control there should be relatively simple. However, when decisions are necessary, they should be made with the following objective in mind: *Avoid idle time at the bottlenecks*. Maintaining the schedule for the bottlenecks helps to avoid blocking and starving the key facilities that determine the factory's capacity. (See Umble and Srikanth 1990 and Pence et al. 1990 for more discussion of ways to accomplish this.)

Buffers for Bottlenecks

Buffers exist to smooth work flow by reducing interference. Bottlenecks must be protected from interference. Therefore, *buffers are most important near bottleneck operations*. To illustrate this point, we modified our simulation of the ''medium variability'' eight-stage factory[9] to create two bottlenecks. The scenario is as follows:

> Process improvements were achieved for six of the stages, shortening their processing times by 20% (the average is now 8 minutes per unit). The two other stages were not improved and are now bottlenecks (average 10 minutes).

With buffer capacities set at 4, average output increased to 6.00 per hour, compared with 5.76 before the improvements. Figure 12-8 shows the average in-

[9]Processing times vary by ±52%. See Figure 12-6 and Table 12-1.

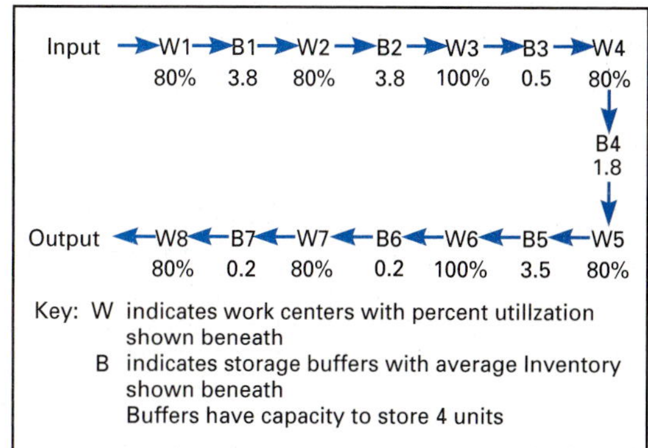

Figure 12-8 Work-Center Utilization and Work-in-Process Inventory in a Serial Facility with Bottlenecks

Table 12-2 Effect of Locating Buffers near the Bottlenecks

Buffer Capacities							Production Rate[a] (units per hour)
B1	B2	B3	B4	B5	B6	B7	
0	1	1	0	1	1	0	5.74
0	2	0	0	2	0	0	5.40
0	0	2	0	0	2	0	5.40

[a]Processing time at each stage varied randomly by ±52% from the mean. Average processing time was 10 minutes at W3 and W6 and 8 minutes elsewhere.

ventory in each buffer and the percent utilization[10] of each work center. (Study the figure to determine which stages are the bottlenecks.)

In a second experiment (not shown) all buffer capacities were reduced to 1. The resulting output was 5.85 per hour, which is still higher than before the improvements.

Three more experiments were run to test the idea of concentrating buffer capacity near the bottleneck operations. In the first experiment all storage was eliminated except buffers before and after each bottleneck. In the second experiment, all storage capacity was concentrated in front of the bottleneck operation, and the third experiment had buffers only downstream of the bottlenecks.

The results, shown in Table 12-2, are clear: *Storage capacity after a bottleneck is just as important as before a bottleneck; storage before and after a bottleneck is better than either one alone.* In fact, 1-unit-capacity buffers surrounding **W3** and **W6** achieve (almost) the same hourly output (5.74) as was possible with 4-unit-capacity buffers before the processes were improved (5.76).

Dispatching Heuristics and Bottleneck Management

In Chapter 11 we described several dispatching heuristics commonly used to control the flow of work in a complex factory. Having said that the nonbottleneck operations should be controlled in a manner that protects the bottlenecks we must also issue a warning: Many (if not most) dispatching rules are either neutral or detrimental toward bottleneck protection.

Some of the more sophisticated heuristics have a look-ahead feature. To decide which job should be worked on first, the remaining time in the shop is estimated, including an allowance for delays due to congestion. Jobs are given priority if they appear likely to be late. But what if there are bottlenecks? Jobs that have future operations on the bottleneck facilities are the ones that will be encountering delays. What good does it do to give priority to jobs that are headed for a traffic jam? That will only make the congestion worse.

There is a parallel in air-traffic control: the gate hold. It is better for a full airplane to wait on the ground before taking off than to arrive at its destination only to fly around in a holding pattern because of congestion. Is the airplane being less efficient because it is sitting on the ground instead of circling among the rain clouds? Besides, if the delay is too long, some passengers may be rerouted to avoid the congested airport.

[10]Utilization is the percentage of the time that the work center is busy. Thus, if a work center is busy, on the average, 48 minutes each hour, its utilization is 80%.

Bottleneck management may call for logic that is opposite to conventional practices. The assignment of priorities should take into account shop congestion, but long queues should be made to repel work rather than to attract congestion. For example, queue buildup might signal the need to reroute some of the jobs to less busy areas, even if those areas are less efficient at the tasks that need to be done.

In this discussion we have focused on using buffers to protect the bottleneck and on reassigning tasks to share the load. Both kinds of improvements help reduce work in process and increase factory output. Bottlenecks should also be the primary targets for process improvement. They are both the cause and the location of in-process inventories, and they determine the capacity of the factory.

REVIEW PROBLEMS

1. A multistage factory has one bottleneck, a machine with a processing capacity of 12 pieces per hour, taking into account downtime for cleaning. All machines operate on a 40-hour week, but are stopped for cleaning every 10 hours. Cleaning requires 30 minutes and is done by an employee trained for that purpose. There are many other production stages in the factory, and the total in-process inventory is 1200 pieces. Last year this firm made a profit of $10 million, before taxes.
   a. Suggest a simple procedural change that would increase the output of the factory by about 5%. Contrast this to your answer to the first review problem in Section 12-1.
   b. Suppose that your suggestion requires paying overtime wages. Show that it is nevertheless very likely to increase profits.

2. In one of the examples of this section, six of the eight stages of a serial-flow factory received process improvements that resulted in 20% faster operation. At those six stages the mean processing time was reduced from 10 minutes to 8 minutes. With buffer capacities of 4, the output of the system increased very little, from 5.76 per hour to only 6.00 per hour.
   a. Explain why a 20% process improvement yielded such a low percentage increase in output.
   b. Predict the output rate if one of the two remaining operations were improved by 20%.
   c. Predict the output rate if both of the remaining operations were improved by 20%. You can make an accurate estimate by drawing an analogy with the results in Table 12-1. (Processing time varies, randomly, by $\pm 52\%$ at each stage.)

Solutions

1. a. For the bottleneck machine only, perform the cleaning operation every eight hours, at night. That increases the capacity of the entire factory by about $0.5/10 = 0.05$ or 5%, assuming that this machine is still the bottleneck after the improvement. In the preceding section, we recommended

moving all cleaning time to after hours. Here we focus on the bottleneck because there should be slack time during the day to clean the other machines.

b. Assume that additional production can be sold at the current price. Current sales are covering fixed plus variable costs of the entire operation and contributing to profit as well. Since the 5% production increase will incur only variable costs, the sales increase should generate at least $500,000 of additional profit (5% of $10 million). This should easily cover the cost of 30 minutes of overtime per day.

2. a. Processing times averaging 10 minutes at the two "unimproved" stages restrict the system's flow to 1 per 10 minutes, or 6 per hour, and that value was achieved. The two bottlenecks are busy 100% of the time. (See Figure 12-8.)

b. 6.0 per hour, for the same reason. One bottleneck remains.

c. All operations average 8 minutes, so each stage has a capacity of 60/8 = 7.5 per hour. However, blocking and starving will prevent that from being achieved. By analogy, the medium-variability system in Table 12-1 achieved 5.76 out of a possible 6.0 per hour; using the same ratio, the improved system should achieve (5.76/6.0)(7.5) = 7.2 per hour. This analogy is valid because processing time varies ±52% from the mean in both cases.

12-3 CONTROLLING JIT PRODUCTION

To operate with very little inventory requires careful planning and flexible control. In this section the concept of a "pull" system is introduced, and the Kanban method for controlling a pull system is described. In a pull system, inventories of material are replaced as they are used. Because little inventory is maintained, the system must be able to respond quickly to avoid interruptions.

Figure 12-9 shows an overview of the planning and control system used at Toyota Motors. The pull system is at the very bottom of the figure and is lowest in the hierarchy of information flow. Planning begins far in advance; production numbers begin flowing to suppliers and plants at least two months in advance. Production sequences are determined at the plants with the goal of leveling the usage of equipment and personnel. Cyclic schedules, similar to those introduced in Chapter 11, are used to determine a production sequence of different models. Detailed daily and weekly schedules are shared with the suppliers. Schedule changes as late as two weeks in advance of actual production are communicated to the suppliers and to the production lines. Last-minute changes go directly to the final assembly line. *It is these minor, last-minute changes that the pull system is designed to handle.*

Communication with suppliers is quite different from a conventional system. This practice, known as JIT purchasing, is discussed later in more detail. Observe that the arrows in Figure 12-9 show at least four levels of communication with successively shorter time frames. None of these constitutes an order. Instead, the company enters long-term arrangements that are, in essence, contracts for a portion of the supplier's production capacity. This is in stark

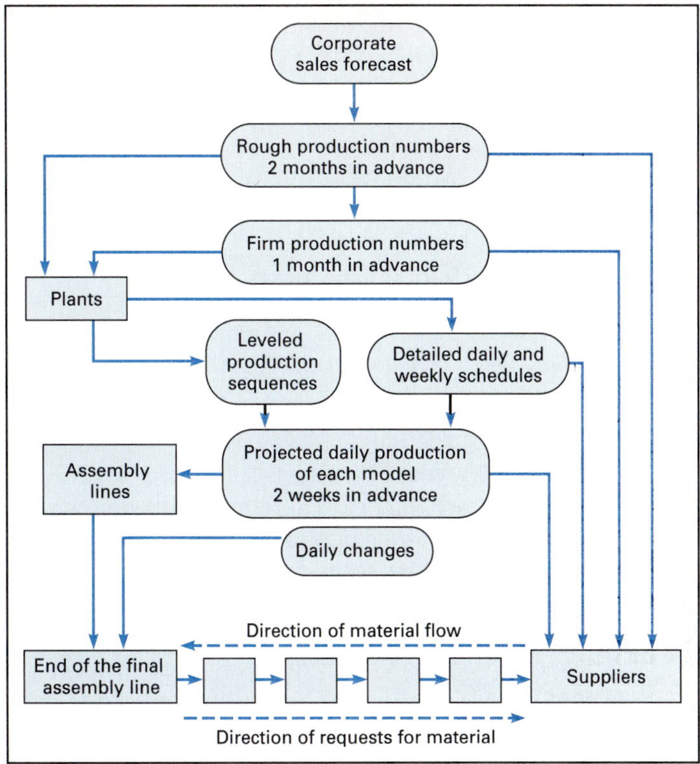

Figure 12-9 Production Planning and Control at Toyota Motors (adapted from Shingo 1989, p. 97). All solid arrows represent flow of information.

contrast with the usual long-range orders for specific quantities of each part. The actual mix of parts to be supplied gradually becomes firmer as actual production time approaches. By the time delivery is imminent, the supplier has been given very nearly exact information about what will be demanded.

However, some customers have special orders, and responding to these requires nearly last-minute changes: "The salesperson informs the head sales office which places the order directly with Toyota Motors. There the order is entered into the computer and relayed to the assembly plant. The car is produced within two days; six days are allowed for delivery, and there is an additional two-day margin" (Shingo 1989, p. 87).

Fortunately, last-minute changes are not important everywhere in the production process. Items that are common to all vehicles, for example, are unaffected by customers' special orders. Processes such as drilling, boring, and machining are examples. "Order-based production becomes essential only at that stage in processing where individual customer requirements must be taken into consideration. This includes, for example, exterior painting and fittings" (Shingo 1989, p. 88). Therefore, the production schedules for processes that are "early" in the manufacture of an automobile are insulated from the vagaries of special ordering.

One of the objectives of JIT in every industry is to design production facilities to resemble assembly lines. For many readers the radical departure from conventional design that we are about to describe will seem merely common sense. (It is!) However, major process improvements are necessary before a company can achieve successful JIT operation. Setup time reduction (Section

12-1) and defect elimination (Chapter 6) are two of the most important, as they allow operation with very low inventory levels.

In this section we will describe methods for smooth factory operation with no stockrooms and very small buffers. In addition, JIT can be applied to the purchasing and delivery of materials, and production plans must be leveled to match production capacity. When all these factors are in place, efficient work flow is possible with little work-in-process inventory.

Kanban: A Pull System for Production Control

A Pull system has only one simple rule: move materials in the production line only when they are needed.

Hernandez, 1989

Picture yourself as a worker in a large factory. You make a component used in a dishwasher. There are eight dishwasher models, and your component, the electro-mechanical controller, is slightly different in each model. Setup time is only a few seconds when you change between models. Mistake-proof bins with automatically controlled lids ensure that only the correct parts are available to you.

To coordinate with the rest of the factory, you need to know which components are needed, in what quantity, and when. Then you need to obtain parts.

In a conventional factory, orders are controlled through a stockroom. The stockroom sends components to the dishwasher assembly line. When inventory runs low, the stockroom clerk issues an order for more. Production control then schedules a run. You (the component maker) find out about this when a work order arrives from production control. The parts you will need arrive at about the same time, presumably. Those parts are controlled and delivered in a similarly complicated manner, requiring considerable coordination and information flow.

Many JIT factories are controlled by a simpler system. Parts are resupplied in standard containers, labeled with the part name or number. When you empty a container, it goes directly to the work center that makes the part (that is, your supplier) and serves as a work order to refill it. The empty container carries three messages: **What** (the part name is on the container's label), **how much** (one container full), and **when** (now).

This is called a pull system because demand triggers movement of items toward the place where the demand occurs. In contrast, a "push" system triggers work orders for parts in anticipation of need; orders are based on a schedule rather than on an impending shortage. The pull mechanism just described is called a *kanban* system. *Kanban* is the Japanese word for "card," referring in this case to the label on the container. (Later we will describe a system in which cards and containers follow different paths.)

If your supplier is right next to you, this system is extremely efficient: Your needs are communicated at the speed of light (your supplier sees the empty container). Of course, the supplier may be busy filling another order, so you may need at least two containers for each part to avoid running out. If the supplier is not nearby, someone has to transport the empty container, and your signal is delayed. In this case additional containers may be needed to avoid shortages.

To this point we have described how you order more parts. How do you

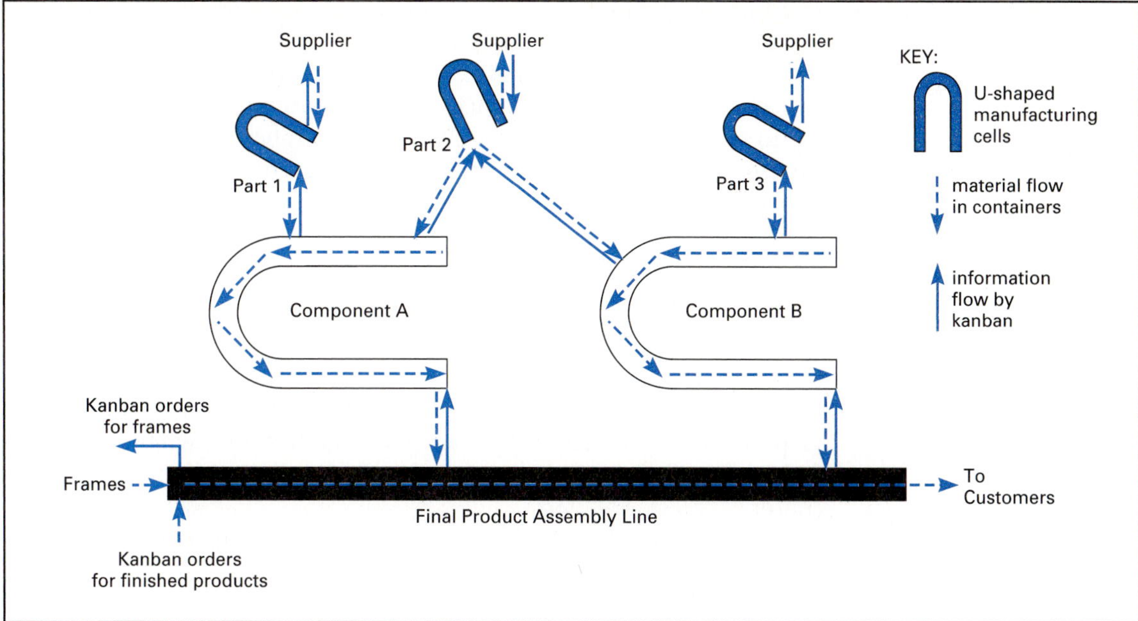

Figure 12-10 Information and Material Flow in a Multistage Factory

know which component to produce? The same method applies, only this time you are the supplier. When your ''customer'' sends you an empty container, the attached kanban tells you what to produce. The same system controls work flow all the way from parts to finished goods.

The information flow in a pull system is opposite to the flow of material. For example, the factory depicted in Figure 12-10 has a final-assembly line that is ''fed'' components from two U-shaped manufacturing cells. Customer orders eventually empty a container, releasing a kanban for finished products; finished-product assembly causes kanban orders for components; component production triggers production of parts; and that causes orders for raw materials and other supplies. The entire production system is activated by customer demand. (More discussion of U-shaped lines and other facility-layout issues is given in Chapter 16.) Similar flows occur in Toyota's production line, represented at the bottom of Figure 12-9. In this way deviations from the scheduled production of final products are communicated back through the facility in a simple, reliable manner.

However, there is inventory in the containers at every link between production areas in the system. The refilled containers will satisfy later demands. The customer who triggered production has already been served. Thus, when operated in this way, pull systems are *just-a-little-early* rather than just-in-time.

One-card, Two-card, and No-card Pull Systems

A kanban is a permanent card that serves as a work order. In the system just described, the card is attached to the container. There are sometimes advantages to separating them. Sending a card to your supplier may be faster than sending an empty container.

In a *one-card system*, there is a kanban attached to each container of parts. When you use all the parts in a container, you detach the card and send it to the appropriate worker, who then makes enough to fill another container, attaches your card to that container, and sends it to you. Empty containers are eventually moved to the appropriate work areas for later use.

A *two-card system* separates *production* orders from *move* orders. When you empty a container of parts, you detach its *move kanban* (or *conveyance kanban*) and send it to your supplier. In this system your supplier has a small buffer of full containers with *production kanban* attached to each of them. A transport worker takes a full container and leaves its production kanban behind as a signal to make more. Your move kanban is attached to the full container and the transport worker brings it to you.

There are two differences between one-card and two-card systems:

1. In a one-card system, the supplier makes parts specifically in response to the arrival of a kanban. In a two-card system, the parts are already waiting when a move kanban arrives. The supplier has made them in response to a production kanban that was detached when a previous order was filled, and that order may have originated from *any* work center that uses the part.
2. In a one-card system, inventory is stored in *input buffers* located at the user(s) of the part. In a two-card system, *both input and output buffers* are maintained. However, the two-card system does not necessarily have more inventory. If several work centers use the same part, the supplier's output buffer may be a more efficient storage location than the user's input buffers.[11]

There are two kinds of *no-card systems*. One uses a mechanical, electrical, or electronic signal to request more parts. The other triggers production whenever there is a place to put it. For example, a spot on the floor can be designated as a *kanban square* for a given component by applying paint or colored tape. Whenever that spot is not full, you have permission to make some more. When the spot is full, you have to stop work.

Inventory in Pull Systems

Each full container is work-in-process inventory. To run a factory under a pull system with near-zero inventory requires that the number and size of containers be minimized. Each of the inventory-reduction techniques from Section 12-1 may be applied to this issue.

Process and supply variability increase the need for inventory. Transport delays are one reason for needing more containers; eliminating pipeline stock is why JIT factories locate suppliers adjacent to users. Product variety increases inventory because each work center needs full containers of all the parts used there; products designed to use the same parts avoid some of this inventory. Eliminating any source of variability reduces the need for buffer inventory and safety stock. Finally, the size of the containers dictates the production-lot size; reducing setup time allows smaller containers.

Coordination between stages is affected by container size. Output containers dictate the production-lot size. Input containers are designed to hold the correct number of parts for one output lot. Avoiding partially full input containers keeps the workplace neat and reduces inventory. It also avoids having to interrupt production to obtain another input container. (Small parts that are used in many products may be delivered in larger quantities.)

---

[11]The supplier's buffer is a queue that is shared by the users. Appendix A gives several examples in which shared queues are more efficient than separate queues.

The quantity of inventory can be changed by adding or removing kanban (Karmarkar 1989). Consider a two-card system. Inventory between two stages is largest if all move cards and all production cards are attached to full containers. Removing a card lowers inventory. This is particularly useful for seasonal items. Replacing the cards for winter items with cards for summer items changes what the factory produces. Care must be exercised in the order of removal so that the system can empty out. Similarly, for an item that is demanded infrequently, temporary kanban may be issued for the item, its part, and its components, so that stock will not be maintained at all times.

Fewer cards cause smaller buffers. In Section 12-1 we saw that larger buffers improve flow by decreasing blocking and starving but also increase inventory and flow time. The same principles apply to pull systems if the number of kanban is viewed as buffer capacity. Bitran and Chang (1987) discuss the design of a kanban system from a mathematical programming perspective.

Responsiveness of Pull Systems

How long will a customer have to wait? In most pull systems small inventories of finished goods are available, so customers experience no delay. If finished-goods inventory is gone (that is, several customers arrive in rapid succession) how long must the next customer wait? If all the necessary components are ready, finished-goods production can begin as soon as a container is emptied. By the time the next customer arrives, production may have been under way for some time. The point is that *the customer of an ideally designed pull system only deals with the last stage* and need not wait for the full chain of events to occur.

For a custom order, the picture is different. The customer must then deal with the flow time through the factory. In the case of automobiles, customization occurs during final assembly; earlier production stages are unaffected. Therefore, low inventory on the final-assembly line assures fast delivery. (Remember Little's law.)

Karmarkar (1989) notes that pull systems are reactive in response to market demand and do not recognize (or anticipate) future events or changes in demand. Pull systems do not function well under extreme variability of lead times or demand. Sometimes it is appropriate to consider hybrids that combine some elements of both push and pull.

Combined Push and Pull Systems for JIT Production

Materials requirements planning (MRP), described in Chapter 10, is an example of a push system. Orders for parts and components are triggered from a schedule of future finished-goods production and ''exploded'' using bills of materials to calculate required quantities. Timing is estimated by ''offsetting'' these requirements (backward in time) from the finished-goods schedule. Start times and due dates are established in this manner, and production control is based on those numbers. As each production step is completed, the products are moved (pushed) to the next step, usually with a stop in a stockroom on the way. Production does not wait for requests from the next workstation.

In theory MRP is a just-in-time system. If all the time offsets are correct, each processing step will occur exactly as planned, and the resulting parts will arrive just as the next step is scheduled to occur. In practice it does not work that way because, as we saw in Chapter 10, the MRP uses *planned* lead times that typically vary from *actual* lead times. According to Karmarkar (1989), ''production lead times vary depending on the degree of congestion or loading within the shop. The fallacy in MRP is that its releases produce the very conditions that determine lead times, but these lead times have already been taken as known and fixed in making the releases.'' In other words, *lead times depend on the work load of the shop, and that is not known until the schedule is computed.* MRP treats lead time and shop load as independent, when they are, in fact, jointly determined.

Unfortunately, the usual response is to use worst-case lead times to make sure that materials will be available. Rather than just-in-time, MRP becomes way-too-early, and large inventories accumulate. Furthermore, MRP is not typically implemented with incentives for continual improvement, which are pervasive throughout the JIT pull approach (Karmarkar 1989).

On the other hand, the typical pull system is embedded in a push framework. For example, reviewing Figure 12-9 reveals that Toyota's JIT system has elements of both push and pull. In the planning stages, bills of materials are used to estimate the required quantities and timing of parts and components. This information is used for capacity planning. It is also used to plan quantities of items that are common to all products. Suppliers make their plans from this same information. The main difference from MRP is that the actual production takes place in a pull environment. Timing and sequence are entirely determined by the kanban mechanism. The planned production quantities are approximately achieved, but they play no direct role on the shop floor.

Karmarkar (1989) describes a scheme for deciding to what extent and in what manner MRP and JIT logic can be combined. He identifies lead-time variability as a major factor. Highly variable lead times are inconsistent with pull control; too much safety stock is required. Lead times are most variable in the case of *custom engineering,* and in that case MRP and push logic should dominate. At the other extreme is *continuous-flow* manufacturing, where control of the rate of production is all that is required. Most discrete-parts manufacturing falls between these extremes. In those cases, push methods such as MRP are most useful for materials planning and order release, but a kanban (or other pull) system may be better suited for real-time shop-floor control.

Both Shingo (1989) and Karmarkar (1989) note that the successful integration of push and pull requires careful leveling of the production load so that the variations felt on the shop floor are within the limits that can be absorbed by the small amounts of inventory in the input and output buffers.

Real-time scheduling systems (described briefly in Chapter 11) are being developed as alternatives to MRP and pull systems. Everything that affects shop capacity is fed into the system, including maintenance schedules, setup times, transport times between stages, and bills of materials. A customer request for finished-goods production triggers requests for capacity on every facility affected by the bill-of-materials explosion. If sufficient capacity is available at all stages in the proper time sequence, the order is accepted. Otherwise it must be rescheduled. The result is a set of start times that are much closer to just-in-time than can be achieved by MRP. Orders are pushed through the shop according to these times.

Real-time scheduling also has an advantage over kanban control systems: No work-in-process inventory is needed. Pull systems need inventory because inventory depletion is the signal to produce. Push systems use schedules and the arrival of materials to trigger production. This is particularly significant when the variety of manufactured goods is high, because maintaining small quantities of thousands of items translates to substantial inventory. Implementation of real-time push systems requires the discipline and dedication to continual improvement demanded by the just-in-time philosophy. Perhaps this will be the future of just-in-time for manufacturers with substantial product variety.

JIT Purchasing

JIT purchasing seeks to extend the fundamental principles of just-in-time to relationships with outside vendors. As with JIT production, JIT purchasing is a philosophy rather than a particular method (Ansari 1990). It calls for frequent small-batch deliveries of high-quality parts. It also requires that close relationships be established with vendors. This is extremely important because operating with low inventory implies a constant risk of shortage: A company must be able to rely on its suppliers just as much as on its internal operations.

Vendor reduction is one method to increase the incentive for vendors to deliver the extremely high quality of service required for JIT. This involves moving away from *multiple sourcing* (purchasing a part from many different suppliers) toward *single sourcing* of purchased parts. The idea is to concentrate more business with fewer vendors so that each vendor will have more to gain by keeping you happy, and more to lose if they do not.

Close association with suppliers carries some risk. For example, with fewer suppliers a company is more susceptible to supply interruptions such as strikes; the risk exposure is focused rather than diversified. Nevertheless, in many cases the advantages have been found to far outweigh the risks. For example, one major U.S. corporation has gone from 8000 suppliers to just 300, and in so doing decreased purchasing costs by nearly 80%. Over a five-year period, the savings have been in the hundreds of millions of dollars.

Successful JIT purchasing requires close, two-way ties with suppliers. This means long-term contracts rather than the ''lowest-cost'' short-term contracts that have been typical. More important, the company needs to ''invest'' in its suppliers by sharing process-, design-, and quality-improvement methods with its vendors. In this way an environment is created in which the company and its vendors share in a codestiny (Hayes 1981) that is mutually beneficial to both parties.

By creating this long-term relationship, both the company and the supplier are able to learn faster about the product and the process, and reap the benefits of a steeper learning curve. Also, if vendor quality becomes as good as that of internal operations, inspection of incoming parts can be eliminated. This is another form of reducing waste, since capacity does not have to be allocated to inspection. Eliminating inspection requires *vendor certification*, a procedure for establishing that the vendor is capable of delivering materials that always conform to specifications (Inman 1990).

Just-in-time delivery poses other special requirements. If material is arriving just before it is needed, any delays such as receiving-area congestion are unacceptable. Receiving must be streamlined, and some of the usual receiving operations may be eliminated altogether. Material delivered in standard containers does not need to be counted, for example. Facility layout may be designed (or changed) to allow *direct delivery* of purchased materials to the factory floor. Work areas that use materials delivered from outside the factory are given exterior locations.

Two problems concerning JIT purchasing often arise in practice. One of these stems from a misunderstanding of the need for JIT purchasing. It is *not* mandatory that JIT purchasing accompany implementation of a JIT system, nor is it required that every purchased part be sourced using JIT purchasing practices. In a study of JIT purchasing, Freeland and Ashby (1989) observed that "common sense does not always mean 'JIT' deliveries." They found that even Japanese practices differed in regard to JIT purchasing, and that criteria such as the physical size of the purchased item, its cost, and the geographical proximity to the supplier affect JIT purchasing practice.

The second pitfall arises from the misconception that JIT *is* JIT purchasing. When JIT was first being introduced in the United States, some manufacturers misunderstood the fundamental concept and assumed that the "solution" was to force their suppliers to deliver JIT. The results were disastrous.

The goal of JIT purchasing is a system in which the vendors are, in essence, part of the factory. A kanban system is often used for communicating requirements to the suppliers, for example. More precisely, kanban are used to communicate *minor variations* in an agreed-upon supply schedule. The purchase contracts are written to allow some degree of flexibility. Deliveries are adjusted based on feedback of actual usage. Thus, suppliers are asked to absorb some of the variation that is inevitable when trying to match supply to demand. They can do this by accumulating inventory or by adjusting their own production rate. If they choose the latter, they need to learn the techniques discussed in this chapter so that they can have small production lots and frequent setups.

REVIEW PROBLEMS

1. Explain why a two-card kanban system need not have more inventory than a one-card system, despite the fact that the former has twice as many work-in-process storage areas.

2. Describe the movements of a production kanban and a move kanban in a two-card system. Which one covers a greater physical distance?

3. What do workers do when no (production) kanban are present?

4. Explain why it is a serious mistake to think of JIT as (just) a kanban control system. You may wish to refer to Figure 12-9 in your answer.

5. Describe three ways to reduce inventory in a kanban-controlled system. Include only methods that will not lower the system's efficiency in the long run.

Solutions

1. In a two-card system, the inventory of a part is distributed between the supplier's output buffer and the input buffers of all the users of that part, rather than stored entirely in input buffers. Holding some inventory at the supplier may actually reduce the number of containers required to avoid disruption.

2. Production kanban never leave the work area. They wait in the output buffer until material is collected by the transport worker, but they stay behind when the container departs, providing a signal to produce more. Move kanban circulate between the input buffer of the user and the output buffer of the supplier, thus traveling a greater distance.

3. Stop. The workers may perform maintenance or cleaning or may practice or improve procedures, but they must not produce.

4. Figure 12-9 shows the kind of planning system that is required to support a pull system. Without planning, there would be nothing to pull: The pipeline would be empty. Also, in addition to pull production control, JIT requires such things as increased quality, reduced setup, and continual improvement.

5. Reduce transport delays by providing more frequent pickup and delivery, faster conveyance, or locating work areas closer together. Eliminate sources of variability such as rework (see *poka-yoke*, mistake-proof operations, in Chapter 6). Reduce setup time, thus allowing smaller production lots and smaller containers.

SUMMARY

JIT sets relentless waste elimination as its goal. Inventory reduction is the primary target, and process improvement is the means. The only way that a system can function well with (almost) zero inventory is if everything works as planned (almost) all the time. Setting this goal for every employee, and giving them the means to work toward the goal, is a strategic move targeted at (a) positioning a company as the low-cost, high-quality supplier and (b) maintaining and improving that position once it is achieved.

Variability is the enemy of JIT production. Smooth flow is most readily achieved when production approaches Henry Ford's ideal of zero variation. Rather than accept no product variety, the JIT approach is to design products and processes for ease of changeover and maximum use of common parts and operations. In addition, variety requires broader training of workers. Reassignment of workers is an effective means of rebalancing when there is a model change, for example. Cross-training is an integral part of many JIT factories.

The transformation to JIT is similar to improving one's personal health regimen. Not only must fat be removed from the system, but also habits must change. Perhaps the most important habit to change is that of using inventory to hide problems. Inventory is, by definition, production earlier than needed, and that is a waste of resources. More pernicious is the fact that many other problems are hidden by the presence of inventory. Identifying and solving those problems leads to long-run savings. The most obvious examples are safety stock to cover for randomly occurring defects, and cycle stock to avoid long setup times. In both cases, getting rid of the cause saves money directly and also allows inventory reduction.

It is surprising how little inventory is needed to maintain smooth work flow. Very small buffers of work-in-process inventory are sufficient to avoid idle time in multistage production systems. In the typical environment, bottleneck operations can be readily identified. Managing these operations is the key to increasing the efficiency of the system. Inventory buffers can be quite effective in avoiding idle time on bottlenecks. Shedding part of a bottleneck's work load can be a low-cost way of adding capacity to the system. Here again standard practices are encountered that are deleterious to system performance. Certain widely used dispatching heuristics actually increase the congestion around bottlenecks, for example.

Careful planning and scheduling can drive out most of the variation in work load. However, small deviations are inevitable, because of special customer orders, for example. To accommodate these deviations, JIT production is often controlled with a pull system based on cards (kanban) and standard containers. Quantity and location of inventory are controlled by the number and placement of cards and the size of the containers. The objective is to eliminate stockrooms altogether, and to maintain only as much inventory as is needed to avoid disruptions. All inventory is stored in the standard containers and kept on the production floor. This requires careful coordination and planning. JIT purchasing extends the JIT philosophy to the delivery of purchased parts. Special relationships with vendors must be formed to allow for JIT delivery. When applied correctly, JIT purchasing yields significant benefits.

On the other hand, advance planning for material flows takes place in a push mode. Standing orders are negotiated based on bills of materials and forecasts of demand. A steady flow of materials is required to make the system work. It is only the last-minute deviations in requirements that are controlled by the pull system exemplified by the use of kanban.

MRP could, in theory, be a just-in-time system, but it has a fatal flaw: It uses fixed lead times. The MRP logic is very useful for advance planning, but other methods are needed for real-time control. Pull systems can serve this purpose. However, new push systems are being introduced that may approach the ideal of zero inventory more closely, particularly when substantial product variety is involved. In the meanwhile, it is safe to say that JIT has forever transformed the way that production systems are viewed.

CASELET

Jenuine Gudgeon Systems Manufacturing, Inc.*

The management of Jenuine Gudgeon Systems Manufacturing (JGSM) is planning a facility to manufacture their new line of gudgeons. The factory is to be a JIT operation, controlled with a kanban system. Through careful design and the use of automation, gudgeon manufacture has been reduced to two operations.

The first operation will use Universal U14 Milerators. In spite of the best engineering efforts, the operation is still highly variable in both cycle time and yield, owing primarily to the inherent variability in the density of the silicon bronze castings. Tests have shown that processing time varies randomly, and is equally likely to be any value between 5 and 11 minutes. This includes time for inspection. Thirty percent of the semifinished gudgeons are defective and are discarded after the first operation. However, U14s are reliable machines, and breakdowns are not expected if the preventive maintenance schedule is followed.

The second operation has been fully automated and will utilize Yamazaki's new MAZAK Gudgeon Gouger, model GG20, which has a nominal

*Modified, with permission, from Thomas et al. 1989.

capacity of 20 gudgeons per hour of run time. Variability in cycle time is negligible, as is the defect rate. However, the Yamazaki engineers have warned of random shutdowns with a mean run time of three hours between failures. Repair requires 30 minutes to replace the gouger module.

The factory will have several U14s feeding a single GG20 in a manner depicted schematically in the following diagram:

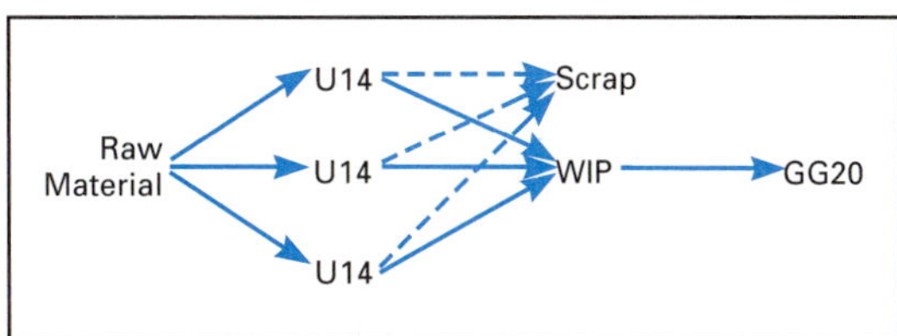

JGSM can afford only one GG20 now, even though they believe that demand is sufficient to justify production of 30 gudgeons per hour. They expect that demand will continue to grow. The U14s are much less expensive than the GG20.

The immediate concern is ordering equipment for the new factory. Several U14s will be required, and some sort of materials-handling system must be designed that allows for the variability of the operations. In a preliminary meeting the planning committee raised a series of questions. Justin Thyme, the vice-president for planning, has asked you to prepare a report that addresses the following issues:

1. How many U14s should be purchased? Exactly matching the capacity of the GG20 will be impossible, but the planning committee is concerned that overcapacity of the U14s could cause enormous quantities of WIP between the two operations.
2. What are the implications of the U14 variability (processing time and scrap)? Will they cause loss of output for the new facility? Will they prevent JGSM from implementing a kanban system to control the movement of materials?
3. What are the implications of the random breakdowns of the GG20? The committee raised the same concerns as in question 2.
4. How much WIP storage space should be provided and where should it be located? Should they use a two-card control system? How should gudgeons be moved from the U14s to the GG20?
5. Universal is designing a new milerator, the U16, that is expected to cost 50% more than the U14. Their design engineers claim to be able to achieve a scrap rate of 15% with JGSM's silicon bronze castings, and processing times that vary from 3 to 7 minutes per piece. If available now, would U16s be a better investment than U14s?

Required: Mr. Thyme wants you to prepare, immediately, a preliminary report giving your reaction based on JIT principles and simple arithmetic. He also wants you to prepare a more complete report in a few days based on a simulation model. (We suggest using the XCELL+ Factory Modeling System. See Conway et al. 1990).

PROBLEMS

1. The equation "present capacity = work + waste" was presented in the introduction to this chapter.
   a. How does this equation relate to the JIT philosophy?
   b. Define "waste" as it is viewed in the JIT philosophy.
   c. It is sometimes said that anything in the production process that does not add value directly to the product is waste and should be eliminated. Explain what is meant by this.
2. Why is inventory viewed as "bad" in the JIT philosophy? Describe examples in which inventory conceals the causes of problems.
3. Explain how Little's law relates to just-in-time manufacturing.

*4. What kinds of problems would be encountered if a kanban system were used to control production in a job shop where the work flow consisted of low-volume, highly customized jobs?

5. Explain why TQM (total quality management) is very important for JIT.

*6. Cross-training of workers in more than one operation is standard procedure in many companies that use JIT. Discuss how cross-trained workers can help keep inventory low and maintain just-in-time production.

7. Summarize briefly the difference between push and pull systems for production scheduling and control.

*8. A company has annual sales of $100 million. They estimate that $10 million is tied up in inventory at any given time.
   a. How much money would this company save if they could reduce inventory to $1 million? (You will have to make some assumptions to answer the question.)
   b. How does this relate to "inventory is waste"?
   c. Estimate the average throughput time (flow time) for this company for each of the two inventory figures. How does reduced flow time benefit the company?

9. A particular machine seems to be prone to failure. On the average it spends 10% of the time in repair.
   a. How can inventory prevent this machine's problem from affecting other work areas?
   b. Besides inventory reduction, what benefits would accrue if the machine's reliability can be improved to near 100%?
10. A work area produces two parts, A and B. Work is controlled by a one-card kanban system. Product A requires very complicated adjustments during setup and hence has a long setup time. Product B's setup is short and easy. To avoid frequent setups of A, the company has specified a large lot size. Production runs of A currently last 8 hours.
    a. Why must the production-lot size for B also be large if A's is?
    b. Why should the transfer-lot size be substantially smaller than 8 hours' worth of production?

---

*Problems with an asterisk have answers in the back of the book.

c. How much inventory of B must there be in the system to avoid disruptions during the production of A? Where will this inventory be located as the production of A begins?

d. This work area is not a bottleneck for the factory. What would happen if A's lot size were reduced without first shortening the setup time of A?

*11. Fallow, Incorporated, manufactures a variety of products from steel tubing. Fallow products are found in most homes around the world. However, the demand for some of these products is highly seasonal. Since a kanban system is used to control production, the seasonal products are added to and deleted from production by inserting or removing their cards. Production occurs in ten stages, arranged serially. When it is time to remove a product from production, in what order should the cards be removed from the system? That is, should kanban be removed from all ten stages at the same time? If so, explain why. If not, suggest a better method.

12. In keeping with the tenet "Set, don't adjust," a drill press has been modified by removing its infinitely-adjustable alignment fence and replacing it with seven standard-width fences that are bolted in place as part of the setup operation. (Figure 12-4 illustrates alignment fences.) This drill press is used for only seven different parts, and this change has eliminated the trial and error involved in moving the fence when changing between parts. However, two problems remain:

a. It still takes 2 minutes to exchange fences. Suggest a method for reducing fence change to a few seconds.

b. Defective parts are sometimes produced because the material is not snugly held against the fence during drilling. Suggest a method for eliminating this source of defects.

13. When preparing to type an examination, a word-processing worker must first establish headers for each page and type a standard set of instructions for the students on the first page. Assuming that the typing is being done on a computer, suggest a method for substantially reducing the time required for this setup operation.

*14. A manufacturer of metal toys uses heated molds to form the bodies of toy trucks. To change between different truck models requires changing the mold, which is very hot and very heavy. This setup operation has been partially mechanized by installing a crane to lift out the mold, move it to its storage area, and pick up another mold and move it into position. Then the mold is heated and the operation resumes. How can they convert most of these operations into external setup time? Give specific suggestions.

*15. In a two-stage manufacturing system, work finished by stage 1 goes to stage 2 for finishing. Four items are made by this system. Between the two stages are four small areas for storage, one for each item. Empty space in an area is like a kanban: The stage-1 worker makes the appropriate item and fills the spot. When all four areas are full, the worker at stage 1 is required to stop. The average time to process a job is 2 hours at stage 1 and 1.8 hours at stage 2. Actual processing time varies from these averages by as much as $\pm 50\%$.

a. What is the maximum rate of output (units per 8-hour day) that this system can achieve, on the average? Explain briefly, stating any assumptions.

b. Explain why idle time must occur in this system if the workers are not cross-trained. Estimate the percent idle time.

c. If the size of the storage area is reduced to near zero, what will the effect be on the output rate of the system? Why?

Careful observation revealed that the difference in processing times was due entirely to differing skill levels of the two workers. Assuming this to be true, the two workers were switched so that the processing time averaged 1.8 hours at stage 1 and 2 hours at stage 2.

d. What happened to the system's output rate as a result of the switch?

e. What happened to the quantity of inventory in the storage space between stages as a result of the switch?

16. The faster worker in the previous problem was reassigned. His replacement requires 2 hours per piece, so now the line is ''balanced.'' Given that a fast worker has been replaced by a slow worker, describe what happened to the average output rate of the two-stage system under the following assumptions:

a. a large storage area between the workers

b. a very small storage area between the workers

17. A four-stage production line is shown in the accompanying diagram. Average processing times are given for each station.

→ W1 →	W2 →	W3 →	W4 →
32 minutes	38 minutes	29 minutes	31 minutes

a. What is the maximum output rate that the line can achieve?

b. Consider where to place a single work-in-process storage area. The candidates are after W1, after W2, and after W3. If only one buffer is allowed, which is the least likely candidate for receiving the storage area? Explain.

c. An engineer is studying stage 2 and claims to be able to decrease its processing time by 50%. What is the maximum output rate the line could then achieve?

d. Disregarding part c, what would the maximum system output rate be if station 1 had a scrap rate of 20%?

*18. In the three-stage system in the accompanying diagram, the final output from W3 is checked for errors by an inspector. Imperfect items are discarded. There is a 10% probability of producing a defect at W1, and the same probability occurs (independently) at W2 and W3. Hence, only 72.9% of the output is error free; the probability of no error is $(0.9)(0.9)(0.9) = 0.729$.

→ W1 →	W2 →	W3 →
20 per hour	10 per hour	20 per hour

a. What is the maximum average output rate of the system, measured in error-free items per hour? Explain.

b. If an inspector is added after W1, what is the system's maximum error-free output rate? (Assume that inspection requires no time.) Explain.

c. What does the difference between answers a and b have to do with the maxim "protect the bottleneck"?

19. The layout of a factory is shown in the accompanying diagram. Arrows indicate the flow of work. For example, all jobs that begin at A go to B, then X. Centers Y and Z are identical and are alternative destinations for every job that emerges from X.

    A controversy has arisen about whether work center X is a bottleneck. Centrally located, X performs one operation on every unit produced by the factory; it is on every routing. The numbers in the diagram show the output capacity of each work area, not the actual amount they produce. At issue is the system's output capacity, measured in the combined production rate of jobs of all types per hour.

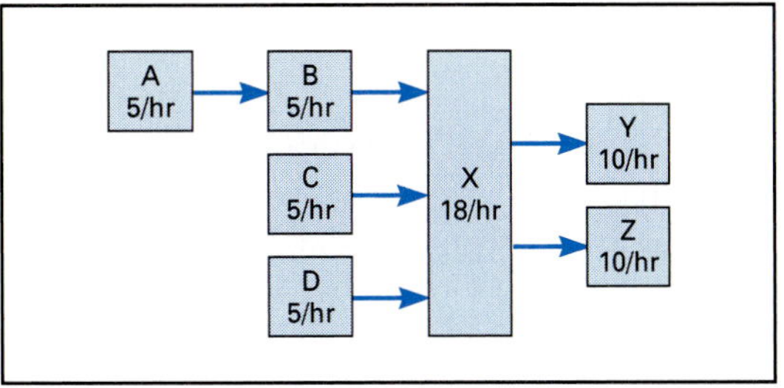

a. Is work center X a bottleneck? Explain.

b. The capacity of 18 per hour for work center X did not take into account the required maintenance that removes it from service for 8 hours out of every 40 hours (i.e., run for 32, then maintenance for 8). Taking this into account, what is the output capacity of the system? Is X a bottleneck?

*20. Many people are puzzled as to why MRP has never been able to schedule production just-in-time. In theory, time phasing and bill-of-materials explosion should produce a schedule in which the needed materials arrive just at the time when production is scheduled to begin. In practice, it is necessary to increase the lead times to make MRP work, and that results in substantial inventory. What is it about MRP that causes this dilemma? (You may need to review part of Chapter 11 to answer this question. Consider the issue of discrete time buckets. Also consider the roles of closed loop MRP and capacity requirements planning.)

21. The Vendor's Lament: Vendors who supply very large JIT companies are often heard to complain that their customers are pushing their inventory back to the suppliers. Toyota's interactions with their suppliers, represented (in part) in Figure 12-9, are typical. Discuss the "vendor's lament" in the context of JIT purchasing.

22. What is meant by the word *codestiny* as it pertains to JIT purchasing? Discuss the benefits and costs (risks) for a company and its suppliers when they undertake JIT purchasing.

REFERENCES

ANSARI, A., *Just in Time Purchasing*, New York: Free Press, 1990.

BITRAN, G., and L. CHANG, "A Mathematical Programming Approach to a Deterministic Kanban System," *Management Science*, vol. 33, no. 4, April, 1987.

BONITO, J.G., "Motivating Employees for Continuous Improvement Efforts," *P&IM Review*, vol. 10, no. 6, June, 1990.

CONWAY, R., W. MAXWELL, J. MCCLAIN, and L.J. THOMAS, "The Role of Work-in-Process Inventory in Serial Production Lines," *Operations Research*, vol. 36, no. 2, March–April, 1988.

CONWAY, R., W. MAXWELL, J. MCCLAIN, and S. WORONA, *User's Guide to XCELL+ Factory Modeling System*, 2nd ed. Redwood City, Calif.: Scientific Press, 1990.

FREELAND, J.R., and H.L. ASHBY, "Some Preliminary Findings of Purchasing Practices in Japan and the United States," Teaching Note UVA-OM-670, Darden Graduate Business School, University of Virginia, 1989.

GOLDRATT, E.M., *The Goal*, revised ed., Croton-on-Hudson, N.Y.: North River Press, 1987.

GOLHAR, D., C. STAMM, and W. SMITH, "JIT Implementation in Small Manufacturing Firms," *Production and Inventory Management Journal*, vol. 31, no. 2, 1990.

HAYES, R.H., "Why Japanese Factories Work," *Harvard Business Review*, July–August, 1981.

HERNANDEZ, A., *Just-in-Time Manufacturing: A Practical Approach*, Englewood Cliffs, N.J.: Prentice-Hall, 1989.

INMAN, R.A., "Quality Certification of Suppliers by JIT Manufacturing Firms," *Production and Inventory Management Journal*, vol. 31, no. 2, 1990.

KARMARKAR, U. "Getting Control of Just-in-Time," *Harvard Business Review*, September–October, 1989.

MELCHER, A., W. ACAR, P. DUMONT, and M. KHOUJA, "Standard-Maintaining and Continuous Improvement Systems: Experiences and Comparisons," *Interfaces*, vol. 20, no. 3, May–June, 1990.

OHNO, T., *Toyota Production System: Beyond Large-Scale Production*, Cambridge, Mass.: Productivity Press, 1988.

OSTOLAZA, J., L.J. THOMAS, and J.O. MCCLAIN, "The Use of Dynamic Line Balancing to Improve Throughput," *Journal of Manufacturing and Operations Management*, vol. 3, no. 2, 1990.

PENCE, N., J. MEGEATH, and J. MORRELL, "Coping with Temporary Bottlenecks in a Several-Stage Process with Multiple Products," *Production and Inventory Management Journal*, vol. 31, no. 3, 1990.

SCHONBERGER, R.J., *World Class Manufacturing*, New York: Free Press, 1986.

SHINGO, S., *A Revolution in Manufacturing: the SMED System*, English ed., Cambridge, Mass.: Productivity Press, 1985.

SHINGO, S., *A Study of the Toyota Production System from an Industrial Engineering Viewpoint*, revised ed., Cambridge, Mass.: Productivity Press, 1989.

SHINGO, S., (ed. A. Robinson), *Modern Approaches to Manufacturing Improvement: The Shingo System*, Cambridge, Mass.: Productivity Press, 1990.

THOMAS, L.J., J.O. MCCLAIN, and D. EDWARDS, *Cases in Operations Management: Using the XCELL Factory Modeling System*, Redwood City, Calif.: Scientific Press, 1989.

TOYODA, E., *Fifty Years in Motion*, New York: Koshida International, 1987.

UMBLE, M., and M. SRIKANTH, *Synchronous Manufacturing: Principles for World Class Excellence*, Cincinnati: South-Western, 1990.

VORA, J., J. SARAPH, and D. PETERSEN, "JIT Implementation Practices," *Production and Inventory Management Journal*, vol. 31, no. 3, 1990.

chapter 13

Scheduling Personnel and Service Systems

One of the unique characteristics of service operations is that production and consumption occur simultaneously. Service cannot be held in inventory in anticipation of future demand. This gives rise to the challenge of planning appropriate levels of capacity to meet peak demand levels—trading off the costs of excess capacity in periods of low demand and insufficient capacity when peak demand occurs. Service organizations, especially high-contact services, must devise and implement strategies that effectively couple capacity management (a production function) and demand management (a marketing function). It is important for management to understand each of these functions and to formulate a strategy that melds them into the overall service concept.

Personnel scheduling is an important part of managing capacity in service operations. Personnel are scheduled in accordance with longer-term capacity plans, which are based on forecasted demand. Schedules that meet these customer demands must also consider the needs of the workers, such as days off and the maximum allowable number of consecutive days worked. Since demand forecasts are rarely perfect, devices such as float pools of personnel or the use of part-time workers can be used to allow for last-minute adjustments in capacity.

Demand management is another way to balance production capability with customer needs. Demand management uses strategies that transfer demand from peak load to periods of low demand and reduce uncertainty in the timing of demand. For example, appointment systems are effective tools for managing demand.

The first two sections of this chapter focus separately on the provider (capacity management) and the consumer (demand management). Section 13-1 explores capacity management in service operations by means of an example that highlights the salient characteristics of the planning decision. We also consider personnel scheduling and discuss methods for determining schedules that meet the needs of customers and workers. Section 13-2 presents several approaches to managing demand. Principles of design for simple appointment systems, including the use of overbooking policies, are also discussed. Finally, in Section 13-3 we discuss situations such as transportation services, in which the timing of both the producer and the consumer are in the control of management.

13-1 CAPACITY MANAGEMENT AND PERSONNEL SCHEDULING

Intermediate-range (aggregate) plans provide initial input into the capacity-management decision. As described in Chapter 9, these plans use forecasts prepared for many months in the future and account for predictable rises and falls in the requirements. The inability of services to carry inventory must be reflected in the intermediate-range capacity-management and planning process. If models of the type defined in Chapter 9 are used, the inventory-based decisions will have to be reduced or eliminated as required by the nature of the service. In the following discussion we consider some important elements of managing capacity in service operations.

Capacity Management

We will use the Yuppie Car Wash Company example of Chapter 2 for illustration. Recall that the Yuppie Car Wash uses a two-stage process. In the first stage the car is washed in one of two identical automatic car-wash (ACW) machines; in the second stage the car's interior is cleaned in one of two interior cleaning centers (ICCs). Yuppie manages ACW capacity by operating one or both ACWs, and it controls ICC capacity by determining the number of workers assigned to the ICCs. The cycle time of each ACW is 2.5 minutes, and the cycle time of each ICC is $6/n$ minutes, where n ($1 \leq n \leq 3$) is the number of workers assigned to each ICC. (For this discussion assume that the same number of workers is assigned to each ICC.) The capacity of each ACW is 24 cars per hour, and the combined capacity of the two ICCs is $20n$ cars per hour.[1]

Yuppie's hours of operation are 9:00 A.M. to 7:00 P.M., Tuesday through Sunday. As is common in service companies, the volume of business differs from day to day and hour to hour. Table 13-1 provides information on average demand. Actual demand levels fluctuate around these averages.

We see that Yuppie's demand exhibits strong seasonal behavior with respect to day of the week and hour of the day. (Seasonality is discussed in Chapter 7.) It is not surprising, for example, that Saturday is the busiest day and that 5:00 to 6:00 P.M. is the busiest hour of the day.

Yuppie must manage capacity to meet this demand. Specifically, management must determine when to operate one or both ACW machines. Since operation of the second machine will incur additional costs (support staff, maintenance, and so on), only one machine should be in operation during certain hours of the week. For instance, 9:00 to 10:00 A.M. Tuesday mornings is a period of low demand. Yuppie must also decide how many workers to schedule in the ICCs over the course of the week.

The ability of a server to meet demand depends on the rate at which demand arrives and the rate at which demand can be processed (that is, the ca-

[1] The cycle time of $6/n$ minutes per car is equivalent to a rate of $60(n/6) = 10n$ cars per hour per ICC, or $20n$ total.

Table 13-1 Seasonal Demand Pattern for Yuppie Car Wash

Average Number of Cars per Day		Daily (Seasonal) Factor
Tuesday	169	0.60 = 169/280
Wednesday	187	0.67
Thursday	235	0.84
Friday	321	1.15
Saturday	410	1.46
Sunday	358	1.28
Average	280	

Average Number of Cars Arriving per Hour		Hourly (Seasonal) Factor
9–10 A.M.	19	0.68 = 19/28
10–11 A.M.	22	0.79
11–12 noon	29	1.04
12–1 P.M.	31	1.11
1–2 P.M.	29	1.04
2–3 P.M.	24	0.86
3–4 P.M.	26	0.93
4–5 P.M.	32	1.14
5–6 P.M.	40	1.43
6–7 P.M.	28	1.00
Average	28	

pacity of the server). One way to measure the ability of (planned) capacity to meet demand is through the calculation of *projected capacity utilization* (*PCU*), where

$$\text{Projected capacity utilization} = \frac{\text{demand}}{\text{capacity}} = \frac{\text{average input rate}}{\text{maximum average output rate}}$$

Projected capacity utilization is closely related to (actual) capacity utilization, defined in Appendix A in the context of queuing theory. (Alternatively, PCU is sometimes referred to as the *traffic intensity*.)

The *actual* capacity utilization of a server measures the fraction of existing capacity that is actually being used; consequently, capacity utilization cannot exceed 1.0. The *projected* capacity utilization, however, measures demand load against a projected capacity and, therefore, may be larger than 1.0. PCU values greater than 1 suggest that projected capacity will be unable to satisfy anticipated demand within the specified time period, even if capacity is utilized 100%. For example, if demand is 70 units per hour and capacity is 50 units per hour, PCU = 140%, meaning that some of the demand will either be processed at a later time or be lost.

Tying this to queuing theory (Appendix A), the length of the waiting line (or *queue*) that forms in front of a server grows dramatically as the actual capacity utilization approaches the value of 1.0. In the long run, if projected capacity utilization exceeds 100%, the queue length will never reach steady state; it will continue to grow.

It is often difficult to assess projected capacity utilization on an absolute scale. For example, if the PCU of an automobile repair shop is 75%, it may not be obvious a priori whether this is good or bad. However, when comparing this with another repair shop that has a PCU of 90%, customers will experience a significantly shorter wait on the average in the shop with lower PCU.[2] Thus, PCU can prove to be extremely helpful when used for comparing two or more facilities on a relative basis. In addition, PCUs that are 100% or greater offer important insight into the inability of supply to meet demand.

Because projected capacity utilization is linked to customer waiting time, it is also useful for considering the trade-off between facility idle time and customer waiting time. The amount of time a customer spends waiting in line is often an important component of the overall level of service provided to the customer (that is, the *service level*). In the automobile repair shop example, on the basis of past experience the shop may determine that a PCU of 75% results in too much mechanic idle time, and although average customer waiting time is low, customers may be willing to wait a little longer for their cars. Thus, the shop might adjust capacity by increasing PCU to 80% and evaluating the resulting service level. An emergency room of a hospital, however, may need to deliberately plan capacity to yield relatively low PCU values, since a high service level is required.

Returning to the Yuppie Car Wash example, to compute the average weekly PCU of the automatic car-wash machines (PCU_{ACW}), assuming that both ACWs are used throughout the week, we first compute the average weekly demand, which is 280 cars per day times 6 days per week, yielding 1680 cars per week. Next, we calculate the weekly capacity (assuming no machine down time). Each ACW requires 2.5 minutes per car. This means that 60/2.5 = 24 cars can be cleaned per hour in each ACW. Since there are two ACWs, each working 10 hours per day, 6 days per week, a total of (24)(2)(10)(6) = 2880 cars can be handled by the ACW machines in a week. Thus, weekly PCU_{ACW} = 1680/2880 = 58.3%.

It appears that on a weekly basis, on the average, Yuppie has sufficient ACW capacity to meet its current demand level. However, because of the inability to inventory the service, Yuppie must also have enough capacity to meet its peak (load) demand requirements. Therefore, it is necessary to examine the PCU of the ACWs during peak demand.

Saturday is the busiest day, with a demand of 410 cars. Since the capacity of two ACW machines is (24)(2)(10) = 480 cars per day, the average capacity utilization on Saturday is PCU_{ACW} = 410/480 = 85.2%, substantially higher than the weekly average of 58.3%. Not surprisingly, projected capacity utilization increases on the busiest day but may still be sufficiently low to provide an adequate service level.

The amount of time required to wash and clean a car is small compared with the length of a day. Also, customers wait for their cars while they are in the car wash. Furthermore, Yuppie has strategically directed its service toward owners of high-priced cars, who may be very sensitive to excessive waiting times. Therefore, not only is it important for Yuppie to determine an appropriate service level, it must also perform peak-demand capacity analysis during the busiest hour of the week.

The busiest hour of the week is Saturday from 5:00 to 6:00 P.M.[3] Yuppie uses both hourly and daily seasonal factors to forecast demand. For example,

---

[2]Even though both shops will have some idle time (since PCU < 100%), waiting occurs because of *variability*. The higher the PCU, the greater the likelihood of delay. See Appendix A for additional discussion.

[3]These calculations assume statistical independence of day of the week and hour of the day. This assumption should be checked when applying this analysis to an actual situation.

using data from Table 13-1,

$$\text{Saturday forecast for 5–6 P.M.} = \begin{pmatrix}\text{Saturday}\\ \text{daily}\\ \text{factor}\end{pmatrix}\begin{pmatrix}\text{5–6 P.M.}\\ \text{hourly}\\ \text{factor}\end{pmatrix}\begin{pmatrix}\text{average}\\ \text{hourly}\\ \text{demand}\end{pmatrix}$$

$$= (1.46)(1.43)(28) = 58.46 \text{ cars}$$

Therefore, $PCU_{ACW} = 58.46/48 = 1.22$ or 122% during the busiest hour of the busiest day of the week.

Because this exceeds 100%, Yuppie does not have adequate capacity to keep the queue of cars from growing during its busiest hour. If this were a one-hour phenomenon, it might be acceptable to Yuppie's customers. However, it is compounded by the carryover of waiting cars from the previous hour. Specifically, the average PCU_{ACW} during the 4:00 to 5:00 hour on Saturday is 97.1%. Thus, there will often be many cars in line before the 5:00 Saturday peak begins.

This illustrates the difficulty, and also some of the nuances, of managing capacity in service operations. Yuppie must decide whether to acquire additional ACW-machine capacity to meet peak demand. This decision will be based on the trade-off between the cost of the additional capacity and the (shortage) cost of not being able to meet peak demand. The cost of additional capacity includes the cost of acquiring it, as well as the cost of maintaining and possibly operating the additional capacity during periods of low demand.

These capacity-management issues must be addressed continually as the service operates on an ongoing basis. The firm must determine how best to manage existing capacity, as well as whether to expand or contract future capacity. It is also necessary, however, to consider the basic trade-offs in the initial design of the operation. In the case of the Yuppie Car Wash, for example, a strategic decision was made to have two ACWs instead of one large one that operates faster. This choice of equipment in the design of the process system allows for flexibility in adjusting capacity to match demand. It also lowers the cost of operating additional capacity during low-demand periods.

Shortage costs arising from the inability to meet peak demand are tied fundamentally to the nature of the service. Because a considerable part of a service is intangible, this capacity decision cannot be made independently from the strategic vision of the service. For example, the cost penalty derived from not being able to serve customers in a timely fashion will be much greater for Yuppie than it would be for a local gas station offering a $1 car wash as a secondary service.

In the second stage of the Yuppie Car Wash, cars go through an interior cleaning center (ICC). If three workers are assigned to each ICC, 60 cars can be cleaned per hour; thus during the peak-demand hour on Saturday, the projected capacity utilization of the ICCs is 97.4%. However, 97.4% substantially overstates the utilization we will observe for the ICCs because their demand arises from the ACW machines, which have a capacity of only 48 cars per hour. Therefore, no matter how many cars arrive at the car wash, no more than 48 per hour will move into the ICCs. Thus for the ICCs, actual utilization will be no more than 48/60 (input rate/output capacity) or 80%, so the ICCs will be idle at least 20% of the time if staffed with three people each.

Unfortunately, this excess ICC capacity does not offset the shortage of ACW capacity: Cars must go through *both* the ACW and the ICC. Since the ACW is the bottleneck, it will not help to have excess capacity in the nonbottleneck ICC operation. As was noted in Chapter 2, this might even irritate customers as they wait a long time for their cars to be washed and see ICC workers "standing around." This emphasizes the need to plan carefully and coordinate the various stages in a multistage process.

Personnel Scheduling

After intermediate-range capacity-management plans have been established, management is then faced with the task of scheduling personnel. It is not straightforward, however, to take aggregate capacity decisions that were derived in response to uncertain demand forecasts and translate them to short-range personnel requirements. For example, when scheduling the nursing staff in a hospital, planned nursing capacity over the next several months may have been established using forecasts of the number of patients, aggregated over different types of patients. These target nursing levels must then be disaggregated according to the type of patient, the specialty of the nurses, and the severity of the need for nursing care.

This requirement for detail, together with the forecast uncertainty, makes it difficult to commit personnel to a schedule except in the short range. Therefore, personnel planning is often done in three stages: annual budgeting, schedule planning (several weeks in advance), and daily assignment. The annual plan is made on an aggregate basis, whereas the schedules are developed for individual workers or groups of workers and are based on more up-to-date forecasts. Last-minute adjustments are made on a daily basis to meet needs created by unplanned absences and variations from the forecasted requirements.

Several methods are in common use for daily adjustments, including *float pools* (groups of people who work where and when they are needed), *call-in personnel* (part timers who are available at short notice), *overtime*, and the *reassignment* of regular staff to balance the work load.

Adjusting personnel assignments on short notice may not be desirable for several reasons: part-time, float, or transfer personnel are sometimes not as well qualified as regular staff; the time and effort required to accomplish a major rebalancing of workers can be substantial; constant large-scale reshuffling of personnel can be upsetting to the work situation, particularly in a setting such as a hospital, where continuity of care is important. Therefore, it is important to achieve a good staffing assignment through careful budgeting and scheduling, so that daily reassignment is kept to a minimum.

A systematic approach is needed to tie together the three stages (budgeting, scheduling, and daily assignment). Kelley and McKenna (1976) describe an integrated nurse-staffing system, which includes the required data-gathering elements for forecasting, scheduling, and daily assignment. An important aspect of the system is the daily projection of the level of work required in each unit of the hospital. This is accomplished by partitioning patient demand, which involves the evaluation and classification of patients, according to the intensity of care required. These requirements are converted to nurse staffing levels through a set of standards, expressed as a table. The system is designed to call attention to variances between the planned and actual staffing levels, an important element of any management control system.

The remainder of this section concentrates on personnel-scheduling methods. This is a vital issue in personnel planning, since it is the means whereby the budget decisions are implemented, and its adequacy determines whether elaborate or simple methods will be used for last-minute personnel changes.

We will begin by describing methods for scheduling a single work shift and then discuss the situation when there is more than one shift per day.

Sundays Off

Detailed scheduling of personnel has two basic objectives: (1) to provide an adequate work force to meet daily operating requirements, and (2) to provide suitable recreation clusters (days off) for the personnel. For example, the New York City Sanitation workers (Beltrami 1977, chap. 2) all have Sunday off and must average two days off per week. The peak garbage load therefore occurs on Monday and is much heavier than average. Ideally, more work crews would be operating on Monday than on other days. However, for forty years, the crews were divided equally among six different schedules, shown in Table 13-2. These assignments were rotated each week, so that a crew would have Sunday and Monday off one week, then Sunday and Tuesday off the following week, and so on. This rotating schedule repeats itself every six weeks and does not allow a heavier work schedule on Monday.

One solution is to have enough workers in each of the six work groups to meet Monday's peak load. By staffing to peak load, however, the other days would exhibit low capacity utilization. Such overstaffing would be quite expensive. Instead, one could allow part of the garbage to remain uncollected for several days, an unsavory solution, indeed! A third solution is to divide the work crews into smaller groups. This would result in a large number of groups (compared with six at present), but the manager could assign fewer groups to the Sunday-Monday days-off pair.

Table 13-3 gives a possible schedule for 30 work groups. Each group follows the same cycle (rotation), but group 1 begins with the week 1 schedule, group 2 begins with the week 2 schedule, and so on. The bottom row of Table 13-3 shows that Monday occurs as a day off only twice in the cycle; thus, the average number of crews not working on Monday is 2/30 = 6.7% of the work force. In contrast, 7/30 = 23.3% of the work force is off on Saturday.

Table 13-2 Six-Week Rotating Schedule of Days Off

Week	Mon.	Tue.	Wed.	Thu.	Fri.	Sat.	Sun.
1	X						X
2		X					X
3			X				X
4				X			X
5					X		X
6						X	X

Table 13-3 Thirty-Week Rotating Schedule of Days Off

Weeks	Mon.	Tue.	Wed.	Thu.	Fri.	Sat.	Sun.
1–2	X						X
3–5		X					X
6–9			X				X
10–16				X			X
17–23					X		X
24–30						X	X
Total days off:	2	3	4	7	7	7	30

In this example the solution to the problem came through modifying a forty-year-old idea by dividing the work force into smaller groups while utilizing the familiar days-off pairs. This can be formulated as a linear programming problem, which allows the inclusion of any desired set of days-off clusters, including three-day weekends, for example. (See Beltrami 1977 for a discussion of how this was done in the sanitation workers example.)

Days-Off Pairs

Telephone exchanges, airline reservation systems, and hospitals are staffed at all times. This rules out a schedule in which everyone has the same day off. One approach is to form schedules based on ''days-off pairs'' so that everyone has two nonworking days per week. Table 13-4 shows all such schedules for which days off are consecutive. The advantage of these schedules is that employees would have two uninterrupted days away from work, even though they may not coincide with a normal weekend.

One way to determine work schedules is to use linear programming (LP), described in Appendix C. Rothstein (1973) gives an example of scheduling hospital personnel. His approach assumes that the number of full-time workers, N, is already known, and that forecasts of work load have been prepared and converted into daily personnel requirements, R_k. The difference N - R_k then represents the number of workers who can have a day off on day k. That is,

N = number of available full-time personnel

R_k = number of personnel required on day k

$n_k = N - R_k$ = number of days off available on day k

If n_k is negative, this indicates that N workers are insufficient on day k, so either N must be increased or part-time or overtime help must be used to decrease R_k. R_k can also be made less than N by shifting some of the work assignments from day k to another day.

The number of available days off must be sufficient to allow *each* of the N employees to have at least two. If the seven different n_k values sum to less than $2N$, again, either N must be increased or R_k decreased. (Reassigning work among days will not help in this case.)

Once these decisions have been made, an LP can be formulated to schedule the work force. However, because the pattern of requirements varies over the week, it may not be possible to assign consecutive days off to everyone. Hence, two kinds of variables are needed:

x_k = number of personnel assigned to the kth day-off schedule in Table 13-4.

Table 13-4 Consecutive-Days-Off Schedules

Schedule	Mon.	Tue.	Wed.	Thu.	Fri.	Sat.	Sun.
1	X	X					
2		X	X				
3			X	X			
4				X	X		
5					X	X	
6						X	X
7	X						X

u_k = number of personnel assigned to an unpaired (nonconsecutive) day off on day k

Three kinds of constraints are needed. The first is

$$\begin{aligned} x_1 + x_2 + u_2 &\le n_2 \\ x_2 + x_3 + u_3 &\le n_3 \\ &\vdots \\ x_6 + x_7 + u_7 &\le n_7 \\ x_7 + x_1 + u_1 &\le n_1 \end{aligned} \qquad (1)$$

In words, the first constraint in (1) focuses on Tuesday, day 2, since x_1 represents Monday and Tuesday off; x_2 represents Tuesday and Wednesday off; and u_2 represents unpaired Tuesdays off. Thus, the constraint assures that the Tuesday work requirements are met by assigning no more than n_2 Tuesday days off.

Constraint 2 makes sure that there are enough days off—two per worker:

$$\sum_{k=1}^{7} 2x_k + u_k \ge 2N \qquad (2)$$

The third type of constraint is a little more complicated:

$$\begin{aligned} u_1 &\le \quad u_2 + u_3 + u_4 + u_5 + u_6 + u_7 \\ u_2 &\le u_1 \quad + u_3 + u_4 + u_5 + u_6 + u_7 \\ &\vdots \\ u_7 &\le u_1 + u_2 + u_3 + u_4 + u_5 + u_6. \end{aligned} \qquad (3)$$

The first constraint in (3) guarantees that unpaired Mondays off, u_1 are not too numerous. We have to give everyone two days off, and if Monday had more unpaired days than the rest of the week combined, someone would require two days off on Monday, which is impossible.

Objectives. Several are possible. The manager must choose one that is appropriate for the situation at hand. Two examples are

$$\text{Max} \sum_{i=1}^{7} x_i \quad \text{(maximize consecutive days off)} \qquad (4)$$

$$\text{Max } x_5 + x_6 + x_7 \quad \begin{pmatrix}\text{maximize consecutive days off} \\ \text{that involve Saturday or Sunday}\end{pmatrix} \qquad (5)$$

Table 13-5 summarizes the solution to Rothstein's example, which was for the 31-person trash-removal crew in a hospital, using objective function 5. The Input Data section shows the uneven daily availability of days off. The center of the table shows the optimal solution, and the last three columns summarize

Table 13-5 Days Off for Hospital Trash-Removal Workers

Input Data		Optimal Solution			Days Off Schedule		
Day	**Available Days Off**	k	x_k	u_k	**Day**	**Unpaired**	**Paired**
MO	12	1	0	0	MO	0	$12 = x_7 + x_1$
TU	1	2	1	0	TU	0	$1 = x_1 + x_2$
WE	10	3	0	9	WE	9	$1 = x_2 + x_3$
TH	0	4	0	0	TH	0	$0 = x_3 + x_4$
FR	16	5	8	8	FR	8	$8 = x_4 + x_5$
SA	10	6	1	1	SA	1	$9 = x_5 + x_6$
SU	13	7	12	0	SU	0	$13 = x_6 + x_7$

how this solution meets the requirements. Thus, the LP recommends using only four of the consecutive-days-off schedules, with one worker having Tuesday and Wednesday (that is, $x_2 = 1$), eight having Friday and Saturday, and so on. On Wednesday, there are $u_3 = 9$ unpaired days off, compared with 8 on Friday and 1 on Saturday. Therefore, eight workers have Wednesday and Friday off, and one will get Wednesday and Saturday.

To use an LP of the type defined by constraints 1 through 3 and objective function 4 or 5, a manager must supply three things: a set of feasible work schedules, such as Tables 13-2 or 13-4, commensurate with the number of work groups; an objective such as (4) or (5); and the allowable numbers of days off. In return the LP delivers two things: a feasible assignment of days off (if one exists), and shadow prices (see Appendix C) to evaluate possible changes in the work requirements. For example, the shadow price associated with the first constraint of type 1 would provide the manager with information on how much the objective-function value would change if management were to alter n_2 (available Tuesday days off), by perhaps adding or deleting part-time personnel. This would change the utilization of the full-time personnel and must therefore be done as a part of overall employment planning.

It is also possible to include additional constraints in the LP. For example, if it is desired to have at least eight Saturday-Sunday days-off pairs, the constraint $x_6 \geq 8$ could be included in the formulation.

There is usually no guarantee that an LP will yield an integer solution. (An LP in which the variables are constrained to assume integer values is called an integer program.) However, Rothstein's original formulation (1973) has been shown to always result in an integral solution, so that management need not concern itself with methods for rounding off the answers. (The inclusion of additional constraints, however, could lead to noninteger solutions. Other employee-scheduling models are described in Ozan 1986 and Wagner 1975, chap. 7.)

Baker and Magazine (1977) discuss work-force scheduling when demand is cyclical and workers have days-off requirements. In their analysis, staffing requirements are permitted to vary according to whether it is a weekend or a weekday. They consider several different days-off policies spanning one- or two-week periods. These include, for example, two days off per week, or in a two-week cyclic schedule, two pairs of consecutive days off (including every other weekend off). In each case they provide a formula for the optimal size of the work force, as well as a procedure for constructing a feasible schedule.

Implementing Personnel-Scheduling Systems

Other examples of personnel-scheduling applications include check encoders in banks (Davis and Reutzel 1981 and Krajewski et al., 1980), and telephone operators for betting (Wilson and Willis 1983). These applications use integer programming formulations (similar in approach to the LP described previously). The problems are solved using heuristics to find good feasible schedules and to choose good combinations from a cost and worker-preference point of view. Bechtold and Jacobs (1990) define an integer programming model for optimal shift scheduling that allows flexible (meal or rest) break assignments.

How does one determine which person is given which days-off schedule? The sanitation workers followed a rotating schedule, so that everyone had the same number of Saturday-Sunday pairs, in the long run. However, it may not be desirable to have such an equal allocation. Some people may have different preferences than others; therefore, unequal assignments may make all parties more satisfied. Arthur and Ravindran (1981) describe nurse-scheduling procedures that allow the nurses to express preferences for different work schedules, and that allocate work assignments in a way that equalizes the nurses' satisfaction in the long run. One method is to construct an *aversion index* for each nurse, which incorporates how well a nurse's schedules have matched his or her preferences in the past, so that a nurse who accepts a bad schedule actually builds up points toward a better schedule in the future.

Developing around-the-clock schedules is based on the same ideas as the LP explained earlier except that the number of alternatives and constraints is considerably greater because of the need to deal with several classes of workers, several shifts per day, rotation among shifts, and choice of days off.

Many organizations operate on more than one shift per day. If each shift is staffed independently, a three-shift operation could be scheduled with three LPs of the kind we have discussed. However, there are two other possibilities: shift rotation and overlapping shifts. In the case of shift rotation, each shift can be viewed as a separate "day," (a seven-day week is thus viewed as twenty one days); however, care must be taken in designing work schedules, to avoid requiring a person to work two consecutive shifts with no rest. This can be accomplished by leaving such schedules out of the set of alternatives, much as we left out three-day weekends in Table 13-4. The number of feasible schedules becomes very large when shift rotation is included; therefore, it is important to choose carefully which ones to include as alternatives.

Overlapping shifts are useful when the requirements vary according to a pattern over a 24-hour period. For example, the police reduce their staffing level some time during the night, but not necessarily at 5:00 P.M. Glover et al. (1984) describe a heuristic scheduling procedure that operates on a personal computer. This condenses about eight hours of manual work into a few minutes to develop weekly work schedules for 100 employees. The method allows for work requirements that vary within a day, overlapping shifts, breaks, lunch periods, requested days off, and limits on available part-time personnel. The automatic scheduler is described as a managerial robot because it actually replaces a manager, freeing him or her for more interesting work. A review problem shows the similarity between overlapping shifts and the consecutive-days-off problem.

REVIEW PROBLEMS

1. In the Yuppie Car Wash example, suppose that on Tuesday mornings from 9:00 to 10:00 management plans to operate one ACW and to place one worker in each ICC. What are the resulting projected capacity utilizations of the ACW and the ICCs?

2. If Yuppie were to acquire a third ACW (identical to the others) to be used during peak demand, how would this affect PCU?

3. The number of police officers needed varies according to the hour of the day. The requirements for one city are as follows:

	A.M.			P.M.		
Hour	2–6	6–10	10–2	2–6	6–10	10–2 A.M.
Staff required	10	40	30	35	15	20

   a. Construct a table similar to Table 13-2 or 13-4 showing all possible eight-hour shifts, using X to denote time on duty (rather than days off, as in previous tables).

   b. Write a constraint that will assure that the requirements for the 6:00 to 10:00 A.M. interval are met.

4. In the hospital trash-crew example (Table 13-5) each of 31 people are assigned days off. There are eight Friday-Saturday pairs, twelve Sunday-Monday pairs, eight Wednesday-Friday pairs, and one each of the pairs Tuesday-Wednesday, Wednesday-Saturday, and Saturday-Sunday. One possible 31-week rotating schedule is shown in the next table, and includes one three-day weekend. The numbers in the body of the accompanying table indicate which of the 31 weeks a given day off corresponds to. For example, the first row has Wednesday and Saturday off as the week-1 pair, and Sunday off as the first part of the week-2 holiday.

Thirty-One-Week Rotating Schedule

Week	Days Off	M	T	W	T	F	S	S
1	WS			1			1	2
2	SM	2						3
3	SM	3						4
4	SM	4						5
	⋮			(Repeat SM until week 13)				
13	SM	13						
14	TW		14	14				
15	WF			15		15		
16	FS					16	16	
17	WF			17		17		
18	FS					18	18	
	⋮			(Repeat WF–FS until week 30)				
29	WF			29		29		
30	FS					30	30	
31	SS						31	31

a. Find the three-day weekend.
b. Identify the work periods that are longer than five consecutive days.
c. What kinds of difficulties might one have in trying to implement weeks 15 to 30?

5. The scheduling methods discussed in this section assume that we know how many personnel are needed.

a. Where would this information come from?
b. What management tools are available to respond to errors in this information?

Solutions

1. On Tuesdays mornings from 9:00 to 10:00, the forecast average demand is (Tuesday factor)(9-10 A.M. factor) (average hourly demand) = (0.60)(0.68)(28) = 11.47 cars. The capacity of one ACW is 24 cars per hour, and ICC capacity is 20 cars per hour (with one worker in each); thus, both stages can handle the arrivals. Therefore, PCU_{ACW} is 11.47/24 = 47.8%, and PCU_{ICC} = 11.47/20 = 57.3%.

2. Peak demand of 58.5 cars per hour occurs from 5:00 to 6:00 P.M. on Saturday. The third ACW would increase ACW capacity to 72 cars/hour. Thus, PCU_{ACW} = 58.5/72 = 81.2%. This would certainly improve Yuppie's ability to handle peak demand. However, management must decide whether the cost of acquiring and operating the extra machine can be justified by the benefit of the increased service level.

3. a.

	A.M.			P.M.		
Schedule	2–6	6–10	10–2	2–6	6–10	10–2 A.M.
1	X	X				
2		X	X			
3			X	X		
4				X	X	
5					X	X
6	X					X
	10	40	30	35	15	20

b. The requirements for the 6:00 to 10:00 A.M. interval can be met through a combination of schedules 1 and 2; thus, we would write

$$x_1 + x_2 + u_2 = 40$$

in which u_2 represents the number of police who are called in for a split shift from 6:00 to 10:00 A.M.

4. a. Saturday, Sunday, and Monday at the end of the first week.
b. Week 13 has seven consecutive workdays beginning on Tuesday and ending with a day off the following Tuesday. There are six-day work pe-

riods beginning on Thursday of week 14, and Saturday 15, 17, 19, 21, . . . , 29, and Sunday of week 30. These are interspersed with short weeks, with split days off.

c. This part of the schedule requires a change every week. This might be viewed as undesirable and confusing. This is all the more important because people rotate through the schedule individually rather than in groups like the New York sanitation workers. Can you imagine trying to arrange a car pool with this schedule?

5. a. Careful forecasts of work requirements are used to prepare the work schedules.

   b. Float pools, call-in personnel, and the reassignment of regular staff are three common tools.

13-2 MANAGING DEMAND

There are many ways to manage the pattern of consumer demand to align it more effectively with service capacity. Pricing and reservation systems are two common ways of altering demand. Fitzsimmons and Sullivan (1982) mention other ways in which demand is managed, namely, *partitioning demand, promoting off-peak demand*, and developing *complementary services.*

Pricing strategies involving discounts or premiums are often used to attract consumers to times when excess service capacity is available, as well as to discourage use during peak demand. For example, telephone companies charge off-peak rates to make use of excess capacity in the evening hours and on weekends. The difference between the regular rate and the discounted rate discourages some users from making calls during the day, when businesses utilize the service extensively. Airlines also offer less expensive fares for travel that does not coincide with business travel.

Reservation or *appointment systems* reduce uncertainty in demand by allowing both the provider of the service and the customer to reserve future capacity. This reduction in uncertainty often leads to lower waiting times for the service. It also enables the organization to make better use of its capacity.

Customer demand can often be broken down into different categories (or segments). For instance, in an automobile repair shop, customers' needs can vary anywhere from an oil change to a major engine overhaul. The nature of the service, and also the length of time required to complete the service, differ dramatically across the various categories of customers. Partitioning demand involves recognizing the various categories of demand and strategically separating them so that both capacity and demand can be better managed.

A hospital emergency room (ER) provides an example of the effective use of partitioning demand. The critical needs of emergency patients require that the ER be adequately staffed to accommodate peak-demand requirements. The costs of maintaining this service level throughout the entire hospital, however, would be prohibitive. By partitioning total patient demand into emergency and nonemergency patients, hospitals can better manage ER capacity. Because some patients visit the ER for nonemergency medical needs, hospitals sometimes maintain the partitioning of demand through differential pricing or insurance reimbursement policies. Also, within the group of patients visiting the ER, demand is further partitioned by a triage function which separates patients into categories, depending on the nature of the illness. This more refined partitioning allows for patients to be scheduled on the basis of their needs and leads to more effective use of ER capacity.

In addition to employing pricing strategies that shift demand away from peak loads, services also promote off-peak demand by identifying other sources of demand that can utilize their service. For example, resort hotels often seek conference business in the off season, and many colleges offer educational and athletic programs for younger students in the summer months.

Service organizations also develop complementary services[4] to facilitate the matching of supply and demand. Many restaurants offer a bar service. In addition to providing an additional source of revenue, the bar serves as a waiting area for the restaurant, allowing demand to be postponed (not for too long). Similarly, airports offer gift shops and newsstands to waiting passengers.

If the firm is able to develop *countercyclical* services, demand can be spread more uniformly throughout the year. For example, a lawn-mower repair shop may repair snowmobiles in the winter to utilize its capacity more effectively year-round.

These strategies seek to overcome the inability to inventory a service by allowing for the management of demand so that it can be better matched with capacity. As the examples illustrate, these strategies are closely related and may be used together. Pricing strategies, for example, can be used in conjunction with partitioning demand, as is the case with first-class and coach service in airline travel.

Appointment Systems

As was noted earlier, appointment systems can be beneficial to both the consumer and the provider of a service. To be efficient, providers must not incur excessive idle time. Unfortunately, this often means that the consumer must accept a delay while waiting for service. Queuing theory models, such as the ones described in Appendix A, are useful in exploring the trade-off between consumer and provider delays. A well-designed appointment system, however, has the capability of reducing delays for both parties, as well as of increasing the productivity of providers with no increase in consumer waiting times.

There are many variables that affect the design of an appointment system. A list of the most significant ones is shown in Table 13-6. Experimentation on alternative appointment systems has relied on both field trials and computer simulation. Fortunately, the results are fairly easy to grasp and implement, although their development was a long and difficult task.

The behavioral characteristics of consumers and providers under different appointment systems are a crucial factor. For example, Rockart and Hofmann (1969) reported that both physicians and patients act more responsibly (more punctual, fewer no-shows) when the appointment system is more personal (customer given definite appointment time, or customer assigned a particular server rather than first available). This is particularly significant because many researchers have found that punctuality and no-show rate have a significant influence on the effectiveness of an appointment system.

The United Hospital Fund of New York (1967) recommended a six-step procedure for designing an appointment system:

1. *Establish the appointment interval.* This is based on the average time

---

[4] This should be distinguished from *complimentary* services.

Table 13-6 Factors Important in Designing an Appointment System

Customer characteristics
Punctuality of customers
Cancellations
No-shows (cancellation without notice)
Walk-in rate (no appointment)
Call-in rate (last-minute appointments)
Categories of customers
Priorities among categories
Properties of arrival rate and service time (variation by time of day, day of week, customer category, etc.)
Provider characteristics
Alternative providers
Punctuality
Service capabilities
Need for breaks
Need for consultation
Absenteeism
System characteristics
Number of services
Appointment interval (every 15 minutes, for example)
Appointment loading (how many customers are given the same appointment time?)
Type of appointment (customer given a time and a server, or only a time and takes first available server)
Priority system (who's next?)
Follow-up visits
Availability of facilities

spent by the server on each consumer, including all matters directly connected with the service being provided, but excluding coffee breaks and the like. Be sure to allow for follow-up visits occurring later in the same day.

2. *Make allowance for nonarrivals.* Calculate an average percentage of cancellations and no-shows, and overbook to allow for this. Strongly consider overbooking the first appointment of the day, since without this redundancy, a no-show or late arrival at this time is guaranteed to leave a server idle. (Overbooking is discussed further presently.)
3. *Establish the number of appointment slots per day.* From the number of server-hours per day, deduct time for breaks and other interruptions, and deduct an estimated amount of time (if any) to be devoted to walk-in customers (those without appointments). Divide the remaining time by the chosen appointment interval to establish how many appointments to make.
4. *Make appointments for the full day.* If properly designed, there will be adequate allowances to avoid overcrowding near the end of the day. Vary the number of appointments by time of day to allow for periods when large numbers of walk-ins are expected, and to allow for same-day follow-up visits.
5. *Maintain appointment order.* Do not use a first-come, first-served rule, as it will encourage people to arrive excessively early, and thereby increase congestion.

6. *Maintain the system*. Management must review system performance, make sure the rules are being followed, and adjust the system as necessary. Without maintenance, the system can fall apart.

The effect of all these rules is to balance the flow of customers with the capabilities of the providers, and to reduce substantially the random fluctuations in work load which lead to both congestion and idle periods.

In many situations walk-in arrivals and no-shows occur in a pattern. Identification of such patterns allows for the effective partitioning of demand. For example, typically there is a time-of-day and a day-of-week pattern for walk-in patients at a health clinic. As a result, the number of appointments should be decreased during the heavy walk-in times and increased at other times to achieve a balance. It is necessary to count the walk-in arrivals during each hour of each day for several weeks to establish the pattern. Careful collection and analysis of data are fundamental to both the design and the control of an appointment system.

Computers are widely used in large-scale appointment and reservation systems. This has been particularly useful in the airline industry and in health clinics. The main advantages of the computer systems are the ease of locating available appointments and of making changes, and the capability of generating reports for management on a regular basis, with a minimum of clerical effort.

Overbooking

Appointments represent future capacity reserved for a specific demand. If a customer does not show up for an appointment, this capacity will be lost. Consequently, many services deliberately overbook customers (that is, make more reservations than can be accommodated) to make the best use of available capacity. The optimal number of customers to overbook depends on the (opportunity) cost of the unused capacity, the shortage cost of having overbooked customers who cannot be served, and the distribution of customer no-shows. The newsperson model discussed in Chapter 8 is useful for calculating overbooking policies.

Assume that we have a probability distribution for the number of no-shows, NS, and let $P(NS \geq X)$ be the probability that $NS \geq X$. If we plan on a certain number of no-shows, and the actual number of no-shows turns out to be less than we planned, we will have too many customers and insufficient capacity to serve them. Let C_S be the shortage cost per customer when this occurs. Alternatively, if the number of no-shows is higher than expected, we will have leftover capacity which will go unused. Let C_U be the (opportunity) cost per customer of this unused capacity. Applying the newsperson formula to this setting, the optimal number of customers to overbook, B, is given by

$$P(NS \geq B) \geq \frac{C_S}{C_U + C_S}$$

where B is the largest value of NS for which the second inequality is satisfied. (If the distribution for NS is continuous, we will be able to find a value of B satisfying $P(NS \geq B) = C_S/(C_U + C_S)$.

Consider the example of an exclusive gourmet restaurant that offers its 7:00 Saturday-evening dinner sitting on a reservation-only basis. The (opportunity) cost to the restaurant of a customer who does not honor a dinner reservation is $100, which is equal to the average contribution margin of a dinner. If a customer has been given a dinner reservation but arrives to find that no table is available, the resulting expected shortage cost is $225. This expected shortage cost represents the cost of providing those customers who choose to wait until the next sitting with complimentary drinks and appetizers, as well as the loss of goodwill resulting from customers being overbooked at a supposedly exclusive restaurant.

The distribution of no-shows is provided in the following table:

Number of No-shows (X)	Probability	$P(NS \geq X)$
0	0.15	1.00
1	0.18	0.85
2	0.19	0.67
3	0.36	0.48
4	0.11	0.12
5	0.01	0.01
≥6	0	0

To determine the optimal overbooking policy, observe that $C_S/(C_U + C_S) = 225/(100 + 225) = 0.69$. Since this is a discrete distribution, the optimal number of customers to overbook, B, is equal to the largest value of no-shows, X, satisfying $P(NS \geq X) \geq 0.69$; hence, $B = 1$. The restaurant should therefore overbook one customer at the 7:00 sitting.

Scheduling Passenger Service

Air, bus, and train passenger systems have three elements to schedule: crews, equipment, and passengers. Unlike an office-based service, these elements physically move. Coordination that involves *where* as well as *when* makes this problem different from professional services such as medical and legal. However, we will see that some of the elements previously described are still useful.

Competition and regulation are key elements in passenger transportation. One aspect of the scheduling decision is to determine the degree to which customer purchasing behavior may be influenced by changing the price structure (special fares for low-travel times) or the service offered (routes, times, movies, etc.).

Airlines have also been successful in partitioning passenger demand by offering standby fares, as well as different classes of discount fares that must be booked a minimum number of days or weeks in advance of the flight. For example, the same flight may have a 30-day (purchased in advance) ''supersaver'' fare as well as a seven-day fare. The lower fares, which must be paid in advance, offer the airlines the opportunity to presell future capacity and, therefore, reduce demand uncertainty. However, only a limited number of each type of advance-purchase fare is offered, since these fares are lower than regular fares sold closer to flight time. Therefore, it is necessary for airlines to identify booking policies that optimally trade off the benefits and costs of special fares. (Glover et al. 1982 describe a system for determining the number of special-fare seats to make available on each segment of 600 Frontier Airline flights. Their system successfully dealt with 30,000 different passenger itineraries. Robinson

1991 defines optimal and approximate airline booking policies when fare classes arrive in sequential blocks.)

One of the difficulties of passenger booking, as with any other appointment system, is last-minute cancellations. This is countered by deliberate overbooking, as was discussed previously. The CAB requires airlines to compensate passengers who are bumped as a result of overbooking. A policy has been instituted whereby airlines ask for volunteers who will accept a fixed compensation in exchange for a change in their tickets. This allows the inconvenience due to cancellations to be transferred to individuals who are not on a tight schedule. To limit the problem, many classes of tickets impose a penalty for cancellation; that is, they are only partially refundable.

Using pricing techniques, in conjunction with offering many fare categories, overbooking, and allowing restricted tickets to be used on a standby basis, constitute what is called *yield management*. Yield management is important to services such as airlines and hotels because of the potential loss of revenue due to low utilization. An airplane flight (or hotel night) represents a nearly fixed cost, and an opportunity to maximize revenue. Empty seats or beds are gone forever. Many papers discuss techniques to maximize revenue using operations management models. (Kimes 1989 gives a discussion and review of yield management.)

When scheduling a passenger service, the three elements (crews, equipment, and passengers) usually have different destinations. Typically a crew will be routed so as to have a round-trip of short duration (one or two days) with appropriate rest periods. The vehicle may have a longer round-trip, involving several different crews and very little time off, until scheduled maintenance is due. The passengers may spend a shorter or longer time with a given vehicle than does the crew; this will generally vary among passengers, depending on their destinations and which other carriers they use on their trips.

Vehicle schedules are based on the type of equipment and its reliability. For example, it is desirable (and perhaps necessary) to avoid landing large-capacity aircraft in low-traffic areas. It is important to have good information readily available to allow rapid decision making in the event of equipment failure. It may be necessary to reassign several aircraft, for example, to take one out of service in Denver, when the nearest spare is in Seattle.

Crew assignments are typically based on seniority. Designing a system of round-trips that cover an entire network is very difficult. There are nearly unlimited combinations, and it is inevitable that some will be less desirable than others. It is sometimes necessary to transport crew members in passenger seats to complete a cycle. Marsten et al. (1979) defined an integer programming-based airline-crew planning process that has been successfully applied in the airfreight industry. Many commercial airlines continue to use effective crew-scheduling models that utilize integer programming models.

The computer has been a blessing to the passenger reservation system. Careful programming and engineering have made it possible to ascertain almost instantly alternative ways to get from point A to point B, the cost, and the availability of seats. (Hopper 1990 discusses the effective use of a computer-based information system in the airline industry.)

Scheduling Extended-Stay Customers

Hotels, hospitals, nursing homes, and other such facilities have a scheduling problem that is unique because most of the customers' time in the system is not in the direct presence of the producer of the service. In fact, it is often convenient to conceptualize a server as a bed, or perhaps a room, rather than the personnel who staff the facility. When this is done, the same scheduling principles apply as in the short-stay situations described previously. Unfortunately, this may overlook one or more of the primary functions of an institution. For example, a resort hotel provides a room, recreational programs, meals, entertainment, and perhaps transportation. A scheduling method that concentrated only on rooms might be disruptive to some of the other functions.

The epitome of this situation is the hospital. Many surgical procedures are not urgent and may be scheduled. This leaves room to schedule for the convenience of patients, doctors, operating-room staff, regular nursing staff, recovery-room staff, admitting department, X-ray, laboratory, and so on. Unfortunately, these various points of view conflict. For example, surgeons like to schedule several operations in a block, to minimize disruption of their other activities. Using a less rigid schedule could require the surgeon to make many trips back and forth between office and operating room while office patients sit and wait.

Operating-room staff also need a regular schedule. The key to this problem is to schedule operations so that utilization of the operating room is fairly uniform. This reduces the idle time of staff and facilities, so that the required procedures can be done without excessive overtime. Weiss (1990) discusses issues pertaining to the scheduling of operating rooms and defines a heuristic procedure that trades off operating-room idle time against physician waiting time.

A hospital-admission scheduling system (see Hancock et al. 1976) anticipates the variation in admissions in several ways. Surgical scheduling gives rise to a day-of-the-week fluctuation in admissions and discharges. Beds must be held empty on Saturday to allow for the expected excess of admissions over discharges that occurs on Sunday, Monday, and Tuesday. An additional allowance is made for the expected number of emergency patients plus a safety margin to assure that all emergencies can be handled. Figure 13-1 show that

Figure 13-1 Patient Types and Hospital Units. Admissions are shown by solid arrows and transfers by dashed arrows.

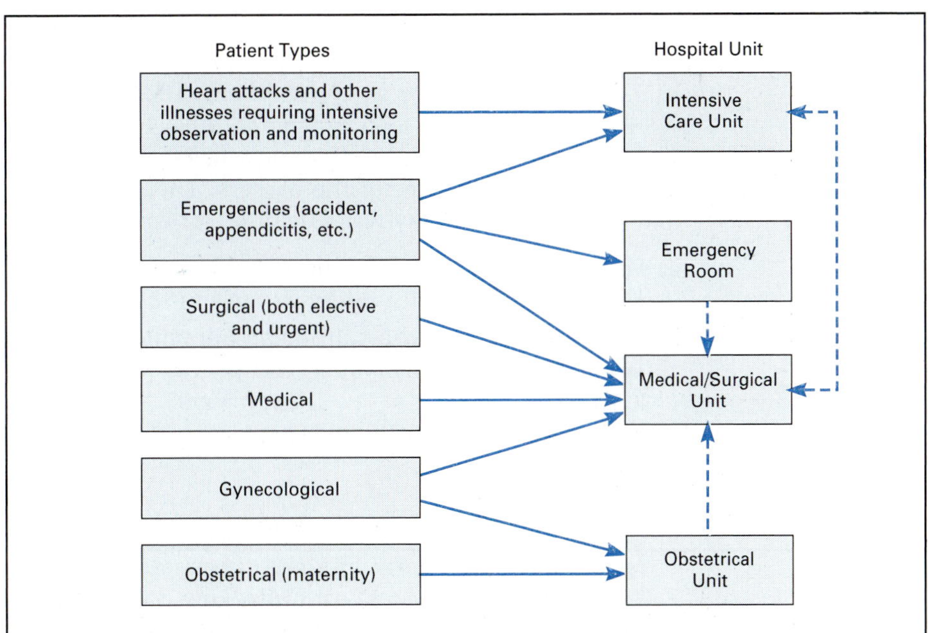

there are many types of patients, and that they can be transferred between departments (units) of the hospital, sometimes for convenience (because of a full unit) or because of medical necessity. For example, the intensive-care unit has an interchange of patients with the medical-surgical unit.

This kind of system gives fixed quotas of admissions to various categories of patients (with the exception of emergencies). It can also incorporate a call-in list of patients who have agreed to be flexible in their date of admission in exchange for an earlier admission. The result is a more reliable pattern of facility utilization than can be achieved with an unplanned admissions program. With proper fine-tuning, admission scheduling can bring about several kinds of improvements. For example, it can increase the uniformity of patient census through the week, and reduce the variation from planned or expected levels. Both these achievements make it easier to obtain low-cost work schedules for hospital personnel, using methods such as those described in the previous section.

As was discussed previously, similar principles can be applied in hotels and other settings in the context of yield management. One of the important aspects of a scheduling system is simplicity of operation. It is vital that the rationale behind the system be understood by those who use it. A hotel manager and a desk clerk, for example, must understand why it is important to retain some empty rooms prior to an unexpected influx such as a convention. If not, they will not use the scheduling system as intended, and the desired improvements will not be achieved.

The key to consumer scheduling consists of good data on when and what kinds of demands will be made, and how long it takes to serve the customers. With these data at hand, simple scheduling systems can be devised that reduce customer delay and increase provider efficiency.

REVIEW PROBLEMS

1. Joe's Barbershop offers only three services: shaves, haircuts, and special haircuts (i.e., hairstyling). Two years ago Joe established an appointment system at the request of some of his longtime customers. Now, about 50% of the customers call for an appointment. There are three barbers, and they work 7 hours per day, after lunch and other breaks are deducted. During a 1-week period (5 days), careful note was taken of the number of customers served and the idle time of the barbers. There were 220 customers served, and 30% of the workday was idle time, for each barber.

   a. From these data, what is the average service time per customer? Is this an appropriate service interval to use in scheduling customers?

   b. Of the customers who call for an appointment, 10% do not keep their appointments. How many appointments should be scheduled (at most) for a given day?

   c. How should these appointments be distributed throughout the hours of the day?

2. a. In the gourmet-restaurant example, suppose that the average cost to the restaurant of each customer who does not show up for a reservation is $120 and the (shortage) cost of booking a reservation but not being able to honor it is $50 per customer. Assuming that the distribution of no-

shows does not change, what is the optimal number of customers to overbook?

b. The gourmet restaurant has decided to implement a policy of overbooking two customers. The cost of each customer who does not show up for a reservation is \$120, and the distribution of no-shows is unchanged. What is the maximum implied shortage cost per customer to the restaurant of not being able to honor a reservation? What is the minimum implied shortage cost?

Solutions

1. a. There were 35 work-hours per barber, or 105 for the week, but only 70% were actually used, or 73.5 hours. Over 220 customers, this averages 0.334 hour, or 20 minutes per customer.

   Since there are three categories of service, one could refine the appointment interval to depend on the work desired. For example, if the appointment interval were 15 minutes, two intervals could be assigned to the special hair cuts. One would need more specific service-time data to do this.

   b. If the appointment interval is 20 minutes, a barber can serve 3 per hour, so the shop can handle 63 per day. If the past is any indication, half of these 63 would be walk-ins, and we would like the other half to be by appointment. Allowing for a 10% no-show rate, we would make up to $(0.5)(63)/(0.90) = 35$ appointments.

   c. If there is any pattern to the walk-in arrivals, the appointments should be concentrated in periods when walk-ins are fewer. Also, one might wish to give more than one appointment per barber at opening time, in case a customer is late or cancels. However, with only a 10% no-show rate, this seems undesirable.

2. a. In this case, $C_S = \$50$ and $C_U = \$120$, so $C_S/(C_U + C_S) = 50/(120 + 50) = 0.29$. The optimal number of customers to overbook is $B = 3$, since $P(NS \geq 3) = 0.48 > 0.29$ and $P(NS \geq 4) = 0.12 < 0.29$.

   b. The restaurant has decided to use $B = 2$. Observe that $P(NS \geq 2) = 0.67$. Since $C_U = \$120$, setting $C_S/(120 + C_S) = 0.67$ and solving for C_S yields $C_S = 243.63$ (rounding down to the nearest penny). This is the *maximum* implied shortage cost per customer. The *minimum* implied shortage cost per customer is found by solving $C_S/(120 + C_S) > P(NS \geq 3) = 0.48$, which yields $C_S > 110.769$. Therefore, 110.77 is the minimum implied shortage cost. All values of C_S between 110.77 and 243.63 cause $B = 2$ to be optimal.

13-3 JOINTLY SCHEDULING CONSUMERS AND PRODUCERS

The examples of personnel scheduling in Section 13-1 assumed that work requirements were known and fixed. In Section 13-2 consumer demands were managed to better accommodate provider capacity. When both consumer and provider are subject to management, scheduling can take into account the preferences and availability of each. This section gives examples that fall into two categories: route selection and conflict avoidance.

Route Selection

The choice of routes can have major cost and revenue effects. In the passenger-service sector, establishing a new link between two cities can affect the traffic on all other links. The new link could lure more traffic from competitors by providing more convenient connections, but it could lower traffic in some parts of the system by providing an alternate route.

The *traveling salesman problem* (*TSP*) is a well-known route-selection problem that is often part of the more complex routing problems discussed presently. Given a set of cities, a *tour* is a path through all the cities that visits each city exactly once. If we are also given distances between pairs of cities, the problem of finding the minimum cost tour is the TSP. The TSP is known to be difficult. Because of its important application, it has been the subject of much research (see Lawler et al., 1985). A recent article in the *Wall Street Journal* (Bishop 1991) reported on the discovery of a new procedure by Miller and Pekny (1991) for solving certain classes of large TSPs. Theoretical advances such as these hold great promise for the future application of TSP to large-scale routing and scheduling problems.

School-bus routes are assigned partly on the basis of the cost of equipment and labor. Although covering a smaller geographical area than airlines or other commercial carriers, the problem is nevertheless very complicated because of the large number of locations for passenger pickup and the desire to keep the time spent on the bus to a minimum. Gochenour et al. (1980) describe a simple heuristic used in selecting school-bus routes. Thomas and Wells (1980) report on a transport system designed to relieve the housing shortage at the University of Manitoba by making larger areas of the city accessible for apartment-dwelling students.

Meals on Wheels is a volunteer service organization that provides hot meals to persons who live at home but cannot cook for themselves. Bartholdi et al. (1983) describe a method of rapidly assigning clients to drivers and establishing a route. The system is based on two Rolodex files and a clear overlay for the city map. Although it is not optimal, the method is quick, easily used, and cuts travel distance by 13%. Adding and deleting clients is a simple matter with this system, in contrast to most optimizing methods in which any change requires a totally new solution.

A number of computerized routing methods have been developed. Stacey (1983) describes VANPLAN applied to a problem with 10,000 to 20,000 customers, 100 to 400 orders per day, and daily rescheduling. Fisher et al. (1982) describe ROVER, an interactive package with color graphics. It was applied to schedule the delivery of consumable supplies to customers of DuPont. The supplies are for use with automatic clinical analyzers, and the customers are located in more than 1000 cities. ROVER determines delivery routes so that each customer can get a shipment every month.

Scheduling to Avoid Conflict

College exams and on-campus employment interviews are examples of services that are scheduled on a one-time basis. (Did you ever consider an exam to be a service?) They differ from appointment systems in that there is a distinct period of time in which all activity is to take place, and the consumer has far less say in the time chosen. All the requirements are known before the schedule is set, and the consumer must accept the assignment. Many other examples exist with similar properties. The general problem is to assign people with the right attributes to perform a set of tasks in a way that optimizes some measure of performance.

Consider the problem of assigning employment interviews (Hill et al., 1983). There are two sets of people: One set represents students seeking jobs and the other set represents interviewers. Students are to be assigned to one or more interviewers, and we wish to be able to specify a (lower and upper) limit on the number of interviewers a student may see, as well as a limit on the number of students an interviewer may see. The objective is to maximize the total utility (benefit) of the employment interviews.

One mathematical formulation of this type of problem uses the variables

$$X_{ij} = \begin{cases} 1 \text{ if student } i \text{ is assigned to interviewer } j \\ 0 \text{ otherwise} \end{cases} \tag{6}$$

The parameters used in the basic formulation include

U_{ij} = utility (benefit) associated with assigning student i to interviewer j

t_i, t_i' = lower and upper limits on the number of interviewers student i may see, respectively

p_j, p_j' = lower and upper limits on the number of students who can be assigned to interviewer j, respectively

The formulation is

$$\text{Max} \sum_i \sum_j U_{ij} X_{ij} \tag{7}$$

subject to

$$t_i \leq \sum_j X_{ij} \leq t_i' \quad \text{for all students } i \tag{8}$$

$$p_j \leq \sum_i X_{ij} \leq p_j' \quad \text{for all interviewers } j \tag{9}$$

$$X_{ij} = 0 \text{ or } 1 \quad \text{for all } i \text{ and } j \tag{10}$$

The utilities of employment interviews (U_{ij}) can be obtained by requiring each student to rank the companies according to the desirability of obtaining an interview. The parameters t_i and t_i' assure that student i is neither shut out of the schedule nor given too many interviews. Similarly, p_j and p_j' specify the minimum and maximum number of students that can be seen by interviewer j.

This problem belongs to a special class of optimization problems known as *network problems*. A network is a graph consisting of a set of *nodes* (or points) and a set of *arcs* (or edges) connecting pairs of nodes. The employment-interview problem is depicted as a network in Figure 13-2. The two sets of nodes correspond to the two sets of people (students and interviewers). The arcs, shown as arrows, represent possible assignments of students to interviewers. The same formulation may be used to allocate a set of tasks to a group of people. (The interviews are the tasks in the preceding example.)

The variable X_{ij} associated with arc (i, j), connecting student i and interviewer j, defines the amount of *flow* shipped along the arc. Since the arc is directed from i to j (as shown by the arrow), flow can only move in this direction. The total flow out of a "student node" represents the number of tasks (interviews) assigned to that student. Similarly, the number of students assigned to interviewer j is the flow into its node. In general, the amount of flow

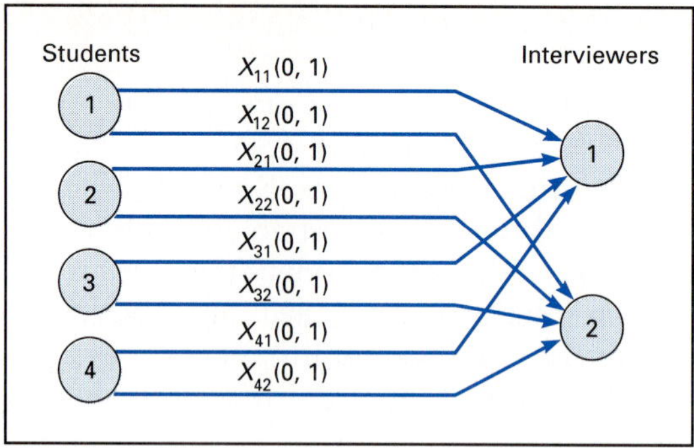

Figure 13-2 The Employment-Interview Problem as a Network

entering (or originating at) a node must equal the amount of flow leaving (or terminating at) the node. This is known as *conservation of flow*. The notation (0,1) on the arcs indicates lower and upper limits on the flows.

If the input data (lower and upper bounds on arc flows, and so forth) is integer, the network formulation will have an optimal solution that has integer values (see Wagner 1975). Thus, the integrality constraints 10 can be replaced by the constraints $0 \leq X_{ij} \leq 1$, for all i and j, and the problem can be solved as a *linear program*. This is a very important property of network models. As was noted in Appendix C, if constraints 10 are required, the problem becomes an *integer program* and is considerably more difficult to solve. Another advantage of a network model is that it can be solved much faster than a general LP. Network algorithms have been devised that are capable of solving large problems quickly.

The special case of the foregoing problem, in which the number of people equals the number of tasks ($t_i = t_i' = 1$ and $p_j = p_j' = 1$) is known as the *assignment problem*. Since it is a network model, the integrality constraints 10 are satisfied automatically. The assignment problem is easily modified to accommodate the situation in which the number of people is not equal to the number of tasks.

In the employment-interview problem suppose that it is also specified that students must satisfy certain traits before being assigned to an interviewer. The network model defined in (7) through (10) can be extended to allow for this, if the traits (k) are mutually exclusive. To model this, let

r_{jk} = the (lower, upper, or exact) limit placed on the students with trait k who are assigned to interviewer j

(For example, interviewer j may want to meet with at least two students who are business majors. In this case k corresponds to business majors and r_{jk} would be the lower limit of two students.) Students' characteristics are then described by the parameters a_{ik}, where

$$a_{ik} = \begin{cases} 1 & \text{if trait } k \text{ is possessed by student } i \\ 0 & \text{otherwise} \end{cases}$$

If some of the interviewers wish to place a lower limit on the number of students with trait k that they interview, the following constraints must then be included in the network model:

$$\sum_i a_{ik}X_{ij} \geq r_{jk} \quad \text{for all interviewers } j \text{ who wish to see a minimum number of students } (r_{jk}) \text{ with attribute } k \tag{11}$$

(Incorporating the traits in the network changes Figure 13-2 substantially. See problem 23.)

Expansion of the network model to include additional constraints that are of a general nature unfortunately interferes with the natural integrality of the solution, and constraints 10 must then be imposed explicitly. The model can no longer be solved as a network problem and must be treated as an integer programming problem. (Mazzola and Neebe 1986 define solution procedures that provide optimal and approximate solutions to assignment problems with additional constraints.)

The interview-assignment situation requires a great deal more than a mathematical model. Great care must be given to collecting accurate information in a timely fashion without an inordinate amount of work. Hill et al. (1983) describe methods for data collection, error checking, and output reporting that are crucial for the successful use of their system. To understand the scope of the effort, consider that they needed 15,000 variables X_{ij} in their model, and each one must have a preference or utility value U_{ij}. To collect such a large volume of data is difficult. To avoid errors in transcribing the data into the computer is practically impossible. To say the least, the implementation of a formal task-assignment method that incorporates preferences requires careful management.

A second example of conflict-avoidance assignment is final-examination scheduling. Here the primary objective is to minimize the number of students who have conflicts such as two exams at the same time or too many exams on the same day. Anderson and Bernhardi (1981) describe a method to develop minimum-conflict schedules based on a mathematical formulation that is very similar to the employment interview problem. Two heuristic (that is, quick but not optimal) solutions were also tried for comparison. An interesting finding was that the heuristics could quickly generate a good starting point for the optimization, making the latter much faster than it otherwise would be.

The preceding examples are all special situations in which the interdependence of consumer and producer schedules is apparent. Reflecting on the first two sections, it is worthwhile to consider how the producer-oriented Section 13-1 and customer-oriented Section 13-2 would be used in practice when both points of view must be adopted. Certainly, some benefits should accrue by taking a broader view than either of those sections implies.

In practice, scheduling consumers and scheduling servers are often separate responsibilities, and coordination between them is loose or missing altogether. One reason for this is that either one alone is extremely complex, and viewing them simultaneously is too difficult. In other cases, the reason is simply tradition: ''That's the way we have always done it!''

As an example of a benefit to be gained by coordination, consider vacation scheduling. There are several times of the year when employees prefer to take their vacations. To grant everyone his or her desired vacation, overtime or part-time hiring may be needed to retain an adequate work force. If it is possible to shift demand away from such intervals, these extra expenses may be avoided. From the other viewpoint, if employees can be encouraged to vacation when demand is low, similar benefits accrue. Thus, joint determination of consumer and producer schedules can be done at the margin even if the responsibilities are separate, and the overall goals of the operation can be better achieved as a result.

REVIEW PROBLEMS

1. How can consumer preferences be accommodated in the selection of school-bus routes? Producer preferences?

2. Consider the network-model formulation of the employment-interview problem. Assume that there are four students and two interviewers, as in Figure 13-2. State the following requirements as mathematical constraints:
   a. Student 1 should not be assigned to more than one interviewer.
   b. At least two students should be assigned to interviewer 2.
   c. Suppose that students 1, 3, and 4 each have at least one year of business experience. Interviewer 1 wants to see at least two students with one or more years of business experience.

Solutions

1. Short bus rides are preferred by both consumers and providers, since they minimize both transportation cost and early rising. Routing to minimize bus mileage will tend to address both concerns. In doing so, there may be one bus route assigned to outlying regions. This bus may take a very long time to complete its tour. The scheduler may wish to introduce a constraint that no one spends longer than a certain amount, while minimizing the average distance of a traveler. (Other answers are possible.)

2. a. $X_{11} + X_{12} \leq 1$.
   b. $X_{12} + X_{22} + X_{32} + X_{42} \geq 2$.
   c. In this case trait k is one or more years of business experience. Since only students 1, 3, and 4 possess this trait, $a_{1k} = a_{3k} = a_{4k} = 1$, and $a_{2k} = 0$. Interviewer 1 wants to see at least two students with work experience, so $r_{1k} = 2$. Therefore, the constraint is

$$X_{11} + X_{31} + X_{41} \geq 2$$

SUMMARY

The production and delivery of a service often require the simultaneous presence of a provider (supply) and a consumer (demand). We have discussed characteristics of services that make it possible to manage both supply and demand in an effective manner that can benefit both parties. However, the design and management of such systems inevitably require that a balance be struck between consumer and provider points of view. For example, the cost of carrying excess service capacity in periods of low demand must be balanced against the cost of not having sufficient capacity in peak-demand periods.

The projected capacity utilization (PCU) provides us with a measure of the ability of capacity to meet demand. The seasonal nature of demand in many services requires that we assess PCU during periods of peak demand. Values of PCU close to or above 100% indicate that the service will not have adequate capacity to meet demand, and long lines will result. PCU provides an index for evaluating the customer-service level, as well as a means for planning capacity.

Both personnel and consumer scheduling systems have several components, ranging from immediate to long-range decisions. Work-force planning requires looking at annual demand patterns, working out vacations, and planning changes in the number of employees, usually on an aggregate basis. Similarly, consumer demand may be managed on a long-run basis by marketing policies such as price promotions.

At the other extreme are the day-to-day decisions involving last-minute changes in work assignments, perhaps using a float pool, and last-minute modification of the consumer schedule, involving cancellations or calling in wait-listed customers.

Between these extremes are scheduling methods. Their objectives vary, but their general function is to work within the annual plans and provide an easily used method that minimizes the amount of last-minute readjustments.

The methods for designing a work schedule range from trial and error (requiring substantial time and effort, and based on rules of thumb and judgment) to sophisticated, computer-based models (easy and inexpensive to use but expensive to develop and implement). We have described a linear programming approach that is useful in some situations and provides the basis for some of the more sophisticated models.

Managing customer demand can be accomplished through the use of strategies involving pricing policies, appointment systems (with or without overbooking), partitioning demand, promotion of off-peak demand, and the development of complementary or countercyclical services. Combinations of these techniques that seek to make effective use of existing capacity fall under the important concept of yield management. Appointment-scheduling systems require attention to fundamental details such as expected service time, punctuality, cancellations, and the arrival of unscheduled customers. Fairly simple rules can incorporate these details. However, the situation becomes much more complicated when the consumer schedules must be merged with the schedules of several categories of providers. We have discussed airlines and hospitals as two illustrations of these difficulties.

Network and assignment models are useful for one-time situations, as is illustrated by employment interviews and exam scheduling. In these two examples the complete schedule can be laid out in advance, and both employers and consumers are required to accept it. Consumer preference and the availability of employees can both be accounted for in these situations, but management has the final say in making the assignment. Most situations are not this clear-cut, but the advantages of coordinating consumer and producer schedules can be substantial.

Behind every scheduling system is an information system, which supplies the data to analyze and forecast demand patterns, and provides other information needed by the personnel who are operating the scheduling system. Airline reservation systems, for example, provide rapid access for ticket agents to information concerning the availability of seats, fares, timing, routes, and so on. They should also be designed to provide management with data on the types and timing of customer demands, to use in exploring schedule changes. This degree of sophistication is not required for every situation, but advancing technology is rapidly bringing computerized scheduling within the reach of even small firms.

PROBLEMS

1. A service differs from a manufactured good in that delivery of the service must occur simultaneously with the demand for it; consequently, the service cannot be inventoried. Explain this statement and provide examples to support your answer.
2. There are many ways to manage a service or product that cannot be inventoried. Define ''capacity management'' and ''demand management,'' and discuss their role in managing such services (or products). In what ways do they complement one another?
3. In a grocery store many of the workers operate as float personnel. Cite two examples.

*4. In an appointment system why is it important to discourage consumers from arriving excessively early for an appointment?

5. Joe's Barbershop has been accepting appointments for haircuts. Most appointments are given during times of the day when walk-in customers are infrequent. Customers are served on a modified first-come, first-served basis; all customers with appointments are served before any walk-in customers. Discuss the advantages and disadvantages of this scheme.
6. The arrival of emergency patients to a hospital is well described by the Poisson probability distribution (Appendix D, Table 5). Suppose that a goal is to make sure that enough beds are available to accommodate all emergency patients with 99% probability, and that the average arrival rate of emergency patients is six per day on Wednesday, when the hospital reaches its peak occupancy.
   a. How many beds should be allocated for emergency arrivals on Wednesday?
   b. If a bed is made available in the emergency room and not used, the cost to the hospital is $50 per bed. To justify a 99% service level in the emergency room, what is the implied cost per emergency patient of not having a bed available? (Hint: Use the newsperson model.)

*7. A large hardware store currently has 14 full-time workers. Management has calculated that 15 workers will be needed on the average during the next 3-month period, but they found that the peak demand during the week will be too high to be handled by a work force of that size. The data are shown in the accompanying table. Full-timers work 5 days per week. Part-time help can be obtained and trained for this kind of work.

Day	Mon.	Tue.	Wed.	Thu.	Fri.	Sat.	Sun.
Workers needed	9.5	12	16	10	10.5	8	8

*Problems with an asterisk have answers in the back of the book.

a. Compare the number of worker-days available from the present work force of 14 people with the amount needed. How many worker-days of part-time help would be needed each week to avoid hiring another full-timer?
b. How many part-timers must be trained to allow for the Wednesday peak with 14 full-timers?
c. Where else during the week would it be logical to use part-timers?
d. Suppose that two part-timers work all day on Wednesday, and part-time help is used to cover the half days on Monday and Friday. One more part-time day must be assigned to some day of the week. What are the advantages and disadvantages of assigning a third part-timer to work a full day Wednesday?
e. Management decided to assign 2 part-timer days to Wednesday, 1 to Tuesday, and 0.5 each to Monday and Friday. Calculate how many days off are available for the full-timers each day of the week, and in total for the week.
f. The union allows the use of part-timers as long as the number of full-timers is 15. How does that change your previous answers?

8. The DJ Sandwich Shop is open six days per week, Monday through Saturday from 10:00 A.M. until 7:00 P.M. The process used for making sandwiches is labor intensive, and capacity is controlled by varying the number of workers scheduled to work throughout the week. The manager can schedule from one to five workers in the sandwich-making area; however, it is too small to handle more than five workers. The number of sandwiches that can be made per hour depends on the number of workers scheduled, as shown in the accompanying table.

Number of Workers	Number of Sandwiches Produced per Hour
1	30
2	60
3	90
4	100
5	120

The average demand for sandwiches, broken down by day of the week and hour of the day, is provided in the following tables:

Average Number of Sandwiches per Day

Monday	320
Tuesday	440
Wednesday	410
Thursday	450
Friday	560
Saturday	520
Average	450

Average Number of Sandwiches per Hour	
10–11 A.M.	20
11–12 noon	60
12–1 P.M.	100
1–2 P.M.	80
2–3 P.M.	30
3–4 P.M.	20
4–5 P.M.	30
5–6 P.M.	70
6–7 P.M.	40
Average	50

a. The manager has hired and trained enough workers to schedule an average of two workers in the sandwich-making area during each hour of the week. What is the resulting weekly projected capacity utilization? Does the sandwich shop have adequate capacity to respond to weekly demand?

b. Identify the hour during the week when peak demand occurs. On the basis of projected capacity utilization, does the sandwich shop have adequate capacity to meet this demand?

c. The preceding table indicates that after a certain point, as the number of workers making sandwiches increases, the number of sandwiches made per worker decreases. Explain why this might occur.

9. Consider the Yuppie Car Wash example of Section 13-1. Suppose that Yuppie is still open six days per week, Tuesday through Sunday; now, however, the hours of operation are 11:00 A.M. to 8:00 P.M., Tuesday through Friday, and 9:00 A.M. to 6:00 P.M. on Saturday and Sunday. Demand data on the average number of cars per day and per hour are provided in the following tables. Because the hours of operation are different on the weekend, separate data are maintained for the average number of cars arriving per hour during the weekend, as indicated in the second table.

Average Number of Cars per Day	
Tuesday	80
Wednesday	95
Thursday	119
Friday	178
Saturday	200
Sunday	156
Average	138

Average Number of Cars Arriving per Hour

	Tuesday–Friday	Saturday, Sunday
9–10 A.M.		12
10–11 A.M.		25
11–12 noon	8	20
12– 1 P.M.	20	35
1– 2 P.M.	12	20
2– 3 P.M.	1	20
3– 4 P.M.	2	10
4– 5 P.M.	10	15
5– 6 P.M.	18	21
6– 7 P.M.	32	
7– 8 P.M.	15	

a. Yuppie can run both ACWs anytime it wishes, and it has hired and trained enough workers to staff each of the two ICCs at an average level of 1.75 workers per hour during the course of the week. Compute the average weekly projected capacity utilization of *each* stage of the car wash. Which stage appears to be more capacity constrained?

b. Assume that management recognizes the hour during the week in which peak demand occurs and has assigned three workers to each ICC during that hour. What is the projected capacity utilization of *each* stage of the process during the peak-demand hour?

*10. In the sanitation workers examples of Tables 13-2 and 13-3, suppose that Spokane, Washington, wishes to form a rotating schedule of the same type. Their weekly trash load is 3500 tons, generated in equal amounts of 500 tons on each of the 7 days of the week. Each collection crew can handle 50 tons per day and works 5 days per week. There are 16 trucks in the fleet but only 15 are available each day because of a rotating maintenance schedule.

a. How many crews are needed?

b. Given your answer to part a, how much uncollected trash will remain after Monday's collection and after Tuesday's collection if none of the crews is permitted to take either Monday or Tuesday off? (Remember that no one works on Sunday. Assume that no trash remains uncollected after Saturday's pick up.)

c. Devise a rotating schedule that minimizes uncollected trash, using your answers to parts a and b and the approach of Table 13-3. Not all of the days-off pairs need be used in your answer.

d. Propose an alternative schedule that has one 3-day weekend but also follows the approach of Table 13-3.

e. Compare the amounts of uncollected trash in parts c and d.

11. (This problem requires a solution to problem 10.) A new neighborhood has been added to Spokane, and their trash of 150 tons is collected on Friday. Part-time workers have been suggested as one way to increase the system capacity by 150 tons per week to adjust to the

new demand. However, as was noted previously, there are only 15 trucks available. Trash can only be collected during the normal working hours.

a. Suggest a method for using part-timers without increasing the amount of uncollected trash, compared with the solution of problem 10, part c.

b. Suggest a schedule that requires only one part-time crew, working more than one day, but that allows the full-timers to have Monday off.

12. Legal Associates, Incorporated (LAI), is staffed by three lawyers and 15 full-time paralegal personnel (PLPs). The PLPs provide service directly to customers in many situations that involve common transactions and standard forms. They also do certain research and other tasks for the lawyers. PLPs work five days per week, and the office is open six days per week (closed Sunday). The demand for PLP services is shown in the accompanying table. Each PLP can handle an average of eight clients per day.

Day	Mon.	Tue.	Wed.	Thu.	Fri.	Sat.	Sun.
Clients	130	100	116	90	144	60	0

Other legal offices provide similar services, so LAI tries to satisfy all demands, to avoid losing customers to their competitors. This sometimes requires that the lawyers take some of the PLP clients.

a. Analyze the demand pattern and show how many full-time PLPs are required each day of the week. How much PLP work is being done by the lawyers?

b. Making assumptions as necessary, decide on how many days off can be taken each day of the week. Remember that PLPs work only full days, five days per week.

c. Devise a days-off schedule similar to Table 13-3 for the PLPs. Not all day-off pairs need be used in your answer.

13. The accompanying table shows the days off available for the 14 employees of a hardware store.

Day	Mon.	Tue.	Wed.	Thu.	Fri.	Sat.	Sun.
Days off	5	3	1	4	4	6	6

a. Formulate an LP that will choose among the schedules in Table 13-4 so as to maximize the number of days-off pairs that are consecutive for the hardware store employees. If you have access to an LP computer program, find the optimal solution.

b. Add a constraint that will assure that the Saturday-Sunday pair will be used at least five times in the schedule. Again, solve it if you can. Compare the solution with part a and explain the similarities and differences.

c. What is wrong with the solution that assigns x_4 = Thursday-Friday = 4, x_6 = Saturday-Sunday = 8, x_1 = Monday-Tuesday = 3, u_1 = Monday (unpaired) = 2, and all other variables equal to 0?

14.

Week	Sun.	Mon.	Tue.	Wed.	Thu.	Fri.	Sat.
1	X	X					
2		X	X				
3			X	X			
4				X	X		
5					X	X	
6						X	X
7	X						X

a. There are two 3-day weekends in this schedule. Find them.

b. How many uninterrupted intervals of workdays are there in this seven-week schedule, and how many days are in each one?

c. How many groups of workers will be on duty each day of the week if this schedule is applied on a rotating basis to seven work groups?

*15. Multiple-shift rotating schedules can be made from the table given in problem 14. (You need not do problem 14 to answer this one.) Suppose that there are 21 work groups and three shifts.

a. Devise a rotating schedule whereby each group works seven weeks of day shift (D), seven of evening (E), and seven of night (N).

b. How many work groups will be on duty each shift?

*16. A brokerage firm wants to establish an appointment system that applies to customers who telephone as well as to those who visit the office. Appointive telephone consultations would be carried out by the broker returning the client's call at the appointed time. The appointments would be limited to people who call for advice and discussion (consultation). Buy and sell orders would still be accepted as they arrive.

The average office visit of a new customer lasts 50 minutes, whereas office visits by established customers average 20 minutes in duration. Phone calls for consultation average 10 minutes duration for all customers. Buy and sell orders require 1 minute of the broker's time on the average, with the balance of the call handled by a clerk. These 1-minute calls do not interrupt office or phone consultations, since the broker usually needs only to approve the clerk's work. If the client wishes to speak to the broker, the call is returned when the broker is free. New customers constitute 40% of office visits, 20% of phone calls for consultation, and no part of buy and sell orders.

There are five brokers in the firm, and the percentages quoted previously vary among the brokers depending on their seniority with the firm, since the more senior brokers have more permanent clients. Office hours are 9:00 A.M. to 6:00 P.M. with 1 hour off for lunch.

There are 150 demands for broker service on the average day, of which 25% are office visits, 25% are phone calls for consultation, and 50% are buy and sell orders.

a. They wish to establish an appointment interval that can be used for phone consultations, with several intervals assigned for each appointment. What is the appropriate appointment interval?

b. How many appointment intervals should there be per day? Be sure to allow for buy and sell calls and for personal time (in the amount of 30 minutes per broker per day).

c. How much idle time will there be per day?

d. What is the maximum number of "new customer" office visits you would recommend scheduling for a given day?

e. Qualitatively, how should the new customer appointments be distributed over the hours of the day? (Should they be concentrated at any particular hours? Are there times to avoid?) How should they be distributed among the five brokers?

*17. The Big-Red Tour Bus Company offers a first-class guided tour of the major sites in historic downtown Podunk. The only tour bus leaves from the train station each day at 1:00 P.M. The tour has become so popular that each tour is easily filled, and seats on the bus are available by reservation only. Reservations are made by telephone, as well as through the major hotels in town. Unfortunately, some tourists reserve seats on the bus but then fail to show up. The tour bus company is trying to determine an appropriate overbooking policy.

Each time a reserved seat remains unfilled, the company experiences an average opportunity cost of $10 due to the lost contribution. If a tourist is overbooked and is unable to participate in the tour because of a lack of seats, the company tries to create an empty seat by offering already seated passengers a complimentary seat on the following day's tour or a free dinner at a local restaurant. On the average, the shortage cost of having an overbooked tourist who cannot be seated is $25. Based on past experience, the distribution of no-shows (NS) is as follows:

Number of No-shows (X)	Probability	P(NS $\geq$ X)
0	0.07	1.00
1	0.11	0.93
2	0.14	0.82
3	0.18	0.68
4	0.17	0.50
5	0.10	0.33
6	0.09	0.23
7	0.07	0.14
8	0.04	0.07
9	0.02	0.03
10	0.01	0.01
$\geq$11	0	0

a. Determine the optimal number of seats to overbook on the tour bus.

b. If the bus company decides to overbook three seats on the bus, in what range would the implied shortage cost of insufficient seating capacity have to fall to justify the overbooking policy.

18. The Sixstar Hotel offers luxurious, first-class service in a major metropolitan area. Rooms are available on a reservation-only basis. (The idea of walking into the lobby and asking whether a room is available would be "unthinkable.") The hotel is consistently able to reserve all rooms on a regular basis.

Despite its select clientele, the Sixstar nonetheless experiences no-shows. So far, the hotel has decided not to overbook rooms. However, the average lost contribution from a vacant room is $150, and management is seriously considering the implementation of an overbooking policy.

According to management, for each guest who arrives at the hotel with a reservation but for whom no room is available, several different costs might ensue. There is a 20% chance that the guest would accept a half-rate room voucher to the nearby Fivestar Hotel (at a cost of $50 to the Sixstar); a 25% chance that the overbooked guest would only accept a full-rate room voucher to the Fivestar (costing the Sixstar $100); a 40% chance that the guest would require a full-rate room voucher to the Fivestar, along with a dinner voucher at the Sixstar (costing the Sixstar a total of $120); and finally, a 15% chance that the customer would not be satisfied by any of these alternatives, in which case the penalty shortage cost to the Sixstar is estimated to be $250, due primarily to the loss of goodwill.

The distribution of no-shows at the Sixstar Hotel is provided in the following table:

Number of No-shows (X)	Probability	$P(NS \geq X)$
0	0.20	1.00
1	0.30	0.80
2	0.25	0.50
3	0.15	0.25
4	0.08	0.10
5	0.02	0.02
≥ 6	0	0

a. Determine the optimal overbooking policy for the Sixstar Hotel.

b. For the current policy of not overbooking any rooms to be justified, what is the *minimum* implied expected shortage cost for each guest who has a reservation but for whom no room is available?

*19. There are 160 certified medical-surgical (MS) beds in Central Hospital, although up to 165 patients can be accommodated. Half the patients are surgical cases, and the other half are admitted for other medical reasons. In each case, half the patients stay three days and half stay six days. One-fourth of all MS patients are classified as emergencies, having problems too urgent to delay admission, whereas the remainder can wait for up to two weeks for an opportune admission appointment.

Currently, among medical patients only emergency patients are admitted on Saturday and Sunday, and the admission pattern is heaviest in the early part of the week. This gives the doctors a better opportunity to minimize their weekend hospital rounds. The surgical admissions follow a similar pattern, except that Friday and Saturday are lowest in admissions, whereas Sunday is a popular day, so that patients may be worked up for Monday surgery.

The hospital administrator has been concerned by the low occupancy on weekends and is trying to convince the doctors to admit more medical patients on the low-admission days. The current and proposed admissions patterns are shown in the first two of the accompanying tables, along with the status of the patients who are in the hospital today, a Thursday.

Current Admissions Pattern

	Sun.	Mon.	Tue.	Wed.	Thu.	Fri.	Sat.	Total
Medical (scheduled)	0	20	20	18	16	10	0	84
Medical (emergency)	4	4	4	4	4	4	4	28
Surgical (scheduled)	20	20	18	16	10	0	0	84
Surgical (emergency)	4	4	4	4	4	4	4	28
	28	48	46	42	34	18	8	224

Proposed Admissions Pattern

	Sun.	Mon.	Tue.	Wed.	Thu.	Fri.	Sat.	Total
Medical (scheduled)	10	14	14	12	12	12	10	84
Medical (emergency)	4	4	4	4	4	4	4	28

(The remainder is the same as the current pattern.)

Patient Status Today (a Thursday) and Probable Status Tomorrow

Days Remaining in Hospital	Number of Patients		
	Thursday (Today)	Friday Admissions	Friday Total
6	17	9	9
5	21		17
4	23		21
3	41	9	32
2	35		41
1	27		35
Total = census	164		155
Discharges	33		27

a. Calculate how many patients will be in the hospital on each of the next seven days using the current admissions pattern. The first day's calculations are shown in the patient status table.

b. Do the same for the proposed patterns. (The new pattern starts tomorrow.)

c. Study the results of part a and criticize the current admissions pattern.

d. Does the proposed pattern allow the hospital to increase its intake of surgical patients? Discuss.

20. (Central Hospital is described in problem 19. It is desirable to have solved problem 19 before doing this one.) The surgeons at Central Hospital wish to keep their admissions pattern unchanged, allowing them to perform most of their surgery Monday through Thursday. At the time an admission is scheduled, a surgeon can predict with fair accuracy (about 75%) whether the patient will have a three-day or a six-day stay. Suggest how the surgeons could reduce the peak census (Thursday's) and increase the weekend census.

*21. In the set of schedules shown here, each of nine work groups follows the pattern from problem 14 (consecutive days off), but they rotate between shifts at different points in the schedule.

a. How many work groups are on duty on each shift during each day of the seven weeks?

b. Show that the groups do not have equal work assignments.

c. What managerial advantages and disadvantages does this schedule have?

	Week 1[a]							Week 2							Week 3							Week 4						
Group	**S**	**M**	**T**	**W**	**T**	**F**	**S**	**S**	**M**	**T**	**W**	**T**	**F**	**S**	**S**	**M**	**T**	**W**	**T**	**F**	**S**	**S**	**M**	**T**	**W**	**T**	**F**	**S**
1			D	D	D	D	D	D			D	D	D	D	D	D			D	D	D	D	D	D			E	E
2	D			E	E	E	E	E	E			E	E	E	E	E	E			N	N	N	N	N	N			D
3	D	D			D	D	D	D	D	D			D	D	D	D	D	D			E	E	E	E	E	E		
4	E	E	E			E	E	E	E	E	E			N	N	N	N	N	N				D	D	D	D	D	
5	D	D	D	D			D	D	D	D	D	D				E	E	E	E	E				E	E	E	E	E
6	E	E	E	E	E				N	N	N	N	N				D	D	D	D	D	D			D	D	D	D
7		D	D	D	D	D				E	E	E	E	E	E			E	E	E	E	E	E			N	N	N
8			N	N	N	N	N	N			D	D	D	D	D	D			D	D	D	D	D	D			D	D
9	N	N			D	D	D	D	D	D			D	D	D	D	D	D			D	D	D	D	D	D		

	Week 5							Week 6							Week 7						
Group	**S**	**M**	**T**	**W**	**T**	**F**	**S**	**S**	**M**	**T**	**W**	**T**	**F**	**S**	**S**	**M**	**T**	**W**	**T**	**F**	**S**
1	E	E	E	E			E	E	E	E	E	E				N	N	N	N	N	
2	D	D	D	D	D				D	D	D	D	D				D	D	D	D	D
3		E	E	E	E	E				N	N	N	N	N	N			D	D	D	D
4			D	D	D	D	D	D			D	D	D	D	D	D			E	E	E
5	E			N	N	N	N	N	N			D	D	D	D	D	D			D	D
6	D	D			D	D	D	D	D	D			E	E	E	E	E	E			E
7	N	N	N			D	D	D	D	D	D			D	D	D	D	D	D		
8	D	D	D	D			E	E	E	E	E	E				E	E	E	E	E	
9		E	E	E	E	E				E	E	E	E	E	E			N	N	N	N

[a]D, day shift; E, evening shift; N, night shift; a blank represents a day off.

22. The M.B.A. class at Corinth University consists of eight students. Three recruiters have agreed to come to campus for employment interviews, but they each have time enough for only four interviews. The placement office wishes to be fair and to please everyone; they want to schedule interviews accordingly. The interviewers have read the résumés of all eight students and have indicated which students they would prefer to interview. Student preferences have been gathered by asking each student to rank the interviewers with rank = 1 indicating the most preferred.

a. Write the constraints of an assignment-type formulation for this problem, following the model of constraints 8 to 10. Some judgment is required to obtain numbers for some of the parameters, such as t_i and p_i. Use your judgment and explain your logic.

b. Several objective functions could be used. Describe at least two and discuss the implications of their use.

23. Consider the application of the network diagram of Figure 13-2 to the assignment of people to tasks. (The set of nodes on the left side of the figure corresponds to people.) Suppose that each task has a (trait) requirement of at least one left-handed and at least one right-handed person. Persons 1 and 2 are lefties, whereas 3 and 4 are righties. Modify the diagram to include these requirements. You will need to add nodes to do this. Indicate a minimum and a maximum flow between two nodes by inserting the two numbers in parentheses on the corresponding arrow.

REFERENCES

ANDERSON, J.M., and R.H. BERNHARDI, "A University Examination Scheduling Model to Minimize Multiple-Examination Days for Students," *Decision Sciences*, vol. 12, no. 2, 1981.

ARTHUR, J.L., and A. RAVINDRAN, "A Multiple Objective Nurse Scheduling Model," *AIIE Transactions*, vol. 13, no. 1, 1981.

BAKER, K.R., and M.J. MAGAZINE, "Workforce Scheduling with Cyclic Demands and Day-Off Constraints," *Management Science*, vol. 24, no. 2, 1977.

BARTHOLDI, J.J., III, K. PLATZMAN, R.L. COLLINS, and W.H. WARDEN III, "A Minimal Technology Routing System for Meals on Wheels," *Interfaces*, vol. 13, no. 3, 1983.

BECHTOLD, S.E., and L.W. JACOBS, "Implicit Modeling of Flexible Break Assignments in Optimal Shift Scheduling," *Management Science*, vol. 36, no. 11, 1990.

BELTRAMI, E., *Models for Public Systems Analysis*, New York: Academic Press, 1977.

BISHOP, J.E., "Mathematicians Find New Key to Old Puzzle," *Wall Street Journal*, February 15, 1991.

DAVIS, S.G., and E.T. REUTZEL, "Joint Determination of Machine Requirements and Shift Scheduling in Banking Operations," *Interfaces*, vol. 11, no. 1, 1981.

FISHER, M.L., A.J. GREENFIELD, R. JAIKUMAR, and J.T. LESTER III, "A Computerized Vehicle Routing Application," *Interfaces*, vol. 12, no. 4, 1982.

FITZSIMMONS, J.A., and R.S. SULLIVAN, *Service Operations Management*, New York: McGraw-Hill, 1982.

GLOVER, F., R. GLOVER, J. LORENZO, and C. MCMILLAN, "The Passenger-Mix Problem in the Scheduled Airlines," *Interfaces*, vol. 12, no. 3, 1982.

GLOVER, F., C. MCMILLAN, and R. GLOVER, "A Heuristic Programming Approach to the Employee Scheduling Problem and Some Thoughts on Managerial Robots," *Journal of Operations Management*, vol. 2, no. 4, 1984.

GOCHENOUR, D.L., JR., E.L. FISHER, and J. BYRD, JR., "Bus Scheduling Revisited: The Monongalia County Experience," *Interfaces*, vol. 10, no. 2, 1980.

HANCOCK, W.M., D.M. WARNER, S. HEDA, and P. FUHS, "Admission Scheduling and Control Systems," chap. III.2 in *Cost Control in Hospitals*, J. Griffith, W. Hancock, and F. Munson, eds., Ann Arbor, Mich.: Health Administration Press, 1976.

HILL, A.B., J.D. NAUMANN, and N.L. CHERVANY, "SCAT and SPAT: Large-Scale Computer-Based Optimization Systems for the Personnel Assignment Problem," *Decision Sciences*, vol. 14, no. 2, 1983.

HOPPER, M.D., "Rattling SABRE—New Ways to Compete on Information," *Harvard Business Review*, May-June, 1990.

KELLEY, T., and W. MCKENNA, "An Integrated Nurse Staffing System," *Proceedings of the Seventh Annual Conference of the Hospital and Health Services Divisions, AIIE*, NCS HME,[5] 1976.

KIMES, S.E., "Yield Management: A Tool for Capacity-Constrained Firms," *Journal of Operations Management*, vol. 8, no. 4, 1989.

KRAJEWSKI, L.J., P. RITZMAN, and P. MCKENZIE, "Shift Scheduling in Banking Operations: A Case Application," *Interfaces*, vol. 10, no. 2, 1980.

LAWLER, E.L., J.K. LENSTRA, A.H.G. RINOOY KAN, and D.B. SCHMOYS, eds., *The Traveling Salesman Problem: A Guided Tour of Combinatorial Optimization*, New York: Wiley, 1985.

MARSTEN, R.E., M.R. MULLER, and C.L. KILLION, "Crew Planning at Flying Tiger: A Successful Application of Integer Programming," *Management Science*, vol. 25, no. 12, 1979.

MAZZOLA, J.B., and A.W. NEEBE, "Resource-Constrained Assignment Scheduling," *Operations Research*, vol. 34, no. 4, 1986.

MILLER, D.L., and J.F. PEKNY, "Exact Solution of Large Asymmetric Traveling Salesman Problems," *Science*, vol. 251, 1991.

OZAN, T.M., *Applied Mathematical Programming for Production and Engineering Management*, Englewood Cliffs, N.J.: Prentice-Hall, 1986.

ROBINSON, L.W., "Optimal and Approximate Control Policies for Airline Booking with Sequential Fare Classes," Working Paper 90-03, Johnson Graduate School of Management, Cornell University, 1991.

ROCKART, J.F., and P.B. HOFMANN, "Physician and Patient Behavior under Different Scheduling Systems in a Hospital Outpatient Department," *Medical Care*, vol. 7, no. 6, 1969.

ROTHSTEIN, M., "Hospital Manpower Shift Scheduling by Mathematical Programming," *Health Services Research*, Spring, 1973.

STACEY, P.J., "Practical Vehicle Routing Using Computer Programs," *Journal of the Operational Research Society*, vol. 34, no. 10, 1983.

THOMAS, R.S.D., and J.M. WELLS, "Multiple-Origin Single-Destination Transit Routing," *Interfaces*, vol. 10, no. 2, 1980.

UNITED HOSPITAL FUND OF NEW YORK, *Systems Analysis of Outpatient Department Appointment and Information Systems*, Training, Research and Special Studies Division, 3 East 54th Street, New York, N.Y. 10022, 1967.

WAGNER, H., *Principles of Operations Research*, Englewood Cliffs, N.J.: Prentice-Hall, 1975.

WEISS, E.N., "Models for Determining Estimated Start Times and Case Orderings in Hospital Operating Rooms," *IIE Transactions*, vol. 22, no. 2, 1990.

WILSON, E.J.G., and R.J. WILLIS, "Scheduling of Telephone Betting Operators—A Case Study," *Journal of the Operational Research Society*, vol. 34, no. 10, 1983.

[5]National Cooperative Services for Hospital Management Engineering, 1200 East Broad Street, Box 36, MRV Station, Richmond, Va. 23298.

chapter 14

Logistics: Managing the Flow of Material

Most large organizations and many small ones have inventory and provide customer service at multiple locations. In this chapter we will present some ways of managing these systems in a coordinated way, to keep cost low and to provide good service. The topics we will discuss are included in the *logistics* function in corporations. Sears, the U.S. Navy, and the Safeway supermarket chain are examples of large logistics systems with inventories produced largely by other organizations. Goodyear, Xerox, and Ford each manage a system containing mostly inventories that they produced themselves. Many other organizations, both large and small, are part of a large production-distribution network.

Logistics is both an old term and a new term. The military has used it for many decades. In business, ''logistics,'' or ''integrated logistics management,'' is replacing ''physical distribution'' and many other phrases, to imply a total-system approach, managing materials throughout the organization. The Council of Logistics Management (CLM), formerly known as the National Council of Physical Distribution Management, uses the following definition:

> Logistics is the process of planning, implementing, and controlling the efficient, cost-effective flow and storage of raw materials, in-process inventory, finished goods and related information from point of origin to point of consumption for the purpose of conforming to customer requirements. (Coyle et al. 1988, p. 6)

These activities form an important part of all national economies. In the United States, as a percentage of GNP, logistics costs have declined owing to the deregulation of transportation (see Coyle et al. 1988). Even so, they constitute over 10% of GNP, similar in size to the health care or education sectors. Of the total of over $500 billion, about 35% is inventory-carrying cost, 60% is transportation cost, and 5% is administrative cost.

Logistics includes the process of delivering the product to the customer.

Customer service is increasingly important in most business. Holding inventory, transporting the product to the customer, and carrying spare parts for maintenance are three logistics functions directly affecting customer service. Survey data show that customer service is the most important marketing variable in the automobile industry, and it ranked third of four, behind ''product'' (quality, breadth of line, etc.) and ''price'' and ahead of ''promotion,'' on the average (Lalonde et al. 1988). The trend is toward customer service being more important.

As with many topics in this book, managers must address the total system in analyzing multilocation distribution systems. One store cannot manage its inventory without knowing the quality (speed, availability) of support it will get from the distribution center (DC). A firm cannot select inventory levels without knowing the mode of transportation it will use or the number of inventory locations and their closeness to customers.

Many types of inventory have been discussed in this book, including anticipation and seasonal inventory (Chapter 9), safety and lot-size inventory (Chapters 8 and 11), and work-in-process inventory (Chapters 2, 10, and 12). Each of these serves a useful purpose, depending on the situation. In this chapter we will discuss in detail another type of inventory, first mentioned in Chapter 8: pipeline inventory. This includes inventory in transit and inventory to cover the time it takes to flow through distribution centers. Just like a physical pipeline, which must be filled to allow water or oil to flow, a distribution system must have inventories to allow a smooth flow of units from producer to consumer. A one-location organization frequently does not own the inventory that is in transit to, or being produced for, the organization. They do not bear the cost of pipeline inventory directly, but they pay for it in the price of the item. A multilocation company usually owns the pipeline stock and must pay the associated inventory cost. Nearly all organizations that manage any materials are part of a large production-distribution system.

14-1 PRODUCTION-DISTRIBUTION SYSTEMS

Many physical goods are produced at one or more plants, shipped through one or more distribution centers, and finally delivered to a customer. Farm Supply Corporation, discussed in Chapter 3, is an example. A schematic representation is shown in Figure 14-1, including the flow of materials from suppliers of raw materials to the final destination for finished goods. When one organization is in control of the distribution center (DC) and either the plant or the retail level or both, it is said to have a *multiechelon distribution system*.

When the distribution-center function is provided by an organization other than either the plant or the retail store, the pejorative term ''middlemen'' is used to describe the distributors. Why do middlemen exist? Consider 100 plants that produce products sold in 1000 retail stores. If each plant is in contact with each retail store, (100)(1000) = 100,000 transportation links must be maintained and managed. If, instead, one distribution center serves the entire system, there will be 100 transportation links from the plants and 1000 transportation links to the retail stores, a total of 1100. This can reduce the cost and increase the effectiveness of the overall system. In some systems cheap transportation methods can be used from the plants to the DC because large quantities flow along those links. For another example, consider air-express companies that maintain contact between producers of rarely used spare parts and the users. In that case

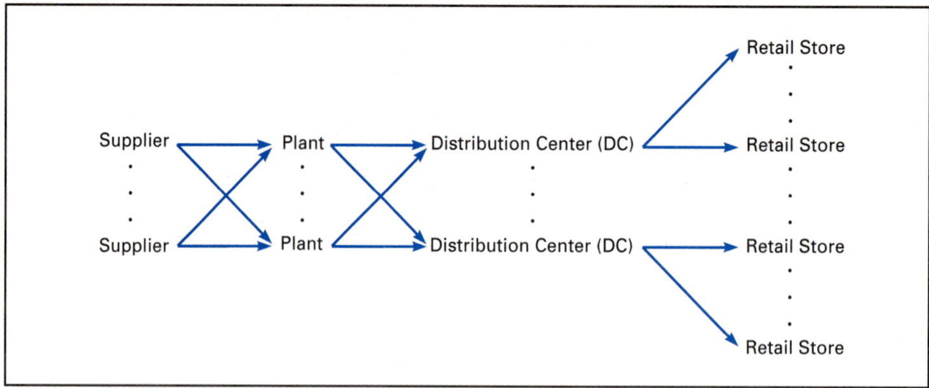

Figure 14-1 Production-Distribution System

transportation cost may increase, but response time is dramatically improved and total inventory can be reduced.

Even when air express is used, each echelon in Figure 14-1 contributes to the total time it takes to respond to customer demands. The time required for shipment may cause slow service, or management may need to maintain inventory sufficient to compensate for that lead time. It is common to refer to the time required between (1) supplier and plant as the *procurement cycle,* (2) plant and DC as the *order cycle,* and (3) DC and retail as the *replenishment cycle.* Table 14-1 lists some causes of these delays for Farm Supply Corporation, a company that owns several plants, a few DCs, and several hundred retail stores.

The total of the three time delays in Figure 14-1 can be several weeks or even months. Reducing those times is crucial to providing better customer service and to reducing the inventory tied up in pipeline stock and safety stock. In fact, pipeline stock equals the sales rate multiplied by any of the times that are related to the physical items (excluding ''identify need,'' ''group orders,'' and ''communicate'' in Table 14-1). To see this, consider the following thought experiment: Place a blue tag on the next item to leave the supplier, and continue placing blue tags until that item arrives on the retail shelf. There will be one day's worth of demand in blue-tagged items for each day of delay. If there were no variability in the lead times, and thus no need for safety stock, this computation would give the total inventory in the system. (This is an application of Little's law, described in Appendix A. Average inventory = arrival rate × average waiting time. Little's law still applies when there is variability in the lead times, but in a more complex way.)

Both pipeline stock and safety stock can be lowered by reducing the times in Table 14-1, but the components of the cycle times have different effects. For one example, Farm Supply may have purchased telecommunications equipment so that zero days of time are involved in communicating orders. This does not affect the pipeline stock directly because inventory enters the pipeline only after the order is received. However, it does reduce the amount of safety stock needed because there are fewer days of uncertain demand to be faced between order and receipt.

For another example, suppose that the firm were to use air freight instead of truck delivery, so that a six-day reduction in transportation time became possible for their replenishment cycle. In this case the units would be in the

Table 14-1 Order Cycle and Replenishment Cycle for Farm Supply Corporation

	Average Time Required (days)
Order cycle	
Identify need at retailer	1
Group orders at retailer	2
Communicate orders to DC	0
Obtain items from stock[a]	1/2
Assemble shipment at DC	1/2
Transport shipment to retailer	3
Receive shipment and restock shelves	1
	8
Replenishment cycle	
Identify need at DC	0
Group orders at DC	1
Communicate orders to plant	0
Produce, purchase, or retrieve items	25
Assemble shipment	2
Transport shipment to DC	7
Receive shipment	1
	36

[a] If the DC is out of stock, which occurs about 6% of the time, this step takes much longer. The item may be "emergency ordered" from a plant or a supplier, depending on the particular item involved.

system six fewer days . Six days of demand for each product would be cut from the pipeline stock. In addition, safety stocks can be reduced for the same reason as in the preceding example. These examples show that different savings can result depending on how a reduction in the cycle time is achieved.

Reducing the order cycle and replenishment cycle also has the benefit of allowing the organization to react to changes in the demand pattern more quickly. A temporary surge in demand at the lowest level usually leads to a much larger swing in the demand seen by the upper levels. This is so because all retail units are likely to place large orders soon after the upswing in retail demand, and the resulting inventories will carry them for a longer time during the downswing. Reducing the cycle times can help to reduce the magnitude of this effect. The oscillation is illustrated in Figure 14-2.

These cycles, induced by information lags, have been blamed for exacerbating recessions. Beman (1981) contrasts the 1974 and the 1980 recession. In the 1974 recession, inventories continued to grow after sales had turned down, and the inventories delayed the rebound. In 1980 inventories were relatively much lower and manufacturers kept them from growing dramatically during the decline. Beman argues that the better control minimized the length and severity of the recession.

Using smaller batch sizes and reducing the order cycle can help management cope with inventory cycles. In addition, detailed information should be maintained on what is happening to retail sales. This information can help the firm to plan its production schedules in advance and avoid the huge swings shown in Figure 14-2. This planning is easiest when the entire system is under one organization's control, but *electronic data interchange* (*EDI*) will allow firms to quickly and easily share information for mutual benefit. EDI is used by a significant fraction of firms now, and it is expected to increase dramatically through the 1990s. Without EDI, a firm may offer to pay for information or offer incentives for long-term contracts. In either case the information system can be a source of competitive advantage for a firm, since it allows the firm to give better customer service. This will be even more true as international customers come to expect and receive the same quality of service offered to domestic customers. (See Copacino 1989 for a discussion of international trends in logistics.)

Fast information and small order quantities can keep plant ''demand'' from fluctuating more than retail demand. However, Chapter 9 discusses aggregate planning, in which demand can be smoothed, depending on the relative cost of inventory and changing production, to create less fluctuation in production than in demand. If this occurs, production should be *less* variable than retail demand. For many years, economists have debated whether this happens. Citing references from 1963 to 1989, Thomas and McClain (1991, Section III A) summarize some of the literature on the ''production-smoothing hypothesis.'' While there is controversy, the empirical evidence suggests that production smoothing still does not occur in the U.S. economy on an aggregate basis.

Clearly, some firms do smooth production. Doing so requires that demand be predictable. While seasonality is likely to be forecastable, macroeconomic fluctuations are more difficult to predict. At the very least, operations managers should develop good information systems and inventory practices to keep fluctuations in production to no more than the fluctuations in retail demand.

Figure 14-2 Effect of Swings in Retail Demand

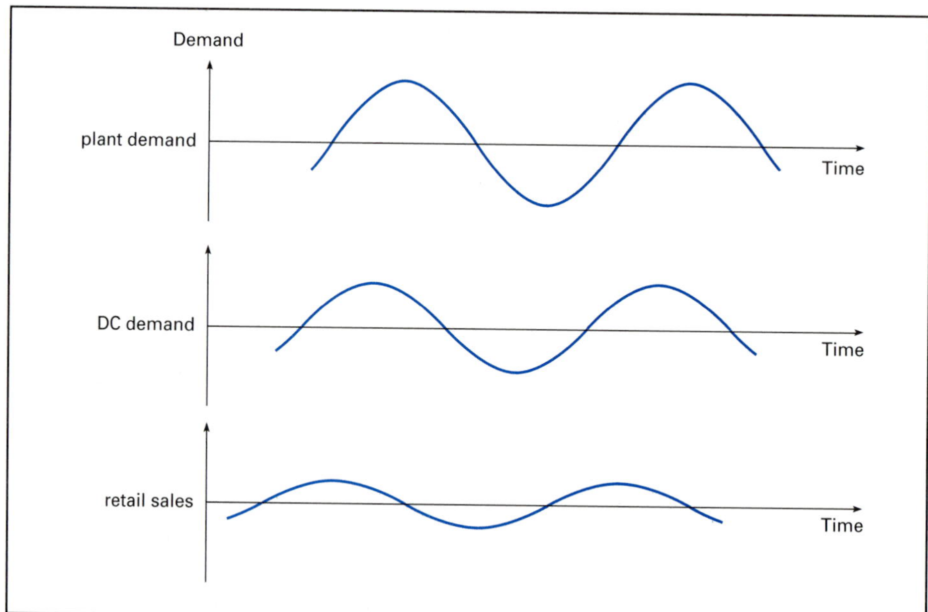

REVIEW PROBLEMS

Farm Supply corporation has a total daily demand rate of $3 million. If they want to fill the pipeline, they must have inventory equal to the sum of the portions of the order and replenishment cycle times that apply to physical items being moved, multiplied by the daily demand rate. Some of this stock is at the store level, and some at the DC level.

1. Estimate the amount of inventory that they need to fill the pipeline.

2. They are considering more frequent shipments. The transport time in both the order cycle and the replenishment cycle would be reduced to one day. The new system will cost $2.4 million more per year than the previous system. Should they change to the new system?

Solutions

1. A total of 4 days, the sum of the first three items in each cycle in Table 14-1, does not apply to items being moved. Thus, we have 36 + 8 − 4 = 40 days that contribute to pipeline stock. (40 days) × ($3,000,000 per day) = $120,000,000.

2. A reduction from 3 + 7 to 1 + 1 transport days results in an inventory reduction of (8)($3,000,000) = $24,000,000. The annual saving would be the inventory carrying cost rate (F_I) multiplied by the inventory reduction of $24,000,000. If F_I exceeds $2,400,000/$24,000,000 = 0.10 = 10%, the firm should use the new system. Common F_I values are in the 15% to 40% range, so the firm probably should use the new system.

14-2 POLICIES AND INCENTIVES

Multilocation inventory systems share many of the problems of other large-scale operations. For example, there is often a diffusion of the responsibility for results. Also, it is difficult to establish service-level goals for upper echelons (as we will see). Finally, it may be true that the incentives faced by individual managers in the system cause them to make decisions that are not good for the entire organization. Dealing with problems such as these is frequently necessary before beginning an analysis of the inventories themselves.

Organization and System Design

Why does an organization choose to have a multiechelon (many-layered) inventory system, with plants shipping to DCs, which in turn ship to the final customer? One reason previously stated is that transportation costs can be reduced by using inexpensive bulk shipment (train carloads, for example) from plants to the DCs. Another reason is that the DC is physically closer to the market than the plant and therefore is a more effective backup stocking point, allowing quicker response to stockouts at the bottom level.

Once it is determined to have a multiechelon system, the designer must decide how many layers to have and how many facilities to have in each layer.

The number and location of facilities is discussed in Chapter 16. The number of layers to have depends on how many final customer locations there are, and how close a support warehouse should be. If there are thousands of lowest-level inventory points (such as repair inventories held by service representatives for computers or copying machines) and if they require close support to provide proper service, as many as 100 support warehouses may be necessary. Then it is possible that another layer can be justified between the support warehouses and the plants, based on transportation cost savings. However, the existence of more than three layers is uncommon. One example of a several-layer system is the U.S. Navy, which has stock on board each ship, in supply ships, in ports, and in large distribution centers that receive shipments from suppliers' plants. Another example is IBM (see Cohen et al. 1990).

Once a system is designed, there are organizational questions to be answered. For example, what authority does the manager of each location have? To what extent should control of the distribution system, including all inventories, be centralized?

The extent of centralization of control is a crucial question with no obvious answer. Many important savings are possible if the distribution system is viewed and controlled in its entirety. Total inventory can be reduced and system-wide trade-offs can be made involving transportation, location, production scheduling, and inventory. (The extent of potential inventory savings is discussed in Sections 14-3 and 14-5). These savings have led some companies to adopt a system for overall control of materials throughout the organization. A director of logistics (or a job with a similar title) would be created to perform this function.

The argument against centralization of the distribution function is that local managers know things that a central manager cannot. Totally centralized control removes one competitive weapon—inventory levels—from division, sales, or product managers. In a profit center a manager must have control over the relevant variables. Some companies feel that establishing responsibility will lead to better management and offset the lost cost-reduction potential of central decision making. There are, of course, intermediate solutions in which staff support is available to local managers on a voluntary basis or in which decisions are made centrally but local managers can override those decisions.

Service Policies

Inventories are used to provide service to the customer. The extent of the inventories is largely governed by the level of service the organization wishes to provide. A policy statement on service might be that "90% of all demands at the retail level will be satisfied immediately, and 8% of the remaining 10% will be satisfied within one day." Another might be, "A demand for a spare part will be satisfied quickly enough that the average downtime due to spares requisition is less than one hour."

A statement of service policy must consider standard practice among competing firms in the industry. In addition, it should consider the cost of meeting the specified level. (This is discussed further in Section 14-4, using "trade-off curves.") Finally, in a multiechelon distribution system the service policy must specify more than a retail service level. There must also be an incentive for upper echelons to quickly support the retail level in an out-of-stock situation. (This is discussed further in Section 14-3.)

It is important to recognize that service measures differ greatly with the situation. Many books concentrate on "percent off-the-shelf service" as a measure. That is, what fraction of the demands are satisfied immediately? In many industries there is no off-the-shelf service; providing the product within four weeks may be considered excellent service. The mathematical approaches must be molded to the service measure, not the reverse. Lalonde et al. (1988) discuss customer service at length. The variety of service measures in different industries is astonishing. For example, on the average, keeping delivery promises is viewed as more important than speed of delivery, in spite of the increasing importance of "time-based competition" (see Stalk 1988).

Accounting in Inventory Management

Several cost accounting questions are crucial to inventory management.[1] We will discuss three of these. First and foremost, what value of the inventory cost is appropriate? The carrying cost, C_I (defined in Chapter 8), is the item value times F_I, the carrying-cost rate. Second, what ordering or setup cost, C_T, is appropriate? Finally, what procedures are appropriate for dealing with obsolete inventory?

The cost of capital, the cost of losses including theft, the marginal cost of physical storage, the cost of obsolescence, and any other costs that vary with the amount of inventory are included in F_I. In a multilocation system these costs vary from location to location, and different F_I values should be used. The cost of obsolescence differs dramatically from item to item, and this difference should be reflected. The cost of obsolescence may vary by location as well. Inventory is more likely to become obsolete the farther out in the system it goes. While centralized, it can be shipped to satisfy demand in many locations and is therefore likely to move out of the system sooner. Finally, the item's value is increased at the lower levels, since transportation cost has been added to the value. This cost may be unimportant in some cases, but it is a large portion of the value for items, such as certain spare parts, that are low in cost but relatively expensive to ship.

The order-transaction or setup cost, C_T, tends to be very small at DCs or retail stores. Pure ordering situations involve a small amount of clerical time and computer time to process an order. Thus, orders at the retail and DC level often are sized to cover a short period of time. (Exceptions to this are caused by price breaks and anticipation of a price increase or a shortage.) For manufacturing, C_T must also include the cost of starting a new production run. Reducing this cost in manufacturing situations is discussed in Chapter 12.

Dead stock is obsolete inventory that is unlikely to be sold. Once inventory items are recognized to be dead stock they can be written off, meaning that inventory assets are reduced by the book value of the inventory. In a company that is making profit, this results in a reduction of income and, therefore, of income tax. For example, a company with a 30% tax rate saves $30 in taxes by writing off $100 of dead stock. The money to be saved by writing off inventory can be substantial.

Rules for determining obsolescence are a source of argument in many firms because individual managers have a reduced profit if their inventory is written off. (The corporation, not the division, gets the tax saving.) Thus, managers do not want to write off inventory. The key to resolving such conflicts lies first in using a charge for holding inventory, F_I per dollar, including a required return on capital and an estimated cost of obsolescence; the total inventory cost is

[1] We will not discuss other accounting issues related to inventories, such as LIFO versus FIFO, because they have little effect on the management of inventories.

subtracted from divisional profits. However, division managers often are promoted within a few years, before inventory costs would exceed the item's value. Thus, policies for declaring items obsolete are also necessary. They must be clear and followed routinely, with exceptions kept to a minimum.

The precise rule to be followed depends strongly on the industry. A company with a fast-changing product line will want to declare items obsolete quickly; a company with slow but steady sales should not. One company has a rule that declares items obsolete once they are held in inventory for six weeks. Another has a rule that declares as obsolete only inventory in excess of five times last year's sales. The rules are different, but both may be appropriate.

System Performance

Four policy questions related to the productivity of distribution inventories are (Muckstadt and Thomas 1983):

1. How is service defined, and what level of service is the standard in the industry?
2. Where will the organization locate inventory, and what mode of transportation will be used?
3. Who is in charge?
4. What measure of inventory performance should be used?

The correct answers depend on the situation, but an organization cannot be efficient if management fails to answer the questions clearly. Our opinion on question 4 is that financial measures should be used. The cost of inventory is subtracted from a manager's profit measure, and the benefit of carrying the inventory (increased sales, lower production cost, and so on) should accrue to the same individual.

REVIEW PROBLEMS

1. A manager has inventory valued at $500,000 (cost) in an item built precisely to one customer's specifications. The items are of zero value to anyone else. The customer will buy 60% of the stock immediately, and she will take the rest in three years. (Assume that there is no doubt about the future sale or its timing.) The company uses $F_I = 0.40$, where the cost of capital is 0.15, the cost of obsolescence (on the average) is 0.15, and the physical cost of storage is 0.10. (All three values are on a before-tax basis. The after-tax cost of capital is 0.09.) Since 0.40 per year times three years is 1.20 (i.e., more than 100%), the manager feels that the $200,000 worth of items should be scrapped now, and new items should be built in three years. Is he right? Why or why not? (Use an after-tax analysis with a tax rate of 0.30. Assume that there will be no inflation. Remember that if they keep the items now, they still get a ''cost of goods sold'' tax deduction in three years.)

2. Summarize the arguments for and against the centralization of all distribution-system functions.

3. To reduce conflict between marketing and production, the controller suggests that marketing be charged with making forecasts that production must meet, and that finished-goods inventory costs be charged to marketing's budget. If a last-minute change in the forecast is necessary, marketing would be

charged for any additional production costs. Production would be responsible for raw material, work-in-process inventories, and costs incurred if they overproduce or are unable to meet the forecast. Is this breakdown reasonable? Why or why not?

Solutions

1. Since the $200,000 cannot be recovered immediately, applying the cost of capital to the full amount is inappropriate. (It was appropriate before the production decision was made.) Also, since we have been assured that the items will not be obsolete, the 0.15 cost of obsolescence is irrelevant. The only marginal cost is the 0.10 physical storage cost. The other costs are sunk. Thus, if the firm keeps the items, there will be only an (0.10)($200,000) = $20,000 cost per year, for physical storage. If the firm scraps the items, they receive $60,000 now, but they must pay $200,000 to build the items in year 3. If they keep the items, they receive a $60,000 ''cost of goods sold'' tax benefit in year 3. The $20,000 and $200,000 costs must be multiplied by (1.0 − 0.30) to put everything on an after-tax basis. Thus, the cash flows are

	Year			
Action	**0**	**1**	**2**	**3**
Scrap	$60,000	0	0	−$140,000
Keep	0	−$14,000	−$14,000	−$14,000+ $60,000

The revenue from the sale of the items is not considered, since it is common to both plans. We want to select the larger of the two discounted cash flows. Discounting to time 0 using the 9% after-tax cost of capital, we obtain -$48,106 and $24,562 for scrap and keep, respectively. The firm should keep the items.

2. Centralization is valuable because large savings are possible by viewing the entire distribution system. On the other hand, individual managers inevitably lose some of their discretionary authority, and the company loses the benefits that can be obtained as a result of that authority.

3. Yes, since the group in charge of the forecast is also in charge of the consequences of the forecast (finished-goods inventory). Production is charged with meeting that forecast as efficiently as possible. (There are many other issues in deciding what responsibilities to give to each and how to measure the performance of production and marketing. For example, if production organizes so that it can respond more quickly than in the past, marketing's forecasting job becomes easier.)

14-3 DETERMINING INVENTORY LEVELS

Determining inventory levels in multilocation inventory systems is difficult because there are so many different situations. Even if demand can be forecast with precision, the problem of planning the flows of information and product is still complicated. There is a dependent relationship between customer demand and demand at warehouses, DCs, or plants. The situation is similar to MRP systems (Chapter 10) for multistage production; decisions made at one level affect all the others. *Distribution requirements planning* (*DRP*) is discussed by Collins and Whybark (1985) and by Bregman (1990), who considers transportation and warehouse constraints as well.

Different methods of using forecasts in inventory decisions are discussed by Zinn and Marmorstein (1990) and by Gardner (1990). Managing multilocation (customer or supplier) relationships in a just-in-time manner is discussed by Chapman and Carter (1990). In this situation inventories are kept small and lead times are both small and carefully managed.

Multilocation inventory decisions must account for the speed of transportation, lot-size decisions, items that are grouped together to share transportation (see Buffa and Munn 1990), and other situational differences. In this section we will not discuss all these topics but rather concentrate on a limited range of cases. We will assume that demand cannot be perfectly forecast, and that stockouts are a serious problem. High-demand situations will be contrasted with low demand. We begin with a discussion of appropriate objectives.

Objectives: Quantifying the Service Policy

The goal of holding inventory is to avoid shortages—to have the right product available where and when the customer wants it. There are several ways to measure the degree of success.

A *stockout-incidents* objective counts the number of times the inventory reaches zero; it ignores the amount of unsatisfied demand and how quickly the system could satisfy the unsatisfied demand. A *backorder-incidents* objective counts the *amount* of demand that cannot be satisfied immediately as a result of a stockout, assuming that the sale is not lost (the item is backordered). If the sale is lost, the percentage of *lost sales* can be measured. The complement of backorder incidents or lost sales is the *fill rate*, which is the percentage of demand satisfied immediately, off the shelf. The foregoing objectives ignore the duration of the shortage from the consumer's point of view. A *time-weighted backorders* objective is one that considers the length of time before a demand is satisfied; in such a system one item backordered for two weeks is assumed to be as costly as two items backordered for one week. For any of these measures, the cost of the shortage can vary from one item to another, depending on factors such as the contribution margin of the item.

The main reason for wanting to avoid stockouts at the upper echelons is that they can lead to a series of stockouts at the organization's lower levels. However, many multiechelon systems have 10,000 or more SKUs (stockkeeping units or different inventory items), and many of these are not carried at the lowest level, owing to low demand. In that situation, a stockout-incidents objective is counterproductive, because every one of these items is perpetually "stocked out" at the lowest level, and service depends on quick response to an order. Unless time weighting is used, there is no incentive to carry these low-demand items at any level in the system. This situation and other similar observations argue for a time-weighted type of objective in any multiechelon system with a large number of low-demand items. (Mathematical methods for implementing two different time-weighted objectives are discussed in Muckstadt and Thomas 1980, along with empirical results.)

In one study of a two-echelon system with fairly large order quantities, a *fill rate* objective was used (see Schwarz et al. 1985). These large order quantities provide substantial inventory at the DC most of the time. As a consequence, very little safety stock is recommended at the DC level. In fact, when fill rate is an appropriate objective, this research seems to indicate that a firm should maintain all its safety stock at the retail level. However, this conclusion may be altered if orders are small and frequent or if the duration of shortages is considered.

Several systems in practice use an objective with different service levels for each echelon. Thus, a system might have a goal of satisfying, without delay, 95% of the demands at the retail stores and 90% of the demands at the DCs. The problem with such an approach is discussed below. In this discussion, we will refer to only two levels, a retail level and a DC level.

In Chapter 8 we gave a formula that can be used to set service levels optimally for one item at one location; namely,

$$\text{Optimal probability of stockout during lead time} = \frac{C_I}{C_B} \times \frac{1}{\text{orders per year}} \tag{1}$$

The reorder level (expected demand during lead time, plus safety stock) is set to the level that satisfies equation 1. The cost of inventory per unit per year is C_I, and C_B is the cost of being out of stock or backordering one unit. In general, the formula shows that the probability of stockout and the level of safety stock *should be different* from item to item because C_I, C_B, and order frequency differ. To achieve an average service level of 95% of the demands satisfied off the shelf at the retail level, some items should have nearly 100% service and some should have a service level far below 95%.

This logic is true when applied to a single echelon, but it falls apart if it is applied to *each level* of a multiechelon system. The same items will have low service levels at both the retail level and the DC, and other items will have safety stock in large quantities at both levels. Thus, there will be excess safety stock (double protection) for some items and no support for other items.

These points can be emphasized as follows:

1. In a one-location system, service levels should vary among items.
2. Service levels should differ across echelons. Items with high safety stock at the retail level need less safety stock at higher echelons, and vice versa.
3. Applying one-location methods to a multiechelon system will lead to decisions counter to point 2. Some system-wide approach must be used.
4. The service level that is appropriate at the retail level depends on the annual demand and its variability, as well as on the values for C_I and C_B.
5. There are ways to modify single-location methods to act as discussed in point 2. These are described next.

Modifying Single-Location Methods

To set safety stocks for a multilocation system, we should take advantage of the system structure. One crucial point is that less total safety stock is needed if it is held at the DC level. This is true because a high demand at one retail outlet can be offset by a low demand at another when stocks are held at a central location, but this cannot occur if each location must protect itself. This phenomenon leads to the establishment of regional blood banks, for example, because the demand for some rare types of blood is low on the average in all locations but occasionally high at some location. Much less blood will be needed if most of the safety stock is centralized and made available by high-speed transport.

The reduction in stock due to centralization is sometimes called "statistical economies of scale." The larger the demand, the more easily predictable (and the less variable) it is. An extreme case of this would be a blood bank in which not more than one unit of type A, negative blood is demanded per year in a region. If we centralize stock at a regional DC, a total of one unit of blood provides perfect protection. However, if we keep stock at each of the eighteen hospitals in the region, eighteen units are required to give perfect protection.

The extent of the benefit available from centralization depends on several characteristics of the system (see Zinn et al. 1989 and Zinn and Marmorstein 1990):

1. The greater the number of locations centralized and the closer they are to being equal in demand, the greater the saving if stock is centralized.
2. If demand is positively correlated across locations, the saving is reduced. If correlation is perfect and positive (+1.0), there is no saving due to centralization. (Positive correlation is likely, as discussed below.)
3. The extent of correlation should be examined using the forecast errors. We call this the "residual correlation" in the data, after trends and seasonal factors, for example, have been removed. (Mathematical models of multilocation inventory, including correlation, are discussed in Erkip et al. 1990.)
4. Locations may have variable but easily forecastable demand, in which case matching flows to the demand (perhaps using DRP) is appropriate, rather than centralization.

Based on experience with many kinds of demand data, the following formula is sometimes used to approximate the amount of safety stock required:

$$\text{Safety stock needed} = kD^a \qquad (2)$$

where

k = safety factor, determined considering C_I and C_B; this will be different for different products

D = total expected demand during lead time

a = exponent derived from data, usually $0.5 < a < 1.0$

Whenever $a < 1.0$, safety stock can be decreased by centralizing stocks. For example, if $a = 0.5$, and there are two locations that each have $D = 100$, we obtain safety stock $= k(100)^{0.5} = k(10)$ at each location, for a total of $k(20)$. For comparison, if stock is centralized at one location, total demand is 200; thus, safety stock $= k(200)^{0.5} = k(14.4)$. The reduction from $20k$ to $14.4k$ is a saving of more than 25%. Values of a between 0.6 and 0.9 are common. Values of a less than 0.5 are possible but unlikely.

The preceding discussion ignores delays; better fill rate may not mean better service if the product will arrive later. Customers may accept delivery delays in some settings, but in other situations delays may be unacceptable. The statistical saving (described previously) provides the manager with one side of the trade-off. With centralized inventory we can be as sure (or even more sure) of having the product on hand, but it will be delivered to the customer later.

The ideal item to centralize is an expensive item that has low and highly variable demand. Many spare parts for items such as computers, aircraft, or copying machines are of this type. The saving due to centralizing some stock may allow an organization to use air freight when a demand occurs. Of course, even with air freight there is some delay. If a computer is running a life-support system, no delay is acceptable. An on-site backup unit should be maintained, even though the cost of the item is high and the need for a backup infrequent. For this reason, some organizations have separate stocking policies for "critical" items.

Some organizations use A-B-C categories (discussed in Chapter 8) to make decisions about stocking levels in multilocation systems. A items (high dollar sales) are stocked to a high service level at the retail level, while C items are centralized. However, this is not the best method, in our opinion. As was discussed previously, an expensive item with low demand is the best candidate for centralization, and it might turn out to be a B item because of its cost. Thus, an A-B-C breakdown based on *unit demands* is preferable for determining stocking levels in a multiechelon system. An even better method would be to form categories of demand-cost groups, such as high unit demand, low cost. The high-demand, low-cost item would have safety stock at the retail level and perhaps only pipeline stock at the others. Low-demand, high-cost items might have stock only at one central location. The important thing is to avoid duplicating safety stocks at all levels. Although a perfect breakdown is difficult to obtain, some attempt at using the structure of the distribution system can reap large benefits. Once the location of safety stock is known, methods from Chapter 8 could be used to set the values.

The methods to be discussed in Section 14-5 can make optimal inventory decisions in some situations. Since they are complex and relatively expensive to implement, modifications of single-location methods are still used in some multiechelon systems. The manager must blend a knowledge of the Chapter 8 methods with an understanding of how to take advantage of the multiechelon structure of the system.

REVIEW PROBLEMS

Suppose that one DC supports 100 identical retail outlets, and consider two items, each having $C_I = 1$ and $C_B = 10$. Item 1 is ordered once a year and item 2 is ordered ten times a year, at the retail level. At each retail outlet, lead-time demand is 10 units for item 1 and 1000 units for item 2. The lead time is the same at the DC as at the retail level, so the DC has a lead-time demand of $(100)(10) = 1000$ units for item 1, and $(100)(1000) = 100{,}000$ units for item 2.

1. What is the optimal probability of stockout for each item using the one-location formula given in equation 1?

2. Using equation 2 with $k = 2.0$ for each item (in spite of the answer to review problem 1) and $a = 0.5$, how much safety stock is needed for each item if safety stock is held at the retail outlets? At the DC?

3. Why might the firm not centralize all safety stock for all items?

Solutions

1. Probability of stockout $= \dfrac{C_I/C_B}{\text{orders per year}}$, which is $(1/10)/1 = 0.1$ for item 1 and $(1/10)/10 = 0.01$ for item 2.

2. At each retail store, safety stock $= kD^a = (2)(D)^{0.5}$. This is $2(10)^{0.5} = 6.32$ for item 1 and $2(1000)^{0.5} = 63.2$ for item 2. The total at all 100 retail units will be $100(6.32) = 632$ for item 1 and $100(63.2) = 6320$ for item 2.

   If safety stock is held at the DC only, D will be 100 times as large. Then we obtain $2(1000)^{0.5} = 63.2$ for item 1 and $2(100{,}000)^{0.5} = 632$ for item 2. As we can see, the total safety stock is reduced significantly. (It is reduced by a factor of $\sqrt{1/100} = 1/10$.)

3. It may be unacceptable to depend on the DC for safety stocks. By the time the stock arrives, it may be too late. Locating stock in a multiechelon setting requires a trade-off between reducing inventory by centralizing stock and providing fast service for the customer.

14-4 TRADE-OFF ANALYSIS FOR INVENTORY MANAGEMENT

In a one-location inventory system, such as a retail store, a manager might like to know how much inventory will be required to provide a 95%, 98%, or 99% service level. This depends on many factors, including the lead time (speed of transportation and information processing), the order quantity, variability of demand, and the definition used for ''service level.'' The optimal service level also depends on the costs of inventory and unfilled demands. The unfilled demand may be back-ordered or may result in a lost sale. We use C_B to denote the cost of shortage per unit. The difficulty of estimating C_B is discussed in Chapter 8. Because of that difficulty, we will use a range of values and generate a *trade-off curve*.

Figure 14-3 is an example of a trade-off curve. It can be used to help a manager select the appropriate amount of inventory to have and the corresponding service level. For example, in Figure 14-3, an inventory of \$2.8 million would result in approximately 1550 stockouts per year. Increasing inventory to \$3.0 million would cut stockouts to about 350, eliminating over three-fourths of the shortages. Adding another \$200,000 of inventory (to \$3.2 million) would have a much smaller effect on the number of stockouts, decreasing them from (roughly) 350 to 75. Trade-off curves always exhibit this decreasing marginal benefit of added inventory investment. The curve does not indicate which inventory level is best, but it gives a manager good information on which to base a decision, without requiring the manager to state an exact value for C_B.

To develop a trade-off curve, we determine a set of C_B values that cover the reasonable range for C_B. For the first C_B value we use equation 12 in Chapter 8 to determine the appropriate number of stockouts per year for each item. The answer is used in equations 7 to 14, Chapter 8, to determine R^* (the reorder level) for each item. Total inventory is estimated as $Q^*/2 + R^* - \overline{U}$, where Q^* is the order quantity and $\overline{U}$ is the expected lead-time demand. Then we sum, over all items, both the number of stockouts and the average inventory. This procedure is repeated for all C_B values, and each repetition gives another point to be plotted on the trade-off curve.

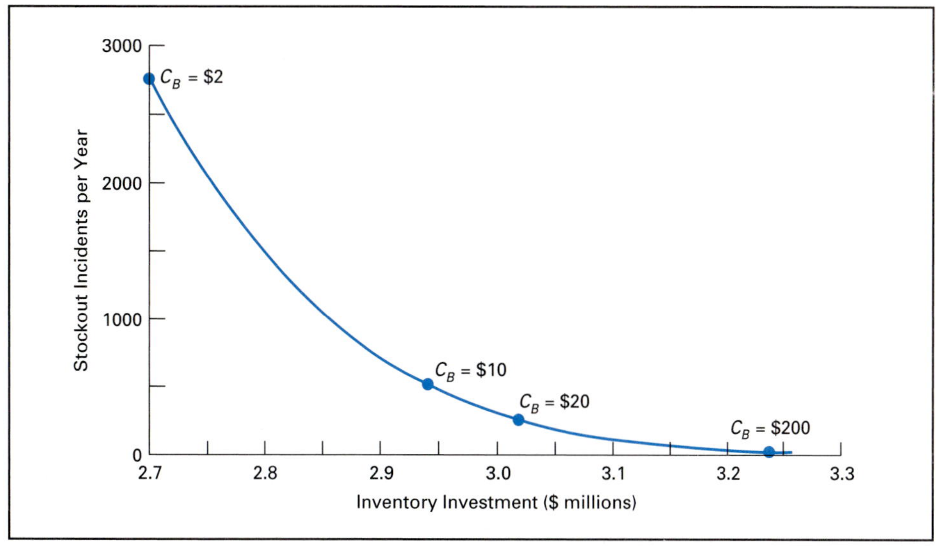

Figure 14-3 Trade-off Curve

A sample of a few hundred items can be used to adequately represent a much larger number of SKUs. Items are chosen to represent different demand and cost situations. This sampling procedure saves thousands of computations. To predict total performance, the stockouts and inventory for each item are multiplied by the number of similar items. In the following example, we will use stockout incidents per year as the service measure. Each stockout occurrence may lead to several unsatisfied requests, which remain backordered until the stock is replenished. Trade-off curves can be developed for other measures such as fill rate, but a few more computations are required.

Suppose that we use only two products to represent a total inventory system. (A much larger sample would be used in practice.) Item 1 has a demand rate of 10,000 per year and is similar to 500 products. Item 2 has a demand rate of 100 per year and is similar to 5000 products. Each item has a value of \$5 per unit, C_I = \$1 per year, C_T = \$50, and lead time is equal to 1/4 year. The standard deviation of demand is equal to the square root of expected demand, over any period of time. The items have normally distributed demand. The following calculations use formulas discussed in Chapter 8 and use C_B = \$10 as the initial value.

Item	Q^* Value	Choose R^* Such That
1	$Q^* = \sqrt{\frac{2(10{,}000)(50)}{1}} = 1000$, so $n = \frac{D}{Q} = 10$	Target probability of stockout per order $= \frac{C_I}{C_B n} = 0.01$, so $z = 2.32$ (see Table 2, Appendix D)
2	$Q^* = \sqrt{\frac{2(100)(50)}{1}} = 100$, so $n = \frac{D}{Q} = 1$	Target probability of stockout per order $= \frac{C_I}{C_B n} = 0.10$, so $z = 1.28$

During the lead time expected demand is one-fourth of annual demand, which is 2500 and 25, respectively. In this case the standard deviation of lead-time demand is $\sqrt{2500} = 50$ and $\sqrt{25} = 5$, respectively. This results in

Item	R^*
1	$R^* = \overline{U} + z\sigma_u = 2500 + (2.32)(50) = 2616$
2	$R^* = \overline{U} + z\sigma_u = 25 + (1.28)(5) = 31.4 \approx 31$

The number of stockouts per year is, at the optimal values, $C_I/C_B = 0.1$ for each item. Finally, we can compute the values of total inventory and stockouts per year by multiplying those values for the two items by the number of similar items each one represents:

Item	Inventory (units)	Stockouts/ Year	Adjusted for Number of Items Represented: Dollars in Inventory	Adjusted for Number of Items Represented: Stockouts/Year
1	$\frac{Q^*}{2} + R^* - \overline{U} = 616$	0.1	(5)(500)(616) = 1,540,000	500(0.1) = 50
2	$\frac{Q^*}{2} + R^* - \overline{U} = 56$	0.1	(5)(5000)(56) = 1,400,000	5,000(0.1) = 500
			$2,940,000	550

This one point (inventory = $2.94 million, stockouts = 550 per year) is shown in Figure 14-3 with the label C_B = $10. Several other points are indicated as well. Each C_B value gives one more point, using the same calculations as the example just completed.

REVIEW PROBLEM

Using $C_B = 2$, compute the exact value of inventory investment and stockouts shown in Figure 14-3.

Solution

When C_B is changed, Q^* and $n = Q^*/D$ values are unchanged. We should choose R^* so that the probability of a stockout is $(C_I/C_B n) = [(1)/2(10)] = 0.05$ for item 1 ($z = 1.65$) and $[(1)/2(1)] = 0.50$ for item 2 ($z = 0$). Then $R^* = 2500 + 1.65(50) = 2582.5 \approx 2582$ for item 1 and $R^* = 25 + 0(5) = 25$ for item 2.

The optimal number of stockouts per year is $C_I/C_B = 0.5$ for each item. This yields the following:

Item	Inventory (units)	Stockouts/ Year	Adjusted for Number of Items Represented: Dollars in Inventory	Adjusted for Number of Items Represented: Stockouts/Year
1	$\frac{Q^*}{2} + R^* - \overline{U} = 582$	0.5	(5)(500)(582) = 1,455,000	(0.5)(500) = 250
2	$\frac{Q^*}{2} + R^* - \overline{U} = 50$	0.5	(5)(5000)(50) = 1,250,000	(0.5)(5000) = 2,500
			$2,705,000	2,750

Therefore, the point labeled $C_B = \$2$ has an inventory of \$2,705,000 and 2750 stockouts per year. Other points on the curve include \$3,022,500 with 275 for $C_B = \$20$ and \$3,237,500 with 27.5 for $C_B = \$200$.

14-5 RESEARCH ON TRADE-OFF CURVES FOR MULTIECHELON SYSTEMS

In a multiechelon system, pipeline inventory is largely determined by the length of the order cycle and of the replenishment cycle. Lot-size inventory may or may not be determined by the use of an economic order quantity. In fact, in many systems most orders are for one unit at a time, and they are used to replenish inventory after each sale. (In a spare-parts system, for example, demand for many of the parts is low, and a replenishment occurs after each demand.) Assuming that pipeline and lot-size inventories have already been determined, we are left with a trade-off between safety stock and backorders.

This problem can be formulated and solved using a technique called the *method of Lagrange multipliers*.[2] In the following example the objective is to minimize a time-weighted backorder measure, and there is a single budget constraint on total system inventory. The trade-off curve is generated by trying different levels of the budget constraint.

$$\text{Minimize} \quad \text{time-weighted backorders at the bottom level} \tag{3}$$

$$\text{subject to} \quad \sum_{i=1}^{n} \sum_{j=0}^{m} (\text{cost of item } i)(\text{stock level at location } j) \leq \text{budget constraint} \tag{4}$$

The formulation uses one DC with m retail stores. Location 0 refers to a distribution center; thus, two levels are considered simultaneously. (The system described by equations 3 and 4 and an application are discussed in Muckstadt and Thomas 1980.) In the optimal solution, very low-demand, high-cost items should be centralized at the DC. Service levels will be very high at the retail level for high-demand, low-cost items. The mathematical approach divides the items into these groups, whereas guesses will frequently be in error. (The review problems at the end of this section will give you a chance to try your hand at guessing.)

[2] Lagrange multipliers are a form of *shadow prices*, discussed in Appendix C. See the references to that appendix, such as Hillier and Lieberman (1986), for a discussion of Lagrange multipliers.

To illustrate the importance of using a multiechelon approach (based on either managerial judgment or a mathematical method) we will reproduce a pair of trade-off curves from an actual inventory system (from Muckstadt and Thomas 1980). The system studied was a spare-parts supply system with low ordering cost and low demand for most items. All orders placed were for one unit, and orders were placed for every demand. This policy is reasonable for this situation.

In addition to the multiechelon approach of equations 3 and 4, a single-echelon approach was tried for comparison. Each level (retail and DC) was examined separately. Several different service levels were used for each of the two levels of the system. Retail service levels of 60%, 75%, 85%, and 95% were coupled with DC-level service levels of 50%, 60%, 75%, 85%, and 95%, for a total of 20 combinations. The service levels were averages, and individual-item service levels were optimally chosen to minimize total investment at the level. This method, however, does not take advantage of the multiechelon structure of the system.

The service-level objective was stated in terms of backorder days per demand. Thus, a 0.50 value implied that, on the average, each customer had to wait for 0.50 day. (Of course, most customers waited for zero time and some waited much longer.) The trade-off curves are shown in Figure 14-4. The higher of the two lines represents the best solution possible using the single-echelon approach and the 20 combinations of service levels.

The saving from using a multiechelon approach is significant. At any level of backorder days (the service-level measure) the single-echelon approach requires about *twice as much* inventory investment. For example, using the multiechelon approach reduces inventory from $31,000 to $15,000, while maintaining average backorder days of 0.4. Part of the saving could be achieved by modifying single-location methods as discussed previously, or by trying other combinations of service levels.

This example has many very low-demand items (spare parts), and uncorrelated demands. Each situation requires different models. We will mention

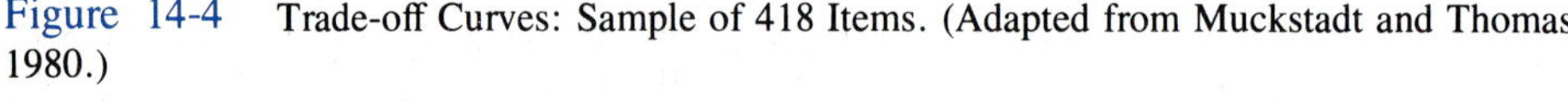

Figure 14-4 Trade-off Curves: Sample of 418 Items. (Adapted from Muckstadt and Thomas 1980.)

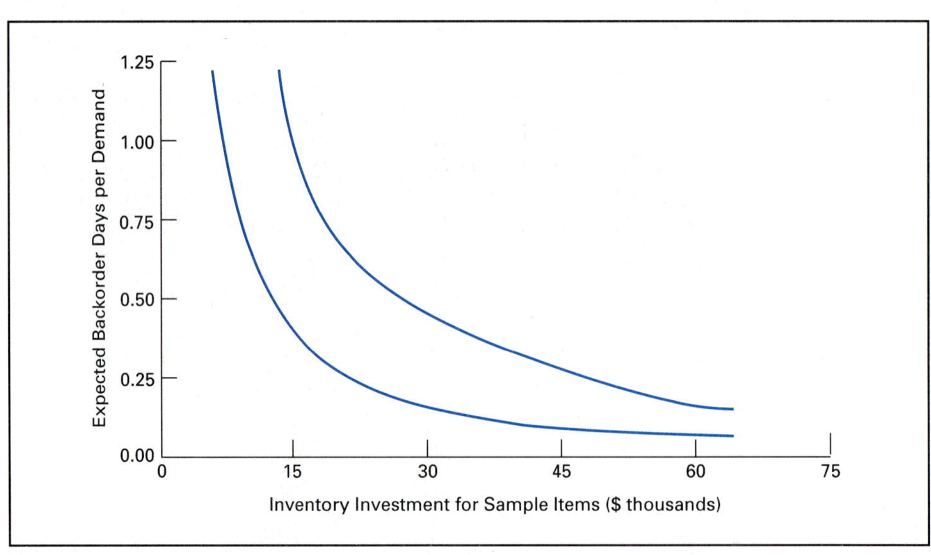

only a few others. However, the main point is that taking advantage of the multiechelon structure can be very beneficial. Once a system-wide view is taken, a manager must make the trade-off. While low cost is always a goal, a lowest-cost distribution system may not give good enough customer service. This may be false economy (see Krenn and Shycon 1983).

Anily and Federgruen (1990) discuss models that include vehicle-routing costs. Jackson (1988) discusses the problem of allocating stock from a central facility to retail outlets at several points in time while waiting for a big shipment. (Some stock should be reserved and released after some demand is observed.) Hausman and Scudder (1982) and Nahmias (1981) examine repairable inventories, such as those found in systems that maintain and support jet aircraft. Cohen et al. (1990) describe the IBM inventory-support system that has many levels in the system, and both high- and low-demand items. Each of these articles contains many other references, as does Schwarz (1981).

REVIEW PROBLEMS

The following table contains eight of the data points used to generate Figure 14-4. At one budget level, the optimal solution centralized three of the eight items, carrying no inventory at the retail level. A fourth item had one unit at each of the 15 retail locations, and a fifth had three units at each retail location. The other three items had retail stock levels of 2. (In preparation for answering the problems, you may wish to compute the expected lead-time demand for each item. Note that expected demand is low.)

Cost and Demand Data for Sample Items

Item	Average Retail Level Daily Demand Rate	Unit Cost	Order Cycle Time (days)	Notes
1	0.04077	$ 69.85	41	highest unit demand
2	0.00380	1.10	41	low unit demand, lowest cost
3	0.00787	9.88	41	low unit demand, medium cost
4	0.03289	5.32	41	high unit demand, low cost
5	0.00207	78.24	41	low unit demand, high cost
6	0.03409	1,376.00	41	high unit demand, highest cost
7	0.02622	15.30	41	high unit demand, medium cost
8	0.00198	34.24	41	lowest unit demand

1. Which three items do you think were centralized? Why?

2. Which item do you think had the largest retail stock level? Why?

Solutions

The expected lead-time demands are found by multiplying the order cycle time of 41 days by the daily demand rate. The results are 1.67, 0.16, 0.32, 1.35, 0.08, 1.40, 1.07, and 0.08.

1. Items 5, 6, and 8 are centralized. Items 5 and 8 have the lowest unit demands, and item 6 is so expensive that the investment in retail inventory is not warranted. Even though demand is low for item 3, its relatively low cost makes the investment for one unit at each store worthwhile.

2. Item 4 has three units at the retail level. It is not the item with the highest demand, but it does have high demand and relatively low cost. From these examples we see that unit demand is a good place to start in determining which items to centralize. After that, a high cost makes us want to centralize.

SUMMARY

There are many kinds of inventories: lot-size or cycle, safety, work-in-process, seasonal, anticipation, pipeline, decoupling, and dead. Any of these can be important in a given situation, and in fact, each constitutes the majority of the inventory investment in some systems. It is important to understand the different purposes served by each of these and how to approach the analysis of each one.

In multilocation inventory systems, pipeline inventories may be large. A trade-off exists between inventory investment and the speed of order processing and of transportation.

The allocation of inventory throughout a multiechelon, multi-item system cannot be handled well using single-location methods. Single-location methods will tend to have too much safety stock for some items and too little for others. The upper echelon should be used to back up the bottom level, not duplicate its pattern of stocking. Centralizing can provide great benefit for some items, at least including items with very low demand and relatively high cost. At the other extreme, high-demand items with relatively low cost should have safety stocks concentrated at the retail level; the service at the distribution center need not be as good. In general, the lower the retail service level, the better the service at the upper echelon should be.

Single-location methods can be modified, using the preceding ideas, to gain some of the advantage available to a multiechelon system. There are mathematical methods that optimize such systems, however, and the increased saving is often significant. The benefit from using a multiechelon approach instead of a single-echelon approach can be great.

Before any analysis is done, questions relating to policies and incentives must be answered. Inventory charges and rules for obsolescence can be used to encourage individual decisions that are good for the overall organization. The degree of centralization of authority (and the potential saving from viewing the overall system) must be balanced against the degree of autonomy that is desirable for individual profit-center managers. Service-policy statements must be appropriate for the industry, and if possible, trade-off analysis can be used in establishing appropriate goals.

Multilocation distribution systems require sound managerial judgment, good system design, and detailed analysis that is often complex. The potential benefit is worth the effort.

PROBLEMS

*1. Define *procurement cycle, replenishment cycle,* and *order cycle.*

2. Why does a reduction of transportation time lower pipeline inventory more than a reduction in order-transmittal time?

*3. A firm that sells $1 million of product per day is considering two proposals for reducing pipeline inventory. The retail-store level carries safety stock equal to three times the square root of lead-time demand, and the current lead time (the order cycle) is 14 days. The two proposals are to reduce transportation time by 2 days at an annual cost of $400,000 or to reduce order-transmittal time by 2 days at a cost of $20,000. If they use $F_I = 0.25$ as a carrying-cost rate (including a 0.15 cost of capital), should they accept one, both, or neither of the proposals?

4. Why would a firm have a multiechelon inventory system? Based on your answer, characterize the type of firm for which a multiechelon system would perform best.

*5. Are the following statements true or false? Why?
   a. F_I may vary dramatically from item to item.
   b. An item's value (as used in making inventory decisions, for example) should not change as it moves through a multiechelon system.
   c. Dead stock never has any value.

6. A firm is using a before-tax inventory-holding-cost rate of $F_I = 0.30$ per year, where the cost of capital is 0.10, the cost of obsolescence is 0.14, and the physical cost of storage is 0.06. The after-tax cost of capital is 0.072 per year. One product is selling steadily at the low rate of ten per month. They believe demand will continue at that rate for ten years or more. They have 1500 units in inventory and the unit cost is $1. The tax rate is 0.30.
   a. Their current policy, which applies uniformly to all items, is to declare obsolete any items that are in excess of five years' forecast of demand. Based only on economic considerations, evaluate the cost of holding one item for five years (ignoring sunk costs) and compare that with the cost of scrapping the item and rebuilding it in five years. Use an after-tax analysis. Remember that if they keep the item, there is a tax benefit at the time of sale.
   b. Again, based only on economic considerations, and ignoring the five-year rule, how many of the 1500 units on hand should they throw away? Either use trial and error to find (approximately) the time at which the two cost formulas are equal or derive a formula to give the answer.

*7. Are the following statements true or false? Why?
   a. Centralizing inventories for all low-demand items is always appropriate.
   b. Centralizing responsibilities for all distribution-system functions

---

*Problems with an asterisk have answers in the back of the book.

will always be financially beneficial to a firm, even though some managers may not like it.

8. a. In a multiechelon inventory system with many items, why should some items be carried only at levels above the retail level?
   b. If a high-demand item has a high fill rate (large safety stock) at the retail level, should the upper levels have zero inventory for that item? Why or why not?
   c. What do parts a and b have to do with using a time-weighted objective function?

*9. A firm has a DC that supports 70 retail outlets. One product has C_I = \$0.42 per year and C_B = \$2.55, and it is ordered once per month. The annual demand at each retail store is 1200 units, and lead time is one month for orders placed by retailers and two months when the DC places an order.
   a. What probability of stockout would be appropriate at the retail outlets, using equation 1?
   b. Given your answer to part a, if demand is normally distributed, what k factor would be appropriate for use in equation 2?
   c. If $a = 0.7$ in equation 2, how much safety stock is needed if the item is carried at each retail store? If the item is carried only at the DC? Use the k factor calculated in part b for both situations.

10. The review problem at the end of Section 14-3 asks you to use k = 2.0 "in spite of the answer to review problem 1."
   a. What k factors are appropriate, assuming that the demand is normally distributed and using the probabilities of stockout, calculated to be 0.1 and 0.01 for the two items?
   b. Using the new k factors (for both the retail outlets and the DC), compute the inventory reduction that would occur if each item is centralized at the DC.

*11. The review problem at the end of Section 14-4 calculates one point on a trade-off curve, the point corresponding to C_B = \$2. The point for C_B = \$10 is calculated in the text of the section. Values are given in the solution to the review problem for C_B = \$20 and C_B = \$200. Verify those two points. For a stockout probability of 0.0005, $z = 3.29$ is used.

12. As F_I, the carrying cost rate selected by management, goes up (down), the optimal amount of inventory to have goes down (up). If management wanted to use the selection of F_I to control total inventory, a trade-off curve of F_I versus inventory could be derived. Briefly say how this could be done and describe any complications that might arise.

13. A manufacturing firm is using three products to represent their total investment—an A item, a B item, and a C item. All three items have a unit value of \$10, C_I = \$2.50 per year, C_T = \$40, a lead time of one month, and a standard deviation of lead-time demand equal to the square root of the expected lead-time demand. The three demand rates are 2000, 300, and 2 per month, and the items are representative of 40, 200, and 5000 items, respectively. Assume that demand is normally distributed.

a. Try C_B = \$10, \$40, and \$200, and plot a trade-off curve similar to Figure 14-4. For a stockout probability of 0.000456, $z = 3.3$ is appropriate.

b. If they currently use C_B = \$10, what one-sentence information might you give them regarding a reduction in the number of stockouts?

*14. a. Describe the type of item that is most appropriate for having centralized stocking in a multiechelon inventory system.

b. What trade-offs are involved in the decision to centralize an item's inventory? That is, what is gained and lost in centralizing the inventory?

15. (This problem is only intended for students who have an understanding of the method of Lagrange multipliers.) Describe how equations 3 and 4 would be solved using a Lagrange multiplier. Why would the problem be separable by item for each Lagrange multiplier value (λ), and what would be the interpretation of the λ value that causes all the budget to be used?

*16. A one-product firm is considering consolidating its three regional DCs into one. They have calculated that by paying \$400,000 more for faster transportation, they would be able to provide the same one-month lead time to customers as the current system does.

The means and standard deviations of monthly demand are as follows (figures are in millions of dollars):

	Mean	**Standard Deviation**
DC1	2.0	0.5
DC2	3.0	0.6
DC3	4.0	0.7

If the demands are independent, the sum of the means and variances will equal the mean demand and variance for the new DC. Thus, we can find

$$\sigma_{1+2+3} = \sqrt{\sigma_1^2 + \sigma_2^2 + \sigma_3^2} = \$1.05$$

a. The firm currently keeps two standard deviations of demand as safety stock, and they would do the same in a centralized DC. How much safety stock can they save by centralizing?

b. Is the inventory saving sufficient to justify the additional transportation cost if the carrying-cost rate of inventory is 0.20?

c. If the demands at the three regional DCs were positively correlated, might that change the answer to part b? Why or why not?

REFERENCES

Anily, S., and A. Federgruen, "One Warehouse Multiple Retailer Systems with Vehicle Routing Costs," *Management Science*, January, 1990.

Beman, L., "A Big Payoff from Inventory Controls," *Fortune*, July 27, 1981.

Bierman, H., T. Dyckman, and R. Hilton, *Cost Accounting: Concepts and Applications*, Boston: PWS-Kent, 1990.

Bregman, R.L., ''Enhanced Distribution Requirements Planning,'' *Journal of Business Logistics*, vol. 11, no. 1, 1990.

Buffa, F.P., and J.R. Munn, ''Multi-Item Grouping Algorithm Yielding Near-Optimal Logistics Cost,'' *Decision Sciences*, vol. 21, no. 1, 1990.

Campbell, J.F., ''Designing Logistics Systems by Analyzing Transportation, Inventory and Terminal Cost Trade-offs,'' *Journal of Business Logistics*, vol. 11, no. 1, 1990.

Chapman, S.N., and P.L. Carter, ''Supplier/Customer Inventory Relationships under Just-In-Time,'' *Decision Sciences*, vol. 21, no. 1, 1990.

Cohen, M., P.V. Kamesam, P. Kleindorfer, H. Lee, and A. Tekerian, ''Optimizer: IBM's Multi-Echelon Inventory System for Managing Service Logistics,'' *Interfaces*, January–February, 1990.

Collins, R.S., and D.C. Whybark, ''Realizing the Potential of Distribution Requirements Planning,'' *Journal of Business Logistics*, vol. 6, no. 1, 1985.

Copacino, W., ''Perspectives on Global Logistics,'' keynote speech at World Trade-Institute/Council of Logistics Management Conference, June 26, 1989.

Coyle, J.J., E.J. Bardi, and C.J. Langley, Jr., *The Management of Business Logistics*, St. Paul, Minn.: West, 1988.

Erkip, N., W.H. Hausman, and S. Nahmias, ''Optimal Centralized Ordering Policies in Multi-Echelon Inventory Systems with Correlated Demands,'' *Management Science*, March, 1990.

Gardner, E.S., Jr., ''Evaluating Forecast Performance in an Inventory Control System,'' *Management Science*, April, 1990.

Hausman, W., and G. Scudder, ''Priority Scheduling Rules for Repairable Inventory Systems,'' *Management Science*, vol. 28, no. 11, November, 1982.

Jackson, P.L., ''Stock Allocation in a Two-Echelon Distribution System or 'What to Do Until Your Ship Comes In,''' *Management Science*, July, 1988.

Kearney, A.T. (consulting firm), *Measuring and Improving Productivity in Physical Distribution*, Council of Logistics Management (formerly NCPDM), Oak Brook, Ill., 1984.

Krenn, J.M., and H.N. Shycon, ''Modeling Sales Response to Customer Service for More Effective Distribution,'' *Proceedings*, NCPDM (now Council of Logistics Management), vol. 2, 1983.

LaLonde, B.J., M.C. Cooper, and T.G. Noordewier, Jr., *Customer Service: A Management Perspective*, Council of Logistics Management, Oak Brook, Ill., 1988.

Muckstadt, J.A., and L.J. Thomas, ''Are Multi-echelon Inventory Methods Worth Implementing in Systems with Low Demand-Rate Items?'' *Management Science*, vol. 26, no. 5, May, 1980.

Muckstadt, J.A., and L.J. Thomas, ''Improving Inventory Productivity in Multilevel Distribution Systems,'' in *Productivity and Efficiency in Distribution Systems*, D. Gautschi, ed., New York: Elsevier North-Holland, 1983.

Nahmias, S., ''Managing Reparable Item Inventory Systems: A Review,'' in *Multi-level Production/Inventory Control Systems: Theory and Practice*, L. Schwarz, ed., New York: Elsevier North-Holland, 1981.

Schwarz, L., ed., *Multi-level Production/Inventory Control Systems: Theory and Practice*, New York: Elsevier North-Holland, 1981.

SCHWARZ, L., B. DEUERMEYER, and R. BADINELLI, "Fill-Rate Optimization in a One-Warehouse N-Identical Retailer Distribution System," *Management Science*, April, 1985.

STALK, G., JR., "Time—The Next Source of Competitive Advantage," *Harvard Business Review*, July–August, 1988.

THOMAS, L.J., and J.O. MCCLAIN, "An Overview of Production Planning," in *Handbook in Operations Research*, S. Graves, A. Rinnooy Kan, and P. Zipkin, eds., Amsterdam: North-Holland, 1991.

ZINN, W., M. LEVY, and D.J. BOWERSOX, "Measuring the Effect of Inventory Centralization/Decentralization on Aggregate Safety Stock: The 'Square Root Law' Revisited," *Journal of Business Logistics*, vol. 10, no. 1, 1989.

ZINN, W., and H. MARMORSTEIN, "Comparing Two Alternative Methods of Determining Safety Stock Levels: The Demand and the Forecast Systems," *Journal of Business Logistics*, vol. 11, no. 1, 1990.

chapter

15

Technological Innovation in Manufacturing and Services

Manufacturing and service processes have benefited continuously from innovations since the Industrial Revolution. During the past twenty-five years, however, significant advances in process technology and automation have made the operations function a critical factor in determining a firm's ability to compete in the global marketplace. This chapter explores innovative techniques and technological developments in operations management, with particular emphasis on automated manufacturing systems.

We begin by defining innovation. Schroeder, Scudder, and Elm (1989) have proposed a definition for innovation in manufacturing; their definition is, however, generally applicable to innovation in business. They define *innovation* as "the implementation of new ideas or changes, big or small, that have the potential to contribute to organizational (business) objectives." This definition is specifically meant to capture the idea that innovation can occur in one large change, as well as in many small (incremental) changes. In addition, by using the phrase "potential to contribute," it is understood that unsuccessful attempts ("failures") can contribute to the learning process and thus to the overall innovative thrust. By linking advances to organizational objectives, we see that innovation leads to benefits such as cost reduction and increased process flexibility.

Jaikumar (1986) discusses the paramount role of technology, process innovation, and in particular, automated manufacturing in the global marketplace. He describes the effective use of flexible manufacturing systems (a particular type of automated system, described in Section 15-1) by Japanese firms, and he contrasts this with the limited implementations encountered in U.S. industry. Jaikumar likens the general area of computer-integrated manufacturing (CIM) to a "battleground for manufacturing supremacy around the globe," and goes on to state: "The battle is on, and the United States is losing badly. It may even lose the war if it doesn't soon figure out how better to use the new technology of automation for competitive advantage."

Jaikumar's comments indicate the importance of understanding the elements of automated manufacturing, as well as how to integrate them. These principles must be mastered and implemented by managers if companies are to compete successfully in this decade and into the next century.

This chapter discusses technological innovations in manufacturing and services. Many other types of innovation have been addressed in this book. In Chapters 10, 11, and 12, for example, we studied MRP, JIT, and hybrid production and scheduling systems, and in Chapter 6 we discussed TQM. Each of these concepts has been innovative and has contributed to improving process objectives. In fact, each chapter in this book contains ideas and concepts that are innovative in their contribution to the technology of operations management.

These innovations seek to increase the effectiveness or the efficiency of the process. This is certainly the case for many of the production planning and scheduling systems we have studied. Another important goal of many process innovations is to strive to obtain the low-cost economies of a flow shop in a job-shop environment. Automated manufacturing holds great promise for achieving this objective.

In Section 15-1 we discuss innovative production systems. As we will see, there are many new terms and an abundance of acronyms that describe the many recent innovations that have occurred. We concentrate initially on manufacturing systems, since considerable advances have been realized in this area. This discussion also considers flexible manufacturing systems (FMSs), and in particular, we discuss the coordination of FMS with a larger production planning and control system, such as MRP. We then focus attention on service processes. Specifically, we consider advances in information technology and the impact these innovations have had on service processes.

Section 15-2 considers the management of automated production systems. It is clear that new technology raises a host of difficult, new issues in human resources, finance, and accounting. It is critical that managers be aware of the many facets and implications of these complex issues.

15-1 INNOVATIVE PRODUCTION SYSTEMS

The study of technological innovation and the management of technology is a well-established subject, on which many books have been written (see, for example, Burgelman and Maidique 1988 or Noori 1990). Understanding the nature of technological innovation requires that we consider both *product innovation* and *process innovation*. Innovations concerning the product (good or service), such as new developments in its concept, nature, design, and structure are product innovations. Process innovations, on the other hand, refer to changes and advances in the production or service-delivery process.

Differentiating between product and process innovation is a convenient way to develop a better understanding of technological innovation. This distinction, however, is not clear-cut. Consider, for example, advances in computer technology. Product innovations have led to more powerful, smaller computers. Some of these product innovations are the direct result of process innovations that have made possible the production of smaller, more reliable computer chips, as well as by the use of computers in the production process. This interrelationship suggests that technological innovation is driven by a complex interaction of process and product innovation.

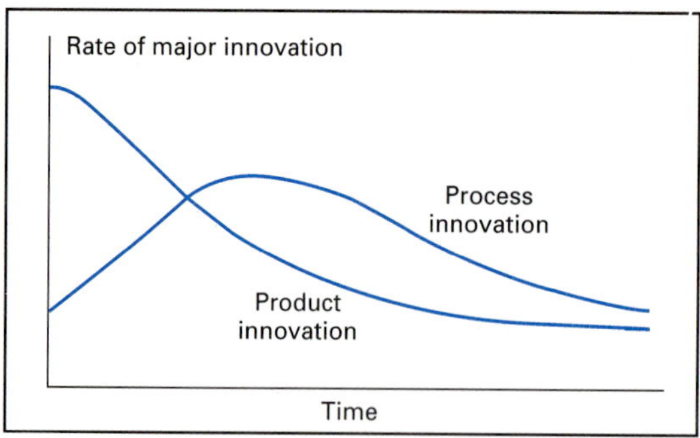

Figure 15-1 Product–Process Innovation. (From W.J. Abernathy and J.M. Utterback, "Patterns of Industrial Innovation," *Technology Review*, June/July, 1978. Reprinted with permission from Technology Review, copyright 1978.)

Abernathy and Utterback (1978) proposed a model of the dynamic relationship of product and process innovation. Their model, depicted in Figure 15-1, incorporates three stages. In the initial stage of its life cycle, the product is subject to significant engineering and design changes, many of which are driven by engineering and market requirements. This *fluid* (or *flexible*) *stage* involves the highest rate of product innovation. At this stage, however, the process experiences a low rate of innovation, since it must remain sufficiently flexible to accommodate rapidly changing product attributes, and investment in dedicated process capability is still risky.

As the product advances in its life cycle, the innovation process moves into the *transitional stage*. In this phase the rate of product innovation decreases substantially, and the rate of process innovation increases. The product is fairly well defined, and investment in process technology is more easily justified. Abernathy and Utterback noted that the production process becomes more rigid and that "islands of automation" may appear for some subprocesses.

In the last phase, the *specific stage*, the rates of both product and process innovation decline. This reflects the common objective of cost reduction, as well as the capital-intensive and rigid nature of the production process.

Understanding the relationship between product and process innovation is critical to establishing the strategic objectives of the firm. The Abernathy and Utterback product–process innovation model links the product and process life cycles in a manner that is analogous to the product-process matrix model of Hayes and Wheelwright (1984; see Chapters 2 and 17). Effectively matching a firm's productive capability with the goods or services it brings to the marketplace, together with an innovative thrust that strives to optimize along these two dimensions simultaneously, can be a formidable competitive strategy. (Strategy is discussed further in Chapter 17.)

We will focus principally on innovations in operations technologies. Noori (1990) considers two different types of operations technologies: those that apply directly to the production process (manufacturing or service) and those that are used in the generation, storage, and transmission of information. We refer to the first type of technology as *process technology* (or *process innovation*). Most of the innovations discussed in the following subsection fall into this category.

The second type is often referred to as *information technology*, encompassing the many innovations that apply to managing information. Advances in communication can also be included in this category. Information technologies are discussed later in this section.

New Manufacturing Methods

Table 15-1 lists some common terms used in connection with modern automation of manufacturing. It also gives references for many of the terms. Def-

Table 15-1 Some New Manufacturing Methods: Terms and Acronyms

Term	Acronym (if any)	Partial List of References
Automation		Groover 1987
Computerized, numerically controlled	CNC or NC	Ayres and Miller 1982
Robot		Kamali et al. 1982
Transfer line		Potter 1983
Artificial Intelligence	AI	
Cellular manufacturing		Taheri 1990 Black 1983
Group technology	GT	Boucher and Muckstadt 1983
Computer-integrated manufacturing	CIM	Mitchell 1991 Foston et al. 1991 Kusiak 1990 Groover 1987
Flexible manufacturing systems	FMS	Luggen 1991 Rhodes 1990 Kusiak 1985 Stecke 1983
Automated storage and retrieval systems	AS/RS	Zisk 1983
Automated guided-vehicle systems	AGVS	Groover 1987
Asynchronous material handling		
Computer-assisted process planning	CAPP	Groover 1987
Computer-aided design	CAD	Groover 1987
Computer-aided manufacturing	CAM	Groover and Zimmers 1984
CAD integrated with CAM	CAD/CAM or CADICAM	

initions will be given presently. We are purposefully vague about the word "new" here, since some of the ideas are not new but simply repackaged or once again fashionable. Still, their common use in manufacturing is relatively new.

The terms listed in Table 15-1 are not all-inclusive, and many of the ideas overlap. For example, a robot is part of an automated system, and cellular manufacturing often accompanies group technology. Finally, there are no standard definitions for these terms, so not everyone uses them in exactly the same way. For these reasons, we will provide a structure for discussing the terms and define them in turn (COMEPP 1982).[1]

There are several motivations behind the new manufacturing thrusts. These are summarized in the following ideas. A manufacturing facility can be

Automated: designed so that machines perform the labor rather than people.

[1]COMEPP is the Cornell Manufacturing Engineering and Productivity Program, of which two of the authors are members. The structure we will use was developed for COMEPP by Professors Maxwell and Muckstadt.

Flexible: designed to allow quick changeovers, small lots, and ease of material handling.

Responsive: designed to allow easy engineering changes, new products, and other responses to the marketplace.

Versatile: designed to have the capability to produce many different items.

The desired characteristics for a manufacturing facility depend on the nature of the demands placed on it. For example, a volatile product line, with many engineering changes, requires a *responsive* system. A large number of products, each produced in small batches, requires a system that is *flexible* and *versatile* whether or not it is *automated*. Using these ideas we can define the terms in Table 15-1. (The references in Table 15-1 can be used for follow-up reading.)

Automation. Automated systems supply machine functions to replace human functions. They reduce labor, accept obnoxious tasks, and provide consistent quality. Versatility and (automated) decision making may be components of an automated system but are not necessarily implied.

A *transfer line* is an automated production line in which parts flow in one direction and are transferred automatically from one workstation to the next.

Industrial robots are automated, but they also include some decision making. They can perform different tasks on different objects. They are also capable of remembering a set of actions and deciding which to use, perhaps based on sensory input. Robots consist of a *manipulator* (a mechanical ''arm''), a *power supply* (hydraulic, electric, or pneumatic), and a *controller* (a ''brain''). Some robots have variable speeds based on feedback (servo robots), whereas others do not. Some robots use *artificial intelligence*, improving their range of possible actions and discretion. They ''think'' in many ways similar to people, learning by experience. (See Kusiak 1990 for a discussion of machine learning.)

Robots currently are used for a variety of tasks, including welding, painting, and loading. Often, robots are used to perform tasks that occur in environments that are either hazardous or unpleasant to humans (see Groover 1987; and Kamali et al. 1982 for a discussion of the advantages and disadvantages in different tasks of robots vis-à-vis human labor).

Designing and building robots to imitate human actions is known as *anthropomorphism*. It is often limiting to think of robots in this way. For example, in designing a robot to perform a simple task such as opening a door, rather than have it emulate the action of the human hand, it might be much more effective to redesign the door handle (NOVA 1985). Also, human actions are limited by the physiology of the human body. For instance, a human wrist can rotate only a limited amount in any direction, whereas a robotic arm is capable of continually rotating 360 degrees. Additional degrees of freedom in movement can lead to more efficient ways of performing tasks (Bylinsky 1987).

Numerically controlled (NC) machines have programmable automation. The instructions are stored on a device such as magnetic tape and are interpreted by a controller unit, which directs the machine. Early forms of NC were incorporated in looms more than a century ago.

Direct numerical control (DNC) is the use of a computer to input the instructions to a number of NC machines.

Computerized numerical control (CNC) is a result of the development of microprocessors, so that each NC machine has its own computer.

Flexible Systems. Job shops, which are designed for low-volume, customized production, typically exhibit *process layouts* in which machines are grouped together according to function. *Cellular manufacturing* involves (partially) modifying the process layout. Instead of having lathes together, grinders together, and so on, one or more manufacturing *cells* are established. These cells contain the variety of machines needed to do most or all of the work for a set of items. Each cell then follows more of a product layout, and flow-shop economies can be sought within the cell.

These can be *manned* or *unmanned* (operated by a robot). With a cellular layout the items do less traveling; consequently, inventory can be reduced and control can be tighter. Workers (or robots) are multifunctional. Since they can perform several tasks, they are less likely to waste time, and productivity is increased.

Schonberger (1986) discusses the importance of cellular manufacturing to the application of just-in-time production systems in environments with many part types and low-volume production. Other benefits will be discussed later for cellular manufacturing and flexible manufacturing systems. Figures 15-2 and 15-3 illustrate manned and unmanned cellular manufacturing units.

Group Technology (GT) refers to methods of analysis for grouping products with similar design and manufacturing requirements. This allows for both design and manufacturing economies. For example, in the design of a new product, by taking advantage of design commonality with closely related existing products, significant benefits can be realized with respect to design efficiencies, quality, and the overall time required to complete the design cycle. Also, upon grouping similar items for production, properly designed manufacturing cells can complete the work for the group of items with minimal time lost for changeovers.

Groups can be formed using a manufacturing plan for the facility and a coding system for the items. There are two basic ways of coding, termed hierarchical and nonhierarchical. The code for a new part must indicate which manufacturing cell will be used. Even if a small amount of work must be done outside the cell, the reduction in total time spent in production can be significant; that is, *flow time* can be reduced dramatically.

A *flexible manufacturing system* (FMS) is a highly automated version of cellular manufacturing. Both material handling and production are automated and integrated by computer control. These systems are expensive, but they allow some of the benefits of fixed-position automation to be gained in a firm with a broad product line and small batch sizes. As we saw in the introduction to this chapter, FMSs hold tremendous promise for changing the nature in which firms compete. Jaikumar (1986) has asserted that this change is well underway. An example of an FMS is provided in Figure 15-4.

There are different types of FMSs, depending on the size, design, and layout of the system, together with the degree of system flexibility, the number of parts that can be produced, the volume of production, and overall system complexity. (See Kusiak 1985 and Noori 1990.) These systems can differ substantially in capability and cost; therefore, it is important to identify the specific type of system when discussing implementation of FMSs.

Many researchers have considered and continue to study design, planning, and control aspects of FMSs. (See, for example, Stecke 1983 and Buzacott and Yao 1986 for terminology, analysis, and a review of analytical models of FMSs.)

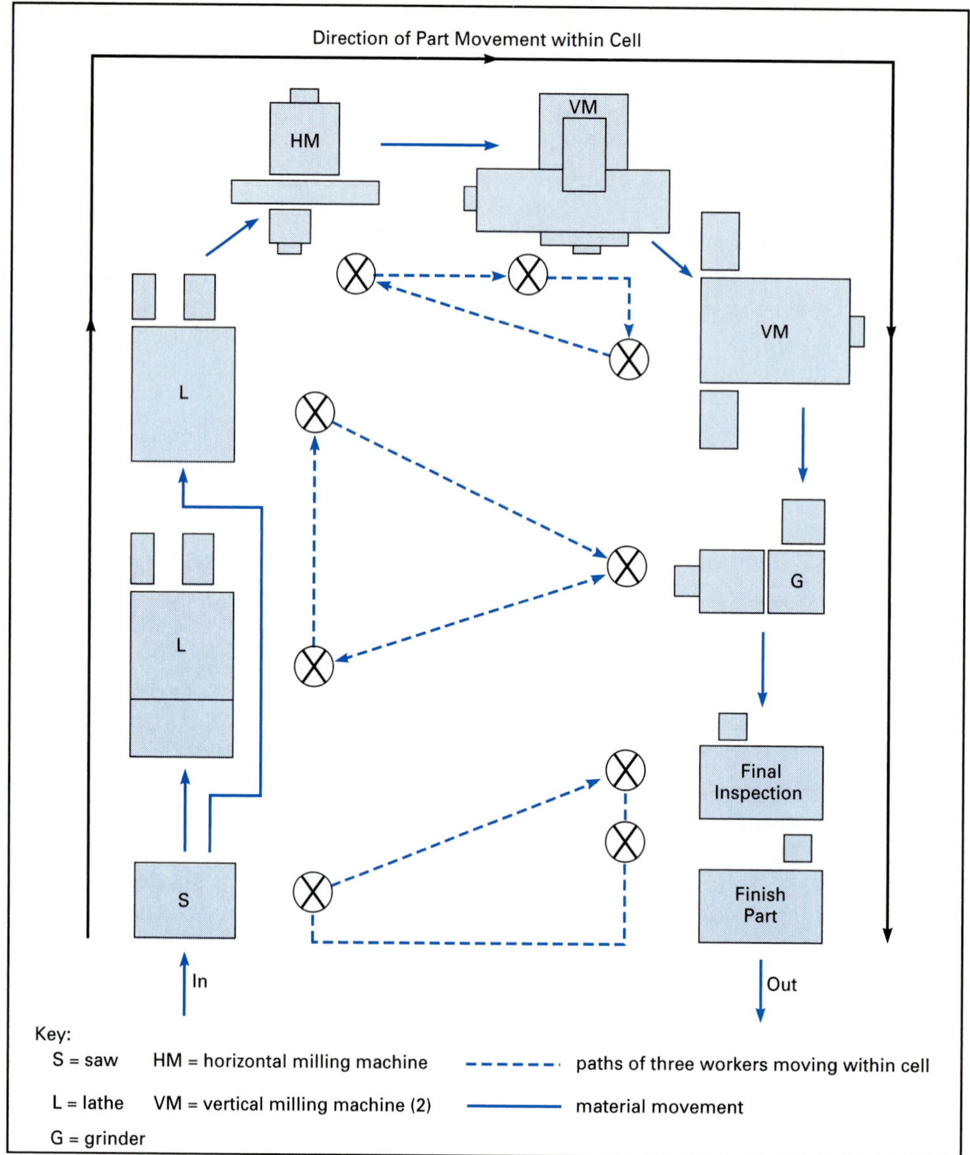

Figure 15-2 Schematic of a Manned Cell Using Conventional Machine Tools—All Laid Out in U-shape and Staffed by Three Multifunctional Workers. (Reprinted from J.T. Black, ''An Overview of Conventional Manufacturing Systems and Comparisons of Conventional Systems,'' *Industrial Engineering*, vol. 15, no. 11 [1983]. Published by the Institute of Industrial Engineers, Atlanta, Georgia. By permission of the Institute.)

Automated storage and retrieval systems (AS/RSs) are computer-controlled high-density storage facilities, such as stacker cranes. AS/RS can feed production and withdraw and store finished products.

Hausman et al. (1976) considered rules for assigning locations to items in an AS/RS. Computerized systems of inventory control are often designed to interface with a warehouse. The Farm Supply caselet, at the end of this chapter, asks the reader to consider the design of a warehouse, including a large stacker crane.

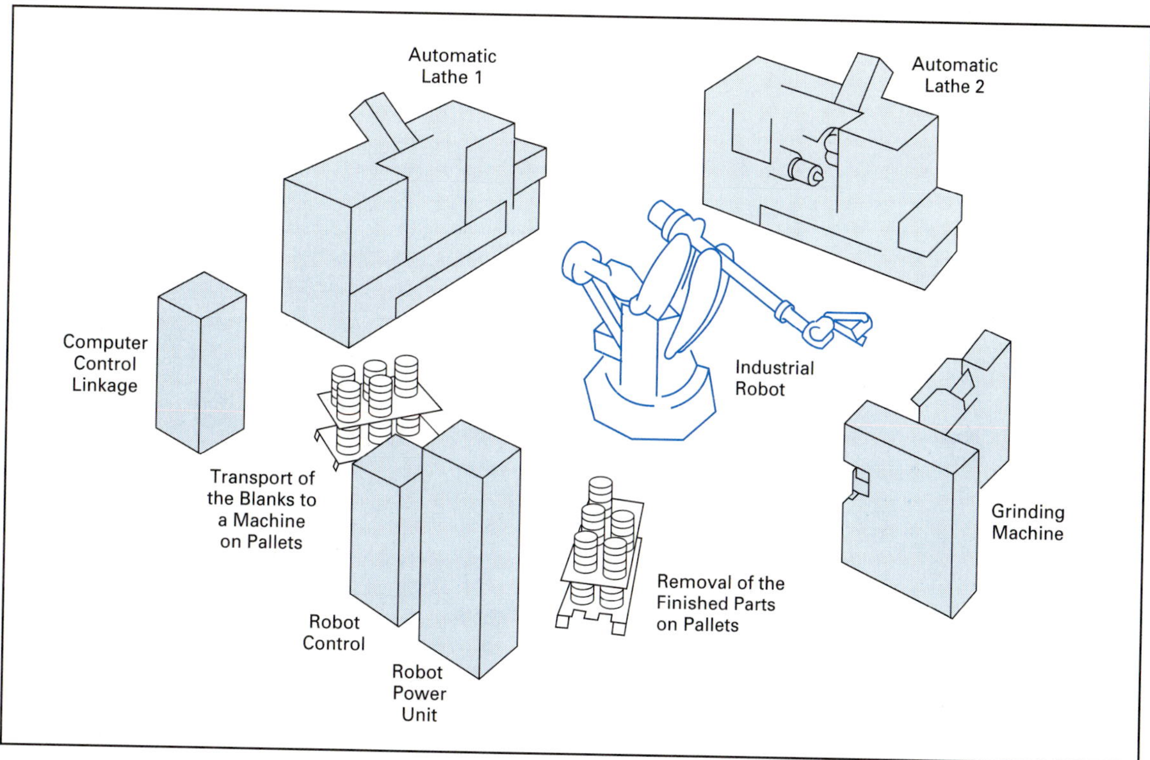

Figure 15-3 Example of Unmanned Cellular Manufacturing System in Which NC Machine Tools and Robot Work Together to Produce Turned and Cylindrically Ground Parts. (Reprinted from J.T. Black, "An Overview of Cellular Manufacturing Systems and Comparisons to Conventional Systems," *Industrial Engineering*, vol. 15, no. 11 [1983]. Published by the Institute of Industrial Engineers, Atlanta, Georgia. By permission of the Institute.)

Automated guided-vehicle systems (AGVSs) are what the name implies: automated vehicles moving work to and from storage and production.

Asynchronous material-handling systems allow different parts of a conveyor to move at different rates. This is important in flexible systems, since different facilities may process items at different rates, and each facility should be supplied with work. A single-speed conveyor can be used for an assembly line, but FMSs process different parts in the same cell. The slowest machine for one part may be the fastest one for the next part. If we always wait for the slowest part, production time will be lost.

Responsiveness to Change. Increasing the ability to respond rapidly to new ideas requires shortening the time needed to convert an idea into a product, as well as having a process that can adapt readily to the production of new products. Important advances in computer-based manufacturing and design technology have contributed significantly toward meeting these requirements. Specifically, three computer-assisted methods fall in this category.

Computer-aided process planning (CAPP) is a computerized method of using group-technology product codes and selecting the process to be used in production.

Computer-aided design (CAD) is a tool for the design engineer. Extensive data bases are developed that allow an engineer to try different designs and

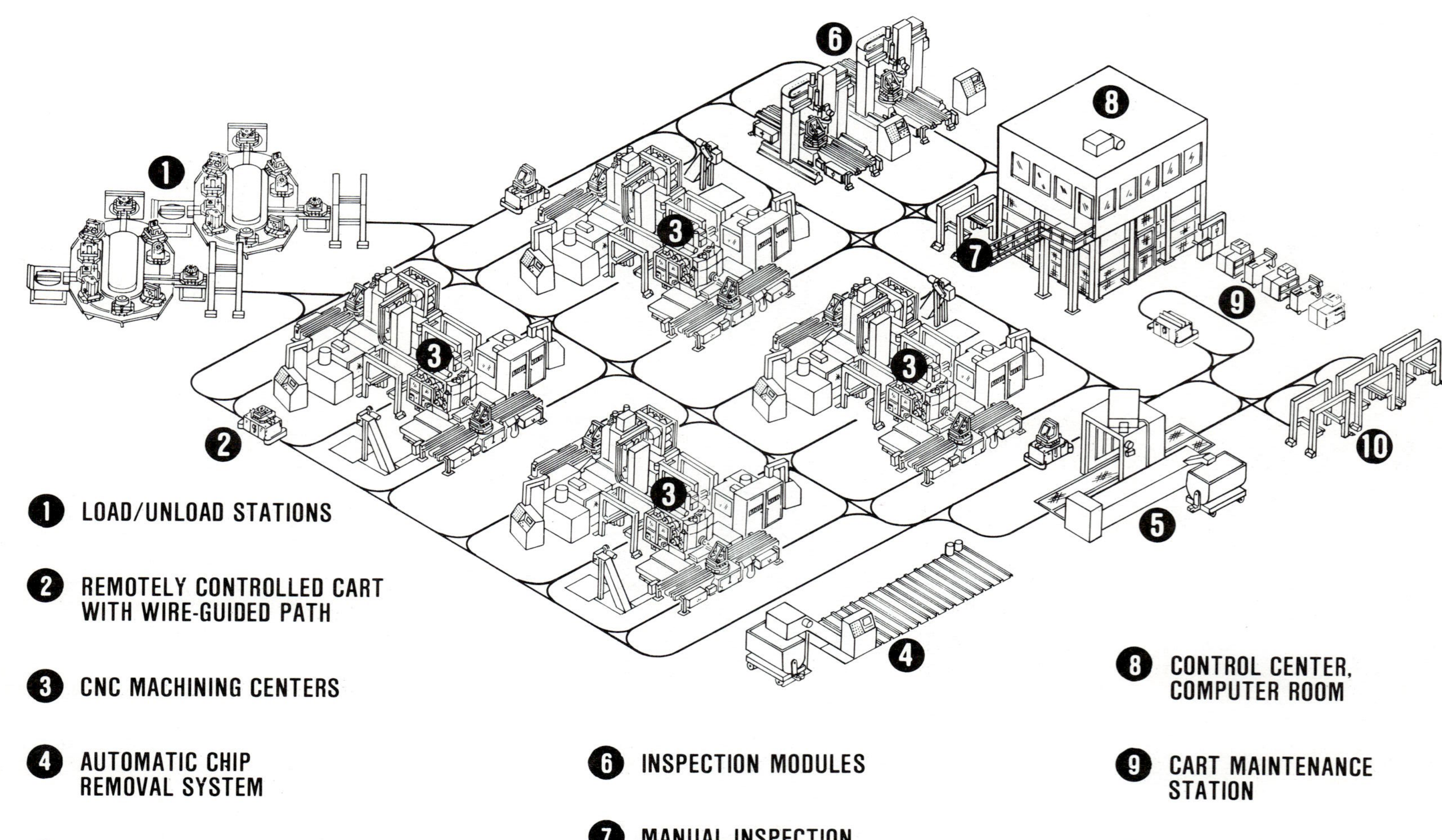

Figure 15-4 A Flexible Manufacturing System. (Courtesy of Cincinnati Milacron.)

test their performance. This substantially reduces the time required to bring an idea into production.

Computer-aided manufacturing (CAM) is a broad term that encompasses the direct use of computers in process control, such as CNC, and indirect means such as cost estimation, work standards, and developing NC input media (see Groover 1987).

CAD/CAM *or* CADICAM, the integration of CAD and CAM, is still in a relatively early stage of development. The ultimate goal is a system that will take the engineer's (computer-assisted) design directly to the (computer-assisted) manufacturing stage. In effect, by pushing a button the picture would become a real object. Less ambitious goals are currently being achieved by integrating data on manufacturing difficulties into the engineering design system.

Development of the IBM LaserPrinter offers a recent example of the promise of CAD/CAM.[2] In designing their new printer, IBM decided to follow the important concept of simplicity. The use of CAD/CAM technology allowed them to test the feasibility of design concepts during product development. They were extremely successful in achieving their objective. In fact, although they had planned for the printer to be assembled by robots, the simplicity of the design allowed for cheaper assembly by hand! This example also provides helpful insight into the benefits that can be derived from the interaction of product and process innovation.

Versatile Systems. A versatile system is one that has the capability to produce many different products. Many of the concepts discussed previously, such as cellular manufacturing, asynchronous material handling, NC machines, CAD, and CAM can contribute to versatility. However, a system can be automated, flexible, and responsive but not versatile. This occurs in the case of a highly automated facility designed specifically to produce a narrow line of high-technology items. It is flexible if production changeovers among the items are easily accomplished. It is responsive if changes in the market for this line of items can be readily accommodated. However, major redesign of the facility might be required to produce a variety of items; thus, the facility would be very limited in versatility.

Although versatility is desirable, it often comes at a cost of reduced productivity. A system that is versatile may be ''jack of all trades, master of none.'' Narrow focus often allows production technology that is highly efficient but single purpose. Thus, a company with versatile facilities will have a competitive advantage in moving between markets, but it may face higher marginal production costs as a result.

Layout Implications

The manufacturing methods and concepts of this section are closely associated with facility layout (Chapter 16). *Process layout* and *product layout* represent two ends of a continuum from small batches to large batches to continuous production (see Chapter 2). The larger the batch and the smaller the product variety, the closer to a continuous process a plant can be designed to be. When quantity is sufficient, this type of plant can have very low unit production costs.

---

[2]''IBM Discovers a Simple Pleasure,'' *Fortune,* May 21, 1990, p. 64.

Cellular manufacturing, group technology, and flexible manufacturing systems attempt to obtain the benefits of product or continuous layout for firms with smaller batches and larger variety. The ability to keep manufacturing cells busy with small batches holds down inventory and production costs. Different layouts and different organizational structures are needed. Figures 15-5 and 15-6 show two layouts for a fictitious two-product firm. The "new" organization uses a cellular manufacturing approach.

Whether a flexible, automated, responsive, or versatile system is appropriate depends on many factors, but two key ones are breadth of product line (variety) and quantity to be produced. The more items, the more flexibility is needed. The larger the volume, the more automation can be justified. Several authors give numerical guidelines for automation decisions (see Ayres and Miller 1982 and Jenkins and Raedels 1983, for example). We prefer to use a detailed financial analysis rather than guidelines. (This is discussed further in Section 15-2.) The idea of matching system capability (and cost) to product-process requirements is captured in Figure 15-7. The figure suggests that high-volume production reduces the need for flexibility. High-volume items can have dedicated production facilities. However, at low volumes there will often be a wide variety of items that share facilities, increasing the need for flexible systems.

Figure 15-5 Common Organization with Common Layout. (Reprinted from R.J. Schonberger. "Integration of Cellular Manufacturing and Just-in-Time Production," *Industrial Engineering*, vol. 15, no. 11 [1983]. Published by the Institute of Industrial Engineers, Atlanta, Georgia. By permission of the Institute.)

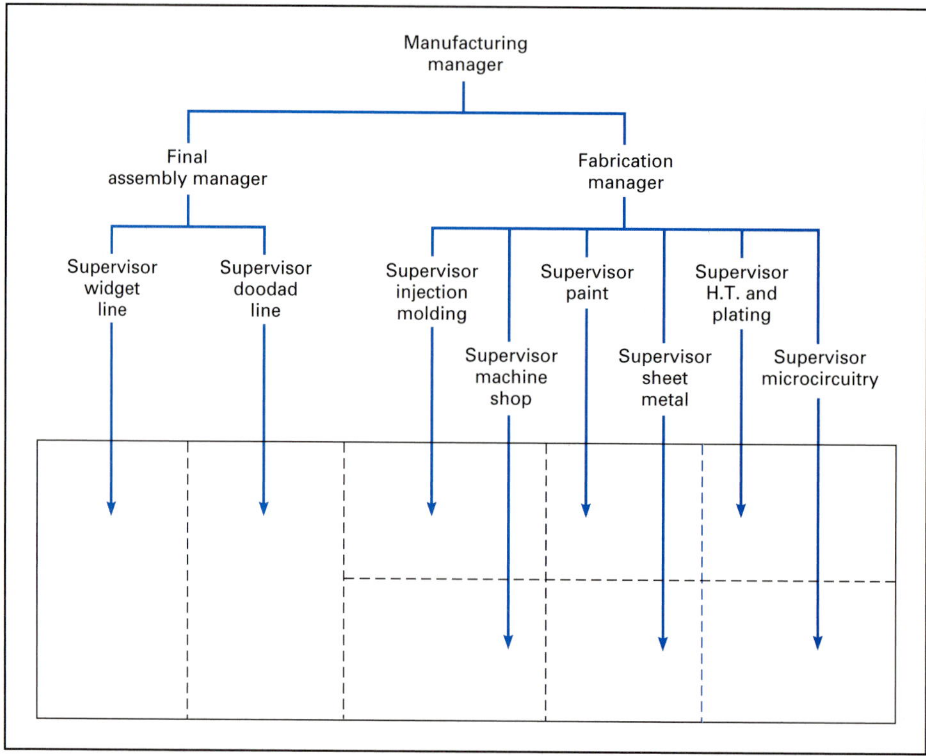

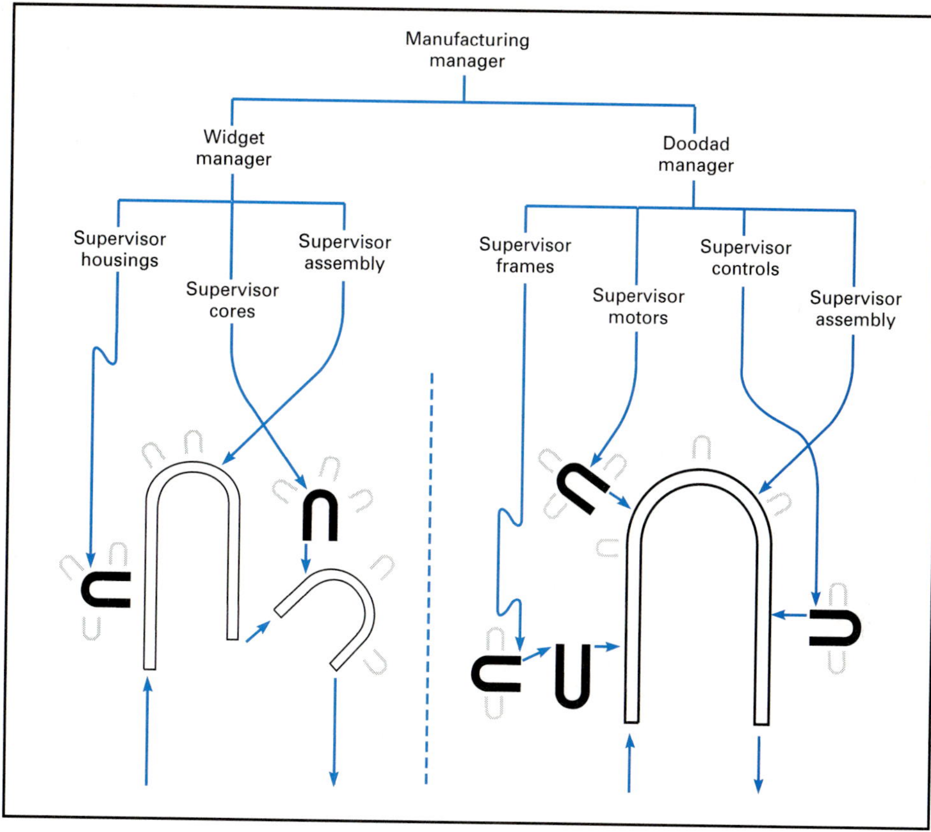

Figure 15-6 New Manufacturing Plant and Organizational Realignment. (Reprinted from R.J. Schonberger, "Integration of Cellular Manufacturing and Just-in-Time Production," *Industrial Engineering*, vol. 15, no. 11 [1983]. Published by the Institute of Industrial Engineers, Atlanta, Georgia. By permission of the Institute.)

Computer Control

Research on automated manufacturing systems continues to advance the technology (see, for example, Mazzola 1990). In our opinion the difficult, unsolved problem is that of overall system control. That is, How do we control the entire facility so that it meets the overall objectives? Klahorst (1981) speaks of three levels of control. Level 1 is simply control of NC machines—to drill a hole of the correct diameter, for example. Level 2 is localized control of parts flow and interface with level 1. Level 3 is a true management information system with decision-making power. Where should parts be sent? When can an order be completed? Systems at levels 1 and 2 are in place and operating. Level 3 remains unsolved, but the topics discussed in Chapters 9 through 12 can be part of an integrated system of control.

Mazzola, Neebe, and Dunn (1989), for example, have proposed a framework for integrating FMS technology into a closed-loop MRP system. The FMS/MRP production planning model, shown in Figure 15-8, provides for system-level MRP planning priorities to induce appropriate production planning and control objectives on the FMS while simultaneously allowing for necessary feedback from the FMS.

As shown in Figure 15-8, this coordinated planning framework is based

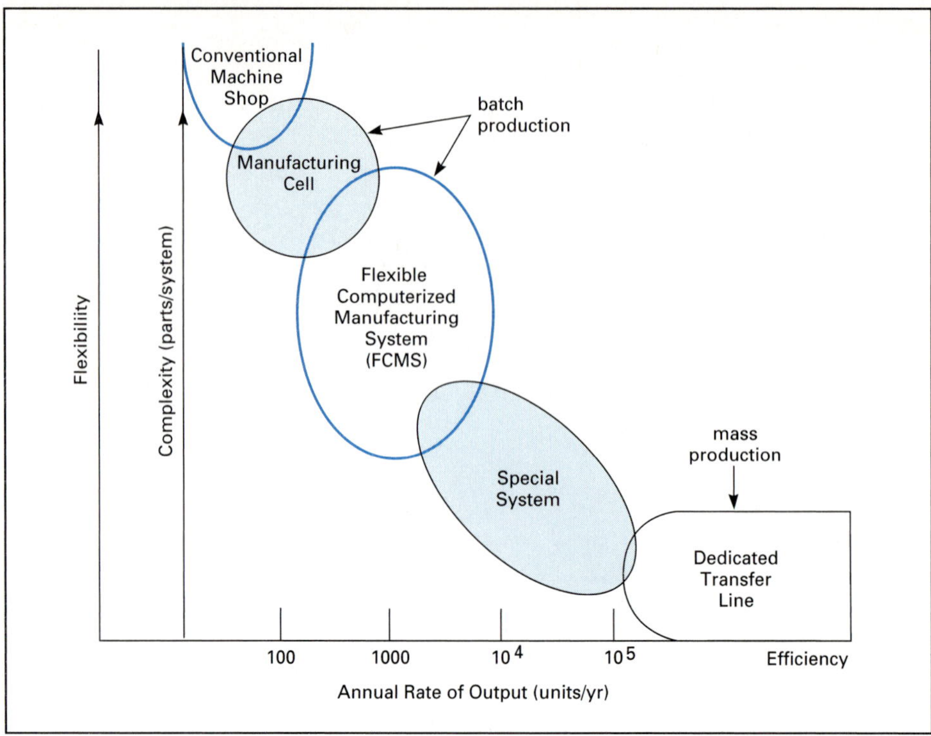

Figure 15-7 Efficiency-versus-Flexibility Trade-Offs. (Reprinted from R. Ayres and S. Miller, ''Robotics, CAM, and Industrial Productivity.'' *National Productivity Review*, vol. 1, no. 1 [1982]. Published by Executive Enterprises Publication Co., Inc., New York. By permission of the publisher.)

Figure 15-8 FMS/MRP Production Planning. (From J.B. Mazzola et al., ''Production Planning of a Flexible Manufacturing System in a Material Requirements Planning Environment,'' *The International Journal of Flexible Manufacturing Systems*, vol. 1, no. 2 [1989]. Reprinted with permission of Kluwer Academic Publishers, Boston, Mass.)

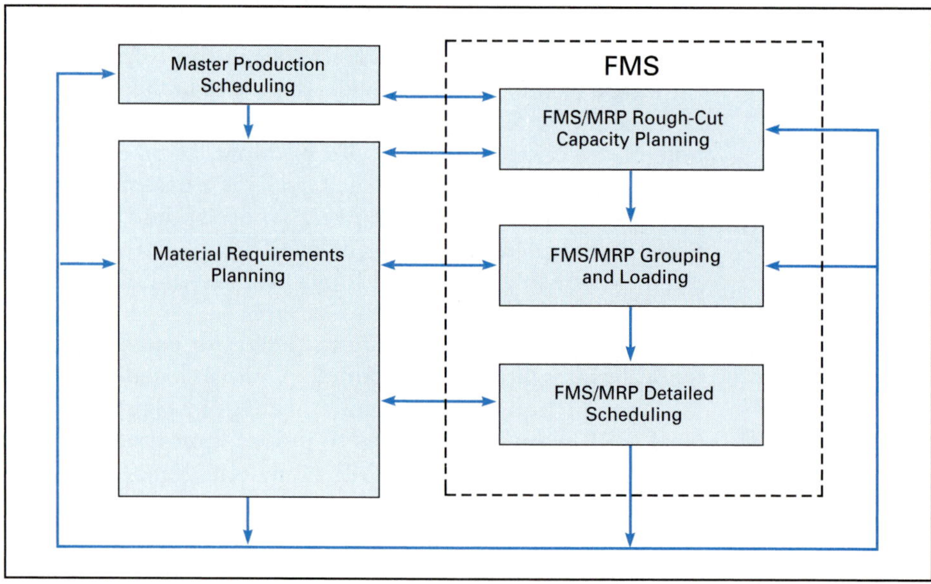

on a hierarchical system involving three levels: FMS/MRP rough-cut capacity planning, FMS/MRP grouping and loading, and FMS/MRP detailed scheduling. Consistent with hierarchical systems (see Chapter 11), decisions made at higher levels determine constraints for lower levels. Information is then fed back to higher levels (in both the FMS and MRP systems) to provide for effective, dynamic operation of the system.

Computer integrated manufacturing (CIM) offers the as yet unrealized dream of an entire automated facility, combining innovative product, process, and information technologies, as well the capability to operate for prolonged periods of time without human intervention. Many manufacturing and consulting firms are trying to be the first to control an entire automated plant well. Several major thrusts have been announced since 1989. Putting the pieces together requires a knowledge of the hardware, excellent computer skills, and, most important in our opinion, a good "feel" for overall systems of production.

Automation and Services

So far our discussion has centered on process technologies in manufacturing operations. In this subsection we consider the application of innovation and new technology to service operations. As we will see, automation offers substantial opportunities for expanding the nature and efficiencies of service operations as well.

Low-contact (or quasi-manufacturing) services are closest to manufacturing operations (see Chapter 2). Consequently, many of the manufacturing innovations discussed previously are already being utilized by such service operations. The Postal Service, for example, is using automated mail-sorting machines to replace labor-intensive sorting operations. The corresponding increases in productivity and quality have been quite impressive. For example, manual sorting has on the average a 4% error rate, and one person can sort about 600 letters per hour. Using automated optical character readers (OCRs), the error rate drops to below 1%, and a two-person crew can sort 35,000 letters per hour.

Increased use of automation is also occurring in medium- and high-contact services. Automatic teller machines (ATMs) at banks are now commonly used to augment teller capacity and extend banking hours. Bylinsky (1987) describes some fascinating applications of robotics in services. Robots, for example, have been developed for use in space and deep-sea exploration. In these applications, the use of robots avoids the additional costs and increased danger of human involvement. In medical applications, physicians have used a robot arm to assist them in delicate brain surgery, and robots are also being used to perform nursing-related activities. Robots have been developed for use in commercial and domestic housekeeping services. In addition to these applications, the military has identified many potential uses of robots. The service-robot industry has a high potential for growth that may even eclipse that for industrial robots.

Advances in information technology have contributed to improvements in service operations. In addition, the timely and efficient management of information is vital to the successful implementation of the manufacturing-process technologies discussed previously. For example, a parts-design database management system can contribute to the implementation of group technology. Table 15-2 lists some important terms in information technology.

Management information systems (MIS) provide users (managers, as well as others) with the capability to access, transform, and report information.

Table 15-2 Information Technologies

Term	Acronym (if any)	Partial List of References
Management information systems	MIS	Zmud 1983
Decision support systems	DSS	
Knowledge systems		Gallagher 1988
Expert systems	ES	
Local area networks	LAN	Marucheck and Sulek 1987
Office automation		
Electronic data interchange	EDI	Milbrandt 1990
Bar codes		Bar Code Survey 1990
Universal product codes (UPC)		
Bar-code scanners		

("MIS" is a term that has been used previously in this book. For example, in Chapter 10 we discussed the usefulness of MRP as an MIS tool.) A *decision support system* (DSS) facilitates human decision making by allowing the decision maker to work interactively with the system in obtaining and analyzing information. (See Zmud 1983 for a more complete taxonomy of computer-based information systems [CBIS].)

An *expert system* (ES) is a form of artificial intelligence in which the system attempts to emulate the human expert by systematically applying a set of stored rules when solving a problem. Expert systems offer promising applications in manufacturing and services. (Examples of applications of expert systems to computer-system configuration, oil-drilling, credit authorization, and tax planning are discussed in Leonard-Barton and Sviokla 1988; see also Murdick et al. 1990.)

The name "expert systems" sometimes implies that the technology is limited to the analysis of complex, difficult problems for which the skills of an expert are required. To expand the application of this technology, the more general term *knowledge-based system* (or *knowledge system*) is now commonly used (see Gallagher 1988).

Management information systems, decision support systems, and expert systems have had a profound impact on virtually all operations, including high-contact services. *Office automation*, for example, has increased dramatically, with the use of photocopying, PCs, word-processing, desk-top publishing, electronic mail, facsimile transmission (FAX), local area networks, and the like. (The use of electronic mail, express mail, and FAX technology helped to reduce critical lead times in the writing of this text.) Many professional services, such as law offices, require the effective implementation of these technologies to remain competitive.

A *local area network* (LAN) is a communication system that links computers, input/output devices, storage devices, and software. LAN technology provides for the rapid exchange of information and the efficient sharing of resources. (See, for example, Marucheck and Sulek 1987.)

Other types of information technology have had a significant effect on operations management. *Bar codes* are used extensively to store pertinent information directly on items. For example, they are used in manufacturing operations to keep track of inventory, especially work-in-process inventory (Karmarkar 1989). Applications of bar codes in service operations are also common. Airlines use bar codes in their baggage-handling operations. Movie video stores use bar-coded identification cards to process and update customer accounts.

Supermarkets use bar-coded information (universal product code, or UPC) in conjunction with UPC scanners to assist at the checkout and to support inventory control and purchasing. McCann and Gallagher (1990) have developed expert systems that use marketing data from UPC information gathered at electronic point-of-sale terminals to provide decision support in advertising strategies and product-promotion and merchandising decisions.[3]

There is tremendous potential for the application of this technology to operations decisions such as facility layout and automated inventory-control systems. Kusiak (1990) discusses the use of knowledge-based systems in manufacturing. Also, the capability to perform sophisticated analysis on demand data can easily lead to innovative approaches to combining marketing and operations in service operations. For example, this technology can facilitate the often difficult task of simultaneously managing demand and service capacity.

Electronic data interchange (EDI) involves the direct exchange of information between computers over a telephone line. Because it is done electronically, EDI provides for the rapid exchange of information and eliminates the need for much of the supporting paperwork. EDI also allows for a reduction in processing errors, since data need not be transcribed several times. EDI can be used to communicate MRP requirements to vendors. In addition, EDI facilitates JIT purchasing, since orders can be quickly, inexpensively, and accurately communicated to suppliers. EDI can also foster close relationships with vendors because of the need to establish mutual EDI capability and delivery standards. Finally, because procurement lead times can be reduced through effective implementation of EDI, retail stores, for example, can benefit by reducing the amount of inventory carried. (See Milbrandt 1990 for a discussion of the benefits of EDI.)

REVIEW PROBLEMS

1. Review Tables 15-1 and 15-2 to be sure that you understand the terms.

2. Why is it necessary to consider the interaction between product and process innovation?

3. Why is cellular manufacturing replacing process layout in some situations?

Solutions

2. The importance of matching process capability with product-manufacturing (or service-delivery) requirements is one of the keys to competing successfully. If product innovation is pursued separately from process innovation, or vice versa, substantial opportunities for achieving a strategic advantage can be lost. The example of the IBM LaserPrinter showed how an unex-

[3]These systems were developed as part of the Marketing Workbench Laboratory at Duke University.

pected but significant process innovation came about as a result of a product innovation.

3. Cellular manufacturing allows many of the production efficiencies of a flow shop to be realized for facilities that produce many different items in small batches.

15-2 MANAGING AUTOMATED SYSTEMS

This section looks at some of the issues that arise in the management of automated production systems. We begin by discussing factors that must be considered when making financial-investment decisions on automated systems. Since their cost can be quite high (FMSs, for example, can cost tens of millions of dollars), it is necessary that financial-justification analysis be extended to include all benefits, both tangible and intangible. We then consider the relationship between automated systems and the cost-accounting and marketing functions. The section concludes with a brief discussion of behavioral and societal issues pertaining to automation and new technology.

Financial Justification

Historically, capital investment decisions have been analyzed using discounted cash-flow analysis (see Chapter 3). This analysis takes into account the time value of money, as well as the costs and benefits of the investment. Kaplan (1986), in discussing financial justification of CIM, notes that discounted cash-flow analysis is still the correct way to approach CIM decisions. Many companies, however, apply this analysis incorrectly. In addition to employing management practices that bias decision making against investment in automated technology, many of the benefits of CIM technology, which extend well beyond labor savings, are often ignored.

Kaplan notes several reasons why companies either misapply discounted cash-flow analysis to CIM investment or bias process investment away from automated technology. In determining the discount rate used in the analysis, for instance, Kaplan claims that many companies impose an arbitrarily high, unrealistic hurdle rate. A project-investment decision should reflect the opportunity cost of capital for investment decisions of the same risk as the project, rather than some generally established (high) target hurdle rate.

A second difficulty noted by Kaplan arises from the tendency on the part of many companies to compare the automated project against the status quo. Typically, it is assumed incorrectly that in the absence of the new investment everything (including market share and cost) will continue as it currently exists. Often this will not be the case, since competitors may adopt the new technology or identify alternative technologies that may have considerable impact on the marketplace. Kaplan quotes Henry Ford's comment, "If you need a new machine and don't buy it, you pay for it without getting it."

In his discussion, Kaplan also observes that many companies bias investment decisions away from large capital investment because of their investment-funding policies. Plant managers often have within their discretion the ability to approve or deny small- to modest-size investment requests. Large capital expenditures, such as those required for many automated manufacturing systems, typically require approval by top-level management or perhaps the board of directors. This practice implicitly reinforces incremental process improvements and discourages larger, possibly more profound process investment.

The analysis of automated-process investment decisions requires the assessment of all the benefits that derive from the new technology. Roger Smith, former chairman of the board of General Motors, once commented: ''Every time the cost of labor goes up $1 an hour, 1,000 more robots become economical'' (*New York Times*, October 14,1981). The main reason given by many managers for automating operations is labor savings. Examining automation only as a labor-savings device is myopic in two very different ways. First, workers will not be committed to a firm if they perceive that the firm is not committed to them. Second, the potential savings (and benefits) extend far beyond labor savings. We will address the second issue first.

Many tangible benefits arise from investment in automated production. Estimates vary dramatically, but most industrial equipment is in productive use only a small fraction of the time. Zisk (1983) mentions 10% to 15%, with a possible increase to 80% to 90% with an FMS. Increased process efficiency can lead to lower levels of work-in-process and finished-goods inventory (Kaplan 1986). The cost savings from lower inventory can be substantial. In addition, if increases in process efficiencies can indeed be realized, total investment in equipment can decline in the long run.

Quality often improves with automation as a result of a machine's precision. Material usage improves; there is less waste. This reduces scrap and rework cost. Better quality may also result in increased sales.

Also, automated production systems often require less factory space than do other configurations. The opportunity cost of this regained space should be reflected in the analysis.

Consistent with the potential for increased processing efficiency in automated systems noted previously, the total time spent in the manufacture of an item can decline dramatically. In many manufacturing companies, items are being physically transformed only 5% of the time. The rest of the time is spent waiting. Thus, huge reductions in total time are possible if the correct parts arrive at the correct machine at the right time. This relates to the reduction in inventory levels mentioned previously. However, it also leads to some extremely important intangible benefits. Response time to customers, for example, can be reduced. This reduction in customer lead time can contribute significantly to the company's competitive position in the marketplace. Kaplan (1986) has observed that CIM also increases system responsiveness to customers by allowing for rapid implementation of design changes.

Automated manufacturing systems can also lead to more flexibility. As in the case of FMSs, automated systems give rise to ''economies of scope,'' that is, the capability for low-cost production of high-variety, low-volume goods (Kaplan 1986). This increased flexibility can also offer a competitive advantage, especially in regard to providing the capability to easily produce replacement parts for old or discontinued models. The flexibility of machines also allows them to serve a backup function in the event of individual machine failure.

If labor cost is reduced, some overhead costs will decline at the same time. Often, the labor that is saved is in operations involving hazardous conditions, so safety improves and insurance costs decrease.

Some additional intangible benefits may also be realized. One benefit is that the first project helps an organization learn how to use automation and to see how operations can be integrated to yield greater total benefits. The initial project is an important first step in moving the company along the automated-process learning curve. Thus, a firm may not meet short-term financial goals on an automation project, but the eventual payoff may be significant.

Another benefit is that automation drives down the marginal cost of a unit of production. A company with a lower marginal cost of production is better able to survive either a price war or simply increased competition. It may be that automation is necessary as a strategic weapon in order to survive.

Many tangible and intangible savings accrue to automated manufacturing, and we do not claim to have captured all of them. When considering an investment of this nature, it is necessary to identify as many as possible. Unfortunately, some of these savings may be hard to quantify. It is important to attempt to estimate them, because, as Potter (1983) noted: ''If [indirect savings] are not used in the justification of a project and the savings truly do exist, the analysis is more incorrect than it would have been if educated estimates had been used.'' Financial analysis can be used to evaluate automation projects; financial analysis can be misused by not including all benefits. Some review problems at the end of this section and some problems at the end of the chapter explore the application of these principles.

Cost Accounting and Marketing

Manufacturing organizations often use direct labor as a basis for generating management accounting numbers. This basis makes no sense if there are few workers. In a highly automated environment, the average direct labor hour could easily generate $1000 worth of cost when overhead is added. Decisions should not be made using such numbers. Machine-hours is a better basis if the capital cost is large, but no simple basis can be as good as a sound economic analysis of the managerial question at hand. (Accounting methods were discussed in Chapter 3.)

Marketing strategy is affected by automation because different processes fit different product lines. Figure 15-7 shows production processes that are appropriate for different numbers of products and annual demand. However, as a matter of strategy, the product line and the factory design (and subsequent modification) should be determined together. The management of product and process innovation should be governed strategically so that the company can strive to obtain maximum benefit from the interaction between these two types of innovation.

In some situations, for example, this might involve limiting the number of finished products, using common parts wherever possible, and limiting engineering changes. A simple product line may improve quality and reduce cost. Customers may buy more of these products, and profits may increase. This is not to say that a small product line is always appropriate. Rather, automation plans and factory design in general should go hand in hand with product-line management.

Automation: Behavioral and Societal Issues

Robots can accept boring, tiresome jobs. They can handle heavy loads and hazardous environments such as spray painting in an enclosed room. (Comparisons of robots and people, with a discussion of the types of jobs best suited for each, is given in Kamali et al. 1982.) Robots can improve safety, reduce boredom, and work odd hours. Yet they are thought of by many workers as a bad thing because they can also reduce the number of jobs.

Introducing any change to an organization is difficult, but a change that can eliminate jobs often causes negative reactions on the part of the work force. For example, in the *Wall Street Journal,* Saga (1983) wrote of the Japanese experience: ''Automation is particularly bad news for older workers. Their traditional skills suddenly obsolete, many find themselves working under the supervision of younger employees.''

Minimizing the difficulties of automation requires planning. Some companies announce that no employees will be laid off as a result of automation. If this can be done, one major concern is eliminated. Even if layoffs are deemed essential, employees should not be kept guessing. Foulkes and Hirsch (1984) have asserted that ''in the interest of maintaining cooperative bargaining relations, the conscientious employer should not wait for the union to request advance notice of new technology but should voluntarily extend this courtesy.''

Once the employment situation is clear, the problem of education must be addressed. The operators must be trained, of course, but the skills of engineering, supervisory, and other support staff may also need to be improved. Learning how to design products, determine production schedules, and monitor quality with automated equipment takes time and commitment. Everyone's help should be solicited, and attention must be paid to all concerned. The implementation process requires not only extensive technical work but also extensive education, communication, and management. Social science and technology must work together to get maximum benefit (see Sonntag 1990).

We conclude this section with a brief discussion of the societal impact of new manufacturing technologies. First, a history lesson. The Industrial Revolution began in the late eighteenth century and had its greatest and earliest effect in the United Kingdom. The technology that received the most attention replaced 200 workers with one worker and one set of machines, in the textile industry. Several groups, including the Luddites, condemned the technology because of its effect on employment. The Luddites went so far as to smash textile machines. However, the increased productivity was so great, and the cost so low that the demand for textiles grew sufficiently to allow total employment in the industry to increase (see Vedder 1982).

This amazing story of increased productivity, demand, and wealth leads many people to believe that the current trends in automation and computerization will also have a beneficial effect. We agree that in the long run, productivity improvements will be good for society. Also, automation will be needed in the early twenty-first century to compensate for a potential labor shortage. (In the United States, the population bulge known as the baby boom will retire, leaving fewer people working.) However, there will be significant pockets of unemployment, for example among older workers in industrial towns and among unskilled workers everywhere. Companies and government will be forced to ameliorate the situation with training programs. It will be in everyone's interest to add value to the work force so that workers can perform the new, more technical tasks.

Finally, automation, and more generally, new technologies, are coming for better or worse, and the potential of new technology will be realized only if the requisite trained work force is in place to facilitate achievement of this goal. Companies that do not use new technology to reduce cost and improve quality will lose sales to those that do. Even so, the best manufacturing and service production facilities will be those that are able to integrate in an effective manner both human and capital resources (see Sheridan 1990).

REVIEW PROBLEMS

1. A company expected that new automated equipment would reduce the total manufacturing time from 10 weeks to 2 weeks. In addition to labor savings, what benefits might the company observe from this change?

2. The APS company produces an item for which the expected monthly cost of sales is $100,000; 70% of this amount is attributable to direct labor. Currently, work-in-process (WIP) amounts to a 4-month supply of inventory. APS is considering whether to replace the current production process with a new automated production system that will reduce labor costs by 40%. In addition, the new system will reduce WIP by 75%.

   a. What is the potential annual labor savings from the new system?
   b. If the new system is implemented and WIP falls immediately, what is the cash inflow from reduced inventory in the first year of operation?
   c. What are some of the other benefits that might arise from the new system?

3. Is automation good or bad for society?

Solutions

1. Work-in-process inventory will be reduced and customer service will improve. We cannot be certain what other benefits would accrue, but quality might improve, waste and finished-goods inventory might be reduced, and the firm might be in a better competitive cost position.
2. a. Annual labor savings = 12(0.4)(0.7)($100,000) = $336,000.
   b. First-year WIP cash inflow = 0.75(4)($100,000) = $300,000.
   c. Another benefit that might result from the new process is higher quality; this can lead to reduced scrap and rework costs and possibly higher sales. In addition to the cash inflow from reduced WIP inventory during the first year, an annual inventory holding-cost saving is realized on the $300,000 reduction in WIP. Many of the other benefits discussed in the chapter may also be realized.
3. It is both good (productivity will increase, thereby adding to total wealth) and bad (some workers will lose jobs and have difficulty being trained for new ones). There are many other points that can be made here. For example, since work helps define people in our society, reducing work may not be good. Also, automation is inevitable, whether it is good or bad.

SUMMARY

The ability to manage technological innovation effectively is a key factor in establishing a competitive position in the marketplace. Innovation requires the implementation of new ideas that have the potential to advance the firm's objectives and occurs as the result of both large and incremental changes. It is helpful to distinguish between product innovation and process innovation, as well as to understand the dynamics of their relationship, which can be linked to the product life cycle.

Technological innovation continues to have a substantial impact on the operations function in both manufacturing and service organizations. Operations technologies can be divided conveniently into two types: process technology, which applies to the production process, and information technology, which applies to managing information.

Manufacturing systems have benefited from a variety of innovative process technologies. These technologies can be classified on the basis of their potential to improve the flexibility, degree of automation, responsiveness, or versatility of the production system. It would not be practical in a text of this nature to attempt to survey in detail the many innovations in technology and equipment that are, and will be, available. Still, we have attempted to introduce important terms for new production (manufacturing and service) technologies.

The effects of new process and information technologies are as profound in the service industries as in manufacturing. Along with dramatic advances in information technology, such process innovations as diagnostic equipment in medical care, automated teller machines in banks, and service robots constitute examples of the effective application of these technologies.

The financial justification of automated production systems requires that we identify all the benefits, both tangible and intangible, that derive from the implementation of the new technology. Traditional discounted cash-flow analysis is still applicable; however, it must be expanded to include quantitative estimates of all the benefits. In addition, firms should avoid investment-justification policies that bias decision making away from automated systems.

Agriculture is a sector that has benefited greatly from improved technology. The fraction of labor involved in agriculture has declined to where a small percentage of the work force feeds us better and more cheaply than ever. The labor force will also decline in manufacturing as new technologies are introduced. Agriculture and manufacturing, however, will remain a key source of wealth creation even as their part of the work force declines.

Technology changes the fabric of our society. As technology advances, changes occur not only in the nature of work but also in the nature of the work force and the way in which jobs are rewarded by society. Different skills are in demand and thus are paid well and respected. In addition to understanding technical issues and methods of strategic, financial, and operational analysis, operations managers must also be sensitive to the human issues in organizations and in society. In the long run, taking care of the work force and the community is good for the entire organization.

CASELET

FARM SUPPLY CORPORATION'S AUTOMATED WAREHOUSE

Farm Supply Corporation (also discussed in Chapters 3 and 14) has three partially automated warehouses, called distribution centers (DCs). They distribute several thousand stock-keeping units (SKUs) through the DCs, including products such as paint, pet food, hardware, small power tools, and gardening items. Each warehouse receives shipments from a few Farm Supply plants and outside vendors. Shipments into the DCs are in full railcar or truckload quantities, and nearly all items are palletized, meaning that they are delivered on 40-by-48-inch wooden pallets for ease of handling.

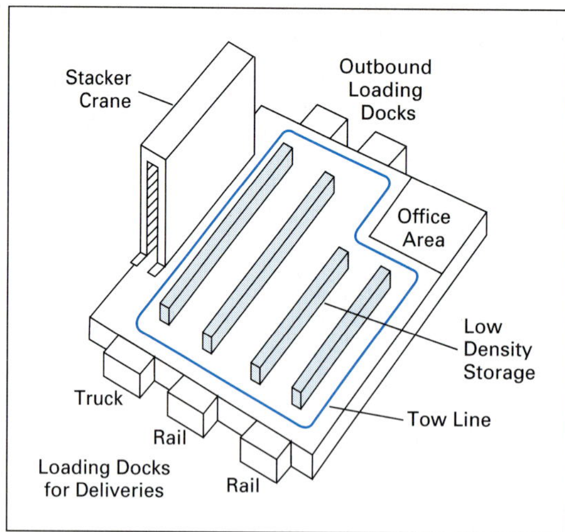

Figure 15-9 Farm Supply Distribution Center

Each DC ships to about one hundred stores. These shipments are in small quantities (less than full pallets) that are loaded into trucks that visit several stores. Each store receives two shipments per week. The truck routes are not always the same, since the demands for truck space vary, and a truck that can satisfy four stores on Monday may be able to satisfy only three stores on Thursday.

Layout. Currently, each DC is composed of three main parts: (1) the office area, including the computer system; (2) the high-density, computer-controlled stacker crane for storing full pallet lots; and (3) a low-rise area with one or two pallets of each item in racks. A schematic diagram is shown in Figure 15-9.

Control and Operation of the DC. All inbound and outbound orders are tracked by computer so that a continuous (perpetual) inventory system is maintained. Orders by the stores are fed into a program that generates picking lists. Items are withdrawn (picked) from low-density storage in the order that they will be loaded into the delivery truck. The tow-line truck is sent around with a list; operators with specialized trucks read the list, then ride the aisles retrieving items.

High-demand items have two pallets in the low-density storage area. Items that are demanded less than once per week (70% of the items) have one pallet. When the last of a pallet is used, another is ordered from the high-density storage. The stacker crane is computer controlled and retrieves only full pallets, automatically. The stacker crane is moving less than 20% of the time, but it is cost-effective as a result of the good physical control of the inventory that it allows.

Costs. Farm Supply has an annual labor cost of operating each DC of approximately $2 million, including all personnel. Equipment maintenance costs roughly $200,000 annually. Finally, each DC has $50 million in inventory. Before automation, these figures were $2 million, $50,000, and $80 million, respectively.

Required

1. Farm Supply is considering automating more of the process. What

might you consider automating, and why? On balance, do you think that your suggestion is a good one?

2. How important is it for Farm Supply to efficiently plan ''stores'' and ''retrieves'' for the stacker crane? Why? At the plant, where shipments are in full pallets and the crane is busy most of the time, is the answer different? Why?
3. Briefly describe an easy heuristic that you might use to determine which stores will be serviced by which trucks.
4. Which category of cost is most important? Why?

PROBLEMS

1. a. What is the difference between product innovation and process innovation? How are they interrelated?
   b. Describe the Abernathy and Utterback model of the dynamic relationship between product and process innovation.
   c. Relate the Abernathy and Utterback product–process interaction model to the Hayes and Wheelwright product–process matrix model (see Chapter 2).

*2. Give an example of the interaction between product and process innovation in a service organization.

3. Review the definitions of *flexible, automated, responsive,* and *versatile* in Section 15-1. How can a manufacturing system be flexible and automated but not versatile? Responsive but not flexible? Automated but not flexible?

4. Define process technology and information technology. What is the difference between them? Provide an example that illustrates the interdependency between these two types of technology.

*5. What is the difference between cellular manufacturing and flexible manufacturing?

6. What is group technology (GT)? Discuss applications of GT to cellular layout and product design.

*7. How can cellular manufacturing be helpful in the application of a just-in-time production system?

8. What are the three levels of computer control proposed by Klahorst for automated manufacturing systems? Briefly discuss the difficulties of implementing level 3.

*9. Discuss Figure 15-7. How is it related to the Hayes and Wheelwright product-process matrix (discussed in Chapter 2)?

10. What is meant by the statement, ''Cellular manufacturing, group technology, and flexible manufacturing systems attempt to obtain the benefits of product or continuous layout for firms with smaller batches and larger variety.''

*11. What are some of the reasons why firms sometimes experience difficulty investing in automated production systems or in justifying financial investment in such systems?

---

*Problems with an asterisk have answers in the back of the book.

12. Describe the tangible and intangible benefits that can result from the implementation of automated production systems. Why is it important to try to capture all these benefits when evaluating a process investment decision?
13. A benefit of automated manufacturing systems arises from the reduction in factory space required for such a system. How can this result in a cost saving for the company? What are the costs that should be used to estimate the opportunity cost of this reclaimed space?

*14. The managers of Widget Manufacturing Company (WIMCO) estimate that a flexible manufacturing system for one of their product lines will cost $20 million. The life of the system is 10 years. The following cost savings are estimated:

Labor: $2 million per year

Material: $600,000 per year

Inventory: $500,000 per year

Added gross margin: $2 million per year (attributable to increased sales)

a. Ignoring taxes and using a 10% discount rate, what is the net present value of the investment if only labor savings are included? (Assume that all cash flows occur at the end of each year, with the exception of the initial investment, which occurs at the beginning of year 1.)
b. If labor and material savings are included?
c. If all benefits are included?
d. What other benefits might occur?

*15. Redo problem 14, part c using a 40% tax rate, an 8% investment tax credit, a 6% after-tax discount rate, and straight-line depreciation over 10 years. (Assume that the investment tax credit is realized at the time of the initial investment.)

16. The FSB Company is considering an automated manufacturing system to replace the existing process. At present the expected monthly cost of sales is $600,000. Direct labor accounts for 75% of this cost. The expected monthly cost of scrap and rework is $80,000. The amount of work-in-process inventory required by the current process is equal to a 3-month supply of inventory. The estimated benefits of the new system are:

    i. 70% reduction in the amount of direct labor
    ii. an increase in quality, resulting in an 80% reduction in the amount of scrap and rework
    iii. a 60% reduction in work-in-process inventory

    If the company were to implement the new process, once the system is fully operational, calculate the cost savings during the first year from the following benefits:

    a. labor savings
    b. reduction in scrap and rework
    c. reduction in work-in-process inventory

17. (This problem continues the automated manufacturing system de-

scribed in problem 16.) The system will cost $15 million. In addition, there is an up-front cost of $2 million for training and additional system software. Ignoring taxes, this investment will be evaluated using a discounted cash-flow analysis over a 10-year period with a discount rate of 10%.

a. Determine the net present value of the investment assuming that all the benefits noted in problem 16 (labor, scrap and rework, and work-in-process savings) are realized. (Assume that all cash flows occur at the end of each year, with the exception of the initial investment and the additional training and software costs, which occur at the beginning of the flrst year.)
b. Using the current process, expected sales, as well as the expected monthly cost of sales, are growing at a compound rate of 5% per year. This is expected to continue under the new system. Determine the net present value of the investment assuming that all the benefits noted in part a are realized. (The expected monthly cost of sales during the first year is $600,000. Assume that scrap and rework cost increases at the same rate that the cost of sales increases.)
c. Identify other benefits that might arise from the new system.

*18. If automation increases wealth and GNP and improves the general economic situation, why might unemployment persist after plants are heavily automated?

REFERENCES

ABERNATHY, W.J. and J.M. UTTERBACK, "Patterns of Industrial Innovation," *Technology Review*, June/July, 1978.

AYRES, R. and S. MILLER, "Robotics, CAM, and Industrial Productivity," *National Productivity Review*, vol. 1, no. 1, 1982.

BAR CODE SURVEY, *Industrial Engineering*, September, 1990.

BLACK, J., "An Overview of Cellular Manufacturing Systems and Comparison to Conventional Systems," *Industrial Engineering*, vol. 15, no. 11, November, 1983.

BOUCHER, T. and J. MUCKSTADT, "The Inventory Cost Effectiveness of Group Technology Production Systems," *Annales de Sciences Economiques Appliquées* (Belgium), vol. 39, no. 1, 1983.

BURGELMAN, R.A. and M.A. MAIDIQUE, *Strategic Management of Technology and Innovation*, Homewood, Ill.: Irwin, 1988.

BUZACOTT, J.A. and D.D. YAO, "Flexible Manufacturing Systems: A Review of Analytical Models," *Management Science*, vol. 32, no. 7, 1986.

BYLINSKY, G., "Invasion of the Service Robots," *Fortune*, September 14, 1987.

COMEPP: Cornell Manufacturing Engineering and Productivity Program, College of Engineering, Cornell University, Ithaca, N.Y., 1982.

FOSTON, A.L., C.L. SMITH, and T. AU, *Fundamentals of Computer-Integrated Manufacturing*, Englewood Cliffs, N.J.: Prentice-Hall, 1991.

FOULKES, F.K. and J.L. HIRSCH, "People Make Robots Work," *Harvard Business Review*, January-February, 1984.

GALLAGHER, J.P., *Knowledge Systems for Business: Integrating Expert Systems and MIS*, Englewood Cliffs, N.J.: Prentice-Hall, 1988.

GROOVER, M.P., *Automation, Production Systems, and Computer-Integrated Manufacturing*, Englewood Cliffs, N.J.: Prentice-Hall, 1987.

GROOVER, M P. and E.W. ZIMMERS, JR., *CAD/CAM: Computer-Aided Design and Manufacturing*, Englewood Cliffs, N.J.: Prentice-Hall, 1984.

HAUSMAN, W.H., L.B. SCHWARZ, and S.C. GRAVES, "Optimal Storage Assignment in Automatic Warehousing Systems," *Management Science*, vol. 22, no. 6, 1976.

HAYES, R.H. and S.C. WHEELWRIGHT, *Restoring our Competitive Edge: Competing through Manufacturing*, New York: Wiley, 1984.

JAIKUMAR, R., "Postindustrial Manufacturing," *Harvard Business Review*, November–December, 1986.

JENKINS, K. and A. RAEDELS, "The Robot Revolution: Strategic Considerations for Managers," *Operations Management Review*, vol. 1, no. 2, 1983.

KAMALI, J., C. MOODIE, and G. SALVENDY, "A Framework for Integrated Assembly Systems: Humans, Automation and Robots," *International Journal of Production Research*, vol. 20, no. 4, 1982.

KAPLAN, R. S., "Must CIM be Justified by Faith Alone?" *Harvard Business Review*, March–April, 1986.

KARMARKAR, U.S., "Getting Control of Just-in-Time," *Harvard Business Review*, September–October, 1989.

KLAHORST, H.T., "Flexible Manufacturing Systems: Combining Elements to Lower Cost and Flexibility," *Industrial Engineering*, vol. 13, no. 11, November, 1981.

KUSIAK, A., "Flexible Manufacturing Systems: A Structural Approach," *International Journal of Production Research*, vol. 23, no. 6, 1985.

KUSIAK, A., *Intelligent Manufacturing Systems*, Englewood Cliffs, N.J.: Prentice-Hall, 1990.

LEONARD-BARTON, D. and J. SVIOKLA, "Putting Expert Systems to Work," *Harvard Business Review*, March–April, 1988.

LUGGEN, W.W., *Flexible Manufacturing Cells and Systems*, Englewood Cliffs, N.J.: Prentice-Hall, 1991.

MARUCHECK, A.S. and J.M. SULEK, "An Algorithm for Technology Choice in Local Area Network Design," *Management Science*, vol. 33, no. 1 , 1987.

MAZZOLA, J.B. (ed.), "Automated Manufacturing Systems," *Annals of Operations Research*, vol. 26, 1990.

MAZZOLA, J.B., A.W. NEEBE, and C.V.R. DUNN, "Production Planning of a Flexible Manufacturing System in a Material Requirements Planning Environment." *International Journal of Flexible Manufacturing Systems*, vol. 1, no. 2, 1989.

MCCANN, J.M. and J.P. GALLAGHER, *Expert Systems for Scanner Data Environments*, Boston: Kluwer, 1990.

MILBRANDT, B., "EDI: A More Efficient Way to Operate," *P&IM Review*, August, 1990.

MITCHELL, F.H., JR., *CIM Systems: An Introduction to Computer-Integrated Manufacturing*, Englewood Cliffs, N.J.: Prentice-Hall, 1991.

MURDICK, R.G., B. RENDER, and R.S. RUSSELL, *Service Operations Management*, Boston: Allyn & Bacon, 1990.

NOORI, H., *Managing the Dynamics of New Technology*, Englewood Cliffs, N.J.: Prentice-Hall, 1990.

NOVA, "The Robot Revolution?" program number 1214, Boston, Mass.: WGBH Publications, 1985.

POTTER, R. "Analyze Indirect Savings to Justify Robot Implementation," *Industrial Engineering*, vol. 15, no. 11, November, 1983.

RHODES, D., "The Critical Imperative in Flexible Manufacturing is Information," *Industrial Engineering*, October, 1990.

SAGA, I., "Japan's Robots Produce Problems for Workers," *Wall Street Journal*, February 28, 1983.

SCHONBERGER, R.J., *World Class Manufacturing*, NewYork: Free Press, 1986.

SCHROEDER, R.G., G.D. SCUDDER, and D.R. ELM, "Innovation in Manufacturing," *Journal of Operations Management*, vol. 8, no. 1, 1989.

SHERIDAN, J. H., "America's Best Plants," *Industry Week*, November 15, 1990.

SONNTAG, V., "Flexible Manufacturing ... from a Different Perspective," *Industrial Engineering*, November, 1990.

STECKE, K.E., "Formulation and Solution of Nonlinear Integer Production Planning Problems for Flexible Manufacturing Systems," *Management Science*, vol. 29, no. 3, March, 1983.

TAHERI, J., "Northern Telecom Tackles Successful Implementation of Cellular Manufacturing," *Industrial Engineering*, October, 1990.

VEDDER, R., "Robotics and the Economy," prepared for the Joint Economic Committee, U.S. Congress, March 26, 1982.

ZISK, B., "Material Transport for Cellular Manufacturing," *Industrial Engineering*, vol. 15, no. 11, November, 1983.

ZMUD, R., *Information Systems in Organizations*, Glenview, Ill.: Scott, Foresman & Company, 1983.

chapter

16

Design and Location of Facilities

Designing a facility, including its capacity, layout, materials-handling patterns, and planned work sequences, often determines how smoothly work can flow, how people feel about their jobs, and how easily the organization can respond to changes in the product line or the product mix. Selecting the set of facility locations to use for plants, distribution centers, or retail outlets often determines a firm's sales, as well as transportation and inventory costs. The design of the facilities in an organization determines how well the production and delivery of goods and services can be accomplished.

In Chapter 1 (see Figure 1-3) we argued that strategy, design, and operations must be coordinated if an organization is to achieve its goals. In several places in the book, including Chapter 11, we presented hierarchies in which higher-level decisions (such as capacity determination) constrain lower-level ones. The lower-level decisions and results are then fed back to the higher level. This chapter addresses facility design (capacity, layout, and location), including the effect on the operational decisions that will follow.

There are many different "design" issues in operations management. *Product design*, for example, has implications for facility design and productivity. A product design with few parts, with clamps instead of screws, and with other ideas from "design for manufacture (DFM)" can simplify the layout and manufacturing process and cause high productivity. *Organizational design* has implications for how plants and offices should be laid out, to encourage communication and effective work teams. In this chapter we will concentrate on *facility design*.

There are many different facility-design issues, depending on the situation. For example, retail stores are placed near customers, and their layout is designed to present merchandise attractively. Warehouses or distribution centers are located to minimize transportation costs and to facilitate quick response to customers. Plant location depends on nearness to customers, labor supply and cost, the availability of materials, government attitudes, and several other factors. The location of landfills, power stations, airports, and other public facilities with negative externalities depends on convincing people that the process used to determine who suffers the bad effects was fair.

Location decisions are part of global business planning. Locating a plant in a country allows the firm to sell there more easily. Low-labor-cost countries have seen growth in manufacturing jobs, particularly for products that have significant labor content. Global firms in the early 1990s bought and built plants in many markets to provide easy access to customers, even in countries or regions with protectionist policies. Some argue that the General Agreement on Tariffs and Trade (GATT) will be ineffective in the 1990s and that trading blocs may appear that have free trade inside and restrictions to outsiders (see Thurow 1990 and Cooney 1989). Location decisions will be at the center of a global firm's competitive strategy in this scenario.

This chapter will not cover all the aforementioned problems and issues, but it will include several different design problems closely related to other topics in this book. We will discuss layout, capacity, and location problems, in Sections 16.1, 16.2 and 16.3, respectively. The use of analytical techniques such as decision analysis, mathematical programming, and computer simulation will be discussed, and several different sets of qualitative issues, for different design decisions, will be described.

16-1 FACILITY LAYOUTS

How should the different pieces of equipment and work areas be arranged? There are many aspects to the design of facilities, including equipment selection, architectural design for function and aesthetics, and limitations imposed by the building or site. Most of these topics are specific to a situation, and they are the province of the manufacturing engineer or architect. Thus, we limit our discussion to layouts. Facility layouts are categorized as *process layout, product layout*, and *fixed-position layout*.

Process layouts are designed around the processes used. All work of a particular type—milling, for example—is done in one place. This arrangement is often used when there is a wide variety of items with different production needs. Product layouts (including assembly lines), designed around the needs of the product, are appropriate when there is a large and continuing demand for a closely related group of products. Since product layouts typically allow faster response to customers and process layouts may allow higher machine utilization, the choice of a layout type depends on the relative costs and on the firm's strategic view of how it will serve customers.

One of the major trends in operations management in the last ten years has been toward the increasing use of product layouts, even when a variety of products is to be produced. The purpose is to extend the low-cost, low-inventory benefits of product layout to other situations. Manufacturing *cells* are collections of a few machines, designed so that a set of products can be produced without having to travel around the plant.

The automated version of manufacturing cells is called flexible manufacturing systems (FMSs; see Chapter 15). They are designed to give fast response times, even for a wide variety of products. The focus is on the strategic need to respond quickly rather than on machine utilization, which may be lower than for a process layout. Layout choice does have a strategic effect, and strategy must be the starting point when designing or redesigning facilities.

To illustrate the difference between product and process layout, consider the physical arrangement of a department that is responsible for designing and producing new products. *Product design* is a service, done for either a manufacturing or a service organization.

Example: The MTM Company

In the MTM Company, the entire job of product design, incorporated in one department, is thought to contain

1. market research, to develop the *product concept*
2. engineering design, to design the product
3. process engineering, to develop the process by which the product will be delivered

This department's output is new product designs. (A similar division of labor could be used for a group that designs new service products, such as a new type of health insurance.)

The MTM Company has six market researchers, nine engineering-design people, and six process engineers. Their offices are all on one floor. Two possible layouts are shown in Figure 16-1.

In the product layout, each design area is a "work cell" (similar in form and benefits to manufacturing cells, discussed in Chapter 15) containing all the functions associated with design, which allows ease of interaction and of transition from one stage of design to another. This type of team approach to design is popular in many companies today. A product layout can reduce the total product flow time and it can be more customer oriented. The process layout, in contrast, groups the workers by function. This helps to foster professionalism within a particular function. Six market researchers will have more ideas to share than two. The significant disadvantages of process layout for a function such as design are that each stage may pass on a design that does not address the needs of the next group. Also, specialization can keep people from focusing on the overall picture and the needs of the customer.

The next three subsections discuss some design methods used for process, product, and fixed-position layouts.

Figure 16-1 Two Layouts for "Design" in the MTM Company

Notes: 1. Each "Design" area has two market researchers, three engineering-design people, and two process engineers.
2. Blank areas contain other functions such as accounting and personnel.

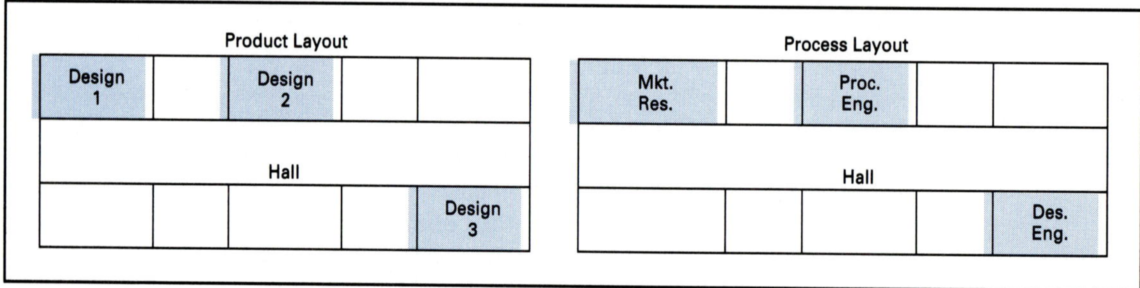

Designing a Process Layout

Patients come to the NIH Clinic[1] for various diagnostic and treatment procedures. The clinic is arranged in a process layout, with separate functional areas. Each area performs a set of tasks that require similar skills or share the same equipment. Patients move among these areas according to their specific needs. Figure 16-2 is a *flow diagram*, showing the functional areas and the typical routes taken by patients in the clinic. The *flow process chart* of Figure 16-3 describes, for a particular kind of patient, the expected sequence of visits and delays.

The flow of people or materials between functional areas is often referred to, in the industrial context, as a *load*. Typically, facility layout is evaluated by the amount of traffic between locations, so that two locations joined by an

[1]This example is an abstraction of a report on the Acute Leukemia Clinic of the National Institutes of Health. See Perrault 1973.

Figure 16-2 Functional-Area Flow Diagram

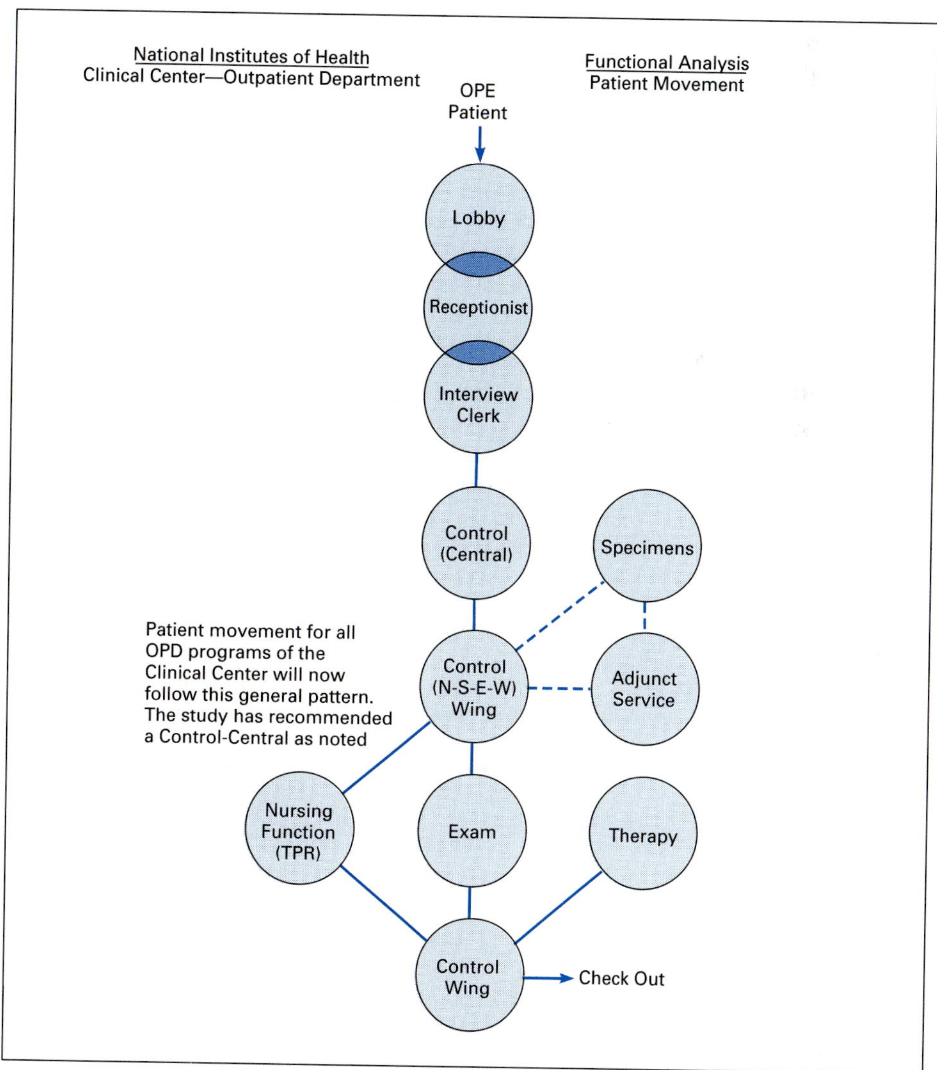

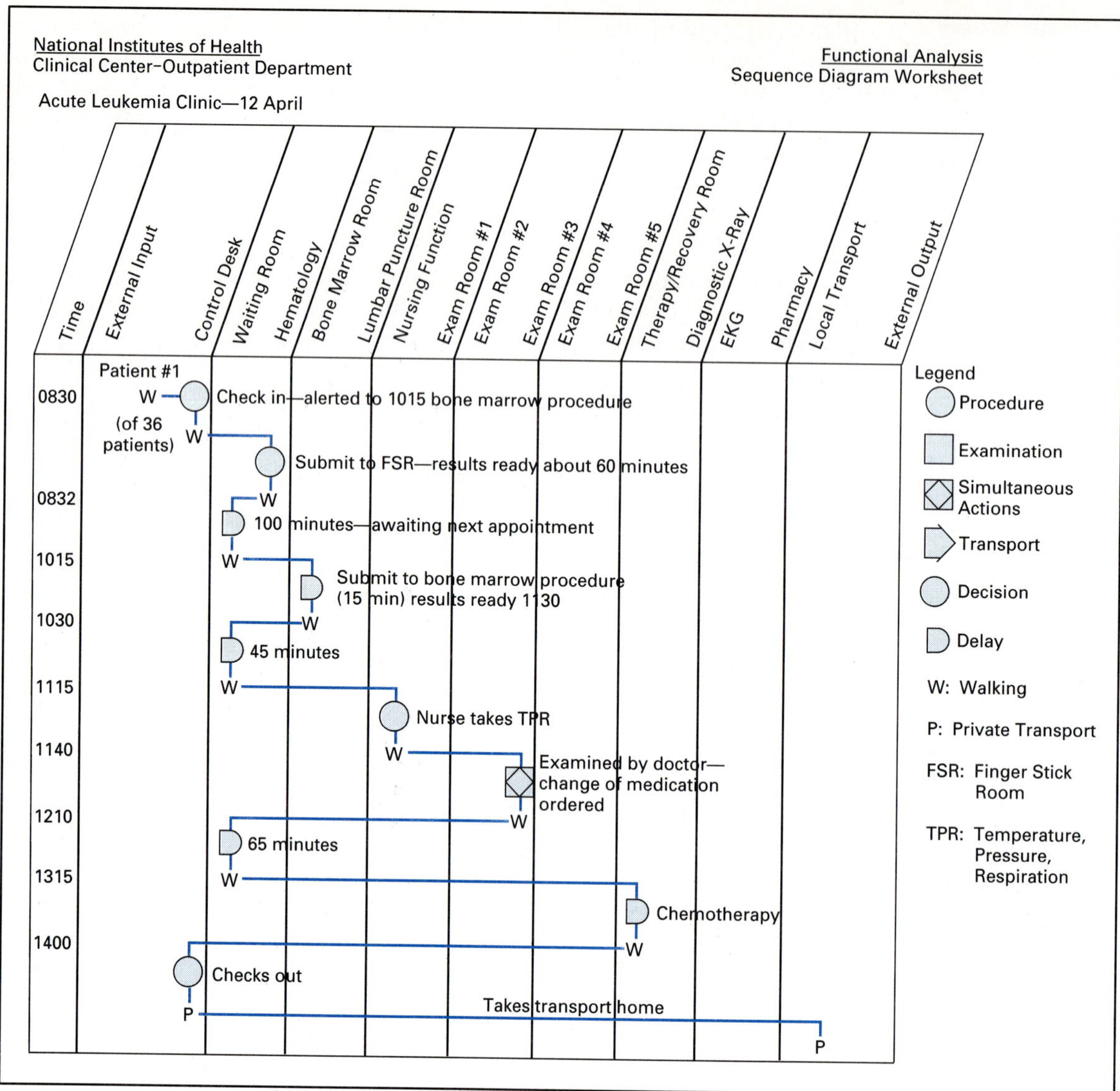

Figure 16-3 Flow Process Chart

especially high flow rate should be located near one another. However, the location analysis must allow for special circumstances, such as the following:

1. An area may be required to be at an exterior door (e.g., a receiving department).
2. A location may be permanently fixed (e.g., a heating and cooling system).
3. There may be absolute requirements concerning proximity (e.g., the control desk must be adjacent to the waiting room).

A *proximity matrix* is used to display these special requirements and their rationale (see Figures 16-4a and 16-4b). For example, Figure 16-4a shows that it

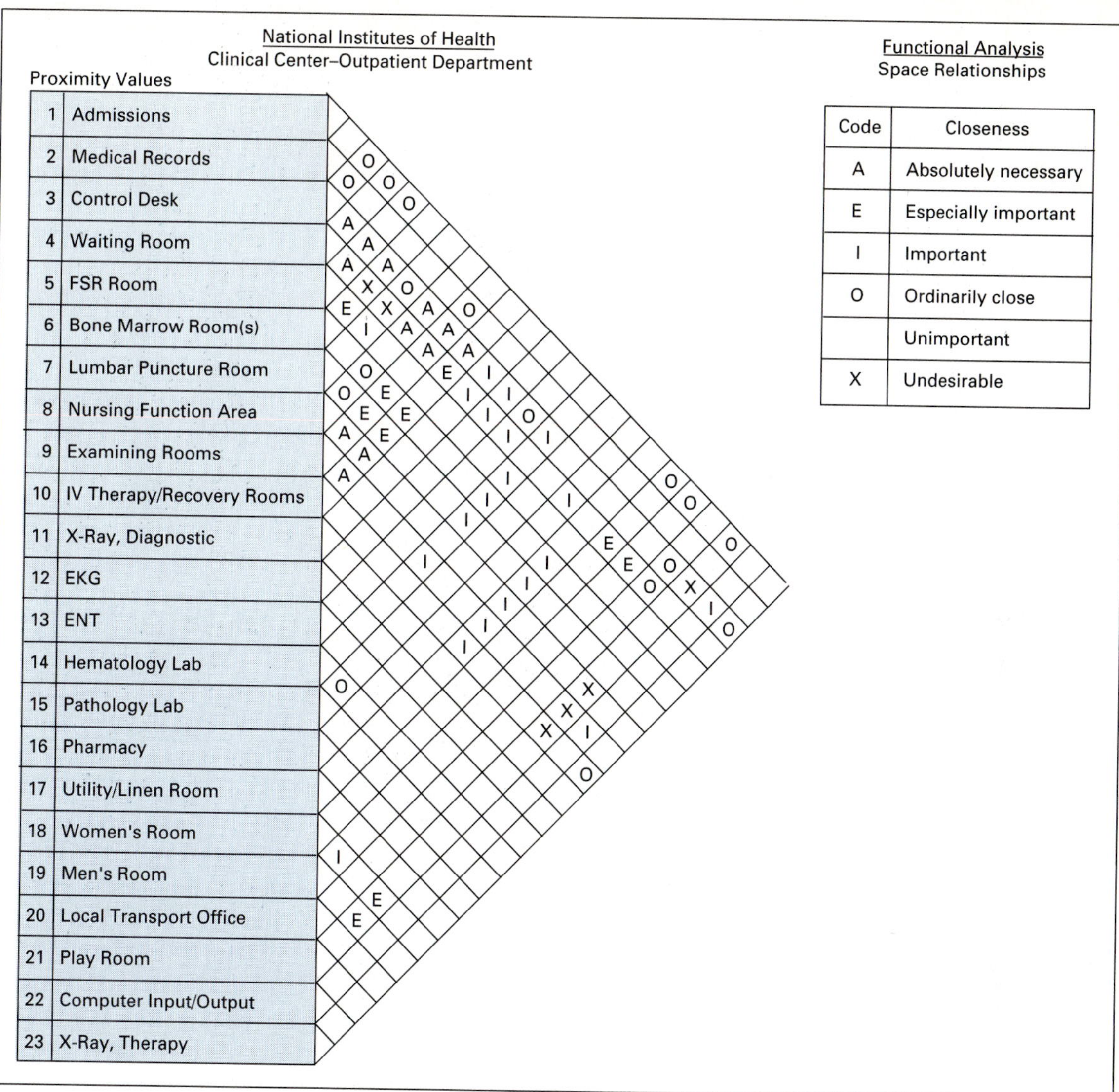

Figure 16-4a Proximity Matrix with Proximity Requirements

is important (but not necessary) for the hematology lab to be near the control desk, and Figure 16-4b indicates that this would promote rapid transfer of test and exam findings.

The matrix in Figure 16-4a is sometimes referred to as an *activity-relationship chart*. Rather than using relationship data, we can create a chart that uses the number of trips between different departments. This is referred to as a *product flow chart*. Then we may try to develop a layout that minimizes the total (distance-weighted) amount of flow. Flow data are more precise, but activity-relationship data can include qualitative factors. The choice of data format should be based on management judgment in the specific situation. (See Schonberger and Knod 1988 for a discussion of the two approaches.) Even if

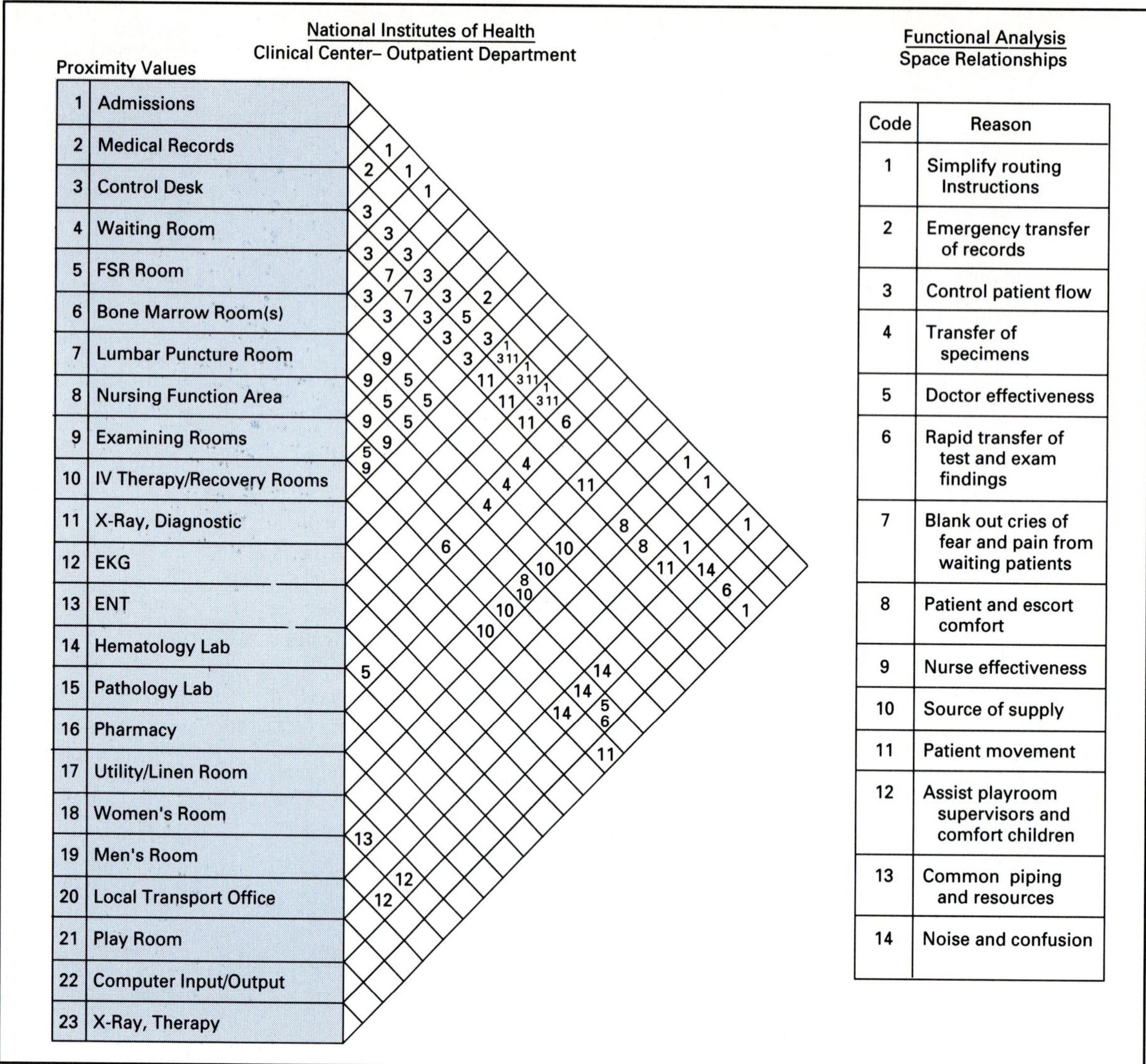

Figure 16-4b Proximity Matrix with Rationale

activity-relationship data are used, a quantitative weight is often used as input to a computerized layout-planning tool, assigning (say) 4 to absolutely necessary, 3 to especially important, and so on, with −1 being used for undesirable.

Trial and error is often used to develop a facility layout using the proximity matrix. Figure 16-5 shows the result of such a procedure. Notice that there is a central core of functional areas that are highly interrelated. This is not unusual, and locating these areas first simplifies the trial-and-error method significantly.

It then remains to fit the functional areas into the actual floor plan in a manner that resembles the schematic diagram but allows proper floor space, hallways, and so on. This is sometimes done with templates, cut from cardboard or plastic, to represent the floor space needed for the work areas. More efficiently, one can use computer graphics that allow changing the design interactively, while the computer keeps track of total distance traveled or other statistics of interest. Using either method, several alternative floor plans can be tried. If an area's size and shape is not completely specified by its function, different building blocks must also be tried. (A room that is 2 meters by 4 meters might be as good as one that is 3 meters by 3 meters.) The value of a visual

Figure 16-5 Rough Schematic Diagram of a Facility Layout

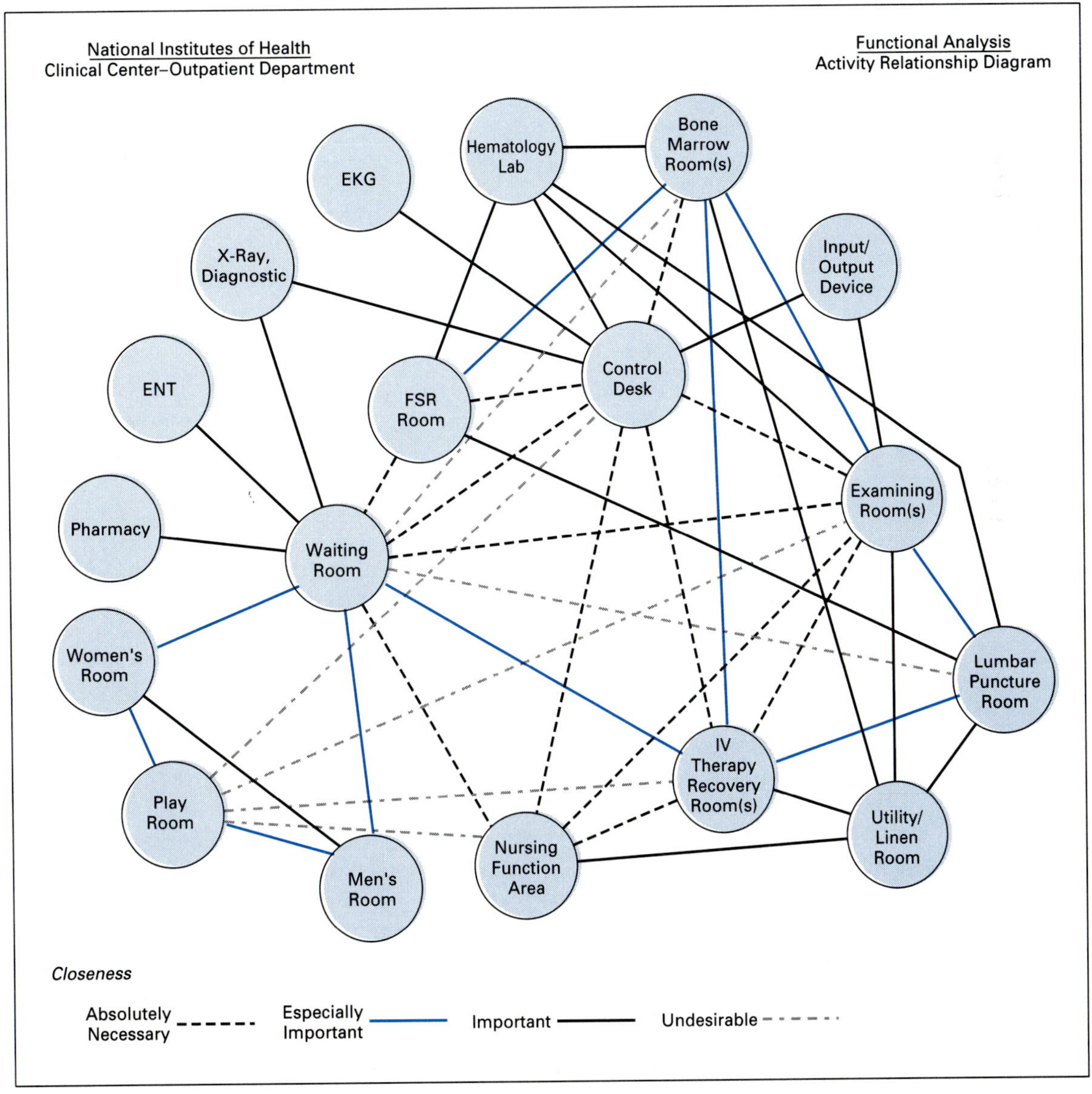

representation, using templates or computer graphics, is that a person obtains a better understanding of the important relationships of the functions and areas. Visual methods are particularly effective when planning minor modifications, such as moving a few departments but leaving most areas as they are.

Another method for creating the rough schematic uses a quantitatively stated objective. As was mentioned previously, we can assign numerical values to the A, E, I, O, U, X designations in relationship data, or we can use product flow data, thereby assuming that all trips of equal distance are equally costly. Costs accrue because of the distance between all pairs of locations. The problem can be formulated as a ''quadratic assignment problem'' (QAP; see Love et al. 1988, chapter 9, for more detail).[2] If we have n areas or facilities (for example, offices or machines) to place in n locations, the formulation can be written as

$$\text{Minimize} \quad \sum_{i=1}^{n} \sum_{k=1}^{n} \sum_{j=1}^{n} \sum_{m=1}^{n} W_{ik} d_{jm} X_{ij} X_{km} \tag{1}$$

$$\text{subject to} \quad \sum_{i=1}^{n} X_{ij} = 1 \qquad j = 1, \ldots, n \tag{2}$$

$$\sum_{j=1}^{n} X_{ij} = 1 \qquad i = 1, \ldots, n \tag{3}$$

$$X_{ij} = \begin{cases} 1 & \text{if facility } i \text{ is assigned to location } j \\ 0 & \text{otherwise} \end{cases} \tag{4}$$

where

W_{ik} = the nonnegative weight reflecting the importance of locating facilities i and k close together

d_{jm} = the distance between locations j and m

Equation 1 multiplies a weight (from either flow data or relationship data) by the distance between each pair of locations selected. A pair is selected only if $X_{ij} = 1$ and $X_{km} = 1$. The problem can be solved by branch-and-bound or heuristic approaches. (See Love et al. 1988, chapter 9. Also, on page 254, references are given to recent survey articles. QAP solutions are also discussed in Francis and White 1974.) The solution is only a beginning because it does not allow for different shapes in the final layout.

Several commercially available computer programs can be used in developing layout designs, particularly ALDEP, CORELAP, and CRAFT (see Francis and White 1974 and Schonberger and Knod 1988 for further discussion). ALDEP and CRAFT are available from IBM Corporation or the IBM Share Library System, and CORELAP can be obtained from Engineering Management Associates of Boston. (Francis and White 1974 also mention other programs.) ALDEP and CORELAP work with relational data, whereas CRAFT works to minimize total travel time, using flow data. All three include more realism than the QAP approach, but they cannot include all options and key factors.

[2] This material can be omitted without loss of continuity. A knowledge of mathematical programming (see Appendix C) is needed.

In our opinion, these programs, and other "optimal" and heuristic methods, should be used as inputs to the decision rather than to make the decision. The programs can and should be used interactively. There are so many factors involved in layouts (personal preferences, safety, appearance, and so on) that they cannot all be included in a computer program. Still, analytical techniques, particularly using interactive graphics, can be very helpful.

One graphics system is Factory Flow (see Tamashunas et al. 1990). This system allows the user to change production levels and part routings interactively, thereby changing the flow data. The model produces a variety of output data, such as materials-handling utilization data, for the manager to use in determining a layout. When more than just the layout is considered (for example, part routings and specific materials-handling equipment used), the term "facilities planning" is used rather than "layout design." (For examples of this broader area, see Stahl 1990, Tamashunas et al. 1990, and Usher et al. 1990. Stahl gives estimated values for office area required per person, percent usable space, and percent aisle space. Also see Tompkins and White 1984.)

Designing a Product Layout

When goods or services are to be produced in large quantities, efficiency gains are attainable using a product layout. The term "product layout" is used because the organization of the work is dictated by the sequence of production or service steps for a product or group of products. An assembly line is the most common type of product layout. Examples include machine shops dedicated to a single product, vaccination clinics, car washes, customs areas in airports, and automobile assembly. Product layouts may or may not be automated, depending on economic variables.

Another example of product layout is a factory designed for *continuous* product flow (often called a continuous process), such as oil refineries. Industries that use continuous processes are called *process industries*, as opposed to batch or discrete-parts production industries. Most of the design considerations for process industries are technical in nature, and we will not discuss them here.

Assembly lines often operate with a "forced" work pace, dictated by the speed of a conveyer on which the jobs are transported between workstations. Careful balancing of tasks is required so that operators are able to finish their tasks in the prescribed amount of time. Some flexibility in job design can be obtained by utilizing conveyers that have provision for the storage of jobs (a queue or *buffer*) waiting to be processed. In this design the important criterion is that the average output rate of each work area be equal, since the between-station queues can absorb short-term deviations from the average. That is, the line must operate *asynchronously*. Asynchronous lines with buffers will be discussed after examining ways to balance the average work in the stations in a line.

Assembly-Line Balancing

An assembly line is said to be perfectly balanced when all workstations (workers and machines) are 100% occupied, working at standard speed, with allowances for errors, personal time, etc. However, it is sometimes neither possible nor desirable to have perfect balance. With an unbalanced line, one has the opportunity to either assign the better workers to more demanding stations, with higher pay, or to rotate people through the easy stations so that everyone has a chance at an easy day now and then.

Example: Kitchen Products Corporation

Kitchen Products Corporation has several major products, one of which is the KPC jingflopper.[3] During assembly each jingflopper is carried on a belt moving past the workers at a steady pace. The desired production rate is 3 per hour. Table 16-1 contains data on the elementary operations needed for assembly of a jingflopper. The operations are designated A to N. The components of the product are designated B-1 to B-11, and subassemblies are designated SA-1 to SA-3. If it were possible for one person to learn all these tasks to 100% proficiency, and to organize all the subassemblies, supplies, tools, jigs, and so on, around a single workstation, one person could assemble one item in 100 minutes, or 0.6 per hour. However, since the desired output rate is 3 per hour, or 1 unit every 20 minutes, five operators would be necessary, each with a complete set of tools and supplies. Most of these tools would be idle most of the time. In contrast, if the assembly were subdivided into five stages, much of the duplication of equipment could be avoided. The jobs would be easier to learn, and because of their repetitive nature, the workers might perform them relatively more quickly. However, as was discussed in Chapter 5, there is a trade-off because the subdivided jobs are probably more boring and might lead to lower self-esteem.

The "Gozinto" chart (assembly chart) of Figure 16-6 shows one possible sequence for the assembly process. Item SA-3 is a subassembly, and item B-8 goes into SA-3, as do B-9 and B-10. Then B-11 is attached and SA-3 goes into the partially completed jingflopper near the end of the assembly sequence.

There are many sequences in which a jingflopper can be assembled, and each sequence can be represented by a Gozinto chart. However, a different

[3] An automated pancake turner, with an optional attachment for turning fried eggs.

Table 16-1 Assembly Operations for a Jingflopper

Operation Label	Time (minutes)	Description	Predecessors
A	2	Inspect frame and place on conveyor	none
B	7	Attach B-4 to frame	A
C	5	Attach B-2 to B-1	none
D	2	Attach B-3 to B-1	none
E	15	Test SA-1	C, D
F	7	Attach SA-1 to frame	A, E
G	6	Attach B-6 to B-5	none
H	4	Attach SA-2 to frame	B, G
I	9	Attach B-7 to frame	A
J	10	Attach B-9 to B-8	none
K	4	Attach B-10 to B-8	none
L	8	Attach B-11 to B-8	J, K
M	6	Attach SA-3 to frame	A, L
N	15	Test item	all others
	Total = 100 minutes		

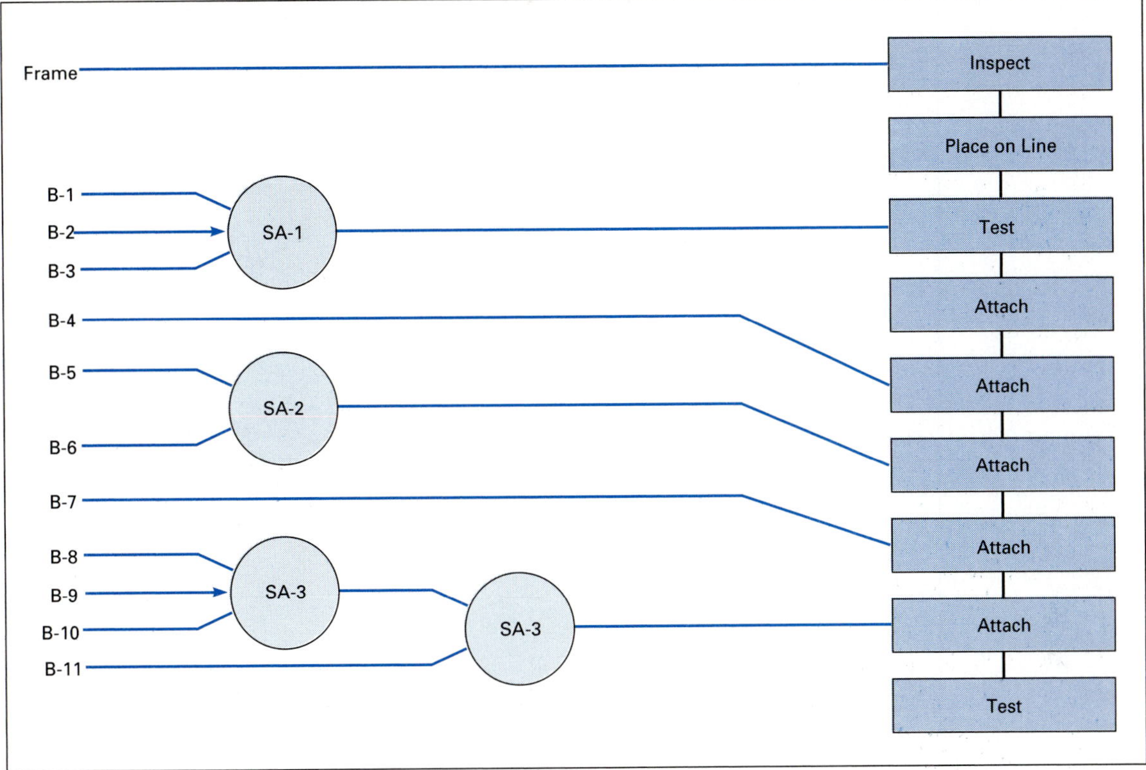

Figure 16-6 Gozinto (Assembly) Chart for a Jingflopper

diagram is more useful in assigning tasks to people in an attempt to balance the production line. Figure 16-7 is a *precedence diagram* for the assembly, showing which sequences are allowed. Each operation is represented by its label (from Table 16-1) and its time. The arrows indicate which operations must come first. To divide the operations among five workers, the simplest method is to draw five loops on the chart, each loop enclosing tasks to be assigned to a workstation, making sure not to violate any of the sequence requirements. The target is five stations with 20 minutes of work per station, to achieve a production rate of 3 per hour.

One possible assignment is shown in Figure 16-8, in which the longest assembly time is 22 minutes at stations 2 and 4. Therefore, the items must be spaced at least 22 minutes apart on the moving belt, and each station has that amount of time. The spacing actually used is called the *cycle time* of the line.

It should now be evident why it may not be possible to achieve a perfect balance. There is a limited number of combinations that satisfy the sequence requirements, and for a given sequence it may not be possible to obtain exactly 20 minutes per station, since the elementary operations are not divisible.

The quality of a solution is measured by the *balance delay*, which is the idle time induced by the imperfect solution. With five workers and a cycle time of 22 minutes at each station, there are (5)(22) = 110 worker-minutes expended per item assembled (including idle time), compared with the required productive time of 100 minutes from Table 16-1. Therefore, the balance delay is 10 minutes of idle time per item, which is 9.1% of the worker's time. Expressed

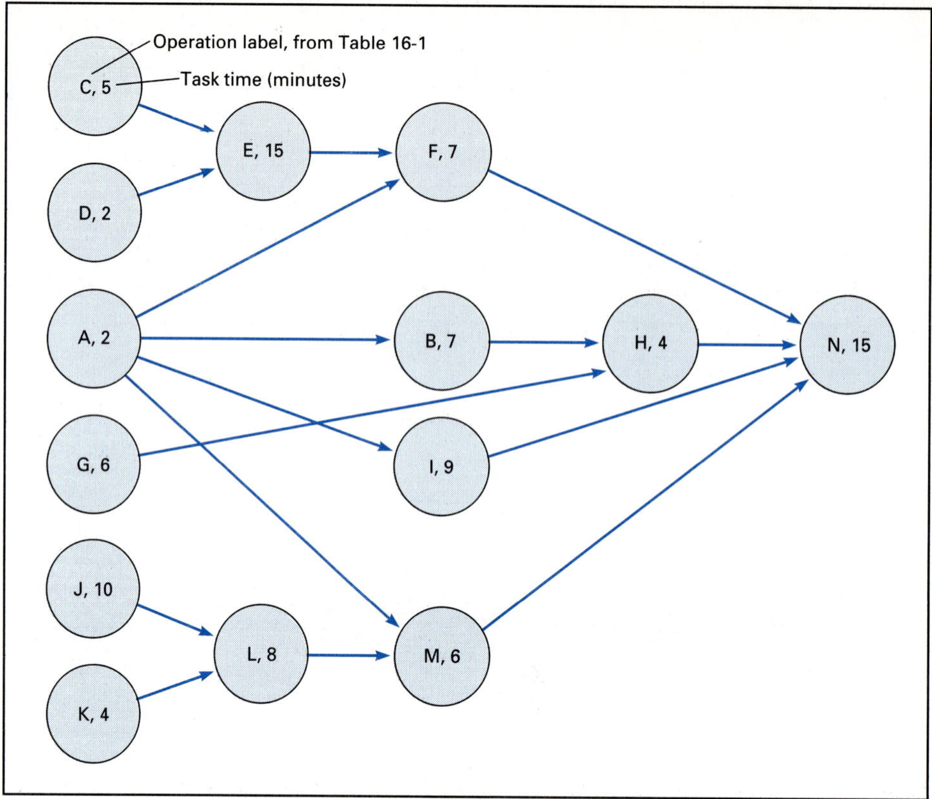

Figure 16-7 Precedence Diagram for the Assembly of a Jingflopper

as a formula, we have

$$\text{Balance delay} = \frac{nc - T}{nc} \tag{5}$$

where

n = number of workstations
c = cycle time = inverse of production rate of the line (c cannot be less than the assembly time required at the slowest station)
T = total amount of work time required per item

Note that the proposed solution does not meet the desired production rate of 3 per hour (cycle time = 22 minutes means production rate = 60/22 = 2.73 per hour). Actually, 3 per hour (one every 20 minutes) would require perfect balance, which we now know is unrealistic to expect. There are four alternatives:

1. Be satisfied with the lower rate.
2. Work overtime.
3. Add another worker (and another workstation).
4. Find some way to increase the line speed.

The line speed could be increased if faster workers were placed at the most difficult workstations. The premium wage necessary to attract and keep such workers can be compared against the costs of the other alternatives.

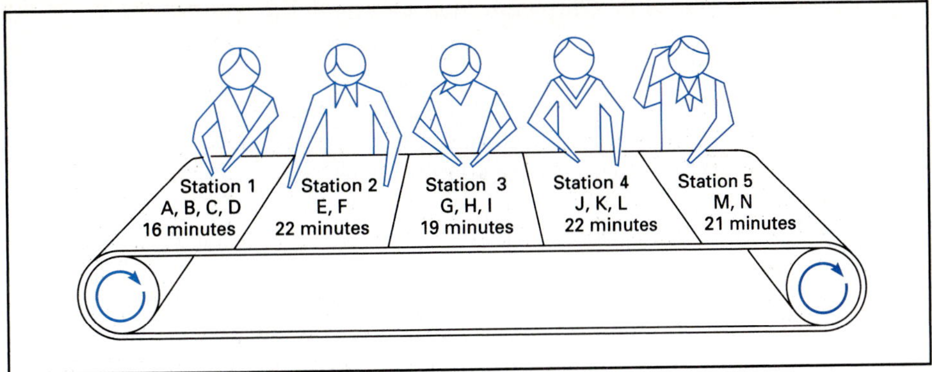

Figure 16-8 Schematic of an Assembly Line

If we add another worker and station and then rebalance the line, an assembly time of 17 minutes can be achieved. (All stations require 17 minutes except the last, which requires only 15 minutes. Problem 9 at the end of the chapter asks you to find this solution.) The desired cycle time of 20 minutes can be attained, and the balance delay of this solution is [(6)(20) − 100]/(6)(20) = 20/120 = 0.1667 or 16.67%. Most of this balance delay occurs because we have an externally imposed cycle time of 20 minutes, slower than the 17 minutes of the slowest station.

If we are free to choose the production rate, we can reduce the balance delay. Equation 5 can be minimized by setting the cycle time equal to the assembly time of the slowest station. Any idle time that still remains is called the *internal balance delay*. In this example the internal balance delay is [(6)(17) − 100]/(6)(17) = 2/102 or 1.96%. This part of the balance delay is due to the indivisibility of the assembly tasks. The rest of the total balance delay, 16.67% − 1.96% = 14.71%, is *external balance delay*.

Finding the best solution to a large line-balancing problem is an immense task because of the many combinations and sequence requirements. (It is, like other problems mentioned earlier, NP-hard, a category of very hard problems.) Baybars (1986) surveys exact algorithms. Hackman et al. (1989) present an excellent review and extension of heuristics that either (a) minimize the number of stations for a given cycle time or (b) minimize the cycle time for a given number of stations. They describe many different heuristics, including the following:

Step 1: Assign a numerical score to each task. (The score is discussed below.)

Step 2: Update the set of available tasks (tasks whose immediate predecessors have been assigned).

Step 3: Assign the available task with the highest numerical score into the first station in which the capacity and precedence constraints will not be violated. Go to Step 2. Proceed until all tasks are assigned.

Hackman et al. (1989) test several numerical scores. For example, one score is the task time. (Put large tasks in place first, then fill in with smaller ones.) Another score is the individual task time plus the sum of task times for all tasks that must follow. In large problems, computing these sums is difficult; however, this score does give slightly better solutions. For example, individual task times (score 1) would rank the items in Table 16-1, highest to lowest, as E, N, J, I, L, B, F, G, M, C, H, K, A, D. Using sums of task times (score 2) produces this ranking: A, C, D, J, E, K, L, B, G, I, F, M, N. In both cases ties are broken by listing the earlier letter in the alphabet first. Initially, the available tasks are those with no predecessors: C, D, A, G, J, and K. From these tasks, the first assignment for the first workstation would be task J if using score 1 and task A if using score 2. The use of these heuristics is illustrated in the problems at the end of the chapter.

An assembly line is only one of several product-layout forms. As was mentioned previously, manufacturing cells are an attempt to bring some of the virtues of product layout to a situation in which many items are made. Many assembly lines today are *mixed-model assembly lines;* the line has tools and parts to make several models of a product rather than just one. (Automobile assembly lines are an example.) Milas (1990) defines two mixed-model situations and discusses the disadvantages of trying to manually balance assembly lines. McCormick et al. (1989) and Yano and Bolat (1989) discuss ways to sequence multiple items on an assembly line, to obtain maximum throughput. In some situations there may be processing alternatives in an assembly-line situation (see Pinto et al. 1983 for models of this type.) Including learning effects in assembly-line models is discussed by Chakravarty (1988).

Layout design is also affected by behavioral factors. To facilitate just-in-time production (see Chapter 12), it helps if workers can see one another's work, so that they can learn from and help each other. A U-shaped assembly area is one way to do this. In a U-shaped assembly area, with the workers in the "middle," it is easy for workers to see how work is proceeding (and provide help if necessary), and it is relatively easy to rebalance the line for more or fewer workers. U-shaped layouts are increasingly common, owing to these advantages.

U-shaped areas make sense if there is variability in the load, the processing times, or the yield. It allows easy reaction to such changes. The line-balancing methods described previously deal with average processing times, ignoring variation. Variation is "the enemy," and it should be driven out, to the extent possible. If significant variation remains, the layout design must account for it. Simulation modeling is necessary to analyze variation in complex situations. XCELL+ is a system that allows easy simulation modeling (see Conway et al. 1990).

When there is processing time variation, asynchronous lines, with small work-in-process buffers, will improve the productivity of a line. Conway et al. (1988) have shown that very small buffers suffice to recover nearly all the output lost through variation. Ostolaza et al. (1990) have analyzed the advantages of having adjacent workers help each other, to smooth out variation in processing times. The punch line here is that simulation can allow specific situations to be analyzed, and small buffers or work-rule changes can produce significant improvements in production capability lost because of variation. Even so, the starting point must be to balance the average work at each station,[4] before analyzing the buffer storage needed to compensate for variation.

---

[4]Some managers argue that one work center should be planned to have more work than the others. This bottleneck may exist because of the cost of a machine. An expensive bottleneck should not have its time wasted. It can be economically appropriate to have "excess" capacity for the other work areas.

Fixed-Position Layouts (Where the Workers Move)

Among many examples where the worker must travel between operations is the warehouse, or *storage layout*. Most service and manufacturing facilities have an area dedicated to the storage of goods. In retail stores, it is common to have most of the inventory displayed in customer self-service areas, designed for maximum marketing appeal. In hospitals, mail-order houses, factories, distribution centers, and military supply depots, the storage areas are designed for minimum cost, with important considerations being rapid access, easy and accurate control, and the possibility for future expansion.

Two-stage systems are used when items are removed from storage in smaller quantities than the containers in which they are received. Open containers are kept in the "pick" area (or central supply), where an individual order is filled by a person who moves through the area. Large-volume distributors use vehicles with personnel lifts to access the appropriate bins quickly. This requires that aisles be one-way and wide enough to maneuver the vehicles. Where distance is a factor, high-volume items will be kept nearest the control area using *turnover-based stocking*. When vehicle congestion is a problem, high-volume items may be kept in more than one location, and aisle lengths are shortened by inserting either perpendicular or diagonal cross-aisles.

The second stage involves the bulk storage area, which has less activity and hence can have fewer aisles. There are two ways to organize such an area: by stock lines or by individual locations. With a stock-line storage layout, each type of item has part of the warehouse allocated to it; thus, the storage area is equivalent to many small warehouses. The main advantage of this layout is ease of control. The operator always knows where to find a given item, and visual inventory inspection is facilitated. However, stock-line layout typically leaves large areas unused as the inventory of each stock-line decreases between replenishments. In contrast, an individual-locations storage layout uses flexible storage assignment. Typically, each location has a label indicating the aisle, a distance down the aisle, and a height (shelf number). A computer record keeps track of the contents of each location, and tells the person (or machine) where to go to find a particular item.

Hausman et al. (1976) and Bozer and White (1990) consider methods of design and rules for assigning locations to items in an *automated storage and retrieval system, AS/RS*. Such systems are capable of generating shopping lists for stock picking, as well as making location and retrieval assignments. The computer may also directly control a stacker crane in the bulk storage area, dispatching these robots-on-rails to store and retrieve items in an efficient manner.

A hospital provides another example where workers move to the work. The majority of the service is provided by nurses, who move among a variety of work areas, including patients' bedsides and nursing stations. The criteria for effective work-area design in such instances include fast response time (the patient should not wait long for service) and high utilization of the server. A circular floor plan, with rooms on the periphery and a central nursing station, is one effective means of achieving both these goals.

In this section we have described three layout types: process, product, and fixed location. Product layouts have low cost and (often) fast response time. Manufacturing cells are an attempt to gain these advantages even when there are many items to be produced. Product layout takes maximum advantage of high volume by subdividing tasks to a level that allows a worker to learn quickly and to be very proficient. This specialization restricts flexibility in job design, as was discussed in Chapter 5.

In process layout, similar operations are grouped together, and jobs may take long and individualized paths through the facility. This is typical when there are low quantities of many job types. In fixed-position layout, the "jobs" hold still and the workers visit the jobs. Many more detailed and elaborate methods are described in the industrial-engineering literature as listed in the references to this chapter.

There is increasing interest in modification of assembly-line and similar operations to allow room for consideration of the worker's needs and desires. At the same time, it is increasingly common for both service and manufacturing operations to move from strictly process layouts toward arrangements that gain some of the advantages of product layout. Most medium-to-high-volume organizations use a combination of the two types of layouts.

REVIEW PROBLEMS

1. Figure 16-8 gives a solution to the line-balancing problem associated with Table 16-1. Find a six-station assignment that can produce an item every 19 minutes or faster. What is the balance delay of the solution?

2. In Figures 16-4a and 16-4b, interpret the proximity values between the waiting area and
   a. the FSR (finger stick room)
   b. the bone marrow rooms
   c. the lumbar puncture room
   d. Are these all well represented in Figure 16-5?

3. What does balance delay mean? Why is it usually impossible to achieve perfect assembly-line balance?

Solutions

1. Many solutions with six stations will achieve 19 minutes or faster. One assignment that will meet a 19-minute cycle time is (J, C, K) for the first station and then (A, D, E), (G, L), (B, I), (F, M, H), and (N) for the other five. The balance delay is $[(19)(6) - 100]/(19)(6) = 0.123 = 12.3\%$. (Note: The heuristics described in this section will find a solution to meet the 19-minute requirement if score 2 is used, but not if score 1 is used.)

2. a. The FSR should be close to the waiting area (code A = absolutely necessary in Figure 16-4a) for purposes of patient control (code 3 in Figure 16-4b).
   b. and c. Both these areas should be located away from the waiting area to prevent unpleasant sounds from disturbing waiting patients.
   d. The layout satisfies these requirements.

3. It is an estimate of the percent idle time attributable to the organization of the assembly line. Sequence requirements and indivisible tasks prevent perfect balance.

16-2 CAPACITY ANALYSIS

Example: The Salt Ridge Bakery Company

The Salt Ridge Bakery Company produces relatively expensive breads for sale through supermarkets. The firm's sales have been growing in recent years and are expected to continue to grow. At the same time, the baking industry has been moving to larger bakeries, to achieve economies of scale; this trend has continued in spite of the resulting higher transportation costs.

The Salt Ridge Bakery needs to expand to meet the increased demand for their product. The vice-president for operations, Sharon Westphal, must decide where to place new plants and how large to make them. In reaching a decision she must consider the forecast of sales in each region of the country, the costs of building and operating each size of plant, the availability of work force and transportation, and the capacity and location of the firm's current facilities.

The forecast must be broken down into different product categories, each category using a different kind of capacity (breads require different mixers than do cookies, for example). Any major changes in the product line must be predicted. Some of these data must be obtained from sources other than the forecasting group.

In determining the *capacity plan*, Westphal must consider company policies concerning their product line and financial decisions. For example, should the plant be designed to provide highest quality, no matter what the cost? Should a new plant earn 15%, 20%, or more, or less on the money invested? Should a plant be tightly designed around the current product mix (a low-cost strategy in the short run), or should it be flexible enough to allow changes with little or no adaptation?

For a profit-making organization such as Salt Ridge, both capacity and location decisions are important parts of their competitive strategy. Production costs, the ability to meet surges in demand, nearness to customers, and distribution requirements are determined by capacity and location decisions. Further, since these decisions are made infrequently, and since they are not easy to reverse, the capacity plan and location decisions must provide flexibility to deal with an uncertain future. Intermediate-horizon decisions (such as hiring plans for the next several months and overtime or extra shifts during that same period) and short-term decisions (such as which products to produce in what quantities and in what order, during the current week) are constrained by the capacity plan. The effect on these shorter-range decisions must be considered in developing the capacity plan.

Nonprofit organizations also face crucial capacity and location decisions. For example, planning the capacity and location of trash-management facilities, such as incinerators and landfills, is a difficult analytical and political problem (see Baetz et al. 1989).

In this section we treat *capacity* as if it were a single number: How many things can we produce per time period? As we saw in Chapters 2 and 12 and Section 16-1, the throughput rate of an assembly line depends on the slowest workstation, called the bottleneck. How much capacity we need depends on how well we manage our resources. Still, there is a strategic decision of how much capacity we should have, and that is the topic for this section.

Example: Salt Ridge Bakery (continued)

Salt Ridge is considering the addition of a new product that would require a capital expenditure, since current capacity is fully utilized and a new type of machine is required. Sharon Westphal is considering expanding one plant and selling the new product in that one region. If the product catches on, a capacity of 5000 units per week will be necessary, and the company will make a net profit of $40,000 per week. (Net profit is taken here to be sales revenue minus all costs of production except the cost of capital tied up in the plant.) If the product does not catch on, a capacity of 2000 units per week will be needed, and the company will make a net profit of $16,000 per week.

A 2000-unit capacity can be built for $800,000. A 5000-unit capacity can be built for $1.5 million. A 2000-unit capacity can be expanded to a 5000-unit capacity for $1 million. Either addition will be of no value after twenty years but will perform until that time. Excess capacity is worthless. After one year of sales, they will know whether the product has caught on.

Initially, Westphal has three possible choices; they are shown in the *decision tree* in Figure 16-9. The boxes in the figure represent decisions to be made by the firm. The circles represent a state of nature, to be observed after a decision is made. (Formulations of this type are discussed in Hamburg 1991.)

A decision tree is useful when there are one or more major uncertainties surrounding a decision problem. We want to see how a decision will perform in each possible situation. A decision may be rejected because it has some chance of losing a lot of money. On the other hand, if the firm can afford the potential loss, it may choose the decision with the highest expected profit. Westphal believes that Salt Ridge should pick the decision with the highest expected profit.

We first note that the net profits occur over time; therefore, time discounting (discussed in Chapter 3) must be used. Thus, we need a discount factor for Salt Ridge. In addition, we need to have a probability of high demand and low demand. Westphal says that the firm wants to earn 25% (before taxes) on invested funds, so the discount rate is 0.25. The probability of high demand, based on other similar new product introductions, is 0.2. The first year's net

Figure 16-9 Decision Tree for the Salt Ridge Capacity Problem

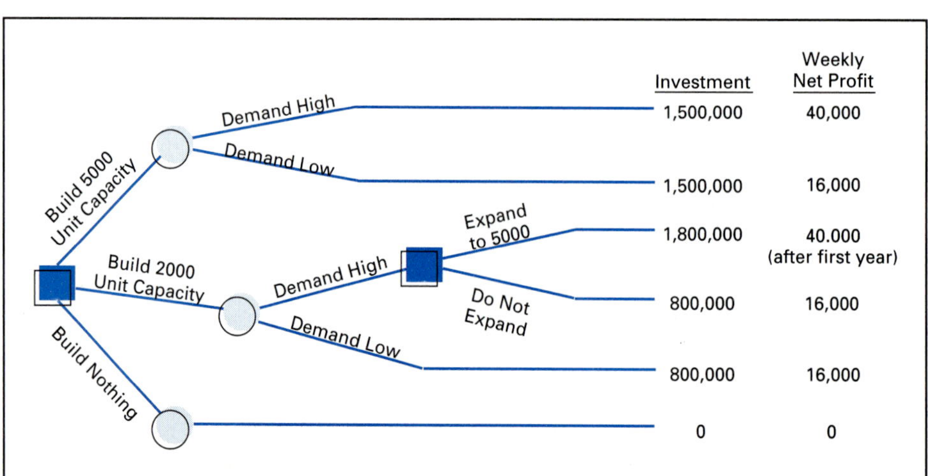

profits occur, on the average, one year after the plant investment is required, for either the original plant or an expansion.

With these data, we can complete the analysis of the Figure 16-9 problem. First, we consider the *second* decision point: If we find out that demand is high, should we expand? (Such problems are always worked "backward.") That is, after 1 year, is it worthwhile to invest an additional $1 million to obtain $40,000 per week instead of $16,000 per week for the remaining 19 years of plant life? The additional net profit due to expansion, calculated as a net present value (NPV) is

$$\text{NPV of additional net profit} = \sum_{j=1}^{19} (40{,}000 - 16{,}000)(52)\left(\frac{1}{1.25}\right)^j$$

This is an annuity of $(24,000)(52) per year for 19 years. An annuity can be evaluated using the formula given in Chapter 3 or using an annuity table. The formula from Chapter 3 gives us

$$A\left[\frac{1-(1+i)^{-T}}{i}\right] = (24{,}000)(52)\left[\frac{1-(1.25)^{-19}}{0.25}\right]$$
$$= (24{,}000)(52)(3.942)$$
$$= \$4{,}920{,}000$$
$$\text{NPV (above investment)} = 4{,}920{,}000 - 1{,}000{,}000 = \$3{,}920{,}000$$

Because the net present value is positive, we conclude that the firm should expand if it finds itself with a low-capacity plant and high demand.

Now Figure 16-9 can be modified to reflect the fact that we know what the second decision will be. Figure 16-10 shows the modification. The net present value can be calculated for each endpoint of the tree. For example, for the branch "build 2000, demand high," the $800,000 investment returns $16,000 per week for 20 years, and in addition, at the end of 1 year, the plant expansion worth $3,920,000 will be undertaken. The net present value is

$$(16{,}000)(52)\sum_{j=1}^{20}\left(\frac{1}{1.25}\right)^j + (3{,}920{,}000)\left(\frac{1}{1.25}\right)^1 - 800{,}000 = \$5{,}626{,}000$$

Figure 16-10 Modified Decision Tree

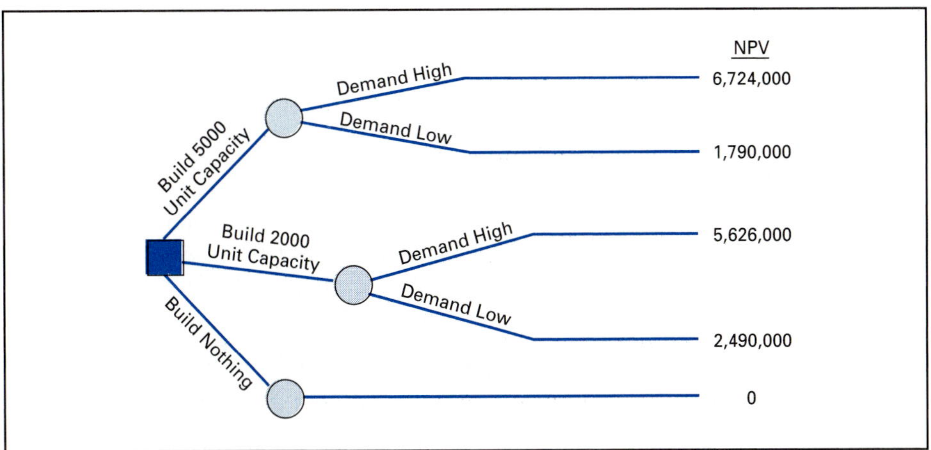

For "build 5000, demand low," the values are

$$(16{,}000)(52) \sum_{j=1}^{20} \left(\frac{1}{1.25}\right)^j - 1{,}500{,}000 = \$1{,}790{,}000$$

The other two values are $6,724,000 for "build 5000, demand high" and $2,490,000 for "build 2000, demand low."

Finally, we can incorporate our estimate of the probability of high demand. We have used a decision tree to formulate the problem and present-value calculations to evaluate the possible outcomes. Now we can use an *expected-value* calculation (see Hamburg 1991) by multiplying each dollar outcome by its probability of occurrence and summing the results.

$$\begin{aligned}
\text{Build 5000:}\quad \text{Expected net present value} &= (0.2)(6{,}724{,}000)\\
+ (0.8)(1{,}790{,}000) &= \$2{,}777{,}000\\
\text{Build 2000:}\quad \text{Expected net present value} &= (0.2)(5{,}626{,}000)\\
+ (0.8)(2{,}490{,}000) &= \$3{,}117{,}200\\
\text{Build nothing:}\quad \text{Expected net present value} &= 0
\end{aligned}$$

This analysis suggests that Westphal should use a small capacity initially and expand it after one year if the demand is high.

The quantitative analysis cannot contain every factor. Analysis like the preceding should be used as an input to the decision. The firm's attitude toward risk, their relationship with local government, and strategic factors might cause them to select any of the three possible decisions.

Strategic Aspects of Capacity Planning

Determining capacity is one of the most important decisions an organization must face. Capacity planning for the long term is a strategic decision. If capacity is too small, an organization may (1) lose customers, (2) allow competitors to enter the market, or (3) be unable to provide timely service. If capacity is too large, an organization may (1) have difficulty controlling the operations, (2) glut the market and drive down the price, or (3) be unable to pay off a loan obtained to build capacity. At the core of good capacity planning is a good long-range forecast, whether we are producing automobiles, generating electricity, or building school buildings. (See Chapter 7 for a discussion of long-range forecasting.) Unfortunately, the forecast depends not only on demand, which is hard enough to forecast several years into the future, but on other factors such as competitors' actions, the price of alternative energy sources, and changes in the average number of pupils per classroom.

Many factors are involved in selecting the capacity for both manufacturing and service organizations. In factories, for example, Skinner (1974) argues that a factory should not be so large that it cannot be given a focused set of tasks. That is, a factory should have a mission that is easy to manage. These ideas have caused some managers to separate a plant into multiple parts for organizational purposes. They believe that there are some diseconomies of scale in coordinating very large plants. This effect has not been verified using cost data, but it appears to be true in some situations. Thus, one strategic question with capacity planning is, can we manage a new, larger facility effectively? If we decide to use smaller factories, the firm still may face the capacity question of deciding how many to build over the next several years.

The main reason for increasing capacity is to have the capability to satisfy market demand. However, this involves more than just a forecast. In some situations additional capacity is used to enable the firm to respond very quickly to customers or to allow the flexibility to change or modify products to maintain a good product line. Of course, capacity greater than the *average* needed is not really excess if its purpose is to allow a more competitive, service-oriented posture in response to variations in demand.

Some organizations increase capacity in an attempt to dominate an industry. Some strategic-planning systems (see Chapter 17) stress the value of dominating the market. One way to do that is to have the largest capacity. If the industry now has only 80% of the needed capacity, building a facility that can saturate the market makes it unprofitable for a competitor to expand. To do so, the competitor would have to cut the price (starting a price war), so that a high return could not be earned. By being first, a company can impose a *barrier to entry*.

Of course, there are risks in increasing capacity strategically. Someone else may have the same idea. If all firms want to dominate a market, they may all add to capacity, systematically ruining their financial health without gaining customers.

Wheelwright (1979) lists an eight-step process for capacity and facilities planning:

1. Assess company situation and environment.
2. Determine available (existing) capacity.
3. Estimate required capacity.
4. Develop alternative plans for matching required and available capacity.
5. Perform quantitative evaluation of the alternatives.
6. Perform qualitative evaluation of the altematives.
7. Recommend a course of action.
8. Implement the course of action.

We feel that this is a good list, focusing as it does on both quantitative and qualitative analysis, and on implementation. Item 3 is complex. ''Estimate'' implies a long-range forecast (discussed in Chapter 7), and that is typically difficult. But ''required capacity'' also involves other factors. We may want excess capacity for marketing purposes or to bar competitors. We may want small capacity so that we can manage it better.

Failure to perform capacity planning can be very costly. The electronics industry was unable to meet demand for personal computers in the first half of the 1980s. But industry-wide expansion led to overcapacity by the end of the decade. The U.S. government supported medical school expansion in the 1960s and 1970s only to face a current surplus of doctors in many specialties (an unthinkable idea a few years ago). Organizations must engage in careful capacity planning, and they must consider the strategic aspects of that analysis.

REVIEW PROBLEMS

1. In the Salt Ridge capacity analysis in Figures 16-9 and 16-10, the decision would change if the probability of high demand were 0.5 instead of 0.2.

   a. Review the financial aspects of the various alternatives and say which alternative you would expect to look more attractive as the probability of high demand increases.

b. Verify your judgment in part a by recalculating the expected net present values.

c. Why is it important to carry out a sensitivity analysis by varying some of the parameters, such as the probability of high demand?

2. Two manufacturing firms in the same industry develop capacity plans. They will each add one plant. Firm A decides to build a plant with capacity less than their forecast of demand and to have it produce only a few products from the line. Firm B decides to build a plant with capacity far in excess of their forecast of demand. How can you explain their plans?

Solutions

1. a. The current solution is to build a small plant and consider an addition next year. If demand is high, this policy would end up with a large plant but expend $300,000 more and lose one year's additional revenue, compared with building a large plant now. The larger the probability of high demand, the more likely this loss. Hence, "Build 5000 unit capacity" will be preferred if the probability of high demand is large enough.

b. The expected values are

Build 5000: Expected net present value = 0.5(6,724,000) + 0.5(1,790,000) = $4,257,000

Build 2000: Expected net present value = 0.5(5,626,000) + 0.5(2,490,000) = $4,058,000

Build nothing: Expected net present value = 0

The decision changes to "Build 5000."

c. The "correct" value is unknown, but trying a range of values reveals how much room there is for error in the estimate. We could determine "crossover points," such as a value where the decision changes from "Build 2000" to "Build 5000." Then the estimation problem becomes, is the probability of high demand above the crossover? This may be easier to address than getting a single-valued estimate.

2. Firm A may want to have a "focused factory" for managerial reasons. Firm B may want to provide a barrier to entry or provide for long-term growth.

16-3 LOCATION ANALYSIS

Locating a Single Facility

Plant location and service-facility location involve different considerations. Much of the labor cost in a manufacturing organization is incurred at the plant. The customer-contact value of a plant is minimal except that because of concern regarding pollution some plants give a negative image to the firm's products.

A customer-service warehouse, on the other hand, must be close enough in terms of shipment time to the final customer to facilitate good customer service. A small portion of the firm's labor costs but a large portion of the transportation costs are incurred at such warehouses.

A retail store must be located to attract customers. Convenience and attraction for retail customers is of paramount importance. The same considerations are important in locating satellite health clinics designed to reach many people.

Location decisions are frequently analyzed by using a checklist to see how a potential location performs on several different criteria. The checklist serves as an aid to the decision maker. The same list might be used for locating many types of facilities, but as was discussed previously, different items become more or less important in different situations. To illustrate this, consider Table 16-2, which lists six items of importance for three different location problems. You are to rank the items by their importance in each of the three situations (that is, place the numbers 1 to 6 in each of the three columns).

Because the actual rankings may vary dramatically from one situation to another, we will not attempt to give "correct" rankings for the table. However, certain points are clear. Most warehouses exist to provide speed of service and to reduce transportation cost. Thus, for the warehouse column, ranks 1 and 2 probably would appear in rows 1 and 4. In contrast, the typical manufacturing plant incurs heavy labor costs, and access to raw materials is vital. Also, construction is more complex and expensive than for warehouses. Thus, items 2, 3, and 5 will probably have the top three ranks for a plant. Finally, for most retail location decisions item 4 is of prime importance. The decision maker considering a retail location will include some measure of the competition in analyzing the attraction to customers. Item 6, the attitude of local governments, can be very important for any location decision, but it is probably most important for a plant, which will have a large presence in the area. In fact, the labor, political, and social situation of the region, community, and even the particular site are very important in selecting a plant location.

Topics such as these have been discussed extensively, particularly for plants and warehouses (see Coyle et al. 1988 and Schmenner 1982), and we will not give a complete discussion here. It is important, though, for us to understand that many considerations are involved. Models that "optimize" the location of one facility typically consider only one or two of the necessary factors. Nevertheless, these models can be used by management as a tool. For example, transportation-cost minimization may be crucial, but other issues must be included, perhaps in a subjective fashion.

Quantitative analysis of the single-facility location problem has a long history (see Love et al. 1988 and Coyle et al. 1988). Love et al. (chapters 2, 3, and

Table 16-2 Some Location Considerations

Item	Rank by Importance For		
	Warehouse	**Plant**	**Retail Store**
1. Transportation and inventory costs	________	________	________
2. Availability, quality, and cost of labor	________	________	________
3. Cost of construction, taxes, and land	________	________	________
4. Convenience to and attraction for the final customers	________	________	________
5. Convenience to raw materials	________	________	________
6. Attitude of local and state governments	________	________	________

4) give extensive discussion of techniques, including location on a plane, on a sphere, and through time, when the single facility may be relocated at a cost. We will discuss only (a) the distance measure to be used and (b) the "grid technique" or "center of gravity approach."

Most location problems can be thought of as if they took place on a plane. (Unless a large fraction of the globe is included, a planar approximation will be fairly accurate.) Recall from plane geometry that the straight-line distance between two points (x_1, y_1) and (x_2, y_2) is $[(x_1 - x_2)^2 + (y_1 - y_2)^2]^{1/2}$. However, real roads are longer than that, by 18% in the United States and 30% in Canada (see Love et al. 1988, page 6). If we were forced to travel only in the direction of one of the axes, we would travel $|x_1 - x_2| + |y_1 - y_2|$ to get between the two points. These two extreme values are special cases of L_p, the distance between two points, (x_1, y_1) and (x_2, y_2):

$$L_p = [|x_1 - x_2|^p + |y_1 - y_2|^p]^{1/p}, \qquad 1 \leq p \leq 2 \tag{6}$$

Estimating p (discussed in Love et al. 1988, chapter 10), results in better distance measures than using $p = 1$ or $p = 2$.

The easiest way to select a location for one facility is to use a center-of-gravity approach. This method attempts to minimize total ton-miles of products shipped. For example, consider a plant location problem. Imagine a map painted on a rigid board, with weights placed at the source of all raw materials and at the location of all customers. The weights equal the tons of product to be shipped times the cost per ton-mile of shipping that product. (Linear cost of shipment and straight-line distances are assumed here. Other versions are discussed in Love et al. 1988.) The *center of gravity* is the point at which we could lift the map and have it balance; it is the plant location that will minimize the sum of all shipping costs, assuming straight-line distances and linear costs. Algebraically, the center of gravity is

$$M = \frac{\sum_{i=1}^{m} r_i d_i \mathrm{RM}_i + \sum_{i=1}^{n} R_i D_i \mathrm{FG}_i}{\sum_{i=1}^{m} r_i \mathrm{RM}_i + \sum_{i=1}^{n} R_i \mathrm{FG}_i} \tag{7}$$

where

equation 7 is computed separately for both the x and y coordinate

r_i, R_i = the rate per ton-mile (or use other appropriate units) to ship raw materials and finished goods, respectively

d_i, D_i = the map coordinate of the location of each raw-material source and finished-goods customer, respectively

RM_i, FG_i = the tons of raw material and finished goods respectively, to be shipped from (to) each location.

This approach would be a first step in the decision process, for reasons discussed previously. (More discussion, with examples, is given in Coyle et al. 1988.)

The foregoing approach treats transportation costs as most important. In retail siting, nearness and attraction to customers is paramount. (A survey of models for retail location is given in Craig et al. 1984.) An interesting example of profit modeling is given by Kimes and Fitzsimmons (1990), who studied site selection for La Quinta Motor Inns.

La Quinta has many existing motor inns; the model looks at the profitability of new sites one at a time. Given a recommended site, a regression model predicts the profitability. Managers then apply judgment to make the final decision whether to invest in that site or not. Kimes and Fitzsimmons modeled profit, not occupancy, since the competitive price can be so low that it is difficult to make money. The model looks at competitive variables (the number of hotel rooms within three miles, for example), demand-generating variables (college enrollment in the area), demographic variables (average family income), and others. As with all regression models, it is difficult to ascertain the exact causality of some relationships. (A high price correlates with profitability, but what allows us to charge a high price?) The authors discuss how LaQuinta uses the model to avoid potential statistical pitfalls.

Systems Analysis of Multilocation Problems

An organization such as Salt Ridge that is considering the location and capacity of several facilities must view the system in a holistic way. Each facility's impact on other facilities must be analyzed, even if we are only considering the location of one more facility to be added to an existing system.

A multilocation system design depends on the type of service that is demanded and the type of transportation used. Off-the-shelf service requires many locations for inventory, close to customers. Service within 24 hours can be achieved either by one location and air freight or by having many locations, probably with less total cost than for off-the-shelf service.

Trading quality of service against cost is particularly difficult for emergency facilities such as fire-fighting units or ambulance facilities. For example, fires often require multiple units to respond, and research has shown that a few minutes difference in response time can make a large difference in both damage and loss of life. (Models of emergency facility location are given by Batta and Mannur 1990 and by Larson and Sadiq 1983.) Different statements of objectives (minimize cost, minimize response time) and constraints (budget constraint, average response time constraint) can lead to very different solutions. Policymakers and managers must carefully consider the objective they select and the constraints they impose.

One analytical technique that can be used with a variety of objectives and constraints is mathematical programming. This technique has been used to help select telemarketing sites (Spencer et al. 1990), to plan multilocation facility modernization (Mason et al. 1990), to design production-distribution systems (Geoffrion and Graves 1974 and Brown et al. 1987), and for general logistics planning (Robinson 1989). Also see Love et al. (1988) for discussion and references. In the next subsection we will give some examples of the use of mathematical programming, using Salt Ridge Bakery as an example.

Mathematical Programming for Capacity and Location Analysis*

The Salt Ridge Bakery Company has a distribution-planning linear program that is used to determine which plants will ship to what market areas. The linear program (LP) is run after capacity changes or when demand patterns have changed enough to warrant a reexamination of the production-distribution pattern. Sharon Westphal would like to know if there are any weaknesses in their current use of the LP, and further, if the LP can be used to help them plan the location and capacity of new plants. To facilitate the discussion, the costs and other information about the LP model are given as follows:

*This subsection requires a knowledge of linear programming, which is described in Appendix C.

Table 16-3 Transportation Costs in Dollars per Pound of Product, Salt Ridge Bakery

From Plant	To Customer in Area 1	2	3	4	5	6	7	8	9	10
A	0.021	0.024	0.019	0.048	0.037	0.029	0.020	0.041	0.050	0.047
B	0.039	0.029	0.040	0.027	0.024	0.023	0.041	0.034	0.034	0.035
C	0.035	0.034	0.029	0.026	0.032	0.041	0.032	0.019	0.018	0.018

Plants: A, B, C (3 different plant locations)
Customer areas: 1, 2, 3, 4, 5, 6, 7, 8, 9, 10
(10 different customer area locations)
Production costs, in dollars per pound of product, and capacities, in pounds per day:
Plant A: $0.347/lb; capacity = 1,800,000 lb/day
Plant B: $0.326/lb; capacity = 4,000,000 lb/day
Plant C: $0.351/lb; capacity = 1,600,000 lb/day

Transportation costs are given in Table 16-3.

Westphal investigated the basis for these cost figures and believes that they are appropriate marginal costs to use in making distribution decisions. (If adding a new plant or retiring an old plant is being considered, the fixed costs of operation must also be included in the analysis.) The cost that is relevant to choosing a plant to use in meeting a certain area's demand is the production cost plus the transportation cost. This means we should add 0.347 to each element in the first row of Table 16-3, 0.326 to each element in the second row, and 0.351 to each element in the third row. These figures are shown in Table 16-4.

The demands per day are fairly constant. Estimates of the demand rates are as follows (in millions of pounds per day):

	AREA 1	2	3	4	5	6	7	8	9	10
Demand (million lb/day)	0.5	0.8	0.5	0.9	0.9	0.8	0.6	0.6	0.8	0.7

There is a total capacity of 7.4 million pounds per day and a total demand of 7.1 million pounds per day. The linear programming formulation that will

Table 16-4 Transportation plus Production Costs ($/lb), Salt Ridge Bakery

From Plant	To Customer in Area 1	2	3	4	5	6	7	8	9	10
A	0.368	0.371	0.366	0.395	0.384	0.376	0.367	0.388	0.397	0.394
B	0.365	0.355	0.366	0.363	0.350	0.349	0.367	0.360	0.360	0.361
C	0.386	0.385	0.380	0.377	0.383	0.392	0.383	0.370	0.369	0.369

find a minimum cost distribution plan is as follows. It is a transportation type of linear program.

Define

X_{ij} = units, in millions of pounds, produced at plant i and shipped to area j; i = A, B, C, and j = 1, 2, . . . , 10

C_{ij} = cost of 1 unit (million pounds) produced at plant i and shipped to area j; for example, C_{A1} = \$368,000, which is 0.368 from Table 16-4, times 1 million pounds per unit.

CAP_i = capacity, in millions of pounds per day, of plant i

DEM_j = demand, in millions of pounds per day, in area j

Then the LP formulation is

$$\text{Minimize} \quad \sum_{i=A}^{C} \sum_{j=1}^{10} C_{ij} X_{ij} \tag{8}$$

$$\text{subject to} \quad \sum_{j=1}^{10} X_{ij} \leq CAP_i \qquad i = A, B, C \tag{9}$$

$$\sum_{i=A}^{C} X_{ij} = DEM_j \qquad j = 1, 2, \ldots, 10 \tag{10}$$

$$X_{ij} \geq 0 \qquad i = A, B, C, \text{ and } j = 1, 2, \ldots, 10 \tag{11}$$

The formulation minimizes total production and transportation costs subject to staying within each plant's capacity and satisfying all demands. The first set of constraints requires that the sum of each plant's total production (the sum of the units shipped to all areas from that plant) must be less than or equal to the plant's capacity. The second set of constraints requires that the total of the units shipped into an area (the sum of the units shipped from all plants to the area) must equal the demand in that area.

The optimal solution to the Salt Ridge Bakery Company problem is as follows:

$X_{A1} = 0.5$ (million pounds) $X_{B2} = 0.8$

$X_{A3} = 0.5$ $X_{B4} = 0.9$

$X_{A7} = 0.6$ $X_{B5} = 0.9$

$X_{C9} = 0.8$ $X_{B6} = 0.8$

$X_{C10} = 0.7$ $X_{B8} = 0.6$

Plant B's capacity is fully utilized. Plants A and C have 0.2 and 0.1 million pounds of slack capacity, respectively. No area is served by more than one plant, but that is a coincidence; it will not necessarily happen in an LP of this type.

Having found a solution, Westphal examined the answers to see if the solution changed any of the cost figures. In particular, she felt that a plant operating at less than 80% capacity would have substantially higher costs per pound. In this case the lowest utilization is 0.89, at plant A, and it is safe to use the solution given. The present use of the LP model seems appropriate. The LP could, in practice, be much larger than the foregoing one, since there might be more plants (perhaps 20) and many more market areas (perhaps as many as 1000). Computer solution of such an LP is easily accomplished.

This LP can help Salt Ridge evaluate alternative capacity and location plans. Salt Ridge is considering three plans for expansion, since plant C needs to be replaced owing to age. Two of the alternative plans are to build a new plant at the plant C site, with either 2 million or 4 million pounds per day of capacity. The other plan is to increase the capacity of plant B to a total of 6 million pounds per day of capacity. The marginal cost of production is 0.326 at the plant B expansion, 0.320 at the 4-million-pound unit at site C, and 0.335 at the 2-million-pound unit at site C. The annual fixed costs of operation must be considered. However, since these are expected to be the same in each of the three cases, we can ignore them. (Westphal calculated that the larger plant's heavier use of automated equipment would lead to a reduction of some overhead costs, with the result that the annual fixed costs of operation are the same as for the smaller plant.) The investment required is $18 million for either of the 2-million-pound-capacity units and $34 million for the 4-million-pound-capacity unit. The firm does have the option of staying with their current capacity. If the old plant C is removed, it has a salvage value of zero.

LP can be used for each of the four possible capacity plans separately. The resulting daily costs can be compared, and the improvement due to the investment can be computed. We can see if the improvement is sufficient to warrant the investment of $18 or $34 million.

To illustrate the method, we initially assume that demand will not change in the near future. Then we have four LPs to run. The capacities were changed appropriately for each LP, and the C_{ij} figures would be calculated using Table 16-3 and the new production cost figures given previously. The total daily costs, taken from the LP solutions, are as follows:

LP1	LP2	LP3	LP4
Original capacities	Close plant C and expand plant B	Build new 2 million pound plant C	Build new 4 million pound plant C
Daily cost = $2,561,600	Daily cost = $2,547,300	Daily cost = $2,533,100	Daily cost = $2,469,700

Several comments should be made about details not reported in the preceding summary of the solutions. In LP2 and LP3, plant A is used only to 55% capacity. In LP4 plant A is not used at all. Also, demand for the product may be increasing. If we set those considerations aside momentarily, we can analyze the investment in new plant capacity. There are 300 working days in one year.

Plant B expansion (LP2) can be eliminated, since the new plant C (2 million pounds) costs the same and gives a lower daily cost.

The 2-million-pound-capacity plant C results in a saving of $2,561,600 − $2,533,100 = $28,500 per day. This is ($28,500)(300) = $8,550,000 per year, for an investment of $18 million. Even with a high discount factor that is a good investment.

The 4-million-pound-capacity plant C results in a further saving (compared with the 2 million pound capacity) of $2,533,100 − $2,469,700 = $63,400 per day. This is (300)($63,400) = $19,020,000 per year, for an additional investment of $16 million. The investment is profitable at any reasonable discount rate. The analysis thus suggests the LP4 plan, with a new 4-million-pound plant C.

However, several important considerations were left out of the foregoing analysis. For example, in LP2 and LP3, the 55% utilization of plant A would almost certainly increase costs, making those plans even less attractive than LP4. Before accepting the LP4 plan, Westphal must consider the benefit or loss of closing plant A. She must also consider the predicted growth in demand and how the new capacity plan will fare when demand grows. In fact, LPs should be run using a five-year or ten-year forecast. It may be that plant A and both 4-million-pound plants will be needed. The analysis is far from complete, but it appears that Westphal and Salt Ridge should invest in the new large plant at site C.

Integer Programming and Plant Capacity

Many problems involving mathematical programs have a structure similar to the problem preceding. A plant is there or it is not. We have 0 or 1 plant of a given capacity at a given site. Such problems can be formulated using *integer variables*, and the technique for solving such problems is called *integer linear programming* (*IP*). A detailed discussion of integer programming is beyond the scope of this text. However, it is important to know that methods very different from LP are used, and that solutions are much more difficult to obtain. Integer programming is discussed briefly in Appendix C.

As an example of a formulation using an integer variable, suppose that we consider the possible expansion of plant B in the Salt Ridge case to be a new plant, D, with the same costs as plant B. Define a new variable, δ_D, which is 1 if plant D is used and 0 if plant D is not used. We can write a new capacity constraint:

$$\sum_{j=1}^{10} X_{Dj} \leq (\delta_D)(2.0) \tag{12}$$

Because δ_D will be 0 or 1, the right-hand side (capacity) is either 0 or 2.0 million pounds. We would also constrain

$$\delta_D = 0 \text{ or } 1 \tag{13}$$

The formulation would be almost identical to the previous one; incorporate plant D in equations 8 to 11, include equations 12 and 13, and add the daily equivalent investment cost times δ_D to the objective function (8). The computer would then have the choice of using the new plant if it would reduce production and transportation costs by more than the investment cost. All four possible capacity plans could be included similarly; the IP would need to have three integer variables, one for each method of increasing capacity.

This brief introduction is not intended to leave you with an understanding of the complex area of integer-programming formulations and solutions. It is intended only to give you a feeling for how such formulations can be written and when they are appropriate. In this example integer variables were used to include or exclude the fixed cost of a new plant, depending on whether the program uses any of the facility. An attempt to do this with continuous variables would allow part of the fixed cost and part of the facility to be included, a serious error in this all-or-nothing situation.

Other Models for Location Analysis

Designing or redesigning a system of warehouse locations requires not only a decision about how many and where, but also a discussion of what type. Public warehouses offer relative ease of entry and exit, whereas company-owned locations are harder to add or delete. Once the type is determined, heuristics (rules of thumb) may be combined with either mathematical programs or simulation models. (Simulation is discussed in Appendix B. See Coyle et al. 1988 for further discussion of how to determine the number and type of warehouses, as well as a discussion of some references for heuristic programming and simulation models.)

These models are expensive to build. The best models are designed to be used interactively, helping the manager to use and extend his or her judgment. For example, demand patterns change with time; therefore, a ''solution'' to warehouse location must be good now, and we must also be able to modify it to be good over time. Also, many authors and managers believe that a location *causes* demand to be higher in the immediate vicinity, through a *presence* effect. The number of warehouses to have is affected by the extent of the presence effect. Finally, depending on who pays for freight costs (and more generally, on how a firm sets its prices), warehouse location can affect the price to the customer as well as the firm's own costs. (Hanjoul et al. 1990 discuss codetermining locations and pricing policy.)

Models can be very useful in determining facility locations, and the use of models, particularly mathematical programming, is on the rise. However, judgment and knowledge of the market must be included in the final system design.

REVIEW PROBLEMS

1. In the formulation given in equations 8 to 10 there are 30 variables and thirteen constraints. Using the cost data from Table 16-4 and the demand and capacity information given in the first part of the chapter, completely write out the objective function and each of the thirteen constraints. That is, write the formulation without using summation notation.

2. If Salt Ridge wanted to solve the LP using a forecast of demand five years hence, which is 40% higher than the current demand rates, and if they wanted to consider using the 4-million-pound-capacity plant C, what would change from your answer to review problem 1? (Do not write the entire formulation; just say what would change.)

3. Why is the design of Salt Ridge Bakery Company's system of plants different from a warehouse-location problem? Briefly give two important differences.

Solutions

1. Minimize
$$\begin{aligned} &368{,}000X_{A1} + 371{,}000X_{A2} + 366{,}000X_{A3} + 395{,}000X_{A4} \\ &+ 384{,}000X_{A5} + 376{,}000X_{A6} + 367{,}000X_{A7} + 388{,}000X_{A8} \\ &+ 397{,}000X_{A9} + 394{,}000X_{A10} + 365{,}000X_{B1} + 355{,}000X_{B2} \\ &+ 366{,}000X_{B3} + 363{,}000X_{B4} + 350{,}000X_{B5} + 349{,}000X_{B6} \\ &+ 367{,}000X_{B7} + 360{,}000X_{B8} + 360{,}000X_{B9} + 361{,}000X_{B10} \\ &+ 386{,}000X_{C1} + 385{,}000X_{C2} + 380{,}000X_{C3} + 377{,}000X_{C4} \\ &+ 383{,}000X_{C5} + 392{,}000X_{C6} + 383{,}000X_{C7} + 370{,}000X_{C8} \\ &+ 369{,}000X_{C9} + 369{,}000X_{C10} \end{aligned}$$

subject to

$$X_{A1} + X_{A2} + X_{A3} + X_{A4} + X_{A5} + X_{A6} + X_{A7} + X_{A8} + X_{A9} + X_{A10} \le 1.8$$
$$X_{B1} + X_{B2} + X_{B3} + X_{B4} + X_{B5} + X_{B6} + X_{B7} + X_{B8} + X_{B9} + X_{B10} \le 4.0$$
$$X_{C1} + X_{C2} + X_{C3} + X_{C4} + X_{C5} + X_{C6} + X_{C7} + X_{C8} + X_{C9} + X_{C10} \le 1.6$$

$$X_{A1} + X_{B1} + X_{C1} = 0.5$$
$$X_{A2} + X_{B2} + X_{C2} = 0.8$$
$$X_{A3} + X_{B3} + X_{C3} = 0.5$$
$$X_{A4} + X_{B4} + X_{C4} = 0.9$$
$$X_{A5} + X_{B5} + X_{C5} = 0.9$$
$$X_{A6} + X_{B6} + X_{C6} = 0.8$$
$$X_{A7} + X_{B7} + X_{C7} = 0.6$$
$$X_{A8} + X_{B8} + X_{C8} = 0.6$$
$$X_{A9} + X_{B9} + X_{C9} = 0.8$$
$$X_{A10} + X_{B10} + X_{C10} = 0.7$$

Even for this small LP, writing out the complete formulation is tedious. That is why we use summation and index notation.

2. The plant C capacity would change from 1.6 to 4.0. All ten plant C costs in the objective function would be reduced by 0.031, owing to the 0.351 to 0.320 production-cost reduction. Finally, all demand figures would be 40% higher; the new values would be (1.4)(0.5) = 0.7, (1.4)(0.8) = 1.12, 0.7, 1.26, 1.26, 1.12, 0.84, 0.84, 1.12, and 0.98.

3. Because the plants incur a much larger labor cost and entail more investment than a warehouse, and because the final customer is a large-scale consumer (a supermarket). Thus, there are no ''local'' delivery costs in the same sense as in many warehouse systems.

SUMMARY

Design is of strategic importance. Design determines what organizations can achieve through day-to-day management. Within operations management, we are concerned about product design, organizational design, and the design of facilities. This chapter deals with the important topic of the design of facilities. Within this area, we discussed the design of individual facilities, including layout and capacity, and facility location.

A process layout is one in which the work is organized by process, grouping similar operations together to allow high utilization. The products move through more slowly than in a product layout. The chapter gives mathematical programming and heuristic methods that minimize travel. Examples include both service and manufacturing organizations, health clinics, and job shops.

In a product layout, the facility is designed around the needs of the product. An assembly line, for example, can allow fast production of an individual product or a set of products. Manufacturing cells are layouts designed to get the speed of response associated with product layout, for a set of machines producing several or many different products. Manufacturing cells were discussed in Chapter 15. In this chapter we discussed methods of balancing assembly lines, allocating work to different workstations.

Any layout method must be the beginning of the solution process, not the end. The layout selected has implications for how employees and customers feel about the organization. (How easy is communication? How varied is the work? How quickly can we respond to customers?) A U-shaped layout, for example, is designed to allow flexible handling of work and ease of communication. A bank must be designed to be attractive and responsive to customers. An analysis that minimizes travel time or maximizes throughput is important, but it does not capture all the important factors. As another example, the assembly-line balancing techniques given here do not consider variation, the possibility of multiple paths for a product, or any of several other realistic enhancements.

Capacity and location decisions typically involve larger investments than any other decision faced by the organization. Capacity determines the organization's ability to deal with changes in the environment, including changes in demand, product line, and competition. Moreover, the scale of operations frequently affects the ambience of the work situation; large plants may be more automated and less personal, for example. In short, these decisions are of prime importance to the organization, whether it is a profit-making or a nonprofit organization.

Location decisions determine the organization's proximity to customers and, thus, the organization's ability to sell its product or service. Also, many of the organization's employees must live near the facility. (This often includes the person who is choosing the location.) Locations can be selected to reduce and control transportation and inventory costs, which are large for many organizations. Location and capacity decisions are frequently tied together, involving the organization's highest-level policies and policymakers. Managers make capacity decisions for many strategic reasons, including controllability, providing barriers to entry, planning for growth, and the ability to respond quickly to customers.

This chapter has discussed a variety of capacity-location problems and ways to approach them. Quantitative techniques have been introduced that deal effectively with the large-scale problems involved. Mathematical-programming models can minimize the production and transportation costs of meeting a specified level of demand. Integer programming can consider the fixed costs of building and operating a new facility. Mathematical programming and other models such as computer simulation and queuing analysis have been used extensively in location-capacity decisions.

A warning—quantitative technique must be used carefully. Because of the importance of the decisions, qualitative as well as quantitative considerations must be included. Further, a static analysis should be avoided; the effect on future decisions and system performance must be considered and is often the determining factor.

Nowhere is the dictum of "solve the right problem" more appropriate than in the design of facilities. An organization's facilities affect employee attitudes and customer service. Minimizing cost, in a narrow sense, can lead to poor performance. Quantitative approaches to these problems are very important; they have been used effectively to solve very large problems. However, the design of facilities must be tied to the organization's strategy, as discussed here and in Chapter 17.

PROBLEMS

1. For each of the following, would the layout be a product, process, or fixed-position layout? Why?
   a. the location of departments or academic fields within the buildings in a large university
   b. a blood donation center
   c. a self-service cafeteria
   d. a building construction site
   e. an airline terminal's customer areas

2. An ethical drug manufacturer must expand plant capacity to meet increasing demand. The company has two alternatives to consider: (a) building a specialized plant with a product layout for its largest-selling product, or (b) building additional capacity using process layout similar to its current facilities. Discuss the possible impact on long-term profits and competitive posture due to this layout decision.

*3. Design a department-store layout using the data in the accompanying figure and table. Begin with a schematic and then develop a rectangular floor plan, 60 feet deep by 100 feet across the front.

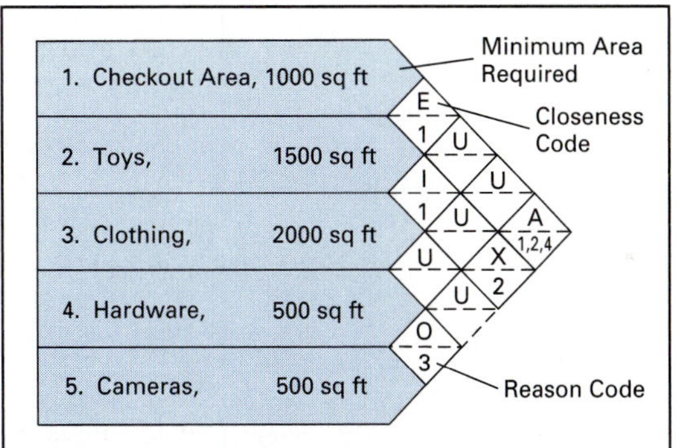

Code	Reason	Code	Closeness
1	marketing	A	absolutely necessary
2	security	E	especially important
3	can share personnel	I	important
4	frequent contact necessary	O	OK
		U	unimportant
		X	undesirable

4. A branch office of a bank[5] has its personnel arranged as shown in the accompanying diagram. The number of trips per day between

*Problems with an asterisk have answers in the back of the book.

[5]This problem is adapted from "Sequoia Bank of California," W. Abernathy and N. Baloff, Graduate School of Business, Stanford University, 1969.

locations was estimated by the assistant manager, who observed the entire office for one day. The result is shown in the form of a proximity matrix, shown in the second diagram. Using her own wristwatch, the assistant manager also estimated the travel time from the bookkeeper to the loans desk as 8 seconds, or 12 seconds from the bookkeeper to the teller. Thus, she estimated that it takes 4 seconds to walk between adjacent desks, and perhaps a little longer to walk diagonally between adjacent desks.

a. Categorize the proximity requirements as A, E, I, O, U, X, based on the number of trips.

b. Suggest an alternative arrangement that allows the operations manager to act as a teller during peak periods and reduces travel time.

c. Estimate the daily time savings of your proposed layout. What impact will it have on customer service? On employee morale?

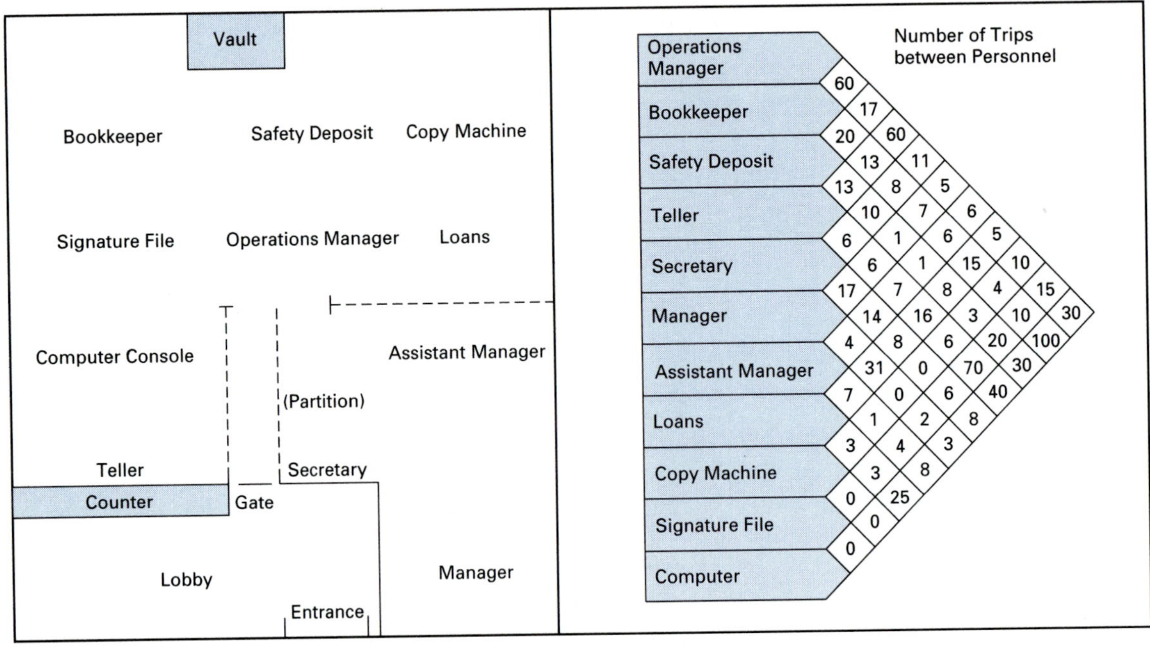

5. Discuss the adequacy of the data-gathering technique in the bank-layout example of problem 4.

*6. A pipe valve has seven parts (see the following list). Prior to final assembly, parts 2 and 3 are combined, as are 4 and 5, into subassemblies. The parts are numbered in order of the assembly operation, and the last step is an inspection. Construct a Gozinto chart for this operation.

i. body
ii. bushing
iii. stem
iv. packing
v. cap
vi. handle
vii. nut to secure handle

7. An assembly line, paced by a single moving belt, has had a history of temporary shutdowns and quality problems. A study showed that of the 54 assembly stations, 51 required only routine, repetitive tasks, but the other three required judgment and a varying amount of time. Each of these three stations performed an inspection and touch-up operation, involving tasks such as adjusting doors to fit tightly and repairing small errors in painting.
   a. How could these three stations be part of the cause of the shutdown and quality problems?
   b. Suggest a solution.

*8. The production line shown here has been producing an average of 720 items per day. The times given are engineering estimates of the normal production time per item at each station. Items are carried on a constantly-moving conveyor.

Station 1	Station 2	Station 3	Station 4
25 seconds	30 seconds	15 seconds	20 seconds

   a. What is the minimum cycle time (in seconds) possible for this line, according to the engineers? Explain.
   b. There are currently seven production hours per day. (i) Given the daily output, what is the actual cycle time? (ii) What is the present balance delay?
   c. Can one worker be eliminated at the present production rate? If so, how? If not, why not?
   d. What is the theoretical minimum number of workers for the present production rate?
   e. What is the maximum production rate possible with the present setup? Explain what you would do *first* if you found it necessary to exceed that rate, without using overtime.
   f. What is the internal balance delay with the present task assignment? Why is zero balance delay unattainable with this assignment?

*9. a. (For this problem use the heuristics described near the end of Section 16-1 to find solutions to the line-balancing problem for assembly of the jingflopper [Table 16-1].) Find two solutions, one for each numerical score described in Section 16-1. The target is 20 minutes per workstation to achieve a production rate of 3 per hour. The number of stations need not be 5.
   b. What is the balance delay for the two station arrangements?
   c. Repeat part a for a target cycle time of 18 minutes, for either one of the numerical scores.
   d. For $n = 6$, the text says that $c = 17$ is possible. Try to find an assignment that accomplishes this, using your own judgment. (The heuristics will not find this solution.)

10. The following is a list of assembly tasks showing sequence restrictions and performance times:

Task	Time (seconds)	Predecessors
A	5	None
B	4	A, E
C	2	none
D	10	E
E	5	none
F	3	C, D
G	5	H, I
H	7	none
I	8	none
J	4	all

a. Develop a diagram showing the sequence requirements.

b. Determine a task grouping that does not violate sequence restrictions and has a cycle-time target of 18 seconds. What method did you use?

c. What is the minimum number of stations needed?

d. What is the balance delay for the arrangement given by the answer to part b?

11. What are the advantages of a U-shaped layout?

*12. Product and process layouts for "design" are shown in Figure 16-1. Describe a product layout for an outpatient clinic that has six doctors (MDs), ten physician's assistants (PAs), six registered nurses (RNs), four licensed practical nurses (LPNs), and four receptionist-bookkeeping personnel. Discuss the advantages and disadvantages of your layout.

13. A firm is considering dramatically reducing its product line, going from 100 products to a few. What layout implications are there? What are a few of the costs and benefits?

14. What considerations are important in locating a single facility, such as a warehouse, a plant, or a retail store?

*15. What considerations are most important in determining the location for a new high school in a city where there are two other high schools that will also be in operation?

16. Table 16-2 gives six location considerations. Describe a type of facility for which item 1, transportation and inventory costs, might be the most important factor. Then do the same for items 2 to 6.

*17. Figure 16-9 shows the returns from the possible Salt Ridge capacity plans, and the problem is analyzed in a before-tax manner in the portion of Section 16-2 that follows Figure 16-9. Use an investment tax credit of 8% of the investment value, a tax rate of 48%, and straight-line depreciation to year 20 (so that the expansion would be depreciated over 19 years).

a. Redo the analysis using a 10% discount rate on an after-tax basis. (After-tax analysis is discussed in Chapter 3.)

b. The probability of ''demand high'' was estimated to be 0.2, but the manager is unsure of that estimate. Over what range for that probability will ''Build 2000'' still be optimal? (That is, what is the breakeven probability?)

*18. The Phrammes Manufacturing Company is planning to locate a new distribution center (DC) to service the three accounts in the western territory. All material will go from the single plant to the DC, and then to the three customers. The locations are shown in the accompanying graph. Customer 1 requires 10 tons of product per month, while each of the other two customers requires 6 tons. The plant will supply all 22 tons of material to the DC each month. The rate per ton-mile is $1 from the plant to the DC and $2 from the DC to any customer.

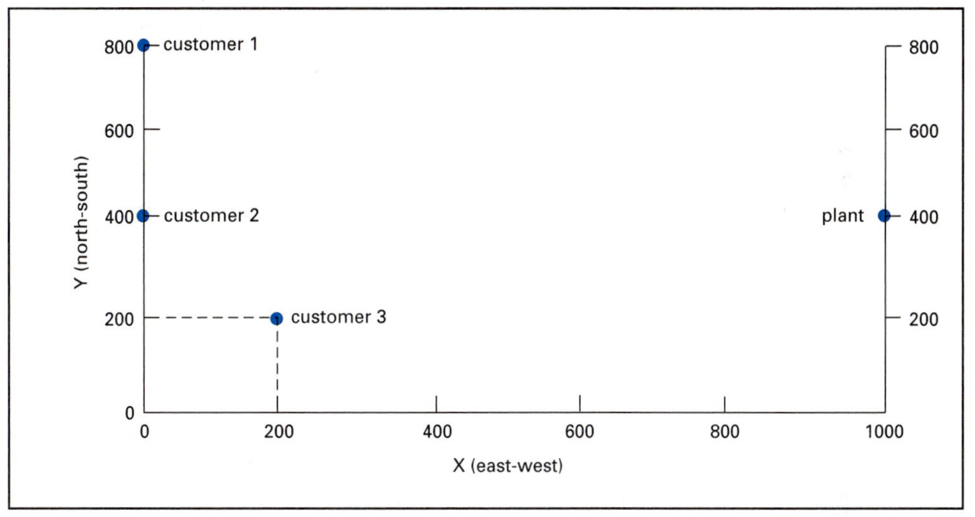

a. Find the center-of-gravity location for the DC, using equation 7 separately for the X and Y coordinates. (Note: The plant is the source of raw materials in the analysis.)

b. If $p = 1.5$ is used in equation 6, what is the expected travel distance over the road from the plant to customer 3? If $p = 1.0$, what is that distance?

*19. A large dairy-products company is redesigning their truck-fleet maintenance department. They want to keep the trucks on the road as much as possible, and in fact, many of the trucks average 14 or more hours of usage per day, 365 days per year.

a. What might ''capacity'' of the maintenance facility mean?

b. What considerations go into determining the appropriate capacity of the maintenance facility?

c. If they need 25 operative trucks to make the daily runs, what information do they need to determine how many extras to have over and above the 25?

20. The following LP is from the chapter text.

$$\text{Minimize} \quad \sum_{i=A}^{C} \sum_{j=1}^{10} C_{ij} X_{ij}$$

$$\text{subject to} \quad \sum_{j=1}^{10} X_{ij} \leq \text{CAP}_i \qquad \text{for } i = A, B, C$$

$$\sum_{i=A}^{C} X_{ij} = \text{DEM}_j \qquad \text{for } j = 1 \text{ to } 10$$

in which X_{ij} = units produced at i and shipped to j.

a. Explain how this LP could be used to evaluate the future returns from an investment in a new plant (denoted plant D) whose location has already been determined.

b. If there are six potential sites for plant D, how can the LP be used?

c. What other major factors must be considered that cannot be included in the LP?

21. Ace Beverage Company produces a regionally sold line of soft drinks. They have two plants (A and B) from which they ship to four market areas. Their sales have been growing dramatically. This year's sales forecast and next year's sales forecast are as follows:

Sales Forecast (thousands of cases)

Area	This Year	Next Year
1	2,000	2,500
2	2,000	3,000
3	4,000	5,000
4	2,000	2,000

The two existing plants each have an annual capacity of 5 million cases (5000 units). The firm has decided to build a new plant that will have the same capacity. Otherwise they will have insufficient capacity next year. The new plant will be at location C or D. The production and transportation costs anticipated for next year are as follows, in dollars per thousand cases.

Production Costs ($/unit)			Transportation Costs ($/unit) To			
Site	**Cost**	**From**	**Area 1**	**Area 2**	**Area 3**	**Area 4**
Plant A	1,200	Plant A	300	200	300	400
Plant B	1,200	Plant B	500	400	350	250
Plant C	1,400	Plant C	500	400	250	400
Plant D	1,200	Plant D	200	300	450	500

a. Write the LP formulation that would minimize cost, meet demand, and indicate what production-shipping pattern to use if plant site C is used. Indicate the changes that would be necessary to consider the plant D location.

b. How would you decide which site to use?

c. Without running an LP, which plant site do you prefer and why? (Assume here that both sites cost the same to build and that cost is the only factor.)

22. In problem 21, we could use an integer linear programming formulation to simultaneously consider both plant sites. Write that formulation. (Refer to problem 21 for cost, demand, and capacity data.)

*23. In Problem 21, suppose that site D is preferred to site C by the LP cost analysis.

  a. What factors might cause a manager to accept plant site C in spite of that analysis?

  b. What information would you need to see if the firm should invest in either plant? That is, how would they decide if the preferred site is a good investment?

24. A distribution manager is going to completely redesign the company's warehousing and shipping patterns, using public warehouses. What information would be needed? Which of the items mentioned in your list would be most difficult to obtain?

25. In the airline industry, the belief has been held that the firm with more capacity (available seats) will have a disproportionate share of the customers.

  a. Why might this be true?

  b. Assume that two companies have equal capacity, with a total of 400 available seats each day. Assume that they are both barely profitable. If one firm decides to change its capacity, describe what might happen in the short run and in the long run.

26. The capacity for a Salt Ridge Bakery plant is analyzed in Figures 16-9 and 16-10, and in the related discussion. The review problem to Section 16-2 asks you to consider a change in the probability of high demand from 0.2 to 0.5.

  a. Using the numbers from the review problem, what probability of high demand is the breakeven value, at which "Build 2000" and "Build 5000" have the same expected payoff?

  b. What competitive aspects of the capacity decision are ignored by part a and by the analysis given in the text?

REFERENCES

BAETZ, B.W., E.I. PAS, and A.W. NEEBE, "Trash Management: Sizing and Timing Decisions for Incineration and Landfill Facilities," *Interfaces*, November-December, 1989.

BATTA, R., and N.R. MANNUR, "Covering Location Models for Emergency Situations that Require Multiple Response Units," *Management Science*, January, 1990.

BAYBARS, I., "A Survey of Exact Algorithms for the Simple Assembly Line Balancing Problem," *Management Science*, vol. 32, no. 8, 1986.

BOZER, Y.A., and J.A. WHITE, "Design and Performance Models for End-of-Aisle Order Picking Systems," *Management Science*, July, 1990.

BROWN, G.G., G.W. GRAVES, and M.D. HONCZARENKO, "Design and Operation of a Multicommodity Production/Distribution System Using Primal Goal Decomposition,'' *Management Science*, November, 1987.

CHAKRAVARTY, A., ''Line Balancing with Task Learning Effects,'' *IIE Transactions*, vol. 20, no. 2, 1988.

CONWAY, R., W. MAXWELL, J. MCCLAIN, and L.J. THOMAS, ''The Role of Work-in-Process Inventory in Serial Production Lines,'' *Operations Research*, vol. 36, no. 2, March–April, 1988.

CONWAY, R., W. MAXWELL, J. MCCLAIN, and S. WORONA, *Users's Guide to XCELL+ Factory Modeling System*, Redwood City, Calif.: Scientific Press, 1990.

COONEY, S., *EC-92 and U. S. Industry*, Washington, D.C.: National Association of Manufacturers, 1989.

COYLE, J.J., E.J. BARDI, and C.J. LANGLEY, JR., *The Management of Business Logistics*, 4th ed., St. Paul, Minn.: West, 1988.

CRAIG, C.S., A. GHOSH, and S. MCLAFFERTY, ''Models of the Retail Location Process: A Review,'' *Journal of Retailing*, vol. 60, no. 1, 1984.

FRANCIS, R., and J. WHITE, *Facility Layout: An Analytical Approach*, Englewood Cliffs, N.J.: Prentice-Hall, 1974.

GEOFFRION, A., and G. GRAVES, ''Multicommodity Distribution System Design by Benders' Decomposition,'' *Management Science*, January, 1974.

HACKMAN, S.T., M.J. MAGAZINE, and T.S. WEE, ''Fast, Effective Algorithms for Simple Assembly Line Balancing Problems,'' *Operations Research*, November–December, 1989.

HAMBURG, M., *Statistical Analysis for Decision Making*, 5th ed., Harcourt, Brace, Jovanovich, 1991.

HANJOUL, P., P. HANSEN, D. PEETERS, and J.F. THISSE, ''Uncapacitated Plant Location under Alternative Spatial Price Policies,'' *Management Science*, January, 1990.

HAUSMAN, W.H., L.B. SCHWARZ, and S.C. GRAVES, ''Optimal Storage Assignment in Automated Warehousing Systems,'' *Management Science*, vol. 26, no. 6, 1976.

KIMES, S.E., and J.E. FITZSIMMONS, ''Selecting Profitable Hotel Sites at La-Quinta Motor Inns,'' *Interfaces*, March–April, 1990.

LARSON, R., and G. SADIQ, ''Facility Locations with the Manhattan Metric in the Presence of Barriers to Travel,'' *Operations Research*, vol. 31, no. 4, 1983.

LOVE, R.F., J.G. MORRIS, and G.O. WESOLOWSKY, *Facilities Location: Models and Methods*, Englewood Cliffs, N.J., Prentice-Hall, 1988.

MASON, L.G., A. GIRARD, and X.D. GU, ''Multilocation Facility Modernization: Models and Heuristics,'' *Operations Research*, May–June, 1990.

MCCORMICK, S.T., M.L. PINEDO, S. SHENKER, and B. WOLF, ''Sequencing in an Assembly Line with Blocking to Minimize Cycle Time,'' *Operations Research*, November–December, 1989.

MILAS, G.H., ''Assembly Line Balancing—Let's Remove the Mystery,'' *Industrial Engineering*, May, 1990.

OSTOLAZA, J., J. MCCLAIN, and L.J. THOMAS, ''The Use of Dynamic (State-Dependent) Assembly-Line Balancing to Improve Throughput,'' *Journal of Manufacturing and Operations Management*, Summer, 1990.

PERRAULT, M.W., ''Facilities Optimization,'' in *Examination of Case Studies in Health Facilities Planning*, Chicago: Hospital Research and Educational Trust, 1973.

PINTO, P., D. DANNENBRING, and B. KHUMAWALA, "Assembly Line Balancing with Processing Alternatives," *Management Science*, vol. 29, no. 7, 1983.

ROBINSON, E.P., JR., "Multi-Activity Uncapacitated Facility Location Problem: A New Tool for Logistics Planning," *Journal of Business Logistics*, vol. 10, no. 2, 1989.

SCHMENNER, R.W., *Making Business Location Decisions*, Englewood Cliffs, N.J.: Prentice-Hall, 1982.

SCHONBERGER, R., and E. KNOD, JR., *Operations Management: Serving the Customer*, 3rd. ed., Plano, TX.: Business Publications, 1988.

SKINNER, W., "The Focused Factory," *Harvard Business Review*, May–June, 1974.

SPENCER, T., III, A.J. BRIGANDI, P.R. DRAGON, and M.J. SHEEHAN, "AT&T's Telemarketing Site Selection System Offers Customer Support," *Interfaces*, January–February, 1990.

STAHL, J.F., "Facility Productivity Today Can Be Planned, Measured, and Controlled—Do It," *Industrial Engineering*, June, 1990.

TAMASHUNAS, V.M., J. LABBAN, and D. SLY, "Interactive Graphics Offer an Analysis of Plant Layout and Material Handling Systems," *Industrial Engineering*, June, 1990.

THOMAS, L.J., J. MCCLAIN, and D. EDWARDS, *Cases in Operations Management: Using the XCELL Factory Modeling System*, Redwood City, Calif.: Scientific Press, 1989.

THUROW, L.C., "GATT is Dead," *Journal of Accountancy*, September, 1990.

TOMPKINS, J.A., and J.A. WHITE, *Facilities Planning*, New York, Wiley, 1984.

USHER, J. S., C.A. CIESIELSKI, and R.A. JOHNSON, "Redesigning an Existing Layout Presents a Major Challenge—And Produces Dramatic Results," *Industrial Engineering*, June, 1990.

WHEELWRIGHT, S., ed., *Capacity Planning and Facilities Choice*, Division of Research, Graduate School of Business Administration, Harvard University, Cambridge, Massachusetts, 1979.

YANO, C.A., and A. BOLAT, "Survey, Development, and Application of Algorithms for Sequencing Paced Assembly Lines," *Journal of Manufacturing and Operations Management*, Fall, 1989.

c h a p t e r

17

Integrating Operations Into the Strategy of Organization

In the area of global competition, organizations "win" by delivering desired goods and services more efficiently. Consumers (all of us) benefit from this process. Operations management is one major factor in becoming a winner.

The operations area is where most of the organization's money is spent and where a large fraction of assets are employed. This causes many managers to concentrate on efficiency, lower cost, and higher utilization when thinking of operations strategy. Skinner (1986) has argued that while productivity is indeed important, focusing only on that factor is inappropriate. In our opinion, operations will be of strategic value only if it produces a broad range of marketing benefits, and marketing can only plan its strategy in conjunction with the long-term strategy for operations. Low cost and high quality are very important; however, firms must go further by *adding value for their customers*. The good or service must be designed, sold, and delivered in a way that the work our firm does benefits the customers more than the cost to us.

Throughout this book we have argued that operations, marketing, finance, and other areas of the firm should be integrated to obtain the benefits of a systems view of the organization. The overall goals, including that of adding value to customers, should be developed at the top of the organization. These objectives should then lead to policy guidelines that mold operational decisions. This chapter will review ways of accomplishing the integration of functions and the development of guiding policies. It is particularly appropriate to discuss these questions here, at the end of the text, where we have an opportunity to integrate many of the topics we have studied.

Chapter 1 introduced three themes for this book.

Theme 1: Organizational strategy must include operations; operations strategy must consider benefits arising outside of operations.

Theme 2: Organizations must integrate strategy, design, and operations.

Theme 3: Quality is fundamental in all activities.

This chapter will expand on these themes. Operations strategy must be part of overall strategy, and operations must, in particular, assist marketing by generating value for the customers. Having a good strategy will be useless unless the design of the facilities allows the firm to achieve the strategic goal, and unless day-to-day management of operations is done with the strategy in mind. Finally, quality must permeate everything we do; even so, quality is not everything a customer wants. Firms must maintain and improve quality while continually finding other ways to add value for the customer.

The main foci for our strategy discussion will be customers and competitors. We make money by doing something the customer values, and by doing it better than our competitors. Chapter 2 introduced several ''ways to compete,'' including cost, customization, innovation, quality, and flexibility. Most firms use more than one of these, and the selection depends on the basic product and what competitors can do. Often, selecting a way to compete implies choosing some customers and ignoring others. Mercedes-Benz, for example, is willing to take a Honda customer, but they do not expect to do so very often. Both financial advisers and discount brokers exist, usually for different clients.

How important is operations? A narrow view would include items such as cost of sales and assets employed. Examining annual reports from many companies, including McDonnell-Douglas, General Motors, Matsushita, Sears Merchandising Group, Marriott, and IBM, we found cost of sales, as a percent, to vary between 40% and 85% (source: 1989 Annual Reports). IBM is at the low end because their large cost of product development, also at least partially an operations responsibility, is accounted for outside of the cost of sales. Inventories, except for Marriott, range from $4 billion to $9.5 billion, and the cost of the inventory exceeds profits in most cases. In the $4000-billion U.S. economy, there are over $800 billion of inventory and over $500 billion of annual plant and equipment expenditures (source: Survey of Current Business, 1990 issues). While these are all large numbers, many managers believe the new plant and equipment number should be larger.

Is operations strategy needed in services? Is the service sector dominating developed economies, making manufacturing obsolete? Both sectors are crucial, and operations strategy must be carefully crafted in both. Cohen and Zysman (1987) have demonstrated why ''manufacturing matters.'' While manufacturing is less than 20% of jobs and GNP, it accounts for nearly 70% of exports, and it creates many service jobs. Still, services account for the bulk of both GNP and employment. Nearly all the topics discussed in this chapter (and book) apply to services. Examples of strategic operations management from both service and manufacturing will be used in this chapter.

17-1 STRATEGIC PLANNING

''If information is plentiful, what is scarce? . . . When information is plentiful, time to attend to it is scarce. Attention is the scarce factor in an information rich society'' (Simon 1988). The key to developing and implementing a successful strategy is deciding what things deserve and receive the most attention.

Basically, firms want to maintain a *sustainable competitive advantage* (see Porter 1985). To do so, firms must add value for some customers, in a more cost-effective way than potential competitors. Customer focus requires that we select customers we can serve well. This may be all customers for a product or service, if we have a sustainable quality or cost advantage, or a segment of customers that need our particular expertise.

Porter (1985) gives three generic strategies: (1) *cost leadership,* (2) *differentiation,* and (3) *focus.* In cost leadership, a firm has the lowest cost for the product category and serves all the customers for that product. This requires not only that the firm have a cost advantage but also that they have an advantage in learning how to reduce costs. (See Lieberman 1989, as well as the discussion of learning or experience curves, Chapter 5, and just-in-time, Chapter 12, in this book.) In differentiation, a firm develops a noncost advantage (such as quality or speed of delivery). Again, a continual improvement program is required if the advantage is to be sustained.

The final generic strategy, focus, requires that the firm select a customer segment and provide more of what that segment needs than broad-based suppliers can. The customers may pay more for a product or service that provides value to them. To implement this strategy we may even turn away business that would cause our operations to lose their focus on the target.

In any of the strategies, the firm must protect its competitive advantage by investing its money and effort. One way to select these investments uses *strategic business units* or *SBUs.*

Selecting Investments Using SBUs

An SBU is a set of products that use similar means and methods of production and are sold to similar types of customers. The number of SBUs must be large enough that significant differences in production or marketing opportunities are not lost by the aggregation of products within each SBU, and small enough that attention can be given to each SBU regarding market-growth predictions, technological forecasting, and competitive-position analysis.

For example, a company that makes athletic shoes might define one SBU as ''high-priced training shoes for runners.'' There would be several styles in that category, and they would be sold both to teams and to individuals. Another SBU would be hiking boots, which would be sold almost entirely to individuals; thus the marketing plans would be very different. Again, there would be several individual styles in the category. Yet another SBU might be the casual shoe market, and an athletic shoe company might have low-priced training shoes in this category. The production process and materials would be different from but similar to that of high-priced training shoes; the marketing plan would be very different. (Reebok grew dramatically in the 1980s by successfully marketing athletic shoes as casual shoes, until ''athletic'' shoes now constitute a majority of shoe sales in the United States.)

Many methods have been suggested to select which SBUs to favor with continued investment. (See Hax and Majluf 1984, for discussion and references.) One method is based on the cost-leadership strategy mentioned previously, in turn based on the learning or experience curve. The argument is that the firm with the highest market share will have a sustainable cost advantage, owing to economies of scale. If we also assume that firms would like to be involved in growing markets, so that the firm can grow, we can characterize SBUs as in Table 17-1.

An SBU identified as type 1 would receive favored treatment in investment dollars, since the firm would be solidifying a position that should reap future benefits. An SBU identified as type 4 would not receive investment funds unless they could promise a very fast return. Type 2 has been called a *cash cow,* meaning that the firm can make money for a long time without investing fur-

Table 17-1 Categorization of SBUs

Market Share (our slice)	Growth of Market (future size of pie)	
	High	Low
High	type 1	type 2
Low	type 3	type 4

ther. Since the market is not growing, it may not be worthwhile to push that SBU for the future. The firm may choose to let market share decline (''harvest'' market share) while generating cash for strategic investments. Type 3 is chosen for major investment only if there is some way to obtain an increased market share.

Concentrating on market share and growth is the essence of a cost-leadership strategy. However, this may be too simplistic. A firm may have a strategic advantage because of experience in a related area. For example, computer control is such a large and growing fraction of the cost of military aircraft that a computer manufacturer might be the principal contractor for a fighter plane, in spite of having no airframe production experience.

Also, in the other two generic strategies discussed previously, a firm may use special expertise to differentiate its products or target its efforts. The firm may in fact enjoy and utilize its smallness. To deal a little better with the complexities of strategic investment, a firm can use something like Table 17-2 to evaluate investment proposals. Table 17-2 is used to answer the question, should this use of capital be approved? In addition to the rate of return projected for the investment, the strategic value is analyzed to keep a firm from losing focus.

Business attractiveness is meant to include several factors. The total industry sales for the product line and the growth rate of that total market would be two of the factors. If the organization is already in the business under study, the current profitability of the line would be a factor in deciding whether to invest more money in that line. Who the competitors are and how likely they are to make a big push in the area are also factors. For some firms with large sales and profit swings owing to seasonal economic cycles, a product (or service) line that is up when the other products are down (countercyclical) would be valuable. Some businesses choose to give each factor a numerical weight, so that business attractiveness can be measured quantitatively.

Fit with organizational strengths is also meant to include many factors, and

Table 17-2 Categories for Operations Investment Proposals

Fit with Organizational Strengths	Business Attractiveness		
	High	Medium	Low
High	best ←		
Medium			
Low			worst

a numerical scale could be developed for it as well. The questions to be considered would include the following:

1. What is the current market share (if the organization is currently making the product)?
2. Can the current sales force or distribution channel market the product (if it is new)?
3. Does the organization have a technological advantage based on technical expertise, previous experience, or special facilities?
4. Are there any special reasons why the organization can produce and distribute the product cheaper or faster than the competition?

The attractiveness-fit approach of Table 17-2 emphasizes the fact that market potential and operations expertise should interact to help form a policy for the allocation of scarce resources. The approach should be viewed as a guideline rather than as the final word for investment decisions. Many other factors must be considered, including the degree and type of risk present in an investment.

Core Competence

Rather than using SBUs as the basis for strategic planning, Prahalad and Hamel (1990) suggest using the idea of a *core competence*. A firm's core competence is the knowledge and ability that gives it an edge, both now and in the future. The competence may be in product or process technology, in methods of serving a set of customers, or in any area that can provide a sustainable advantage. A frozen-food manufacturer with a core competence in distribution might use that competence to add other firms' frozen foods to its line of distributed products, for example.

Using this idea to guide strategic investments, some products must be protected because they allow the firm to continue to build the knowledge about the core area in the firm. Direct investment in R&D is also guided by what the core area is. *Core products* that build on the core competence must be developed. For example, GE used its competence in new materials as an important part of its effort to develop improved major appliances in the 1980s. GE clearly also has competence in distributing and selling consumer products, but it used a very different competence (materials) to enhance that position. L.L. Bean sells high-quality products, but it uses world-class customer service and distribution to increase sales.

Many core competences are technological in nature, and companies need a clear view of their position to protect it in the long term. A product advantage can be overcome by a firm with either the basic technology (DRAMs[1] as opposed to computers) or processing technology. To be effective, a core competence must provide a key part of the firm's sustainable advantage. (Ways to develop a technology strategy are discussed in MacAvoy 1988.)

Core competence can also be organizational, such as possessing the ability to develop new automobiles quickly. Clark and Fujimoto (1989) have claimed

[1]DRAMs, dynamic random access memory chips, are a basic component of computers.

that this gives some Japanese automakers an advantage over those in Europe and the United States. Core competences should be thought of broadly, to include basic technology, product and process technology, and organizational skills. The key core competences must then be selected and defended by investment of both effort and money.

The Value Chain

The final strategic planning topic to be discussed here is the *value chain* (Porter 1985). Porter suggests examining the entire process of adding value to a product, and selecting portions of that chain that are crucial to maintaining competitive advantage. Figure 17-1 (a modification of Figure 2-2 from Porter 1985) shows a generic value chain. Each *primary activity* is a link in the chain.

The value chain allows the firm to focus on where the money is spent and to consider which portions of the chain are essential to competitive strategy. For example, if inbound logistics accounts for the majority of the cost (through purchases), the firm may decide either to integrate vertically or to form a long-term partnership with suppliers, to ensure supply and control of that cost. Figure 17-1 can also help the firm focus on what groups in and out of the company must interact to maintain competitive advantage. Using inbound logistics again, the operations and procurement groups must manage those costs together.

Finally, Figure 17-1 highlights the importance of operations in strategic planning. Although operations is only one of the five primary activities, our view is that operations management includes all but marketing and sales, and the interaction of operations with marketing and sales is one of the key foci of this chapter. Further, the support activities of procurement, technology development, and human-resource management should all involve operations managers. The next section analyzes operations strategy specifically, applying concepts from this section.

Figure 17-1 A Generic Value Chain. Reprinted with permission of The Free Press, a Division of Macmillan, Inc. from COMPETITIVE ADVANTAGE: Creating and Sustaining Superior Performance by Michael E. Porter. Copyright © 1985 by Michael E. Porter.

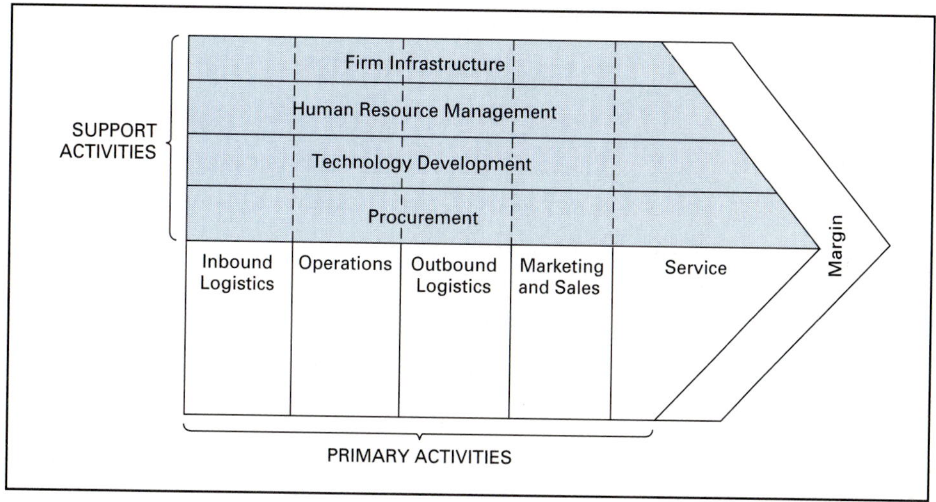

REVIEW PROBLEMS

Consider the strategy of a private, expensive, and well-known business school.

1. Name three SBUs that the school might have.
2. Which of the three generic strategies best fits this organization?
3. What core competence should this organization seek to maintain and build on, in your opinion?

Solutions

1. M.B.A., B.A., and Ph.D. graduates are SBUs, as are research output (articles and books) and executive education.
2. Differentiation fits best. Cost leadership is not viable because several large competitors (state schools) receive government subsidies. Focus would characterize a school that, for example, gives only M.B.A.'s, or a school that has decided to concentrate most of its resources in executive education.
3. Many answers are possible (and are reviewed frequently in faculty meetings). One competence would be the ability to generate innovative ideas through research, thereby guaranteeing a flow of new course material.

17-2 OPERATIONS STRATEGY

A strategy for the operations area of a firm cannot be developed without knowing the overall strategy. However, the overall strategy should be developed in conjunction with operations managers, considering current and possible future capabilities. Also, strategy is only useful if it is used to guide both long-term and day-to-day management decisions. This section will discuss operations strategy and the connections to corporate strategy and implementation. (More complete discussions, oriented toward manufacturing, are given in Gunn 1987, Hayes et al. 1988, Hill 1989, and other references at the end of the chapter.)

There are many books and articles on manufacturing strategy, but few on *service operations strategy*. Thus, we will refer to many manufacturing-strategy books and articles and discuss manufacturing more than services. But we will demonstrate the applicability of many of the concepts to services.

The most important idea is that operations must be customer oriented; the firm must provide value to the customer and build the capability to continue doing so. Chase and Garvin (1989) have gone so far as to suggest that a plant should be a *service factory*. Hausman and Montgomery (1990) discuss ways of "making manufacturing market driven." This requires good communication among many groups. The clearest part of the communication must be related to what performance is needed in the marketplace. Also, there will be alternative ways to deliver the same performance.

As one example of communication between marketing and manufacturing, consider the problem of product design. If marketing sets the specifications and passes them to engineering, who in turn design the product and pass the design to manufacturing, there may be specifications that are both costly and not basic to the product's function. Back and forth communication, achieved using a design team composed of all three groups, can produce a lower-cost, customer-oriented product. *Quality function deployment* (*QFD*) is a technique that helps all parties to focus on the key product concepts: What is this product supposed to do for the customer? (See Denton 1990 and Chapter 6.) Strategy can guide the separate groups and facilitate communication.

As an example of different ways of achieving the same goal, consider a firm that must deliver spare parts to repair copying machines in any major city in the European Community within twenty-four hours. One way is to maintain an inventory of all parts in each city. Another is to keep inventory in one location and use airfreight from a central facility. Strategy should set the goal, and operations should determine how to meet it. Operations should also provide information on how much it would cost (or save) to improve on the goal, so that the strategic goal can be reconsidered. (See Chapter 14.)

Three Key Questions In Operations Strategy

The following three questions will be used to focus our discussion for the rest of this chapter.

QUESTION 1: What business are we in, and who are the customers and competitors?

The answer to this question should come from the company's strategy. If operations managers are to be customer oriented, they must have clear answers to Question 1. As the strategy and marketing literature shows, the answers are often unclear. Cross Pens are really more a ''gift'' (especially ''corporate gift'') than a writing implement. The customers are both corporations, which give pens with a corporate logo to their customers, and individuals. In the corporate-gift category, the competition includes a wide variety of firms and products other than pens.

The classic example of the wrong answer to Question 1 is the U.S. railroad industry. In the early twentieth century, those companies thought they were in the railroad business. In fact, they were in the transportation business with trucking firms as effective competitors. They ignored their customers' need for point-to-point transportation. In answering Question 1, managers must consider how to serve the customer's real needs and deal with new competitors who may be able to serve those needs.

QUESTION 2: How can operations produce ''order winners?''

The phrase *order winners* is from Hill (1989), who focuses on how manufacturing (or more generally, operations) can actively stimulate customers to buy the product (good or service). Hill separates order winners from *qualifying criteria*, which are characteristics necessary to be considered for the order. For example, many customers now think of outstanding product quality as essential, and they select a high-quality product on the basis of other criteria such as speed and reliability of service. In this case, the quality of the item is a qualifying criterion and the quality of service is the order winner.

An order winner must differentiate the product (good or service). As time

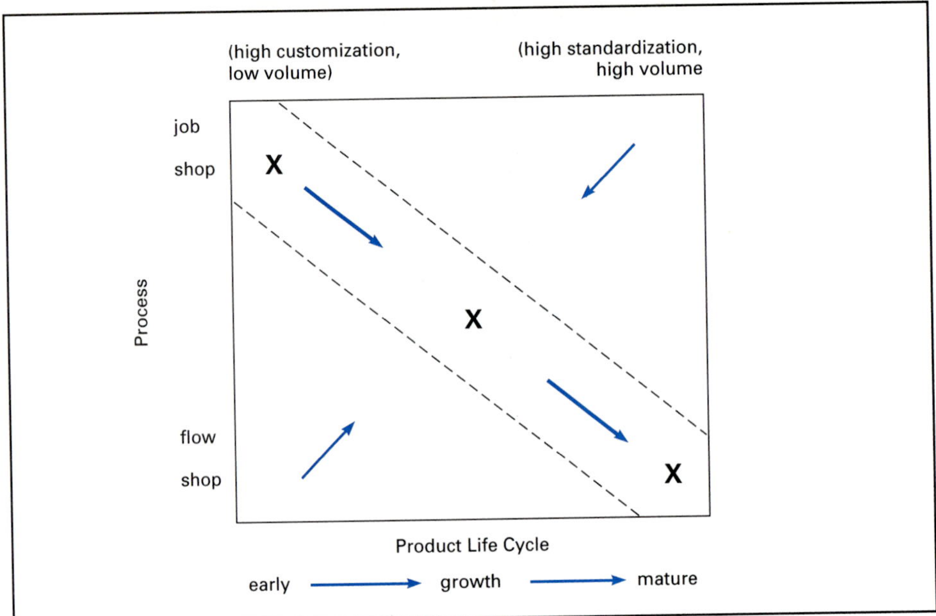

Figure 17-2 Product–Process Matrix. (From R. Hayes and S. Wheelwright, *Restoring our Competitive Edge: Competing through Manufacturing*, New York: John Wiley & Sons, 1984.)

passes, competitors respond, and an order-winning characteristic often becomes a qualifying characteristic. Hence, new order winners may be continually needed. For example, at different stages of a product's life cycle, the order winners may change from "new and innovative" to "price."

The competitive requirements for the product in the marketplace must be consistent with the manufacturing process and infrastructure. To obtain a strategic fit, the process must be able to deliver the necessary order winners. In Chapter 2, Figure 2-4, we discussed the product–process matrix from Hayes and Wheelwright (1984). This figure, reproduced here as Figure 17-2, gives suggested product life cycle and process pairs.

During the early part of the life cycle, a production facility with high flexibility (a job shop) can generate order winners such as customization. For a mature product, a dedicated facility (a flow shop) can produce high quality and low cost, the order winners for many, but not all, mature products.

Hill (1989) discusses *product profiling* as a means to align process choice and market needs. Incremental decisions made independently in marketing or operations can result in a product–process mismatch. Constant surveillance is needed to maintain facilities and technologies that can continue to produce order winners.

QUESTION 3: How can we coordinate strategy (S), System design (D), and day-to-day operations (O)?

Operations will be a competitive weapon only if the foregoing three levels of decisions are coordinated. A firm cannot have a strategy of being flexible in meeting customer's needs if they have inflexible facilities, or if they measure plant managers only on obtaining low cost. Figure 1-3, reproduced here as Figure 17-3, illustrates the connections necessary among strategy, design, and operations (SDO).

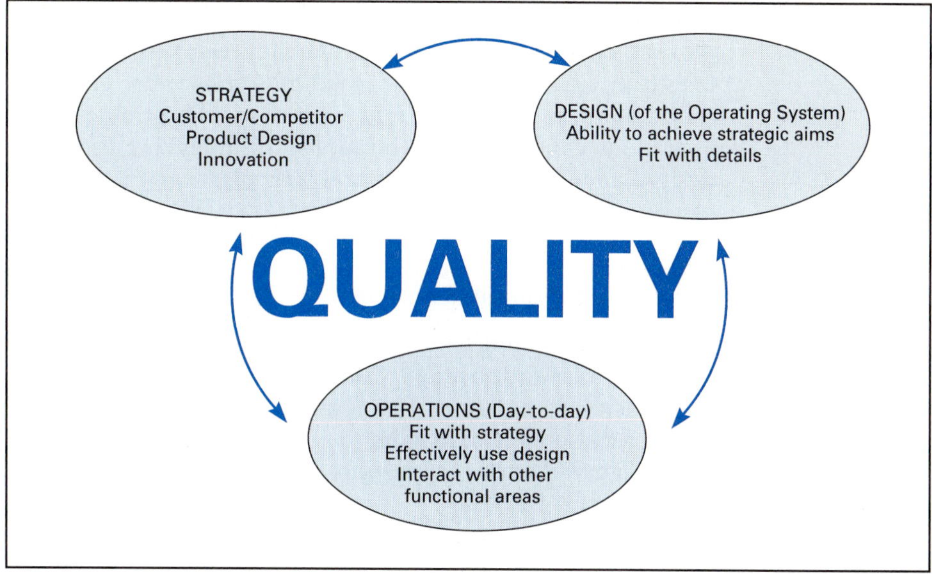

Figure 17-3 Integrating Strategy, Design, and Operations

In Chapter 1 we discussed an example of a firm that had a strategy of flexibility; thus, they used a factory design with a flexible manufacturing system. However, the plant manager was measured on the fraction of ''uptime'' (when the system is working on a product), thereby discouraging frequent changeovers or attempts to learn new things that can be produced by the system. There was a lack of coordination of SDO. In Section 17-4 we will give examples of good coordination.

Several tools and concepts are available for integrating strategy with design. Quality function deployment (QFD), discussed in Chapter 6, helps managers to match strategy (based on market needs) with product design. This is done by concentrating on the product concept, which considers the basic customer needs to be met by the product. Hill's (1989) product-profiling technique allows the market needs and the process capabilities to be consistent with each other. Regular attention can halt the natural drift toward inconsistency that comes with the many independent marketing and production decisions made through time.

Hayes and Wheelwright's product–process matrix (Figure 17-2) suggests different facility capabilities at different stages of the life cycle, with each stage having a different strategic need. An organization with many facilities may have some that focus on new products while others focus on mature products, each using the appropriate processes. Occasionally a portion of a facility (a factory within a factory) may be focused on a particular type of activity. (Skinner 1974 argued that ''focused factories'' can meet strategic goals better than large, general-purpose ones. Many firms in our experience use this concept, although they use several different names for it.)

Maintaining the consistency of strategy and design is important, but it will lead nowhere unless the day-to-day operations are handled consistently with the strategy. The main tools to be used are (1) communication, and (2) performance measurement. First and foremost, we believe that employees should know and understand both the corporate strategy and how their activity can contribute to it. Empowering employees (see Chapter 5) only works if the employees have a clear view of what they need to do. Second, as discussed at length in Chapter 5, performance measures must encourage cross-functional cooperation and be consistent with corporate strategy. Finally, the details of operations can be the starting point for analyzing the integration of strategy, design, and operations. If we are particularly good at some operations, a strategy can be formed that takes advantage of that.

How to Begin Implementation

The implementation of an operations strategy begins with an analysis of the firm's current position. Chase and Aquilano (1989) give two *audit questionnaires,* one for manufacturing (based on Skinner's work) and one for services. Each of these asks managers to investigate the current and desired status in four major categories (each with five to eleven subcategories). The four major categories are

product
technology of transformation
operating control system
work force

In each of these major categories, subcategories can be written for a particular firm. Then a ''percentage degree of fit of actual versus desired'' can be derived. For example, under product, the product line could be ''standardized, mixed, or customized.'' The range of products could be ''few, intermediate, or many.'' Skinner's list includes the extent of coordination among engineering, marketing, and manufacturing in this category, with ''little, some, much'' as the three levels.

We prefer to include an additional category, *competitive analysis,* that is implied by the preceding four categories. We also include *coordination* among engineering, marketing, and manufacturing as an important item, particularly as it relates to new product introduction. Finally, our list contains some more detailed information about the production process, product line, planning process, and competitive situation, based on our own experience and *diagnostic analysis* (see Hax et al. 1980). In addition to analyzing the competitive situation in the marketplace, we analyze the *cost drivers* and *time drivers,* that is, where the cost and lead times are greatest.

Our six major categories, with several subcategories, are shown in Table 17-3.

Strategy implementation can begin (and be reconsidered) by using Table 17-3 to assess the firm's present situation, compared with competitors. Then a strategy must be selected that is based on a sustainable competitive advantage. This can lead to an ideal state for each item in Table 17-3. Action plans must be formulated to move the firm toward the ideal states, concentrating on the most important items first. Finally, progress should be regularly monitored.

The items in Table 17-3 are written for a manufacturing organization, but most of them apply to services as well. However, we believe that each situation, manufacturing or service, may require that some items be added or deleted. And each organization must select those items that are most important in their business. Examples are given in Section 17-4.

Table 17-3 Analyzing Competitive Position

Product line
- A-B-C analysis
- Stable/unstable demand pattern
- Make-to-order, make-to-stock, assemble- (or finish-) to-order, or engineer-to-order
- Number of items at each stage of production (product structure)
- Lead time and value added at each stage of production
- Stability of design through time

Coordination
- Engineering, marketing, manufacturing
- New product introduction: frequency
- New product introduction: efficiency

Facilities
- Degree of flexibility
- Degree of automation
- Number of plants and distribution centers
- Location advantages and disadvantages
- Clarity of mission for each facility

Operating control system
- Information: quality and speed
- Forecasts: quality of forecasts of different horizons
- Planning horizons: for aggregate planning and for production scheduling
- Quality control system
- Operations management organization
- Inventory: amount, location, and control of

Work Force
- Worker skills and training procedures to add skills
- Worker autonomy
- Consistency of stated policies with practice
- Nature of tasks

Competitive analysis
- Current and future competitors, and ability to meet the threats
- Quality and cost comparisons
- Comparative service policies and performance

The Current Situation

Before leaving this section, we will discuss the current situation in the practice of operations strategy. This is done with trepidation because ''current'' ideas change quickly. However, we believe that the basic idea of knowing your customers and adding value for them (gaining mutual benefit) will not change for a very long time.

The years since the 1950s have seen some companies change their focus many times, from cost to customization to quality, with interludes in which financial legerdemain mattered more than products and services. In reaction, operations managers have looked for eternal truths, ideas that can focus and energize all members of the organization. To imply unchanging attention to certain issues, the word *total* or *totally* has been used.[2]

Total employee involvement, total productive maintenance, total quality management, and *total customer service* are important phrases that tell us to have a

[2]*Totally* was a key word in the short-lived U.S. slang ''Valspeak'' (Valley talk), as in ''totally awesome.''

broader view of the issue in question and to maintain attention. For example, quality is not just quality of products but of everything done by the organization. Total quality management (TQM) should guide all actions. Total employee involvement (TEI) means that all employees should utilize their education, intelligence, and energy to further the organization's strategic goals, not just to do their job in a narrow sense. In each case managers must take a broad view of the strategic value of quality (for example) *and* pay attention to the details as well.

The danger in any slogan is that we may not be prepared to move beyond it quickly enough. Attention to product quality has turned many companies around, as was discussed in Chapters 1 and 6. But there is evidence (see Miller and Kim 1990 and Stalk 1988) that it is time to work toward other goals in addition to the quality of the item. Speed of response or flexibility in meeting customer needs may be the next form of competition. Product quality will continue to be necessary—at least a qualifying criterion in Hill's terminology—but the order winner may change.

The fundamental point is that operations strategy must be planned by constantly reevaluating the customers' needs and the competitors' capability. No idea is at the top of the list forever, and we can change the list by providing something new to our customers. A focus on employees and their contribution will always be a potential source of competitive advantage. Wiggenhorn (1990) discusses the value of building an asset in the people who work for Motorola. Developing a learning organization (Lieberman 1989 and Hayes et al., 1988) is one key part of building this asset. Similarly, quality and customer service should be part of every strategic plan. Managers must be forward-looking in how they define and create quality, employee involvement, and customer service.

The following characteristics set apart world-class-operations organizations in our opinion, at the current time:

1. clarity of strategy guiding strategic investments and the following points:
2. good relationships across functions (manufacturing-marketing-engineering) and with suppliers
3. total quality management, throughout the organization
4. caring about the details (measures, job design, inventory, and so on) with strategic focus
5. information availability to allow speed of response
6. developing and utilizing human resources, and creating a learning organization

This list does not include global strategy, particularly global alliances, which are discussed in the next section. Quality is prominently displayed, but it is not alone. Customers and quality will remain, but no list of key items is forever, including ours.

REVIEW PROBLEMS

1. Consider the strategy of one of the "top ten" business schools.

   a. The customers include students who select the programs, companies who hire the graduates, and the academic and business communities who use the research output of the school. For the students and companies, what are some of the order winners that cause them to come to the school?

b. Describe one way in which an inconsistency might exist among the strategy, design, and operations in this school.

2. Why should airlines consider telecommunications companies as potential competitors for business customers?

Solutions

1. a. For students: economic value of the degree, as measured by starting salaries; low tuition for state schools; quality of instruction including educational content; facilities.
   For companies: prestige of the school; quality (education, drive, and personality) of the students they hire; fit of the students' skills with their needs.
   b. Because research contributes directly to society and indirectly to teaching quality, by keeping faculty members current and innovative, many schools' strategy stresses excellence in both teaching and research. The performance-measurement system will be consistent with this strategy only if both research and teaching are evaluated.

2. The service of facilitating face-to-face meetings can be delivered by arranging a video conference, saving both time and money. By contrast, the airlines should be more secure with the vacation travel segment. Given current technology, we want to send our bodies, not just our image, on vacation.

17-3 GLOBAL MANUFACTURING STRATEGY

Manufacturing is a crucial part of international trade. It accounts for two-thirds of total U.S. exports, for example, even though it is only one-fifth of GNP. The amount of international trade in manufactured goods is increasing, and the nature of the competition is changing. Especially in manufacturing, but increasingly in services as well, a global strategy is necessary for success.

A *global manufacturing strategy* involves selling one's products in many (international) markets, and being willing to compete aggressively in both the organization's home market and the competitor's home market. This may deny a competitor "cross-subsidization," that is, using large home-country profits to support aggressive price competition in other markets (see Hamel and Prahalad 1985). A global company has a clear mission for each of its facilities so that they know how to contribute to the overall strategy (see Ferdows 1989). As part of the analysis leading to these mission statements, a global company designs an international supplier network and builds relationships with the suppliers (see Carter et al., 1988). Finally, and most importantly, a global company utilizes human resources fully, in each country in which it does business (see Pucik et al., 1989). We will now discuss the first and third of these points further.

Facility Missions in an International Network

Building an international network of factories and other facilities requires a clear mission statement for each one. Ferdows (1989) has suggested six ge-

STRATEGIC PURPOSE	TECHNICAL ACTIVITY: High	TECHNICAL ACTIVITY: Low
Access to Low-cost Inputs	Source	Offshore
Use of Technological Resources	Lead	Outpost
Proximity to Market	Contributor	Server

Figure 17-4 Six Generic Roles. (From Ferdows, 1989.)

neric roles for factories in a global firm. These six are based on (a) the level of technical activity and (b) the strategic purpose for the site. Ferdows characterizes technical activity as high or low and presents three strategic purposes: access to low-cost inputs, the use of local technological resources, and proximity to market. Figure 17-4 presents the six combinations and the name given by Ferdows to each.

A factory that simply utilizes a low-cost input such as inexpensive labor is an *offshore plant*. Examples include *maquiladora* plants in Mexico, which produce items with high labor content such as wiring harnesses for automobiles. A *lead plant* is designed to tap into local technological capability, for their own use or use throughout the corporation. Many of IBM's sites around the world, for example, develop, obtain, and use technology. The facilities are not just factories. Lead plants often have primary product-development capability for some products.

Increasingly, access to low-cost labor is not a sufficient reason to locate a factory. Spreading an information net for technology or maintaining a presence to help sell products is also important. A local presence can be used to fight a competitor in that market (see Hamel and Prahalad 1985).

A clear, forward-looking global strategy must include the markets we intend to concentrate on, and the mission of each facility in that overall strategy. Analytical techniques, such as mathematical programming, can be used to analyze production-shipping patterns to minimize transportation, production, and tax costs, once the network is established. But the solution must be implemented using judgment, based on the strategic analysis that established that network.

Using Human Resources in a Global Company

A global strategy requires the talents of managers, workers, and technical people from all countries of operation. Most companies have some difficulty with this, because the headquarters' managers must trust people that are in some important ways different from themselves.

Pucik, Hanada, and Fifield (1989) have described five stages of internationalization and relate them to human-resource strategy. (Their study focused on Japanese-owned U.S. corporations.) The five stages are

1. export orientation
2. localization
3. internationalization
4. multinationalization
5. globalization

In stage 1, a one-country firm seeks international markets. Stage 2 sees the beginning of multicountry production, and stage 3 may link different offshore units together. Decision making still resides in the host country. In stage 4 decentralization begins, with subsidiaries making some important decisions without the direct involvement of the home country. Many senior managers have lived and worked in several countries during their career. A global company (stage 5) virtually has no home country. Senior executives can be drawn from many different countries. A common culture may exist, but it will not be identified solely with the country of origin.

Each stage represents increasing trust in local managers. In stage 5, ideas, technology, and people can flow across borders, as well as products. The key is to utilize the talents and energy available in each country with an appreciation of the local culture. If people are well utilized in all countries, all the national economies involved can benefit. In addition to the flow of technology and ideas, global companies can achieve economies of distribution and production through operations analysis. The same ideas extend to building an international supplier network (see Carter et al., 1988) or building a human-resource asset in suppliers, as well as to reducing the costs of purchasing, transportation, and production.

The Current Situation

Three current trends are important to consider. First, as was mentioned in Chapter 1, geographic trading regions (the EEC and North America, for example) appear to be forming. Trade will be easier within these regions, and they will be harder to penetrate from the outside. (Cooney 1989 discusses ways that the EEC may affect U.S. manufacturing.) Many companies are trying to locate in the EEC to protect against the risk of being an outsider.

Second, direct labor cost is becoming less important, as direct labor declines as a percentage of cost (see National Research Council 1990). This is true even though there are huge differences in labor costs—from $1 to $20 per hour between various countries—because direct labor is often less than 10% of cost. The efficiency of labor is very important, and Lieberman (1989) has argued that learning how to learn (to reduce costs) is a major source of the advantage held by the Japanese automobile industry.

Finally, managers must now learn how to cooperate as well as compete. Organizations must interact well with the work force and across departments (as was discussed in Chapter 5). They must also cooperate closely with suppliers, to mutual benefit (as was discussed in Chapter 12). Also, the current trend is for companies to form *alliances* with other companies, even with competitors. Alliances may be utilized to share technology or to get one's products into new markets. (Harrigan 1987 and Ohmae 1989 discuss the value of alliances, and Bowersox 1990 discusses alliances in the logistics area.)

There are notes of caution about alliances. One survey indicated that U.S. managers feel ill at ease in alliances (*Wall Street Journal Reports* 1989). A study done for the EEC revealed that European countries have engaged in fewer joint ventures than U.S. or Japanese companies, and have fared poorly when they have done so (Cohendet et al., 1988).

We do believe that the manager of the 1990s must understand global businesses and appreciate different cultures; he or she must be prepared to be cooperative in a variety of ways, as well as to recognize the intense competition that will characterize this decade, even if the manager is employed by a one-country organization.

REVIEW PROBLEMS

Select a company, with which you are familiar, that is engaged in international business.

1. Which stage of internationalization best characterizes its present position, in your opinion? Briefly state the reasons for your selection.

2. Select a facility owned by the company and place it in one of the six categories of Figure 17-4.

3. Does the company have any alliances with other companies? What purposes might such alliances serve?

Solutions

We will use the Ford Motor Company as an example. Even if you select the same company, the answers may be different, since the issues are partly matters of opinion.

1. Multinationalization. Ford Europe operates largely independently and has often been the major source of profit for the firm. Still, senior executives at headquarters are nearly all U.S. nationals, so we would not place it in Stage 5.

2. Ford recently purchased Jaguar. Several Jaguar facilities could be placed in the contributor category, since Jaguar gives Ford access to the "luxury-Europe" market. Since Ford is working on sending technology and designs in both directions between the United States and Europe, some facilities could be characterized as lead facilities.

3. Their alliance with Mazda has several purposes, one of which is to improve the design process of both firms.

17-4 EXAMPLES

Worldwide Metal Products Producer

A producer of a wide variety of metal products has been slipping in market share and profitability. "European Metals" is the third largest firm for its products in the European market and is considering divesting that business. Their customer service is poor. The largest competitor delivers products within four weeks. European Metals promises six-week delivery but is able to keep the promise only half the time. Because of this, their market share has declined in recent years. Information on income and market share is given in Table 17-4.

Their production cycle time is ten weeks; therefore, they have large amounts of inventory. The firm produces 500 semifinished items, but because of accessories that are used in finishing the products they have a total of 20,000 finished items. They always are able to produce a finished product from a semifinished product in less

Table 17-4 Income and Market Share Data for European Metals

Income Statement for European Metals (EM)

	Year				
	1986	**1987**	**1988**	**1989**	**1990**
Sales	101.6	103.8	112.7	119.2	126.5
Cost of sales	67.1	70.1	78.0	82.1	91.0
Selling and admin. expense	21.2	21.3	24.0	25.0	25.3
Other costs	8.1	8.4	9.1	10.1	11.1
Net income	5.1	4.0	1.6	2.0	(0.3)

Market-Share Data for EM and Competitors

	Share in Year				
Company	**1986**	**1987**	**1988**	**1989**	**1990**
A	29.0	29.5	30.0	31.0	32.0
B	23.0	23.0	22.9	22.3	22.5
EM	19.4	19.3	19.0	18.9	17.6
C	12.4	12.1	12.1	11.9	12.0
Others	16.2	16.1	16.0	15.9	15.9

than two weeks. Table 17-5 depicts the production process and current inventory situation.

Of the 500 semifinished items, 50 of them accounted for 66.5% of sales in 1990, while the 300 lowest-demand items accounted for

Table 17-5 The Manufacturing Process of European Metals

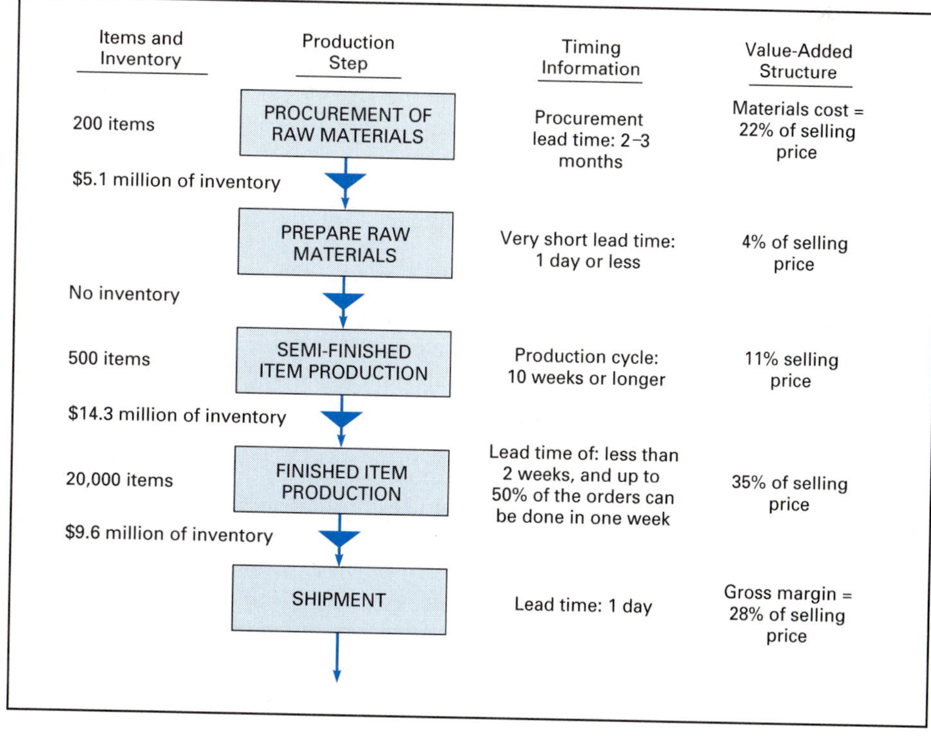

only 8.4%. None of the 20,000 finished items is a high-volume item, since many lengths and fixtures are customer specific.

European Metals is considering a $14,250,000 investment that would allow them to operate a two-week production cycle for semifinished items. This set of machines would reduce setup time and production time. (Currently, setup time occupies 45% of the 10-week cycle and production time, 55%.) It would also improve quality slightly, although the current level of quality is as good as that of any of the competitors.

This example makes several points pertinent to the topics of this chapter. First, consider the analysis of competitive position outlined in Table 17-3. Based on the preceding material, European Metals

1. has many very-low-demand items at both semifinished and finished stages
2. follows a mixture of make-to-stock and finish-to-order, even though there is an explosion of the number of items at the finishing stage
3. has a value-added pattern that is largest at the finishing stage
4. has a large amount of inventory for a company this size, with just over four inventory turns per year (if revenue/inventory is used), and just over three turns (if cost of sales/inventory is used)
5. has similar cost and quality but worse service than the largest competitor

Next, consider Questions 2 and 3 from Section 17-2. It is reasonable to assume that one order winner is speed of service. (European Metals should either know this for sure or verify it before proceeding.) Company A has gained while EM has lost share. This argues that the strategy should include meeting or beating the best service in the industry if EM is to remain in the business.

If the Strategy includes four-week service, the design and operations (Figure 17-3) must be consistent. There are several ways to ensure this.

The product structure and value-added pattern suggest that maintaining finished-goods inventory should be avoided if possible, using a finish-to-order approach (see Chapter 10). The four-week service goal allows this. Without detailed analysis we cannot know how much semifinished inventory will be needed.

How would strategy, design, and operations (SDO) fit together if European Metals invests the $14,250,000? The strategy would still be focused on four-week service. The design of the factory would include significant new machinery and changes in work flow. The day-to-day operations would change dramatically. With a two-week production cycle, a make-to-order approach could be used if raw materials are always available. The goal of fast service can be achieved while changing the basic method of meeting demand, if the factory design includes the new set of machines.

Is the $14,250,000 expenditure justified? A detailed analysis must be done, but the benefits will include eliminating most of the $14,300,000 of semifinished inventory. This is true because semifinished inventory is not needed when we have a two-week cycle; the firm can make semifinished items and then finish them within the four-week service time. (A little inventory will be maintained to smooth demand on the semifinished production facility.) The $9,600,000 of finished goods should also be cut, but that should occur even without the new machines. (Currently, the firm could finish to order.) Basically, an inventory asset can be traded for machines. Second, fast service should stop the market-share erosion and even regain some of it. (The firm estimates a 2% share gain within one year.) Inventory saving plus the value of extra sales more than justify the expenditure.

Are there other ways to achieve fast (four-week) service? Perhaps. For example, it may be possible to reduce setup times using the methods discussed in Chapter 12. Also, we should consider dropping a large number of C items from the product line. As was discussed in Chapter 3, low-demand items often are not profitable. (They may, however, be required to maintain our image as a full-line supplier.) The important thing is to select a strategy appropriate for this industry and to coordinate the design and operations with that strategy. In managing the operations we must ensure that the performance measures used include the achievement of four-week service, and that other measures do not cause managers to lose track of speed of service.

A Manufacturer of Personal Computers

Apple Computer in 1983 faced the decision of where to put a new plant to produce the Macintosh. Two choices were Dallas, Texas, and the San Francisco Bay Area, California (see Swanger 1984). If Dallas were the choice, a "conventional build" process would be used. In the Bay Area, an automated facility would be used.

Many issues were involved in the decision, including labor cost (lower in Dallas) and using available technical talent (in the Bay Area, Apple engineering staff). The Bay Area was finally selected. Its major advantages included enhanced communication between technical staffs and the plant and learning new manufacturing technology.

The Bay Area plant could be justified because the order winners in computer hardware include innovation in design and manufacturing. Selecting a site and organizational design that facilitates innovation fits with the strategic aim of constantly producing state-of-the-art machines. In Ferdows' (1989) facility mission categorization, the Bay Area plant is a lead plant, working with local technological resources at a high-technology facility. Apple does have an international network, including Ireland (to gain access to the European market—a contributor plant) and Singapore (for productive, low-cost labor—a source plant).

A Health Planning Agency

A state health-planning agency has reviewed the usage of acute cancer-care wards (and some other facilities) in the state. They found that many such facilities were utilized less than 50% of capacity, while others were over capacity. They felt that they had two options: (1) impose a rule requiring that any proposed acute cancer-care ward must be approved by the state agency, which would approve only wards with expected usage above a minimum level, or (2) allow each hospital to act independently.

The considerations are almost endless, and the future of the health-care system will be affected in a major way. Some of the arguments against central controls are as follows: Fully utilized facilities will tend to be in the cities, so access will not be as easy for many rural patients. Some rural patients may even refuse to go to the city; thus, the quality of care will be unequal. Further, doctors may prefer to practice in hospitals with many advanced facilities; therefore, hospitals that are not allowed advanced facilities may have trouble attracting medical staff.

On the other side of the argument, the American Medical Association and the specialty groups within it publish utilization figures (number of cases) that are necessary, in their opinion, to provide enough experience to maintain the skill levels of the staff. If the state agency allows hospitals to proceed on their own, low quality may occur as a result of underutilization. Also, it is expensive from society's viewpoint to duplicate high-priced medical facilities, especially when they will not be fully utilized.

The state agency must first determine a strategy for the system. What type of service do they want to give? How important is economic efficiency? If they decide that efficient utilization and the quality of care associated with that are more important than closeness to the customer, they must have a system design (set of facilities) consistent with that strategy. They must also manage day to day, using a strong referral system or advertising, perhaps with subsidized transportation, to minimize the disadvantage that rural patients face.

REVIEW PROBLEMS

Suppose that European Metals wanted to achieve four-week service largely through dropping C items, but also with some reduction of setup time, to avoid spending the $14,250,000.

1. How does our view of the customer and competitor change, and what are the order winners?

2. Briefly describe the strategy, design, and operations in this case.

3. What would you worry about if this approach is followed?

Solutions

1. The "customer" is limited to customers who want high-demand items. This may exclude both some small customers and some orders from large customers. The competitors are unchanged. They are acting as if the order winner is fast (four-week) service. Also, if they drop C items, they must believe that being a full-line supplier is not an order winner.

2. The strategy is to provide four-week service, but only to a portion of the market. The design includes the current facilities, but some new performance measures and organizational changes will be necessary. In particular, low-demand-item sales will be discouraged, and sales people will be rewarded for concentrating on A items. The operations manager will be rewarded not only for cost but also for setup-time reduction.

3. Will we lose big customers because we do not supply all their needs? Can we achieve a two-week cycle in this way? Currently, setup time takes 45% of 10 weeks. To reduce setup time to around one week of a two-week cycle will require an aggressive combination of dropping items and setup-time reduction. Finally, what if we are successful and demand grows: Can we

reduce setup time further, to add more production? Still, this approach is worth considering because it can achieve both service goals and inventory reduction without spending the $14,250,000.

17-5 THE FUTURE

Operations strategy has received increasing attention in recent years. More companies and researchers are concentrating on the importance of operations, particularly in manufacturing firms. (Recent edited volumes with interesting research and managerial articles include Ettlie et al. 1990, Ferdows 1989, Moody 1990, and Sheth and Eshghi 1989. Swamidass 1989 and Anderson et al. 1989 present hundreds of references on manufacturing and operations strategy.) It is a surprise-free prediction that this area will continue to receive attention in the future, leading to the development of new, useful ways of formulating and implementing operations strategy.

Predicting the economic climate for the remainder of this century is more difficult. In this section we will very briefly examine a few trends that we believe operations managers must understand and use to develop their strategies.

In our global economy, competition will be tougher than ever before. In this competition operations managers must be both efficient and innovative in finding ways to add value for customers, for mutual benefit. Global competition will increase in both services and manufacturing, and service organizations must make productivity gains at a pace more comparable to that which manufacturing has achieved in the past. The competition implies hard work for operations managers, but good news for average consumers. All countries can benefit but will do so only if their managers are up to the challenge.

Technology, including automation, will continue to be important. A country's standard of living will depend on its pace of technological development. However, countries will depend even more on the quality of their overall work force, since technology transfer occurs fairly quickly at the present time.

Obtaining, developing, and utilizing human resources may be the most important managerial task. In our opinion, there are three key challenges in this area: First, organizations must be able to utilize and reward people from different backgrounds at all levels of the organization. This includes the influx of women and minorities in the U.S. job market, as well as the changing work force in each country of a multinational firm. Second, organizations must foster cooperation as well as competition. Cooperation will be important across managerial functions, between management and labor (the line may blur between them), and among organizations (both with suppliers and with other business partners). Both managerial style and the use of information technology (electronic data interchange [EDI] with customers and suppliers, for example) can assist in this effort. Finally, everyone's talents must be fully utilized. To enable fast response, this means that everyone will be a decision maker. To ensure that decisions are good, the organization's strategy must be clearly understood and accepted, and managers must train and support employees as well as make decisions and give direction.

Societal issues will grow in importance. Being a good corporate citizen has always been important, but concerns for the environment, education, and social problems will take center stage. Operations managers must deal with these issues, even though the exact benefits are hard to quantify. Mintzberg

(1982) argued that although *efficiency* is a value-free word in theory (one can and should efficiently achieve social goals), in fact the measurability of cost and the lack of measurability of quality of life means that a drive for efficiency really becomes a drive for low cost. Operations managers must counteract this tendency, using their judgment to include crucial qualitative factors in their decisions.

Finally, as a systems view of problems and organizations is taken, managers will include more factors in their decision making. The interaction of marketing and production will be analyzed; the flow of materials will be designed using an overall view from raw materials to consumer goods, and sociopolitical effects of doing business in an international setting will be within the realm of many operations managers. In complex situations such as these, a mathematically optimal solution will have little meaning, but managers can use analytical methods to help them find a satisfactory one. Quantitative techniques will not (and should not) become less common; they are highly valuable decision aids. But they will be used for decision support rather than to make the decisions.

Operations managers will be necessary in each of these views of the future, and they will be doing things similar to what they do now. They may be in the service industry rather than in manufacturing; they may be more supportive than directive; they will have access to more sophisticated information processing; but the heart of most manufacturing and service industries will still be the production and delivery of goods and services. As a red-bearded professor once said: ''There's making it and selling it; and everything else is just keeping score.''

PROBLEMS

*1. Why is the operations area of strategic importance in:
   a. hospitals?
   b. a construction company?
   c. an automobile manufacturer?

2. Select a large manufacturing company and examine its annual reports for the past three years. Write a brief report commenting on the relative size of the cost of sales, inventories, and plant and equipment, as well as any trends in those variables over the three-year period. What possible explanations are there for unusually high values?

3. Following the pattern described in problem 2, perform a comparative analysis for three or four large firms in the same manufacturing industry. (For example, examine Chrysler, Ford, General Motors, and Toyota, or Goodyear, Bridgestone, and Michelin.) Which company seems to have the best operations management? What makes you think so?

4. Why is manufacturing an important part of the U.S. economy, even though it is less than 20% of GNP?

*5. The Health Care Agency example of Section 17-4 bears some resemblance to the question of whether to centralize certain spare parts, discussed in Chapter 14. Discuss the similarities and differences.

*Problems with an asterisk have answers in the back of the book.

6. Some business schools have established either degree programs, executive education centers, or both, in countries outside their home country. Which of Ferdows' six generic roles (see Figure 17-4) do these facilities fulfill, in your opinion? Explain.

*7. a. What is an SBU and what is the purpose of using SBUs?
   b. Give some possible SBUs in (i) an automobile manufacturer, (ii) a bank, and (iii) a furniture manufacturer.

8. What considerations are included in Table 17-2 that are not included in Table 17-1? What considerations are not adequately included in either one, in your opinion?

9. Several automobile companies have recently started major new lines of cars (Acura, Lexus, Infiniti, Saturn). Suppose that the next new line to be introduced in the United States has as one of its main strategic goals to be able to accept an individualized order and deliver that automobile to the customer in five working days or less. Describe one of the issues arising in answering the three key questions raised in Section 17-2, if the firm is to do this.

10. In review problem 2 of Section 17-2, an airline example is used, suggesting that telecommunications companies may be future competitors for airlines. Further, one response to that threat is to concentrate on the vacation market. Allegis (parent company of United Airlines) tried that strategy in the 1980s, by vertically integrating to obtain tie-ins with resorts, offering complete vacation opportunities. In your opinion, is it a good idea for airlines to concentrate on vacationers? Even if this strategy makes sense, why might it not have worked well in the 1980s?

*11. Consider the Health Planning Agency example of Section 17-4. List the pros and cons of limiting the number of cancer-care facilities.

12. In the future of operations management,
   a. why will changes in information processing be important? In what industries do you think the effect will be largest?
   b. why does a trend toward automation not necessarily imply a high rate of unemployment?

*13. Many hospitals, both not-for-profit and for-profit organizations, try to increase sales, to allow them to reduce average costs and thereby serve their customers better. They face some new competition from ''wellness'' programs offered by health clubs, corporations, and many other organizations. These programs are designed to keep people from becoming ill. What strategies can hospitals use to respond to this competition? Discuss the new view of customers and competitors that is required.

14. Universities are engaged in competition. You are to select a particular university and help them develop a competitive strategy.
   a. What potential changes in their customers do you foresee in the next 10 years? Include both research and teaching products.
   b. How can they reach some of the new customers for both research and teaching products?
   c. What new competitors do they face?
   d. How can they face global competition?

e. At which stage of internationalization (Section 17-3) is the university, in your opinion? Explain.

15. Select a company with which you are familiar and discuss their competitive strategy, focusing on the three key questions raised in Section 17-2.

REFERENCES

ANDERSON, J.C., G. CLEVELAND, and R.G. SCHROEDER, "Operations Strategy: A Literature Review," *Journal of Operations Management*, vol. 8, no. 2, 1989.

BOWERSOX, D., "The Strategic Benefits of Logistics Alliances," *Harvard Business Review*, July–August, 1990.

CARTER, J.R., R. NARASIMHAN, and S.K. VICKERY, *International Sourcing for Manufacturing Operations*, Monograph No. 3, Operations Management Association, Waco, Tex., 1988.

CHASE, R.B., and D.A. GARVIN, "The Service Factory," *Harvard Business Review*, July–August, 1989.

CHASE, R., and N. AQUILANO, *Production and Operations Management: A Life Cycle Approach*, 5th ed., Homewood, Ill.: Irwin, 1989.

CLARK, K.B., and T. FUJIMOTO, "Overlapping Problem Solving in Product Development," in K. Ferdows, ed., *Managing International Manufacturing*, Amsterdam: North-Holland, 1989.

COHEN, S., and J. ZYSMAN, *Manufacturing Matters*, New York: Basic Books, 1987.

COHENDET, P., M.J. LEDOUX, J. VALLS, and R. SCHWARZ, "Europe-USA-Japan: Triad or Pacific Axis: Analysis of Recent Collaborative Ventures" (in French), Commission of the E.E.C., Program Fast-II, Contract F5Z-0164-F, 1988.

COONEY, S., *EC-92 and U.S. Industry*, National Association of Manufacturers, Washington, D.C., February, 1989.

DENTON, D.K., "Enhance Competitiveness and Customer Satisfaction . . . Here's One Approach!" *Industrial Engineering*, May, 1990.

ETTLIE, J.E., M.E. BURSTEIN, and A. FEIGENBAUM, *Manufacturing Strategy: The Research Agenda for the Next Decade*, Boston: Kluwer, 1990.

FERDOWS, K., "Mapping International Factory Networks," in K. Ferdows, ed., *Managing International Manufacturing*, Amsterdam: North-Holland, 1989.

GUNN, T., *Manufacturing for Competitive Advantage: Becoming a World Class Manufacturer*, Cambridge, Mass.: Ballinger, 1987.

HAMEL, G., and C.K. PRAHALAD, "Do You Really Have a Global Strategy?" *Harvard Business Review*, July–August, 1985.

HARRIGAN, K.R., "Managing Joint Ventures Part 1," *Management Review*, February, 1987.

HAUSMAN, W.H., and D.B. MONTGOMERY, "Making Manufacturing Market Driven," Research Paper 1003, Department of IE and EM, Stanford University, 1990.

HAX, A., and N. MAJLUF, *Strategic Management: An Integrative Perspective*, Englewood Cliffs, N.J., Prentice-Hall, 1984.

HAX, A., N. MAJLUF, and M. PENDROCK, "Diagnostic Analysis of a Production and Distribution System," *Management Science*, September, 1980.

HAYES, R.H., and S.C. WHEELWRIGHT, *Restoring our Competitive Edge*, New York: Wiley, 1984.

HAYES, R.H., S.C. WHEELWRIGHT, and K.B. CLARK, *Dynamic Manufacturing: Creating the Learning Organizations*, New York: Free Press, 1988.

HILL, T., *Manufacturing Strategy: Text and Cases*, Homewood, Ill., Irwin, 1989.

LIEBERMAN, M.B., ''Learning, Productivity, and U.S.-Japan Industrial Competitiveness,'' in K. Ferdows, ed., *Managing International Manufacturing*, Amsterdam: North-Holland, 1989.

MACAVOY, T., ''Technology Strategy,'' Darden Graduate Business School, University of Virginia, UVA-OM-656, 1988.

MILLER, J.G., and J.S. KIM, *Beyond the Quality Revolution: U.S. Manufacturing Strategy in the 1990's*, B.U. Manufacturing Roundtable, Boston, 1990.

MINTZBERG, H., ''A Note on that Dirty Word 'Efficiency',,'' *Interfaces*, vol. 12, no. 5, 1982.

MOODY, P., *Strategic Manufacturing*, Homewood, Ill.: Dow-Jones-Irwin, 1990.

NATIONAL RESEARCH COUNCIL, *The Internationalization of U.S. Manufacturing: Causes and Consequences*, Washington, D.C.: National Academy Press, 1990.

OHMAE, K., ''The Global Logic of Strategic Alliances,'' *Harvard Business Review*, March–April, 1989.

PORTER, M.E., *Competitive Advantage*, New York: Free Press, 1985.

PRAHALAD, C.K., and G. HAMEL, ''The Core Competence of the Corporation,'' *Harvard Business Review*, May–June, 1990.

PUCIK, V., M. HANADA, and G. FIFIELD, *Management Culture and the Effectiveness of Local Executives in Japanese-Owned U.S. Corporations*, University of Michigan, Ann Arbor, 1989.

SHETH, J., and G. ESHGHI, *Global Operations Perspectives*, Cincinnati: South Western, 1989.

SIMON, H.A., ''Managing in an Information-Rich World,'' in *Competing Through Productivity and Quality*, Y.K. Shetty and V.M. Buehler, eds., Cambridge, Mass.: Productivity Press, 1988.

SKINNER, W., ''The Productivity Paradox,'' *Harvard Business Review*, July–August, 1986.

STALK, G., JR., ''Time—The Next Source of Competitive Advantage,'' *Harvard Business Review*, July–August, 1988.

SURVEY OF CURRENT BUSINESS, U. S. Department of Commerce, Washington, D.C., several issues, 1990.

SWAMIDASS, P., ''Manufacturing Strategy: A Selected Bibliography,'' *Journal of Operations Management*, vol, 8, no. 3, 1989.

SWANGER, C., ''Apple Computer, Inc.—Macintosh (A),'' Stanford Graduate School of Business, Stanford, Calif., 1984.

WIGGENHORN, W., ''Motorola U.: When Training Becomes an Education,'' *Harvard Business Review*, July–August, 1990.

''WORLD BUSINESS,'' *Wall Street Journal Reports*, September 22, 1989.

appendix

A

Probabilistic Models of Service and Waiting Facilities

When customers arrive, the capability to satisfy their demands for goods or services depends on the availability of personnel, equipment, and supplies. Customers seldom arrive at a uniform rate, and the time required to perform the service can also vary. Consequently, a typical service system will have periods of idle capacity, interspersed with periods when customers outnumber servers, forming a waiting line, or *queue*.

This feast-or-famine effect is observed even if arrivals are more or less steady, as in a dentist's office where patients arrive according to a schedule. The usual cause of delay is the difference in service times among the customers. A very long service time overlaps with the time allotted for the next service, and thereby causes a waiting line that persists until shorter service times reduce it. This discussion points out a general principle of waiting lines:

> *Waiting lines are caused by variability in either the rate of arrivals or the rate of service, or both. Therefore, over the long run, a service system will exhibit both idle capacity and waiting lines.*

A *stochastic waiting-line model* is a set of mathematical equations that use probability distributions to (1) describe the variability in arrival and service rates and (2) predict the resulting effects on both servers and customers. Thus, the input to a stochastic model includes probability distributions of arrival and service rates, and the output includes probability distributions of busy servers and waiting customers. These outputs are the mathematical version of the feast-or-famine effect in real systems. The study of the behavior of waiting lines is known as *queuing theory*.

There are many examples of *stochastic processes* in management, and many of them may be characterized as customer meets server, which places them within the realm of queuing theory. In the most obvious examples, customers and servers are people (retail stores, doctors' offices, hamburger stands). However, machines or other inanimate objects are sometimes the server (automatic tollbooths, computer systems, telephones) or the customer (cars waiting for repair, jobs waiting to be done). Also, it is not necessary for the customers to form a physical waiting line in front of a stationary server. For example, if an ambulance service receives too many calls, the patients are placed on a waiting list, which constitutes a queue even though the patients are dispersed throughout the city.

As a consequence of this generality, stochastic models are used in several chapters of this book. In this appendix we shall limit our examples to those involving people. The first section explains and illustrates some important planning concepts which may be understood on an intuitive basis. These concepts deal with averages (such as the average utilization of servers) and do not require any notions of probability distributions. The second part presents formulas for predicting the size of the waiting line, based on the use of the Poisson and exponential probability distributions.

A-1 PLANNING PRINCIPLES: SYSTEMS IN STEADY STATE

There are a number of properties that are useful for planning the capacity of a service system. The ones discussed here require the important assumption that the system is in steady state.

> *Definition: A system is said to be in steady state if (1) the number of servers, the average arrival rate, and the average service capacity are not changing; (2) the average arrival rate is less than the average service capacity times the number of servers; and (3) these conditions have existed for a substantial period of time. (See the following discussion.) The opposite of steady state is transience, which refers to the behavior of the system during the period following some change.*

The *pipeline principle* states that the steady-state average rate of flow through a system must be equal to the intake rate in the long run. Thus, for example, the number of college admissions equals the graduates plus dropouts, in the long run. This may seem so simple as to be trivial, but it is sometimes overlooked. During the transient period following an increase in the size of the entering college class, the admission rate exceeds the graduation plus dropout rate, but steady state is restored by the time the first of the larger classes has reached graduation.

Figure A-1 shows a typical service system with a single waiting line. The pipeline principle is incorporated in this diagram by making sure that the average inflow equals the average outflow at each point in the system. For example, the rate at which customers demand service (λ) equals the rate at which they join the queue ($\bar{\lambda}$) plus the turnaway rate (unmet demand). Furthermore, the departure rate (after service) equals the rate of joining the queue (before service), on the average. We will use this principle to develop a series of useful relationships.

Maximum Input Rate. In the model of Figure A-1, customers either join the queue and wait for service or depart without joining the queue (unmet demand.) Since λ represents all of demand and $\bar{\lambda}$ represents those who join the queue, it follows that

Average input rate to queue $\le$ average demand from calling population

$$\bar{\lambda} \le \lambda$$

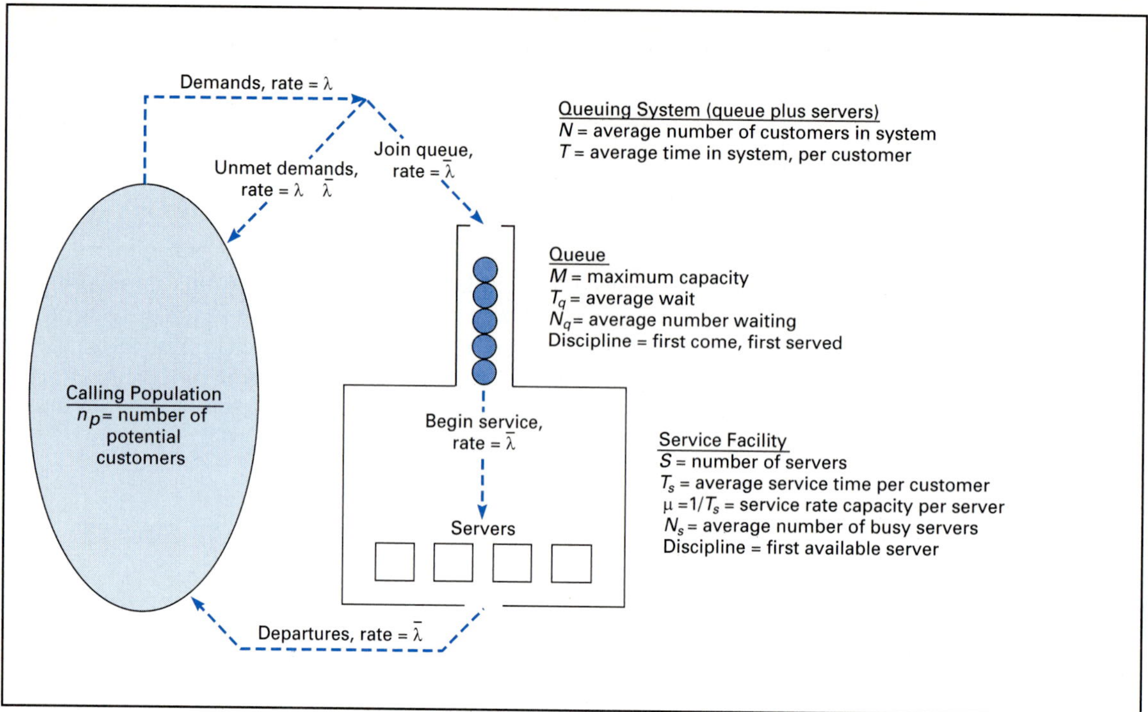

Figure A-1 Schematic of a Queuing Process with a Single Waiting Line

Service Capacity. The *service capacity*, μ, measures how many customers one server can serve per unit time, on the average. The average service time per customer, T_s, is sometimes easier to measure than the service capacity. However, the two are related by the following, which can be taken as the definition of μ:

$$T_s = \frac{1}{\mu} \quad \text{or} \quad \mu = \frac{1}{T_s}$$

Although μ is often called the *service rate*, the term *service capacity* is more accurate because μ represents the server's capability, to be distinguished from actual performance. That is, μ would be the average output rate if the server were busy all the time.

We assume here that all servers are identical; thus, the service capacity of a facility with S servers is $S\mu$. Although output cannot exceed capacity in the long run, it may be less than capacity. When that occurs there will be periods of idle time for some or all of the servers. In fact, according to the pipeline principle, the average output rate must equal the average input rate, $\bar{\lambda}$. Putting these two facts together,

$$\text{Average input rate} \leq \text{service capacity of facility}$$

$$\bar{\lambda} \leq S\mu$$

Utilization. The *utilization* of a facility is the fraction of capacity actually used. Since $\bar{\lambda}$ is both the input and the output rate, and $S\mu$ is the service capacity (which places a limit on the output rate), a general formula for utilization is

$$\text{Average utilization} = \frac{\text{average input rate}}{\text{average service capacity}} = \frac{\bar{\lambda}}{S\mu}$$

and the average fraction of time that is *not* used productively is (1 − average utilization).

The Greek letter ρ is used to denote the *traffic intensity*, or the *utilization factor*. It measures the demand for the service *relative to the capacity to supply the service*.[1] That is,

$$\text{Utilization factor (or traffic intensity)} = \frac{\text{average demand rate}}{\text{average service capacity}}$$

$$\rho = \frac{\lambda}{S\mu}$$

There is an important difference between the average utilization and the utilization factor: *The utilization factor (ρ) can exceed 1.0, whereas the average utilization cannot*. That is, ρ reflects λ, the *potential* demand from the calling population, whereas the average utilization uses $\bar{\lambda}$, the *actual* rate at which service is provided, which may be lower. In general,

$$\text{Average utilization} \leq \rho$$

and the two are equal only if all demand is met (no turnaways, $\lambda = \bar{\lambda}$).

Minimum Number of Servers. Since average utilization cannot exceed 1.0 in the long run, $\bar{\lambda}/S\mu \leq 1.0$, which may be rearranged as

$$\text{Number of servers} \geq \frac{\text{average input rate}}{\text{average service capacity per server}}$$

$$S \geq \frac{\bar{\lambda}}{\mu}$$

Occupied Servers. There are S servers. Since $\bar{\lambda}/S\mu$ is the fraction of time each server is occupied, we can multiply by S to obtain the average *number* of busy servers, denoted N_s.

$$\text{Average number of busy servers} = \frac{\text{average input rate}}{\text{average service capacity per server}}$$

$$N_s = \frac{\bar{\lambda}}{\mu}$$

Customers Being Served. Since there is one customer for each busy server, on the average the number of customers in the process of being served *is the same as the number of busy servers*, N_s.

Each of the preceding formulas can be stated in terms of T_s rather than μ. For example, $N_s = \bar{\lambda}T_s$, average utilization $= \bar{\lambda}T_s/S$, and $\rho = \lambda T_s/S$.

---

[1]In the discussion of capacity management of service operations (Chapter 13), the utilization factor is based on forecasts of demand and capacity and is referred to as the projected capacity utilization (PCU).

Customers in the Queue. The average waiting time per customer, T_q, is related to the average queue length, N_q, by

Average queue length = (average rate of joining queue)(average waiting time)

$$N_q = \bar{\lambda} T_q.$$

Of course, if there is a maximum queue length, M, the average cannot exceed the maximum, and $\bar{\lambda}$ is less than λ to account for customers who are not able to join the queue. This would apply in the case of a drive-in bank if cars are turned away when the line backs up into the street.

Customers in the System. The queuing system consists of the queue(s) and the service facility. As a consequence, the average number of customers in the system, N, and the average time (waiting plus service) per customer in the system, T, are given by

$$N = N_q + N_s$$

and

$$T = T_q + T_s = T_q + 1/\mu$$

It also follows that the total number of customers in the system is related to the total time in the system by the simple formula[2]

$$N = \bar{\lambda} T$$

In summary, we have assumed that S identical servers are always available. Both arrivals and service may be random. However, the *average* service capacity of each server does not change with time, nor does the average rate of arrivals. The resulting steady-state analysis has given us the following formulas:

$$\begin{array}{ccccccc} \text{Average utilization} & = & \dfrac{\text{average input rate}}{\text{service capacity of facility}} & = & \dfrac{\text{average number of busy servers}}{\text{total number of servers}} & \le & \text{utilization factor} \\ \text{Average utilization} & = & \dfrac{\bar{\lambda}}{S\mu} & = & \dfrac{N_s}{S} & \le & \rho \quad (\text{or } \lambda/S\mu) \end{array} \qquad (1)$$

$$\begin{array}{ccccc} \text{Demand arrival rate} & \ge & \text{input rate of customers joining queue} & \le & \text{service rate capacity} \\ \lambda & \ge & \bar{\lambda} & \le & S\mu \quad (\text{or } S/T_s) \end{array} \qquad (2)$$

$$\begin{array}{ccccc} \text{Number of servers} & \ge & \text{average number of occupied servers} & = & \left(\begin{array}{c}\text{average}\\ \text{input}\\ \text{rate}\end{array}\right)\left(\begin{array}{c}\text{average}\\ \text{service}\\ \text{time}\end{array}\right) \\ S & \ge & N_s & = & \bar{\lambda} T_s \quad (\text{or } \bar{\lambda}/\mu) \end{array} \qquad (3)$$

[2]This property is sometimes referred to as *Little's law* (Little 1961). The equations $N_q = \bar{\lambda} T_q$ and $N_s = \bar{\lambda} T_s$ are versions of the same principle. If there are no unmet demands, the demand arrival rate is equal to the rate at which customers join the queue (i.e., $\lambda = \bar{\lambda}$), and this formula takes on its more familiar form $N = \lambda T$.

$$\begin{array}{ccccc} \text{Maximum queue size} & \geq & \text{average queue size} & = & \begin{pmatrix}\text{average}\\ \text{input}\\ \text{rate}\end{pmatrix}\begin{pmatrix}\text{average}\\ \text{time in}\\ \text{queue}\end{pmatrix} \\ M & \geq & N_q & = & \bar{\lambda} T_q \end{array} \tag{4}$$

$$\begin{array}{ccccccc} \text{Average time in system} & = & \text{average time in queue} & + & \text{average service time} & \\ T & = & T_q & + & T_s & (\text{or } T_q + 1/\mu) \end{array} \tag{5}$$

$$\begin{array}{ccccc} \text{Space for customers in the system} & \geq & \text{average number of customers in the system} & = & \begin{pmatrix}\text{average}\\ \text{input}\\ \text{rate}\end{pmatrix}\begin{pmatrix}\text{average}\\ \text{time in}\\ \text{system}\end{pmatrix} \\ M + S & \geq & N = N_q + N_s & = & \bar{\lambda} T \end{array} \tag{6}$$

These formulas hold for any service system in steady state, no matter what probability distributions govern the variability of arrivals and service time.[3] However, there is a missing link between equations 1 and 4: The average waiting time must be related to the average utilization of the service facility, since waiting lines become a serious problem in facilities that are very busy. Formulas for that relationship are given in the next section. Before pursuing those relationships, we will consider a few applications in the review problems.

REVIEW PROBLEMS

1. The average car spends 10 seconds in the toll station on Murkey Turnpike. There are three tollbooths. How much traffic can the station handle?

2. A 450-bed hospital expects to admit 18,250 patients next year, each averaging 8 days of hospital stay. Is there a sufficient number of beds? On the average, how many beds will be empty? What would happen to hospital utilization if 10 more beds were added?

3. An airline telephone-reservation service has been designed to hold calls whenever a clerk is not available. The design goal is an average waiting time of less than 3 minutes. Approximately 200 calls per hour are to be handled. How many calls must the system be able to place on hold?

4. On Murkey Turnpike (review problem 1) the maximum rate of traffic flow is 20 cars per minute, occurring between 5:15 and 5:30 P.M. on Friday. The rate is 17 per minute during the 15-minute periods before 5:15 and after 5:30 P.M. Describe the transient behavior of the tollbooth waiting line during the peak.

5. A five-story building has two elevators. How can this be viewed as a queuing system?

[3]Steady-state queuing theory models assume that customer arrivals are distributed about a constant mean; this is known as stationary arrivals. When the arrival pattern exhibits time-varying behavior, as in the case of the Yuppie Car Wash discussed in Chapters 2 and 13, it is technically appropriate to use nonstationary-arrival queuing models, which are considerably more complex than stationary-arrival models. Approximating nonstationary arrivals with stationary models can offer helpful insight into the behavior of the queuing system. See Green and Kolesar (1991) and Green, Kolesar, and Svoronos (1991).

Solutions

1. Since the average service time is 10 seconds, the capacity of each booth is $\mu = 1/T_s = 1/10$ car per second, or 6 cars per minute. With $S = 3$ booths, the capacity of the station is $S\mu = (3)(6) = 18$ cars per minute.

2. Since each bed may be viewed as a server, $S = 450$. $\bar{\lambda} = 18{,}250/365 = 50$ per day, and $T_s = 8$ days. Therefore, from equation 3, $N_s = (50)(8) = 400$ beds occupied, on the average, leaving an average of 50 empty. These 50 beds constitute a safety margin, since the *actual* hospital census will vary daily. Using equation 1, utilization will average 400/450, or 89%. If there are 10 more beds, there will still be $N_s = 400$ occupied, unless either admissions or length of stay changes; thus, utilization will average 400/460 or 87%.

3. If all customers are willing to wait, $\bar{\lambda} = 200$ per hour, or 3.333 calls per minute. Using equation 4, $N_q = \bar{\lambda} T_q = (3.33)(3) = 10$ calls waiting, on the average. The actual number waiting will vary from this average, so the queue capacity must be larger than 10. (The next section gives information on the extra margin of safety.)

4. During the peak period, the arrival rate (20 per minute) exceeds the service capacity (18 per minute) by 2 cars per minute; consequently, the waiting line grows at this average rate. The number of cars waiting increases by about (2)(15) = 30 over the 15-minute peak interval, on the average. This additional queue will dissipate once the arrival rate drops again.

5. The elevators are the two servers and people waiting on different floors are the customers. To some extent the system operates first come, first served. However, the elevator control mechanism supplements this with a scheduling rule that keeps the elevator moving in the same direction until it reaches the highest or lowest floor with customers waiting.

A-2 WAITING TIME: A QUEUING-THEORY APPROACH

Waiting time can be caused by variability in arrivals and service. Accordingly, we must explicitly model these two random variables to predict waiting time. The derivation of the relationships is too involved for this appendix. Instead, we will state a few of these results without proof and give examples to show how they can be used. They are based on the assumptions that (1) arrivals per unit time follow the Poisson probability distribution (as before, the mean arrival rate = λ), and (2) service times are governed by the exponential probability distribution (with mean $T_s = 1/\mu$).[4] Together, we will refer to these assumptions as the *Markov property*. The third assumption is (3) that all servers are identical, which was also assumed in the previous section. The fourth assumption is (4) that customers are served on a first-come, first-served basis (within one or more specified priority classes).

[4]The Poisson and exponential probability distributions are closely related in that they provide different ways of describing the same stochastic process. Specifically, when the number of arrivals per unit time follows a Poisson distribution with mean arrival rate λ, the time between consecutive arrivals (i.e., the *interarrival time*) follows an exponential distribution with mean $1/\lambda$. See Appendix D, Tables 4 and 5, for more information on these distributions.

These assumptions are made for convenience; without them, the analysis becomes very cumbersome, if indeed not even impossible. Because they are fairly restrictive assumptions, the models to be described are often not accurate in the strictest sense. Nevertheless, the models do have substantial value for several reasons: (1) Together with the steady-state formulas of the previous section, the queuing-theory models often provide a reasonable approximation; (2) the results usually provide an upper-bound estimate of average waiting time, even if the assumptions of the model are not realistic; and (3) the general nature of the trade-off between service capacity and queue length can be studied with these limited models, demonstrating several general principles.

Figure A-2 summarizes the kind of system that we will study. (The results of the preceding section are also included in the diagram.) The three elements are (1) the calling population of potential customers (often referred to as the service population), (2) the queue, and (3) the service facility. We will discuss each of these in turn.

When the *calling population* is large compared with the number of customers in the queue and service facility ($n_p >> N = N_q + N_s$), the demand rate varies randomly about the mean value λ, regardless of the actual number in the queue. This is referred to as an *infinite-population* ($n_p = \infty$) *model*. In contrast, suppose that n_p is only twice as large as N; then on the average the calling population is reduced by half (the other half are waiting for service or being served), so the arrival rate is also down by 50%. *Only the infinite-population model is considered here*. However, it is reasonable to use such a model as long as $N < 0.01\ n_p$ (which implies that less than 1% of the population is in the service system, on the average).

Since the population is infinite, there is no theoretical limit to the length of the waiting line unless a maximum queue capacity (M) is specified. In that

Figure A-2 Schematic with Summary of Steady-State Relationships

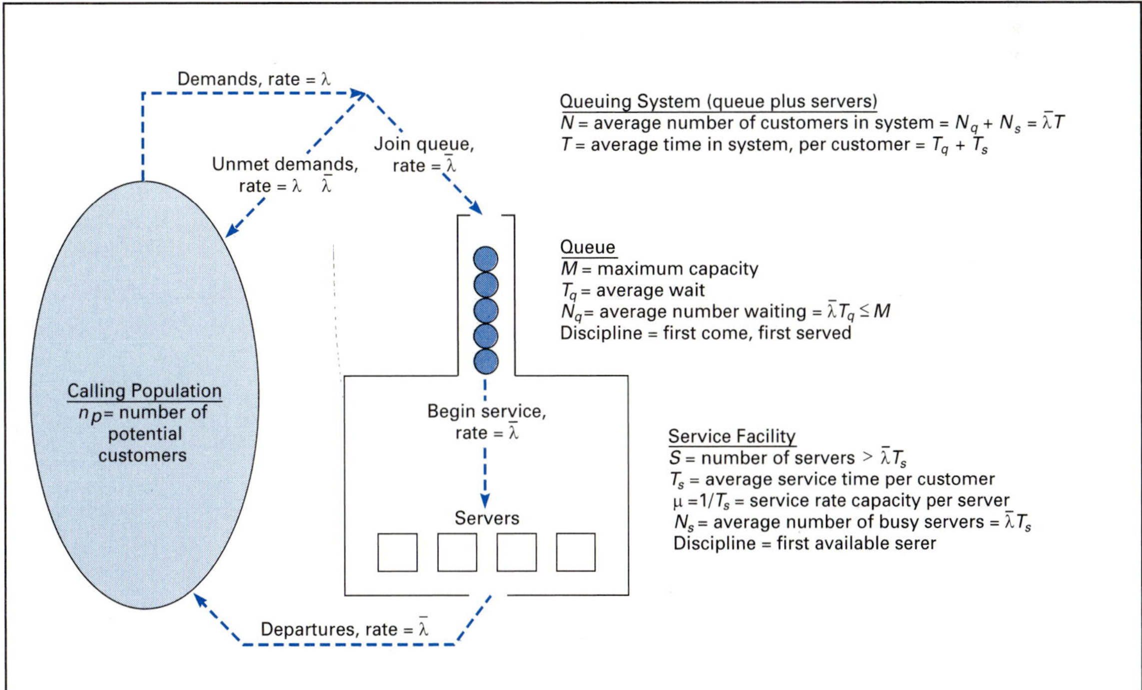

case we have a *finite-queue model*. When the queue reaches the maximum capacity of the waiting area, it is assumed that arrivals are turned away. These customers are lost to the system. When the waiting area once again has space available, arrivals resume at the same average rate as before (no loss of goodwill). This occurs, for example, in telephone reservation systems. Callers are placed on hold when "all service representatives are busy." Once a certain number have been placed on hold, new callers receive a busy signal and are denied access to the system. In this situation the average rate of joining the queue ($\bar{\lambda}$) is lower than the demand rate (λ).

In many situations there is no practical limit on the size of the queue. This is true, for example, when the queue is really a list of names of people waiting to be called for service. It is also true for many service facilities, which are carefully designed to have substantial excess capacity in the waiting room. This is referred to as an *infinite-capacity queue*. For the infinite-capacity queue, $\lambda = \bar{\lambda}$ because no demands are turned away.

In the *service facility* are S identical servers ($S = 1$ if there is a single server). Servers are fed by a common queue. Each serves one customer at a time, averaging T_s time units per customer (not including idle time). The service capacity per server, denoted μ, is simply $1/T_s$.

The *queue discipline* refers to the sequencing rule(s) used to determine the order in which customers are served. Customers may be served on a priority basis, with K classes of customers, each class having a separate queue. Class 1 has top priority for the next available server, and class 2 is not served unless the class 1 queue is empty, and so on for the remaining classes. Within each priority class, customers are served on a first-come, first-served basis. (The diagram in Figure A-2 depicts only one priority class.)

Networks of queues, such as the example in Figure A-3, are analyzed one at a time with the output of one subsystem supplying input to one or more succeeding subsystems. Of course, the total output of each facility must equal its input (the pipeline principle).

Figure A-3 Service Network: A Clinic with a Screener Who Decides Whether Walk-in Patients Should See the Doctor (Probability P_1), a Nurse (Probability P_3), or Nobody, (Probability P_2)[a]

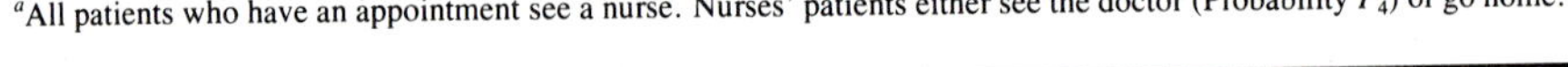
[a]All patients who have an appointment see a nurse. Nurses' patients either see the doctor (Probability P_4) or go home.

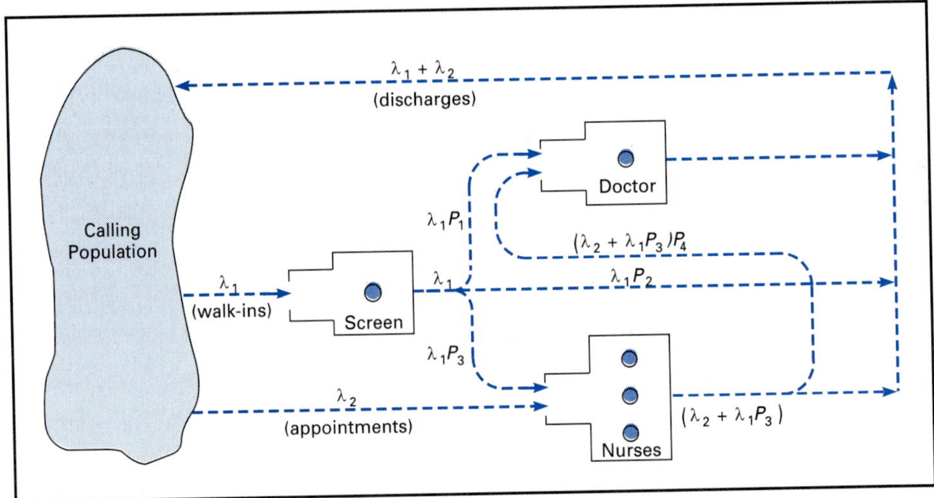

Table A-1 Summary of Some Queuing Formulas Based on the Markov Property

Model	Rate of Joining Queue ($\bar{\lambda}$)	Average Number (N_q)	Time (T_q) in Queue
I: *Single server ($S = 1$), infinite queue capacity, infinite population*			
	$\bar{\lambda} = \lambda$	$N_q = \dfrac{\rho^2}{1 - \rho}$	$T_q = \dfrac{N_q}{\lambda}$
II: *Multiple servers ($S \geq 1$), infinite queue capacity, infinite population*			
	$\bar{\lambda} = \lambda$	$N_q =$ value from Table A-2	$T_q = \dfrac{N_q}{\lambda}$
III: *Multiple servers ($S \geq 1$), finite queue with capacity = M, infinite population*			
	$A = \dfrac{\rho/(1 - \rho)}{N_q \text{ from Table A-2}}$	$N_q = \dfrac{\rho}{1 - \rho}\left\{\dfrac{1 - \rho^M(M - M\rho + 1)}{A - \rho^{M+1}}\right\}$	$T_q = \dfrac{N_q}{\bar{\lambda}}$
	$P_{\text{full}} = \dfrac{\rho^M(1 - \rho)}{A - \rho^{M+1}}$		
	$\bar{\lambda} = \lambda(1 - P_{\text{full}})$		
IV: *Multiple servers ($S \geq 1$), infinite queue capacity, infinite population, K priority classes*			
	$\lambda_k =$ Class k arrival rate	$N_q =$ value from Table A-2	$T_q = \dfrac{N_q}{\lambda}$
		(The preceding values describe the queue without regard to priority class. The following give values by priority class.)	
	$\bar{\lambda} = \lambda = \sum_{k=1}^{K} \lambda_k$	$A = \dfrac{\rho/(1 - \rho)}{N_q \text{ from Table A-2}}$	
	$\rho_k = \dfrac{\lambda_k}{S\mu}$	$N_{qk} = \dfrac{\rho_k}{AB_{k-1}B_k}, \quad k = 1, \ldots, K$	$T_{qk} = \dfrac{N_{qk}}{\lambda_k}$
	$B_0 = 1.0$		
	$B_k = B_{k-1} - \rho_k, \quad k = 1, \ldots, K$		

Notes: For all models: $\rho = \dfrac{\lambda}{S\mu}$.

For Model III: P_{full} = probability that the queue is full (i.e., has M customers).

For Models III and IV: The number A has no physical meaning; it is just an intermediate calculation.

For Model IV: The B_k values are also intermediate calculations that have no meaning.

The formulas for various queuing systems are contained in Table A-1. Although they may look difficult, most of the work is eliminated by reference to Table A-2. The rest of the computations are easy to perform with a hand calculator.

Example: The City Walk-In Clinic

Three categories of patients are treated at City Clinic, arriving at a rate of 10, 15, and 20 per 8-hour day, respectively. All patients are walk-ins, since this clinic does not accept appointments. Service capacity is 25 patients per day for each of the two nurse practitioners who staff the clinic. The first category of patients is the primary target population for the facility. However, all patients are currently served on a first-come, first-served basis, regardless of category. Some thought has been given to limiting access by reducing the waiting

Table A-2 Average Number in Waiting Line (N_q), with Ninety-Fifth and Ninety-Nineth Percentiles[a] for Model II, Table A-1

	Utilization Factor ($\rho = \lambda/S\mu$)												
Servers	**0.10**	**0.20**	**0.30**	**0.40**	**0.50**	**0.60**	**0.70**	**0.75**	**0.80**	**0.85**	**0.90**	**0.95**	**0.98**
1	0.011	0.050	0.129	0.267	0.500	0.900	1.633	2.250	3.200	4.817	8.100	18.050	48.020
	0 0	0 1	1 2	2 4	3 5	4 8	7 11	9 15	12 19	17 27	27 42	57 88	147 226
2	0.002	0.017	0.059	0.152	0.333	0.675	1.345	1.929	2.844	4.426	7.674	17.587	47.535
	0 0	0 1	0 2	1 3	2 5	4 7	6 11	8 14	11 19	16 26	26 42	56 88	146 226
3	0.000	0.006	0.030	0.094	0.237	0.532	1.149	1.703	2.589	4.139	7.354	17.233	47.160
	0 0	0 0	0 1	1 2	2 4	3 6	6 10	8 14	11 18	16 26	26 41	56 87	146 226
4	0.000	0.002	0.016	0.060	0.174	0.431	1.000	1.528	2.386	3.906	7.090	16.937	46.844
	0 0	0 0	0 1	0 2	1 4	3 6	6 10	8 13	11 18	16 26	26 41	56 87	146 225
5	0.000	0.001	0.009	0.040	0.130	0.354	0.882	1.385	2.216	3.709	6.862	16.678	46.566
	0 0	0 0	0 0	0 1	1 3	3 6	5 10	7 13	10 17	15 25	25 41	55 87	145 225
6	0.000	0.000	0.005	0.027	0.099	0.295	0.784	1.265	2.071	3.536	6.661	16.446	46.314
	0 0	0 0	0 0	0 1	0 3	2 5	5 9	7 13	10 17	15 25	25 40	55 86	145 225
7	0.000	0.000	0.003	0.018	0.076	0.248	0.702	1.161	1.944	3.383	6.480	16.235	46.084
	0 0	0 0	0 0	0 1	0 2	2 5	5 9	7 12	10 17	15 25	25 40	55 86	145 224
8	0.000	0.000	0.002	0.012	0.059	0.209	0.631	1.071	1.831	3.245	6.314	16.039	45.870
	0 0	0 0	0 0	0 0	0 2	2 5	4 9	6 12	9 17	15 24	25 40	55 86	145 224
9	0.000	0.000	0.001	0.008	0.046	0.178	0.571	0.991	1.729	3.118	6.161	15.857	45.669
	0 0	0 0	0 0	0 0	0 2	1 4	4 8	6 12	9 16	14 24	24 40	54 86	144 224
10	0.000	0.000	0.000	0.006	0.036	0.152	0.517	0.920	1.637	3.003	6.019	15.686	45.480
	0 0	0 0	0 0	0 0	0 1	1 4	4 8	6 11	9 16	14 24	24 39	54 86	144 224
11	0.000	0.000	0.000	0.004	0.028	0.130	0.471	0.856	1.553	2.895	5.886	15.525	45.300
	0 0	0 0	0 0	0 0	0 1	1 4	3 8	6 11	9 16	14 24	24 39	54 85	144 224
12	0.000	0.000	0.000	0.003	0.022	0.112	0.429	0.798	1.475	2.796	5.760	15.371	45.129
	0 0	0 0	0 0	0 0	0 1	0 3	3 8	5 11	8 16	14 23	24 39	54 85	144 223
13	0.000	0.000	0.000	0.002	0.018	0.097	0.392	0.746	1.404	2.702	5.642	15.226	44.965
	0 0	0 0	0 0	0 0	0 0	0 3	3 7	5 11	8 15	13 23	24 39	54 85	144 223
14	0.000	0.000	0.000	0.001	0.014	0.084	0.359	0.698	1.338	2.615	5.530	15.086	44.808
	0 0	0 0	0 0	0 0	0 0	0 3	3 7	5 10	8 15	13 23	23 39	53 85	143 223
15	0.000	0.000	0.000	0.001	0.011	0.072	0.329	0.654	1.277	2.533	5.424	14.952	44.656
	0 0	0 0	0 0	0 0	0 0	0 3	2 7	5 10	8 15	13 23	23 38	53 85	143 223
16	0.000	0.000	0.000	0.001	0.009	0.063	0.303	0.614	1.220	2.455	5.322	14.824	44.510
	0 0	0 0	0 0	0 0	0 0	0 2	2 7	4 10	8 15	13 23	23 38	53 84	143 223
17	0.000	0.000	0.000	0.000	0.007	0.055	0.278	0.577	1.166	2.381	5.225	14.700	44.369
	0 0	0 0	0 0	0 0	0 0	0 2	2 6	4 10	7 15	13 23	23 38	53 84	143 223

18	0.000	0.000	0.000	0.000	0.006	0.048	0.256	0.542	1.116	2.312	5.132	14.580	44.232
	0 0	0 0	0 0	0 0	0 0	0 2	2 6	4 10	7 14	12 22	23 38	53 84	143 222
19	0.000	0.000	0.000	0.000	0.005	0.041	0.236	0.511	1.069	2.245	5.043	14.465	44.099
	0 0	0 0	0 0	0 0	0 0	0 1	1 6	4 9	7 14	12 22	22 38	53 84	143 222
20	0.000	0.000	0.000	0.000	0.004	0.036	0.218	0.481	1.024	2.182	4.957	14.353	43.970
	0 0	0 0	0 0	0 0	0 0	0 1	1 6	4 9	7 14	12 22	22 38	52 84	142 222
25	0.000	0.000	0.000	0.000	0.001	0.019	0.148	0.362	0.836	1.905	4.571	13.839	43.371
	0 0	0 0	0 0	0 0	0 0	0 0	0 5	3 8	6 13	11 21	22 37	52 83	142 221
30	0.000	0.000	0.000	0.000	0.000	0.010	0.102	0.276	0.691	1.680	4.243	13.386	42.834
	0 0	0 0	0 0	0 0	0 0	0 0	0 4	2 7	5 12	10 20	21 36	51 82	141 221
35	0.000	0.000	0.000	0.000	0.000	0.005	0.072	0.213	0.577	1.491	3.957	12.979	42.344
	0 0	0 0	0 0	0 0	0 0	0 0	0 3	1 6	4 11	10 20	20 35	50 82	141 220
40	0.000	0.000	0.000	0.000	0.000	0.003	0.051	0.166	0.485	1.331	3.704	12.609	41.892
	0 0	0 0	0 0	0 0	0 0	0 0	0 2	0 5	3 11	9 19	20 35	50 81	140 220
50	0.000	0.000	0.000	0.000	0.000	0.001	0.026	0.102	0.348	1.075	3.275	11.953	41.075
	0 0	0 0	0 0	0 0	0 0	0 0	0 0	0 4	2 9	8 18	18 34	49 80	139 219

[a]Key: The decimal numbers are N_q values, and the integers are $q(95)$ and $q(99)$. That is, the probability is >95% that the queue is $\leq q(95)$, and similarly for $q(99)$.

$$N_q = \frac{\rho/(1-\rho)}{1 + (1-\rho)S! \sum_{n=0}^{S-1} \frac{(S\rho)^{n-S}}{n!}}$$

$$\text{P(queue} > q) = (1-\rho)(N_q)\rho^q$$

$$\text{P(wait} > t) = \left(\frac{1-\rho}{\rho}\right)(N_q)e^{(\lambda - S\mu)t}$$

room to a capacity of 10 patients and sending overflow patients to a neighboring clinic.

Analysis 1 (No Priorities, Infinite-Capacity Queue). Under current policy, there are no priorities and no stated limit on queue size or population. Since there are $S = 2$ servers, this matches Model II in Table A-1, with $\lambda = \bar{\lambda} = 10 + 15 + 20 = 45$ admissions per day, $\mu = 25$ per day per server. The utilization factor is $\rho = \lambda/S\mu = 45/[(2)(25)] = 0.9$. With the infinite queue capacity, no customers are lost ($\bar{\lambda} = \lambda$); thus, the average utilization is equal to ρ. This means that the two nurse practitioners are busy 90% of the time.

To find the average number in the queue, we look in Table A-2, in the row for $S = 2$ servers. Reading across the top, we find the column for which $\rho = 0.90$. Where the $S = 2$ row and the $\rho = 0.9$ column intersect, we find $N_q = 7.674$ patients waiting, on the average. The average patient waiting time is $T_q = N_q/\bar{\lambda} = 7.674/45 = 0.1705$ day $= 1.36$ hours at 8 hours per day. This very high waiting time indicates why they are considering limiting the arrivals.

When we found $N_q = 7.674$ in Table A-2, there were two other numbers, 26 and 42, immediately below. These are the ninety-fifth and ninety-ninth percentile points, respectively, from the probability distribution of the waiting line. Consequently, we know that there is about a 5% chance that the waiting line will exceed 26 people; therefore, their suggested policy of limiting the line to 10 people will have a large effect.

Analysis 2 (Finite Queue). With a queue limit of $M = 10$, Model III of Table A-1 gives a formula for the percent of patients who are turned away.

$$P_{\text{full}} = \frac{\rho^M(1-\rho)}{A - \rho^{M+1}}, \qquad \text{in which } A = \frac{\rho/(1-\rho)}{N_q \text{ from Table A-2}}$$

Now, from Analysis 1, we know that $\rho = 0.9$, and the N_q value from Table A-2 is 7.674. Plugging these into the preceding equations, the result is

$$A = \frac{0.9/0.1}{7.674} = 1.173, \qquad \rho^M = 0.9^{10} = 0.3487$$

$$P_{\text{full}} = \frac{\rho^M(1-\rho)}{A - \rho^{M+1}} = \frac{0.3487(0.1)}{1.173 - (0.9)(0.3487)} = \frac{0.03487}{0.8591} = 0.0406$$

Thus, the queue is full 4.06% of the time. Therefore, about 4% of arrivals will be turned away. According to Model III, the rate at which customers join the queue is

$$\bar{\lambda} = \lambda(1 - P_{\text{full}}) = 43.2 \text{ per day}$$

which is 4% below the demand rate of 45. Therefore, the average utilization will be $\bar{\lambda}/S\mu = 43.2/50 = 0.864$, which is 4% lower than the utilization factor, $\rho = 0.9$.

Finally, Table A-1 indicates that the average number in queue is

$$N_q = \frac{\rho}{1-\rho}\left\{\frac{1 - \rho^M(M - M\rho + 1)}{A - \rho^{M+1}}\right\} = \frac{0.9}{0.1}\left\{\frac{1 - 0.3487(10 - 9 + 1)}{0.8591}\right\} = 3.17$$

and the average wait is $T_q = N_q/\bar{\lambda} = 3.17/43.2 = 0.073$ day $= 0.59$ hour. Thus, the model predicts that the small (4%) reduction in arrivals, caused by limiting the queue to 10 or fewer, will decrease the average waiting time by almost 60%

(from 1.4 to 0.6 hour). *This surprisingly large decrease is because the patients turned away would have had long waits, since their arrivals occur when the line is 10 or more.*

Analysis 3 (Priorities). The three categories of City Clinic's patients might be given different priorities. Category 1 is the primary target population. If the clinic wished to give top priority to these patients, second priority to category 2, and third to category 3, Model IV of Table A-1 applies. Using $K = 3$ priorities, we follow the instructions in the table. First, the three arrival rates are $\lambda_1 = 10$, $\lambda_2 = 15$, and $\lambda_3 = 20$ patients per day. $A = 1.173$ (from Analysis 2), and we calculate the factors ρ_k, B_k, and N_{qk} as follows:

k	$\rho_k = \frac{\lambda_k}{S\mu}$	$B_k = B_{k-1} - \rho_k$	$N_{qk} = \frac{\rho_k}{AB_{k-1}B_k}$	$T_{qk} = \frac{N_{qk}}{\lambda_k}$ (days)
0		$B_0 = 1.0$		
1	$\frac{10}{50} = 0.2$	$B_1 = B_0 - \rho_1 = 0.8$	$\frac{0.2}{(A)(1)(0.8)} = 0.213$	$\frac{0.213}{10} = 0.0213$
2	$\frac{15}{50} = 0.3$	$B_2 = B_1 - \rho_2 = 0.5$	$\frac{0.3}{(A)(0.8)(0.5)} = 0.640$	$\frac{0.640}{15} = 0.0427$
3	$\frac{20}{50} = 0.4$	$B_3 = B_2 - \rho_3 = 0.1$	$\frac{0.4}{(A)(0.5)(0.1)} = 6.821$	$\frac{6.821}{20} = 0.341$
			Total = 7.674	

We note from these computations that the average number waiting is still 7.674 (Analysis 1), unchanged by the priority system, but *the waiting line is disproportionately category 3 patients*. That is, even though category 3's proportion in the queue is 6.82/7.67 = 89%, its proportion of arrivals is only λ_3/λ = 20/45 = 44%. The waiting times may be converted to hours by multiplying by 8 hours per day. The results are 0.17 hour for category 1, 0.34 hour for category 2, and 2.73 hours for category 3.

Conclusions for City Clinic. We have no evidence that the Markov property accurately describes the arrivals and service times; therefore, these analyses must be viewed as only approximate. The two proposals to deal with the unacceptably long waits may be contrasted as egalitarian (Analysis 2 turns away patients from *all* categories) versus selective (Analysis 3 makes life miserable for category 3 patients). Note, however, that the egalitarian approach results in a loss of 4% of patient revenues.

A very important *principle of waiting time versus idle time* is that waiting times can be reduced either by reducing the arrival rate or by increasing the number of servers or their work pace (service rate). Each of these actions will increase the average idle time of the servers. The analysis of City Clinic with a finite queue illustrates the effect of reducing the arrival rate by turning away customers. Next we will analyze the effects of extra servers and of a lower rate of demand.

Optimization

The cost trade-off between idle time and waiting time may be illustrated by considering two options for decreasing patient congestion at the City Clinic:

(1) Increase the number of nurse practitioners or (2) decrease the number of patients served. To keep the analysis simple, we will assume an infinite-capacity queue without priority classes. Because option 2 varies the size of the population served, the analysis is done on a cost-per-arrival basis.

The *cost of the clinic* is assumed to have three components: fixed cost (F), cost per additional server (C_s), and marginal cost per patient served (C_p). The cost per server includes the salaries of the nurse practitioners and the variable overhead for supporting them. The marginal cost per patient served is very small, mostly attributable to supplies and record keeping. Fixed cost refers to the fixed overhead of the clinic, also small in comparison with the cost per additional server. The total daily cost of the clinic is

$$F + SC_s + \bar{\lambda}C_p$$

and the average cost of the clinic per arrival is

$$\text{AC} = \frac{F + SC_s}{\bar{\lambda}} + C_p$$

The *opportunity cost to the consumer* is assumed to be proportional to the time spent in the clinic (since type and quality of service are assumed fixed, as are location, hours of operation, and so on). Therefore, if C_w is the cost to the consumer per hour of waiting and T_q is the average wait measured in hours, C_wT_q is the average consumer's opportunity cost per arrival. Thus, the *total average cost per arrival* is

$$\text{TCA} = \frac{F + SC_s}{\bar{\lambda}} + C_p + C_wT_q$$

For City Clinic, we will use F = \$200 per day, C_s = \$150 per server per day, and C_p = \$6 per arrival. The two values C_w = \$2 per hour and C_w = \$10 per hour are used to provide a range for this hard-to-measure parameter.

Table A-3 shows the total average cost per arrival. Assuming that all the costs are passed on to the consumer, if the consumer's waiting time is valued at \$2 per hour, the current policy of $\bar{\lambda} = \lambda = 45$, $S = 2$ is better than the others,

Table A-3 Costs of Operation and Waiting at City Clinic

Cost of Clinic			Cost of Waiting						
						Cost		Total Cost per Arrival (TCA)	
Servers (S)	Patients per Day (λ)	Average Cost per Arrival (AC)	ρ	Queue (N_q)	Wait (T_q, hours)	$C_w = 2$	$C_w = 10$	$C_w = 2$	$C_w = 10$
2	45	17.11	0.9	7.674	1.364	2.73	13.64	19.84	30.75
3	45	20.44	0.6	0.53	0.094	0.19	0.94	20.63	21.38
4	45	23.78	0.45	0.11	0.020	0.04	0.20	23.82	23.98
2	40	19.25	0.8	2.84	0.568	1.14	5.68	20.39	24.93
2	35	22	0.7	1.34	0.306	0.61	3.06	22.61	25.06
2	30	25.67	0.6	0.67	0.179	0.36	1.79	26.03	27.46
2	25	30.8	0.5	0.33	0.106	0.21	1.06	31.01	31.86

since it achieves the lowest total cost of \$19.84 per visit. However, the conclusion is different when C_w = \$10 per hour, for which the lowest-cost number of servers is three; the cost of adding the third server is more than offset by the reduction in waiting-time costs.

Apparently the policy of reducing the number of patients served is not a good idea. The reduction in waiting time is substantial, but the cost per patient increases because the fixed cost is spread over fewer individuals. (This is the case for both values of C_w.)

Sensitivity Analysis

A disproportionate reduction in waiting time occurs when changes are made to a system that is near saturation. For example, in Table A-3 an increase from two to three servers (50%) cuts waiting time from 1.364 to 0.094 hour (93%), and a reduction in the demand rate from 45 to 40 (11%) cuts the delay by 0.8 hour (or 58%). This is a very important phenomenon to remember: *The long-run average size of a waiting line can be very sensitive to small changes in the system parameters, especially if there is very little slack capacity*. For infinite-capacity queues, a heavily utilized (say ≥95%) system will have a very long waiting line, on the average, in the long run. Under these circumstances customer service can be improved substantially by providing small amounts of additional capacity.

Many services are provided on an appointment basis, which reduces the randomness in the arrival process. Moreover, some services can be delivered in a fixed amount of time, or with only small variation. How does this affect the waiting line? The answer is that shorter average waits result whenever randomness is reduced in either arrivals or service time. Therefore, the use of the formulas presented here represents a conservative analysis, in that waiting times should be smaller than calculated when appointment systems are present.

There are many queuing situations in which mathematical models are difficult or impossible to derive. When a more precise model is needed, simulation is often used (see Appendix B).

REVIEW PROBLEMS

1. What is the difference between a finite-queue model and a finite-population model?

2. Which gives larger N_q values, finite or infinite population models? Why?

3. The average car spends 10 seconds in a toll station on Murkey Turnpike. There are three tollbooths in the station.

   a. What is the average number of cars in the waiting line when the traffic flow averages 14 cars per minute? 16? 18? 20?

   b. If the average flow peaks at 16.2 cars per minute, suggest how large the toll-plaza capacity should be for waiting cars.

4. A typist works for five executives, each of whom generates an average of five dictated (tape-recorded) jobs per hour.

a. Explain why this is not a finite-population model with $n_p = 5$ potential customers.

b. Assuming that this is an infinite-capacity queue, what must the typist's service rate average, in the long run?

Solutions

1. Finite-queue models place a limit on the length of the waiting line, regardless of the number of potential customers. Finite-population models explicitly take into account the reduction in the number of potential customers as some of them join the queuing system.

2. Infinite. In a finite-population model, the arrival rate slows down as the queue builds up simply because there are fewer potential customers in the calling population (they are in the queuing system instead).

3. a. There are $S = 3$ tollbooths. $T_s = 10$ seconds per car, so $\mu = 1/10$ car per second, or 6 per minute per tollbooth. For $\lambda = 14$ per minute, $\rho = \lambda / S\mu = 14/[(3)(6)] = 0.78$. From Table A-2, with $S = 3$ and a utilization factor of 0.78, we find that N_q is between 1.7 and 2.6 cars. Interpolation yields 2.2 cars waiting, on the average. For $\lambda = 16$, $\rho = 0.89$, and $N_q = 6.7$ cars. There is no steady-state solution for 18 and 20 cars per hour, since ρ is no longer less than 1.00.

   b. At 16.2 cars per minute, $\rho = 0.9$, and the average line is 7.4 cars. The length of the line will exceed 26 cars less than 5% of the time, and 41 cars less than 1% of the time. Therefore, the waiting area should hold about 40 cars if the peak rate is one that persists for any length of time.

4. a. The population is not the executives. It is the jobs they generate. The rate of arrival of those jobs is not affected by the typist's queue of tapes. However, it might be a finite-queue model if there is a limit on the number of available tapes.

   b. The average service capacity must be greater than (5)(5) = 25 per hour.

SUMMARY

The formulas in this appendix represent only a small part of the body of available queuing-theory models. We have concentrated on steady-state models, which describe systems that are unchanging in their service capabilities and are subjected to randomly varying streams of inputs (customers) whose service time needs are also randomly varying. Because of the restrictive assumptions entailed in the Markov property, these models are very seldom more than a rough approximation. (For further discussion of queuing theory see, for example, Cooper 1981, Eppen et al. 1991, or Hillier and Lieberman 1986.)

In an article about attempts to apply queuing theory, Byrd (1978) described a series of frustrations in matching up the assumptions against reality. The examples he chose were diverse: a bookstore, a pinball parlor, a drugstore, a stop light, and so on. In each case, the textbook models seemed inadequate. In a rejoinder to that piece, Bhat (1978) pointed to a huge body of literature on applications of queuing theory. However, he also made a significant point: "If a better solution is unnecessary for the problem at hand, one should not hesitate to stop with a 'quick and dirty' one." The applications of queuing theory in this text follow that philosophy. The models help us to gain useful insight into many applications in operations management, but we must remember to interpret the output of the models within the limits of the restrictive assumptions.

PROBLEMS

Note: In those of the following problems that require assumptions beyond the general steady-state properties discussed in Section A-1, use the basic assumptions of Section A-2, including the Markov property.

*1. Identify which of the following statements are accurate descriptions of a system in steady state. For each false statement, explain why it is false.
   a. Arrivals are not varying in frequency.
   b. The number of servers is constant.
   c. The service time is the same for all customers.
   d. The waiting line has achieved its ultimate level and is no longer changing.
   e. The average input rate equals the average output rate.

2. This problem is intended to point out the nonlinear nature of queuing theory models. Use an infinite-queue-capacity, infinite-population model.
   a. For $S = 5$ servers, look up the average number waiting for the ρ values 0.1, 0.3, 0.5, 0.7, 0.8, and 0.9, and plot N_q against ρ.
   b. Interpret what you see in your plot, remembering that ρ represents the utilization of the servers.
   c. For a given number of servers, there are only two ways that the utilization factor can be altered. What are they?
   d. A five-server system currently has a work load that keeps the servers occupied 70% of the time. Suppose that the work load increased so that the utilization became 90%. From your answer to part a, what is the percentage increase in the average waiting line? Compare that with the percentage increase in the work load, and comment.
   e. What might a fast-food restaurant do to increase the service rate, μ?

*3. The U.R. Trukin Company manufactures shirts, and employs one person to inspect and perform any necessary rework. The inspector can operate at the rate of 10,000 shirts per month.
   a. Using Model I in Table A-1, compute the average number of shirts waiting for inspection if the production rate is 8000 per month.
   b. What is the percentage of idle time for the inspector?
   c. Answer parts a and b if the production rate is 9000.
   d. Compare the increase in the work load (λ) with the increase in the waiting line between parts a and c.
   e. Do you think the Markov property holds for this example? Which of its two assumptions is more questionable for this example?

---

*Problems with an asterisk have answers in the back of the book.

f. Given your answer to part d, in which direction are your estimates of the averge queue biased? Why?

4. A public health agency in Venezuela is providing free polio vaccinations. Arrivals of people seem to be random throughout the day, with an average of 288 per day. The public health nurse can provide up to 360 doses per day. The clinic is open 6 hours a day, but they give doses to all persons waiting at closing time.
   a. How large should their waiting area be? Explain your answer.
   b. The service time is not actually random. In fact, the service always takes *exactly* 1 minute. In what direction does this change your answer?
   c. Criticize your answer to part a from the point of view of the steady-state assumption.

*5. A service system has $\lambda = 40$ arrivals per hour, and $\mu = 15$ customers can be served per hour by each server. Each server costs $12 per hour in wages and fringe benefits.
   a. What is the theoretical minimum number of servers?
   b. How many servers are required to keep waiting time to less than 5 minutes on the average? (Trial-and-error is required to answer this.)
   c. Express your answer to part b as a payroll cost per customer served.
   d. If customers value their own time at $8 per hour, would they prefer that the system have three servers or four? (Assume that the savings of having fewer servers is passed on to the customer.)

6. One of the workstations in the Duke Manufacturing Company shop is manned by Pete Salt. He is a specialist in machine parts finishing and receives jobs from many departments of the company, on an irregular basis. He receives an average of 10 jobs per day, and the pileup of unfinished jobs awaiting his attention amounts to 8 jobs, on the average.
   a. Estimate his idle time (percent; use either the Model I formulas or Table A-2, and solve for ρ. *Note:* If you cannot answer part a, assume that the answer is 10% and continue.)
   b. Estimate Pete's service rate capability, μ.
   c. If a new job arrives for Pete (with no special priority), how long will it be before he begins to work on the job?
   d. What would be the average number of jobs in the waiting line if another equivalent worker were permanently assigned to work in the station next to Pete's, and jobs were fed to both stations by a common queue?

7. Two professors each have private secretaries (don't we wish) who can type four pages per hour. The professors each generate three pages of work per hour. What benefit would there be if they pooled their typing between the two secretaries? Explain why this difference occurs.

*8. A barbershop has two barbers, each of whom can serve five customers per hour. A total of eight customers per hour arrive at the shop on the average.

a. If 60% of the customers want barber 1, 40% want barber 2, and no customer will accept a barber other than their preferred barber, how long does the average customer wait?

b. If all customers would take the next available barber, how long would the average customer wait?

c. In words, why is the average customer waiting time in part b less than in part a? Suppose that the customer preferences were divided equally. Would "next available barber" still yield shorter customer waiting time?

*9. A hospital admits an average of 10 new patients per day, with an average stay of 8 days. A first-come, first-served waiting list is used for patients categorized as urgent admissions, as opposed to emergency patients and elective admissions. About 20% of patients are admitted through the waiting list, whereas the other 80% are either scheduled or admitted immediately. The average urgent patient waits 2 days for admission. The following questions can be answered by using equations 1 to 4, without reference to any of the models in Table A-1.

a. How many beds does this hospital probably have?

b. How many beds are full, on the average?

c. How many names are on the waiting list, on the average?

10. A bank has one drive-in window. The average drive-in customer spends 4 minutes at the window. There are 13.5 customers per hour who wish to use the drive-in window. What is the average size of the waiting line if

a. there is no limit on the number of cars allowed in line?

b. there is a limit of four cars?

11. Tasty Bakers has 10 mixing machines that are in almost constant use. They are operated by one person, who adds the appropriate ingredients, sets the timer, and then departs to load other mixers. When the timer stops the mixer, the operator empties the contents and cleans the machine, if necessary. This service requires an average of 1 minute in total. The amount of mixing time averages 19 minutes.

a. What is the rate of demand for service, per machine?

b. What is the total hourly demand rate?

c. Using Model I, Table A-1, what is the average number of mixers waiting for service?

d. Is the infinite-population assumption of Model I adequate in this case? Discuss.

*12. In a job shop there are two priority classes, normal orders and hot orders. Usually, 10% of orders are classified as hot, and when such an order arrives at a machine center, it is processed on the first available machine, regardless of how many normal orders are waiting. If two or more hot orders are in the queue, the hot orders are processed in the order in which they arrived. (This is also the case with two or more normal orders.)

a. First, assume that the hot-order priority system is *not* in use. Estimate the average waiting time at a machine center with $S = 10$

identical machines, when $\lambda = 18$ jobs per day, $\mu = 2$ jobs per day per machine.

b. Estimate the average wait for hot orders and for normal orders when the hot-order priority system is in use.

13. The Skunk Hollow Service Station is the only supplier of gasoline for the friendly community of Skunk Hollow. The station has been open 12 hours per day, serving an average of 14 customers per hour with one gas pump. During a recent gas shortage, customers began to ''top off the tank'' for fear of being caught short of gasoline if and when SHSS ran out. The net effect was to *double the frequency of visits* to the service station, but each visit required only *half of the usual amount of gasoline.*

a. Using the following data, calculate the length of the waiting line before and during the crisis.

Before the Gas Crisis

Time to take the customer's order = 10 seconds
Time to pump gas = 2 minutes (average)
Time to receive payment and write up credit card slip = 50 seconds (average)
Arrival rate = 14 per hour (average)

Changes during the Gas Crisis

Time to pump gas = 1 minute (average)
Arrival rate = 28 per hour (average)

b. What would be the effect on the waiting line of adding another gas pump during the crisis? Be sure to state your assumptions about the arrangements for waiting customers. (Assume that there are enough attendants to avoid delay between customers.)

14. The Yuppie Car Wash Company[5] has two automatic car-wash machines. To be cleaned, a car need only go through one of the machines. Each machine can handle one car at a time. Yuppie has the option of operating one or two machines, depending on the expected volume of business. When both machines are operating, they are fed by a common queue. Cars are serviced according to a first-come, first-served priority. There is ample room in the large parking lot for cars to wait to enter the car wash.

Yuppie Car Wash is considering running only one machine on Wednesday afternoons because the expected arrival rate is only 19.2 cars per hour at that time. Each machine requires a constant amount of time to wash a car. However, before washing, some adjustments must be made to accommodate the specific type of car. This, together with varying times required for positioning the cars, introduces variability into the total cleaning time per car. The mean total service time for each machine (including drive through, machine adjustment, and washing) is 2.5 minutes per car.

[5]The Yuppie Car Wash Company was introduced in Chapter 2 as a two-stage process. This question considers only the first stage, consisting of the automatic car-wash machines.

a. Assume that Yuppie schedules only one car-wash machine for use on Wednesday afternoons.

(i) What is the expected number of cars in the car wash (i.e., waiting in queue and being serviced)?

(ii) How long, on average, will a car wait in line before entering the car wash?

b. Answer the questions for part a assuming that both car-wash machines are used on Wednesday afternoons.

15. The Quik Job Shop currently has four employees and 20 machines. All employees are expert on each of the twenty machines. Each job involves several steps, each requiring a different machine. An employee is assigned to each job, moving with it through the shop and performing all of its processing steps. The wide variety of jobs leads to a wide variety of processing times (total time required to finish a job). The average is about 2.7 hours per job. Quik employees work 8-hour days. There are approximately eight new jobs each day.

a. Estimate the average flow time (time from receipt of order until finish of job).

b. List the assumptions that you must make to get an answer to part a.

c. One employee will retire in 2 weeks. What will happen to the average flow time in the weeks following her departure, assuming that she is not replaced?

*16. A family-practice medical clinic employs a receptionist, a nurse clinician (NC), and a physician (MD). The receptionist has been trained to screen patients with regard to whether they should see the NC or the MD. There are, of course, some errors, so the NC sees some patients who must then go to the physician. The accompanying diagram shows the flow of patients.

λ = arrival rate of patients = 30 per hour

P_1 = fraction who go to nurse clinician = 2/3

P_2 = fraction of NC patients who must also see the physician = 0.15

μ_S = service rate of the receptionist-screener = 40 per hour

μ_D = service rate of the MD = 15 per hour

μ_N = service rate of the NC = 30 per hour

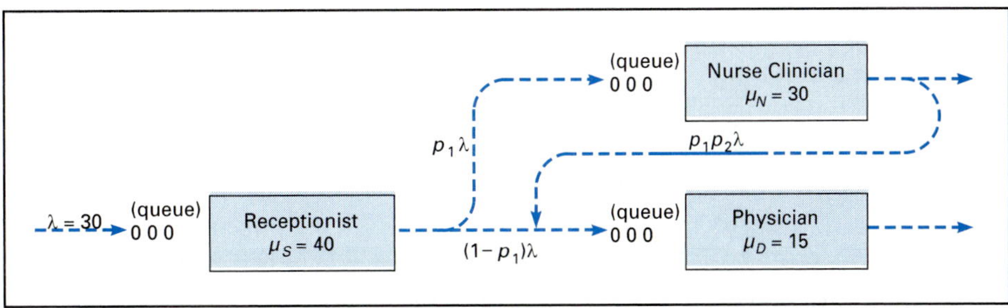

Using queuing theory, calculate:

a. the average waiting time in each queue
b. the average time in the entire system for each of the three patient paths
c. the overall average time in the system
d. the idle time of each server, per hour
e. the impact of having two physicians instead of one, sharing the same queue on a ''first MD available'' basis

17. A community has ten ambulances. It is now considering reorganizing (decentralizing) its ambulance service into three districts, each with three ambulances, rather than continuing the present arrangement with a central dispatching location. This would reduce the number to nine ambulances.

Under the present arrangement, when an ambulance is available, it can answer and complete a call in 30 minutes (average), from time of dispatch until final arrival at the emergency room. Under the proposed system, carefully dividing the districts into units with equal populations, ambulances will be able to answer and complete calls in 20 minutes, on the average. Both estimates include an average of 6 minutes on the scene (loading the patient) and 8 minutes travel time to the nearest emergency center.

There are presently ten calls (demands) per hour. This is not expected to change in the near future. However, under the new district arrangement, district A has 3.0 calls per hour, and B and C each have 3.5. The city officials realize that they cannot split an ambulance, and the traffic arrangements make it impossible to have three districts with equal call rates. Medical experts are pressing for decentralization because they believe the 10-minute reduction in travel time will significantly reduce deaths and injuries.

Would you recommend decentralizing and eliminating one ambulance? A criterion for measuring the effectiveness of a system should emphasize the response time. The accompanying diagram was constructed to show the major events in an average call for an ambulance.

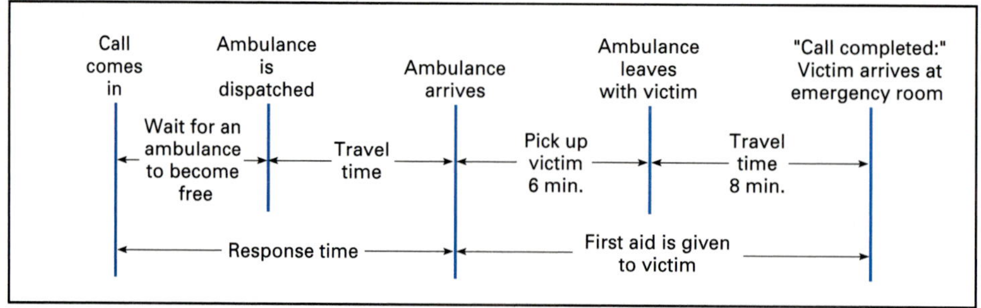

REFERENCES

BHAT, U.N., ''The Value of Queuing Theory: A Rejoinder,'' *Interfaces*, vol. 8, no. 3, 1978.

BYRD, J., "The Value of Queuing Theory," *Interfaces*, vol. 8, no. 3, 1978.

COOPER, R.B., *Introduction to Queuing Theory*, 2nd ed., New York: Elsevier North-Holland, 1981.

EPPEN, G.D., F.J. GOULD, and C.P. SCHMIDT, *Introductory Management Science*, 3rd ed., Englewood Cliffs, N.J.: Prentice-Hall, 1991.

GREEN, L. and P. KOLESAR, "The Pointwise Stationary Approximation for Queues with Nonstationary Arrivals," *Management Science*, vol. 37, no. 1, 1991.

GREEN, L., P. KOLESAR, and A. SVORONOS, "Some Effects of Nonstationarity on Multiserver Markovian Queueing Systems," *Operations Research*, vol. 39, no. 3, 1991.

HILLIER, F.S. and G.J. LIEBERMAN, *Operations Research*, 4th ed., San Francisco: Holden-Day, 1986.

LITTLE, J.D.C., "A Proof of Queueing Formula: $L = \lambda W$," *Operations Research*, vol. 9, no. 3, 1961.

appendix

B

Simulation

You have seen simulation before. Television news used animated simulations to describe the Voyager spacecraft's trip to the planets. Automobile commercials show engineers designing and testing new body shapes on a video screen. And then there are the ubiquitous video games that simulate journeys through imaginary landscapes.

Simulation is also widely used in operations management. Its greatest value is to study changes that could be very beneficial if done correctly but extremely disruptive if done poorly. For example, city planners use simulation to study the flow of traffic under different arrangements of one-way streets, or to compare different methods of timing the stoplights. Many different alternatives may be tried; when a bad idea is simulated, the only drivers that suffer gridlock are the simulated drivers inside a computer program.

Simulation has been called management's laboratory. It gives managers the capability to experiment with new ideas at relatively low cost. Perhaps even more important, the experiments are done in private. No one knows about the ideas that prove ineffective. Only changes that are shown to represent real improvements ever get beyond closed doors.

Simulation is used in a wide variety of situations: manufacturing, service, military and environmental analysis; investigating inanimate systems such as computer networks, biological systems such as rivers and lakes, and human systems such as hospital maternity wards. Questions addressed through simulation range from the mundane (who gets Saturday off next week?) to the grandiose (when will the world's population stop increasing?).

The increasing power of microcomputers has dramatically accelerated the availability and use of simulation. User-friendly tools such as the XCELL+ Factory Modeling System (Conway et al., 1990) and spreadsheet simulation (Cornwell and Modianos 1990) make simulation accessible to managers who have neither the time nor the inclination to write a computer program. Examples of the kind of problems suitable for special-purpose tools like XCELL+ will be discussed later. More powerful simulation tools include general-purpose simulation languages like GPSS, SIMSCRIPT, and SLAM. (These are described in Bratley et al. 1987 and Law and Kelton 1982, but we will not discuss them here.)

This appendix begins with an example, showing how a manager can quickly gain understanding of a system by experimenting with a simulation model. Section B-2 then introduces the basic concepts through elementary examples. The Monte Carlo method, used to include the element of randomness in a simulation model, is described in Section B-3. Analysis of the information produced by a simulation is the topic of Section B-4, followed by discussions of model validity and the appropriate managerial use of a simulation model.

B-1 SIMULATION USING A PERSONAL COMPUTER: TEJAS OUTFITTERS

Tejas Outfitters sells sporting goods by mail. Their volume is very large, and the operation strongly resembles a factory. Orders are entered into the computer, which prints out a ''pick list'' showing the quantity and the name of each item along with its location in the warehouse. The list goes to a ''picker'' who finds the items and places them in a cart similar to a grocery basket. Baskets are delivered to the packing and shipping area for final processing before mailing.

Sally Skyrunner is responsible for operation of the packing and shipping area. It is organized in two stages, packers and shippers. The packer chooses an appropriate box size and places the items from one basket into the box. A conveyor takes the box to the shipper who inspects the contents against the original order, makes sure that appropriate care has been taken to prevent damage, seals the box, and attaches a printed mailing label. The box is then weighed and appropriate postage is applied.

The flow of work is not smooth. The time required to pack a box varies from 0.5 to 1.5 minutes. The shipper uses from 0.75 to 2.0 minutes. Often there is a logjam of jobs between the two stages.

Figure B-1 shows the screen of a personal computer during an XCELL simulation (Conway et al. 1987) of packing and shipping. For a first experiment, Sally placed only one worker in packing (w1) and one worker in shipping (w2), even though she has several packing-shipping lines. In the figure, r1 represents the point where the baskets enter the packing and shipping area. The packer (w1) takes a basket from r1, packs the contents into a box, and passes the box to a storage buffer, b1. The shipper (w2) takes boxes from b1 and prepares them for shipping. Boxes ready for shipping leave the system through s1.

In designing the simulation, Sally assumed that the packer's processing times were equally likely to take on any value between 0.5 and 1.5 minutes, with the choice being made at random by the computer for each simulated order. The same kind of assumption was made for the shipper, but the limits were 0.75 and 2.0 minutes.

Figure B-2 shows what happened during the first 50 simulated minutes. The top diagram is a plot of the number of orders in temporary storage between the packer and the shipper. You can see what happened. The buffer quickly filled to capacity. The bottom diagram is a Gantt chart showing how the two simulated workers spent their time. Except for a brief period at the beginning, the shipper (w2) is busy all the time. The packer, however, fell idle (''blocked''

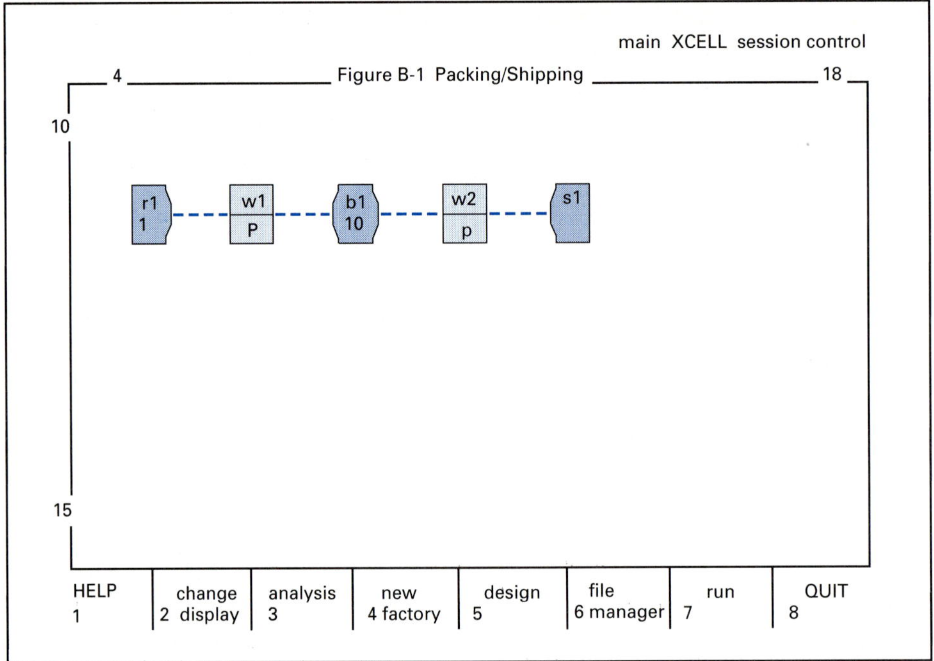

Figure B-1 An XCELL Model of Packing and Shipping at Tejas Outfitters

in the Gantt charts) for brief periods beginning at about 30 minutes into the simulation. What caused this idle time to occur?

Sally quickly realized that the packer is simply faster than the shipper. The line is not balanced. When the storage buffer fills up, the packer has no choice but to stop working and give the shipper time to finish a job. The packer is ''blocked.''

Figure B-3 shows a model that Sally used to test a change that she was considering: having more than one shipper draw from the same storage buffer. This would require a different layout because the current conveyor moves packages directly from one packer to one shipper, but she thought that a more flexible system might avoid some of the current logjam. The numbers below the workers in Figure B-3 are the average percentage of the time that they were busy during 1000 simulated minutes. Both w2 and w3 (the shippers) have substantial idle time; they are utilized only 62% and 76% of the time, respectively. And the buffer contents averaged only 0.05 boxes, so it was empty most of the time. Apparently, two shippers are faster than one packer.

Sally's third experimental model, shown in Figure B-4, tries to balance the work load by using two packers to ''feed'' three shippers. She found these results to be more satisfactory. Average idle time is less than 10% for the shippers, the packers are busy all the time, and very little inventory accumulates. The average throughput rate at the shipping area (s1) is 2 per minute. Figure B-5 shows that the inventory during 1000 simulated minutes varies randomly, reaching a maximum of 6 boxes on three occasions, but mostly remaining at 0, 1, or 2 boxes.

To this point, Sally had invested less than one hour of her time designing and running the simulations. She went on to test many other alternative arrangements for her packers and shippers. Among the ideas she tested was leav-

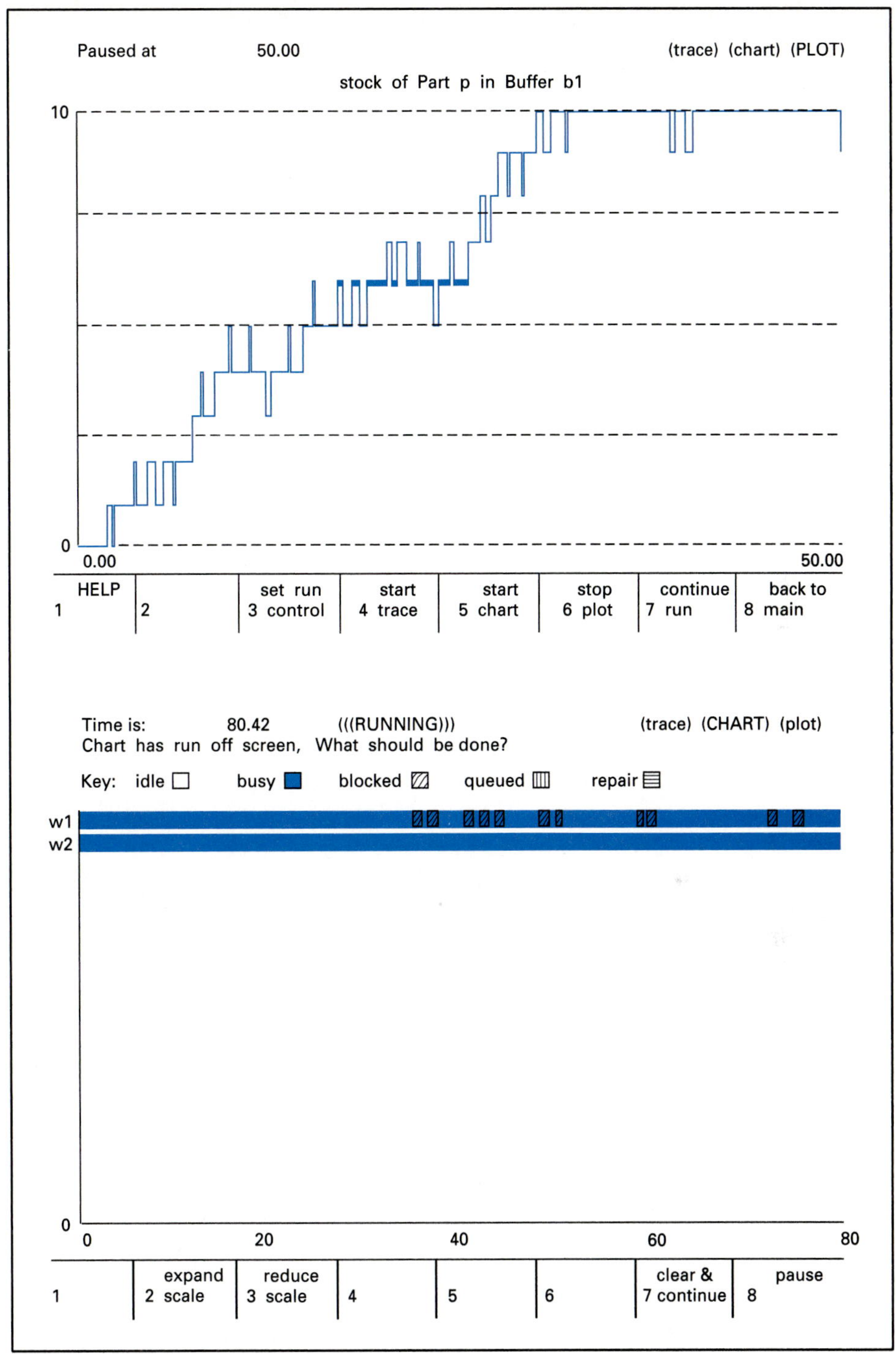

Figure B-2 Inventory and Worker Utilization In Packing and Shipping

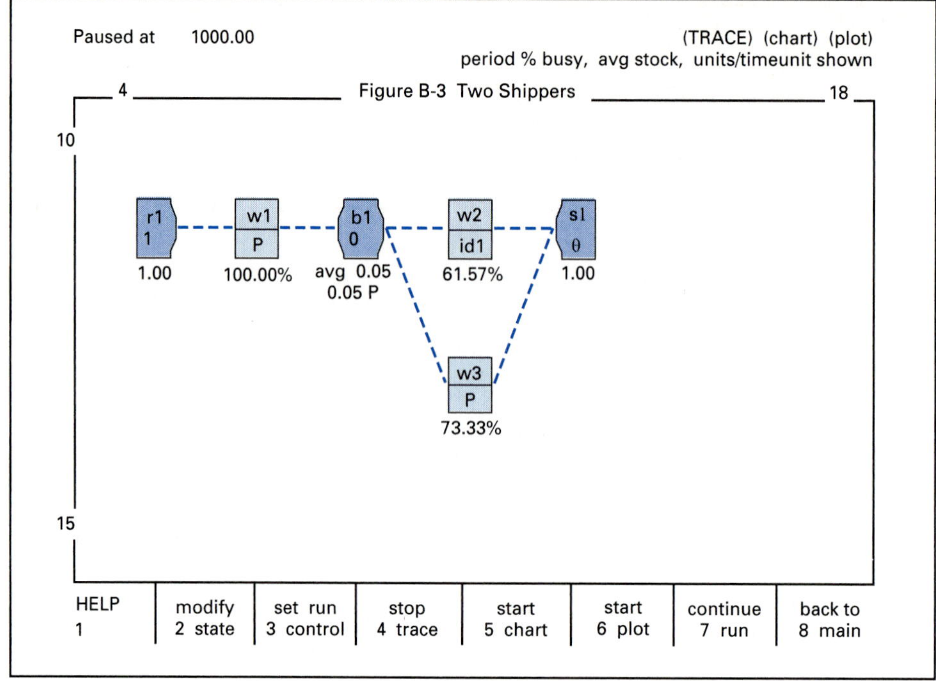

Figure B-3 One Packer Feeding Two Shippers

Figure B-4 Two Packers Feeding Three Shippers

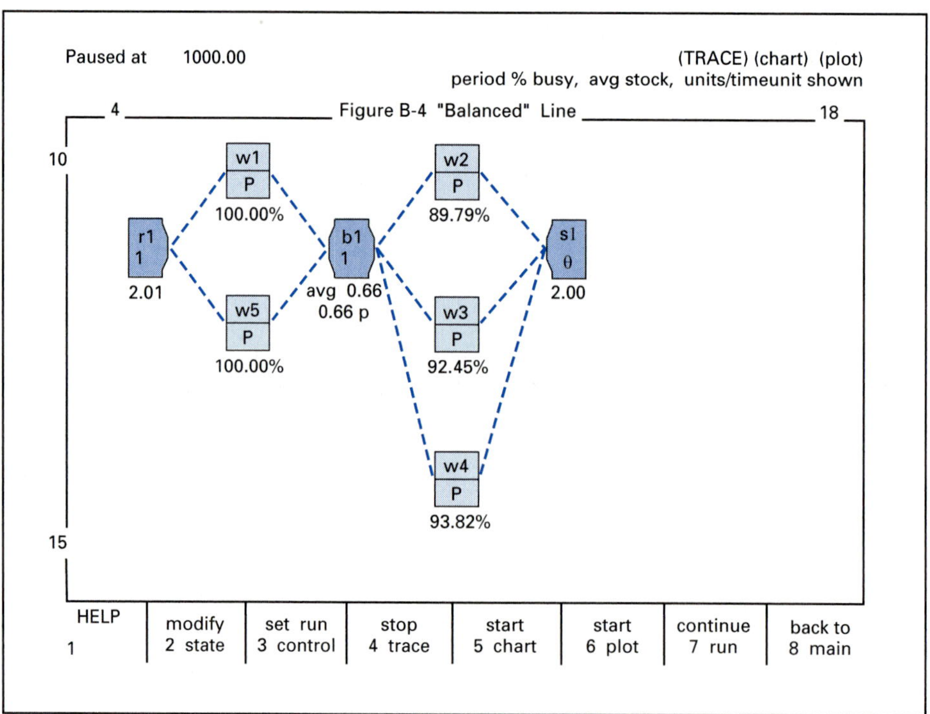

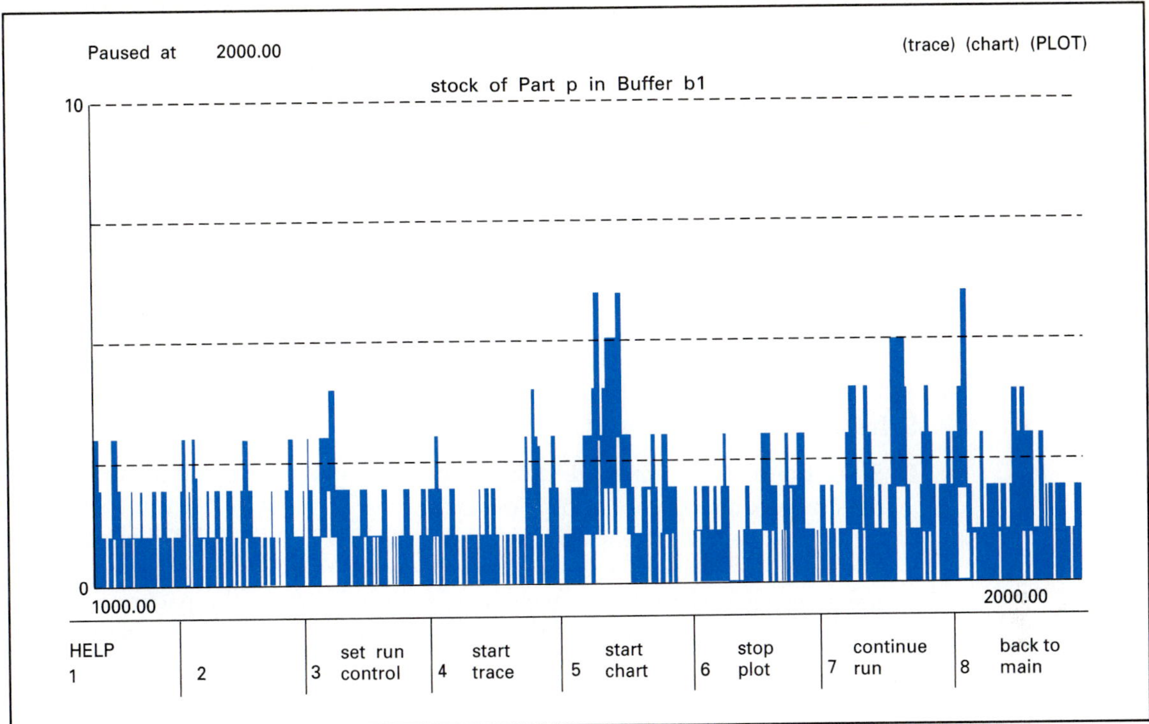

Figure B-5 Inventory with Two Packers and Three Shippers

ing the current layout in place (like Figure B-1) but having the workers help each other as needed. When the shipper falls behind, Sally assumed, the packer would do part of the shipper's job on each box. This would temporarily slow the packer down and speed the shipper up, relieving the logjam. (This is called dynamic line balancing. See Ostolaza et al. 1990.)

Special-purpose simulation packages are designed for ease of use. For example, in XCELL there are only five building blocks for designing a factory simulation model: receiving areas, work centers, storage buffers, shipping areas, and maintenance centers. A more advanced version, XCELL+, includes automated guided vehicles (AGV) to simulate materials handling. Any of these may be created or copied with a single keystroke and are easily modified to suit the situation. Running and collecting data are equally simple, making use of animation and graphics as well as numerical summaries.

Ease of use has a price, however. There are many situations that are difficult or impossible to model with a package like XCELL+. Nonetheless, the attractiveness of a microcomputer package that is easy to learn and use makes this approach to simulation a valuable one. More special-purpose simulation packages are becoming available all the time.

REVIEW PROBLEMS

1. Compute the average processing time per box for the packing operation, and also for the shipping operation. Use these two numbers to explain Sally's first results, shown in Figure B-2.

2. How many boxes per minute can one packer pack, on the average? One shipper ship? Use these answers to explain the ''near balance'' achieved in Figure B-4.

3. Since three shippers are faster than two packers, one might expect that no inventory would occur in the model of Figure B-4, yet Figure B-5 shows that this is not true. Explain why inventory occurs even though boxes can be removed from the buffer faster than they come in, on the average.

4. Based on the simulation results, how large should the storage buffer between two packers and three shippers be? How could the simulation model be used to shed light on this question?

Solutions

1. Since the packing times are uniformly distributed between 0.5 and 1.5 minutes (according to the description), the average must be 1.0 minutes. Similarly, the average time for the shipper is (0.75 + 2.0)/2 or 1.375 minutes per box. This confirms that the shipper is slower than the packer. In fact, the imbalance is 0.375 minutes per box, which is 37.5% of the packer's average time. So the packer must stop eventually, and spend a fair portion of time doing nothing.

2. Packer: 1 minute per box is 1 box per minute. Shipper: 1.375 minutes per box is 1/1.375 = 0.7273 box per minute. Two packers can do 2 boxes per minute, whereas 3 shippers can do 3(0.7273) = 2.1818 boxes per minute. Thus, the shipping stage is faster, and must be idle part of the time. Their average utilization should be 2.0/2.1818 = 0.9167. (See Appendix A: Utilization = arrival rate divided by service rate.) This is very near the numbers in Figure B-4.

3. Randomness of processing times is the key. These processing times vary by as much as 50%, so we can expect that the slower stage will sometimes get done before the faster stage. When this happens, inventory occurs. The random variation is apparent in Figure B-5.

4. Figure B-5 suggests that there is no need for capacity larger than 6 boxes. In fact, since inventory reaches 6 very briefly, it would be interesting to know whether capacity for storing 5 boxes would be just as good. Another simulation run, with a capacity-5 buffer, could answer that question. In fact, a series of simulations with various buffer capacities would show how much effect reduced buffer capacity would have on the output rate of this system.

B-2 MANUAL SIMULATION USING HISTORICAL DATA: CARTHAGE MEDICAL CLINIC

Simulation is so easy that we are going to do it rather than explain how it is done. Through the example of the Carthage Medical Clinic, you will learn the basics of how a simulation is actually carried out. The main difference between this example and simulation models you might someday use is size; most realistic models are larger.

Table B-1 The First Ten Patients on Three Days at Carthage Clinic

	Day 1[a]		Day 2		Day 3	
Patient	T^b	T_S[c] (minutes)	T	T_S	T	T_S
P1	1:05 P.M.	15	1:00	20	1:15	5
P2	1:15	15	1:05	15	1:20	20
P3	1:20	10	1:15	10	1:30	15
P4	1:30	10	1:15	15	1:35	15
P5	1:45	15	1:25	10	1:50	20
P6	1:45	5	1:40	15	1:50	10
P7	1:50	10	1:45	5	2:05	N
P8	1:55	5	2:00	N	2:20	N
P9	2:05	N[d]	2:15	N	2:25	N
P10	2:10	N	2:15	N	2:30	N

[a]Opening time = 1:00 P.M. and closing time = 2:00 P.M.
[b]T = arrival time.
[c]T_S = service duration.
[d]Arrived after clinic closed. Not served.

The data in Table B-1 were collected on three days of the first week of January 1990 at the Carthage Medical Clinic. (Much more data were actually collected. We are keeping it small here to be merciful to the reader.) On those days, the arrival times of all patients were noted as they walked in the door. Service times were noted as follows: ''Begin service time'' was recorded when a patient met with a doctor, and ''end service time'' occurred when the doctor was free to see another patient. Service time was calculated as ''end service'' minus ''begin service.''

With these data, several questions were addressed concerning the operation of the clinic. The focus of the investigation was the punctuality of the doctors. The clinic opens at 1:00 P.M. but the doctors arrive somewhat later. This causes delays in the schedule for the rest of the clinic session.

PROBLEM 1: *How many patients are already present when the doctors arrive?*

PROBLEM 2: *The clinic closes its doors at 2:00, but the clinic ''session'' does not officially end until all patients present at 2:00 have been seen by a doctor. How late do the sessions end, and how is that affected by the punctuality of the doctors?*

PROBLEM 3: *How many minutes must patients wait, and how does this change when the doctors are late?*

Analysis of Problem 1: Patients Present When Doctors Arrive

The answer to problem 1 is readily apparent from Table B-1, if you know what time the doctors arrived. For example, if the doctors arrived at 1:30, how many patients would already be there on each day? The answers are 4 on day 1, 5 on day 2, and 3 on the last day. The average is 4.00 patients, with a range from 3 to 5.

Now, suppose that they were to arrive at 1:15 instead. The answers are 2, 4, and 1 patients present on the respective days, for an average of 2.33 and a range from 1 to 4.

This is probably the simplest simulation you will ever see, but it serves to illustrate four points. First, *data from a simulation do not give an absolutely certain answer*. Just like in real life, there is a random element, so we need statistics to describe the results. And we need to pay attention to sample size. Only three days of data gives us only three observations. To increase the accuracy of the averages that we calculated, we could (presumably) collect more data.

Second, *the purpose of a simulation is to answer "what if" questions*. What if the doctors arrive at 1:15? At 1:30? Accordingly, the results of the simulation are not usually final answers to the real question (such as what time the doctors should get there) but rather part of the information needed to answer a larger question. What else would we need to know to address the question of when the doctors should arrive? Does it matter that they may be coming to the clinic from the hospital where they were treating seriously ill patients?

Figure B-6 shows a typical format for reporting the results of a set of simulation experiments. It shows how "sensitive" the number of patients is to the lateness of the doctors. The average number waiting increases almost linearly with the doctors' lateness. The upper and lower limits are one way to illustrate how variable the operation is. Thus, in one picture we have captured our first two points: variability and "what if."

The third lesson from the clinic example is that *all models are based on a set of assumptions*. Here we have assumed that the patient arrival pattern is not influenced by the doctors' punctuality. The same patient arrival pattern was used when the doctors were 15 minutes late as when they were 30 minutes late. We have also assumed that the data on patient arrivals are somehow representative of what will happen in the future. Are data collected in the first week of January representative? Probably not, because of the proximity of the New Year's holiday.

In general, simulation models are based on assumptions that do not exactly capture reality, for a simple reason: if you ever want to finish building the simulation model, you have to simplify reality in some way. To answer the questions posed, we do not need to know the age distribution of the patients, for example.

The final point concerns the operation of a simulation. By scanning the data, we can tell when, for example, the first patient will arrive each day. However, it would be "unfair" to use that information to schedule the arrival of the doctors, since they have no way of knowing exact patient-arrival times. The

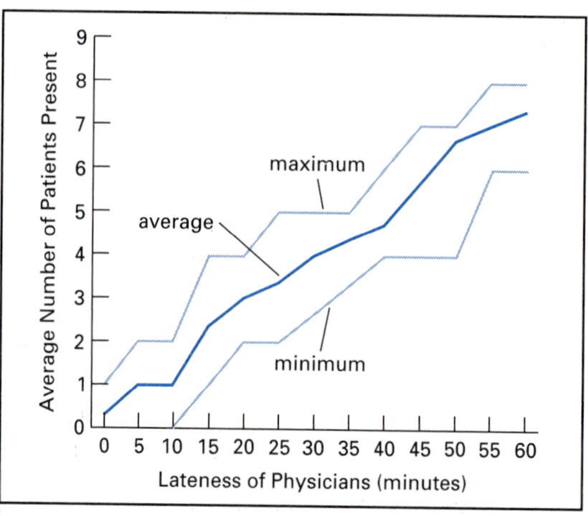

Figure B-6 Number of Patients Present When the Doctors Arrive

table of arrival times is the simulation's "calendar of future events." The point is that *this calendar may only be used to keep track of events, not to simulate decisions* such as the doctors' choices of when to show up for work.

Analysis of Problem 2: When Can We Go Home?

This question addresses the closing portion of the clinic session. As a consequence, the simulation must continue for a longer simulated time period. To simulate a complete session, we must know how many doctors there are, their arrival times, and which patients they can see. We will assume that there are two doctors—one arrives at 1:15 and the other at 1:30—and that either doctor will see any patient on a first come, first served basis.

Figure B-7 depicts simulating the first day. The first patient, P1, arrives at 1:05. The first doctor and the second patient both arrive at 1:15. Doctor 1 sees P1 while P2 waits. The third patient, P3, joins the queue at 1:20 and both patients wait until 1:30 before being seen. And so on. At 2:00, when the doors close, P7 is still with doctor 1, and P8 is in the waiting room. The session ends at 2:05 on this day.

The same method can be used to show that day 2 and day 3 both end at 2:10. Therefore, based on this small sample, we estimate that the average session ends at 2:08.33 ranging from 2:05 to 2:10, if doctors arrive as we assumed.

How would you generate a graph like Figure B-6 to help finish this problem? We must run more simulations with different lateness patterns for the physicians. However, allowing one doctor to arrive at 1:15 and the other at 1:30 raises another question. What is lateness? In our example, the average lateness was 22.5 minutes (halfway between 15 and 30). Would we get the same result if both doctors showed up at 1:22.5? Probably not.

This is an example of a difficulty with all modeling efforts. It has been whimsically labeled "the curse of dimensionality." The more dimensions a problem has (to make it more realistic), the harder it is to study. Here we faced the difficulty of presenting the results graphically, but there is also the issue of how many experiments to run.

For example, Table B-2 shows 28 combinations of lateness. To evaluate them all would require 28 simulations. Now suppose that we have identified five different arrival rates of patients, one for each day of the week. This could multiply the number of runs by 5. Clearly things have quickly gotten out of hand.

There are many ways to deal with the curse of dimensionality, and we do not have space to discuss them here. "Experimental design" is the topic if you wish to pursue it further.

Figure B-7 Simulation of Day 1 at the Carthage Medical Clinic

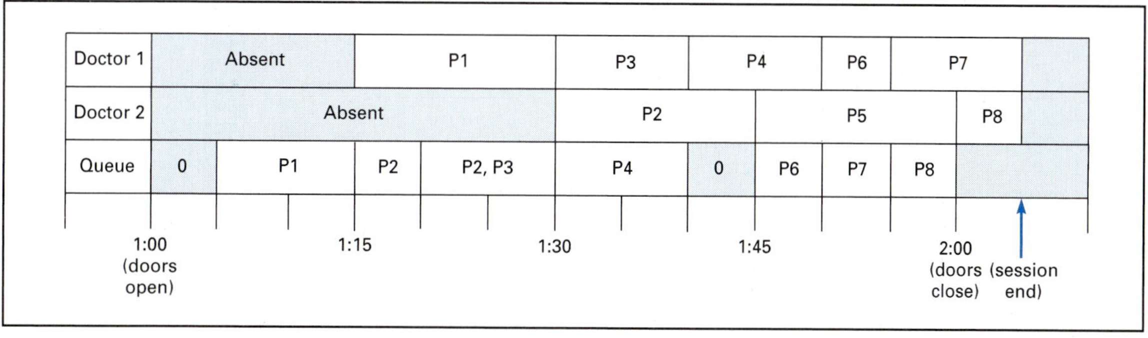

Table B-2 Possible Experiments to Study Physician Lateness

Lateness of Doctor 2	Lateness of Doctor 1 (minutes)						
	0	5	10	15	20	25	30
0	X	X	X	X	X	X	X
5		X	X	X	X	X	X
10			X	X	X	X	X
15				X	X	X	X
20					X	X	X
25						X	X
30							X

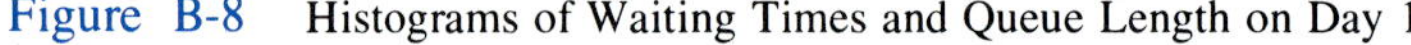

Analysis of Problem 3: Waiting Times

The third question concerns waiting time throughout the clinic session. The information we need is back in Figure B-7. The bar labeled "queue" shows that P1 waited 10 minutes (from 1:05 to 1:15), P2 waited 15 minutes (1:15 to 1:30), and so on. The waiting times, in order of patient arrival, are 10, 15, 10, 10, 0, 5, 5, and 5. Early arrivals waited longer than late arrivals. Is that a general pattern? This is only the result for one day. We should examine the results for the other two days to see if there is a similar pattern. Again the issue of sample size is important. We should simulate many more days before drawing any conclusions.

Figure B-8 summarizes the waiting times in another manner, a histogram. It shows that most patients waited either 5 or 10 minutes on day 1, and that no one waited longer than 15 minutes. Again, this figure would be much more satisfactory with more data.

The queue can be analyzed in another way: How many patients are waiting at a given time? Once again we can glean the necessary data from Figure B-7. There are three 5-minute intervals with no patients in queue. Beginning at 1:20 there are two intervals with two waiting patients. The rest of the intervals have one lonely patient in the waiting room. The histogram of these results is included in Figure B-8. It shows that the waiting room was empty 23% of the time, contained one patient 62% of the time, and two patients 15% of the time.

Figure B-8 Histograms of Waiting Times and Queue Length on Day 1

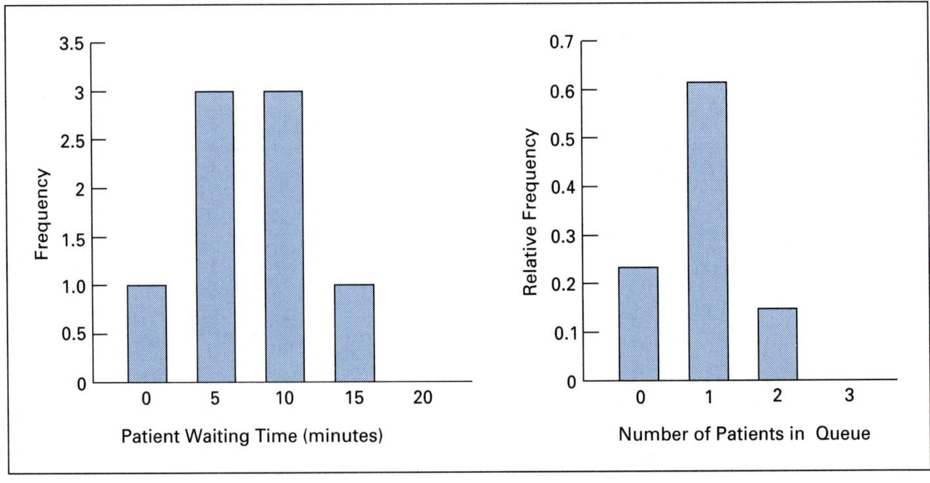

Entities, Attributes, Events, and Timing

A brief introduction to some of the basic elements of simulation will conclude this section. *Entities* are the things being simulated—doctors and patients in the Clinic simulation. *Attributes* are properties that describe the entities, listed as follows for Carthage Clinic:

Patient Attributes

arrival time

location in clinic (waiting room, examination room)

service duration

Doctor Attributes

arrival time

status (absent, idle, serving patient *n*)

time until free (if currently serving a patient)

An *event* occurs when something changes in the system, typically some attribute. In the list that follows, see if you can explain why some events are determined outside the simulation and others are determined by the progress of the simulation:

Externally Determined (Exogenous) Events	*Internally Determined (Endogenous) Events*
Clinic opens	Patient's service begins
Patient arrives	Patient's service ends, patient departs
Doctor arrives	Doctor departs
Clinic doors close	Clinic session ends

To see the external-versus-internal distinction, consider "Doctor arrives" versus "Doctor departs." In our examples, we decided ahead of time when the doctors were going to show up for work, but we had to simulate a full day of operation to figure out when they would be able to leave. If we changed something about the way the simulation operates, the internal event might be affected but the external one would not. For example, if the second doctor were removed from the simulation, the first doctor's arrival would be unaffected, but he or she might be very late for supper.

Timing refers to how we keep track of the simulation. In the clinic example we simply move the simulated clock forward 5 minutes and look to see whether anything is supposed to happen. For example, Figure B-7 showed that many events happened at 1:30: Doctor 2 and patient 4 arrived, patient 1 departed, and patients 2 and 3 began their consultations with the doctors. Having marked all of these changes, the simulation advances to 1:35 and finds that nothing happens, so the clock jumps another 5 minutes to 1:40, and so on. This is called a time-step simulation.

Event-step is another way of controlling the timing. The difference is that after processing all events at 1:30, the simulation would be programmed to scan a calendar of future events and simply jump to the next relevant time, which would be 1:40 in this case. The difference is minor in our example, but can be important. Event-step can simulate continuous time, whereas time-step requires discrete time periods.

Manual simulation is very tedious. (You should arrange for someone else to do it!) If you are going to pass the job to someone else, it is vital to explain

Table B-3 Instructions for the Carthage Clinic Simulation

1. Begin day. t = 1:00 P.M., all doctors are absent, queue empty.
2. If any patients have just arrived, enter their ID numbers in the queue list.
3. If any doctors have just arrived, change them from absent to idle.
4. If any patients are to depart now, change their doctors from busy to idle.
5. If there are both idle doctors and waiting patients, remove the next patient from the queue and place with an idle doctor. Note the patient's (future) departure time by adding service time to t. Change doctor from idle to busy.
6. Repeat step 5 until queue is empty or all doctors are busy.
7. $t = t + 5$ (move clock forward 5 minutes).
8. Repeat steps 2 to 7 until closing time.
9. After closing time, repeat steps 4, 5, 6, and 7 until all patients have departed, sending idle doctors home when the queue is empty.

exactly what you want done. Table B-3 lists a set of instructions that one could follow, either to continue the simulations in the same manner or to program a computer to do the job. Steps 3, 4, and 5 all refer to entities, particularly to changes in their attributes. That is, those steps simulate events. Step 7 is the time-step clock.

REVIEW PROBLEMS

1. If both doctors arrive at 1:40, how many patients would be present? Give an answer for each of the three days represented in Table B-1 and compare your results with Figure B-6.

2. a. Use Figure B-7 to identify arrival and departure times, as well as the time when service begins (patient and doctor meet) for every patient on day 1.
   b. Compute waiting times for each patient. Use your results to verify the histogram in Figure B-8.
   c. Why do patient departures occur in a different order than patient arrivals?

3. In the clinic simulation, we assumed that the arrival time of the doctors would not influence the arrival times of the patients. Discuss the adequacy and usefulness of this assumption in reality.

4. What new entities, attributes, and events would be introduced if a physician's assistant (PA) were used in the Carthage Clinic instead of one of the doctors? (A PA can serve most patient needs but must consult with the doctor periodically and might turn a patient over to the doctor if the case is too complicated.)

5. Follow the instructions in Table B-3 and see if the events match the chart in Figure B-7. Use the patient arrival times for day 1, given in Table B-1. Simulate all events that occur through time 1:15.

6. What limitations does the Carthage Clinic simulation have because we are using historical data (real, not simulated) to simulate patient arrival times?

Solutions

1. 4 on day 1, 6 on day 2 and 4 on day 3. The average is 4.67, the minimum is 4, and the maximum is 6, just as in Figure B-6 for lateness of 40 minutes.

2. a.

Patient	Arrives	Service Begins	Departs	Waiting Time
P1	1:05	1:15	1:30	10
P2	1:15	1:30	1:45	15
P3	1:20	1:30	1:40	10
P4	1:30	1:40	1:50	10
P5	1:45	1:45	2:00	0
P6	1:45	1:50	1:55	5
P7	1:50	1:55	2:05	5
P8	1:55	2:00	2:05	5

b. Waiting times = ''service begins'' minus ''arrives'' in the foregoing table. Frequencies: 0 occurs once, 5 occurs three times, 10 occurs three times and 15 occurs once, just as in Figure B-6.

c. P3 leaves before P2 because P3 had a shorter service time, and they started service at the same time.

3. If doctors are habitually late, the patients may adjust their arrival patterns accordingly. However, we have no way of knowing whether this would, in fact, occur. It is useful to ignore this effect, since that allows us to get some approximate answers about the effects of physician lateness.

4. New entity: Physician's assistant.

New attributes: Patient status now includes ''interrupted'' and ''transferred,'' as well as ''waiting'' and ''being served.'' A new attribute is whether the patient's needs can be met by the assistant. Doctor and assistant status both now include ''in consultation.''

New events: Service halts temporarily.
Service resumes.
Patient transferred from assistant to doctor.

5. The steps are shown in the following table. Notice that there are events that do not appear in Figure B-7. For example, at 1:15 when doctor 1 arrives, he or she is temporarily assigned the status ''idle'' in step 2. Then, step 4 moves the patient P1 into the examination room with the doctor and changes the doctor to ''busy,'' still at 1:15. The doctor was idle for zero time. This is just a convention used in the instructions. These zero-time situations have no effect on the results.

Time	Step Number (Table B-3)	Action
1:00	1	Opening
	2	Nothing
	3	Nothing
	4	Nothing
	5	Nothing
	6	Nothing
	7	t = 1:05
1:05	2	P1 arrives, joins queue
	3–6	Nothing
	7	t = 1:10
1:10	2–6	Nothing
	7	t = 1:15
1:15	2	P2 arrives, joins queue
	3	Doctor 1 arrives, idle
	4	Nothing
	5	Doctor 1 begins with P1
	6	P2 remains in queue
	7	t = 1:20

6. Historical data may be irrelevant. For example, arrival rates may be increasing if the clinic is gaining customers. There could be seasonal patterns, in which case we would need to collect data from several different times of the year. Most important, it will be impossible to simulate thousands of time periods (as Sally did in the previous section, using XCELL) because we would not have that much data, nor would it be appropriate to spend our time collecting that data. See the next section for an alternative, using the Monte Carlo method.

B-3 SIMULATING WITH ARTIFICIAL DATA: MONTE CARLO

One purpose of simulation is to experiment with ideas and situations that have never occurred before. Obtaining historical data is impossible in such circumstances, but it is often possible to describe an unknown situation by using a probability distribution. For example, one might study the pattern of occurrences of traffic accidents and conclude that the number of accidents per hour has the Poisson probability distribution,[1] with a mean value that varies with the time of day, the day of the week, and weather conditions. Simulating the occurrence of accidents ten years in the future would then involve forecasting the average rate and using the *Monte Carlo* method to generate simulated data with all the patterns of today's accidents, but using a rate corresponding to the 10-year forecast and randomness that is governed by the Poisson probability distribution. The same method could generate a series of simulated equipment failures to test a proposed maintenance system or a series of demands to test a new inventory control system.

The idea of Monte Carlo is quite simple. The first step is to find or create

[1]Four probability distributions are described in Appendix D, Tables 2 through 5.

a device, like a roulette wheel, that takes on different states randomly (where it stops, nobody knows). A coin is the simplest device, and is quite an effective simulator of the boy-or-girl outcome in childbirth. This device is not perfect, of course, since the heads-or-tails outcomes are equally likely, whereas more boys are born than girls.

The second step in Monte Carlo is to match the outcomes of the random device with the outcomes of the process being simulated. This must be done in such a way that the simulated events will have the correct probability of occurring.

Suppose that we randomize with a wheel of fortune, with 100 pegs arrayed with perfect symmetry about the periphery and a single pointer fixed in position. This device has 100 equally likely outcomes, which may be divided up any way we wish, to mimic a real process. Consider the probability distribution of daily demand for hot dogs at Joe's Corner Hot Dog Stand (Table B-4), which was derived from a study of historical sales. We could simulate daily demands by painting the wheel of fortune as shown in Figure B-9 (making certain to use weightless paint). There should be 30 pegs in the sector labeled "0 hot dogs," 40 pegs in the "1 hot dog" sector, and so on.

If each peg is labeled with a two-digit number (from 00 to 99), one convenient assignment of pegs to "hot dogs demanded" is shown in Table B-4. There are two important relationships between the peg numbers and the probabilities in Table B-4. First, one peg = 1% of probability (since there are 100

Table B-4 Probability Distribution of Daily Hot Dog Demands

Hot dogs	0	1	2	3	4
Probability	0.30	0.40	0.20	0.07	0.03
Peg numbers (Figure B-9)	01–30	31–70	71–90	91–97	98–00

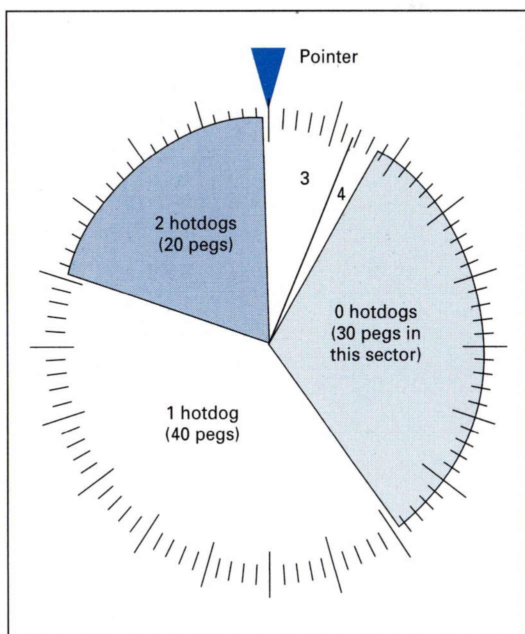

Figure B-9 Wheel of Fortune With 100 Pegs: A Random Generator of Hot Dog Demands

equally likely pegs); thus, 30 pegs were assigned to achieve a 30% probability of zero demand, and so on. Second, the peg numbers correspond to the cumulative probability of hot dog demand. That is, the probability of one or fewer hot dogs is 0.30 + 0.40 = 0.70, the same as the last peg number assigned to "one hot dog." This comes about because of the way we arranged the peg assignment, and it can always be done that way. We will use this *cumulative probability assignment* again, as soon as we have divested ourselves of the rather awkward wheel of fortune.

Physical devices have many drawbacks as random-number generators. One of the main drawbacks is that they do not fit into a computer very well. Fortunately, mathematical formulas are commonly available to generate *pseudo-random numbers,* which can be made to appear completely random for long periods of time. These numbers are decimal fractions uniformly distributed between 0 and 1, exactly fitting the requirements of our cumulative probability assignment method. A computer performs Monte Carlo by generating a pseudo-random number and matching it against the cumulative probability. Table B-5 shows the same random-number assignment as Table B-4 except that a decimal notation (rather than peg numbers) is used to represent the painted areas on the wheel. Suppose that the pseudo-random-number generator spewed forth the following five numbers: 0.53076, 0.67675, 0.11682, 0.80779, and 0.18002. The first number, 0.53076, falls in the "1 hot dog" interval in Table B-5, so Joe sells one simulated hot dog on the first simulated day. The second day also has 1 sale, and the remaining days have sales of 0, 2, and 0 hot dogs, respectively.

Continuous variables may also be simulated by the cumulative probability method. Recall, for a moment, the Carthage Medical Clinic simulation. Time was treated as a discrete variable, moving in five-minute increments. That was done for convenience (allowing us to use the time-step method of simulation), but continuous time can also be simulated. Figure B-10 shows a cumulative probability distribution of the time between customer arrivals at Joe's Corner Hotdog Stand, with an illustration of how to convert a random number to a simulated interval:

> First, obtain a random number from a table or pseudo-random-number generator (0.74217 in the example). Next find that value on the vertical axis. Then move straight over to the curve, and from there, straight down. In this case, the result is 6.1 minutes between customers.

These two methods (table and graph) of using cumulative probabilities are equivalent. Finding the random number on the vertical axis is the same as looking it up in the cumulative probability table. Other methods for continuous variables, using mathematical formulas, are illustrated in problems 6, 7 and 8.

Manual simulations can also take advantage of Monte Carlo by using tables of random digits such as Table 1 in Appendix D. One merely reads successive numbers from the table, rather than spinning the wheel of fortune.

Looking back, we see that Monte Carlo simulation requires two things:

Table B-5 Random-Number Assignment by the Cumulative Probability Rule

Hot dogs	0	1	2	3	4
Probability	0.30	0.40	0.20	0.07	0.03
Random numbers	0–0.3	0.3–0.7	0.7–0.9	0.9–0.97	0.97–1.0

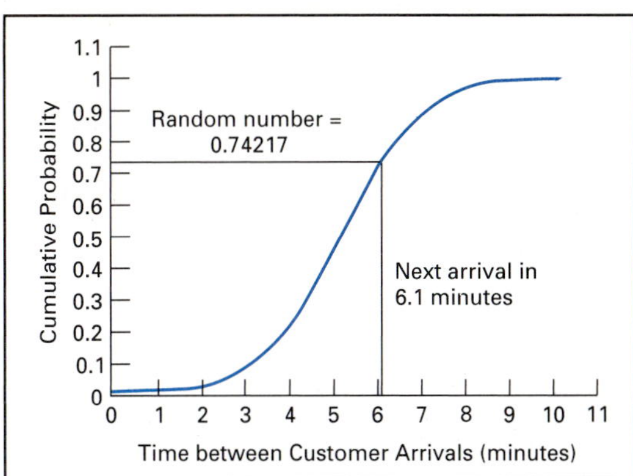

Figure B-10 Cumulative Distribution Method for a Continuous Random Variable

random numbers and a probability distribution. Random numbers are easily obtained, either from tables like Table D-1 or from a random-number generator in a computer. The probability distribution must be obtained by the simulator (you) in one way or another. At the beginning of this section one method was mentioned: identifying a known probability distribution (such as Poisson or normal) from historical data and modifying it as necessary to fit the situation being simulated. Sometimes only an opinion is available. For example, a foreman may be able to give an estimate of how long a job will take, and may also be able to give optimistic and pessimistic time estimates. There are several methods for incorporating such rough data into a simulation, which we will not pursue.

The data generated by the Monte Carlo method can be used in exactly the same way as the real data in the examples of Section B-2. Monte Carlo can therefore be viewed as a method for generating enough realistic data so that adequate experimentation can be done with a simulation model.

REVIEW PROBLEMS

1. The accompanying table gives a list of random digits and probabilities for times between arrivals and service times for patients at the Carthage Clinic. Generate five patients' arrivals, recording an arrival time and a service time for each. (Remember, the doors open at 1:00 P.M.)

Time between Arrivals		Service Duration	
Time (minutes)	Probability	Time (minutes)	Probability
0	0.17	0	0.00
5	0.40	5	0.20
10	0.20	10	0.23
15	0.23	15	0.37
20	0.00	20	0.20

Random numbers for arrivals: 3513 6976 9847 1622 3874

Random numbers for service times: 2883 0882 4311 2741 2020

2. Use the simulated times you generated in review problem 1 to simulate the first five arrivals, using a Gantt chart like Figure B-7 to keep track of the simulated activities.

3. Use the first five random numbers from problem 1 to simulate five arrivals to Joe's Corner Hotdog Stand, using the continuous distribution in Figure B-10. Assume that an arrival last occurred at 4:00 P.M. and that you are simulating the next five.

Solutions

1. First, construct random-number-assignment tables using cumulative probabilities:

Time between Arrivals		Service Duration	
Time	**Random Numbers**	**Service Time**	**Random Numbers**
0	0001–1700	5	0001–2000
5	1701–5700	10	2001–4300
10	5701–7700	15	4301–8000
15	7701–0000	20	8001–0000

Next, use the random numbers to generate arrivals and service times. (Note that the simulated time between arrivals for P2 is 10 minutes, so P2 arrives at 1:15, 10 minutes *after* P1.)

Patient	Random Number	Interarrival Time	Arrival Time	Random Number	Service Time
P1	3513	5	1:05	2883	10
P2	6976	10	1:15	0882	5
P3	9847	15	1:30	4311	15
P4	1622	0	1:30	2741	10
P5	3874	5	1:35	2020	10

2.

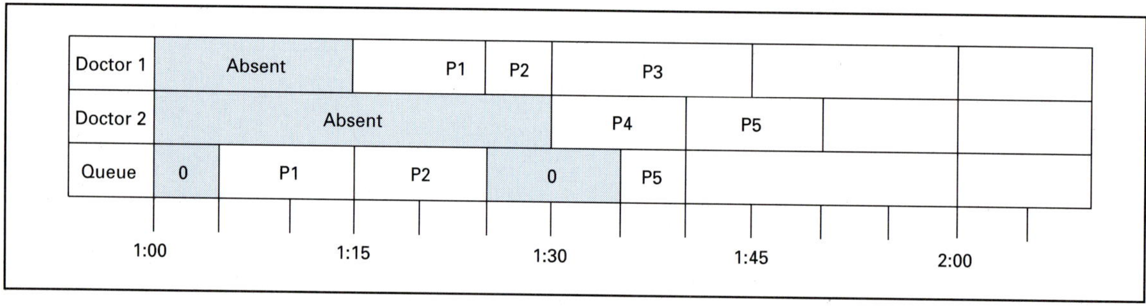

3. Since it is difficult to read the figure accurately, we used only the first two digits of the random numbers.

Random Number	Time (minutes)	Arrival Time
35	4.6	4:04.6
69	5.9	4:10.5
98	8.2	4:18.7
16	3.6	4:22.3
38	4.7	4:27.0

B-4 RELIABILITY AND VALIDITY

How do you know if a simulation is any good? In this section, we will address two aspects of this question: Is the model valid? Is the data from the simulation reliable?

Validity: Is The Model Real Enough?

Validity is the first priority in model building. If the model cannot be trusted, it will be of no use. However, validity comes in degrees, and it is not practical to strive for a perfect model (if there is such a thing), since development time and effort would be unjustifiably expensive. Validity must be defined and evaluated in relationship to the intended use of the model.

Evaluation of model validity, often called validation, may be visualized as consisting of three stages (Law and Kelton 1982, chapter 10):

1. Compare the assumptions of the model to existing theory, known research findings, and intuition. (Choose the best possible building blocks for the model.)
2. Subject these assumptions, one at a time, to empirical (statistical) tests, whenever possible.
3. Test the overall model's performance and its predictive power when compared with management intuition and a variety of real data.

The first two stages refer to the details of model construction, whereas the third involves a look at the performance of the complete model. These three stages are applied repeatedly during model development and testing, prior to any decision making based on the model.

Theoretically, model-improvement efforts should continue until the cost of further improvement exceeds the gain that a better model would make possible. Practically speaking, you never know exactly when this balance occurs. The decision maker should be involved throughout the development of a model, passing judgment on the adequacy of assumptions as they are incorporated in the model.

As an example of the three stages of validation, consider the Carthage Medical Clinic from Section B-2. One of the assumptions was that patients, once in the waiting room, do not get angry and leave if waiting time becomes lengthy. One could appeal to research findings on this question, if they exist, or one could ask someone who works in the clinic how often they believe people leave. (That would be a stage-1 validity test.) If it seems to be a significant issue, one could conduct an on-site experiment (a stage-2 validity test) to observe the circumstances under which, and the likelihood that, people leave.

A third approach would be to incorporate, in the model, a probability of leaving the queue. Because it is difficult or impossible to accurately estimate such a probability value from real data, one should carry out a sensitivity analysis; that is, vary the probability of departure and see how influential it is on the results and on the decisions we might make based on the model. This is a stage-3 analysis, because it focuses on overall model performance.

Stage 3 for the clinic example would also include a test to see whether the model behaves like a real system. One method would be to configure the model to mimic the existing clinic and test whether the simulated waiting times were similar to the actual waiting times.

It is also desirable to put the model through its paces by trying out many different ideas, and seeing whether the model's predictions make sense. For example, does an increase in the doctor's lateness result in an increase in patient delays? Does a reduction in the variability of patient arrivals reduce idle time? Or, in general, does the model behave like the real system, in the judgment of the manager? A formal version of this approach is called a Turing test, in which a knowledgeable manager is presented with two sets of data and required to decide which one came from a model and which from a real system. The manager is allowed to ask for more data. If the manager cannot tell the difference, the model passes the test.

If a model fails a validity test, one must consider the possible sources of error:

1. model design
2. model programming or execution
3. data input (including the random-number generator, if one is used)
4. interpretation of the results
5. use of the model

It is easy to lose sight of error sources 4 and 5. It may happen, for example, that the model is rejected because its results contradict the intuition of the manager. Two possibilities should be investigated. Were the results improperly presented? Are there alternative explanations of the unexpected findings that were not fully explored? One should also ask whether the model is being used improperly, in a way not intended by its designers. It is always worthwhile to consider these possibilities before beginning a detailed investigation of the sort suggested by error sources 1, 2, and 3.

Reliability: Was The Model Run Correctly?

Run length is how long you run a simulation. The clinic simulation was run for three simulated days (or less) in Section B-2, but that resulted in a very small amount of data. Just how long should the run length be? The answer depends on how you are using the model.

In Section B-1 Sally Skyrunner used her XCELL simulation model in several different ways. First, she simulated a short time period so that she could get a feeling for what was going on between the packers and the shippers. Figure B-2 showed very clearly the imbalance between them: Inventory quickly increased until the buffer was full. Later, she simulated 1000 time periods to

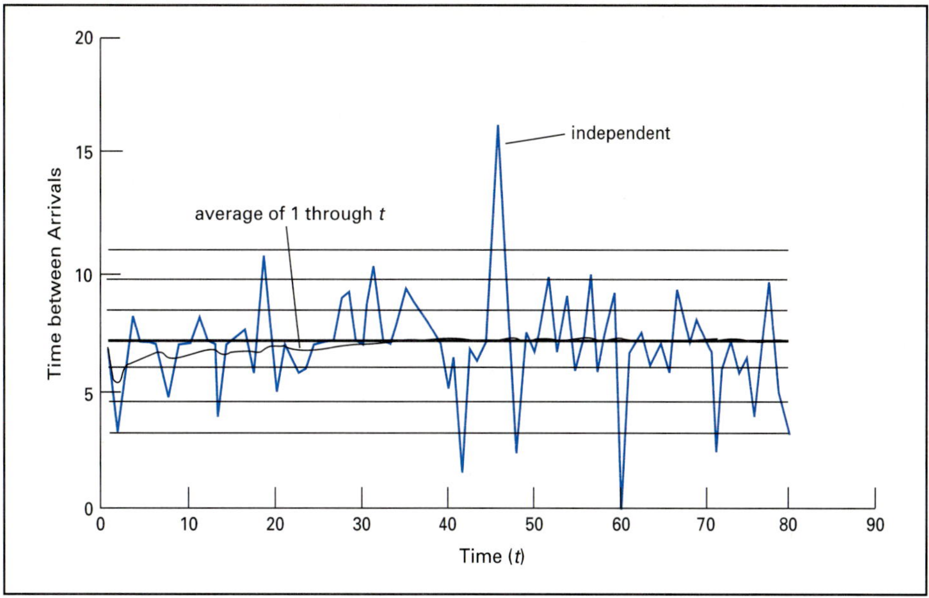

Figure B-11 Behavior of the Average of Independent Observations

get an accurate measure of the average ''busy time'' of the workers when the line was more nearly balanced (Figure B-4).

Long-run averages are often of interest. For example, Sally Skyrunner wanted to know the average amount of partly finished jobs in the buffer. The longer a simulation runs, the more accurate the estimate. Figure B-11 illustrates this point when the data consist of statistically independent observations. Notice that the cumulative average of periods 1 through *t* (plotted as a solid black line) changes substantially during the first thirty observations but remains relatively constant thereafter. Statisticians convey this property through the standard error:

$$\text{Standard error of a sample average} = \sigma/\sqrt{n} \tag{1}$$

in which σ is the standard deviation of the individual observations and n is the number of observations. This equation shows that the error gets smaller as n increases.

In a simulation the run length often, but not always, determines the sample size. However, there is a catch, and it is called autocorrelation (or serial correlation). The number of people in a queue is an example. If there are 10 people in queue at 1:05 P.M. there will probably still be about 10 at 1:06 P.M. That is, the queue length at one time is correlated with the queue length at another time; the queue length is correlated with itself, hence the term autocorrelation.

Figure B-12 illustrates the difference between statistically independent observations and autocorrelated observations. Notice that these two series have the same mean, in the long run, but the autocorrelated one takes long excursions away from the mean. This has several implications.

First, one could be badly misled by the first 30 observations of the autocorrelated series. They seem to indicate a low mean with a downward trend, but the remainder of the picture is entirely different. The sample of 30 autocorrelated observations is not nearly as representative as 30 independent ones.

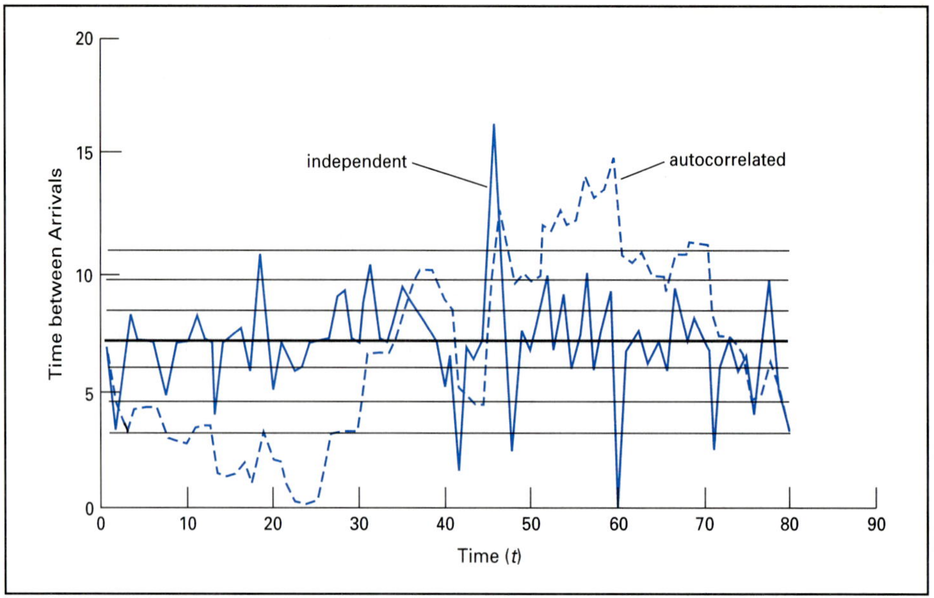

Figure B-12 Independent versus Autocorrelated Observations

Second, the run length required to accurately estimate the long-run average is much greater with autocorrelation. Figure B-13 illustrates that the average does not settle down rapidly, at all. (Compare with Figure B-11!) The formula for standard error (equation 1) does not hold for autocorrelated observations.

Finally, autocorrelation is not bad; it is simply a fact in some aspects of a system. It is helpful to know when this property exists in the simulation, because it probably also exists in the real system you are modeling. Why do you need to know this? Suppose that, wanting to test the validity of your model, you go to the real system and measure the average queue size. How many observations would you need from the real system to compare it with the simulation? If the simulation has already taught you that the data are autocorrelated, you can apply that knowledge in deciding how to collect data from the real system.

How do you know if autocorrelation is present? One way is to look at the data, watching for patterns similar to the solid black line in Figure B-11. Another way is to consult a statistician. There are many ways to test for autocorrelation, and sophisticated statistical methods for dealing with it. A third way is to think about the system you are modeling. If there any reason to believe that your observations are not statistically independent? In the example of queue length, the queue at 1:05 P.M. is part of the cause of the queue at 1:06 P.M., so they must be related. In any case it is important to understand that autocorrelation is common in real systems as well as simulated ones, and that the reliability of your analysis is affected by its presence.

To this point we have discussed run length and the estimation of long-run averages. A related issue is use of a *run-in period*. This is typically a span of time at the beginning of a simulation run; data from this time span are ignored. Consider the Tejas Outfitters example of Section B-1 again. Sally obtained, in her last simulation run, an estimate of the average inventory in the buffer between the packer and the shipper. However, when the simulation first

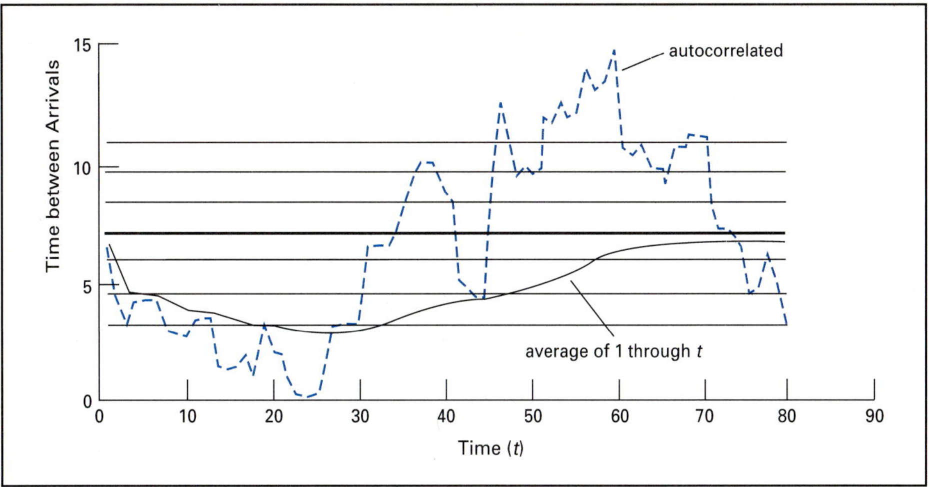

Figure B-13 Behavior of the Average of Autocorrelated Observations

begins, the entire operation is empty and idle. It will take some time before the system achieves a state that is more typical of the real operation. A run-in period is used for this purpose. For example, Sally could run the simulation until (say) 100 boxes had been completed, and then begin to take data on the inventory and idle time in the system. Long-run averages of continually operating systems are measures of "steady-state" behavior, and typically require a run-in period.

"Transient behavior" refers to operation during short intervals, in which the starting (or ending) conditions are important. Ignoring the data during a run-in period may be a mistake for transient measures. The Carthage Medical Clinic is a case in point. Every day at 1:00 the real system begins in an "empty and idle" mode. One hour later the doors close, but the system doesn't stop until it is once again empty and idle. In a sense, only the run-in period is of any interest at all in this example. Getting accurate statistics depends on many repetitions, each beginning with an empty system, rather than on allowing the simulation to run continuously for 1000 simulated minutes as Sally Skyrunner did for Tejas Outfitters.

We have discussed validity (designing) and reliability (running) as two separate topics, but it should now be clear that they are interdependent. One way you can tell whether your model is valid is to run it and compare the results with what you expect. But this comparison requires reliable data, so the issues of run length, autocorrelation, and run-in must be faced. One usually goes back and forth between design and run many times in the course of a project involving simulation. (Further discussion may be found in Kleijnen 1987, in which a number of statistical tools for simulation are described.)

REVIEW PROBLEMS

1. In the three stages of validity testing, what is the major characteristic that sets stage 3 apart from stages 1 and 2?

2. If the output of a simulation model does not make intuitive sense to a manager, what next?

3. The following averages were collected from a simulation of a production line. Four experiments were run to determine the effect of sample size on the accuracy of the answers. The underlying data were examined and found to be statistically independent (no autocorrelation). Calculate the standard error of each sample average. Compare the standard errors of the four experiments. Does doubling the sample size also double the accuacy of the sample average?

	Number of Observations	Average of the Observations	Standard Deviation
Experiment 1	100	10.61	1.25
Experiment 2	200	10.35	1.31
Experiment 3	300	10.47	1.14
Experiment 4	400	10.43	1.20

4. Why should Sally Skyrunner use a run-in period for the Tejas Outfitters simulation? Why would it be a mistake to use a run-in period for Carthage Medical Clinic?

5. Why is "queue length" autocorrelated? Is this true for real waiting lines or only simulated ones?

Solutions

1. The first two stages consist of tests of parts of the model, whereas the final stage looks at the performance of the model as a whole.

2. The model should not (and will not) be used in making decisions until the manager trusts it. Thus, either the model must be improved or the manager's intuition will change because of insights provided by the model, or else the whole thing will be junked.

3. Using equation 1 the standard errors are 0.0125, 0.0926, 0.0658 and 0.0600. No; to double the accuracy (cut the standard error in half) we would have to go from 100 to 400 observations, a fourfold increase. The reason is the square root in equation 1.

4. The first few minutes, when the shipper has nothing to do, are not of interest to Sally. She wants to know how the system behaves under continual operation. In contrast, all the questions about Carthage Clinic focus on the issue of how the session *begins*, so it would be silly to ignore the first few minutes.

5. Suppose there are 10 people in queue when customer 17 arrives. The possible queue sizes when customer 18 arrives are 11, 10, 9, . . . , 0, and the numbers near 10 are more likely than those near 0. Obviously, this autocorrelation occurs in actual waiting lines as well.

SUMMARY

Simulation is in daily use by manufacturers, the military, health planners, engineers, utility companies, and many others. The models range from simple and hand-computed to very complex computer programs. Even the most complex situation is composed of fairly simple elements. However, the difficulty of interpreting the results can be substantial, because of the many possible sources of randomness and the complexity of interactions when many variables are put together.

To make effective use of a simulation model, a manager must be willing to invest time in its design and development. Trade-offs must be made between the degree of detail and the cost (size) of the model. Since these decisions require an understanding both of the model and of its intended use, they must be made by an intended user, who must develop a good understanding of the model during its development.

Access to simulation becomes increasingly convenient as computer systems improve. Quick response to a manager's request is an important attribute of any management tool, and simulation is no exception. This requires careful attention to programming. Input should be easy and output should be readily understandable. Computer graphics have proven particularly useful in this regard, and simulation packages for desktop computers commonly make use of this method of communication.

Because randomness is an integral part of Monte Carlo simulation, the analysis of simulated data usually requires statistical methods. The techniques may be either simple or sophisticated, depending on the complexity of the model and the number of different inputs and outputs. In using a simulation to search for an optimal solution, careful attention to the rules for selecting which alternatives to simulate (and which to ignore) can have a dramatic effect on the cost of the search.

Simulation has been used in many of the areas covered in this book. Most notable are warehouse location, manufacturing-system design and control, and the design of service facilities.

PROBLEMS

1. The following table describes the probability distribution of service times at a hamburger stand. Use the following random numbers to simulate service times for three customers: 0.06248, 0.92317, 0.45473, and 0.51124.

Minutes	5	10	15	20	25
Probability	0.15	0.3	0.25	0.2	0.1

2. At Harry's Barbershop, 40% of the customers will accept only barber 1, 30% want barber 2, and 30% will accept either barber. Generate five customers, using Monte Carlo to determine which category each belongs to, using the following random numbers: 0.567, 0.246, 0.979, 0.895, and 0.098.

*3. Haircuts take a varying amount of time. The following data describe

*Problems with an asterisk have answers in the back of the book.

the experience at Harry's Barbershop:

Haircut time (minutes)	15–20	20–25	25–30	30–35
Number of customers	121	134	130	115

a. Convert these data to relative frequencies (probabilities) and set up a random-number assignment table similar to Table B-5.
b. Generate five simulated haircut times, using the random numbers 0.784, 0.611, 0.874, 0.200, and 0.798.
c. Plot the cumulative probability from your table, following the format of Figure B-10. Draw a smooth curve through the points you have plotted.
d. Use the five random numbers from part b to generate five simulated haircut times from your graph, using the method shown in Figure B-10.

4. An orange-juice stand has demand for oranges and orange juice with the following probability mass function:

Orange Demand (oranges per customer)	Probability	Juice Demand (cups per customer)	Probability
1	0.3	1	0.1
2	0.3	2	0.5
3	0.2	3	0.1
4	0.2	4	0.3

a. Set up random-number assignment tables for simulating demand for oranges and for juice.
b. Twenty percent of the customers buy only oranges, 70% buy only juice, and 10% buy both. Simulate three customers. First simulate whether the purchase is oranges, juice, or both. Then generate the simulated quantity or quantities. Use the following random numbers: 0.351, 0.697, 0.984, 0.162, 0.387, 0.288, 0.088, and 0.431.
c. Of what use could this type of simulation be to the owners of the stand? What additional data would be needed?

*5. (This problem refers to the PERT/CPM method from Chapter 4.) The accompanying PERT diagram describes a very simple project consisting of three activities. The activities have been done many times before. The probabilities in the accompanying table are a summary of historical activity times.

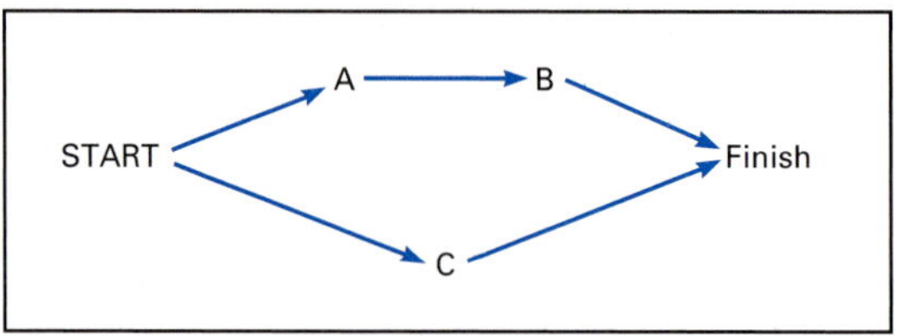

Activity Time (weeks)	Probabilities		
	Activity A	**Activity B**	**Activity C**
1	0.0	0.2	0.0
2	0.4	0.6	0.0
3	0.4	0.1	0.2
4	0.1	0.1	0.4
5	0.1	0.0	0.4
Expected value (weeks)	2.9	2.1	4.2

a. Using the following random numbers (read down the columns), simulate the entire project once. (i) What was the completion time of the project? (ii) What was the critical path?

Random Numbers

0.96589	0.88727	0.72655
0.03477	0.29528	0.63956
0.72898	0.32411	0.88861
0.39420	0.94211	0.58042
0.47743	0.60156	0.38037

b. Repeat part a four more times and use the results to estimate the *expected* completion time of the project. Draw a histogram of project completion times.

c. You have been asked to find a completion time deadline that you can be 80% certain of meeting. How would you use the simulation to find such a deadline?

d. What are the most important assumptions you are making in using this simulation?

*6. The normal probability distribution may be simulated by using the cumulative probability method. The random-number assignment may be done by using the normal probability table, Table 2, Appendix D.

a. Look up the z values corresponding to each of the following random numbers, treating the random numbers as cumulative probabilities: 0.885, 0.274, 0.998, 0.036, and 0.655.

b. The diameter of machined parts from a certain process is normally distributed with a mean of 10 centimeters and a standard deviation of 0.0010 centimeter. Convert the z values from part a into simulated diameters using the formula: $x = \text{mean} + z\sigma$.

7. If a variable has the exponential probability distribution, and its mean value is μ, the cumulative probability function is

$$\text{Probability of } x \text{ or less} = 1 - e^{-x/\mu}$$

In using the Monte Carlo method, the variable x is simulated by using the cumulative probability function as in Figure B-10. This is the same as solving for x in the following equation, in which RN stands for random number:

$$\text{RN} = \text{probability of } x \text{ or less}$$

a. Solve this equation for x using the exponential probability distribution. (Hint: Use logarithms.)

b. Generate five service times from the exponential distribution if the average service time is 10 minutes per customer, using the random numbers 0.567, 0.246, 0.979, 0.895, and 0.098.

*8. a. The average life of an incandescent bulb is 1200 hours, with a standard deviation of 50 hours. Using the random number 0.9342, generate a simulated bulb lifetime, assuming that bulb life is normally distributed. (Use the method described in problem 6.)

b. The process of part a was repeated forty times; the average simulated bulb life was 1160 hours and the standard deviation was 52 hours. Is there any reason to believe that the random numbers are not random? Explain.

9. The history of machine breakdowns was simulated under two different repair policies. Policy 1 had scheduled maintenance twice a month, whereas policy 2 had weekly maintenance. The simulated numbers of breakdowns per week are listed in the following table. They were generated using the same sequence of random numbers for each policy.

	Breakdowns	
Week	**Policy 1**	**Policy 2**
1	20	19
2	23	21
3	18	14
4	14	15
5	20	17

a. Compute the average number of breakdowns per week for each policy. Also compute the standard error for each average.

b. Are the results statistically significantly different at the 95% level of confidence? (This part assumes some knowledge of statistics.)

*10. A simulation model of a waiting-line with four servers was designed to compare several different working schedules. Before using the simulation, a simple test of validity was devised, in which all servers were given identical characteristics and the simulated customers arrived according to a Poisson process, with exponential service times. The simulation could then be compared with a queuing theory model. (See Appendix A.) Suppose that the simulation gave a queue length 10% lower than the queuing theory model. What two questions must you ask before you may make a judgment about the accuracy of the simulation?

11. The following data (see accompanying table) were taken from an XCELL simulation of a simple waiting line. There is a single server, and customers are served on a first come, first served basis. However, there is a limit to the number of waiting customers. In this simulation run, the limit is 100. That is, at any time that there are 100 customers in the waiting line, arrivals stop (no new customers join the queue) until space becomes available. (In Appendix A, this is a single-server, finite-capacity queue.)

    The simulation was stopped every 100 time units and the results were recorded in two ways (see table). First, Period Data contains averages for each 100-time-unit interval. Second, Cumulative Data contains averages from the beginning of the run. For example, at time 700, the average number in queue was 1.80 for the simulated period between time 600 and time 700, whereas the average was 10.98 from time 0 to 700.

	Period Data		Cumulative Data	
Time	Average Utilization of Server	Average Queue Size	Average Utilization of Server	Average Queue Size
100	0.969	21.21	0.969	21.21
200	1.000	31.31	0.985	26.26
300	1.000	10.37	0.990	20.96
400	0.892	3.21	0.965	16.53
500	0.821	2.90	0.936	13.80
600	0.950	6.09	0.939	12.52
700	0.803	1.80	0.919	10.98
800	0.904	15.84	0.917	11.59
900	1.000	41.25	0.927	14.89
1000	1.000	36.78	0.934	17.08

a. Plot the "period data" for the average number in the queue. Do they appear to be "independent observations" or "autocorrelated"? Explain your answer.

b. Based on the simulation results, give a numerical estimate of the long-run average number of customers in the waiting line.

c. In the simulation the average time between customer arrivals was set to be 0.9 minutes unless the queue was full; when the queue was full (contained 100 customers) the arrivals stopped until space became available. The average time required to serve a customer was set to be 1.0 minutes. Based on this information, explain why the average-queue-length data cannot be correct, in the long run. That is, 17.08 cannot be the long-run average queue length for the system being modeled. Why?

d. The following data were collected from the same simulation model with a run length of 10,000 time units between observations. Is 10,000 units long enough for a run-in period? Explain.

	Period Data		Cumulative Data	
Time	Average Utilization of Server	Average Queue Size	Average Utilization of Server	Average Queue Size
10,000	0.993	80.03	0.993	80.03
20,000	1.000	89.73	0.997	84.88
30,000	1.000	87.94	0.998	85.90
40,000	1.000	89.71	0.998	86.85
50,000	1.000	88.00	0.999	87.08

e. Explain why 87.08 (cumulative data at time 50,000) should not be used to estimate the average number of customers in the waiting line. Calculate a better estimate from the data given, and explain why it is better.

12. (Problem 11 should be done before this one.) The figures below show a plot of the actual (not average) number in queue for the first 1000 time units of two simulations. The first plot is the simulation in problem 11. The second plot is for a simulation with the waiting line's capacity reduced to 10 customers. The average interval between arrivals was 0.9 minutes in both simulations, and the average service time was 1.0 minute. As before, arrivals are halted when the waiting line is filled to capacity.

a. Explain how these diagrams show that 1000 time units is a very small sample of observations when the capacity of the waiting line is 100 but is a much more reasonable sample size for a capacity of 10.

b. Plot the following average queue size "Period Data" and compare it with the plot in part a of the previous question. Which plot shows a greater degree of autocorrelation of the observations? Explain.

	Period Data		Cumulative Data	
Time	Average Utilization of Server	Average Queue Size	Average Utilization of Server	Average Queue Size
100	0.969	6.11	0.969	6.11
200	0.939	4.18	0.954	5.15
300	0.755	2.15	0.888	4.15
400	0.902	3.71	0.891	4.04
500	0.840	3.79	0.881	3.99
600	0.924	5.10	0.888	4.17
700	1.000	8.53	0.904	4.80
800	0.880	4.60	0.901	4.77
900	0.997	6.37	0.912	4.95
1000	0.960	5.06	0.917	4.96

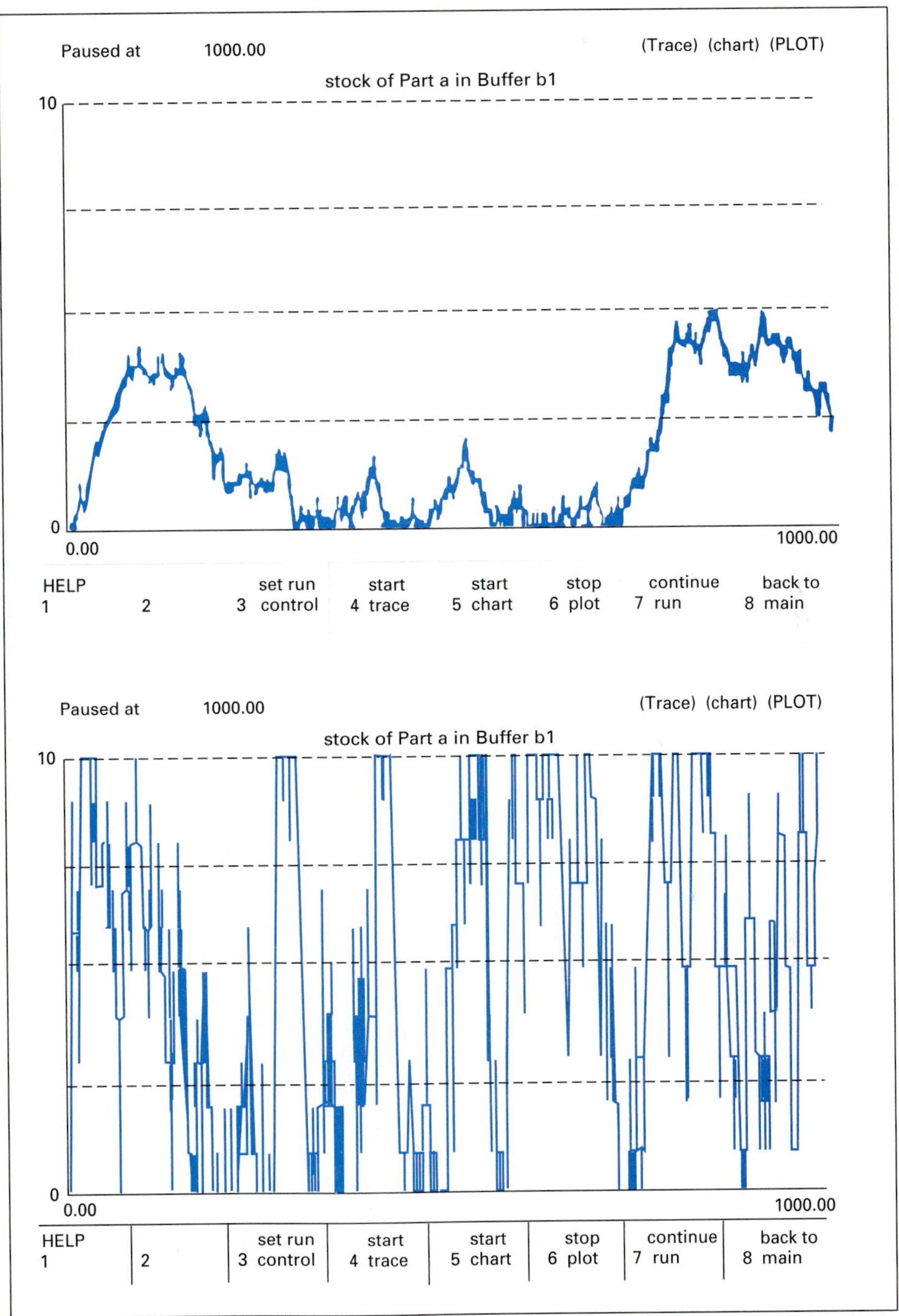

Paused at
1000.00
(Trace) (chart) (PLOT)
stock of Part a in Buffer b1
10
0
0.00
1000.00
HELP 1
2
set run 3 control
start 4 trace
start 5 chart
stop 6 plot
continue 7 run
back to 8 main
Paused at
1000.00
(Trace) (chart) (PLOT)
stock of Part a in Buffer b1
10
0
0.00
1000.00
HELP 1
2
set run 3 control
start 4 trace
start 5 chart
stop 6 plot
continue 7 run
back to 8 main

c. The following data were taken for a variety of waiting-line capacities. Draw a graph similar to Figure B-6 that shows the relationship of average queue size to the capacity of the queue.

	Queue Capacity			
Time	**10**	**20**	**50**	**100**
10,000	5.65	11.90	36.22	80.03
20,000	5.87	12.27	39.72	89.73
30,000	5.74	11.79	37.96	87.94
40,000	5.72	12.45	39.70	89.71

*13. At Silver Shirt Corporation, an inspector is stationed at the end of the production line. Shirts arrive at 2-minute intervals, and the inspector assigns them to one of three categories: good (no further work needed), rework (minor touch-up required), and reject (major repair needed). The inspector spends the least amount of time on rejects, since they are usually easy to discover and are then set aside. The greatest amount of time is spent on the rework shirts, since the inspector does the touch-up. The accompanying table shows the relative frequency of each category, and the time per shirt.

Category	Frequency (%)	Time per Shirt (minutes)
Good	85	1.8
Rework	10	2.3
Reject	5	1.0

a. Use Monte Carlo to generate 10 simulated shirts. Use the following random numbers: 0.567, 0.246, 0.979, 0.895, 0.098, 0.784, 0.611, 0.874, 0.900, and 0.798.

b. Simulate the arrival and processing of these 10 shirts, and show the results on a Gantt chart, similar to Figure B-7.

c. Write a set of instructions describing this simulation as was done in Table B-3.

d. How would the simulation be altered if the times given in the table were averages per shirt and we had a probability distribution of times for each category of shirt?

14. High Rise Ski Association is planning a new ski area. As part of the planning process, they have contracted with you to build a simulation model to determine the congestion to be anticipated at the bottom of the ski lifts. As the first step in this job, you were asked to concentrate on a single lift. The congestion is known to vary with the time of day, and to increase when the lift has to be stopped. The lift almost never breaks down, but it stops whenever a customer makes a serious error in entering or leaving a chair.

a. What data do you need?

b. List in English phrases the major blocks in the simulation.

15. Following a recent college convocation there was a reception. At the reception a queuing problem arose that will have to be solved prior to next year's convocation. In particular, the punch and cookie service was much too slow throughout the reception, particularly in the first half hour. The data are as follows:

 i. There are three punch and cookie tables (two nonalcoholic punches, one alcoholic; cookies are available at all three.)

 ii. During the first half hour, service at any table takes 1/2 minute without cookies (10% of customers), or 1 minute with cookies (90% of customers). During the remaining 1 hour, service takes the same time, but only 60% of customers want cookies.

 iii. During the first half hour, the number of people who arrive every minute is as follows:

Arrivals	6	7	8	9	10	11
Probability	0.2	0.3	0.2	0.1	0.1	0.1

 During the remaining 1 hour the probabilities change to

Arrivals	0	1	2	3
Probability	0.2	0.4	0.2	0.2

 Seventy five percent of customers choose the nonalcoholic punch. Those who choose the nonalcoholic punch go to the shorter of those two lines. Customers are served on a first come, first served basis.

a. What are the entities and their attributes?

b. Set up all random-number assignment tables.

c. Indicate how the simulation would proceed (i.e., in what order would various steps of the simulation be taken?). Briefly, what differences are there between the first half hour and the last hour? What time unit should be used, and why?

16. A typing pool consists of four typists and one supervisor-typist. They receive a variety of work, which is sorted into two priorities by the supervisor. The top-priority work is done on a first come, first served basis, but the second-priority jobs are performed by selecting the shortest job first. At the beginning of each day, the waiting pile of priority-2 work is searched. Any job that has waited longer than 7 days is moved to priority 1, where it joins the first come, first served queue according to the date it was received by the pool. Work arrives each hour as follows:

Jobs per hour	0	1	2	3	4
Probability	0.2	0.3	0.2	0.2	0.1

One-fourth of the jobs are top priority, on the average. The estimated job length is normally distributed with a mean of 1.5 hours and a standard deviation of 0.5 hour.

a. Set up random-number assignment tables and formulas, and demonstrate how each one works using the following random numbers: 0.82338, 0.29840, 0.55626, 0.60977, and 0.35137. (Note: The method for simulating normally distributed variables is given in problem 6.)

b. List the important events for a simulation of the pool, with a brief English description of what occurs in the simulation at each event.

c. At time (hour) 10, there are 6 jobs present in the queue and the typists have just arrived for work and have no partially finished jobs left from the previous day. The data for the jobs in queue is given in the accompanying table. Use a Gantt chart similar to figure B-7 to simulate the first hour. Use the random numbers as needed, reading row by row. Round job lengths to one decimal place.

Job	Priority	Length
J1	2	1.8
J2	1	2.1
J3	2	1.4
J4	2	0.9
J5	2	1.5
J6	2	1.6

Random Numbers

82	33	82	98	40	55	62	66
09	77	35	13	71	49	83	33

*17. OJ is an orange juice stand at Girdle Beach. Each evening, the owners place an order for the number of oranges to be delivered on the following morning. Each morning, they squeeze some of the oranges into juice, two oranges per cup. During the day, they sell both oranges and juice. If their supply of juice runs out, they squeeze additional oranges on demand. This slows down their service rate by 50%, and sometimes causes long waiting lines. At the end of the day, leftover juice is disposed of, and leftover oranges are stored until the following day. If OJ runs out of both oranges and juice, they close for the day, and their competitors gladly take the thirsty customers.

A computer simulation program was written, with the objective of helping to decide on the following two issues: how many unsqueezed oranges to stock at the beginning of the day, and how much juice to squeeze before opening.

a. What information should the computer report to aid in this decision?

b. What information must be given to the computer for it to perform the simulation?

18. The chief administrative officer of Midvale General Hospital has read about simulation and believes the maternity unit can be simulated. The present layout is as shown in the accompanying diagram.

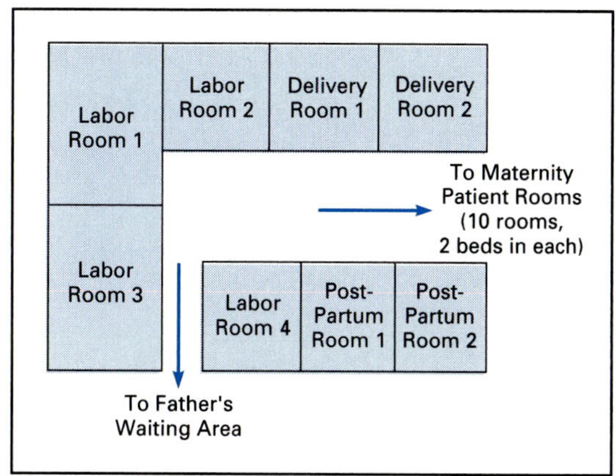

Given

i. Delivery room 2 can handle either cesarean or vaginal deliveries. Delivery room 1 can handle only vaginal delivery.

ii. Labor rooms and postpartum recovery rooms can be used interchangeably, but the administration prefers not to do so.

Objectives

i. Minimize the number of times that a delivery must be performed in a postpartum recovery room.

ii. Minimize the number of times postpartum recovery must be done in a room not designed for that purpose.

iii. Minimize the number of times a patient in labor cannot be assigned to a labor or recovery room because they are full.

iv. Minimize cost.

The hospital administrator thinks that the first three objectives may be inconsistent with the fourth, and is considering the following plans, most of which will require capital expenditures.

Plan A: Prepare delivery room 2 for cesarean deliveries—cost, $40,000.

Plan B: Prepare labor room 4 so that it can serve as either a labor room or a postpartum room—cost, $20,000.

Plan C: Convert one maternity patient room to a postpartum room—cost, $40,000.

Plan D: Eliminate the waiting area (visitors would wait in the main lobby and be paged), creating two new rooms, one labor room and one postpartum room—cost, $60,000.

Plan E: Leave the system as it is—no cost.

As a consultant to the administrator, you are to do the following:

a. Describe (using a flow chart or numbered steps) the simulation.

Be sure to show what output would be required. Fine detail is not necessary.

b. Show how random numbers would be used to generate values of each random variable.

c. Starting with no rooms filled, simulate 2 hours of operation. Begin by listing entities and attributes. You have the following data:
   (i) Vaginal delivery time is normally distributed with an average of 1 hour and a standard deviation of 0.2 hour.
   (ii) Cesarean delivery time is normally distributed with an average of 2 hours and a standard deviation of 0.3 hour.
   (iii) The number of arrivals is Poisson distributed with a mean of 0.5 per quarter hour, or 2 per hour. Assume that arrivals occur at the beginning of the quarter hour, and use 15 minutes as the time unit (i.e., round other occurrences to the nearest 15-minute interval). Always assign patients to rooms on a first come, first served basis.
   (iv) One of every 10 arrivals is for a cesarean delivery.
   (v) Time in the labor room (prior to vaginal delivery) is normally distributed with mean = 5, σ = 1. (Assume that there is no false labor.) Cesareans spend exactly 1 hour in a labor room.
   (vi) Time in the postpartum room is 1 hour for 80% of the patients, and 2 hours for the remaining 20%.

d. Comment on the validity of assumptions, approximations, and the data. Also, how useful would the first day's simulated data be?

e. Suppose that the output of the simulation is as follows:

	Objective Number			
Plan	**i**	**ii**	**iii**	**iv**
A	0.04	5.0	12	40,000
B	0.10	4.0	16	20,000
C	0.10	3.0	11	40,000
D	0.01	3.0	8	60,000
E	0.10	5.0	12	0

where (i), (ii) and (iii) are yearly averages for the first three objectives, and (iv) is the additional cost of the plan. Which plan do you choose? Why?

f. Are the data useful if we want to consider doing two of the plans?

g. In addition to building plans, could we use the simulation to test anything else?

19. The Stazo Corporation makes a series of handmade items in a job-shop setting. Their machine shop layout is shown in the accompanying diagram. WIP stands for a work-in process inventory, and M^c stands for a machine and its operator.

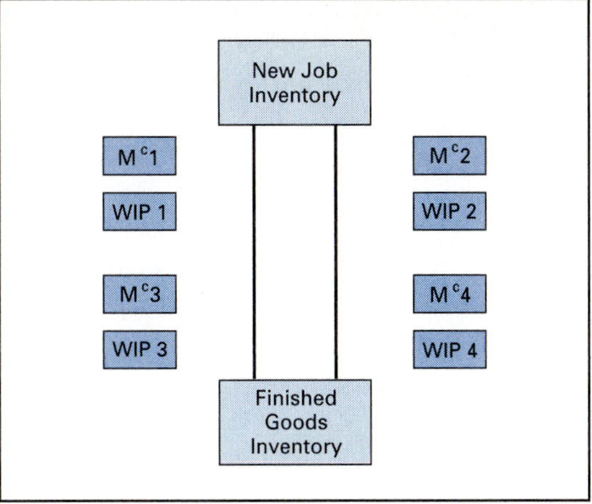

For example, after M^c1 finishes a task, the item is placed in WIP 1. Then the operator examines the new-job inventory and each of the WIP inventories and selects a critical job or the job with the shortest expected operating time. When a job is complete, it is moved to finished-goods inventory, where it eventually is shipped to the customer.

A job, upon arrival, is assigned a routing (path) that it must take through the shop. Processing times are random variables owing to the complicated nature of the work; sometimes a job's processing time is several times larger than the expected duration. Routing and processing time information for one job type is shown in the following table. M^c3 is not used on this job type.

	Machine	Operation Time
First operation	M^c2	2 (probability = 0.7) 6 (probability = 0.3)
Second operation	M^c4	4 (constant)
Third operation	M^c1	normally distributed with $\mu = 3$, $\sigma = 1$

At the present time, only jobs of the preceding type are in the shop. Job J1 is in WIP 4, ready to go to M^c1 to receive its last operation. Job J2 is in WIP 2, has been finished at M^c2, and is ready to go to M^c4. Job J3 is in the new-job inventory.

a. Generate activity times for all tasks required to finish these three jobs. Six task times are necessary (two of them are not random). Use the random numbers 0.27085, 0.81016, 0.27412, and 0.89304. Use the first two random numbers to generate the task times for jobs J1 and J2 on M^c1, and the last two for job J3.

b. Using an event-step simulation, show the timing of job movements through the system until all three jobs reach finished-goods inventory.

REFERENCES

BRATLEY, P., B. FOX, and L. SCHRAGE, *A Guide to Simulation*, 2nd ed., New York: Springer-Verlag, 1987.

CONWAY, R., W. MAXWELL, J. MCCLAIN, and S. WORONA, *User's Guide to XCELL+ Factory Modeling System*, 2nd ed., Redwood City, Calif.: Scientific Press, 1990.

CONWAY, R., W. MAXWELL, and S. WORONA, *User's Guide to XCELL Factory Modeling System*, Redwood City, Calif.: Scientific Press, 1987.

CORNWELL, L.W., and D.T. MODIANOS, "Management Tool: Using Spreadsheets for Simulation Models," *Production and Inventory Mangement*, vol. 31, no. 3, 1990.

HENRICKSEN, J.O., "The Integrated Simulation Environment (Simulation Software of the 1990s)," *Operations Research*, vol. 31, no. 6, 1983.

HOOVER, S.V., and R.F. PERRY, *Simulation: A Problem-Solving Approach*, New York: Addison-Wesley, 1989.

KLEIJNEN, J.P.C., *Statistical Tools for Simulation Practitioners*, New York: Dekker, 1987.

LAW, A.M., and W.D. KELTON, *Simulation Modeling and Analysis*. New York: McGraw-Hill, 1982.

MILLER, R.K., *Manufacturing Simulation*, Lilburn, Ga.: Fairmont, 1990.

MORGENTHALER, G.W., "The Theory and Application of Simulation in Operations Research," in *Progress in Operations Research*, vol. 1, R.L. Ackoff, ed., New York: Wiley, 1961.

OSTOLAZA, J., J. MCCLAIN, and L.J. THOMAS, "The Use of Dynamic Line Balancing to Improve Throughput," *Journal of Manufacturing and Operations Management*, vol. 3, no. 2, 1990.

SCHRUBEN, L., "Confidence Interval Estimation Using Standardized Time Series," *Operations Research*, vol. 31, no. 6, 1983.

SHANNON, R.E., *Systems Simulation: The Art and Science*, Englewood Cliffs, N.J.: Prentice-Hall, 1975.

SHANTHIKUMAR, J.G., and R.G. SARGENT, "A Unifying View of Hybrid Simulation/Analytic Models and Modeling," *Operations Research*, vol. 31, no. 6, 1983.

appendix

C

Linear Programming

Linear programming (LP) is an important mathematical tool that can be used in the solution of a wide variety of large, complex managerial problems. For example:

> An oil refinery can vary its product mix by its choice among the different grades of crude oil available from various parts of the world. The selection of process is also important, since parameters such as temperature will affect the yield. As prices and demands vary, an LP recommends which inputs and processes to use to maximize profits.
>
> Livestock gain in value as they grow, but the rate of gain depends in part on their feed. The choice of the proper combination of ingredients to maximize the net gain in value can be modeled as an LP.
>
> A firm that distributes products over a large territory faces an unimaginably large number of choices in deciding how best to meet demand from its network of warehouses. Each warehouse has a limited stock of items, and demands often cannot be met from the nearest warehouse. If there are 25 warehouses and 1000 customers, there are 25,000 possible matchups between customer and warehouse. Management must choose among more than 10^{40} combinations of these matchups. LP can quickly recommend shipping quantities and destinations that minimize the cost of distribution.

These are just a sample of the managerial problems that have been addressed successfully by linear programming. A few others are described throughout this text. Project scheduling can be improved by allocating funds appropriately among the most critical tasks so as to reduce the overall project duration (Chapter 4). Production costs can be reduced by using overtime and inventory to control changes in the size of the work force (Chapter 9). In the short run, personnel work schedules must take into account not only the production schedule but also assigned vacations, absenteeism, worker preferences for days off, and other considerations (Chapter 13).

Besides recommending solutions to problems such as these, LP can supply useful information for other complex managerial decisions. In Chapter 16, for example, production capacity and facility-location decisions were discussed. Because of the variety of nonquantifiable factors involved, models such as LP do not make the final decision. However, models can be extremely useful in evaluating particular aspects of the decision. For example, one aspect of the capacity-location decision is the future operating cost as demands change and new plants are brought on line. LP can be used to simulate how the firm would operate under various scenarios.

The *simplex algorithm* and its successors are commonly used methods for solving LP problems. Commercially available computer programs can solve problems with thousands of variables. However, the emphasis of this appendix is not on solution methods but rather on formulation and managerial use of the solutions. Therefore, the description of the simplex method is brief. (See Wagner 1975 or Hillier and Lieberman 1986 for a more detailed discussion of the simplex method.)

The goal of this appendix is to explain the two most important aspects of LP for a manager: *formulation* (converting managerial problems into LPs) and *interpretation* of the solution (including sensitivity analysis). This requires at least an intuitive grasp of the method of solution. Solutions are not decisions. Models seldom capture enough of reality to be trusted without careful scrutiny. Changes are often required to bring the model's recommendations into line with reality. Without a feeling for the way an LP will respond to changes, a manager would be ineffective in such interactions.

To develop this intuition, Section C-1 introduces LP with a simple example that can be solved on a graph. This shows how LP finds a solution that satisfies all the restrictions (or *constraints*) specified by the user while simultaneously maximizing profits or minimizing costs. Equally important, it demonstrates how the answer changes when modifications are made to the constraints or other model parameters. This is called *sensitivity analysis* and forms the basis for managerial use of LP.

Section C-2 explains the simplex algorithm. The first two subsections, ''Standard LP Format'' and ''Slack and Surplus Variables,'' should be read carefully, but the rest of the section may be skipped without loss of continuity. Section C-2 also introduces sensitivity analysis from the point of view of the simplex method.

Formulating managerial problems as LPs is the topic of Section C-3, using a manufacturing example. Given the large number of constraints to be embodied in the LP, a classification scheme is presented to help assure that all important constraints are captured.

Section C-4 describes the output typically available from a computer LP package and shows how a number of important managerial questions can be approached using this information. As Geoffrion (1976) pointed out, the so-called optimal solution produced by an LP is only part of its value; LP can also be used by a manager to develop insight into the problem, and to modify the solution in light of information that could not be included in the LP model.

Linear programming is encompassed within the broader field of *mathematical programming*. In the final section we discuss some other topics in mathematical programming. Specifically, we review some recent developments in solution methods for LP, including a new technique that has received coverage in the popular press. We also briefly discuss the nature and application of *integer programming* problems.

C-1 GRAPHICAL INTRODUCTION TO LINEAR PROGRAMMING

Managerial problems can often be characterized as *constrained-optimization problems;* that is, an attempt is made to optimize one or more objectives (or goals) subject to constraints arising from physical restrictions, existing policy, and the like. Many of the problems that we face daily can be cast in this framework.[1] Linear programming models have both an objective function and a set of constraints. Maximizing profits or minimizing costs are common objectives, but others are often used. There can be an enormous number of constraints in an LP, and each one represents either a restriction or a goal specified by the manager. The resulting mathematical model may require several pages of formulas to represent the decision situation.

There are two criteria that a problem must satisfy in order to qualify as an LP. First, the objective and the constraints must be expressed as *linear* equations. Second, the variables must be continuous (fractional values must have some meaning). Many applications violate the second criterion, but rounding off often suffices. For example, if an LP recommends production of 4123.7 units of an item, it probably makes little difference whether we make 4123 or 4124. The following example illustrates the formulation and solution of an LP.

Example: Tasty Toothpaste Company

The Tasty Toothpaste Company manufacturers two kinds of toothpaste in quantities measured in units equivalent to 1000 five-ounce tubes. Formula X is sold to discount stores under several house brands at a net profit of $50 per unit,[2] whereas formula Y is Tasty's own brand, which nets $60 profit per unit. Monthly sales are forecasted to be no more than 50,000 units for X and no more than 10,000 units for Y. Both these figures would normally be accepted as feasible sales goals. Management needs to make production-quantity decisions for each product. Therefore, the *decision variables* are x = quantity produced (in thousands of units) of X, and y = quantity (thousands) of Y.

There is a temporary but critical shortage of the secret ingredient that gives Tasty its taste. There are only 100,000 ounces available for use in producing next month's toothpaste. Product X requires 2 ounces of flavoring per unit, whereas Y uses 4 ounces per unit. Thus, for example, production of 50,000 units of X and 10,000 of Y would require $2x + 4y = (2)(50) + (4)(10) = 100 + 40 = 140$ thousand ounces of flavoring. Since only 100,000 are available, we must decide on the best compromise between the two products, and the solution must satisfy a constraint:

$$2x + 4y \leq 100 \quad \text{(flavor limit)} \tag{1}$$

[1]When presenting this topic to students, one of the authors claims that: "Life is a series of constrained-optimization problems." While some students may not immediately appreciate the significance of this statement, it is not uncommon to hear this quote repeated frequently during final-exam week!

[2]Technically, this figure is the *contribution margin* of the item because it represents revenue minus variable cost and omits fixed cost. For the purpose of this discussion, however, we refer to it as net profit.

The term ''flavor limit'' has been added as a label to describe the constraint for future discussion.

There are standing contracts for 40,000 units of X per month. This represents a lower limit on production. The market strategy of the company is to emphasize the house brands, a market segment in which they wish to strengthen their position. Therefore, the company has specified that the amount of Y (Tasty's own brand) produced should not exceed one-fourth of the total production beyond the 40,000-unit minimum. The mathematical expression of this is

$$y \leq \frac{1}{4}(x + y - 40)$$

in which $x + y$ represents the total production; thus, $x + y - 40$ is the amount of production beyond 40,000 units.

The standard format of a linear programming constraint has all the variables on the left-hand side of the inequality. The policy constraint on product mix can be rearranged into the required format as follows:

$$4y \leq x + y - 40$$

$$4y - x - y \leq -40$$

$$x - 3y \geq 40 \quad \text{(policy limit)} \tag{2}$$

LP assumes that all variables are constrained to take on nonnegative values. Most LP software packages handle these nonnegativity constraints automatically. (It is necessary to employ a specific modeling technique to allow for variables to assume negative values.) In the context of the Tasty Toothpaste Company problem, nonnegativity of the decision variables ($x \geq 0$, $y \geq 0$) is consistent with the physical constraint that production cannot occur in negative quantities. It is good practice to include the nonnegativity constraints in the problem formulation.

The lower limit on production resulting from the standing contracts can be represented by another constraint, $x \geq 40$. However, constraint 2 already forces x to equal or exceed 40. To see this, rewrite (2) as $x \geq 40 + 3y$, which together with the nonnegativity constraint $y \geq 0$ implies that $x \geq 40$. Hence, the constraint $x \geq 40$ is not needed and is referred to as a *redundant* constraint.

We now face six restrictions or constraints in finding the best compromise solution for the upcoming month. They consist of the inequalities 1 and 2, and the following upper and lower limits:

$$x \leq 50 \quad \text{(market limit)} \tag{3}$$

$$y \leq 10 \quad \text{(market limit)} \tag{4}$$

$$x \geq 0 \quad \text{(nonnegativity limit)} \tag{5}$$

$$y \geq 0 \quad \text{(nonnegativity limit)} \tag{6}$$

Constraints 1 through 6 can be conveniently summarized on a graph, since there are only two variables. Figure C-1 shows all the constraints discussed so far. For example, constraints 5 and 6 imply that we need only consider the nonnegative quadrant in the plane. Constraint 1 is plotted by first graphing the straight line defined by the underlying equation $2x + 4y = 100$, which is done by finding two points on the line, as follows: (a) If we set $x = 0$, then $2x + 4y = 0 + 4y = 100$, so $y = 100/4 = 25$; (b) setting $y = 0$, $2x + 4y = 2x + 0 = 100$,

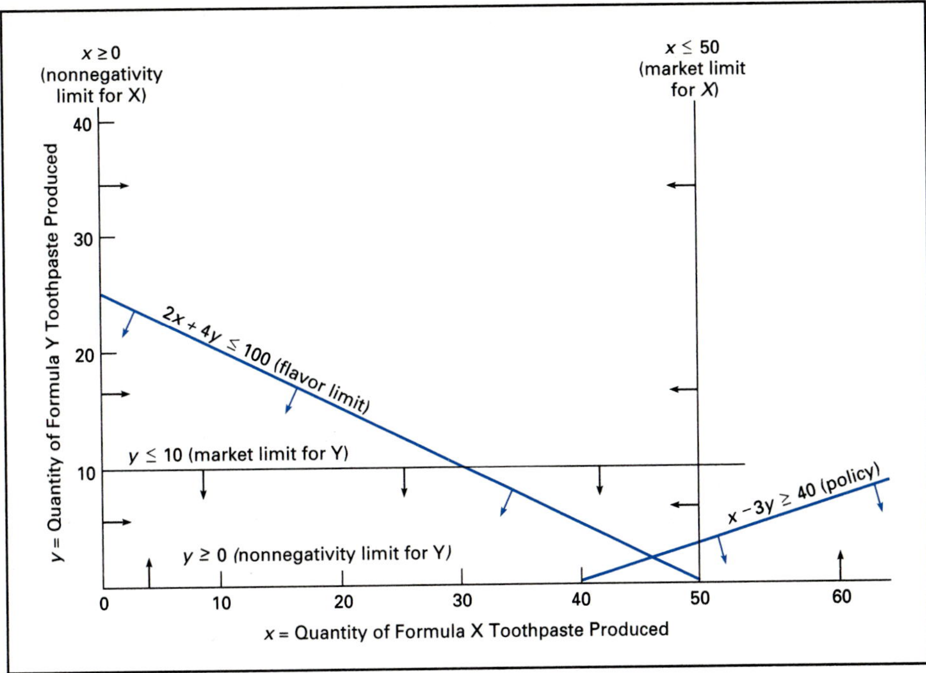

Figure C-1 Graph of Tasty Toothpaste's Problem

so $x = 100/2 = 50$. Thus, the flavor-limit line passes through the y-axis at $x = 0$, $y = 25$, and through the x-axis at $x = 50$, $y = 0$. Next, the linear inequality $2x + 4y \leq 100$ defines a *half space* (or in two-dimensional space, a *half plane*); that is, it defines all the points lying on the line, together with all the points on one (specific) side of the line. To determine whether the inequality defines the upper or lower half plane, we see that the origin $x = 0$, $y = 0$ has $2x + 4y = 0 + 0 = 0$, which is certainly ≤ 100; thus, the origin lies in the half plane defined by the inequality. This is indicated by the arrows pointing downward from the flavor-limit line.

A solution must satisfy all the constraints. In Figure C-2 we have shaded all the areas *excluded* by the constraints, paying careful attention to the direction of the arrows in Figure C-1. The remaining area is a small triangle, indicating that x will be between 40 and 50, and y will be 2 units or less. This area is called the *feasible region*. (It is *not* always a triangle, as will be seen in the review problems.)

The *objective function* in this example is the total profit, which is \$50 for each unit of X and \$60 for Y, or

$$\text{(Maximize)} \quad 50x + 60y = \text{profit} \tag{7}$$

For this problem, the *optimal solution* will be a point in the feasible region that maximizes profit. (In other applications, however, the objective function may be minimized, as in the case of minimizing cost.) Equation 7 represents another straight line, but unlike the constraints the objective function can move. For example, two profit lines have been plotted as dashed lines in Figure C-2. The one labeled "profit = 1000" was obtained by arbitrarily selecting a profit of 1000, inserting 1000 on the right side of equation 7, and plotting the resulting equation, $50x + 60y = 1000$. As this profit line does not intersect the feasible

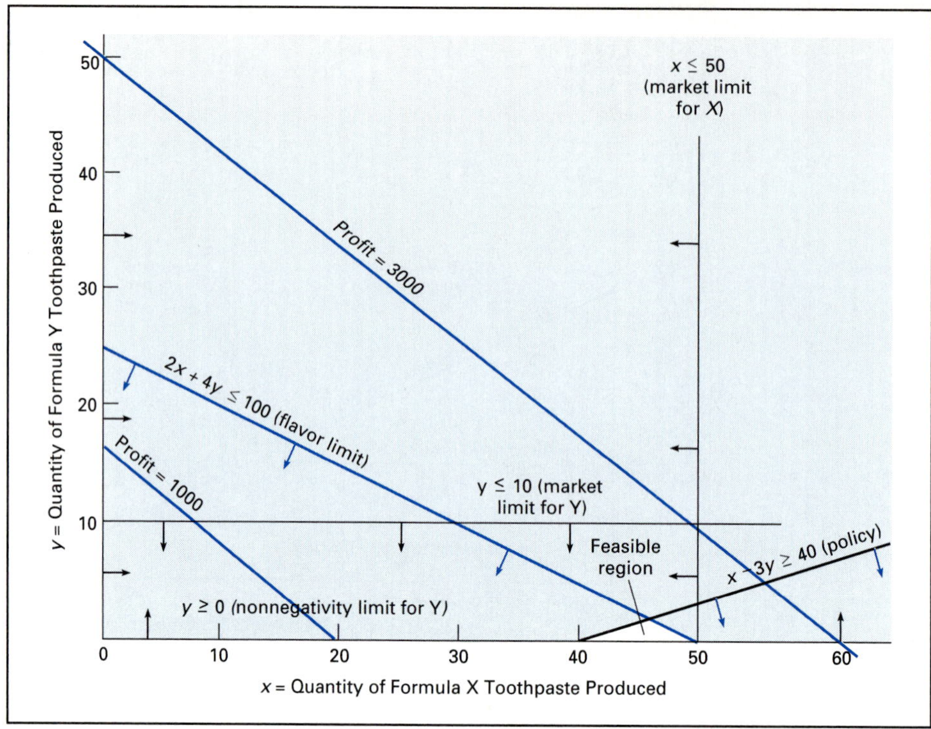

Figure C-2 Feasible Region and Two Profit Lines

region, there is no point that satisfies all the constraints and simultaneously yields a profit of \$1000. A second profit line, with a value of 3000 is also graphed. This line, labeled "profit = 3000," overshoots the feasible region.

Before seeking the optimal solution, let us examine these two profit lines. First, they are parallel. When we try another profit line, it will be parallel to these two. Second, the higher profit is the line that is to the upper right. Therefore, we want to find a profit line that passes through the feasible region, remains parallel to the two already plotted, and is as far to the upper right as possible. By visual inspection, we can see that the optimal solution will be at the rightmost corner of the feasible region, where $x = 50$, $y = 0$, yielding a profit of $(50)(50) + (60)(0) = 2500$ thousand dollars (recall that x and y are stated in thousands of units).

Discussion

Every two-variable LP can be graphed. The feasible region always has straight sides, although it is sometimes open in one direction. Improvements in the objective function correspond to moving a straight line across the graph in a parallel manner. Moving in one direction will minimize the objective function, whereas the opposite direction maximizes.

Because we want to move the objective function line as far as we can, but still have at least part of it in the feasible region, *one of the corners will always be an optimal solution* except in unusual circumstances. This indicates a great shortcut: In most cases we can limit our search for an optimal solution to the *corner points* (or *extreme points*) of the feasible region.

Sometimes an entire side of the feasible region can be optimal, as is illustrated in problem 3. In that case there are at least two optimal corner points and many other *alternative optimal solutions*. It is also possible that there may be no optimal solution, or no solution at all. The first case occurs when the feasible region has an opening in a direction such that the objective function can improve indefinitely. This is referred to as an *unbounded solution* and usually indicates that the formulation does not accurately capture the real-world problem. The second case happens if inconsistent constraints are given, so that there is no feasible region. This indicates that the formulation may be incorrect, or as sometimes happens in practice, constraints are imposed by management without regard to underlying consistency.

Which corner point or points are optimal depends on the slope of the objective function and the shape of the feasible region. This interaction between objective function and constraints can lead to unexpected (or counterintuitive) results. For example, the Tasty Toothpaste LP appears very simple:

$$\text{Maximize } 50x + 60y$$

subject to

$$2x + 4y \leq 100$$

$$x - 3y \geq 40$$

$$x \leq 50$$

$$y \leq 10$$

and the nonnegativity constraints $x \geq 0$ and $y \geq 0$. At first glance it would seem appropriate to produce as much Y as possible because it has the higher net profit. Nevertheless, the optimal solution is $x = 50$, $y = 0$. This is optimal because Y requires twice as much of the scarce flavor ingredient.

In general, the solution to an LP depends as much on the constraints as on the objective function. Because the solution depends so heavily on the constraints, it is prudent to study how changes in the constraints will affect the answer. This is called sensitivity analysis; the review problems provide examples of the type of questions that can be addressed. We will return to this topic in Sections C-2 and C-4.

Realistic problems often involve hundreds or thousands of variables, precluding the use of the graphical approach. There may be thousands of constraints, making it difficult to find any solution, let alone an optimal one. Fortunately, computer programs are widely available to do the job (see, for example, Schrage 1981). Much like the graphical method, computer programs that use the simplex method consider only corner points, but they operate in a "hyperspace" with dimensions equal to the number of variables in the problem. The constraints are "hyperplanes" rather than lines. Interpreting computer output is discussed in Section C-4.

As we have observed, optimal LP solutions can be found at corner points, which occur at the intersection of lines, or in higher dimensions, planes or hyperplanes. However, the corner points of the feasible region will often have fractional values for the variables. Therefore, LP answers must often be rounded off to obtain whole-number (integer) answers. Usually, these changes are minor. However, there are many problems in which rounding off can give bad or even meaningless answers. Linear programming problems with integer variables are called *integer programming problems*, which are discussed briefly in Section C-5.

REVIEW PROBLEMS

1. The optimal solution to Tasty Toothpaste was $x = 50$, $y = 0$. Locate this point in Figure C-1, and mark it with a small circle.
   a. The market limit for Y was 10,000 units. What would happen to the optimal solution if this were changed to 5000? 15,000?
   b. The market limit for X was 50,000. What would happen if this were changed to 48,000?
   c. What effect does the policy limit constraint (2) have on the optimal solution?

2. Suppose that management changed the policy limit constraint by dropping the limitation on y, but retaining 40 as a lower limit for x. Draw the new feasible region.

3. Suppose that the objective function were $50x + 200y$. Find the optimal solution to the problem as modified in review problem 2.

4. Answer review problem 1 for the solution to review problem 3.

Solutions

1. a. The $y = 10$ line does not touch the feasible region. Moving it up or down by 5 units will not affect the feasible region (and hence the optimal solution) at all. Had this constraint been absent, the solution would have been the same. This is a redundant constraint for all three constraint limits, 5, 10, or 15 (thousand).
   b. Moving the market limit of X to 48 would clip off the right-hand corner of the feasible region. The new solution would occur where the line $x = 48$ intersects the flavor limit. Since we know that x is 48 at the intersection, to find y we can solve equation 1: $2(48) + 4y = 100$, so $y = (100 - 96)/4 = 1$. The new corner point would be $x = 48$, $y = 1$; this solution will yield the highest profit. The profit would be $50(48) + 60(1) = 2460$, a drop of 40 attributable to the 1-unit decrease in the market limit for X.
   c. None. The optimal solution occurred at the intersection of the flavor limit, the market limit for X, and the nonnegativity limit for Y. As long as we use this objective function and the other constraints, the same solution would be optimal even if the policy-limit constraint were omitted.

2. The new feasible region is shown in the following graph:

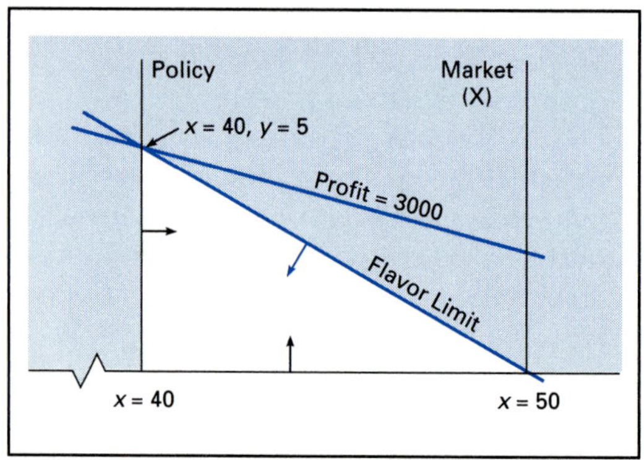

3. The profit = 3000 line is now much nearer the horizontal, running from $x = 0$, $y = 15$ to $x = 60$, $y = 0$. This line is plotted in the solution to review problem 2. Profit increases as the line moves upward, so optimal profit occurs at the peak of the triangle, which is $x = 40$, $y = 5$, for a profit of (50)(40) + (200)(5) = 3000 (thousand) dollars.

4. a. Same as review problem 1, part a.
   b. $x \leq 50$ now has no effect, since the optimal solution has changed to a new corner point of the feasible region.
   c. The policy constraint is now crucial. If we change it at all, the peak of the triangular feasible region would move.

C-2 THE SIMPLEX METHOD FOR SOLVING A LINEAR PROGRAM

LP is a type of constrained-optimization problem. The solution can be found by the *simplex method*, which is based on the same concepts as the simultaneous solution of two or more linear equations. The goal of the simplex method is to find the best (optimal) solution. It accomplishes that goal by limiting the search to corner points that improve the solution. How this is done is the subject of this section. Readers who are not interested in the details of the simplex method should read the first two subsections and then skip to Section C-3.

Standard LP Format

Standard LP format requires that all the variables appear only on the left-hand side of each constraint (equation or inequality). In this section the reason for that requirement will become clear as we introduce the idea of a tableau for LP computation. As a definition:

> *An LP in* standard format *has linear constraints (equations or inequalities) arranged with all variables on the left-hand side and a nonnegative constant on the right. It also has a linear objective function (with no constant term). All variables are constrained to be nonnegative.*

The policy constraint on product mix provided an example of rearranging so that variables are on the left. Achieving nonnegative right-hand sides (abbreviated RHS) is a little trickier. Consider, for example, a constraint

$$x + y \geq -20$$

To get rid of the negative right-hand-side constant, we multiply both sides of the constraint by -1. In the preceding example this changes the constraint to

$$-x - y \leq 20$$

Multiplying by -1 changes the *sense* of the inequality. In this case, $\geq$ becomes $\leq$.

Now consider an objective function with a constant. Suppose that the objective were to minimize a cost function that has a fixed element. For example, minimize $9x - 2y + 150$ has a fixed element of 150. The standard LP format requires that we delete the 150. This is of little concern to us because a solution that minimizes the variable costs $9x - 2y$ also minimizes the cost function with fixed cost added. When we get the solution, we can add 150.

Slack and Surplus Variables

The simplex method works only with equations; thus, our first task is to convert all inequality ($\leq$ and $\geq$) constraints to equalities. Continuing with the Tasty Toothpaste example, constraints 1 and 2 were

$$2x + 4y \leq 100 \tag{1}$$

$$x - 3y \geq 40 \tag{2}$$

In inequality 1, if the left-hand side is less than the right-hand side (which is allowed by $\leq$), the difference is termed *slack*. That is, if we define w to be the *slack variable* for constraint 1,

$$w = 100 - (2x + 4y)$$

Rearranging this to get the variables on the left side, the result is

$$2x + 4y + w = 100 \tag{8}$$

We made constraint 1 an equality by explicitly including a slack variable. To ensure that the left-hand side never exceeds the right-hand side, the slack variable w must be nonnegtive. For example, if $w = -5$, $2x + 4y = 105$, which is not allowed in the original constraint (1). Thus, constraint 1 can be replaced by equality 8 and the nonnegativity requirement $w \geq 0$.

Constraint 2 may also be replaced by an equality, but this time we must subtract a slack variable, since the left side is allowed to be greater than the right side. For $\geq$ constraints, the difference between the two sides is called *surplus* (or negative slack). Let v be the *surplus variable* for (2). Then (2) is replaced by two requirements:

$$x - 3y - v = 40 \tag{9}$$

$$v \geq 0$$

The general rule is to convert each $\leq$ constraint to $=$ by adding a slack variable, and to convert each $\geq$ to $=$ by subtracting a surplus variable. Slack and surplus variables must be constrained to be nonnegative.

Slack and surplus variables have real meanings within the context of the problem setting. For example, the slack variable in equation 8 represents the quantity of the secret flavor ingredient left unused by our choice of production quantities x and y. The surplus variable in equation 9 represents the amount by which the policy limit on product mix is exceeded (oversatisfied). It is important to keep these interpretations in mind.

At corner points, the constraints that intersect have zero slack or surplus. For example, in Figure C-2 the point $x = 50$, $y = 0$ has zero slack for the two constraints $x \leq 50$ and $2x + 4y \leq 100$, whereas the policy constraint and the market limit for y do not pass through this point; their slack and surplus variables are positive.

In the review problems, we found that changes in some of the constraints affected the optimal solution, whereas changes in other constraints had no effect on the solution. *The solution is sensitive to changes in any constraint that has zero slack or surplus, and not sensitive if the slack or surplus exceeds zero.* Constraints that have zero slack or surplus are said to be *binding* (or *active*) constraints.

The Tableau

We will continue the Tasty Toothpaste LP example but, for convenience, drop the two constraints $x \leq 50$ and $y \leq 10$. (As we saw in the graphical solution, these two constraints do not affect the optimal solution.) The resulting LP, including slack and surplus variables, may be summarized in standard LP format as

$$\text{Max} \quad 50x + 60y \tag{7}$$

s.t.

$$2x + 4y + w = 100 \tag{8}$$

$$x - 3y - v = 40 \tag{9}$$

$$x, y, w, v \geq 0 \tag{10}$$

in which *Max* means to maximize (we use *Min* if the objective is to minimize) and *s.t.* means "*subject to* the following constraints being satisfied." Constraint 10 indicates that each of the variables is to assume a nonnegative value.

For computation, the problem data are displayed in a *tableau*. An LP tableau is a table with numbers arranged in horizontal rows and vertical columns. Table C-1 is a tableau corresponding to the LP equations 7 to 9. Each row in the tableau corresponds to a constraint except row 1, which corresponds to the objective function. Each column (except the last) represents a variable. The RHS column contains the constants from the right-hand sides of the equations.

The property that makes LP difficult to solve is that all the constraints must be satisfied simultaneously rather than one at a time. The tableau makes it easy to find these solutions. As computations proceed, the tableau is changed. The columns always represent information about the variables, but the rows and the RHS column are altered in their interpretation, as we will see later.

Notice that the nonnegativity constraints (10) are not represented as rows in the tableau. Instead, these constraints are handled by not allowing the values in the RHS column to become negative. To see how the tableau captures this, consider row 2, which corresponds to equation 8. If we set $x = 0$ and $y = 0$ (the reason for doing this will soon become apparent), the resulting equation implies $w = 100$. By not allowing the value in the RHS column to become negative, the nonnegativity of w is maintained.

If we examine this explanation more carefully, we will see that the column in the tableau labeled w has an important property; namely, all but one of the entries in this column are 0, and the only nonzero entry is a 1. A column of this type is called a *unit column* or (*unit vector*). Note that if the nonzero entry had been some other positive number, we could have multiplied the entire row by the reciprocal of the number, which would create a 1 in the desired location.

Table C-1 Tableau for Tasty Toothpaste

Eq. No.	Row No.		x	y	w	v	RHS
7	1	(Max)	50	60	0	0	
8	2		2	4	1	0	100
9	3		1	−3	0	−1	40

Because the row corresponds to an equation, multiplication by the reciprocal preserves the equality; since the reciprocal is a positive number, the sign of the RHS will not change. (This, in fact, is one of the tableau operations we will discuss later.)

The advantage of having a unit column in the column for w is that only one row (equation) contains the variable w. This means that choosing a quantity for w will have no effect on any equation other than row 2. If each equation could be solved in this manner, simultaneous solution would be a breeze.

Since it is helpful to have unit columns, we begin the simplex method by creating a unit column corresponding to each row (with the exception of the objective function row, row 1). The unit column in the column labeled w corresponds to row 2 because the unique entry of 1 in the column appears in row 2.

Now consider row 3, which arises from equation 9. The surplus variable v was used to make this constraint an equality. The column in the tableau corresponding to v, however, is not a unit column. If we try to make it a unit column by multiplying row 3 by -1, the entry in the RHS column will become negative; that is, if we set $x = 0$ and $y = 0$ in equation 9, $v = -40$, which violates nonnegativity. One way to avoid this difficulty is to introduce a new, temporary variable, called an *artificial variable*.

Augmenting the Initial Tableau: Artificial Variables

Artificial variables differ from slack and surplus variables in one important way: They have no meaning in the original problem and therefore are required to be 0 in the final solution. An artificial variable can be interpreted as the amount by which the constraint is violated. That is why it must be 0 when we are finished.

Equation 9 is changed by adding the artificial variable A:

$$x - 3y - v + A = 40 \tag{11}$$

We can now solve this equation as easily as we solved (8); that is, if $x = 0$, $y = 0$, and $v = 0$, $A = 40$. This solution, however, does not satisfy equation 9. We will somehow have to drive the artificial variable A to 0 in future solutions because when A is 0, equations 9 and 11 are identical.

Table C-2 shows the augmented tableau. Notice that the artificial variable A looks like a unit column corresponding to row 3 except for the large negative coefficient in the objective function. Since the objective is to maximize row 1, the artificial variable has been given an objective coefficient that is so negative that an optimal solution method will drive it to 0.

From this we see that artificial variables look very much like slack variables in the tableau; however, artificial variables have coefficients in the objective row that make them unattractive with respect to the direction of op-

Table C-2 Augmented Tableau for Tasty Toothpaste

Eq. No.	Row No.		x	y	w	v	A	RHS
7	1	(Max)	50	60	0	0	−10,000	
8	2		2	4	1	0	0	100
11	3		1	−3	0	−1	1	40

timization. There is no need to introduce an artificial variable for a $\leq$ constraint, since the slack variable will supply the necessary unit column. In summary:

> *Each equation that has no slack variable must be given its own artificial variable. They are needed only for = and $\geq$ constraints. In a maximization problem, the objective function coefficients for artificial variables are large (in absolute value) and negative. For a minimization problem, they are large and positive.*

Once the tableau has been augmented by the appropriate artificial variables and columns, the initial solution is obtained simply by setting each slack and artifical variable equal to its corresponding RHS quantity. For Table C-2 the solution is $w = 100$, $A = 40$. All the other variables are 0 in this solution.

The "Net Change" Objective Function

We are preparing to move from the initial solution ($w = 100$, $A = 40$, $x = y = v = 0$) to an optimal one, using the objective function as a guide. To do so requires that we know how much the objective function would improve if we increase x, y, or v. Consider, for example, increasing x. The objective function is $50x + 60y + 0w + 0v - 10{,}000A$, so the direct effect of increasing x is to increase the objective function by 50. However, there is an indirect effect that (in this case) is far greater: The artificial variable A will decrease. In equation 11, or row 3 in Table C-2, $x - 3y - v + A$ must remain equal to 40; if x increases by one unit with no change in y or v, A will decrease by one unit from 40 to 39, yielding $x - 3y - v + A = 1 - 0 - 0 + 39$, which is still 40, as required. Lowering A by one unit increases the objective function by 10,000; thus, the *net change* of a one-unit increase in x is its direct effect of 50 plus the indirect effect of 10,000, or 10,050.

To transform the objective function to show net changes, we multiply row 3 of the tableau in Table C-2 by 10,000 and add the result to row 1. This has the effect of eliminating A from row 1; its effects are now entirely reflected in the other variables. (Note that adding a multiple of one equation to another is one of the steps for solving simultaneous equations.) Algebraically,

row 1:	$50x + 60y + 0w + 0v - 10{,}000A$
(10,000)(row 3):	$10{,}000(x - 3y - v + A) = 10{,}000(40)$
sum:	$10{,}050x - 29{,}940y + 0w - 10{,}000v + 0A = 400{,}000$

The result is shown as row 1 in Table C-3. Note that variable A now has a unit column in the tableau.

The first-row entry for x is now 10,050, reflecting the fact that adding one unit of x yields 50 in direct profits and 10,000 indirectly by reducing A. Variable y now looks like a terrible investment, since the gain of 60 has been offset by a loss of 30,000, because to increase y by one unit requires *increasing* A by 3.

Table C-3 First Simplex Tableau for Tasty Toothpaste

Row No.		x	y	w	v	A	RHS
1	(Max)	10,050	−29,940	0	−10,000	0	400,000
2		2	4	1	0	0	100
3		1	−3	0	−1	1	40

The RHS column in C-3 has an entry of 400,000 for row 1. Its interpretation will be given presently. The tableau is now in a form suitable for optimization by the simplex method. Hence, it is called the *first simplex tableau*.

Interpreting a Simplex Tableau

The simplex tableau should be thought of in a new way: It represents a solution. The tableau in Table C-3 represents the solution $w = 100$, $A = 40$, profit $= -400{,}000$. Notice that the RHS column contains these numbers, with the exception of row 1, which is the negative of the profit. That is, 100 units of v at 0 return and 40 of A at a return of $-10{,}000$ is $0 + (-10{,}000)(40) = -400{,}000$, compared with $+400{,}000$ in row 1. Henceforth, as we move through simplex iterations:

The RHS column contains the current solution.

As we discussed earlier, with the possible exception of the objective-function row, the RHS values *must* be kept nonnegative to preserve the nonnegativity of the solution.

It is easy to identify which variables correspond to the RHS values ($w = 100$ and $A = 40$). Simply determine the unit column corresponding to each row. In this solution, w and A are referred to as the *basic variables* because they alone define the solution. The rest of the variables are 0. In general:

The basic variables have unit columns. Each RHS is the current solution for its corresponding basic variable.

In this new interpretation the basic variables have taken possession of the rows. As we will see, all the numbers in the tableau tell us something about the basic variables.

The rest of the variables are called *nonbasic*. They are all 0 in the solution represented by the tableau. However, the tableau contains information about the nonbasic variables. For example, as we saw previously:

The first row contains the net rates of increase in the objective function that would result from increases in the nonbasic variables.

This information is vital if we want to know how to improve the solution. But changing a variable affects more than the objective function. It also affects the basic variables. (That is why we need *net* changes in row 1.) As we will illustrate:

If a nonbasic variable is increased, its column contains the net rates of substitution (decrease) of the basic variables.

Now that a tableau has been identified with a current solution, it remains to show how to find the best solution. If the solution is to be improved, it is by changing the nonbasic variables.[3] One way of carrying this out is the simplex method.

The Simplex Method

Row 1 of Table C-3 shows that x is the most profitable variable in the tableau. However, it is currently nonbasic and therefore equal to 0. We desig-

[3] There is one basic variable per row. Therefore, there is only one solution for a given set of basic variables. New solutions are found by selecting a nonbasic variable and exchanging it for a basic variable.

nate x as the *entering variable* because we want to bring it into the solution. We have just used

> *The Simplex Criterion for Optimality: As long as there are any positive coefficients in the first row of a maximization problem, the solution can be improved. If all row 1 coefficients are zero or negative, the solution is optimal. (The opposite signs apply for minimization.)*

The next task is to find a solution that includes x. The method uses two columns: the x column and the RHS. Consider the possibility of increasing x from its current value of 0. Reading down the x column, it is apparent that each unit increase in x would require two units of RHS from row 2 and one unit from row 3.

How far can we increase x? The RHS values represent basic variables; therefore, we must stop increasing x before any RHS becomes negative.

Consider row 2. The RHS is 100 and each unit of x substitutes for two of these. Therefore, if x increases by $100/2 = 50$, the RHS will decrease to 0. Any further increase in x would drive the RHS negative, which is not allowed. Similarly, in row 3 the allowable range of increase for x is $40/1 = 40$. Therefore, to avoid negative RHS values in both rows, x cannot exceed either 40 or 50 and is thus limited to the smaller of the two numbers, or 40.

When $x = 40$ is reached, the RHS of row 3 is reduced to 0, and the variable that it represents becomes nonbasic. Since A is basic in row 3, it is the *departing variable*. In short, 40 units of x have displaced A as a basic variable. The objective function should improve by 10,050 for each unit of x, or $(40)(10{,}050) = 402{,}000$.

This example has shown how to improve the solution. A formal statement of this procedure is as follows:

Simplex step 1: To find the entering variable, choose any variable with a + sign in row 1 for maximization, or a − sign for minimization.

Simplex step 2: To find the departing variable, do the following:

(a) Divide each RHS value (except row 1) by the corresponding entry in the column of the entering variable. Ignore ratios for which the entering-variable column entry is zero or negative.

(b) Find the row with the smallest ratio.[4] Call that the departing row. The basic variable for that row is the departing variable.

(c) If all rows have negative or zero denominators, abandon the problem. There is no limit on the entering variable, so the solution is unbounded.

Once the entering and departing variables have been identified, a new tableau is needed to represent the new solution. This requires a bit of algebra. First, we define

> *The pivot element: the number at the intersection of the column of the entering variable and the row of the departing variable.*

[4]In step 2b, the possibility exists that a "tie" will occur in the selection of the departing variable. For the purpose of this discussion, break such a tie arbitrarily. This occurrence, however, gives rise to the possibility that the simplex method could then cycle among the same set of tableaus. Bland (1977) discusses pivoting rules that avoid cycling.

In our example, we wish to make x a basic variable in row 3. The pivot element is therefore the number 1 in the x column.

To make x basic, we must give it a unit column with a 1 in row 3. There is already a 1 in row 3 of the x column. (If not, we would divide each number in row 3 by the pivot element.) Now to get the 0s for the rest of the unit column. For row 1, this is done as follows:

$$\text{New row 1} = \text{old row 1} - (10{,}050)(\text{new row 3})$$

That is:

	x	y	w	v	A	RHS
Old row 1 =	10,050	−29,940	0	−10,000	0	400,000
10,050 (new row 3) =	10,050	−30,150	0	−10,050	10,050	402,000
Subtract to get	0	210	0	50	−10,500	−2,000

The same procedure is used to process row 2:

$$\text{New row 2} = \text{old row 2} - (2)(\text{new row 3})$$

The results are shown in Table C-4.

In deriving the new tableau we have performed the third simplex step:

Simplex step 3: The *pivot step:*

(a) Divide each number in the departing row by the pivot element. Call the result the new departing row.

(b) Process all the remaining rows starting with row 1. That is, for each row i except the departing row,

(i) in the column of the entering variable, locate the number in row i (call it B)

(ii) multiply the new departing row by B and subtract the result from row i (that is, new row i = old row i − (B)[new departing row])

The three simplex steps constitute the simplex method. When step 3 is completed, there is a new tableau; thus, steps 1, 2, and 3 can be repeated. This continues until there is no variable that meets the condition in step 1; that is, no variable can improve the objective function. Then the simplex criterion is satisfied and the algorithm terminates.

Table C-4 Second Simplex Tableau for Tasty Toothpaste

Row No.		x	y	w	v	A	RHS
1	(Max)	0	210	0	50	−10,050	−2,000
2		0	10	1	2	−2	20
3		1	−3	0	−1	1	40

Possible Outcomes for the Simplex Method

OUTCOME 1: *No feasible solution* (artificial variables remain in the solution). *Problem:* The constraints are inconsistent, and the problem is *infeasible. Example:* $x + y = 10$ and $x + y = 20$ are inconsistent, because $x + y$ cannot be both 10 and 20 at the same time. *Remedy:* Either give up in despair or reformulate the problem.

OUTCOME 2: *The solution is unbounded* (all entering-variable column entries [below the objective-function row, row 1] are either negative or zero). *Problem:* The constraints are not sufficient to prevent the optimum from being positive or negative infinity. *Example:* Maximize $z = x + y$ with the constraint $x - y = 10$. Note that $x = 100{,}010$, $y = 100{,}000$ is feasible, as are any numbers such that x exceeds y by 10 units. *Remedy:* You have probably left out a real-world constraint on available resources. Reformulate the problem.

OUTCOME 3: *An optimal solution is found.* This is the desired outcome. Although the final basic solution is optimal, there may be more than one optimal solution. This may be ascertained by looking at the final objective-function row.

(a) If there exists a nonbasic variable that (i) has a coefficient of 0 in the final objective-function row, and for which (ii) the resulting departing row for this variable (if it were to be pivoted [or brought] into the set of basic variables) has a nonzero value in the RHS column,[5] the solution reported by the LP is only one of an infinite number of optimal solutions.

(b) All these optimal solutions achieve the same value of the objective function; therefore, we can choose among them based on facts not included in the LP formulation.

(c) The alternative optimal solutions are found by "bringing in" any of the nonbasic variables that satisfy the conditions in (a).

Sensitivity Analysis of the Optimal Solution

If an LP formulation is changed, it stands to reason that the optimal solution will also change. Sensitivity analysis explores the link between the problem and its optimal solution. This is important because values used in the formulation may be estimates or may be changed by management action. Section C-4 describes sensitivity analysis based on the output from a typical LP computer program. The following discussion briefly illustrates how sensitivity information is obtained from the simplex tableau.

For purposes of illustration, we will consider forcing a nonoptimal (nonbasic) variable into the solution. (This could be necessary if, on reflection, a

[5]The occurrence of one or more 0s in the RHS column of the tableau (below the objective-function row) gives rise to a *degenerate solution*. The simplex method can handle degeneracy; however, degeneracy is not considered further in this appendix.

manager required the production of an unprofitable item to round out a product line.) The analysis follows from simplex step 2. Increasing an entering variable has *linear* effects on the objective-function value and on the basic variables. Simplex step 2 will also yield a departing variable, so the effect is linear over a limited range; it ends when one of the basic variables is driven to 0.

The rates of change are given in the column of the nonbasic variable in the optimal simplex tableau. Row 1 is the *rate* at which the objective-function value changes. This is called the *reduced cost*. The other rows are the net rates of substitution for the basic variables.

There are many other questions that a manager might wish to address using sensitivity analysis. Some of them use the idea just explained for nonbasic variables. For example, changing a RHS value can be shown to be equivalent to forcing a nonbasic slack into the solution. Section C-4 describes the most common sensitivity outputs from computer LP packages and their application.

Discussion

Computer programs are widely available to do the work discussed in this section (and more). Many of these programs are based on the simplex method, which operates by (1) moving from one basic solution to another, and (2) using the simplex criterion to assure that each move improves the solution. The program stops when no more improvements are possible and reports an optimal, feasible, basic solution (if one exists). The tableau that accompanies the solution contains necessary information to study modifications of that solution.

The Tasty Toothpaste LP was graphed in Figure C-2 in the previous section. We have now generated two tableaus, and each is a solution. The first, Table C-3, has both x and y equal to 0 (they are nonbasic). This corresponds to the origin in Figure C-2. The second, Table C-4, has $x = 40$ and $y = 0$, which corresponds to the lower left corner of the feasible region in the graph. *The basic solutions generated by simplex tableaus correspond to the corner points of the graph. If all artificial variables are 0, a tableau solution is a corner point of the feasible region. Thus, the simplex method solves the LP by moving from corner point to corner point.*

REVIEW PROBLEMS

1. What is the solution given by Table C-4? (How much of each variable and at what profit?)

2. According to simplex step 1, which variables in Table C-4 are candidates to be the next entering variable? Which one would you choose? Why?

3. Let v be the entering variable. Using simplex step 2, determine the departing variable.

4. Using simplex step 3, find a new tableau.

5. Is this solution optimal? How can you tell?

6. Locate the solution to review problem 4 in Figure C-2 in the preceding section. Does this confirm your answer to review problem 5?

7. How much would profit drop if we forced the LP to produce one unit of Y?

Solutions

1. The basic variables are $x = 40$ and $w = 20$. The nonbasic variables are $y = 0$ and $v = 0$. The net profit is 2000. (The artifical variable $A = 0$ is a nonbasic variable as desired.)

2. The candidates for the entering variable are v and y because this is a maximization problem, and they have positive values in row 1. The net profit of y is 210 per unit, which is higher than that of v; hence, it is a reasonable choice for the entering variable.

3. Despite the answer to review problem 2, we have chosen v as the entering variable. Perform simplex step 2 by first checking row 2: the ratio is $20/2 = 10$. The column entry is negative (-1) for row 3, so we ignore the ratio. Thus, the departing row is row 2, and the departing variable is w.

4. The pivot element is 2. The new tableau is shown in Table C-5. Note the role played by the column of the entering variable v: in Table C-4, the number 2 is the pivot element, and the numbers 50 and -1 play the role of B when rows 1 and 3 are processed in simplex step 3b, respectively.

5. This solution is optimal because all row 1 coefficients are negative or zero. (If we had introduced y first, v would still have a positive coefficient; it would enter in the next iteration and y would depart.)

6. Table C-5 corresponds to $x = 50$, $y = 0$, the lower right point in the feasible region of the graph. This does confirm the solution to review problem 5 because we proved graphically that this is the optimal solution.

Table C-5 Third Simplex Tableau for Tasty Toothpaste and the Formulation with Slack, Surplus, and Artificial Variables

Row No.	x	y	w	v	A	RHS
1	0	−40	−25	0	−10,000	−2,500
2	0	5	0.5	1	−1	10
3	1	2	0.5	0	0	50

$$
\begin{aligned}
\text{Max} \quad & 50x + 60y - 10{,}000A \\
\text{s.t.} \quad & 2x + 4y + w = 100 \\
& x - 3y - v + A = 40 \\
& x, y, w, v \geq 0
\end{aligned}
$$

7. If y were the entering variable, the objective function would drop at a rate of $40 per unit (the reduced cost in row 1).

C-3 LINEAR PROGRAMMING FORMULATIONS

There are a number of standard LP formulations, and many of them are used in this text. For the convenience of the student interested in practicing the important art of formulation, and for the instructor who wishes to include more examples, here is a directory of LP formulations in this text.

Transportation and distribution problem: Section 16-3 (which includes a mixed-integer programming formulation), and problems 20 to 23 in Chapter 16. Also, see problems 15 and 21 in this appendix.

Multiple-period production planning: Section 9-5, problems 16 and 20 in Chapter 9, and the Handicraft Jewelry Company caselet.

Personnel scheduling: Section 13-1 and problem 13 in Chapter 13.

Assignment problem: Section 13-3, and problems 22 and 23 in Chapter 13.

Product mix: this section and problems 12, 13, 16, 18, and 19.

Blending: problem 17 and the Red Brand Canners caselet in this appendix.

Nonlinear objective functions with diseconomies of scale: problems 14 and 15 in this appendix.

This section addresses the questions asked most frequently by people faced with using LP for the first time. The case of the Rockwell Stone Corporation is used to bring most of the questions to a practical level. Although it is a simplified version of the allocation of resources to production, it has complications of the kind often encountered in full-scale problems. It is also large enough that one is pleased to use a computer for its solution. Rockwell Stone is an example of a multistage production-planning problem, of the type discussed in Chapter 10.

Example: Rockwell Stone Corporation

The Rockwell Stone Corporation makes two models of rock crushers. Sales of these two products and spare crusher blades (they do not sell any parts other than crusher blades) are handled through an internal sales department. Forecasts of the demand for the upcoming quarter are as follows:

Item	Description	Selling Price	Demand Forecast (next quarter)
BS1	rock crusher, light	$14,000	250
BS2	rock crusher, heavy	46,000	150
P2	crusher blade, replacement	3,400	5,000

In the fabrication area of the plant, raw materials are processed into parts that then go to the assembly area, where they are stored until needed. In addition to the fabricated parts, the assembly of a rock crusher requires two subassemblies, which are purchased from an outside supplier. Another supplier offers P4 for sale, but Rockwell currenty makes all the P4 it needs. Whether to make or buy this part is currently being considered. The fabrication and assembly requirements, listing the materials required for the assembly of each of the two products and the manufacture of each part, are as follows:

	RAW MATERIALS REQUIRED PER PART		
Part	RM1	RM2	Labor-Hours per Part
P1	25	0	0.1
P2	37	700	2.0
P3	0	12	2.0
P4	0	170	25.0

	PARTS REQUIRED PER ROCK CRUSHER				SUBASSEMBLIES		
Crusher Model	P1	P2	P3	P4	SA1	SA2	Labor
BS1	3	2	4	2	1	0	0.3
BS2	6	5	4	1	2	1	1.0

For items that may be purchased, the prices and availabilities are as follows:

Item	Price	Purchase Limit
P4	$ 1,035	no limit
SA1	3,150	450
SA2	18,000	no limit
RM1	5	750,000
RM2	5	no limit
LABOR	$8.50/hr	no limit

Although the data seem to indicate maximum sales of 250 + 150 = 400 rock crushers, there is some degree of substitutability between the two models. Maximum total sales have been estimated to be 360. The firm has set a minimum production goal of 300 rock crushers. The purchasing manager has been give a budget of $7.2 million, from which the required subassemblies and raw materials must be purchased. The budget restriction would not apply to the purchase of P4.

Formulating the Multistage Production LP

The remainder of the section is devoted to understanding the formulation of this problem.

How Does One Decide What the Decision Variables Should Be? Variables are created for every decision or recommendation that is to come from the LP. Rockwell Stone wants to know what quantity of each part to fabricate, how many subassemblies and raw materials to purchase, and how many rock crushers to assemble. They further desire a recommended quantity of P2 to fabricate for sale, and of P4 to purchase from the outside supplier. We will use Rockwell's notation wherever possible, so that BS1 will stand for the quantity of model-1 rock crushers to be produced, P1 the quantity of type-1 parts to be fabricated, and so on. In addition, the number of part type 2 to be sold as spares will be designated SPARE, and BUY will be the quantity of type-4 parts purchased from the outside.

How Are Objectives and Constraints Formulated? The first step is to list, verbally, all the restrictions that the solution must satisfy. Each of these restrictions will be represented by one (or sometimes more than one) equation or inequality. Management must also specify its objectives, first verbally, then quantitatively.

There is a convenient categorization scheme that helps the user determine whether the LP formulation contains all the necessary components. The categories are (1) accounting constraints, (2) facts-of-life constraints, (3) policy constraints, and (4) objective function.

1. *Accounting constraints.* These are equations that tie the variables together. Without these constraints, the LP might recommend producing rock crushers but no type-1 parts. To prevent such a ridiculous recommendation, we must account for the parts that will be required in the production of rock crushers. In words, and then in mathematical terms, the constraint for type-1 parts (P1) is

$$\text{Type-1 parts required} = 3 \text{ for each BS1} + 6 \text{ for each BS2}$$

$$\text{P1} = 3\ \text{BS1} + 6\ \text{BS2} \tag{12}$$

To see if this prevents the aforementioned error, set BS1 = 10 and BS2 = 20, and note that this gives us P1 = (3)(10) + (6)(20) = 150, which is just enough type-1 parts to produce 10 model-1 rock crushers and 20 of model 2.

For part type 2 (P2) there are three uses: in the assembly of two types of rock crushers and in sales for spare parts. Equation 13 will account for the type-2 parts used in the assembly of BS1 and BS2 crushers and will also require production of the quantity required for spares. Equations 14 and 15 give the accounting constraints for P3 and P4.

$$\text{P2} = 2\ \text{BS1} + 5\ \text{BS2} + 1\ \text{SPARE} \tag{13}$$

$$\text{P3} = 4\ \text{BS1} + 4\ \text{BS2} \tag{14}$$

$$\text{P4} = 2\ \text{BS1} + 1\ \text{BS2} - 1\ \text{BUY} \tag{15}$$

2. *Facts-of-life constraints.* Because of a limited market for rock crushers, we can sell no more than 250 of type 1 and 150 of type 2. Therefore, upper limits must be placed on BS1 and BS2:

$$\text{BS1} \leq 250 \tag{16}$$

$$\text{BS2} \leq 150 \tag{17}$$

Another fact-of-life constraint is that no more than 360 rock crushers can be sold in total because they are partial substitutes for one another. This is formulated as

$$BS1 + BS2 \leq 360 \tag{18}$$

Although these examples of facts-of-life constraints are inequalities, this is not always so. For example, a permanent contract to produce an exact quantity of an item would be an equality constraint. Also, the numbers used in these constraints may sometimes be more appropriately termed guesses, as the actual fact may not be known. (The market constraint is an example of an educated guess.)

3. *Policy constraints.* A budget is an example of a policy constraint imposed on the solution by a management decision. The following expresses the budget for the purchase of raw materials and subassemblies:

$$3150\ SA1 + 18{,}000\ SA2 + 5\ RM1 + 5\ RM2 \leq 7{,}200{,}000 \tag{19}$$

Notice that an inequality has been used to express the budget as an upper limit. A slack variable for this inequality would represent budgeted funds not used in the LP solution.

Company policy also requires a minimum output of at least 300 rock crushers. Therefore, another policy constraint is

$$BS1 + BS2 \geq 300 \tag{20}$$

4. *The objective function.* If the objective is to maximize the total contribution to fixed cost and profit, the objective function is

$$\begin{aligned}(\text{MAX})\quad & 14{,}000\ BS1 + 46{,}000\ BS2 + 3400\ SPARE \\ & -1035\ BUY - 3150\ SA1 - 18{,}000\ SA2 - 5\ RM1 \\ & -5\ RM2 - 8.50\ LABOR\end{aligned} \tag{21}$$

Table C-6 summarizes the Rockwell Stone LP formulation, including all the constraints just discussed and several others that were formulated from the verbal description. (The constraints are shown in standard format.)

How Are Constraints Tested? Equation 12 was tested earlier in this section by plugging numbers in for each variable, and seeing whether the results matched the verbal description. This is an important step, because it is very easy to write constraints incorrectly or backward. For example, the statement "Each BS1 takes three P1, two P2, four P3, and two P4" might be written, erroneously, as

$$BS1 = 3\ P1 + 2\ P2 + 4\ P3 + 2\ P4$$

To see why this is wrong, plug in P1 = 3, P2 = 2, P3 = 4, and P4 = 2 and see if you get BS1 = 1. (You don't!) The correct formulation requires four equations, one for each part. They are equations 12 to 15. When the same numbers are plugged in, each of the four equations balances.

How Can the Entire Formulation Be Checked? This is a very important question, because it is the interaction of the many variables and constraints that makes a large-scale problem difficult to solve. Checking the constraints one at a time does not guarantee that the formulation is complete and accurate. Final testing of the model is done by running the computer program and examining

Table C-6 Formulation for Rockwell Stone Corporation

Equation Number	Row Number		
21	1	Max	14,000 BS1 + 46,000 BS2 + 3400 SPARE − 1035 BUY − 3150 SA1 − 18,000 SA2 − 5 RM1 − 5 RM2 − 8.50 LABOR
12	2		P1 − 3 BS1 − 6 BS2 = 0
13	3		P2 − 2 BS1 − 5 BS2 − SPARE = 0
14	4		P3 − 4 BS1 − 4 BS2 = 0
15	5		P4 − 2 BS1 − BS2 + BUY = 0
	6		SA1 − BS1 − 2 BS2 = 0
	7		SA2 − BS2 = 0
	8		RM1 − 25 P1 − 37 P2 = 0
	9		RM2 − 700 P2 − 12 P3 − 170 P4 = 0
	10		LABOR − 0.3 BS1 − 1.0 BS2 − 0.1 P1 − 2 P2 − 2 P3 − 25 P4 = 0
18	11		BS1 + BS2 ≤ 360
20	12		BS1 + BS2 ≥ 300
19	13		3150 SA1 + 18,000 SA2 + 5 RM1 + 5 RM2 ≤ 7,200,000
16	14		BS1 ≤ 250
17	15		BS2 ≤ 150
	16		SPARE ≤ 5000
	17		SA1 ≤ 450
	18		RM1 ≤ 750,000

the results. It is at this stage that errors of omission are often discovered. For example, if one or more accounting constraints have been omitted, the LP will recommend an impossible solution such as ''Produce 200 rock crushers and sell them all, but minimize costs by not buying any subassemblies.'' Such a solution would result if rows 6 and 7 in Table C-6 were omitted.

How Can We Tell Whether the Output Makes Sense? Understanding the LP answer is the subject of the next section. This question requires us to go beyond learning how to read the answer; we must learn how to determine the implications of answers that appear unreasonable, because LP solutions may radically alter one's view of the problem.

Summary

An LP user must go through a rather involved process to translate a problem into mathematical terms that a computer can understand. The variables for the LP correspond to every detailed decision. Some constraints correspond to restrictions caused by facts of life and policies, and others must tie the variables together in a way that accounts for all the interactions among the decisions. One should check each constraint individually by plugging in reasonable values of the decision variables. The entire formulation is tested by examining the output to determine whether it makes sense, and changing the formulation if necessary.

To complete a formulation, the numbers used in the equations must be obtained. These include the technological coefficients which express the formula or recipe for the products, and the constants that appear on the right-hand side of the equations. Some of these numbers may require substantial effort to collect. Estimation will often have to suffice, especially if the linear equations are only approximations to the real situation. The next section deals with methods of determining how crucial these estimates are, and how influential the resulting errors may be on the solution.

REVIEW PROBLEMS

1. Test equation 15 by plugging in BS1 = 10, BS2 = 20, and BUY = 15. Would this be sufficient to produce 10 BS1 and 20 BS2? How many type-4 parts would be fabricated, according to (15)?

2. What are the accounting constraints (other than equations 12, 13, 14, and 15) in the Rockwell Stone problem (Table C-6)? Select one of these constraints; state it in words and then mathematically.

3. MacChamps produces a tasty hamburger known as the Champburger. Each Champburger takes three slices of bread, two beef patties, and one pickle. Show that the following constraint is not correct, and write a correct expression (or set of expressions).

$$\text{CHAMP} = 3\ \text{BREAD} + 2\ \text{BEEF} + 1\ \text{PICKLE}$$

Solutions

1. P4 = 2 BS1 + 1 BS2 − 1 BUY
   P4 = (2)(10) + (1)(20) − (1)(15) = 20 + 20 − 15 = 25.
   Yes. Each BS1 takes 2 P4, so 20 are needed there, and 20 are also needed for producing 20 BS2, for a total of 40. However, 15 are procured through purchasing (BUY = 15), so 25 is a sufficient number to fabricate.

2. In Table C-6, rows 6 to 10 are accounting constraints. For row 6, the constraint is, "The number of SA1 needed is 1 for each BS1 and 2 for each BS2." Mathematically, this is

$$\text{SA1} = 1\ \text{BS1} + 2\ \text{BS2}$$

   which is transformed to row 6 in Table C-6 by subtracting 1 BS1 and 2 BS2 from both sides.

3. If the formula were correct, then BREAD = 3, BEEF = 2, and PICKLE = 1 should lead to CHAMP = 1.

$$1 \stackrel{?}{=} (3)(3) + (2)(2) + (1)(1) = 9 + 4 + 1 = 14$$

   Since this does not check, the constraint is wrong. The correct constraints are

$$\text{BREAD} = 3\ \text{CHAMP}$$

$$\text{BEEF} = 2\ \text{CHAMP}$$

$$\text{PICKLE} = 1\ \text{CHAMP}$$

which read "The number of bread slices equals 3 for each Champburger, the number of beef patties equals 2 for each Champburger," and so on. Checking these formulas, we have

$$3 = (3)(1)$$

$$2 = (2)(1)$$

$$1 = (1)(1)$$

C-4 MANAGERIAL USE OF LP SOLUTIONS

The Rockwell Stone LP was formulated by a manager named Tom Dirk. The optimal solution for Rockwell Stone is shown in Table C-7. The objective function value (total contribution) is \$280,315. (Again, for simplicity, we will refer to this as "profit.") The recommended production quantities are (see the column labeled SOLUTION) BS1 = 250 type-1 rock crushers, BS2 = 100 of type 2, SPARE = 0 crusher blades to be produced as spares, and so on.

There are two controversial recommendations. First, P4 = 0 and BUY = 600 indicate that all parts of type P4 should be purchased from the outside supplier. Second, SPARE = 0 suggests going out of the business of supplying spare crusher blades. Tom realized that management would object to these solutions because they violate a long-standing policy, "We service what we sell."

This puts Tom in a difficult position. Having proposed that the LP can solve Rockwell Stone's production-planning problem, he must either justify these recommendations or change them. He decided to talk the situation over with Dean Smalley, a friend who had been with the company five years longer than he.

Dean: The boss sure isn't going to like this solution. We have always produced spare crusher blades. It is part of our image. You had better change your model if you want to get anywhere.

Tom: Well, I could add a constraint such as SPARE $\geq$ 10 and run the LP again. Maybe I'll do several runs with different values of SPARE and make a graph of net profits as a function of the level of production of SPARE.

Dean: That would be a good idea, but the news of your LP has already leaked out and started a controversy over going out of the business of spare blades.

Tom: So now I'm the center of a controversy. Maybe I ought to look for some ideas that could improve my image with top management. According to the LP output (Table C-7) the market limit of 250 for Rock Crusher model BS1 has been reached in the solution. I wonder if we could make more money if this market were larger? Should I recommend that Rockwell Stone undertake a marketing promotion for model BS1?

Sensitivity Analysis

As the conversation continued, Tom realized that there were many things he would like to know about the LP recommendations. Sensitivity analysis is a method of analyzing a solution, and LP is one of a very few management

Table C-7 Optimal Solution and Sensitivity Analysis for Rockwell Stone Corporation

OBJECTIVE FUNCTION VALUE = 280,315.00

			OBJECTIVE COEFFICIENT RANGES		
VARIABLE	SOLUTION	REDUCED COST	CURRENT COEF.	ALLOWED INCREASE	ALLOWED DECREASE
BS1	250	0.00	14,000	INFINITY	146.20
BS2	100	0.00	46,000	292.40	1,083.40
SPARE	0	302.00	3,400	302.00	INFINITY
BUY	600	0.00	−1,035	INFINITY	27.50
SA1	450	0.00	−3,150	INFINITY	541.70
SA2	100	0.00	−18,000	292.40	1,083.40
RM1	70,750	0.00	−5	7.90	3.23
RM2	716,800	0.00	−5	0.16	0.31
LABOR	5,110	0.00	−8.5	1.10	52.21
P1	1,350	0.00	0.0	INFINITY	180.57
P2	1,000	0.00	0.0	292.40	216.68
P3	1,400	0.00	0.0	INFINITY	73.10
P4	0	27.50	0.0	27.50	INFINITY

			RIGHT-HAND-SIDE RANGES		
ROW	SLACK/ SURPLUS	DUAL PRICES	CURRENT RHS	ALLOWED INCREASE	ALLOWED DECREASE
2	0	−125.85	0	358.00	1,350.00
3	0	−3,702.00	0	12.14	1,000.00
4	0	−77.00	0	745.83	1,400.00
5	0	−1,035.00	0	INFINITY	600.00
6	0	−3,691.70	0	100.00	2.39
7	0	−18,000.00	0	2.49	100.00
8	0	−5.00	0	8,950.00	70,750.00
9	0	−5.00	0	8,950.00	716,800.00
10	0	−8.50	0	INFINITY	5,110.00
11	10	0.00	360	INFINITY	10.00
12	50	0.00	300	50.00	INFINITY
13	44,750	0.00	7,200,000	INFINITY	44,750.00
14	0	146.20	250	20.00	4.17
15	50	0.00	150	INFINITY	50.00
16	5,000	0.00	5,000	INFINITY	5,000.00
17	0	541.70	450	2.05	100.00
18	679,250	0.00	750,000	INFINITY	679,250.00

science techniques in which sensitivity analysis is directly available in the output. For example, the marketing promotion is an option that did not occur to Tom when formulating the LP. Sensitivity analysis can help to decide whether the effort and expense of such a campaign would be justified.

In this section sensitivity analysis is defined as changing one element of the problem and watching what happens to the optimal solution. Even with this one-at-a-time restriction, a rich variety of questions can be addressed. The following symbols are used to simplify the description:

X = variables
C = objective-function coefficients (one for each X)
RHS = constants on the right-hand side of the constraints
Z = value of the objective function
Z^*, X^* = optimal values of Z and X, respectively

The Sensitivity Game

Sensitivity analysis can be viewed as a game between a manager and an LP. First, the manager specifies a problem formulation and the LP solves it. Then the manager changes the problem. The LP's response is to find a new optimal solution. Sensitivity analysis is an attempt to anticipate the LP's next move. Becoming adept at this game allows one to answer many interesting questions with very little work.

As in chess, each player has a set of pieces to move. The manager's pieces are the coefficients of the model, such as the RHS and C values. The LP's pieces are the optimal X^* values and the optimal objective function value, Z^*. *The manager is allowed to change only one parameter of the problem at each move, but the LP is allowed to change any or all of the variables in its response.*

The manager has two additional moves that can be very powerful: adding a new constraint or a new variable to the formulation. However, LP's ability to modify all the variables at once allows it to make very complex responses that are difficult to anticipate.

The object of the game for the LP is to maintain the best solution possible (either the highest or lowest Z^*). The manager has many goals and plays the game to get a solution that satisfies them as well as possible. Among the manager's goals are testing different opportunities, such as changes in selling prices or marketing campaigns to increase demand. Playing the sensitivity game allows the manager to evaluate the marginal benefits or costs of future plans. Of particular interest is the opportunity cost associated with an action (or lack of action).

Shadow Prices and Opportunity Costs

Profits and losses are usually given by the optimal objective-function value, Z^*. An opportunity cost is a potential improvement in Z^* if management were able to ease one of the restrictions. Linear programs give a great deal of information about opportunity costs, which is usually stated in (somewhat standard) LP-specific terminology. DUAL PRICE and REDUCED COST are examples. A generic term for this concept is *shadow price.*

> *The shadow price is the* net *rate of change of Z^* in response to a change in the formulation. Shadow prices are opportunity costs.*

The word *net* is emphasized as a reminder that the LP is allowed to change all X^* values in order to achieve a new Z^*. This section is devoted to finding shadow prices in the LP output and learning how to apply them to managerial problems.

Modifying Constraints

Tom spent the first part of the meeting explaining the LP formulation (Table C-6) to Dean. Then they began to work on questions concerning the solution (Table C-7).

Dean: The LP said to produce 250 BS1 rock crushers. More production is impossible because of the market constraint of 250 (row 14 of Table C-6). The way I look at it, your idea of expanding the market for BS1 should be of interest, since the LP recommends making as much as the market will bear. But your model has other restrictions. For example, the supply of RM1 is restricted to 750,000 units (row 18). Which would be more profitable, promoting BS1 sales or buying additional RM1?

Tom: I think we can solve this one quickly. The LP output (Table C-7) shows no slack in row 14 and a slack of 697,250 in row 18. Since there are tons of RM1 left over, we don't want to buy more right now. My textbook calls this the principle of *complementary slackness:*

PRINCIPLE 1: *Constraints that have slack in the optimal solution must have zero shadow prices. And constraints with nonzero shadow prices must have zero slack.* A constraint with zero slack is called a *binding (or active) constraint. (This principle also holds for constraints with surplus variables.)*

Dean: Yes, I agree with that. But how do we decide whether to go for more BS1 sales? How much more profit can be generated?

Tom: There are several ways to find opportunity costs in LP. Here's the way for constraints:

PRINCIPLE 2: *DUAL PRICES are shadow prices for the constraints.*

The DUAL PRICE for row 14 is 146.20 in the output; that is the opportunity cost of this market limit. Additional sales of BS1 would increase profits at a rate of up to $146.20 per unit sold. The cost of the promotion would have to be paid for from this increase.

Dean: Some of the DUAL PRICES are negative. Does this indicate that profits decrease?

Tom: Yes. But there is a way to tell whether a given change is going to be bad or good without getting confused by the signs of the shadow prices.

PRINCIPLE 3: *Changes that reduce the size of the feasible region cannot be favorable. Changes that increase the feasible region cannot be harmful.* The feasible region becomes smaller if you reduce the RHS of a $\leqslant$ constraint or increase the RHS of a $\geqslant$ constraint.

It helps to reflect on the graphs in Section C-1. If part of the feasible region is chopped off by moving a constraint, there are two possibilities. If the optimal solution was in the portion chopped off, the LP is forced to find a new solution in the smaller feasible region, and it must choose one that it had previously rejected! Thus, whether minimizing or maximizing, the solution will be worse than before. The other possibility is that the chopped-off segment does not contain the optimal solution, in which case the previous solution remains optimal. The only way that an improved solution can be found is if new area is added to the feasible region.

Dean: I think I get it. Adding BS1 demand would give the LP more choices. The LP could still choose 250 if that were optimal, so adding demand can't hurt. So the shadow price of increasing demand must represent higher profit or lower cost. But how far can we increase sales at a unit gain of $146.20?

PRINCIPLE 4: *Z* changes linearly as a RHS value is changed within a limited range.* The RIGHT-HAND-SIDE RANGES section of the output shows these limits. The shadow price (DUAL PRICE) indicates the rate of change.

Tom: For the BS1 market (row 14) the ALLOWED INCREASE is 20. Therefore, the first 20 units (or less) of additional demand will increase profits by $146.20 per unit.

Dean: I see that the ALLOWED DECREASE is 4.17. Does this mean that the first 4.17 BS1 sales lost to competitors would reduce profit at a rate of $146.20 per unit?

Tom: Yes. The opportunity cost of a constraint is the same in both directions. The only difference is that profits go up if sales of BS1 increase, and down if sales decrease.

Dean: But what if the change exceeds the range?

Tom: Even though the shadow price is not valid beyond the range, a limit can be given:

PRINCIPLE 5: *If the shadow price (DUAL PRICE) indicates that a RHS change is favorable within the specified range, it is less favorable beyond. Or, if it is unfavorable, going beyond the range makes it worse.*

Thus, if the promotion would increase demand by 30 units, profits would increase by *no more than* ($146.20)(30) = $4386. If that is not high enough to justify the effort, no more analysis is needed. But if $4386 is more than the cost of the promotion, we would want to run the LP again with a higher BS1 market limit to see how much profits actually increase.

Dean: So the shadow price (DUAL PRICE) is an optimistic estimate. Is that always true? It seems pretty risky to assume that one rule applies in every situation.

Tom: It always applies in LP problems. The reasoning behind principle 5 is as follows: In the sensitivity game, the LP attains the best possible response to management's move. Available resources and production quantities of all the products are juggled until the best way to produce more BS1 within the given constraints is found. Therefore, 146.2 is the highest return that can be attained on additional sales of BS1. At the end of the range, the LP has exhausted the optimal strategy it was using. To meet additional BS1 demand the LP must use an inferior strategy, so returns will be lower.

Dean: Let me try to summarize. BS1's upper limit of 250 is binding; it is restricting the optimal solution and has no slack. Its shadow price (DUAL PRICE) of 146.2 is the opportunity cost of this limit as long as demand is between 250 − 4.17 = 245.83 and 250 + 20 = 270. Above 270, the shadow price is an upper limit on profits from additional demand. Below 245.83 the shadow price is a lower limit on lost profits.

Tom: That's right. You can also examine the limit on RM1 given in row 18 in the same way. Its DUAL PRICE is zero and its slack is 679,250. If you look at the range, you will see that this zero shadow price holds as long as there is slack.

Dean: Yes. That was your complementary slackness notion. When the slack is gone, there can be a nonzero shadow price. Right?

Tom: Right.

Modifying the Nonnegativity Constraints

Dean: Let's quit beating around the bush. What about spare crusher blades? The LP says to make none. How do I find the shadow price for changing that one? RM1 and BS1 were easy because they had upper limits in the constraints, so we just looked at the DUAL PRICES. But SPARE doesn't have a limit.

Tom: Actually, it does. It has a lower limit of zero, and that is binding.

PRINCIPLE 6: *REDUCED COSTS are the shadow prices for the nonnegativity constraints.* Because the nonnegativity constraints are $\geqslant$, increasing them makes Z^* worse.

Thus, for every spare produced, profits will decrease by at least \$302. That's the REDUCED COST of SPARE in the output.

Dean: That doesn't seem correct. We sell them for \$3400 and that is supposed to cover the costs of materials and labor and still allow for a profit margin.

Tom: The \$3400 does not take into account the fact that some of the materials used to make spares might be needed for making something else that is more profitable. But the shadow price does take other products into account. The LP prices things according to their most profitable use. We can force production by adding a constraint such as SPARE $\geqslant$ 10, and the LP will recommend a different solution. It might even change all the production quantities. Whatever it does will obtain the highest possible profits, but they will still be lower by at least \$302 per spare produced.

Dean: What about the range? How do we know how many spares could be produced at an opportunity cost of \$302?

Tom: The output in Table C-7 does not give the range over which the REDUCED COST is valid. This information could be provided, but it's common for LP software to omit it. There is a range, however, and if SPARE is increased too far, the REDUCED COST changes in a way that is less favorable (principle 5). Since the LP is maximizing profits in this case, the loss per unit would increase if SPARE goes beyond the range.

The Two Meanings of a Shadow Price

Dean: OK, let's say that you are right; profits would decrease at a rate of \$302 per unit by producing spares. I have two reasons why we should produce them anyway. First, a loss of \$302 is small compared with the price of \$3400, and it's probably worth it to be able to offer the service. Second, if that's all it takes, I'll bet that we could get approval for a price increase so that sales cover costs. What would your LP say to that?

Tom: If the selling price of spares is increased more than \$302, that would offset the opportunity cost and the LP would recommend production. I can't tell you how many spares it would recommend, but the LP would no longer see it as a losing proposition. You can see in the output that the ALLOWED INCREASE in the OBJECTIVE COEFFICIENT of SPARE is 302.

Dean: Yes, I see that in the table (Table C-7). So a new price of \$3400 + \$302 = \$3702 would make SPARE break even.

Tom: That's right. The \$302 has two meanings. It is the opportunity cost of forcing the LP to produce spares by adding a constraint, and it is also the (minimum) price increase that would make it optimal to produce spares.

Dean: That makes sense. If someone offered to compensate me for my loss, I would be willing to go along with production of a financial loser. But what about the ALLOWED DECREASE column? Why does it say INFINITY?

Tom: It means that we can decrease the price as much as we want without changing the optimal solution. Cutting the selling price would only make spare blades less profitable, so the LP would still recommend against production.

Dean: That makes sense too. Now I want to follow up on the two meanings of REDUCED COSTS. You said that it is an opportunity cost of producing more spares than optimal, and it is also the price change that would make it optimal to produce more. Right?

Tom: Right.

Dean: Do all the shadow prices have two meanings? Take the DUAL PRICE of the BS1 market limit (row 14). If the opportunity cost of this limit on the RHS is $146.20, is that the maximum price I would pay to increase the market limit by 1?

Tom: That is a good way to put it. Every shadow price has two meanings, one as an opportunity cost and the other as a price change. In the BS1 example, the price change applies to a variable that is not in the LP at the moment, namely a variable to represent the demand generated by a promotion. If it were included, and its cost were less than $146.20, the LP would take advantage of it. If the cost exceeded $146.20, its optimal quantity would be zero, and there would be no promotion.

Modifying the Variables

Having learned how to evaluate changes in SPARE and BS1, it occurred to Dean that there may be a great opportunity for additional profit with the other major product, BS2. In the formulation, its selling price of $46,000 is by far the highest of any product. Even so, its optimal production quantity is 100 units, which is 50 units less than its market limit in row 15. Unlike BS1, the market limit for BS2 has a zero opportunity cost (DUAL PRICE, row 15) because there are 50 units of slack in the constraint.

Dean: Leaving 50 units of unmet demand in the BS2 market could be bad for the corporate image. Why is BS2 production below the market? What would happen if we increase it? In the table its REDUCED COST is zero. Does that mean that we can increase it at no cost?

Tom: No. Remember principle 6. The REDUCED COST tells us what happens if the RHS of the nonnegativity constraint BS2 $\geqslant 0$ is increased. Since BS2 is already 100, changing BS2 $\geqslant 0$ has no effect, so the REDUCED COST is zero.

Dean: Then how can we evaluate an increase in BS2?

Tom: Let's see what we can learn from the OBJECTIVE COEFFICIENT RANGES.

PRINCIPLE 7: *Changes to an objective coefficient within the allowed range have no effect on the optimal quantities, X^*.* In maximization problems, increasing an objective coefficient, C, more than the ALLOWED INCREASE causes the corresponding X^* to increase; decreasing C more than the ALLOWED DECREASE will reduce X^*. (In minimization problems, the opposite is true.) Within the range, if dC is the change in C, the change in Z^* is $(X^*)(dC)$, and there is no change in X^*.

The coefficient for BS2 is its selling price of $46,000. If that goes up by more than the ALLOWED INCREASE of $292.40, the LP will choose a new solution that has greater production of type-2 rock crushers.

Dean: I see what you are saying, but I can't for the life of me understand where that number came from.

Tom: It's not easy. The LP is always looking for the most profitable way to use the resources. It has evaluated alternatives to the optimal solution. The $292.40 comes from knowing the next-best alternative.

Graphically, changing one objective coefficient tilts the objective function. A small tilt often has no effect on the choice of the optimal corner point. The increase of 292.4 is just enough to make the LP indifferent between the current solution and producing more BS2.

Dean: I'll take your word for it. But I still want to know the same information about BS2 as we learned about SPARE. We lose profits at the rate of $302 per unit to produce SPARE, and the same $302 could be added to the selling price to motivate the LP into producing spares. Does the same idea work for BS2?

Tom: Yes. The price changes in the OBJECTIVE COEFFICIENT RANGE section are also shadow prices. The optimal production of BS2 is 100. If we added the constraint BS2 $\geqslant$ 101, the extra unit would cost us at least $292.40 in lost profits. The new solution's objective function would be lower by $292.40, or more.

Dean: So the $292.40 is both the opportunity cost of producing more BS2 than is optimal, and the price change required to make it optimal to produce more BS2. Right?

Tom: Right. And all the other OBJECTIVE COEFFICIENT ALLOWED INCREASES and DECREASES have double meanings, too.

Dean: This opportunity cost must hold for a range of BS2 values, but I don't see the range in the output.

Tom: Some computer programs give you the range for this kind of sensitivity analysis. The one I used does not. So we have to use principle 5. That's why I said it would cost *at least* $292.40 per unit.

Dean: You are telling me that all shadow prices are optimistic estimates of the opportunity cost if the range is exceeded.

Tom: That's right. It holds for DUAL PRICES, REDUCED COSTS, and the shadow prices we have just found in the OBJECTIVE COEFFICIENT RANGES.

Dean: What about decreasing BS2? If more BS2 costs $292.40 per unit, then if we produced less we would *gain* $292.40 per unit. Right?

Tom: No. The LP chose BS2 = 100 to maximize profits, so profits cannot get better if we impose a different solution.

PRINCIPLE 8: *Forcing a variable away from its optimal quantity, X^*, cannot improve Z^*.*

Think of it this way. If the selling price drops by more than the ALLOWED DECREASE of \$1083.40, the optimal BS2 production will decrease. Why does the price have to decrease so far to get a reduction in output? Because the last unit of BS2 generated a net profit of \$1083.40; that is the opportunity cost of decreasing production.

Dean: OK. The opportunity cost of increasing BS2 is \$292.40, and the opportunity cost of decreasing it is \$1083.40. And these same figures are the price changes that would make it optimal to increase or decrease BS2 production.

Tom: That's right.

Dean: Those numbers seem to be pulled out of a hat. How does the LP know that we would lose \$1083.40 if we produced less BS2?

Tom: It finds the best way to use the resources that would become available if BS2 production were reduced. My textbook summarizes it this way:

PRINCIPLE 9: *The shadow price for a new constraint to change X^* is numerically equal to the OBJECTIVE COEFFICIENT ALLOWED INCREASE or DECREASE that would encourage a change in the same direction; or, the opportunity cost of a forced change is the same as the price adjustment needed to motivate the change.*

This is complicated enough to make it worthwhile to list the four cases to which it applies.

For maximization,

shadow price for new constraint increasing X^*	=	OBJECTIVE COEFFICIENT ALLOWED INCREASE
shadow price for new constraint decreasing X^*	=	OBJECTIVE COEFFICIENT ALLOWED DECREASE

For minimization,

shadow price for new constraint increasing X^*	=	OBJECTIVE COEFFICIENT ALLOWED DECREASE
shadow price for new constraint decreasing X^*	=	OBJECTIVE COEFFICIENT ALLOWED INCREASE

In keeping with principle 8, each of these shadow prices represents a rate at which Z^* is *worsened.*

Dean: I'm trying to apply the same reasoning to the other product, BS1, but the table (Table C-7) seems confusing. To find the price change that would cause an increase in BS1, I look at the OBJECTIVE COEFFICIENT ALLOWED INCREASE, but the table says that it is INFINITY. Is that really true?

Tom: When you see an INFINITY, it means that you are up against some problem constraint. Remember that for SPARE, there was no price decrease large enough to motivate less production because production was already zero. The nonnegativity constraint stops SPARE from going lower, regardless of price.

Dean: I get it. The market constraint for BS1 was 250 units (row 14 in Table C-6) and even an infinite price increase is not large enough to make the LP violate that constraint.

Tom: That's right.

Dean: Now I've got you trapped. At the beginning of this meeting we decided that a promotion could increase the market for BS1, and the opportunity cost of not doing the promotion was the DUAL PRICE of \$146.20. But now principle 9 tells us that the OBJECTIVE COEFFICIENT ALLOWED INCREASE is supposed to equal the opportunity cost, and that is INFINITY, not \$146.20. How do you explain that?

Tom: That's a tough one. But there is an explanation. Sensitivity analysis assumes that we change only one part of the formulation at a time. Principles 2, 3, and 4 assumed that we changed one RHS value. Row 14 was the one that affected the BS1 market limit. Principle 7 assumes that we change one objective coefficient. The price of BS1 is an example.

Principle 9 assumes that we add one new constraint, such as BS2 $\geqslant$ 101, and leave all the original constraints as they are. But we cannot add a constraint to force BS1 above 250 without violating row 14.

Dean: I don't see what's so different. Can't we just add a constraint like BS1 $\geqslant$ 255 to get more BS1 production?

Tom: No. Not without changing the existing constraint (row 14), because BS1 cannot be both greater than 255 and less than 250 at the same time. That is why the opportunity cost of increasing BS1 is infinity. If you go above 250, *there is no solution.*

Dean: The LP seems simpleminded if it doesn't know that it must change the upper limit if a new constraint is added.

Tom: It is simpleminded in that respect. Some LP packages are more sophisticated in the way that upper limits are handled. But it really doesn't matter. The information we wanted about BS1 was there. We just had to remember to look in row 14 where the market limit was.

Thanks for your help. You have given me some ideas for my report. I am going to prepare cost trade-offs for spare blades, different levels of BS2 output, and for the idea of promoting BS1 sales.

Dean: Glad to help. While you are at it, why don't you look at the possibility of producing extra units of P1? I understand that there is a market for it, too.

Interpreting Equality Constraints

We have used a number from every section of Table C-7, and most of them have been used twice! However, the principles have not dealt with equality constraints. Principle 3 has warned us to expect shadow prices of opposite direction for $\geqslant$ constraints compared with $\leqslant$. It turns out that = constraints can have DUAL PRICES of either sign. How can we tell whether an increase in the RHS of an equality is good or bad?

In the formulation of Table C-6, rows 2 to 10 are the accounting constraints that tie together the products, components, parts, subassemblies, raw materials, and labor. In the solution of Table C-7, the SLACK is 0 for each of these rows; equalities have no slack!

Row 2 has a DUAL PRICE of −125.85. DUAL PRICE relates to changes in the RHS, so consider what it would mean if the RHS of row 2 were increased from 0 to 1. Then it would read

$$\text{Row 2:}\quad \text{P1} - 3\ \text{BS1} - 6\ \text{BS2} = 1$$

In words, production of part type 1 is now required to exceed the assembly requirements by 1 unit. Therefore, the DUAL PRICE of −125.85 is the opportunity cost of producing extra units of P1. If management wishes to have an extra supply of P1 (perhaps for repairs), each unit produced would lower profits by $125.85. If these parts are sold as spare parts, the selling price should exceed $125.85 per unit to cover costs.

In this example, it was obvious that additional P1 must represent a cost rather than a profit, since there is no provision in the formulation for selling it. In other cases it may not be so obvious whether a change will be advantageous or detrimental to the objective function.

PRINCIPLE 10: *By convention, a positive DUAL PRICE represents an improvement in the objective function when the RHS is increased.* (This does not apply to REDUCED COSTS.)

Therefore, to be consistent with principle 3 the DUAL PRICE should be positive for $\leqslant$ and negative for $\geqslant$. If you encounter an output with the signs reversed for $\leqslant$ and $\geqslant$ DUAL PRICES, reverse the signs of all DUAL PRICES and use principle 10. Before applying a shadow price, it is always wise to examine what the change means, as in the preceding example.

Summary

The Rockwell Stone example has illustrated that a large number of relevant management issues can be addressed through LP. Understanding the output can save a great deal of work. The shadow prices may be used as opportunity costs to evaluate changes in the formulation such as increased demand or decreased supply of material. Even beyond their valid ranges, the shadow prices can be used to obtain limits on the change in Z^*.

Opportunity costs associated with the restrictions of the problem are called shadow prices. Shadow prices represent the rate of change of the optimal objective function value, Z^*. Ignoring the signs, DUAL PRICES are shadow prices for changing the RHS values, and REDUCED COSTS are shadow prices for the nonnegativity constraints.

A RHS value usually represents some resource that is in limited supply or a goal that management has set. The shadow price evaluates the opportunity cost of staying within the constraint and at the same time is an upper limit on how much management should be willing to pay to relax the constraint.

The nonnegativity constraints affect only the variables that have an optimal value of zero. Their shadow prices tell us how much the objective-function value will be worsened by introducing a nonoptimal variable into the solution. The shadow price also equals the change in the objective coefficient that would make it optimal to bring that variable into the solution.

Changing a RHS value affects Z^* and X^* linearly over a range. Changes in one direction improve Z^*, and the other direction makes Z^* worse. The same shadow price applies to both directions. This is also true for the nonnegativity constraints, although the ranges are not given in the output.

A constraint can be added to the formulation to force a variable X to move away from its optimal value, X^*. Either increasing or decreasing X leads to *worse* values for Z^* (lower if maximizing, higher if minimizing). The shadow price for increasing X is different than for decreasing it. The ranges are not given in the LP output shown in this text.

In every case, if a change goes beyond the range in which the shadow price is valid, the shadow price provides an optimistic estimate of the effect on Z^*.

The objective coefficients C can vary over a range given in the output without affecting X^*. Beyond the range, X^* will change in the direction that is motivated by the change in C. For example, to increase a particular X^*, we could increase its profit (or decrease its cost) by more than the allowable change.

Commercially available LP packages allow one to design the output to suit the application. This is particularly important because many applications are so large that output such as Table C-7 would be voluminous. As with any aid to decision making, the report should be designed to present the most relevant material only and in a format that is easy to understand.

REVIEW PROBLEMS

1. Interpret the output in Table C-7 for row 12.

2. What would happen to the solution if the cost of labor were to decrease by 0.5? 2.0?

3. The LP recommended that Rockwell Stone purchase 450 units of SA1, which is all of the available supply. If additional units of SA1 are available from another source, how much should Rockwell be willing to pay, and how many units should be purchased at that price? How would the additional units be used?

4. Rockwell is considering putting some of the 450 SA1 units aside for use as spare parts. Use the shadow price of row 6 to determine how much this will cost.

5. Use principle 9 to find the cost per unit of decreasing SA1 from its optimal purchase quantity. Why is this answer different from that for review problem 3?

Solutions

1. Row 12 is a lower limit of 300 on production of rock crushers. It is the only $\geqslant$ constraint in the formulation (other than the nonnegativity constraints). The entry 50 in the SLACK/SURPLUS column means that the limit of 300 in row 12 is exceeded by 50 units. The DUAL PRICE is 0 over a range determined by the SURPLUS. (This is consistent with the complementary slackness property stated in principle 1.)

2. If the objective coefficient of LABOR is between $-8.5 - 52.21 = -60.71$ and $-8.5 + 1.1 = -7.4$, there will be no change in the production quantities. Lowering costs by 0.5 increases the coefficient from -8.5 to -8.0, which is within this range; therefore, X^* does not change. However, the optimal so-

lution calls for 5110 hours of LABOR; therefore, lowering its unit cost by 0.5 would increase profits by (0.5)(5110) = 2555. If the labor cost decreases by 2.0, its objective coefficient falls outside the range, so a new solution will result, using more LABOR.

3. The limit of 450 units for SA1 is given in row 17. The DUAL PRICE of row 17 is $541.70, which is valid if the available quantity increases by 2.05 units or less. However, the objective function includes the current purchase price of $3150; thus, we would be willing to pay up to $3150 + $541.70 or $3691.70 per unit for two additional units of SA1. These units would be used to increase production of BS2 rock crushers, since BS1 is already at its upper limit of 250.

4. Increasing the RHS of row 6 would mean that more units of SA1 are to be purchased than are used for assembly. The difference can be set aside for use as spares (or for any other use). Row 6 of Table C-7 indicates that the objective function will decrease by $3691.70 per unit for the first 100 units that are set aside in this way. The reason for the decrease is that there will be less production of rock crushers if some of the SA1s are set aside. (Note the close relationship between this answer and that to review problem 3.)

5. The shadow price of decreasing SA1 is the OBJECTIVE FUNCTION ALLOWED DECREASE = 541.70. In this case, we save (avoid) the purchase cost of $3150, which is not true in review problem 3.

C-5 OTHER TOPICS IN MATHEMATICAL PROGRAMMING

We have seen that LP is a useful tool for modeling complex, real-world problems. In addition to offering an optimal solution to the problem formulation, its greatest benefit stems from its ability to deepen understanding and sharpen managerial insight into the nature of the problem and its many parameters. In this section we briefly discuss some additional aspects of mathematical programming. First, we review some new developments concerning solution methods for LPs. We then briefly discuss integer programming.

A New Solution Method for Linear Programming

A front-page article in the *New York Times* recently reported:

> a startling theoretical breakthrough in the solving of systems of equations that often grow too vast and complex for the most powerful computers. . . .
>
> The discovery . . . has also set off a deluge of inquiries from brokerage houses, oil companies and airlines, industries with millions of dollars at stake in problems known as linear programming (Gleick 1984)

News of this discovery also appeared in other well-known newspapers and magazines, such as *The Wall Street Journal* and *Business Week* (see Guyon 1986 and Wild and Port 1987).

These articles covered the development of a new solution procedure (or *algorithm*) for LP (Karmarkar 1984). This algorithm, now widely referred to as the *interior-point method*, is important in the field of mathematical programming for several reasons. In addition to representing an innovative solution approach to LP, it also provides an efficient way to solve LPs—both theoretically and computationally. A brief review of the history of solving LPs will help us to appreciate the significance of this discovery.

The simplex method was developed in 1947 by George Dantzig and has been the principal algorithm for solving LPs since that time. (See Dantzig 1963 for a discussion of the early history of LP.)

Interestingly, from a theoretical perspective, the simplex method is not an efficient algorithm. Recall that the simplex method solves LPs by moving from corner point to corner point in its search for an optimal solution. In a worst-case scenario, the simplex method can visit a very large (exponential) number of extreme points in solving an LP. This means that in the worst case, to solve a large problem the simplex method could require an inordinate amount of time—years, or even centuries! Fortunately this rarely occurs in practice, and the simplex method has proven to be a useful and robust problem-solving tool.

For a long time it was not known whether LP problems were intrinsically difficult to solve; that is, it might not be possible for anyone to develop an efficient algorithm to solve the problem. If that were the case, the simplex method might have been as efficient as could be expected. However, Khachian (1979) discovered a new solution method, "the ellipsoid algorithm," that did not require a worst-case exponential effort to solve LPs. This was an important mathematical discovery, since the inherent difficulty of LP had been established. Unfortunately, the ellipsoid algorithm did not turn out to be a good way to solve LPs in practice. Despite its nice theoretical properties, its exacting computational requirements did not make it competitive with the simplex method when actually solving problems.

The interior-point method provides another theoretically efficient solution approach to solving LPs. However, it also appears to be competitive with the simplex method in the actual solution of many classes of real-world problems. Computational testing suggests that it may run faster than the simplex method on some classes of large problems.

Figure C-3 illustrates the basic difference between the solution approaches taken by the simplex and interior-point methods. The simplex method operates

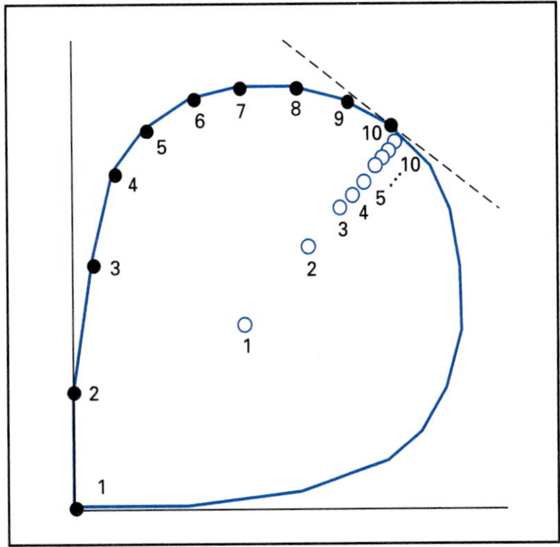

Figure C-3 Simplex Method (•) and Interior-Point Method (○) Approaches to the Optimal Solution of a Small LP. (Reprinted by permission of J.N. Hooker, "Karmarkar's Linear Programming Algorithm," *Interfaces*, vol. 16, no. 4 (July–August, 1986). Copyright 1986 the Operations Research Society of America and The Institute of Management Sciences, 290 Westminster Street, Providence, Rhode Island 02903 U.S.A.)

on the surface of the feasible region, moving among corner points. As its name suggests, the interior-point method moves among points lying strictly inside the feasible region (interior points) as it converges toward the optimal solution. Like the simplex method, the interior-point method is an iterative algorithm, meaning that it follows a repetitive sequence of steps. In each iteration the interior-point method employs a projective technique that transforms the feasible region in a way that maintains the essential properties of the region while allowing the algorithm to make substantial progress toward the optimal solution when moving to the new interior point. Hooker (1986) provides an excellent introduction to the interior-point method.

Commercial software packages are already including versions of the interior-point method. A possible disadvantage of the interior-point method is that it does not readily provide the sensitivity-analysis information of the type discussed in Section C-4. As Hooker (1986) notes, however, it is possible to use a simplex-method procedure as a follow-on to the interior-point method. In this way, the material covered in Section C-4 would be directly applicable to interior-point-method solution of LPs.

Integer Programming

In section C-1 we noted that LP requires that fractional values of the decision variables be acceptable. Many LP applications require that some or all of the decision variables take on integer values. As was mentioned earlier, if the optimal quantities are large, it is often acceptable to round them to integer values without significantly affecting solution quality. However, when the decision variable is limited to a small number of integer values, rounding is usually not acceptable.

Suppose, for example, that a particular machine can be used to produce an item and that the machine has a setup cost of $250. However, there are alternative, less efficient ways to produce the item. This is frequently modeled by using a variable that takes on the value of 1 if the machine is to be used in the production of the item, in which case the setup cost of the machine will be incurred, or that takes on a value of 0 (if the machine is not used). If we solve this application as an LP, a fractional value for the setup variable is meaningless.

Integer programming (*IP*) problems are constrained-optimization problems in which some or all of the variables are restricted to take on integer values. A variable, such as the one described in the preceding paragraph, that must assume a value of either 0 or 1 is called a *0-1 variable* (or a *binary variable*). 0-1 variables are useful because they allow us to incorporate logical conditions into the optimization model. (For example, the setup cost of $250 is incurred if and only if the machine is used.)

Appropriately, constrained-optimization problems involving 0-1 variables are called *0-1 integer programming problems*. If an optimization model contains both continuous and integer variables, it is called a *mixed integer programming problem*.

Applications of integer (and mixed integer) programming models arise in many areas of operations management. Scheduling problems, of the kind discussed in Chapters 11 and 13, can often be formulated as integer programming problems. This also applies to production-planning problems (Chapters 9, 10, and 12), inventory problems (Chapter 8), as well as to facility location and layout (Chapter 16). In Section 16-3 a mixed integer formulation of a plant-location problem was briefly discussed.

Not surprisingly, mathematical programming has proven to be an extremely important tool for solving operations management problems. This is particularly true for integer programming. IPs, however, are much more difficult to solve than LPs. An "efficient" algorithm (in the computer-science sense) for IP has not been discovered. Unlike the simplex method for LP, there is no general solution method that consistently works well on large problems in practice. The existence of an efficient algorithm for IP is still the subject of inquiry among mathematicians and computer scientists, some of whom conjecture that an efficient algorithm cannot be found.

Researchers, however, have developed general solution procedures for IP problems. These algorithms perform reasonably well on small problems but run the risk of requiring an excessive amount of time on even medium-size problems. A 100-variable IP problem, for example, might be solved on a microcomputer in a matter of minutes, whereas another IP of the same size could possibly require years to solve on a supercomputer!

Despite the seeming intractability of integer programs, significant advances have been made in the solution and application of useful problem classes. Researchers are sometimes able to take advantage of the special problem structure exhibited by these classes of integer programming problems in designing solution procedures. Although the underlying problem is still difficult, these specialized algorithms can be extremely effective in obtaining optimal or near-optimal solutions to real-world–size problems in a reasonable amount of time.

Shapiro (1991) describes the use of mathematical programming models in production-planning and scheduling problems and discusses applications of mixed integer programming models to problems in purchasing and production planning. These models have been successful in large-scale applications. Shapiro notes that much remains to be accomplished in extending the tractability and application of mathematical programs, especially mixed integer programming model formulations. As the technology advances, mathematical programming models hold considerable promise for future application. (See Nemhauser and Wolsey 1988 for a discussion of IP.)

The purpose of this appendix has been to explain the basics of LP, as well as to provide a brief glimpse into the field of mathemtical programming and to highlight the importance of this methodology in solving operations management problems. As computing capability grows more powerful and cheaper, it will be essential that managers be familiar, even comfortable, with the effective use of these tools in their organization.

CASELET

RED BRAND CANNERS*

On Monday morning, Mr. Mitchell Gordon, vice-president of operations, asked the controller, the sales manager, and the production manager to meet with him to discuss the amount of tomato products to pack that

*Reprinted from *Stanford Business Cases 1977* with permission of the publishers, Stanford University Graduate School of Business. Copyright 1977 and by the Board of Trustees of the Leland Stanford Junior University.

season. The tomato crop, which had been purchased at planting, was beginning to arrive at the cannery, and packing operations would have to be started by the following Monday. Red Brand Canners was a medium-size company that canned and distributed a variety of fruit and vegetable products under private brands in the western states.

Mr. William Cooper, the controller, and Mr. Charles Myers, the sales manager, were the first to arrive in Mr. Gordon's office. Dan Tucker, the production manager, came in a few minutes later and said that he had picked up Produce Inspection's latest estimate of the quality of the incoming tomatoes. According to their report, about 20% of the crop was grade-A quality and the remaining portion of the 3-million-pound crop was grade B.

Gordon asked Myers about the demand for tomato products for the coming year. Myers replied that they could sell all the whole canned tomatoes they could produce. The expected demand for tomato juice and tomato paste, on the other hand, was limited. The sales manager then passed around the latest demand forecast, which is shown in Exhibit 1. He reminded the

Exhibit 1 Sales Data

Product	Selling Price per Case	Demand Forecast (cases)
Whole tomatoes	$4.00	800,000
Tomato juice	4.50	50,000
Tomato paste	3.80	80,000

group that the selling prices had been set in light of the long-term marketing strategy of the company, and potential sales had been forecast at these prices.

Bill Cooper, after looking at Myers' estimates of demand, said that it looked like the company ''should do quite well (on the tomato crop) this year.'' With the new accounting system that had been set up, he had been able to compute the contribution for each product, and according to his analysis the incremental profit on the whole tomatoes was greater than for any other tomato product. In May, after Red Brand had signed contracts agreeing to purchase the grower's production at an average delivered price of 6 cents per pound, Cooper had computed the tomato products' contributions (see Exhibit 2).

Dan Tucker brought to Cooper's attention the fact that although there was ample production capacity, it was impossible to produce all whole tomatoes, as too small a portion of the tomato crop was grade-A quality. Red Brand used a numerical scale to record the quality of both raw produce and prepared products. This scale ran from 0 to 10, the higher number representing better quality. Rating tomatoes according to this scale, grade-A tomatoes averaged 9 points per pound and grade-B tomatoes averaged 5 points per pound. Tucker noted that the minimum average input quality for canned whole tomatoes was 8 and for juice it was 6 points per pound. Paste could be made entirely from grade-B tomatoes. This quality-point requirement meant that whole tomato production was limited to 800,000 pounds.

Gordon stated that this was not a real limitation. He had been recently solicited to purchase 80,000 pounds of grade-A tomatoes at 8.5 cents per pound and at that time had turned down the offer. He felt, however, that the tomatoes were still available.

Exhibit 2 Product Item Profitability (per case)

Product	Whole Tomatoes	Tomato Juice	Tomato Paste
Selling price	$4.00	$4.50	$3.80
Variable costs			
Direct labor	1.18	1.32	0.54
Variable OHD	0.24	0.36	0.26
Variable selling	0.40	0.85	0.38
Packaging material	0.70	0.65	0.77
Fruit	1.08	1.20	1.50
Total variable costs	3.60	4.38	3.45
Contribution	0.40	0.12	0.35
Less allocated OHD	0.28	0.21	0.23
Net profit	0.12	(0.09)	0.12

Product usage is as follows:

Product	Pounds per Case
Whole tomatoes	18
Tomato juice	20
Tomato paste	25

Myers, who had been doing some calculations, said that although he agreed that the company "should do quite well this year," it would not be canning whole tomatoes. It seemed to him that the tomato cost should be allocated on the basis of quality and quantity rather than by quantity only as Cooper had done. Therefore, he had recomputed the marginal profit on this basis (see Exhibit 3), and from his results, Red Brand should use 2 million

Exhibit 3 Marginal Analysis of Tomato Products

Z = cost per pound of grade-A tomatoes in cents

Y = cost per pound of grade-B tomatoes in cents

$$(1)\ (600{,}000 \text{ lb} \times Z) + (2{,}400{,}000 \text{ lb} \times Y) = (3{,}000{,}000 \text{ lb} \times 6 \text{ cents/lb})$$

$$(2)\ \frac{Z}{9} = \frac{Y}{5}$$

Z = 9.32 cents per pound

Y = 5.18 cents per pound

Product	Canned Whole Tomatoes	Tomato Juice	Tomato Paste
Selling price	$4.00	$4.50	$3.80
Variable cost (excluding tomato costs)	2.52	3.18	1.95
	$1.48	$1.32	$1.85
Tomato cost	1.49	1.24	1.30
Marginal profit	($0.01)	$0.08	$0.55

pounds of grade-B tomatoes for paste, and the remaining 400,000 pounds of grade-B tomatoes and all the grade-A tomatoes for juice. If the demand expectations were realized, a contribution of $48,000 would be made on this year's tomato crop.

Required

1. Check Myers' production plan to see if his $48,000 figure is correct.
2. Formulate an LP that allocates the 3-million-pound crop to the three products.
3. The objective is to maximize total contribution. Decide on objective-function coefficients based on cost-accounting principles, keeping in mind Cooper's and Myers' cost-allocation schemes.
4. Solve the LP if you have a computer package available.
5. Whether or not you solve the LP, discuss how LP can help them to decide on the option for 80,000 more grade-A tomatoes.

PROBLEMS

*1. Consider the following LP:

$$\begin{aligned} &\text{Minimize} && X_1 + X_2 \\ &\text{subject to (2)} && X_1 + 2X_2 \leqslant 12 \\ &\text{(3)} && 2X_1 + X_2 \leqslant 10 \\ &\text{(4)} && X_1 + 3X_2 \geqslant 4 \\ &\text{(5)} && 3X_1 + X_2 \geqslant 5 \\ &\text{(6)} && X_1, X_2 \geqslant 0 \end{aligned}$$

a. Check each of the following solutions for feasibility. (Are the constraints satisfied?)

Solution 1: $X_1 = 0, X_2 = 0$ Solution 5: $X_1 = 5, X_2 = 0$
Solution 2: $X_1 = 0, X_2 = 5$ Solution 6: $X_1 = 1, X_2 = 1$
Solution 3: $X_1 = 0, X_2 = 6$ Solution 7: $X_1 = 2, X_2 = 2$
Solution 4: $X_1 = 4, X_2 = 0$ Solution 8: $X_1 = 4, X_2 = 4$

b. Find the objective-function value for each of the feasible solutions shown in part a.

c. Plot the constraints on a graph similar to Figure C-1. Be sure to include the arrows to indicate which side of each line satisfies the inequality.

d. Plot the points from part a,and verify your answer to a.

e. Plot the objective function for the two values $X_1 + X_2 = 1$, and $X_1 + X_2 = 10$. Then find the optimal solution, remembering that this is a minimization problem.

2. Consider the LP in problem 1.

a. Insert slack or surplus variables to convert all constraints to equalities.

*Problems with an asterisk have answers in the back of the book.

b. Calculate the quantities of each slack or surplus variable for each solution given in part a of problem 1.

c. Is it true that a negative value of a slack or surplus variable occurs if and only if an inequality constraint is violated? Show how you know.

*3. Consider the following LP.

$$\begin{array}{lrcl} \text{Maximize} & 2X_1 + 2X_2 & & \\ \text{subject to (2)} & 2X_1 + X_2 & \leqslant & 20 \\ \text{(3)} & X_1 + X_2 & \leqslant & 12 \\ \text{(4)} & X_1 + 2X_2 & \leqslant & 20 \\ \text{(5)} & X_1, X_2 & \geqslant & 0 \end{array}$$

a. Check the following solutions for feasibility and give their objective-function values: $X_1 = 8$, $X_2 = 4$; $X_1 = 6$, $X_2 = 6$; and $X_1 = 4$, $X_2 = 8$.

b. What two properties do all these solutions have in common?

c. Graph the constraints, plot the three points from part a, and plot the objective function at $2X_1 + 2X_2 = 30$.

d. Verify that all three solutions from part a are optimal.

e. If you had the final tableau from a simplex solution to this problem, how would you know that more than one optimal solution exists?

4. a. Solve the following LP graphically:

$$\begin{array}{lrcl} \text{Maximize} & N + M & & \\ \text{subject to (2)} & 2N + 0.5M & \leqslant & 200 \\ \text{(3)} & N + M & \leqslant & 200 \\ \text{(4)} & 0.05N + 0.25M & \leqslant & 20 \\ \text{(5)} & N, M & \geqslant & 0 \end{array}$$

b. Identify which of the constraints can be changed with no effect on the optimal solution.

c. Change the right-hand side of constraint 2 to 220 and estimate the amount of change in the objective function.

5. Consider the following LP:

$$\begin{array}{lrcl} \text{Maximize} & 10X_1 + 9X_2 & & \\ \text{subject to (2)} & 0.7X_1 + X_2 & \leqslant & 630 \\ \text{(3)} & 3X_1 + 5X_2 & \leqslant & 3600 \\ \text{(4)} & 3X_1 + 2X_2 & \leqslant & 2124 \\ \text{(5)} & X_1 + 2.5X_2 & \leqslant & 1350 \\ \text{(6)} & X_1, X_2 & \geqslant & 0 \end{array}$$

a. Solve this LP graphically.

b. Include an additional constraint, (7): $X_1 + X_2 \geqslant 1000$, on your graph and comment on the resulting set of feasible solutions (i.e., the feasible region).

6. What follows is the computer output and a graph of a two-variable LP that minimizes a cost function. The purpose of this problem is to see how sensitivity analysis looks on a graph.

MIN $X + 4Y$
SUBJECT TO
(2) $2X + Y \geqslant 3$
(3) $4X + 5Y \geqslant 10$

OBJECTIVE FUNCTION VALUE = 2.5

			OBJECTIVE COEFFICIENT RANGES		
VARIABLE	SOLUTION	REDUCED COST	CURRENT COEF.	ALLOWED INCREASE	ALLOWED DECREASE
X	2.50	0.00	1.00	2.20	1.00
Y	0.00	2.75	4.00	INFINITY	2.75

			RIGHT-HAND-SIDE RANGES		
ROW	SLACK/ SURPLUS	DUAL PRICES	CURRENT RHS	ALLOWED INCREASE	ALLOWED DECREASE
2	2.00	0.00	3.00	2.00	INFINITY
3	0.00	−0.25	10.00	INFINITY	4.00

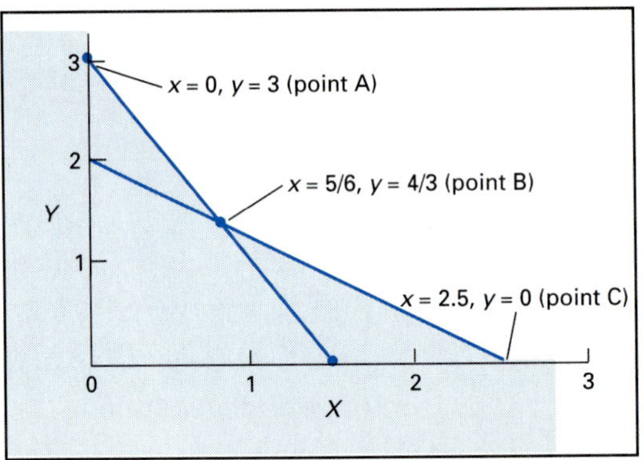

a. The optimal objective-function value (cost) is 2.5. Plot the objective-function equation $X + 4Y = 2.5$. What are the optimal values of X and Y?

b. The ALLOWED INCREASE of the objective coefficient of X is 2.2, which would increase the unit cost of X from 1.0 (now) to 3.2. The objective-function value would be $3.2(2.5) + 4(0) = 8.0$ for the current X and Y solution. Plot the new objective function $3.2X + 4Y = 8$. What are the optimal values of X and Y? What would happen if the coefficient of X were 3.21? (No need to plot.) Explain what the ALLOWED INCREASE = 2.2 means based on this exercise.

c. Instead of changing the objective coefficients, how else could we force the solution $X = 5/6$ to be optimal by adding a $\leqslant$ constraint? What would the objective-function value be? Based on this, compute the opportunity cost per unit change in X. Compare your answer with part b and comment on principle 9 of Section C-4.

d. Ignoring parts b and c, consider decreasing the RHS of row 3. Use principle 3 of Section C-4 to predict whether this will be good or bad. According to the output, what effect will this have? Over what range?

e. Change the RHS of constraint 3 to 8.0; plot it on the graph and compute the new optimal solution. How much has it changed per unit change in RHS? Compare with part d.

f. Repeat part e for a RHS of 4 and use your results to comment on principle 5 in Section C-4.

g. Without computation (and ignoring the foregoing) explain what would happen if we forced Y to increase by imposing a constraint such as $Y \geqslant 1$. What would happen to cost (quantitative)? What would happen to X (qualitative, referring to the graph)?

h. Using the same approach as in part g, explain what happens if the RHS of row 2 is increased.

*7. Consider the following LP:

$$
\begin{array}{lrl}
\text{Maximize} & & 10X_1 + 9X_2 \\
\text{subject to} & (2) & 0.7X_1 + X_2 \leqslant 630 \\
 & (3) & X_1 + 5X_2 \leqslant 3600 \\
 & (4) & 3X_1 + 2X_2 \leqslant 2124 \\
 & (5) & X_1 + 2.5X_2 \leqslant 1350 \\
 & (6) & X_1, X_2 \geqslant 0
\end{array}
$$

We are going to evaluate a particular basic solution to see whether it is feasible and whether it is optimal.

a. Change all constraints to equalities by inserting slack or surplus variables. Call them S_1, S_2, S_3, and S_4.

b. Write a tableau for this problem.

c. Interpret the solution implied by the tableau.

d. What are the quantities of the nonbasic variables?

e. Is the solution feasible?

f. Is it optimal?

g. Would it be optimal if the objective were minimization?

8. Problem 7 should be done before this one. All equation numbers refer to the LP developed in that problem, with slack variables having been added to each constraint. We are going to bring X_1 into the basis and eliminate S_1. This is not the choice that the simplex method would make, and we will see why.

a. Using X_1 as the entering variable and S_1 as the departing variable, carry out simplex step 3 on the objective function and row 2.

b. Is the simplex criterion for optimality satisfied?

c. What are the quantities of X_1 and X_2 in this solution?

d. Substitute your answer from part c into the original LP equations and explain why this is not the optimal solution to the LP.

e. What should the departing variable have been instead of S_1?

*9. Use the simplex method to show that the optimal solution to the LP in problem 7 is $X_1 = 540$, $X_2 = 252$. (Note that this exercise is solved graphically in problem 5.)

10. Solve the following LP using the simplex method. (This is identical to the problem solved graphically in problem 4.)

$$\begin{aligned}
\text{Maximize} \quad & N + M \\
\text{subject to} \quad & 2N + 0.5M + SP = 200 \\
& N + M + SC = 200 \\
& 0.05N + 0.25M + ST = 20 \\
& N, M, SP, SC, ST \geqslant 0
\end{aligned}$$

11. Use the simplex method to solve the minimization LP in problem 6.

*12. Blizzard's Clam Chowder comes in two varieties, New England and Manhattan. The ingredients are as follows for 1 liter of soup.

New England: 2 potatoes, 1 clam, 0.85 liter water, 0.05 liter tomato sauce.

Manhattan: 0.5 potato, 1 clam, 0.65 liter water, 0.25 liter tomato sauce.

Clams cost $0.10 each, tomato sauce costs $0.60 per liter, potatoes cost $0.03 each, and water is so cheap that we can ignore it in this problem. At Blizzard, the current stocks of ingredients are 200,000 potatoes, 200,000 clams, 20,000 liters of tomato sauce, and unlimited water.

The two varieties of soup sell for the same price, and their current stock will not saturate the markets.

a. Select a one-letter symbol for each ingredient and each product. Define them in words.
b. Write the constraints that account for the ingredients used.
c. Test your constraints in part b using the quantities of ingredients for 1 liter of New England and 1 liter of Manhattan.
d. If Blizzard were planning a production run of New England chowder only, how many liters could they make using only the current stock of ingredients? Which ingredients would be left over?
e. Answer part d for a run of Manhattan chowder, assuming that no New England chowder is made.
f. Assuming that all leftover ingredients must be discarded, how could Blizzard get the most profit out of their current stock without purchasing additional ingredients? (Formulate an LP to help them with this decision, but do not solve it.)

*13. (This problem requires data from, but not a solution to, problem 12.) The management of Blizzard's Clam Chowder Company found the linear programming approach interesting, but it did not solve their real problem. They plan production on a quarterly basis. At the end of each quarter, any leftover soup is deducted from the demand forecast for the next quarter. Then production plans and purchasing decisions are made based on not allowing production to exceed the modified demand forecast. Current prices and current inventories of ingredients left from the previous period also enter the decision. However, these plans are never precisely carried out because Blizzard procures the ingredients by contracting to purchase the entire harvest (of potatoes, clams, or tomatoes) from farmers and clammers in the region, and the delivered quantities usually vary from expectations. Furthermore, production plans are modified whenever the demand deviates significantly from the forecast. As a consequence, it is not uncommon to have leftover ingredients or leftover soup as the new planning period approaches. Leftover ingredients are treated as free (no cost) resources in their quarterly plan.

The clam chowder demand forecast for the upcoming quarter is 500,000 liters of New England and 450,000 liters of Manhattan, to sell at \$1.05 and \$1 per liter, respectively. Data on ingredient prices and stocks are given in problem 12. There are 50,000 liters of leftover Manhattan and no leftover New England Clam chowder.

a. In an LP formulation for clam chowder production planning, why is it important to use a different variable for potatoes to be purchased than for potatoes to be used from current stocks?

b. Carefully define the variables for this problem, giving a one- or two-letter symbol for each one.

c. Write the constraints and state them in words.

d. What objective function should be used? Why? Formulate and explain it.

e. Categorize each constraint as either accounting, fact of life, or policy (see Section C-3) and discuss briefly.

f. There is an obvious optimal solution to this problem. Can you find it? Explain.

14. (This problem requires a solution to Problem 13.) At a meeting of all the management personnel of Blizzard's Clam Chowder Company, the purchasing manager pointed out that the company cannot obtain unlimited supplies of potatoes at \$0.03 each. Often they will have to go as high as \$0.05 to obtain the required quantities. In the upcoming quarter, it is estimated that up to 150,000 potatoes can be obtained at \$0.03, and an additional 300,000 potatoes will be available at \$0.05.

a. As the inventor of the LP in problem 13, explain how you could incorporate this consideration in your formulation. (Hint: Consider your answer to part a of problem 13, treating the \$0.03 potatoes as a limited resource.)

b. This is an example of a nonlinear function in LP, since the slope of the cost function for potatoes *changes* from 0.03 to 0.05 at 300,000 potatoes. If all ingredients had nonlinear prices and limited quantities, why may the solution "produce enough to satisfy all demand" not be optimal?

*15. The Acme Company has three plants and four warehouses. The following data have been obtained for aggregate planning for the coming quarter; all figures are in units of one thousand unless otherwise specified.

Plant	Unit Production Cost	Plant Capacity	Warehouse	Demand
A	\$1.00	1200	1	700
B	1.20	1200	2	400
C	0.90	500	3	600
			4	500

Average selling price = \$1.50/thousand at all warehouses.

Unit Transportation Cost				
	To			
From	**1**	**2**	**3**	**4**
A	$0.10	$0.15	$0.40	$0.30
B	0.50	0.20	0.25	0.20
C	0.25	0.45	0.30	0.25

a. Suppose that the objective is to minimize cost, with upper limits on production due to the plant capacities, and upper limits on amounts shipped so that each warehouse receives no more than the expected demand. Explain why the optimal solution to that problem is zero, i.e., produce nothing. How should the demand constraints be stated to prevent this from happening?

b. Suppose that the objective is to maximize contribution to fixed cost and profit. What kind of constraint should be used to relate demand to production: equality, upper limit, or lower limit? Explain.

c. Formulate this problem as an LP to maximize contribution, using the variables A1, A2, and so on, to represent the quantities produced at plant A and shipped to warehouse 1 and warehouse 2, and so on, for all 12 combinations of plant-to-warehouse shipments.

d. The company does not wish to spend more than $400,000 on transportation. Incorporate this budget in your LP.

e. Up to 50,000 units of additional capacity are available at plant C at an additional cost of $0.05 per unit actually used. Modify your LP to allow it to choose whether to use the additional capacity.

16. The SFWP corporation produces 500 different products. Group 42 consists of four departments: stamping, forming, welding, and painting. Three different products are produced in Group 42, and the company is interested in reevaluating the production mix. Their aggregate production plan has set upper limits on the production rate in these departments by specifying the number of employees and not allowing extra shifts or overtime during the current month. However, the demands for these items, as estimated from sales trends, are increasing.

    a. Formulate an LP to recommend the daily production of each item, using the data in the accompanying tables.

    b. Management is considering shifting some workers between departments in Group 42. How could the LP output be used to help select desirable exchanges? (Not a new LP, just the solution of the LP in part a.)

    c. Would your answer for part b also hold for personnel exchanges between groups within the company? Explain.

Item	Time Required per Item Produced (seconds)				Marginal Contribution to Profit
	Stamping	Forming	Welding	Painting	
A	6	15	10	10	$0.020
B	3	5	20	8	0.030
C	10	6	8	25	0.025

Available Manpower (50 Minutes per Hour, 8 Hours per Shift)		
Department	Employees	Time Available (seconds)
Stamping	1.5	36,000
Forming	2	48,000
Welding	2	48,000
Painting	2.5	60,000

17. Four kinds of grain are mixed for cattle feed, with the goal of maximizing net dollar gain per month, defined as value of the beef minus the cost of the feed. Certain nutrients must be held within prespecified allowances, some by law, and others for the health of the animals. Formulate an LP to recommend the proportions to be used in the feed mix, using the following data for nutrients A, B, and C:

Grain Types	Cost per Pound	Nutrient Content (units per pound)			Dollar Value of Weight Gain Contribution (per pound of feed)
		A	B	C	
1	$0.10	0.1	0.05	0.3	$2.00
2	0.20	0.6	0.01	0.2	3.00
3	0.25	0.4	0.2	0.1	5.00
4	0.30	0.5	0.03	0.1	7.00

Nutrients	Minimum Units per Pound of Feed Mix	Maximim Units per Pound of Feed Mix
A	0.3	none
B	none	0.1
C	0.2	0.25

*18. The Seemore Cement Company makes two grades of cement. Each grade has a minimum production quantity to satisfy a contract they have with Smidt Builders. The minimums are 5000 tons of grade A and 4000 of grade B. Each ton of grade A is composed of 0.5 ton of ingredient 1, 0.3 ton of ingredient 2, and 0.2 ton of ingredient 3. The composition of grade B is 0.4, 0.2, and 0.4 of ingredients 1, 2, and 3, respectively. Each ton of grade A sells for $200 and costs $20 to manufacture, exclusive of raw materials. Grade B also costs $20 to manufacture, but sells for $170 per ton. Cement ingredients 1 and 3 are available in unlimited quantity, but 2 is available only up to 15,000 tons.

a. Formulate an LP with the preceding information. Be sure to define your variables.
b. This LP formulation is incomplete. What information would be needed to complete it?
c. Using either numbers (you make them up) or letters (math symbols) complete the formulation.

19. A farm family owns 100 acres of land and has $15,000 in funds available for investment. Its members can produce a total of 3500 worker-hours of labor during the winter months and 4000 worker-hours during the summer. If any of these worker-hours are not needed, younger members of the family will use them to work on a neighboring farm for $3.80 per hour during the winter months and $4.10 per hour during the summer.

Cash income may be obtained from three crops and two types of livestock: dairy cows and laying hens. No investment funds are needed for the crops. However, each cow will require an investment outlay of $400, and each hen will require $3. Each cow will require 1.5 acres of land, 100 worker-hours of work during the winter months, and another 50 worker-hours during the summer (150 total for the year). Each cow will produce a net annual cash income of $400 for the family. The corresponding figures for each hen are 0 acres, 0.6 worker-hour during the winter, 0.3 worker-hour during the summer (0.9 total for the year), and an annual net cash income of $2. The chicken house can accommodate a maximum of 3000 hens, and the size of the barn limits the herd to a maximum of 32 cows.

Estimated worker-hours and income per acre planted in each of the three crops are as follows:

	Soybeans	Corn	Oats
Winter worker-hours	20	35	10
Summer worker-hours	50	75	40
Net annual cash income ($)	175	300	120

The family wishes to determine how much acreage should be planted in each of the crops and how many cows and hens should be kept to maximize their net cash income.

a. Formulate an LP to help them with this problem.
b. Based on the results of your LP (if the output were available), how could they decide whether to consider expansion of the cow barn?
c. What advice could you give them based on the shadow price of the constraint on available land?

*20. The accompanying table shows the solution to the Blizzard's Clam Chowder problem. (It is useful, but not necessary, to have done problem 12 before this one. Data for this problem are described there.)

NENG = thousands of liters of New England Clam Chowder produced

MNHTN = thousands of liters of Manhattan Clam Chowder produced

MAX NENG + MNHTN

SUBJECT TO

(2) 2 NENG + 0.5 MNHTN ≤ 200 (potatoes)

(3) NENG + MNHTN ≤ 200 (clams)

(4) 0.05 NENG + 0.25 MNHTN ≤ 20 (tomato sauce)

OBJECTIVE FUNCTION VALUE = 147.37

VARIABLE	SOLUTION	REDUCED COST	OBJECTIVE COEFFICIENT RANGES: CURRENT COEF.	ALLOWED INCREASE	ALLOWED DECREASE
NENG	84.21	0	1.00	3.00	0.80
MNHTN	63.16	0	1.00	4.00	0.75

ROW	SLACK/ SURPLUS	DUAL PRICES	RIGHT-HAND-SIDE RANGES: CURRENT RHS	ALLOWED INCREASE	ALLOWED DECREASE
2	0	0.421	200	125.00	160.00
3	52.63	0	200	INFINITY	52.63
4	0	3.158	20	16.67	15.00

a. What is the optimal solution? How much of each ingredient is left over? (Notice that all variables are in thousands.)

b. Suppose that 20,000 more potatoes were available at no cost. How much more soup could be produced?

c. Repeat part b for 20,000 additional clams, and again for 20,000 liters of tomato sauce, each time assuming that only one ingredient is increased.

d. Disregarding parts b and c, suppose that a recount of the potato inventory yielded only 180,000. What should the change in total output be?

e. Repeat part d, assuming 200,000 potatoes and 180,000 clams, then 140,000 clams, then 70,000 clams.

f. Ignoring parts b to e, suppose that the market for New England chowder will only allow sales of 50,000 liters. What will the optimal total production be, and how many liters of Manhattan does this imply?

g. Ignoring parts b to f, suppose that the selling price of New England is $1.05 per liter, compared with $1 for Manhattan. Is the solution in part a optimal? Explain.

21. (Problem 15 should be done prior to this one, although it is not absolutely necessary.) The accompanying table shows the solution to the Acme Company's production and distribution problem without considering the possibility of additional capacity at plant C.

MAX .4 A1 + .35 A2 + .1 A3 + .2 A4 − .2 B1 + .1 B2
+ .05 B3 + .1 B4 + .35 C1 + .15 C2 + .3 C3 + .35 C4

SUBJECT TO

$$
\begin{aligned}
A1 + A2 + A3 + A4 &\le 1200 \quad (2)\\
B1 + B2 + B3 + B4 &\le 1200 \quad (3)\\
C1 + C2 + C3 + C4 &\le 500 \quad (4)\\
A1 + B1 + C1 &\le 700 \quad (5)\\
A2 + B2 + C2 &\le 400 \quad (6)\\
A3 + B3 + C3 &\le 600 \quad (7)\\
A4 + B4 + C4 &\le 500 \quad (8)
\end{aligned}
$$

$$
\begin{aligned}
&.1\,A1 + .15\,A2 + .4\,A3 + .3\,A4 + .5\,B1 + .2\,B2 \quad (9)\\
&+ .25\,B3 + .2\,B4 + .25\,C1 + .45\,C2 + .3\,C3 + .25\,C4 \le 400
\end{aligned}
$$

OBJECTIVE FUNCTION VALUE = 632

			OBJECTIVE COEFFICIENT RANGES		
VARIABLE	**SOLUTION**	**REDUCED COST**	**CURRENT COEF.**	**ALLOWED INCREASE**	**ALLOWED DECREASE**
A1	700	0	0.40	INFINITY	0.24
A2	400	0	0.35	INFINITY	0.18
A3	0	0.06	0.10	0.06	INFINITY
A4	100	0	0.20	0.18	0.06
B1	0	0.06	−0.20	0.60	INFINITY
B2	0	0.18	0.10	0.18	INFINITY
B3	40	0	0.05	0	0.05
B4	400	0	0.10	0.06	0
C1	0	0.24	0.35	0.24	INFINITY
C2	0	0.42	0.15	0.42	INFINITY
C3	500	0	0.30	INFINITY	0
C4	0	0	0.35	0	INFINITY

			RIGHT-HAND-SIDE RANGES		
ROW	**SLACK/ SURPLUS**	**DUAL PRICES**	**CURRENT RHS**	**ALLOWED INCREASE**	**ALLOWED DECREASE**
2	0	0.080	1200	100.00	100
3	760	0	1200	INFINITY	760
4	0	0.240	500	33.33	300
5	0	0.300	700	100.00	400
6	0	0.240	400	100.00	300
7	60	0	600	INFINITY	60
8	0	0.060	500	50.00	75
9	0	0.200	400	15.00	10

a. What is the optimal plant-to-warehouse distribution pattern?
b. Are there any other optimal solutions? Explain.
c. What is the net contribution for the quarter?
d. Would a larger transportation budget allow higher net quarterly profits? Would that be a good investment? How much would you recommend adding to or deleting from the transportation budget?
e. How much more profit would Acme obtain if the capacity of plant C were expanded by 50,000 units? Would this be a good opportunity if each unit of increased capacity costs $0.05 each quarter?
f. The shipment of 700 units from plant A to warehouse 1 was criticized as being excessive. If A1 is forced to be smaller, will profits increase or decline? At what rate?

REFERENCES

BLAND, R.G. "New Finite Rules for the Simplex Method," *Mathematics of Operations Research*, vol. 2, no. 2, 1977.

DANTZIG, G.B., *Linear Programming and Extensions*, Princeton, N.J.: Princeton University Press, 1963.

EPPEN, G.D., F.J. GOULD, and C.P. SCHMIDT, *Introductory Management Science*, 3rd ed., Englewood Cliffs, N.J.: Prentice-Hall, 1991.

GEOFFRION, A.M., "The Purpose of Mathematical Programming Is Insight, Not Numbers," *Interfaces*, vol. 7, no. 1, 1976.

GLEICK, J., "Breakthrough in Problem Solving," *New York Times*, November 19, 1984.

GUYON, J., "Karmarkar Algorithm Proves Its Worth," *Wall Street Journal*, July 18, 1986.

HILLIER, F.S., and G.J. LIEBERMAN, *Operations Research*, 4th ed., San Francisco: Holden-Day, 1986.

HOOKER, J.N., "Karmarkar's Linear Programming Algorithm," *Interfaces*, vol. 16, no. 4, 1986.

KARMARKAR, N., "A New Polynomial-Time Algorithm for Linear Programming," *Combinatorica*, vol. 4, no. 4, 1984.

KHACHIAN, L.G., "A Polynomial Algorithm in Linear Programming," *Doklady Akademii Nauk SSSR*, vol. 244, translated in *Soviet Mathematics—Doklady*, vol. 20, no. 1, 1979.

NEMHAUSER, G.L., and L.A. WOLSEY, *Integer and Combinatorial Optimization*, New York: Wiley, 1988.

SCHRAGE, L., *Linear Programming Models with LINDO*, Palo Alto, Calif.: Scientific Press, 1981.

SHAPIRO, J.F., "Mathematical Programming Models and Methods for Production Planning and Scheduling," in *Handbook in Operations Research*, S.C. Graves, A.H.G. Rinnooykan, and P. Zipkin, eds., Amsterdam, North-Holland, 1991.

WAGNER, H., *Principles of Operations Research*, 2nd ed., Englewood Cliffs, N.J.: Prentice-Hall, 1975.

WILD, W.G., JR., and O. PORT, "The Startling Discovery Bell Labs Kept in the Shadows," *Business Week*, September 21, 1987.

appendix

Appendix D Tables

TABLE 1 RANDOM NUMBERS

09 18 82 00 97	32 82 53 95 27	04 22 08 63 04	83 38 98 73 74	64 27 85 80 44
90 04 58 54 97	51 98 15 06 54	94 93 88 19 97	91 87 07 61 50	68 47 66 46 59
73 18 95 02 07	47 67 72 62 69	62 29 06 44 64	27 12 46 70 18	41 36 18 27 60
75 76 87 64 90	20 97 18 17 49	90 42 91 22 72	95 37 50 58 71	93 82 34 31 78
54 01 64 40 56	66 28 13 10 03	00 68 22 73 98	20 71 45 32 95	07 70 61 78 13
08 35 86 99 10	78 54 24 27 85	13 66 15 88 73	04 61 89 75 53	31 22 30 84 20
28 30 60 32 64	81 33 31 05 91	40 51 00 78 93	32 60 46 04 75	94 11 90 18 40
53 84 08 62 33	81 59 41 36 28	51 21 59 02 90	28 46 66 87 95	77 76 22 07 91
91 75 75 37 41	61 61 36 22 69	50 26 39 02 12	55 78 17 65 14	83 48 34 70 55
89 41 59 26 94	00 39 75 83 91	12 60 71 76 46	48 94 97 23 06	83 48 34 70 55
				94 54 13 74 08
77 51 30 38 20	86 83 42 99 01	68 41 48 27 74	51 90 81 39 80	72 89 35 55 07
19 50 23 71 74	69 97 92 02 88	55 21 02 97 73	74 28 77 52 51	65 34 46 74 15
21 81 85 93 13	93 27 88 17 57	05 68 67 31 56	07 08 28 50 46	31 85 33 84 52
51 47 46 64 99	68 10 72 36 21	94 04 99 13 45	42 83 60 91 91	08 00 74 54 49
99 55 96 83 31	62 53 52 41 70	69 77 71 28 30	74 81 97 81 42	43 86 07 28 34
33 71 34 80 07	93 58 47 28 69	51 92 66 47 21	58 30 32 98 22	93 17 49 39 72
85 27 48 68 93	11 30 32 92 70	28 83 43 41 37	73 51 59 04 00	71 14 84 36 43
84 13 38 96 40	44 03 55 21 66	73 85 27 00 91	61 22 26 05 61	62 32 71 84 23
56 73 21 62 34	17 39 59 61 31	10 12 39 16 22	85 49 65 75 60	81 60 41 88 80
65 13 85 68 06	87 64 88 52 61	34 31 36 58 61	45 87 52 10 69	85 64 44 72 77
38 00 10 21 76	81 71 91 17 11	71 60 29 29 37	74 21 96 40 49	65 58 44 96 98
37 40 29 63 97	01 30 47 75 86	56 27 11 00 86	47 32 46 26 05	40 03 03 74 38
97 12 54 03 48	87 08 33 14 17	21 81 53 92 50	75 23 76 20 47	15 50 12 95 78
21 82 64 11 34	47 14 33 40 72	64 63 88 59 02	49 13 90 64 41	03 85 65 45 52
73 13 54 27 42	95 71 90 90 35	85 79 47 42 96	08 78 98 81 56	64 69 11 92 02
07 63 87 79 29	03 06 11 80 72	96 20 74 41 56	23 82 19 95 38	04 71 36 69 94
60 52 88 34 41	07 95 41 98 14	59 17 52 06 95	05 53 35 21 39	61 21 20 64 55
83 59 63 56 55	06 95 89 29 83	05 12 80 97 19	77 43 35 37 83	92 30 15 04 98
10 85 06 27 46	99 59 91 05 07	13 49 90 63 19	53 07 57 18 39	06 41 01 93 62
39 82 09 89 52	43 62 26 31 47	64 42 18 08 14	43 80 00 93 51	31 02 47 31 67
59 58 00 64 78	75 58 97 88 00	88 83 55 44 86	23 76 80 61 56	04 11 10 84 08
38 50 80 73 41	23 79 34 87 63	90 82 29 70 22	17 71 90 42 07	95 95 44 99 53
30 69 27 06 68	94 68 81 61 27	56 19 68 00 91	82 06 76 34 00	05 46 26 92 00
65 44 39 56 59	18 28 82 74 37	49 63 22 40 41	08 33 76 56 76	96 29 99 08 36
27 26 75 02 64	13 19 27 22 94	07 47 74 46 06	17 98 54 89 11	97 34 13 03 58
91 30 70 69 91	19 07 22 42 10	36 69 95 37 28	28 82 53 57 93	28 97 66 62 52
68 43 49 46 88	84 47 31 36 22	62 12 69 84 08	12 84 38 25 90	09 81 59 31 46
48 90 81 58 77	54 74 52 45 91	35 70 00 47 54	83 82 45 26 92	54 13 05 51 60
06 91 34 51 97	42 67 27 86 01	11 88 30 95 28	63 01 19 89 01	14 97 44 03 44
10 45 51 60 19	14 21 03 37 12	91 34 23 78 21	88 32 58 08 51	43 66 77 08 83
12 88 39 73 43	65 02 76 11 84	04 28 50 13 92	17 97 41 50 77	90 71 22 67 69
21 77 83 09 76	38 80 73 69 61	31 64 94 20 96	63 28 10 20 23	08 81 64 74 49
19 52 35 95 15	65 12 25 96 59	86 28 36 82 58	69 57 21 37 98	16 43 59 15 29
67 24 55 26 70	35 58 31 65 63	79 24 68 66 86	76 46 33 42 22	26 65 59 08 02
60 58 44 73 77	07 50 03 79 92	45 13 42 65 29	28 78 08 36 37	41 32 64 43 44
53 85 34 13 77	36 06 69 48 50	58 83 87 38 59	49 36 47 33 31	96 24 04 36 42
24 63 73 87 36	74 38 48 93 42	52 62 30 79 92	12 36 91 86 01	03 74 28 38 73
83 08 01 24 51	38 99 22 28 15	07 75 95 17 77	97 37 72 75 85	51 97 23 78 67
16 44 42 43 34	36 15 19 90 73	27 49 37 09 39	85 13 03 25 52	54 84 65 47 59
60 79 01 81 57	57 17 86 57 62	11 16 17 85 76	45 81 95 29 79	65 13 00 48 60

SOURCE: Reproduced by permission from tables of the RAND Corporation in A Million Random Digits with 100,000 Normal Deviates (New York: Free Press, 1955).

TABLE 2 NORMAL DISTRIBUTION (UPPER TAIL)

Areas under the Normal Curve from Z to ∞

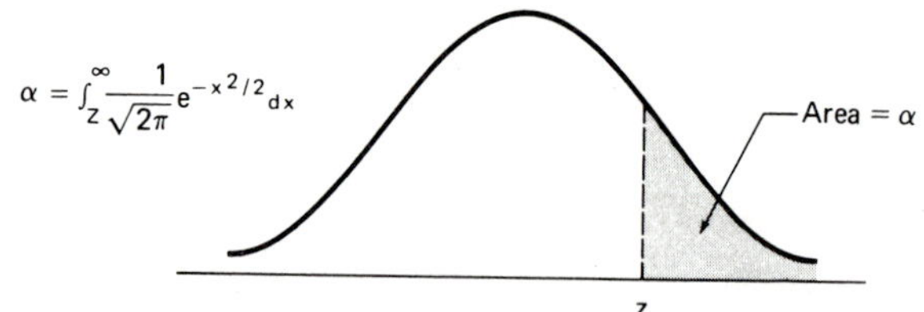

z	0.00	0.01	0.02	0.03	0.04	0.05	0.06	0.07	0.08	0.09
0.0	0.5000	0.4960	0.4920	0.4880	0.4840	0.4801	0.4761	0.4721	0.4681	0.4641
0.1	0.4602	0.4562	0.4522	0.4483	0.4443	0.4404	0.4364	0.4325	0.4286	0.4247
0.2	0.4207	0.4168	0.4129	0.4090	0.4052	0.4013	0.3974	0.3936	0.3897	0.3859
0.3	0.3821	0.3783	0.3745	0.3707	0.3669	0.3632	0.3594	0.3557	0.3520	0.3483
0.4	0.3446	0.3409	0.3372	0.3336	0.3300	0.3264	0.3228	0.3192	0.3156	0.3121
0.5	0.3085	0.3050	0.3015	0.2981	0.2946	0.2912	0.2877	0.2843	0.2810	0.2776
0.6	0.2743	0.2709	0.2676	0.2643	0.2611	0.2578	0.2546	0.2514	0.2483	0.2451
0.7	0.2420	0.2389	0.2358	0.2327	0.2296	0.2266	0.2236	0.2206	0.2177	0.2148
0.8	0.2119	0.2090	0.2061	0.2033	0.2005	0.1977	0.1949	0.1922	0.1894	0.1867
0.9	0.1841	0.1814	0.1788	0.1762	0.1736	0.1711	0.1685	0.1660	0.1635	0.1611
1.0	0.1587	0.1562	0.1539	0.1515	0.1492	0.1469	0.1446	0.1423	0.1401	0.1379
1.1	0.1357	0.1335	0.1314	0.1292	0.1271	0.1251	0.1230	0.1210	0.1190	0.1170
1.2	0.1151	0.1131	0.1112	0.1093	0.1075	0.1056	0.1038	0.1020	0.1003	0.0985
1.3	0.0968	0.0951	0.0934	0.0918	0.0901	0.0885	0.0869	0.0853	0.0838	0.0823
1.4	0.0808	0.0793	0.0778	0.0764	0.0749	0.0735	0.0721	0.0708	0.0694	0.0681
1.5	0.0668	0.0655	0.0643	0.0630	0.0618	0.0606	0.0594	0.0582	0.0571	0.0559
1.6	0.0548	0.0537	0.0526	0.0516	0.0505	0.0495	0.0485	0.0475	0.0465	0.0455
1.7	0.0446	0.0436	0.0427	0.0418	0.0409	0.0401	0.0392	0.0384	0.0375	0.0367
1.8	0.0359	0.0351	0.0344	0.0336	0.0329	0.0322	0.0314	0.0307	0.0301	0.0294
1.9	0.0287	0.0281	0.0274	0.0268	0.0262	0.0256	0.0250	0.0244	0.0239	0.0233
2.0	0.0228	0.0222	0.0217	0.0212	0.0207	0.0202	0.0197	0.0192	0.0188	0.0183
2.1	0.0179	0.0174	0.0170	0.0166	0.0162	0.0158	0.0154	0.0150	0.0146	0.0143
2.2	0.0139	0.0136	0.0132	0.0129	0.0125	0.0122	0.0119	0.0116	0.0113	0.0110
2.3	0.0107	0.0104	0.0102	0.00990	0.00964	0.00939	0.00914	0.00889	0.00866	0.00842
2.4	0.00820	0.00798	0.00776	0.00755	0.00734	0.00714	0.00695	0.00676	0.00657	0.00639
2.5	0.00621	0.00604	0.00587	0.00570	0.00554	0.00539	0.00523	0.00508	0.00494	0.00480
2.6	0.00466	0.00453	0.00440	0.00427	0.00415	0.00402	0.00391	0.00379	0.00368	0.00357
2.7	0.00347	0.00336	0.00326	0.00317	0.00307	0.00298	0.00289	0.00280	0.00272	0.00264
2.8	0.00256	0.00248	0.00240	0.00233	0.00226	0.00219	0.00212	0.00205	0.00199	0.00193
2.9	0.00187	0.00181	0.00175	0.00169	0.00164	0.00159	0.00154	0.00149	0.00144	0.00139

z	0.0	0.1	0.2	0.3	0.4	0.5	0.6	0.7	0.8	0.9
3	0.00135	$0.0^{3}968$[a]	$0.0^{3}687$	$0.0^{3}483$	$0.0^{3}337$	$0.0^{3}233$	$0.0^{3}159$	$0.0^{3}108$	$0.0^{4}723$	$0.0^{4}481$
4	$0.0^{4}317$	$0.0^{4}207$	$0.0^{4}133$	$0.0^{5}854$	$0.0^{5}541$	$0.0^{5}340$	$0.0^{5}211$	$0.0^{5}130$	$0.0^{6}793$	$0.0^{6}479$
5	$0.0^{6}287$	$0.0^{6}170$	$0.0^{7}996$	$0.0^{7}579$	$0.0^{7}333$	$0.0^{7}190$	$0.0^{7}107$	$0.0^{8}599$	$0.0^{8}332$	$0.0^{8}182$
6	$0.0^{9}987$	$0.0^{9}530$	$0.0^{9}282$	$0.0^{9}149$	$0.0^{10}777$	$0.0^{10}402$	$0.0^{10}206$	$0.0^{10}104$	$0.0^{11}523$	$0.0^{11}260$

z	PROBABILITY	
1.282	0.100	Most frequently encountered probabilities
1.645	0.050	
1.960	0.025	
2.326	0.010	
2.576	0.005	

[a] Note: $0.0^{3}968$ means three zeros before the 968, or 0.000968.

TABLE 3 STUDENT *t* DISTRIBUTION (UPPER TAIL)

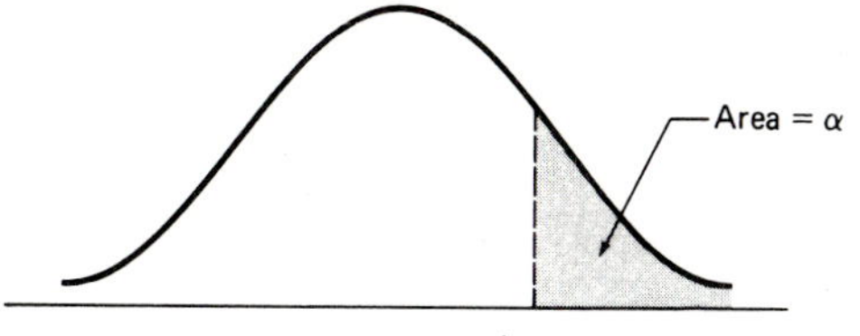

Areas under the Student Curve from to to ∞, for a Specified Number of Degrees of Freedom

The following table provides the values of *t* that correspond to a given probability (area) between *t* and +∞ (or −*t* and −∞) for a specified number of degrees of freedom.

Degrees of Freedom	ONE-TAIL PROBABILITY (AREA) 0.40	0.25	0.10	0.05	0.025	0.01	0.005	0.001
1	0.325	1.000	3.078	6.314	12.706	31.821	63.657	318.31
2	0.289	0.816	1.886	2.920	4.303	6.965	9.925	22.326
3	0.277	0.765	1.638	2.353	3.182	4.541	5.841	10.213
4	0.271	0.741	1.533	2.132	2.776	3.747	4.604	7.173
5	0.267	0.727	1.476	2.015	2.571	3.365	4.032	5.893
6	0.265	0.718	1.440	1.943	2.447	3.143	3.707	5.208
7	0.263	0.711	1.415	1.895	2.365	2.998	3.499	4.785
8	0.262	0.706	1.397	1.860	2.306	2.896	3.355	4.501
9	0.261	0.703	1.383	1.833	2.262	2.821	3.250	4.297
10	0.260	0.700	1.372	1.812	2.228	2.764	3.169	4.144
11	0.260	0.697	1.363	1.796	2.201	2.718	3.106	4.025
12	0.259	0.695	1.356	1.782	2.179	2.681	3.055	3.930
13	0.259	0.694	1.350	1.771	2.160	2.650	3.012	3.852
14	0.258	0.692	1.345	1.761	2.145	2.624	2.977	3.787
15	0.258	0.691	1.341	1.753	2.131	2.602	2.947	3.733
16	0.258	0.690	1.337	1.746	2.120	2.583	2.921	3.686
17	0.257	0.689	1.333	1.740	2.110	2.567	2.898	3.646
18	0.257	0.688	1.330	1.734	2.101	2.552	2.878	3.610
19	0.257	0.688	1.328	1.729	2.093	2.539	2.861	3.579
20	0.257	0.687	1.325	1.725	2.086	2.528	2.845	3.552
21	0.257	0.686	1.323	1.721	2.080	2.518	2.831	3.527
22	0.256	0.686	1.321	1.717	2.074	2.508	2.819	3.505
23	0.256	0.685	1.319	1.714	2.069	2.500	2.807	3.485
24	0.256	0.685	1.318	1.711	2.064	2.492	2.797	3.467
25	0.256	0.684	1.316	1.708	2.060	2.485	2.787	3.450
26	0.256	0.684	1.315	1.706	2.056	2.479	2.779	3.435
27	0.256	0.684	1.314	1.703	2.052	2.473	2.771	3.421
28	0.256	0.683	1.313	1.701	2.048	2.467	2.763	3.408
29	0.256	0.683	1.311	1.699	2.045	2.462	2.756	3.396
30	0.256	0.683	1.310	1.697	2.042	2.457	2.750	3.385
40	0.255	0.681	1.303	1.684	2.021	2.423	2.704	3.307
60	0.254	0.679	1.296	1.671	2.000	2.390	2.660	3.232
120	0.254	0.677	1.289	1.658	1.980	2.358	2.617	3.160
∞	0.253	0.674	1.282	1.645	1.960	2.326	2.576	3.090

SOURCE: E. S. Pearson and H. O. Hartley, Biometrika Tables for Statisticians, Vol. 1, 1966, London, by permission.

TABLE 4 EXPONENTIAL DISTRIBUTION (LOWER TAIL)

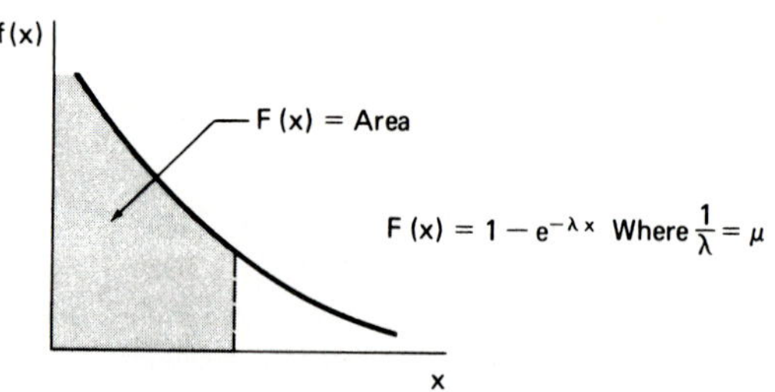

Area under the Exponential Curve between 0 and X

λx	$F(x)$	λx	$F(x)$	λx	$F(x)$	λx	$F(x)$
0.0	0.00	1.0	0.63	2.0	0.86	4.0	0.982
0.1	0.10	1.1	0.67	2.2	0.89	4.5	0.989
0.2	0.18	1.2	0.70	2.4	0.91	5.0	0.993
0.3	0.26	1.3	0.73	2.6	0.92	5.5	0.996
0.4	0.33	1.4	0.75	2.8	0.94	6.0	0.998
0.5	0.39	1.5	0.78	3.0	0.95	6.5	0.9985
0.6	0.45	1.6	0.80	3.2	0.96	7.0	0.9991
0.7	0.50	1.7	0.82	3.4	0.97	8.0	0.9997
0.8	0.55	1.8	0.83	3.6	0.97	9.0	0.9999
0.9	0.59	1.9	0.85	3.8	0.98	10.0	0.99995

TABLE 5 POISSON DISTRIBUTION

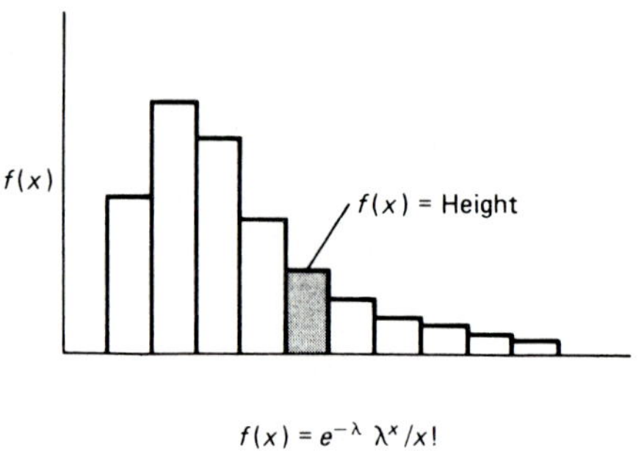

$f(x) = e^{-\lambda}\lambda^x/x!$

The table gives the probability of exactly x occurrences for given expected value λ.

x	λ = 0.005	0.01	0.02	0.03	0.04	0.05	0.06	0.07	0.08	0.09
0	.9950	.9900	.9802	.9704	.9608	.9512	.9418	.9324	.9231	.9139
1	.0050	.0099	.0192	.0291	.0384	.0476	.0565	.0653	.0738	.0823
2	.0000	.0000	.0002	.0004	.0008	.0012	.0017	.0023	.0030	.0037
3	.0000	.0000	.0000	.0000	.0000	.0000	.0000	.0001	.0001	.0001

TABLE 5 (continued)

x	λ 0.1	0.2	0.3	0.4	0.5	0.6	0.7	0.8	0.9	1.0
0	.9048	.8187	.7408	.6703	.6065	.5488	.4966	.4493	.4066	.3679
1	.0905	.1637	.2222	.2681	.3033	.3293	.3476	.3595	.3659	.3679
2	.0045	.0164	.0333	.0536	.0758	.0988	.1217	.1438	.1647	.1839
3	.0002	.0011	.0033	.0072	.0126	.0198	.0284	.0383	.0494	.0613
4	.0000	.0001	.0002	.0007	.0016	.0030	.0050	.0077	.0111	.0153
5	.0000	.0000	.0000	.0001	.0002	.0004	.0007	.0012	.0020	.0031
6	.0000	.0000	.0000	.0000	.0000	.0000	.0001	.0002	.0003	.0005
7	.0000	.0000	.0000	.0000	.0000	.0000	.0000	.0000	.0000	.0001

x	λ 1.1	1.2	1.3	1.4	1.5	1.6	1.7	1.8	1.9	2.0
0	.3329	.3012	.2725	.2466	.2231	.2019	.1827	.1653	.1496	.1353
1	.3662	.3614	.3543	.3452	.3347	.3230	.3106	.2975	.2842	.2707
2	.2014	.2169	.2303	.2417	.2510	.2584	.2640	.2678	.2700	.2707
3	.0738	.0867	.0998	.1128	.1255	.1378	.1496	.1607	.1710	.1804
4	.0203	.0260	.0324	.0395	.0471	.0551	.0636	.0723	.0812	.0902
5	.0045	.0062	.0084	.0111	.0141	.0176	.0216	.0260	.0309	.0361
6	.0008	.0012	.0018	.0026	.0035	.0047	.0061	.0078	.0098	.0120
7	.0001	.0002	.0003	.0005	.0008	.0011	.0015	.0020	.0027	.0034
8	.0000	.0000	.0001	.0001	.0001	.0002	.0003	.0005	.0006	.0009
9	.0000	.0000	.0000	.0000	.0000	.0000	.0001	.0001	.0001	.0002

x	λ 2.1	2.2	2.3	2.4	2.5	2.6	2.7	2.8	2.9	3.0
0	.1225	.1108	.1003	.0907	.0821	.0743	.0672	.0608	.0550	.0498
1	.2572	.2438	.2306	.2177	.2052	.1931	.1815	.1703	.1596	.1494
2	.2700	.2681	.2652	.2613	.2565	.2510	.2450	.2384	.2314	.2240
3	.1890	.1966	.2033	.2090	.2138	.2176	.2205	.2225	.2237	.2240
4	.0992	.1082	.1169	.1254	.1336	.1414	.1488	.1557	.1622	.1680
5	.0417	.0476	.0538	.0602	.0668	.0735	.0804	.0872	.0940	.1008
6	.0146	.0174	.0206	.0241	.0278	.0319	.0362	.0407	.0455	.0504
7	.0044	.0055	.0068	.0083	.0099	.0118	.0139	.0163	.0188	.0216
8	.0011	.0015	.0019	.0025	.0031	.0038	.0047	.0057	.0068	.0081
9	.0003	.0004	.0005	.0007	.0009	.0011	.0014	.0018	.0022	.0027
10	.0001	.0001	.0001	.0002	.0002	.0003	.0004	.0005	.0006	.0008
11	.0000	.0000	.0000	.0000	.0000	.0001	.0001	.0001	.0002	.0002
12	.0000	.0000	.0000	.0000	.0000	.0000	.0000	.0000	.0000	.0001

TABLE 5 (continued)

	λ									
x	3.1	3.2	3.3	3.4	3.5	3.6	3.7	3.8	3.9	4.0
0	.0450	.0408	.0369	.0334	.0302	.0273	.0247	.0224	.0202	.0183
1	.1397	.1304	.1217	.1135	.1057	.0984	.0915	.0850	.0789	.0733
2	.2165	.2087	.2008	.1929	.1850	.1771	.1692	.1615	.1539	.1465
3	.2237	.2226	.2209	.2186	.2158	.2125	.2087	.2046	.2001	.1954
4	.1734	.1781	.1823	.1858	.1888	.1912	.1931	.1944	.1951	.1954
5	.1075	.1140	.1203	.1264	.1322	.1377	.1429	.1477	.1522	.1563
6	.0555	.0608	.0662	.0716	.0771	.0826	.0881	.0936	.0989	.1042
7	.0246	.0278	.0312	.0348	.0385	.0425	.0466	.0508	.0551	.0595
8	.0095	.0111	.0129	.0148	.0169	.0191	.0215	.0241	.0269	.0298
9	.0033	.0040	.0047	.0056	.0066	.0076	.0089	.0102	.0116	.0132
10	.0010	.0013	.0016	.0019	.0023	.0028	.0033	.0039	.0045	.0053
11	.0003	.0004	.0005	.0006	.0007	.0009	.0011	.0013	.0016	.0019
12	.0001	.0001	.0001	.0002	.0002	.0003	.0003	.0004	.0005	.0006
13	.0000	.0000	.0000	.0000	.0001	.0001	.0001	.0001	.0002	.0002
14	.0000	.0000	.0000	.0000	.0000	.0000	.0000	.0000	.0000	.0001

	λ									
x	4.1	4.2	4.3	4.4	4.5	4.6	4.7	4.8	4.9	5.0
0	.0166	.0150	.0136	.0123	.0111	.0101	.0091	.0082	.0074	.0067
1	.0679	.0630	.0583	.0540	.0500	.0462	.0427	.0395	.0365	.0337
2	.1393	.1323	.1254	.1188	.1125	.1063	.1005	.0948	.0894	.0842
3	.1904	.1852	.1798	.1743	.1687	.1631	.1574	.1517	.1460	.1404
4	.1951	.1944	.1933	.1917	.1898	.1875	.1849	.1820	.1789	.1755
5	.1600	.1633	.1662	.1687	.1708	.1725	.1738	.1747	.1753	.1755
6	.1093	.1143	.1191	.1237	.1281	.1323	.1362	.1398	.1432	.1462
7	.0640	.0686	.0732	.0778	.0824	.0869	.0914	.0959	.1002	.1044
8	.0328	.0360	.0393	.0428	.0463	.0500	.0537	.0575	.0614	.0653
9	.0150	.0168	.0188	.0209	.0232	.0255	.0280	.0307	.0334	.0363
10	.0061	.0071	.0081	.0092	.0104	.0118	.0132	.0147	.0164	.0181
11	.0023	.0027	.0032	.0037	.0043	.0049	.0056	.0064	.0073	.0082
12	.0008	.0009	.0011	.0014	.0016	.0019	.0022	.0026	.0030	.0034
13	.0002	.0003	.0004	.0005	.0006	.0007	.0008	.0009	.0011	.0013
14	.0001	.0001	.0001	.0001	.0002	.0002	.0003	.0003	.0004	.0005
15	.0000	.0000	.0000	.0000	.0001	.0001	.0001	.0001	.0001	.0002

TABLE 5 (continued)

x	λ = 5.1	5.2	5.3	5.4	5.5	5.6	5.7	5.8	5.9	6.0
0	.0061	.0055	.0050	.0045	.0041	.0037	.0033	.0030	.0027	.0025
1	.0311	.0287	.0265	.0244	.0225	.0207	.0191	.0176	.0162	.0149
2	.0793	.0746	.0701	.0659	.0618	.0580	.0544	.0509	.0477	.0446
3	.1348	.1293	.1239	.1185	.1133	.1082	.1033	.0985	.0938	.0892
4	.1719	.1681	.1641	.1600	.1558	.1515	.1472	.1428	.1383	.1339
5	.1753	.1748	.1740	.1728	.1714	.1697	.1678	.1656	.1632	.1606
6	.1490	.1515	.1537	.1555	.1571	.1584	.1594	.1601	.1605	.1606
7	.1086	.1125	.1163	.1200	.1234	.1267	.1298	.1326	.1353	.1377
8	.0692	.0731	.0771	.0810	.0849	.0887	.0925	.0962	.0998	.1033
9	.0392	.0423	.0454	.0486	.0519	.0552	.0586	.0620	.0654	.0688
10	.0200	.0220	.0241	.0262	.0285	.0309	.0334	.0359	.0386	.0413
11	.0093	.0104	.0116	.0129	.0143	.0157	.0173	.0190	.0207	.0225
12	.0039	.0045	.0051	.0058	.0065	.0073	.0082	.0092	.0102	.0113
13	.0015	.0018	.0021	.0024	.0028	.0032	.0036	.0041	.0046	.0052
14	.0006	.0007	.0008	.0009	.0011	.0013	.0015	.0017	.0019	.0022
15	.0002	.0002	.0003	.0003	.0004	.0005	.0006	.0007	.0008	.0009
16	.0001	.0001	.0001	.0001	.0001	.0002	.0002	.0002	.0003	.0003
17	.0000	.0000	.0000	.0000	.0000	.0001	.0001	.0001	.0001	.0001

x	λ = 6.1	6.2	6.3	6.4	6.5	6.6	6.7	6.8	6.9	7.0
0	.0022	.0020	.0018	.0017	.0015	.0014	.0012	.0011	.0010	.0009
1	.0137	.0126	.0116	.0106	.0098	.0090	.0082	.0076	.0070	.0064
2	.0417	.0390	.0364	.0340	.0318	.0296	.0276	.0258	.0240	.0223
3	.0848	.0806	.0765	.0726	.0688	.0652	.0617	.0584	.0552	.0521
4	.1294	.1249	.1205	.1162	.1118	.1076	.1034	.0992	.0952	.0912
5	.1579	.1549	.1519	.1487	.1454	.1420	.1385	.1349	.1314	.1277
6	.1605	.1601	.1595	.1586	.1575	.1562	.1546	.1529	.1511	.1490
7	.1399	.1418	.1435	.1450	.1462	.1472	.1480	.1486	.1489	.1490
8	.1066	.1099	.1130	.1160	.1188	.1215	.1240	.1263	.1284	.1304
9	.0723	.0757	.0791	.0825	.0858	.0891	.0923	.0954	.0985	.1014
10	.0441	.0469	.0498	.0528	.0558	.0588	.0618	.0649	.0679	.0710
11	.0245	.0265	.0285	.0307	.0330	.0353	.0377	.0401	.0426	.0452
12	.0124	.0137	.0150	.0164	.0179	.0194	.0210	.0227	.0245	.0264
13	.0058	.0065	.0073	.0081	.0089	.0098	.0108	.0119	.0130	.0142
14	.0025	.0029	.0033	.0037	.0041	.0046	.0052	.0058	.0064	.0071
15	.0010	.0012	.0014	.0016	.0018	.0020	.0023	.0026	.0029	.0033
16	.0004	.0005	.0005	.0006	.0007	.0008	.0010	.0011	.0013	.0014
17	.0001	.0002	.0002	.0002	.0003	.0003	.0004	.0004	.0005	.0006
18	.0000	.0001	.0001	.0001	.0001	.0001	.0001	.0002	.0002	.0002
19	.0000	.0000	.0000	.0000	.0000	.0000	.0000	.0001	.0001	.0001

TABLE 5 (continued)

	λ									
x	7.1	7.2	7.3	7.4	7.5	7.6	7.7	7.8	7.9	8.0
0	.0008	.0007	.0007	.0006	.0006	.0005	.0005	.0004	.0004	.0003
1	.0059	.0054	.0049	.0045	.0041	.0038	.0035	.0032	.0029	.0027
2	.0208	.0194	.0180	.0167	.0156	.0145	.0134	.0125	.0116	.0107
3	.0492	.0464	.0438	.0413	.0389	.0366	.0345	.0324	.0305	.0286
4	.0874	.0836	.0799	.0764	.0729	.0696	.0663	.0632	.0602	.0573
5	.1241	.1204	.1167	.1130	.1094	.1057	.1021	.0986	.0951	.0916
6	.1468	.1445	.1420	.1394	.1367	.1339	.1311	.1282	.1252	.1221
7	.1489	.1486	.1481	.1474	.1465	.1454	.1442	.1428	.1413	.1396
8	.1321	.1337	.1351	.1363	.1373	.1382	.1388	.1392	.1395	.1396
9	.1042	.1070	.1096	.1121	.1144	.1167	.1187	.1207	.1224	.1241
10	.0740	.0770	.0800	.0829	.0858	.0887	.0914	.0941	.0967	.0993
11	.0478	.0504	.0531	.0558	.0585	.0613	.0640	.0667	.0695	.0722
12	.0283	.0303	.0323	.0344	.0366	.0388	.0411	.0434	.0457	.0481
13	.0154	.0168	.0181	.0196	.0211	.0227	.0243	.0260	.0278	.0296
14	.0078	.0086	.0095	.0104	.0113	.0123	.0134	.0145	.0157	.0169
15	.0037	.0041	.0046	.0051	.0057	.0062	.0069	.0075	.0083	.0090
16	.0016	.0019	.0021	.0024	.0026	.0030	.0033	.0037	.0041	.0045
17	.0007	.0008	.0009	.0010	.0012	.0013	.0015	.0017	.0019	.0021
18	.0003	.0003	.0004	.0004	.0005	.0006	.0006	.0007	.0008	.0009
19	.0001	.0001	.0001	.0002	.0002	.0002	.0003	.0003	.0003	.0004
20	.0000	.0000	.0001	.0001	.0001	.0001	.0001	.0001	.0001	.0002
21	.0000	.0000	.0000	.0000	.0000	.0000	.0000	.0000	.0001	.0001

	λ									
x	8.1	8.2	8.3	8.4	8.5	8.6	8.7	8.8	8.9	9.0
0	.0003	.0003	.0002	.0002	.0002	.0002	.0002	.0002	.0001	.0001
1	.0025	.0023	.0021	.0019	.0017	.0016	.0014	.0013	.0012	.0011
2	.0100	.0092	.0086	.0079	.0074	.0068	.0063	.0058	.0054	.0050
3	.0269	.0252	.0237	.0222	.0208	.0195	.0183	.0171	.0160	.0150
4	.0544	.0517	.0491	.0466	.0443	.0420	.0398	.0377	.0357	.0337
5	.0882	.0849	.0816	.0784	.0752	.0722	.0692	.0663	.0635	.0607
6	.1191	.1160	.1128	.1097	.1066	.1034	.1003	.0972	.0941	.0911
7	.1378	.1358	.1338	.1317	.1294	.1271	.1247	.1222	.1197	.1171
8	.1395	.1392	.1388	.1382	.1375	.1366	.1356	.1344	.1332	.1318
9	.1256	.1269	.1280	.1290	.1299	1306	.1311	.1315	.1317	.1318
10	.1017	.1040	.1063	.1084	.1104	.1123	.1140	.1157	.1172	.1186
11	.0749	.0776	.0802	.0828	.0853	.0878	.0902	.0925	.0948	.0970
12	.0505	.0530	.0555	.0579	.0604	.0629	.0654	.0679	.0703	.0728
13	.0315	.0334	.0354	.0374	.0395	.0416	.0438	.0459	.0481	.0504
14	.0182	.0196	.0210	.0225	.0240	.0256	.0272	.0289	.0306	.0324

TABLE 5 (continued)

15	.0098	.0107	.0116	.0126	.0136	.0147	.0158	.0169	.0182	.0194
16	.0050	.0055	.0060	.0066	.0072	.0079	.0086	.0093	.0101	.0109
17	.0024	.0026	.0029	.0033	.0036	.0040	.0044	.0048	.0053	.0058
18	.0011	.0012	.0014	.0015	.0017	.0019	.0021	.0024	.0026	.0029
19	.0005	.0005	.0006	.0007	.0008	.0009	.0010	.0011	.0012	.0014
20	.0002	.0002	.0002	.0003	.0003	.0004	.0004	.0005	.0005	.0006
21	.0001	.0001	.0001	.0001	.0001	.0002	.0002	.0002	.0002	.0003
22	.0000	.0000	.0000	.0000	.0001	.0001	.0001	.0001	.0001	.0001

	λ									
x	9.1	9.2	9.3	9.4	9.5	9.6	9.7	9.8	9.9	10.0
0	.0001	.0001	.0001	.0001	.0001	.0001	.0001	.0001	.0001	.0000
1	.0010	.0009	.0009	.0008	.0007	.0007	.0006	.0005	.0005	.0005
2	.0046	.0043	.0040	.0037	.0034	.0031	.0029	.0027	.0025	.0023
3	.0140	.0131	.0123	.0115	.00107	.0100	.0093	.0087	.0081	.0076
4	.0319	.0302	.0285	.0269	.00254	.0240	.0226	.0213	.0201	.0189
5	.0581	.0555	.0530	.0506	.0483	.0460	.0439	.0418	.0398	.0378
6	.0881	.0851	.0822	.0793	.0764	.0736	.0709	.0682	.0656	.0631
7	.1145	.1118	.1091	.1064	.1037	.1010	.0982	.0955	.0928	.0901
8	.1302	.1286	.1269	.1251	.1232	.1212	.1191	.1170	.1148	.1126
9	.1317	.1315	.1311	.1306	.1300	.1293	.1284	.1274	.1263	.1251
10	.1198	.1210	.1219	.1228	.1235	.1241	.1245	.1249	.1250	.1251
11	.0991	.1012	.1031	.1049	.1067	.1083	.1098	.1112	.1125	.1137
12	.0752	.0776	.0799	.0822	.0844	.0866	.0888	.0908	.0928	.0948
13	.0526	.0549	.0472	.0594	.0617	.0640	.0662	.0685	.0707	.0729
14	.0342	.0361	.0380	.0399	.0419	.0439	.0459	.0479	.0500	.0521
15	.0208	.0221	.0235	.0250	.0265	.0281	.0297	.0313	.0330	.0347
16	.0118	.0127	.0137	.0147	.0157	.0168	.0180	.0192	.0204	.0217
17	.0063	.0069	.0075	.0081	.0088	.0095	.0103	.0111	.0119	.0128
18	.0032	.0035	.0039	.0042	.0046	.0051	.0055	.0060	.0065	.0071
19	.0015	.0017	.0019	.0021	.0023	.0026	.0028	.0031	.0034	.0037
20	.0007	.0008	.0009	.0010	.0011	.0012	.0014	.0015	.0017	.0019
21	.0003	.0003	.0004	.0004	.0005	.0006	.0006	.0007	.0008	.0009
22	.0001	.0001	.0002	.0002	.0002	.0002	.0003	.0003	.0004	.0004
23	.0000	.0001	.0001	.0001	.0001	.0001	.0001	.0001	.0002	.0002
24	.0000	.0000	.0000	.0000	.0000	.0000	.0000	.0001	.0001	.0001

TABLE 6A PRESENT VALUE OF A SINGLE PAYMENT OF $1 AT THE END OF PERIOD *T*

	DISCOUNT RATE														
T	1%	2%	4%	6%	8%	10%	12%	14%	15%	16%	18%	20%	22%	24%	25%
1	0.990	0.980	0.962	0.943	0.926	0.909	0.893	0.877	0.870	0.862	0.847	0.833	0.820	0.806	0.800
2	0.980	0.961	0.925	0.890	0.857	0.826	0.797	0.769	0.756	0.743	0.718	0.694	0.672	0.650	0.640
3	0.971	0.942	0.889	0.840	0.794	0.751	0.712	0.675	0.658	0.641	0.609	0.579	0.551	0.524	0.512
4	0.961	0.924	0.855	0.792	0.735	0.683	0.636	0.592	0.572	0.552	0.516	0.482	0.451	0.423	0.410
5	0.951	0.906	0.822	0.747	0.681	0.621	0.567	0.519	0.497	0.476	0.437	0.402	0.370	0.341	0.328
6	0.942	0.888	0.790	0.705	0.630	0.564	0.507	0.456	0.432	0.410	0.370	0.335	0.303	0.275	0.262
7	0.933	0.871	0.760	0.665	0.583	0.513	0.452	0.400	0.376	0.354	0.314	0.279	0.249	0.222	0.210
8	0.923	0.853	0.731	0.627	0.540	0.467	0.404	0.351	0.327	0.305	0.266	0.233	0.204	0.179	0.168
9	0.914	0.837	0.703	0.592	0.500	0.424	0.361	0.308	0.284	0.263	0.225	0.194	0.167	0.144	0.134
10	0.905	0.820	0.676	0.558	0.463	0.386	0.322	0.270	0.247	0.227	0.191	0.162	0.137	0.116	0.107
11	0.896	0.804	0.650	0.527	0.429	0.350	0.287	0.237	0.215	0.195	0.162	0.135	0.112	0.094	0.086
12	0.887	0.788	0.625	0.497	0.397	0.319	0.257	0.208	0.187	0.168	0.137	0.112	0.092	0.076	0.069
13	0.879	0.773	0.601	0.469	0.368	0.290	0.229	0.182	0.163	0.145	0.116	0.093	0.075	0.061	0.055
14	0.870	0.758	0.577	0.442	0.340	0.263	0.205	0.160	0.141	0.125	0.099	0.078	0.062	0.049	0.044
15	0.861	0.743	0.555	0.417	0.315	0.239	0.183	0.140	0.123	0.108	0.084	0.065	0.051	0.040	0.035
16	0.853	0.728	0.534	0.394	0.292	0.218	0.163	0.123	0.107	0.093	0.071	0.054	0.042	0.032	0.028
17	0.844	0.714	0.513	0.371	0.270	0.198	0.146	0.108	0.093	0.080	0.060	0.045	0.034	0.026	0.023
18	0.836	0.700	0.494	0.350	0.250	0.180	0.130	0.095	0.081	0.069	0.051	0.038	0.028	0.021	0.018
19	0.828	0.686	0.475	0.331	0.232	0.164	0.116	0.083	0.070	0.060	0.043	0.031	0.023	0.017	0.014
20	0.820	0.673	0.456	0.312	0.215	0.149	0.104	0.073	0.061	0.051	0.037	0.026	0.019	0.014	0.012
21	0.811	0.660	0.439	0.294	0.199	0.135	0.093	0.064	0.053	0.044	0.031	0.022	0.015	0.011	0.009
22	0.803	0.647	0.422	0.278	0.184	0.123	0.083	0.056	0.046	0.038	0.026	0.018	0.013	0.009	0.007
23	0.795	0.634	0.406	0.262	0.170	0.112	0.074	0.049	0.040	0.033	0.022	0.015	0.010	0.007	0.006
24	0.788	0.622	0.390	0.247	0.158	0.102	0.066	0.043	0.035	0.028	0.019	0.013	0.008	0.006	0.005
25	0.780	0.610	0.375	0.233	0.146	0.092	0.059	0.038	0.030	0.024	0.016	0.010	0.007	0.005	0.004

TABLE 6B PRESENT VALUE OF AN ANNUITY CONSISTING OF $1 PAYMENTS AT THE END OF EACH OF THE NEXT *T* PERIODS

	DISCOUNT RATE														
T	1%	2%	4%	6%	8%	10%	12%	14%	15%	16%	18%	20%	22%	24%	25%
1	0.990	0.980	0.962	0.943	0.926	0.909	0.893	0.877	0.870	0.862	0.847	0.833	0.820	0.806	0.800
2	1.970	1.942	1.886	1.833	1.783	1.736	1.690	1.647	1.626	1.605	1.566	1.528	1.492	1.457	1.440
3	2.941	2.884	2.775	2.673	2.577	2.487	2.402	2.322	2.283	2.246	2.174	2.106	2.042	1.981	1.952
4	3.902	3.808	3.630	3.465	3.312	3.170	3.037	2.914	2.855	2.798	2.690	2.589	2.494	2.404	2.362
5	4.853	4.713	4.452	4.212	3.993	3.791	3.605	3.433	3.352	3.274	3.127	2.991	2.864	2.745	2.689
6	5.795	5.601	5.242	4.917	4.623	4.355	4.111	3.889	3.784	3.685	3.498	3.326	3.167	3.020	2.951
7	6.728	6.472	6.002	5.582	5.206	4.868	4.564	4.288	4.160	4.039	3.812	3.605	3.416	3.242	3.161
8	7.652	7.325	6.733	6.210	5.747	5.335	4.968	4.639	4.487	4.344	4.078	3.837	3.619	3.421	3.329
9	8.566	8.162	7.435	6.802	6.247	5.759	5.328	4.946	4.772	4.607	4.303	4.031	3.786	3.566	3.463
10	9.471	8.983	8.111	7.360	6.710	6.145	5.650	5.216	5.019	4.833	4.494	4.192	3.923	3.682	3.571
11	10.368	9.787	8.760	7.887	7.139	6.495	5.937	5.453	5.234	5.029	4.656	4.327	4.035	3.776	3.656
12	11.255	10.575	9.385	8.384	7.536	6.814	6.194	5.660	5.421	5.197	4.793	4.439	4.127	3.851	3.725
13	12.135	11.343	9.986	8.853	7.904	7.103	6.424	5.842	5.583	5.342	4.910	4.533	4.203	3.912	3.780
14	13.004	12.106	10.563	9.295	8.244	7.367	6.628	6.002	5.724	5.468	5.008	4.611	4.265	3.962	3.824
15	13.865	12.849	11.118	9.712	8.559	7.606	6.811	6.142	5.847	5.575	5.092	4.675	4.315	4.001	3.859
16	14.718	13.578	11.652	10.106	8.851	7.824	6.974	6.265	5.954	5.669	5.162	4.730	4.357	4.033	3.887
17	15.562	14.292	12.166	10.477	9.122	8.022	7.120	6.373	6.047	5.749	5.222	4.775	4.391	4.059	3.910
18	16.398	14.992	12.659	10.828	9.372	8.201	7.250	6.467	6.128	5.818	5.273	4.812	4.419	4.080	3.928
19	17.226	15.678	13.134	11.158	9.604	8.365	7.366	6.550	6.198	5.877	5.316	4.844	4.442	4.097	3.942
20	18.046	16.351	13.590	11.470	9.818	8.514	7.469	6.623	6.259	5.929	5.353	4.870	4.460	4.110	3.954
21	18.857	17.011	14.029	11.764	10.017	8.649	7.562	6.687	6.312	5.973	5.384	4.891	4.476	4.121	3.963
22	19.660	17.658	14.451	12.042	10.201	8.772	7.645	6.743	6.359	6.011	5.410	4.909	4.488	4.130	3.970
23	20.456	18.292	14.857	12.303	10.371	8.883	7.718	6.792	6.399	6.044	5.432	4.925	4.499	4.137	3.976
24	21.243	18.914	15.247	12.550	10.529	8.985	7.784	6.835	6.434	6.073	5.451	4.937	4.507	4.143	3.981
25	22.023	19.523	15.622	12.783	10.675	9.077	7.843	6.873	6.464	6.097	5.467	4.948	4.514	4.147	3.985

Solutions to Starred Problems

CHAPTER 1[1]

1. Check clearing; credit operations; facility design to allow customer interface as well as smooth operations; worker scheduling; cost control.
3. The agency can perform more or improved services if it is efficient.
6. Services cannot be inventoried in the usual sense of the word. Thus supply-demand coordination is achieved in different ways.
8. Frequent pick-ups and deliveries improve service but increase costs. More collection points provide easier access (better service) but at an increased cost.
10. Air-conditioning manufacturing; Christmas card production.
11. Minimize cost; provide a wide range of services; maintain good community relations; maintain high quality. The first goal conflicts with the others.
15. a. To provide cost, feasibility, and quality information.
    b. Projected sales volume and its seasonality, sales price, and distribution information.
    c. In addition to (a), lead times to first shipment, production quantities possible, source and quality of material supply, packaging information.

[1]There are many questions for which more than one answer is possible. Rather than making that statement every time it is appropriate, we have made it once, here. Further, the answers given here will be very brief, and therefore, on occasion will be incomplete.

CHAPTER 2

2. a. Multiple-bottleneck processes occur when two or more work centers are limiting resources.

   b. The location of bottlenecks can indeed shift in the process. If different types of products are made, changes in the production mix can cause a shift in the bottlenecks. Also, bottlenecks can change as the capacities of work centers are changed by adjusting the number of workers or machines.

3. Recall that automatic car-wash-machine capacity is 48 cars/hour.

   a. 1 worker/ICC: ICC capacity is 60(1/6)(2) = 20 cars/hour; process capacity is min {48, 20} = 20 cars/hour. Bottleneck: ICCs.

   b. 3 workers/ICC: ICC capacity is 60(3/6)(2) = 60 cars/hour; process capacity is min {48, 60} = 48 cars/hour. Bottleneck: ACW machines.

7. a. Ordinarily we would expect to see some work-in-process inventory, since the work centers operate independently, and some parts might have to await processing of remaining parts before assembly can begin. As we will see in the rest of this question, the nature of the production process will determine the size of this work-in-process inventory.

   b. Make-to-stock process:

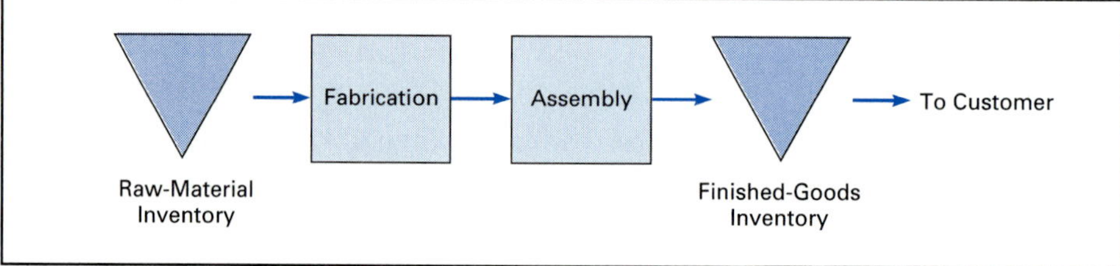

   Characteristics: Large (planned) finished-goods inventory. Some planned raw-material inventory. Although work-in-process inventory will occur between fabrication and assembly, it is not depicted separately, since it is not a key planned feature of the make-to-stock process.

   c. Assemble-to-order process:

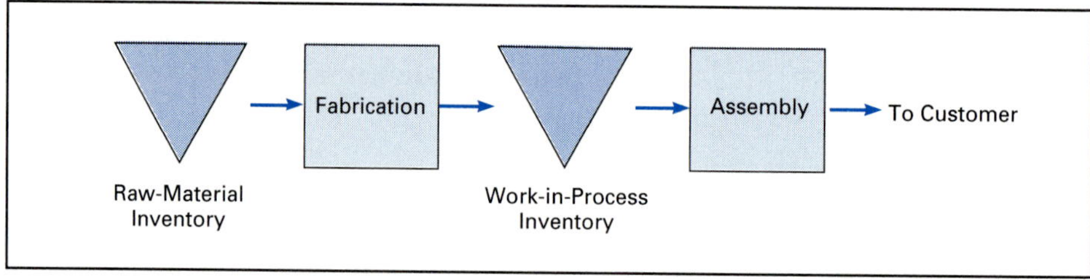

   There is a large planned work-in-process inventory of fabricated parts so that products can be assembled to customer order.

d. Make-to-order process:

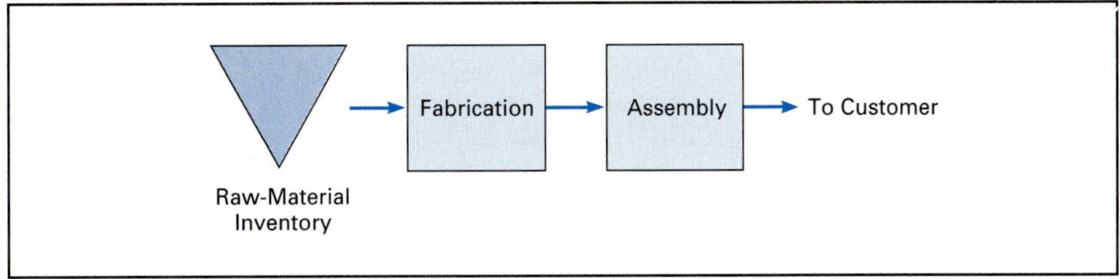

No planned work-in-process or finished-goods inventory. Raw-material inventory shown here can reduce product lead time.

19.

Number of Workers	ICC Cycle Time (min)	ICC Capacity (cars/hr)	Process Capacity (cars/hr)	Bottleneck
1	6	10	10	ICC
2[a]	3	20	20	ICC
3	2	30	30	ICC
4	3/2	40	40	ICC
5	6/5	50	48	ACW[b]
6	1	60	48	ACW

[a]Includes all combinations of workers in ICC1 and ICC2 that add up to 2; i.e., (2, 0), (1, 1), (0, 2).
[b]Automatic car-wash machine.

CHAPTER 3

1. One store, since one layout has little effect on the rest of the system.
6. Trucking expense will increase, but inventories and emergency orders will decline.
9. They should choose 200; TC (200) = 125.0
11. The computer could minimize cost by satisfying none of the demand. (Set all $X_{ij} = 0$.)
16. 12.78 ≈ 13 is the breakeven point; the firm should find out who their customers might be and try to estimate the average return more carefully.
18. $120,408.
19. Buy the trucks; present value of rental payments = $6,549,000.
21. a. More attractive since there is one additional value component. (The salvage value will exceed the loss of tax savings due to reduced depreciation.)
    b. More attractive since the tax saving is received earlier and thus has a larger present value.
25. a. Product costs: IBM = $2.45; TCT = $3.96; RF = $1.98
    Gross Margins: IBM = $0.55; TCT = $0.54; RF = $0.52
    b. Product Cost: IBM = $1.98; TCT = $6.32; RF = $2.72
    Gross Margin: IBM = $1.02; TCT = $−1.82; RF = $−0.22

CHAPTER 4

3. a. Activity C is shown as starting later than its ES.
   b. B and D are most worrisome (no slack). A has 2 units of slack and is probably least worrisome.
4.

Activity	ES	EF	LS	LF	Slack
E	0	5	5	10	5
F	0	4	7	11	7
G	0	9	3	12	3
A	5	10	10	15	5
B	4	8	11	15	7
C	9	17	12	20	3
D	10	15	15	20	5

   b. Critical path = G, C for 9 + 8 = 17 days.
   c. Path E—A has less slack than F—B, and is therefore probably more likely to delay D.
   d. 17 days. Probably too low because it doesn't recognize that the critical path might shift. Time estimates may be wrong.
6. a. Critical path includes activities 3, 4, and 6, completed at time 9 (i.e., week 45).

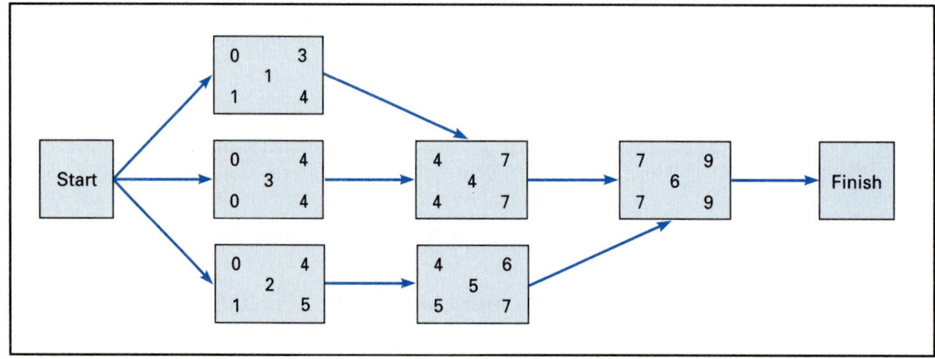

   b. 9 is too low. Variability in student progress will slow down the average.
8. a. Activities B, F, H and I have 3 days of slack, the smallest for non-critical activities.
   b. More than 2 days, 5 days and 5 days, respectively.
   c. (i) F (up by 2) and H (up by 2)
   (ii) none
10. a. Activity F has 7 days of slack.
   b. 5 days
   c. No. The LS for D is 14.
   d. Break H into two parts, (HA, 6) and (HB, 8). Activity HA can start at time 0. HB has predecessors HA and G, can start at time 21, and can finish at 29. The critical path is B—D—A, and activity HB has one unit of slack. Project completion is 5 days earlier.

e. G is no longer on the critical path. Shortening G has no effect on project completion. Forget that option.

11. a. 32 hours

    b. 24 hours at \$310

12. a. Critical path is C—E—F for 35 days. D and B have slack of 4 days.

    b. If the Cobalt unit is shut down when the accelerator is delivered, speed electricians up by 2 days, saving \$200.

15. a. $\bar{x} = 27$, $\sigma = 2.867$

    b. 85%

    c. Actual probability is probably lower than 85%.

CHAPTER 5

1. a. An individual programmer may respond inappropriately if measured on KLOC/PY. For a large department with a standard mix of projects, the measures can be a useful guide.

   b. The average time to develop a program measures our ability to innovate in the marketplace. Using quality and market measures should keep us from focusing only on "more."

   c. One improvement would be to measure the "function" performed by the program rather than the lines of code.

4. "Stopwatch" measures activity times. "Work sampling" estimates "proportion of time spent in each category of activity."

6. a. 0.20

   b. 0.1012

   c. 1537 in total, or 1477 more than the pilot study.

9. Two examples are to guarantee that no one will lose jobs or pay and to give cash awards for good ideas.

11. a. 1.04

    b. The product may have changed; the labor force may be different; they may have new capital equipment.

12. a. 20 P1's and 6⅔ P2's. (The fraction would be a partially completed unit.)

    b. P2 may be more profitable; they may want to maintain a significant presence in both market segments.

16. Group incentives can be directed more easily toward the goals of the organization, and people have a need to belong to and contribute to a group. Individual goals may be preferred because the individual can see the immediate reward and because it is easier to see how to improve vis-à-vis that incentive.

17. Airlines might have some techniques that could be applied in the university setting. The university might try to reduce time required by the customer and mistakes in the records.

18. a. At $i = 200$, A's advantage is 65.4 to 67.0. At $i = 100$, A's advantage is 38.9 to 52.5.

    b. To solve for cumulative breakeven, set $360i^{0.678}/(0.678) = 150i^{0.848}/(0.848)$. The result is $i = 642.8$.

CHAPTER 6

4. a. Acceptance sampling is applied to a large batch of finished goods. Process control occurs while production is still underway.
   b. Process control.
   c. If costs of defective items are very high, 100% inspection is appropriate. If cost of inspection is very high, ''zero'' inspection is best.
8. a. Customers value fast service and accurate charges. This is an example of a process improvement combined with mistake-proofing. It eliminates searching for and reading price tags, punching in prices, looking up prices if tag is missing, remembering or double-checking coupons against items, and punching in or calculating coupon value.
   b. The computer applies the correct price. Also, higher productivity lowers prices in the long run.
   c. Some computer systems report the item name and price out loud.
11. a. Prompt and reliable delivery of the new employee (product) to the manager (customer) is a measure of quality of this service. The company may be paying overtime or suffering a reduction in productivity until the position is filled.
   b. The SOURCES branch refers to the methods for locating suitable candidates. The bushy twig lists four sources that may be affected by lack of close working relationship with sources.
   c. A less attractive position will have fewer applicants and take longer to fill. Also, the higher the probability of accepting the offer, the less likely another round of interviews will be needed.
15. In addition to the 1% normally outside the limits, the process will be ''out of control'' sometimes, and then a much higher percentage of points will fall outside the limits.
17. a. AQL = 1% and LTPD = 5%.
   b. $\alpha = 10\%$ and $\beta = 2.5\%$ (i.e., $1 - 0.975 = 0.025$).
   c. $c = 3.69 \rightarrow 4$, and $n = 234.4 \rightarrow 234$
   d. Inspect 234 roller-bearings from each batch, and reject if 5 or more are defective. A rejected batch should either be returned to the vendor or fully inspected.
   e. $n = 244$, $c = 5$ with $p_c = 0.0225$. The larger sample is needed to lower the error probability. Increasing p_c decreases the probability of rejecting a good batch.
22. a. No. C_{ins} lies between $f_{min}C_{def} = \$0.20$ and $f_{max}C_{def} = \$1.60$.
   b. Using 0.04 as f_{max}, we get $f_{max}C_{def} = \$0.80$, so zero inspection is suggested.
27. a. The center line is 30, 3-Sigma control limits are 19.27 and 40.73, 2-Sigma limits are 22.84 and 37.16, and 1-Sigma limits are 26.42 and 33.58. We are assuming that the given data represent the accident rate when things are ''in control.''
   b. Centerline is 18.61 and the limits are 1-Sigma = 11.70 and 25.52, 2-Sigma = 4.78 and 32.43, and 3-Sigma = 0 and 39.34.

c. Daily observations should use $30 \pm 3(8) = 6$ and 54 as the 3-Sigma limits, (plug in 2 or 1 for the others). These would be accurate *in this case* because we were told that daily values have the normal distribution.

d. *Weekly:* The same limits would apply because of the central limit theorem. *Daily:* They could still use a daily chart but the control limits would not be accurate.

29. No. The general rule is that $n = 5$ is sufficient to detect shifts of 2σ or more. If the process mean increases by 2σ (0.006 mm), 9.18% of roller bearings will be faulty, an unacceptably high fraction.

30. a. Using equation (13) the upper limit should be 0.0152.

b. High variability in the size of the bearings is unacceptable.

CHAPTER 7

3. Mary wins. Her forecast has almost completely discounted the (now irrelevant) data from before the drop in demand.

5. a. $S_1 = 18.4$; $\text{MAD}_1 = 3.87$

b. They should use a high α value for a while. Sales personnel may have "grass roots" information that could improve the forecast.

6. a. 183 ± 25

b. 189.6 ± 28.5

9. a. Sales dropped rapidly during periods 1 to 6; the regression estimates are $a_6 = 129.5$ and $b_6 = -16.9$.

b. Ignoring periods 1 to 5, $a_6 = 110.7$ and $b_6 = 5.0$

c. Using the initialization procedure with $m = 6$, the recommended values are $R_a = 4/8 = 0.5$, and $R_b = (0.5)^2 = 0.25$.

d.

t	6	7	8	9	10	11	12
D_t		120	110	130	140	130	140
a_t	110.7	117.9	117.0	124.8	135.0	136.4	140.5
b_t	5.0	6.1	2.6	5.2	7.7	4.5	4.3
$a_t + b_t$	115.7	124.0	119.6	130.0	142.7	140.9	144.8

11. a. $\bar{x} = 6.5$, $\Sigma x^2 = 650$, $\Sigma xy = 5137$, $\bar{y} = 62.0$, $n = 12$, $b = 2.105$, $a = 48.318$

b. The sum of the absolute errors is 33.6, so MAD = 33.6/12 = 2.8.

13. a. 1.097

b. Use an exponentially weighted average of the Wednesday centered averages.

14. a.

Month	Sept.	Oct.	Nov.	Dec.	Jan.
Cake	99,000	108,000	126,000	117,000	72,000
Frosting	57,200	63,600	75,600	71,500	44,800

b. The final quarter is Oct.-Dec., so the forecast is (108,000 + 126,000 + 117,000) = 351,000 for cake mix and 210,700 for frosting.

c.

	Cake	Frosting
Deseasonalize:	94,000/1.1 = 85,455	52,727
e_t =	85,455 − 90,000 = −4,545	727
a_t =	90,000 + (0.1)(−4,545) = 89,546	52,073
b_t =	0	1,000 + 0.01(727) = 1,007
$a_t + b_t$ =	89,546	53,080
Multiply times Oct. seasonal:	107,455	63,696

d. Average the two seasonal factors. One might want to weight the individual factors by sales volume.

16. Using equation (17), forecast = 6.52. But this is the forecast of the natural logarithm of registrations, in thousand. Thus

$$\text{forecast} = e^{6.52} = 679 \text{ thousand}$$

20. a. $S_t = \alpha D_t + (1 - \alpha) S_{t-1} = \alpha D_t + S_{t-1} - \alpha S_{t-1}$
$= S_{t-1} + \alpha D_t - \alpha S_{t-1}$
$= S_{t-1} + \alpha(D_t - S_{t-1})$

b. $a_t = a_{t-1} + R_a e_t = a_{t-1} + R_a(D_t - \{a_{t-1} + b_{t-1}\})$
When $b_{t-1} = 0$, this becomes $a_{t-1} + R_a(D_t - a_{t-1})$.

c. In both cases you get 100 + 0.1(110 − 100) = 101.

21. a. Deseasonalized sales = 452/0.798 = 566.4,
$e_7 = 13.2$, $a_7 = 556.5$, and $b_7 = 2.31$.

b.

t:	Trend projections:	Seasonalized Forecasts:
8	556.5 + 1(2.31) = 558.8	(558.8)(1.196) = 668.3 (4th quarter)
9	556.5 + 2(2.31) = 561.1	(561.1)(1.053) = 590.8 (1st quarter)

c. The forecasts were revised upward because the sales in period 7 were higher than had been predicted.

CHAPTER 8

7. a. Larger orders last longer, yielding less frequent transactions.
b. Larger orders increase cycle stock, $Q/2$.
c. Do a Q^+ type of approach, as in Section 8-3.

9. a. $Q^* = 1000$ lb.
b. $Q^* = 223.6$ lb, $D^\$ = \$200{,}000$ per year, TVC = \$894.4 per year, and $n = 22.4$ orders per year.
c. Higher inventory cost for titanium implies smaller Q.

11. At the cheaper price, $C_I = \$3.90$ and $Q^* = 277$, which exceeds 200 and is therefore optimal.

13. a. Both items have the same costs, but different demands D, so they cannot have the same Q^*.
b. Perhaps, although some other considerations, such as quantity discounts, might be present.

15. Using equation 19, $Q = 250$ items, which should be placed on the last order before the price increase.

17. a. $Q^* = 400$.
    b. $n = 4000/400 = 10$ per year.
    c. Safety stock $= z\sigma_u = (2.33)(48) = 112$.
    d. (C_I)(safety stock) $= \$280$.
    e. Cutting $\overline{\text{LT}}$ by 50% saves nothing *in this case*, since σ_u is not affected. Cutting σ(LT) by 50% saves half of \$280, or \$140.
22. a. $\sigma_u = 80$, $z = (600 - 400)/80 = 2.5$, Probability $= 0.0062$, and $n =$ 10 orders per year, so there are $(10)(0.0062) = 0.062$ stockout per year.
    b. Using $C_B \approx \$350$ in equations 12, 13, and 14, $R = 664$.
24. a. Let c = cost. Then optimal stockout probability $= (c - 0.9c)/(0.3c + 0 + c - 0.9c) = 0.25$. Therefore, the rule is to stock enough to meet all demand 75% of the time.
    b. Using Table 5, Appendix D, the order should be for 13 loaves to keep the cumulative stockout probability below 0.25. (The cumulative probability is $0.0729 + \cdots + 0.0001 = 0.2085$ for demand of 13 or more.)
    c. This is not a one-shot opportunity. Future demand may depend on keeping a high service level.
26. a. $1649/6 = 274.83$ per week, so $D = 14{,}291$ per year.
    b. Orders placed on Tuesday of week 1, Wednesday of week 3, and Tuesday of week 5. Orders arrive on Tuesday of week 2, Wednesday of week 5. Shortage of 22 on Tuesday of week 5.
    c. No shortages. Orders for 533 on Monday of week 1, 542 on Monday of week 3, 528 on Monday of week 5. Orders received on Monday of weeks 2 and 5.
    d. $R - \bar{u} = 550 - (2)(274.83) = 0.33$ or 0, so the (Q, R) system has no safety stock in part b. $\text{TI} - (T)(\bar{d}) - \overline{U} = 1100 - 2(274.83) - 2(274.83) = 0.66$, so there is also none in part c.

CHAPTER 9

2. By backlogging demand, scheduling consumers, using price promotions to level demand, and diversifying product line.
5. a. Inventory cost of bottles (not wine), additional production equipment, additional warehouse space.
   b. Second-shift startup and premium wage, and frequent changeovers due to low inventory.
   c. Oversupply.
   d. Shortages.
7. a. 40 units.
   b. Average requirements change for June to December only. The new values are 4.76, 4.71, 4.38, 4.48, 4.46, 4.50, and 5.04 for June through December, respectively, and 5.04 is the highest.
   c. 40 units causes horizon to jump to December.
   d. No change.
9. a. Cumulative requirements = 130, 240, 380, 480.
   b. Yes.

c. Peak output would be reduced (may save some overtime). Inventory is less in month 2 and the same elsewhere. Yes, this is an improvement.

10. a. Steepest production curve in months 5 and 6.
    b. 18.75 units per month.
    c. Month 10.
    d. Follow given plan in months 1 to 4. Then follow a constant production rate through month 10, meeting the same ending inventory. This reduces inventory cost, reduces peak production rate, and saves a layoff at end of month 6.

13. a. Produce 5875 per month. Total cost = \$1,428,000, consisting of \$1,260,000 for holding inventory and \$168,000 for overtime.
    b. \$1,270,000, consisting of \$1,000,000 for holding inventory, \$50,000 for hiring and firing, and \$220,000 for second shift.
    c. Part b leaves 3000 more units of inventory than part a. If this difference is carried one month, the cost advantage of part b virtually disappears.

15. a. m^* = 5 months (largest integer in 5.38). Therefore, $2(m^* + 1) = 12$, and seasonal layoffs can be used (rule 1 in Table 9-3).
    b. Beginning of month 11 at the earliest (rule 4).
    c. At least 6 months (rule 6).
    d. Layoffs at end of month 4 (rule 3) and hiring at end of month 10 (see part b).
    e. Current work force can produce (5000)(4) = 20,000 through month 4, whereas demand = 21,000.
    f. Hiring/firing is a cheaper way to increase production for periods above $l^* = 1.0$ month.
    g. Hire fewer workers, earlier, because there will be a layoff in period 5 (rule 6).
    h. Plan 1 = \$2560; plan 2 = \$1830; plan 3 = \$2760.
    i. Plan 2 violates this principle but is \$730 cheaper than plan 1.

17. a. (61 − 5)/6 = 9.33 per month.
    b. Backlog exceeds 15 in period 5.
    c. MCP = produce 9.4 per month for first 5 months, which stays within specified bounds.
    d. The violation of the minimum backlog by 1 truck in month 3 seems a small price to pay for keeping the work force steady.

22. a. [8(3750)]/[15(8)(20)] = 12.5 months.
    b. $b = 0.2345$; $a = 7184.51$; $Y_{17} + \ldots + Y_{24} = 28{,}358.04$. 28,358.04/[15(8)(20)] = 11.8 months.

CHAPTER 10

2. MRP uses dependent demand to calculate quantities and timing of components parts. It provides a planned completion time and an order-release time for each part. Used in conjunction with capacity-requirements planning, MRP can also determine potential bottlenecks.

The effects of a trial master production schedule can be observed, and if necessary, changes can be made to the schedule, as well as to allocation of resources.

4. a. Safety time.
   b. External independent demand for a component or because a reject allowance is needed.
   c. Yes, so that frequent shortages will not cause constant replanning of the master schedule.
7. The finished product may have many different options, with color, fabric, or special features added on a make-to-order basis. If this is the case, the plant may choose to master schedule at the subassembly level. Finished units can then be assembled to customer order. Alternatively, a plant may only produce subassemblies, which are then transported to another plant.
9. (i) dependent-demand components
   (ii) work-in-process inventory that occurs in discrete, identifiable parts
   (iii) a master production schedule known well in advance
   (iv) a multistage manufacturing process
   (v) lead times that are not highly variable
   (vi) small reject allowances
12. a. Immediately prior to month 1, we must have on hand 400 units of TM75, 600 units of TM112, and 3200 units of RM1. (Note that an additional 4000 units of RM1 will be in-process in the TM products).
    b. Since there is less uncertainty in RM1 delivery, we will not have to plan for as much safety stock or safety time. Also, we will not have to wait as long as 4 months. The lead time is now 3 months, however, (it has been as low as 1 month in the past), so we will not be able to react as quickly to changes.
14. a. Level 0 contains A, level 1 contains C and D, level 2 contains B and F, and level 3 contains E.
    b. 600 of B, 400 of C, 100 of D, 1900 of E, and 1100 of F.
    c. 1200 units in week 4 and 700 units in week 6.
17. a. The figure has six levels with SYS1 and SYS2 on level 0; SUB1, SUB2, and SUB4 on level 1; RM2, SUB3, and COMP4 on level 2; COMP1 and COMP3 on level 3; COMP2 on level 4; and RM1 and RM3 on level 5. There are 25 entries on level 5, 13 for SYS1 and 12 for SYS2.
    b. 86
18. a. The planned order releases (quantity, week) for each of the items are as follows:
    SYS1: (1000, 14)
    SYS2: (2000, 4), (2000, 14)
    SUB1: (2090, 2), (3100, 12)
    SUB2: (2064, 2), (5080, 12)
    SUB4: (1029, 12)
    SUB3: (3067, 2), (2060, 12)

b. Planned order-release quantities could be scaled upward to allow for rejects, and the computer would then be programmed to ''receive'' only usable goods (90% for finished items and 80% for subassemblies).

19. All answers are in order for SYS1, SYS2, SUB1, SUB2, SUB3, and SUB4.
    a. 100, 200, 310, 508, 309, 103
    b. 245, 400, 431, 552, 352, 185
    c. 2, 2, 1, 1, 1, 2 (to the nearest week). Runs should be made more often for finished items (every 2 weeks), and components should be scheduled in a lot-for-lot manner.
20. a. The labor-hours needed per week during the first 17 weeks are 0, 5054.7, 5054.7, 1800, 1800, 0, 0, 0, 0, 0, 0, 7888.3, 7888.3, 2700, 2700, 0, 0.

CHAPTER 11

1. Rework causes uncertainty in run lengths. Bad input parts may cause shortages. In general, poor quality causes timing of production to change, thus ruining the schedule. Long production runs cause long lead times, which means more uncertainty in demand that can cause schedule changes.
5. a. Lot size is the quantity of an item produced in a single run.
   b. Run length is the time required to produce the lot.
   c. Production interval is the time between successive start times.
   d. Runout time is the forecasted time that a quantity of an item will satisfy demand.
   e. Setup time is the time required to prepare for production of an item.
   f. All have the same meaning for a family. However, a family may have a major setup time in addition to the minor setups for each item.
7. a. 9,000 per year.
   b.

Lots each per year:	1	2	5	10	20	50
Maximum output:	9900	9800	9500	9000	8000	5000
Q = Lot Size:	4950	2450	950	450	200	50

   c.

Setup time:	5	10	20	50	100
Maximum output:	9900	9800	9600	9000	8000

   d. Inventory cost may drop. Shorter setups may improve scheduling. Quality may improve with smaller batches. Other answers are possible.
10. a. 29,597
    b. 37.0 days
    c. 74.0 days
    d. 21,472; 2.686; 53.7.
    e. EOQ formula gives 20,928. Nearly equal if D is much smaller than P.

12. a. Since supervisors have other productive tasks, an opportunity cost should be assigned to their time spent on changeovers.
    b. Increase, since C_S will increase.
14. a. 0.674 week.
    b. 202 of A, 135 of B, and 67 of C.
    c. 0.202 week.
17. a. Yes. Idle capacity is 30 per week or 12%.
    b. T_{min} = 6 weeks. The frequencies (n) are 6/6 = 1, 14/6 = 2.33 or 2, and 10/6 = 1.67 or 2. N_{max} = 2. The multiples (m) are 2/1 = 2, 2/2 = 1, and 2/2 = 1. Cycle length = (N_{max})(T_{min}) = (2)(6) = 12 weeks. Production quantities must average 12 times the weekly demand, or 840, 240, 360, 240, 480, and 480. Divide by P = 250 to get the run times per cycle of 3.36, 0.96, 1.44, 0.96, 1.92, and 1.92.
    c. Because family A is to be run twice each cycle (m = 2 for that family), we will use ABAC as the repeating family sequence and divide run time by 2 for items in family A. The sequence of items is 1, 2, 3, 4, 1, 2, 5, 6, and the start times are 0.00, 1.68, 2.16, 3.60, 4.56, 6.24, 6.72, 8.64.

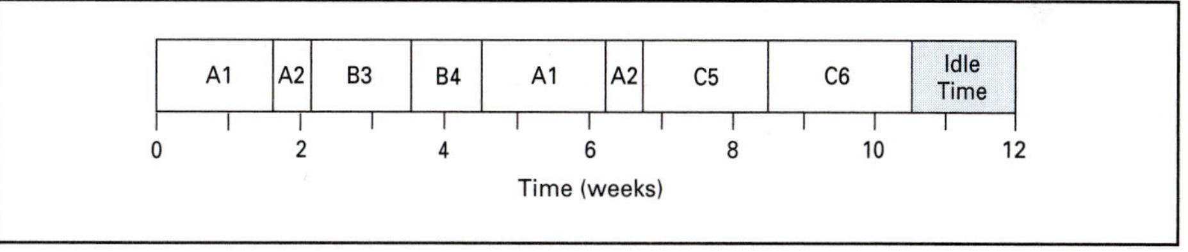

    d. No. Using equation (18), the cycle length must be at least 4/(1 − 220/250) = 4/0.12 = 33.3 weeks.
19. a. T_{min} = 10, the smallest of the T* values.

Family	A	B	C	D	E
T^*/T_{min}	3	1	1.2	1.125	1.5
n	4	1	1	1	2
m	1	4	4	4	2

    b. One production sequence is ABCD BCDE BCD BCDE.
    c. To satisfy annual demand of 150,000 in 250 production days requires daily production capacity of at least 600.
    d. A schedule is shown in the table and chart below.

Start Times by Family:

A	B	C	D	E
0.0	2.0	3.5	6.0	
	8.0	9.5	12.0	14.0
	16.0	17.5	20.0	
	22.0	23.5	26.0	28.0

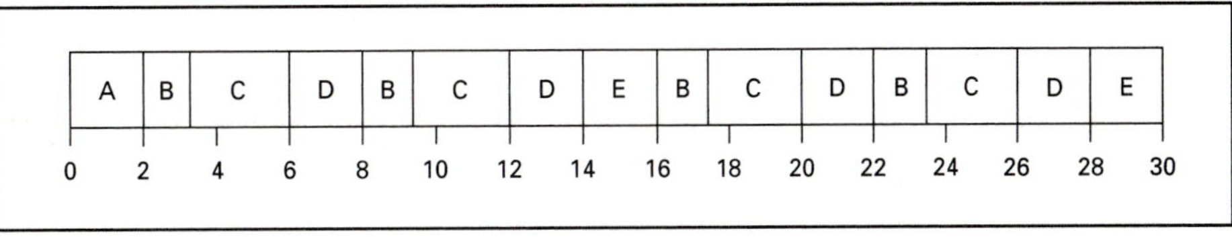

21. a. 2.6 weeks
    b. Production is −60, 1140, 980, 440 for fruity, wintergreen, spearmint, and bubblegum. The −60 indicates production should be zero for that item.
    c. Perhaps one of the flavors has more variation in usage, and therefore needs a larger safety margin. Or, if there is one mainstay flavor, CCC may wish to give it an extra margin of safety. Either of these would translate to a longer runout time for the item.
24. a. No
    b. J1 starts on M1 and J2 starts on M2, at time zero. At time 4 both remaining tasks are started and makespan is reduced to 8.
    c. 8
26. a. Type M2, since one of each of J1, J2, and J3 would require 13 days on M2, but 6 and 7 on M1 and M3, respectively.
    b. All jobs can be done by day 20. In our chart, the new machine will work on J2, 2 (second job of type J2), then J1, 2 and J3, 2, finishing its work at day 19. The old M2 is done on day 14.
28. a. i. ABCDE; A is 1 hour late and E is 5 hours late.
       ii. CBDAE; A is 4.5 hours late and E is 5 hours late.
       iii. AEBCD; A is 1 hour late, E is 1.5 hours late, and C is 0.5 hour late.
    b. FCFS or SOT
    c. DS/RO
    d. Results apply to this set of jobs.
30. a. 2 per day per machine
    b. $N_q = 16.678$
    c. The Markov assumption, steady state, FCFS discipline, single waiting line, infinite population, and arrival and service rates independent of queue size.
    d. Lower, since SOT moves jobs through more quickly.

CHAPTER 12

4. Storing small quantities of every part and component might cause too much inventory.
6. A cross-trained worker who is "starved" for material can help his supplier "catch up." Workers trained in maintenance and repair can reduce delays due to breakdowns.
8. a. Assuming $F_I = 20\%$, saving = 0.2($9 million) = $1.8 million per year.
   b. Wasting $1.8 million per year, inventory also allows other wasteful activities to continue.
   c. Little's law: flowtime $= \dfrac{\text{Inventory}}{\text{Output Rate}} = \dfrac{\$10\text{ million}}{\$100\text{ million/yr}}$ or 0.1 year.
   With inventory of $1 million, average flowtime would be 0.01 year. Benefits include a more responsive system.

11. To allow the system to "empty out," kanban removal should begin at the raw materials end and progress eventually to finished goods.
14. Have two cranes, one for removing and the other for installing. Fetch the new mold during the previous production run and pre-heat it.
15. a. Four jobs per 8 hours of operation of the slower machine.
    b. The faster worker will average about 10% idle time.
    c. Lower. Blocking and starving become more likely.
    d. Nothing.
    e. Inventory increases between stages.
18. a. W2 is the bottleneck; (10)(0.729) = 7.29 nondefectives per hour.
    b. The system can produce (10)(0.9)(0.9) = 8.1 nondefectives per hour.
    c. Not giving defective items to W2 avoids wasting any of its capacity on items that are already defective.
20. The *planned* lead times are inaccurate because they are assumed to be constant and known in advance, when (in reality) lead times depend on the facility loading. Discrete time buckets exacerbate the problem since lead times must be expressed in multiples of the time bucket.

CHAPTER 13

4. They increase congestion.
7. a. Total demand = 74 workdays per week, compared to (14)(5) = 70 available. Thus we need 4 days of part-time help.
    b. At least 2.
    c. Pick up the half days on Monday and Friday.
    d. Advantage is that the entire full-time crew would *not* be present on any day. Disadvantage is that 3 different part-timers need to be trained.
    e. Days off Monday through Sunday = 5, 3, 0, 4, 4, 6, 6 = 28 total.
    f. Only Wednesday requires part-time help.
10. a. 3500/250 = 14 crews.
    b. 300 Monday, 100 Tuesday.
    c. Days off are: Weeks 1 and 2 have Wed. and Sun., weeks 3–6 have Thurs. and Sun., weeks 7–10 have Fri. and Sun., and weeks 11–14 have Sat. and Sun.
    d. Same as (c) except week 1 is Mon. and Sun. instead of Wed. and Sun.
    e. Solution (d) leaves an extra 50 tons uncollected at the end of Monday and Tuesday.
15. a. Groups 1–7 take weeks 1–7 day shift, groups 8–14 do the same but evenings, and 15–21 the same but nights. Rotate after finishing week 7 of the schedule.
    b. 5
16. a. 10 minutes, with 2 and 5 intervals allocated to established and new customer office visits, respectively.

b. If you allow 30 minutes per broker for breaks, etc., there would be (2400 − 150 − 75)/10 = 217 intervals, or more if we allow for no-shows.

c. Total demand = 1650 minutes, so idle time = 750 minutes per day or 150 per broker per day.

d. Allowing 150 minutes personal time, (750 − 150)/50 = 12 (or fewer) in addition to the 15 already allocated in part c.

e. Away from heavy demand times. Toward the junior members, as they have fewer established customers.

17. a. $C_S = \$25$; $C_U = \$10$; $C_S/(C_U + C_S) = 25/(10 + 25) = 0.71$. The bus company should overbook $B = 2$ seats on each bus, since $P(NS \geq 2) > 0.71 > P(NS \geq 3)$.

b. If $10 < C_S \leq 21.25$, an overbooking policy of 3 seats will be optimal.

19. a. Fri. through Thurs. = 155, 128, 115, 131,152, 163, 164.

b. 157, 140, 137, 146, 156, 156, 155.

c. The current pattern is above certified capacity on Thursday, and leaves only a one-bed safety margin.

d. Yes. Up to 4 more patients can be in the hospital without exceeding 160.

21. a. *Day shift:* 3 on duty every day except 4 on duty during week 1 (Thurs.-Sat.), week 2 (Sun., and Fri.-Sat.), week 3 (Sun., Mon. and Sat.), week 4 (Sun.-Tues.)

Evenings: 2 every day except 3 during week 5 (Mon.-Wed.) and week 6 (Tues.-Thurs.).

Nights: 1 every day except 2 during week 7 (Wed.-Fri.).

b. Groups 1 and 6 have 5 nights, and the other groups have 6. There are also differences in evenings and days.

c. Advantage—regularity. Disadvantage—vacation planning and uneven work loads by day of week do not fit in. May need part time help because of this.

CHAPTER 14

1. All three cycles are time lags between needing an item and having it available. Procurement—material supplier and plant. Replenishment—plant and DC. Order—DC and retail outlet. See Section 14-1 for discussion.

3. Only proposal 1 is justified. Net annual saving = \$100,208.

5. a. True, because the risk of obsolescence and several costs depend on the nature of the item.

b. False, since the value added in transportation may be significant.

c. False, since dead stock may be claimed as a tax loss.

7. a. False, since the carrying cost may be very low or instant service may be required.

b. False, because revenue may be lost due to lack of product availability.

9. a. 0.0137

b. 2.21

c. 3,885 at retail; 1,765 at the DC.

11. C_B = $20. Inventory is 629 and 58 units for items 1 and 2 respectively. Stockouts per year is 0.05 for both items. Total values are $3,022,500 in inventory and 275 stockouts per year. C_B = $200. The corresponding value are 665; 63; 0.005; $3,237,500; and 27.5.

14. a. High-cost, low-demand items where a slight delay is not too costly.

 b. Inventory is reduced. Response time may increase, and/or transportation cost may rise.

16. a. 3,600,000 − 2,100,000 = $1,500,000

 b. No, since $400,000 > (0.2)(1,500,000).

 c. No. The inventory saving would be even lower.

CHAPTER 15

2. The education of business school students provides an interesting example of the interrelationship between product and process innovation. During the last ten years, significant advances in microcomputer technology have affected the "product" (i.e., the student), as well as the process (the curriculum and the classroom). Students are becoming increasingly more proficient in computer analysis and application of software. The educational process has seen considerable application of computer technology, both in the classroom and in the preparation of classroom materials. Innovations of one type lead to innovations of the other.

5. Flexible manufacturing can be viewed as a highly automated version of cellular manufacturing.

7. Cellular manufacturing provides for the limited implementation of just-in-time (JIT) production systems in a job-shop environment. JIT is not directly applicable to job-shop production. By producing similar parts in a production cell, however, JIT may then be implemented within the cell, allowing JIT benefits to accrue.

9. Figure 15-7 and the Hayes-Wheelwright product-process matrix share the common fundamental principle of effectively matching process capability with product requirements. The production systems mentioned in Figure 15-7 are situated along the main diagonal, matching process with product and proceeding from low volume, high flexibility and high complexity (conventional machine [job] shop) to high volume, low flexibility and low complexity (dedicated transfer line).

11. The misapplication of discounted cash-flow analysis and biasing the investment-decision process often make it difficult to invest in, or financially justify investment in, automated systems. Common examples include setting an unrealistically high hurdle rate, investment-funding policies that discourage large capital investments, failing to capture many of the benefits (both tangible and intangible), and comparing the investment against the status quo.

14. a. −$7,710,866 (or, using Table 6b in Appendix D, −$7,710,000)

 b. −$4,024,126 (or −$4,023,000)

 c. +$11,337,292 (or $11,339,500)

d. Other possible benefits include improved quality, less factory space, improved response time to customers, increased flexibility, improved safety, and so forth.

15. +$10,009,936 (or, using Table 6b in Appendix D, $10,009,600)

18. The jobs created may not be designed for the people who lost jobs. Some industrial cities may have a permanently lower number of jobs. Training and relocation programs may be insufficient.

CHAPTER 16

3.

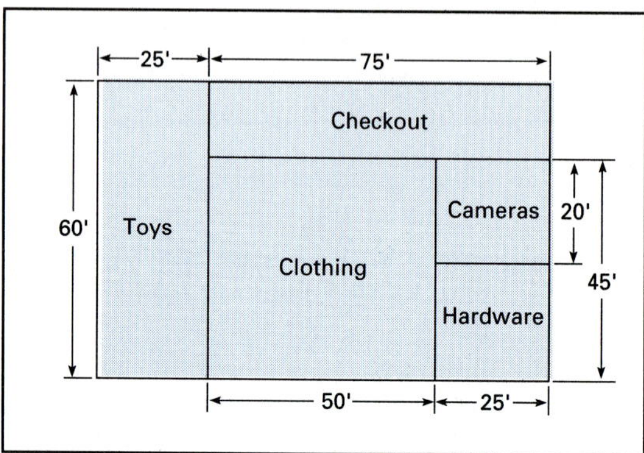

6.

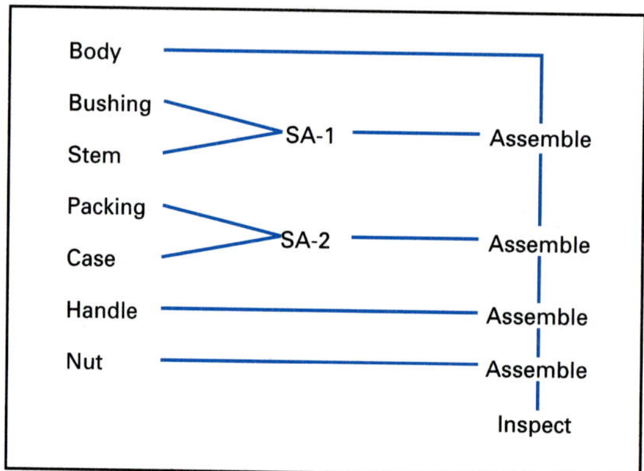

8. a. 30 seconds

   b. 7 hours/760 items or 35 seconds per item, for a balance dalay of 35.7%.

   c. Yes. Combine stations 3 and 4.

   d. 3

   e. 2 per minute. To improve, try to transfer a task from station 2 to station 3.

   f. 0.25; because the stations cannot be made to have identical cycle times.

9. a. Score 1 is the individual task times. Score 2 is the sum of the individual task times and the times of all tasks that must follow. The

numerical values are:

Task:	A	B	C	D	E	F	G	H	I	J	K	L	M	N
Score 1:	2	7	5	2	15	7	6	4	9	10	4	8	6	15
Score 2:	50	26	42	39	37	22	25	19	24	39	33	29	21	15

The assignments are:
Score 1: (J,G,K), (C,L,A,D), (I,B,H), (M), (E), (F), and (N).
Score 2: (A,C,D,J), (E,K), (L,B), (G,I,H), (F,M), and (N).

b. Balance delay is 28.6% for Score 1 and 16.7% for Score 2.

c. The two scores are the same as in part (a). The assignments for $c = 18$ minutes are:
Score 1: (J,G,A), (C,K,L), (I,B,D), (M,H), (E), (F), and (N).
Score 2: (A,C,D,K), (J,L), (E), (B,G,H), (I,F), (M), and (N).
For both assignments, the balance delay is 20.6%.

d. With $c = 17$, the following assignment, with 6 stations, has a balance delay of less than 2%. The heuristics cannot find this solution. It is interesting to consider formalizing a heuristic that would find this solution *and* be easy to implement in large problems. (J,C,A), (D,E), (G,K,F), (L,I), (B,M,H), (N).

12. A product (or cellular) layout might include four cells with doctors, physicians' assistants, nurses, and practical nurses. A central reception area would funnel patients to one of the cells, where, for most patients, their entire needs would be fulfilled. The advantage is less travel time for patients and perhaps better privacy. A disadvantage is that specialization may not be easy to incorporate.

15. Property and construction cost; system-wide transportation costs; socioeconomic composition of the three schools; usefulness of the new site for community activities.

17. a. Build 2000, expand if demand is high. Expected net present value = $3,968,000

b. Break-even probability = 0.405

18. a. X, Y coordinates are 370 and 485 respectively.

b. For $p = 1.5$, distance = 865 miles.
For $p = 1.0$, distance = 1000 miles.

19. a. Number of truck bays, number of trucks, or throughput capability.

b. Cost of the facility and of operating the facility; number of spare trucks needed to maintain readiness; overtime cost if regular throughput capacity is insufficient.

c. The trucks' regular repair and breakdown rates; time to perform maintenance of various types; costs mentioned in (b).

23. a. Prediction of future demand patterns, construction and operating costs; the ''presence'' effect of either plant.

b. Consider net contribution attributable to the new plant. Without it, the firm will lose some sales. Do an investment analysis.

CHAPTER 17

1. a. Facilities are very expensive, so utilization must be high if costs are to be controlled.

b. Idle time must be kept low (by proper scheduling) to meet completion time and cost contract values.

c. The operations area spends the money; cost and quality determine both short-run and long-run profitability.

5. Money can be saved by centralizing the assets, to utilize them better, in either case. Customer service, in the sense of immediate availability, can be degraded by centralizing, in either case. Many differences can be listed. For cancer care, the customer is moved to the facility, rather than the reverse. Better quality of the product may be obtained by centralizing health care.

7. a. A set of products that uses similar technology and is sold to a specific type of customer; SBUs are used to help plan strategic operations and marketing efforts.

   b. i. Subcompact inexpensive cars; compact inexpensive cars; compact luxury cars.

      ii. Associate degrees with bookkeeping skills; bachelor's degrees with technical training in (say) accounting; Ph.D.s with research skills.

      iii. Expensive traditional dining room furniture; expensive modern dining room furniture; inexpensive traditional dining room furniture.

11. a. PROS: Better care because of higher volume; lower cost.
    CONS: Poor access for some people and for some physicians.

    b. The physicians will have less practice, but the patients might be more comfortable closer to home. The total effect is hard to predict.

13. One important way is to offer wellness programs themselves since they have doctors and other facilities that give them some advantage. "Wellness" requires that every person be a potential customer, whereas most current hospital services consider only people with health problems as the customer. Competitors are much broader also, in that almost any group can compete for this portion of the market.

APPENDIX A

1. a. False. Arrival frequency *varies* according to the Poisson probability distribution. Only the *mean* arrival rate is assumed constant.

   b. True.

   c. False. Same argument as (a).

   d. False. Same argument as (a).

   e. True, over the *long run*.

3. a. $N_q = 3.2$ shirts.

   b. 20%

   c. 8.1 shirts and 10%

   d. 12.5% increase in shirts leads to 153% increase in queue.

   e. No. Shirts probably arrive at a fairly uniform rate.

   f. The answers are too high, since there is less variability than assumed.

5. a. 3.
   b. For $S = 4$, $T_q = 1.2$ minutes.
   c. (4)(12)/40 = \$1.20 per customer.
   d. Four is preferred. Three servers increases T_q by 8.9 minutes per visit, which is more expensive at \$8 per hour than the additional \$0.30 per visit needed to pay the extra server.
8. a. $T_q = 4.8$ hours for barber 1 and 0.36 hours for barber 2, for an average of $(0.6)(4.8) + (0.4)(0.36) = 3.02$ hours.
   b. $T_q = 0.36$ hours.
   c. If they were equally popular, there would still be instances in part (a) when one of the barbers is idle while customers are waiting for the other. This does not occur under "first available server," so the average wait will be lower in part b.
9. a. More than 80. $S \geq \bar{\lambda}T_s = 80$.
   b. $N_s = \bar{\lambda}T_s = 80$.
   c. $\bar{\lambda} = (0.2)(10) = 2$ per day; $N_q = \bar{\lambda}T_q = 4$ patients.
12. a. $S = 10$, $N_q = 6.019$, $T_q = 0.334$ day.
    b. Use Model IV with $K = 2$. $N_{q1} = 0.066$, $N_{q2} = 5.954$, $T_{q1} = 0.037$ day, and $T_{q2} = 0.37$ day, so hot orders wait one-tenth as long as regular orders.
16. a. T_q values at the receptionist = 4.5 minutes, nurse clinician = 4.0 minutes, and physician = 26 minutes.
    b. Count T_q and T_s.
       Path 1: (NC only) = 12 minutes.
       Path 2: (NC, MD) = 42 minutes.
       Path 3: (MD only) = 36 minutes.
    c. 23 minutes.
    d. Receptionist is idle 0.25 hour per hour, NC = 0.33, and MD = 0.13.
    e. Reduces T_q to 0.9 minute for MD, but increases MD idle time to 1.13 doc-hours per hour (0.567 each).

APPENDIX B

3. a.

Time (minutes)	15–20	20–25	25–30	30–35
Random numbers	.001–.242	.243–.510	.511–.770	.771–.000

   b. Customer 1 = 30–35; 2 = 25–30; 3 = 30–35; 4 = 15–20; 5 = 30–35
   c. The plot is zero out to $t = 15$ minutes, then a nearly-straight line from ($P = 0$ at $t = 15$) to ($P = 1.0$ at $t = 35$), then a horizontal line at $P = 1.0$ beyond $t = 35$.
   d. 31 minutes, 28 minutes, 32, 19 and 31.
5. a. 5 weeks for A, 1 week for B, 5 weeks for C. Critical path = A—B requiring 6 weeks.
   b. A = 2, B = 2, C = 5 for completion in 5 weeks.
      A = 2, B = 2, C = 5, same result.
      Similarly, the last two runs give 5 and 6.
      Average = (6 + 5 + 5 + 5 + 6)/5 = 5.4
   c. Repeat 100 times and find the 80th percentile.

d. Activity times are statistically independent; historical distributions are accurate for the future.

6. a. $P = 0.885$ corresponds to $z = +1.2$; 0.274 implies $z = -0.6$, and the other 3 are +2.9, −1.8 and +0.4.
   b. Part 1 = 10 + z(0.0010) = 10.0012, and the rest are 9.9994, 10.0029, 9.9982 and 10.0004.
8. a. $z = 1.5$, so life = 1200 + 1.5(50) = 1275.
   b. Using equation (1), $1160 \pm 1.96(52)/\sqrt{40}$ does not include 1200, so the simulated value is suspiciously low.
10. Queuing model assumes steady state; did the simulation? Is 10% statistically significant?
13. a. Good = .001 to .850; rework = .851 to .950; reject = .951 to .000. Shirt 1 = good, 2 = G, 3 = reject, 4 = rework, 5 = G, 6 = G, 7 = G, 8 = rework, 9 = rework, 10 = G.
    b.

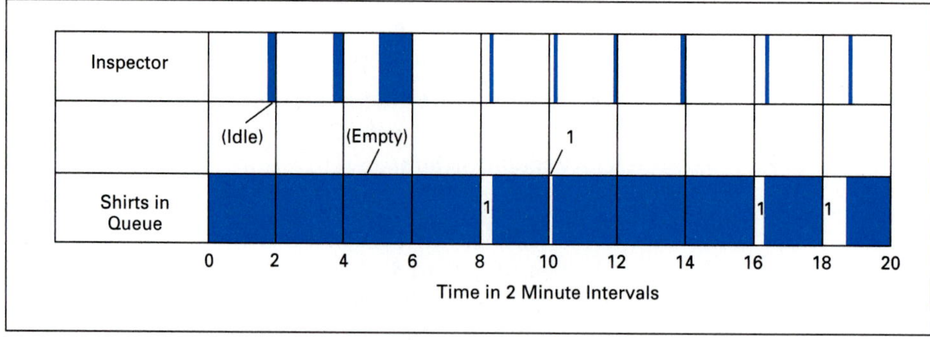

c. 1. Set clock at zero ($t = 0$), inspector = idle, queue = empty.
   2. Add 1 shirt to queue.
   3. If Inspector is idle and queue is empty, go to step 6.
   4. If Inspector is idle and queue is not empty, take shirt from queue and compute time when inspector will finish (that is, t + inspection time). Write this down as an attribute of the inspector.
   5. If Inspector is busy but will be finished before next arrival, then move clock forward to time when inspector is finished and go to step 3.
   6. Move clock to next shirt arrival and repeat steps 2–6.

d. After each shirt's category is generated, as in part (a), a second random number would be used to generate its processing time from the probability distribution corresponding to the category.

17. a. Means and standard deviations of sales, waste, procurements, lost sales, waiting line.
    b. Probability distributions of demands by time of day, and service times.

APPENDIX C

1. a. Solutions 1, 6, and 8 are infeasible.
   b. Solution 2, Z = 5. Solution 3, Z = 6. Solution 4, Z = 4. Solution 5, Z = 5. Solution 7, Z = 4.

c, d and e.

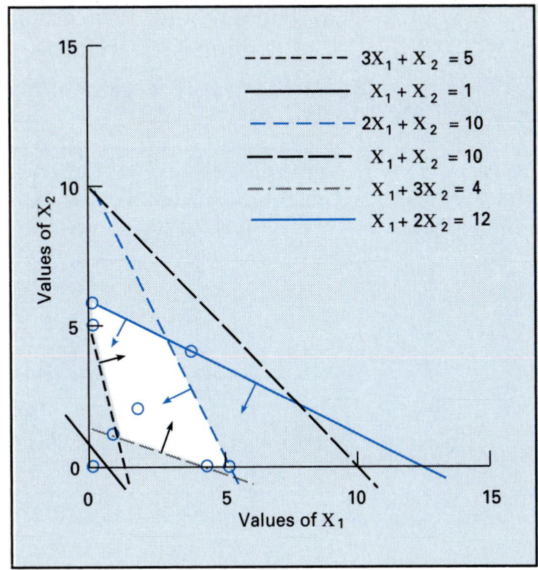

The optimum (minimum) occurs at the lower left corner, at the intersection of the two lines $3X_1 + X_2 = 5$ and $X_1 + 3X_2 = 4$. Solving them simultaneously (or carefully reading the graph) yields the solution $X_1 = 1.375$ and $X_2 = 0.875$, for an objective-function value of 2.25.

3. a. All feasible. Z value is 24 for each solution.
   b. Same Z and same value (of 12) for constraint 3.
   c.

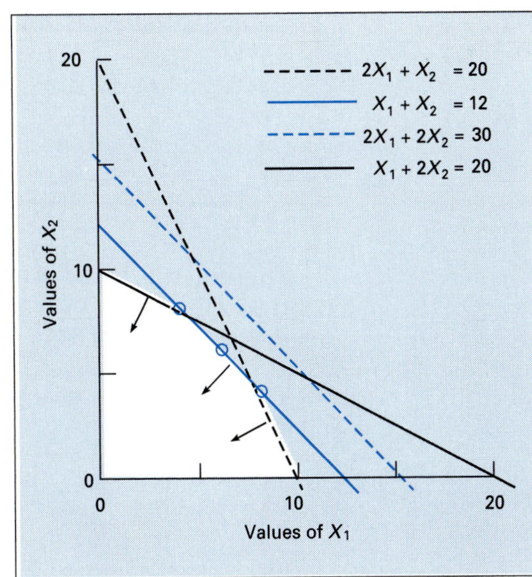

   d. The objective function is parallel to the constraint $X_1 + X_2 = 12$, and so all points on that line have the same objective-function value. The objective function is increasing as we move up to the right, so all three points are optimal.

e. There would be a zero among the objective function coefficients of the nonbasic variables.

7. a and b: Only slacks are needed.

Row No.		X_1	X_2	S_1	S_2	S_3	S_4	RHS
1	(Max)	10	9	0	0	0	0	0
2		0.7	1	1	0	0	0	630
3		3	5	0	1	0	0	3600
4		3	2	0	0	1	0	2124
5		1	2.5	0	0	0	1	1350

c. Objective-function value = 0, S_1 = 630, S_2 = 3600, S_3 = 2124, S_4 = 1350.

d. $X_1 = 0$, $X_2 = 0$ are nonbasic.

e. Yes. All variables including slacks are nonnegative.

f. No. Two positive numbers in row 1.

g. Yes. No negative numbers in row 1.

9. Working from the tableau in Problem 7, let X_1 be the entering variable. The ratios of RHS/"X_1 column" are as follows. Row 2: 630/0.7 = 900, row 3: 3600/3 = 1200, row 4: 2124/3 = 708, row 5: 1350/1 = 1350. The minimum is 708, so row 4 is the departing row and S_3, being basic in row 4, is the departing variable. The pivot element is in the X_1 column, row 4, or 3.0.

Row No.	X_1	X_2	S_1	S_2	S_3	S_4	RHS
1	0	2.333	0	0	−3.333	0	−7080
2	0	0.533	1	0	−0.233	0	134.4
3	0	3	0	1	−1	0	1476
4	1	0.667	0	0	0.333	0	708
5	0	1.833	0	0	−0.333	1	642

X_2 is the entering variable now. The ratios are as follows. Row 2: 134.4/0.533 = 252, row 3: 492, row 4: 1062, row 5: 350.2, so row 2 and S_1 are departing, and 0.533 is the pivot element.

Row No.	X_1	X_2	S_1	S_2	S_3	S_4	RHS
1	0	0	−4.3750	0	−2.31250	0	−7668
2	0	1	1.8750	0	−0.43750	0	252
3	0	0	−5.6250	1	0.31250	0	720
4	1	0	−1.2500	0	0.62500	0	540
5	0	0	−3.4375	0	0.46875	1	180

12. a. P = number of potatoes used in production. C = same, for clams, and T = same, for liters of tomato sauce. N = liters of New England Chowder produced, M = same for Manhattan.
    b. $P = 2N + 0.5M$, $C = N + M$, $T = 0.05N + 0.25M$.
    c. Using $N = 1$ and $M = 1$, we get $P = 2.5$ potatoes, $C = 2$ clams and $T = 0.3$ liter, which is just what is needed.
    d. 100,000 liters of N, with 100,000 clams and 15,000 liters of sauce left over.
    e. 80,000 liters of M with 160,000 potatoes and 120,000 clams left over.
    f. All costs are sunk and revenue is equal for both products, so maximize total production $= N + M$, subject to constraints in part b and $P \le 200{,}000$, $C \le 200{,}000$, and $T \le 20{,}000$.
13. a. They have different prices.
    b. LP, LC, LT = leftover potatoes, clams,and tomato sauce used in production. PP, PC, PT = purchased potatoes (etc.) used. N = liters of New England produced. M = same, Manhattan.
    c. $\text{LP} + \text{PP} = 2N + 0.5M$, $\text{LC} + \text{PC} = N + M$, $\text{LT} + \text{PT} = 0.05N + 0.25M$, $\text{LP} \le 200{,}000$, $\text{LC} \le 200{,}000$, $\text{LT} \le 20{,}000$, $N \le 500{,}000$, $M \le 400{,}000$.
    d. Maximize $1.05N + 1.00M - 0.03\text{PP} - 0.10\text{PC} - 0.60\text{PT}$
    e. The first 3 are accounting, the next 3 are facts of life, and the last 2 are both policy and facts of life.
    f. With the prices given, both products have a positive net return. Buy as much as is needed for production to meet demand.
15. a. This solution achieves zero cost. Change the demand constraints to "equalities."
    b. Upper limit, allowing the LP to select product mix.
    c. Maximize $.40\ A1 + .35\ A2 + .10\ A3 + .20\ A4 - .20\ B1 + .10\ B2 + .05\ B3 + .10\ B4 + .35\ C1 + .15\ C2 + .30\ C3 + .35\ C4$, Subject to $A1 + A2 + A3 + A4 \le 1200$; $B1 + B2 + B3 + B4 \le 1200$; $C1 + C2 + C3 + C4 \le 500$; $A1 + B1 + C1 \le 700$; $A2 + B2 + C2 \le 400$; $A3 + B3 + C3 \le 600$; $A4 + B4 + C4 \le 500$
    d. $.10\ A1 + .15\ A2 + \cdots + .25\ C4 \le 400$
    e. Y = additional capacity; $Y \le 50$ and change the plant C constraint to $C1 + C2 + C3 \le 500 + Y$, and add $-0.05Y$ to the objective function.
18. a. X_A = tons of cement A (similarly X_B); Y_1 = tons of ingredient 1 (similarly Y_2, Y_3). Maximize $180X_A + 150X_B$ subject to $Y_1 = 0.5X_A + 0.4X_B$; $Y_2 = 0.3X_A + 0.2X_B$; $Y_3 = 0.2X_A + 0.4X_B$; $Y_2 \le 15{,}000$; $X_A \ge 5000$; $X_B \ge 4000$.
    b. Upper limits on sales, and costs of ingredients.
    c. Maximize $180X_A + 150X_B - C_1X_1 - C_2X_2 - C_3X_3$ subject to $X_A \le U_A$; $X_B \le U_B$; and the constraints in (a).
20. a. 84,210 liters of New England and 63,160 of Manhattan. Leftovers = 52.63 thousand clams.
    b. $(0.421)(20) = 8.42$ thousand liters of chowder.
    c. Additional clams are of no use. An additional 20 thousand liters of

tomato sauce exeeds the range of the shadow price, so *no more than* (3.158)(20) = 63.16 thousand liters.

d. Decrease by (0.421)(20) = 8.42 thousand liters.

e. i. No change. ii and iii. Cannot tell because the change exeeds the ALLOWED DECREASE.

f. The shadow price for decreasing NENG is 0.80, so the objective function (chowder output) decreases by at leat (0.8)(84.21 − 50) = 27.37, so the new output would be 147.37 − 27.37 = 120 or less. Since NENG = 50, MNHTN = 120 − 50 = 70 or less.

g. Yes, it is still optimal. The ALLOWED INCREASE of NENG's objective coefficient is 3.0.

Index